BUSINESS LAW IN SCOTLAND

THIRD EDITION

BUSINESS LAW IN SCOTLAND
THIRD EDITION

General Editor
Gillian Black
Senior Lecturer in Law, University of Edinburgh

Josephine Bisacre
Associate Professor of Business Law,
Heriot-Watt University

David Cabrelli
Senior Lecturer in Commercial Law,
University of Edinburgh

Elizabeth Campbell
Senior Lecturer in Criminal Law and Evidence,
University of Edinburgh

James Chalmers
Regius Professor of Law,
University of Glasgow

Jane Cornwell
Lecturer,
University of Edinburgh

Stuart Cross
Professor of Law,
University of Dundee

Alan Delaney
Director,
Maclay Murray & Spens LLP

Cowan Ervine
Honorary Teaching Fellow,
University of Dundee

Alex Gibb
Lecturer in Law,
North East Scotland College

Greg Gordon
Senior Lecturer in Law,
University of Aberdeen

Fiona Grant
Lecturer in Law,
University of Abertay, Dundee

Angus McAllister
Solicitor, Emeritus Professor of Law,
University of the West of Scotland

Frankie McCarthy
Senior Lecturer in Private Law,
University of Glasgow

Amy Pairman
Trainee Solicitor,
Brodies LLP

Dominic Scullion
Senior Solicitor,
Anderson Strathern LLP

Andrew R. Wilson
Editor of SCOLAG Legal Journal

Hong-Lin Yu
Reader in Law,
University of Stirling

W. GREEN

THOMSON REUTERS

Published in 2015 by W. Green, 21 Alva Street,
Edinburgh EH2 4PS
Part of Thomson Reuters (Professional) UK Limited
(Registered in England & Wales, Company No 1679046.
Registered Office: 2nd Floor, 1 Mark Square, Leonard Street,
London EC2A 4EG

Typeset by YHT Ltd, Middlesex
Printed and bound in Great Britain by Printed and bound in Great Britain
by CPI Group (UK) Ltd, Croydon, CR0 4YY

ISBN 978-0414-03673-4

A catalogue record for this title is available
from the British Library

Foreword

Laws and regulations significantly impact on business and it is essential that those in business or those advising business, including Chartered Accountants ("CAs"), have a level of understanding of the legal framework within which they operate. Businesses operating in Scotland are impacted not only by Scots law but also by legislation from both the UK and European Parliaments.

Obtaining knowledge of business law can be difficult due to the diverse range of legal topics and the difficulty of accessing and deciphering the law itself. This 3rd edition of *Business Law in Scotland* makes this a much easier task by providing a summary of the various laws affecting business in Scotland. It covers a wide range of topics which impact on daily business life, including: business regulation; the sale of goods and services, including e-commerce; contract law; employment law; intellectual property; and the specific laws relating to different forms of business entity such as companies and partnerships.

In qualifying as a Chartered Accountant ("CA"), it is essential to have an understanding of the broad range of legal topics related to business and is an important element in the CA qualification. *Business Law in Scotland* will be an invaluable support and reference for individuals in business, in the profession and those studying business law, even if part of a wider area of study.

Michelle Crickett
Director of Research
ICAS

July 2015

Introduction

Law, like business practice, does not stand still, and this third edition of *Business Law in Scotland* reflects considerable changes in the legal and regulatory framework for businesses over the last four years. In particular, consumer protection and e-commerce have seen significant new regulation, while contract and company law continue to keep the courts and legislature busy. To reflect the increasing importance of limited liability partnerships, we are delighted to include a new chapter in this edition, which focuses on this important business vehicle.

As with the previous editions of this book, our aim remains to provide a clear summary of the law in relation to those core areas which are relevant to current business practice. Anyone in business in Scotland needs to know a little about the law. Whether running a web-based start-up as a sole trader or an established company with hundreds of employees, the law will affect your business. And while the services of a solicitor may be available, it is essential to have a basic understanding of areas of law as diverse as contract, employment, delict and insurance. This book aims to provide an introduction to those areas of law which are most relevant to people in business in Scotland—and in particular, to help readers identify legal issues at an early stage in order to minimise inconvenience and delay, by seeking professional advice in good time.

The book is organised in five sections. The first (Chs 1–3) provides an introduction to the Scottish legal system, sources of law, and a guide to business regulation. The second section (Chs 4–13) covers core areas of Scots private law, including contract, delict and property law. Section three (Chs 14–21) addresses those areas of commerce that most organisations will usually, at some time or other, have to deal with, whether it is company regulation, partnership agreements, insurance, security and insolvency. In section four (Ch.22), the focus switches to dispute resolution in Scotland—what to do if it all goes wrong. This includes seeking redress in the courts as well as alternative methods of resolving problems, such as arbitration. The final section (Ch.23) is a guide to legal writing and problem solving, to help apply the law in problem scenarios, not least when answering exam questions.

In compiling this edition, we have again sought to reflect the current "business law" syllabus set down by the Institute of Chartered Accountants for Scotland ("ICAS") for accountants on the Chartered Accountant programme in Scotland. We hope that *Business Law in Scotland* will provide a useful resource to those students following the ICAS CA qualification, as well as those on business law courses across Scotland. We are particularly pleased that Michelle Crickett, Director of Research at ICAS has contributed the Foreword.

All references to websites are correct as at May 15, 2015.

Finally, on behalf of all the contributors, I should like to thank Kirsty Swain, Kathy Pauline and the staff at W. Green for their hard work in bringing this book together—their support and guidance has been much appreciated.

Gillian Black
Edinburgh, June 2015

Contents

Table of Contents

CHAPTER 8: EMPLOYMENT LAW

CHAPTER 9: AGENCY

CHAPTER 10: DELICT

CHAPTER 14: CHOICE OF BUSINESS MEDIUM

CHAPTER 15: THE LAW OF PARTNERSHIP

CHAPTER 22: DISPUTE RESOLUTION

CHAPTER 23: INTRODUCTION TO LEGAL WRITING AND PROBLEM SOLVING TECHNIQUES

Table of Cases

Table of United Kingdom Statutes

Table of Scottish Statutes

Table of United Kingdom Statutory Instruments

Table of Scottish Statutory Instruments

Chapter 1 Introduction to the Nature and Sources of Scots Law

Josephine Bisacre[1]

▶ CHAPTER OVERVIEW

This chapter is concerned with the nature and sources of Scots law. It **1–01** looks first at fundamental issues of what we mean by law and the difference between legal and non-legal rules. It then traces the development of Scots law from the period before the Roman occupation to modern times, highlighting the important events that shaped the modern legal system. It explains various ways in which law can be categorised in order to understand it better. The remainder of the chapter is concerned with the formal sources of Scots law, the most important of which are legislation and case law (judicial precedent).

✓ OUTCOMES

At the end of this chapter you should be able to: **1–02**

- ✓ understand the difference between legal and non-legal rules;
- ✓ have an awareness of the historical reasons for the relationship between Scots and English law today;
- ✓ make use of different classifications of law to aid understanding of the various branches of law;
- ✓ understand the relationship between European legislation and legislation of the UK and Scottish Parliaments;
- ✓ describe the procedure for enactment of an Act of the UK Parliament and an Act of the Scottish Parliament and for the making of delegated legislation;
- ✓ describe the requirements for a precedent from an earlier court to be binding on a later court;
- ✓ display awareness of the minor formal sources of law: the institutional writers, custom and equity; and
- ✓ distinguish the formal sources of Scots law from secondary sources.

---

[1] Associate Professor of Business Law, Heriot-Watt University.

INTRODUCTION

1–03 Businesses operate within a legal framework which gives them a set of rules that are known in advance, and are kept up-to-date. If there are business disputes, or someone is injured by business activities, disputes can be brought before the court and remedies obtained. There are also criminal laws to try to ensure that businesses adopt safe business practices. There are legal rules which provide different business structures, such as the partnership or the registered company described in Chs 14–17. Managers and employees of businesses need some knowledge of the law: they need to know when their business is bound in a contract, and if a contract has been breached, what remedies may be sought; they need to know what the legal implications are if an employee injures a member of the public while working; and every business that takes on even one employee needs to know something about employment law. The important thing for managers of businesses to bear in mind is that while no one would expect them to have an encyclopaedic knowledge of law they need to have a working knowledge of the most important aspects of business law, and they need to be able to ask the right questions when seeking legal advice from professional lawyers. Accountants also have a role in advising business managers on aspects of law, and are often the first port of call for such advice.

Legal rules and non-legal rules

1–04 Legal rules may appear similar to non-legal rules. For example, I may regard it as imperative that I honour an arrangement to turn up at a particular venue on a certain day and have dinner with a friend. However, if my friend decides not to turn up and goes to a football match instead, I would not be able to exercise any legal remedy, nor would the State exact any punishment. All legal systems have to draw a line between areas of behaviour that are covered by legal rules and areas of behaviour that are best regulated only by codes of moral and social behaviour. This dividing line may differ from society to society and may change over time. For example, in Scotland, it used to be the case that *sponsiones ludicrae* (gambling contracts) would not be enforced by the courts as being too trivial for their consideration. However, that has now changed and these contracts are now enforceable.[2] Talking on a mobile phone, other than a hands-free instrument, while driving a car has recently become a criminal offence for which the penalty has been increased to £100 with three penalty points on the licence.[3] Following the death in Scotland of a small child who was killed by the discharge of an air rifle, the Scottish Parliament sought to regulate these weapons and obtained new devolved powers to legislate in this area in s.10 of the Scotland Act 2012. At the time of writing the Air Weapons and Licensing (Scotland) Bill is making its way through the Scottish Parliament. The difference between a legal

---

[2] As a result of s.335 of the Gambling Act 2005.
[3] Road Safety Act 2006 s.26.

rule and a non-legal rule lies in whether the rule is regarded as having the authority of the State behind it: it may provide for an enforcement mechanism granting a remedy should the rule be breached (civil law), or may provide for State-backed punishment for transgression of the rule (criminal law).

Scots law and English law

Scotland, although part of the UK, has its own distinct legal system with **1–05** many rules of law that differ from those in the rest of the UK, including separate courts. However, as this chapter goes on to discuss, in some areas of business law the law across the UK is the same or very similar. In sale and supply of goods, consumer protection, employment law, agency, partnership and company law, and intellectual property law, the law in the different parts of the UK is largely the same. Parts of contract law and the law of delict are similar, although not identical. However, there are significant differences in criminal law, property law, the law of trusts and in the law on rights in security, the reasons lying in their different historical development.

The History and Development of Scots Law

The two major influences on Scots law over the centuries have been **1–06** English law and Roman law. Because of this, modern Scots law can be said to be a mixed system of law combining elements of the deductive reasoning characteristic of the civil legal systems derived from Roman law,[4] which apply principles to the solution of factual cases, with the inductive approach of the English common law,[5] which does the opposite, using inductive reasoning to develop principles from concrete cases.

The Celtic period

Little is known about the laws applying in Scotland before the Roman **1–07** occupation between 79AD and about 400AD. Scotland at that period was inhabited by various Celtic tribes who would have had their own separate customary laws, which were probably unwritten. When the Romans arrived in Scotland they made attempts to subdue the tribes, but they were never fully successful and Roman law was resisted in Scotland.

After the Roman occupation ended, Scotland was inhabited by four peoples: the Picts who inhabited the area from the Forth to the Pentland Firth; the Britons in Strathclyde; the Scots in Dalriada (modern Argyllshire); and the Angles based in the Lothians between the Tweed and the Forth. The Picts, Britons and Scots were all Celtic races who came to Scotland originally from Gaul, whereas the Angles were originally a

---

[4] Principally the countries of Western Europe, although the civil legal tradition has been exported to Louisiana in the US and South Africa.
[5] The common law approach applies in the US, Australia and Canada and other former colonies of the UK.

Teutonic race who moved into Scotland from England. Around 843AD
Kenneth MacAlpin, King of the Scots, united the Picts and the Scots in a
kingdom called Scotia. It is known that Norse invaders started to arrive
in Orkney, Shetland and the Western Isles in the ninth century bringing
with them Norse law, traces of which remain to this day in udal law in
Orkney and Shetland.[6] However, there is little evidence of lasting legal
influence on modern Scots law from this period, except the office of Lord
Lyon King of Arms in relation to nobiliary law, which remains to this
day.[7]

The middle ages to the union of the Parliaments

1–08 In 1016 Scotland was unified into one kingdom when Malcolm II, King
of Scots, together with Owen the Bald, King of Strathclyde, defeated the
Angles at the Battle of Carham.

The feudal system of land ownership arrived in Scotland around the
same time as the Norman Conquest in England in 1066. This system
survived in Scotland until it was abolished by the Abolition of Feudal
Tenure etc. (Scotland) Act 2000, one of the early Acts of the new Scottish
Parliament. Under the feudal system land was held by a vassal from a
feudal superior, who in turn held his rights from the King. Feudal tenure
involved obligations, initially including military service.

In the early middle ages, the King was the source of justice, which was
dispensed by the King's Council, which combined the functions of a
Court and a Parliament. Justiciars dispensed civil and criminal justice at
twice-yearly Justice Ayres held in spring and autumn in various locations.
The modern High Court of Justiciary traces its name from the Justiciars.
Sheriffs were also introduced in this period to dispense local justice in
civil and criminal matters, and combined this function with that of collecting taxes. There were also barony courts as part of the feudal system.
In the early mediaeval period a person could be tried by ordeal, under
which an accused could face a duel, but this gave way to trial by jury
during the reign of Alexander II.

In the twelfth and thirteenth centuries the burghs rose to prominence
and burgh courts were introduced presided over by the Chamberlain. A
legal text the *Leges Quattuor Burgorum* or Laws of the Four Burghs
(Edinburgh, Berwick, Roxburgh and Stirling) was written in the thirteenth century codifying the customary and legal rules used in the four
burghs to dispense justice. Other important early legal works which have
survived were the *Regiam Majestatem* and the *Quoniam Attachiamenta*
(both named after the first words in the text) which may date from the
fourteenth century or possibly earlier.

1–09 Before the Reformation, canon law (the law of the Roman Catholic
Church) was very important in Scotland. Churchmen were among the

---

[6] A system of land tenure that applied in Orkney and Shetland, and of which some aspects
still survive.
[7] T.B. Smith, *A Short Commentary on the Law of Scotland* (Edinburgh, W. Green, 1962),
p.4.

best educated in the land, and canon law was influential upon the development of family law in Scotland. It was churchmen who first travelled to continental European universities and brought back ideas borrowed from Roman law. Church courts were held in this period up to the Reformation, to decide on matters where canon law was influential. An example of the influence of canon law on modern Scots law is the binding nature of gratuitous promise in Scots law.

Some areas of business law can trace their origin to the middle ages. Merchants from different countries used to meet at major trade fairs across Europe and also at the seaports. This was an opportunity for the exchange of ideas and a European law merchant or mercantile law developed from the eleventh century onwards, as distinct from local laws. Since trade is conducted across national borders, it is important to have a degree of uniformity in commercial law. In Scotland, a Court of the Admiral of Scotland met in seaside burghs, and courts were also held at trade fairs to decide disputes between merchants. Some modern legal concepts trace their origin to this period, such as negotiable instruments, the use of simplified methods of execution for commercial documents and marine insurance.

Wars of Independence took place between Scotland and England after the death of Alexander III in 1286, ending with an uneasy peace in 1328 negotiated in the Treaty of Northampton, by which England recognised Robert the Bruce as king of an independent Scotland. The cold war between England and Scotland during and after this period meant that the only outside influence on Scots law in this period came from Roman law as taught and applied in continental Europe.

In the fifteenth century the Universities of St Andrews (1411), Glasgow **1–10** (1451) and Aberdeen (1494) were founded and began to teach law. However, because the standard of law teaching was higher in continental Europe, it became common for scholars to study civil law initially at French and Italian universities and latterly at universities in the Netherlands, where they could study civil law in Latin. As a result, legal scholars returned home to Scotland bringing with them ideas from Roman law to fill in the gaps in the developing legal system. Parts of the law of obligations and the law on corporeal moveable property derive from Roman legal concepts. Many of the legal scholars in the seventeenth and eighteenth centuries were held in such esteem that their works were elevated to the status of being considered themselves to be formal sources of law.[8] This period of rapid development of Scots law coincided with the Scottish Enlightenment, a period in Scottish history of particularly fruitful development of ideas across the fields of science, economics, philosophy and law, during which thinkers and scientists such as Adam Smith, James Watt, and David Hume were exerting an influence in Scotland and beyond.

In the sixteenth century, the most notable development was the

---

[8] The most prominent example is James Dalrymple, Viscount Stair whose most authoritative work is his *Institutions of the Law of Scotland*, 1681. See paras 1–52—1–53 towards the end of this chapter where the Institutional Writers are discussed.

founding of the College of Justice in 1532 (the Court of Session), which was a collegiate civil court of 15 professional judges based in Edinburgh. Law reporting began to develop in rudimentary form in Practicks from this period. Another decisive event was the Reformation in 1559–1560, which ended the church courts and the application of canon law.

The beginning of the seventeenth century witnessed the Union of the Crowns, when James VI of Scotland became king of England in 1603. Although James desired complete union between the two kingdoms, public opinion in neither country was in favour. An important legal landmark in this period was the creation of the General Register of Sasines in 1617, which provided a single register of landownership for Scotland, a register which continued until it was gradually replaced by the Land Register only towards the end of the twentieth century. Another legal landmark was the setting up of the High Court of Justiciary in 1672 as a criminal court, replacing the Justice Ayres. It was a circuit court, to try the most serious crimes throughout Scotland, and existed in this form until its personnel were consolidated with those of the Court of Session in the nineteenth century.

The union of the Parliaments to the twenty-first century

1–11 The union of the Scottish and English Parliaments in 1707 was precipitated by various events: discord about the eventual succession to the throne if Queen Anne should die without surviving children; by Scotland's weak economic state after the collapse of the disastrous attempt to establish a colony in Darien, Panama; and by the likelihood of war between England and France and the undesirable prospect from the English point of view of Scotland again coming to the aid of France, under the Auld Alliance.

Acts of both Parliaments were passed to enact the provisions of the Treaty of Union. The Treaty provided that the two kingdoms would become Great Britain with a common coinage, and recognition of the Hanoverian succession to the throne. The two Parliaments were to be succeeded by one Parliament of Great Britain. There would be free trade between Scotland and England. The Treaty retained the separate system of courts in Scotland. The Treaty states that Scottish criminal cases could no longer be appealed to English courts, but does not explicitly so state in respect of civil appeals.[9] The Treaty provided that public law should be uniform throughout Great Britain, but that Scottish private law could not be altered, "except for the evident utility of the subjects within Scotland".[10]

The pre-1707 Scottish Parliament was much less powerful than its

---

[9] Union with England Act 1707 art.XIX. The House of Lords continued to hear appeals on civil matters on points of law from Scottish courts thereafter—see *Greenshields v Magistrates of Edinburgh* (1710–1711) Rob 12. The Supreme Court, which has replaced the House of Lords as a final court of appeal, has the power to act as a final court of appeal on civil matters from Scottish courts. This is discussed later in this chapter in para.1–43.

[10] Union with England Act 1707 art.XVII.

English counterpart. In the middle ages, the Scottish Parliament had been made up of clergy and barons, but by the time of Robert the Bruce (1274–1329) representatives from the Burghs were added (the Three Estates). However, it was never a fully democratic Parliament. It also served as a court, and as an organ of the government. From the fifteenth century it was dominated by a committee called the Lords of the Articles who controlled the business of the Parliament. The Acts of the old Scots Parliament had a characteristic not shared by its successor, whereby they could lose the force of law by desuetude (discontinuance through lack of use) without having to be expressly repealed if a long period of contrary usage could be demonstrated.[11] A few statutes of the old Scots Parliament are still in force today, the oldest being the Royal Mines Act 1424 which reserves gold and silver mines to the Crown.[12] After the Union of the Parliaments, the Parliament at Westminster enacted separate statutes for Scotland in those areas of law where Scots law differed from English law and uniform statutes (sometimes with some separate sections for Scotland), where the law was the same or similar.

After the Treaty of Union, Scots law was increasingly influenced by English law. One of the major reasons was because civil appeals could be taken to the House of Lords, and these were often heard by a bench of English judges. However, since 1876 there was always at least one Scottish Law Lord assigned to a Scottish case, and this remains true of the new Supreme Court. Also, being a much larger legal system, England offered a fruitful source of case law, which was increasingly well documented in law reports. English influence on the law of Scotland can also be seen in the enactment of unified statutes for Scotland and England on important aspects of business law at the end of the nineteenth century relating to the sale of goods, bills of exchange, and partnership.[13] The influence of Roman law also declined as continental legal systems were gradually codified, reducing the amount of Roman law taught at continental universities, and because during the period of the Napoleonic Wars, travel was difficult.

In the nineteenth century, Parliament became the Parliament of the United Kingdom with the inclusion of Ireland in 1800, and this was changed by a further treaty in 1920 to include Northern Ireland only, after the Republic of Ireland was created. The Court of Session was reorganised into the modern structure of the Inner and Outer House with the Inner House divided into two Divisions, and its personnel was consolidated with those of the High Court of Justiciary.[14] The Scottish Office

---

[11] A recent case that discussed desuetude was *Secretary of State for Business Enterprise and Regulatory Reform v UK Bankruptcy Ltd*, 2010 S.L.T. 1242, in which the College of Justice Act 1532 was found not to be in desuetude, which meant that a company director was not allowed to represent the company in court in relation to proceedings for compulsory liquidation.

[12] Acts of the old Scots Parliament that are still in force can be found on *http://www.legislation.gov.uk* [Accessed May 15, 2015], the legislation service of the National Archives, covering UK, Scottish, Welsh and Northern Irish legislation.

[13] The Bills of Exchange Act 1882 and the Partnership Act 1890 apply to this day.

[14] See Ch.2, "Structure of the Scottish Legal System".

was created in 1885 to govern Scotland in those areas of government where separate rules applied. This system continued until devolution when the Scotland Act 1998 created a Scottish Parliament and a government for Scotland. Some further powers were devolved in 2012, and in September 2014 there was a referendum in Scotland on the question whether Scotland should become an independent country, in which there was a 55 per cent / 45 per cent vote in favour of remaining part of the UK. Following that referendum, there has been a subsequent review (the Smith Commission) that recommended that further powers should be devolved to the Scottish Parliament.

The twentieth century saw the creation of the European Convention on Human Rights, the European Community (now the European Union), as well as the Scottish Parliament. Finally, the Supreme Court replaced the House of Lords as the final court of civil appeal from UK courts, and as the final court of criminal appeal from the courts in England, Wales and Northern Ireland in October 2009.

The European Convention on Human Rights and Fundamental Freedoms

1–12 A major constitutional development immediately after the Second World War was the drawing up of the European Convention on Human Rights and Fundamental Freedoms by the Council of Europe in 1949.[15] The aim of this Convention was to prevent abuses of human rights by the State recurring in Europe, by providing fundamental human rights and remedies for their abuse. Although the UK has been bound by this Convention since 1950, its citizens have only since 1966 had the right to take a case to the Court of Human Rights in Strasbourg, on the grounds of violation of human rights by a public body. Because of difficulties and delays in taking a case to the court in Strasbourg, the Human Rights Act 1998 and the Scotland Act 1998 embedded the European Convention on Human Rights and Fundamental Freedoms into national law in the UK, which means that remedies against public bodies can now be sought before the domestic courts. As the courts are public bodies, their procedures must be compliant with the Convention, as must those of all other public bodies. The legislation of the new Scottish Parliament is ineffective if not compliant.[16] By contrast, because the UK Parliament is a sovereign parliament, non-compliant legislation from the UK Parliament is not invalid, but would be a breach of the Convention. For these reasons, all legislation must be scrutinised in advance for compliance. In the case of the Westminster Parliament, there is a procedure for amendment of statutes by delegated legislation to make them compliant.

---

[15] The Council of Europe, despite the similarity of its name with one of the organs if the European Union, is a different body with broader membership than the EU. It has 47 members comprising all European countries including Turkey and Russia. See *http://www.coe.int/en/* [Accessed May 15, 2015].

[16] The Scotland Act 1998 s.29.

The European Union

Another major legal development of the twentieth century was the creation **1–13**
of the European Community, which was originally concerned with European integration and the development of an internal market and later
developed into a more extensive European Union. The European Community has existed since 1956, as an economic community of six Member
States, which the UK joined in 1973. As of 2015 there are 28 Member
States and the organisation has expanded its areas of competence so that it
is now a customs union, has a foreign and security policy, provides common citizenship rights, and provides police and judicial co-operation. Since
the Lisbon Treaty came into force on December 1, 2009, the EU now has
legal personality. The organisation has an institutional infrastructure in the
European Council, European Commission, the Council of the European
Union, the European Parliament and the European Court of Justice. It has
the power to legislate and European legislation must be applied within the
Member States in priority to national law, within its sphere of competence.

The Scottish Parliament

The final years of the twentieth century saw another major constitutional **1–14**
change for Scotland. As has already been mentioned, after 1707, legislation for Scotland was enacted by the Westminster Parliament. Lack of
parliamentary time for Scottish legislation caused dissatisfaction. Too
often legislation on disparate matters was crammed into Law Reform
(Miscellaneous Provisions) (Scotland) Acts, or long overdue reforms
were delayed. Also, government through the Scottish Office was
unpopular in periods when the government of the day did not represent
the politics of the majority of the electorate of Scotland, as was the case in
the 1980s. For these reasons, after the failure to secure a sufficient
majority in a referendum in 1979, another referendum was held in 1997
which led to the establishment of the Scottish Parliament and a Scottish
Executive (now Scottish Government). The Scottish Parliament is a
unicameral Parliament and is based at Holyrood in Edinburgh. It currently has 129 Members of the Scottish Parliament ("MSPs"). Its power
to legislate is devolved from the UK Parliament, and is limited to legislating within those powers not reserved to the Westminster Parliament.
Its powers to legislate were added to by the Scotland Act 2012, which
granted it the power to set a rate of income tax for Scotland and the
power to levy a tax on transactions involving land. The new land and
buildings transaction tax started being levied from April 1, 2015, and as
stated above, more powers are likely to be devolved to the Scottish
Parliament following the referendum decision in 2014 that Scotland
should remain part of the UK. It is important to emphasise that the new
Scottish Parliament is not a re-creation of the pre-1707 Scottish Parliament, but a completely new Parliament.[17] Even in the few years since it

---

[17] For information about the Scottish Parliament see its website *http://www.scottish.par-
liament.uk* [Accessed May 15, 2015].

came into existence, it has passed some major statutes such as the Abolition of Feudal Tenure etc. (Scotland) Act 2000 which changed the system of land ownership in Scotland, and the Bankruptcy and Diligence etc. (Scotland) Act 2007 which is designed to encourage an enterprise culture in Scotland by shortening the period of bankruptcy from three years to one year, after which an application can be made for discharge.

CATEGORIES OF LAW

1–15 Law imposes itself on most areas of human activity, and even on relations between States themselves. The branch of the law covering the treaties and conventions entered into between States is known as "public international law".

There are other classifications of law, some of which cut across each other and in which the same terms have different meanings, which can be confusing.

Public law and private law

1–16 Public law relates the relationship between the State and the citizen including legal persons such as partnerships and companies, while private law concerns itself with regulating relationships between citizens.

Public law can itself be divided into *constitutional law*, *administrative law* and *criminal law*. Constitutional law is concerned with a State's constitution, written or unwritten, and the operation of the organs of the State: the legislature (Parliament), the executive (government) and the judiciary (the courts). Administrative law provides a framework regulating the exercise of power by the government, to protect its citizens from abuse of power. Criminal law provides prescriptive rules to try to ensure acceptable behaviour by the citizens. A State decides which behaviour should be penalised, and this may change as society changes. If behaviour breaches these rules, the State will prosecute the alleged offender in the criminal courts and if convicted, State-sanctioned punishment will follow.

Most of the substantive law that affects businesses covered in this book is private law. Private law includes the law of contract, law of delict, family law, law of trusts, commercial law, company law, insolvency law, parts of employment law, and the law of property, plus remedies for breach of the relevant legal rules.

Public law	Private law
Constitutional law Administrative law Criminal law	Contract Delict Family law Law of trusts Commercial law Company law Insolvency law Parts of employment law Law of property Remedies

Civil law and criminal law

Law can also be classified into *civil* and *criminal law*. This distinction **1–17** relates to the courts that hear the cases. Civil cases are cases where one party is in dispute with another and seeks a remedy, which is obtained from a civil court. Where a person has been charged with commission of a crime, a prosecutor will bring the case before a criminal court, seeking a sentence (punishment). This classification of law cuts across the previous one, in that cases on constitutional law in the UK are brought before the civil courts as there are no separate constitutional courts in this country, and cases on some aspects of administrative law are also brought before the civil courts, although there are some separate administrative tribunals in the UK. Cases on private law are always brought before the civil courts.[18]

Civil law and common law

This is a completely different use of the term "civil law". In this sense it **1–18** refers to Roman law and the legal systems derived from it. The distinction is made between civilian legal systems and common law systems. The civil systems of law derive from Roman law, and make use of codes containing general principles of law which are applied to cases. Many of the States of Western Europe developed their legal systems from Roman law, as has already been described earlier in this chapter. Common law is judge-made law and originated in England, from where it has been exported to England's colonies including the US, Canada and Australia. Scots law is often described as being a mixed system.

Common law and statute law

Common law is also distinguished from statute law or legislation. As will **1–19** be seen in the next part of this chapter, every legal rule has a formal source from which it derives its authority as law, which may lie in a piece of primary or subordinate legislation. If it does not, it derives from the

---

[18] See Ch.2, "Structure of the Scottish Legal System".

common law, which consists of legal rules that have been declared by the judges in case law, plus legal rules stemming from other minor formal sources. While the most important formal source of law in Scotland is statute law, the common law remains an important formal source of the law of contract, delict, criminal law and the law of agency. The rest of this chapter is concerned with these formal sources of law.

THE FORMAL SOURCES OF SCOTS LAW

1–20 In order for laws to have their binding quality, rules of law must derive from a formal source. This is what differentiates legal from non-legal rules.

Key Concept

The formal sources of Scots law are:

- Legislation.
- Judicial precedent.
- The Institutional Writers.
- Custom.
- Equity.

There is a ranking in authority between these formal sources, with legislation in the first place, followed by judicial precedent. The other formal sources are of limited importance nowadays.

LEGISLATION

1–21 Legislation is enacted by the UK Parliament or by a body to whom the UK Parliament has delegated the power to legislate. The Crown also has some residual power to legislate.

Key Concept

Legislation that is binding in Scotland comes from four sources:

- The European Union.
- The UK Parliament.
- The Scottish Parliament.
- The Royal Prerogative.

European legislation

There are four types of European legislation that have binding force: **1–22**
Treaties, Regulations, Directives and Decisions.

Treaties are the primary legislation of the EU and are entered into
between the Member States, to create the ground rules for the union.
Since the Treaty of Rome in 1957, there have been many other treaties,
admitting new members and adding new spheres of competence. Provisions in the treaties themselves may have direct effect within Member
States, despite contrary national law. The latest treaty is the Lisbon
Treaty which came into force on December 1, 2009, which made some
structural changes to the European Union such as the creation of an EU
President of the European Council and a High Representative for Foreign Affairs and gave the EU legal personality.

Article 288 of the Treaty on the Functioning of the European Union
empowers organs of the EU to make secondary legislation in the form of
Regulations, Directives, and *Decisions.* Recommendations and opinions
can also be issued but these have no binding force. For the EU to have
legislative competence, authority to legislate has to be found in an article
in one of the treaties. In some areas of business law (for example,
employment law and company law), national laws have been approxi-
mated or harmonised in certain areas in order to provide a level playing
field for business to prevent unfair competition and exploitation of
workers.[19]

Regulations are binding on Member States and their citizens and have
direct effect, which means that they do not need to be enacted into
national law.[20]

Directives are instructions to Member States to amend their laws and
are binding as to the results to be achieved. They may provide various
legislative options. They have been used extensively in company law and
employment law to try to make national laws comparable although not
identical. If Directives are not fully translated into national law, they can
have direct effect, enabling affected citizens to seek a remedy against the
Member State from the European Court of Justice.[21] Directives take
effect when notified to Member States, and usually provide a period for
their implementation into national law.

Decisions of the Commission or the Council are only binding upon the
Member States to whom they are addressed.

How European law is made

Various organs of the EU are involved in the creation of European leg- **1–23**
islation: the European Commission, the Council of the European Union,
the European Council, and the European Parliament. The European
Commission is the "government" of the EU and is composed of a

---

[19] Articles 114–115 of the Treaty on the Functioning of the European Union allows for the
approximation of national laws to create the common market.
[20] Article 288 of the Treaty on the Functioning of the European Union.
[21] *Francovich v Italy* Case 6/90 and 9/90 [1991] ECR I-5357.

President, 7 Vice-Presidents and 20 Commissioners (i.e. 1 commissioner per Member State). The Council of the European Union is one of the law-making bodies along with the European Parliament, it has a role in making treaties, and the EU budget has to be approved by it as well as by the European Parliament. It is composed of a minister from every Member State, with different ministers attending according to the topic under discussion. It has a six-monthly rotating presidency, with each Member State taking this role in turn. The European Council (a body with a confusingly similar name to the Council of the European Union) decides the political direction and the priorities of the EU. It is made up of heads of State in the 28 Member States, the president of the European Council[22] and the president of the European Commission. All these bodies are based in Brussels.

The European Parliament, despite its name, is not a Parliament in the normal sense of being the body that initiates and enacts European law. Instead it is largely a forum for debate and a consultative body. However, following recent treaties, its powers have grown and it now has an increased role in legislation, as well as in the approval of the appointees to European Commission, and has power to approve the EU budget. It meets in Brussels and in Strasbourg.

The ideas for secondary legislation are formulated by the European Commission. It drafts a proposal for legislation which may be circulated widely for consultation and commented upon. The proposal is then put to the Council of the European Union, from whence it goes to the European Parliament and is considered by a committee of the Parliament which may propose amendments, which are voted on by the Parliament. The proposal is then scrutinised by one of the working groups of the Council, and a text is either agreed by all the Member States or voted on by the Council generally by qualified majority voting (taking into account both the number of Member States and the number of EU citizens reflected in the voting). There are some variations on this legislative procedure, which give greater or lesser powers to the European Parliament, depending on the subject of the legislation.

Legislation of the UK Parliament

1–24 The UK Parliament is a sovereign Parliament, and has legislative competence over Scotland, England, Wales and Northern Ireland, despite devolved powers in differing degrees having been granted to Scotland, Wales and Northern Ireland. This means that, in theory at least, it can pass laws on anything it likes without limit. It can be argued that the UK Parliament has ceded some of its sovereignty to the EU, since, as we have seen, it has allowed some EU law to be recognised as superior to its own statutes in its areas of competence. However, the UK Parliament is still sovereign in the sense that it could repeal its own legislation that

---

[22] At the time of writing, this post was held by Donald Tusk.

enacted the various treaties of the EU into UK law. The legal validity of acts of the UK Parliament cannot be challenged in court.[23]

The Queen has an important ceremonial role in that all Bills have to receive the Royal Assent before they can become law. The Queen also gives the Queen's Speech at the State opening of each session of Parliament in November, when she reads out the government's proposed legislative programme for the session.

The UK Parliament has two legislative chambers, the House of Commons and the House of Lords. The House of Commons is made up of 650 elected Members of Parliament ("MPs"), 59 of them from Scotland. This figure will reduce to 600 as a result of s.11 of the Parliamentary Voting System and Constituencies Act 2011 which came into force on February 16, 2011, though the boundary review that would bring that into effect has been delayed to 2018. The House of Lords is currently composed of around 760 members, mainly appointed by the political parties, Included in their number are 26 bishops and 92 elected hereditary peers. Recent proposals for reform of the House of Lords have come to little because of differences of opinion. However, the House of Lords Reform Act 2014 has been enacted, which allows members to resign or retire and provides for those who do not attend Parliament or who are convicted of serious offences to be removed.

Acts of the UK Parliament can be divided into public general statutes which apply to us all, and private, local or personal statutes, which apply only to those who are the subject of the legislation. There are some hybrid Bills which are a mixture of the two.

Acts of the UK Parliament all start off as Bills. Most Bills are proposed by government departments as part of the government's legislative programme, although in every session of Parliament some bills will come forward as private members' bills. These are public bills which are proposed by MPs of any party who are selected by ballot.[24] Although private members' bills can be starved of Parliamentary time by the government if it does not like them, they are nevertheless an important part of the democratic process.

How a Bill becomes an Act of the Westminster Parliament

Ideas for legislation may be included in a party's election manifesto. **1–25** Other ideas may be a reaction to events, such as the UK's recent anti-terrorism laws, which were enacted in the aftermath of 9/11. Some ideas are extensively discussed in advance, to ensure that there is a measure of assent to the legislation and that unforeseen difficulties will not arise.

A government Bill will be drafted by the Parliamentary Counsel Office of the Cabinet Office. The Bill then goes through various stages in both

---

[23] Lord Campbell in *Edinburgh and Dalkeith Railway v Wauchope* (1842) 1 Bell App. Cas 252 at 279.
[24] An example of a private members' bill is the Abortion Act 1967 which legalised abortion in the UK, which was proposed by David Steel MP when he was a backbench MP before becoming leader of the Liberal Party and later the Presiding Officer of the Scottish Parliament at its inception.

Houses of Parliament before it becomes an Act—the First Reading, Second Reading, Committee Stage, Report Stage and Third Reading— after which it will receive the Royal Assent and become an Act of Parliament. Bills may be introduced first into either House. At various stages amendments may be proposed and voted on.

The First Reading is a formality: the short title of the Bill is read out and a date is set for the Second Reading. The Bill will be printed. Before the Second Reading, the Minister in charge of a government Bill makes a declaration that the Bill is compatible with the Human Rights Act 1998,[25] or that the government wishes to proceed with the Bill anyway.[26] At the Second Reading there will be a debate on the general principles of the Bill. The Bill then enters the Committee Stage when it goes to a Standing Committee (House of Commons) or a Committee of the Whole House (House of Lords). The composition of a Standing Committee is in accordance with the share of the vote of the different parties in the House. Bills of "first class constitutional importance" such as the Bill that preceded the Scotland Act 1998 are normally heard by a Committee of the Whole House in the House of Commons as well. At the Committee Stage the Bill is examined clause by clause, and this is the stage at which most amendments take place. At the Report Stage, the Committee reports back to the House, and if the Committee Stage took place before a Select Committee, there may be further debate on the provisions of the Bill, and further amendments. The Third Reading allows for a final debate on the principles of the Bill, followed by a vote. After the Bill has passed through all these stages in one House, it then goes to the other House where it goes through the same stages, and if approved receives the Royal Assent and becomes an Act.[27]

Acts do not generally come into force at once, but are usually brought into force later by the use of delegated legislation.

The legislative powers of the House of Lords are inferior to those of the House of Commons. Legislation on taxation and expenditure ("money bills") cannot be rejected by the House of Lords, but only delayed for one month. Under the Parliament Acts 1911 and 1949, other Bills that the House of Lords does not want to pass can be delayed for one year over two sessions of Parliament only. The Parliament Acts have not often been invoked, but were invoked in relation to the Hunting Act 2004.

---

[25] See earlier in this chapter, where the European Convention on Human Rights and Fundamental Freedoms is discussed.

[26] Since the UK Parliament is a sovereign Parliament, it can proceed with non-compliant legislation, though this is clearly undesirable.

[27] You can track the progress of a Bill through Parliament on Parliament's website *http://www.parliament.uk* [Accessed May 15, 2015].

What an Act of the UK Parliament looks like

An Act of Parliament has a short title by which the Act is popularly **1–26** known, e.g. "the Companies Act 2006". It has a chapter number, which reflects the chronological order in which statutes were enacted in a particular year. For example, the chapter number of the Companies Act 2006 is "c.46". Acts are divided into sections and subdivided into subsections. Some statutes have supplementary material in schedules at the end. Sections of statutes may be divided into parts and chapters if it is helpful to group them in that way. At the start of an Act of the UK Parliament there may be an arrangement of the sections. Acts have a long title as well as a short title to provide an indication of the purpose of the legislation. The date when the Act received the Royal Assent is given. Every section nowadays has a marginal note, though these are not part of the Act as enacted by Parliament. The enactment wording of an Act of the UK Parliament is expressed in wording that sounds rather archaic to modern ears:

> "Be it enacted by the Queen's most Excellent Majesty, by and with the advice and consent of the Lords Spiritual and Temporal, and Commons, in this present Parliament assembled, and by and with the authority of the same, as follows."

Acts of the UK Parliament or sections within Acts may extend to the whole of the UK or to parts of the UK only. If a statute does not extend to the whole of the UK, it will have a section towards the end stating its extent. Even within the areas of legislative competence of the Scottish Parliament, to be discussed later in this chapter, much legislation for Scotland had already been enacted prior to the creation of the Scottish Parliament and will remain in force unless and until it is repealed. Also, the Scottish Parliament sometimes chooses to have legislation made for it by the Parliament at Westminster, generally to ensure uniformity between provisions that apply also to the rest of the UK. An example of this is the Corporate Manslaughter and Corporate Homicide Act 2007 where criminal provisions for Scotland on corporate homicide are enacted alongside provisions for the rest of the UK, despite the fact that criminal law is an area of legislative competence devolved to the Scottish Parliament.

If society's needs change, a later statute can be passed to amend parts of the earlier statute. If a statute is not needed at all, it can be repealed, whereupon all parts of that statute will cease to be a formal source of law. Acts of the UK Parliament normally continue in force unless repealed, except where an Act specifies an expiry date—this used to be the case with anti-terrorism legislation for Northern Ireland which used to have to be voted on annually.

How to find legislation

1–27 Once a statute has been enacted, it is printed and sold by Her Majesty's Stationery Office. It is also published in a series called *Public General Statutes and Measures*. Legislation is also published in electronic form on the website of the National Archives, maintained for the government, which gives most legislation with updates included,[28] or on the subscription databases such as Westlaw, LexisLibrary, Lawtel or Justis.

Legislation of the Scottish Parliament

1–28 As has been mentioned earlier in this chapter, Scotland had her own Parliament prior to the Union of the Parliaments in 1707. A few of the Acts of that Parliament are still in force, most having ceased to apply because they were repealed, or fell into desuetude.[29]

The modern Scottish Parliament is a different institution from the pre-1707 Scottish Parliament. Its parent legislation is the Scotland Act 1998, and it has been granted legislative competence in all areas not reserved to the Westminster Parliament.[30] Reserved matters include constitutional law, taxation, large parts of business law such as data protection, company law and the law of business associations generally, intellectual property law, consumer law and employment law. However, the Scottish Parliament is still left with a large area of legislative competence. In the field of business law this includes criminal law, legislation on the law of bankruptcy, the law of rights in security, the law of diligence (enforcement of claims), property law and the law of trusts. The Scottish Parliament is not a sovereign Parliament, unlike its Westminster counterpart, and can only legislate within its sphere of competence, since its legislation could be challenged for being in excess of its powers as laid out in the Scotland Act 1998.[31] These challenges are nowadays taken to the Supreme Court, which has jurisdiction to hear devolution issues, having taken over this responsibility from the Judicial Committee of the Privy Council in 2009. All Scottish legislation is therefore really a kind of delegated legislation.[32] Not only may the Scottish Parliament not legislate in those areas reserved to the Westminster Parliament, but in addition it may not legislate in ways that are incompatible with the European Convention on Human Rights and Fundamental Freedoms or with EU law, it may not enact legislation with extra-territorial scope, or legislate to remove the Lord Advocate as head of the system of criminal prosecution or investigation of deaths in Scotland.[33]

The same distinction is made for Acts of the Scottish Parliament between public general Acts and private Acts.

---

[28] See *http://www.legislation.gov.uk* [Accessed May 15, 2015].
[29] See earlier in this chapter under "The History and Development of Scots Law" at para.1–11.
[30] Scotland Act 1998 ss.28–30 and Sch.5.
[31] Scotland Act 1998 s.54.
[32] See later in this chapter, paras 1–31—1–35.
[33] Scotland Act 1998 s.29(2).

How a Bill becomes an Act of the Scottish Parliament

As in the Westminster Parliament, legislation starts off as Bills which are **1–29**
proposed either by the Scottish Government (formerly Scottish Executive) or by individual Members of the Scottish Parliament ("MSPs") or
by one of the Parliament's Committees (Committee Bills). There is no
Queen's Speech as in the Westminster Parliament, but the Scottish
Government has always outlined its legislative programme soon after
each general election. As the Parliament is not sovereign, a Bill first has to
be checked in advance to ensure that it comes within its legislative
competence. The proposer of the Bill must so certify, and the Presiding
Officer of the Scottish Parliament must also state whether or not he
considers that the Bill is within its legislative competence. If a Bill appears
not to be compliant, the Advocate-General for Scotland,[34] or the Lord
Advocate[35] can refer the Bill to the Supreme Court[36] under s.33 of the
Scotland Act 1998 for a ruling as to competence.

At stage 1 in the enactment of a Bill, it goes to a lead committee which
reports back to the Scottish Parliament. A general debate takes place in
the Parliament on the main points of the Bill in conjunction with the
committee report. If the Parliament approves the Bill at this stage, it goes
back to the lead committee or to another committee or a Committee of
the Whole House for a detailed consideration of the clauses of the Bill for
stage 2 and the Bill is voted upon. Stage 3 is normally a formal stage at
which the Bill is presented to the full Parliament and will normally be
passed without further discussion, although it is possible for further
amendments to be made at this stage.[37]

Because of the necessity to ensure that the Parliament does not exceed
its legislative competence, the Royal Assent cannot be given immediately,
but is delayed for four weeks, to provide time for further checking of
legislative competence. As stated above, in this period the Advocate-
General for Scotland, the Lord Advocate, or the Attorney-General[38] may
refer the Bill to the Supreme Court for a decision on competence.[39] The
Westminster government also has the power to issue an order prohibiting
the Presiding Officer of the Scottish Parliament from submitting the Bill
for the Royal Assent if it considers that the Bill has exceeded its
competence.

Even once Acts of the Scottish Parliament have entered into force, they
may still be challenged for having exceeded their legislative competence.
"Devolution issues", i.e. issues of whether an Act of the Scottish Parliament has strayed beyond its sphere of competence may be raised by

---

[34] Law Officer for the Crown who advises the government at Westminster on matters of
Scots law. See Ch.2, "Structure of the Scottish Legal System".
[35] Law Officer for the Crown, responsible for advice to the government in Scotland and
head of the criminal prosecution service in Scotland.
[36] The structure and functioning of the Supreme Court will be explained in Ch.2, "Structure of the Scottish Legal System".
[37] Scotland Act 1998 s.36.
[38] The Principal Law Officer of the Crown in England.
[39] Under s.33 of the Scotland Act 1998.

either the Lord Advocate or the Advocate-General for Scotland,[40] they may arise in the context of other proceedings in court, and may also be raised by affected persons who fulfil the requirements of the Scotland Act 1998 in the civil and criminal courts anywhere in the UK. Appeals concerning devolution issues may be made to the Supreme Court.

What an Act of the Scottish Parliament looks like

1–30 Acts of the Scottish Parliament look very similar to Acts of the Westminster Parliament. They have a short title, which includes the word "Scotland" in brackets and the date, for example the Courts Reform (Scotland) Act 2014. Each Act has a chronological serial number, in this case an "asp number" which stands for "Act of the Scottish Parliament". In all other respects they look the same as acts of the UK Parliament. The enactment wording of an Act of the Scottish Parliament is rather simpler than the wording used in the UK Parliament, as one might expect with a recently-created Parliament. Acts include the statement, "[t]he Bill for this Act of the Scottish Parliament was passed by the Parliament on (date) and received the Royal Assent on (date)".

As is the case with Acts of the Westminster Parliament, Acts of the Scottish Parliament continue in force unless repealed and desuetude does not apply to them. The same rules on publication apply to Scottish primary legislation as to Acts of the Westminster Parliament.

Delegated legislation

1–31 Delegated (or subordinate or secondary) legislation is made by a body other than Parliament in exercise of powers given to that body by Parliament in a parent statute. Delegated legislation as a method of legislating has the following points in its favour:

> (1) It saves parliamentary time, which is limited. Parliament could never manage to legislate on all the matters covered by delegated legislation. In 2014, 30 Acts were passed by the Westminster Parliament, compared with several thousand statutory instruments ("SIs"). In Scotland in 2014, there were 19 Acts of the Scottish Parliament and several hundred Scottish Statutory Instruments ("SSIs").
>
> (2) Delegated legislation can be put in place faster than primary legislation. It can be used respond rapidly to emergencies, such as the outbreak of foot and mouth disease in 2007, as delegated legislation can be put in place very quickly and can be amended quickly.
>
> (3) Experts can be involved in the framing of delegated legislation in areas which are technically complex.
>
> (4) Delegated legislation can be used to phase in a large piece of new primary legislation slowly. Different parts of a statute can be

---

[40] Scotland Act 1998 s.98 and Sch.6.

introduced at different times by the relevant government minister issuing commencement orders. This was done with the introduction of provisions of the Companies Act 2006.

However, the use of delegated legislation brings with it some undesirable effects as well:

(1) Delegated legislation is sometimes criticised for being undemocratic, in that there is much less advance consultation with sections of the public than is generally the case with Acts of Parliament. Most delegated legislation is issued by the government of the day and although Parliament may be able to vote on the delegated legislation, MPs have no influence on the contents.

(2) Although the internet has been very helpful in making it easier for the public to discover the existence of delegated legislation that is relevant to them, people are generally less well aware of delegated legislation than of primary legislation.

(3) There is concern that in some cases the parent statute may itself lack detail and allow excessively wide powers of delegation. This makes the task of scrutiny of the parent statute in its passage through Parliament very hard, as MPs do not know at the time of the passage of the Bill what the implications of the legislation will be. An example of this is the Financial Services and Markets Act 2000 which provided for extensive delegated legislation in implement of its provisions.

(4) Some statutes contain powers which allow the person to whom the powers are delegated to amend other pieces of legislation, which further removes the possibility for parliamentary scrutiny—so called "Henry VIII clauses". One example is s.113(5) and (6) of the Scotland Act 1998, which delegates powers to amend other statutes. It should be noted that the Legislative and Regulatory Reform Act 2006 gives increased power to the UK government to issue legislative reform orders to amend primary legislation so as to remove "burdens" imposed by legislation, subject to certain preconditions. This wide-ranging power further removes the democratic control of Parliament over legislation.

Ultra vires and delegated legislation

Because the powers to make delegated legislation are laid down in the **1–32** parent Act of Parliament or Act of the Scottish Parliament, delegated legislation may not exceed these boundaries. Like legislation of the Scottish Parliament, delegated legislation may be challenged in court if it is ultra vires (beyond the powers) of the body to whom legislative power was delegated.

Forms of delegated legislation

1–33   The overwhelming majority of delegated legislation is made by the government. Governments issue Orders, Regulations, Rules, Schemes or Directions which are all forms of delegated legislation. Local authorities also make use of delegated legislation to create bylaws or management rules for their local areas, such as the bans on drinking in public places in Glasgow, Dundee, Aberdeen and Edinburgh and many other local authority areas in Scotland. Delegated legislation is also used by the supreme courts in Scotland to make their own procedural rules by Acts of Sederunt (Court of Session) and Acts of Adjournal (High Court of Justiciary). Some statutory bodies such as railway companies have delegated powers to make their own rules. The Privy Council[41] also holds some delegated powers including delegated power to issue Orders in Council amend the constitutions of Scottish Universities, and power to issue Orders in Council to regulate the fisheries on the Tweed and Esk Rivers in the borders of Scotland and England.[42]

1–34   Some delegated legislation must be in the form of a statutory instrument ("SI") or Scottish statutory instrument ("SSI"). If this is the case, the parent Act will say so. All Orders in Council must be in this form. The Statutory Instruments Act 1946 lays down rules for SIs, to ensure they receive some measure of scrutiny and publicity. SIs must be dated, given a unique identifying number, printed, published and sold. Depending on the parent statute, they may have to be laid before Parliament three weeks before coming into effect and in other cases a draft must be laid before Parliament. A SI may be examined by the Joint Committee on SIs of the two Houses of Parliament to ensure compliance with these rules. Although the Committee has no power to reject a SI, it may refer it to either House on a variety of grounds, including being ultra vires (beyond the powers) of its parent statute. Even if it is referred, the contents of the SI may be debated but not amended. The parent statute may provide for the SI to be voted on by either or both Houses of Parliament. The vote may be either by negative or affirmative resolution. A negative resolution allows Parliament to reject the SI, while an affirmative resolution means that the SI will only come into effect if it is approved. However, although these procedures provide a veto to Parliament, they do not provide any mechanism for amendment. Some parent statutes provide for other methods of Parliamentary scrutiny.

In the case of delegated legislation in Scotland where the parent statute is an Act of the Scottish Parliament, the Scotland Act 1998 requires that government delegated legislation takes the form of a SSI. The Scotland Act 1998 lays down 11 different regimes for parliamentary approval, depending on the subject of the delegated legislation. The different

---

[41] This body is made up of certain government ministers and senior members of the opposition and senior judges.
[42] Scotland Act 1998 s.111.

procedures call for resolutions of the Scottish Parliament and/or of both or either House of the Westminster Parliament.[43]

How to find delegated legislation

Because there is much more of it, delegated legislation is harder to locate **1–35** than Acts of Parliament. As has been mentioned, every SI and SSI has a sequential number, and it is essential to know this number. As well as the name and year, every SI and SSI has a citation which contains the name and sequential number, for example the Bankruptcy (Scotland) Regulations 2014 (SSI 2014/225). They can be found on the website of the National Archives at *http://www.legislation.gov.uk* which is the official legislation website, and by using subscription databases such as Westlaw, LexisLibrary, Justis or Lawtel.

Legislation under the royal prerogative

The Crown (the sovereign as represented by the government) has various **1–36** special law-making powers which it exercises without recourse to Parliament. These include the power to ask ministers to form a government, the power to dissolve Parliament, the power to sign treaties and declare war, and power to legislate for the colonies. Since the Constitutional Reform and Governance Act 2010, the royal prerogative on treaty-making is subject to the fact that treaties must be laid before Parliament before they can be ratified, and for Parliament to indicate its disapproval of ratification, although there is a mechanism in s.20 for treaties to be ratified even if Parliament does not approve them.

JUDICIAL PRECEDENT

The formal source of some parts of Scots law comes not from legislation **1–37** but from prior decisions of the Scottish courts (judicial precedent). In these parts of Scots law, the decisions of past cases may be binding on later courts. The major areas of Scots business law where the formal source is in case law are the law of contract (voluntary obligations),[44] the law of delict (involuntary obligations),[45] parts of criminal law,[46] the law of agency,[47] parts of the law of property,[48] parts of the law of rights in security[49] and parts of the law of trusts.[50]

It is important to draw a distinction between areas of law where judicial precedent is a formal source of law, and those areas where the formal source is statutory, but where cases are referred to court to apply

---

[43] Scotland Act 1998 s.115 and Sch.7.
[44] See Ch.4.
[45] See Ch.10.
[46] See Ch.3.
[47] See Ch.9.
[48] See Ch.11.
[49] See Ch.21.
[50] See Ch.13.

or interpret the statute. In these circumstances the case is not the formal source of law but an application of it.

Treating judicial precedent as binding rather than as persuasive (*stare decisis* or "to stand upon decisions") is a characteristic of common law systems of law and not of the civil law systems of continental Europe or of the European Court of Justice and the European Court of Human Rights. Before the Union of the Parliaments in 1707, precedent in Scotland used to be more loosely applied, so that it was only a series of identical decisions that was binding on the courts and individual cases were regarded as evidence of the law rather than as a formal source of the law. However, by the nineteenth century, the Scottish courts had adopted the English doctrine of binding precedent.

T.B. Smith in his *Short Commentary on the Law of Scotland*[51] describes judicial precedent as, "a good servant and a bad master". The doctrine can bring certainty, but there are dangers in over-reliance on precedents.

1–38   *Stare decisis* or binding precedent brings the following benefits:

(1) Going to court should not be a lottery. It accords with people's sense of justice that like cases should be treated alike.

(2) It makes for a more efficient legal system. Potential litigants can be given legal advice prior to bringing a case on the likelihood of success or failure in court, and can decide accordingly. One test case which establishes a legal precedent may allow other identical cases to be settled out of court.

(3) It provides some flexibility to the law, in enabling it to develop incrementally as society and the economy develop. For example, the delictual liability of a ginger beer manufacturer for negligence at common law was first established in the "neighbour" principle in the House of Lords case *Donoghue v Stevenson*, 1932 S.C. H.L. 31. It has been extended by later courts incrementally and by analogy to other areas such as the liability for professional negligence of a surveyor who made errors in a survey of a house instructed by a mortgage lender.[52]

Judicial precedent brings with it also certain disadvantages:

(1) A precedent may take the development of the law up a blind alley from which only new legislation can rescue it. An example of this comes from the law of occupiers' liability where the Occupiers' Liability Act 1957 and the Occupiers' Liability (Scotland) Act 1961 had to be enacted to overturn an unsatisfactory precedent from the House of Lords.

(2) Precedents can slow the development of the law if an old precedent suitable to a by-gone age has to be followed.

---

[51] T.B. Smith, *A Short Commentary on the Law of Scotland* (Edinburgh: W. Green, 1962), p.34.

[52] See *Martin v Bell Ingram*, 1986 S.C. 208, discussed in Ch.10, "Delict".

(3) In a country with a relatively small population such as Scotland, there is a lack of case law on many issues. This has led to reliance on English cases in areas where the law between England and Scotland is the same.

(4) It is sometimes hard for a court to decide when a precedent must be applied, especially where this would lead to an undesirable result. This is the case where there are conflicting precedents of equal weight. This may lead to an arbitrary decision by a court as to whether a precedent should be applied.

(5) A precedent may be hard to discover: a case may not be reported at all or be badly reported, with important issues missing from the law report. Or a case may be reported years after the case was heard.

(6) All relevant precedents must be cited to the court regardless of whether or not they have been reported. With the advent of electronic databases of case law such as Westlaw, the courts may at times be presented with too many cases, which may in the end lead to a retreat from binding precedent, as is being seen in the USA today.

When must a precedent be followed?

The European Court of Human Rights in Strasbourg and the European **1–39** Court of Justice in Luxembourg do not apply binding precedent, since their rules are not based on the common law tradition. However, if a court in Scotland makes a request to the European Court of Justice for a preliminary ruling in an issue of the interpretation of European law, the court in Scotland must apply the decision of the European Court of Justice. Also, in cases in Scotland where an issue of the interpretation of European law arises, the court in Scotland must apply precedents from the European Court of Justice.

Key concept

Not every prior case has to be followed by a later court.
The precedent must be:

- in point; and
- binding.

---

(1) In point

Not everything that judges say has to be followed. The binding element is **1–40** the ratio decidendi or reason for the decision. This is the precise issue of law (not fact) on which the case was decided. Everything else that the judge said that is not essential to the disposition of the case is obiter dicta or things said by the way, which are never binding, though they may be persuasive on later courts.

It is for the judges in the later case to determine the ratio decidendi in the earlier case. This may be difficult, as judges do not clearly signpost them as such in their judgments, and a judge may have come to the judgment by more than one route (multiple ratios). Also, different judges in an appeal case may have advanced different legal arguments in their judgments. Cases may be badly reported so that it may be difficult to ascertain the ratio.

(2) The precedent must also be binding

1–41 The issue of which court in Scotland binds which other courts in Scotland has itself been decided by precedent, and the civil courts and criminal courts form into two hierarchies.[53]

In relation to both the civil and criminal courts in Scotland, when the Supreme Court is deciding on devolution issues, its decisions are binding on the lower courts.[54]

The civil courts

1–42 Judicial precedent is strictly applied by the civil courts in Scotland. As a general rule, appellate courts bind courts of first instance, and larger courts bind smaller.

The Supreme Court

1–43 The Supreme Court replaced the House of Lords as the highest court in the UK in 2009.[55] Its role will be discussed in Ch.2, "Structure of the Scottish Legal System". Decisions of the Supreme Court in Scottish appeals bind all the civil courts of Scotland including on devolution issues and issues of compatibility of legislation and the acts of public authorities with the European Convention on Human Rights and Fundamental Freedoms and EU law. If the precedent is not a Scottish case, but is from another part of the UK, and concerns an area of law where Scots law is the same as the law applying in the earlier case, the prior decision may be binding on the later case.[56] Other Supreme Court civil appeals are persuasive only.

Before 1966, the House of Lords considered itself bound by its own prior decisions. However, in that year, the Lord Chancellor issued a Practice Direction, stating that although normally the House of Lords would continue to adhere to its prior decisions in the interests of certainty, it reserved the right to depart from its prior decisions, when it considered it right to do so. This power has been used sparingly, but was used by the House of Lords in the Scottish case of *Dick v Falkirk Burgh*.[57] This also applies to the Supreme Court.

---

[53] For more information on the civil and criminal courts in Scotland, see Ch.2, "Structure of the Scottish Legal System".
[54] Section 103 of the Scotland Act 1998. See ss.1–28 earlier in this chapter.
[55] It was created by s.40 of the Constitutional Reform Act 2005.
[56] *Glasgow Corporation v Central Land Board*, 1956 S.C. (H.L.) 1.
[57] 1976 S.C. (H.L.) 1.

The Court of Session and the Sheriff Court

Although this court is divided into the Inner House (a court of appeal) **1–44** and the Outer House (a court of first instance) it is a collegiate court which allows for the convening of a larger court to decide difficult cases. Decisions of the Supreme Court bind both the Inner House and the Outer House. A Division of the Inner House (normally three judges) is probably bound by a prior decision of either Division of the Inner House and by a court of five or more judges. A court of five or more judges can overrule a previous decision of a Division of the Inner House.

A Lord Ordinary sitting in the Outer House is bound by the Supreme Court and by a Division of the Inner House, but is not bound by a decision of another Lord Ordinary, although where prior decisions are not followed, reasons are usually given.

Sheriffs are bound by decisions of the Supreme Court in a Scottish appeal and by decisions of a Division of the Inner House of the Court of Session, but there are differing views as to whether they are bound by the decision of a Lord Ordinary in the Outer House of the Court of Session. They are certainly bound by decisions of sheriff principals in their own sheriffdoms, but not by other sheriff principals or fellow sheriffs.

Decisions of the Judicial Committee of the Privy Council on civil appeals from UK colonies are persuasive only on Scottish courts in later cases.

The criminal courts

Precedent is applied more flexibly in the criminal courts than in the civil **1–45** courts, because liberty is potentially at stake, and also because in the case of courts that go out on circuit, it was difficult to get hold of all the law reports everywhere that the court might sit.

The Supreme Court

The Supreme Court has no jurisdiction to hear appeals in Scottish **1–46** criminal matters.[58]

The High Court of Justiciary

The High Court of Justiciary like the Court of Session is a collegiate **1–47** court, which allows for larger courts to be convened, to hear appeals on difficult legal issues. The High Court of Justiciary sitting as a Court of Criminal Appeal is not bound by its former decisions, except, perhaps, those of the full court.[59] It has the power to convene a larger court to

---

[58] Supreme Court Practice Direction 12 *Criminal Proceedings*, para.12.1.6. However, the Supreme Court can hear appeals from the High Court of Justiciary on issues relating to the European Convention on Human Rights, or of compatibility of Scots criminal law with EU law, with leave to appeal from the High Court of Justiciary, failing which leave can be applied for from the Supreme Court.

[59] *Sugden v HM Advocate*, 1934 J.C. 103.

overrule its previous decisions. In *Webster v Dominick*,[60] an appeal was
made to the High Court of Justiciary sitting as a Court of Criminal
Appeal that shameless indecency should no longer be a crime in Scots law
because it contravened the European Convention on Human Rights and
Fundamental Freedoms by being too ill-defined in scope. A bench of five
judges was convened, which held that shameless indecency should no
longer be a crime in Scotland, but the offence should be redefined as
public indecency, which should be assessed not with reference to whether
the behaviour was liable to deprave and corrupt others but according to
whether, if viewed objectively, the conduct would cause offence to public
order judged against the social standards of the day. An earlier precedent
was overruled.

A decision of a single judge in the High Court of Justiciary (as a court
of trial) is bound by the High Court of Justiciary sitting as a Court of
Criminal Appeal.

The Sheriff Court

1–48 A sheriff is bound by decisions of the High Court of Justiciary sitting as a
Court of Criminal Appeal. It used to be that sheriffs were thought not to
be bound by decisions of the High Court of Justiciary as a court of trial.
However, in *Jessop v Stevenson*,[61] the High Court of Justiciary in an
appeal from the sheriff court held that sheriffs were so bound.

The Justice of the Peace Court

1–49 The Justice of the Peace Court (formerly the District Court), the lowest
criminal court in Scotland, is concerned with minor offences, and predominantly with questions of fact rather than law. The Justice of the
Peace Court is bound by decisions of the High Court of Justiciary as a
Court of Criminal Appeal, and is probably also bound by decisions of the
High Court of Justiciary as a court of trial, and possibly also the sheriff
court.[62]

How a precedent may be handled in subsequent cases

1–50 If a precedent is both in point (as regards its point of law), and binding
(as coming from a superior court) it must be followed. If either of these
elements is lacking, it need not be followed.

A court may be able to avoid having to follow a precedent by resorting
to the following:

> (1) It may be able to *distinguish* a precedent, which involves showing
> that it is not in point, perhaps because it was not fully argued in
> the earlier case.

---

[60] 2005 1 J.C. 65.
[61] 1988 J.C. 17.
[62] The fact that the predecessor of the Justice of the Peace Court, the district court is
probably bound by the sheriff court is asserted by D.M. Walker, *Scottish Legal System*,
8th edn (Edinburgh: W. Green, 2001), p.447.

(2) If there are conflicting precedents of equal authority the court may *follow* one and not follow the other.

(3) Where the precedent is both a very old one and a long time has elapsed since it was last relied on, the court may *doubt* a precedent.

(4) Where the court considers that the prior decision was made *per incuriam* (i.e. in error because all the legal issues were not fully considered), it is not regarded as binding. Judges are reluctant to take this course because it reduces the certainty of the common law.

(5) Where the court considers that a legal rule has ceased to apply because the reason for the rule no longer exists (in Latin *cessante ratio cessat ipsa lex*), the precedent is not binding. Courts are reluctant to use this reason for not following a precedent, because it reduces the certainty of the common law, and feel that it is better for Parliament to legislate for a change in the law than for them to amend the law by creatively ignoring a precedent.

The role of law reporting in judicial precedent

A system of judicial precedent depends for its efficacy on a good system **1–51** of law reporting, in order to be aware of all the precedents, and to weigh up whether they are in point. In the early law reports, such as Sinclair's Practicks (1540–1549) law reports were a few lines long and did not report the judges' words verbatim. Today cases are systematically reported both in hard copy and electronically, and are quickly available after the cases take place.

Edited series of law reports summarise the facts and the decision of the case in headnotes at the beginning of the report. They may cover the arguments of counsel before the court. They then give the opinions of the judges verbatim, and state how the case has been disposed of.

Nowadays the courts themselves report their judgments later on the day they are issued using the World Wide Web.[63] The principal edited series of law reports in Scotland are the *Session Cases*, the *Scots Law Times*, the *Scottish Civil Law Reports*, and the *Scottish Criminal Case Reports*.

INSTITUTIONAL WRITERS

Although legislation and judicial precedent are by far the most important **1–52** formal sources of Scots law, there are other less important formal sources, one of which consists of the works of certain very influential writers on Scots law. The debt that Scots law owes to these writers has

---

[63] Decisions of the Scottish courts are available on the Scottish Courts website at *http://www.scotcourts.gov.uk/search-judgments* [Accessed May 15, 2015]. Supreme Court decisions are available at *https://www.supremecourt.uk/decided-cases/* [Accessed May 15, 2015].

been referred to earlier in this chapter as part of the history and development of Scots law.[64] These writers played a big part in the creation of a modern legal system in Scotland, as they did their work during a period of rapid development of the law when it was being crafted into a modern legal system out of the mix of customary law, mediaeval writings such as the *Regiam Majestatem,* Acts of the old Scots Parliament and the decisions of the courts as published in the Practicks, added to by borrowings from Roman law. These writers are often referred to as "institutional writers" because their works were modelled on the late Roman texts they studied, and principally Justinian's *Institutes.* They are also known as authoritative writers. Most of them were judges and/or academic lawyers. Such was their influence on the courts in the nineteenth century that their works were regarded as themselves a formal source of law, rather than as a secondary source, as would be the case with a modern textbook, however eminent the author.

Whether a writer should be included among the institutional writers depends on whether his work has been treated as such by the courts, and not every work by one of these writers might so qualify, but the list would normally include the following writers and works:

(1) Sir Thomas Craig of Riccarton (*Jus Feudale,* 1603, but published in 1655, a work on property law, published after his death).

(2) Sir George Mackenzie (*The Laws and Customs of Scotland in Matters Criminal,* 1678). Mackenzie earned the nickname "Bloody Mackenzie" from his career as a criminal prosecutor.

(3) James Dalrymple, Viscount Stair (*The Institutions of the Law of Scotland,* 1681). Stair is the most influential of the institutional writers, and his work covered wide areas of civil law, including the law of obligations, property and succession. Stair had first been a lecturer at the University of Glasgow, who went on become Lord President of the Court of Session in 1671, but was forced to resign 10 years later because he refused to swear an oath recognising the supremacy of the King over the church, and fled to the Netherlands where his work was influenced by Roman law. He returned to Scotland in 1688 when William of Orange ascended the throne, and became Lord President of the Court of Session again in 1689.

(4) Andrew McDouall, Lord Bankton (*An Institute of the Laws of Scotland,* 1751).

(5) Henry Home, Lord Kames (*Principles of Equity,* 1760).

(6) John Erskine of Carnock (*Principles of the Law of Scotland,* 1754, and *An Institute of the Law of Scotland,* 1773).

(7) Baron David Hume (*Commentaries on the Law of Scotland Respecting Crimes,* 1797).

---

[64] See paras 1–08—1–10 earlier in this chapter.

(8) George Joseph Bell (*Commentaries on the Law of Scotland and on the Principles of Mercantile Jurisprudence*, 1810, and *Principles of the Law of Scotland*, 1829).

How much importance should be placed on the Institutional Writers?

In *Drew v Drew*, Lord Benholm stated: **1–53**

"When on any point of law I find Stair's opinion uncontradicted, I look upon that opinion as ascertaining the law of Scotland."[65]

T.B. Smith, writing much later, evaluated the influence of the institutional writers as, "approximately equal to that of a Division of the Inner House of the Court of Session".[66]

In any event, whatever the level of their authority might have been, it is now declining steadily with the passage of time, as the points of law for which their work was authoritative are gradually affected by legislation, or by developments in case law.

Legal writers of varying levels of authority are cited today in court and referred to in judicial opinions. However, it is important to bear in mind that modern academic writings on law are never more than secondary sources of legal rules, i.e. they are *about* the law rather than *being* the law.

CUSTOM

Before the Roman occupation of Scotland, law was largely customary **1–54** and different rules will have applied in different parts of Scotland in the period before Scotland became one kingdom. Gradually customary laws were written down in works such as the *Regiam Majestatem*. In the period before the system of binding precedent was adopted in Scotland in the nineteenth century, custom was a major formal source of the law. The customs among merchants were a very important formal source of commercial law in mediaeval times.

Nowadays, custom is still regarded as a source of law, although it has diminished greatly in importance, as it is steadily replaced by legislation and by judicial precedent.

Some customs are regarded as already being part of the law, and these customs do not need to be proved in court. These customs are more a historical source than a formal source of the legal rule, as they will have been enacted into legislation or can be found in a judicial precedent. For example, the legal rights of a spouse and children to inherit part of the deceased's estate come from customary law but have been legislated for in the Succession (Scotland) Act 1964. Also, much of the common law of

---

[65] (1870) 9 M. 163 at 167.
[66] T.B. Smith, *A Short Commentary on the Law of Scotland* (Edinburgh: W. Green, 1962), p.32.

leases in Scotland comes from customary law, but is now found in decisions of the courts.

In cases where no legislation or judicial precedent or institutional writing can be cited as the formal source of a legal rule, it is possible to use custom as a formal source of law. To do so, the custom must be proved to the satisfaction of the court. It has to be proved that the custom:

(1) has been acquiesced in for a long though undefined period of time as representing the law;
(2) is definite and certain;
(3) is fair and reasonable; and
(4) is consistent with legal principle. In *Bruce v Smith*,[67] landlords in Shetland failed to prove a local custom by which they claimed to be entitled by customary law to one-third of the caaing whales killed by their tenants on the foreshore as the custom, though it did appear to exist, failed the test of reasonableness.

Custom can also be used as a source of contractual rules that have not been expressly provided for in the contract, though in this sense it is not a formal source of law.

EQUITY

1–55 Scotland never had a system of equity separate from law as was the case in England, where separate courts of equity existed at one time. In England, separate courts of equity had developed from the fourteenth century to counteract the growing rigidity and lack of remedies inherent in the common law, and served the purpose of plugging gaps in the common law. Eventually the two sets of remedies could be claimed in the same court. Although Scotland never had a separate system of equity, as in England, parts of the common law of Scotland owe their origin to equitable considerations, an example being the constraints on the use of specific implement as a contractual remedy.[68]

Also, the Inner House of the Court of Session and the High Court of Justiciary both have an extraordinary equitable jurisdiction called the *nobile officium* (noble office) to fill in the gaps in the law so as to provide a remedy if one is not otherwise available. These powers are rarely used and must not be used to defeat the intention of Parliament. The Inner House has used its powers in relation to public trusts, if the purposes have to be varied and there is no other means of doing so. The High Court of Justiciary has a declaratory power to declare behaviour which was not hitherto regarded as criminal, to be so. A modern example is *Khaliq v HM Advocate*,[69] in which the High Court of Justiciary declared

---

[67] (1890) 17 R. 1000.
[68] See *Moore v Paterson* (1881) 9 R. 337.
[69] 1984 J.C. 23.

the sale of glue-sniffing kits to children to be a criminal act, as being the "wilful supply of potentially noxious substances".

Reminder on formal sources of law

In this book, the student of business law will be introduced to a range of **1–56** areas of substantive business law. When students are called on to write about the law in essays and examinations, it is essential always to give authority for every assertion about the law. Where the student is speaking about a legal rule, the formal source must be given, which will normally be a piece of legislation or a case. Students must remember that a textbook, however helpful, is not a primary source of law, and should only be referred to if the textbook writer gave a useful insight that is original and worth referring to in its own right. A textbook should never be referred to as a lazy substitute for a reference to a primary source.

▼ CHAPTER SUMMARY

INTRODUCTION TO LAW

(1) A working knowledge of key areas of business law is important for **1–57** business managers, as decisions with legal implications are taken all the time in business. Accountants also need a good knowledge of business law, as they often have to give advice to business managers which includes legal issues.

(2) Legal and non-legal rules often appear similar. It is essential to be able to distinguish between them, as only legal rules provide for enforcement if they are breached.

HISTORY AND DEVELOPMENT OF SCOTS LAW

(1) The two biggest influences on Scots law over the centuries have been English law and Roman law. As a result Scots law is a mixed system between the common law and civil law traditions.

(2) The feudal system of land ownership began in Scotland in the middle ages and continued up to the year 2000.

(3) Some modern commercial law concepts trace their origin to the law merchant in mediaeval times. These include bills of exchange and marine insurance.

(4) The Court of Session was founded in 1532 as a permanent civil court.

(5) The Union of the Crowns took place in 1603, when James VI of Scotland became James I of England.

(6) The General Register of Sasines was founded in 1617 to provide a central register of transactions relating to land. It has only recently been replaced by a new system of land registration.

(7) The High Court of Justiciary was founded in 1672.

(8) The Union of the Parliaments took place in 1707. The Act of Union guaranteed that separate Scottish courts should be retained and that Scots private law could not be altered, "except for the evident utility of the subjects within Scotland".

(9)   The period roughly from 1600–1830 was a period of development of Scots law through the influence of the institutional writers, (authoritative writers) when Roman law concepts were received into Scots law.

(10) After 1800, the major influence on Scots law was from English law.

(11) European legislation has been an important source of law since the UK joined the European Community (now the EU) in 1972.

(12) Since the Scotland Act 1998, Scotland has again had a separate Parliament, with power to legislate within a defined area of devolved competence, and separate government which operates within its area of devolved competence.

CATEGORIES OF LAW

(1)   Public law and Private law: Public law regulates the relationship between the State and the citizen, while private law regulates the relationship between citizens.

(2)   Civil law and Criminal law: Civil cases are heard in the civil courts and criminal cases are heard in the criminal courts.

(3)   Civil law and Common law: Civil systems of law are developed from Roman law, while common law systems are developed from English law.

(4)   Common law and Statute law: Statute law = legislation. Common law consists of the legal rules that stem from the other formal sources of law: judicial precedent, the institutional writers, custom and equity.

THE FORMAL SOURCES OF SCOTS LAW

They are, in the following order:

(1) Legislation.
(2) Judicial Precedent.
(3) The Institutional Writers.
(4) Custom.
(5) Equity.

LEGISLATION

(1)   Legislation may be made by the EU, by the UK Parliament, it may be made under the Royal Prerogative, it may be made by the Scottish Parliament, and delegated legislation can be made by bodies using powers delegated by Parliament.

EUROPEAN LEGISLATION

(1)   There are four types of European legislation that have binding force: Treaties (primary legislation), Regulations, Directives and Decisions (secondary legislation).

THE UK PARLIAMENT

(1) The UK Parliament is a sovereign parliament and can enact legislation on anything it likes.

(2) A Bill has to go through five stages in both Houses in order to become an Act: First Reading, Second Reading, Committee Stage, Report Stage, and Third Reading. It can then receive the Royal Assent and become an Act.

THE SCOTTISH PARLIAMENT

(1) The Scottish Parliament holds devolved power to pass Acts of the Scottish Parliament in areas of competence not reserved to the UK Parliament.

(2) A Bill goes through the following stages in the Scottish Parliament in order to become an Act: It first must be scrutinised to ensure it is within the Scottish Parliament's legislative competence. Stage 1—the Bill goes to the lead committee, and the main points of the Bill and the committee's report are debated in Parliament. Stage 2—there is a detailed consideration of the Bill by committee and a vote. Stage 3—the Bill is presented to the full Parliament for final consideration and a vote. Four weeks must elapse before can then receive the Royal Assent and become an Act to allow for checking of legislative competence.

(3) Acts of the Scottish Parliament can be challenged in court for exceeding their legislative competence.

DELEGATED LEGISLATION

(1) Delegated (or subordinate) legislation is made by a body other than Parliament under powers delegated to it by Parliament in a parent statute.

(2) Delegated legislation can be challenged in court if it has exceeded the powers delegated to it (ultra vires).

LEGISLATION UNDER THE ROYAL PREROGATIVE

(1) The Crown holds certain residual powers to legislate.

JUDICIAL PRECEDENT

(1) The formal source of parts of Scots law is judicial precedent, i.e. certain prior decisions of the courts must be followed in a later case.

(2) For a later court to have to follow an earlier decision, the previous case must be: (a) in point; and (b) binding.

(3) The ratio decidendi (reason for the decision) is the exact point of law in the previous case on which the decision was based.

(4)   Obiter dicta (things said by the judge by the way) are other remarks
      that were not part of the ratio decidendi and therefore do not bind the
      later court.

INSTITUTIONAL WRITERS

(1)   The works of a select group of writers on law who wrote during a
      seminal period for the development of Scots law between 1600–1820
      which are still regarded as being a formal source of law.
(2)   The authority of these writers is diminishing over time as the legal
      content of their works is gradually changed by legislation or devel-
      opments in case law.
(3)   The works of modern writers are not regarded as being a source of law.

CUSTOM

(1)   A custom can be regarded as a formal source of law:

      (a) if it has been regarded as law for a long period;
      (b) if it is definite and certain;
      (c) if it is fair and reasonable; and
      (d) if it is consistent with legal principle.

EQUITY

(1)   Equitable principles can be found in Scots law, e.g. the remedy of
      specific implement.
(2)   The Court of Session and the High Court of Justiciary have an
      extraordinary equitable jurisdiction (*nobile officium* or noble office) to
      fill in gaps in the law, which they use sparingly, and the High Court of
      Justiciary has a declaratory power to declare immoral conduct to be a
      crime.

? QUICK QUIZ

-   Why is it important that a business or accountancy student
    should know something about business law?
-   What is the essential difference between public law and private
    law?
-   Explain the procedure for the enactment of a public Bill in the
    UK Parliament.
-   If you wanted to look up a section of an Act of the UK Parlia-
    ment, where would you look?
-   What are the provisions in the Scotland Act 1998 which fix the
    boundaries of the legislative competence of the Scottish
    Parliament?

- Name one new area of legislative competence granted to the Scottish Parliament in the Scotland Act 2012.
- What role do the UK Parliament and the Scottish Parliament play in relation to delegated legislation?
- What are the advantages and disadvantages of having a system of binding precedent?
- In what circumstances must a later court follow the decision of an earlier court in Scotland?
- To what extent are the institutional writers still of relevance to the decisions of the courts today?
- In what circumstances is custom regarded as a formal source of Scots law?
- Explain what is meant by the *nobile officium* of the Court of Session and High Court of Justiciary.
- When writing about the law in an essay or an examination, you have to give the formal source of a legal rule. Why would it not normally be correct to refer to a textbook as your authority?

FURTHER READING

➤ A book that covers most of the material in this chapter but in much more depth, and is available in an up-to-date edition is H. MacQueen, R. White and I. Willock, *Scottish Legal System*, 5th edn (Edinburgh: Bloomsbury Professional, 2013). See also D. Walker, *The Scottish Legal System*, 8th edn (Edinburgh: W. Green, 2001).

➤ The formal sources of Scots law are covered in depth in the contributions of R.B. Ferguson, G. Maher and T.B. Smith, and D. Sellar, and the historical sources are covered in depth by the contributions of T.D. Fergus and G. Maher in the *Stair Memorial Encyclopaedia: The Law of Scotland,* Vol. 22 (The Law Society of Scotland/Butterworths, Edinburgh, 1987) (and updates).

RELEVANT WEBLINKS

➤ The UK Parliament: *http://www.parliament.uk* [Accessed May 15, 2015].
  You can learn about how Parliament works on this website, find out what Bills are before Parliament, and track their progress.
➤ The Scottish Parliament: *http://www.scottish.parliament.uk* [Accessed May 15, 2015].
  This site is a similar resource to the UK Parliament site.
➤ Decisions of the Scottish Courts: *http://www.scotcourts.gov.uk/search-judgments* [Accessed May 15, 2015].
➤ Decisions of the Supreme Court: *https://www.supremecourt.uk/decided-cases/* [Accessed May 15, 2015].

> The European Convention of Human Rights and Fundamental Freedoms: *http://www.coe.int* [Accessed May 15, 2015]. This link takes you to the Council of Europe website, where you can find the text of the Convention.

> The European Union: *http://europa.eu* [Accessed May 15, 2015]. This is a portal that allows you to learn about the EU and its various institutions, and to access European legislation.

> Legislation: website offered by the National Archives: *http://www.legislation.gov.uk* [Accessed May 15, 2015].
This database gives updated texts of most statutes of the UK Parliament, the Scottish Parliament, the National Assembly for Wales and the Northern Ireland Assembly plus unamended SIs and SSIs, and SIs (or equivalent) from the other regional assemblies.

Chapter 2   Structure of the Scotttish Legal System

ANDREW R. WILSON[1]

▶ CHAPTER OVERVIEW

This chapter is concerned with the essential composition of the legal 2–01
system of Scotland. It starts by detailing the two systems of our civil and
criminal courts. The chapter then outlines the tribunals system and
publicly appointed ombudsmen. It closes by summarising the personnel
working in the Scottish legal system: the two legal professions; the judiciary; and the law officers.

✓ OUTCOMES

At the end of this chapter you should be able to: 2–02

- ✓   appreciate the difference between civil and criminal courts;
- ✓   identify the different courts;
- ✓   understand the differences in jurisdiction between the various courts;
- ✓   identify and understand the route of appeals in civil and in criminal cases;
- ✓   understand the nature and function of administrative tribunals;
- ✓   identify and understand the nature and function of ombudsmen; and
- ✓   identify the different aspects and key offices of the Scottish legal professions.

INTRODUCTION

Scotland has its own system of courts legal professions, judges and law 2–03
officers. These existed prior to the Treaty of Union with England in 1707,
have been maintained since and, for the most part, have developed
separately from the other jurisdictions in the UK.[2] It is a process of

---

[1] Editor of *SCOLAG Legal Journal*.
[2] The UK has three separate jurisdictions whose laws and legal systems vary from one
another: England & Wales; Northern Ireland; and Scotland.

development which continues today. At the time of writing a number of changes to the courts, tribunals and judiciary in Scotland are due to be brought into effect. Where these are significant they are included to ensure readers will be aware of imminent changes.

Jurisdictions

2–04 Any court may only hear cases that fall within its jurisdiction, that is to say, within the limits of the power it may exercise. Jurisdiction may be limited by geographical boundaries, subject matter of the legal issue in the case or the type or size of order the particular court can award.[3]

In Scotland the civil courts are empowered to hear civil law cases following civil court procedure. Similarly, criminal cases are a matter for the criminal courts following criminal procedure. Although at times they bear the same names and can even be presided over by the same judges it is important to appreciate the difference between criminal and civil law,[4] the different courts, the procedures they will follow and the powers they exercise.

Fact and law

2–05 A further distinction it is important to appreciate is the difference between fact and law. In both civil and criminal cases the differing parties put forward arguments of fact and of law. They present evidence as to the facts in the case and set out legal arguments on their interpretation of the rules of the law with which the case is concerned. What the true facts of a case are is decided by the jury if there is one, or the judge if there is no jury. However, decisions of law are always a matter for the judge in the case.

THE CIVIL COURT SYSTEM

2–06 Civil law covers a wide range of legal issues. These relate largely to legal issues of rights and duties between persons, as opposed to criminal matters which are between a person and the State. It is important to note here that in legal terms "person" means any one or thing with legal personality—that may be an individual, a company or other legal entity. Some writers may distinguish between "natural legal persons"—i.e. individual human beings—and "artificial legal persons" such as limited companies, trusts and unincorporated associations.

In civil cases the person bringing the action is called the pursuer. The person against whom the action is brought is the defender. Different terms are used in other jurisdictions, for example in English courts the parties are termed "claimant" and "defendant" respectively.

---

[3] Amounts, such as maximum prison terms but particularly fines or financial limits, will change over time. They are almost always set in secondary legislation, which is easier and faster to draft and enact.

[4] See "Categories of law" above at para.1–15.

At present the civil courts of Scotland are the Sheriff Court, the Court of Session and the Supreme Court of the United Kingdom. From early 2016 the Sheriff Appeal Court will also operate as a civil court. Both the Sheriff Court and the Court of Session are further divided into different jurisdictions and procedures. The Sheriff Court includes small claims, summary cause procedure, and ordinary cause procedure (small claims and summary cause are due to be replaced by simple procedure, expected to be operating from Spring of 2016). The Court of Session comprises the Outer House and the Inner House.

Key Concepts

Civil law relates to legal rights and duties between persons.
Person means any one or thing with legal personality.
A pursuer is the person who brings a civil action.
A defender is the person against whom an action is brought.
Privative jurisdiction: cases which can only be brought in a particular court.

Sheriff Court

The major part of civil judicial business in Scotland is conducted in the sheriff court. It is the only inferior court exercising first instance jurisdiction in civil matters. The sheriff courts exercise a civil jurisdiction within their respective territories which is very wide, being almost concurrent with that of the Court of Session. **2–07**

The sheriff court can be defined according to the geographical area, persons and subject matter involved in the particular case.

Organisation

Organisationally, Scotland is divided into six sheriffdoms. They are: **2–08**

- Glasgow and Strathkelvin.
- Grampian Highland and Islands.
- Lothian and Borders.
- North Strathclyde.
- South Strathclyde, Dumfries and Galloway.
- Tayside, Central and Fife.

Each is presided over by its own sheriff principal. Sheriffdoms are generally further divided into districts, each of which is served by a particular sheriff court. There are currently 39 sheriff courts in Scotland.[5]

---

[5] As of February 1, 2015: the Sheriff Court Districts Amendment Order 2013 (SSI 2013/152)

Jurisdiction

2–09 The civil jurisdiction of the sheriff court has been repeatedly extended over the years. It can be defined by three criteria: location; persons; and subject matter. The first of these is simply the territory of the particular sheriffdom (not just the particular sheriff court district).

Persons

2–10 For the court to hear a case it must have jurisdiction over the defender (*actor sequitur forum rei*—the pursuer follows the court of the defender). The sheriff court will have jurisdiction over the defender if they:

- are resident or domiciled within the sheriffdom;
- carry on business in the sheriffdom; or
- own heritable property in the sheriffdom which is the subject of the action.

Subject matter

2–11 As well as the territory of the sheriffdom and persons within it, the jurisdiction of the court may be determined by the subject of the case:

- In cases concerning a contract, the court for the place the contract is to be performed has jurisdiction.
- In cases relating to delict, the court for the place where the harmful event occurred has jurisdiction.
- In ordinary cause cases, the sheriff has discretion whether to remit the cause to the Court of Session.
- Certain actions are reserved to the Court of Session, e.g. applications for judicial review, actions for reduction, petitions for winding up of a company if the paid-up capital exceeds £120,000.[6]
- Certain actions are reserved to specialist courts, e.g. questions over the right to bear a coat of arms are reserved to the Court of the Lord Lyon.

The sheriff court's jurisdiction over actions for debt or damages is without financial limit. In such cases where the value does not exceed £5,000[7] the jurisdiction of the court is privative, that is to say such an action must be brought in the sheriff court and cannot be raised in the Court of Session.[8]

---

[6] Insolvency Act 1986 s.120.
[7] The Sheriff Courts (Scotland) Act 1971 (Privative Jurisdiction and Summary Cause) Order 2007 (SSI 2007/507) art.2.
[8] This limit is due to be increased to £100,000 by s.39 of the Courts Reform (Scotland) Act 2014 (not yet in force).

Procedures

There is generally no jury in civil cases in the sheriff court and trial is **2–12** usually by a sheriff sitting alone. The only exception is in cases where an employee seeks damages against their employer in respect of injuries sustained in the course of their employment.

There are three types of proceeding conducted in the sheriff court. The difference between them is largely the financial value of the cause.

Ordinary cause

Ordinary cause procedure is not a distinct process defined in statute. **2–13** Rather, it is the standard form of process and procedure carried out in any civil case brought in the sheriff court which cannot be taken as a summary cause.

The jurisdiction of the sheriff court is very wide both in terms of the cases it can hear and the powers it can exercise. Actions brought before the court cover a wide range of activities including repayment of debt, claims for damages, actions in bankruptcy, implementation of a contract, orders relating to parenting, separation, divorce and adoption. Some will involve complex issues and important points of law. In ordinary cause cases the sheriff has discretion whether to remit the action to the Court of Session.

Summary cause

Summary cause procedure was introduced to simplify and speed up court **2–14** actions brought in respect of relatively small amounts of money. It is applicable to any civil action for payment of money not exceeding £5,000[9] (exclusive of interest and expenses owed on the subject amount) and actions for implement of an obligation or the recovery of heritable or moveable property (unless there is an alternative or additional crave for payment of a sum exceeding £5,000).

A summary cause action does not normally involve written pleadings and evidence led at the hearing is not recorded. In undefended actions for payment the parties are not required to appear in court. A summary cause action may be raised by any person but most often actions are raised by commercial organisations, public sector creditors such as local authorities and public utilities, and debt recovery agencies.

Small claims

Small debt cause or "small claim" is a process used for a summary action **2–15** where the value does not exceed £3,000.[10] It is designed to be a simple process that is less formal and easier for non-lawyers to access. It is intended to encourage the parties to appear on their own behalf rather

---

[9] As per the Sheriff Courts (Scotland) Act 1971 (Privative Jurisdiction and Summary Cause) Order 2007 (SSI 2007/507) art.3.

[10] Small Claims (Scotland) Order 1988 art.2 (as amended by the Small Claims (Scotland) Amendment Order 2007 (SSI 2007/496)).

than being represented by a lawyer and, consequently, legal aid is not available to pursue or defend a small claim. Further to this end, only limited expenses may be claimed in respect of a small claim (a maximum of £150 where the value of the claim is £1,500 or less; or 10 per cent of the value if the claim exceeds £1,500).[11]

The Scottish Courts Service produces a series of guidance notes on small claims which are available on its website.[12]

Imminent change: simple procedure

2–16 Both small debt cause and summary cause procedure are due to be replaced by a single procedure. This will be simple procedure which will apply to actions of a value not exceeding £5,000.[13] The change is expected to take effect in early 2016. From then on sheriff courts will operate just two procedures—simple and ordinary.

Appeals

2–17 There are two routes of appeal from a decision of the sheriff court. Which route is taken will depend on the type of procedure under which the case was heard. The judgment of a sheriff may be appealed to the sheriff principal unless excluded by statute. However, if the case is not a summary cause then appeal may either be made to the sheriff principal, from whom appeal lies to the Court of Session, or be made directly to the Inner House. In most instances appeals will first be made to the sheriff principal as it presents a speedier and less expensive option.

Imminent change: Sheriff Appeals Court

2–18 The previous two routes for appeals from the sheriff are due to be replaced by a single route to the Sheriff Appeal Court.[14] This is due to start hearing appeals in criminal cases in late 2015 and in civil cases from early 2016.

The Court of Session

2–19 Apart from cases in which the sheriff court has sole jurisdiction or where the Court of Session has privative jurisdiction, the pursuer has a choice of initiating his claim in the appropriate sheriff court or in the Court of Session. The Court of Session holds jurisdiction over the whole of Scotland. Accordingly, all persons ordinarily resident in Scotland, businesses based in Scotland and contractual and delictual activity carried out in Scotland fall within the court's jurisdiction. The court also exercises the equitable power of *nobile officium* whereby, in exceptional

---

[11] Small Claims (Scotland) Order 1988 art.4 (as amended by SSI 2007/496).
[12] *http://www.scotcourts.gov.uk/rules-and-practice/guidance-notes/small-claim-guidance-notes* [Accessed May 15, 2015].
[13] Courts Reform (Scotland) Act 2014 s.72 (not yet in force)
[14] Courts Reform (Scotland) Act 2014 ss.46–62 (not yet in force).

circumstances, the court may fulfil the objects of justice by providing a remedy where none otherwise exists in law.

The Court of Session is Scotland's supreme civil court. It sits in Parliament House, in Edinburgh. It has extensive power to regulate its own practice and procedure which it does by Acts of Sederunt, a form of secondary legislation.

The court is both a court of first instance and an appellate court. For the purposes of hearing cases, the court is divided into the Outer House and the Inner House.

Outer House

The Outer House of the Court of Session is solely a court of first instance **2–20** in which the Lord Ordinary, the judge, sits alone or in some cases with a civil jury of 12 persons (e.g. in defamation cases).[15] It hears cases on practically every area of civil law including, for example, those dealt with in subsequent chapters of this book including contract, company law, delict and property. As well as disputed cases the court considers many uncontested petitions of an administrative nature such as the appointment of new trustees or the winding up of a company.

Appeal from a decision of a Lord Ordinary may be made to the Inner House of the Court of Session. Appeals are rarely made on points of fact; most usually they are on points of law only.

Inner House

The main task of the Inner House is to sit as an appeal court, although in **2–21** a small range of cases it may act as a court of first instance.[16] The Inner House is divided into the First and Second Division. The divisions are of equal authority and presided over by the Lord President and Lord Justice-Clerk respectively. Each division is made up of six judges. When the pressure of business demands it, which is increasingly frequently, an Extra Division of three judges will sit.

Generally the court will sit in basic quorum with a bench of three judges. However, if a case is particularly important or if it is necessary to consider a previous decision of the court then a larger bench of five or more may be convened.

Appeal against a decision of the Inner House may be made to the Supreme Court of the United Kingdom.

Supreme Court of the United Kingdom

Historically, the House of Lords formed the highest civil court for all **2–22** three UK jurisdictions, a function which embodied an ancient right of ultimate appeal to Parliament that justice be done. However, from October 1, 2009 the appellate jurisdiction of the House of Lords and the

---

[15] Court of Session Act 1988 s.11.
[16] For example, "special cases" where parties agree as to the facts and the court considers solely a question of law, or petitions to the *nobile officium*.

devolution jurisdiction of the Judicial Committee of the Privy Council both transferred to a new Supreme Court of the United Kingdom.[17] The establishment of the new court created a clear separation of powers between the legislature and the judiciary for the first time in British constitutional history.

Leave to appeal, that is permission from the court, is not normally required for Scottish appeals which may proceed directly to the Supreme Court provided that two Scottish counsels have certified the reasonableness of the appeal. If the case originated in the sheriff court then an appeal to the Supreme Court can only be on a point of law.[18] This position will however soon change when a requirement will be introduced for an appellant to have either the leave of the Inner House or of the Supreme Court in order to appeal to the Supreme Court.[19]

The Court is comprised of 12 judges,[20] who are Justices of the Supreme Court of the United Kingdom, and by Royal Warrant are accorded the courtesy title of "Lord" or "Lady". They are appointed by the monarch on the advice of the Prime Minister who receives recommendations from a selection commission convened by the Lord Chancellor[21] (an office which is no longer judicial[22] but held by the Secretary of State for Justice). Qualification for appointment is to have held high judicial office for at least two years or to have had right of audience in the superior courts for at least 15 years.[23] Of the 12 Justices, two are normally appointed from Scotland and one from Northern Ireland. Generally both of the Scottish Justices will sit on an appeal from Scotland. The Supreme Court usually sits as a panel of five Justices, although in more significant cases a larger number may be convened. The minimum quorum is three, and to be duly constituted in its proceedings the Court must consist of an uneven number of Justices.[24]

In addition to its civil law jurisdiction the Supreme Court serves a constitutional function in respect of devolved powers under the Scotland Acts 1998 and 2012.[25] Of such cases, most have related to the requirement that the devolved powers are exercised in compliance with rights protected under the Human Rights Act 1998. This has had an impact on Scots criminal cases in that such devolved functions include most of our criminal law, policing, prisons and the system of criminal prosecutions.

---

[17] Constitutional Reform Act 2005 ss.23 and 40.
[18] Court of Session Act 1988 s.32(5).
[19] Courts Reform (Scotland) Act 2014 s.117 (not yet in force), which will amend the Court of Session Act 1988 s.40.
[20] Constitutional Reform Act 2005 s.23(2).
[21] Constitutional Reform Act 2005 s.26.
[22] Constitutional Reform Act 2005 ss.2–22.
[23] Constitutional Reform Act 2005 s.25.
[24] Constitutional Reform Act 2005 s.42.
[25] Constitutional Reform Act 2005 s.40(4).

Other courts

As mentioned above, there are also a number of specialist Scottish courts 2–23
which exercise jurisdiction in specified areas of civil law. The best known
of these is probably the Children's Hearings system, which hears a range
of civil and criminal matters relating to children. However, below is an
outline of the specialist courts more relevant to businesses or corporations in Scotland.

Scottish Land Court

The Scottish Land Court's jurisdiction is set firmly within the context of 2–24
Scottish farming. It has authority to resolve a range of disputes, including
between landlords and tenants in agriculture and crofting. The court is
based in Edinburgh, but holds hearings throughout Scotland.

Lands Tribunal for Scotland

The Lands Tribunal for Scotland has statutory power to deal with var- 2–25
ious specific types of dispute involving land or property. Its main areas of
work include: tenants' rights to purchase their public sector houses;
disputed compensation for compulsory purchase of land or loss in value
of land caused by public works; and valuations for rating on non-
domestic premises. The functions of the Tribunal are due to be transferred into the reformed Scottish Tribunals in due course.[26]

Court of the Lord Lyon

No armorial bearings (more commonly known as a coat of arms) may be 2–26
used in Scotland unless they are on record in the Public Register of all
Arms and Bearings in Scotland. The Lord Lyon King of Arms has jurisdiction on questions of heraldry and may grant arms to Scottish people,
businesses or organisations. The court administers the Public Register of
All Arms and Bearings in Scotland. Appeal from a decision of the court
lies with the Court of Session.

THE CRIMINAL COURT SYSTEM

Criminal law is concerned with the determination of guilt and punish- 2–27
ment for conduct that is outlawed by the State. While civil law deals with
the legal relationships between persons, criminal law is part of public law
and provides a body of rules of proper behaviour for persons: both
individuals and corporations. Further examination of criminal law and
the aspects of it most relevant to business can be found in Ch.3, "Business
Regulation".

 Criminal prosecutions in Scotland are almost exclusively brought on
behalf of the State by the Crown Office and Procurator Fiscal Service

---

[26] Tribunals (Scotland) Act 2014 s.27 and Sch.1 (not yet in force)

either in the name of the Lord Advocate or local procurator fiscal. The person prosecuted for a crime is termed the accused or the pannel.

The criminal courts of Scotland are the Justice of the Peace Court, Sheriff Court and the High Court of Justiciary. These are due to be joined, from late 2015, by a new Sheriff Appeal Court.[27] Both the Sheriff Court and the High Court of Justiciary are further divided into different jurisdictions and procedures. The Sheriff Court may try summary or solemn cases. The High Court of Justiciary sits both as a trial court of the most serious crimes and as the ultimate court of criminal appeal.

Criminal jurisdiction is divided into two: summary and solemn. Summary trials are heard and determined by a judge, sheriff or justice of the peace sitting alone. Solemn cases, however, are tried by a judge or sheriff and a jury of 15 persons. In the case of statutory offences the legislation may specify whether the offence is to be tried summarily, on indictment or either way. Most common law crimes may be tried by either procedure. Except for those crimes which are privative to the High Court, the choice of procedure and court is made by the prosecution according to the seriousness of the case and the penalty sought.

Which court tries a criminal case will depend upon where it is alleged to have been committed, the seriousness of the crime and the corresponding severity of the punishment appropriate.

Key Concepts

Criminal law is concerned with determining guilt and punishment for conduct outlawed by the State.
Criminal jurisdiction is divided into **summary** and **solemn**.
Except for crimes privative to the High Court, the choice of procedure and court is made by the prosecution according to the seriousness of the case and the penalty sought.

The Justice of the Peace Court

2–28 The Justice of the Peace Court ("JP court") is the lowest in the hierarchy of criminal courts and deals only with summary cases. There are currently 34 JP courts across Scotland. Coming under the authority of the relevant sheriff principal and administered by the Scottish Courts Service,[28] they replaced the system of district courts which were administered by local councils, a move which unified the administration of Scotland's courts and ensures clear separation and independence from other arms of the State.

Justice of the Peace Courts are generally presided over by a Justice of the Peace ("JP") sitting alone or as a bench of three.[29] JPs are lay judges

---

[27] Courts Reform (Scotland) Act 2014 ss.46–62 (not yet in force).
[28] Criminal Proceedings etc. (Reform) (Scotland) Act 2007 ss.59–66.
[29] Criminal Procedure (Scotland) Act 1995 s.6(2).

not lawyers and are assisted on points of law and procedure by a legally qualified clerk to the court.[30] On the advice of the relevant sheriff principal the Scottish Ministers may appoint a legally qualified stipendiary magistrate to sit in the JP Court.[31] To date, however, Glasgow and Strathkelvin is the only sheriffdom to have appointed stipendiary magistrates and the office is due to soon be abolished as part of the wider reforms of the courts and summary justice.[32]

The jurisdiction of the JP court is primarily the area of the sheriff court district within which it is situated but extends to the entire sheriffdom.[33] The JP court may grant warrants and in sentencing may make orders as well as impose fines up to level 4 on the standard scale (£2,500)[34] or a period of imprisonment up to a maximum of 60 days.[35] A JP court may impose a community payback order with one or more requirements in respect of offender supervision, compensation, residence, conduct, and unpaid work or other activity.[36] A stipendiary magistrate, on the other hand, may exercise the same sentencing powers as a sheriff in summary sitting.[37]

In part because of the limits on sentencing powers, the JP court deals only with the most minor of crimes. However, prosecutions for more serious crimes are also precluded from being tried in the JP court and are restricted to the sheriff court or to the High Court of Justiciary.[38]

Appeal from the JP court, either against sentence or conviction, lies with the High Court of Justiciary sitting as a Court of Appeal.[39] This is due to change in late 2015 when the newly established Sheriff Appeal Court will assume jurisdiction for all appeals relating to all summary criminal proceedings from both the JP court and the sheriff court.[40]

Sheriff Court

The sheriff court has a criminal jurisdiction to hear both summary and **2–29** solemn cases, and is the busiest of the criminal courts. Its criminal jurisdiction extends throughout the sheriffdom but prosecutions for a number of serious crimes are reserved to the High Court of Justiciary.

Summary procedure

In summary cases the sheriff sits alone and decides both points of law and **2–30** questions of fact. In addition to a full range of statutory orders available to him, the sentencing power of a sheriff when sitting summarily extends

---

[30] Criminal Proceedings etc. (Reform) (Scotland) Act 2007 s.63(3), (4) and (5).
[31] Criminal Proceedings etc. (Reform) (Scotland) Act 2007 s.74.
[32] Courts Reform (Scotland) Act 2014 s.128 (not yet in force).
[33] Criminal Proceedings etc. (Reform) (Scotland) Act 2007 s.62(1).
[34] Criminal Procedure (Scotland) Act 1995 s.225.
[35] Criminal Procedure (Scotland) Act 1995 s.7(6).
[36] Criminal Procedure (Scotland) Act 1995 s.227A(5).
[37] Criminal Procedure (Scotland) Act 1995 s.7(5).
[38] Criminal Procedure (Scotland) Act 1995 s.7(4) and (8).
[39] Criminal Procedure (Scotland) Act 1995 s.175.
[40] Courts Reform (Scotland) Act 2014 s.118 (not yet in force).

to imposing fines of up to £10,000[41] or a term of imprisonment of up to 12 months,[42] although sentence for statutory offences may be lower.

Solemn procedure

2–31 Solemn procedure is reserved for more serious offences. It is more costly, more time consuming and imposes harsher penalties. In solemn cases the sheriff sits with a jury of 15 people drawn from the local community. The role of the sheriff is to preside over the court and act as a judge of law, whereas the jury alone decides questions of fact.

Upon conviction by solemn procedure a sheriff may impose a custodial sentence of up to five years' imprisonment,[43] or a fine for any amount, even in excess of any limit specified for a statutory offence.[44] In addition, if a sheriff considers his powers to be inadequate in a particular case he may refer the case to the High Court for sentencing.

In criminal appeals there is no role for the sheriff principal; in criminal law he has the same status as any other sheriff. Appeal from the sheriff court, against sentence or verdict, lies with the High Court of Justiciary sitting as a Court of Appeal. It is planned that from late 2015 the Sheriff Appeal Court will assume jurisdiction for all summary criminal appeals; appeal in solemn procedure cases will still lie with the High Court of Justiciary.

High Court of Justiciary

2–32 The High Court of Justiciary is Scotland's supreme criminal court. It has jurisdiction over the whole of Scotland and over all crimes, unless expressly excluded by statute. It sits as a trial court and as a court of appeal as well as having a supervisory jurisdiction over inferior courts. Like its civil counterpart, the High Court of Justiciary has extensive power to regulate its own practice and procedure, which it does by a form of secondary legislation known as Acts of Adjournal.[45]

The trial court (first instance)

2–33 The High Court of Justiciary tries the most serious crimes and has privative jurisdiction over some, such as murder, treason, rape and serious sexual offences.[46] The trial court is a circuit court and may sit in various large towns and cities around Scotland. It also sits permanently in Edinburgh, Glasgow, and Aberdeen.

Trials are generally conducted by a single judge with a jury of 15. In difficult cases more than one judge may sit. In sentencing a prisoner who has been convicted in the sheriff court a single judge alone will usually sit.

Where the panel is convicted of a statutory offence, the maximum term

---

[41] Criminal Procedure (Scotland) Act 1995 s.5(2)(a), read with s.225(8).
[42] Criminal Procedure (Scotland) Act 1995 s.5(2)(d).
[43] Criminal Procedure (Scotland) Act 1995 s.3(3).
[44] Criminal Procedure (Scotland) Act 1995 s.211(1) and (2).
[45] Criminal Procedure (Scotland) Act 1995 s.305.
[46] Criminal Procedure (Scotland) Act 1995 s.3(6).

of imprisonment allowed is generally limited by the relevant statute. Whether the offence is a common law or a statutory one a judge may impose an unlimited fine.[47] Similarly, there is no limit on the prison term the High Court of Justiciary may impose in relation to common law offences: it may specify a sentence of imprisonment for any fixed period or for life. One limitation on the sentencing discretion of the High Court is that any person convicted of murder must be sentenced to life imprisonment.[48] In passing a life sentence the judge must fix and state at the time of sentence the period of time ("the punishment part") the person must serve in prison before they may be considered for release on licence.[49]

The appeal court

The High Court of Justiciary sitting as a Court of Appeal is the ultimate **2–34** court of criminal appeal in Scotland. There is no route of appeal beyond the High Court. The appeal court sits in Edinburgh. Three judges usually sit on an appeal, although more may do so if it is an exceptionally difficult case or a particularly important point of criminal law.

In addition to hearing appeals, the Lord Advocate may refer a point of law which arises in the course of a case to the High Court for an opinion (a "Lord Advocate's Reference"). This allows the High Court of Justiciary to give directions which set out the law for future similar cases.

Extraordinary powers

Declaratory power

The jurisdiction of the High Court of Justiciary is unlimited at common **2–35** law and it also possesses the power to declare particular conduct to be contrary to the criminal law. That power has never been removed by statute, although it is doubted whether the court would seek to exercise it today. In a modern democracy the power of declaring and defining new offences is generally regarded as best exercised by the legislature.

Nobile officium

"The Court of Justiciary has the exclusive power of providing a **2–36** remedy for all extraordinary or unforeseen occurrences in the course of criminal business, whether before themselves or any inferior Court. Akin to the well known nobile officium of the Court of Session, is a similar power enjoyed by the Justiciary Court."[50]

The application of this power of intervening in extraordinary circumstances for the purpose of preventing injustice or oppression is limited and rare. It cannot be invoked when to do so would conflict with statute.

---

[47] Criminal Procedure (Scotland) Act 1995 s.211(1) and (2).
[48] Criminal Procedure (Scotland) Act 1995 s.205(1).
[49] Prisoners and Criminal Proceedings (Scotland) Act 1993 s.2.
[50] A. Alison, *Practice of the Criminal Law of Scotland* (Edinburgh: Blackwood, 1833), p.23.

TRIBUNALS

2–37 The size and nature of the modern State expanded considerably after the Second World War. Whether for the provision of education, welfare support, health services or the collection of taxation, the State intervenes in the lives of citizens in numerous ways and on many occasions. Having to rely on expensive and lengthy court action to resolve conflicts in all of these areas would be impracticable, the courts simply could not deal with the sheer volume of cases generated. Tribunals are widely utilised to resolve disputes or apply the law as they tend to be cheaper, faster, less formal, more expert and generally more accessible than are the courts of law.

Tribunals operate in a number of areas of law and both Scotland's separate legal system and more recent devolution within the UK mean that there are two different sets of tribunals operating in Scotland. The larger part are "reserved" tribunals operating in UK law, that is to say, areas of law which are reserved to the UK Parliament and which do not differ between the three jurisdictions of the UK. The other set may be termed "devolved" tribunals which operate in areas of governance devolved to the Scottish Parliament. Tribunals as a whole may be termed "administrative" as they generally deal with grievances individuals have with administrative decisions of the state, for example in awarding or withholding welfare benefits, or granting a foreign national leave to remain in the UK. The notable exceptions to this administrative character are employment tribunals, which deal with disputes between persons—namely employers and their employees—and employment tribunals still sit slightly apart from other reserved tribunals. Nevertheless, the jurisdictions of all tribunals are established and defined by legislation and are largely tasked with resolving disputes arising under legislation: hence they may also be called "statutory tribunals".

Like the functions of the State, to which they relate, tribunals developed unsystematically in a rather haphazard manner and varied in composition and process However, reforms, first of reserved tribunals and more recently of devolved tribunals have sought to create simplified statutory frameworks for each set of tribunals and bring the various tribunals within each of them under unified overarching structures, each with greater similarity in appointments, function and appeals.

Key Concepts

Tribunals are not courts but widely used to resolve disputes or apply the law.

They are mostly **administrative** but always **statutory**.

Tribunals deal with **large numbers of cases**. They are generally speedier, less costly, less formal, more expert and more accessible than courts of law.

Reserved tribunals operate in relation to reserved areas of

governance, whereas **devolved Scottish tribunals** deal with issues devolved to Scotland.
Recent reforms aim to simplify and harmonise the organisation of tribunals and their operation.

Nature and composition

Although they exercise a judicial or quasi-judicial function, tribunals are **2–38** not part of the court system. They tend to be less adversarial in nature and more inquisitorial. Tribunals operate in fields where the adjudicating body is required to have a certain level of expertise in the subject matter. Members may be required to have certain professional qualifications and tribunals will generally be presided over by a legally qualified chairperson.

Reserved tribunals

Most tribunals were unified within a common two level framework **2–39** established by the Tribunals, Courts and Enforcement Act 2007. The First-tier Tribunal consolidates 20 previously separate tribunals of first instance into one, with appeals from its decisions generally being dealt with by the Upper Tribunal. Some important tribunals still operate outwith this unified system. This is because, instead of wholesale replacement of all tribunals, the course of reform has been the establishment of the two tiers, into which separate tribunals could then integrate in time.

The First-tier Tribunal

The size and variety of the First-tier Tribunal's workload would be **2–40** unwieldy without being organised into sub-divisions. Thus, the separate remits of the former tribunals now constitute whole or part of the various "jurisdictions" which in turn are grouped into a number of chambers. Each chamber encompasses a particular area of work of the Tribunal.

Examples of First-tier jurisdictions

The following are jurisdictions of the First-tier Tribunal dealing with **2–41** aspects of administrative justice of particular relevance to commercial businesses:

The First-tier Tribunal: General Regulatory Chamber

This is the broadest jurisdiction and has a remit which covers the deci- **2–42** sions and actions of regulatory bodies which are not allocated to the Health, Education and Social Care Chamber or to the Tax Chamber.[51] This includes competence that was formerly covered by a number of tribunals including the Consumer Credit Appeals Tribunal and the

---

[51] The First-tier Tribunal and Upper Tribunal (Chambers) Order 2010 (SI 2010/2655) art.3.

Information Tribunal. It has particular relevance to businesses as it hears appeals from notices issued by the Information Commissioner under the Data Protection Act; the Freedom of Information Act; the Privacy and Electronic Communication Regulations; and the Environmental Information Regulations. See "Information Commissioner", below at para.2–54.

The First-tier Tribunal: Tax Chamber

2–43 This jurisdiction hears appeals made against decisions of Her Majesty's Revenue and Customs. It covers much of the remit of five formerly separate finance and tax tribunals. It deals with a range of matters involving direct and indirect taxation including income tax, PAYE, customs duties, corporation tax, VAT, capital gains tax and excise duties.

Other First-tier jurisdictions

2–44 The seven chambers of the First-tier Tribunal and those jurisdictions which are most relevant to businesses are as follows:

(1) The General Regulatory Chamber:

(a) Claims Management Services.
(b) Consumer Credit.
(c) Environment.
(d) Estate Agents.
(e) Information Rights.
(f) Transport.

(2) Social Entitlement Chamber:

(a) Social Security and Child Support.

(3) Immigration and Asylum Chamber:

(a) Immigration and Asylum.

(4) Property Chamber
(5) Tax Chamber:

(a) First-tier Tribunal (Tax).

(6) Health, Education and Social Care Chamber.
(7) War Pensions and Armed Forces Compensation Chamber.

The Upper Tribunal

2–45 The Upper Tribunal is a superior court of record. The greater part of its work is to hear appeals from and enforce decisions of the First-tier Tribunal. Its decisions are binding on the First-tier Tribunal and public authorities below, and it has powers to enforce both its own procedures and the procedures of the First-tier Tribunal.

In addition it decides some cases that do not go through the First-tier

Tribunal and may exercise powers of judicial review in certain circumstances.

The Upper Tribunal is divided into four chambers. They are:

(1) Administrative Appeals.
(2) Tax and Chancery.
(3) Lands.
(4) Immigration and Asylum.

Employment and Employment Appeal Tribunals

Undoubtedly the largest and most significant area of law dealt with by **2–46** tribunals, that is of greatest relevance to business, is employment. As it stands, Employment and Employment Appeal Tribunals are still separate from the First-tier and Upper Tribunal structure of other reserved tribunals.

Employment tribunals

Employment tribunals ("ETs") are arguably the most important tribu- **2–47** nals for businesses to be familiar with. An ET hears claims about a wide variety of matters in relation to employment brought by employees against their employer. These include unfair dismissal, redundancy, unfair discrimination and claims relating to wages.

An ET is generally comprised of a panel of three: a legally qualified chairman and two lay members. One of the lay members will have experience of employment issues in representing the interests of employees; the other will have experience of being an employer. Either party in a hearing before an ET may arrange for representation by a lawyer, trade union official or advice worker. Legal Aid may be available for an ET hearing in Scotland, but generally not in England and Wales or Northern Ireland.

For further details see Ch.8, "Employment law". Information is also available online from the Employment Tribunals' website.

The Employment Appeal Tribunal

The Employment Appeal Tribunal ("EAT") sits in London and Edin- **2–48** burgh. Its main function is to hear appeals from decisions made by Employment Tribunals. An appeal to the EAT must be on a point of law. The EAT will not normally re-examine issues of fact established by the ET.

EAT hearings are conducted by a judge alone or by a judge and two lay members. The judge is normally a Court of Session judge or an English High Court or circuit judge. The lay members have practical experience in employment relations: one on the employers' side and one on the employees' side.

Further appeal, from a decision of the EAT, lies to the Court of Session on any question of law arising from any decision or order of the

EAT sitting in Scotland, with the leave of the tribunal or the Court of Session.

Reserved tribunal organisation

2–49 Her Majesty's Courts and Tribunals Service ("HMCTS") is an executive agency of the Ministry of Justice of the UK Government. It is responsible for the administration of the criminal, civil and family courts all tribunals in England and Wales and non-devolved tribunals in Scotland and Northern Ireland.

Devolved tribunals

2–50 The Scottish Tribunal Service, a unit of the Justice Directorate of the Scottish Government, currently administers devolved Scottish tribunals. These include, among others, the Lands Tribunal for Scotland, the Private Rented Housing Panel the Scottish Charity Appeals Panel, Council Tax Reduction Review Panel, and the Pensions Appeal Tribunal Scotland. However, much will change in the coming years. Changes to UK tribunals (including abolition of The Administrative Justice & Tribunals Council), reform of the civil courts and judiciary in Scotland as well as the continuing process of devolving powers to the Scottish Parliament have all influenced reform of the devolved tribunals in Scotland. The Tribunal (Scotland) Act 2014 is not yet in force but it provides for a unified two-tier tribunal structure similar to that for UK tribunals. It will be administered by an amalgamated Scottish Courts and Tribunals Service with tribunals supervised by a new office of President of Scottish Tribunals, under the leadership of the Lord President of the Court of Session.

As with the reform of reserved tribunals, the recent legislation will create a framework into which separate tribunals can integrate over time. It is expected that the first changes will come into effect in 2015 and continue to roll on for almost a decade.

OMBUDSMEN

2–51 The use of ombudsmen is relatively new to the UK, but has developed significantly since the establishment of the Parliamentary Commissioner for Administration in 1969. There are an increasing number of ombudsmen or commissioners who perform important roles in remedying grievances. Yet ombudsmen are not part of the courts system, nor are they part of the system of administrative justice which includes tribunals and enquiries.

The key function of ombudsmen is the resolution of complaints made against particular bodies. An ombudsman does not function as an advocate or representative of the complainer, nor does he simply sit in judgment over evidence presented by two sides of a complaint. An ombudsman has significant investigatory powers and fulfils an inquisitorial role. As well as the authority to demand the presentation of evidence and documents, comparable to a court, an ombudsman will also have powers to enter premises and search and seize any evidence thought relevant to the complaint in question.

Most ombudsmen deal exclusively with complaints relating to administration by public bodies. A select few also have considerable powers in respect of private persons.

Major ombudsmen

Parliamentary ombudsman

The parliamentary ombudsman ("PO") was the first and, arguably, most **2–52** significant of ombudsmen in the UK, established by the Parliamentary Commissioner Act 1967. The PO considers complaints in respect of the administrative functions of a relevant public body, which are referred to her by a Member of Parliament on behalf of a member of the public who claims to have sustained injustice in consequence of maladministration.

The key concept in defining the jurisdiction of the PO (and other public sector ombudsmen) is that of "maladministration". The term is not defined in statute. During the passage of the original Bill it was suggested that "maladministration" would cover "bias, neglect, inattention, delay, incompetence, ineptitude, perversity, turpitude, arbitrariness and so on".[52] While "maladministration" has been criticised for uncertainty, it has nevertheless also been found to be, "clearly open-ended, covering the *manner* in which a decision is reached or discretion is exercised; but excluding the *merits* of the decision itself".[53]

The PO is appointed by the Monarch to hold office during good behaviour and can only be removed from office by the Monarch at their own request or following addresses by both Houses of Parliament. The Ombudsman is accountable to Parliament, producing an annual report and on occasion special issue reports, as she sees fit. All such reports enjoy absolute privilege. The PO is overseen by the Public Administration Select Committee of the House of Commons.

The PO has all the investigatory power available to a court in calling written and oral evidence under oath. However, the PO has no powers to enforce decisions; the only sanction being the publication of the findings and presentation to Parliament.

---

[52] H.C. Deb., Vol.754, col.51 (1966)—Often referred to as the "Crossman catalogue" after the then Leader of the House, Richard Crossman MP, who introduced the Bill.

[53] *R v Local Commissioner for Administration for the North and East Area of England, Ex p Bradford Metropolitan City Council* [1979] Q.B. 287 CA, per Denning M.R. at 312.

Scottish Public Services Ombudsman

2–53 The creation of the Scottish Parliament necessitated the creation of an
equivalent to the PO with competence over the actions of the Scottish
Executive, Administration and public bodies in devolved issues.[54] After
consultation the Scottish Parliament decided to go considerably further
and consolidate a number of ombudsmen into a "one-stop shop". The
Scottish Public Services Ombudsman[55] ("SPSO") replaced the Scottish
Parliamentary and Health Service Ombudsman, Local Government
Ombudsman for Scotland and Housing Association Ombudsman for
Scotland. Subsequently it has also replaced the Scottish Prisons Com-
plaints Commissioner.[56]

The SPSO is appointed by the Monarch on nomination by the Parliament and deals with complaints in respect of Scottish Parliament and
Scottish Government, colleges and universities, the health services, local
government, registered social landlords and a multitude of public bodies
listed in the 2002 Act. The SPSO also works with such authorities to
promote good practice in the administration of public services in
Scotland.

In the conduct of an investigation the SPSO has the same power as the
Court of Session in calling written and oral evidence under oath.
Obstruction of an SPSO investigation is actionable on petition to the
Court of Session as contempt against the court.

The SPSO has no powers to make awards or enforce a recommendation. Its sole sanction is public publication of its report and presentation
to the Scottish Parliament, with the expectation that the matter be
addressed.

Information Commissioner

2–54 The Information Commissioner ("IC") is a particularly important
ombudsman with which any businesses should be familiar. It is a UK-
wide independent public body set up to protect personal information and
promote public access to official information. In addition to important
functions in respect of public bodies regarding Freedom of Information
and Environmental Information Regulations, the IC deals with data
protection and privacy and electronic communication regulations.[57]
These latter two directly affect a great many businesses.

Data protection relates to the gathering, holding and processing of any

---

[54] "Scottish Executive" is the term specified in the Scotland Act 1998 (s.44) for senior
ministers and used during the first two terms of devolution from 1999 for the whole of
the Scottish Government. "Scottish administration" has wider meaning (see s.126 of the
1998 Act) and includes non-ministerial offices and the civil service. Though "Scottish
Executive" is still the legally correct term, the first SNP administration stopped using it
in 2007, rejecting it in favour of "Scottish Government" in all publicity materials,
documents and signage.

[55] Scottish Public Services Ombudsman Act 2002.

[56] Scottish Parliamentary Commissions and Commissioners etc. Act 2010 Sch.3 para.20.

[57] Freedom of Information issues in relation to devolved bodies are dealt with by the
Scottish Information Commissioner (see para.2–55).

information by which individuals can be identified. Privacy and Electronic Communication Regulations are rules for people who wish to send electronic direct marketing, for example email and text messages. These and other areas of business regulation are covered in Ch.3, "Business Regulation".

In the course of investigations the Commissioner can seek a warrant from the court to enter premises, inspect and seize any equipment found there which is used or intended for processing personal data. The IC may also issue an information notice requiring a person or business to supply information relevant to an investigation, or an enforcement notice directing them to carry out specified action to comply with data regulations. Providing a false statement or failure to comply with a notice from the IC is an offence, punishable by a fine (up to a maximum of £10,000 upon summary conviction, or unlimited fine upon solemn conviction) and documents or material used in the processing of data may be forfeited, destroyed or erased.[58]

Scottish Information Commissioner

The Scottish Information Commissioner exercises considerable authority **2–55** under the Freedom of Information (Scotland) Act 2002. The Commissioner has substantial powers to enforce the right of citizens to access information held by public bodies. She issues codes of practice and monitors adherence to them. She investigates and adjudicates applications from any person claiming a body has failed to comply with its duties under the Act.

The Commissioner is appointed by the Monarch on the nomination of the Scottish Parliament and reports directly to the Parliament. She can only be removed from office at his own request, being retired at the end of the year in which she reaches the age of 65, or by a resolution of the Parliament passed with a two-thirds majority.

Scottish Legal Complaints Commission

The Scottish Legal Complaints Commission ("SLCC"), which replaced **2–56** the Scottish Legal Services Ombudsman, deals with complaints about legal practitioners in Scotland. It acts as a gateway for all complaints against practitioners. If a complaint relates to the service received by the client the Commission may choose to investigate the matter itself, but issues relating to the conduct of a practitioner will be referred on to the relevant professional body. The Commission also oversees how the professional bodies investigate and prosecute instances of misconduct or unsatisfactory conduct. Established under the Legal Profession and Legal Aid (Scotland) Act 2007, the SLCC is not a court, nor a government agency but an independent corporate body. Its members are appointed for a term of five years by the Scottish Ministers, on the advice of the

---

[58] Data Protection Act 1998 s.60.

Lord President of the Court of Session. Members of the SLCC may also be removed only by the Lord President.

The SLCC has the same authority as a sheriff court to issue an order that the practitioner rectify the error made at their own expense. Where the Commission considers that the complainer has been directly affected by the inadequate professional services, the SLCC may direct the practitioner to pay compensation of up to £20,000 to the complainer for loss, inconvenience or distress resulting from the inadequate professional services.

Financial Ombudsman Service

2–57 The Financial Ombudsman Service ("FOS") is appointed and run by the Financial Conduct Authority ("FCA") under powers conferred in the Financial Services and Markets Act 2000 (as amended).

The job of the FOS is to help resolve individual disputes between consumers and businesses providing financial services including banks, building societies, insurance firms and financial advisers. It also covers—for their financial services activities—many businesses that offer financial services as a secondary activity to their main business (e.g. motor dealers).

The FOS could be said to lack complete independence, in that within a particular complaint a failing may lie with the FSA itself. While it does not have the powers of investigation properly associated with an ombudsman, the FOS may ask the court to compel a party to a complaint to produce relevant evidence. If the party cannot give reasonable excuse for its refusal to comply with the FOS request, the court will then order the evidence in question to be handed over.

In making a decision on a complaint the FOS may make an award of money to compensate a complainer for financial loss or damages, or in respect of costs incurred. If not complied with, such an award will be enforced by an order of the Court of Session.

"Non Ombudsmen"

2–58 There has been a marked tendency for many public bodies to set up their own adjudicators which are often termed "ombudsman", much to the chagrin of the PO.[59] Generally they lack the statutory powers and independence from the subject organisation that is necessary to truly meet the notion of ombudsmen.

For example, the Prisons and Probation Ombudsman for England and Wales is directly appointed by the Secretary of State for Justice. Additionally, there are a number of state appointed offices termed "ombudsmen" that deal with the private sector—for example the Housing Services Ombudsman (England and Wales). Again, many such offices may lack the political independence and/or the range of investigatory powers and statutory authority necessary for a true ombudsman.

---

[59] 1993–1994 H.C. 33.

> **Key Concepts**
>
> **Ombudsmen** are not consumer advocates but impartial inquisitors. They mostly investigate grievances arising from **maladministration**.
> True ombudsmen are statutory, impartial, independent and have substantial powers of investigation.

THE LEGAL PROFESSION

The term "lawyer" is a generic one which covers a multitude of different **2–59** occupations of people working in and with the law. The legal profession, on the other hand, refers to legal practitioners who are accredited by and subject to the rules of a professional body, to advise and represent the legal interests of paying clients. In Scotland the legal profession is divided into two mutually exclusive branches: those of solicitors and advocates. Both branches of the profession are accorded specific responsibilities and rights, recognised in law and subject to strict regulation.

Solicitors

Solicitors are effectively the "general practitioners" of the legal profes- **2–60** sion. They may be hired directly by members of the public to provide legal advice or representation. Indeed, solicitors' offices are a regular feature of high streets in towns and cities throughout Scotland.

There are currently over 11,000 solicitors in Scotland certified to practice and who are regulated by the Law Society of Scotland, which is established and empowered under statute to govern the profession. Solicitors may work as sole practitioners or in partnership with other solicitors. Most work in partnerships, offering a wide range of general legal advice and services such as drafting and administering of wills and trusts, facilitating the sale of property or company formation. Solicitors may offer advice in respect of court action and represent clients in the lower courts—the JP court in criminal cases or the sheriff court in either criminal or civil cases.

In addition to those working in private practice, large corporations may employ their own in-house solicitors to deal with much of the particular organisation's legal work. Large commercial businesses such as banks or insurance companies as well as public bodies such as local councils will often have their own legal departments, which will include a number of solicitors.

The Law Society of Scotland accredits universities awarding LLB (Bachelor of Laws) degrees in Scots law. Such degrees form part of the qualification process and exempt graduates from having to complete the Society's entrance examinations. After gaining an LLB in Scots law or passing the Society's entrance exams, a would-be-solicitor must complete a 26-week course and attain Professional Education and Training stage 1, or "PEAT 1" (commonly known as the Diploma in Legal Practice), before then going on to complete a two-year traineeship ("PEAT 2") with a practising solicitor in Scotland. Only upon successful completion of each of those elements of professional training will they qualify for and be granted the practising certificate necessary to work as a solicitor.

In addition to overseeing entrance to the profession, the Society also regulates the on-going training solicitors must complete throughout their career. A practising solicitor is currently required to complete a minimum of 20 hours' continuing professional development ("CPD") in each practice year.

Notary Public

2–61 In many other jurisdictions the position of Notary Public is a distinct legal profession. However, in Scotland only solicitors may become notaries, and most, but not all, are. The chief role of a notary is bearing witness to and certifying the validity of certain legal documents. These include where a document requires the administration of an oath or the receipt of an affidavit or solemn affirmation, as well as the making of affidavits and affirmations, and the making or certifying of documents for use in foreign jurisdictions requiring execution or certification before a Notary.

Solicitor-advocate

2–62 A solicitor-advocate is a practising solicitor who by additional training and experience has applied for and been granted rights of audience in one or more of the Supreme Courts (i.e. the Court of Session and the High Court of Justiciary).

Advocates

2–63 Advocates form the second branch of the Scottish legal profession— collectively referred to as "the bar". The bar is a specialised branch of the profession. Advocates have rights of audience in all the courts of Scotland, including the Court of Session, the High Court of Justiciary and the Supreme Court of the United Kingdom. They represent clients in court or provide expert advice, generally in respect of litigation.

There are around 460 advocates practising in Scotland. Counsel are self-employed, each working on their own account: partnerships or agreements to share work or profits are not allowed. Most operate within the Faculty of Advocates, headquartered in Parliament House in Edinburgh.

In order to become an advocate it is necessary to attain a law degree and PEAT 1 (or Diploma in Legal Practice), pass a year-long traineeship with a solicitor and pass an examination in evidence and procedure and then complete a nine-month period of "devilling", training as the pupil of experienced advocates the Faculty has approved as "devilmasters". A "devil" will be assessed by their devilmasters on their oral and written advocacy skills before being admitted to the Faculty and granted the right to appear before the court.

Advocates cannot be employed by members of the public directly. Traditionally and most commonly, an advocate is instructed by a solicitor on behalf of their client. However, since 2006 wider direct access has been granted to a larger number of professional bodies and organisations. Those now able to approach and instruct counsel include foreign lawyers, professional bodies, public limited companies, voluntary organisations, public authorities, trade unions, employers' associations and any person or body on the FCA Register.

Queen's Counsel

Queen's Counsel ("QC") is a title awarded to advocates and solicitor- **2–64** advocates with at least 13 years' experience, who are considered to have achieved distinction in full-time practice. "Taking silk", as becoming a QC is commonly known, is in the gift of the Monarch and is exercised through the First Minister upon recommendation by the Lord Justice-General.

Advocate deputes

Advocate deputes are advocates employed by the Crown Office and **2–65** Procurator Fiscal Service to prosecute cases in the High Court. The advocate deputes, together with the Lord Advocate and Solicitor General, comprise Crown Counsel.

Judiciary

With the exception of Justices of the Peace, judges in Scotland are drawn **2–66** from the legal profession. Most appointments are made by the Monarch on the advice of the First Minister according to recommendations made to him by the Lord President and the Judicial Appointments Board for Scotland.

Justices of the Peace

Justices of the Peace are members of the local community appointed by **2–67** the Scottish government. Appointment is based on recommendation submitted by the Justice of the Peace Advisory Committee for the relevant sheriffdom. JPs are lay justices, i.e. they are not legally qualified.

JPs are appointed by the Scottish Ministers for a term of five years.[60] Re-appointment is automatic unless the person declines, has reached the age of 69, is disqualified, or the sheriff principal recommends to the ministers that the person not be re-appointed. A JP must live in or within 15 miles of the sheriffdom.

A JP must retire upon reaching 70 years of age and is disqualified if they become or are bankrupt. A JP may only removed from office by order of a tribunal appointed by the Lord President of the Court of Session.

---

[60] Criminal Proceedings etc. (Reform) (Scotland) Act 2007 ss.67–73, and 76.

Stipendiary magistrates

2–68 Currently, a stipendiary is a permanent, legally qualified judge employed to sit in the JP court. A stipendiary may be appointed by the Scottish Ministers if, on the advice of a sheriff principal, they consider that the appointment is necessary or expedient for the purposes of the efficient administration of any or all of the JP courts in that sheriff principal's sheriffdom. The appointee must be a solicitor or advocate with at least five years' experience.[61]

Part-time magistrates may be appointed for a term of five years. Full-time magistrates are appointed for an indefinite term. However, the office of stipendiary magistrate is due to be abolished.[62]

Sheriffs

2–69 There are currently over 140 full-time sheriffs in service. To be appointed a sheriff a person must be and have been an advocate or solicitor for at least 10 years.[63] Those appointed should be practitioners of standing, whether Queen's Counsel, advocates or solicitors with considerable court experience. Before appointment, the person will in many cases have some experience of the shrieval bench as a part-time sheriff.

Once appointed a sheriff may remain in office until the compulsory retirement age, which is 70. Sheriffs may, if they wish, retire at any time after reaching the age of 60. A sheriff may be required to live in or near the town in which he or she has the main or only court.

A sheriff can only be removed from office by statutory instrument, laid before the Scottish Parliament by the First Minister. Such instrument may only be laid following the recommendation of the Lord President of the Court of Session, having undertaken an investigation into the said sheriff.

Summary sheriff

2–70 An important imminent change yet to take effect is the creation of the office of summary sheriff. Qualification and the process of appointment will be the same as that for a sheriff.[64] In general, a summary sheriff will have only the competence and jurisdiction to preside in summary civil and criminal proceedings.[65] The process of removal of a sheriff or summary sheriff from office remains similar as to before, being only by an order laid before the Scottish Parliament by the First Minister after investigation and the hearing of an independent tribunal.[66]

---

[61] Criminal Proceedings etc. (Reform) (Scotland) Act 2007 s.74.
[62] Courts Reform (Scotland) Act 2014 s.128 (not yet in force).
[63] Sheriff Courts (Scotland) Act 1971.
[64] Courts Reform (Scotland) Act 2014 s.14 (not yet in force).
[65] Courts Reform (Scotland) Act 2014 ss.44 and 45 respectively (not yet in force).
[66] Courts Reform (Scotland) Act 2014 s.25 (not yet in force).

Sheriffs principal

There are six sheriffs principal in Scotland. Each presides over a parti- **2–71** cular sheriffdom and discharges a number of administrative functions in respect of the courts in that sheriffdom. A sheriff principal sometimes sits in criminal courts or conducts major fatal accident inquiries. Currently, a sheriff principal's judicial business is primarily as an appellate judge who sits alone to determine appeals from the decisions of sheriffs in civil matters. That function will change once the Sheriff Appeal Court begins operation. Appointment, service and removal for the office of sheriff principal is as that for sheriffs.[67]

Judges of the Supreme Courts of Scotland

Since 1836 the judiciary of the highest criminal and civil courts in Scot- **2–72** land have been unified. While individual judges will sometimes specialise in particular areas or types of law, as a rule a judge of the Supreme Courts in Scotland may sit on both criminal and civil cases in the respective courts. Each judge will cover a broad spectrum of cases. However, particular judges may be designated to hear cases relating to specific areas of law where certain experience or knowledge is advantageous. For example a judge may be designated to hear intellectual property, judicial review or commercial cases.

There are currently 34 judges of the Supreme Courts.[68] Those eligible for appointment as a judge of the Supreme Courts include experienced advocates, usually QCs, or a sheriff principal, sheriff or solicitor-advocate with a minimum of five years' experience.

A judge of the Supreme Courts may resign at any time, and must retire upon reaching the age of 75. However, a judge of the Supreme Courts can only be removed from office by the Monarch upon the recommendation of the First Minister and with the agreement of the Scottish Parliament following a proper investigation and report on whether the judge is unfit for office by reason of inability, neglect of duty or misbehaviour.[69]

Senators of the College of Justice

Judges of the Court of Session are termed "Senators of the College of **2–73** Justice" or "Lords of Council and Session". A judge takes the courtesy title of "Lord" or "Lady" followed by their surname or a territorial title: for example, Lady Clark of Calton (Lynda Clark); Lord Bracadale (Alastair P. Campbell). When sitting in the Outer House the judge may also be called a Lord Ordinary.

Generally, 22 judges sit as Lords Ordinary in the Outer House. A further 12 sit in the Inner House: six, including the Lord President sit in the First Division; six, including the Lord Justice Clerk, sit in the Second

---

[67] Sheriff Courts (Scotland) Act 1971.
[68] The number may well reduce once the Sheriff Appeal Court is in operation if the pressure of appellate business on the Supreme Courts reduces.
[69] Scotland Act 1998 s.95(6)–(8).

Division. However, the exact numbers are subject to change according to new appointments, retirements and occasionally the formation of an extra division of the Inner House.

Lord Commissioners of the High Court of Justiciary

2–74 Judges of the High Court of Justiciary are called "Lord Commissioners of the High Court of Justiciary". Sitting generally reflects that of the Court of Session—Lords Ordinary presiding over criminal trials in the High Court and the members of divisions in the Inner House of the Court of Session generally forming a bench to hear appeals in the High Court of Justiciary sitting as a Court of Appeal.

Lord President and Lord Justice-General

2–75 The offices of Lord President and Lord Justice-General are the highest judicial offices in Scots civil and criminal law respectively. These two titles are now held by a single judge, dual title dates from the amalgamation of civil and criminal judiciary in the nineteenth century.

Appointment is by the Monarch, on the advice of the Prime Minister according to recommendations made by the First Minister, after consulting the serving Lord President and Lord Justice-General.[70]

Lord Justice-Clerk

2–76 The Lord Justice-Clerk is the second most senior judge in Scotland, behind the Lord President of the Court of Session. The holder has the title in both the Court of Session and the High Court of Justiciary and is in charge of the Second Division of the Inner House of the Court of Session. The office is one of the Great Offices of State in Scotland.

Complaints

2–77 Complaints about practising lawyers are dealt with by the Scottish Legal Complaints Commission (see above, at para.2–56) and the professional bodies—the Law Society of Scotland or the Faculty of Advocates.

LAW OFFICERS

2–78 Reference to "the Scottish law officers" means the Lord Advocate and Solicitor General. However, as a result of devolution there is also the Advocate General—a UK law officer with dedicated powers and responsibilities of particular relevance to Scotland.

Lord Advocate

2–79 The Lord Advocate is the senior law officer in Scotland. The office dates back to at least 1483.

---

[70] Scotland Act 1998 s.95(1)–(3).

Today the Lord Advocate fulfils four major legal roles. As head of the Crown Office and Procurator Fiscal Service ("COPFS") the Lord Advocate is in charge of the system of prosecution and investigation of deaths. The Lord Advocate is also a member of the Scottish Executive and is the chief legal adviser to the Scottish Government. The Lord Advocate also represents the Scottish Executive in civil proceedings and represents the public interest in a range of statutory and common law civil functions.

The Lord Advocate is appointed by the Monarch, on the advice of the First Minister with the agreement of the Scottish Parliament. Unlike other Ministers, however, they cannot be removed from office by the First Minister without the approval of the Parliament.[71]

Solicitor General

The Solicitor General is the deputy of the Lord Advocate in the prose- **2–80** cution system. In the absence of a Lord Advocate in office he takes over full responsibility for the exercise of the functions of the Lord Advocate.

Procurators fiscal

Area and district procurators fiscal work within the Crown Office and **2–81** Procurator Fiscal Service. They prosecute crimes locally in the lower courts throughout Scotland on behalf of the Lord Advocate.

Advocate General

The office of Advocate General was established as a result of devolution. **2–82** Appointed by the Prime Minister, the Advocate General advises the UK Government on issues of Scots law with respect to UK legislation and governance not devolved to Holyrood under the Scotland Act 1998.

The Advocate General also has statutory functions under the Act relating to ensuring the devolved institutions act intra vires. He can refer Bills of the Scottish Parliament to the Supreme Court of the United Kingdom for decisions on their competence or raise proceedings in the courts on devolution issues arising from actions of the Scottish Government or Scottish Parliament. He is also given notice of any devolution issue raised in the courts and can intervene in such cases.

▼ CHAPTER SUMMARY

THE CIVIL COURTS

    (1) Sheriff court: **2–83**

        (a) Ordinary cause.

        (b) Summary cause.

        (c) Small claims.

---

[71] Scotland Act 1998 s.48(1).

    (d) "(b)" and "(c)" soon to be replaced by simple procedure.

(2) Sheriff Appeal Court (expected 2016).
(3) The Court of Session (Outer House).
(4) The Court of Session (Inner House).
(5) The Supreme Court of the United Kingdom.

Jurisdiction can be defined according to place, person or subject matter.
    The pursuer follows the defender.
    The jurisdiction of the Sheriff Court and Court of Session largely overlap, but each still has its privative jurisdiction.
    The choice of court and procedure will depend on the cost of the action and the nature and size of the remedy the pursuer seeks.

The Criminal Courts

(1) JP court.
(2) Sheriff Court:

    (a) Summary.
    (b) Solemn.

(3) Sheriff Appeal Court (expected late 2015)
(4) The High Court of Justiciary.
(5) The High Court of Justiciary Court of Appeal.

Criminal law is public law.
    Prosecutions are brought by the Crown Office and Procurator Fiscal Service.
    The courts vary in composition, jurisdiction and gravity of penalties they can impose.
    The court is chosen by the prosecution, according to the seriousness of the offence and the penalty sought.

Tribunals

(1) Mainly administrative, always statutory.
(2) Are utilised for certain benefits in resolving disputes:

    (a) Less costly than the courts.
    (b) Speedier resolution.
    (c) Expert adjudication.
    (d) Less formal.
    (e) More accessible.

(3) Most deal with issues of public administration, such as:

    (a) Social Security.
    (b) Asylum and Immigration.

(4) Some deal with vital business matters:

    (a) Information Rights.
    (b) Tax.
    (c) Employment.

OMBUDSMEN

(1) Established by statutes to resolve complaints in respect of maladministration by particular bodies.
(2) Act as impartial inquisitors.
(3) Most act in the public sector:

    (a) Parliamentary Ombudsman.
    (b) Scottish Public Services Ombudsman.
    (c) Scottish Information Commissioner.

(4) Some act in the private sector or across both public and private:

    (a) Information Commissioner.
    (b) Scottish Legal Complaints Commission.
    (c) Financial Ombudsman Service.

(5) True ombudsmen are:

    (a) Statutory.
    (b) Impartial.
    (c) Have powers of investigation.
    (d) Backed by the powers of court orders.

THE LEGAL PROFESSION

(1) Divided into two branches:

    (a) Solicitors.
    (b) Advocates.

(2) Each regulated by professional bodies.
(3) Judiciary:

    (a) JPs.
    (b) Summary sheriff (expected 2015).
    (c) Sheriff.
    (d) Sheriff principal.
    (e) Senators of the College of Justice.
    (f) Lord Commissioners of Justiciary.
    (g) The Lord President and the Lord Justice-General.
    (h) The Lord Justice Clerk.

THE LAW OFFICERS

(1) Lord Advocate.
(2) Solicitor General.
(3) Procurators Fiscal.
(4) Advocate General.

? QUICK QUIZ

- What does "privative jurisdiction" mean?

- What three criteria define the civil jurisdiction of the sheriff court?
- Which court hears applications for judicial review?
- What is the maximum prison sentence that can be imposed by the JP court?
- How many years must a JP have practised as a lawyer?
- What is the ultimate court of civil appeal?
- What is the ultimate court of criminal appeal?
- What is the maximum fine a sheriff can impose after conviction in a solemn trial?
- How many people sit in a Scottish criminal jury?
- What is a judge of the High Court called?
- What does an Advocate Depute do?
- Name the offices of the highest civil and criminal judiciary in Scotland?

? FURTHER READING

> *Stair Memorial Encyclopaedia* (Civil Procedure); (Constitutional Law); (Courts and Competency (Vol.6)); (Criminal Procedure); (Employment); (Tribunals).
> R.S. Shiels, *Law Basics: Scottish Legal System*, 3rd edn (Edinburgh: W. Green, 2011).
> H.L. MacQueen, R.M. White & I.D. Willock, *Scottish Legal System*, 5th edn (Haywards Heath, West Sussex: Bloomsbury Professional, 2013).

RELEVANT WEBLINKS

Courts

> Scottish Courts Service: *http://www.scotcourts.gov.uk* [Accessed May 15, 2015].
> UK Supreme Court: *https://www.supremecourt.uk* [Accessed May 15, 2015].
> Scottish Government, Modernising the civil court and tribunal systems: *http://www.gov.scot/Topics/Justice/policies/civil-courts* [Accessed May 15, 2015].

Tribunals

> Reserved tribunals: *http://www.justice.gov.uk/tribunals/* [Accessed May 15, 2015].
> Scottish Tribunal Service: *http://www.gov.scot/Topics/Justice/policies/civil-courts/tribunal-system/Tribunals* [Accessed May 15, 2015].

Ombudsmen

> ➤ The Ombudsmen Association: *http://www.bioa.org.uk* [Accessed May 15, 2015].
> ➤ Scottish Public Services Ombudsman: *http://www.spso.org.uk* [Accessed May 15, 2015].
> ➤ Information Commissioner website: *https://ico.org.uk* [Accessed May 15, 2015].

Legal personnel

> ➤ Law Society of Scotland: *http://www.lawscot.org.uk* [Accessed May 15, 2015].
> ➤ Faculty of Advocates: *http://www.advocates.org.uk* [Accessed May 15, 2015].
> ➤ Judiciary of Scotland: *www.scotland-judiciary.org.uk* [Accessed May 15, 2015].
> ➤ Crown Office and Procurator Fiscal Service: *http://www.copfs.-gov.uk* [Accessed May 15, 2015].
> ➤ Office of the Advocate General: *https://www.gov.uk/government/organisations/office-of-the-advocate-general-for-scotland* [Accessed May 15, 2015].

Chapter 3   Business Regulation

Liz Campbell, Greg Gordon and Michael Plaxton[1]

▶ CHAPTER OVERVIEW

3–01 This chapter is concerned with the measures adopted by the law in order to regulate businesses. It is divided into three main sections. As the criminal law is one of the most important tools used in business regulation, the chapter commences by introducing the reader to the purpose and general principles of the criminal law. It then goes on to consider a number of offences which are of particular relevance to business. Finally, it examines a number of regulatory regimes which parliament has enacted to control a range of business activities.

✓ OUTCOMES

3–02 By the end of this chapter you should be able to:

- ✓ understand the nature and purpose of the criminal law;
- ✓ appreciate criminal offences generally require both actus reus and mens rea while recognising that in the case of strict liability offences, only an actus reus is required;
- ✓ be aware that criminal liability can in certain situations be incurred both by art and part and vicariously, and understand the difference between those terms;
- ✓ appreciate the difficulties in holding corporations criminally liable, and understand the circumstances in which corporations are and are not criminally liable;
- ✓ be able to describe the essential features of a number of common law crimes of dishonesty relevant to business, namely theft, embezzlement, fraud, uttering and extortion;
- ✓ understand the various statutory offences in the Bribery Act 2010;
- ✓ understand what regulatory offences are, and appreciate that criminalisation is just one of a range of responses used by the state to regulate modern business practice;

---

[1] Liz Campbell is Senior Lecturer in the School of Law, University of Edinburgh, and Greg Gordon is Senior Lecturer in the School of Law, University of Aberdeen. Michael Plaxton is an Associate Professor in the College of Law, University of Saskatchewan.

✓ be in a position to describe the regulatory regimes which the state has put in place in relation to occupational health and safety, corporate homicide, the misuse of data and competition between businesses; and

✓ have an understanding of the breath of scope of environmental regulation currently in force within the UK, and be in a position to describe some of its key features.

THE CRIMINAL LAW—ITS PURPOSE AND GENERAL PRINCIPLES

Introduction

At times, the public interest in the criminal law appears to be insatiable. **3–03** The media reports continually on the outcome of criminal trials, crime novels fill the shelves of bookshops and crime reconstruction programmes are broadcast regularly on television. Thus, even readers who have never formally studied the criminal law will have built up at least some degree of awareness of its contents. It will therefore come as no surprise to learn that the criminal law prohibits forms of behaviour which society regards as serious wrongs. However, what might be less apparent is precisely *how* the criminal law defines such prohibited wrongs, and *why* certain forms of blameworthy conduct are treated as worthy of criminal prohibition while others are not. We shall consider these (and other) issues in the paragraphs which follow.

The nature of criminal law

There is a common perception that the purpose of the criminal law is to **3–04** achieve "justice for the victim"—that it aims to punish the offender in the name of the individual harmed. This, however, is a mistaken view of the criminal law's function. Such an analysis would see harmful conduct as a private wrong directed exclusively towards the victim. However, criminal law is not a branch of private law, but of public law. In other words, it is not principally concerned with the legal relationship between individuals but between the State and the individual. A crime is regarded as an affront to the community at large, not just to the individual victim. The public interest in preventing, resolving and punishing harmful behaviour that falls within the scope of the criminal law is reflected in the fact that prosecutions are generally taken on the part of the State. This is why, when the most serious criminal allegations come to court, the parties to the litigation are the accused and "Her Majesty's Advocate", the latter of whom pursues the case in the name of the sovereign and on behalf of the State.[2] None of this is to say that the victim of a crime will have no legal remedy against the wrongdoer. The Scottish criminal courts have the

---

[2] Her Majesty's Advocate prosecutes all cases that take place in front of a judge and jury and which are conducted under what is known as solemn procedure: see further para.2–27, above. Less serious crimes are prosecuted by local public prosecutors known as "procurators fiscal."

power to issue a compensation order, requiring the wrongdoer to make at least some degree of payment for the benefit of the victim.[3] Often, however, the sum which can be paid to the victim in this way will be inadequate to fully compensate him. In such cases, the victim has the right to seek further compensation through alternative branches of the law.[4]

Elements of criminal offences

3–05 A crime is generally described as comprising both an external element— typically some manner of conduct or behaviour (such as a positive act, an omission or the bringing about of a particular state of affairs)—and a mental aspect (namely a blameworthy state of mind such as intention, recklessness, or the possession of knowledge). The Latin maxim *"actus non facit reum nisi mens sit rea"* encapsulates this notion, stating as it does that behaviour cannot amount to a crime unless carried out with a blameworthy state of mind. This axiom provides the terms actus reus, which refers to the external element of a crime, and mens rea, which describes the mental element. Generally speaking, an individual can only commit a criminal offence by engaging in a course of conduct that the law regards as wrongful, while simultaneously possessing a blameworthy state of mind. This proposition holds true for all common law crimes such as assault, murder and theft. However, and crucially, an exception is made in the context of what are known as "strict liability" offences. These require only an actus reus for their commission; mens rea is not required. Some offences which have been created by statute or delegated legislation ("statutory offences") are crimes of strict liability. A variety of statutory offences which are relevant to the State's regulation of business activities are discussed at paras 3–30 to 3–54, below.

Actus reus

3–06 The external element (actus reus) of a given offence may be an act or an omission. For example, the actus reus for assault is an "attack" (which is itself a legal term of art referring to conduct causing injury or fear of injury).[5] In the usual case, one person can attack another only by performing a positive act, for instance, by punching the victim or brandishing a knife.

Omissions may be divided into two categories: (a) pure omission; and (b) commission by omission. It can be difficult, in practice, to say that any

---

[3] In solemn cases, the amount of compensation which can be awarded is unlimited. In summary cases, there are strict limits on the amount of compensation that the court can order: Criminal Procedure (Scotland) Act 1995 s.249.

[4] Delict, or occasionally contract law, may provide a remedy for the wronged party. Delict is discussed in Ch.10 of this book; the law of contract is the subject of Ch.4. In certain cases, victims of physical violence may also be entitled to claim compensation from the state through the Criminal Injuries Compensation Scheme—see *https://www.gov.uk/ government/organisations/criminal-injuries-compensation-authority* [Accessed May 15, 2015].

[5] *Gilmour v McGlennan*, 1993 S.C.C.R. 837.

given omission is either one or the other. In principle, though, the distinction rests upon the insight that a person may act without moving. For instance, commission by omission is evident in the English case of *Fagan v Metropolitan Police Commissioner*,[6] where the accused inadvertently parked his car on another's foot. When he realised what he had done, he refused to move the vehicle. Under the circumstances, the accused's failure to move the car may be viewed as an "attack", such that it would satisfy the actus reus of assault. Broadly speaking, where the accused has acted without moving this represents a case of "commission by omission". In such cases, the "omission" is treated as a positive act.

"Pure omission" is where the accused has not acted at all. Scots criminal law has traditionally hesitated to impose liability on individuals for pure omissions. The mere fact that the accused in a given case had a *moral* duty to act is not enough. For example, it may be highly immoral to stand by and permit a child to drown in a pool when they could be rescued with no risk to oneself, but unless a special duty of the type described in the following paragraph exists, it is not criminal[7]: an accused can satisfy the actus reus of a criminal offence through inaction only if he had a legal duty to act.

At common law, courts have recognised a legal duty to act in only a small range of circumstances: (1) where the accused has a particular kind of relationship with the victim (for example, a parental or spousal relationship)[8]; (2) where the accused has assumed responsibility for the victim[9]; (3) where the accused owes a public duty by virtue of some official position[10]; or (4) where the accused herself created the danger.[11] Beyond this narrow range, the courts have taken the view that it should fall to Parliament to impose positive duties to act on citizens. One example of a statutory crime of pure omission is failing to stop a motor vehicle or bicycle when requested to do so by a police officer.[12]

Causation

The actus reus of an offence may or may not require proof that the **3–07** accused caused a certain result to occur. For example, murder requires proof that the accused caused the death of the victim, and assault requires proof that the accused caused injury or fear of injury. By contrast, the crime of breaching the peace does not require proof that the accused caused any particular result at all. Where an offence does demand proof that the accused caused a given result, the Crown will usually discharge that burden if it shows that, but for the accused's conduct, the result would not have occurred. There are limits to this "but for" liability. On

---

[6] [1969] 1 Q.B. 439.
[7] In some other legal systems, a different approach is taken. For instance, French law recognises the crime of deliberately failing to provide assistance to endangered persons.
[8] See *R v Gibbins and Proctor* (1918) 13 Cr. App. R. 134.
[9] See, e.g. *R v Instan* [1893] 1 Q.B. 450.
[10] See, e.g. *Bonar and Hogg v MacLeod*, 1983 S.C.C.R. 161.
[11] See, e.g. *MacPhail v Clark*, 1983 S.C.C.R. 395.
[12] Road Traffic Act 1988 s.163.

occasion, something so unforeseeable will happen between the accused's conduct and the result that it may be unjust to hold the accused liable for that result. In such cases, there has been an intervening act (or novus actus interveniens) which has "broken the chain of causation". Suppose, for example, that A deliberately pushes B into a soft pile of leaves during a thunderstorm. At that moment, B is struck by a bolt of lightning, and he is killed. It seems clear that A, by pushing B, has assaulted him. It also seems clear that, but for the push, B would not have been in a position to be struck by the lightning bolt. Nonetheless, it seems wrong to say that A has caused B's death; it was so unforeseeable that a lightning bolt would strike that location at that moment, that the lightning bolt could be described as a novus actus interveniens which severs A's liability for B's death.

To sever the causal link the novus actus interveniens must supersede the original act. The circumstances in which this will occur are very limited in practice. For example, poor or incorrect medical treatment, also known as *malregimen*, rarely breaks the chain of causation unless the treatment is palpably wrong or grossly negligent.[13] In addition, an adult victim's voluntary and deliberate consumption of controlled drugs does not necessarily break the chain so as to exculpate the accused who recklessly supplied the drugs for the injury/death which ensued.[14] Moreover, intervention by a third party will not necessarily break the causal chain.[15] It seems that if the intervening act was a foreseeable one, then the causal connection is unbroken, and the initial action will be deemed to have caused the result.

The courts have also established that not even every unforeseeable circumstance will break the chain of causation. Suppose that A punches B, who, unbeknownst to A, suffers from a condition which makes him unusually vulnerable to the blow, and B dies. In that case, the apparent unforeseeability of the existence of a condition capable of transforming an ordinary blow into a fatal injury will not sever the chain of causation.[16] The accused must "take his victim as he finds him", a principle sometimes referred to as the "egg-shell skull rule". It seems that such an approach is adopted on the grounds of public policy, on the basis that the initial criminal act ought not to have occurred in the first instance, and so this principle may serve as a deterrent. The rule is well-established but controversial: though we surely want to deter people from attacking each other, it can seem harsh to say that A has "caused" B's death, when we might just as easily say that it was B's condition that killed him.

---

[13] Such criteria were satisfied in *R v Jordan* (1956) 40 Cr. App. R. 152; *R v Smith* [1959] 2 All E.R. 193.

[14] *MacAngus v HM Advocate*, 2009 S.L.T. 137.

[15] *People v Fowler* 174 Pac. 892 (1918).

[16] *Bird v Her Majesty's Advocate*, 1952 J.C. 23.

Background state of affairs

Finally, the actus reus of an offence may require proof of some back- **3–08** ground state of affairs. For example, the actus reus of theft is, "appropriation of corporeal property belonging to another without the owner's consent".[17] It is not enough for the Crown to show that an accused has appropriated property—it must in addition prove that the property belonged to someone else, and that the owner did not consent to the appropriation.

On occasion, the Crown may prove the actus reus of an offence by showing nothing more than that a state of affairs existed—i.e. without showing that the accused did anything in particular. These offences generally are what are called "status offences" in that they hold a person liable for what he *is*, rather than what he *does*. For example, s.11 of the Terrorism Act 2000 makes it a criminal offence to be a member of a terrorist organisation, whether or not one advances an actual act of terrorism.

Mens rea

As we have already seen, for the most part, criminal liability is not **3–09** attributed to an individual merely because he has fulfilled the actus reus of an offence. Generally speaking, before a person is declared guilty of a particular offence, it must be proved that he has an appropriately blameworthy mental state.[18] The three types of mens rea that tend to arise most frequently are: (a) intention; (b) recklessness; and (c) knowledge.

Intention

Some crimes require proof that the accused had a particular intention at **3–10** the time of engaging in the criminal conduct. As previously noted, assault requires proof of an intention to cause injury or fear of injury.[19] Similarly, theft requires proof of an intention to deprive the owner of her property,[20] and fraud requires proof of an intention to deceive.[21] The law generally considers someone to be acting intentionally when he acts with purpose. So, returning to example of assault, if A walks up to B in a park and hits him in the face with a cricket bat, this would provide a strong example of A acting with criminal intent. However if A is playing cricket in the park and, while swinging the bat to play a shot, happens to strike B in the face as he passes while walking his dog, A does not have the requisite mens rea for assault. He has acted deliberately only in the sense that he did mean to swing the bat. However, he did this for the purpose of hitting the ball, not for the purpose of attacking B. If, by swinging the bat when he did, A acted with a complete disregard for the consequences of

---

[17] See *Black v Carmichael*, 1992 S.C.C.R. 709.
[18] As has already been noted, offences of strict liability form an important exception to this rule. Strict liability is considered at para.3–15, below.
[19] See *Smart v HM Advocate*, 1975 S.L.T. 65.
[20] See *Black v Carmichael*, 1992 S.C.C.R. 709.
[21] See *Mackenzie v Skeen*, 1971 J.C. 43.

his action, he will have behaved recklessly. That will not satisfy the mens rea requirement for assault, but is sufficient to establish the mens rea for the separate crime of reckless injury.[22]

It should be noted, however, that although proof of intention may be required for some offences, motive is generally irrelevant to criminal liability.[23] Thus, returning to the example of A, B and the cricket bat, if the court is satisfied on the basis of the evidence put before it that A intended to attack B with the bat—that is enough. The prosecution do not need to prove why A acted as he did, only the assault took place and that A intended that.

Recklessness

3–11 A large number of offences require or permit mens rea to be established through the proof of mere recklessness: for example, the offences of reckless injury, reckless endangerment or involuntary culpable homicide. To say that someone has acted "recklessly" is to say that he has not paid due regard to the consequences of his actions. However, the same could be said of someone who has acted carelessly or negligently. Recklessness is conceptually related to carelessness and negligence, but it refers to an especially inadequate regard to the consequences. Hence, recklessness has been described as "gross negligence" or a *complete* disregard for the consequences of one's actions.[24]

Knowledge

3–12 Some offences require proof that the accused had knowledge of some state of affairs. For example, the crime of reset requires proof that the accused knew that the goods he possessed were stolen.[25] This does not mean that an individual can avoid liability for knowledge-based offences simply by shutting his eyes to the circumstances around him; if the circumstances were such that it would have been blameworthy for him not to make inquiries, knowledge may be imputed to him.

Mens rea: objective or subjective?

3–13 Case law is inconsistent as to whether the Crown can establish the mens rea of an offence only by adducing proof of the accused's actual state of mind, or whether the Crown can do so by arguing that a reasonable man would have had that state of mind had he been in the accused's shoes at the time he acted. The former approach to proof is "subjectivist", whereas the latter is "objectivist". The subjective approach involves an examination into the state of mind of the particular accused at the time he carried out the actus reus, while the objective approach adopts a

---

[22] *HM Advocate v Harris*, 1993 S.L.T. 963.
[23] See *Palazzo v Copeland*, 1976 J.C. 52. Motive can be important in the context of certain defences, but is otherwise irrelevant. See further the discussion on defences at para.3–20, below.
[24] See *Paton v HM Advocate*, 1936 J.C. 19.
[25] See *Latta v Herron* (1967) S.C.C.R. (Supp.) 18.

reasonable man standard and may involve the presumption of intention on the basis of the act.

Intention-based offences are typically subjectivist—that is, the inquiry is to whether the accused actually had the requisite intention (for example, in cases of theft, the intention to deprive). It does not matter that, in principle, no reasonable person would have done as the accused did unless he had an intention to deprive; it remains open to the court to conclude that the accused did not himself have that intention and that he cannot, therefore, be convicted of theft. In other words, the subjectivist approach precludes the assumption that, because the accused acted as he did, he must have had a particular intention.

Recklessness-based offences, on the other hand, are typically thought to be objectivist. This means that the Crown does not need to prove that the accused actually perceived the risk he was running by engaging in his course of conduct; it is enough that a reasonable person *would* have perceived the danger. Ultimately, this concerns the issue of whether the accused's conduct reflects a level of care falling *far below* that expected of reasonable people. (A point often missed is that the Crown must do more than show that reasonable people would not act as the accused did, since this will demonstrate only carelessness or negligence. In practice, this leaves ample room for disagreement as to whether an accused's conduct was reckless or merely negligent.) There is good reason to think that knowledge-based offences, too, are objectivist inasmuch as the trier of fact can infer knowledge from the circumstances surrounding the accused's conduct.

Error

Certain kinds of error are relevant to whether an accused has the requisite **3–14** mens rea for a given offence; others are not. Mistakes of fact can be relevant, but this is not always so. Consider, for example, a case involving an accusation of rape. The mens rea of rape is satisfied where the accused A knows that the other person B is not consenting or at any rate is reckless as to whether B is consenting.[26] If the accused believed that the other was consenting and if that belief was reasonable then he lacks the mens rea for the offence.

Many non-lawyers will have, at some point, heard that "ignorance of the law is no excuse". That is only partly true. An accused cannot successfully argue that he should be acquitted on the basis of an honest but mistaken belief that what he was doing was not criminal.[27] However, some errors of *civil* law may negate the mens rea for certain offences. For example, as we shall see at para.3–22 below, theft requires proof of an intention to deprive the owner of his property. An accused can only have such an intention if he believes that the property in question belongs to someone else; if the accused believes that the property belongs to him, then he lacks the requisite mens rea. Similarly, in *Gould*, the accused was

---

[26] Sexual Offences (Scotland) Act 2009 s.1(1).
[27] *Brown v Frame*, 2005 S.L.T. 744.

acquitted of bigamy because he honestly but mistakenly believed that his first marriage had been dissolved before he entered into his second marriage.[28]

Strict liability

3–15 As we have already seen,[29] all common law offences require proof of both an actus reus and a mens rea. However, while some statutory offences follow the same pattern and require both actus reus and mens rea, not all do. Some statutory offences do not require proof of mens rea. Often the wording of the statutory provision creating the offence will itself let the reader know whether or not a particular offence is intended to be one of strict liability. If the statute states that the offence can only be committed "knowingly", "wilfully", "intentionally" or "recklessly", then it is apparent that mens rea is required. Equally, if the statute expressly states that the offence is one of strict liability, or that mens rea is not required for the offence's commission, then again the matter is clear. However, if the statute does not expressly deal with the issue, the courts will need to determine what Parliament intended. The courts will commence by presuming that mens rea is required. However, the presumption can be overcome if the statute creating the offence is directed towards an issue of social concern, such as public safety, and, "if the creation of strict liability will be effective to promote the objects of the statute by encouraging greater vigilance to prevent the commission of the prohibited act".[30]

Key Concepts

A crime has two specific elements: an actus reus (the physical element) and mens rea (the mental element). The exception to this is a strict liability crime, which requires only proof of an actus reus.
The actus reus usually takes the form of an act however in some specific cases an omission may constitute an actus reus.
Mens rea (or "guilty mind") is most often defined in terms of intention, knowledge or recklessness.

Art and part liability

3–16 The principle of art and part liability concerns participation or involvement in a crime, and provides that any person who participates in the commission of an offence may be held criminally responsible. There are two requirements for art and part liability, as delineated in case law.

---

[28] *R v Gould* [1968] 2 Q.B. 65.
[29] See para.3–05, above.
[30] *Gammon Ltd v Attorney-General of Hong Kong* [1985] A.C. 1, per Lord Scarman at 17.

First, there must be a common purpose,[31] and second, the accused must participate in the criminal enterprise.[32]

Vicarious liability

In the criminal context,[33] vicarious liability arises when criminal liability **3–17** is imputed to one person or company on the basis of what *another* person did (or failed to do), even though the actors do not share a common purpose. Vicarious liability does not arise at common law: one cannot be held vicariously liable for a common law crime. However, vicarious liability is quite commonly imposed in statutes establishing regulatory offences. In such offences, the employer or proprietor of a business may be criminally liable for the criminal conduct of his employees or agents if (and only if) the conduct takes place within the scope of the employment or agency agreement.[34]

Vicarious liability is imposed in one of two circumstances. First, it may be imposed by the express terms of a statute. For example, the Licensing (Scotland) Act 1976 permits the license-holder to be vicariously liable for a range of offences committed by his employees or agents. For instance, the license-holder is guilty of an offence if the license-holder's employee sells alcohol to a person who is younger than 18 years of age.[35] However, the statute also provides the license-holder with a "due diligence" defence—in other words, the license-holder can escape liability if he can persuade the court that he took appropriate steps to avoid the commission of the offence.[36] It will often be the case that the legislature will mitigate the apparent harshness of an express provision for vicarious liability by granting some sort of statutory defence on which the employer or principal may rely.

Secondly, where the statute itself does not expressly permit an employer or principal to be found vicariously liable, the courts may nonetheless read such a possibility into the regulatory regime. This occurs only where the employer or principal could be said to have shared responsibility for the function performed by the employee or agent, i.e. where the employer could be said to bear some degree of fault for the lack of conformity to the regulations in question.

Corporate liability

Corporate liability differs from vicarious liability in that it refers to **3–18** situations where a corporate entity—generally a company, but sometimes another entity having a legal identity separate from its consistent members—has *itself* engaged in criminal conduct and is accordingly held criminal responsibility for its *own* acts or omissions. Thus, as outlined in

---

[31] *HM Advocate v Lappen*, 1956 S.L.T. 109.
[32] See *HM Advocate v Kerr* (1871) 2 Coup. 334.
[33] Vicarious liability also arises in other contexts, most notably, in the law of delict.
[34] See *City and Suburban Dairies v Mackenna*, 1918 J.C. 105 at 110.
[35] Licensing (Scotland) Act 1976 s.68(1).
[36] Licensing (Scotland) Act 1976 s.71.

the preceding section, a corporation may in certain circumstances be vicariously liable for the criminal conduct of its employees; alternatively, it may be directly liable for its own criminal conduct.

Historically, it was believed that corporate bodies could not themselves commit criminal offences.[37] However, Scottish courts now take the view that corporate bodies can be held liable for statutory offences and some common law crimes. There are two dominant issues in the attribution of liability to a corporate entity, stemming from the fact that such an entity is not a physical person. The first issue is a simple matter of practicality: some offences can be punished only with a term of imprisonment and an incorporeal entity cannot be imprisoned. This means that a corporate entity cannot be convicted of any offence where the minimum punishment is imprisonment. Murder is the classic example of such a crime.

The second issue is more complex. As we have seen, for all common law offences, the Crown must prove both actus reus and mens rea. A corporation, however, has no brain and, therefore, no mental state of its own. Before criminal liability can be assigned to a corporation, a sensible way must be established of identifying its mental state. In Scotland, this is done by reference to the "controlling mind" of the company.[38] The "controlling mind" must be an individual person within the corporation who is in a position to set agendas and policies. The conduct and mens rea of the controlling mind of the company can then be attributed to the company. The problem, however, is that very often corporations act in dishonest or harmful ways, not as a result of decisions being taken by senior personnel who are in a position to set agendas and policies, but as a result of the way that the company is being run by managers operating at a lower level of the corporate structure, or of employees involved in the company's day to day business. Thus a successful prosecution is often impossible, particularly in the case of large companies with a complex management structure, because the controlling mind of the company may be wholly uninvolved in these matters. It is generally easier for large companies to be prosecuted for breaches of regulatory offences, particularly where these are offences of strict liability. The practical difficulties associated with bringing successful prosecutions for manslaughter or culpable homicide against large companies has led to the creation of a new corporate homicide offence, discussed at para.3–42, below.

Inchoate offences

3–19   Under s.294 of the Criminal Procedure (Scotland) Act 1995, any attempt to commit a crime is itself criminal. A person has "attempted" a particular offence when he has ceased to prepare to commit the offence and has begun to perpetrate it.[39] Reasonable people can disagree about whether a given accused has moved from preparation to perpetration; it

---

[37] See, e.g. Mackenzie, *Laws and Customs of Scotland in Matters Criminal* (Edinburgh: James Glen, 1678), i, i, 9.

[38] See *Purcell Meats (Scotland) Ltd v McLeod*, 1987 S.L.T. 528.

[39] See *HM Advocate v Camerons*, 1911 S.C. (J.) 110.

certainly appears that an accused can be said to "attempt" a crime before moving to the *final* stages of perpetration.

In *Cawthorne*, the High Court held that the mens rea for an attempted crime is the same as the mens rea for the completed offence.[40] Thus, one can be convicted of attempted murder only by acting with "wicked intention" or "wicked recklessness with intention to do bodily harm".[41] Likewise, one can be convicted of attempted theft only if the Crown proves an "intention to deceive". The holding in *Cawthorne* is peculiar inasmuch as it means that, in some cases, a person can be said to attempt something recklessly. This is a strange way to use the word "attempt": if A has not intended to do something, it would not ordinarily be said that she has attempted to do it at all. Nonetheless, this remains the state of the law in Scotland.

Substantive defences

Numerous defences exist in Scots law, including mental disorder defen- **3–20** ces,[42] automatism,[43] self-defence, coercion (the defence that the accused was forced to commit a crime against his will by another person), necessity (the defence that the accused was forced to commit a crime as a result of circumstances beyond his control) and provocation. These defences, if successful, will either lead to an outright acquittal or a conviction for a lesser offence. A further defence possibility is simple denial of some aspect of the actus reus, perhaps by means of the presence of an alibi, where the accused claims to be elsewhere at the time of the offence. In practice, common law defences generally are most commonly pled in the context of classic *malum in se* crimes like murder or assault in an attempt to excuse or justify the accused's actions. They occur in the business law context only relatively rarely and we will therefore pay no close attention to them here.

CRIMES RELEVANT TO BUSINESS

When we read media reports about the trial for murder of an alleged **3–21** serial killer or the assault and robbery of an elderly lady, the criminal law seems quite unrelated to the world of business. However, business covers

---

[40] See *Cawthorne v HM Advocate*, 1968 J.C. 32.

[41] *HM Advocate v Purcell*, 2008 J.C. 131.

[42] The defence once called "insanity", now referred to as the criminal responsibility of persons with mental disorder, is pled when an accused contends that he behaved in a way which would otherwise have been criminal because he was unable by reason of mental disorder to appreciate the nature or wrongfulness of the conduct: s.51A Criminal Procedure (Scotland) Act, as inserted by Criminal Justice and Licensing (Scotland) Act 2010 Pt 7.

[43] Non-insane automatism arises where the accused has suffered a total alienation, but not as a result of an internal factor, such as a mental illness, but as a result of an external factor: for instance, where the accused contends that someone has "spiked" his drink with hallucinogenic drugs. Voluntary intoxication is not a defence in Scots law (*Brennan v HM Advocate*, 1977 J.C. 38).

the broadest possible range of human activities and as such those engaged
in business can, from time to time, come into contact with large areas of
the criminal law, either as victims or the accused. Anyone personally
conducting a business which involves interaction with the general public
needs to know when he is entitled to use force legitimately to eject drunk
or troublesome customers, and the degree of force that may be used.
Those who are involved in potentially dangerous businesses (for instance,
the transportation of passengers, or of explosive or dangerous substances) need to know the circumstances in which they can be charged
with reckless injury or even murder or culpable homicide in the event that
something goes wrong and passengers or bystanders are killed or injured.
It is, however, outside the scope of this work to provide a full account of
all the common law crimes which businesses might possibly encounter.
The common law crimes of greatest relevance to business are those
typically categorised as crimes of dishonesty: theft, embezzlement, fraud,
uttering and extortion. In this section we will briefly examine each of
these common law offences.

Theft

3–22 The actus reus for theft is, "appropriation of corporeal moveable[44]
property belonging to another without the owner's consent".[45] Thus one
cannot steal property belonging to oneself, and something which is not
owned—for instance, a wild animal—cannot be stolen. However, the
mere fact that property has been lost or apparently abandoned does not
in law mean that it is ownerless: in Scots law, one can be found guilty of
theft by taking possession of an item that one finds. It is not necessary for
the Crown to show that the accused physically carried away property in
order to prove that the accused appropriated it; the accused has
"appropriated" property once he starts to make use of it as if he was its
owner.[46] Moreover, the Crown need not show that the accused appropriated the goods in question for any particular length of time: temporary
appropriation is sufficient.[47]

As theft applies only to corporeal property, pure knowledge or information cannot be stolen. Thus I do not steal trade secrets from my
employer by remembering the information and carrying it around in my
head. However, the physical media on which information is recorded can
be stolen. Thus, a piece of paper or a memory stick may be stolen, but the
information contained on the paper or the memory stick cannot.

---

[44] "Corporeal movable" property is property that is physically tangible but which is not
land or permanently fixed to land. A car, a television or a pet dog would be examples of
corporeal moveable property. Such property can be distinguished from immovable
(sometimes known as "heritable") property and incorporeal property (such as intellectual property). For a further discussion of the different classes of property see paras 11–
04 to 11–05, below. In *Grant v Allan*, 1988 S.L.T. 11 the accused could not be found
guilty of theft as the information which he had "stolen" was not corporeal.

[45] See *Carmichael v Black*, 1992 S.L.T. 897.

[46] See G.H. Gordon and M.G.A. Christie, *The Criminal Law of Scotland*, 3rd edn (Edinburgh: W. Green, 2001), p.13.

[47] *Fowler v O'Brien*, 1994 S.C.C.R. 112.

The mens rea for theft is an "intention to deprive". It is not necessary for the Crown to prove that the accused intended to deprive the owner permanently.[48] Thus, where the accused intends merely to "borrow" goods belonging to another, without first obtaining the owner's consent, the accused has the mens rea for theft.

Key Concept

The appropriation of another person's corporeal moveable property without his consent combined with an intention to deprive that person of his property form the key elements of the crime of theft. Temporary deprivation is sufficient to constitute the actus reus and satisfaction of the mens rea requirement does not demand proof that the accused intended to permanently deprive the owner of his property.

Embezzlement

Embezzlement is conceptually related to theft. The actus reus of **3–23** embezzlement is the dishonest appropriation of property that one already possesses using the authority of another person, to whom one is bound to account.[49] However, theft and embezzlement differ in several key respects. The most important distinction is that non-corporeal property—like, for example, information—may be embezzled, but it cannot be the object of a theft. Secondly, theft can be committed by someone who was not already in possession of the goods when he appropriated them, whereas embezzlement cannot. Thirdly, embezzlement presupposes that the thief and the owner have some pre-existing relationship; that the owner authorised the possession of the goods ultimately appropriated. Theft does not.

The mens rea for embezzlement is the same as that for theft: an intention to deprive.

Fraud

The actus reus of fraud is the use of a false pretence that: (a) deceives **3–24** another; and (b) causes a definite practical result.[50] Usually, fraudsters deceive others in order to obtain a financial benefit: for instance, a dishonest art dealer may make a false pretence by claiming that a painting he is showing to a client is by a famous artist. If the client believes him, he has been deceived, and if as a result he buys the painting for more than it is worth, then a definite practical result has been achieved and the actus reus of the crime has been committed. A "definite practical result" is achieved so long as the deceived party acts in a way she would not have

---

[48] See *Carmichael v Black*, 1992 S.L.T. 897.
[49] *Allenby v HM Advocate*, 1938 J.C. 55.
[50] *MacDonald v HM Advocate*, 1996 S.L.T. 723; 1996 S.C.C.R. 663.

acted but for the accused's deception. In the example given, the definite practical result is the sale of the painting for a higher price than the client would otherwise have paid. However, it is not necessary for the Crown to show that the accused derived any financial or other benefit from the deception. Thus, in the case of *James Paton*, the court held that the accused could be convicted of fraud even though his false pretence did not produce any financial windfall for him: he had artificially manipulated the appearance of livestock which he then entered into an agricultural exhibition in order to increase his chances of winning. However, winning the show brought no prize money, merely the glory of victory.[51] It is important to remember that the Crown must prove that the false pretence *caused* the definite practical result: the mere fact that the accused deceived another with the false pretence will not be enough to establish fraud unless the Crown can also show that the deceived party would have otherwise acted differently. So returning to the example of the art dealer, there is fraud only if the pretence caused the purchaser to buy the picture at an inflated price; if the evidence is that he would have bought it at the price requested without knowing who it was by, causation cannot be established.

The actor has the necessary mens rea for fraud if he has: (a) knowledge of the deception; and (b) an intention to deceive. Thus, it is not enough for the Crown to show that the accused has asserted a falsehood, that another has believed it, and that a definite practical result was caused by it; the Crown must establish that the accused knew the assertion was false, and intended to deceive others by making the assertion. This is clear from the decision in *MacKenzie v Skeen*.[52] In that case, the accused worked for a slaughterhouse that sold offal according to weight. The accused's job was to weigh the offal. The accused used a faulty system to do so and, as a result, someone was presented with a false bill. The court held that, even if the false pretence deceived another and led to a definite practical result (i.e. the paying of an inappropriately high or low sum of money), the accused could not be convicted unless he knew that his method of calculating the weight of the offal was faulty.

In addition to the common law offence of fraud, there are many specific types of fraud prohibited by statute. Some of these statutory offences will be discussed in Ch.6, "Consumer Protection", below.

Uttering

3–25 The offence of uttering is committed where a person: (a) deliberately exposes a forged document to another person as if it was genuine; (b) the exposure is to the prejudice of the person whose name was forged; and (c) the forged document passes beyond the control of the person uttering it. Importantly, there is no need for the Crown to show that the accused forged the document himself—it is enough that he "transmits" it.[53]

---

[51] *James Paton* (1858) 3 Irv. 208.
[52] *MacKenzie v Skeen*, 1971 J.C. 43, 1972 S.L.T. 15.
[53] See *Barr v HM Advocate*, 1927 J.C. 51.

Furthermore, there is no need for the Crown to show that anyone was deceived by the forgery; there is no requirement of proof of a "definite practical result". This distinguishes the offence of uttering from that of fraud.

To commit the offence of uttering, an individual must expose a forged document *as if it were genuine*; it is not enough that the accused simply showed the document to another. Thus, if the accused showed a forged cheque to another, saying "this is a forged document," he could not be convicted of uttering. Moreover, the act of uttering is not complete unless and until the forged document passes beyond the control of the utterer: even if the accused shows a forged cheque to another, pretending that it was genuine, he commits no offence unless and until he hands the cheque over (and therefore loses the opportunity to undo the attempt at deception). The courts have held that a document passes beyond one's control once it has been posted.[54] (This is so even though it is now quite possible for someone to expose the falsity of the document after it has been posted—for instance, by making a phone call or even driving to the addressee—but before it could possibly reach its destination.)

The case of *John Smith* states that the utterance must be to the prejudice of the person whose name has been forged.[55] Subsequent authorities do not mention this requirement. If the requirement still exists, the Crown must show that the exposure of the forged document would, *if believed*, work to the disadvantage of the person whose name was forged. The Crown does not need to show that there was any actual disadvantage. (Again, remember that the crime of uttering does not require any definite practical result.) Thus, the exposure of a forged cheque will work to the prejudice of the person whose signature has been forged, since the amount stated on the cheque will be removed from the bank account of that person.[56] On the other hand, the exposure of a forged signature on an otherwise plain piece of notepaper cannot, even if others believe that the signature is genuine, work to the detriment of the individual whose name was forged.

The mens rea for uttering is: (a) knowledge that the document is forged; and (b) an intention to deceive another.

Extortion

Extortion is the use of a "threat to concuss a person into paying a **3–26** demand".[57] It is typically thought that extortion must involve a demand for money, but this is not so—the demand may be for anything. Furthermore, it does not matter whether the accused has demanded something which is lawfully owed. Consider, for example, the circumstances in *Carmichael v Black*.[58] There, a vehicle was parked on private property without permission. The accused clamped the vehicle and placed a notice

[54] *William Jeffrey* (1842) 1 Broun 337.
[55] *John Smith* (1871) 2 Coup. 1.
[56] *John Smith* (1871) 2 Coup. 1.
[57] *Alex Crawford* (1850) Shaw 309 at 322; *Carmichael v Black*, 1992 S.L.T. 897.
[58] *Carmichael v Black*, 1992 S.L.T. 897.

on the windshield advising the owner of the car that, unless £45 was paid, the clamp would not be removed. The court held that the accused could not enforce a debt through any means other than a civil suit. The demand for £45, backed up with the threat of not unclamping the vehicle, could therefore satisfy the actus reus of extortion. This illustrates a second point worth noting: the threat need not be one of physical violence, and indeed can be a threat to do something which one is legally entitled to do. Thus, in *Rae v Donnelly*, the accused's conviction for extortion was upheld after he threatened to expose an illicit affair between two of his employees if one of the people involved in the affair did not drop a lawsuit which she had initiated against him.[59] While the accused was legally entitled to expose the affair if he chose to, he was not entitled to *threaten to expose it* in order to force his victim to give up her claim against him.

Bribery

3–27 In the world of business, there is the potential for unethical behaviour and corrupt practices, in a bid to gain competitive advantage. So, the criminal law prevents and punishes acts of bribery. The law in this respect has been reformed quite recently by the Bribery Act 2010, repealing the Public Bodies Corrupt Practices Act 1889, the Prevention of Corruption Acts 1906 and 1916. The 2010 Act, which applies across the UK, provides for the offences of bribing another person[60] (active bribery), being bribed[61] (passive bribery), and bribing foreign public officials.[62] Bribing involves offering, promising or giving a financial or other advantage to another person, where the briber intends this to induce a person to perform improperly a relevant function or activity, or to reward a person for such improper performance, or where the briber knows or believes that the acceptance of the advantage would itself constitute such improper performance.[63] The Act also introduced the offence of failure of commercial organisations to prevent bribery of someone on their behalf.[64] An organisation will have a defence if it can prove it has adequate procedures in place to prevent persons associated with it from bribing.

The Act applies to such actions in the UK and abroad, in both the public and private sectors. The replacement statutory offences do not differ greatly from their predecessors, except for extension of the offences to the private sector, a development which is questioned by Horder and

---

[59] *Rae v Donnelly*, 1982 S.C.C.R. 148.
[60] Bribery Act 2010 s.1.
[61] Bribery Act 2010 s.2
[62] Bribery Act 2010 s.6.
[63] Bribery Act 2010 s.1.
[64] Bribery Act 2010 s.7.

Aldridge for arguably overlooking the distinct moral significance in public sector wrongdoing.[65] Nonetheless, as noted in the *Joint Prosecution Guidance of The Director of the Serious Fraud Office and The Director of Public Prosecutions*,[66] there is a clear focus on commercial bribery in the Act, though it covers all forms of bribery. Bona fide hospitality and promotional expenditure that seeks to improve the image of a commercial organisation is recognised as a legitimate and important dimension of business and will not be criminalised, unless such behavior fits the relatively narrow statutory definition.

Key Concept

It is an offence to bribe another person, to bribe a foreign public official, and to be bribed. It is an offence for a commercial organisation to fail to prevent bribery of someone on their behalf. An organisation will have a defence if it can prove it has adequate procedures in place to prevent persons associated with it from bribing.

REGULATORY LAW AND REGULATORY OFFENCES

Introduction

In the modern, highly-developed state, the criminal law is used frequently **3–28** not just in the conventional sense of punishing conduct that is clearly wrongful and harmful, but also as a convenient means of putting in place legally enforceable rules intended to ensure that certain minimum standards and policies are adhered to. The body of law whereby public authorities seek to exercise control over activities that are of importance to the community is known as regulatory law. Much of regulatory law is directed towards business. Thus, those who engage in the sale of food, medical drugs and alcohol are made subject to certain positive duties designed to protect the public from some of the risks attached to the consumption of such products: those who drive motor vehicles are subject to various positive duties which protect pedestrians and other drivers from the risks attached to the dangerous use of such vehicles; landlords have positive duties designed to mitigate the risks associated with living in unsafe homes; employers have a range of duties to protect employees from the risks associated with certain working environments; companies engaged in industrial activities bear positive duties designed to minimise detrimental environmental impact. With the sort of behaviour covered by classic or conventional crimes like murder, the reasons for the law

---

[65] Jeremy Horder and Peter Alldridge (eds), *Modern Bribery Law Comparative Perspectives* (Cambridge: CUP, 2013), p.3.

[66] *http://www.cps.gov.uk/legal/a_to_c/bribery_act_2010/index.html* [Accessed May 15, 2015].

responding as it does are usually fairly obvious. Deliberately attacking and killing someone obviously involves the infliction of the most serious form of harm; it is not hard to see why the criminal law prohibits it. By contrast, the various activities listed above—selling food, renting out houses, employing people so that will carry out work—are not invariably harmful; indeed, more often than not, these activities are good things. We need to be able to gain access to food, housing and an opportunity to earn our living. In seeking to regulate these activities, the law therefore cannot simply ban them: it needs to put in place a system of rules which permit the valuable activity to continue, while removing or minimising some of the risks or problems that are associated with it.

The criminal law is therefore not the only means of enforcing regulatory law; a variety of approaches are taken. Occasionally, the State takes the view that "self-regulation" is appropriate. This is the approach which has been utilised traditionally for the regulation of the professions: for instance, complaints of professional misconduct against professional people are commonly investigated by the relevant professional body, and then adjudicated upon by an independent tribunal.[67] Alternatively, the state may require that a licence be obtained before one can undertake certain activities. Thus individuals need a licence to drive, and businesses large and small require a range of licences to undertake activities as run-of-the-mill as operating a taxi or selling alcohol, or as sophisticated as operating a telecommunications network, drilling for oil or operating a nuclear power plant. Sometimes, legislation establishes a public body with the specific remit of overseeing and enforcing a given area of regulatory law. Thus occupational health and safety law is enforced by the Health and Safety Executive and data protection law by the Information Commissioner's office.

Even where these other approaches are utilised, however, the criminal law remains present in the background. Where licences are required, operating without one is almost invariably a criminal offence, and operating with a licence but in breach of its terms is also an offence. Lying to, or otherwise obstructing the investigations of, members of statutory inspectorates is often criminal, as is failing to comply with any orders which they make.

Where the criminal law is the vehicle by which regulatory law is enforced, as we have already seen, regulatory offences are commonly (but by no means invariably) "strict liability offences". In such instances, the

---

[67] In the case of accountants, for instance, complaints are first dealt with by the particular professional body of which the accountant complained against is a member (e.g. the Association of Chartered Certified Accountants or the Institute of Chartered Accountants of Scotland). If, on the facts, it appears that there may have been misconduct and that the case raises serious matters of public interest in the UK, the matter will be referred to the Financial Reporting Council ("FRC"), where it will be investigated by the FRC's Executive Counsel. If satisfied there is a case to answer, the Executive Counsel will file a complaint which will be heard by a Tribunal appointed by the FRC. If the complaint is upheld, sanctions include a reprimand, a fine or an order that the accountant's practicing certificate be withdrawn. See *https://www.frc.org.uk/Our-Work/Conduct/Professional-discipline.aspx* [Accessed May 15, 2015].

Crown can establish guilt without proof of mens rea. The Crown need only adduce evidence that the accused person or company failed to discharge its duty to act: criminal liability will follow directly from the establishment of that fact (unless the accused is entitled to a defence).

Selected regulatory regimes and regulatory offences

It would be a mistake to imagine that regulatory law is an entirely new **3–29** thing. The biblical exhortation, "when you build a new house, make a parapet around your roof so that you may not bring the guilt of bloodshed on your house if someone falls from the roof"[68] can be seen as an early example of health and safety regulation. Germany's laws governing the purity of beer dated back to 1516,[69] while the UK has regulated workplace health, safety and welfare since 1802, when the first of the Factories Acts was introduced.[70] However, it undoubtedly is the case that the number of regulatory laws with which businesses have to comply has expanded dramatically over the last 50 years or so. Indeed, organisations which represent the interests of businesses in the UK frequently protest that the law has become too bureaucratic: they contend that there is simply too much regulation, and that the costs associated with complying with it are out of proportion to any benefits the regulation brings. The British Chambers of Commerce estimated that the total cost of the major sets of regulations with which businesses require to comply exceeded £88.3 billion in the period between 1998 and 2010.[71] When Gordon Brown became prime minister in 2007, a former chairman of the Confederation of British Industry identified the reduction of the regulatory burden as one of the most important tasks facing him.[72] The Conservative-Liberal coalition Government elected in 2010 have sought to lessen the burden of regulation, particularly for small businesses.[73] But while it is possible to have too much regulation, too little can also be deeply problematic. Lax regulation of the financial markets is one of the

---

[68] Deuteronomy 22, 8.
[69] The *Reinheitsgebot*; this was abolished in 1987 and replaced with a new set of regulations as the old law was unduly restrictive and contravened EU law.
[70] Albeit the level of protection afforded by the Factories Act 1802 looks very minimal by modern standards.
[71] This data is taken from British Chambers of Commerce, *Burdens Barometer* (2010), which could formerly be downloaded from the British Chambers of Commerce's website. It is no longer available from there but can still be downloaded from *http://www.thamesvalleychamber.co.uk/uploads/Policy/BurdensBarometer2010.pdf* [Accessed May 15, 2015]. The British Chambers of Commerce has not published the Burdens Barometer since 2010.
[72] "From day one, it is vital that simpler and better regulation of wealth and job creation takes the place of excessive red tape. Bureaucracy is a serious problem in the private sector." Sir Digby Jones, "A Manifesto for Gordon Brown", *Independent*, June 28, 2007.
[73] See, e.g. Mark Prisk MP, Minister for State for Business and Enterprise, "Creating the Most Entrepreneurial Decade", available at *https://www.gov.uk/government/speeches/creating-the-most-entrepreneurial-decade-2* [Accessed May 15, 2015]. See also the work of the Better Regulation Executive, a Government body which seeks to identify and "weed out" ineffectual and unnecessary regulations: *https://www.gov.uk/government/policies/business-regulation* [Accessed May 15, 2015].

factors which led to the credit crunch and financial crisis of 2007–2010. The Deepwater Horizon blowout and oil spill of April 20, 2010 could potentially have been prevented, or its effects reduced, if the US offshore regulatory regime had been more effective.[74] Striking the balance between having enough regulation to mitigate the risks or problems inherent in an activity without making that activity unnecessarily difficult or expensive to undertake is an inherently difficult thing to do.

It is not possible in this section to detail all of the regulatory provisions with which businesses require to comply. However, a selection of the more important regulatory provisions are discussed below.

Regulatory provisions designed to secure health and safety

Health and safety at work

3–30 Health and safety law in the UK adopts what might be described as a two-step approach. First, the leading piece of legislation in the field, the Health and Safety at Work etc. Act 1974 ("HSWA"), sets out a number of over-arching duties. These are expressed in very general terms and all employers have to comply with them. However, the detailed regulations which make up the greater part of UK health and safety law are set out in a large number of Statutory Instruments. Some of the regulations contained in these Instruments are of broad application—for instance, every employer and self-employed person in the UK has to comply with the Management of Health and Safety Regulations 1999, which, as we shall see, require risk assessments to be carried out. Other regulations, however, are sector-specific—they apply only to businesses engaged in a particular industry. As one might expect, potentially hazardous industries are subjected to a greater degree of sector-specific health and safety regulation than more mundane activities. For instance, the construction and offshore oil and gas industries are subjected to especially close regulation.

Principal duties imposed by HSWA upon employers

3–31 HSWA imposes a number of principal duties upon employers. Breaching these duties is a criminal offence and may alternatively or in addition give rise to enforcement proceedings against the employer.[75]

Employer's duty to ensure the health, safety and welfare of employees

3–32 Section 2(1) HSWA provides that, "it shall be the duty of every employer to ensure, so far as is reasonably practicable, the health, safety and welfare at work of all his employees". Section 2(2) HSWA lists five areas to which this duty extends in particular. These are:

---

[74] National Commission on the BP Deepwater Horizon Oil Spill and Offshore Drilling, *Report to President: The Gulf Oil Disaster and the Future of Offshore Drilling* (2011), available for download from *http://www.gpo.gov/fdsys/pkg/GPO-OILCOMMISSION/pdf/GPO-OILCOMMISSION.pdf* [Accessed May 15, 2015].

[75] See para.3–41 below.

(a) the provision and maintenance of plant and systems of work that are, so far as is reasonably practicable, safe and without risks to health;

(b) arrangements for ensuring, so far as is reasonably practicable, safety and absence of risks to health in connection with the use, handling, storage and transport of articles and substances;

(c) the provision of such information, instruction, training and supervision as is necessary to ensure, so far as is reasonably practicable, the health and safety at work of his employees;

(d) so far as is reasonably practicable as regards any place of work under the employer's control, the maintenance of it in a condition that is safe and without risks to health and the provision and maintenance of means of access to and egress from it that are safe and without such risks; and

(e) the provision and maintenance of a working environment for his employees that is, so far as is reasonably practicable, safe, without risks to health, and adequate as regards facilities and arrangements for their welfare at work.

Employer's duty to prepare a written health and safety at work policy

Section 2(3) HSWA requires anyone who employs more than five persons **3–33** to prepare and keep updated a written statement of his general policy with respect to the health and safety at work of his employees and the organisation and arrangements for carrying out that policy, and to bring the statement and any revision of it to the notice of all his employees.

Employer's duty to ensure the health and safety of non-employees

Section 3(1) HSWA provides that it shall be the duty of every employer **3–34** to ensure, so far as is reasonably practicable, that persons not in his employment but who may be affected by things done in the course of the employer's activities are not exposed to risks to their health or safety. An employer could be prosecuted under this section if, for example, he invited members of the public to tour a factory which contained dangerous machinery, and therefore exposed them to the risk of injury. Section 3(2) HSWA imposes similar duties on the self-employed.

Employee's own responsibilities under HSWA

It is not just the employer who is made subject to responsibilities by **3–35** HSWA; the Act also imposes some duties upon employees. In particular, s.7 HSWA provides that every employee is, while at work, under an obligation:

(a) to take reasonable care for the health and safety of himself and of other persons who may be affected by his acts or omissions at work; and

(b) as regards any duty or requirement imposed on his employer or any other person by or under any of the relevant statutory provisions, to cooperate with him so far as is necessary to enable that duty or requirement to be performed or complied with.

As was the case with the obligations imposed upon employers, it is a criminal offence to breach these obligations. Thus employees can be prosecuted for jeopardising the health and safety of either themselves, their colleagues or others who may be affected by their actions at work.[76] In practice, however, such prosecutions are very rare.

Health and safety regulations

3–36 There are so many health and safety regulations in force regulating so many different aspects of the operation of businesses that it is impossible to even briefly describe them all here. We will, however, briefly cover a selection of the more commonly encountered regulations.

The Management of Health and Safety at Work Regulations 1999

3–37 Regulation 3 of the Management of Health and Safety at Work Regulations 1999 (usually described as the "Management Regulations") is one of the cornerstones of UK health and safety law. This regulation requires every employer and self-employed person to undertake (and, when necessary, repeat the undertaking of) a suitable and sufficient assessment of the risks which his business poses to the health and safety of his employees and anyone else who might be affected by it. Other important duties imposed upon employers by the Management Regulations are the obligations to plan, organise, control, monitor and review their health and safety provision,[77] to appropriately survey the health of his employees[78] and to establish appropriate procedures to be followed in the event of serious and imminent danger to persons in the workplace.[79]

The Provision and Use of Work Equipment Regulations 1998

3–38 These regulations are designed to prevent employees from being injured by being provided with dangerous equipment. They require employers to ensure that equipment provided to workers is suitable for its intended purpose,[80] maintained in efficient working order and in good repair[81] that maintenance is appropriately recorded[82] and that equipment is regularly inspected to ensure its safety.[83]

---

[76] See *Skinner v HM Advocate*, 1994 S.C.C.R. 316. In this case, an employee who had overall responsibility for the undertaking of a particular set of roadworks was convicted of a breach of s.7 when he failed to adequately warn motorists of the existence of the roadworks.

[77] Management of Health and Safety at Work Regulations 1999 (SI 1999/3242) reg.5.

[78] Management of Health and Safety at Work Regulations 1999 (SI 1999/3242) reg.6.

[79] Management of Health and Safety at Work Regulations 1999 (SI 1999/3242) reg.8.

[80] Provision and Use of Work Equipment Regulations 1998 (SI 1998/2306) reg.4.

[81] Provision and Use of Work Equipment Regulations 1998 (SI 1998/2306) reg.5.

[82] Provision and Use of Work Equipment Regulations 1998 (SI 1998/2306) reg.5.

[83] Provision and Use of Work Equipment Regulations 1998 (SI 1998/2306) reg.6.

The Manual Handling Operations Regulations 1992

These regulations place employers under an obligation, so far as is rea- **3–39** sonably practicable, to avoid the need for his employees to undertake any manual handling operations at work which involve a risk of their being injured.[84] Where it is not reasonably practicable to avoid such manual handling work altogether, the employer is under an obligation to make a suitable and sufficient risk assessment of the handling operation,[85] to take appropriate steps to reduce the risk of injury to his employees,[86] and to provide information to employees about the total weight and weight distribution of each load.[87]

The Health and Safety (Display Screen Equipment) Regulations 1992

These regulations oblige employers to assess the suitability of work-sta- **3–40** tions[88] and train their users on their safe use,[89] permit workers who use computer screens in the course of their employment to demand free eye tests and any necessary treatment,[90] and state that the work patterns of workers using computer screens must be planned so as to ensure that they are given periodic breaks and changes of activity.[91]

Enforcement

Section 10 of the HSWA created the Health and Safety Commission and **3–41** the Health and Safety Executive. Initially, the Commission was tasked with overseeing occupational health and safety policy from a strategic standpoint and the Executive was involved in the day to day enforcement of the health and safety regime. Since April 1, 2008, however, the two bodies have been merged and both of these functions are now undertaken by the Health and Safety Executive. Local Authorities also have the duty to enforce health and safety law in certain types of business premises.[92] The HSWA provides safety inspectors with extensive powers: for instance, inspectors may enter premises, examine premises and their contents, take measurements and photographs, remove samples of sub-stances found, dismantle or test any apparently dangerous equipment, interview witnesses and make copies books or documents.[93] If an inspector reaches the conclusion that health and safety law is being breached, he can serve an improvement notice requiring that the con-travention be remedied within a given period.[94] Moreover, if an inspector forms the conclusion that there is an immediate risk of serious personal

---

[84] Manual Handling Operations Regulations 1992 (SI 1992/2793) reg.4(1)(a).
[85] Manual Handling Operations Regulations 1992 (SI 1992/2793) reg.4(1)(b)(i).
[86] Manual Handling Operations Regulations 1992 (SI 1992/2793) reg.4(1)(b)(ii).
[87] Manual Handling Operations Regulations 1992 (SI 1992/2793) reg.4(1)(b)(iii).
[88] Health and Safety (Display Screen Equipment) Regulations 1992 (SI 1992/2792) reg.2.
[89] Health and Safety (Display Screen Equipment) Regulations 1992 (SI 1992/2792) reg.6.
[90] Health and Safety (Display Screen Equipment) Regulations 1992 (SI 1992/2792) reg.5.
[91] Health and Safety (Display Screen Equipment) Regulations 1992 (SI 1992/2792) reg.4.
[92] See *http://www.hse.gov.uk/lau/* [Accessed May 15, 2015].
[93] HSWA s.20.
[94] HSWA s.21.

injury, he may issue a prohibition notice, directing that the dangerous activity be stopped immediately.[95] Alternatively, the inspector can choose not to utilise either the improvement or prohibition notice process and to instead report the employer to the procurator fiscal, recommending prosecution for the breach of health and safety law. This is commonly done in the case of a serious breach of the law. Failing to implement either an improvement or prohibition notice is also a criminal offence.

The courts take the contravention of health and safety law seriously, particularly when the risks wrong by the wrongdoer were obvious or where death or serious injury has resulted. Some of the largest fines ever handed down by courts in UK have been for breaches of health and safety law.[96]

Key Concept

The Health & Safety at Work etc. Act imposes a number of principal duties upon employers. A breach of these duties will constitute a criminal offence and may result in proceedings against the employer.

Corporate homicide

3–42   The problems which have been experienced in convicting corporations—particularly large companies—of the common law offence of corporate homicide have already been discussed.[97] In an attempt to address these difficulties, the Corporate Manslaughter and Corporate Homicide Act 2007 ("Corporate Homicide Act") created a new offence of corporate homicide. A corporation commits this offence if:

> "[T]he way in which its activities are managed or organised—(a) causes a person's death, and (b) amounts to a gross breach of a relevant duty of care owed by the organisation to the deceased."[98]

The fatality must be substantially attributable to the policies and strategies devised by the entity's senior management;[99] i.e. those who make, "decisions about how the whole or a substantial part of [the corporation's] activities are to be managed or organised" or manage or organise all or a substantial part of those activities.[100] The legislation continues to

---

[95] HSWA s.22.
[96] In 2005, Transco Plc, the company which administers the gas pipelines network in the UK, was fined £15 million for a series of health and safety failings which led to the death of a family of four in a gas explosion. In 2010, a consortium of oil companies were fined £5.35 million for health and safety breaches which led to an explosion at the Buncefield oil storage depot in Hertfordshire.
[97] See para.3–18, above.
[98] Corporate Manslaughter and Corporate Homicide Act 2007 s.1(1).
[99] Corporate Homicide Act s.1(3).
[100] Corporate Homicide Act s.1(4)(c).

attribute liability to the corporation on the basis of the conduct and mens rea of those who function as its "controlling mind".[101]

The Crown must prove that the corporation caused death by breaching "a relevant duty of care". Section 2(1) stipulates that the relevant duties of care include those owed to "employees or to other persons working for the organisation or performing services for it"; to persons for whose safety the organisation is responsible as an occupier of premises; and those owed in connection with the supply of goods or services, construction or maintenance operations, any other activity on a commercial basis, and the use or keeping of any plant, vehicle or other thing. The breach of such a duty must be "gross", that is, falling, "far below what can reasonably be expected of the organisation in the circumstances".[102] The test, in other words, is one of recklessness.

In determining whether the corporation was criminally reckless, the jury may have regard to whether it failed to comply with health and safety legislation, and decide whether any such violation was serious or especially risky.[103] The jury may also consider whether the corporation failed to actively foster a culture in which compliance with health and safety laws is treated by employees as something to be encouraged and enforced.[104] The number of convictions remains in low single figures.[105] There has yet to be a prosecution in Scotland under the 2007 Act.

Key Concept

The Corporate Manslaughter and Corporate Homicide Act 2007 introduced the possibility that a corporation may incur criminal liability in relation to a death.
Liability will be attributed to the corporation based on the actions and mens rea of those identified as its "controlling mind".

The protection of consumers from misleading information

We have already seen that the common law crime of fraud is committed **3–43** when a person makes a false pretence and causes a definite practical result. There are, in addition, a number of statutory provisions which also prohibit certain kinds of false pretence. These are fully discussed in Ch.6, "Consumer Protection", below.

---

[101] See the commentary by Peter Ferguson QC, "Corporate Manslaughter and Corporate Homicide Act 2007", 2007 S.L.T. (News) 251 at 252–253.
[102] Corporate Homicide Act s.1(4)(b).
[103] Corporate Homicide Act s.8(2).
[104] Corporate Homicide Act s.8(3).
[105] See for example *R v Cotswold Geotechnical Holdings Ltd* [2011] EWCA Crim 1337; *R v JMW Farms Ltd* Unreported May 8, 2012 (Crown Ct (Belfast)); *R v Lion Steel Equipment Ltd* Unreported July 20, 2012 (Crown Ct (Manchester)).

Regulatory requirements relative to the misuse of data

Computer Misuse Act 1990

3–44 Section 1 of the Computer Misuse Act 1990 ("CMA") states:

> (1) A person is guilty of an offence if—
>
> > (a) he causes a computer to perform any function with intent to secure access to any program or data held in any computer;
> > (b) the access he intends to secure is unauthorised; and
> > (c) he knows at the time when he causes the computer to perform the function that that is the case.
>
> (2) The intent a person has to have to commit an offence under this section need not be directed at—
>
> > (a) any particular program or data;
> > (b) a program or data of a particular kind; or
> > (c) a program or data held in any particular computer.

Though the CMA was primarily designed to thwart remote-access computer hacking, one can commit the offence simply by physically standing at another person's computer and causing the computer to perform any function with intent to access, without authorisation, programs or data contained in that computer.[106] The wording of s.1(1)(a) suggests that actual access to the program or data is not required; it is enough that the accused causes the computer to perform a function in an attempt to access that program or data. Access to any program or data is "unauthorised" if it is accessed by a person who is not entitled to control access to it or has not been given access by someone so entitled.[107] The question in a given case will be whether the accused had authorisation to access the *actual* data or programs involved, not whether he had authorisation to access the *kind* of data or programs involved. Thus, a person who has authorisation to access the computer files of a particular group of customers does not necessarily have authorisation to access the computer files of other customers even though all the files contain the same kind of information.[108] If the accused has authorisation to access the program or data in question, however, it appears that she does not lose that authorisation merely because she has an inappropriate reason for accessing it.[109]

In addition, s.3 provides that:

> A person is guilty of an offence if—

---

[106] *Attorney-General's Reference (No.1 of 1991)* [1992] 3 W.L.R. 432 (CA).

[107] CMA s.17(5).

[108] See *R. v Bow Street Metropolitan Magistrates, ex parte US Government* [1999] 3 W.L.R. 620.

[109] See *DPP v Bignell* (1998) 1 Cr. App. R. 1, approved in *Bow Street Magistrates*.

> (a) he does any act which causes an unauthorised modification of the contents of any computer; and
> (b) at the time when he does the act he has the requisite intent and the requisite knowledge.

The accused has the requisite intent if she intends to modify the contents of a computer program for the purpose of impairing the operation of the computer, preventing or impairing access to any program or data on the computer, or impairing the operation of any program or the reliability of data.[110] The accused has the requisite knowledge if she knows that the modifications in question are unauthorised.[111]

A person is also guilty of an offence under s.3A of the CMA if he "makes, adapts, supplies or offers to supply" any "article"—an expression defined so as to include either physical devices or computer programs or data—intending it to assist in the commission of offences under ss.1 or 3. Thus, for example, the author or user of computer malware will himself commit a crime if it can be established that he intended it to be used in the commission of a s.1 or s.3 offence.

Data Protection Act 1998

Following concern, both domestically and at the level of international **3–45** law,[112] about the possibility that the growing amount of personal data held on computer databases could be being misused, laws regulating the retention and use of personal data were first introduced in the UK by the Data Protection Act 1984. This Act was replaced by the Data Protection Act 1998 ("DPA"), which implements the European Data Protection Directive 95/46/EC and which both expands the scope of the UK's data protection regime (meaning that for the first time some paper based records, as well as those held electronically, are regulated) and fortifies the data rights available to individuals.

Definitions

The DPA is ultimately concerned with the regulation of the processing of **3–46** personal data. Broadly speaking, data is "processed" when it is obtained, recorded, held or when a variety of operations are carried out upon it: examples include organising, accessing, altering, disclosing or erasing the data. The DPA defines "data" primarily as information held by equipment operating automatically in response to instructions given for that purpose (in practice, this means information held on computer and

---

[110] CMA s.3(2).
[111] CMA s.3(3).
[112] Council of Europe, *Convention for the Protection of Individuals with regard to Automatic Processing of Personal Data*, Strasbourg, January 28, 1981, 20 I.L.M. 317. The Data Protection Act 1984 implemented the UK's obligations under this treaty.

accessible by programs).[113] The person about whom the information is held is known as the "data subject". The person holding the information about the data subject is known as the "data controller". "Personal data" is data which relates to a living person who can be identified either directly from those data, or from those data and other information held or likely to come into the possession of the data controller. Information such as a person's name, address, age and the like will be "personal data". "Sensitive personal data" is also defined by the DPA and is given some specific protections not afforded to regular personal data. "Sensitive personal data" is defined as information which relates to a data subject's racial or ethnic origin, political opinions, religious or similar beliefs, membership (or non-membership) of a trade union, physical or mental health or condition, sexual life and police or criminal record.[114]

This multitude of definitions serves to demonstrate that the DPA is drafted in a rather convoluted and technical manner. This is unfortunate, given that its purpose is to provide "the man or woman in the street" with a set of rights. However, despite the DPA's apparent complexity, once the definitions which it uses are understood, its core principles not unduly hard to follow.

The data protection principles

3–47 The DPA contains eight data protection principles which apply to all instances of data processing, other than processing which falls within the scope of an exemption. (In practice, the majority of the exemptions relate to the domestic use of information and the public sector and a limited number of professions, including the legal profession and journalism; exemptions are not more generally available in the business context.) The most detailed principle is the first principle, which states:

> (1) Personal data shall be processed fairly and lawfully and, in particular, shall not be processed unless one or more of the following conditions is met:
>
> - the data subject has given his consent to the processing[115];
> - the processing is necessary for the performance of a contract to which the data subject is a party or for the taking of steps at the request of the data subject with a view to entering into a contract;
> - the processing is necessary for compliance with any legal obligation to which the data controller is subject, other than an obligation imposed by contract;

---

[113] Certain records, including health and education records, are also included in the definition whether held on computer or not. See DPA s.1(1)(d) read with s.68 and Sch.11 and 12. All recorded information held by public authorities also qualifies as "data": DPA s.1(1)(e).

[114] DPA s.2.

[115] As we shall see, in practice this is the easiest and safest way for a data controller to comply with the DPA.

- the processing is necessary in order to protect the vital interests of the data subject;
- the processing is necessary for the administration of justice, or for the exercise of any functions:
  — of the Houses of Parliament;
  — conferred on any person by or under any enactment;
  — of the Crown, a Minister of the Crown or a government department;
  — of a public nature exercised in the public interest by any person;

- The processing is necessary for the purposes of legitimate interests pursued by the data controller or by the third party or parties to whom the data are disclosed, except where the processing is unwarranted in any particular case by reason of prejudice to the rights and freedoms or legitimate interests of the data subject; he Secretary of State may by order specify particular circumstances in which this condition is, or is not, to be taken to be satisfied.

Given the lack of certainty inherent in some of the above conditions,[116] in practice a sensible data controller will always seek to obtain the consent of a data subject to the controller's proposed processing. It is for this reason that when, for instance, one is purchasing goods off the internet, immediately before to completing the purchase, one will generally be presented with a set of "tick boxes", offering the option to agree or not agree to what the seller proposes to do with your personal data.

In the case of "sensitive personal data" only, in addition to one of the above conditions, one of a further set of additional conditions must also be met if the first principle is to be satisfied. Among this additional set of conditions are the following:

- the data subject has given his explicit consent to the processing of the personal data;
- the processing is necessary for the purposes of exercising or performing any right or obligation which is conferred or imposed by law on the data controller in connection with employment;
- the information contained in the personal data has been made public as a result of steps deliberately taken by the data subject;
- the processing is necessary for the purpose of, or in connection with, any legal proceedings or the obtaining of legal advice;

---

[116] It can be difficult, for example, for a data controller to demonstrate that it was "necessary" to process information, as opposed to it being merely "desirable" or "convenient" for him to do so.

- the processing is necessary for medical purposes and is undertaken by a health professional or other person owing the data subject an effectual duty of confidentiality; and
- the processing is of sensitive personal data consisting of information as to racial or ethnic origin and is necessary for the purpose of identifying or keeping under review the existence or absence of equality of opportunity or treatment between persons of different racial or ethnic origins, with a view to enabling such equality to be promoted or maintained.[117]

The remaining data protection principles are set out in paras 2–8 of Sch.1 to the DPA, as follows:

(2) Personal data shall be obtained only for one or more specified and lawful purposes, and shall not be further processed in any manner incompatible with that purpose or those purposes.

(3) Personal data shall be adequate, relevant and not excessive in relation to the purpose or purposes for which they are processed.

(4) Personal data shall be accurate and, where necessary, kept up to date.

(5) Personal data processed for any purpose or purposes shall not be kept for longer than is necessary for that purpose or those purposes.

(6) Personal data shall be processed in accordance with the rights of data subjects under this Act.

(7) Appropriate technical and organisational measures shall be taken against unauthorised or unlawful processing of personal data and against accidental loss or destruction of, or damage to, personal data.

(8) Personal data shall not be transferred to a country or territory outside the European Economic Area ("EEA") unless that country or territory ensures an adequate level of protection for the rights and freedoms of data subjects in relation to the processing of personal data.[118]

Enforcement (1): the rights of data subjects

3–48 Data subjects have a variety of rights under the DPA; these can be used by the individual in order to enforce the data protection principles. In particular, data subjects have the right to know whether any personal data relating to them is held by a particular data controller and, if so, to receive a copy of it.[119] This is known as a subject access request. If the personal data held by the data controller is inaccurate, the data subject is entitled to have the information corrected, blocked, erased or destroyed

---

[117] The full list of conditions can be found in Sch.3 to the DPA.

[118] The EEA comprises the Member States of the EU and the States of Iceland, Norway and Lichtenstein.

[119] DPA s.7. The data controller is entitled to demand that the request be made in writing and to levy a small fee for providing the copy.

and may go to court for an order to that effect if the data controller will not voluntarily alter the information held.[120] If the data subject is likely to suffer substantial and unwarranted distress or damage through the processing of his personal information, he is entitled to serve a notice on the data controller, demanding that he stop processing the data.[121] Data subjects are also entitled to demand that data controllers stop sending direct marketing materials to them.[122] Data controllers who breach any of the data subject's rights and thereby cause a data subject to suffer a loss are liable to pay compensation to the data subject.[123]

Enforcement (2): enforcement by the State

In addition to the data subject's own right to take an interest in the **3–49** personal data held about him, the DPA provides the Information Commissioner's office ("ICO") with a broad range of powers designed to enforce compliance with the DPA. Any organisation which is not exempt must notify the ICO that it is processing personal data[124]; failure to do so is a criminal offence. In addition, the ICO has the power to:

- enter upon premises and conduct searches to ensure that organisations are complying with the DPA[125];
- serve information notices requiring organisations to provide the ICO with specified information within a certain time period with a view towards assessing whether the data protection principles are being properly complied with;
- serve enforcement notices where there has been a breach of the DPA, compelling organisations to take action in order to comply with the law;[126]
- prosecute those who commit criminal offences under the DPA. Breaching a data protection principle is not of itself a criminal offence: however the DPA does create a number of criminal offences. For instance, failing to notify the ICO of processing is an offence of strict liability[127]; failing to comply with an enforcement or other notice issued by the ICO is also an offence of strict liability, albeit the data controller has the benefit of a "due

---

[120] DPA s.14.
[121] DPA s.10.
[122] DPA s.11.
[123] DPA s.13.
[124] DPA s.17.
[125] DPA s.50 read together with Sch.9.
[126] For instance, on November 18, 2014 an enforcement order was served on Grampian Health Board after patients' medical records were found lying unattended in public on six separate occasions. The Commissioner considered this to be a breach of the seventh data protection principle and served a notice upon the Health Board, requiring it to improve its practices. Copies of enforcement orders are available for download from *https://ico.org.uk/action-weve-taken/enforcement/* [Accessed May 15, 2015].
[127] DPA s.17 read together with s.21.

diligence" defence[128]; and it is an offence to knowingly or recklessly obtain or disclose personal data without the consent of the relevant data controller, or to procure another to do so[129];

- conduct audits to assess whether organisations' processing of personal data follows good practice; and
- report to Parliament on data protection issues of concern.

Key Concept

The use of data in the commercial environment is regulated by the Computer Misuse Act 1990 and the Data Protection Act 1998. The Computer Misuse Act is primarily designed to criminalise computer hacking but the offences it creates are broader than that. The Data Protection Act restricts the circumstances in which data may be held and processed and imposes particularly tight restrictions on the processing of personal data.

Competition law

3–50   Competition between businesses generally is perceived to be a good thing. The fact that businesses have to fight amongst each other for customers is believed to lead to the "survival of the fittest" and to act as an incentive for businesses to lower prices (because if they don't, consumers will buy from business rivals that do), increase quality (as otherwise consumers will buy better goods from business rivals) and generally reduce waste and perform more efficiently: factors which are thought to work to the benefit both of the economy and the individual consumer.

Competition might be good for the consumer and the economy in general, but it can be said to be inconvenient for individual businesses who may find that in a competitive marketplace they require to work harder and for less profit than would be the case in a less competitive marketplace. There is, therefore, a natural temptation for businesses to seek to reduce the amount of competition which they face. However, given the benefits which competition is thought to bring, it will come as no surprise to learn that attempts to eradicate competition or distort the free market are taken very seriously, and most jurisdictions have developed a body of law that regulates such behaviour.[130] Both UK and EU laws exist to prohibit anti-competitive practices. UK law is currently governed principally by the Competition Act 1998 ("CA"); EU law by

---

[128] DPA s.47.

[129] DPA s.55. Substantial fines were imposed, for instance, on ICU Investigations Limited, one of its directors and several of its employees after private investigators employed by the company tricked a number of data controllers into disclosing personal data without the consent of the data subject: see *http://www.bbc.co.uk/news/uk-england-27162574* [Accessed May 15, 2015].

[130] In America, where modern competition law first emerged, this body of law is known as "antitrust" law.

arts 101 and 102 the Treaty on the Functioning of the European Union ("TFEU"). There were formerly significant differences between UK and EU competition law but the sets of law have by and large become harmonised into one set of rules.[131] Both UK and EU law contain two main prohibitions: businesses[132] must not engage in anti-competitive agreements or practices, and they must not seek to abuse a dominant market position. In addition, competition law seeks to control mergers between large corporations which would have the effect of threatening competition.

The regulation of anti-competitive agreements and behaviour

Chapter 1 of the Competition Act 1998 and art.101 of TFEU both **3–51** prohibit arrangements between businesses which have the capacity to:

- affect trade in the UK or EU; and
- have, as their object or effect, the restriction of competition in the UK or EU.

A variety of such agreements have been found to exist over the years. Perhaps the classic examples of such agreements are price-fixing and market-sharing agreements, but others also exist: orchestrated customer boycotts, trade association rules and mergers which have the effect of significantly impeding competition have all on occasion breached Chapter 1 or art.101. For our purposes it is sufficient to focus on price-fixing and market-sharing agreements.

Price fixing

Price fixing occurs when trade competitors agree that they will set either **3–52** the purchase or selling price of goods or services, or that they will similarly fix other important terms on which they do business. For obvious reasons, the price is usually set at a level which is higher than would be achievable in a truly competitive market. Such agreements will not breach competition law if they will have only a minimal effect upon competition.[133] In all other cases, they are prohibited.

There have been a number of notable examples of such agreements. For instance, in 2006, the Court of Appeal concluded that the well-known sports shop, JJB Sports, had been involved in fixing the price of

---

[131] Some differences of detail remain, particularly with regard to investigatory powers and the procedure for dealing with complaints about competition, but it is outside the scope of this work to discuss them.

[132] In fact, the prohibition is imposed upon "undertakings", a term which includes all vehicles commonly used for business purposes in this country and also includes state bodies and trade organisations.

[133] In the case of trade competitors, if the aggregate market share of all the parties involved in the agreement is less than 10% of the market affected by the agreement it will be considered to fall outside the ambit of the prohibition on the basis that it is an "agreement of minor importance".

Umbro football shirts.[134] In the same case, the toy and game manufacturer Hasbro and retailers Argos and Littlewoods were found to have
entered into an agreement fixing the retail sale price of a number of
Hasbro products.[135] Civil penalties of £6.7 million had been imposed on
JJB and £17.28 million on Argos. The Court of Appeal found that these
penalties were appropriate and refused to overturn them on appeal.
Similarly, in 2009, a large number of companies active in the English
construction industry received a civil penalty of £129.5 million for a
variety of price fixing activities.[136]

Market-sharing agreements

3–53 The most straightforward example of a market-sharing agreement is
where two competitors agree that they will stay out of a particular area:
e.g. that one will operate within the Highlands of Scotland and the east
coast, and the other within the south-west and the Borders. This sort of
arrangement may be efficient from the standpoint of the businesses,
because it may save them from the expense of setting up a sales infrastructure in areas where they have not traditionally done business. It is,
however, inefficient from the standpoint of the consumer, as it means that
he does not have the opportunity to buy from the company who has
agreed not to sell within the part of the country in which he resides.
Again, such agreements breach Chapter 1 of the Competition Act 1998
and art.101 of TFEU.

Abuse of a dominant market position

3–54 Chapter 2 of the Competition Act 1998 and art.102 of TFEU both
prohibit conduct which:

- amounts to abuse of a dominant position; and
- affects trade in the UK or EU.

By definition, businesses can only contravene this rule by having a
dominant position. Dominance is assessed by considering the business's
market power: this in turn usually involves having regard to the business's level of market share. Generally, a company with a market share of
40 per cent is at risk of being found to be in a dominant position; a
company with a market share of 50 per cent will be presumed to be in a
dominant position, although this presumption may be rebutted by the
leading of evidence.[137]

It is not, however, the mere possession of a dominant market position

---

[134] *Argos Ltd and JJB Sports Ltd v Office of Fair Trading* [2006] U.K.C.L.R. 1135. The
investigation into the price fixing practices was reportedly triggered by a tip-off provided
by the chief executive of a rival sports shop company after he was told by a senior
executive of JJB that, "there is a club in the North, son, and you're not part of it".

[135] Ironically, one of the products concerned was the board-game, Monopoly.

[136] See *http://www.telegraph.co.uk/finance/newsbysector/constructionandproperty/6216928/
OFT-fines-103-construction-firms-129.5m-for-bid-rigging.html* [Accessed May 15, 2015].

[137] See *AKZO Chemie BV v Commission (C-62/86)* [1991] E.C.R. I-3359.

which is problematic, but the *abuse* of that dominance. Abuse of a dominant position may occur in a number of ways: predatory pricing (i.e. the practice of selling goods or services at a lower price than they are worth in order to "kill off" competition) and offering rebates to loyal customers are examples of the kind of conduct which will be seen as abusive. A good example of such conduct occurred in the case of *Aberdeen Journals Ltd v Director General of Fair Trading.*[138] Here, Aberdeen Journals was found to have abused the dominant position which it held within the newspaper advertising market in Aberdeen by greatly reducing the cost of advertising in its newspapers to below cost price in advance of the launch of a new competitor newspaper, the Aberdeen Independent.

Enforcement of prohibitions on anti-competitive agreements and abuses a dominant market position

In the UK, investigations into anti-competitive agreements and abuses of **3–55** dominant positions (whether under UK or EU law) are now carried out by the Competition and Markets Authority ("CMA").[139] The CMA has extensive powers to carry out investigations, including the right to enter into and search business premises. If anti-competitive behaviour in breach of the CA or TFEU is established, the principal enforcement mechanism is the imposition of a penalty, similar to a fine but in fact recoverable under civil law and procedure, rather than under the criminal law. Such a penalty will be imposed in first instance by the CMA but if the penalised business believes the penalty to be excessive it may appeal to the Competition Appeals Tribunal ("CAT"). The CMA is empowered to impose penalties as high as 10 per cent of a company group's worldwide turnover. In addition, while the criminal law has not traditionally played a role in the enforcement of UK competition law, individuals who are guilty of the most serious anti-competitive practices such as price-fixing commit an offence and, if convicted, a maximum sentence of five years imprisonment and/or an unlimited fine. Company directors found to have been involved in anti-competitive practices may be disqualified for up to 15 years. In *R v Whittle, Brammar and Allison*, three executives who had been involved in a long-standing price fixing cartel were imprisoned for a total six years and two months and disqualified from acting as company directors for a total of 17 years.[140] Moreover, anti-competitive agreements are void and unenforceable, and persons who can demonstrate that they have suffered a loss as a result of another's breach of competition law may be entitled to compensation.[141] Thus it can be seen that the consequences of breaching competition law can potentially be very severe indeed.

---

[138] [2003] CAT 11.
[139] Formerly these activities were undertaken by the Office of Fair Trading and the Competition Commission.
[140] [2008] EWCA Crim 2560; [2009] U.K.C.L.R. 247.
[141] CA s.47(A).

Merger control

3–56 The merger of large corporate entities can also have an impact upon competition, even if that is not the main reason why the parties have decided to enter into the merger. Mergers that have a "European Community dimension"—generally speaking, mergers of business organisations having very large turnovers (i.e. those measured in many thousands of millions of Euros) will be governed by the EU under and in terms of the Merger Regulation (EC/139/2004). Smaller UK mergers will be dealt with under UK law, which is now contained in the Enterprise Act 2002 ("EA") as amended by the Enterprise and Regulatory Reform Act 2013. This provides that the CMA has a duty to investigate any proposed merger where the company targeted for acquisition has an annual turnover in excess of £70 million, and/or the merged companies would between them supply at least 25 per cent of the goods of services of a particular type either within the UK, or within part of the UK.[142] If the CMA concludes, on the basis of a preliminary or "Phase 1" investigation, that such a merger may have the effect of causing a "substantial lessening in competition", it must either conduct a more detailed "Phase 2" investigation or receive undertakings from the companies who intend to merge which satisfy it that the reconfigured company would not substantially lessen competition.[143] If, following Phase 2 investigation, the CMA is satisfied that the merger may substantially lessen competition, it may prohibit the merger,[144] approve it subject to conditions, or approve it subject to the receipt of undertakings from the companies party to the merger. For instance, in the case of the acquisition by Cineworld of City Screen Limited, the CMA considered the merger may be anticipated to result in a substantial lessening of competition in three locations— Aberdeen, Bury St Edmunds and Cambridge. The CMA was willing to approve the merger, subject to Cineworld's signing a binding undertaking to sell those particular cinemas within an agreed timescale.[145]

Key Concept

Anti-competitive practices are currently governed principally in domestic law by the Competition Act 1998 and in EU law by arts 101 and 102 of TFEU. The law makes conduct such as price fixing and abusing a dominant position criminal and regulates the circumstances in which companies who both enjoy significant market share may merge.

---

[142] EA s.23.

[143] EA s.73.

[144] As in the Akzo Nobel N.V. / Metlac Holding S.r.l. merger inquiry, where the CMA was satisfied that the proposed merger would lead to a significant lessening in competition in the beer and beverage can industry in the UK: see *https://www.gov.uk/cma-cases/akzo-nobel-n-v-metlac-holding-s-r-l-merger-inquiry* [Accessed May 15, 2015].

[145] See CMA, Cineworld / City Screen merger inquiry, available at *https://www.gov.uk/cma-cases/cineworld-city-screen-merger-inquiry* [Accessed May 15, 2015].

Environmental law

Environmental regulation is a very substantial body of law which **3–57** encompasses a wide range of situations ranging from the unauthorised release of genetically modified organisms[146] to the protection of rare offshore marine habitats from offshore oil and gas activities.[147] Given the scope of the subject, it is not possible here to offer more than a brief introduction.[148] A broad range of regulatory approaches are also taken within the field, ranging right along the spectrum from what is known as "procedural regulation" through a licensing/permissioning approach up to the imposition of criminal liability.

"Procedural regulation" is where the law is not concerned with the outcome of a given regulatory process, but requires only that a particular process be gone through before a decision is reached. This is a feature of environmental impact law. Certain large-scale projects of a nature such that they are likely to have a significant effect upon the environment must be the subject of an environmental impact assessment ("EIA") before the state is permitted to approve them. However, matters end there. The law does not prescribe what is to happen in the event that the EIA suggests that the project should not go ahead. Instead, it seeks to ensure that the potential impact upon the environment is borne in mind when the decision on whether or not to proceed with the project is being taken.[149]

So far as licensing is concerned, those involved in the waste disposal business require a licence authorising their operations from the local waste regulation authority.[150] Such licences may be suspended or revoked if the holder ceases to be a fit and proper person to hold such a licence, or if the continuation of the activities authorised by the licence would cause serious levels of pollution.[151]

Criminal liability is imposed in a number of environmental law regulations. For instance, it is an offence for a company which supplies water to provide water that is unfit for human consumption. The offence is one of strict liability, but the water company is entitled to a due diligence defence; it is also a defence for it to prove that it had no reasonable grounds for suspecting that the water would be used for human consumption.[152]

---

[146] Regulated by Pt VI of the Environmental Protection Act 1990.

[147] On which see, e.g. the Habitats Directive (EC/92/43) and the Offshore Petroleum Activities (Conservation of Habitats) Regulations 2001.

[148] For an excellent account of environmental law and policy see S. Bell, D. McGillivray and O. Pedersen, *Environmental Law*, 8th edn (Oxford: OUP, 2013).

[149] See C. Reid, *Nature Conservation Law*, 3rd edn (Edinburgh: W. Green, 2009), para.8.3.14.

[150] Environmental Protection Act 1990 s.35.

[151] Environmental Protection Act 1990 s.38.

[152] Water Industry Act 1991 s.70.

▼ CHAPTER SUMMARY

THE CRIMINAL LAW

3–58

(1) Generally an individual can only commit a criminal offence by engaging in a course of conduct which the law regards as wrongful (the actus reus) while simultaneously possessing a blameworthy state of mind (the required mens rea).

(2) An important exception to this is a strict liability crime where proof of the relevant actus reus is sufficient to secure a conviction.

(3) The actus reus usually takes the form of an action but in some specific cases may result from an omission.

(4) Where an offence requires proof that the accused caused the given result (the requirement of causation), the Crown must prove that "but for" the accused's actions the result would not have occurred.

(5) Where an intervening act (novus actus interveniens) occurs between the accused's conduct and the result this may "break the chain of causation" thereby making it unjust to hold the accused liable for the result.

(6) The three types of mens rea that tend to arise most frequently are: (a) intention; (b) recklessness; and (c) knowledge.

(7) A corporate body can be guilty of a criminal offence. Where an offence requires mens rea it must be proved that those identified as the "controlling mind" of the company possessed the necessary "guilty mind".

(8) Art and part liability concerns participation or involvement in a crime. Any person who participates in the commission of an offence may be held criminally responsible.

(9) Vicarious liability arises when criminal liability is imputed to one person or company on the basis of what *another* person did (or failed to do), even though the actors do not share a common purpose.

THEFT

(1) The appropriation of another person's corporeal moveable property without his consent combined with an intention to deprive that person of his property form the actus reus and mens rea of theft.

(2) Temporary deprivation is sufficient to constitute the actus reus, and satisfaction of the mens rea requirement does not demand proof that the accused intended to permanently deprive the owner of his property.

EMBEZZLEMENT

(1) The actus reus of embezzlement is the dishonest appropriation of property which, while belonging to another, is already in one's possession. The mens rea of the crime is the intention to deprive the owner of his property.

(2) Non-corporeal property, such as information, may be embezzled, but it cannot be the object of a theft.

FRAUD

(1) The actus reus of fraud is the use of a false pretence that deceives another and causes a definite practical result.
(2) The mens rea is satisfied by proof of knowledge of the deception along with an intention to deceive.

UTTERING

(1) In the crime of uttering it is not necessary for the Crown to prove that the accused forged the document himself. It is sufficient to show that the accused transmitted the document in the knowledge that the document was forged and with the intention of deceiving another.

EXTORTION

(1) Extortion is constituted by the use of a threat in pursuit of a demand.
(2) The demand may be for something other than money.

BRIBERY

(1) It is an offence to bribe another person, to bribe a foreign public official, and to be bribed. It is an offence for a commercial organisation to fail to prevent bribery of someone on their behalf. An organisation will have a defence if it can prove it has adequate procedures in place to prevent persons associated with it from bribing.

REGULATORY LAW

(1) The criminal law is only one method used to enforce regulatory law. Other approaches include:

    (a) self regulation through a professional body;
    (b) requirement for state controlled licences; and
    (c) regulation through by a public body established by legislation.

(2) An important piece of legislation which impacts on all businesses is the Health and Safety at Work etc. Act 1974.
(3) The HWSA 1974 imposes a number of principal duties upon employers. A breach of these duties will constitute a criminal offence and may result in proceedings against the employer.

CORPORATE HOMICIDE

(1) The Corporate Manslaughter and Corporate Homicide Act 2007 was introduced in order to increase the chances of a corporation incurring a form of criminal liability which the public will recognise as seriously blameworthy in relation to a death.

(2) The actus reus of the crime is causing a person's death; its mens rea is doing so through a gross breach of a relevant duty of care. This in turn requires recklessness

(3) Liability will be attributed to the corporation based on the actions and mens rea of those identified as its "controlling mind".

MISUSE OF DATA

(1) The use of data in the commercial environment is regulated by the Computer Misuse Act 1990 and the Data Protection Act 1998. The Computer Misuse Act is primarily designed to criminalise computer hacking but the offences it creates go broader than that. The Data Protection Act restricts the circumstances in which data may be held and processed and imposes particularly tight restrictions on the processing of personal data.

COMPETITION LAW

(1) Anti-competitive practices are currently governed principally in domestic law by the Competition Act 1998 and in EU law by arts 101 and 102 of TFEU. The law makes conduct such as price fixing and abusing a dominant position criminal and regulates the circumstances in which companies who both enjoy significant market share may merge.

ENVIRONMENTAL LAW

(1) Regulation in this area of the law extends from licensing requirements to imposition of criminal liability through strict liability crimes.

? QUICK QUIZ

- Is the criminal law a branch of public or private law?
- What are the elements of a common law offence?
- What kinds of state of mind are capable of satisfying the requirement of mens rea?
- What is strict liability?
- What is vicarious liability?
- Can corporations be found guilty of a crime?
- What is the mens rea of theft?
- What are the elements of the crime of fraud?
- How can a business defend itself against a charge of failing to prevent bribery?
- What does the expression "regulatory law" mean?
- The Health and Safety at Work etc. Act 1974 is the main piece of occupational health legislation in the UK. What are the essential features of HSWA?

- What is the purpose of the Corporate Manslaughter and Corporate Homicide Act 2007?
- What are the essential features of the Data Protection Act 1998?
- Why do we regulate competition between businesses? Which anti-competitive behaviours are regulated by competition law? What are the consequences of breaching the prohibitions?

📖 FURTHER READING

- ➤ C. Gane, C. Stoddart and J. Chalmers (eds), *A Casebook on the Criminal Law of Scotland*, 4th edn (Edinburgh: W. Green, 2009) (a good reference source containing extracts from cases of particular importance).
- ➤ G. Gordon and M. Christie, *The Criminal Law of Scotland*, 3rd edn (Edinburgh: W. Green, 2005) (the most authoritative modern text; excellent and comprehensive but as a result very detailed complex at points).
- ➤ *Tolley's Health and Safety at Work Handbook 2015*, 27th edn (London: LexisNexis, 2015) (provides a good practical account of health and safety law).
- ➤ R. Baldwin and M. Cave, *Understanding Regulation: Theory, Strategy and Practice,* 2nd edn, (Oxford: OUP, 2011) (theoretical in approach; complex but thought-provoking).
- ➤ T. Jones and M. Christie, *Criminal Law*, 5th edn (Edinburgh: W. Green, 2012) (an excellent concise guide).
- ➤ S. Bell, D. McGillivray and O. Pedersen, *Environmental Law*, 8th edn (Oxford: OUP, 2013) (an excellent introductory account).
- ➤ R. Whish and D. Bailey, *Competition Law*, 7th edn, (Oxford: OUP, 2012) (an excellent and comprehensive guide to the subject; note, however, that it is out of date in that the abolition of the OFT and CC and introduction of the CMA post-date this edition).

🖱 RELEVANT WEBLINKS

- ➤ Scottish Courts Website (database of criminal cases): *http://www.scotcourts.gov.uk/search-judgments/high-court* [Accessed May 15, 2015].
- ➤ Health and Safety Executive: *http://www.hse.gov.uk* [Accessed May 15, 2015].
- ➤ Information Commissioner's Office: *https://ico.org.uk/* [Accessed May 15, 2015].
- ➤ Competition and Markets Authority: *https://www.gov.uk/government/organisations/competition-and-markets-authority* [Accessed May 15, 2015].

Chapter 4   The Law of Contract

GREG GORDON[1]

▶ CHAPTER OVERVIEW

4–01 This chapter is concerned with the law of contract. It begins by looking at the definition of a contract and then examines the process by which contracts are formed. The chapter then proceeds to consider important aspects relating to the legal content of a contract and then turns to the issue of defective contracts. Remedies for breach of contract are then considered and, finally, the various circumstances under which contractual obligations may become extinct are discussed.

✓ OUTCOMES

4–02 After studying this chapter you should:

✓ be able to describe what a contract is and be able to differentiate contracts from:

- non-binding agreements; and
- unilateral gratuitous promises.

✓ understand the process by which contracts are formed and, in particular, be aware of the legal significance of both *consensus in idem* and intention, and understand the following concepts:

- offer;
- acceptance (including the problems associated with the communication of acceptance);
- counter-offer; and
- battle of the forms

✓ appreciate that while formalities are not normally required for the creation of a contract there are exceptions to this general rule, most notably, those contained in the Requirements of Writing (Scotland) Act 1995 ("RWSA");

✓ be aware that the legal content of a contract is contained in its terms and have some appreciation of some of the key terms of some of the more important contracts encountered in business;

---

[1] Senior Lecturer in Law, University of Aberdeen.

✓ understand that terms may be:

- expressly agreed;
- incorporated by reference or by a course of dealing; or
- implied by the law.

✓ be aware that the Unfair Contract Terms Act 1977 and the Consumer Rights Act 2015 regulate the use of unfair terms in contracts, and understand the key features of both of those regulatory instruments;

✓ appreciate that not all attempts to enter into a contract will be successful and understand the meaning and significance of the terms "void", "voidable" and "unenforceable" contract;

✓ be aware of the circumstances in which a person will lack legal capacity to enter into a contract and understand the meaning and significance of the terms "force and fear", "facility and circumvention" and "undue influence";

✓ understand the legal effect that errors (including misrepresentations) can have upon parties' attempts to enter contractual relations;

✓ understand what is meant by, and what sorts of situations will qualify as, "*pacta illicita*":

- in connection with the above, be able to describe when a court will and will not enforce a restrictive covenant or solus agreement.

✓ understand what a "breach of contract" is, differentiate the various different types of breach (anticipatory, material, simple) from each other and be able to describe the main remedies available in the event of breach;

✓ recognise that only the parties to a contract may usually sue or be sued for a breach of contract, but that in exceptional circumstances a *jus quaesitum tertio* (third party right) will exist;

✓ understand the circumstances in which contractual obligations come to an end.

WHAT IS A CONTRACT?

"Business" could be defined in many ways, but at the heart of the concept **4–03** is the provision of goods and services with a view towards profit. Contract law is the legal lynchpin of those activities. It is therefore important for students of business law to have a firm grasp of the essential features of the law of contract.

Even if one has never given much thought to the law of contract, the fact remains that we all enter into contracts on a daily basis. Every time we travel by bus or pay to park a car, the law of contract is involved. Similarly, we conclude a contract every time we buy ourselves a newspaper, pay to watch a sporting event or buy a meal in a cafe. The same principles of the law of contract are also involved when we carry out less commonplace transactions, like when we buy insurance or purchase a home.[2] Contract law is therefore part of the everyday flow of our lives.

In the classic book on the Scots law of contract, Gloag defined a contract as, "an agreement which creates or is intended to create a legal obligation between the parties to it".[3] This definition could be criticised for being rather simplistic: other writers have defined contract at greater length.[4] However the strength of Gloag's definition is that it allows us to focus on two concepts which lie at the heart of contract law: the idea of agreement, and the need for an intention to create legal obligations.

Agreement

The need for two or more parties

4–04 Contracts are by their nature bilateral or multi-lateral: there needs to more than one party to a contract. This is a logical consequence of the fact that contracts are ultimately about agreement. It would be nonsense to talk about "agreeing" with oneself.

The general lack of need for particular formality

4–05 In Scots law there is in general no need for an agreement to take a particular form before it will be recognised by the courts as a legally enforceable contract. In particular, there is usually no need for a contract to be in writing.[5] One sometimes hears people say something like, "the person who fixed my roof ripped me off but there's nothing I can do about it because I didn't have a contract". This is not correct. If a tradesman has received an instruction to attend at a householder's home, go onto his roof, assess what is wrong and fix it and has then proceeded to carry out this work then there *is* a contract in place. It is not necessarily the most advantageous contract that the householder could have entered into: there would have been less potential for disagreement between the parties if there had been more specific agreement on exactly what the roofer's scope of work was, the quality of the materials he was to use in doing it, and exactly what he was going to charge. But none of this affects the fact that a contract has, as a matter of law, come into existence.

In addition we should note that the "doctrine of consideration", which

---

[2] Note that although the general principles of contract remain the same, these principles are supplemented by the addition of further legal rules in the case of certain types of contracts. For instance, contracts for the purchase of land (including houses) are made subject to the RWSA, discussed further at para.4–29, below.

[3] W. Gloag, *The Law of Contract*, 2nd edn (Edinburgh: W. Green, 1929), p.8.

[4] H. MacQueen and J. Thomson, *Contract Law in Scotland*, 3rd edn (Haywards Heath: Bloomsbury Professional Limited, 2012) (hereinafter "MacQueen and Thomson") at para.1.9: "Contract can be defined as an agreement between two or more parties having the capacity to make it in the form demanded by law to perform on one side or both acts which are not trifling, indeterminate, impossible or illegal".

[5] There are a limited number of exceptions to this general rule. The most important such exception relates to contracts for the transfer of land; these are discussed at para.4–29, below. Certain types of consumer credit agreement also require to be in a particular form before they will be fully legally enforceable: see Ch.6, "Consumer Protection", below.

adds a range of technical complications to English contract law, is not recognised in Scots law.[6] The doctrine states that for an enforceable contract to come into effect between the parties, something known as "valuable consideration" must pass between them. Valuable consideration means money or money's worth. In practice, this means that agreements entered into without consideration on both sides—for instance, an agreement to donate money to a charity—cannot be considered to be contracts in English law. This doctrine forms no part of Scots law.

When is agreement reached?

The particular circumstances in which the courts will hold that an agreement has been reached will be discussed in greater detail at paras 4–11—4–27, below. **4–06**

Intention to create legal obligations

As we have seen, before a contract can be formed, there must be an agreement between two or more people. However, not *all* agreements are contractual in nature: only those which are intended to create legal obligations will constitute a contract. Perhaps the most common examples of an agreement not intended to create legal relations are social and domestic arrangements. **4–07**

Social and domestic arrangements

If two friends agree to meet in order to play squash and one of them changes his mind and fails to turn up, this will not ordinarily be a breach of contract. The law presumes that people who enter into arrangements of this kind intend them not to be legally binding. A similar presumption is made in the case of domestic arrangements.[7] Thus if a husband and wife agree that he will do the ironing if she dusts the house, these obligations will not ordinarily be legally enforceable. In such situations, we generally go ahead and do the thing that we agreed to do not because the law says we must, but because we think it is the right thing to do, perhaps because we actively want to or perhaps because we have promised to do so and do not want to go back on our word. **4–08**

Agreements made in the commercial context

By contrast, when we move from the social sphere to the business or commercial context—for instance, when we agree to buy or sell things, or to provide services in exchange for payment—the law assumes that we *do* intend our agreements to be legally binding. Thus, such agreements are generally contracts. Again, however, this is not an absolute rule of law **4–09**

---

[6] *Carlyle v Royal Bank of Scotland plc* [2015] UKSC 13, per Lord Hodge at [35].
[7] This presumption is, however, rebuttable: if it is clear that the parties both accepted that the agreement was to be legally binding, then even a social or domestic arrangement can be the subject of an enforceable contract.

but merely a rebuttable presumption, and there are certain types of commercial agreement which the courts recognise may not be intended to be binding. For instance, when a business decides that it wishes to lease commercial premises such as an industrial unit from a landlord, the parties will commonly enter into a "heads of terms" agreement. This is done because contracts of commercial lease are generally very lengthy documents and negotiations relating to them can become very time-consuming and complicated. It is generally thought to assist the parties' negotiations if they are able to agree some key principles of the deal at a relatively early stage of the process. Such "heads of terms" agreements are not generally intended to be legally binding. Outside of this particular context, non-binding commercial agreements are rare. However, the courts will occasionally be persuaded that a commercial agreement was not intended to be legally binding. A notable instance where this occurred is discussed below.

Rose and Frank Company v J.R. Crompton and Brothers Ltd
[1925] A.C. 445

An American firm ("RF") entered into an agreement with an English company ("C") whereby RF were appointed the only company permitted to sell C's products in North America. C became dissatisfied with the level of service provided by RF and decided to terminate the agreement with immediate effect and appoint other American agents. RF sued, contending that they had a binding contract and that C could only lawfully end it by doing so in accordance with its termination clause. If RF had been correct in this, it would have meant that C would have been held to have breached the contract, and RF would have been entitled to damages. However, the House of Lords held that the agreement between the parties was not a contract, and was therefore not legally enforceable. This was so because the contract contained a provision expressly stating that it was not a "formal or legal agreement" but was:

"[O]nly a definite expression and record of the purpose and intention of the parties concerned, to which they each honourably pledge themselves, with the fullest confidence that it will be carried through with mutual loyalty and friendly co-operation."

> **Key Concept**
>
> A contract is an agreement entered into between two or more par-
> ties, which the parties intend to be legally binding.
>
>   The courts will presume that the parties to social or domestic
> agreements do not intend their agreement to be binding, and will
> assume that parties to commercial or business-related agreements
> do intend their agreements to constitute contracts. In both cases,
> however, these presumptions are rebuttable in the face of clear
> evidence to the contrary.

Unilateral gratuitous promise

As we have already seen at para.4–05, above, Scots law does not recog- **4–10**
nise the doctrine of consideration. As a consequence, in Scots law, contracts whereby one party gives a benefit and in exchange receives nothing
of financial value are enforceable. Moreover, it means that a unilateral
promise to do something is also binding in Scots law, but only if the
promise is made:

- in formal writing[8]; or
- in the course of business.[9]

Declaring that one will make a gift at a future time is the classic example
of a promise. Such a declaration will be binding in Scotland as long as
one of the two criteria set out immediately above is satisfied. Thus if A
promises to give his sister B a television, he will not be legally bound to
do so unless he commits the promise to a formal writing. By contrast, if
C, the owner of a television shop, broadcasts a radio advertisement
offering to give a free TV to the 100th person to enter his shop on a
particular day, that customer is legally entitled to demand delivery of the
TV. An offer to pay a reward in exchange for the provision of information or the return of an item of property can also be characterised as a
promise,[10] as can an undertaking to keep an offer open for a period of
time in order to allow the person to whom the offer has been made to
have some time in which to consider it.[11]

  The distinction between a promise and a contract can sometimes be

---

[8] For example, in writing and signed by the promiser. For a further discussion of what is
meant by "formal writing", see para.4–29, below.

[9] The RWSA s.1(1).

[10] *Petrie v Earl of Airlie* (1834) 13 S. 68. In this case, a sign were anonymously posted
attacking the Earl's character after he refused to support a particular Bill before parliament. The Earl issued a proclamation offering a reward for information leading to the
conviction of the people who had produced the sign. Petrie provided information
implicating his brother and another. The Court of Session held that it the Earl was
legally bound to pay the reward.

[11] *Littlejohn v Hadwen* (1822) 20 S.L.R. 5.

elusive. In *Woolman on Contract*, Black provides a useful analysis of the essential distinctions:

- A contract arises out of the will of two (or more) parties. A promise is the product of one person's intention alone.
- In the case of promise, no acceptance is required to create a binding obligation.
- An offer is revocable until accepted. A promise is binding and irrevocable from the moment it is made.
- A promise places an obligation on one person alone. By contrast, contracts place obligations on both parties to the contract. In theory this is true even of gratuitous contracts. For instance, if A offers to gift a statue to his local council and it accepts, the council is under an obligation to take the statue. In the case of a promise, the council would have a right to reject the statue.[12]

Key Concept

A unilateral gratuitous promise is not a contract as it is not an agreement made between two or more parties. However, such promises are legally binding in Scots law either if they are written down and signed by the promisor, or if they are made in a business context.

FORMATION OF CONTRACTS

Introduction

4–11   Contracts are formed when the parties reach what is known as *consensus in idem* or a "meeting of the minds". This is achieved by the parties expressly or impliedly communicating their consent to be bound by the terms of the agreement. At that moment a contract comes into existence.[13] Generally, the question of whether the parties have reached *consensus in idem* is analysed in terms of offer and acceptance.[14] We shall

---

[12] G. Black, *Woolman on Contract*, 5th edn (Edinburgh: W. Green, 2014) (hereinafter Black, *Woolman on Contract*), para.4–02.

[13] Always assuming that there is no impediment preventing the parties from entering into contractual relations. Such impediments are discussed at paras 4–51—4–55, below.

[14] W. McBryde, *The Law of Contract in Scotland*, 3rd edn, (Edinburgh: SULI / W. Green, 2007) ("McBryde, *Contract*"), para.6.04. McBryde goes on to note that this approach can be somewhat artificial in circumstances where the contract has come into effect not as a result of express negotiations but through performance. Consider the following example. A customer goes into a shop, picks up a magazine, proceeds to the check-out and gives the magazine over to be scanned. The purchase price appears on the till's display screen; the customer hands over the price and exits with the magazine. It is difficult to identify exactly which of these acts constitutes an offer and which the acceptance. There has nevertheless clearly been a meeting of the minds resulting in a contract of sale and purchase.

commence this section by considering *consensus in idem* in greater detail before expanding on what we mean by "offer" and "acceptance" and concluding by examining some important issues that arise as a result of the law's conceptualisation of contract in terms of offer and acceptance.

Key Concept

A contract is formed when the parties reach *consensus in idem*—a meeting of the minds. This is generally achieved when an offer is met by an unconditional acceptance.

Consensus in idem (1): what needs to be agreed before consensus is reached?

It is important to understand precisely what needs to be agreed between **4–12** the parties before it can be said that a *consensus in idem* has been achieved. It is not the case that every minute detail of the contract requires to be specifically agreed. For a contract to be constituted, only its essential elements need to have been settled upon. What is "essential" will vary as between different types of contract, but in the case of contracts for the sale of goods, for example, the subject-matter of what is being sold and its price will be considered to be essential.

Consensus in idem (2): resolving disputes about essentials—the objective nature of the test

Sometimes, a dispute will arise between the parties about one of the **4–13** essentials of the contract. One might think that this would automatically mean that there was no agreement: how can there be *consensus* if the parties are arguing about an essential matter? Nevertheless, a contract may very well still exist in such circumstances. The courts assess the question of whether consensus in idem has been reached not *subjectively*, but *objectively*. In other words, the courts determine the matter not by assessing what the parties actually thought they had agreed (which would be a subjective approach) but by considering what an objective person who happened to witness the parties' contractual negotiations would have understood the parties to have agreed. *Muirhead and Turnbull v Dickson* provides a good example of the objective approach in operation.

Muirhead and Turnbull v Dickson
(1905) 7 F. 606

Muirhead and Turnbull ("MT") were piano sellers who entered into an agreement with Dickson ("D") that he would take a piano from them at a price of £26, payable in monthly instalments. D took delivery of the piano and paid his first five instalments. He then stopped paying. MT sued, arguing that the contract between it and

D was one of hire purchase and that as a result D was under an obligation to return the piano, which was still owned by MT, and that MT were entitled to treat the money paid by D as payments towards the hire of the piano. D defended the action on the basis that it was not a contract of hire purchase at all, but a credit sale. On that analysis, ownership of the piano had passed to D upon delivery: as such, while MT could claim the balance due on the purchase price, they could not reclaim the piano from him. When the case was argued in court, there was evidence that MT's usual practice was to sell on hire purchase terms. However, MT was not able to establish that D had been made aware that this was what they intended in this particular case. Indeed, there had been no express agreement between the parties and it appeared that MT and D were at cross-purposes as to the nature of the agreement which they were entering into. Nevertheless, the court held that that there had been *consensus in idem* between the parties. In emphasising the objective nature of the test which is used, Lord President Dunedin stated that, "commercial contracts cannot be arranged by what people think in their inmost minds. Commercial contracts are made according to what people say". The parties had said and done enough to lead an objective bystander to conclude that they were agreeing a credit sale.

The objective nature of the test also means that there will be occasions where courts will hold that there is no contract, even when the parties thought there was one and have proceeded to implement the obligations that they thought had been agreed. This is exemplified by *Mathieson Gee (Ayrshire) Ltd v Quigley.*

Mathieson Gee (Ayrshire) Ltd v Quigley
1952 S.L.T. 239

Mathieson Gee ("MG") offered to hire Quigley ("Q") equipment for the removal of silt which had built up in a large pond at his home. Q purported to accept their offer to remove and dispose of the silt. The equipment was delivered and a part-payment of the contractual price was made. A dispute then arose as to what precisely had been agreed, and the parties went to court. There, the parties contended that there was a contract between them and asked the court to adjudicate on whether it was one for the provision of equipment only, or one for the carrying out of the job of removing the silt. The court declined to do so, on the basis that an analysis of the evidence in the case demonstrated that the acceptance did not meet the terms of the offer: as such, there had therefore been no consensus in idem, and no contract could therefore have come into existence.

Thus if a party delivers goods, performs work or incurs expense in the erroneous belief that a contract has come into existence, it can make no use of the law of contract, as no contract has come into effect. It may, however, be able to establish a remedy under a separate branch of law known as unjustified enrichment.[15]

Key Concept

Consensus in idem is reached when an objective bystander observing the parties discussions, correspondence and behaviour would come to the conclusion that they had agreed on all of the essential elements of the contract.

Offers

An offer is both a proposal by one party to enter into a legally binding **4–14** agreement with another and a statement of the terms which the offeror (i.e. the person making the offer) proposes should govern that agreement. The essential feature of an offer, and the thing that distinguishes it from certain other types of proposal which may also be involved in the lead-up to a contract, is that it must "contemplate acceptance". This means that, to qualify as an offer, the proposal must be of such a nature that if it were met with an unqualified acceptance, a contract would be formed without the need for further negotiation. In other words, to qualify as an offer, a proposal must contain at least the essential terms on which the offeror intends to do the deal.

Offers may come in many forms. In general, they can be written or verbal or, in some instances, they can be inferred from the circumstances.[16]

Non-offers

Not every statement or proposal concerning a potential supply of goods **4–15** or services will in law constitute an offer. It is important to be able to distinguish between offers and other proposals which, while they may superficially resemble offers, are not considered by the courts to contain an offer's essential legal characteristics.

---

[15] Unjustified enrichment is a highly technical area of law that falls outside the scope of this book. For a good introductory account, see H. MacQueen, *Unjustified Enrichment*, 2nd edn (Edinburgh: W. Green, 2009). For a detailed discussion, see R. Evans-Jones, *Unjustified Enrichment* (Edinburgh: SULI / W. Green, 2013), Vols I and II.

[16] This is the general principle; however, the law imposes some formalities concerning the form which both an offer and an acceptance must take in some, limited, situations. See paras 4–28—4–29, below.

Statements of future intent

4–16 A broad statement of future intent will not be considered to be an offer. Thus the statement "I am going to sell my car" is not an offer. At this stage, too much is unknown for the statement to contemplate acceptance. We do not know which car is being spoken about, when the transaction will take place or what the price will be. The essential features of an offer are therefore absent.

Invitations to treat

4–17 Invitations to treat more closely resemble offers and require fuller consideration.[17] An invitation to treat is not an offer but merely an announcement that one would like others to come forward and make an offer. For instance, invitations to tender are commonly used in major construction and engineering projects. In such a case, the party wishing work carried out will invite interested parties to tender the price they would charge for the job, and the terms and conditions on which they would do it. Invitations to tender are generally invitations to treat. Where this is so, the party hosting the tender will be under no liability to accept the best-value tender received.[18] Consequently, the tenders received as a result the exercise will not be acceptances concluding a contract, but merely offers which the party who announced the tender is at liberty to accept or decline. Advertisements, too, are presumed to be invitations to treat, although this presumption will be overcome (and the advertisement therefore treated as an offer) if the advertisement makes it clear that the advertiser intends to be bound by an acceptance. The case of *Carlill v Carbolic Smoke Ball Company* provides a famous example of such an advertisement.

Carlill v Carbolic Smoke Ball Company
[1893] 1 Q.B. 256

The Carbolic Smoke Ball Company ("CSBC") took out a number of newspaper advertisements extolling the virtues of its "carbolic smoke ball," a product which, when, lit, gave off fumes which CSBC claimed had medical benefits. CSBC's advertisement offered to pay £100 to anyone who contracted influenza after buying and using one of their carbolic smoke balls in accordance with its printed instructions. CSBC also stated that it had deposited £1000 with a named bank, "in order to demonstrate their sincerity in the matter". Impressed by the advertisement, Mrs Carlill

---

[17] "Treat" in this context has a rather archaic legal meaning. "To treat" in this sense means "to enter into a contract". "Treaty"—meaning an agreement between two or more governments—also stems from this sense of the word.

[18] This does, however, depend on the precise terms of the invitation to tender. If this contains a clear undertaking to accept the best bid, then in Scots law at least the inviting party will be bound, not under the law of contract, but promise, discussed earlier at para.4–10, above.

purchased one of the balls from her local chemist and diligently used it. She caught flu and sued CSBC, arguing that their advertisement was an offer which she had impliedly accepted by purchasing one of the balls. The court concluded that, in the very particular circumstances of the case, CSBC's advertisement was indeed an offer. In practice, advertisements in such terms are very rarely encountered nowadays and in the majority of cases an advert will constitute an invitation to treat.

Further examples of an invitation to treat are the exhibition of items for viewing in advance of an auction sale or the display of goods in a shop or on the internet.[19] An unusual but striking example of this is seen in *Fisher v Bell*.[20] Here, a shopkeeper displayed a flick-knife for sale in his shop window with a price-tag next to it. He was prosecuted under legislation which made it an offence to "sell or offer to sell a flick-knife". The shopkeeper was found not guilty of the charge on the basis that displaying the flick-knife was not an offer to sell, but merely an invitation to treat.

Communication of offers

Offers must be communicated before they become effectual: "an offer is **4–18** nothing until it is communicated to the offeree".[21] Thus if an offer is formulated in a person's mind but not articulated, or written down but not passed to the offeree, it is ineffectual. Additionally, if an offer is transmitted to an offeree without the offeror's authorisation, that, too, is ineffectual.

In *Burr v Police Commissioners of Bo'ness*,[22] B was employed by the Commissioners as a sanitary inspector. Following a dispute between the parties about work which B contended he had been required to carry out without adequate payment, the Commissioners passed a resolution increasing B's salary but requiring him to work under the supervision of another. The Commissioners did not intimate this resolution to B, but news of it was it was informally "leaked" to him. B protested at being required to work under supervision. The Commissioners responded by cancelling the part of the resolution which increased B's salary. B sued, contending he was entitled to be paid at the higher rate, but lost his claim on the basis that the offer had never been legally communicated to him.

Offers can be (and frequently are) made only towards a specified person. Where this is so, others are not entitled to intercept the offer and accept it; it may only be accepted by the person to whom it was addressed. Offerers can, however, make offers on a more open basis if

---

[19] *Chwee Kin Keong v Digilandmall.com Pte Ltd* (2004) 2 S.L.R. 594. For further discussion of e-commerce, see Chapter 7.
[20] [1961] 1 Q.B. 394.
[21] *Thomson v James* (1855) 18 D. 1 per the Lord President (McNeill) at 10.
[22] (1896) 24 R. 148.

they choose, stating that they can be accepted by a particular class of persons (for instance, members of a particular trade union or alumni of a particular university). Indeed, in appropriate cases the courts will hold that an offer has been addressed to the world at large, and that anyone is entitled to accept it if they so choose: see *Carlill v Carbolic Smoke Ball Company*[23] and *Hunter v General Accident Fire and Life Assurance Corporation*,[24] in which the court stated:

> "[W]hen a general offer addressed to the public is appropriated to himself by a distinct acceptance by one person, then it is be read in exactly the same way as if it had been addressed to the individual originally."

Key Concepts

Not all discussions or proposals made during the course of a contractual negotiation are offers. The identifying feature of an offer is that it must "contemplate acceptance." Statements of future intent and invitations to treat are not offers and therefore cannot be accepted by the offeree.

Revocation of offer

4–19 Unlike a unilateral promise, which takes legal effect as soon as it is made,[25] offers can be revoked or withdrawn at any time before acceptance unless the offeror provides otherwise.[26] However, the revocation of the offer must be communicated to the person to whom the offer was made.

Lapse of offer

4–20 Quite apart from the possibility of revocation, offers will automatically lapse in certain circumstances. Once an offer has lapsed, it no longer legally exists and the offeree is therefore no longer able to accept it. The circumstances in which an offer will lapse are:

- through passage of time. If a time-limit imposed by the offeror passes without the offer being accepted, the offer lapses. If no time-limit is imposed by the offeror, the offer will remain open for a reasonable period of time. What is reasonable will depend on the facts and circumstances of the case: for instance, where the offer concerns perishable goods such as a truck-load of cut

---

[23] [1893] 1 Q.B. 256, discussed at para.4–17, above.
[24] 1909 S.C. (H.L.) 30.
[25] See para.4–10, above.
[26] The offeror can, if he or she chooses, state that the offer is open for a certain period of time, or indeed that it is irrevocable—in other words that the offer cannot be withdrawn by the offeror, and will only fall when it lapses through the operation of law (see para.4–20).

flowers, the offer may very well lapse more quickly than if it concerns goods which are not subject to the risk of deterioration, such as a load of gravel. Similarly, offers concerning commodities with volatile prices will stay open for a shorter period than those the price of which is more stable;

- upon rejection of the offer, or the making of a counter-offer[27];
- upon the death of either party or in the event of the offeror becoming bankrupt or insane;
- upon the destruction or material alteration of the subject-matter of the offer; or
- in the event of supervening illegality.[28]

Acceptance

MacQueen and Thomson define acceptance particularly succinctly: **4–21**

> "An acceptance is the final unqualified assent by the offeree to the terms stipulated in the offer."[29]

As we have already seen, an acceptance will only give rise to *consensus in idem* if it coincides with the offer. Thus if (as in *Mathieson Gee (Ayrshire) Ltd v Quigley*,[30] discussed at para.4–13, above) the offeree purports to accept something that the offeror did not offer, no contract is formed. In addition, a purported "acceptance" that seeks to introduce new terms into the contract is not an acceptance at all, but a counter-offer.

Key Concept

The identifying feature of an acceptance is that it must be an unqualified agreement to the offer put forward by the offeree.

As with offers, acceptances come in a variety of guises. Express acceptances may be made verbally or in writing.[31] Silence *on its own* is not sufficient to serve as an acceptance.[32] Thus if a self-employed gardener puts notes through various householders' letter boxes saying that unless he hears from them by 17.00 the following day, he will proceed to mow their lawn at a cost of £20, and hears nothing from them, he cannot insist upon mowing their lawns and demanding payment. The courts will, however, be willing in appropriate cases to infer an implied acceptance

---

[27] Counter-offers are discussed at para.4–23, below.

[28] For a discussion of what is meant by "supervening illegality" see para.4–109, below.

[29] MacQueen and Thomson, para.2.23.

[30] 1952 S.L.T. 239.

[31] For example, either in traditional writing, or by modern equivalent means such as by fax or email.

[32] Although in rare cases, the surrounding circumstances may occasionally cause the court, "to infer that a party, through his silence, has assented to be bound by a proffered contract": see *Shaw v James Scott Builders* [2010] CSOH 68 at [50].

from an offeree's behaviour. Such acceptance—known as acceptance by performance—is perfectly valid. So if the example given above were changed so that a householder offered the gardener £20 to mow his lawn, and the gardener then proceeded to mow the lawn, his actions would amount to acceptance by performance, and he would be entitled to claim his payment.

In general, any of these forms of acceptance is valid, and there is no need for the acceptance to be in the same medium as the offer: a written offer does not, as a matter of law, have to be accepted in writing. However, the offeror is entitled to stipulate the form of acceptance in the offer itself, and where this is done, the offeree must accept in the medium demanded.

Non-acceptance

Rejection

4–22 The rejection of an offer causes it to lapse. As a lapsed offer ceases to be, rejection cannot be undone. If the offeree subsequently regrets rejecting an offer, he cannot change his mind and issue a legally binding acceptance; he can do no more than go back to the offeror and seek to re-open negotiations.

Counter-offer

4–23 A response to an offer which, while not expressly rejecting the offer, seeks to qualify it by deleting some of the offer's terms and/or imposing new conditions is known as a "counter-offer" or "qualified acceptance". Despite the fact that it is not expressed as an outright rejection, a counter-offer has the effect, first, of rejecting the offer to which it is a response and then of making a fresh offer for the party who was originally the offeror to consider. A good example of counter-offer in operation is seen in *Wolf and Wolf v Forfar Potato Co Ltd*.[33]

Wolf and Wolf v Forfar Potato Co Ltd
1984 S.L.T. 100

FPC offered to sell a consignment of potatoes to WW, a firm of potato merchants. The offer was open for acceptance by 5pm the following day. On the following morning, WW sent what purported to be an acceptance of FPC's offer. However, this so-called acceptance sought to add a number of new terms and conditions to those which had been proposed by FPC. During a telephone conversation, FPC made it clear that the new conditions were not acceptable and thereafter WW sent a further document, purporting to accept FPC's original offer. FPC did not respond and did not supply the potatoes. WW sued, arguing that FPC were in breach of

---

[33] 1984 S.L.T. 100.

contract. The court held that WW's first "acceptance" was a counter-offer. As a matter of law, this rejected FPC's offer, and put in place a fresh offer which FPC had rejected. As FPC's offer had lapsed upon rejection, WW's second attempt at issuing an "acceptance" to the original offer could not conclude the contract either. Instead, it was a fresh offer which FPC had chosen not to accept. There was therefore no contract between the parties.

The battle of the forms

As some contractual negotiations can be quite protracted it is possible for **4–24** there to be a large number of counter-offers before a contract is eventually concluded by a simple acceptance. This can lead to a particular problem known as the "battle of the forms". This occurs when two parties agree that they wish to enter into a contract with each other, but where each wants their own standard terms and conditions to govern the contract. This is most readily illustrated by way of example. Company A orders goods from Company B. A wants the contract to proceed on the basis of its standard terms and conditions of purchase, so it incorporates them into the purchase order which it sends B.[34] B receives the order. It wants to sell the goods to A, but in accordance with its own standard terms and conditions of business.[35] It sends an order confirmation form in which it incorporates its own standard terms and conditions. A couple of days later, it despatches the goods, which are accepted by Company A. It is clear that the parties wish to contract with each other, but how does the law ascertain which set of terms and conditions prevail? The answer is that the law does not look at this matter from the standpoint of what would be an acceptable compromise to impose upon the parties. It looks at the matter in terms of offer, counter-offer (or counter-offers) and acceptance. The party who wins the battle of the forms is the one which succeeds in making the last counter-offer before acceptance. It is sometimes said that that party has "fired the last shot" in the battle of the forms, but this is potentially misleading. It must be stressed that it is last set of conditions proffered *before acceptance* which wins the "battle". Thus, any sets of conditions put forward once the contract has been concluded by acceptance are irrelevant. The point is well illustrated in *Continental Tyre and Rubber Co Ltd v Trunk Trailer Co Ltd.*[36]

---

[34] Company A may wish to this because it is familiar with what its legal rights and liabilities are under its own standard terms and conditions are. It may also be that A has slanted its standard conditions of purchase in its own favour. For instance, these terms might seek to impose strict obligations on the seller about the quality of the goods, or to give A an unusually long time in which to pay for the goods.

[35] It may want to do this because B's conditions are biased in B's favour: for instance, B may wish to restrict A's rights to the lowest allowable under the law, or to be able to choose when he delivers the goods, or to compel A to pay for the goods very quickly.

[36] 1987 S.C.L.R. 58.

Continental Tyre and Rubber Co Ltd v Trunk Trailer Co Ltd
1987 S.C.L.R. 58

TTCL placed an order for tyres from CTRC. The order was printed on TTCL's standard order form, which contained the company's standard terms and conditions of business. CTRC proceeded to supply the tyres in a number of batches. Each batch was accompanied by a delivery note and followed a few days later by an invoice. Both the delivery note and the invoice contained CTRC's terms and conditions, which differed markedly from those of TTCL. TTCL became dissatisfied with the tyres, which they considered wore out more quickly than should be the case, and sued. CTRC defended the action on the basis that the contract has been concluded on their terms and conditions, and measured against those, there was no breach. The court found in favour of TTCL: the contract had been concluded by performance when the first batch of tyres was delivered. CTRC's attempts to have their own terms and conditions govern the contract therefore came too late.

Communication of acceptance

4–25 As with offers, acceptances must usually be communicated before they take effect, although the offeror can, if he chooses, frame his offer in such a way that the requirement for communication of acceptance is dispensed with.[37]

It is important to know at which particular moment in time the law will consider an acceptance to have been communicated. This is particularly so when the offeror seeks to revoke his offer at or around the same time as the offeree purports to accepts the offer, or where an offer is subject to a time-limit and a dispute arises as to whether or not the offeree's acceptance has come in on time.

In relation to contracts concluded in Scotland or between a party located in Scotland and another located elsewhere in the UK, the law recognises two distinct categories of communication of acceptances: instantaneous and delayed.[38] Different sets of rules apply to each, so it is important to be able to differentiate between the two.

---

[37] This is competent, but occurs only rarely. In *Carlill v Carbolic Smoke Ball Company* [1893] 1 Q.B. 256, CSBC argued that, even if their advertisement were to be considered an offer, there could be no contract as C had never communicated an acceptance to them. The court held that by wording their advertisement as they did, CSBC had dispensed with the need for communication: acceptance took place when C purchased smoke ball and used it in accordance with its instructions.

[38] This distinction is not widely recognised outside the Anglo-American legal world. Most continental systems operate on the basis of the rules for instantaneous communication. This can make resolving these questions in cross-border contracts rather difficult, but such considerations fall outside the scope of this work.

Instantaneous communication

The classic example of instantaneous communication is meeting someone **4–26**
and having a conversation with that person face to face. Telephone
conversations are also instantaneous (give or take a couple of seconds
satellite delay if one happens to be talking with someone on the other side
of the world). Although they take time to prepare, telexes and faxes are
also considered to be instantaneous because, at the moment when they
are sent, one is in direct communication with the other party, and so if
anything goes wrong with the attempted transmission one realises that
more or less instantly and can attempt to transmit the information again.
Similarly, live-time instant message conversation using platforms such as
Skype is instantaneous form of communication. So too is sharing
information over the internet in order to make a purchase from a fully
integrated sales website like those operated by the major airlines and
companies such as Amazon or iTunes.

For all of these forms of communication, the rule is as set out in
Entores Ltd v Miles Far East Corporation. There, Lord Denning
observed:

> "Suppose that I make an offer to a man by telephone and, in the
> middle of his reply, the line goes 'dead' so that I do not hear his
> words of acceptance. There is no contract at that moment. The other
> man may not know the precise moment when the line failed. But he
> will know that the telephone conversation was abruptly broken off.
> If he wishes to make a contract, he must therefore get through again
> so as to make sure that I heard. Suppose next, that the line does not
> go dead, but it is nevertheless so indistinct that I do not catch what
> he says and I ask him to repeat it. He then repeats it and I hear his
> acceptance. The contract is made, not on the first time when I do not
> hear, but only the second time when I do hear."[39]

It is not enough, therefore, to try to communicate an acceptance and fail.
The acceptance must be received. It is the person who is trying to communicate the acceptance who has the burden of ensuring that the message
has got through.

Delayed communication

The rules concerning delayed communication of acceptances evolved to **4–27**
accommodate the widespread use of the postal system in contractual
negotiations from the 1800s onwards. Even assuming that one's letter is
not lost or unduly delayed, once committed to the post it will not be
delivered instantly but will take at least a day to work its way through the
system. Similarly, sending a telegram is a delayed communication. Email
is also thought of as a delayed communication. Although email systems
will often deliver messages very quickly, one is not in direct

---

[39] *Entores Ltd v Miles Far East Corporation* [1955] 2 Q.B. 327 at 332 to 333.

communication with the recipient of the message and, when for some
reason a message is not successfully delivered, it can take a significant
period of time for the system to generate a message warning the sender of
that fact.

When the rule on delayed communications was being formulated, the
courts had to attempt to balance the competing interests of the person
sending an acceptance by post with those of the person receiving it. Once
the sender has posted his acceptance, he has no control over what happens to it: it therefore seems unfair if a delay which is outside of his
control acts to his prejudice. Equally, however, it may be harsh upon
someone awaiting an acceptance if he is deemed to receive the acceptance
days or even weeks before it actually lands on his doorstep. In *Dunlop v
Higgins*[40] it was held that the interests of the sender should be preferred to
that of the recipient: the rule on delayed communications is therefore that
the acceptance is "effective on dispatch". Once a properly-addressed
letter is placed into the postbox, the acceptance takes effect, even if the
letter is delayed, although in Scots law it appears that if the letter is lost in
the postal system and is therefore not delivered the acceptance will not be
deemed to have been effectual.[41]

The rule has been subjected to criticism and can have some fairly
startling consequences. For example, if an offer must be accepted by
17.00 on a particular day, the acceptance is effectual if it got into the
postbox at 16.57 notwithstanding the fact that the other party is not
going to receive the letter until early on the following day at the earliest.
On the other hand, if one continually tries to phone through an acceptance from at 16.45 onwards but cannot get through until 17.05, the
deadline has been missed. For this reason, offerors will commonly disapply the postal rule, stating that their offer is only available for acceptance to be received by the offeror before [*whenever they set the deadline to
be*]. When parties choose to exclude the postal rule from operation, it
would appear that a letter becomes effectual at the point when it comes
into the recipient's possession, not at the point when it is actually read. In
Carmarthen Developments Ltd v Pennington,[42] a case where the postal rule
did not apply, a question arose as to when the letter had been "delivered"
and became effective. The court held that delivery of the relevant letter
took effect when the recipient collected his sack of mail from the post
office at 8.50am, not when the letter was actually read, later on in the
morning. Additionally, the fact that offers and revocations of offers are
not subject to the postal rule but are effectual only upon receipt also has
the potential to produce peculiar results: if an offeror decides to revoke
his offer and puts a letter to that effect in the post, the revocation does not
take effect until received by the offeree. So if the offeree gets a letter of
acceptance into the post before the revocation of offer is delivered to him,

---

[40] (1848) 6 Bell's App. 195.
[41] *Mason v Benhar Coal* (1882) 9 R. 883. The position in England is to the contrary: even if
the letter is lost in the post and never makes its way to the offeror, the contract is
nevertheless concluded: *Household Fire Insurance v Grant* (1879) L.R. Ex. D. 216.
[42] [2008] CSOH 139.

the contract is concluded, even if the letter of acceptance was dispatched hours or days after the dispatch of the revocation.

Key Concepts

An acceptance, like an offer, does not take effect until it is communicated. In the case of instantaneous methods of communication an acceptance will not be communicated until it is actually heard by the other party. In the case of delayed methods of communication, communication is "effective on despatch".

CONTRACTUAL FORMALITIES

Introduction

As has already been explained, there is, in general, no requirement to **4–28** comply with particular formalities when one is making a contract. So in the ordinary course of events contracts may be concluded verbally, in writing, by implication or through some combination of these.

There are, however, a limited number of exceptions to this rule. Situations therefore exist where the law imposes particular formalities. The most significant set of technical formalities is contained in the RWSA (discussed immediately below). Other examples also exist, most notably, in the field of consumer protection law.[43]

The Requirements of Writing (Scotland) Act 1995 ("RWSA")

The RSWA commences by confirming the general principle that, subject **4–29** to the provisions of RSWA itself and any other enactment, writing is not required for the constitution of a contract, unilateral obligation or trust.[44] It then goes on to list in s.1(2) the particular types of contracts and other legal instruments which do require formal writing in order to be legally valid. These are:

   (a) the constitution of—

      (i) a contract or unilateral obligation for the creation, transfer, variation or extinction of an interest in land;
      (ii) a gratuitous unilateral obligation except an obligation undertaken in the course of business; and
      (iii) a trust whereby a person declares himself to be sole trustee of his own property or any property which he may acquire;

   (b) the creation, transfer, variation or extinction of an interest in land otherwise than by the operation of a court decree, enactment or rule of law; and

---

[43] See, e.g. the discussion in Ch.6, "Consumer Protection", below.
[44] RWSA s.1(1).

(c) the making of any will, testamentary trust disposition and settlement or codicil.

Thus contracts and promises relative to land,[45] gratuitous unilateral
obligations, "sole trustee" trusts and wills all need to be constituted in
accordance with the formalities demanded by RWSA if they are to be
binding.[46] What, then, are the Act's formalities? Any legal instrument of
the type set out in s.1(2) of the Act need to be both in writing and signed
at the end of the document ("subscribed") by all the persons intended to
be bound by it.[47] If the document is intended to be "probative"—in other
words, if it is to be presumed to be authentic without the need for producing evidence on matters such as the fact that the signature on the
document truly is that of the person who purports to have signed it—the
document should also be signed by a witness.[48] Thus it is not, as a matter
of pure law, necessary for the subscription to be witnessed but if it is not,
then evidence will have to be led to the effect that the signature is that of
the person who purported to sign. This is potentially expensive and time-
consuming and (if, in the interim, the grantor disappears, becomes insane
or dies) may become practically impossible to do.

The only exception to the need for the legal instruments listed in s.1(2)
to be in writing and subscribed is contained in s.1(3) and 1(4) RWSA.
These provide that where an agreement exists which is not in the correct
form[49] (e.g. it is verbal; or it is in writing but not signed) the obligor (i.e.
the party obliged to perform under the agreement) will be legally bound
by the agreement if the obligee (the person getting the benefit of the
obligation under the defective agreement) has:

- acted or refrained from acting in reliance upon the contract and
  with the knowledge or acquiescence of the obligor (the person
  giving the obligation); and
- as a result, the obligee has had a material change of position; and
- the interests of the obligee would be adversely affected to a
  material extent if the other party were allowed to withdraw from
  the obligation.

---

[45] But not the creation of leases for less than one year: these are excluded by RWSA s.1(7).
[46] Gratuitous unilateral obligations (promises) have already been discussed at para.4–10,
above. Trust law is discussed in Ch.13, below. Wills are the legal writings whereby a
person specifies what they wish to happen to their property upon their death.
[47] RWSA s.2.
[48] RWSA s.3. This presumption can be overcome, but the burden of proof lies on the party
challenging the authenticity of the signature.
[49] Note that before the statutory rule can take effect, the party seeking to rely on it must be
able to demonstrate that there was a firm agreement between the parties. It is not enough
for him to establish that the parties were close to agreeing, or that he had been assured
that agreement would be reached at some point in the future: see, e.g. *Aisling Developments Ltd v Persimmon Homes Ltd*, 2009 S.L.T. 494.

THE CONTENTS OF A CONTRACT: CONTRACTUAL TERMS

Introduction

Just as important as a consideration of how a contract comes to be **4–30** formed is the question, what are the contents of this agreement, once it comes into existence? Or to put matters another way, what legal rights are provided, and which legal duties imposed, by the contract? The rights and obligations imposed by a contract are known as its terms (or sometimes, terms and conditions).

Illustrative examples of typical contractual terms

Contracts cover the whole range of commercial activities: different types **4–31** of contract will contain different terms, and we cannot possibly list and discuss the kind of terms that one would expect to see in each and every type of contract. Nevertheless, it is still useful to consider some illustrative examples of the terms which one encounters in certain types of contract.

Sale of goods

Perhaps the most important business contract is a contract for the sale **4–32** and purchase of goods. Such contracts need to deal with a range of issues such as:

- What is the identity of the goods being sold?
- Price: at what price are the goods being sold? In a lump sum, or by instalments? When is it payable?
- Delivery: when are the goods being handed over the purchaser? If in the future, when? What are the rights and obligations of the parties if the goods are delayed, lost or damaged in transit?
- What are the rights and obligations of the parties if the goods turn out to be unfit for the purpose for which they are sold, defective, or if, on reflection, the purchaser decides that he simply doesn't want them?

The Consumer Rights Act 2015 ("CRA") governs the vast majority of such contracts. This aspect of the CRA is considered in detail at Ch.5, below.

Contracts for the provision of services

Another commonly encountered business contract is a contract for the **4–33** provision of services. These contracts differ from sales in that they are not concerned with the transfer of items of corporeal property, but with the carrying out of work by one person for another. Contracts with professionals such as accountants or lawyers are contracts for the provision of services; so, too, are the contracts we make with airlines or

railway operators to carry us from one place to another,[50] insurance
contracts[51] and contracts with tradesmen for the carrying out of activities
such as fitting a kitchen. Such contracts will contain terms intended to
answer the following kinds of questions:

- What is the nature of the service being provided?
- Does it have to be carried out personally, or can the service
  provider delegate the provision of the service to someone else?
- How much will the services cost? It the job being carried out for a
  fixed price, or at an hourly or daily rate?
- When must the job be finished? What are the legal consequences if
  it is not finished in time?
- To what standard are the services to be carried out? What are the
  rights and obligations of the parties if the services are not carried
  out to that standard?

How do terms find their way into contracts?

4–34 There are three ways in which terms can find their way into a contract.
These are:

- expressly, by agreement;
- by incorporation from an outside source; and
- by implication.

Each will be considered in turn.

Express agreement

4–35 The most obvious way in which terms can find their way into a contract is
for them to be expressly agreed by the parties. Subject to any specific
restrictions imposed by statute,[52] such agreement may be verbal or in
writing. As we shall see below, there are a number of statutory provisions
and rules of common law which restrict the legal enforceability of certain
types of contractual terms. Generally speaking, however, the courts will
enforce terms that have been expressly agreed between the parties. Where
the contract is a written one which the offeree has signed, the offeree will
in general be held to have agreed to the terms of the contract, even if he
has not read or understood them.

The incorporation of terms

4–36 Terms may be incorporated into a contract either by reference or through
a prior course of dealings.

---

[50] Such contracts are commonly described as contracts of carriage, but they are just a
particular type of contract for the provision of services.
[51] Insurance contracts are discussed further in Ch.18, below.
[52] Such as the RWSA, discussed above.

Incorporation by reference

Instead of producing a lengthy written contract fully setting out the terms **4–37** of the contract, a seller of goods or a service provider might offer a customer a brief document which deals with key issues such as the nature of the goods or services to be provided and the price of those goods or services but which otherwise refers the customer to standard terms and conditions of business. These terms and conditions might either be printed on the back of the contract, enclosed as a separate document or available elsewhere: perhaps from a website, or by post on request from the company's head office. Is an attempt to incorporate terms in this way valid? In a series of decisions, the courts have held that terms can by incorporated into a contract by reference, but only if certain conditions are met.

Incorporation by signature. Where the reference to the terms is con- **4–38** tained in a document signed by the offeree at or before the point of creation of the contract, then the courts have traditionally held (albeit sometimes with marked reluctance[53]) that the offeree is bound by the terms even if he has neither read them nor had a ready opportunity to do so. Signature in such cases is considered to act as agreement to the terms.

Incorporation in other cases. Where the reference is not contained in a **4–39** document signed by the offeree, a number of conditions require to be met before the courts will accept that the conditions have been validly incorporated into the contract.

- The offeror must bring the offeree's attention to the conditions timeously, which is to say, at or before the time contract was concluded. This may be done by way of a notice displayed or in a document given to the offeree. Any attempt to impose terms after the contract has been concluded will be unsuccessful. In *Olley v Marlborough Court Hotel*,[54] Mrs Olley, a guest at the hotel, left her fur coat in a locked store room for safe keeping. The coat was stolen. She sued the hotel, who defended on the basis that, in every room of the hotel, there was a notice stating that the hotel would not be liable in the event that guests' property was stolen. The court held that the hotel's reference to the notice came too late to be effectual: the contract had been concluded at the reception desk.
- If the terms and conditions are contained in a document presented to the offeree, as opposed to a public notice, then the document must be one which the offeree would reasonably have understood to be contractual in nature. Not every piece of paper handed over during the course of a contractual negotiation is of such a nature.

---

[53] As in *McCutcheon v MacBrayne*, 1964 S.C. (H.L.) 28. See, in particular, the comments of Lord Devlin at 39–40.
[54] [1949] 1 K.B. 532.

Invoices, receipts and acceptance notes for goods supplied have been held in a string of cases not to be contractual in nature, and, while tickets issued in contracts of carriage[55] are viewed as contractual, not all tickets are: some are viewed as mere receipts or vouchers. In *Taylor v Glasgow Corporation*,[56] Mrs Taylor slipped and fell down the stair when visiting public baths run by the Corporation. In defending the action, the Corporation sought to rely upon a clause printed on the ticket which Mrs Taylor had received when paying her admission fee: this notice disclaimed liability for, "any loss, injury or damage sustained by persons entering this establishment". The court held that this ticket was no more than a voucher—a receipt indicating that the holder had paid the requisite price and was entitled to make use of the facility. As such, it could not impose contractual terms.

● The offeror must in addition take adequate steps to bring the terms to the notice of the offeree. A notice stating that the terms on which services are being provided may be obtained from the offeror's head office will probably be valid if printed on the front of a contractual document, but not if printed on the back.[57] Similarly, a public notice posted up in the offeror's office stating the terms on which he does business will be sufficient only if the offeree has been in the office at or before the acceptance of the contract, and then only if it was plainly visible from the parts of the office open to the public.[58]

Key Concepts

In the case of terms incorporated by reference, if, at or before the time of entering into the contract, the offeree signs a legal document which states on the face of it that the contract is to be governed by terms which can be seen elsewhere, the courts will usually hold that the offeree is bound by those terms. If the offeree has not signed such a document, a number of conditions must be satisfied before a court will hold the terms incorporated into the contract. The terms must be:

● brought to the offeree's attention at or before the conclusion of the contract;
● contained in a document which the offeree would reasonably have understood to be contractual in nature; and
● adequately brought to the attention of the offeree.

---

[55] For example, contracts for the transportation of a person from one place to another. See, e.g. *Thomson v London Midland and Scottish Railway Co* [1930] 1 K.B. 41.
[56] 1952 S.C. 440.
[57] *Parker v SE Railway Co* (1877) 2 L.R. C.P.D. 416.
[58] *McCutcheon v MacBrayne*, 1964 S.C. (H.L.) 28.

Incorporation by a course of dealing

Quite apart from incorporation by reference, it is also possible for terms **4–40** to be incorporated into a contract by a prior course of dealing. For this to occur, the hypothetical objective observer must be in a position to conclude that when these parties do business, they invariably do so on a particular set of terms. There must therefore be a number of prior transactions between the parties and evidence that a set of conditions has been both consistently referred to and accepted (or at least, not objected to).

Terms implied by law

Not all contractual terms find their way into contracts because they have **4–41** been expressly agreed to, or incorporated into the contract by the parties. Terms may also be implied into the contract. This is necessary because often the parties will say very little about what the terms of the agreement are going to be. Taking the example of a contract of sale, sometimes the only things expressly agreed between the parties are what is being sold, who is selling it to whom and the price. Everything else may be left unsaid. However, this does not mean that such a contract will contain no terms: a whole host of detailed provisions are implied into the contract by the CRA.[59] Terms can also be implied into contracts by the common law. At common law, a term will be implied into a contract in the circumstances described in *William Morton & Co v Muir Brothers & Co*[60]:

> "If the condition is such that every reasonable man on the one part would desire for his own protection to stipulate for the condition, and that no reasonable man on the other part would refuse to accede to it, then it is not unnatural that the conditions should be taken for granted in all contracts of the class without the necessity of giving it formal expression."

For example, when a professional person such as a solicitor or an accountant agrees to do some work for a client, a contract for the provision of services is formed under which the law will imply a duty on the part of the professional person to carry out the services in accordance with the degree of care which could ordinarily be expected of a member of that profession.

Interpretation of contractual terms

As we have already seen, very few contracts *need* be in writing in order to **4–42** be legally binding. However, in practise, very many contracts will be in writing and, generally speaking, recording one's contract in writing is a good idea. It simplifies the process of proving that a contract existed between the parties, and often helps remove doubt about the precise legal

---

[59] The CRA is discussed in detail in Ch.5, below.
[60] 1907 S.C. 1211, per Lord McLaren at 1224.

obligations that the parties have undertaken. But reducing the contract to writing does open up the possibility that the parties will come to disagree about what the wording in the document means. If a home-owner ("A") and a builder ("B") enter into a contract whereby B is to extend A's home, A might very well want to make it a term of the contract that B will be legally responsible for any damage that B causes to A's house. If the contract contains such a clause and B accidentally puts a ladder through A's window, it is clear that B will be liable. But is B contractually liable if the building works sever the roots of A's beloved apple tree, which is situated in the garden, and causes it to die? Where disputes arise about what the wording of a particular contractual provision means, the courts have to be able to interpret (or "construe" or "construct") what those words mean. In the example given, it would depend on what is meant by the word "house"—can the word be interpreted widely enough to include "garden"?

The English law of contractual interpretation was restated by Lord Hoffmann in the landmark case of *Investor Compensation Scheme Ltd v West Bromwich Building Society*.[61] Here, the House of Lords held that the formerly rather restrictive English rules of contractual interpretation should be liberalised. The law, argued Lord Hoffmann, should adopt a less literal and more contextual approach and lay emphasis upon the "factual matrix" or surrounding circumstances in which the words were used.[62] Lord Hoffmann's restatement has proven to be controversial in English law, and has not been unequivocally accepted into Scots law, with some judges seeming more sympathetic to it than others.[63] There is, therefore, a degree of uncertainty as to the direction that the law of contractual interpretation will take in Scots law in the future. It is, however, possible to state some general principles of modern Scots contractual interpretation:

- The ordinary meaning of the words used will be court's usual starting point.[64] Any deviation from the dominant meaning of the words used in the contract will have to be justified. Returning to the example given above, the word "house" usually means a building or structure intended for habitation. That will be the court's starting point in the current case; if the word is to mean something different on this occasion, there must be strong justification.

---

[61] [1998] 1 W.L.R. 896.

[62] In other words, less emphasis should be laid on what a word has been held to mean in previous court decisions and greater weight attached to what an objective bystander would have understood the parties to have intended the word to mean in the facts and circumstances of the present case.

[63] See, e.g. Black, *Woolman on Contract*, paras 8–01—8–15. The Hoffmann approach was subjected to considerable criticism by the Inner House of the Court of Session in *Multi-Link Leisure Developments Ltd v North Lanarkshire Council* [2009] CSIH 96; 2010 S.C. 302. However the Supreme Court did not make any such criticism when it considered the case: *Multi-Link Leisure Developments Ltd v North Lanarkshire Council* [2010] UKSC 47.

[64] *Bank of Scotland v Dunedin Property Investment Co Ltd*, 1998 S.C. 657.

- "An essentially objective exercise." Before Lord Hoffmann's restatement, contractual interpretation was an essentially objective exercise. In other words, the court was concerned to identify what an impartial bystander would understand the contractual wording to mean, not what the parties themselves subjectively believed the words meant. This continues to be the case; however it is now clear that the objective bystander is called upon to assess the words of the contract within the broader context in which they were used.[65] So returning to the example above, it is irrelevant if A can prove he has always understood the word "house" to include "garden". That proves only what he subjectively thought. However, if there is evidence that both A and B understood "house" to include "garden" then that would point towards B being liable for the damage to the tree.
- "Contractual document to be read as a whole." The disputed words are not to be read in isolation, but within the context of the contract as a whole. Thus, in truth, the issue for the court is not what the disputed words mean, but what the document means. Returning to the example above, imagine that A and B's contract provides that, as well as building the extension, B is going to carry out some renovation work on A's house, and among the things that are listed for B to do is "lay gravel along garden path". The fact that work to be carried out in the garden is described as work on A's house would tend to support his argument that these parties intended the word "house" to include "garden".
- "Different approaches for different types of contract." There is growing support in Scotland for the proposition that different contracts might require different treatment. Where a contract is a formal one prepared by lawyers and which uses technical legal language, the courts are reluctant to base their decision upon the "factual matrix". Here, they are likely to use the words in their technical legal sense.[66] However, where the court is called upon the interpret a less formal contract, it is much more likely to be willing to use the context in which the words were used as an aid to construction. Returning to the example above, a relatively low-value construction contract entered into between a householder and a small-scale builder would be likely to be the kind of contract in which the surrounding context would be considered admissible by the court.
- "Construction, not reconstruction." Finally, it should be noted that the purpose of the exercise is to ascertain the true intent of the parties, not to come to the aid of someone who has had the misfortune to enter into a contract which is detrimental to his

[65] *Luminar Lava Ignite Ltd v Mama Group Plc* [2010] CSIH 1.
[66] *Multi-Link Leisure Developments Ltd v North Lanarkshire Council* [2009] CSIH 96; 2010 S.C. 302; *Credential Bath Street Ltd v Venture Investment Placement Ltd* [2007] CSOH 208.

interests.[67] So if the court concludes that, on analysis, the parties did not intend damage to the garden to be included in the contract, it will not add in new words or give "house" an expanded meaning because it feels sympathy for the unfortunate householder.

THE LEGAL REGULATION OF CONTRACTUAL TERMS

Introduction

4-43 As we have seen, contracts are ultimately about agreement. One might therefore think that the purpose of contract law would be to give effect to what the parties have agreed, and often, the law does just that. However, the law has also come to recognise that there are situations where it is profoundly unfair to give effect to the terms of the contract as agreed by the parties. This is particularly so in consumer contracts.[68] These are contracts where a consumer of goods or services contracts with an entity whose business it is to provide goods or services. In some cases, the contract may be made between a 16 year old who might be wholly unused to commerce and one of the largest companies in the world.[69] In such cases, there is clearly a disparity in the sophistication and bargaining power of the two parties. Indeed, on a daily basis, consumers face contract by ultimatum: they will be presented with the company's standard term contract and told that these are the only terms on which the company does business; the consumer must "take it or leave it".

Exemption clauses

4-44 Sometimes, contracts will contain what are known as exemption clauses. These are clauses by which one party seeks to exclude or limit liability it would otherwise incur. A contractual term stating that a hotel does not accept liability for the theft of guests' property is an example of an *exclusion* clause, as it excludes liability for such a claim. A term stating that in the event of theft, the hotel will not be liable for damages in excess of £100 would be a *limitation* clause. Such clauses certainly have a legitimate place when knowingly entered into by sophisticated business organisations in order to implement informed choices which they have made on how best to allocate risk.[70] However, in other contexts—such as

---

[67] *Credential Bath Street Ltd v Venture Investment Placement Ltd* [2007] CSOH 208.

[68] It also has the potential to occur in other contexts too, such as where a large and sophisticated business organisation enters into a contract on standard terms with a much smaller business.

[69] As when a school-leaver buys an airline ticket from, e.g. British Airways in order to travel to university for the first time.

[70] In the specific context of the oil and gas industry, for instance, parties to oilfield service contracts frequently re-allocate their prospective liability for certain types of loss. See, e.g. G. Gordon, "Risk Allocation in Oil and Gas Contracts" in G. Gordon, J. Paterson and E. Usenmez (eds), *Oil and Gas Law: Current Practice and Emerging Trends*, 2nd edn, (Dundee: Dundee University Press, 2011) at p.443.

when they are incorporated by signature into a contract by a consumer who has not read, far less understood what he is signing—they have the potential to be grossly unfair.

Common law control of unfair contract terms

The common law provided some measure of protection for the unwary by **4–45** imposing rules on the circumstances in which terms could be incorporated into a contract. It also developed a rule which stated that, in the event that an exemption clause was ambiguous, it would be interpreted in the way least favourable to the interests of the party who had imposed the clause upon the other.[71] However, the courts were unwilling to declare unambiguous, properly incorporated terms to be unenforceable.[72]

Statutory and regulatory control of unfair contracts

In the middle part of the twentieth century there developed a growing **4–46** awareness that the common law's response was not adequate in itself to address the problem.[73] The Unfair Contract Terms Act ("UCTA") was enacted in 1977 in order to control the use of exemption clauses. The Act was followed in due course firstly by the Unfair Terms in Consumer Contracts Regulations 1994 and then by the Unfair Terms in Consumer Contracts Regulations 1999 ("UCTTR"). These Regulations provided consumers with a broader range of protections, but—rather confusingly—the provisions of the Regulations in some instances duplicated and in others differed from UCTA. This rather untidy situation has now been resolved by Pt 2 of the CRA, which provides that UCTA will no longer have any application to consumer contracts, repeals the Unfair Terms in Consumer Contracts Regulations 1999, and replaces those regulations with a comprehensive set of protections against unfair contract terms which will apply only to consumer contracts. The CRA received Royal Assent on March 26, 2015 and is expected to enter into force in October 2015. This chapter will proceed on the basis that the CRA has fully entered into force.

The Unfair Contract Terms Act 1977 ("UCTA")

As noted above, the Unfair Contract Terms Act no longer applies to **4–47** consumer contracts. However, UCTA continues to be relevant to contracts between businesses. UCTA's primary function is to regulate attempts by businesses to exclude or limit their liabilities through the use of exemption clauses. The Unfair Contract Terms Act applies to a broad range of contracts, including contracts for the sale or supply of goods, employment contracts, contracts for the provision of services and

---

[71] This is known as the *contra proferentem* rule.
[72] See MacQueen and Thomson, para.7.1.
[73] The common law approach has not been abolished, but is now supplemented by the statutory provisions discussed in the paragraphs that follow.

contracts permitting persons to enter onto land.[74] However, it should be noted that some significant types of contract are excluded from the Act's ambit. In particular, UCTA does not apply to contracts of insurance, contracts for the sale of land or contracts relative to the formation of dissolution of any form of business organisation.

Section 16 of UCTA contains two important provisions. Section 16(1)(a) of UCTA provides that any exemption clause that limits or excludes a business's liability for death or personal injury resulting from its negligence or other breach of duty is void and unenforceable. This is so because Parliament considered that the most abusive use of such clauses was to seek to evade or limit lawful liability for unlawfully causing injury to others. By contrast, s.16(1)(b) of UCTA states that any other exemption clause which limits or excludes a business's liability for negligence or other breach of duty is enforceable only if it is fair and reasonable for the term to have been included in the contract and for it to be relied upon in the circumstances. Thus, if a business's negligence or breach of duty has not caused someone to be injured or killed but has, for instance, caused property to be lost or damaged, the exemption clause will be ineffectual only if unfair and unreasonable. Among the range of factors that the court will take into account in determining whether the clause is fair and reasonable is the relative strength of the bargaining position of the parties.[75]

Section 17 UCTA provides a further set of protections for the benefit of businesses forced, due to their poor bargaining power relative to another business, to enter into a contract on another party's standard terms. Section 17 provides that in such situations, any term of a contract which either allows a party to exclude or restrict liability for breach of contract or permits a party to render no performance or to render a performance substantially different from that which was reasonably expected from the contract will be enforceable only if fair and reasonable. The provisions of s.17 differ from those of s.16 in that they are provided even where (as will often be the case) the breach or different performance of the contract has nothing to do with negligence or fault.[76]

---

[74] An example of the last-mentioned form of contract is the one by which a football club permits a spectator to enter a stadium to watch a football match.

[75] UCTA s.24(2) and Sch.2.

[76] If a builder fails to complete a job in the time agreed, he will have breached a contract *irrespective of whether or not he was negligent*. The builder's work may have been unavoidably delayed by poor weather or the non-availability of essential plant and materials: Black, *Woolman on Contract*, para.9–09.

Key Concepts

UCTA is concerned principally with a particular class of unfair terms known as exemption clauses. Its provisions no longer apply to consumer contracts but have the potential to apply to many contracts entered into between businesses, and:

- render unenforceable exemption clauses which purport to exclude or limit liability for death or personal injury caused as a result of negligence or other breach of duty;
- state that exemption clauses which exclude or limit liability for other sorts of losses caused as a result of negligence or other breach of duty will only be enforceable if they satisfy a fair and reasonable test; and
- make all exemption clauses contained in standard-form contracts subject to a fair and reasonable test.

The Consumer Rights Act 2015 ("CRA")

CRA Part 2 applies to contractual terms in consumer contracts. For these **4–48** purposes, a contract is a consumer contract if it has been entered into between a trader and a consumer and is not a contract of employment or apprenticeship.[77] CRA s.2 defines what is meant by a "trader" and a "consumer". "Trader" means a person acting for purposes relating to that person's trade, business, craft or profession, whether acting personally or through another person acting in the trader's name or on the trader's behalf, while "consumer" means an individual acting for purposes that are wholly or mainly outside that individual's trade, business, craft or profession. In broad terms, Part 2 of the CRA[78] has two main purposes: to encourage the use of plain and intelligible language in written consumer contracts; and to regulate the use in consumer contracts of certain terms which have the potential to be unfair. The first of these objectives is implemented by s.68, which provides that businesses must ensure that any written contractual term is "transparent", meaning that it must be expressed in plain, intelligible language and be legible. Section 69 provides that if there is any doubt about the meaning of a written term, the interpretation which is most favourable to the consumer shall prevail.

Turning now to the issue of unfairness, an important limitation to scope of the CRA is that neither contractual provisions which specify the main subject matter of the contract or which determine the price to be paid under the contact may be assessed for fairness. Thus the unfair contract terms provisions of the CRA will not provide protection for someone who, after entering into a contract, discovers that he has paid an inflated price for goods. The CRA permits the fairness of all other

---

[77] CRA s.61.
[78] Other provisions of the CRA are dealt with elsewhere in this work.

provisions in consumer contracts to be scrutinised. CRA s.62 provides that a term will be unfair "if, contrary to the requirement of good faith, it causes a significant imbalance in the parties' rights and obligations under the contract to the detriment of the consumer". Any provision of a consumer contract that is found to be unfair will not be binding on the consumer[79]: however, if the consumer, for some reason, wishes to rely on the term, he may do so[80]; and if a term is declared to be non-binding by the court, the rest of the contract shall continue to have legal effect if it is capable of continuing in existence without the unfair term.[81]

The CRA adopts a three-stage approach to assessing unfairness. First, some contractual provisions are "blacklisted"; if they are challenged by a consumer, the court *must* hold to be unfair. Included in this category are trader's attempts to exclude or restrict liability for negligently-caused death or personal injury.[82] Thus the long-standing prohibition on such exclusions and limitations first contained in UCTA is carried forward into the new law: such provisions are effectively deemed to be contrary to good faith, significantly imbalanced and detrimental to the consumer. Secondly, some contractual provisions are included on a "greylist" contained in Pt 1 of Sch.2 to the CRA. This list contains an "indicative and non-exhaustive list of terms of consumer contracts that may be regarded as unfair".[83] Thus, unlike the blacklisted provisions, these provisions will not automatically be held to be unfair; the court will have to consider the full facts and circumstances of the individual case in coming to a decision on whether the term meets the definition of unfairness contained in s.62. The statutory greylist approach was introduced by UCTTR, but the CRA has added a number of new provisions to the greylist. Among the 20 types of provision now included on the greylist are provisions which:

- impose disproportionately high charges in situations where the consumer decides not to conclude or perform the contract or for services which have not been supplied;
- allow the trader to unilaterally determine the characteristics or subject matter of the contract after the consumer is bound by the contract, or which allow the trader to unilaterally determine the price after the consumer is bound;
- permit the seller or supplier to retain sums paid by the consumer where the latter decides not to conclude or perform the contract;
- enable the seller or supplier to terminate a contract of indeterminate duration without reasonable notice except where there are serious grounds for doing so;

---

[79] CRA s.62(1).
[80] CRA s.62(3).
[81] CRA s.67.
[82] Also included in this category are attempts by traders to provide that the consumer bears the burden of proof with respect to compliance by a distance supplier or an intermediary with an obligation under any enactment or rule implementing the Distance Marketing Directive. The law on distance selling is discussed further at Chapter 7, below.
[83] CRA s.63(1).

- irrevocably bind the consumer to terms with which he had no real opportunity of becoming acquainted before the conclusion of the contract;
- enable the business to alter the terms of the contract unilaterally without a valid reason that is specified in the contract; or
- exclude or hinder the consumer's right to take legal action or exercise any other legal remedy.[84]

Thirdly and finally on the question of unfairness, it should be remembered that CRA s.62 is not restricted to situations where the term in question is contained on the statutory blacklist or greylist. It is drafted in general terms. As a result, any non-excluded provision in a consumer contract[85] may be found to unfair "if, contrary to the requirement of good faith, it causes a significant imbalance in the parties' rights and obligations under the contract to the detriment of the consumer". So if a trader manages to dream up a contractual provision which provides him with a new and ingenious way of unfairly taking advantage of a consumer, the provision may still be declared to be unfair, even if it does not appear on the statutory black-or greylist.

The CRA continues the practice first introduced by UTCCR of appointing a statutory overseer of the effectiveness of the law and enforcer and overseer of the law. CRA s.70 provides that this role will be undertaken by the Competition and Markets Authority ("CMA").[86] The CMA may consider complaints about terms that have been used or are proposed to be used in consumer contracts and, if he considers any of the terms to be unfair, may take court action preventing the continued use of these terms. This was an important innovation when first introduced by UTCCR. One of the weaknesses of UCTA was that, while as a matter of law it makes certain types of exclusion clauses unenforceable, it did not contain a mechanism preventing businesses from purporting to include such clauses in their contracts. Thus, consumers in a dispute with a business might see the clause in their contract and just assume that because it was in the contract it could not be challenged. Having a public body in an overseeing role has the potential to "clean up" contracting practice by ensuring that the legal effect of clauses of dubious legality are tested and unenforceable clauses removed from consumer contracts. Following high levels of complaints relative to the contracting practices of certain industries, the Office of Fair Trading, which is the public body which previously had oversight of unfair contractual terms, issued a

---

[84] For the full list listing, see CRA Sch.2 Pt 1.
[85] i.e. any provision which does not specify the main subject matter of the contract or determine the price to be paid under the contact.
[86] A number of other qualifying bodies also have enforcement powers for certain purposes. These include local trading standards agencies, the Information Commissioner and the Financial Services Authority. See CRA Sch.3.

number of guidance documents providing companies active within these industries with an indication of the OFT's principal areas of concern.[87]

Key Concepts

Unlike UCTA, Part 2 of the CRA provides protection only for the benefit of consumers contracting with businesses. Like UCTA, the CRA renders unenforceable clauses which purport to exclude or limit liability for negligently-caused death or personal injury. In addition, it seeks to regulate any form of unfairness which may act to the detriment of the consumer. It does this by:

- providing incentives for businesses to contract in plain and readily understandable language;
- providing that terms which, contrary to the requirement of good faith cause a significant imbalance in the parties' rights and obligations under the contract to the detriment of the consumer are unfair and unenforceable against the consumer, and providing the consumer and the court with the benefit of an illustrative list of contractual terms and practices which may, depending on the facts and circumstances of the case, be thought likely to be unfair; and
- providing CMA with an enforcement and overseeing role which and permits that body to issue guidance and to take court action demanding that organisations stop using unfair terms in their contracts.

DEFECTIVE CONTRACTS

Introduction

4-49 As we have already seen, contracts come about when the parties agree to enter into a legally binding arrangement between themselves. Sometimes, however an attempt by the parties to enter into a contract may go wrong. There may be some sort of defect or impediment which makes a contract "void", "voidable" or "legally unenforceable". It is important to appreciate that these expressions are not interchangeable. They mean quite distinct things.

---

[87] These documents may be linked to from at the CMA's website, available at *https://www.gov.uk/government/collections/cma-consumer-enforcement-guidance* [Accessed May 15, 2015]. Among the businesses for whom sector-specific guidance has been produced are the care home industry, the package holiday industry and the fitness and health club industry.

"Void", "voidable" and "unenforceable" explained

A "void contract" is an absolute nullity; it has no legal effect whatsoever. **4–50** Nothing requires to be done to bring a void contract to an end as it never came into being in the first place. Contracts will generally be considered void if they suffer from a fundamental defect, for instance, if one or more to the parties does not have legal capacity to enter into a contract.

A "voidable contract", on the other hand, does come into existence, but suffers from an underlying defect which means that either of the parties can petition the court, asking for it to be "annulled" or "reduced". As we shall see below, a contract will be declared voidable if someone has been tricked into entering it by the provision of false information, or if there is problem (other than a fundamental problem) with a party's legal capacity. Crucially, however, the right to reduce a contract will be lost if:

- the party seeking to reduce the contract has delayed unreasonably before commencing proceedings to have the contract set aside, or behaves in such a way as to lead the other party to believe that the contract is not going to be challenged;
- a third party has since innocently acquired rights that it would be unfair for the court to interfere with; or
- restitutio in integrum can no longer be effected. The law requires that if a contract is going to be reduced, it must be physically possible to put the parties back in the position that they occupied before the contract was entered into. This cannot always be done, as the following case demonstrates.

Boyd and Forrest v Glasgow and South West Railway Company
1915 S.C. (H.L.) 20

BF entered into a contract with GSWRC to build a railway line. BF duly started the job and proceeded to blast railway cuttings into the countryside, move earth and commence laying the line. Having done so, they discovered that information they had received from GSWRC about the geological characteristics of the area in which they were working was incorrect; the contract was therefore voidable. They attempted to reduce the contract, but the court held that they could not do so. The engineering work which they had carried out could not readily be undone. In these circumstances, restitutio in integrum was impossible.

An "unenforceable agreement" is different again; here the courts, without giving consideration to whether the contract is void or voidable, simply say that the contract is of a nature that they will not enforce it. Courts will hold a contract unenforceable if it is contrary to public policy or pursues an immoral objective.

The distinction between these expressions can have significant consequences. As we have already seen, the right to annul a voidable contract may be lost; void or unenforceable contracts, by contrast, remain void or unenforceable come what may. Another particularly important consequence is seen in the context of contracts for the sale of goods. If a void contract purports to transfer property, no title to that property passes and any subsequent sale or disposal is ineffectual. With a voidable contract, the position would be different. As a voidable contract exists until such time as it is reduced by the court, if property is transferred under a voidable contract that has not yet been set aside then a good title to the property is passed. This in turn means that the person who purchased the property can pass a valid title on to a third party.

Key Concepts

Not all attempts to create a contract will be successful. Defects may emerge which render either a contract or a particular term within a contract void, voidable or unenforceable.

There is legal significance in the distinction between void, voidable or unenforceable contracts. In particular, the right to reduce a voidable contract can be lost in certain circumstances. This issue does not arise with void or unenforceable contracts.

Instances of defects in contracts

Lack of legal capacity

4–51 As a matter of law, certain categories of people are not permitted to enter into contracts. Such people are said to lack legal capacity to enter into agreements. Any purported contract entered into by a person lacking legal capacity will be void. There are a number of situations where a person will lack legal capacity. Each will be considered in turn.

Non-age

4–52 The law seeks to protect the interests of children and young persons by providing that before they attain a certain age, they cannot enter into a legally binding contract. There is no automatic cut-off point in place after which an elderly person automatically loses legal capacity, but as we shall see, vulnerable elderly people are protected in other ways.[88] The rules related to non-age in Scotland are contained in the Age of Legal Capacity (Scotland) Act 1991 ("ALCSA"). The ALCSA divides the young person's capacity to act into three periods, namely:

> (1) A period from birth to the last day on which a young person is aged 15.

---

[88] For example, the discussion of facility and circumvention at para.4–58, below.

During this period, a young person is in general deemed to have no capacity to enter into a contract,[89] and any contracts relating to the young person will generally require to be entered into by his or her legal guardian (generally, his or her parents).[90] The only exception to this rule is that a young person may enter into a binding agreement so long as:

(a) it relates to a transaction is of a kind commonly entered into by persons of that age; and
(b) the terms of the transaction are reasonable.[91]

(2) A period lasting from the day when the age of 16 is attained until the last day on which a young person is aged 17.

Upon reaching the age of 16, a person is deemed to be capable of looking after his own legal affairs and therefore attains legal capacity.[92] He or she may therefore enter into binding legal contracts. 16 and 17-year olds are, however, given the benefit of a statutory protection from prejudicial transactions. If such a person enters into a prejudicial transaction, he is entitled to make an application to the court to have that transaction set aside. The ALCSA defines a "prejudicial transaction" as one which a reasonably prudent adult would not have entered into, and which has caused or is likely to cause substantial prejudice to the young person.[93] Any such application must be presented to the court before the young person reaches 21 years of age. The ALCSA also contains a provision which allows an application to be made to the court to have a transaction made by someone between 16 and 18 ratified by the court.[94] If the court is satisfied that the transaction is not prejudicial, then it will issue a judgment confirming this. Any transaction so confirmed cannot later be challenged on the grounds that it was prejudicial.

(3) A period commencing upon the attainment of 18 years of age.

On one's 18th birthday, one continues to have legal capacity but ceases to enjoy the benefit of the protection provided by s3 ALCSA.[95]

Insanity

The law seeks to protect the interests of the insane by stating that such **4–53** persons lack legal capacity; any contracts entered into by such persons

---

[89] ALCSA s.1(1)(a).
[90] ALCSA s.5.
[91] ALCSA s.2(1).
[92] ALCSA s.1(1)(b).
[93] ALCSA s.3. Any such application must be presented to the court before the young person reaches 21 years of age.
[94] ALCSA s.4.
[95] The court's protection can still be sought in relation to contracts entered into while one was 16 or 17, but no protection is afforded for contracts entered into from one's 18th birthday onwards.

are therefore void.[96] This does not mean that every person suffering to any extent from a mental illness is prevented from entering into a contract. Before someone will be said to lack mental capacity as a result of insanity, he must be suffering from a mental illness or disorder sufficiently severe to mean that he has no understanding of the nature of the obligations which he is offering to undertake. Procedures exist for the appointment of guardians to look after the interests of insane persons. As the law is concerned with the mental state of the person at the time that he entered into the contract, and not at any other point, it is believed that someone who suffers from a mental condition the effects of which become more or less acute from time to time may enter into a contract during a lucid interval. Arguably, the law does not, at present, do enough to protect the legal interests people who suffer from mental illnesses which produce symptoms falling short of the present test for insanity.[97]

Intoxication

4-54 If someone is so intoxicated by drink or (presumably[98]) drugs that they are unaware of the nature of the obligations which they are offering to undertake, then they will lack the capacity to enter into a contract. Any contracts the person purports to enter into whilst in that condition will therefore be void. However, the law will not lightly permit people to escape their contractual obligations by pleading intoxication and if such an argument is to be successful there must be compelling evidence that the contract was entered into in a state of extremely advanced intoxication. In *Pollock v Burns*,[99] P signed a document committing him to pay a sum of money to B in relation to a race-horse which P had bought from him. A dispute arose as to the enforceability of the document and the court was asked to rule on its validity. P led evidence that he had been drinking heavily for days prior to signing the document and that he had no recollection of signing it. However, there was other evidence which showed that although he had been drinking, P was still in a position to converse with B, sign the document and then to help B put on his coat as

---

[96] As an exception to this general rule, someone providing the necessities of life to an insane person may recover a reasonable price (which may not necessarily the contract price, particularly if the provider is profiteering at the expense of the insane person) for so doing: SGA 1979 s.3(2).

[97] Bipolar disorder, for instance, can lead to periods of intense excitement during which a person may, while still aware at some level of what they are doing, act in a disinhibited way. This may cause such a person to enter into contracts which they would not generally have wished to enter into. See, for instance, T. Leven, "Bipolar Disorder and Debt", *Guardian*, October 28, 2006, available for download from *http://www.guardian.co.uk/money/2006/oct/28/accounts.saving* [Accessed May 15, 2015].

[98] The reported cases, almost all of which come from the Victorian era, are concerned with the effects of alcohol rather than illicit or prescription drugs but in principle the rules developed in the one context would appear to be application in the other. One relatively recent case which considered (but did not decide) the issue was *X v BBC* [2005] CSOH 80, where Ms X attempted to reduce a contract on the grounds of incapacity, both through age (she was 17) and intoxication. She averred she had consumed a bottle of Buckfast and 15 tablets of valium.

[99] (1875) 2 R. 497.

he was leaving. The court held that in these circumstances it was not satisfied that P had been utterly intoxicated, and the obligation to pay therefore stood.

Corporations

Corporations such as companies have legal personalities separate from **4-55** those of their members. However, as corporations are persons in only legal, and not a natural sense, they are generally established by documents which set out and determine the extent of their legal powers. At common law, any act on the part of the corporation which goes outside those powers is void. However, these common law rules have, at least for companies, been somewhat overtaken by statutory provisions in the Companies Act 2006 which provide at least some measure of protection for persons entering into contractual relations with companies: these are further discussed in Ch.16, "Company Law", below.

Improper negotiations and abuse of position

Scots law recognises that sometimes conduct on the part of one of the **4-56** parties unfairly induces the other party to enter into an agreement that they would not otherwise have concluded. It permits such contracts to be challenged in certain circumstances. These are discussed below.

Force and fear

A contract will be rendered null and void if it was entered into in cir- **4-57** cumstances so extreme that a person was entirely unable to exercise free will as a result of his fear of the threat or use of force. In such circumstances, the objective bystander would take the view that there was no real *consensus in idem*. History provides us with some notable examples of force and fear. Perhaps the most celebrated is *Earl of Orkney v Vinfra*,[100] in which the Earl took offence at V's refusal to sign a legally binding document and threatened to stab him through the head if he did not put pen to paper. V duly signed, but the Earl's triumph was short-lived; the court held that the document was null and void. However, of greater day to day relevance today is the fact that other, lesser threats will be sufficient to have a contract rendered voidable if the pressure exerted by the threats is sufficient to mean that the consent was not given freely. In order to establish this, a party must show that an illegitimate threat has been made which is of such a nature that the objective bystander would conclude that the victim's consent was not freely given.[101] The threat may be against the victim or someone closely connected to him. However, only threats which are unlawful will be considered to be illegitimate. Threats of physical violence clearly qualify, but so, too, do threats to spread malicious and untrue rumours about someone,[102] or a threat to breach a

---

[100] (1606) Mor. 16481.
[101] *Euan Wallace and Partners v Wescot Homes Plc*, 2000 S.L.T. 327.
[102] Such threats constitute the delict of defamation.

pre-existing contract. By contrast, a threat to put someone into insolvency in respect of a debt which is lawfully due is not illegitimate.[103]

Facility and circumvention

4–58 The expression "facility" describes a weakened state of mind. A facile person continues to have some understanding of their actions, but is suggestible and susceptible to influence. Facility may arise in many ways, for instance as a result of old age, mental illness short of insanity,[104] or physical frailty leading a person to be psychologically dependant upon another.[105] However the mere fact that a person is suffering from a serious (or even terminal) illness does not of itself make a person facile; there must in addition be evidence of a diminution of the person's mental powers.[106] Facility need not be a permanent state of mind but can be a transient condition: someone recovering from the administration of a general anaesthetic may be facile today but in a more robust frame of mind tomorrow. "Circumvention" occurs when someone:

- takes dishonest advantage of the other person's facile condition and thereby induces them to enter into a contract with them, or make a promise; and
- the transaction causes the facile person a loss.

A contract entered into as a result of facility and circumvention is voidable.

Undue influence

4–59 A contract may be attacked on the basis of undue influence where:

- the person alleged to have exercised an undue influence is in a relationship of trust or influence over the other party; and
- the party in that position of trust or influence abuses it and thereby induces the other party to enter into an arrangement to the detriment of the trusting party.

When established, the plea of undue influence permits a party to reduce a contract. In practice, undue influence arises most commonly in relationships of parent and child,[107] between spouses,[108] or as between professional persons and their clients.[109]

---

[103] *Wolfson v Edelman*, 1952 S.L.T. (Sh. Ct.) 97.
[104] As we have already seen, if someone is insane, they will in any event lack legal capacity on that ground.
[105] See, e.g. *Horne v Whyte* [2005] CSOH 115.
[106] *Pirie v Clydesdale Bank Plc*, 2007 S.C.L.R. 18.
[107] See, e.g. *Forbes v Forbes' Trs*, 1957 S.C. 325.
[108] See, e.g. *Royal Bank of Scotland Plc v Etridge (No.2)* [2002] 2 A.C. 773.
[109] See, e.g. *Anstruther v Wilkie* 1856 18 D. 405.

Error

Parties sometimes purport to enter into a contract whilst one or more of **4–60** them are labouring under some kind of misapprehension. In such cases, the courts have to steer an awkward course between the competing interests of the parties. Considerations of fairness to the party who has made the mistake might lead the court to wish to release that party from the (possibly very onerous) consequences of its error. But equally it would undesirable if large numbers of contracts were capable of being challenged on the basis that one of the parties did not fully understand what it was doing when entering into it: considerations of certainty, therefore, would make the courts lean towards upholding the contract notwithstanding the error. Against this background, the common law has sought (and often struggled[110]) to evolve a system of categorisation whereby different treatment is offered to different types of error.[111]

Black has recently argued that it is "possible to identify five questions **4–61** that can help determine whether a contract resulting from error is enforceable or not."[112]

The questions are:

(1) Is the error so serious that it prevents *consensus in idem*?
(2) Is the error "in the substantials"?
(3) Is the error unilateral or bilateral?
(4) Has there been "error plus"?
(5) Has the error been induced by the other party to the contract?

Black has also produced a useful flowchart (reproduced below) illustrating the legal consequences of how the questions are answered. Black's framework provides a useful guide through this difficult area of law and is adopted here. The commentary which follows is to be read in conjunction with the flowchart.[113]

---

[110] The courts have found it difficult to lay down a coherent and consistent set of rules relative to error. Some of the elderly cases on this area have to be treated with great care. Moreover, different writers offer different theories as to how error should be conceptualised. In *Wills v Strategic Procurement (UK) Limited* [2013] CSOH 26, Lord Malcolm noted that, "[t]he effect of error on the validity of a contract is one of the most uncertain areas in our private law." For further discussion see Black, *Woolman on Contract*, paras 6–15—6–42.

[111] Apart from the common law's rules, a statutory process exists to correct certain types of error. The Law Reform (Miscellaneous Provisions) (Scotland) Act 1985 s.8 introduced a process known as rectification. This empowers the court to correct any document which was intended to express or give effect to an agreement but which failed to "express accurately the common intention of the parties". Thus if, for example, A and B reach a verbal agreement then attempt to put that agreement into writing, but make an error in recording the contracts' terms, they can use the process of rectification to correct the error in the written agreement.

[112] Black, *Woolman on Contract*, para.6–16. See also G. Black, "Error Reduced" (2015) 19 Edin. L.R. 140.

[113] Flowchart originally published in Black, *Woolman on Contract*, 5th edn (Edinburgh: W. Green, 2014), p.88; paragraph references in the flowchart are to that work.

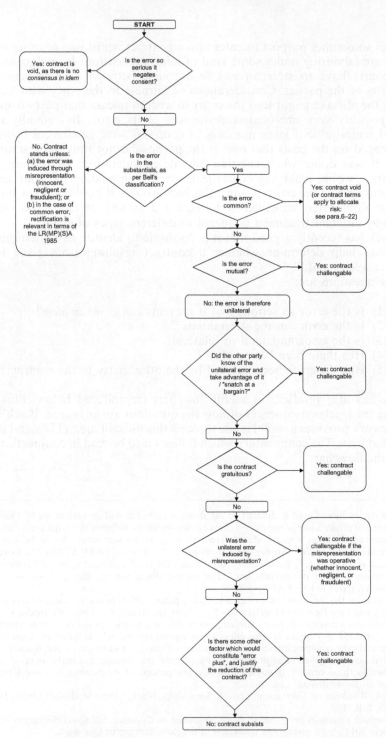

(1) Is the error so serious that it prevents *consensus in idem* and there is, therefore, no contract at all?

As we have already seen, contracts are formed when a *consensus in idem*– **4–62** a meeting of the minds–is reached. If an error is so serious that it means that the parties have not truly reached agreement, then no contract can be said to have come into existence. We have already seen an example of this in the discussion of *Mathieson Gee (Ayrshire) Limited v Quigley*,[114] where the parties were at cross-purposes as to the subject-matter of the contract and as a result no contract was formed. A further example can be seen in *Stuart & Co v Kennedy*.[115] Here, building material was sold at a rate of 1 shilling and nine pence per foot. However, the seller considered himself to be selling by the superficial foot, a unit of area, while the purchaser considered himself to be buying by the lineal foot, a unit of length. The price calculated on the basis of the pursuer's understanding was more than double the price calculated on the defender's understanding. The court held that in the circumstances there was no *consensus in idem*.

(2) Is the error "in the substantials"?

Trivial or peripheral errors are not sufficiently fundamental to allow a **4–63** party to escape from the consequences of entering into a contract. They have no effect upon the validity of a contract. Thus if I buy a second-hand bicycle believing it to be black when it is in fact a very dark blue, the contract will stand. Only errors which are sufficiently significant to "go to the root" of a contract are relevant. An error will go to the root of a contract if it can be demonstrated that, were it not for the error, one or more of the parties would have declined to enter into the agreement.[116] Such errors are sometimes described as "errors in the substantials".[117]

An error in the substantials is necessary but not sufficient to invalidate a contract. In other words, an error which is not in the substantials can have no effect upon the validity of the contract, but making an error which *is* in the substantials will not in and of itself lead to the contract being declared invalid. For this to happen, the error in the substantials must be combined with some other factor; see further the discussion below.

(3) Is the error unilateral or bilateral?

Unilateral errors involve only one party to the contract. Unless the error **4–64** is so fundamental that it has resulted in there being no *consensus in idem*, and unless "error plus" or misrepresentation is involved,[118] the courts will normally consider such an error to be a legal irrelevance, and will decline to reduce a contract entered into as a result of this kind of mistake. So if a man seeks to impress his wife by purchasing two seats for her favourite

---

[114] 1952 S.C. (H.L.) 38.
[115] (1885) 13 R. 221
[116] *Menzies v Menzies* (1893) 20 R. (H.L.) 108.
[117] Bell, *Principles*, s.11.
[118] These issues are further discussed below.

theatrical show off eBay at an inflated price, mistakenly believing the "grand circle" to contain the best seats in the house when it in fact contains very poor views and limited leg-room, he cannot take any action to reduce the contract.[119]

Bilateral errors, by contrast, involve both parties (or, where there are more than two parties, all parties) to the contract. Such errors may be sub-categorised as common or mutual. An error is "common" when all parties to the contract make the same mistake. For instance, in a contract for the sale of a painting, if both parties think the painting continues to be in existence whereas in fact it was destroyed by a fire moments before the contract came into existence, that would be a case of a common error.[120] In such a case, if the common error relates to an essential element of the contract, the contract will be void. Less material common errors have no effect upon the validity of the contract.

A bilateral error is described as "mutual" when each party mis-understands the other party's intentions. As we have already seen, sometimes this misunderstanding will be so fundamental as to prevent the parties from achieving *consensus in idem*. Other mutual errors have no effect upon the validity of the contract.

(4) Has there been "error plus"?

4-65 The doctrine of "error plus" was advanced by Professor McBryde, who, in *The Law of Contract in Scotland*, argued that a unilateral error will not be sufficient in itself to invalidate a contract.[121] For a contract to be invalidated, an error in substantials must either be mutual or a unilateral error operating in conjunction with some additional factor. McBryde's analysis has started to receive considerable judicial support.[122] It would seem that there is no set and final list of "plus" factors that may be combined with error in order to invalidate a contract. Perhaps the most important such situation in practice is the situation where a party has entered into a contract in reliance upon a misrepresentation from the other party to the contract; this situation is discussed in greater detail below. Other situations where the courts have been willing to set aside a contract on the basis of "error plus" are where the party not in error is aware of the other party's mistake and deliberately takes unfair

---

[119] This example is taken from unhappy personal experience.
[120] This example is taken from Black, *Woolman on Contract*, para.6–22.
[121] McBryde, *Contract*, paras 15.23–15.39.
[122] See, e.g. *Parvaiz v Thresher Wines Acquisitions Ltd* [2008] CSOH 160; *Wills v Strategic Procurement (UK) Limited* [2013] CSOH 26.

advantage of it in order to "snap up a bargain"[123] or obtain some other unjust advantage,[124] or where the contract is gratuitous in nature.[125] A contract is gratuitous when one party undertakes obligations without receiving anything any reciprocal performance or payment from the other party.

(5) Has the error been induced by the other party to the contract?

The law of misrepresentation developed significantly throughout the **4–66** twentieth century and most cases on error are now pursued on this ground. A misrepresentation is a misleading statement made by one person to another. A person who is induced to enter into a contract as a result of a misrepresentation will be entitled to some manner of legal remedy if:

- the statement complained of was made by the other contracting party or someone acting on his behalf[126]; and
- the misrepresentation was not trivial and was made in a context where the objective observer would conclude it was intended to be a serious statement of fact.

The precise nature of the remedy available will depend upon two further factors:

- the degree of blameworthiness attaching to which the person who made it: in other words, did they mislead the other party fraudulently, negligently, or innocently?; and
- the significance of the misrepresentation: does it relate to a material matter, or to an essential one?[127]

Fraudulent misrepresentation. A fraudulent misrepresentation is one **4–67** which is made with a deliberate intention to deceive.[128] In practice, it is difficult to prove a dishonest intent in all but the most extreme of circumstances and cases of fraudulent misrepresentation are relatively rare.

---

[123] *Steuart's Trustees v Hart* (1875) 3 R. 192. In this case, the seller of land thought that as a matter of law, after the sale, he would be entitled to receive from the purchaser a significant annual land charge. He therefore did not insist upon a high purchase price for the property. The true position was that the seller was entitled to receive only a small fraction of the annual charge that he imagined he would receive. The purchaser was aware of the true position and knew that the seller was mistaken. The court held that that the contract could be set aside as this was an error in substantials which had been unfairly taken advantage of by the purchaser.

[124] *Wills v Strategic Procurement (UK) Limited* [2013] CSOH 26.

[125] *Hunter v Bradford Property Trust Ltd*, 1970 S.L.T. 173.

[126] Thus, if I enter into a mortgage agreement with a particular bank because a friend says that bank offers the best rates available, when in fact a mortgage with that bank is offered only on very expensive terms, my contract with the bank is not capable of being annulled. The position would be different if the person giving me the misleading information was a mortgage advisor employed by the bank.

[127] Essential error is discussed at para.4–12, above.

[128] *Derry v Peek* (1889) 44 L.R. App. Cas. 337.

Where fraud is established, the legal effect of the misrepresentation will depend upon whether the misrepresentation relates to an essential or merely a material matter.[129] If the misrepresentation induces an essential error, the contract will be void. If the misrepresentation brings about a material error, the contract will be voidable. In both cases, damages will in addition be available to the party to whom the misrepresentation was made if it can prove it has suffered a loss as a result of the misrepresentation.

4–68 Negligent misrepresentation. A negligent misrepresentation occurs when a person makes a misleading statement having failed to take reasonable care to ensure its accuracy. Such misrepresentations only give rise to legal consequences if the misrepresenter owes a "duty of care"[130] to the party to whom the misrepresentation is made; this criterion will usually be established when the parties are engaged in contractual negotiations.[131] If a negligent misrepresentation induces an essential error, the contract will be void. If it brings about a error in substantials, the contract will be voidable. In both cases, damages will in addition be available to the party to whom the misrepresentation was made if it can prove it has suffered a loss as a result.[132]

4–69 Innocent misrepresentation. A statement will be considered an innocent misrepresentation if its maker honestly but mistakenly believed it to be true, and if he made the statement in circumstances which would not entitle the court to conclude he had been negligent in saying what he did. Innocent misrepresentations render a contract voidable, but damages are never available where a misrepresentation is innocent. Thus, the only remedy available to a person who enters into a contract as a result of an innocent misrepresentation is to reduce the contract and, as we have already seen, the right to reduce a contract can in certain circumstances be lost.

Key Concepts

Parties sometimes enter into contracts on the basis of some kind of misapprehension (error). The legal effect of an error on a contract depends upon a combination of factors: whether the error is bilateral or unilateral; what the error is about; whether it has been made by the party itself or; whether the case involves error alone or "error plus"; and whether or not the error arose as a result of a

---

[129] As we have already seen, if the misrepresentation relates only to a trivial matter, it is of no legal significance and no remedy is available at all.
[130] The legal concept of "duty of care" is discussed in greater detail in Ch.10, "Delict", below.
[131] *Esso Petroleum Co v Mardon* [1976] Q.B. 801; *Cramaso LLP v Viscount Reidhaven's Trustees* [2014] UKSC 4.
[132] Law Reform (Miscellaneous Provisions) (Scotland) Act 1985 s.10.

misrepresentation by the other party. Taking all these factors together we can say that:

- An error which is so fundamental that it prevents the parties from reaching consensus in idem will prevent a contract from coming into existence;
- Trivial errors have no effect upon the legal validity of the contract;
- Errors which are not sufficiently fundamental as to prevent consensus in idem but which relate to the substantials of the contract fall into an intermediate category.
  —They are not sufficient, in themselves, to affect the validity of a contract but if they are either mutual or are unilateral errors operating in conjunction with another factor ("error plus") the contract may be set aside.
  —The "error plus" requirement is most commonly fulfilled in cases of misrepresentation, but the courts have also recognised situations where one party knowingly takes advantage of the other party's error and gratuitious contracts as being enough to constitute "error plus."

Pacta illicita

Introduction

There are certain contracts which the courts will not enforce, even if the **4–70** parties themselves intend them to be enforceable. At common law, at least, such contracts are not void or voidable; the courts simply take the view that they will not allow the parties to enforce them.[133] These contracts are known by the Latin expression *pacta illicita*. The direct translation of this expression is "illegal contracts" but as we shall see often the term is used more broadly than this would suggest: the term encompasses not just contracts to carry out unlawful acts, but also contracts which would be contrary to the public interest, possibly on the grounds that the contract promotes immorality or is an unjustifiable restraint of free trade. The principal examples of *pacta illicita* are outlined below.

Contracts to commit crimes

The clearest example of *pacta illicita* is an agreement to commit a crime. **4–71** An agreement to carry out a murder entered into between a mafia boss and a contract killer will not be enforceable in the courts; nor will a contract for the purchase of cocaine entered into between a drug user and his dealer. For the very obvious reason that to pursue a claim under such a contract would necessarily involve publicly confessing that one has been involved in criminality, such cases very rarely appear before the courts.

---

[133] The position can be different in the case of statutory *pacta illicita*: see para.4–75, below.

Contracts to commit delicts

4–72 Contravening the criminal law is not the only way one can commit a legal wrong. The commission of a delict, too, is unlawful.[134] A contract whereby the parties agree that one of them will breach the law of delict is therefore also *pactum illicitum*. The delict of inducing a breach of contract occurs when one person (A) knowingly, intentionally and without justification induces another person (B) to breach the terms of a pre-existing contract with a third party (C).[135] So if A knowingly, intentionally and without justification entered into a contract with B compelling B to breach his pre-existing contract with C, the contract between A and B be a *pactum illicitum*.

Contracts which promote immorality

4–73 The court will not give effect to agreements which promote or further immoral behaviour. A contract for the provision of sexual services by way of prostitution, for instance, will not be enforceable. In *Hamilton v Main*,[136] H granted a bill of exchange—essentially a cheque—for £60 to M, an inn-keeper, in order to pay for the drink consumed by him and the hire of a prostitute provided by M during what appears to have been a rather rumbustious stay at M's inn.[137] The court held that the bill of exchange was not enforceable in full: M was entitled to charge a reasonable price for the alcohol which had been consumed, but could not receive payment for the services of the prostitute.

Contracts which are contrary to public policy

4–74 The courts will also decline to enforce any contract which is contrary to public policy. Numerous contracts have been declared contrary to public policy: for example, contracts to perpetrate a fraud against a court.[138] For a long time *sponsiones ludicrae*—contracts relating to gambling—were also considered to be contrary to public policy. However, the rule against such contracts was abolished when the law relating to gambling was modernised.[139] Gambling agreements are now, therefore, generally legally enforceable. Attempts to unjustifiably interfere with free trade are also strictly speaking examples of contracts that are unenforceable because they are contrary to public policy but these of such great practical importance that they deserve to be given separate treatment. They are discussed at paras 4–76—4–79, below.

---

[134] The law of delict is discussed in Ch.10, below.
[135] See, e.g. *BMTA v Gray*, 1951 S.C. 586.
[136] (1823) 2 S. 356.
[137] According to the case report, during the seven days that M and his lady friend lodged at the inn, they between them consumed, "113 bottles of port and Madeira wine, besides a large quantity of spirituous and malt liqueurs".
[138] *Walker v Walker*, 1911 S.C. 163.
[139] Gambling Act 2005 s.334. The change came into effect on September 1, 2007.

Statutory pacta illicita

Parliament may declare by statute that certain types of contract, or **4–75**
certain terms within a contract, are illegal. Sometimes parliament will
state that such terms or contracts are unenforceable; sometimes it will
state that they are "null" or "void". We have already seen an example of
such a provision when discussing s.16(1) of UCTA, and the equivalent
provisions of the CRA which make clauses which purport to exclude
liability for death or personal injury as a result of negligence, void.[140]

Contracts and contractual terms in restraint of free trade

The courts are, in general, hostile to contracts which restrict one of the **4–76**
parties' ability to work to earn a living, or otherwise act as a restraint
upon free trade. This is because there is believed to be a very strong
public interest in free trade. We will examine the courts' approach to two
particular types of contract which have the effect of restricting free trade:
restrictive covenants and *solus* agreements.

Restrictive covenants. A restrictive covenant is a term by which one **4–77**
party to the contract agrees that for a period of time he will refrain from
doing certain things which would involve him commercially competing
with the other party. Restrictive covenants are commonly inserted into
contracts for the sale of a business or contracts of employment. In the
context of the sale of a business, the seller of the business might enter into
a covenant in something like the following terms:

> "Seller hereby undertakes and covenants not to set up any business
> within [X] miles of [the location of the business sold] for a period of
> [Y] years from the date hereof."

A restrictive covenant in an employment contract intended to prevent the
employee from working for a trade competitor might look something like
this:

> "Employee hereby undertakes and agrees that he will not accept any
> work, whether as an employee, contractor or in any other manner
> whatever, for a business which is:
>
> (a) to any extent whatever a competitor of Employer; and
> (b) located within [X] miles of [the location of Employee's
>   present place of employment]
>
> for a period of [X] months/years after the date of termination of this
> agreement."

---

[140] See paras 4–47 and 4–78.

A contract of employment might alternatively or in addition contain a separate restrictive covenant designed to prevent the employee from undertaking work for the customers of his former employer.

The leading case of *Nordenfelt v Maxim Nordenfelt*[141] provides that a restrictive covenant will be unenforceable unless the person seeking to enforce the restriction can demonstrate that the clause:

- Protects a legitimate interest of his. The desire to protect confidential information (so-called "trade secrets") is a commonly given example of a legitimate interest.[142] This includes information about the names and addresses of customers and the pricing structure of products or services. The preservation of a business connection is another example which could be given. Thus when an employee has had extensive client contact, the court may very well accept that it is legitimate to include a clause forbidding the employee from approaching those clients and trying to take them with him if he leaves the company. This has arisen in cases involving employees as diverse as currency traders[143] and milkmen.[144] Other examples could be given, but the courts will never consider a mere desire to avoid fair competition to be legitimate;
- Is reasonable in the circumstances. What is "reasonable" will depend upon a range of factors including the length of the restriction, the geographical area involved and the precise nature of the restriction imposed.[145] The issue of whether the clause was reasonable is determined by considering the facts and state of knowledge of the parties at the time that the contract was entered into, not with the benefit of hindsight; and
- Is in the public interest. In practice, when the first two criteria are satisfied, it is most unusual for the courts to hold that the restriction is contrary to the public interest.

The courts apply this test somewhat differently as between restrictive covenants imposed relative to the sale of a business and those imposed in contracts of employment. Each will be discussed separately, below. In the meantime, it should be noted that when assessing the reasonableness of a restrictive covenant, the court will look at the covenant as it stands. The court will not "water down" an unreasonable covenant to the point where it becomes reasonable—they will either enforce the covenant as it stands, or strike it out. So if a restrictive covenant is stated in an agreement to last for five years and to cover a radius of 50 miles from the employer's place of business and the court considers that only a six month duration relative to a radius of one mile was justified, the covenant

---

[141] [1894] A.C. 535.
[142] See, e.g. *Bluebell Apparel v Dickinson*, 1980 S.L.T. 158.
[143] *Associated Foreign Exchange Limited v International Foreign Exchange (UK) Ltd and Abbassi* [2010] EWHC (Ch) 1178.
[144] *Scottish Farmers Dairy Co (Glasgow) Ltd v McGhee*, 1933 S.C. 148.
[145] See further Black, *Woolman on Contract*, paras 12–33—12–34.

will be declared unenforceable.[146] However, if there are a number of separate restrictive covenants within a contract, the court may take the view that some of them are unenforceable while some others are capable of being enforced.[147]

In general, the courts will be more accepting of a broad restriction in a contract for the sale of a business than it will be in the context of an employment context. Where someone is selling his business and the purchaser has paid money for the good-will of the business, the purchaser obviously has a strong interest in ensuring that his investment is protected. This is dramatically demonstrated by *Nordenfelt v Maxim Nordenfelt*.

Nordenfelt v Maxim Nordenfelt
[1894] A.C. 535

N sold his arms business to a new limited company ("MN") for a very significant price. It was agreed that he would act as the new company's Managing Director for five years, and N also entered into a restrictive covenant under which he undertook that, for a 25 year period, he would not, "engage except on behalf of the company either directly or indirectly in the trade or business of a manufacturer of guns, gun mountings or gunpowder, explosives or ammunition". The clause therefore had no geographical limit whatever and, if it was enforceable, effectively meant that N could not engage in the arms trade anywhere in the world for the rest of his working life. In due course, N left the new company and started selling guns, in apparent breach of his covenant. Relying upon the restrictive covenant, MN took N to court, seeking an order to prevent him continuing to trade. The House of Lords upheld the covenant. N's business was a world-wide one—"he had upon his books almost every monarch in every state of any note in the habitable globe"—and as he had been paid for the goodwill of his business, the restraint was reasonable.

A more recent example of the court being willing to enforce a restrictive **4–78** covenant drawn in broad terms can be seen in *Agri Energy v McCallion*.[148] M sold his domestic oil supply and recycling business, which was primarily based in the North East of Scotland, to AE for £200,000. M agreed to be bound by a restrictive covenant which prevented him competing against AE anywhere within Scotland for a period of five years. M established a rival business around three years later. M argued that as his business had been based in the North East of Scotland, a

---

[146] See, e.g. *MacFarlane v Dumbarton Steamboat Co Ltd* (1899) 1 F. 993 discussed at para.4–78, below.
[147] *Mulvein v Murray*, 1908 S.C. 528.
[148] [2014] CSOH 14.

restriction preventing him from competing with AE anywhere within the country was excessively broad. However, the court disagreed, holding that it would not be necessary for M's business to be located within the North East of Scotland for him to deal with his former customers; he could simply send vehicles direct to their premises from anywhere in the country. However, the court will not always uphold a restriction contained in a contract for the sale of a business. In *MacFarlane v Dumbarton Steamboat Co Ltd*[149] a restrictive covenant which sought to prevent the seller of a business which carried goods between Dumbarton and Glasgow from operating as carriers anywhere within the UK within 10 years of the date of the sale was struck down. The critical factor that the court relied upon in deciding the case was the inherently local nature of the ferry business. If MacFarlane were to operate a ferry from, say, Tayport to Dundee, this could have no impact whatever upon the volume of traffic carried on the Dumbarton to Glasgow crossing. As a result, a nationwide restriction was wholly unreasonable.

As was noted above, the courts will in general be less accepting of a broad restriction in an employment contract than in one for the sale of a business. This is so because, while the courts are prepared to order someone who has received money from a purchaser for the goodwill of his business not to work in direct competition, it is rather less willing to prevent employees from earning a living. The courts will carefully scrutinise the duration of the restriction and precisely what it is that the employee is being prevented from doing. Thus in *Associated Foreign Exchange Ltd v International Foreign Exchange (UK) Ltd and Abbassi*,[150] the employer sought to protect sensitive price information by preventing the employee from working for a competitor for a year. The court held that in a fast-moving market such as the currency market, such information quickly lost its sensitivity, and so a one-year duration was too long. No more than six months could have been justified. In *Rentokil Ltd v Hampton*,[151] the court held that a clause preventing employees from marketing, selling or supplying products or services in competition to Rentokil was too broad. Rentokil's business was wide-ranging. The defender was a timber infestation surveyor but this clause would prevent him from earning a living selling fly-killing apparatus or mouse-traps. However, if the employee has worked in a senior position and has been privy to sensitive trade secrets and/or has had an opportunity to build up close personal relationships with the employer's customer base, the courts may be prepared to recognise that the employer has a legitimate interest to protect.[152] Where this is so, a skilfully prepared clause which imposes

---

[149] (1899) 1 F. 993.
[150] [2010] EWHC (Ch) 1178.
[151] 1982 S.L.T. 422.
[152] See, e.g. *Dallas MacMillan & Sinclair v Simpson*, 1989 S.L.T. 454; *Prosoft Resources v Griffiths*, 1999 S.L.T. 1255.

only the minimum restrictions necessary to protect the employer's legitimate interests will be upheld.[153]

Solus agreements. A *solus* agreement is one whereby a seller of goods **4–79** agrees to sell only or predominantly the products of a particular supplier. This restriction is normally granted in exchange for some degree of financial support from the supplier, typically to offset the start-up costs of the business, and these arrangements are most commonly seen in the public house and petrol retail businesses. Like restrictive covenants, *solus* agreements will be declared unenforceable unless the restrictions upon free trade which they impose are reasonable in all the circumstances.[154]

BREACH OF CONTRACT

Introduction

If either party fails without justification to fulfil an obligation it has **4–80** undertaken in the contract, then that party is in breach of contract.[155] The party not in breach is generally referred to as the innocent party.

Breaches of contract can take many forms. By way of example, in a contract for the sale of goods, if the purchaser fails to pay the price on time, he is in breach of contract. If the seller fails to deliver the goods, or if delivers them and they are not of the same quality as was described in the contract, then that too would be a breach of contract.

Some breaches are more significant than others. A significant breach of contract—one which "goes to the root of the contract"[156]—is known as a material breach. Examples of a material breach would be failing to perform one's obligations under a contract at all, or performing them in a seriously defective way, for instance by delivering goods significantly different from what the parties had contracted for. So: A orders a new "state of the art" fridge freezer; B delivers a second-hand budget model, a material breach has occurred. Less significant breaches are not material, and may be referred to as "ancillary" or "simple" breaches. The distinction between material breaches and simple breaches is important and has a bearing on the legal remedies for breach of contract which the innocent party may seek from the party in breach. Remedies for breach of contract are discussed at paras 4–82—4–96.

---

[153] See, e.g. *Stewart v Stewart* (1899) 1 F. 1158; *Dallas MacMillan & Sinclair v Simpson*, 1989 S.L.T. 454.
[154] *Petrofina (Great Britain) Ltd v Martin* [1966] Ch. 146.
[155] The best example of a situation where a party is justified in not carrying out an obligation under the contract is where the other party has itself already failed to carry out one or more of its obligations under the contract. This topic will be discussed further under the heading of retention, at para.4–85, below.
[156] *Wade v Waldron*, 1909 S.C. 571, per the Lord President (Dunedin) at 576.

> **Key Concepts**
>
> If either party fails without justification to fulfil an obligation it has
> undertaken in the contract, that party is in breach of contract. Par-
> ticularly significant breaches—material breaches—give the innocent
> party a greater range of legal remedies than less significant brea-
> ches of contract.

Anticipatory breach

4–81 A type of breach of contract which requires particular consideration is
anticipatory breach (sometimes known as repudiation). This occurs when
the party who is due to make performance under a contract informs the
innocent party that he is not going to fulfil his side of the bargain. An
innocent party faced with such a declaration from the repudiating party
may elect to do one of three things:

- The innocent party is entitled to take the other party's statement
  at face value, accept that the contract is not going to be performed, declare the repudiating party in material breach of contract, rescind the contract[157] and, always assuming that the
  repudiating party's decision not to perform has caused the
  innocent party a loss, bring a court action for damages.
- The innocent may decide to simply wait for the time for performance to come around. If the repudiating party decides, on reflection, to go ahead and carry out its obligations under the contract,
  there is no breach. However, if the repudiating party fails to perform its obligations at the appointed time, the innocent party is then
  entitled to declare a material breach, rescind and sue for damages.
- If the innocent party is in a position to carry out its side of the
  bargain without any further co-operation from the repudiating
  party, it can choose to ignore the repudiation, carry out its
  obligations under the contract, and demand payment of the price
  under the contract.[158]

Note, however, that the third option will only rarely be open to the
innocent party, as in the usual course of events the innocent party will not
be able to carry out its obligations without at least some measure of co-
operation from the repudiating party.[159] Consider the following examples:

---

[157] Rescission is discussed at para.4–84, below.
[158] *White and Carter (Councils) Ltd v McGregor*, 1962 S.C. (H.L.) 1.
[159] In *White and Carter (Councils)*, the facts were unusual. The pursuer was an advertising
agency. It entered into a contract with the defender to post certain advertisements on his
behalf. The defender changed his mind almost immediately after concluding the contract,
and repudiated. The pursuers refused to accept his repudiation and, as they required no
assistance from the defender in order to post the advertisements up around the town,
went ahead and carried out their obligations under the contract. They were held to be
entitled to recover the full contract price.

- A agrees to buy a television from B with delivery to be in a weeks' time.
- C agrees to fit a kitchen in D's house a month from now.

Neither A, B, C or D will be in a position to unilaterally carry out their side of the bargain in the event that the other party repudiates the contract. A cannot physically get a hold of the TV without B's co-operation; similarly B cannot physically compel A to take delivery of the TV if A refuses to; C cannot get into D's house to carry out the work unless D unlocks the door; and D cannot physically make C carry out the work against C's will.

Remedies for breach of contract

Where a contract has been breached, the innocent party will be able to **4–82** pursue one or more remedies against the party who has breached the contract.

Self-help remedies

Self-help (sometimes called "defensive") remedies are ones which the **4–83** innocent party is entitled to take without having to have recourse to the courts. These remedies are available only in the case of material breach. Only the courts can provide remedies for simple breaches of contract. The principal self-help remedies are discussed below.

Rescission

Rescission occurs when the innocent party, faced with a material breach **4–84** by the other party to the contract, decides not to continue with the contract and brings it to an end (rescinds it). A person who buys a new car that is found to be suffering from significant defects is entitled to rescind the contract and demand the repayment of the purchase price.[160] This is often the most powerful remedy available to the innocent party and, if the innocent party suffers a loss which is not adequately compensated by rescission alone, he will in addition be entitled to sue for damages.

Retention

Retention is where the innocent party with-holds payment or perfor- **4–85** mance of its obligations until the party in breach performs its obligations under the contract. A "rent-strike" is a good example of retention. If a landlord permits a property let to a tenant under a contract of lease to fall into a dilapidated state, the tenant may choose to with-hold payment of a proportion of the rent until such time as the landlord effects the necessary repairs. The remedy is only partial, in the sense that the innocent party

---

[160] *Lamara v Capital Bank Plc* [2006] CSIH 49. If the defects are not significant but trivial then rescission is not available as the breach will not be material.

continues to be under a legal liability to carry out its obligations once the party in breach performs its obligations.[161] It can nevertheless be a very useful way of encouraging the breaching party to remedy its breach.

Lien

4-86 When an innocent party happens to have lawfully within its possession goods or documents belonging to the party in breach, it may retain possession of that property (exercise a lien over it) until the party in breach performs its obligations under the contract. Solicitors who are owed money by a client can generally refuse to deliver to the client any legal documents which they hold on his behalf until such time as they are paid,[162] as can accountants. Similarly, mechanics or jewellers who have carried out repairs upon a customer's property are entitled to decline to return the items until their bill is paid.

Judicial remedies

4-87 Judicial remedies are available only by order of the court. The principal judicial remedies are discussed below.

Action for debt

4-88 One of the most commonly-encountered breaches of contract is a failure to pay money due under the contract. The classic example of this concerns the purchase of goods[163] on credit terms. The purchaser buys goods which are delivered; the contract states that the purchaser has a period of, say, 30 days in which to pay; the purchaser does not make payment. Upon the expiry of the period of credit, the purchaser is in breach of contract and the seller may raise a court action demanding payment of the purchase price.

Specific implement

4-89 Conceptually, specific implement is similar to an action for debt in so far as the innocent party raises a court action demanding that the party in breach carries through a contractual obligation. The difference between the two remedies is that the specific implement concerns situations arising where, "a positive act of performance other than the payment of money is sought from the contract breaker".[164] Perhaps the classic example of specific implement is an action for delivery of an item bought but not yet delivered.

Parties are not always entitled to demand specific implement. In particular, the courts will not grant a decree of specific implement if:

---

[161] For example, in the example given, the tenant will have to pay the arrears of rent to the landlord once the property has been adequately repaired.
[162] See A. Paterson and B. Ritchie, *Law, Practice and Conduct for Solicitors* (Edinburgh: W. Green, 2006), para.11.12.
[163] The same principle is equally applicable to contracts for the provision of services.
[164] MacQueen and Thomson, *Contract Law in Scotland*, para.6.6.

- performance is impossible, perhaps because the subject-matter of the contract has been stolen or accidentally destroyed;
- the insistence upon specific implement would cause the party in breach hardship or loss out of all proportion to the benefit which would accrue to the innocent party;
- the subject matter of the contract is of no particular significance and damages would provide adequate compensation. This would be the case, for example, where the seller of readily available, mass-produced consumer goods such as a TV set fails to deliver the goods contracted for. However, this rule would not prevent someone from seeking delivery of a rare or unusual item such as an antique, a work of art of a specially-commissioned item of furniture; or
- the contract involves a significant degree of personal relationship. Contracts of employment and partnership fall into this category. If an employee walks out on a contract of employment without giving the notice period required by the contract, the courts will not insist that he or she returns to their place of work to see the contract out.

The fact that the court will not allow specific implement in these circumstances does not mean that someone can just breach their contract and "get away with it". Other remedies—for instance, damages—will continue to be available to the innocent party.

Interdict

An interdict is essentially the converse of a decree for specific implement. **4–90** Whereas a decree of specific implement is a judicial demand that someone does something, an interdict is an order not to do something. Interdicts are used to prevent the occurrence of legal wrongs which are about to be committed, or to bring an end to ongoing legal wrongs. In the contractual context, interdict is most commonly used in an attempt to prevent or stop parties from breaching restrictive covenants.[165]

Damages

Actions for the payment of damages rank along with actions for the **4–91** recovery of debt as the most commonly utilised judicial remedies for breach of contract. When an innocent party raises an action for damages against the party in breach, he in effect asks the court to award a sum of money in order to make good the losses suffered by the innocent party as a result of the breach. Depending on the circumstances of the breach, damages may be:

---

[165] For a discussion on restrictive covenants, see paras 4–77—4–78, above.

- available in conjunction with another remedy (for instance, an innocent party may rescind and demand damages, or seek interdict and damages);
- pursued as an alternative to another remedy (an innocent party unsure if she is as a matter of law entitled to specific implement may demand that remedy which failing, damages); or
- the only remedy available.

4–92 The compensatory nature of damages. In Scots law, at least, the purpose of damages is invariably to compensate the innocent party for losses suffered as a result of the breach.[166] The purpose is not to punish the party who is in breach. As a result, the award of damages is intended to put the innocent party back in the position that he or she would have been in had the breach not occurred. However, only certain types of losses are recognised as legally recoverable. In general, damages are available only to compensate personal injuries damage to property and economic losses. In a standard commercial contract, the courts will not award damages for any hurt feelings, annoyance or distress occasioned by the breach of contract.[167]

4–93 The requirement of causation. Damages are only recoverable for loss which can be proved to have been caused by the breach of contract. In other words, the person claiming damages must be able to link the breach of contract complained about to the loss suffered. If, while a building is being renovated, a house collapses after a builder knocks down an internal wall which he had not been asked to demolish, the owner cannot sue the builder *just because* he breached the terms of his contract. The home owner must be able to prove on the balance of probabilities that the building fell down as a direct result of the builder's breach of contract.

4–94 The duty to mitigate loss. When a contract is breached, the innocent party is, in general, under a legal obligation to take steps to mitigate his or her loss.[168] However, this is a relatively "soft" duty: the innocent party is not under an obligation to take all steps which could conceivably be taken to mitigate his or her loss. The obligation is to take reasonable steps only. Thus, the innocent party will not be expected to incur substantial expenses or take large commercial risks in order to mitigate his or her loss, but where the innocent party does incur the expenses associated

---

[166] This is not the case in every legal system. Many American legal systems, for example, permit an innocent party to seek punitive damages when the breach is a particularly flagrant or disgraceful one. In these cases, the party in breach is made to pay significantly more than the innocent party lost, as a deterrent and a punishment.

[167] However, in contracts which are essentially about relaxation or enjoyment rather than commerce, this rule will not apply: *Farley v Skinner* [2001] 3 W.L.R. 899. The courts have. therefore. held that damages for distress, annoyance and hurt feelings are available when contracts for the provision of holidays or wedding services are breached.

[168] The rule in *White and Carter (Councils) Ltd v McGregor*, 1962 S.C. (H.L.) 1, discussed at para.4–81, above, provides an exception to this rule.

with taking appropriate steps to re-advertise goods or services refused by the party in breach, such expenses are recoverable.

Remoteness of loss. A further limitation which the law places on the **4–95** damages that can be recovered by the innocent party is that damages will not be awarded for any loss which is "too remote". The classic statement of remoteness is found in the English case of *Hadley v Baxendale*.[169] Here, it was held that damages payable under contract:

> "[S]hould be such as may fairly and reasonably be considered as either arising naturally ie according to the usual cause of things, from such breach of contract itself or such as may reasonably supposed to have been in the contemplation of both parties at the time they made the contract as the probable result of the breach."

The Scottish case of *Balfour Beatty Construction v Scottish Power Plc* provides a good example of the test in operation.

Balfour Beatty Construction v Scottish Power Plc
1994 S.C. (H.L.) 20

BB won a tender to build a length of road. BB operated a work-site next to the road at which preparatory construction works were carried out, and entered into a contract with SP for the provision of electricity to the site. BB needed to build a concrete aqueduct to carry the Union Canal over the new road. In order to be structurally sound, the aqueduct needed to be created in one continuous pour of concrete. This in turn required an uninterrupted electricity supply. However, the electricity supply failed during the course of the pour and as a result the first attempt at building the aqueduct had to be demolished and reconstructed at significant cost. BB sued SP for damages for breach of contract. SP defended on the basis that while they had been in breach, they could not be expected to foresee the unusually severe consequences of failing to maintain the power supply. The House of Lords held that they were not liable for this loss. The consequences did not naturally flow from the failure of an electricity supply, and SP had not at the time of entering into the contract been made aware that this damage would occur if the supply were interrupted, so it could not be said that it was within SP's contemplation at the time of entering into the contract.

Liquidate damages. A liquidate damages clause is one which attempts **4–96** to set out at the start of the parties' contractual relationship the level of damages which will be paid upon the occurrence of a specified type of

---

[169] (1854) 9 Exch. 341.

breach of contract. Such clauses are often used in, for example, the construction or engineering industry to determine the amount of damages which will be payable to the innocent party if the contract is not completed on time.

The courts will enforce a liquidate damages clause if they are satisfied that the clause represented a genuine and reasonable pre-estimate of the innocent party's loss.[170] However, because, as was noted above, the Scottish courts view damages as essentially compensatory in nature, the courts will not enforce a liquidate damages clause if it is a penalty. In assessing whether a clause is a penalty, the courts will have regard to the true nature of the clause, not the label attached to it by the parties.[171] Thus a clause which the parties described in the contract as a "penalty clause" will be enforced if, on analysis, the court is satisfied that it is not punitive in nature while a clause described by the parties as a "liquidate damages clause" will be ruled unenforceable if it *is* punitive in nature. The courts will use a number of tests in order to ascertain the true nature of the clause. These were set out in *Dunlop Pneumatic Tyre Co v New Garage Motor Co*[172] as follows:

- A clause will be held to be a penalty if the amount stipulated to be paid is "extravagant and unconscionable".
- A clause will be penal if the breach consists only in not paying a sum of money, and the clause stipulates for a sum greater than the sum which was originally due to be paid.
- A clause is presumed penal when a single lump sum is made payable by way of compensation on the occurrence of one or more or all of several events, some of which may occasion serious damage but others of which are of little significance.
- A clause will not be penal simply because the consequences of the breach cannot be easily ascertained. Indeed, the courts accept that, "that is just the situation when it is probable that pre-estimated damage was the true bargain between the parties".

WHO MAY SUE WHEN A CONTRACT IS BREACHED?

The general rule: privity of contract

4–97 Contracts create legal relations between the parties to the contract, not between those parties and the world at large. This concept is sometimes described as the doctrine of privity of contract. In general, therefore, only a party to the contract may sue or be sued in the event of a breach.[173] We can illustrate this point by way of example. Suppose A, a supplier of computer processors, enters into a contract with B, one of the world's

---

[170] *Dunlop Pneumatic Tyre Co v New Garage Motor Co* (1915) A.C. 79.
[171] *Lord Elphinstone v The Monkland Iron and Coal Co Ltd* [1883] 13 R. (H.L.) 98.
[172] [1915] A.C. 79 at 86.
[173] *Finnie v Glasgow and South West Railway Co* (1857) 20 D. (H.L.) 2.

largest computer manufacturers, to supply components at a fraction of the normal price. If the contract is honoured, it will enable B to pass on a significant saving to customers all over the world. However, in the event, A breaches the contract and fails to supply the processors. B can sue A for A's breach of contract. However, the many thousands of consumers who, instead of being able to buy computers at a reduced price, are going to have to pay the full price for them are unable to sue, as they were not party to the contract between A and B.

An exception to the rule: jus quaesitum tertio

As an exception to the rule that only parties to the contract may sue or be **4–98** sued in the event of a breach, Scots law will permit third parties (i.e. someone not party to the contract) to acquire the right to enforce the contract if certain qualifying criteria are satisfied. The law does this because occasionally, parties will enter into a contract which is not for their own purposes, but for the benefit of a third party (i.e. someone who is not party to the contract). When this occurs, the courts will give effect to the intentions of the parties. Enforceable third party rights are known by the Latin expression, *jus quaesitum tertio*.

Two very important points need to be recognised in relation to *jus quaesitum tertio*:

- The courts will only permit the parties to a contract to convey a *benefit* upon a third party. *Jus quaesitum tertio* cannot be used to impose a *burden* upon it. Thus, parties A and B may between them agree that A is going to pay B to carry out work for C's benefit, and if B is duly paid by A and does not carry out the work, then C may sue him. However, A and B cannot agree that B will carry out work for A's benefit and C will pay.
- The courts will only recognise a *jus quaesitum tertio* if it is clear that the contracting parties intended to be firmly bound by their agreement. If it appears to the court that the contracting parties wished to be in a position to change their minds about the arrangement, then no *jus quaesitum tertio* will come into existence.[174] The seriousness of the parties' intent will be confirmed by their carrying out actions such as, for example, delivering a copy of the contract to the third party, so it can see the nature of the right for itself, or publicly registering the document.

An example of *jus quaesitum tertio* in operation may be found in the case of *Mortons Trustees v The Aged Christian Friends Society of Scotland*.[175] Here, M wished to make a donation to a charity. However the situation

---

[174] This aspect of the present law has the effect of significantly limiting the range of situations where a *jus quaesitium tertio* can come into existence. The Scottish Law Commission has suggested that this requirement should be relaxed, but it is not yet clear if or when this recommendation will become law. Scottish Law Commission, *Discussion Paper No.157 on Third Party Rights in Contract* (2014), p.77.

[175] (1899) 2 F. 82.

was complicated by the fact that the charity had not yet legally come into existence. M therefore entered into a contract with the members of a provisional committee involved in setting up the charity. The contract clearly stated that M would pay annual instalments to the charitable society for a period of 10 years. During M's lifetime, the obligation was honoured. However, when M died, the trustees on her estate refused to continue to make the payment. The charity successfully sued for payment: in the circumstances, it enjoyed a clear *jus quaesitum tertio*.

EXTINCTION OF CONTRACTUAL OBLIGATIONS

Introduction

4–99 Contractual obligations do not last forever. It would clearly be nonsensical, 10 years after the day when a newsagent sold you a newspaper, to say that you and the seller are still in a contractual relationship relative to that sale. Contractual obligations come to an end in a number of ways. We shall consider the most common instances below

Performance

4–100 One of the most commonplace ways in which a contractual relationship will come to an end is upon performance. Once the obligations on both sides of the contract have been performed in full, the contract's purpose is at an end and it simply "withers away" into legal nothingness. So if A takes out a contract of loan with B in order to buy a car, the contract will ordinarily come to an end when A makes his or her final repayment. Similarly, if C purchases a new television which comes with a two year warranty from D, then the contract between the parties will come to an end when the warranty period expires. It is, however, possible for a contract apparently brought to an end by performance to revive if the apparent performance proves to be defective. Thus in *Leggat Bros v Gray*,[176] the defender paid a debt due under a contract by cheque, which subsequently "bounced". The court held that despite the apparent performance by the defender at the point of the, the debt revived when the cheque was dishonoured.

Discharge by consent

4–101 A contract may be brought to an end by discharge by consent. This occurs when the parties agree that all existing performance and obligations under the contract is to be waived. This may occur for a number of reasons: for instance, if A owes B a sum of money under a contract, B may agree to write off the debt either as a gesture of goodwill or because A has recommended B's services to someone else. In either such case, A's initial obligation to pay the purchase price is discharged by consent.

---

[176] 1908 S.C. 67.

Compensation

Another way in which certain forms of obligations can come to an end it **4–102** through a process called compensation. The law's use of the term "compensation" is perhaps unfortunate, because that expression is used in other legal contexts to mean something quite different. In this context, compensation describes the setting off of one obligation against another. If A owes B £100 in relation to one transaction and B owes A £150 in relation to another, the two obligations can be set off against each other with the net effect that B would owe A £50.

Compensation applies only to monetary obligations and so if an electrician and a plumber agree that the electrician will rewire the plumber's house in exchange for the plumber installing a new bathroom at the electrician's, the law will not permit set-off of the obligations. In that case, the law would require each party to pay the other for the work which has been done. Moreover, for compensation to operate, both of the monetary obligations must be both "current" and "liquid". The requirement that both obligations be current means that one cannot set an existing obligation off against one which has not yet come into being. The word "liquid" is used here not in its popular sense but in much the same way when the term is used in the expression "liquidate damages": in other words, the money obligation must be one which is for a certain, or at least, readily ascertainable, sum of money. The purchase price of goods bought under a contract of sale is a good example of a liquid debt: one knows precisely what the price is; it has been the subject of agreement between the parties. A claim for damages for breach of contract, by contrast, is a claim for an illiquid sum of money, as the precise value of the claim is not readily ascertainable. Until the court rules on the matter and fixes the amount of damages sue, it is impossible for the parties to say exactly how much one is due to the other.

Novation

Novation occurs where an original obligation is extinguished and **4–103** replaced by a new obligation. This occurs commonly in practice. Parties to a contract may find that it is not working to their satisfaction and decide to re-negotiate its terms. Where this occurs, the new set of contractual obligations will supersede the old set.

Confusion

Confusion occurs when the same person becomes both the debtor and the **4–104** creditor in relation to a legal obligation. A person cannot be under an obligation to his or her-self; where the same legal person simultaneously has both the right to enforce and the obligation to perform an obligation, the obligation itself cases to be. One might wonder how confusion could ever occur in practice: people are hardly likely to try to enter into contracts with themselves. However, confusion can occur because in practice the right to enforce obligations under contracts are sometimes sold or otherwise transferred. For instance, A, a company which is experiencing cash flow problems and which is in immediate need of a large lump sum, might sell all of the debts which it is entitled to recover from its customers to B, a financial institution, in exchange for, say 60 per cent of those debts' aggregate value. If one of the debts transferred is one which was originally owed by B to A, then we can see that as a result of this transaction, B has become both the debtor and the creditor in this obligation. The obligation will therefore be extinguished by confusion.

Prescription

4–105 Prescription is the branch of law which is concerned with the creation or extinction of legal obligations through the passage of time. This is a complex area of the law relevant not only to contract but also delict and property law. Prescription is relevant to contract law as it provides one of the circumstances in which contractual obligations to pay a debt may be extinguished. People who are owed money for performing obligations under a contract have only a finite amount of time in order to take action to recover the debt due to them. Two prescriptive periods are potentially relevant to contractual obligations: the so-called short negative pre-scription period of five years from the date when the obligation became enforceable[177] and the long negative prescription of 20 years.[178] The great majority of contractual obligations fall into the five-year period, but the 20-year period is the relevant one for contracts relating to land. The period stops running either on the date when a writ asserting the pur-suer's claim is stamped by the court and then legally served upon the defender, or if the defender makes a "relevant acknowledgement" of the claim.[179]

Frustration (impossibility)

4–106 The obligations under a contract will be brought to an end as a result of the doctrine of frustration if, after the contract has been concluded but before the contract is performed, an event which is outside the control of the parties makes performance either:

- physically impossible;
- practically impossible; or
- impossible to perform which breaking the law.

Each category of impossibility shall be discussed in turn.

---

[177] Prescription and Limitation (Scotland) Act 1973 ("PLSA") s.6.
[178] PLSA s.7.
[179] A relevant acknowledgement takes place where there has either been part-performance of the obligation such as "clearly indicates" that the obligation still exists, or where the debtor has provided an "unequivocal written admission clearly acknowledging" that the obligation is still in existence: PLSA s.10. These are restrictive criteria and if the creditor is any doubt about whether they have been satisfied, the only safe course of action is to serve appropriate court papers upon the defender before the prescriptive period expires.

Physical impossibility—rei interitus

Frustration by physical impossibility (sometimes known as "*rei inter-* **4–107** *itus*") will arise when a supervening event outside the control of either party destroys the subject-matter of the contract. A good example of this occurred in *Taylor v Caldwell*.[180] C, the owner of the premises used as a music hall, agreed to let it to a theatrical impresario, T, for four dates. T arranged for impressive programmes of entertainment to take place on each of the dates. However, one week before the first concert, the music hall burned down through no fault of either of the parties. T sued for the loss of the profit which he would have made had the venture proceeded as planned. The court held, however, that the parties' obligations under the contract had been brought to an end by the destruction of the subject-matter of the contract.

A contract will also be brought to an end by frustration by physical impossibility upon the death of a party who has been chosen to carry out a contract because of his personal characteristics or skills. Such contracts are known as contracts *delectus personae*. Not all contracts are of this nature: the purchase of standard consumer products, for example, does not raise such issues. However, if one specifically commissions someone to manufacture a stained glass window or a one-off, hand-made item of furniture, *delectus personae* is present. Contracts of employment are commonly encountered examples of contracts *delectus personae*.

Practical impossibility

Practical impossibility is another event that can frustrate a contract. This **4–108** arises when an event has occurred which, while not inevitably making the contract physically impossible to perform, makes performance "something radically different from what the parties contemplated when they entered into it".[181] The most famous example of a contract being frustrated for practical impossibility is the so-called "coronation case", *Krell v Henry*.[182] Here, rooms affording a clear view of Pall Mall were let out at high prices to permit affluent members of the public to see the procession marking Edward VII's coronation. In the event, however, the King fell ill and the coronation was cancelled. It was held that the contract had been frustrated: its commercial purpose was not the hire of the room, but the hire of a location from which to see the parade. However, the courts will not lightly accept that performance of a contract has become practically impossible, and in particular, the mere fact that the change in circumstances makes it impossible for someone selling goods or providing a service to make a profit is irrelevant.[183] In *Tsakiroglou & Co Ltd v Noblee Thorl GmbH*,[184] the parties entered into a charter of a boat to carry a cargo of nuts from Port Sudan on the east coast of Africa to Hamburg, in

---

[180] (1863) 3 B. & S. 826.
[181] *Paal Wilson & Co v Blumenthal* [1983] 1 A.C. 854.
[182] [1903] 2 K.B. 740.
[183] *Davis Contractors v Fareham Urban District Council* [1956] A.C. 696.
[184] [1962] A.C. 93.

Germany's northern coast. In entering into the contract, both parties assumed that the ship would proceed by the shortest route, which involved passing through the Suez Canal, but nothing about the route to be taken was expressly stated in the contract. The Suez crisis of 1956 intervened and the Egyptian government closed the canal. This meant that the ship would have to undertake its voyage round the Cape of Good Hope, adding thousands of miles to the distance the ship would have to travel and more than doubling the cost of fuel and crewing costs of the vessel. The court held that the contract had not been frustrated; although the voyage was longer and more expensive than was envisaged, an alternative route existed; the contract therefore stood.

Supervening illegality

4–109 A contract will also be frustrated if its performance becomes illegal after the contract has been formed, but before it is performed. This may occur, for instance, if legislation is passed in the intervening time which makes it illegal for a person situated within the jurisdiction to trade with certain named individuals, organisations or states.[185] It can also occur as a result of the outbreak of war. In *Cantiere San Rocco SA v Clyde Shipbuilding & Engineering Co Ltd*,[186] a Scottish engineering company entered into a contract with an Austrian company for the provision of ship's engines. Before the contract could be fully performed, the First World War was declared. As the UK was at war with (among other nations), Austria, it was illegal (under the common law doctrine of enemy alien) for UK-based companies to maintain trading arrangements with Austrian-based organisations. The contract was therefore declared frustrated as a result of supervening illegality.

▼ CHAPTER SUMMARY

WHAT IS A CONTRACT?

4–110 A contract is an agreement entered into between two or more parties, which the parties intend to be legally binding.

The courts will presume that the parties to social or domestic agreements do not intend their agreement to be binding, and will assume that parties to commercial or business-related agreements do intend their agreements to constitute contracts. In both cases, however, these presumptions are rebuttable in the face of clear evidence to the contrary.

A unilateral gratuitous promise is not a contract as it is not an agreement made between two or more parties. However, such promises are legally binding in Scots

---

[185] A time of writing, UK financial institutions are prevented by statutory instrument from providing certain goods and/or services to a range of people and organisations associated with, e.g. Al-Quaeda and the Taliban, North Korea, a number of African states and parts of the former Soviet Union. The particular prohibitions vary from case to case. For up to date information, see *https://www.gov.uk/current-arms-embargoes-and-other-restrictions* [Accessed May 15, 2015].

[186] 1923 S.C. (H.L.) 105.

law either if they are written down and signed by the promisor, or if they are made in a business context.

HOW IS A CONTRACT FORMED?

A contract is formed when an *offer* is met by an *unconditional acceptance* leading to *consensus in idem*—a meeting of the minds.

Consensus in idem is reached when an objective bystander observing the parties discussions, correspondence and behaviour would come to the conclusion that they had agreed on all of the essential elements of the contract.

In general, the law does not require contracts to be in a particular form (e.g. in writing). As a result, offers may generally be made orally, in writing or even by implication from the factual circumstances. Exceptionally, the law requires that some contracts need to be in a particular form (i.e. in writing) before they will be valid.

Not all discussions or proposals made during the course of a contractual negotiation are offers. The identifying feature of an offer is that it must "contemplate acceptance". Statements of future intent and invitations to treat are not offers and therefore cannot be accepted by the offeree.

An offer is not effectual until it is communicated to the offeree.

Offers may only be accepted by the person to whom they are addressed but it is possible for an offeror to address an offer to one person, a category of people or the world at large.

An offer may be revoked before acceptance unless the offeror has undertaken to leave his offer open for acceptance for a period of time: where the offeror does so, the undertaking will be enforceable if it satisfies the criteria for the making of a unilateral promise.

Offers automatically lapse upon the occurrence of a number of events, namely: passage of time, rejection (including the making of a counter-offer), death of either party or the bankruptcy or insanity of the offeror, the destruction or material alteration of the subject-matter of the contract or in the event of supervening illegality.

Unless: (a) the offeror has demanded that acceptance has to be made in a particular way; or (b) the contract is one of the few types of agreement which the law demands be made in a particular form, an acceptance may be communicated in any medium of the offeree's choosing.

The identifying feature of an acceptance is that it must be an unqualified agreement to the offer put forward by the offeree.

A reply to an offer which agrees to some or even most of the terms advanced by the offeror but which seeks to introduce new legal terms into the deal is a counter-offer, not an acceptance.

A counter-offer has the legal effect of rejecting the initial offer and presenting a new offer that may, in its turn, be either accepted or rejected by the other party.

A "battle of the forms" can occur when both parties to a negotiation seek to contract upon their preferred own terms and conditions. The "battle" will be won by the party who presents the final set of terms and conditions before legal acceptance.

An acceptance, like an offer, does not take effect until it is communicated. In the case of instantaneous methods of communication an acceptance will not be communicated until it is actually heard by the other party. In the case of delayed methods of communication, communication is "effective on despatch".

Formalities: RWSA

Contrary to the general rule (which states that formalities do not need to be observed when one enters into a contract), some contracts do require to be entered into in a particular way if they are to be effectual. The most important practical example is a contract for the sale or transfer of ownership of land. RWSA provides that such contracts need to be made in writing and require to be signed. It is strongly advisable for them to in addition be witnessed.

Contractual Terms

The content of a contract is found in its terms. Contracts cover a broad range of commercial activities, and different types of contract will contain different types of terms. But in general, the terms of a contract will set out the obligations that each party is to undertake: who is doing what for whom, when, how and in exchange for what?

Terms may find their way into contract by express agreement, by incorporation from an external source either by reference or by a prior course of dealings, or by implication.

In the case of terms incorporated by reference, if, at or before the time of entering into the contract, the offeree signs a legal document which states on the face of it that the contract is to be governed by terms which can be seen elsewhere, the courts will usually hold that the offeree is bound by those terms. If the offeree has not signed such a document, a number of conditions must be satisfied before a court will hold the terms incorporated into the contract. The terms must be:

- brought to the offeree's attention at or before the conclusion of the contract;
- contained in a document which the offeree would reasonably have understood to be contractual in nature; and
- adequately brought to the attention of the offeree.

Terms are commonly implied into contracts by the law, rather than the parties themselves. This may be done by statute (e.g. the SGA) or by the common law. A term will be incorporated at common law if it is of such a nature that a reasonable man would himself want for his own protection, and no reasonable man would refuse to accept it.

Interpretation of Contractual Terms

Where contracts are in writing, disagreements can develop between the parties as to what the wording of the contract means. In resolving such disputes, the courts will bear the following principles in mind:

- The words should be given their ordinary meaning unless there is a strong justification for departing from that interpretation.
- The interpretation exercise is an objective one, not a subjective one, but the fictitious impartial bystander will be deemed to know the broader context within which the words were used.

- The disputed words are not to be read in isolation, but within the context of the contract as a whole.
- Formal legal contracts may be read more literally and less contextually than less formal commercial agreements.
- The purpose of the exercise is to ascertain the true intent of the parties, not to come to the aid of someone who has had the misfortune to enter into a contract which is detrimental to his interests.

LEGAL REGULATION OF UNFAIR TERMS

Historically, many parties have adopted the practice of contracting on terms and conditions which are heavily biased in their favour. Over the years, this led to much unfairness. The problem was seen at its most acute when consumers contracted with large commercial organisations. The common law's response to this problem came to be seen as inadequate.

Unlike UCTA, Pt 2 of the CRA provides protection only for the benefit of consumers contracting with businesses. Like UCTA, the CRA renders unenforceable clauses which purport to exclude or limit liability for negligently-caused death or personal injury. In addition, it seeks to regulate any form of unfairness which may act to the detriment of the consumer. It does this by:

- providing incentives for businesses to contract in plain and readily understandable language;
- providing that terms which, contrary to the requirement of good faith, cause a significant imbalance in the parties' rights and obligations under the contract to the detriment of the consumer are unfair and unenforceable against the consumer, and providing the consumer and the court with the benefit of an illustrative list of contractual terms and practices which may, depending on the facts and circumstances of the case, be thought likely to be unfair; and
- providing CMA with an enforcement and an overseeing role which and permitting permits that body to issue guidance and to take court action demanding that organisations stop using unfair terms in their contracts.

DEFECTIVE CONTRACTS

Not all attempts to create a contract will be successful. Defects may emerge which render either a contract or a particular term within a contract void, voidable or unenforceable.

There is legal significance in the distinction between void, voidable or unenforceable contracts. In particular, the right to reduce a voidable contract can be lost in certain circumstances. This issue does not arise with void or unenforceable contracts.

A contract will be void if it is entered into by someone who lacks legal capacity. A person may lack legal capacity by reason of:

- Non-age.
- Insanity.
- Intoxication.

- Being a corporation; corporations are legal persons established for certain purposes and do not, in general, have the legal capacity to enter into contracts outwith those purposes (albeit certain statutory protections exist to protect innocent third parties dealing with companies).

A contract will also be void if entered into by someone unable to exercise free will as he was in immediate peril of his life. This is the most extreme form of the doctrine of force and fear.

In other, lesser, examples of force and fear, a contract will be voidable. A contract will also be voidable if entered into as a result of facility and circumvention or the undue influence of another.

Parties sometimes enter into contracts on the basis of some kind of misapprehension (error). The legal effect of an error on a contract depends upon a combination of factors: whether the error is bilateral or unilateral; what the error is about; whether it has been made by the party itself or; whether the case involves error alone or "error plus"; and whether or not the error arose as a result of a misrepresentation by the other party. Taking all these factors together we can say that:

- An error which is so fundamental that it prevents the parties from reaching consensus in idem will prevent a contract from coming into existence;
- Trivial errors have no effect upon the legal validity of the contract;
- Errors which are not sufficiently fundamental as to prevent consensus in idem but which relate to the substantials of the contract fall into an intermediate category.
  — They are not sufficient, in themselves, to affect the validity of a contract but if they are either mutual or are unilateral errors operating in conjunction with another factor ("error plus") the contract may be set aside.
  — The "error plus" requirement is most commonly fulfilled in cases of misrepresentation, but the courts have also recognised situations where one party knowingly takes advantage of the other party's error and gratuitious contracts as being enough to constitute "error plus."

A further category of defective contract is *pacta illicita*. These are illegal contracts. Such contracts are unenforceable. Some examples of *pacta illicita* are:

- Contracts to commit crimes.
- Contracts to commit delicts.
- Contracts which promote immorality.
- Contracts which are contrary to public policy.
- Contracts rendered illegal by statute. Contrary to the general rule, these will not always simply render a contract unenforceable but may declare a particular contract or term of a contract void.

Contractual terms in restraint of trade require separate discussion. Such contractual terms may be public policy. However, not all such terms will be considered unenforceable: these clauses are assessed on a case-by-case by the courts. In particular, a restrictive covenant (an especially important example of a contractual term in restraint of trade) will be upheld by the court if it:

- protects a legitimate interest of the party seeking to enforce it;
- is reasonable in the circumstances; and
- is in the public interest.

A restrictive covenant which cannot satisfy these criteria will be declared unenforceable.

BREACH OF CONTRACT

If either party fails without justification to fulfil an obligation it has undertaken in the contract, that party is in breach of contract. Particularly significant breaches—material breaches—give the innocent party a greater range of legal remedies than less significant breaches of contract.

A variety of self-help and judicial remedies are available to the innocent party in the event of breach. Self-help remedies are available only in the case of a material breach. Judicial remedies are not subject to this restriction.

Among the main self-help remedies are rescission, retention and lien. The main judicial remedies are actions for the recovery of debt, specific implement, interdict, damages and liquidate damages.

Damages are imposed solely for the purpose of compensating the innocent party, not to punish the party in breach. In contract law, damages are generally available only to compensate personal injuries, and damage to property and economic losses.

In order to claim damages, the innocent party must be in a position to demonstrate that the breach of contract has caused him loss. The innocent party must also take reasonable steps to mitigate his loss, and will not be able to recover damages in respect of losses which the law deems to be too remotely connected to the breach of contract for it to be reasonable to merit compensation.

Liquidate damages are awards of damages made in accordance with a clause in the parties' contract which specifies the level of damages which will be paid upon the occurrence of a specified type of breach of contract. Such a clause is unenforceable if its true purpose is to punish the party in breach. However, if its true purpose is to provide a reasonable pre-estimate of what the innocent party stands to lose in the event of breach, the clause will be enforceable.

WHO MAY SUE WHEN A CONTRACT IS BREACHED?

In general, Scots law follows the doctrine of privity of contract. This is means that generally only the parties to a contract may sue or be sued on it.

An important exception to this principle is made in the case of *jus quaesitum tertio*, which provides that a person not party to the contract will have the right to sue (but not be sued) under it if the parties to the contract clearly intended that person to have an enforceable legal right.

EXTINCTION OF CONTRACTUAL OBLIGATIONS

Contractual obligations do not last forever but come to an end in a number of different ways.

- When the obligations due to be performed under the contract are carried out, the contract itself ceases to exist.
- In addition, obligations may be discharged:

  - by mutual consent;
  - by compensation (or "set-off");
  - by novation; or
  - by confusion.

- After a certain period of time (usually five years in the case of contractual obligations), an obligation will expire unless the innocent party initiates court proceedings relative to the obligation or receives a relevant acknowledgement of claim.
- Finally, a contract may also be brought to an end by frustration. This occurs when, after the contract has been concluded but before the contract is performed, an event which is outside the control of the parties makes performance either:

  - physically impossible;
  - practically impossible; or
  - impossible to perform which breaking the law.

? QUICK QUIZ

- What is a contract?
- Are all agreements contractually binding?
- Is a unilateral gratuitous promise a contract?
- What is *consensus in idem*? What is its legal significance?
- What kind of test do the courts use to assess if a *consensus in idem* has been reached?
- What is the identifying feature of an offer?
- What is an intention to treat? Give examples of common invitations to treat.
- Does an offer not stated to be subject to a time-limit remain open indefinitely?
- What is the identifying feature of an acceptance?
- What is the legal effect of a counter-offer?
- When will the law consider an acceptance to have been effectually communicated to the offeror?
- "Contracts relating to [*blank*] form the most significant exception to the rule that contracts do not require to be in writing." What is the missing word?
- A and B intend to enter into a contract. A brings a document containing contractual terms and conditions to B's attention before the contract is concluded. B doesn't understand what the terms mean, but reckons that as long he doesn't sign anything they can't become part of the contract anyway. Is B's analysis correct?
- Name the major statutory and regimes which regulate unfair contractual terms. Outline their essential features.

- Is a contract entered into between a record company and an 8-year-old child prodigy legally binding? What about one between a record company and a 17 year old?
- If a person suffering from a mental illness, while on a euphoric high, decides to spend £100,000 on designer clothes, is the contract of purchase they have apparently entered into legally binding?
- A is a fan of the band Fleet Foxes. He learns from friends that "The Foxes" are to be appearing live at SECC, and phones the ticket hotline to buy a ticket for the event. When the ticket arrives, he sees that it is for a concert being given by a different band simply called "The Foxes", who he hadn't heard of before and doesn't wish to go and see. Is A bound by the contract?
- A places a large bet on a horse-race. His horse loses. Disappointed, he decides to cheer himself up by buying a knighthood from a corrupt public official. Happy now, A celebrates by buying a case of vintage champagne and some cocaine for recreational use. How many binding contracts has A entered into in this sequence of events?
- What is a restrictive covenant? Will such contractual terms be enforced by the courts?
- What is a material breach of contract? Which contractual remedies available to someone suffering a material breach of contract are not available to the innocent party in the case of a non-material breach?
- What is meant by "the duty to mitigate loss"?
- What is meant by "remoteness of damages"?
- What are liquidate damages, and are they legally enforceable?
- After what period of time will the right to enforce a contractual obligation be lost?
- In which circumstances will a contract be brought to an end by "frustration"?

📖 FURTHER READING

➤ G. Black, *Woolman on Contract*, 5th edn (Edinburgh: W. Green, 2014) (an excellent introductory text).
➤ H. MacQueen and J. Thomson, *Contract Law in Scotland*, 3rd edn (Haywards Heath: Bloomsbury Professional Ltd, 2012) (more detailed than *Woolman on Contract*; a very good intermediate text).
➤ W. McBryde, *The Law of Contract in Scotland*, 3rd edn (Edinburgh: W. Green, 2007) (an excellent reference work but very detailed and complex).
➤ J. Huntley et al, *Contract: Cases and Materials*, 2nd edn (Edinburgh: W. Green, 2003) (a useful source of legal cases and authorities).

⌨ RELEVANT WEBLINKS

➤ Scottish Courts and Tribunals, Judgments: *http://www.scot-courts.gov.uk/search-judgments* [Accessed May 15, 2015]. (A very useful source of Scottish caselaw, judgments from most recent cases of significance can be found here.)

➤ The Supreme Court of the United Kingdom: *https://www.supremecourt.uk/decided-cases/* [Accessed May 15, 2015]. (Judgments from cases which have been appealed from the court system in Scotland to the Supreme Court may be found here.)

➤ The National Archives, Legislation: *http://www.legislation.gov.uk* [Accessed May 15, 2015]. (A useful source of primary legislation and statutory instruments; the full text of relevant statutes such as the Consumer Rights Act 2015 may be accessed by searching this site.)

➤ Competition and Markets Authority, Consumer Enforcement Guidance: *https://www.gov.uk/government/collections/cma-consumer-enforcement-guidance* [Accessed May 15, 2015]. (See here for guidance on the CMA's approach to unfair terms in consumer contracts.)

Chapter 5 Commercial Sale and Supply of Goods

COWAN ERVINE[1]

► CHAPTER OVERVIEW

This chapter deals with various contracts by which goods can be trans- **5–01**
ferred from one person to another. It is limited to commercial transactions that is, transactions between businesses or B2B as they are
sometimes called. This is because purchases by consumers are now subject to their own legislation, the Consumer Rights Act 2015. Consumer
transactions are covered in Chapter 6, "Consumer Protection". The most
common contract under which goods are transferred is known as the
contract of sale. This is a contract governed by the Sale of Goods Act
1979 ("SGA 1979") and involves the transfer of ownership of goods for a
money consideration called the price. There are other ways in which
goods can be transferred such as hire-purchase, barter or, where services
are also being provided, as when a car is being serviced and a part is
replaced. These have in common that the buyer becomes the owner.
These are regulated by other pieces of legislation such as the Supply of
Goods (Implied Terms) Act 1973 and the Supply of Goods and Services
Act 1982. Most attention will be paid to the contract of sale. There are
rules about when ownership is transferred which are also connected with
who takes the risk of the goods being lost or damaged during the
transaction. A key part of the contract of sale is the part dealing with
terms about description and quality which are implied in all such contracts. Similar terms are also implied into the other contracts for the
supply of goods. Both seller and buyer have legal obligations and there
are remedies available if one party breaches an obligation. These contracts have in common that the buyer becomes the owner. The contract of
hire is different in that the customer only gets temporary possession of the
goods. It is governed by the Supply of Goods and Services Act 1982. It
has similar implied terms about description and quality.

✓ OUTCOMES

After studying this chapter you should know: **5–02**

---

[1] Honorary Teaching Fellow, University of Dundee.

✓ which contracts involve the supply of goods;
✓ the main characteristics of the contract of sale;
✓ the terms implied in various contracts for the supply of goods; and
✓ the right and duties of suppliers and buyers of goods.

INTRODUCTION

5–03 This chapter is called "Commercial Sale and Supply of Goods" because there are several different ways in which someone can acquire goods. The most common type of contract is the contract of sale and we shall concentrate on it. However, goods can be bought by paying instalments and one way of doing that is to buy on hire purchase. Goods may also be obtained by hiring them as where machinery is rented for a short period to do a particular job. Hire in the form of a finance lease is often used in business where the economic effect is very similar to sale. Though it is not very common, goods are sometimes bartered with one product being exchanged for another or in part exchange where a product and cash are exchanged for a product. Legally these transactions involve different types of contract and different Acts of Parliament apply to them. As the contract of sale is the most important we shall concentrate on it but reference will also be made to the others.

THE CONTRACT OF SALE

5–04 For more than a century the contract of sale has been governed by an Act of Parliament. The current version is the SGA 1979. Section 2 of the Act defines a contract of sale as:

> "A contract by which the seller transfers or agrees to transfer the property in goods to the buyer for a money consideration, called the price."

There are several points to notice about this definition:

- **"Transfers or agrees to transfer"**: the Act applies not just where the goods are being handed over but also where there is only an agreement to do so in the future. In other words, there can still be a contract of sale where the buyer and seller have only agreed to hand over the goods in exchange for payment at some time in the future.
- **"Property"**: in this context property means legal title or ownership.
- **"Money consideration"**: this is what distinguishes sale from barter or a gift. Cases where a person directly swaps one good for another are covered by the Supply of Goods and Services Act

1982. Monetary consideration includes not just cash but cheques and payment by credit card.

- **"Transfer the property":** the hiring of goods is not covered because the definition refers to the transfer of title (ownership) whereas goods that are on hire do not belong to the person using them but to the person who is hiring them out.

The definition of "goods"

Goods, for the purposes of the SGA 1979 are defined as: **5–05**

"All corporeal moveables except money; and in particular 'goods' includes industrial growing crops and things attached to or forming part of the land, which are agreed to be severed before sale or under the contact of sale."

This definition means that property such as houses and flats are not goods nor are the fixtures, but the fittings are goods. Goods include all tangible things and whilst money itself is not goods, coins or banknotes that have a greater value than their legal tender value are. Goods include crops, which are sown and intended to be harvested, but not wild crops.

Section 5 states that the goods that are the subject of a contract may be existing goods, owned or possessed by the seller, or goods to be manufactured or acquired by the seller after the contract of sale. Goods not already in existence or requiring to be manufactured are called *future goods* in the Act. A contract where the seller is trying to sell future goods at that moment operates as an agreement to sell.

So we can see that "goods" covers a huge range of things from books to buses and a great deal in between.

Key Concept

Goods in the context of SGA 1979 are defined as corporeal moveables including things growing on or in the land. Property and land are not goods for the purposes of the Act. Money is also excluded from this definition except in relation to antique coins and banknotes.

Price

A monetary consideration called the price distinguishes sale from some **5–06** other transactions. The price can be fixed by the contract or can be determined in a manner agreed by both parties, for example a valuation by a third party. If no price is agreed between buyer and seller, the buyer must pay a "reasonable" price.

Formation of the contract

5–07 The normal rules about the formation of contracts apply to the contract of sale and there are usually no special formalities that need be complied with. Commercial sellers need to keep in mind that when dealing with consumer buyers the Consumer Contracts (Information, Cancellation and Additional Charges) Regulations 2013[2] require that certain information must be given. Failure to do so can result in the contract being unenforceable.

When does property pass from the seller to the buyer?

5–08 Sale is about transferring the "property" or ownership in the goods and the SGA 1979 defines when that occurs. It is important to know when this happens particularly if either the seller or buyer has become insolvent. If the seller has become insolvent before he has given up ownership of goods those goods are assets of his which are available to pay his creditors. Knowing when ownership has been transferred can also be important in deciding whether it is the buyer or seller who bears the risk of the goods being damaged or lost. Sections 16–18 of the Act deal with this issue.

To understand these sections it is first essential to know what "specific goods" and "unascertained goods" are. Section 61 defines "specific goods" as "goods identified and agreed on at the time a contract of sale is made". An example would be the purchase by a farmer of a tractor where the farmer goes to a showroom and agrees to buy a particular vehicle indentified by make and registration number. "Unascertained goods" are not defined in the Act but it is clear that the term is used in contra-distinction to specific goods. It covers three situations:

- goods are to be manufactured or grown;
- generic goods, e.g. a ton of coal; and
- an unidentified part of a specific whole, e.g. a case of Beaujolais Nouveau from the shipment in a particular wine merchant's warehouse.

The starting point for working out when ownership passes is s.16, which states that until goods are "ascertained" ownership cannot be transferred. Goods are unascertained until they are allocated to a particular contract. An example might be a roll of carpet—the goods are unascertained until the correct length is cut off the roll for a particular order.

There is one exception to this rule and it applies to sales from part of an identified bulk. It is quite common for traders in commodities such as oil or cereals to buy and pay for part of a cargo or a consignment being stored in a warehouse which would be known as a sale from bulk. Until that part has been identified it is not *ascertained*. To avoid unfairness that could arise in these situations if the seller became insolvent before the

---

[2] SI 2013/3134. For detailed discussion of these Regulations see Ch.7, "E-commerce".

goods were ascertained, the law was altered in this situation. Section 20A of the Act provides that traders who have paid in advance for a specified quantity of goods which are part of a bulk which has been identified acquire an undivided share in the bulk and become owners in common with the other buyers or with the seller.

For goods that are ascertained or specified, s.17 states that property in **5–09** the goods passes when the buyer and seller intend it should pass. The trouble is that it may be far from clear what they intended. If that is the case, s.18 of the Act comes to the rescue by setting out a number of rules to assist in working out what their intention must have been. These rules are set out in s.18.

Rule 1. In an unconditional contract for specific goods in a deliverable state, property passes when the contract is made, and it is immaterial whether the time of payment or the time of delivery, or both, be postponed.

An example of this is *Dennant v Skinner*[3] where at an auction a bid was accepted by the auctioneer. The buyer was then given a form saying that ownership would not pass until the buyer's cheque cleared. It was held this was not a term of the contract and rule 1 applied.

Rule 2. In a contract for specific goods where the seller has to do something to the goods before delivery (put them in a deliverable state), property passes when that has been done and the buyer has been informed.

Rule 3. In a contract for the sale of specific goods where they are in a deliverable state but the seller has to weigh, measure, test, etc. to find the price, property does not pass until that is done and the buyer is informed.

Rule 4. If goods are sent on approval or sale or return, property passes when buyers show their approval or acceptance or do something inconsistent with someone else's ownership, or if buyers retain the goods and there is no fixed time for the return then property passes after a reasonable length of time.

For example, in *Kirkham v Attenborough*,[4] a manufacturer of jewellery sent some pieces on a sale or return basis to X who then pawned them to Attenborough and did not pay Kirkham. It was held under rule 4 that property had passed to X when he had pawned the jewellery because this was a way of showing that he was accepting the goods.

Rule 5. Where there is a contract for the sale of unascertained or future goods by description, and goods of that description and in a deliverable state are unconditionally appropriated to the contract, either by the seller with the assent of the buyer, or by the buyer with

---

[3] [1948] 2 K.B. 164.
[4] [1897] 1 Q.B. 201.

the assent of the seller, the property in the goods thereupon passes to the buyer. Such assent may be express or implied, and may be given either before or after the appropriation is made.

Philip Head and Sons Ltd v Shop Fronts
[1970] 1 Lloyds Rep. 140

Philip Head Ltd had agreed to supply and lay some carpet in a new office development. They arranged for the delivery of the carpet to the site but before they could lay it someone stole it. Who was to bear the loss? Was it Philip Head Ltd or their customer? Whoever was the owner would have to bear the loss. The judge decided that it was Philip Head Ltd and he reached this conclusion by applying this rule. He said that lying on site but not fitted it could not be said to be in a deliverable state.

Key Concept

Where goods are unascertained, no property in the goods can be transferred to the buyer until the goods are ascertained—SGA s.16. Where goods are specific or ascertained property in the goods passes when the parties intended the property to pass—SGA s.17. In the absence of clear evidence of the intention of the parties to the contract the rules contained in SGA s.18 will be applied.

Section 19 allows the seller to impose terms governing when property will pass under a contract and property will not pass until they are fulfilled. This permits retention of title clauses which allow a seller to protect himself against the danger of the buyer becoming insolvent before payment has been made. This was established in *Armour v Thyssen Edelstahlwerke AG*.[5]

Does the seller have the right to sell?

5–10　Questions may arise about the right of the seller to sell the goods and difficult questions may arise involving the buyer, the person from whom the goods were acquired, and the true owner. Such problems often arise where the original owner has been tricked into parting with his goods by a rogue. In contracts of sale the starting point is the implied terms that are at the heart of the SGA 1979. Section 12 of the Act has terms relating to title or ownership. Section 12(1) provides that there is an implied term that the seller has a right to sell the goods. Section 12(2) provides that there is also an implied term that the goods are free from any charge or encumbrance not disclosed or known to the buyer before the contract is

---

[5] [1991] 2 A.C. 339.

made and that the buyer will enjoy quiet possession of the goods except so far as it may be disturbed by the owner or other person entitled to the benefit of any charge or encumbrance which was disclosed.

> ### McDonald v Provan (of Scotland Street) Ltd
> ### 1960 S.L.T. 231
>
> *McDonald v Provan (of Scotland Street) Ltd* demonstrates the operation of s.12. McDonald bought a car from Provan Ltd, who in turn had bought it in good faith. Three months after the sale the car was taken from McDonald by the police because at least part of it was stolen property. It appeared that the car consisted of parts of two separate cars, one of which had been stolen, that had been welded together. McDonald sued for damages for breach of the implied term about title in s.12 and it was held that he was entitled to succeed if he could prove the assertions on which he relied.

The seller does not have the right to sell: nemo dat quod non habet

Section 12 protects the buyer from someone who has not had the right to **5–11** sell the goods. If the true owner takes back the goods he or she can sue for breach of this implied term. Often in these situations the seller cannot be traced so it becomes important to try to show that the buyer did get a good title. The barrier to this is the general principle that those who transfer goods to others cannot confer a better title than they themselves have. For example, a thief has no title to what has been stolen so when he or she purports to sell the goods the buyer, however innocent, does not become the owner. This principle is set out in s.21 of the Act. However, it can work very unfairly so a number of exceptions have grown up often referred to as the exceptions to the *nemo dat* rule. This is a reference to the Latin phrase at the top of this paragraph which means: you cannot give a title that you do not have.

The exceptions

Personal bar

This exception is found in s.21 just after it states the general rule. The **5–12** section goes on that the owner of goods can be precluded from denying the seller's authority to sell because of his conduct. An example comes from the English case of *Eastern Distributors Ltd v Goldring*.[6] Mr Murphy, the owner of a van, signed hire purchase forms in blank, so that a car dealer who was assisting him to finance the purchase of a Chrysler car could sell it to a hire purchase company. It had been agreed between them that the dealer would only sell the van if the dealer was able to arrange

---

[6] [1957] 2 Q.B. 600.

finance for the purchase of the Chrysler from the hire purchase company. This did not prove to be possible but the dealer still sold the van to the hire purchase company, Eastern Distributors Ltd. Meantime, Mr Murphy who still had possession of the van sold it to Mr Goldring. So now he and Eastern Distributors claimed to be the owners. It was held that Eastern Distributors, not Mr Goldring, were the true owners because they had bought in good faith from the car dealer whom Mr Murphy had put in a position to sell his van.

Sale by a mercantile agent

5–13 Section 2(1) of the Factors Act 1889 states that:

> "Where a mercantile agent is, with the consent of the owner, in possession of goods or of the documents of title to goods, any sale, pledge, or other disposition of the goods, made by him when acting in the ordinary course of business of a mercantile agent, shall, subject to the provisions of this Act, be as valid as if he were expressly authorised by the owner of the goods to make the same; provided that the person taking under the disposition acts in good faith, and has not at the time of the disposition notice that the person making the disposition has not authority to make the same."

Examples of mercantile agents are shops, auctioneers and warehousemen so this exception is of considerable everyday importance.

Sale under a voidable title

5–14 A voidable title to goods is one which is valid until it is successfully challenged. It is to be distinguished from a *void* title which is one which has never been valid and so cannot confer rights. Where a seller has a voidable title the person in possession of the goods can pass a good title until steps have been taken by the true owner to avoid that title. A classic example is provided by the case of *MacLeod v Kerr*.[7]

MacLeod v Kerr
1965 S.C. 253

Kerr had advertised his car for sale in a newspaper and sold it to a man who came to see it. He accepted a cheque in payment and permitted the man to take the car away together with the registration document. The man had given a false name and paid with a cheque from a stolen cheque book. On discovering that he had been tricked Kerr immediately informed the police. Meanwhile, the rogue sold the car to a Mr Gibson who knew nothing of these events. The rogue was not worth suing and the question in the case was which of two people who had been duped by him was the

---

[7] 1965 S.C. 253.

legal owner of the car. It was held by the Court of Session that the rogue's fraudulent misrepresentation resulted in him obtaining a voidable title. Informing the police was not sufficient to upset this title so the rogue was still able to give Gibson ownership. Mr MacLeod, incidentally, was the procurator fiscal who had custody of the car while the dispute between Mr Kerr and Mr Gibson was resolved and took no part in the case though his name had to appear for procedural reasons.

Sale by a seller in possession after a sale

It will sometimes happen that after a sale has been completed and the **5–15** buyer has become the owner of the goods they will remain in the possession of the seller. Should the seller purport to sell them to someone else that person will get a good title. This is the effect of s.24 of the Act which applies where the person to whom the goods were sold the second time does not know of the original sale and is acting in good faith. Although the original purchaser will have lost the goods to the new purchaser, he will have a right against the seller for breach of contract.

Sale by a buyer in possession after a sale

This is the converse of the previous situation. Before becoming the legal **5–16** owner the buyer has obtained possession of the goods. Nevertheless, as a result of s.25 of the Act such a person can give a good title to someone acting in good faith who does not know of the original seller's rights. A good example comes from the case of *Archivent Sales & Development Ltd v Strathclyde Regional Council*[8] which also demonstrates that this exception can override a retention of title clause.

Archivent
1985 S.L.T. 154

Archivent delivered building materials to the site where a contractor was building a school for the regional council. The contract between Archivent and the contractor included a clause reserving title in the materials to them until payment was made in full. The contract between the contractor and the council provided that the materials should become the property of the council when they were delivered to the site. The contractor became insolvent before Archivent had been paid. The council had acted in good faith throughout and had been unaware of the clause reserving title until after the insolvency. The issue was who owned the goods and in the circumstances it was decided that it was the council by virtue of s.25.

---

[8] 1985 S.L.T. 154.

Sales of motor vehicles subject to hire purchase or conditional sale

5–17 Someone who buys goods by means of hire-purchase or conditional sale, which is very similar, does not become the owner of them until all the instalments have been paid and thus cannot pass a good title to anyone else. Unfortunately, it is not uncommon for those buying cars on hire purchase and conditional sale to try to do so. To combat the hardship to unsuspecting purchasers from such people ss.27–29 of the Hire Purchase Act 1964 were passed. These apply only to motor vehicles and result in a private purchaser acting in good faith and without notice of the hire purchase or conditional sale agreement getting as good a title as the true owner (usually a finance company) has. It should be emphasised that this applies only to hire purchase and conditional sale and not to pure hire.

When does the risk pass?

5–18 Various problems may arise where the goods have been destroyed or damaged around the time of the contract. Section 6 of the SGA 1979 provides that where there is a contract for the sale of specific goods, and the goods without the knowledge of the seller have perished at the time when the contract is made, the contract is void. This might apply where the seller and buyer have agreed that the seller will sell a specific car identified by make and registration number. If, unknown to either, it was destroyed in a fire on the day before the contract was made the contract would be a nullity.

Section 7 deals with a slightly different situation. Like s.6 it applies to a sale of specific goods, but here the destruction occurs, without any fault on the part of the seller or buyer, after the contract has been entered into but before risk passes to the buyer. In this situation the sale is avoided.

In the case of unascertained goods the scope for them to perish in a legal sense is more limited. An agreement to sell purely generic goods cannot be frustrated by the destruction of the goods and it is of no concern to the buyer that the seller had a particular source in mind as Asquith L.J. explained in *Monkland v Jack Barclay Ltd*[9]:

> "Suppose A has contracted to sell to B unascertained goods by description for example, 'a' Bentley Mark VI (not 'this' Bentley Mark VI), and suppose, further, that the seller expects to acquire the goods from a particular source, which may, indeed, be the only source available, the bare fact, without more, that when the time for delivery comes that source has dried up and that the seller cannot draw on it, does not absolve the seller. He is still, in the absence of some contractual term excusing him, liable for non-delivery."

Other situations are covered by s.20 of the Act. This provides that the risk of damage to or destruction of the goods is with the owner. This is another reason why the rules discussed earlier about when ownership passes are important. This rule is subject to some important exceptions.

---

[9] [1951] 2 K.B. 252.

First, the parties may have decided otherwise. It is common in retention of title clauses to provide that though the goods remain in the ownership of the seller the buyer bears the risk of damage or destruction. Also, where delivery has been delayed because of the fault of one of the parties the party responsible for the delay bears the risk of loss which would not have occurred had delivery been on time. There is also an important exception for the benefit of consumers which is discussed in the next chapter.

Duties of the seller

(a) Delivery

Section 27 provides that it is the seller's duty to deliver the goods and s.29 **5–19** explains that whether it is up to the seller to send the goods or the buyer to take delivery depends on the interpretation of the contract. If the contract does not say where delivery is to be made the same section provides that it is to be the seller's place of business or, where he or she has no place of business, his or her residence. However, if the contract is for the sale of specific goods which the parties knew at the time of the contract were somewhere else delivery should be made at that other place. If the contract requires the seller to send the goods to the buyer but does not say when this is to be done, s.29(3) provides that this must be done within a reasonable time and delivery must be at a reasonable hour. In *Hartley v Hyams*[10] it was held that time is prima facie of the essence in a commercial contract and so failure to deliver on time will justify the buyer in rescinding the contract.

Section 30 deals with delivery of the wrong quantity of goods. Where too few goods are delivered but the shortfall is not material the buyer may not reject the delivery but must pay for what is delivered at the contract rate. If too many goods are delivered the buyer may only reject the delivery if the excess is material. If it is material the buyer may choose to reject only the excess, or keep the whole delivery, paying at the contract rate.

(b) Duty to pass a good title

This has already been discussed under the heading of the right to sell. **5–20**

(c) Duty to provide goods of the correct description

Section 13 of 1979 Act provides that where there is a sale by description **5–21** there is an implied term that the goods will correspond with the description. If the sale is by sample, as well as by description, it is not sufficient that the bulk of the goods correspond with the sample if the goods do not also correspond with the description. Sales are by description in a wide range of situations. An obvious example is provided by mail order purchasing where the buyer relies on the description in a

---

[10] [1920] 3 K.B. 475.

catalogue or an advertisement in a newspaper or magazine. As s.13(3) makes clear, the fact that the goods are seen and selected by the buyer does not prevent the sale being one by description. Many goods are packaged and the buyer relies on the label or packaging for identification of the product. *Beale v Taylor*[11] extended this to a situation where the purchaser had examined the goods.

Beale v Taylor
[1967] 1 W.L.R. 1193

Mr Taylor had placed an advertisement for a car in a newspaper, describing the car as "Herald, convertible, white, 1961". After examining the car, Mr Beale decided to buy it. In fact, the car was an amalgamation of a 1961 Herald and another of a different year which had been welded together and was in a very dangerous condition. As this was a private sale, Mr Beale could not rely on the quality terms in s.14, so he had to resort to s.13. The English Court of Appeal held that the words "1961 Herald" formed part of the description which had not been complied with.

The modern tendency is to draw a distinction between disputes about quality, which should be reserved for s.14, and those about the identity of the goods, which are appropriate to s.13. This point was made in *Border Harvesters Ltd v Edwards Engineering (Perth) Ltd*[12] where the buyers were dissatisfied with the performance of a drying machine. Their attempt to argue that this could be brought within s.13 failed, the judge pointing out that they got what they bargained for namely, a drying machine of a certain type.

As *Beale v Taylor*[13] demonstrates, almost any words describing the goods will be regarded as part of the description. Strict compliance with description has been enforced in some cases.[14] However, as the unusual facts of *Harlingdon and Leinster Enterprises Ltd v Christopher Hull Fine Art Ltd*[15] demonstrate, there are limits. This case resulted from the sale of a painting which the defendants had purchased some time earlier when it had been described as being by the German artist, Munter. On the claimant, a specialist in German art, expressing interest in it the defendant emphasised that he did not know much about it, his particular expertise being in a different school of painting. The Court of Appeal held that it must be the intention of the parties that the description should be relied on. On the facts of this case that could not be said to have occurred.

---

[11] [1967] 1 W.L.R. 1193.
[12] 1985 S.L.T. 128.
[13] [1967] 1 W.L.R. 1193.
[14] See *Arcos v E.A. Ronaasen & Son* [1933] A.C. 470.
[15] [1990] 1 All E.R. 737.

(d) Duty to provide goods of satisfactory quality

A central aspect of any contract for the sale of goods will be the quality of **5–22** the goods. Section 14 provides that there is an implied term that goods must be of satisfactory quality. Before looking at what exactly this means some preliminary points need to be noted. This implied term only applies to sales in the course of a business: private sales are not covered. A wide meaning is given to a sale in the course of a business as *Stevenson v Rogers*[16] demonstrates.

Stevenson v Rogers
[1999] Q.B. 1028

Mr Rogers was a commercial fisherman who decided to sell his fishing boat and buy another one. The buyer alleged that there was a defect in the boat and Mr Rogers countered by arguing that as the sale was not in the course of a business the implied quality term did not apply. The English Court of Appeal disagreed. They pointed out that the boat was part of Mr Rogers' equipment as a fisherman and thus when he sold he was doing so in the course of his business.

Another important point is that it does not matter that the seller was not in any way to blame for the defect. A classic example is *Frost v Aylesbury Dairy*.[17]

Frost v Aylesbury Dairy
[1905] 1 K.B. 608

The dairy had supplied Mr Frost and his family with milk that contained typhoid germs, which caused the death of his wife. The evidence showed that the dairy's processes were extremely careful and that typhoid germs could only be detected by prolonged investigation. Nevertheless, it was held that there was an implied term that the milk would be reasonably fit for consumption. It was irrelevant that the defect could not have been discovered at the time of sale.

It can also be important that the term applies, to quote s.14(1), to, "goods supplied under a contract of sale". This means that the labelling and packaging of goods are part of the product as are instructions. This was important in *Wormell v RHM Agricultural (East) Ltd*[18] where it was

---

[16] [1999] Q.B. 1028.
[17] [1905] 1 K.B. 608.
[18] [1986] 1 All E.R. 769.

deficiencies in the instructions that rendered the product of unsatisfactory quality. It also means that material that was not intended to be included with the goods can also render them unsatisfactory. For example, in *Wilson v Rickett Cockerell & Co*[19] a bag of coal which contained a detonator rendered the consignment of unsatisfactory quality.

Section 14(2C) sets out two situations where the test of satisfactory quality does not apply. These are:

(1) Defects "specifically drawn to the buyer's attention before the contract is made". It is important to note that the factor must be specifically brought to the buyer's attention. In *Turnock v Fortune*[20] it was held by the sheriff principal that a strong recommendation from a third party not to buy a car did not amount to specifically drawing attention to its unroadworthiness, and thus did not prevent the car from being regarded as unmerchantable, the predecessor of satisfactory quality.
(2) If a buyer has examined the goods before the contract was made nothing which "that examination ought to reveal" can be relied on to demonstrate that the goods are not of satisfactory quality.

The definition of satisfactory quality

5–23 Section 14(2A) of the Act starts with a general definition of satisfactory quality and then later subsections go on to set out some criteria for judging when goods are of satisfactory quality. Section 14(2A) states:

"For the purposes of this Act, goods are of satisfactory quality if they meet the standard that a reasonable person would regard as satisfactory, taking account of any description of the goods, the price (if relevant) and all the other relevant circumstances."

The standard is objective: not what the particular buyer considers but what the hypothetical reasonable person would consider reasonable. The reasonable person is not an expert, to quote the English Court of Appeal in *Jewson Ltd v Boyhan*.[21] In coming to a decision such a person must take into account the description attached to the goods. One cannot expect a second-hand car to be in as good a condition as a new one; but if a product is described as designed to the highest standards one is entitled to expect more from it than from a run-of-the-mill product. In *Clegg v Andersson* Hale L.J. pointed out that the buyer of a very expensive, brand new, ocean-going yacht is entitled to expect it to be "perfect or nearly so".[22]

Price is an ambiguous indicator of quality so it is to be taken into account only if relevant. Sometimes a lower price indicates lower quality

---

[19] [1954] Q.B. 598.
[20] 1989 S.L.T. (Sh Ct) 32.
[21] [2003] EWCA Civ. 1030 at [78].
[22] [2003] 1 All E.R. (Comm) 721 at [73].

but it may simply indicate a desire to sell items faster. In *Thain v Anniesland Trade Centre*,[23] for example, stress was put on the price together with the fact that the car was second-hand, not new, and had a high mileage as factors that lowered the level of quality that could be expected. At the other end of the scale, payment of a high price, as the observation of Hale L.J. in the previous paragraph demonstrates, will raise the standard of quality that can be expected.

In addition to these factors, "all the other relevant circumstances" are to be considered. In *Britvic v Messer*[24] this seems to have been important. The case involved the sale of carbon dioxide by the manufacturer to a soft drinks firm that added it to its products. It had been contaminated with minute traces of benzene which is carcinogenic. Despite the fact that the levels were well below the levels that were considered unsafe it was decided that the carbon dioxide was not of satisfactory quality because of the commercial fact that consumers would not be prepared to buy products to which it had been added.

Although it was probably unnecessary, subss.(2D)–(2F) were recently added to the section making it clear that public statements by "seller, the producer or his representative, particularly in advertising or on labelling" are relevant circumstances. *Lamarra v Capital Bank Plc*[25] makes it clear that the fact that new cars come with a manufacturer's warranty is not a relevant circumstance.

In addition to the general definition, s.14(2B) states that: **5–24**

"The following (among others) are in appropriate cases aspects of the quality of goods—

(a) fitness for all the purposes for which goods of the kind in question are commonly supplied,
(b) appearance and finish,
(c) freedom from minor defects,
(d) safety, and
(e) durability."

The first factor is that the goods are fit for all the purposes for which goods of the kind in question are commonly supplied. This is clearly an important factor. If a kettle does not boil water or a car breaks down frequently, no-one would think it of satisfactory quality. If goods have more than one purpose and the seller intends his product to fulfil only one of those purposes it will be necessary to make this clear. This may be done explicitly or, in some circumstances, other factors such as the price may indicate this fact.

The case of *Jewson Ltd v Boyhan*[26] shows that the implied term of

---

[23] 1997 S.L.T. (Sh Ct) 102.
[24] [2002] EWCA Civ 548.
[25] 2007 S.C. 95.
[26] [2003] EWCA Civ 1030.

satisfactory quality is not the appropriate one where the buyer has a particular purpose in mind.

Jewson Ltd v Boyhan
[2003] EWCA Civ 1030

The buyer was a property developer who purchased from Jewsons a number of electric central heating boilers for installation in flats that he was constructing. He discovered that these boilers had poor energy ratings according to government approved tests and feared that the flats would therefore be difficult or impossible to sell. This caused him to abandon the project and, when Jewsons sued him for the price of the boilers, he counterclaimed for several hundred thousand pounds based on his loss of profit and increased costs resulting from the installation of the boilers, as opposed to boilers with better energy ratings. He argued that among the purposes for which the boilers had to be fit was ensuring that they would not render the flats in which they were to be installed difficult or impossible to sell. In effect, the Court of Appeal did not accept that this was one of "the purposes for which goods of the kind in question are commonly supplied". As one of the judges put it, "[the buyer] got exactly what he had bargained for: twelve boilers which worked perfectly well".[27]

5-25 Appearance and finish, and freedom from minor defects are also to be taken into account in determining whether goods are of satisfactory quality. The application of this test will, of course, depend on the facts. Second-hand goods may be expected to have some minor marks or defects while, usually, new goods should not. Hale L.J. pointed out in *Clegg v Andersson*, a consumer case, that: "[i]n some cases, such as a high priced quality product, the customer may be entitled to expect that it is free from even minor defects, in other words perfect or nearly so".[28] However, certain kinds of product such as earthenware, pottery or natural products may be expected to have minor inconsistencies and blemishes and these may well not render them of unsatisfactory quality.[29] In some cases this test will have no application at all as in the case of cars sold as scrap and loads of manure.

There has never been any doubt that unsafe goods were not of the quality demanded by law[30] and this is explicitly recognised in the definition. Safety was the central factor in *Clegg v Andersson*.[31] A new ocean-going yacht costing £250,000 was delivered to the buyer with a keel which

---

[27] [2003] EWCA Civ 1030 at [79].

[28] [2003] 1 All E.R. (Comm) 721; [2003] EWCA Civ 320; [2003] 2 Lloyd's Rep. 32 at [72].

[29] In one case, granite gravestones were held to be of satisfactory quality since the blemishes were part of the natural stone: *Bon Accord Granite v Buchan*, 2005 G.W.D. 28-531.

[30] *Godley v Perry* [1960] 1 W.L.R. 9, CA; *Lambert v Lewis* [1982] A.C. 225.

[31] [2003] 1 All E.R. (Comm) 721; [2003] EWCA Civ 320; [2003] 2 Lloyd's Rep. 32.

was substantially heavier than the manufacturer's specification. Technical evidence showed that this would render the rigging unsafe and, in the circumstances, the Court of Appeal had no difficulty in finding that the yacht did not meet the standard of satisfactory quality.[32]

The final factor is durability. It is important to realise that this term is to be satisfied at the time of delivery and not at some later date. Later events may be relevant in determining whether, at the time of sale, the goods were durable.[33] This factor was important in the first case to discuss the new satisfactory quality term, *Thain v Anniesland Trade Centre*.[34]

> ### Thain v Anniesland Trade Centre
> #### 1997 S.L.T. (Sh Ct) 102
>
> Ms Thain had paid £2,995 for a second-hand Renault 19 car that had travelled about 80,000 miles and was about six years old. Two weeks after she purchased it an intermittent droning noise was noticed and this proved to be a failing differential bearing in the automatic gear box. The sellers refused to replace the gear box. Eventually, after about nine to ten weeks, the car was unusable and Ms Thain rejected it. The sheriff principal upheld the sheriff's decision that the car was of satisfactory quality observing:
>
> > "The sheriff's conclusion can only be described as that of the reasonable person. Even a negligible degree of durability may not represent unsatisfactory quality where the second-hand car supplied is as old and as heavily used as the Renault had been. The plain fact is that, given the Renault's age and mileage when supplied, its durability was a matter of luck. Durability, in all the circumstances, was simply not a quality that a reasonable person would demand of it."[35]

(e) Duty to provide goods to fit a particular purpose specified by the buyer

Section 14 of the Act has another separate implied term about quality in **5–26** s.14(3). This states that where goods are sold in the course of a business and the seller "expressly or by implication, makes known" to the seller, "any particular purpose for which the goods are being bought, there is an implied term that the goods supplied under the contract are reasonably fit for that purpose, whether or not that is a purpose for which such goods are commonly supplied, except where the circumstances show that the buyer does not rely, or that it is unreasonable for him to rely, on the skill or judgment of the seller".

---

[32] [2003] 1 All E.R. (Comm) 721 at [49] and [73].
[33] *Crowther v Shannon Motor Co Ltd* [1975] 1 W.L.R. 30.
[34] 1997 S.L.T. (Sh Ct) 102; 1997 S.C.L.R. 991.
[35] 1997 S.L.T. (Sh Ct) 102 at 106.

This term only applies if the buyer has made it clear that the goods are wanted for a particular purpose. That does not have to be spelt out in the case of goods which have only one purpose such as a kettle or a hot water bottle. Where goods might be used for several purposes the term can only be relied on if the particular purpose that the buyer has in mind has been made clear to the seller. The result may then be that goods which are of satisfactory quality will not satisfy this term. Take the example of someone who needs paint to paint a wooden fence. He or she asks the seller for suitable paint for this job and is advised to buy a certain tin of paint. On applying the paint it soon peels off. It turns out that this is because it is paint which is suitable only for painting metal work. The seller would be in breach of this implied term although the paint is perfectly good paint for its proper purpose.

Flynn v Scott[36] makes clear that the particular purpose must be clearly specified. There, the subject of the sale was a lorry which could have been used for a number of different functions, though the buyer intended to use it to transport furniture and livestock. A claim for breach of the implied term of fitness for purpose failed because it was not shown that the buyer had communicated his particular purpose.

If the customer has some susceptibility, this must be communicated to the seller. *Griffiths v Peter Conway Ltd*[37] is an example.

Griffiths v Peter Conway Ltd
[1939] 1 All E.R. 685

Mrs Griffith developed a very severe attack of dermatitis as a result of wearing a tweed coat purchased from the defendants. Her skin was unusually sensitive and the evidence showed that there was nothing in the cloth that would have affected a normal person's skin. As Mrs Griffiths had not informed the sellers of her sensitivity they were not liable.

(f) Duty to provide goods matching sample

5–27 Goods may often be sold by reference to a sample. Consumer sales of wallpaper and carpets are examples where the buyer chooses the particular design from a book of samples. In this situation s.15(2) provides that:

> "In the case of a contract for sale by sample there is an implied term—
>
> (a) that the bulk will correspond with the sample in quality;

---

[36] 1949 S.C. 442; 1949 S.L.T. 399.
[37] [1939] 1 All E.R. 685, approved in *Slater v Finning Ltd*, 1996 S.L.T. 912; [1996] 3 All E.R. 398, HL.

(c) that the goods will be free from any defect, making their quality unsatisfactory, which would not be apparent on reasonable examination of the sample."

Key Concepts

In contracts of sale there are usually *express* terms which are clearly spelled out in the contract and *implied* terms which are not.
   The Sale of Goods Act ss.12, 13, 14 and 15 provide for implied terms in relation to the duties of the seller. These terms apply whether the seller has been at fault or not, *Frost v Aylesbury Dairy* (1905).

Seller's remedies

(1) Action for the price—s.49

If the property in the goods has passed to the buyer and he has not paid the seller's principal remedy is to sue for the price. **5–28**

(2) Damages for non-acceptance—s.50

Section 50 deals with the situation where the buyer refuses to take delivery of the goods. The seller can sue for non-acceptance and s.50(2) states that the measure of damages (i.e. how damages are assessed) is, in principle, "the estimated loss directly and naturally resulting, in the ordinary course of events, from the buyer's breach of contract". If there is a market for the goods in question, this will be the difference between the contract price and the market price. **5–29**

(3) Other remedies

In commercial transactions the sellers may discover that they are not going to be paid at a point where they still have control of the goods. This gives them useful powers as follows: **5–30**

(a) Right of lien over goods—ss.39(1)(a) and 41

This is a right to retain the goods until they have been paid for. **5–31**

(b) Stoppage in transit—ss.44–46

If the seller learns that the buyer has become insolvent while the goods are being transported, s.44 gives a right to retake possession of them and keep them until payment is received. **5–32**

(c) Right of resale—ss.39(1)(c) and 48

Where goods are perishable or the unpaid seller gives notice of intention to resell, this may be done within a reasonable time. **5–33**

Buyer's remedies

5–34 If it is the seller who is in breach of the contract, the buyer has a number of possible remedies. Remember that the buyer must be able to demonstrate that in some way the seller has failed to carry out the terms of the contract. This may be a failure to honour an express term or one of the implied terms. For example, if the buyer considers that the goods are not of good quality, it is necessary to show that they do not meet the standard of satisfactory quality in s.14. It is only then that the buyer can start to consider which of the following remedies he or she wishes to pursue.

Right to reject

5–35 Section 15B of the SGA 1979 provides that, where the seller is in breach of any term of a contract the buyer is entitled to claim damages and, if the breach is material, to reject the goods and treat the contract as repudiated. This is what was called "rescission".

As Hale L.J. pointed out in the English case of *Clegg v Andersson*[38]:

> "The customer has a right to reject goods which are not of satisfactory quality. He does not have to act reasonably in choosing rejection rather than damages or cure [and the fact that this remedy] may be thought to be disproportionate by some is irrelevant."

While the customer does not have to act reasonably, he or she must show that there was a "material" breach and act fairly quickly. What is "material" depends on the circumstances of the particular case.

Conditions for rejecting

5–36   (i) You must tell the seller that you are rejecting, though, unless the contract says so, you need not return the goods—see s.36.
   (ii) The goods must not have been accepted. The right to reject ceases to be available when the consumer has accepted the goods in the legal sense. When goods are accepted is defined in s.35 of the SGA 1979. It occurs in three circumstances:

   (1) The buyer has intimated to the seller that he has accepted the goods. If the buyer says that the goods have been accepted, rejection is no longer possible.
   (2) On receiving delivery, the buyer does an act inconsistent with the seller's ownership. In commercial transactions, the most common situation where this arises is in the re-sale of goods. For a Scottish case involving a consumer, see:

---

[38] [2003] 1 All E.R. (Comm) 721.

Hunter v Albancode Plc
1989 G.W.D. 39-1843

Mrs Hunter bought a suite of furniture which proved to be defective and she purported to reject it. When it was not uplifted by Albancode, Mrs Hunter continued to use it as she could not afford to replace it until she obtained a refund. The Sheriff held that continuing to use the goods amounted to an act inconsistent with the seller's ownership and thus the right to reject had been lost.

Section 35(7) makes clear that agreeing to a repair does not amount to an act inconsistent with the seller's ownership.

(3) After the lapse of a reasonable time, the buyer retains the goods without intimating to the seller that he has rejected them. What is a reasonable time is a question of fact and will vary from product to product, being longer for more complex products. In *Clegg v Andersson* which we looked at on another point above, the buyer of the yacht took delivery in August. He did not reject the goods until the following March. This was not too late. This lengthy period is explained by the fact that he was entitled to delay his decision to accept or reject the yacht until the seller had provided him with the necessary technical information to make a decision. When he got that information he then made up his mind to reject with three weeks after consulting his technical advisers. *Douglas v Glenvarigill Co Ltd*[39] concerned an Audi car that developed serious faults which did not become obvious until over a year after delivery and rejection was not intimated for another 15 months. Despite having sympathy for the plight of the buyer the judge observed that, "rejection is a relatively short term remedy, and is simply not available when a latent defect manifests itself for the first time more than a year after delivery; in no reported case has rejection been permitted after such a period".

Other aspects of rejection

Section 35A of the SGA 1979 deals with partial rejection. Where a buyer **5–37** has the right to reject goods but is prepared to retain some of them and reject only the remainder, the right to reject is not lost by retaining some of them. Where goods are delivered by instalments, the right to reject a non-conforming instalment is not lost by having accepted another instalment.

Where the seller delivers too few goods, or too many, s.30 provides that rejection is only possible where the excess or shortfall is material.

---

[39] [2010] CSOH 14.

Damages

5–38 Section 15B provides that damages is also a remedy where a contract of sale is breached. This may be the only remedy for the non-material breach of an express term, or may be the remedy which must be used where the right to reject has been lost through acceptance.

The SGA 1979 applies the normal contract rule that the damages should be such as result naturally from the breach in the ordinary course of events. Where the breach is the failure of the seller to deliver the goods, s.51 goes on to say that where there is an available market for the goods, the measure of damages is, prima facie, to be ascertained by the difference between the contract price and the market or current price of the goods at the time that they ought to have been delivered.

Where the seller delivers the goods but is in breach of one of the terms of the contract regarding quality, s.53A states how the buyer's loss is to be calculated. The measure of damages for the seller's breach of contract is the estimated loss directly and naturally resulting, in the ordinary course of events, from the breach. The general rule is set out in subs.(1) and states that the damages are to be "the estimated loss directly and naturally resulting, in the ordinary course of events, from the breach". Subsection (2) goes on to deal with the specific case of the breach consisting of failure to deliver goods of the right quality. Here it is "the difference between the value of the goods at the time of delivery to the buyer and the value they would have had if they had fulfilled the contract". In addition, other damage may have resulted to the buyer or his or her property. In *Godley v Perry*[40] a defective catapult resulted in the purchaser losing an eye, and the claim for breach of contract was mainly for damages for this injury.

Specific implement

5–39 Specific implement is an order of a court to do something. Recall your general contract law. From that it will be clear that this remedy will rarely be of any importance as one of the remedies in commercial contracts for sale of goods. This is because courts will not normally force one party to carry out the contract if damages would be an alternative. In most cases of sale of goods that will be the case. Only where the goods were unique would be specific implement be ordered.

The additional consumer remedies

5–40 Consumers are able to invoke a different set of remedies and these are discussed in Chapter 6, "Consumer Protection".

---

[40] [1960] 1 W.L.R. 9.

OTHER CONTRACTS FOR THE SUPPLY OF GOODS

Part 1A of the Supply of Goods and Services Act 1982 provides implied **5–41** terms and remedies for certain types of contract by which goods can be obtained.

The categories of contracts affected

(a) Contracts for the transfer of goods (s.11A)

Section 11A defines these as those, "under which one person transfers or **5–42** agrees to transfer to another the property in goods, whether or not services are also provided, other than an excepted contract", i.e.:

- contract of sale;
- hire purchase contract;
- contract where there is no consideration; and
- contract operating by way of mortgage, pledge, charge or security.

Examples of contracts within this definition would be: barter; contracts for work and materials; goods exchanged for tokens or coupons.

What terms are implied?

- s.11B—terms about title.   **5–43**
- s.11C—a term about description.
- s.11D—terms about quality and fitness for purpose.
- s.11E—correspondence of sample with bulk.

As these are virtually a carbon copy of those found in the SGA 1979, they are not reproduced here.

Remedies

Section 11F sets out the remedies in language appropriate to Scots law. It **5–44** is a copy of s.15B of the SGA 1979.

(b) Contracts of hire

Contracts of hire are defined by s.11G of the Supply of Goods and **5–45** Services Act 1982 as contracts, "under which one person ('the supplier') hires or agrees to hire goods to another whether or not services are also to be provided whatever the nature of the consideration other than hire purchase contracts".

Examples are rentals, e.g. television or short-term hire of machinery, leasing, finance leasing, and contract hire.

What terms are implied?

- s.11H—Terms about title.   **5–46**
- s.11I—A term about description.

- s.11J—Terms about quality and fitness for purpose.
- s.11K—Correspondence of sample with bulk.

Remedies

5–47 These are not set out in the Act. The common law remedies therefore apply.

EXCLUSION OF LIABILITY

5–48 Suppliers of goods will often attempt to exclude or limit their legal liability to the buyer. This topic is covered in detail in Ch.4 on contract law to which reference should be made and is only briefly dealt with here. Section 20(1) of the Unfair Contract Terms Act 1977 provides that in commercial contracts of sale and hire purchase terms purporting to exclude or limit the implied terms about title are void. Section 21(3A) achieves the same result for such terms in other contracts for the transfer of goods. The various terms about description, quality, fitness for purpose and sale by sample in commercial contracts can only be excluded if it can be shown to be fair and reasonable.[41]

▼ CHAPTER SUMMARY

5–49
(1) One of several contracts can be involved when goods are supplied. These include sale, hire-purchase, barter and goods supplied when services are also performed.
(2) The most common supply of goods contract is the contract of sale and it is governed by the SGA 1979.
(3) A contract of sale is one the seller transfers or agrees to transfer the property in goods to the buyer for a monetary consideration, called the price (SGA 1979 s.2(1)).
(4) The Act has rules about when legal title to the goods passes from the seller to the buyer (SGA 1979 ss.16–18).
(5) These rules are also important in deciding who bears the risk if something goes wrong during a transaction.
(6) A seller can only sell what he owns and if he tries to sell something that is not his, the buyer generally does not become the owner (SGA 1979 s.21).
(7) To this rule there are several exceptions:

    (a) personal bar;
    (b) sale by a mercantile agent;
    (c) if a seller has a voidable title, and that title is not reduced by the time of sale to a purchaser who buys in good faith without notice of the defect in title, the purchaser may keep the goods;
    (d) SGA 1979 s.23—*Macleod v Kerr* (1965);

---

[41] In relation to contracts of sale and hire purchase see the Unfair Contract Terms Act 1977 s.20(2); and for other contracts for the transfer of goods see s.21.

    (e) buyer or seller in possession after sale (SGA 1979 ss.24 and 25)—
        Archivent Sales and Developments Ltd v Strathclyde Regional Council (1985);

    (f) sales of motor vehicles subject to hire purchase or conditional sale (Hire Purchase Act 1964 ss.27–29).

(8) The heart of the SGA 1979 is a series of sections which implies various terms into all contracts of sale. (Note that these terms apply whether the seller has been at fault or not, see *Frost v Aylesbury Dairy* (1905).) They are:

- The seller has the right to sell the goods (s.12(1)).
- There is no charge or encumbrance over the goods (s.12(2)(a)).
- The buyer will enjoy quiet possession of the goods (s.12(2)(b)).
- The seller will not be liable for the charge or encumbrance if the charge or encumbrance is disclosed (s.12(3), (4) and (5)).
- Goods will correspond with their description (s.13). See *Beale v Taylor* (1967).
- Goods sold must be of satisfactory quality (s.14(2)).

Important cases on satisfactory quality are *Clegg v Andersson* (2003), *Thain v Anniesland Trade Centre* (1997) and *Lamarra v Capital Bank Plc* (2007).

- Goods must be reasonably fit for a purpose which has been specified by the buyer (s.14(3)). See *Griffiths v Peter Conway* (1939).
- The terms in s.14 apply only to sales in the course of a business. See *Stevenson v Rogers* (1999).
- The bulk will correspond with any sample (s.15).

(9) Breach by the seller of these implied terms entitles a purchaser to various remedies. These are:
EITHER:

    (a) to reject the goods and get his or her money back;
    (b) damages; or
    (c) specific performance (rare).

Rejection must be made fairly quickly (SGA 1979 s.35).
    Damages is a sum of money that represents the loss to the person making the claim (SGA 1979 s.53A). Normal contract rules about damages apply.

(10) If it is the buyer who has broken the contract the seller has the following remedies:

    (a) Action for the price—s.49.
    (b) Damages for non-acceptance—s.50.
    (c) Other remedies:
        (i)   Right of lien over goods—ss.39(1)(a) and 41.
        (ii) Stoppage in transit—ss.44–46.
        (iii) Right of resale—ss.39(1)(c) and 48.

(11) Other contracts for the supply of goods.

    (a) There are similar implied terms in the contracts of barter or where goods are transferred when services are also being rendered (Sale and Supply of Goods Act 1982 Pt 1A).

(b) The Contract of Hire. The Supply of Goods and Services Act 1982 ss.11H–11K implies terms into hire contracts.

? QUICK QUIZ

- Name three types of contract dealing with the supply of goods.
- Which Act of Parliament governs commercial contracts of sale?
- How is a contract of sale different from other contracts for the supply of goods?
- There are exceptions to the rule that someone who is not the legal owner of goods cannot pass on a good title to them. State two of them.
- What terms are implied in contracts of sale?
- When are goods of satisfactory quality?
- When does the satisfactory quality test not apply?
- What remedies are available to a purchaser who buys defective goods?
- What remedies are available to a seller if the buyer breaks the contract?
- What terms are implied in contracts for the transfer of goods governed by the Supply of Goods and Services Act 1982?

FURTHER READING

➢ P.S. Atiyah, J. Adams and J. MacQueen, *The Sale of Goods Act*, 12th edn (Oxford: Pearson, 2010).

RELEVANT WEBLINKS

➢ Department of Business, Innovation and Skills: *https:// www.gov.uk/government/organisations/department-for-business- innovation-skills* [Accessed May 15, 2015].

Chapter 6   Consumer Protection

Cowan Ervine[1]

▶ CHAPTER OVERVIEW

This chapter deals with four major aspects of consumer protection. After **6–01** pointing out that other chapters deal with some facets of the topic it considers first with how consumers are protected when they buy goods and digital content. We also purchase many services from those of hairdressers to solicitors and these are dealt with next. The third area is the provision of consumer credit and the various methods by which credit can be provided are explained. Consumer credit is largely governed by the Consumer Credit Act 1974, which has been updated by the Consumer Credit Act 2006 and the Financial Services and Markets Act 2000. More recently, statutory instruments have made more changes to ensure that UK law complies fully with the EU's 2008 Consumer Credit Directive. The special terminology that the Act uses is discussed, as well as the various methods by which consumers are protected. This involves a system permitting only "authorised" firms to enter the industry and requirements to provide consumers with information so that they know what they are letting themselves in for. There are special protections for consumers of credit such as connected lender liability where the credit provider can be liable for the failings of the supplier of the goods or services. The courts have special powers to deal with consumers who run into difficulties with their credit agreements. The final part of the chapter deals with the control of various trade practices. This section concentrates on the Consumer Protection from Unfair Trading Regulations 2008 which implement the EU's Unfair Commercial Practices Directive. This is designed to deal with various practices which may harm consumers. These may appear in advertising or sales promotions. The regulations create a duty not to trade unfairly. There is a general ban on unfair trade practices as well as bans on misleading actions, misleading omissions and aggressive practices. In addition there is a list of specific practices which are always deemed unfair. The Competition and Markets Authority ("CMA") (which has taken over many of the roles of the Office of Fair Trading) and local trading standards officers enforce these regulations using various methods both criminal and civil.

In addition to the Consumer Protection Regulations there are the Consumer Contracts (Information, Cancellation and Additional

---

[1] Honorary Teaching Fellow, University of Dundee.

Charges) Regulations 2013 which regulate various selling methods. These are discussed in Ch.7, "E-commerce".

6–02 After studying this chapter you should:

> ✓ be aware of the range of ways in which consumers are protected;
> ✓ know in more detail how supply of goods and digital content, consumer credit and trade practices are controlled;
> ✓ in relation to the supply of goods and digital content know that the major statute is the Consumer Rights Act 2015;
> ✓ in relation to credit know that:
>
> > ● the major statutes are the Consumer Credit Act 1974 and the Financial Services and Markets Act 2000;
> > ● the authorisation system is important;
> > ● consumers are entitled to information before making credit agreements;
> > ● there are special protections during the agreement;
> > ● credit granters can be liable for what the suppliers of goods and services say; and
> > ● sheriffs have wide powers to deal with breaches of agreement.
>
> ✓ know how users of services are protected;
> ✓ in relation to trade practices know that:
>
> > ● there are new regulations making major changes in their control;
> > ● these regulations introduce a duty not to trade unfairly; and
> > ● they are enforced in a number of ways.

INTRODUCTION

6–03 The term consumer protection is a convenient name for a range of legal rules which are designed to protect individuals who purchase goods or services for their own personal use or consumption. Some of its rules are closely related to areas of law that you will have touched on in other chapters of this book. For example, in the Ch.4 on "The law of contract" you will have seen that the control of exclusion clauses and other potentially unfair terms in business to business transactions are controlled by the Unfair Contract Terms Act 1977 and in business to consumer transactions by Pt 1 of the Consumer Rights Act 2015. Ch.7 on E-commerce discusses how consumers purchasing by means of modern technology get special protection. The contract rules about misrepresentation and undue influence can also be important in the protection of consumers. In Ch.10, "Delict", the important case of *Donoghue v Stevenson* is discussed in detail. This is one of the most important consumer protection cases of all time. The same chapter discusses strict liability for defective products contained in Pt 1 of the Consumer Protection Act 1987, another very important piece of consumer protection legislation. This chapter deals with two other important areas of consumer protection: consumer credit and the control of unfair trading practices.

Supply of Goods and Digital Content and Services

This section deals with contracts which involve consumers acquiring **6–04** goods and what is called digital content, i.e. things like music or video content whether on DVD or CD or as streamed material such as Netflix, computer programs, apps and games. The commercial supply of goods has been dealt with separately in Ch.5. This is because the Consumer Rights Act 2015 ("CRA 2015") has set out the rights of consumer buyers of goods and digital content. It also deals with the supply of services. Each of these contracts is dealt with in a separate chapter of Part 1 but as CRA 2015 s.1(4) makes clear "in each case the Chapter applies even if the contract also covers something covered by another Chapter". Such contracts are called "mixed contracts" by that subsection. Previously the law had developed piecemeal and was located in a number of Acts of Parliament.

In the case of the supply of goods it had developed from legislation, the Sale of Goods Acts, which was originally designed for business transactions. It had become complex with various additions mainly to include protections for consumers. Modern technological developments had not been taken on board and the law in this area was uncertain. Pt 1 of the CRA 2015 brings together and harmonises the law relating to consumer purchases. It is drafted in clearer language using modern techniques to assist the reader to make sense of it. For example, before the sections of the Act which set out the rights of a consumer who buys goods there is a sub-heading *"What statutory rights are there under a goods contract?"*. One of those rights is to get goods of satisfactory quality and at the end of s.9 which defines what this means the final subsection points to a later section which sets out a consumer's rights if a trader does not provide goods of the right standard.

What CRA 2015 Part 1 covers

There are various types of contract that involve the transfer of the **6–05** ownership or possession of goods as we saw in relation to commercial transactions. The same may be said of digital content but that will be dealt with separately later as will contracts for services. Perhaps the commonest is the contract of sale where goods are purchased in return for money. Goods are sometimes exchanged for other goods in a contract of barter, in return for vouchers, bought on various forms of credit and, sometimes, even given away. One of the weaknesses of the previous law was that what were economically similar transactions were regulated by

different statutes. Part 1 of the CRA 2015 deals with the legal consequences of what it refers to collectively as contracts to supply goods.[2]
The Act defines which contracts it deals with and then sets out what legal
consequences follow in relation, for example, to the quality that can be
expected, when ownership is transferred and who bears the risk of
something going wrong while the goods are being delivered and what
remedies are available where a contract is broken.

To be a consumer contract an agreement musts be one between a
trader and a consumer whether the contract is written or oral or implied
from the parties' conduct.[3] A trader is defined in s.2 as "a person acting
for purposes relating to that person's trade, business, craft or profession,
whether acting personally or through another person acting in the trader's name or on the trader's behalf". "Person" is used in the legal sense
of any entity recognised by the law so it covers not just individuals but
companies and other organisations. "Business" includes "the activities of
any government department or local or public authority"[4] so it will cover
not only conventional shops and Internet traders but not-for-profit
organisations, such as charities, mutuals and cooperatives which often
sell goods for profit. The reference to acting "through another person
acting in the trader's name or on the trader's behalf" is a useful clarification of the law. Examples would be a trader which subcontracts part
of a building contract or a company for which the employees make
contracts with customers. In both situations it is the trader who is liable
for proper execution of the contract.

A "consumer" is "an individual acting for purposes which are wholly
or mainly outside that individual's trade, business, craft or profession".[5]
The use of the term individual excludes corporate entities such as limited
liability companies but could apply to those operating as sole traders and
partnerships governed by the Partnership Act 1890.[6] This might cover
situations such as that in *R & B Customs Brokers Co. Ltd. v United
Dominions Trust Ltd.*[7] involving the purchase of a car for use both in the
business and as the trader's family car.

For the purposes of this part of the Act "goods" means "any tangible
moveable items, but that includes water, gas and electricity if and only if
they are put up for supply in a limited volume or set quantity".[8] So,
"goods" are anything physical which you can move thus excluding
purchases of land or a house. Water, gas and electricity are included but
only gas sold in cylinders, not gas piped into a home. Similarly, with
water it is only bottled water that is included not water delivered through
the mains.

---

[2] CRA 2015 s.3(4).
[3] CRA 2015 s.1(1) and (2).
[4] CRA 2015 s.2(7).
[5] CRA 2015 s.2.
[6] See recital 17 of the EU's Consumer Rights Directive, which Pt 1 of the CRA 2015
implements.
[7] [1988] 1 W.L.R. 321
[8] CRA 2015 s.2(8).

The four contracts to supply goods

There are four types of contracts to supply goods: a sales contract; a **6–06** contract for the hire of goods; a hire-purchase contract; and a contract for transfer of goods. Section 3(5), makes clear these contracts include those involving the transfer of a share in the goods, whether between current owners or the owner of a share and a third party. Certain transactions that might otherwise come within the definition of a contract to sell goods are excluded. These are: contracts to supply coins or notes for use as currency, though this does not cover sales of notes or coins as collectors' items; goods sold under court orders; those intended to operate as a mortgage, pledge, charge or other security; and gifts.[9] For most purposes Pt 1 does not apply to purchases at auctions but this means traditional auctions where second hand goods are sold and individuals have the opportunity of attending in person. This rules out facilities such as eBay.

Sales contracts

Sales contracts are those where a trader transfers or agrees to transfer **6–07** ownership of goods to a consumer who agrees to pay the price. Ownership means "the general property in goods, not merely a special property".[10] This "general property" is the right over goods which an absolute owner has in contrast to the more limited "special property" in a thing which means that a person can only put the item to a particular use rather than having absolute rights of ownership. This Act makes clear that this includes two common situations. It is a sales contract where a trader agrees to manufacture or produce goods for a consumer who agrees to pay the price. This could cover the purchase of furniture where the consumer sees a particular model in a showroom but what he or she buys is that model modified by, for example, having different material and the addition of special castors and anti-stain treatment. The other is "conditional sales contracts" where goods are paid for in instalments and the trader retains ownership of them until the conditions in the contract have been met, whether the consumer has possession of the goods in the meantime or not. The point of this from the trader's point of view is that he or she has security for payment of the price as they are still the owners.

One area where the separation of commercial and consumer transactions breaks down is in relation to the ownership of goods in sales contracts. Determining the time at which ownership is transferred from the trader to the consumer is less important than it was under the original Sale of Goods Act because becoming owner is no longer linked to the transfer of the risk of something going wrong with the goods. Nevertheless, it can be important where the seller becomes insolvent. If ownership (or the "property" as the Sale of Goods Act 1979 calls it) has passed to the consumer the goods are theirs and not available to pay

---

[9] CRA 2015 s.3(3).
[10] CRA 2015 s.4(1).

creditors. If not, even though the consumer has paid for the goods, they are available to pay off the creditors and the consumer has only a worthless right to sue the trader for breach of contract. The Sale of Goods Act has rules about how the passing of ownership is determined. These are discussed in Ch.5, paras 5–08 and 5–09, above.

Contract of hire

6–08 Section 6 clearly explains that:

> "A contract is for the hire of goods if under it the trader gives or agrees to give the consumer possession of the goods with the right to use them, subject to the terms of the contract, for a period determined in accordance with the contract."

This is what might be called simple hire and renting a car for the weekend is a good example. It is also used sometimes on a longer term basis as a means of financing the acquisition of a car when it is known as car leasing or contract hire. Here the lease is for a fixed period at a rent equivalent to the sale price of the goods and the cost of credit.

Hire-purchase

6–09 Hire-purchase agreements are a sort of hybrid between simple hire and sale. There are two conditions: the goods are hired in return for periodical payments by the consumer; and secondly ownership of the goods will be transferred to the consumer if the terms of the contract are complied with and the consumer exercises an option to buy or some other event set out in the contract occurs.[11] The typical h-p contract involves consumers paying a number of monthly or weekly instalments and one final, often quite small, optional payment at which point they become the owners of the goods. This is a form of selling on credit for until the final option payment is made the trader is the owner of the goods and thus has security for the payment of the price. It looks very similar to the conditional sale but in conditional sale the buyer must become the owner on paying all the instalments whereas in h-p, theoretically, the buyer must exercise an option to purchase before becoming owner.[12]

Contracts for transfer of goods

6–10 There can be other transactions where the exchange is not for money or, for some other reason, it is not a sales contract or an h-p agreement. An obvious example would be barter where one object is exchanged for another or the purchase of goods by means of vouchers. In the past there has been some doubt whether trading-in, common in the car trade, was sale or some other kind of transaction legally. This is of little importance under the CRA 2015.

---

[11] CRA 2015 s.7.
[12] CRA 2015 s.7(4) underlines the difference.

What are a consumer's statutory rights?

The answer to this question is found in ss.9–18 of the CRA 2015. The **6–11** rights are similar to those relating to commercial contracts so it will be possible to refer back to the discussion in Ch.5 at a number of points. In the Sale of Goods Act 1979 these rights are referred to as implied terms. They apply although the parties have not expressly said anything about them. The CRA 2015 does not speak of implied terms; instead it refers to supply of goods contracts including certain terms. The language is different but the concept is the same. Section 18 points out that apart from the terms about quality and fitness for purpose in these sections there are no other such terms unless they are express terms.

Satisfactory quality

Section 9 of the CRA 2015 states that "Every contract to supply goods is **6–12** to be treated as including a term that the quality of the goods is satisfactory". Like the same term in the Sale of Goods Act 1979, it applies despite the fact that there was no fault on the part of the seller. For a case illustrating this point look at *Frost v Ayslebury Dairy* in Ch.5 para.5–22. The term will not apply if, before the contract was made, the defect in the goods was specifically drawn to the consumer's attention or it was one which when the consumer examined the goods the examination carried out ought to have revealed.

The definition of satisfactory quality in the CRA 2015 and the 1979 are the same subject to some minor drafting points. Section 9(2) of the 2015 contains the basic definition (see 1979 Act s.14(2B)) and this is expanded on in the next subsection of each Act by setting out a list of aspects of satisfactory quality. These are fitness for purpose, appearance and finish, freedom from minor defects, safety and durability. You should refer to the discussion of this definition in Ch.5, paras 5–23 to 5–25.

Fitness for a particular purpose

Section 10 of the 2015 Act means that all contracts to supply goods **6–13** include a term that where the consumer makes known to the trader (expressly or by implication) any particular purpose for which the goods are wanted they must be reasonably fit for that purpose. It does not matter whether that is a purpose for which goods of that kind are usually supplied. You should refer to the discussion in Ch.5 para.5–26 of similar term in the 1979 Act.

Goods to be as described

Section 11 of the CRA 2015 includes a term in contracts to supply goods **6–14** by description that they will match that description. This is the equivalent of s.13 of the 1979 Act and you should refer to Ch.5 para.5–21.

Pre-contract information

6–15 The Consumer Contracts (Information, Cancellation and Additional Charges) Regulations 2013 require a trader to provide certain types of information to consumers before they make purchases. This applies in slightly different ways to sales in shops, off trade premises or by electronic means. Section 11(4) of the CRA 2015 makes information about the main characteristics of the goods which these regulations require terms of the contract. Section 12 has the same effect in relation to other pre-contract information such as price, delivery terms and, where applicable complaints handling procedures and after sales service.[13]

Goods to match sample

6–16 Goods such as carpets and wallpaper are frequently bought after being selected by looking at swatches of material. Section 13 of the CRA 2015 says that it is a term of the contract that the sample will match the goods except to the extent that any differences between the sample and the goods are brought to the consumer's attention before the contract is made. The goods must also be free from any defect that makes their quality unsatisfactory and that would not be apparent on a reasonable examination of the sample.

Goods to match model

6–17 Goods must also match any model by reference to which they were bought. This is slightly different from the previous term which deals with cases where the consumer has seen only a part of what is later bought. Here the consumer has seen a complete version of the product, perhaps a computer on display in a showroom. The computer that he acquires will often not be the one he or she has seen but one brought from the storeroom.

Trader to have right to supply the goods

6–18 Section 17 provides that the seller must have the right to supply the goods. In the case of hire this is only the right to transfer possession not ownership. All that the consumer needs in hire is the right to use the goods undisturbed by anyone else's claims. The trader can provide this without necessarily being the owner. He may have hired his own stock of goods to hire to others. In the case of sale and the other contracts to supply goods it is ownership that the trader must transfer. In addition, the trader undertakes that no other person should have rights over the goods such as a right to use them unless the consumer is made aware of this before making the contract. There is also a right that the consumer's possession of the goods should not be disturbed by anyone with rights over the goods.[14]

---

[13] In relation to E-commerce see Ch.7.
[14] CRA 2015 s.17(2).

Other issues with the right to sell in sales contracts

Section 17 means that the trader must have the right to transfer owner- **6–19** ship where there is a sales contract. Should this not be case and the true owner takes back the goods the consumer can sue for breach of this right. However, problems can arise where the seller cannot be traced or is not worth suing. It can, therefore, be important to try to show that the consumer has got ownership. The barrier to this is the general principle that those who transfer goods to others cannot confer a better title to ownership than they themselves have. This principle is set out in s.21 of the Sale of Goods Act 1979 which is still relevant to consumer sales contracts. It can work unfairly so various exceptions have been created and are usually referred to as exceptions to the *nemo dat* rule, *nemo dat* being an abbreviation for a Latin phrase meaning that you cannot give a title that you do not have. You should go back to Ch.5 paras 5–12 to 5–17 to see the various exceptions to the *nemo dat* rule. Although these are in the 1979 Act they still apply to consumer sales contracts.

What are the consumer's remedies for breach of the terms of the contract?

The CRA 2015 sets out a series of remedies which are available to a **6–20** consumer who has acquired goods which, to quote s.19 of the Act, "do not conform to the contract". Goods do not conform to the contract if:

- they are not of satisfactory quality, fit for purpose, match description, sample and model;
- have been installed incorrectly (where that was the trader's responsibility under the contract)[15];
- digital content is included in the goods and it does not conform[16]; and
- they fail to meet express terms of the contract.

The point at which goods must conform is the date of delivery but it is assumed that they did not conform at that date if they fail to do so at any time within six months of delivery unless the trader can show that they did conform during that time or the rule is incompatible with the nature of the goods. For example, the six-month rule will not help someone who tries to claim that fresh vegetables or meat do not conform by showing that they have gone off a month after purchase.[17]
The remedies are:

- short term right to reject;
- repair or replacement;
- price reduction or final right to reject.

---

[15] This is set out in CRA 2015 s.15.
[16] See CRA 2015 s.16.
[17] CRA 2015 s.19(14) and (15).

Short term right to reject

6–21 The CRA 2015 preserves what has always been the consumer's main right where goods have not met contractual standards—the right to reject. It is a very powerful remedy allowing a consumer to return the goods and demand the price back. While powerful, it is only available for 30 days after delivery. In practice, often what a consumer who has received defective goods wants is not money back but a working product either by having the faulty one repaired or replaced. To encourage such a solution the 30 day rejection period will be extended to the later of seven days after "the waiting period" or the original end of the 30 days plus the waiting period. The "waiting period" starts with the date on which the consumer requests or agrees to repair or replacement and ends when he or she receives the repaired or replacement article.[18]

To exercise the right to reject consumers need only indicate clearly that they are rejecting the goods and treating the contract as at an end.[19] The trader then has a duty to refund the price without undue delay and, in any event within 15 days,[20] and the consumer must make the goods available for collection by the trader or if agreed, return the rejected goods to the trader.[21] Where a refund is to be provided and the original payment (or part of it) was made with money, the consumer is entitled to money back not a substitute such as store vouchers or a credit note. If money was not used to pay the refund would be a return of whatever the consumer gave in exchange for the goods.[22] In hire contracts and h-p and conditional sale contracts the right to a refund only applies to anything paid for a period when the consumer got no use of the goods.[23] No fee can be imposed for making a refund.[24]

Only some of the goods may be faulty, or as the Act puts it, do not conform to the contract. Were a consumer to buy several bags of vegetables but those in one bag were rotten and the rest in good condition all the vegetables could be rejected. Section 21 allows the buyer to reject some or all of the goods that do not conform but may not reject any that do. Similarly, if the goods are being sold in instalments and some of the goods in one instalment are defective he or she may choose to reject some or all of the non-conforming goods though all the goods that do conform must be retained. This does not apply where the goods form what is called a "commercial unit". This is where division of the unit would materially impair the value of the goods or the character of the unit. A set of encyclopaedias would be a commercial unit so all or none may be rejected. The same provisions about the exercise of the right to reject partially as apply to rejection under s.20 are set out in s.21.

---

[18] CRA 2015 s.22(9).
[19] CRA 2015 s.20(5) and (6).
[20] CRA 2015 s.20(15).
[21] CRA 2015 s.20(7).
[22] CRA 2015 s.20(9)–(12).
[23] CRA 2015 s.20(13) and (14).
[24] CRA 2015 s.20(17).

Repair or replacement

A consumer may prefer to have the goods repaired or replaced or may **6–22** have to rely on this remedy because the 30-day period for rejection has expired. Section 23 requires the seller to carry out the buyer's preferred option "within a reasonable time but without causing significant inconvenience to the consumer".[25] A reasonable time or significant inconvenience depends on the nature of the goods and the purpose for which they were acquired. The seller must "bear any necessary costs incurred in [repair or replacement] (including in particular the cost of any labour, materials or postage)".[26]

The seller cannot be forced to carry out one of these remedies if it is not possible to do so or if the cost of doing so would be "disproportionate" either to carrying out the other remedy, offering a price reduction or rescinding the contract. Section 23(4) offers guidance on when one remedy is disproportionate to another. This will be the case where the cost of a remedy is unreasonable taking into account the value of the goods if they conformed to the contract, the significance of the defect and whether the alternative remedy could be effected without significant inconvenience to the buyer. This might mean that if there is a cosmetic defect on a part of a washing machine which will not be visible when it is installed, it will be difficult to insist on a repair which might be quite expensive in comparison to giving a reduction in price. Similarly, where the value of the product is low and the cost of repair would exceed that value it is unlikely that repair could be insisted upon when replacement would be a cheaper option.

Price reduction or final right to reject

If the first two remedies cannot be, or have not been, carried out price **6–23** reduction or the final right to reject may be tried. They apply where: one repair or replacement of the original goods has resulted in goods that still do not conform to the contract; repair or replacement does not work because it is impossible or disproportionate to other remedies; or the trader has failed to carry out the consumer's request for a repair or replacement within a reasonable time and without significant inconvenience to the consumer.[27] For the purposes of determining when one repair has been carried out s.24(7) states that, where the repair is carried out on the consumer's premises, the repair is not complete until the trader indicates to the consumer that the repairs are finished so a "single repair" might involve more than one visit, without triggering the right to a price reduction or the final right to reject.

Price reduction will not be available if anything transferred in return for the goods cannot be given back in its original state or cannot be divided up to provide the appropriate reduction.[28] The only guidance on

---

[25] CRA 2015 s.23(2).
[26] CRA 2015 s.23(2)(b).
[27] CRA 2015 s.24(5).
[28] CRA 2015 s.24(4).

how to calculate the price reduction is that it should be "by an appropriate amount" which can be the full price or whatever the consumer is required to transfer in return for the goods.[29]

Where the consumer's remedy is the final right to reject the process is the same as for the short term right to reject discussed above apply.[30] The consumer will only get a full refund where the right is exercised less than six months after ownership or possession of the goods has been transferred, they have been delivered and, where appropriate, been installed.[31] For motor vehicles the six-month rule does not apply at all and a deduction can be made for any use.[32] In no case may a deduction be made to take account of use in any period when the consumer had the goods only because the trader failed to collect them at an agreed time.[33] How the deduction is to be calculated is not stated.

Delivery of the wrong quantity

6–24 Where the wrong quantity of goods is delivered the whole delivery may be rejected. Should a consumer choose to keep the goods the contract rate must be paid for that amount. If more is delivered than was contracted for, the consumer has the additional option to reject the excess and keep the contracted amount.[34]

Other remedies

6–25 The CRA 2015 recognises that there may be circumstances where other remedies will be more appropriate either on their own or in conjunction with those just discussed. These could be one of the following:

- claiming damages;
- seeking an order for specific implement;
- rely on the breach to defend a claim by the trader for the unpaid price; or
- for breach of an express term, exercising a right to treat the contract as at an end.

The most common of these remedies is damages. A classic example from earlier sale legislation is *Godley v Perry* [1960] 1 W.L.R. 9.

A small boy bought a catapult which proved to be defective resulting in the loss of one of his eyes. His claim was for breach of what would now be the terms about satisfactory quality and fitness for purposes in ss.9 and 10 of the CRA 2015. It was not the trivial price of the catapult that was in issue but substantial damages to compensate for a serious personal

---

[29] CRA 2015 s.24(2).
[30] See CRA 2015 s.20.
[31] CRA 2015 s.20(8), (10) and (11).
[32] CRA 2015 s.20(10). Section 20(14) gives the Secretary of State power to extend the goods to which this exemption can apply.
[33] CRA 2015 s.20(9).
[34] CRA 2015 s.25.

injury which was a consequence of breach of contract. It is possible that damages for distress might be awarded on appropriate facts. In *Jackson v Chrysler Acceptances Ltd*[35] the trader knew that the buyer was about to go on a foreign holiday in his new car. When it proved to be faulty and spoilt the holiday by breaking down frequently damages were awarded for the distress and disappointment.

In theory an order of specific implement is possible: in practice this will be very rare as the remedy is only granted when damages are not sufficient which will not normally be the case in consumer sales. If the consumer has not paid for the defective goods he or she will not be prepared to pay for them and if the trader chooses to sue the remedy will be to set up the breach of contract as a defence.

Excluding liability

Liability for breach of the various terms included in contracts to supply **6–26** goods by the CRA 2015 cannot be excluded or restricted.[36] Excluding or restricting liability has an extended meaning and includes limiting the remedies available, imposing onerous conditions on invoking them, putting a consumer at a disadvantage as a result of pursuing a remedy or excluding or restricting the rules of evidence or procedure.[37]

Buying digital content

Digital technologies are of enormous importance. Many appliances **6–27** depend on digital technology such as mobile phones, DVD players, washing machines and car engines. "Digital products" comprise computer software, videos, films, music, games, e-books and apps amongst others. They can be supplied by means of a physical device such as music on a CD, film on a DVD or software on a disc. In addition, software is frequently downloaded over the internet and it is common to stream music or films over the same medium. Despite its importance, the legal rights of purchasers of digital products have been far from clear. The CRA 2015 improves the situation by providing a legal structure for what it terms "digital content" which is modelled on that for contracts for the supply of goods. The Consumer Contracts (Information, Cancellation and Additional Charges) Regulations 2013 ("CC Regulations") also regulate contracts for this content by requiring consumers to be given pre-contract information and cancellation rights[38] and they are discussed in Ch.7, "E-commerce".

---

[35] *Jackson v Chrysler Acceptances Ltd* [1978] R.T.R. 474.
[36] CRA 2015 s.31(1).
[37] CRA 2015 s.31(2).
[38] See Ch.7, "E-commerce".

What is digital content?

6–28 Section 2(9) uses the definition of "digital content" in the Consumer Rights Directive. It "means data which are produced and supplied in digital form". Recital 19 of the Directive shows that a wide meaning was intended as it states that the definition covers "data which are produced and supplied in digital form, such as computer programs, applications, games, music, videos or texts, irrespective of whether they are accessed through downloading or streaming, from a tangible medium or through any other means". Chapter 3 of Pt 1 of the Act deals specifically with contracts to provide digital content. It applies to contracts between traders and consumers[39] where there is agreement to pay for the content with money or where digital content (which is not otherwise available free) is supplied free with goods, digital content or services for which the consumer has paid a price. This would cover free software given away with a paid-for magazine. In both cases price includes payment by means of facilities for which money has been paid. This covers payment with virtual currency such as Bitcoins, tokens or vouchers. It does not apply merely because the trader supplies a service by which digital content reaches the consumer such as such as the film downloading site Netflix or the music streaming site Spotify.

The consumer's rights

Trader's right to supply digital content

6–29 There is a term that the trader has a right to supply the content or will have by the time it is to be supplied.[40] It refers to a right to supply rather than to transfer ownership because digital content contracts do not usually transfer ownership of any intellectual property rights to the content to the consumer who does not become the owner in the sense that a consumer purchasing goods under a contract of sale does. Normally, the trader passes on a limited right to use the digital content in certain defined circumstances, and ownership of any rights to the content usually remains with the originator of the digital content. This term cannot be excluded or restricted.[41]

Other pre-contract information included in contract

6–30 Section 37 establishes that information mentioned in Schs 1 or 2 to the Consumer Contracts (Information, Cancellation and Additional Charges) Regulations 2013[42] which does not relate to the main characteristics of the goods also forms part of the contract between the trader and the consumer.

---

[39] See para.6–05 for the meaning of these terms.
[40] CRA 2015 s.41.
[41] CRA 2015 s.47.
[42] SI 2013/3134.

Satisfactory quality

Section 34 is a carbon copy of s.9 except that in subs.(3) appear and finish **6–31** are, for obvious reasons, not included in the list of aspects.

Fitness for purpose

Section 35 mirrors s.10. **6–32**

Content to match description

Section 36 includes a term that digital content will match any description **6–33** applied to it and where a consumer has examined a trial version before buying the content must match or be better than the trial version.

Information about main characteristics, functionality and compatibility required by the CC Regulations

The other pre-contract information required by these regulations relating **6–34** to main characteristics and functionality is also included in the contract.[43]

Digital content is different from goods in that it is often possible for the manufacturer to modify it after making it available to a consumer. Section 40 sanctions this but subject to the terms about quality and description in ss.34–36 applying to the modification.

Remedies

To have a remedy a consumer must show that the digital content does not **6–35** conform to the contract. This means that it is not of satisfactory quality, fit for purpose or does not match its description. If this is the case there are two remedies: repair or replacement; and price reduction. There is no right to reject and obtain a refund as there is with goods. This is because it is not possible in any meaningful way to return digital content at least where it is not contained on some tangible medium such a disk or DVD. If it is contained on a disk there will be a contract to supply goods so rejection will apply but by virtue of s.16 because the defect in the data renders what is a contract for the supply of goods non-conforming. The right to repair or replacement follows the same pattern as that for goods and must be achieved within a reasonable time and without significant inconvenience to the consumer.[44] The right to price reduction is also similar to that for goods applying where neither repair nor replacement can be insisted upon or repair or replacement have not been carried out. The time limits and the method of refund are the same and no fee may be charged. There is one difference in that there is no limit on the number of attempts at repair. This is necessary because of the nature of some types of software which tend to come with some "bugs" which often are dealt with by updates. To limit sellers to one repair might encourage some consumers to abuse their rights.

---

[43] CRA 2015 s.37.
[44] CRA 2015 s.42.

Other remedies are also available as is the case with supply of goods contracts. These are:

- claiming damages;
- seeking an order for specific implement;
- relying on the breach to defend a claim by the trader for the unpaid price; and
- for breach of an express term, exercising a right to treat the contract as at an end.

Damage to a device or other digital content

6–36 Digital content may contains viruses that corrupt other data contained on a consumer's device or damage the device itself. If it can be shown that the digital content caused damage to the consumer's device or other digital content and was caused through the trader's failure to use reasonable care and skill to prevent it, the consumer is entitled to a remedy. This can be repair, if that can be done within a reasonable time and without significantly inconveniencing the consumer, or financial compensation. The conditions about time limits and the absence of fees apply. What constitutes "reasonable care and skill" will be judged against the standards of the profession.

Exclusion of liability

6–37 The terms about satisfactory quality, fitness for purpose, description and the right to supply cannot be excluded or restricted. Exclusion and restriction have an extended meaning.

Services

6–38 An important part of modern economies are services industries. These include professional services such as those of solicitors, accountants and doctors and the services of plumbers, joiners, electricians, hairdressers and motor mechanics. Some of these services are what might be termed pure services in that what one gets is purely the skill of the practitioner and there is nothing tangible. This is the case with a lawyer where the client is seeking advice. In other cases the services entails the exercise of skill as well as the production of something tangible. The services of a car mechanic would be an example. Mechanics use their skill to diagnose the condition of a car but completing the job will usually involve the provision of parts. Such types of service are referred to as contracts for work and materials or, in the terminology of the CRA 2015, "mixed contracts".[45] Despite their importance the law relating to services has been much less accessible than that on supply of goods. Where the latter has been set out in statute for many years, until recently, the law relating to services has been found in the common law decisions of the judges. With the enactment of the CRA 2015 that has changed. Part 1 of Ch.4 of that

---

[45] See CRA 2015 s.1(4).

Act does for contracts for services what the Sale of Goods Acts did for goods contracts.

The CRA 2015 applies to contracts for traders to supply services to consumers. "Consumer" and "trader" are defined in the same way as for the other contracts covered earlier in this chapter. Contracts of employment and apprenticeship are not included and there is power for the Secretary of State to add further exceptions.[46] The structure of Pt 4 is to set out the terms that are included in contracts to supply services and then provide remedies where these terms are not observed.

Information about the trader or service to be binding

The first issue where there are disputes about a service can often be about **6–39** what exactly was agreed to be done. Section 50 goes some way to addressing this problem by including as a term of the contract anything said or written to the consumer by or on behalf of the trader about the trader or the service which the consumer took into account in deciding to contract. Similarly, things taken into account after the service started which influenced decisions about the service are terms. These things include the pre-contract information required by the CC Regulations 2013.[47]

Service to be performed with reasonable care and skill

The person carrying out the service must do so with reasonable skill and **6–40** care. This is the level of competence of the reasonable practitioner of the particular trade or profession. A simple example is provided by *McIntyre v Gallacher*.[48] Mr Gallacher was a Glasgow plumber who had been employed to carry out plumbing work in a row of tenements including sealing off some pipes. One of the pipes was not properly sealed off and water leaked causing damage to property on lower floors for which the landlord, Mr McIntyre, was liable. Evidence proved that the proper and workmanlike method of sealing a pipe was to solder it. In this case Mr Gallacher, or one of his workmen, had only hammered the end of the lead pipe together and it eventually leaked. He was thus liable for failing to carry out the job with the requisite level of skill.

Reasonable price to be paid

It is not uncommon for the parties to a contract for services to have failed **6–41** to agree a price in advance. If this is the case s.51 fills the gap by stating that the contract is to be treated as including a term that a reasonable price is to be paid.

---

[46] CRA 2015 s.47(5).
[47] See Ch.7 on E-commerce.
[48] *McIntyre v Gallacher* (1883) 11 R. 64.

Service to be performed in a reasonable time

6–42 Another common source of friction in service contracts is the time for completion of the work. Ideally, this ought to be set out in the contract but if it is not s.52 provides that the contract is treated as including a term that the service must be performed within a reasonable time.

Remedies

6–43 There are two main remedies for failure to carry out the contract: repeat performance; and price reduction. They are available where the contract has not been carried out with reasonable skill and care or terms relating to the performance of the contract which s.50 includes in the contract have been broken.[49] Section 50 also includes in the contract terms that do not relate to the performance of the contract such as the identity of the seller. If such terms are broken the remedy is price reduction as also is the case where the contract is not carried out within a reasonable time.[50] Where a consumer has the right to ask the trader for repeat performance the trader must redo all or part of the service as needed to bring it into conformity with the contract within a reasonable time and at the trader's expense.[51] Where the consumer has the right to a reduction in price, the refund must be made without undue delay and in any event within 14 calendar days of the date when the trader agreed that a refund was appropriate. It must be made using the same means as the consumer used to pay for the service unless he or she expressly agrees to a different method and no fee may be imposed for making it.[52]

The Act does not prevent other remedies being sought instead of, or in addition to, the remedies discussed above such as damages, recovery of money paid where the consumer has got nothing in return for a payment, specific implement or using the trader's breach as a defence. Damages may well be an appropriate remedy and if they are sought the normal rules about contractual damages will apply. The general rule is that damages are intended to put the consumer in the same position as if there had not been a breach. In relation to contract to supply services there may well be exceptions to the principle that damages are not normally recoverable for injury to feelings occasioned by a breach of contract.[53] It does not apply when the purpose of the contract is to provide pleasure and a classic example is the case of *Diesen v Samson*.[54] A photographer failed to turn up to take photographs of the pursuer's wedding and damages were awarded for the disappointment that this caused. Such damages have also been awarded where package holidays have failed to live up to the claims made in the brochure[55] and a firm of solicitors failed

---

[49] CRA 2015 s.54(2).
[50] CRA 2015 s.54(4).
[51] CRA 2015 s.55(2).
[52] CRA 2015 s.56.
[53] *Addis v Gramophone Co Ltd* [1909] A.C. 488.
[54] *Diesen v Samson*, 1971 S.L.T. (Sh. Ct.) 49.
[55] *Jarvis v Swans Tours Ltd* [1973] 1 Q.B. 233; *Jackson v Horizon Holidays Ltd* [1975] 1 W.L.R. 1468.

to take appropriate legal action to prevent the plaintiff's husband harassing her in breach of an injunction.[56] In *Farley v Skinner*[57] the House of Lords held that damages could be awarded on this basis but that amounts should not normally exceed £10,000.

Exclusion clauses

It is not possible for a trader to exclude liability for breach of the terms **6–44** about reasonable care and the information required to be included by s.50 as well as those on price and time. This extends beyond straightforward attempts to exclude liability to subtler ways of reducing a consumer's rights as discussed above in relation to contracts to supply goods.[58]

CONSUMER CREDIT

As a walk down any high street will show, credit is very important. On all **6–45** sides consumers are being urged to borrow money or purchase goods on credit. Credit comes in many forms. Banks and finance companies offer overdrafts and personal loans, shops sell goods on hire purchase and other forms of credit and goods and services can be paid for by credit cards. Pawnbrokers and moneylenders are also sources of credit. Because of its importance economically and the problems that it can cause for consumers, credit is heavily regulated by law. The principal controls are found in the Consumer Credit Act 1974 ("the 1974 Act") which has been amended by the Consumer Credit Act 2006, and the Financial Services and Markets Act 2000. It has also been amended more recently by regulations to make it comply with the EU's Consumer Credit Directive.

The Consumer Credit Act 1974

The 1974 Act regulates a wide range of credit transactions. However, it **6–46** should be realised that aspects of the ordinary law of contract, such as the law on formation and misrepresentation still apply, and the 1974 Act does not apply to all credit contracts, as we shall see below.

The 1974 Act applies to two types of agreement:

- credit agreements; and
- hire agreements.

---

[56] See *Heywood v Wellers (A Firm)* [1976] Q.B. 44.
[57] *Farley v Skinner* [2001] UKHL 49; [2002] 2 A.C. 732.
[58] CRA 2015 s.57.

> **Key Concept**
>
> Consumer credit is governed by the Consumer Credit Act 1974 and the Financial Services and Markets Act 2000. It covers both consumer credit and consumer hire agreements. A key idea in the Act is that of the "regulated agreement". With few exceptions, it is only regulated agreements that are covered by the Act.

Credit agreements

6–47 The 1974 Act applies to what it calls "regulated" credit agreements. To qualify an agreement must be:

> (i) with an individual; and
> (ii) either:
>
>> a debtor-creditor-supplier agreement; or
>> a debtor-creditor agreement;
>
> (iii) not be exempt.

(i) Individuals

6–48 "Individual" here means human beings as well as partnerships of not more than three partners (not more than one of whom is a limited company) and unincorporated bodies such as clubs as long as they do not consist entirely of bodies corporate and are not partnerships.

(ii) Debtor-creditor-supplier agreements

6–49 A debtor-creditor-supplier agreement can arise in three ways.[59] It occurs where a restricted use credit agreement is made to finance a transaction between a debtor and a creditor. An example would be a hire purchase or credit sale agreement where the supplier provides the finance. Where, as is probably more common, a third party provides restricted use finance this, too, is a debtor-creditor-supplier agreement if made under pre-existing arrangements, or in contemplation of future arrangements between the creditor and the supplier. The typical hire purchase arrangement, where the finance is provided by a finance company, is a good example, but credit card and check trading transactions provide further examples. The third situation deals with the case where a third party provides unrestricted use credit under pre-existing arrangements with the supplier in the knowledge that the credit is to be used to finance a transaction between the debtor and the supplier. This brings within the ambit of debtor-creditor-supplier agreements situations where a supplier, such as a retailer, has agreed to refer customers to a finance company that will

---

[59] Consumer Credit Act 1974 s.12.

provide them with loans which, although technically not limited to the purchase of a specific product, all parties know will be so used.

(iii) Debtor-creditor agreements

Restricted use credit agreements which would be debtor-creditor-supplier **6–50** agreements but for the fact that there are no pre-existing arrangements between the creditor and the supplier are known as debtor-creditor agreements. Restricted use credit arrangements to refinance any existing indebtedness of the debtor are in the same category. So are unrestricted use credit agreements which are not made by the creditor under pre-existing arrangements with a supplier.[60] Examples are bank overdrafts, moneylenders' advances and loans from pawnbrokers.

Consumer hire agreements

Section 15 of the 1974 Act defines a consumer hire agreement. It is: **6–51**

- made by an individual (the "hirer");
- for the hiring of goods to the hirer;
- not a hire purchase agreement; and
- capable of lasting for more than three months.

Typical examples of hire agreements are TV rentals. Cars are sometimes acquired in this way through what are known as finance leases. Short-term car hire for a weekend or a holiday will not be included because of the requirement to be capable of lasting for more than three months.

Exempt agreements

Agreements that would come within the definition are exempt. Most of **6–52** these are set out in the Financial Services and Markets Act 2000 (Regulated Activities) (Amendment) (No.2) Order 2013[61] ("RAO 2013") arts 60C–60H. They are:

(1) Agreements where the creditor is a local authority, building society or one of a number of other organisations listed in the section where the loan is secured on land.

(2) Agreements financing purchases of land which do not gain exemption under the previous exemptions will be exempt if the number of payments to be made does not exceed four.[62]

(3) A debtor-creditor-supplier agreement for fixed sum credit which is not hire purchase or conditional sale where the number of payments to be made by the debtor in respect of the credit does not exceed four and must be made within 12 months of the date of the agreement.

---

[60] Consumer Credit Act 1974 s.12.
[61] SI 2013/1881.
[62] Consumer Credit (Exempt Agreements) Order 1989 (SI 1989/869) art.3(1)(b).

(4) A debtor-creditor-supplier agreement which is not for hire purchase or conditional sale and provides running account credit where the whole of the credit is repayable in one instalment.

(5) A low interest exemption for debtor-creditor agreements, low being defined as an APR which does not exceed 1 per cent above the highest base rate of an English or Scottish clearing bank in the 28 days prior to the making of the agreement.[63]

(6) Some agreements with a "high net worth" person. This allows someone who is wealthy to agree not to have the protections of the Act presumably because they are thought to know how to look after themselves.

(7) Credit exceeds £25,000 or hire payments are more than £25,000 if the agreement is entered into by the debtor or hirer wholly or predominantly for the purposes of a business.

Partially regulated agreements

Small agreements

6–53 A consumer credit agreement for credit not exceeding £50 which is not a hire purchase or conditional sale agreement, a regulated consumer hire agreement that does not require the hirer to make payments exceeding £50; and a non-commercial agreement are only subject to some of the controls in the Act.

Controlling business activities

6–54 Various parts of the 1974 Act regulate the way in which those in the credit industry can carry on their businesses. In addition to the authorisation system there are controls on advertising, canvassing for business, the marketing of credit cards and the operation of credit reference agencies.

The authorisation system

6–55 The licensing system operated under the OFT has been abolished and firms in the credit industry must comply with the requirements of the Financial Services and Markets Act 2000 which requires those in the financial services industry to be "authorised" by the Financial Conduct Authority ("FCA"). There is a "general prohibition" on carrying on regulated activities unless a business is authorised or exempt in s.19 of the 2000 Act. Various activities are specified and those relating to consumer credit are to be found in the RAO 2013.[64] The list is very similar to that under the Consumer Credit Act licensing system. They are:

- lending;
- hiring;

---

[63] Consumer Credit (Exempt Agreements) Order 1989 (SI 1989/869) art.4.
[64] See RAO 2013 arts 36A to 36G, 36H to 36IA, 39D to 39L, 60B to 60K, 60N to 60R and 89A to 89D.

- credit broking;
- operating an electronic system in relation to lending;
- debt-adjusting;
- debt-counselling;
- debt-collecting;
- debt administration;
- credit information services; or
- credit reference agency.

The authorisation system is operated by the FCA is more rigorous than the previous licensing system. Firms must meet "threshold conditions", which are minimum standards set out in the Financial Services and Markets Act 2000. These involve examination of the legal status of the business, its resources, the location of its offices, the suitability of its controllers, and its business model. These requirements will be applied less rigorously in the case of firms applying for limited permission than for those seeking full permission. Limited permission activities are those where lending, credit-broking or hiring is a secondary activity or debt related activities are not for profit. An example would be a high-street retailer whose main business is selling goods. Such a retailer will often have arrangements with a finance company to provide customers with credit and will put them in touch with the finance company from which credit will be obtained. Under the legislation the retailer is a credit-broker and needs to be authorised. As selling goods is the main business and broking is a secondary activity to help finance the purchase only a limited permission authorisation is necessary. Other examples are not-for-profit debt counselling and debt adjusting, not-for-profit credit information services and some local authority lending.

Advertising controls

Advertising is regulated by the FCA as one aspect of its rules on financial **6–56** promotion. The source of its jurisdiction is s.21 of the 2000 Act but the detailed rules are in its Consumer Credit Source Book section 3 ("CONC3").[65] The principal rule of CONC3 is that all financial promotions are clear, fair and not misleading but this is supplemented by more specific rules and examples of practices that are likely to contravene the clear, fair and not misleading rule. Credit and hire advertising is also regulated by the Consumer Protection from Unfair Trading Regulations 2008 discussed below and by the self-regulatory system operated by Advertising Standards Authority ("ASA") through the British Code of Advertising Practice.

---

[65] See *https://fshandbook.info/FS/html/FCA/CONC/3* [Accessed May 15, 2015].

Canvassing

6–57 Canvassing debtor-creditor agreements (of which the most common type will be personal loans) off trade premises is a criminal offence. So is soliciting the entry of an individual into such an agreement during a visit carried out in response to a request made on a previous occasion, if the request was not in writing and signed by the person making it.

Circulars to minors

6–58 In line with the policy of protecting vulnerable consumers, the 1974 Act makes it a criminal offence to send to a person under 18 years old, with a view to financial gain, any document inviting him or her to borrow money, obtain goods or services on credit, hire goods, or even apply for information about doing any of these things.

Credit reference agencies

6–59 Credit reference agencies play an important part in the credit industry by providing information to credit granters about consumers. This often involves a credit score based on this information. Given the importance of credit scoring and access to credit, the accuracy of the information held by credit reference agencies is vital. Their existence also raises other issues related to privacy. For this reason, as well as being authorised under the 2000 Act, the 1974 Act contains protections for consumers. Section 157 imposes a duty on a creditor, owner or negotiator who turns down a credit application on the basis of information obtained by the creditor from a credit reference agency to inform the consumer of this fact and give details of the source of the information. In other cases credit providers have a duty to respond within seven working days[66] to a written request for the name and address of any credit reference agency from which information has been sought about the customer's financial standing. This obligation is complemented by s.7 of the Data Protection Act 1998 which allows consumers to see files relating to them.[67]

Key Concept

The ways in which those in the credit industry do business is heavily regulated. Of the methods used the most important is the authorisation system.

Pre-contract information

6–60 There has been widespread concern that some consumers have availed themselves of credit without fully realising what they are taking on. The legislation seeks to ensure that they are given adequate information

---

[66] See Consumer Credit (Credit Reference Agency) Regulations 2000 (SI 2000/290) reg.3.
[67] For further details on the Data Protection Act 1998, see Ch.3, "Business Regulation".

before committing themselves to a credit agreement. The Consumer Credit (Disclosure of Information) Regulations 2010 require that consumers intending to sign a credit agreement should be given a great deal of information. This includes the type of agreement, its length, the cost of credit and basic information about the lender. In addition, s.55C entitles them to request a copy of the draft agreement.

Form and content of agreements

In a further attempt to ensure that consumers know exactly what they are **6–61** doing, the form and content of regulated agreements are closely regulated.[68] The debtor or hirer must be made aware of:

- the rights and duties conferred or imposed on him by the agreement;
- the cost of credit;
- the protection and remedies available under the 1974 Act; and
- any other matters which it is desirable that creditors should know.

The Consumer Credit (Agreement) Regulations 2010[69] ("the Regulations") set out in great detail the form, content, legibility and signature of documents containing regulated consumer credit and hire agreements. Different types of agreement require different types of information to be given and the Regulations set out the requirements for each type in schedules. These have in common the fact that the kind of information which must be given falls into six main categories:

(1) heading on the first page of the document prominently stating the legal nature of the agreement;
(2) name and address of each party;
(3) financial information, such as the timing and amount of payments;
(4) the cost of credit, including the APR;
(5) other information such as details of any security provided and charges payable on default;
(6) remedies available under the Act.

The Regulations also require that there should be a signature box in an agreement and go into detail on exactly how this is to be set out. In the case of credit-token agreements the name, address and telephone number of the person to whom notice is to be given of loss or misuse must be included.

---

[68] The 1974 Act s.60.
[69] SI 2010/1014.

Proper execution of an agreement

6–62 Execution of an agreement is the technical term for the signing of it by both parties. To be properly executed, as the Act calls it, the following requirements must be complied with:

(1) the document must be in the prescribed form containing all the prescribed terms and conform to the agreement regulations;
(2) it must contain all the terms of the agreement apart from the implied terms;
(3) it must be legible;
(4) the requirements of ss.62 and 63 about supplying copies;
(5) the cancellation provisions of s.64 or the special provisions of s.58 for a consideration period where there is a heritable security;
(6) it must be signed in the prescribed manner by the debtor and the creditor or owner.[70]

Copies of the agreement

6–63 The debtor or hirer must get at least one copy of an agreement and ss.61A–63 of the 1974 Act have detailed rules about this. If the debtor signs an agreement at the same time as the creditor, a copy of the executed agreement must be given to the debtor then and there. Where an unexecuted agreement is presented to the debtor and he or she signs it but the creditor does not sign at that time, the debtor must then and there be given a copy of the unexecuted agreement. In addition, within seven days of the agreement being signed by the creditor a further copy must be sent. Where an agreement is sent to the debtor a copy must also accompany it. If the agreement has already been signed by the creditor and so becomes an executed agreement on the debtor signing it, no further copy need be sent. If, however, the creditor has not signed it at that stage a copy of the executed agreement must be sent within seven days of being signed by the creditor.

Consequences of improper execution

6–64 Where an agreement has not been properly executed it can only be enforced against a creditor or hirer by an order of the sheriff court.[71]

Withdrawal

6–65 Where the debtor or hirer has signed the agreement before the creditor has done so they will have an opportunity to withdraw what is, legally speaking, an offer. Section 57 says that no special wording is required; all that is required is that it, "indicates the intention of the [consumer] to withdraw from a prospective regulated agreement".[72] The notice of withdrawal can be written or oral and can be given to the creditor or

---

[70] Requirements 1–3 and 6 are found in the 1974 Act s.61.
[71] The 1974 Act s.65(1).
[72] The 1974 Act s.57(2).

hirer, a credit broker or supplier who is the negotiator in antecedent negotiations and any person who, in the course of a business carried on by him, acts on behalf of the debtor or hirer in any negotiations for the agreement.[73] Withdrawal has the same effect as cancellation and is discussed below.

Cancellation

As a result of the European Consumer Credit Directive, s.66A of the 1974 **6–66** Act provides a 14-day "cooling-off" period during which a consumer can, without giving any reason, cancel a consumer credit agreement. This does not apply to consumer hire agreements and some consumer credit agreements so the earlier cancellation provisions are still relevant. These cancellation rules are set out in ss.67–73 of the 1974 Act. They apply where two conditions are met:

- oral representations have been made in the presence of the debtor or hirer during the course of antecedent negotiations; and
- the subsequent agreement must not have been signed by the debtor or hirer at trade premises.

The "cooling-off" period begins when the debtor or hirer signs the unexecuted agreement. It ends five days after the second statutory notice or copy is received by the debtor or hirer. To exercise the right to cancel, a notice must be served within the cancellation period on one of a number of people. This notice, unlike a notice that one is withdrawing from a prospective agreement, must be in writing. If it is posted it is deemed to be served on the recipient at the time of posting, whether or not it ever arrives.[74] The notice can be given to the same people to whom an intention to withdraw from a prospective agreement may be sent, as well as anyone specified in the statutory cancellation notice.[75] The effect of a notice of cancellation is to cancel the agreement and any linked transaction; and to withdraw any offer by the debtor or hirer, or a relative, to enter into a linked transaction.

During the agreement

Implied terms

Credit contracts relating to goods will be contracts of sale to supply **6–67** goods governed by Pt 1 of the Consumer Rights Act 2015 discussed in Ch.6, "Sale and Supply of Goods and Digital Content". The terms included in such contracts by that Act will therefore apply.

---

[73] The 1974 Act s.175 provides that the deemed agent is under a contractual duty to the creditor or owner to transmit the notice to him forthwith.
[74] The 1974 Act s.69(7).
[75] The 1974 Act s.69(1).

Connected lender liability

6–68 When consumers are buying goods on credit they will often deal only with the supplier, for example, a shop. They will not have any contact with the finance company or bank providing the credit. Despite this, where there is a relationship between the supplier and the provider of the credit the latter may be liable for the acts or omissions of the supplier.

Section 56: liability for antecedent negotiations

6–69 Section 56 makes the finance provider liable for the statements of the supplier of the goods. It applies where a debtor-creditor-supplier transaction is involved. A typical example would arise where the consumer buys using hire purchase. The consumer will see the goods in a shop and if he or she decides to buy using hire purchase the goods are sold to the finance company and, technically, it is the finance company that sells them to the consumer. The shop drops out of the transaction. Although it will probably have known nothing about the transaction in the shop the finance company is liable for any claims made there.

Regulation 62 of the Payment Services Regulations 2009[76] provides that except where the consumer has acted fraudulently, he or she is not liable for any losses incurred in respect of an unauthorised payment transaction.

Equal liability: sections 75 and 75A

6–70 Section 75 gives consumers valuable protection in certain situations. Where it applies the consumer can make the same claims against the company providing the credit for breach of contract and misrepresentation that it can make against the supplier of the goods or services. However, four conditions must be met:

- the cash price of the goods or service being supplied must exceed £100 but not be more than £30,000 (including VAT);
- there must be a debtor-creditor-supplier agreement regulated by the 1974 Act, an agreement where credit is advanced to an individual and which is not exempt under the Act;
- the provider of the credit is in the business of giving credit and the credit agreement is made in the course of that business; and
- the credit is advanced under pre-existing arrangements, or in contemplation of future arrangements, between the provider of credit and the supplier.

One of the most common situations where connected lender liability applies is a credit card transaction such as Mastercard or Visa. Suppose that someone arranges a package holiday but after the cost has been paid but before the holiday has been taken the holiday company becomes insolvent. If the cost has been paid by credit card the consumer can look

---

[76] SI 2009/209.

to the credit card company for reimbursement. It would also apply where a consumer wished to buy a car from a motor dealer and the dealer arranged finance with a finance company with which he had pre-existing arrangements. It would not apply where the consumer wished to buy the car and went to his bank and arranged a personal loan, even where the bank was aware that the loan was specifically for the purchase of the car. In this case the credit is not advanced under pre-existing arrangements between the supplier and the bank and there is not a debtor-creditor-supplier agreement.

It has been decided by the House of Lords in *OFT v Lloyds TSB Bank Plc*[77] that this protection applies where a credit card is used abroad.

For many years the Scottish courts took the view that s.75 meant that the consumer could not only rescind the supply contract but also the credit contract. The Inner House of the Court of Session decided in *Durkin v DSG Retail*[78] that this was not possible by means of s.75 and the Supreme Court agreed but decided that it could be achieved in a different way. To quote Lord Hodge:

> "... the law implies a term into such a credit agreement that it is conditional upon the survival of the supply agreement. The debtor on rejecting the goods and thereby rescinding the supply agreement for breach of contract may also rescind the credit agreement by invoking this condition."[79]

With effect from February 1, 2011, s.75A of the 1974 Act has given similar protection where goods or services costing between £30,000 and £62,260 have been purchased. Unlike s.75, the consumer must first make reasonable efforts to resolve the dispute with the supplier before making a claim against the credit provider.

Termination

Regulated hire purchase and conditional sale agreements may be termi- **6–71** nated by the debtor at any time before the final payment falls due by giving notice to anyone who is entitled to receive payments under the agreement. To this right there are two exceptions, both relating to conditional sale agreements. Such an agreement relating to land, title to which has passed to the buyer, or one relating to goods where the property has vested in the debtor who has transferred the goods to someone else, cannot be terminated. On termination the debtor must pay the difference between what has been paid and half the total price of the goods. In making this calculation any installation charge is deducted first and the whole of that charge added as it is clearly reasonable that such a charge should be payable. It is possible that the amount due could be less if it can be shown that the creditor's loss is less.

---

[77] [2007] UKHL 48.
[78] [2010] CSIH 49.
[79] [2014] UKSC 21 at [26].

In the case of a consumer hire agreement there is also a right to terminate, but the earliest time at which this can occur is 18 months after the making of the agreement. Notice of not less than the shorter of the shortest payment interval or three months must be given. Because early termination can cause hardship to the owner there are three circumstances in which the right is not available. These are: where the total payments, ignoring sums payable on breach, exceed £1,000 in any year; where the goods are let out for the hirer's business and were selected by him and acquired by the owner at his request from a third party; and, finally, where the hirer requires the goods to re-let them in the course of business.

Early settlement

6–72 At any time during a regulated consumer credit agreement the debtor may give notice to the creditor of an intention to complete payments early.[80] This is only economic if there is a rebate on the total charge for credit and the regulations prescribe how this is to be calculated.[81]

Default

6–73 A consumer who breaks the terms of a credit agreement is said to be in default. A simple example would be where the buyer paying for goods on hire purchase fails to keep up the instalments. As credit agreements often have harsh terms which come into operation in this situation there are various protections for consumers in the 1974 Act.

Before a creditor can take action against a debtor, s.76 states that a default notice must be served specifying:

- the breach;
- what action needs to be taken to remedy it;
- if it is not capable of remedy the compensation required; and
- the date by which this must be paid has to be stated.

Where a debtor has paid one-third or more of the total price of the goods, and the property in the goods remains in the creditor, the goods are known as "protected goods". This means that the creditor is not entitled to recover possession from the debtor except on an order of the sheriff court.

Judicial control

Enforcement orders

6–74 In some cases a credit agreement can only be enforced by the creditor by getting a court order. When this has to be done ss.135 and 136 give wide powers to the sheriff to vary agreements.

---

[80] The 1974 Act s.94.
[81] See Consumer Credit (Early Settlement) Regulations 2004 (SI 2004/1483).

Time orders

Where a creditor is taking action to enforce a credit agreement, s.129 of **6–75** the 1974 Act gives wide powers to the sheriff to make time orders. These are orders which permit the sheriff to adjust the rate and time of payments of instalments by debtors, hirers or sureties. In addition, they can be used to specify the time within which a breach of an agreement, other than non-payment of money, should be rectified. There are parallel powers in relation to hire agreements in s.132.

Special powers relating to hire purchase and conditional sale agreements

In cases of hire purchase or conditional sale agreements, s.133 of the 1974 **6–76** Act contains special provisions involving "return orders" and "transfer orders". Such orders may be made where an application for an enforcement order or time order has been made, or where the creditor has brought an action to recover possession of goods. They allow a sheriff to adjust the transaction where more than one product is being bought and payments covering at least part of them have been made.

Unfair credit relationships

The power in the original Consumer Credit Act to reopen extortionate **6–77** credit bargains has been replaced by new provisions dealing with unfair credit relationships. From April 6, 2008 powers in ss.140A and 140B will apply where the relationship is unfair because of its terms, the way the creditor has exercised its rights or in any other way. A sheriff will have wide powers to alter the original agreement.

Key Concept

The Consumer Credit Act 1974 provides sheriffs with wide powers to deal with breaches of credit and hire agreements (ss.132–136). In addition to these provisions, ss.140A–140D enable sheriffs to reopen unfair credit bargains.

THE CONSUMER PROTECTION FROM UNFAIR TRADING REGULATIONS 2008

Overview of the Regulations

The Consumer Protection from Unfair Trading Regulations 2008[82] **6–78** ("CPRs") bring about a major change in the way that UK law deals with unfair trade practices directed at consumers. These practices cover a wide range of things such as misleading advertisements, high pressure selling

---

[82] SI 2008/1277.

and various scams such as misleading and dishonest mailings to people informing them that they have won prizes in lotteries. The regulations are necessary to implement a European Directive, the Unfair Commercial Practices Directive.[83] Some idea of the scale of the change may be gained by noting that it has been necessary to repeal several important pieces of existing legislation. Of these the best known is the Trade Descriptions Act 1968.

The approach of the Directive is to create what may be called a duty on traders not to trade unfairly. The Directive and the implementing Regulations start by creating a general duty prohibiting unfair practices. This is expected to act as a safety net because there are more specific rules in the directive which are expected to catch most unfair practices. The purpose of the general prohibition is to ensure that resourceful traders do not get away with dubious practices that do not fall within the letter of the other parts of the Regulations. In addition to the general duty, the Regulations ban misleading acts and misleading omissions as well as aggressive practices. There is in addition a list of 31 practices which are regarded as so serious that they are always to be considered to be unfair.

Scope of the Regulations

6–79 The Regulations principally protect consumers against unfair commercial practices. A recent amendment of the term "consumer" to mean "an individual who is acting for purposes that are wholly or mainly outside that individual's business results in some limited protection for sole traders.[84] A commercial practice:

> "[M]eans any act, omission, course of conduct, representation or commercial communication (including advertising and marketing) by a trader, which is directly connected with the promotion, sale or supply of a product to or from a consumer, whether occurring before, during or after a commercial transaction in relation to a product."

It should be noted that "product" means not just goods but also immovable property and services as well as digital content and rights and obligations and demands for payment. The definition covers practices occurring before, during and after the purchase of a product. For example, high pressure selling techniques are used by some sellers and will be covered by this definition. Practices occurring after a product has been acquired such as after sales services promised on the sale of a car or the activities of debt collectors are covered. Because the practice is to be "directly connected" to the promotion, sale or supply of a product, manufacturers' practices can be caught. The OFT's draft guidance on the

---

[83] 2005/29/EC.
[84] CPRs reg.2 as substituted by reg.2(3) of the Consumer Protection (Amendment) Regulations 2014 (SI 2014/870) in relation to contracts entered into, or payments made, on or after October 1, 2014.

regulations, *Guidance on the Consumer Protection from Unfair Trading Regulations 2008*, gave the following example:

Example

A trader makes and sells processed cheese slices to supermarkets. Although the trader does not sell directly to consumers, any labels they produces must be compliant with the CPRs as they are directly connected with the promotion and sale of the cheese slices to consumers.

The Regulations cover not only the sale or supply of a product *to* a consumer they also cover sale or supply by a consumer to a trader. This would catch the situation that arose in the Trade Descriptions Act 1968 case of *Fletcher v Budgen*[85] where a second-hand car dealer made false statements about a car which was traded-in in order to offer a lower price for it. The purpose of the Regulations is to protect the economic interests of consumers. They are not concerned with questions of taste or decency.

Key Concept

The Consumer Protection from Unfair Trading Practices Regulations 2008 protects consumers rather than businesses (with a minor exception for sole traders) against unfair commercial practices. A consumer is an individual who is acting wholly or mainly for purposes which are outside business.

Unfair practices

Regulation 3 is the key to the regulations. It states that, "[u]nfair com- **6–80** mercial practices are prohibited" and then goes on to set out four situations when practices are unfair. These are:

- aggressive practices;
- breaches of the general prohibition (reg.3(3));
- misleading actions;
- misleading omissions; and
- banned practices.

Because the general prohibition is the least likely to be relevant in practice and the practices on the banned list the most likely it is useful to look at these categories in reverse order.

---

[85] [1974] 1 W.L.R. 1056.

Schedule 1: banned practices

6–81 Schedule 1 to the Regulations sets out 31 practices which are considered unfair in all circumstances. There is an outright ban on these practices. The first four involve false claims about involvement in trade organisations or schemes such as being a member of a code of conduct, that a code has been endorsed by a public body when it has not or that the trader or its products have been endorsed by someone when they have not. An example would be a claim by a plumber that he was on the Gas Safe Register of tradespeople qualified to work on gas appliances when he was not.

"Bait advertising" and "bait and switch" advertising are on the list. These are advertisements about products that the seller does not intend to sell. Also included are false claims that a product can legally be sold, that it will be available for only a limited time, that consumers' legal rights are a distinctive feature of an offer or that the trader is about to close down. Various marketing scams are included such as pyramid schemes, bogus prize schemes and "free" gifts which involve further payments beyond the cost of responding or collecting the product. The CPRs were successfully used to deal with misleading premium-rate prize draw scratch-card promotions in the first reported case on the CPRs, *Office of Fair Trading v Purely Creative Ltd.*[86] False claims that a product can facilitate winning at games of chance, cure illnesses, dysfunctions or malformations or that an after sales service is available outside the state in which it has been sold or will be available are all banned as is failing to honour an undertaking to provide after-sales service to consumers in a language other than that in which the trader has communicated with those consumers.

Direct appeals to children to buy advertised products or persuade their parents to do so are banned. Creating the impression that the consumer cannot leave the premises until a contract is formed, a practice associated with time-share marketing, conducting personal visits to the consumer's home, ignoring the consumer's request to leave or not to return, and making persistent and unwanted solicitations by telephone, fax, email or other remote means are also prohibited. Traders pretending not to be selling as traders are also included as are unsolicited product scams where goods are sent to someone who has not ordered them and then followed up with demands for payment. Using editorial content in the media to promote a product where a trader has paid for the promotion without making that clear, sometimes referred to as "advertorials", and promoting a product of a particular manufacturer in such a way as to mislead consumers to think that it is that of another manufacturer are also on the banned list.

---

[86] [2011] EWHC 106.

Misleading practices

Misleading actions (regulation 5)

Misleading action occurs when a practice misleads through the infor- **6–82** mation it contains, or its deceptive presentation, and causes or is likely to cause the average consumer to take a different decision. For instance, if a trader falsely tells a consumer that his boiler cannot be repaired and he will need a new one, he will have committed a misleading action.

There are three ways in which actions can be misleading:

    (i) misleading information generally;
   (ii) creating confusion with competitors' products; and
  (iii) failing to honour firm commitments made in a code of conduct.

(i) Misleading information generally. These are actions that mislead **6–83** because:

- they contain false information or they deceive or are likely to deceive the average consumer (even if the information they contain is factually correct);
- the false information, or deception, relates to one or more pieces of information in a list (see below); and
- the average consumer takes, or is likely to take, a different decision as a result. This is called a "transactional decision" in the regulations.

The false information must relate to various things set out in reg.5(4). The most important of these are likely to be the price and the main characteristics of the product. The "main characteristics" comprise a long list set out in reg.5(5), which is not unlike the list of features of a trade description contained in s.2 of the Trade Descriptions Act 1968. These include such things as the availability of the product, its benefits, risks, composition and accessories, fitness for purpose, quantity, origin, expected results from use and the results of tests carried out on it.

This is the part of the Regulations that will catch the common practice of "clocking" a car, that is, turning back the odometer or mileage recorder. This could come under "usage" in reg.5(5) or could more generally be within the general meaning of "main characteristic". Remembering that the Regulations cover services as well as goods, another example could involve a package holiday. Suppose that a holiday brochure says that the hotel has a swimming pool and that when customers arrive there it is still under construction. This will be an example of false information about a main characteristic.

A claim does not have to be false if the overall effect is deceptive. An example could be a jar of moisturising cream sold in jars which have false bottoms and are substantially larger in appearance than required to hold the amount of cream. Even though the weight of the contents is accurately printed on the jar it could well be that this form of packaging would amount to a misleading practice.

6–84 (ii) Creating confusion with a competitor's products. The second way in which a practice may amount to a misleading action is where it is marketed in a way which creates confusion with any products, trademarks, trade names or other distinguishing marks of a competitor. This is designed to deal with practices such as copycat marketing where a manufacturer tries to benefit from the popularity of a successful product by producing one that looks similar to it. Again it must be shown that the average consumer would be likely to take a different decision.

6–85 (iii) Failing to honour firm commitments made in a code of conduct. The third kind of misleading actions arise where a trader who has undertaken to be bound by a code of conduct indicates that he is bound by it but fails to comply with a firm and verifiable commitment in it.

Example[87]

A trader is a member of a code of practice that promotes the sustainable use of wood and uses the code's logo in an advertising campaign. The code of practice contains a commitment that its members will not use hardwood from unsustainable sources. However, it is found that the product advertised by the trader contains hardwood from endangered rainforests. This practice is a breach of a firm and verifiable commitment.

This misleading action must be likely to cause the average consumer to make a different decision.

Misleading omissions (regulation 6)

6–86 Practices may be misleading not only because they positively mislead by giving false information but also by failing to give consumers the information they need to make an informed choice. Regulation 6 deals with this aspect of unfair practices. A practice will be misleading by omission if it:

- omits material information;
- hides material information;
- provides material information in a manner which is unclear, unintelligible, ambiguous or untimely; or
- fails to identify its commercial intent.

It must also be shown that the average consumer would take a different decision as a result.

When deciding whether a practice misleads by omission, the courts will take account of the context and reg.6(2) says that certain factors should be taken into account. These are the features and circumstances of the

---

[87] The OFT's *Guidance on the Consumer Protection from Unfair Trading Regulations 2008.*

commercial practice, the limitations of the medium used to communicate the commercial practice, and where the medium used to communicate the commercial practice imposes limitations of space or time, any measures taken by the trader to make the information available to consumers by other means. Where, for example, a cereal bar wrapper contained an offer of a t-shirt at a low price as a promotional offer it might be difficult to include comprehensive information. An indication that full details of the offer could be found on the manufacturer's website might prevent a breach of the Regulations.

The missing information must be "material" which means information that the average consumer needs, in the context, to make informed decisions. It includes any information required by European derived ("EU") law, such as the Package Travel, Package Holidays and Package Tours Regulations 1992[88] and the Consumer Protection (Distance Selling) Regulations 2000.[89] What information is required may range from a very small amount of information for simple products, to more information for complex products.

If a commercial practice is what is called an "invitation to purchase" it must provide certain information or there will be a misleading omission. An "invitation to purchase" is "a commercial communication which indicates characteristics of the product and the price in a way appropriate to the means of that commercial communication and thereby enables the consumer to make a purchase".[90] It is not to be confused with the idea of an invitation to treat found in contract law though in some circumstances there may be overlap.

There will be many kinds of invitations to purchase. Newspaper advertisements containing prices will be examples as would an interactive TV advertisement through which consumers can place orders and restaurant menus. On the other hand, many advertisements which are designed to promote the trader's brand will not be. Newspapers, magazines and billboards often contain advertisements which merely draw attention to a product or company without giving specific details about price or the characteristics of products.

Where an advertisement is an invitation to purchase, reg.6(4) requires further information to be provided. Subject to the same considerations about the context and the limitations of the communication medium as we have seen apply to misleading omissions generally, the information must be provided in a clear, unambiguous, intelligible and timely manner.

The information that is deemed to be material in invitations to purchase includes:

- the main characteristics of the product;
- the identity of the trader;
- the trader's address;
- the price of the product (including taxes);

---

[88] SI 1992/3288.
[89] SI 2000/2334.
[90] CPRs reg.2(1).

- any arrangements for payment, delivery or performance; and
- complaint handling that differ from consumers' reasonable expectations.

Aggressive practices (regulation 7)

6–87 Regulation 7 sets out the circumstances in which a practice will be regarded as aggressive. There are three requirements:

- that harassment, coercion or undue influence has been used by a trader;
- that this has significantly impaired or is likely significantly to impair the average consumer's freedom of choice; and
- that this has caused or is likely to cause the average consumer to take a different decision.[91]

The aggressive practices which might be regarded as aggressive will be numerous and varied. In *Office of Fair Trading v Ashbourne Management Services Ltd*[92] the English High Court found that because agreements for gym memberships were not consumer credit agreements the threat to report customers to a credit reference agency could be seen as aggressive because no credit agreement had been breached. The draft guidance on the regulations given by the OFT cites the example of a mechanic who has a consumer's car at his garage and has done more work than agreed, and who refuses to return the car to the consumer until he is paid in full for the work. The mechanic did not check with the consumer before he went ahead with the extra work. As he has the car, he has power over the consumer's decision to pay for the unauthorised work. He has exploited his position of power, by demanding payment for doing more than was agreed and refusing to return the vehicle until the consumer has paid for all the work.

The exploitation of specific misfortune is one of the factors to be taken into account in deciding if a practice is aggressive. This could arise where staff working in a funeral parlour put pressure on a recently bereaved relative, who is deciding on a coffin, to buy a more expensive coffin as a better mark of respect. This might be seen as coercion or undue influence. An example of harassment might arise where a debt collector persistently telephones a debtor late at night or telephones the debtor at his workplace.

The general clause

6–88 Regulation 3(1) and (3) of the CPRs set out the general prohibition on unfair business to consumer commercial practices. This can catch practices which are neither misleading nor aggressive and are not on the list of banned practices.

---

[91] CPRs reg.7(1).
[92] [2011] EWHC 1237.

To come within the general prohibition a practice must:

- contravene the requirements of professional diligence; and
- materially distort the economic behaviour of the average consumer.

Professional diligence is defined (in reg.2) as:

"The standard of special skill and care which a trader may reasonably be expected to exercise towards consumers which is commensurate with either:

(a) honest market practice in the trader's field of activity, or
(b) the general principle of good faith in the trader's field of activity, or both."

This general clause is designed as a safety net to catch practices which cannot be brought within one of the other categories. In this way it is hoped that the regulations will not be circumvented by devious traders.

Who is the "average" consumer?

Whether commercial practices are generally unfair or unfair because they **6–89** are misleading or aggressive depends on their effect on the "average consumer". It has no application to the practices in the banned list in Sch.1. It is important, therefore, to know what is meant by the "average consumer". There are three different applications of the test. First, it means the, "average consumer whom it reaches or to whom it is addressed", to quote the Directive on which the regulations are based. We know from the recitals to the directive that this means someone, "who is reasonably well-informed and reasonably observant and circumspect, taking into account social, cultural and linguistic factors".

This might not work very fairly in some circumstances so, "when a commercial practice is directed to a particular group of consumers" it is the average member of that group that is to be taken as the benchmark. For example, if a television advertisement were shown during a children's programme the test would be its effect on an average child.

Another variation of the test applies where a practice is aimed at, "a clearly identifiable group of consumers who are particularly vulnerable to the practice or the underlying product because of their mental or physical infirmity, age or credulity in a way which the trader could reasonably be expected to foresee".[93] An example might be elderly infirm people in relation to advertisements about stair lifts. In that case the test would be the effect on the average elderly consumer.

---

[93] CPRs reg.2(4) and (5).

> **Key Concept**
>
> Commercial practices are unfair if they are misleading actions, misleading omissions or one of those on the list of banned practices. In addition, a practice can be unfair because it contravenes the requirements of professional diligence. With the exception of the practices on the banned list unfairness is judged by the effect on the "average customer".

Enforcement

6–90 The CPRs will be enforced using a number of techniques invoking both civil and criminal law. In the least serious cases no formal action may be necessary and it may be more a matter of guidance and education or issuing warning letters. In more serious cases enforcers have formal options. Regulation 20(4) directs enforcers to, "have regard to the desirability of encouraging control of unfair commercial practices by such established means as it considers appropriate having regard to all the circumstances of the particular case". For example, if an enforcer is satisfied that a problem with an advertisement can be adequately dealt with by the Advertising Standards Authority which has a well-established record of dealing with complaints about advertisements it could refer the complaint to that body.

Where an informal approach or reference to established means is not appropriate, enforcers may take civil enforcement action in respect of any breach of the CPRs as community infringements under Pt 8 of the Enterprise Act 2002. Under this procedure, enforcers may apply to a court for an enforcement order to prevent community or domestic infringements. Breach of an enforcement order could be contempt of court which could lead to up to two years' imprisonment and/or an unlimited fine. This procedure is discussed in detail later in this chapter.

Breach of the regulations in almost all cases will be criminal offences. They fall into two broad categories: those involving proof of mens rea (guilty intent) and those that are strict liability offences. Regulation 8 is the mens rea offence making traders criminally liable for breach of the general duty not to trade unfairly contained in reg.3. To prove this offence it must be shown that the trader "knowingly or recklessly" engaged in a commercial practice which contravenes the requirements of professional diligence; and "the practice materially distorts or is likely to materially distort the economic behaviour of the average consumer (within the meaning of reg.3(4)) with regard to the product".

The other offences are strict liability offences of the kind that have been common in consumer protection statutes. All that is required is that the prohibited conduct is proved; it is not necessary to show any form of mens rea or guilty mind. The apparent harshness of this is ameliorated by providing certain due diligence defences. Regulation 9 makes it an offence to engage in a commercial practice which is a misleading action except for breaches of commitments in codes of conduct. Misleading omissions are offences under reg.10 and reg.11 makes aggressive practices criminal offences as well. Regulation 12 makes most of the commercial practices listed in Sch.1 criminal offences. The exceptions are the offence, in para.11 of the Schedule, of promoting a product in editorial content in the media without revealing that the material has been paid for and, somewhat surprisingly, the offence in para.28 of including in an advertisement a direct exhortation to children to buy advertised products or persuade their parents or other adults to buy advertised products for them.

The enforcement action described above is taken by the Competition and Markets Authority and district councils. An amendment to the Regulations has added Part 4A which gives consumers a private right of action which is discussed below.

Civil remedies for misleading and aggressive practices

There are common law remedies for misleading and aggressive practices **6–91** but they are of little value to consumers because, as the Law Commissions observed, "... consumers can become lost in a bewildering array of remedies, all with their own complexities and uncertainties."[94] Victims of misleading and aggressive practices can now bring civil claims for loss arising from most, but not all of the misleading and aggressive practices using remedies set out in Pt 4A of the CPRs. They do not apply to breach of the general clause or to misleading omissions.

"Products"

The remedies apply to products as defined in the way outlined in para.6– **6–92** 79. Regulation 27C(4) excludes immoveable property except an assured tenancy within the meaning of Pt 2 of the Housing (Scotland) Act 1988, i.e. most residential lettings except social housing and student accommodation, and leases of holiday accommodation. In addition, the new rights do not apply to most financial services such as pensions, mortgages, insurance and banking. Most credit agreements are also excluded except, a "restricted-use credit agreement".[95] This covers situations where the credit provided is used to finance a specific transaction between the borrower and lender, for example hire-purchase, or to finance a transaction between the borrower and a supplier, other than the lender. The reason for these exclusions is that both areas are already highly regulated.

To qualify for a remedy a consumer must meet three conditions:

Condition 1

The first condition is that the consumer has: **6–93**

---

[94] The Law Commission and the Scottish Law Commission, Joint Report on *Consumer Redress for Misleading and Aggressive Practices* (March 2012), Law Com. No.332 and Scot. Law Com. No.226, Cm 8323 para.4.2.

[95] As defined in the Financial Services and Markets Act 2000 (Regulated Activities) Order 2001 (SI 2001/544) art 60L(1).

- entered into a contract with a trader for the trader to sell or supply a product[96];
- contracted with a trader to sell or supply a product to the trader[97]; and
- made a payment to a trader for the supply of a product.

Condition 2

6–94 The consumer must show that a trader has engaged in a "prohibited practice". This can take two forms: either the trader has engaged in the practice; or a *producer* has done so and the trader is, or could reasonably be expected to be, aware of it. A *producer* is a manufacturer of goods or digital content or an importer of such things. A "prohibited practice" for the purpose of the civil remedy has a more restricted meaning than in the rest of the regulations. It means either a misleading action as defined in reg.5 or an aggressive practice as defined in reg.7.[98] There is no civil remedy for misleading omissions. The practice must also result in a decision by the consumer to enter a contract for the sale or supply of a product from the trader, for the sale of goods to a trader or the making of a payment to a trader for the supply of a product.[99] It does not cover other decisions such as wasted visits to a shop in response to an advertisement or continuing to spend time browsing on a website which would be covered under the main version of the definition under reg.2.

Condition 3

6–95 The third condition is that the prohibited practice is a significant factor in the consumer's decision to enter into the contract or make the payment.

Remedies

6–96 There are two tiers of remedies: the tier 1 or standard remedies are the right to unwind the transaction or obtain a discount on the price; and the tier 2 remedies are damages for indirect economic losses and distress and inconvenience. The right to unwind means that the consumer receives a refund of money paid and is released from any future obligations. If unwinding is not possible the consumer may receive a discount on the purchase price on a sliding scale from 25–100 per cent. The tier 1 remedies apply on a strict liability basis with the amount being based on the price paid and without the need for evidence of loss. Tier 2 remedies, on the other, hand apply only if the consumer proves loss and are subject to a due diligence defence for the trader. The remedies as they apply to business to consumer and consumer to business transactions as well as improper payments are discussed in more detail below.

---

[96] CPRs reg.27A(2)(a).
[97] CPRs reg.27A(2)(b) Excluded from this category is a transaction where the trader is also supplying or agreeing to supply a product to the consumer, as well as paying a sum of money for the consumer's product.
[98] CPRs reg.27B.
[99] CPRs reg.27(B)(2).

Tier 1

Unwinding business to consumer transactions

The right to unwind allows the consumer to undo the transaction they **6–97**
entered into, restoring the consumer to the position he or she was in
before entering the contract or making the payment. The consumer must
indicate within 90 days ("the relevant period") that he or she is rejecting
the product and this can be done in any manner that is clear".[100] The 90-
day period starts running from the latest of:

- when the goods or digital content are first delivered;
- when the performance of the service begins;
- when the lease begins; or
- the right is first exercisable.[101]

The right to unwind can only apply if the product is capable of being
rejected so, if the goods have been fully consumed, or the service was fully
performed, it is no-longer possible to restore the parties to the position
they were in before the misleading or aggressive practice, and the right to
unwind cannot apply. However, it is enough that it is possible to return
some element of the product. In respect of services which cannot be
returned in a meaningful way it is enough that the consumer rejected
some element of the service before it is fully performed and in the case of
a right that it has not been fully exercised.

The effect of establishing a right to unwind is that "the contract comes
to an end so that the consumer and the trader are released from their
obligations under it".[102] Money paid by the consumer must be refunded
and there is normally no allowance for use of the product that the consumer may have had. However, if the contract was for the continuous or
regular supply of goods or services and the consumer has consumed the
goods or services for more than one month there can be a deduction
reflecting the value that the consumer has received.[103]

Where the contract is for the sale or supply of goods the consumer
must make the goods available for collection but does not have to take
them back to the trader. In some situations, the trading-in of a car would
be a common example, the consumer may have paid over money and
transferred non-monetary items. Here the trader, in addition to refunding
the money, must return the non-monetary items transferred prior to the
unwinding of the contract.[104] If it is not possible to substitute the same
thing that was transferred the consumer is entitled to receive back
whatever was transferred, in its original state, for example a traded-in

---

[100] CPRs reg.27E(2).
[101] CPRs reg.27E(4).
[102] CPRs reg.27F(1)(a).
[103] CPRs reg.27F(7).
[104] CPRs reg.27F(4).

vehicle.[105] If this is not possible, then the consumer has to be paid the market price of the transferred item when the product was rejected.

Unwinding consumer to business contracts

6–98 Where a consumer has sold goods to the trader as a result of a misleading or aggressive practice the remedy of unwinding operates slightly differently. The 90-day time limit does not apply. The consumer has to give a clear indication that the contract has ended[106] and both the trader and consumer are released from their obligations.[107] If it is possible for the trader to return the consumer's goods in the same condition as when sold by the consumer, the consumer can get the goods back and has to refund the trader any sum the trader had paid for the goods.[108] If return of the goods, in the same condition, is not possible and the market price of the goods sold to the trader exceeds the price paid by the trader, the consumer is entitled to be paid the excess amount.[109]

Unwinding improper payments

6–99 There is also a right to unwind an improper payment which a consumer has been pressured into making and again the 90-day limit does not apply. This remedy only applies to payments which were not owed either in full or in part. It does not apply where a payment is due as where a consumer has bought goods and paid following misleading statements or threats. There may be a right to tier 2 damages remedies under reg.27J discussed below where there is evidence of distress or other financial loss.

A discount

6–100 If the right to unwind is no longer available either because the 90-day limit has expired or the product has been consumed there is still the possibility of compensation by way of a cash discount. Discounts apply where the cost of the product is not more than £5,000. Where payments have been made "the relevant percentage" can be ordered to be repaid and where they have yet to be made can be reduced. The relevant percentage is a series of bands: 25 per cent if the malpractice is more than minor; 50 per cent if it is significant; 75 per cent if it is serious; and 100 per cent if it is very serious. A minor transgression does not qualify for any reduction.

Where the cost of the product is over £5,000, the consumer paid more than the market price for the product and there is clear evidence of the difference between the market price and the contract price the discount percentage is the percentage difference between the market price and the contract price.[110] Suppose that a "clocked" car is sold for £10,000 when

---

[105] CPRs reg.27(5).
[106] CPRs reg.27G(2) and (3).
[107] CPRs reg.27G(1)(a).
[108] CPRs reg.27G(5).
[109] CPRs reg.27G(6).
[110] CPRs reg.27I(6) and (7)

the market price of the car showing the real mileage would have been £6,000. The percentage difference between these prices is 40 per cent so the consumer would be entitled to a discount of £4,000.[111]

Tier 2 remedy: damages

6–101

In addition to the tier 1 remedies discussed above, a consumer may be able to obtain compensation for two other forms of loss which resemble traditional damages. These are consequential financial loss and damages for alarm, distress or physical inconvenience. These second tier remedies for indirect losses are provided only if the consumer can prove that the practice caused actual loss, meeting a "but for" test of causation.[112] The consumer must also show that the loss was reasonably foreseeable when the prohibited practice occurred[113] which applies the usual test for the recovery of damages for breach of civil obligations.

The Law Commissions suggested that examples of such indirect financial losses might include the costs of installing goods, or disposing of an existing product as where a consumer who is sold a new bed in an aggressive way then throws away the old bed to make room for it.[114] Damages for distress and inconvenience are also available in the same way as they are currently available for breach of contract. The most likely occasion for such damages will be where there has been an aggressive practice. A novel feature of the damages remedy is that there is a due diligence defence.[115] It operates where traders can show that a misleading or aggressive practice was due to a mistake, reliance on information supplied to them by another person, the act or default of a person other than the trader, an accident, or another cause beyond the trader's control, and the trader took all reasonable precautions and exercised all due diligence to avoid the occurrence of the prohibited practice.

Timeshare

6–102

Timeshare is a right to use accommodation at a holiday development or resort for a specified number of weeks each year over a specified period of time or in perpetuity. To acquire this right an "owner" pays a lump sum to a "developer". In addition, there are usually annual service charges and there may also be optional annual fees for participation in a scheme to exchange timeshares with others. There have been many complaints about sharp practice in the timeshare market and as a result the UK timeshare industry was first specifically regulated by the Timeshare Act

---

[111] For other examples of the operation of the discount rules see Department of Business Innovation and Skills, *Misleading and Aggressive Commercial Practices—New Private Rights for Consumers Guidance on the Consumer Protection (Amendment) Regulations 2014* (August 2014), p.13.

[112] CPRs reg.27J(1).

[113] CPRs reg.21J(2).

[114] Law Commission (Consultation Paper No.199) and the Scottish Law Commission (Discussion Paper No.149), *Consumer Redress for Misleading and Aggressive Practices—A Joint Consultation Paper* (2011), para.14.58.

[115] CPRs reg.27J(5).

1992 with amending legislation being introduced to implement the first EC Timeshare Directive. Since then, the provision of timeshare has evolved and new long term holiday products requiring similar levels of cost and commitment by consumers have appeared on the market. These new holiday products and certain other services related to timeshare, such as resale contracts and exchange contracts were not regulated under EC law or domestic law. With effect from February 23, 2011 the Timeshare, Holiday Products, Resale and Exchange Contracts Regulations 2010[116] regulate this area. They were necessary to implement the second EU Timeshare Directive of 2008 and repeal the earlier legislation.

The approach of the new regulations is similar to the earlier legislation. They first try to ensure that consumers make a properly informed decision to buy a timeshare or other product known as "holiday accommodation contracts", and then to give a period for reflection during which they can cancel the arrangement. To further the first objective Pt 3 of the regulations requires sellers to provide anyone who requests it with information about the accommodation. Failure to do so is a criminal offence. If the consumer purchases a timeshare this information is deemed to be a term of the contract. To combat the many complaints about high pressure selling methods Pt 5 of the regulations state that a cooling-off period must be provided during which the consumer can choose to cancel the contract. Consumers who have entered into a holiday accommodation contracts must be given a notice informing them of this right and the cooling-off period must be at least 14 days from the date of the contract. Not only may consumers withdraw from the contract during the cooling-off period, the operator cannot enforce the agreement during that period. That means, for example, that the seller may not ask for or accept any money from the consumer during it. The 14-day cooling-off period will be extended to three months and 10 days if the operator fails to include certain information which must be given under Pt 3 about the contract. Contracts will often have been financed by credit agreements and the Regulations provide that on cancellation the credit agreement automatically comes to an end at no cost to the consumer.

6–103   **Estate agency**

Estate agency has been the subject of much criticism over many years because of the sharp practices of a minority of those involved in it.[117] The Estate Agents Act 1979 ("the 1979 Act") controls certain aspects of the work of estate agents. Following the abolition of the OFT it is enforced by a "lead enforcement authority", currently the National Trading Standards Estate Agency Team of Powys County Council.[118] The 1979 Act does not control entry into the profession: instead, it creates a system

---

[116] SI 2010/2960.
[117] See the Office of Fair Trading, *Estate Agency: A report by the Director-General of Fair Trading* (March, 1990).
[118] See Estate Agents Act 1979 ss.3 and 26(1).

of negative licensing. The lead enforcement authority is given powers to ban persons from acting as estate agents if it finds that they are unfit to do so. The grounds which may render a person unfit include convictions for fraud, dishonesty or violence; convictions for breach of the 1979 Act; failure to comply with other obligations under the 1979 Act; and discrimination.

In addition, ss.12–21 impose duties on estate agents. They must give certain information about their charges and when these are payable. There is a duty to declare any conflict of interest or personal interest in the transaction. Where deposits are taken from a purchaser, there are duties relating to keeping the money in a clients' account. Failure to observe the duty to provide the client with information about charges results in the contract being unenforceable without the approval of the sheriff.[119] Section 23A of the 1979 Act requires estate agents to be members of a redress scheme approved by the Secretary of State and three such schemes exist.

Enforcement orders

6–104

Under Pt 8 of the Enterprise Act 2002, the CMA, trading standards authorities, regulators of particular industries such as gas, electricity and telecommunications and other designated enforcement bodies such as the consumer organisation *Which?*, can apply to the courts to stop traders infringing a wide range of consumer protection legislation. This power is not designed to deal with the complaints of individual consumers. To obtain an enforcement order it must be shown that the conduct of the trader is harming the "collective interests of consumers". These orders are known as enforcement orders. Breach of an enforcement order is a contempt of court and could result in a fine or imprisonment.

Enforcers can also use enforcement orders to clamp down on traders who fail to carry out a service with reasonable care and skill. The CMA is responsible for co-ordinating enforcement action under the regulations.

Who can seek enforcement orders?

6–105

Under Pt 8 of the Act there are three types of enforcers, outlined below.

(i) General enforcers

In addition to the CMA, the Trading Standards Service.

(ii) Designated enforcers

- the Civil Aviation Authority;
- the Director General of Electricity Supply for Northern Ireland;
- the Director General of Gas for Northern Ireland;
- Ofcom;
- the Office of Communications;

---

[119] The 1979 Act s.18(6).

- the Water Services Regulation Authority;
- the Gas and Electricity Markets Authority;
- the Information Commissioner;
- the Office of Rail Regulation;
- the Financial Conduct Authority; and
- Consumers' Association (*Which?*).

(iii) Community enforcers

Community enforcers are entities from other EEA States that are listed in the Official Journal of the European Communities. These enforcers may apply for injunctions in other Member States.

▼ CHAPTER SUMMARY

6–106

(1) Consumer credit is governed by the 1974 Act and the Financial Services and Markets Act 2000. It covers both consumer credit and consumer hire agreements

(2) A key idea in the Act is that of the "regulated agreement". With few exceptions, it is only regulated agreements that are covered by the Act.

(3) A regulated consumer credit agreement is (see s.15) one:

    (i) with an individual;

    (ii) either:

        a debtor-creditor-supplier agreement; or

        a debtor-creditor agreement; and

    (iii) not exempt.

"Individual" here means human beings as well as small partnerships.

(4) A regulated consumer hire agreement (see s.16) is:

- made by an individual (the "hirer");
- for the hiring of goods to the hirer;
- not a hire purchase agreement;
- capable of lasting for more than three months.

(5) Consumers are protected in several ways.

    (a) Control of business practices:

- Those in the credit industry must be authorised by the FCA.
- Advertising is controlled.
- Loans cannot be sold door-to-door.
- Credit cards can only be sent to those who request them.

    (b) Controls on making a credit agreement:

- Credit documents must be in the right form.
- Copies must be given to the consumer.
- In some cases there is a cooling-off period allowing a consumer to have second thoughts (ss.67–73).

    (c) Protection during the agreement:

- Connected lender liability—see ss.56 and 75.
- On s.75 see *OFT v Lloyds TSB Bank Plc* (2007).

- Right to terminate (ss.99–104).
- Early settlement (ss.94–97).

(d) Protection of those in financial difficulty:

- Goods on hire purchase cannot be repossessed if "protected" (s.90).
- Creditors can only take action against a consumer who is in breach of an agreement if a default notice has been served.
- Sheriffs have wide powers to deal with breaches of credit and hire agreements (ss.132–136).
- These include power to reopen unfair credit bargains (ss.140A–140D).

(6) A wide range of trading practices is prohibited by the Consumer Protection from Unfair Trading Regulations 2008.

What the CPRs call "commercial practices" will be considered unfair if:

- a misleading action;
- a misleading omission;
- aggressive;
- one of a number of specific practices; and
- does not meet the standard of "professional diligence" expected of traders.

Unfairness is generally tested by asking if an "average consumer" would be misled.

Unfair practices in many cases are criminal offences but are more likely to be dealt with by administrative action by the Competition and Markets Authority or local trading standards officers.

? QUICK QUIZ

- Which Act would you consult if you bought digital content which turned out to be defective?
- What are your remedies if a TV you have bought has a fault?
- Which are the main statutes governing consumer credit?
- Which two categories of agreement do the Acts referred to in the previous question cover?
- Name two ways in which the activities of traders in the credit industry are controlled.
- Who runs the system of authorising firms in the credit industry?
- What is connected lender liability?
- Why were the Consumer Protection from Unfair Trading Regulations 2008 introduced?
- As well as a general ban on unfair practices the CPRs ban four different types of unfair practice. Name them.
- Describe a specific practice banned by the CPRs.
- What is meant in the CPRs by the "average consumer"?
- What methods are used to enforce the Consumer Protection from Unfair Trading Regulations 2008?

- Name other legislation controlling a trade practice.

📖 FURTHER READING

➢ Cowan Ervine, *Consumer Law in Scotland*, 5th edn (Edinburgh: W. Green, 2015).

🖱 RELEVANT WEBLINKS

➢ Department for Business Innovation and Skills: *https:// www.gov.uk/government/organisations/department-for-business-innovation-skills* [Accessed May 15, 2015].
➢ Competition and Markets Authority: *www.gov.uk/government/ organisations/competition-and-markets-authority* [Accessed May 15, 2015].

Chapter 7   E-commerce

GILLIAN BLACK AND AMY PAIRMAN[1]

► CHAPTER OVERVIEW

Electronic commerce, or e-commerce, is the term usually applied to **7–01** commercial transactions concluded online or by way of email. Typically this will refer to buying and selling goods and services over the internet, and this chapter will focus on the legal regulation of such transactions. These regulations apply both where the goods or services are provided online, such as software or music downloads, and where they are provided in real-time, such as the physical delivery of books, DVDs, or other purchases ordered online. The chapter will start with a short introduction to e-commerce and the need to regulate it, and then look at two areas: (i) the Electronic Commerce (EC Directive) Regulations 2002[2]; and (ii) the Consumer Contracts (Information, Cancellation and Additional Charges) Regulations.[3]

This chapter will not discuss the new Consumer Rights Act 2015. Instead the focus will be on e-commerce as regulated by the two above mentioned pieces of legislation. For a more general discussion of Consumer Protection, and the potential impact of the new Consumer Rights Act 2015, Chapters 5 and 6 should be consulted.

✓ OUTCOMES

By the end of this chapter you should: **7–02**

- ✓ understand the significance of e-commerce in an economic and political context;
- ✓ understand the legal regulation of contracts concluded online;
- ✓ be familiar with the obligations imposed on service providers by the Electronic Commerce (EC Directive) Regulations 2002;
- ✓ know what traders must do to comply with their obligations under the Consumer Contracts (Information, Cancellation and Additional Charges) Regulations 2013; and

---

[1] Senior Lecturer in Law, University of Edinburgh, and Trainee Solicitor, Brodies LLP.
[2] SI 2002/2013.
[3] SI 2013/3134.

✓ understand the protection given to consumers under the Consumer Contracts (Information, Cancellation and Additional Charges) Regulations 2013.

INTRODUCTION

Why regulate e-commerce?

7–03 When the internet first came to prominence (in the early to mid-1990s) there was some question as to whether it was possible or desirable to regulate its use, particularly the World Wide Web.[4] Early users of the internet saw it as a global, unregulated space. However, with increasing use of the internet in everyday life, especially in commerce, the need for regulation increased. Governments had a vested interest in ensuring safe access to the internet, in order to promote business interests and protect consumers. Recognising the excellent opportunity provided by the internet to promote the freedoms of the EU, particularly regarding the provision of goods and services, the EU has led the way in promoting consumer confidence and opening up the internal market online. Thus, a small trader in rural Spain can now access over 500 million people in 28 Member States. The same trader can combine traditional retail practices with online e-tailing (known as "bricks and clicks") or can operate purely online, either independently or through a third party site, such as eBay, for example.

The main advantages of trading online for businesses are access to a wider (and far-flung) customer base; the opportunity to offer more specialised or tailored goods or services; the low start-up costs, especially with regard to physical premises; and the ability to market and promote products and services at a relatively low cost. For consumers, the primary benefits are the much wider range of goods and services available, which can be accessed with ease through online searches; the quantity of information and ability to compare different goods and services, and to compare the same goods and services provided by different e-tailers; and the "open all hours" availability of the web. Additionally, the cost-savings afforded to suppliers by operating online can be passed onto the consumer through lower prices.

Although figures for the value of e-commerce vary widely, recent data from the Office for National Statistics indicates that online retailing made up 11.3 per cent of total retail sales in the UK in December 2014.[5] This is the equivalent of £741.9million per week, on average. These figures can be compared with those from April 2007, when online sales amounted to

---

[4] The internet is the term for the world-wide network which enables computers to communicate, and which hosts, among other things, the World Wide Web. The internet also enables email communication. The Web, or WWW, is probably the best known element of the internet, and consists of billions of webpages which provide information, and enable global research and commerce on an unprecedented scale.

[5] Office for National Statistics, *Statistical Bulletin*, Retail Sales, December 2014. Available at: *http://www.ons.gov.uk/ons/dcp171778_392208.pdf* [Accessed May 15, 2015].

£159.9million per week, and comprised only 3.1 per cent of total retail sales. This growth from 2007 to 2014 illustrates the ever-increasing significance of e-commerce to the UK economy.

While e-commerce is important to the UK economy, this has to be balanced against consumers' need for protection when shopping online. When consumers shop online they are at a particular disadvantage vis-à-vis their high-street counterparts: online consumers cannot inspect the goods prior to purchase; they run the risk of non-delivery; and they will not have met their supplier. In particular, the internet can grant traders much greater anonymity.[6] Given that most online purchases involve advance payment, a consumer needs protection from a potentially anonymous supplier receiving payment but failing to perform. Intervention is therefore required to protect consumers while shopping online.

Concluding contracts electronically

If persons are to trade electronically, the most important question to consider is whether, and if so, how, contracts can be concluded electronically. Scots contract law only requires a formal written contract in limited situations, most notably contracts relating to land.[7] However, the Requirements of Writing (Scotland) Act 1995 has now been amended to provide that contracts which require formal validity can be concluded electronically, where the granter has authenticated the electronic document by adding his digital signature, and this digital signature is certified in accordance with the Act.[8] This means that all contracts under Scots law can be entered into electronically, where there has been compliance with the provisions of the 1995 Act as amended. **7–04**

In all other cases, a wholly or partially verbal contract is sufficient in Scots law. Email, being similar to a telephone conversation which is written down, or a fax, is therefore sufficient to conclude a contract, albeit not one that requires formal validity.[9]

In addition to these specific provisions regarding conclusion of contracts electronically, it is important to remember that all other principles of contract law still apply in the online world. Thus, both parties to the contract must have capacity, and the validity of the contract could be challenged where there is evidence of force and fear or undue influence, for example.[10]

However, life is undeniably more complex in online transactions. There are two European Directives which regulate commercial transactions executed online, and impose additional obligations on traders who wish

---

[6] A website owner can easily be disguised. Even ".uk" websites may not be owned or operated from the UK.

[7] Requirements of Writing (Scotland) Act 1995 s.1(1) and 1(2), and Ch.4 on contract law.

[8] See ss.1(2A), 2A and 3A of the Requirements of Writing (Scotland) Act 1995, as amended by the Automated Title of Land (Electronic Communications) (Scotland) Order 2006 (SSI 2006/431), made under s.8 of the Electronic Communications Act 2000.

[9] See *Baillie Estates v Du Pont* [2009] CSIH 95 and, in England, *Proton Energy Group v Orlen Lietuva* [2013] EWHC 2872 for examples of contracts concluded via email.

[10] For further detail on these principles, see Ch.4, on contract law.

to take advantage of the internet. The next section of the chapter will examine the Electronic Commerce Directive, while the section following will consider the Consumer Contracts (Information, Cancellation and Additional Charges) Regulations.

THE ELECTRONIC COMMERCE REGULATIONS

Introductory matters and defined terms

7–05 The Electronic Commerce Directive[11] has been implemented in the UK as the Electronic Commerce (EC Directive) Regulations 2002[12] ("E-Commerce Regulations"). These Regulations are undeniably complex to interpret and apply, partly because they are heavily reliant on a number of defined terms, which are not immediately familiar to Scots lawyers. For example, the E-Commerce Regulations regulate providers of "information society services", a rather wide-ranging term which covers:

> "any service normally provided for remuneration, at a distance, by means of electronic equipment for the processing (including digital compression) and storage of data, and at the individual request of a recipient of the service."[13]

The Directive itself provides some guidance, explaining the two key concepts within the definition.[14] "At a distance" is said to require that the service be provided without the parties being simultaneously present, whilst "by electronic means" means that that the service is sent initially and received at its destination by a means of electronic equipment.

This broad concept, therefore, covers most online commercial activities,[15] including: (i) the online sale of goods and services; (ii) the activities of internet service providers ("ISPs") and email providers, who enable access to the internet and email; (iii) online or email advertising; and (iv) services which are not remunerated by those who receive them but by other parties (an example would be a free email account, which is paid for by way of advertising from third parties). Two recent cases from the European Court of Justice have highlighted the breadth of the concept with both eBay[16] and Google,[17] as an "internet referencing service", being brought within the definition. However, the cases also emphasise that for the E-Commerce Regulations to apply, all elements of this definition

---

[11] Directive 2000/31/EC of the European Parliament and of the Council of 8 June 2000 on certain legal aspects of information society services, in particular electronic commerce, in the internal market.

[12] SI 2002/2013.

[13] As defined in E-Commerce Regulations, reg.2, with reference to recital 17 of the Electronic Commerce Directive.

[14] E-Commerce Directive art.1(2).

[15] See recital 18 of the E-Commerce Directive for a detailed list of the sorts of activities covered.

[16] *L'Oreal v eBay* [2012] All E.R. (EC) 501.

[17] *Google France SARL, Google Inc v Louis Vuitton Malletier SA* [2011] Bus. L.R. 1.

must be fulfilled.[18] Face-to-face transactions will therefore be excluded by virtue of the need for the "distance" service provision. Services which are not provided at the individual request of the recipient will also be excluded, such as those broadcast television channels which are provided to all users simultaneously and not on demand.

It is very important to note that the E-Commerce Regulations extend to commercial contracts between businesses ("B2B") as well as between businesses and consumers ("B2C"). Any B2B contracts will therefore be protected, as well as B2C contracts. Service providers must ensure they comply with the E-Commerce Regulations in all their dealings, not merely consumer contracts.

However, the E-Commerce Regulations do not apply to all electronic activities conducted at a distance. The activities of a public notary and the defence of a client's interests before the courts are excluded, as are betting, gaming or lotteries where there is a financial stake involved.[19] In addition, the E-Commerce Regulations do not apply in respect of taxation, data protection matters, or any practices governed by cartel law.[20]

A further introductory point is that the E-Commerce Regulations aim **7–06** to ensure that Member States do not hinder the creation of an internal market by imposing legal barriers to cross-border online activities. Accordingly, the E-Commerce Regulations create a "coordinated field", and operate within that field. This coordinated field is defined as the field of legal regulation relating to online provision of information, advertising, shopping and contracting, and those legal requirements which concern the behaviour of the service provider and its services.[21] However, the coordinated field does not include legal requirements directed towards "goods as such", for example the regulation of the sale of goods or safety standards.[22]

Regulation 4 states that where a service provider is affected by legal requirements in the coordinated field then the applicable legal requirement shall be that of its home jurisdiction, irrespective of where the actual information society services are provided.[23] Under this provision, a service provider based in Scotland would come under the jurisdiction of Scots law, even where the services were provided in France or Italy, for example. However, regulation 4(4) states that this rule shall not apply to

---

[18] See *Google France SARL, Google Inc v Louis Vuitton Malletier SA* [2011] Bus. L.R. 1.
[19] E-Commerce Regulations reg.3(1)(d).
[20] E-Commerce Regulations reg.3(1)(a), (b), and (c).
[21] E-Commerce Regulations reg.2.
[22] This point came under discussion in a case involving sales of contact lenses online: the Directive applied in relation to the act of selling the lenses via the internet, which was within the coordinated field, whereas national rules applied in relation to the supply of lenses concerning health and safety: *Ker-Optika bt v ANTSZ Del-dunantuli Regionalis Intezete* (C-108/09) [2011] 2 C.M.L.R. 15.
[23] This is known as the "country of origin" principle, that is to say the governing law is that of the supplier's home state. Matters of jurisdiction and choice of law are very complex in cross-border transactions, because each party usually wishes to litigate in his home state. The area of law which deals with jurisdiction and choice of law is known as "international private law". This chapter will not deal with this in any detail, except to note specific principles in the various laws, where relevant.

those fields listed in the Schedule to the E-Commerce Regulations, and the Schedule includes consumer contracts.[24] Accordingly, consumer contracts must comply with the relevant laws in the *consumer's* home state, even where the activities of the service provider fall within the coordinated field.

In regulating service providers, the E-Commerce Regulations do two things. First, they impose obligations as to the provision of information and related communications (regs 6–15) and secondly, they exempt service providers from liability in certain circumstances relating to the transfer, caching and hosting of third party information (regs 17–19).

The obligations of service providers: regulations 6–15

7–07 One of the concerns with online trading is that the trader is (or can be) largely anonymous. Consumers and other businesses may not be able to discern whether the online business is a multi-national firm or is being run out of someone's kitchen.[25] Similarly, it is not always possible to tell where the online business is based.[26] The EU response to this has been to require those trading online to provide certain information to their customers, to increase transparency and accountability, and therefore increase consumer confidence.

The necessary information specified in reg.6(1) of the E-Commerce Regulations is:

(1) the name of the service provider;
(2) the geographic address at which the service provider is established;
(3) contact details of the service provider, including email address, which make it possible to "contact him rapidly and communicate with him in a direct and effective manner"[27];
(4) details of any trade register in which the service provider is registered and means of identifying him in that register;
(5) details of the relevant supervisory authority where the service provider is subject to authorisation;
(6) where the service provider exercises a regulated profession, details must be provided informing the customer of any professional body with which the service provider is registered,

---

[24] The other excluded areas under the Schedule are: "Copyright, neighbouring rights, rights referred to in Directive 87/54/EEC and Directive 96/9/EC and industrial property rights; The freedom of the parties to a contract to choose the applicable law; ... Formal validity of contracts creating or transferring rights in real estate where such contracts are subject to mandatory formal requirements of the law of the member State where the real estate is situated; The permissibility of unsolicited commercial communications by electronic mail."

[25] In the words of the famous New Yorker cartoon by Peter Steiner, "On the Internet, nobody knows you're a dog."

[26] The "top-level" domain, the ".uk" or ".ie" or ".ca" part of the url indicates where the url was registered, but does not necessarily mean the business is located there. For example, the top-level domain of Tuvalu is popular with television stations, as it is ".tv".

[27] E-Commerce Regulations reg.6(1)(c).

including jurisdiction, and reference to the professional rules applicable in that jurisdiction. Thus, a chartered accountant registered in Scotland would need to make reference on his website or in commercial communications to the Institute of Chartered Accountants of Scotland, as the relevant professional body; and

(7) finally, where the service provider is VAT registered, its identification number must be stated.

Obviously, the precise information to be provided by a service provider will depend on its circumstances, so that items 4–7 above will not be applicable in all cases. The information required by items 1–3 will, however, be relevant to all service providers, as will the further requirement in reg.6(2), which requires any pricing information to be indicated clearly and unambiguously. Specifically, the service provider must make it clear whether the price stated includes any taxes and delivery costs.

In making this information available, the service provider must comply **7–08** with the terms of reg.6, which require the information to be provided "clearly and unambiguously" and in a form which is "easily, directly and permanently accessible." This may require the service provider to provide the information separately from, or in different format to, the information society services. For example, the services may be provided by text message, but this is unlikely to fulfil the separate requirement of "permanent accessibility" in this regulation. Service providers may therefore have to take further steps to provide the reg.6 information in a form that complies with the E-Commerce Regulations.

Regulations 7 and 8 also impose requirements in relation to "commercial communications". These are defined in the E-Commerce Regulations as a communication "in any form, designed to promote, directly or indirectly, the goods, services or image of any person pursuing a commercial ... activity".[28] This would cover, for example, an email to previous customers to promote a new product. Regulation 7 requires that all commercial communications must be clearly identifiable as such and identify the person on whose behalf they are made, together with any promotional offers and the terms and conditions of those offers. Where it is an unsolicited commercial communication (for example, spam emails), it must be "clearly and unambiguously identifiable as such as soon as it is received" according to reg.8.[29] Anyone who receives spam regularly will testify to the fact that this provision is not often observed, perhaps due to the large proportion of spam which originates from outside the European Economic Area ("EEA").

---

[28] E-Commerce Regulations reg.2(1). Where the communication consists only of an address or webpage address or where it has been prepared independently of (and not at the expense of) the person that it promotes, then it is excluded from the definition of commercial communication, and is not regulated by the E-Commerce Regulations.

[29] Unsolicited commercial communications, typically spam, are also regulated by the Privacy and Electronic Communications (EC Directive) Regulations 2003 (SI 2003/2426).

Perhaps the most critical regulation in the E-Commerce Regulations is that which relates to the conclusion of electronic contracts, under reg.9. This applies to all B2C contracts, and to those B2B contracts where the parties have not agreed otherwise.[30] It is therefore possible for a service provider to contract out of reg.9 in its B2B dealings, but not its B2C contracts. Where the E-Commerce Regulations do apply, however, and where a contract can be concluded online, then the service provider is under a number of obligations pre- and post- conclusion.

7–09   To deal with the pre-contractual obligations first, these constitute a further information requirement. The most important of these is the obligation in reg.9(1)(a) to provide the customer with details of "the different technical steps to follow to conclude the contract". This is an attempt to provide some certainty as to when both parties become bound by legal obligations. In the past, this has been notoriously difficult, as witnessed by a number of high profile disputes in the last decade between consumers and e-tailers. These typically arise where goods are displayed online at incorrect prices, which offer consumers a bargain. A recent example is the Repricer Express software glitch that occurred on December 12, 2014 causing hundreds of items to be displayed for sale at 1p on Amazon. Where a customer orders one (or, frequently, several) of these erroneously priced goods, and the e-tailer then refuses to deliver, the question then arises whether the initial order was sufficient to conclude a contract, creating a legal obligation, or whether it was simply an offer by the customer capable of rejection by the e-tailer.[31]

However, although e-tailers must make the contractual steps clear, no further guidance is given in the E-Commerce Regulations as to when this moment of conclusion occurs. Issues of principle therefore remain unresolved. For example, a standard online transaction can be broken into four constituent parts, as follows:

Consumer browses website

↓

Consumer places order for goods and submits credit card details

↓

Supplier acknowledges order

↓

Supplier takes payment and despatches goods

In legal terms, these facts and actions could be analysed in a number of ways, such as:

---

[30] E-Commerce Regulations reg.9(1).
[31] This has been the subject of litigation in Singapore, where purchasers tried to take advantage of erroneously posted prices online: *Chwee Kin Keong v Digilandmall.com Pte Ltd* [2004] 2 S.L.R. 594.

Fact/Action	Legal Analysis I	Legal Analysis II	Legal Analysis III	Legal Analysis IV
Website on public display	No legal significance	Invitation to treat	Invitation to treat	Offer
Consumer places order	Invitation to treat	Offer	Offer	Acceptance of offer: **Contract Concluded**
Supplier acknowledges order	Offer	Acceptance of offer: **Contract Concluded**		
Supplier performs: takes payment and despatches goods	Consumer accepts goods on delivery: **Contract Concluded**		Acceptance of offer: **Contract Concluded**	

From this, it can be seen that the different legal steps could be met by a number of different actions: the offer could be constituted by the website, the consumer's order or the supplier's acknowledgment. Conversely, the legal status of these different elements remains unclear: are goods for sale on a website an invitation to treat or an offer? Is the consumer's order an invitation to treat, an offer or an acceptance of prior offer?

The E-Commerce Regulations do not clarify the legal consequences of each step, but they do place the onus on the supplier to make the contractual steps known to the consumer. The legal provision in the E-Commerce Regulations is therefore not as effective as it might otherwise have been, and can be seen as a lost opportunity to clarify legislatively the moment at which an online contract is concluded.

As well as making clear the mode of concluding a contract, the service **7–10** provider must also inform the customer whether or not the concluded contract will be filed by the service provider and whether it will be accessible (reg.9(1)(b)); how any input errors can be identified and corrected prior to the placing of the order (reg.9(1)(c)); and the languages offered for the conclusion of the contract (reg.9(1)(d)). Where the service provider subscribes to any codes of conduct, it must make these known to the customer, together with details of how to consult those codes (reg.9(2)). Where the terms and conditions which govern the contract are made available by the service provider, they must be accessible to the customer, such that the customer can store and reproduce them (reg.9(3)).

Many of these requirements can be met by an automated email sent to the customer following the receipt of the order, which provides the information in a clear and unambiguous manner. However, the most critical element of reg.9 will require some consideration by the service provider, to ensure that the steps to be followed to conclude the contract are made explicitly clear prior to the customer placing the order. There are two main ways this can be done, either through a step-by-step "breadcrumb trail", being a visual representation of the stages at the top of the webpage,[32] or a contract formation clause in the terms and conditions.[33]

Service providers should also note that reg.10 expressly states that the provisions of reg.9 are supplemental to other information requirements under EU law, and are not optional extras. Thus, e-tailers must also take account of the Consumer Contracts (Information, Cancellation and Additional Charges) Regulations 2013, discussed below, for example.

Once the order has been placed, the requirements of reg.11 take effect, to oblige service providers to acknowledge receipt of the order "without undue delay" (reg.11(1)(a)), while reg.11(1)(b) reiterates the requirement to enable the customer to identify and correct any input errors prior to the placing of an order by technological means. Regulation 11 also clears up any doubt over when "receipt" happens electronically: the order and acknowledgement shall "be deemed to be received when the parties to whom they are addressed are able to access them." (reg.11(2)(a)). It is therefore not sufficient to show that the order or acknowledgment was sent: it must have been *received* to take effect.[34] However, in the case of an electronic order for information society services, such as ISP services, the acknowledgement can take the form of the provision of the service that has been paid for (reg.11(2)(b)).

Both regs 9 and 11 confirm that their information provisions do not apply where the contracts are concluded exclusively by email (or its technical equivalent). This would exclude email negotiations, but would apply to online purchases made using the e-tailer's standard order form. Further technical legal clarification is given by reg.12 which confirms that the "order" placed by the customer may equate to the formal "offer" for the purposes of contract law, but that it need not. Thus, the service provider is free to stipulate which stage of the electronic communication constitutes the offer and acceptance in the contract formation process, which accords with the terms of reg.9, allowing the service provider to stipulate the steps necessary to conclude the contract.

Liability of service providers

7–11   Regulations 13–15 deal with aspects of liability and compliance. Regulation 13 states that any recipient of the information society services may raise an action against the service provider for damages for breach of statutory duty, in order to enforce regs 6, 7, 8, 9(1) and 11(1)(a). Although direct action against the service provider is often the most persuasive remedy for recipients, this right is limited to breach of the listed regulations only. In addition, it may prove impractical for

---

[32] For example, see *www.amazon.co.uk* [Accessed May 15, 2015].
[33] For example, see *www.topshop.com* [Accessed May 15, 2015].
[34] Contrast this with the postal acceptance rule in Ch.4.

recipients (especially consumer recipients) to raise a court action where the service provider is located in a different jurisdiction.

Where the service provider fails to comply with reg.9(3), the recipient shall be entitled to seek a court order to enforce this provision, in accordance with reg.14. Regulation 9(3) would be breached where the supplier provides terms and conditions but fails to make them available for storage and reproduction by the recipient. Although the right under reg.14 does have the benefit of direct redress for the customer, it is difficult to envisage many customers (whether business or consumer) taking the necessary court action, with its associated expense, to enforce it, simply to gain access to the terms and conditions. Further, there is no suggestion that any compensation for resulting loss will be available.

Perhaps the most practical remedy, and the one with the most serious consequences for the service provider, is set out in reg.15, which provides the customer with an opportunity to rescind the contract (i.e. to bring the contract to an end) where there has been a breach of reg.11(1)(b). (Regulation 11(1)(b) obliges the service provider to give the customer the opportunity to identify and correct any input errors prior to placing the order.) Although this is a powerful remedy for the customer, it is severely limited because it can only be exercised for breach of one sub-regulation. Further, since rescission operates to bring the contract to an end, it may not be a desirable solution for the customer, who may not want to cancel the contract.

Protection for intermediaries: regulations 17–19

In recognition of the fact that many service providers (such as ISPs) may **7–12** well act as intermediaries, and deal with information and data for which they are not directly responsible, the E-Commerce Regulations provide a number of safeguards for these providers.[35] Although these safeguards are not necessarily an integral part of online commerce, they are an important part of the E-Commerce Regulations and it is helpful to mention them briefly.

Regulation 17 deals with the transmission of information by the service provider, where this is done on behalf of the ISS recipient, and the service provider is a "mere conduit". Where the service provider simply transmits information provided by a recipient of the service, the service provider shall not be liable for any damages (or indeed any criminal sanction) which results from the transmission of this information. An example would be where a defamatory statement is sent by email: the ISP or email provider will not be liable for the defamation that results from this information. The service provider can only take advantage of this exclusion of liability if it can show that it was not responsible for: initiating the transmission; selecting the receiver of the transmission; and selecting or modifying the information transmitted. Effectively, the service provider must be acting as a "mere conduit" for the information,

---

[35] E-Commerce Regulations reg.20, however, provides that the parties can contract out of these safeguards, and agree other terms if they wish to do so.

and where the pursuer can show that there was a more active involvement by the service provider, liability will arise.

Similarly, reg.18 deals with the problems faced by service providers who temporarily cache information—usually to improve the speed and efficiency of their service. Search engines or ISPs, for example, may make a temporary cache of webpages to enable faster retrieval the next time the page is searched for. Caching is therefore a temporary storage of data, and service providers will not be liable for any damages or criminal sanctions resulting from their cache of information, where this storage is automatic, temporary and undertaken solely for the purpose of improving the efficiency of the service for future users. The exclusion from liability is not absolute however: a service provider can only take advantage of the exclusion where it has not modified the cached information and where it has acted expeditiously to remove the cached information once it obtains actual knowledge that the original information has been removed.[36]

Regulation 19 provides the third category of relief from liability, which arises where the service provider has provided hosting or storage services. Examples of hosting or storage services might be a blog site and a webspace hosting site. Where a recipient has used this service to upload material in breach of copyright, perhaps to his blog or personal website for example, the service provider will not be liable so long as it was unaware of the breach, or acted expeditiously to remove the offending information once the breach comes to its attention. In *L'Oreal v eBay*[37] the European Court of Justice suggested that when considering whether a service provider has become aware of the breach the court must ask whether a "diligent economic operator would have identified the illegality and acted expeditiously".

THE CONSUMER CONTRACT (INFORMATION, CANCELLATION AND ADDITIONAL CHARGES) REGULATIONS

Scope of the Regulations

7–13 When trading online, suppliers need to be aware of their obligations under the Consumer Rights Directive.[38] The Directive was passed as part of the EU's "e-commerce action plan", and has been implemented in the UK as the Consumer Contracts (Information, Cancellation and Additional Charges) Regulation 2013 (the "CC Regulations").[39] The CC

---

[36] The detailed terms of the qualification for exclusion are set out in E-Commerce Regulations reg.18(b).

[37] *L'Oreal v eBay* [2012] All E.R. (EC) 501 at [120].

[38] Directive 2011/83/EU of the European Parliament and the Council of 25 October 2011 on consumer rights amending Council Directive 93/13/EEC and Directive 1999/44/EC of the European Parliament and of the Council and repealing Council Directive 85/577/EEC and Directive 97/7/EC of the European Parliament and of the Council.

[39] SI 2013/3134.

Regulations govern contracts entered into on or after June 13, 2014,[40] and in doing so they replace the Consumer Protection (Distance Selling) Regulations 2000.[41] It is important to note that the CC Regulations are not retrospective, meaning contracts entered into prior to June 13, 2014 will still come under the Distance Selling Regulations.[42]

When considering the new Regulations the first question must be: when will a contract be governed be the CC Regulations?

In order to fall within the scope of the CC Regulations a contract must satisfy two distinct definitional categories. The first considers how and where the contract is formed, whilst the second focuses on the nature of the contract itself. The protection given to consumers, and the obligations imposed on traders, will only apply if the contract in question falls within **both** of these categories.

How and when was the contract formed?

Turning then to the first definitional category: the "when and how" of the **7–14** contract. The contract must be an "off-premises" contract, an "on premises" contract or a "distance contract".

"Off-premises contracts"

Very few e-commerce based transactions will be able to satisfy the first of **7–15** these categories. This is because the definition requires there to be "simultaneous physical presence" between the trader and the consumer, and e-commerce by its online nature lacks this. The only exception to this physical requirement is where the contract is concluded: "immediately after the consumer was personally and individually addressed in a place that was not the business premises [of the trader]".[43] This could happen where a trader comes to the home of the consumer. However, the need for the consumer to have been "personally and individually" addressed, and the contract concluded "immediately" thereafter means only a handful of e-commerce based contracts will ever fall into this category.

"On premises contracts"

Next, an "on premises contract" is defined as "a contract which is neither **7–16** a distance contract nor an off-premises contract". The width of this definition is no doubt designed to provide a catch-all provision for consumers to rely on.[44] Rather than rely on this imprecise category, most e-commerce contracts will, however, come under the more structured definition of a "distance contract". Distance contracts, and the regime under the CC Regulations governing them, will therefore, be the focus of the remainder of the chapter.

---

[40] CC Regulations reg.1(2).
[41] SI 2000/2334.
[42] CC Regulations reg.2(a). For further detail on the previous regulations, see the second edition of *Business Law in Scotland* (2nd edn, Edinburgh: W. Green, 2011), Ch.7.
[43] CC Regulations reg.5.
[44] CC Regulations reg.7(4) and reg.27(3).

"Distance contracts"

7–17 "Distance contracts" are defined by reg.5 as:

> "a contract concluded between a trader and a consumer under an organised distance sales or service-provision scheme without the simultaneous physical presence of the trader and the consumer, with the exclusive use of one or more means of distance communication up to and including the time at which the contract is concluded".

This definition can be broken down into five elements, all of which must be fulfilled before the CC Regulations can apply:

(1) First, there must be a **contract**. Therefore the standard rules of Scots contract law (such as offer and acceptance, and capacity) must be satisfied.[45]

(2) Secondly, the contract must be between a "**trader**" and a "**consumer**". The effect of this is that, unlike the E-Commerce Regulations, the CC Regulations do not apply to business to business contracts.

Both terms are given a specific meaning under the CC Regulations:

"A consumer" is:

> "an individual acting for purposes which are wholly or mainly outside that individual's trade, business, craft or profession".[46]

Thus, it is not possible for a juristic entity (for example a company) to qualify as a consumer under the Regulations, and instead only "individuals" will be protected. This restriction follows the EU trend of limiting consumer protection to natural persons. The UK has, however, amended the original text of the Directive by adding the concept of "mainly outside" the individual's trade, business craft or profession. This was done in response to concerns that the EU approach was too narrow.[47] The effect of the addition is that protection is extended to individuals who are contracting for a mixed purpose—that is to say partly within and partly outside their trade, business, craft or profession.

This raises the question: how mixed can a contract be with the individual still retaining the label of "consumer"? Some guidance may be taken from the recitals of the Directive. For although the Directive does not use the concept of "mainly outside" in this context, it does recognise the possibility of a contract having a "dual purpose"—one consumer based, the other trade. Recital 19 suggests that the test is whether or not

---

[45] See Ch.4 for an account of the general principles of Scots contract law.

[46] CC Regulations reg.4.

[47] The Law Commission and the Scottish Law Commission, "Report on: Consumer Redress for Misleading and Aggressive Practises" (Law Com. No.332) (Scot Law Com. No.226), 2012 at para.6.13.

the trade purpose has become predominant in the overall context of the contract.[48] For example, an individual buying a laptop mainly for playing games but also with the intention of sending some work emails would still qualify as a consumer.[49]

A "trader" is then defined as:

> "a person acting for purposes relating to that person's trade, business, craft or profession, whether acting personally or through another person acting in the trader's name or on the trader's behalf".

This definition captures a wide range of actors ranging from the unincorporated sole trader to the multi-national company. The key distinction to "consumers" being that, here the regulation refers to "persons" not "individuals"; as such, juristic entities can be (and usually are) the trader. The scope is widened further by the idea of the purpose "*relating to* that person's trade, business, craft or profession". This allows activities leading up to or otherwise relating to the trade to bring the actor under the definition of "trader". The second part of the definition then refers to acting through another. Thus, where a trader acts through an agent or subcontractor they remain liable.

(3) The third element of a "distance contract" requires there to be an **"organised distance sales or service-provision scheme"**. Unfortunately, this concept is not defined in the Regulations. Nevertheless, it is likely that an 'organised sales of service-provision scheme" would exclude a one-off or occasional contract: the EU Directorate-General for Justice gives the example of a trader who only exceptionally concludes a contract with a consumer by email.[50]

(4) The fourth requirement is that the contract must be concluded **without the simultaneous physical presence** of the trader and consumer. It is here that the distance contract definition comes into its own in relation to e-commerce, for it is the lack of physical presence which typifies (and indeed leads to many of the problems associated with) electronic commerce.

(5) Finally, the contract must be concluded exclusively by the use of one or more means of **distance communication**. This reinforces the fourth requirement and the need for there to be no physical contact between the consumer and the trader. Both requirements do, however, only apply up to and including the time at which the contract is concluded. From this it can be inferred that any face-to-face contact thereafter does not affect the distance selling status of the contract, for example where the consumer orders

---

[48] Recital 19 of the Directive.
[49] An example given by the Law Commissions' Report (2012), para.6.10.
[50] Directorate-General for Justice of the European Commission, *DG Guidance Document concerning the Consumer Rights Directive* (June 13, 2014) (hereafter the "DG Guidance Document"), p.30.

online but then collects in store. It should also be remembered that the parties can use a combination of several different means of distance communication, and still fall within the definition—such as beginning the contract online but making payment by telephone.

Unlike the previous Distance Selling Regulations, the new CC Regulations do not include an indicative list of what amounts to a "distance communication". Nevertheless, it is safe to assume both the internet and email communication (which form the focus of this chapter) will be a means of distance communication.[51] An advantage of not including an exhaustive list of distance communication is that the Regulations are, to some extent, future-proofed. If a new method of distance communication is developed it will still be covered by the CC Regulations without the need for any legislative intervention.

Therefore, if a contract has all five of the following elements then it will be a "distance contract" under the Regulations and the first "when and how" definitional threshold will be reached:

    (i) it is a contract under Scots law;
   (ii) it is concluded between a "trader" and a "consumer";
  (iii) there is a "organised distance sales or service-provision scheme";
  (iv) there is no simultaneous physical presence; and
   (v) only distance communication is used.

The nature of the contract

7–18 The next step in understanding the scope of contracts covered by the CC Regulations is to consider the second definitional category used, based on the nature of the contract. This amounts to the question of whether the contract can be said to be a services, sales or digital content contract. Few contracts will, however, fail to fall into one of these categories. Instead the importance of the distinction becomes apparent when considering the different and specific rules that affect each. For example, the calculation of the time period in which a consumer can cancel the contract will vary depending on the nature of the contract. It is therefore important to understand the three different types of contract.

Sales or service contract?

7–19 Both service and sales contracts are defined in reg.5, with a service contract being:

> "a contract, other than a sales contract, under which a trader supplies or agrees to supply a service to a consumer and the consumer pays or agrees to pay the price".

---

[51] Recital 20 of the Consumer Rights Directive.

A sales contract is:

> "a contract under which a trader transfers or agrees to transfer the ownership of goods to a consumer and the consumer pays or agrees to pay the price, including any contract that has both goods and services as its object".

The first thing to notice is that neither a sales nor a service contract can be gratuitous, and therefore the consumer must pay or agree to pay a price.[52] The guidance issued by the EU Directorate-General for Justice suggests that "price" relates solely to payment in money, but would include vouchers, gift cards or loyalty points with a specific monetary value.[53]

Secondly, the distinguishing feature of a sales contract is the transfer of ownership of the goods in question. In a service contract no such transfer takes place, and instead a service is performed or is agreed to be performed by the trader.

There is, however, a degree of overlap between the two concepts, as a sales contract is defined as including: "any contract which has both goods and services as its object". On the face of it this suggests that when a contract contains both goods and services (a mixed contract) it should always be considered, and dealt with, as if it were a sales contract. This would, however, sadly be an oversimplification.

Both the UK Department for Business Innovation & Skills[54] ("BIS") **7–20** and the EU Directorate-General for Justice[55] outline that such mixed contracts should be classified based on their real purpose. Therefore, if the main purpose of the contract is the transfer of ownership it should be considered a sales contract, even if it also relates to a service provided by the seller. For example, the purchase of new kitchen units which includes the installation in the consumer's home would be likely to be classed as a sales contract. Where, however, transfer of ownership is not the main purpose it should be considered to be a service contract, despite the fact it also contains sale elements. An example here could be attending a cookery class, where the price also includes the ingredients, but the main purpose is the provision of services, being the cookery tuition. Interestingly the guidance offered by the EU Directorate-General for Justice recommends that when assessing the main purpose of a mixed contract

---

[52] This of course reflects the requirement for a consideration in English contract law, although it is a requirement which is not contained within the general principles of Scots contract law. Nevertheless, a distance sales or service contract will only be covered by the CC Regulations where there is a price. To this extent, it mirrors the Sale of Goods Act 1979, which also requires the buyer to pay a price for the goods, as per s.2(1).

[53] *DG Guidance Document* (June 13, 2014), p.8.

[54] UK Department for Business Innovation & Skills ("BIS"), *Implementing Guidance on Consumer Contracts (Information, Cancellation and Additional Charges) Regulations* (December 2013), p.6.

[55] *DG Guidance Document* (June 13, 2014), p.6.

no reference should be made to the relative value of the goods or service.[56]

Finally, it must be noted that the definition of a sales contract explicitly refers to the transfer of ownership from a trader to a consumer, meaning the Regulations will not apply where the scenario is reversed and the consumer is acting as seller.

Digital content contract

7–21 The third type of contract under the Regulations are contracts for the supply of digital content when not supplied on a tangible medium. This recognition of digital content contracts as a distinct category shows the growing importance of instantly available digital content in the consumer market. It must be realised, however, that it only relates to such content when it is not supplied on a tangible medium, which is to say not on a CD or DVD.[57] If the content is delivered in such a tangible form, it will be dealt with as a sales contract under the Regulations.

Unfortunately, however, the precise scope of this new concept is not clear, as the Regulations do not define: "digital content contract". Instead only the term "digital content" is defined in isolation. Regulation 5 simply states that digital content means "data which are produced and supplied in a digital form". This reluctance to provide a precise definition creates some difficulty in distinguishing between a service contract where the service in question is the supply of digital content, and a contract for the supply of digital content not on a tangible medium. This difficulty is compounded by the conflicting guidance being offered by BIS and by the recitals accompanying the Directive.

The UK BIS guidelines suggest that a digital content contract concerns the situation where data are supplied through downloading or streaming,[58] which would suggest that when the data are being accessed but not downloaded or streamed it is a service contract. One example would be a subscription to an online newspaper where the data is only accessed. However, this conflicts with recital 19 which suggests that:

> "Digital content means data which are produced and supplied in a digital form, such as computer programmes, applications, games, music, videos or texts, *irrespective of whether they are accessed through downloading or streaming ...*".[60]

This suggests that downloading/streaming is only one means of accessing the data rather than the indicative test of whether it is a digital content contract or a service contract.

7–22 The importance of being able to identify a contract as either a service contract or a contract for the supply of digital content is highlighted when the cancellation rights in relation to each are considered. The

---

[56] *DG Guidance Document* (June 13, 2014), p.6.
[57] See Recital 19 of Directive.
[58] BIS, *Implementing Guidance* (December 2013), p.6.

cancellation rights for consumers are more generous in relation to service contracts than for digital content contracts, as will be explored further below.[59]

One final point to note in relation to digital content contracts is the lack of reference to the need for a price to be paid. As noted above the definitions of both a service and a sales contract explicitly state that the consumer must pay or agree to pay a price. As no precise definition exists for digital content contracts no such stipulation is made. This potentially widens the scope of the Directive considerably, as it brings free online digital content, such as the millions of free downloadable apps, within the scope of the Regulations. One method of limiting the impact of this would be to deem these free digital content contracts to be service contracts. Hence, without the payment of a price they would be outwith the "service contract" definition and thus the scope of the CC Regulations. However, until the courts have a chance to consider how the distinction is to be drawn between these two types of contract in practice, it is always possible that free online downloads will be covered by the CC Regulations as digital content contracts.

Therefore to summarise: the second definitional category contained in the CC Regulations requires the nature of the contract to be considered. The contract in question must be identified as a sales, service or digital content contract to fall within the scope of the Regulations.

Limitations

Even where a contract satisfies the requirements of both: (i) the "when and how"; and (ii) the nature of the contract, the CC Regulations do not always automatically apply. This is because reg.6 sets out a list of limitations, and if the contract falls within one of these the CC Regulations will not apply.[60] **7–23**

The following contracts are **excluded** from the scope of the CC Regulations:

(1)   a contract for gambling within the meaning of the Gambling Act 2005 (which includes gaming, betting and participating in a lottery)[61];

(2)   a contract concerning financial services, that is to say for services of a banking, credit, insurance, personal pension, investment or payment nature[62];

(3)   a contract for the creation of immoveable property or a right in immoveable property[63];

---

[59] See below on cancellation rights under the CC Regulations.
[60] CC Regulations reg.6(1).
[61] CC Regulations reg.6(1)(a)(i).
[62] CC Regulations reg.6(1)(b).
[63] CC Regulations reg.6(1)(c).

(4)　　a contract for rental of accommodation for residential purposes,[64] but note it does not exclude rental of accommodation
for non-residential purposes[65];

(5)　　a contract for the construction of new buildings, or the construction of substantially new buildings[66];

(6)　　a contract for the supply of foodstuffs, beverages or other
goods intended for current consumption in the household and
which are supplied by a trader on frequent and regular rounds
to the consumer's home, residence or workplace[67];

(7)　　a contract for package travel, package holidays and package
tours.[68] "Package" meaning a pre-arranged combination of at
least two different elements, such as transport, accommodation
or other tourist services when sold or offered for sale at an
inclusive price; either with an overnight stay or for a period of
more than twenty four hours[69];

(8)　　a contract in respect of certain aspects of timeshares, long term
holiday products, resale and exchange contracts within the
meaning of Directive 2008/122/EC of the European
Parliament[70];

(9)　　a contract concluded by means of automatic vending machines
or automated commercial premises[71];

(10)　a contract concluded with a telecommunications operator
through a public telephone for the use of the telephone[72];

(11)　a contract concluded for the use of one single connection, by
telephone, internet or fax, established by a consumer.[73] For
example this exception would exclude a contract with an
internet café for a single internet session, but not a contract for
continuing wifi services[74]; and

(12)　a contract under which goods are sold by way of execution or
otherwise by authority of law.[75]

Contracts concluded at auction do not appear in this list of excluded
contracts. Under the previous Distance Selling Regulations 2000[76] much
confusion was created by reg.5(1)(f) which simply stated that the Regulations did not apply to "any contract concluded at auction". This
raised the question of whether a distance contract concluded by way of an

---

[64]　CC Regulations reg.6(1)(d).
[65]　Recital 26 of the Directive.
[66]　CC Regulations reg.6(1)(e).
[67]　CC Regulations reg.6(1)(f).
[68]　CC Regulations reg.6(1)(g).
[69]　For more information as to the precise scope of this exclusion see 90/314/EEC of 13 June
1990 on package travel, package holidays and package tours.
[70]　CC Regulations reg.6(1)(h).
[71]　CC Regulations reg.6(2)(a).
[72]　CC Regulations reg.6(2)(b).
[73]　CC Regulations reg.6(2)(c).
[74]　*DG Guidance Document* (June 13, 2014), p.11.
[75]　CC Regulations reg.6(2)(d).
[76]　Consumer Protection (Distance Selling) Regulations 2000 (SI 2000/2334).

online auction site, such as eBay, would be within the scope of those regulations. With no UK case law considering the matter,[77] it was left to academics to debate the point,[78] with no clear answer emerging. Thankfully the CC Regulations have laid the matter to rest. Auctions are generally not excluded from falling within the regulations; instead only certain restrictions are applied to "contracts concluded at public auction".[79] It is the definition given to "public auction" which provides the most clarity in relation to online auctions. Regulation 5 requires that the consumer attend or be given the possibility to attend in person in order for the contract to be considered to be concluded at a public auction. As such, online auctions such as eBay, will not come under this exclusion. Therefore, as long as all other definitional requirements are met, contracts concluded by way of an online auction will gain the full protection of the CC Regulations.[80]

As well as the listed exclusions under reg.6, a number of other partial **7–24** exclusions are spread throughout the CC Regulations limiting the information obligations placed on traders and the consumers' right to cancel. These will be considered in relation to the relevant rights and obligations affected.

In summary, when faced with an e-commerce situation there are three main questions to consider when deciding if the CC Regulations apply to the contract(s) involved:

(1) When and how was the contract concluded? In most cases this will require analysis of the five elements of the "distance contract" definition contained in reg.5.
(2) What is the nature of the contract: is it a sales, services or digital content contract?
(3) Does the contract fall within one of the reg.6 excluded contracts?

The information requirements

Having considered when the CC Regulations will apply, it is now possible **7–25** to discuss the rights and obligations they impose. As far as the consumer is concerned, the main thrust of the CC Regulations is the trader's obligation to provide certain information and the consumer's right to cancel, also known as the "cooling off period".

To take the information provision obligations first: Part 2 of the Regulations sets out the information requirements which a trader must comply with. The relevant Regulations in relation to distance contracts

---

[77] The point was discussed in *L'Oreal SA v eBay International AG* [2009] EWHC 1094, per Arnold J at 471 but not decided.

[78] See: A. Nordhausen in "Distance Marketing in the European Union", at p.247, in Edwards (ed), *The New Legal Framework for E-Commerce in Europe* (Oxford: Hart Publishing, 2005); C. Riefa, "To be or not to be an auctioneer? Some thoughts on the legal nature of online "eBay" auctions and the protection of consumers", (2008) 31 J.C.P. 167.

[79] Under CC Regulations reg.28(g) the right to cancel does not apply.

[80] As confirmed by recital 24 of the Directive.

are regs 13–18. These information requirements can be broken down into two main categories: (1) information which must be provided before making a distance contract; and (2) confirmation of the contract.

Information which must be provided before making a distance contract

7–26 Regulation 13 sets out the two main information obligations which must be satisfied by a trader before making a distance contract: the information contained in Sch.2, and provisions of the model cancellation form.

Schedule 2 information

7–27 First, the trader must give or make available all the information listed in Sch.2 to the Regulations.[81] This includes[82]:

(1) the main characteristics of the goods, service or digital content;
(2) the identity of the trader;
(3) the address and contact details of the trader, and where available the telephone number, fax number and email address;
(4) the total price of the goods, services or digital content inclusive of taxes, or how it will be calculated if the subject matter means it cannot be calculated in advance;
(5) where applicable, any additional delivery charges and any other costs or, if they cannot be calculated in advance the fact that they may be payable;
(6) payment, delivery and performance arrangements;
(7) the trader's complaints handling policy;
(8) the contract's duration and conditions for terminating it;
(9) where the right to cancel exists, the conditions, time limits and procedures for exercising that right;
(10) where there is no right to cancel or the right may be lost the consumer must be informed of this;
(11) that, in relation to a contract for services, if the consumer exercises the right to cancel after having requested the service be performed before the expiry of the cancellation period that the consumer is liable to pay for the services received, up to that point; and
(12) where applicable, the consumer must be informed that they will have to bear the cost of returning the goods.

Regulation 13 then goes on to explain how this information, and the remainder of the information listed in Sch.2 must be provided.

First, the trader is under an obligation to "give or make available" the information.[83] Regulation 8 explains that something is "made available" to the consumer if "the consumer can reasonably be expected to access

---

[81] CC Regulations reg.13(1)(a).
[82] For the full list see Sch.2.
[83] CC Regulations reg.13(1)(a).

it". The effect of this is that the trader can comply with its obligation even if the information has not actually been accessed by the consumer, so long as they can reasonably be expected to know how to access it. How the courts will assess whether or not a consumer reasonably knows how to access information remains to be seen.

Secondly, the information must be given or made available in a "clear and comprehensible manner",[84] meaning the trader must not use confusing terminology. It is, however, unclear whether "clear and comprehensible" also extends to the manner in which the information is conveyed: if the relevant information is clear and comprehensible yet hidden in the midst of a lengthy contract, would the trader have complied with their obligations under reg.13? Arguably this would not be within the spirit of the Regulations, nor the Directive it implements, and as such it is suggested that traders should avoid hiding the required information in the small print.

The CC Regulations do also provide specific guidance as to how the information surrounding the right to cancel and any ensuing costs should be conveyed. The trader is given the option of using the model instructions on cancellation set out in Pt A of Sch.3.[85]

The model cancellation form

The second main information obligation placed on the trader, in relation **7–28** to pre-contractual information, again deals with the consumer's right to cancel. Under reg.13(1)(b) if a right to cancel exists, the trader must give or make available to the consumer the cancellation form as set out in Pt B of Sch.3 to the Regulations.[86] This requirement is in addition to the trader's obligation to inform the consumer that the right to cancel exists as set out in Sch.2 (usually done by way of the model instructions in Pt A of Sch.3). Therefore the trader must provide both the form and inform the consumer of their rights.

Whilst the trader is under an obligation to supply the form in Pt B of Sch.3, they are not obliged to require the consumer to use it; nor can the consumer be forced to do so.[87] Moreover, the trader is free to provide a different form for the consumer to use, as long as it is in addition to the model form as set out in Pt B.[88] This leaves the consumer in the rather bewildering situation of possibly being faced with two cancellation forms and, whilst they are not obliged to use either this is not a straightforward approach for consumers, and is not likely to enhance consumer confidence.

---

[84] CC Regulations reg.13(1)(a).
[85] CC Regulations reg.13(3).
[86] CC Regulations reg.13(1)(b).
[87] CC Regulations reg.32(3) establishes that the consumer can either use the form or make any other clear statement.
[88] Law Commissions' Report (2012), para.6.2.

Providing the required information when there is limited space

7–29 Finally, the CC Regulations recognise that there may be limited space or time to display the required pre-contractual information when using some forms of distance communication.

Regulation 13(4) states that as long as the following information is given, or made available to, the consumer in a clear and comprehensible manner:

(i) the main characteristic of the goods;
(ii) the identity of the trader;
(iii) the total price and costs of the contract;
(iv) the information about the consumer's right to cancel; and
(v) the contract's duration and conditions for terminating it,

then the other information required under Sch.2 may be provided in "another appropriate way".

This raises the question of what amounts to "another appropriate way"? Whilst the Regulations themselves do not expand upon this idea, recital 36 of the Directive does. It suggests that the information could be provided by giving a toll free telephone number or a hyperlink through which the information would be available.

One matter that remains unresolved is whether the model cancellation form can be provided in "another appropriate manner" or whether it must form part of the initial limited distance communication. The guidance issued by the EU Directorate-General for Justice suggests that the model cancellation form must be provided in the limited means of communication,[89] but the actual text of the regulation states that all information required by reg.13(1)—which includes the model cancellation form—may be provided in another appropriate manner. Until the courts have a chance to consider this, the safest option is for the trader to include the cancellation form even when the means of communication is limited.

Effect of failing to provide the required pre-contractual information

7–30 The importance of the trader's pre-contractual information obligations lies in the consequences for the trader in failing to comply. The ramifications are threefold:

(1) First, all the information (even that provided in another appropriate manner in relation to limited distance communications) must be provided, "before the consumer is bound by a distance contract".[90] It is important to realise, however, that the Regulations do not say the contract is not formed: the reference is to the consumer not yet being bound. This suggests that the

---

[89] *DG Guidance Document* (June 13, 2014), p.33.
[90] CC Regulations reg.13(1).

protection is (rightly) one-sided, and as such the contract can still come into existence and be enforced by the consumer against the trader, but not vice versa. Thus, until the trader provides this information, he may be bound by the contract, but be unable to enforce it against the consumer. This provides a major source of protection for the consumer, as until they are bound by the contract they have no obligation to pay, or to accept the goods, services or digital content.

(2) Secondly, under reg.13(5) if the trader has failed to provide the information required in relation to any additional charges and costs, and where applicable the consumer's obligation to pay to return the goods, the consumer will not bear the costs of these charges.

(3) Thirdly, and as will be expanded upon in the next section, under reg.31 the consumer is given a longer cancellation period to reflect the lack of information provided.

Additional requirements for contracts concluded by "electronic means"

The Regulations provide additional pre-contractual requirements for **7–31** distance contracts concluded by electronic means. Although "electronic means" is not defined in the Directive, both the nature of the requirements and the guidance given by the EU Directorate-General suggest it should be interpreted as including websites.[91] This is, therefore, a key supplementary provision in relation to e-commerce.

Under reg.14 the online trader is required to do three things:

(1) First, before the ordering process begins the consumer must be informed clearly and legibly of any delivery restrictions and the means of payment which are accepted.[92]

(2) Secondly, before the consumer places their order the trader must ensure that they have been made aware of the information listed in paragraph (a), (f), (g), (h), (s) and (t) of Sch.2.[93] Of course if the trader has complied with reg.13 they will have already made this information available.

(3) Finally, the trader must ensure that when placing an order the consumer explicitly acknowledges that the order implies an obligation to pay.[94] Moreover, if there is a button which must be pressed then it must be labelled with the words "order with an obligation to pay" or a similarly unambiguous phrase. Interestingly, the guidance given by the EU Directorate-General for Justice suggest that "order now" would not be sufficient as it does not effectively convey the obligation to pay.[95]

---

[91] *DG Guidance Document* (June 13, 2014), p.31.
[92] CC Regulations reg.14(6).
[93] CC Regulations reg.14(2).
[94] CC Regulations reg.14(3).
[95] *DG Guidance Document* (June 13, 2014), p.32.

The result of failing to comply with this final requirement is extreme: the consumer is not bound by the contract or order.[96] In fact, failure to comply means the contract can never be enforced against the consumer.[97] Thus, traders would do well to check that their final confirmation button complies with this new requirement, particularly those who are using the potentially unacceptable "order now" formulation.

Confirmation of the contract

7–32   Having complied with the pre-contractual information requirements the trader must then ensure that they satisfy the second information obligation and confirm the contract in accordance with reg.16.[98] This requirement applies to all contracts falling within Pt 2, not just those concluded by electronic means.

In confirming the contract the trader is required to include all the information contained in Sch.2,[99] being the same information required to be given to the consumer at the pre-contractual stage under reg.13. The only difference is that, under reg.16, the information must be supplied on a "durable medium".

A durable medium includes paper or email, or any other medium that allows the information to be addressed personally to the recipient and enables the recipient to store it in a way accessible for future reference.[100] The aim of this measure is to provide both parties with a record of what has been agreed, and convey the formality of what has been done. If, however, the trader has already provided the information in such a form when complying with reg.13 they need not give it again.[101] If not, then the trader must send this information on a durable medium within a reasonable time after the conclusion of the contract, but no later than the time of delivery or the performance of the service.[102]

Limitations on the information obligations

7–33   Before moving on to discuss the second main arm of the CC Regulations, the right to cancel, it is necessary to consider the partial exclusions which apply to Pt 2 and thus limit the above information requirements. First, under reg.7, Pt 2 does not apply to a contract for the supply of medicinal product by administration, by a prescriber or under a prescription. Nor does it apply to a contract for the supply of a product by a health care professional where that product is available free or by prescription.[103]

---

[96]   CC Regulations reg.14(5).
[97]   This can be contrasted with failure to comply with reg.13 (above), which can be "cured" by the trader, and the contract enforced.
[98]   CC Regulations reg.16(1).
[99]   CC Regulations reg.16(2).
[100] CC Regulations reg.5.
[101] CC Regulations reg.16(2).
[102] CC Regulations reg.16(4).
[103] CC Regulations reg.7(2).

Secondly, it does not apply to contracts for passenger transport services.[104] Given that transport services, particularly train and air fares, are one of the most common online purchases this exclusion has the potential to weaken the protection given to consumers by the Regulations. This has, however, been somewhat mitigated by the fact that the exclusion does not apply to reg.14(1)–(5) (contracts concluded by electronic means). Thus, the trader is still required to provide some of the information contained in Sch.2 and ensure that the activation button explicitly acknowledges the obligation to pay.

Therefore, to summarise: Pt 2 of the Regulations place certain information provision obligations on a trader. These can be broken down into two parts:

(1) Pre-contractual information.
(2) Confirmation.

Both concern the information listed in Sch.2 to the Regulations, the main difference being that under "confirmation" the information must be provided in a durable medium.

The right of cancellation

The consumer's right

Part 3 deals with the consumer's right to cancel the contract. This right to **7–34** cancel, sometime referred to as the "cooling off period", is arguably the strongest measure of protection given to consumers under the CC Regulations and one of their most effective remedies.

The basic right is that all consumers are entitled to cancel a distance contract, within the cancellation period, without giving reason or incurring any liability.[105] However, this right is not absolute. As with the information requirements, the CC Regulations contain a number of partial exceptions. The Regulations are again limited in relation to medicinal products and transport services[106] in the same manner as in Pt 2. The restrictions on the right to cancel do, however, go further: reg.28 sets out a number of situations in which Pt 3 will not apply.

Pt 3 will not apply when:

(1) The price for the supply of goods or services (other than the supply of water, gas, electricity or heating) is dependent on fluctuations in the financial market which cannot be controlled by the trader and which may occur in the cancellation period.
(2) When the goods have been made to the consumer's specification or are clearly personalised. For example a particular component for a computer which has been individually made for the consumer and is not generally available. If, however, the consumer

---

[104] CC Regulations reg.7(3).
[105] CC Regulations reg.29(1).
[106] CC Regulations reg.27.

has chosen the components for the product from a pre-set list of generally available options this would not fall under the exception, for example selecting a colour option.[107]

(3) The supply of goods which deteriorate or expire rapidly. This exception will act to bar most contracts concerning food stuffs from falling within the scope of the regulation.

(4) The supply of alcoholic beverages, but only where (i) the price has been agreed at the time of the conclusion of the contract; (ii) the delivery takes place after 30 days; and (iii) their value is dependent on fluctuations in the market which cannot be controlled by the trader.

(5) Contracts where the consumer has specifically requested a visit from the trader for the purpose of carrying out urgent repairs.

(6) The supply of a newspaper, periodical or magazine, unless they are subscription contracts. The effect being a contract to purchase a newspaper from your local shop is not affected by Pt 3 of the Regulations, but the contract governing a subscription for such a publication is.

(7) Contracts concluded at public auctions.[108]

(8) The supply of accommodation, transport of goods, vehicle rental services, catering or services relating to leisure activities, if the contract provides for performance on a specific date or in a specified period.

7–35 Regulation 28 then goes on to detail three situations in which, although the right to cancel initially affects the contract it ceases to be available[109]:

(1) in the case of a contract for the supply of sealed goods which are not suitable for return due to health protection or hygiene reasons, the right to cancel is lost after they are unsealed after delivery;

(2) in the case of a contract for the supply of sealed audio or sealed video recordings or sealed computer software, if the goods are unsealed after delivery; and

(3) in the case of any sales contract, if the goods become mixed inseparably with other items after delivery.

In all of these cases the trader would be at a clear disadvantage if the consumer were able to cancel the contract and return the goods. For example, after goods have been customised, have perished or become inseparably mixed with other goods their re-sale value will diminish significantly. This does not, however, mean the consumer is left with no remedy in law. Rather, they will have to fall back on other consumer protection measures such as those in the Sale of Goods Act 1979, which

---

[107] *DG Guidance Document* (June 13, 2014), p.54.
[108] See above for discussion on how this affects online auction sites such as eBay.
[109] CC Regulations reg.13(3).

provides a remedy where, for example, the goods arc not of "satisfactory quality".[110] Moreover, the new Consumer Rights Act may also provide alternative protection in such circumstances.[111]

Calculating the cancellation period

Assuming the contract in question does not fall under one of the exclusions the consumer will have the automatic right to cancel within the cancellation period. It is therefore necessary to know when the cancellation period both begins and ends. **7–36**

When does it begin?

Under reg.29(2) the cancellation period begins "when the contract is entered into". On the face of it this is a sensible and clear provision, as it gives the consumer the right to cancel from the moment the contractual agreement is made. Such simplicity does, however, hide a rather unsettled reality. **7–37**

As discussed in relation to the E-Commerce Regulations, the moment of contract formation in standard online transactions is not always clear. There are in fact four different points at which it could be possible to say "the contract is entered into". Unfortunately, as with the E-Commerce Regulations, the CC Regulations have done little to clarify the situation. For whilst the Consumer Rights Directive maintains that that it does not affect national contract law in relation to formation,[112] the wording of two of the provisions within the CC Regulations appear to suggest an approach to the moment of formation. The problem is these two approaches are different.

First, as discussed above, reg.14 places an obligation on the trader to make the consumer aware that: "placing the order entails an obligation to pay the trader".[113] This suggests that in placing the order the consumer is accepting the trader's standing offer and as such the contract is formed at this point. This is because in Scots law until the actual point of formation no obligations exist. Therefore if the consumer has an "obligation to pay" on pressing the button, the contract must be formed at this point—meaning the trader's offer is being accepted.

Regulation 29(3), however, states that the right to cancel does not affect "the consumer's right to withdraw an *offer* made by the consumer to enter a distance contract". This suggests that it is the consumer who is making the offer, and as such the contract is not entered into until the trader accepts—a point in time which will be later than when the consumer places the initial order.

It is not possible, therefore, to say exactly when the cancellation period begins. Until these questions are resolved, consumers and traders will

---

[110] Sale of Goods Act 1979 s.14.
[111] See further Chs 5 and 6.
[112] Consumer Rights Directive art.5(3).
[113] CC Regulations 14(4).

have to make do with the principle that the cancellation period beings: "when the contract is entered into". Thankfully, greater clarity can be found in relation to the when the cancellation period ends.

When does it end?

7–38 There are two possibilities here: either the "normal cancellation period" will apply, or an extended period, and each will be considered in turn.

The normal cancellation period

7–39 The normal cancellation period is governed by reg.30. For sales contracts the normal cancellation period ends 14 days after the day on which the goods come into the physical possession of the consumer (or a person identified by the consumer to take possession).[114] In the case of the service[115]/digital content contracts, where there are no physical goods to transfer, the period ends 14 days after the day the contract is entered into.[116] Obviously, this raises the same problems discussed above about when the period begins.

It is important to note that the clock starts running the day after delivery/commencement of the contract. This means, for example, if goods were delivered on August 1 the cancellation period would end on August 16.

There are, however, three modifications to this general rule in relation to contracts for sale. First, if multiple goods are ordered by the consumer in one order and are delivered on different days, the cancellation period in respect of **all** the goods ends the 14th day after the day on which the last of the goods is delivered.[117] Secondly, if the goods consist of multiple lots or pieces of something which are delivered on different days the cancellation period ends at the end of the 14th day after the day on which the last of the pieces is delivered.[118] Finally, if the contract is a contract for the regular delivery of goods during a defined period of more than one day, the cancellation period ends at the end of the 14th day after the day on which the first of the goods are delivered.[119]

The extended cooling off period

7–40 In some cases, however, the consumer will be entitled to a longer "cooling off" period. Under reg.31, if the trader has not supplied the consumer with the information contained in para.(l) of Sch.2 to the Regulations (regarding the right to cancel) the cancellation period will be extended. In failing to provide this information the trader is breaching the pre-contractual information requirements contained in reg.13(1). How long

---

[114] CC Regulations reg.30(3).
[115] CC Regulations reg.30(3)(a).
[116] CC Regulations reg.30(2)(b).
[117] CC Regulations reg.30(4).
[118] CC Regulations reg.30(5).
[119] CC Regulations reg.30(6).

the period is extended for depends on how long the trader remains in breach.

The basic rule is that the cancellation period will be extended to 12 months after the day on which the cancellation period should have ended had reg.13 been complied with (the basic 14 days).[120] Again it is important to note that it is the day after it should have ended under reg.13, thus the cancellation period would end 12 months and 15 days after the day the contract was entered into or the goods were delivered.

The trader does, however, have the ability to shorten the extension by providing the consumer with the necessary information about their right to cancel.[121] If the trader provides this information within 12 months then the cancellation period will end 14 days after the information is received. The clock for the 12-month period starts when the normal cancellation period should have begun under reg.30 (so either when the consumer took physical possession or in terms of service/digital content contracts, when the contract was entered into). Therefore, if the normal cancellation period should have begun on August 1, 2015 and the trader informs the consumer of their right to cancel on July 31, 2016 the cancellation period will end 14 days after this.

Before moving on to explain how the consumer actually cancels the contract, and the effects of doing so, there are two supplementary points that need to be considered in relation to calculating the cancellation period. First, what counts as a "day"? The Regulations do not expand on whether this refers to all calendar days or just business days, but the Directive does. In contrast to previous legislation (including the Distance Selling Regulations) the Directive sets out that "days" means calendar days and includes public holidays, Sundays and Saturdays, save where these are expressly excepted by the particular contract.[122] However, if the last day of the appropriate cancellation period is a public holiday, Sunday or Saturday the period shall expire on the last hour of the next working day.[123] Secondly, it should be noted that a trader is free to offer a longer cancellation period than that stipulated under the regulations, as the aim of the Directive is not to prevent a trader offering better protection.[124]

Exercising the right to cancel

Under reg.29 the consumer has a right to cancel the contract within the **7–41** "cancellation period". Regulation 30 sets out when this cancellation period begins, and the normal length of it. Regulation 31 then details how this period can be extended, should the trader fail to inform the consumer about their right to cancel. How the consumer then exercises their right to cancel is set out in reg.32: the simple requirement being that they must

---

[120] CC Regulations reg.31(3).
[121] CC Regulations reg.31(2).
[122] Consumer Rights Directive art.3(3).
[123] Consumer Rights Directive art.3(4).
[124] Consumer Rights Directive art.3(6).

inform the trader of their decision to cancel.[125] In order to do so the consumer may either use the cancellation form provided by the trader (the form contained in Pt B of Sch.3 as discussed above), or make any other clear statement setting out the decision to cancel.[126] This statement does not have to be in writing or even on a durable medium, and as such a telephone call could suffice.[127] Indeed even if the trader supplies a form on their website the consumer cannot be forced to use it.[128] However, the consumer cannot withdraw by simply returning the goods or refusing delivery without an accompanying clear statement.

Finally, the withdrawal becomes effective from the moment it is sent, rather than when it is received[129]; thus so long as it is sent before the cancellation period ends it will be effective.[130] If a dispute arises it will be the consumer who bears the burden of proof of showing the contract was cancelled within the cancellation period and in accordance with the Regulations.[131] Hence it may be advisable for the consumer in this instance to use a durable medium.

If the contract is cancelled in accordance with the CC Regulations, the effect is to end any future obligations on the parties to perform the contract.[132] This means that the consumer must cancel the whole contract, and cannot opt for partial cancellation. This would potentially undermine the value of the right to the consumer, by forcing him into an "all or nothing" situation. However, there is no judicial guidance on this point and it may be that traders would accept a partial cancellation where relevant.

Residual obligations once the contract is cancelled:

7–42 Whilst the parties may no longer have any future obligations under the contract once cancellation becomes effective, they do have residual responsibilities under the Regulations. These relate to: reimbursement; return of any goods delivered; and payment for any services or digital content provided.

Reimbursement

7–43 Under reg.34, the trader must reimburse all payments received from the consumer, including any charges for delivery. In relation to delivery, if the trader has offered a range of delivery methods, they only have to refund what the consumer would have paid had the least expensive and generally accepted method had been used. For example if the consumer

---

[125] CC Regulations reg.32(1)
[126] CC Regulations reg.32(3).
[127] Consumer Rights Directive recital 44.
[128] CC Regulations reg.32(4).
[129] Much like the postal acceptance rule in Scots contract law.
[130] CC Regulations reg.32(5).
[131] CC Regulations reg.32(6).
[132] CC Regulations reg.33(1).

paid extra for next day delivery, they will only receive back the cost of standard delivery.

The reimbursement for all the payments must be made without undue delay and in the case of a sales contract no later than 14 days after the trader receives the goods or evidence is supplied that the consumer has sent them.[133] The consumer cannot, therefore, force the trader to reimburse them until they have relinquished control of goods. This is evidently in the trader's favour, as it means they can prevent the situation occurring where the consumer has both the money and the goods. If the trader has offered to collect the goods however, the consumer must be reimbursed by the end of the 14th day after the day on which the trader was informed of the consumer's decision to cancel the contract.[134]

The trader must make such reimbursement using the same means of payment the consumer used for the initial transaction, unless they consumer specifically agrees otherwise.[135] This means reimbursement cannot be by way of voucher or store credit unless the consumer consents. Moreover, the trader cannot impose a fee on the consumer in respect of the reimbursement.[136]

Whilst traders are prohibited from imposing a fee for reimbursement, the CC Regulations do allow them to deduct from the reimbursement, or demand a separate payment, in some situations. This typically arises in relation to any use of the returned goods which goes beyond use that was necessary to establish their nature, characteristic and functioning.[137] The aim of this provision is to prevent a consumer using the goods and then exercising their right to cancel and return them for a full refund.

It remains to be seen what extent of use the courts will judge as "beyond necessary". However, it seems that the trader should not be allowed to deduct for the removal of the packaging to inspect the item, but they can deduct when the item has been used rather than checked.[138] They also make clear that establishing the functioning of the goods is different from assessing whether they are fault free in every respect.[139] So, for example, the consumer would be able to try on a dress but not wear it and then seek to return it.[140] There is, however, one caveat to the trader's power to deduct: if the trader has failed to provide the consumer with the required information about their right to cancel in para.(l) of Sch.2 no deduction for use, regardless of whether it is necessary or not, can be made.[141]

---

[133] CC Regulations reg.34(5).
[134] CC Regulations reg.34(6).
[135] CC Regulations reg.34(7).
[136] CC Regulations reg.34(8).
[137] CC Regulations reg.34(9) and (12).
[138] BIS *Implementing Guidance* (December 2013), p.12.
[139] *DG Guidance Document* (June 13, 2014), p.47.
[140] Consumer Rights Directive recital 47.
[141] CC Regulations reg.34(11).

Return of goods

7–44 It is necessary to consider how and when the goods have to be returned. The default position is that the responsibility for returning the goods lies with the consumer[142] and they must bear the costs of doing so.[143] However, if the trader has failed to inform the consumer (as he is required to under reg.13) that they will face this cost, then the consumer will not be required to pay. Moreover, if the trader offers to collect the goods any cost will lie with them.[144]

Partial performance of a service contract

7–45 In the case of a distance contract for the supply of services slightly different rules apply, reflecting the inherent problem in "returning" services after they have been partially provided. Under reg.36 the trader is prohibited from beginning to supply a service before the cancellation period has ended,[145] allowing the consumer the full use of the cooling off period to change their mind. The consumer can, however, expressly request that the service be provided early. The right to cancel will be retained unless the consumer acknowledges that the consequences of early performance is the loss of their cancellation right once performance is complete.[146]

This does, however, create the situation where the consumer may cancel the contract once performance has begun but before it is completed. What is the situation where there has been partial performance? If a consumer has (i) requested performance within the cancellation period; (ii) been informed by the trader about their right to cancel; and (iii) been made aware that they would have to pay the costs up to the point of cancellation, then they must pay for the services provided.[147] How much they must pay is based on the price of the whole contract in comparison to the proportion of what was provided.[148] For example if the full service cost £100 but the consumer cancelled after 25 per cent had been received they would have to pay £25.

However, if the price of the contract as a whole is considered excessive, on the basis of the market value of the service, then the amount payable will be calculated by comparing the equivalent price for such services supplied by other traders.[149] If the trader in question were charging £700 for the full service but others in the sector were only charging around £300 this £300 figure would be used by the courts to reassess the amount the consumer in question has to pay.

---

[142] CC Regulations reg.35(2).
[143] CC Regulations reg.35(5).
[144] CC Regulations reg.35(5).
[145] CC Regulations reg.36(1).
[146] CC Regulations reg.36(2).
[147] CC Regulations reg.36(6).
[148] CC Regulations reg.36(4).
[149] CC Regulations reg.36(5).

Payment for digital content

Regulation 37 provides specific rules to deal with the situation where, **7–46** under a contract for the supply of digital content, data are transferred within the cancellation period. Again from the outset the trader is prohibited from supplying such digital content within the cancellation period unless the consumer specifically requests it and acknowledges the consequences of doing so.[150] In this case, the consequence for the consumer is that the right to cancel is lost as soon as performance is begun.[151] This is because, unlike traditional services, the supply of digital content is immediate and, in most cases, absolute—meaning that there is not the same possibility for partial performance. The result is that if the consumer consents to early performance, acknowledges that their right to cancel will be lost, and the trader confirms this consent and acknowledgment on a durable medium,[152] then the consumer will have to pay the full contract price for the digital content which was supplied. Moreover, unlike service contracts there is no provision for modification of an excessive price in relation to digital content under the Regulations.

In summary, when a consumer exercises their right to cancel a contract it is important to remember that the story does not end there. Instead it is necessary to consider:

(1) The consumer's right to be reimbursed under reg.34.
(2) The return of any physical goods to the trader under reg.35.
(3) Payment for any partial performance of a service contract under reg.36.

Cancellation: ancillary contracts

The final residual matter that needs to be considered when a consumer **7–47** exercises their right to cancel is the question of ancillary contracts. An ancillary contract is a contract which is related to the main contract but is subsidiary to it. For example, an insurance contract in relation to a contract for the sale of jewellery, or a credit agreement in relation to a television purchase.[153] In accordance with reg.38, if the consumer cancels the main contract then any ancillary contracts associated with it are also terminated.[154] This does not, however, apply to all ancillary contracts. Regulation 38(3) limits it those ancillary contract where the goods or services are either being supplied by the same trader as the main contract, or by a third party on the basis of an agreement with the main trader.

---

[150] CC Regulations reg.37(1).
[151] CC Regulations reg.37(2).
[152] CC Regulations reg.37(4).
[153] BIS *Implementing Guidance* (December 2013), p.7.
[154] CC Regulations reg.38(1). The value of having this right clearly set out can be illustrated by the case of *Durkin v DSG Retail Ltd*. The consumer was granted relief only after the Supreme Court clarified that an ancillary contract under the Consumer Credit Act 1974 could be set aside. However, this result only came after many years of litigation and expense, which not many consumers could afford to undertake. See *Durkin v DSG Retail Ltd* [2014] UKSC 21.

Thus if the consumer has approached a third party independently, any contract agreed would not be deemed "ancillary" under the Regulations, and hence would not be automatically terminated. Of course it may well be that the ancillary contract falls under the CC Regulations in its own right, meaning the consumer would have the right to cancel it so long as it was still within the cancellation period.

It is notable that a contract can be deemed ancillary even if it relates to financial services,[155] despite the fact such contracts are usually outwith the scope of the regulations. This reflects the reality that the majority of the ancillary contracts that consumers will enter into will be of a financial nature, usually by way of a credit agreement.

The CC Regulations also make it clear that the only cost the consumer must bear in relation to the cancelled ancillary contract are those relating to (i) any enhanced delivery option chosen; (ii) any diminution in value based on handling of the goods beyond what was necessary; (iii) any cost for returning goods; or (iv) payment in relation to services rendered in the cancellation period. All of these exceptions are governed by the same provisions that affect such costs in relation to the main contract and have been discussed above.

One question not dealt with by the CC Regulations is who is responsible for refunding the consumer for any costs associated with the ancillary contract. BIS suggests that if the payment for the ancillary contract was made to the trader of the main contract then the trader must refund it and then recoup the costs from the third party. If, however the payment was made to the third party directly then that party must refund. The problem with this second option is that there is no explicit obligation under the Regulations for the third party to make such a refund. The more consumer-friendly interpretation of the Regulations would therefore be to see the main trader's obligation under reg.34(1) to refund all payments as including any payment, including those relating to ancillary contracts.

Performance of the contract

7–48 If the consumer does not cancel the contract, then the obvious next step is for the trader to perform and supply the goods, services or digital content contracted for. Somewhat curiously, however, there is no express obligation under the CC Regulations by which the trader must perform. Instead the Regulations only make provision for the "delivery of goods" in relation to sales contracts under reg.42. This means that the consumer will have to rely on the ordinary principles of Scots contract law, and the provisions of the specific contract in question, when looking to compel performance under a services or digital content contract.

In relation to sales contracts, if the contract is not cancelled, then the supplier is obliged to deliver the goods to the consumer.[156] This must happen without undue delay and, unless otherwise agreed, no more than

---

[155] CC Regulations reg.38(3).
[156] CC Regulations reg.42(2).

30 days after the day on which the contract is entered into.[157] In terms of what amounts to delivery, the Regulations talk of the voluntary transfer of possession from one person to another.[158] This is expanded upon in the recitals of the Directive, which suggest that the goods should be treated as delivered when the consumer, or a third party indicated by them, has access to the goods to use them as owner or the ability to resell them.[159]

If the trader fails to deliver the goods within the 30 days, the consumer may "treat the contract as at an end"[160] if:

(1) the trader has refused to deliver the goods;
(2) the delivery of the goods in the agreed time was essential taking into account all the relevant circumstances at the time the contract was entered into; or
(3) the consumer told the trader, before the contract was entered into, that delivery in the agreed time was essential.

The term "essential" is not defined in the CC Regulations, but it probably reflects the broader Scots concept of materiality.[161] Whether or not delivery within 30 days or the agreed period will be essential (or material) will depend on the specific contract. To give an example, the need for a wedding dress to be delivered by the wedding day would be essential.[162]

If it cannot be shown that delivery was "essential" and the trader has **7–49** not refused to deliver the goods (that is to say none of the three conditions apply) the consumer has a second option: they may specify a new time for delivery.[163] If the trader then fails to deliver the goods within this new period, regardless of whether it was essential or not, the consumer may treat the contract as at an end.[164]

This raises the question: what is meant by "treating the contract at an end"? The CC Regulations do not explain what is meant by this. Is the contract automatically rescinded or must the consumer communicate his intention to terminate to the trader? It is likely to be the latter.[165] If the consumer does choose to treat the contract as at an end, either because one of the three conditions is met or delivery has not occurred in the new specified period, the trader must reimburse the consumer all payments made under the contract, without undue delay.[166]

It is important to realise that treating the contract at an end is not the only choice the consumer has, however. The CC Regulations make clear that it is something the consumer may do, at his option. Thus, should the

---

[157] CC Regulations reg.42(3).
[158] CC Regulations reg.5.
[159] Consumer Rights Directive recital 51.
[160] CC Regulations reg.42(6).
[161] See para.4–80 in Ch.4.
[162] See Consumer Rights Directive recital 42.
[163] CC Regulations reg.42(7).
[164] CC Regulations reg.42(8).
[165] Consumer Rights Directive recital 52 states that, without prejudice to national law, the consumer should notify the trader of his will to terminate.
[166] CC Regulations reg.42(9).

consumer wish to continue with the contract they may do so, despite late delivery. In doing so, the consumer would not affect their right to cancel the contract under regs 30 or 31, nor any other remedies available,[167] for example under the Sale of Goods Act 1979.

Finally, when considering delivery of goods it is necessary to know with whom the risk lies. That is to say, who is responsible for the goods and who must bear any loss resulting from their destruction? The CC Regulations make it clear it is the trader: Regulation 43 states that until the goods come into the physical possession of the consumer, they remain at the trader's risk.

Surcharges, additional payments and charges for customer helplines

7–50 Having considered Pts 2 and 3 and the rights and obligations they impose, it is now possible to turn and briefly consider Pt 4 of the Regulations: "Protection from inertia selling and additional charges".

A major concern in relation to e-commerce is the hidden charges levied on consumers by traders. The Consumer Rights Directive tried to tackle three of the main problem areas, namely payment surcharges, additional payments, and charges for customer helplines.

Payment surcharges

7–51 A payment surcharge is a charge imposed on a consumer when they use a particular payment method, most notably a credit card. In 2011, an Office of Fair Trading ("OFT") investigation showed that certain sectors were imposing high payment surcharges on consumers. As a result the Government chose to implement the relevant aspects of the Consumer Rights Directive ahead of schedule through the Consumer Rights (Payment Surcharges) Regulations 2012,[168] which came into force on April 6, 2013. The effect of the 2012 Regulations is that a trader must not charge consumers fees that exceed the cost borne by the trader for the use of that means of payment.

Additional charges

7–52 The CC Regulations also implement the Directive's initiatives in relation to additional charges. Thus, a consumer cannot be forced to pay any additional charge above the agreed contract price, unless they expressly consent.[169] Moreover, such consent cannot be obtained through an opt-out option, the prime example being a pre-ticked box on a website.[170] This means, for example, the trader cannot offer a gift wrap service costing an additional £5 and require the consumer to deselect a box if they do not want it. This applies even if the additional charge relates to financial

---

[167] CC Regulations reg.42(1).
[168] SI 2012/3110.
[169] CC Regulations reg.40(1).
[170] CC Regulations reg.40(2).

services which would normally be outwith the CC Regulations. Whilst it does not mean that the financial service contract itself becomes governed by the Regulations, it does prevent it being entered into through an unsuspecting add-on. If the trader does receive such an additional payment, the contract is to be treated as containing an implied term that the trader must reimburse the consumer,[171] and failure to do so places the trader in breach of contract.

Telephone helplines

The CC Regulations establish that if the trader operates a telephone helpline for consumers to use to contact them about a contract they have entered into, the trader cannot charge more than the basic rate for the call.[172] **7-53**

Enforcement

Given that the CC Regulations impose a number of obligations on the trader, it is important to consider how these are to be enforced, as the Regulations will only benefit consumers if they can be enforced to their benefit. **7-54**

One of the main problems in relation to enforcement is that consumers are simply not aware of their rights. For example in relation to the Distance Selling Regulations which the CC Regulations replace, an OFT market study showed that 56 per cent of consumers were oblivious of their right to cancel an online contract.[173] Nevertheless, whilst there may be relatively low levels of awareness, the success or otherwise of these new CC Regulations will depend on the success of the enforcement mechanisms provided.

Part 6 of the CC Regulations deals with the critical matter of enforcement. The first point to note is that the explicit method of enforcement is through complaints to the "enforcement authority".[174] An enforcement authority is deemed to be every local weights and measures authority in Great Britain,[175] and in Scotland such functions are exercised by local councils.[176] These authorities are placed under a duty to consider any complaint made about a contravention of the CC Regulations, so long as it is not frivolous or vexatious. Where a valid complaint is made, the enforcement authority may apply for an interdict or order of specific implement against such persons who appear to be in contravention.[177] The enforcement authorities must also notify the Competition and

---

[171] CC Regulations reg.40(4).
[172] CC Regulations reg.41(1).
[173] The report, "Internet Shopping" was published in June 2007 and is available at: *http://webarchive.nationalarchives.gov.uk/20140402142426/http://www.oft.gov.uk/shared_oft/reports/consumer_protection/oft921.pdf* [Accessed May 15, 2015].
[174] CC Regulations reg.44(1).
[175] CC Regulations reg.44(3).
[176] In accordance with the Local Government etc (Scotland) Act 1994 s.2.
[177] CC Regulations reg.45(1).

Markets Authority ("CMA"), which replaces the now abolished OFT, of the outcome of any such order made against the trader.[178]

7–55 Although consumers have the right to raise a complaint with the relevant local council as "enforcement authority", they have no direct right to bring an action against the trader on the basis of breach of the Regulations. Whilst the consumer may not have standing to bring an action under the CC Regulations there is scope to raise an action based on their contract with the trader. This is due to the fact that the CC Regulations make a large number of their provisions (and the trader's compliance with them) an implied term of the contract. Hence, if the trader fails to comply with the implied term, the consumer may raise an action for breach of contract based on the normal principles of contract law. The most important implied terms in the CC Regulations are: (i) reg.18 which makes it an implied term the trader has complied with the information requirements in relation to distance contracts in regs 13, 14 and 16; and (ii) reg.34(13) which makes the trader's obligation to reimburse sums due on cancellation an implied term.

Therefore, the main method of enforcement under the new CC Regulations is, in fact, not a mechanism within the Regulations themselves but the traditional principles of Scots contract law—an action for breach of an implied term in law.

Conclusion

7–56 A closing observation on the CC Regulations is to question whether the aim of increasing consumer confidence is actually achieved. The evidence of a widespread lack of awareness would suggest that most consumers trade online even without the reassurance provided by legislation. It is also not clear how much comfort can be derived from the provision of information, which is the primary obligation under the CC Regulations. The cooling off period does redress the balance, by allowing consumers a chance to change their mind, yet even this has its drawbacks, most notably the complications involved in returning goods after they have been delivered. In many cases, consumer confidence will be generated through experience and familiarity, rather than legislative intervention.

THE RELATIONSHIP BETWEEN THE CC REGULATIONS AND THE E-COMMERCE REGULATIONS

7–57 This chapter has considered the rights and obligations given, and imposed on, parties acting online under both the E-Commerce Regulations and the Consumer Contracts (Information, Cancellation and Additional Charges) Regulation 2013 ("CC Regulations"). Both sets of Regulations discussed impose information obligations upon traders. The final aspect that therefore needs to be considered is how these two sets of rules interact.

---

[178] CC Regulations reg.46.

Article 6(8) of the Consumer Rights Directive sets out that the information requirements under it are in addition to those in the E-Commerce Directive. Nevertheless should the two differ in relation to "content and the manner in which the information is to be provided", the article states that the Consumer Rights Directive is to prevail. From this starting point the first thing to note is that some (but not all) of the information to be supplied is the same.

Traders must, however, be aware that in satisfying the new CC Regulations they are not automatically satisfying all the requirements under the E-Commerce Regulations. The E-Commerce Regulations require more information about the trader themselves, for example his trade or public registration and his VAT number, information about promotional offers and importantly information about the technical steps required to conclude the contract.

Further, the two sets of Regulations apply to different situations. The E-Commerce Regulations only deal with online commerce but cover B2B as well as B2C relationships. In contrast the CC Regulations are much wider in scope, applying to on-premises and off-premises contracts as well as distance contracts. At the same time, however, the CC Regulations are narrower since they only apply to B2C transactions and not B2B dealings.

▼ CHAPTER SUMMARY

The key points from this chapter on e-commerce are: **7–58**

WHY REGULATE E-COMMERCE?

(1) Government and EU recognition of e-commerce is necessary to help boost consumer confidence and open up the Internal market for both suppliers and customers.
(2) Trading online brings advantages for both suppliers and customers, including greater choice, wider markets, and cost savings.

CONCLUDING CONTRACTS ELECTRONICALLY

(1) The Requirements of Writing (Scotland) Act 1995 (as amended) enables all contracts in Scots law to be formally concluded electronically.
(2) The exact point of conclusion is, however, uncertain; there are four potential points at which the contract may be formed.

THE ELECTRONIC COMMERCE (EC DIRECTIVE) REGULATIONS

(1) The Electronic Commerce Directive (2000/31/EC on certain legal aspects of information society services, in particular electronic

commerce) has been implemented in the UK as the Electronic Commerce (EC Directive) Regulations 2002 (SI 2002/2013).

(2) The Electronic Commerce (EC Directive) Regulations govern the provision of "information society services" and cover B2B and B2C contracts.

(3) Under the E-Commerce Regulations, the service provider may choose to have his contracts governed by the laws of his home jurisdiction, unless the customer is a consumer, in which case the laws of the consumer's jurisdiction apply.

(4) The E-Commerce Regulations impose information requirements on service providers, in regs 6–15.

(5) Part of the information that suppliers are required to provide is details of how the contract is concluded online, as per regs 9–11.

(6) Regulations 17–19 provide protection for intermediaries who transmit, cache, host or store information which gives rise to liability, for example defamatory statements.

THE CONSUMER CONTRACTS (INFORMATION, CANCELLATION AND ADDITIONAL CHARGES) REGULATIONS 2013

(1) The Consumer Contracts (Information, Cancellation and Additional Charges) Regulations 2013 (SI 2013/3134) implement the Consumer Rights Directive (2011/83/EU on consumer rights), and replace the Consumer Protection (Distance Selling) Regulations 2000 (SI 2000/2334) in relation to contracts entered into on or after June 13, 2014.

(2) The Consumer Contracts (Information, Cancellation and Additional Charges) Regulations govern B2C contracts for goods or services, or digital content concluded either "on premises", "off–premises" or at a "distance".

(3) Regulations 13, 14 and 16 impose pre- and post-contractual information obligations on the trader.

(4) Regulation 29 gives consumers the right to cancel the contract within a 14-day period, although this period can be extended if the consumer is not notified of this right by the trader.

(5) Enforcement of the Consumer Contracts Regulations is the responsibility of the Competition and Markets Authority and local authorities, although consumers may bring an action for breach of contract based on the implied terms imposed by the Regulations.

? QUICK QUIZ

- Can a contract be concluded electronically in Scots law? What is your authority for this?
- When is the contract concluded?
- What are "information society services"?
- What legislation regulates the provision of information society services?
- What obligations are imposed on providers of information society services? (Hint: what information is required?)

- What is a "distance contract"? (Your definition should contain five elements.)
- What legislation regulates distance contracts?
- What is a sales contract? Give an example.
- What is service contract? Give an example.
- When is a contract a contract for the supply of digital content not on a tangible medium?
- What information must be provided by sellers under a distance contract? (Hint: don't forget the additional requirements when the contract is concluded by "electronic means".)
- When does the consumer's right to cancel arise? How does this cancellation affect ancillary contracts?
- How can the CC Regulations be enforced by a consumer?

📖 FURTHER READING:

- ➤ R. Kadir, "The rules of advertisement in an electronic age" (2013) 55(1) *International Journal of Law & Management* 42.
- ➤ E. Hall, G. Howells and J. Watson, "The Consumer Rights Directive—An Assessment of its Contribution to the Development of European Consumer Contract Law" (2012) 1 *European Review of Contract Law* 138.
- ➤ H. Eidenmuller, "Why Withdrawal Rights?" (2011) 1 *European Review of Contract Law* 4.
- ➤ John Adams and Hector MacQueen, *Atiyah's Sale of Goods*, 12th edn (Oxford: Pearson, 2010).
- ➤ Lilian Edwards and Charlotte Waelde (eds), *Law and the Internet*, 3rd edn (Oxford: Hart Publishing, 2009).
- ➤ Lilian Edwards (ed), *The New Legal Framework for E-Commerce in Europe* (Oxford: Hart Publishing, 2005).
- ➤ Chris Reed, *Internet Law Texts and Materials*, 2nd edn (Cambridge: Cambridge University Press, 2004).

🖱 RELEVANT WEBLINKS

- ➤ UK legislation: *www.legislation.gov.uk* [Accessed May 15, 2015].
- ➤ Europa, Ensuring Safe Shopping Across the EU: *ec.europa.eu/consumers/cons_int/safe_shop/index_en.htm* [Accessed May 15, 2015].
- ➤ BIS Implementing Guidance on the Consumer Contracts Regulations, available at:
- ➤ *https://www.gov.uk/government/uploads/system/uploads/attachment_data/file/310044/bis-13-1368-consumer-contracts-information-cancellation-and-additional-payments-regulations-guidance.pdf* [Accessed May 15, 2015].

Chapter 8   Employment Law

ALAN DELANEY[1]

▶ CHAPTER OVERVIEW

8–01 This chapter is concerned with employment law. It begins by looking at the appropriate test to identify a contract of employment. Terms and conditions are considered before moving onto the termination of employment. The chapter then turns to look at rights in relation to unfair dismissal and redundancy payments, before concluding with a brief overview of discrimination legislation and the introduction of employment tribunal fees.

✓ OUTCOMES

8–02 By the end of this chapter, you should be able to:

✓ identify the key ingredients for a contract of employment;
✓ discuss the main sources of terms and conditions of employment;
✓ explain the means by which an employment contract might be terminated;
✓ understand the key principles of unfair dismissal; and
✓ outline what is meant by direct and indirect discrimination and harassment.

THE CONTRACT OF EMPLOYMENT

Introduction

8–03 Modern-day employment law is essentially a mixture of common law (especially contract law) and a minimum level of statutory employment rights. Generally employment tribunals have exclusive jurisdiction to hear claims based on statutory rights. Claims based on a breach of contract must usually be brought before the civil courts (although the employment tribunal has limited jurisdiction for certain breach of contract claims). It should also be noted that EU law has played an increasingly important role in setting minimum employment standards, particularly in the discrimination field. Those employed by "emanations

---

[1] Director, Maclay Murray & Spens, LLP.

of the State" may also be able to rely directly on the provisions of a Directive, so long as they are unconditional and sufficiently precise.[2] Other legislation such as the Human Rights Act 1998 and the Data Protection Act 1998 are also having a gradual influence on employment law which is likely to continue in the future.

Identifying a contract of employment

Many significant employment rights are restricted to employees (includ- **8–04** ing, for example, rights to maternity benefits, redundancy payments and not to be unfairly dismissed). It is therefore important to be able to identify a contract of employment.

It should be a simple matter to identify a contract of employment. In practice, however, it can be difficult in some cases. The starting point is the Employment Rights Act 1996 ("ERA 1996") which defines an "employee" as an individual who has entered into or works under a "contract of employment". This in turn is defined as a contract of service or apprenticeship, whether express or implied, and (if it is express) whether oral or in writing.[3] The focus in most cases will be on being able to establish a "contract of service".

Over the years, courts and employment tribunals have grappled with the question of what gives rise to a "contract of service". Various tests have been applied at times, none of which has emerged as pre-eminent, other than what is sometimes known as the "multiple" test, requiring consideration of a variety of different factors. Essentially, there is a need to consider: (a) whether certain fundamental criteria are satisfied on the facts; and (b) all other relevant characteristics of the relationship, to ascertain if they are consistent or not with a "contract of service".[4]

First, a minimum level of mutual obligations between the parties requires to be demonstrated. An employee needs to establish that the employer is under an obligation to provide work to them, and that they are under an equivalent obligation to perform that work. Without this "mutuality", a contract of employment does not arise.

Carmichael v National Power
[2000] I.R.L.R. 43, HL

Mrs C worked as a power station guide for N on a "casual as required" basis. She was paid only for the hours worked by her from time to time. There were occasions where N offered work to Mrs C which she chose not to accept. Along with another guide, Mrs L, they brought claims alleging a failure to provide written statements of employment particulars. This in turn required them to

[2] *Gibson v East Riding of Yorkshire Council* [2000] I.R.L.R. 598.
[3] ERA 1996 s.230(2).
[4] *Ready Mixed Concrete (South East) Ltd v Minister of Pensions and National Insurance* (1968) 2 Q.B. 497, HC.

establish that they were employed over the course of their work for
N.

HELD: the House of Lords found that as both Mrs C and Mrs L
were able to choose not to work when contacted by N and had
done so on various occasions, there were insufficient mutual
obligations to create a contract of service. The tribunal had been
entitled to find from the documents and surrounding circumstances
that the intention of the parties was not to have their relationship
governed by contract during the periods when the tour guides were
not working.

Mutuality by itself, however, is not enough. The employee in most cases
will also have to perform the work personally in exchange for wages or
remuneration, under the control or supervision of the employer. The
ability to arrange for a substitute to perform the work will usually be
fatal, unless there are exceptional circumstances.[5]

Finally, the other provisions of the contract need to be consistent with
employment. Certain provisions can point towards this, including fixed
hours of work, eligibility for benefits generally reserved for employees
(such as sick pay, maternity pay and pensions), application of disciplinary and grievance procedures, statutory notice provisions, and
other similar obligations.

As well as the above, employment tribunals and courts will have regard
to a number of factors including:

- how the parties view the relationship (the "label" given to the
  relationship by the parties will be taken into account but will not
  be determinative);
- who assumes the financial risk (does the employer assume the
  financial risk and the reward of the business—apart from any
  employee incentive benefits);
- whether equipment is provided by the employer or not (provision
  of equipment by an employee is fairly uncommon); and
- payment of tax and national insurance (seldom a key factor, since
  this will be determined by HMRC obligations).

---

[5] Compare *Express & Echo Publications Ltd v Tanton* [1999] I.R.L.R. 367, CA (right to
provide substitute inconsistent with contract of employment) with *Macfarlane v Glasgow
City Council* [2001] I.R.L.R. 7 (gymnastic instructor with limited right if unable to attend
to arrange replacement from employer-maintained list could still be consistent with
employment).

> **Key Concept**
>
> **Employee status**
>
> - Establishing a "contract of service" generally requires demonstrating certain fundamental criteria.
> - There has to be mutuality of obligations between the parties to the contract (typically an obligation on the employer to provide work and on the individual to perform that work personally—although some very limited right to arrange a substitute may not be fatal).
> - There also needs to be a sufficient level of control by the employer over the individual in relation to the work performed.
> - Other characteristics of the relationship (e.g. terms of the contract) should be consistent with a "contract of service".

Workers

Some statutory rights go further and benefit "workers", a wider category **8–05** which includes employees, but also extends to others who work under a contract (whether express or implied, oral or in writing) to personally undertake work or services for another party, whose status is not that of a client or customer of the person's profession or business. In other words, the law seeks to exclude from these rights only those who are genuinely self-employed. Examples of legislation extending to workers includes the right not to suffer unauthorised deductions from wages[6] and rights that arise in relation to working time and paid annual leave under the Working Time Regulations 1998. It should be similarly noted that discrimination law is also wider in scope such that most workers are protected, as with certain other categories of person.

Agency workers

The status of "agency workers" has been a specific problem area in recent **8–06** years. This often tripartite relationship is at its most straightforward where an individual (A) contracts with an agency (B) to provide work to an end-user (C). Such individuals can be engaged on fairly long-term arrangements yet deprived of the basic employment rights which require employee status, leading to a fundamental absence of job security.

Most attempts in this scenario to assert unfair dismissal rights by an individual against the agency have been unsuccessful, on the ground that the agency typically assumes no obligation to offer work to the individual, and where an offer of work is made, it does not need to be accepted or performed by the person. In the absence of mutuality (as well as sufficient day-to-day control or supervision), it is difficult to establish employment.[7]

Similarly, the fundamental problem faced by the individual seeking to

---

[6] ERA s.13.
[7] *Montgomery v Johnson Underwood Ltd* [2001] I.R.L.R. 269, CA.

argue employment by the end-user is typically the lack of any direct legal obligations between them. Whilst one case sought to imply a contract of employment as between the individual and end-user, this challenge to the status quo appears not to have established itself.[8]

Subsequent cases have stressed the need for there to be "necessity" before a contract will be implied. This is unlikely to arise where the existing relationship can be adequately explained by the contracts already in place (usually between the individual and the agency and separately between the agency and the end-user). Whilst the courts recognise that this places agency workers in a vulnerable position, they have generally stressed that this is a matter for Parliament to address.[9]

Some legislation is now in place to protect agency workers. The Conduct of Employment Agencies and Employment Businesses Regulations 2003 sets down certain minimum requirements including an obligation to provide information to individuals and end-users as to employment status. In addition, the Agency Workers Regulations 2010 provide a right for agency workers to no less favourable terms and conditions relating to basic pay and working conditions, subject to a 12-week qualifying period.

Company directors

8–07 The other group of individuals who can give rise to uncertainty as to "employment status" is that of executive directors. It is not inconsistent to be both a director and an employee (often such directors will work under a "service agreement"). The extent of shareholding is a relevant but not a decisive matter. Even a controlling shareholding can still be consistent with employment, if this genuinely reflects the reality of the situation and is not a sham.[10] This issue is most commonly encountered in the context of insolvency, when a director wishes to claim payments from the National Insurance Fund, which requires "employee" status to be established.[11]

TERMS AND CONDITIONS OF EMPLOYMENT

Formation

8–08 There is no need for a contract of employment to be in writing, although this is highly advisable for reasons of clarity and evidence. Terms can be oral or in writing, and express or implied by custom and practice.

---

[8] *Dacas v Brook Street Bureau (UK) Ltd* [2004] I.R.L.R. 358.
[9] *James v London Borough of Greenwich* [2007] I.R.L.R. 168 (upheld by the Court of Appeal [2008] I.R.L.R. 302).
[10] *Secretary of State for Trade and Industry v Bottrill* [1999] I.C.R. 592; *Nesbitt & Nesbitt v Secretary of State for Trade and Industry* [2007] I.R.L.R. 847.
[11] ERA ss.182–190.

Written statement of particulars

An employer is required by statute to provide a written statement of **8–09**
employment particulars to an employee within two months of employment commencing.[12] This statement must contain:

- names of the employer and employee;
- date when employment began (as well the date from which any
  continuous service is recognised);
- remuneration details (rate/scale and when payment is to be
  made);
- hours of work;
- terms and conditions in relation to holidays, sick pay, pension
  entitlement;
- notice entitlements;
- job title or a description of duties;
- place or places of work;
- if a fixed-term contract, when it is envisaged to end;
- details of any collective agreement which applies to the
  employment;
- details of disciplinary or grievance procedures which apply (or
  reference to where they can be found); and
- certain further information where work requires to be performed
  outside the UK for more than one month.

Some of this information can be provided via other documents. An
employee who does not receive a statement can bring a claim to an
employment tribunal, which has power to confirm or amend particulars.
An employer is generally required to update changes to this statement
within one month of the change having effect. Whilst the written statement is unilaterally given by the employer and therefore not contractual,
it can of course be influential in establishing what the agreed terms are
between the parties.

Collective agreements

Collective agreements can be a further source of terms and conditions. **8–10**
Such agreements are made by or on behalf of one or more trade unions
with one or more employers or employers' associations and relate to one
or more of the following:

- terms and conditions of employment or the physical conditions in
  which any workers are required to work;
- engagement or non-engagement, or termination or suspension of
  employment or the duties of employment, of one or more
  workers;
- matters of discipline;

---

[12] ERA s.1.

- a worker's membership or non-membership of a trade union;
- facilities for officials of trade unions; and
- machinery for negotiation or consultation, and other procedures relating to any of the above matters.

Whilst collective agreements are presumed by law to be unenforceable between the parties[13] (i.e. trade union and employer) this does not prevent terms within a collective agreement, which relate to terms and conditions of individual employees, from becoming incorporated within contracts of employment and as such enforceable within that contract. Once incorporated within contracts of employment, such terms will survive the termination of the underlying collective agreement.[14]

Wages

8–11 The contract of employment will determine the level and extent of wages payable by the employer to the employee. In addition, employers must comply with the National Minimum Wage Act 1998 which currently requires employers to pay a standard rate of £6.50 per hour (for those aged 21 or above) or a development rate of £5.13 per hour (for those aged 18–20 or 21 or over but undergoing accredited training in the first six months of employment). These rates are correct as at October 1, 2014 but are subject to annual review in October each year.

Workers are given statutory protection against unlawful deductions from their wages.[15] Employers can only make deductions where: (a) required or authorised by statute or a relevant provision of the contract of employment; or (b) the worker has given prior written consent to the deduction being made. Exceptions apply where there has been an overpayment of wages or expenses, and in certain other narrow circumstances. The onus is on an employer to consider the circumstances in which they may require to make a deduction from wages and to get written consent in advance from workers. Those working in retail employment receive some additional protection as to the level of deductions that can be made which arise from cash shortages or stock deficiency, even where consent has been obtained. Where an unlawful deduction has taken place, workers can complain to an employment tribunal within three months of the relevant deduction (or series of deductions).

Hours

8–12 Hours are regulated by the contract of employment subject to statutory limits set out in the Working Time Regulations 1998. The Regulations provide for an average maximum weekly limit of 48 hours across a standard reference period of 17 weeks. Failure to comply with this limit is a criminal offence for employers. It is open to employers to either

---

[13] Trade Union and Labour Relations (Consolidation) Act 1992 ("TULR(C)A") s.179.
[14] *Gibbons v Associated British Ports* [1985] I.R.L.R. 376.
[15] ERA s.13.

negotiate a change to the length of the reference period with workforce representatives, or to enter into individual opt-out agreements with workers in relation to this upper limit on average working hours. Other key provisions of the Regulations include entitlement to paid annual leave (currently 5.6 weeks), daily rest of 11 hours in each 24-hour period, weekly rest of 24 hours in every 7 day period (or at the employer's option 48 consecutive hours in a 14-day period), and the right to a rest break of 20 minutes where an employee is working a shift longer than six hours. There are also provisions in relation to night work and in relation to young workers. Some entitlements can be varied either by collective or workforce agreements and certain exemptions apply in relation to particular activities (e.g. where there is a need for continuity of service or production).

Maternity and family-friendly rights

It is not possible to provide detailed coverage of the many family-friendly **8–13** statutory employment rights that are relevant to the contract of employment. The main rights can be summarised as follows, some of which require specific eligibility criteria to be met:

- A right to 26 weeks' ordinary maternity leave and a further 26 weeks of additional maternity leave (all employees eligible, subject to notification requirements).
- A right to 39 weeks' statutory maternity pay (which the Government aims to increase to 52 weeks in due course).
- A right to return from maternity leave to the same job (or, where the full 52 weeks has been taken and this is not practicable, to an alternative which is suitable and appropriate and on no less favourable terms and conditions).
- A right of up to two weeks' paternity leave and paternity pay.
- A right of up to 13 weeks' unpaid parental leave.
- A right to ordinary/additional adoption leave and adoption pay.
- A right to request flexible working.
- A right to reasonable time off for dependants in certain circumstances.

Note that in relation to babies due or children placed for adoption on or after April 5, 2015, eligible parents may now elect to share statutory maternity leave and pay (except the first two-week compulsory leave period) and also adoption leave and pay.

Implied duties

Certain obligations are implied by common law into every contract of **8–14** employment. An employee, for example, is under a duty to give faithful service, to obey lawful and reasonable orders and to exercise reasonable skill and care. Similarly, an employer is under an implied duty to provide work, take reasonable care in relation to health and safety at work, and not to exercise a discretion under the contract (e.g. in relation to a flexibility or mobility clause) in such a manner as to render performance of the contract impossible. Similarly, a key implied term is that the employer is required not to engage in conduct likely to undermine mutual trust and confidence, without reasonable and proper cause for doing so.

> ### United Bank v Akhtar
> #### [1989] I.R.L.R. 507
>
> A was employed by U as a clerical worker in Leeds. Relying on a mobility clause in his contract of employment, U required A to transfer from Leeds to Birmingham on six days' notice and without financial assistance. A's request for a three-month postponement to make personal arrangements was refused and he ultimately resigned and claimed constructive dismissal.
> HELD: U had breached A's contract of employment—there is an implied duty to give reasonable notice in such circumstances and by failing to do so U had made it impossible for A to move. Employers are under a duty not to exercise contractual terms in such a manner as would be likely to breach mutual trust and confidence without reasonable or proper cause.
> See also: **Malik v Bank of Credit and Commerce International SA** [1997] I.R.L.R. 462, HL.

Transfer of undertakings

8–15 It should also be noted that there is specific statutory protection of terms and conditions of employment in relation to a transfer of an undertaking or a service provision change in terms of the Transfer of Undertakings (Protection of Employment) Regulations 2006.

TERMINATION OF EMPLOYMENT AND WRONGFUL DISMISSAL

Notice rights

8–16 The parties to a contract of employment will generally agree appropriate notice periods to apply. If no specific provision is made, a reasonable period of notice can be implied at common law, based on the employee's role and seniority. In any event, every employee who has been continuously employed for one month or more is entitled to a statutory minimum period of notice, when an employer wishes to terminate the contract of employment. A sliding scale applies as follows:

- one week's notice where continuous employment is between one month and two years;
- one week's notice per year where continuous service is between two years and 12 years; and
- 12 weeks' notice where continuous service is 12 years or longer.

An employer is entitled to only one week's statutory notice from an employee who has been continuously employed for one month or more (contractually, more notice is usually required). An employee may also elect to receive a payment in lieu of statutory notice entitlement.

Breach of contract and wrongful dismissal

The rights to contractual or statutory minimum notice do not apply **8–17** where a party is entitled to terminate the contract because of the other party's conduct. Thus, an employer might opt to summarily dismiss an employee who is guilty of serious misconduct or other act which amounts to a material or fundamental breach of contract. Where an employer terminates the contract in breach of contract, for example by not giving proper notice, or failing to follow a contractual disciplinary procedure, an employee will be able to claim damages for wrongful dismissal. Similarly, an employee might choose to resign without giving notice in circumstances where an employer has acted in a manner which amounts to a material or fundamental breach of contract. This may arise from breach of either an express term (such as the duty to pay wages) or an implied term (such as the duty not to damage mutual trust and confidence without reasonable or proper cause).[16] An employer can also pursue damages from an employee who resigns without giving notice in circumstances which do not involve a material or fundamental breach of contract. It should also be noted that aside from cases involving termination of employment, a breach of contract by the employer will not itself operate to terminate the employment contract, and the employee in such cases may be able to continue working and pursue damages for breach of contract from the employer (or a claim for wages, if appropriate).[17]

Other termination

An employment contract can become "frustrated" and terminate auto- **8–18** matically by operation of law, where unforeseen circumstances arise which render future performance impossible. Examples include the death of either party and historically have included the imposition of a substantial custodial sentence, or a sudden medical trauma which renders the employee permanently unable to work. As courts and employment tribunals tend to be reluctant to find an employment contract to be frustrated, the argument tends to be little used in practice.

Similarly, a contract of employment is terminated in certain but not all insolvency situations (a court order winding up a company is the main example of an order which does operate to terminate such contracts).

---

[16] *Malik v Bank of Credit and Commerce International SA (In Liquidation)* [1997] I.R.L.R. 462, HL.
[17] *Rigby v Ferodo Ltd* [1987] I.R.L.R. 516, HL.

UNFAIR DISMISSAL

Who has the right?

8–19 Section 94 of the ERA 1996 confers one of the most important rights within employment law: not to be unfairly dismissed. The right is generally restricted to employees who have minimum continuous service of two years with their employer. There are exceptions to this service requirement—which apply in relation to dismissals for certain automatically unfair reasons, including those relating to pregnancy, childbirth, maternity or other statutory family-related leave, as well as dismissals arising from making protected disclosures (whistle-blowing) or taking certain actions in relation to health and safety or trade union activities.[18]

What is a dismissal?

8–20 "Dismissal" is given a statutory meaning, and extends beyond termination of an employment contract by an employer. Section 95 provides that a dismissal arises in relation to:

- termination by the employer (with or without notice);
- termination of a limited-term contract by virtue of the limiting event and which is not renewed (the expiry of a fixed-term contract is the main example); and
- termination by the employee in circumstances where he is entitled to do so without notice by reason of the employer's conduct (i.e. "constructive" dismissal).

Constructive dismissal requires an employee to have resigned in response to a fundamental or material breach of contract by the employer, as discussed above. It should be noted that where an employer is too hasty in accepting the resignation of an employee which is either ambiguous or which is unambiguous but given in the "heat of the moment" or in circumstances of apparent emotional stress, this may amount to termination by the employer, rather than constructive dismissal.[19]

Potentially fair reasons for dismissal

8–21 Unless an employee establishes dismissal for an automatically unfair reason (in which case a finding of unfair dismissal is made), the employer is under an onus to establish that the dismissal was for one (or more) potentially fair reasons. These relate to:

- capability or qualifications (e.g. the employee is no longer capable or qualified to perform the role);

---

[18] ERA s.108.
[19] *Kwik-Fit Ltd v Lineham* [1992] I.R.L.R. 156, EAT.

- conduct of the employee (e.g. the employee is guilty of gross misconduct or has been dismissed for further misconduct after a series of warnings);
- redundancy;
- inability to continue working without contravening an enactment (e.g. a person employed as a driver who is subsequently banned from driving); or
- some other substantial reason of a kind such as to justify the dismissal (this is intended to be a residual category to cover dismissals for other substantial reasons not falling within the other headings).

Retirement as a potentially fair reason for dismissal was abolished with effect from April 6, 2011. The employer needs to provide a minimum level of evidence in each case before a tribunal will accept a potentially fair reason to exist. For example, in a redundancy case, the employer is required to establish at this stage that a genuine redundancy situation existed and that this was the potentially fair reason for dismissal.

Reasonableness

Once an employer establishes a potentially fair reason, a tribunal must **8–22** determine whether or not the dismissal was fair or unfair. This requires the tribunal to have regard to whether in the circumstances (including the size and administrative resources of the employer) it has acted reasonably or unreasonably in treating the reason for dismissal as sufficient. Courts have interpreted this requirement such that a tribunal has to ask whether the decision to dismiss fell within the "band of reasonable responses" open to a reasonable employer faced with the same circumstances. It is not appropriate for a tribunal to substitute its own view as to what action it would have taken.[20] It must objectively assess the decision to dismiss against the scope for one reasonable employer to take one approach but another reasonable employer to take a different approach. Only where the dismissal is outside the "band of reasonable responses" will the dismissal be unfair.

What a tribunal will generally look for will depend on the potentially fair reason being relied upon. In a capability dismissal, it will usually be necessary as a minimum to show that the employee was given sufficient warning of shortcomings and a genuine opportunity to improve (or in cases of ill-health that there has been adequate investigation of the medical position and regular consultation with the employee throughout). In a conduct dismissal, as a minimum, unless guilt is admitted, the employer will have to believe the employee is guilty, on reasonable grounds, after as much investigation as is reasonable.[21] Employers are also expected to follow a procedure which is fair and reasonable. In addition, the Advisory, Conciliation and Arbitration Service ("Acas")

---

[20] *Iceland Frozen Food v Jones* [1993] I.C.R. 17.
[21] *British Home Stores v Burchell* [1978] I.R.L.R. 379.

statutory code of practice on disciplinary and grievance procedures (which came into force on April 6, 2009) applies to situations involving misconduct and/or poor performance. A failure to follow the code in itself does not give rise to any specific liability but employment tribunals will take such a failure into account in appropriate cases and have power to increase any award made by up to 25 per cent where an employer unreasonably fails to follow the code. It does not apply to dismissals on grounds of redundancy or the non renewal of fixed term contracts on their expiry.[22] In redundancy cases, tribunals will consider issues such as the selection process for redundancy, the consultation process with employees, and whether means of avoiding the redundancy dismissal (such as alternative employment) were explored by the employer.

Polkey v AE Dayton Services Ltd
[1988] I.C.R. 142, HL

This case has long been a key decision in stressing the importance of procedural safeguards as part of a fair dismissal process. The case involved a redundancy which was unfair due to a lack of consultation with the employee before the decision was made by the employer. Lord Bridge in his judgement referred to the potentially fair reasons and said this:

"An employer having prima facie grounds to dismiss for one of these reasons will in the great majority of cases not act reasonably in treating the reason as a sufficient reason for dismissal unless and until he has taken the steps, conveniently classified in most of the authorities as 'procedural', which are necessary in the circumstances of the case to justify that course of action. Thus, in the case of incapacity, the employer will normally not act reasonably unless he gives the employee fair warning and an opportunity to mend his ways and show that he can do the job; in the case of misconduct, the employer will normally not act reasonably unless he investigates the complaint of misconduct fully and fairly and hears whatever the employee wishes to say in his defence or in explanation or mitigation; in the case of redundancy, the employer will normally not act reasonably unless he warns and consults any employees affected or their representative, adopts a fair basis on which to select for redundancy and takes such steps as may be reasonable to avoid or minimise redundancy by redeployment within his own organisation."

---

[22] A copy of the statutory code of practice together with a wide range of other guidance published by Acas can be found at *http://www.acas.org.uk* [Accessed May 15, 2015].

Complaints

A claim of unfair dismissal requires to be lodged within three months of **8–23** the effective date of termination of employment.[23] On upholding a claim of unfair dismissal the tribunal can order: (a) such compensation as is just and equitable in the circumstances; and/or (b) reinstatement; or (c) re-engagement.[24] Compensation for unfair dismissal breaks down into two elements: (i) a basic award (which is equivalent to a statutory redundancy payment—capped from April 6, 2015 at £14,250); and (ii) a compensatory award (which is generally design to reflect loss of earnings—capped from April 6, 2015 at the lesser of £78,335 or 12 months' gross pay). No maximum limit on the compensatory element applies to a dismissal for certain health and safety reasons or on the grounds of making a protected disclosure (whistle-blowing). In cases where an employer fails to comply with a reinstatement or re-engagement order, a further "additional award" can be made (capped from April 6, 2015 at £24,700). It is open to employers to argue that re-employment is not practicable in the circumstances. In practice, compensation tends to be the main remedy for unfair dismissals.

Key Concepts

Unfair dismissal

- The statutory meaning of "dismissal" includes: (a) termination by the employer; (b) the expiry of a limited-term contract; and (c) resignation by the employee in circumstances where the employee is entitled to do so by reason of the employer's conduct ("constructive dismissal").
- The right to claim unfair dismissal is restricted to employees who generally must establish continuous service of two years with the employer.
- There are exceptions to the minimum service requirement for certain automatically unfair reasons, including those relating to pregnancy, childbirth, maternity or other statutory-related leave, as well as dismissals arising from making protected disclosures or taking certain actions in relation to health and safety or trade union activities.
- An Acas statutory code of practice applies to situations involving misconduct and/or poor performance. A failure to follow the code will be taken into account by an employment tribunal who may increase any award made by up to 25 per cent where an employer has unreasonably failed to comply.
- In addition, any dismissal requires to be "potentially fair" reason

---

[23] ERA s.111.
[24] ERA ss.112–126.

> and otherwise reasonable in the circumstances in terms of s.98 of
> the ERA 1996.
> ● The remedies for unfair dismissal are compensation, re- instate-
> ment and re-engagement.

REDUNDANCY PAYMENTS

Who has the right?

8–24   The right to a redundancy payment arises where an employee is dismissed
on grounds of redundancy, or alternatively, in certain other limited
situations involving lay-off or short-time working.[25] To be eligible, an
employee needs to have two years' continuous service as at the relevant
date of termination.[26] Those who volunteer in redundancy situations are
generally looked upon as being dismissed on redundancy grounds, unless
there is evidence to the contrary.

What is redundancy?

8–25   For the purpose of redundancy payments, a dismissal on grounds of
redundancy will be established where the dismissal is wholly or mainly
attributable to[27]:

- the fact that an employer has ceased or intends to cease: (a) to
  carry on the business for the purposes of which the employee was
  employed; or (b) to carry on that business in the place where the
  employee was employed; or
- the fact that the requirements of that business: (a) for employees
  to carry out work of a particular kind; or (b) for employees to
  carry out work of a particular kind in the place where the
  employee was employed, has in either case, ceased or diminished,
  or are expected to cease or diminish.

The focus can be seen to be on a disappearing role, workplace or a
cessation or diminution of work. Note that the definition of redundancy
is sufficient to permit what is known as "bumping", typically where one
employee with long experience but whose role no longer exists, displaces
a newer employee who has recently joined. The reason for dismissing the
newer employee is still on grounds of redundancy.[28] Place of employment
is generally approached by looking at where the employee actually
worked in practice, rather than looking at where their contract might
oblige them to work, if requested by the employer.[29]

---

[25]   ERA s.135.
[26]   ERA s.155.
[27]   ERA s.139.
[28]   *Murray v Foyle Meats* [1999] I.R.L.R. 563.
[29]   *High Table v Horst* [1997] I.R.L.R. 513.

How is a redundancy payment calculated?

A statutory redundancy payment is calculated by reference to weekly **8–26** pay, age and length of service. A maximum limit is placed on "weekly pay" for this purpose (currently £475 from April 6, 2015). Essentially, the payment is calculated at the rate of 1.5 weeks' pay for a year of employment when the employee was aged not less than 41; otherwise at the rate of one week's pay for a year of employment when the employee was aged not less than 22 and finally at the rate of a .5 week's pay for each year of employment below this age. The maximum period for calculation purposes is 20 years, with no account taken of any earlier year.

> **Example:**
>
> X is made redundant from XYZ Limited on April 6, 2015 after 25 complete years employment, aged 45 and earning £800 per week. His payment is calculated as follows:
>
> Years not less than 41 = 4 x £475 (maximum weekly pay) x 1.5 (multiplication factor) = £2,850
>
> Years between 22 and 41 = 16 (limited to last 20 years) x £475 x 1 = £7,600
>
> Total = £2,850 + £7,600 = £10,450

Alternative employment

An employee who receives an offer of alternative employment in a **8–27** redundancy situation is entitled to a statutory four-week trial period (which can be extended by agreement between the parties where training is required) to determine whether the job is suitable, without losing the right to claim a redundancy payment.[30] Conversely, an employee who unreasonably refuses an offer of suitable alternative employment made prior to the date on which the dismissal for redundancy takes effect (or within four weeks of that date) will lose their right to a redundancy payment.[31]

Right to time off

An employee who is given notice of dismissal on grounds of redundancy **8–28** is entitled to be permitted by an employer to take reasonable paid time off during working hours in the notice period to: (a) look for new employment; or (b) make arrangements for training for future employment. An employee not afforded such rights can bring an employment tribunal claim within three months of the failure.

---

[30] ERA s.138(2).
[31] ERA s.141(4).

Claim for redundancy payment

8–29 Where an employer has failed to make a statutory redundancy payment, an employee can bring a claim to an employment tribunal for such a payment within six months of the relevant date (usually termination of employment).

Other considerations

Enhanced redundancy

8–30 An employee may be contractually entitled to a payment over and above the minimum statutory redundancy payment. Many employers offer more generous schemes which offer payments that are inclusive of the statutory element. The employee needs to establish a contractual right to the payment, rather than simply one-off or adhoc situations in the past where the employer has chosen to pay more than the statutory minimum. A failure by an employer to pay an enhanced redundancy payment will entitle an employee to bring a claim for breach of contract. This can be brought in an employment tribunal (subject to an upper limit of £25,000 damages) or can be brought in the ordinary civil courts within the normal limitation period for breach of contract claims.

Collective consultation requirements

8–31 A statutory duty arises to consult trade union or other elected representatives where an employer is proposing to dismiss as redundant 20 or more employees at one establishment within a period of 90 days or less.[32] Such consultation must begin in good time and at least 30 days before the first of the dismissals takes effect unless the employer proposes to dismiss 100 or more within that period, in which case it must begin in good time and at least 45 days before the first of the dismissals takes effect. There are detailed statutory provisions which set out various obligations in relation to this requirement to collectively consult with representatives. A failure to comply by an employer may on application to an employment tribunal trigger a protective award being made of up to 90 days pay per employee.[33] An employer is also required in collective redundancy situations to notify the Secretary of State in advance within similar prescribed periods (commonly done in practice on a HR1 form).

---

[32] TULR(C)A s.188.
[33] TULR(C)A s.189. It is important to note that these provisions are also triggered on dismissals and re-engagement on new terms and conditions: see *GMB v MAN Truck & Bus UK Ltd* [2000] I.R.L.R. 636.

DISCRIMINATION

Introduction

This chapter can do no more than scratch the surface of existing dis- **8–32** crimination law and provide a very brief outline of the statutory provisions. Prior to the main provisions of the Equality Act 2010 ("the Act") coming into force on October 1, 2010, discrimination law was located across a number of different pieces of legislation, much of which was intended to implement EC Directives.[34] The Act seeks to consolidate and replace this legislation and attempts to harmonise variations in coverage which existed under the old law.[35] The Equality and Human Rights Commission ("EHRC") plays a vital role in seeking to eliminate discrimination and has certain powers and duties under the Act. A detailed explanation of the provisions of the Act can be found in the EHRC Code of Practice on Employment, which is essential reading for employers seeking to understand their responsibilities.[36] Tribunals and courts must take into account any part of the Code that appears to them relevant to any question arising in any proceedings. Public authorities also have a specific equality duty under the Act which they must have regard to in the exercise of their functions.[37]

Scope

The Act restates the provisions on equal pay previously found in the **8–33** Equal Pay Act 1970 which require equality of pay as between men and women in relation to: (a) like work; (b) work rated as equivalent; or (c) work of equal value. It is open to an employer to defend an equal pay claim by showing that the difference in pay is due to a genuine material factor between the man and the woman, other than gender.[38] The equal pay provisions are otherwise beyond the scope of this chapter.

The Act renders discrimination unlawful in relation to one of the following "protected characteristics":

- Age.
- Disability.
- Gender reassignment.
- Marriage and civil partnership.
- Pregnancy and maternity.
- Race.

---

[34] See the Framework Directive (2000/78/EC), the Race Directive (2000/43/EC) and the Equal Treatment Directive (2006/54/EC).
[35] Separate protection remains in relation to part-time and fixed-term status: see the Part-time Workers (Prevention of Less Favourable Treatment) Regulations 2000 (SI 2000/1551) and the Fixed-term Employees (Prevention of Less Favourable Treatment) Regulations 2002 (SI 2002/2034).
[36] EHRC, *Equality Act 2010 Code of Practice on Employment* (The Stationary Office, 2010), available from *http://www.equalityhumanrights.com* [Accessed May 15, 2015].
[37] Equality Act 2010 s.149.
[38] Equality Act 2010 ss.65–69.

- Religion or belief.[39]
- Sex.
- Sexual orientation.

The main types of prohibited conduct applying to most of these protected characteristics under the Act are direct discrimination, indirect discrimination, harassment and victimisation.

Disability discrimination

8-34 A person is considered to have a "disability" for the purposes of the Act if they have a physical or mental impairment which has a substantial and long-term adverse effect on their ability to carry out normal day-to-day activities.[40] There is detailed guidance issued by the Office for Disability Issues which is to be taken into account for the purpose of determining questions relating to the definition of "disability", which can often be a complex matter.[41]

Certain conditions are deemed as disabilities without the need to satisfy this test including cancer, HIV infection and multiple sclerosis.[42]

It should be noted that disability discrimination goes further than other areas of discrimination and also allows two unique types of claims to be brought.

The first is where A treats B unfavourably because of something arising in consequence of B's disability, which A cannot show to be a proportionate means of achieving a legitimate aim.[43] Cases might arise under this heading, for example, in relation to how employers operate sickness absence policies in the workplace, where the alleged treatment is not due to the fact of disability but to absence arising from the disability.

The second is a duty on employers to make reasonable adjustments where a physical feature of premises, or a provision, criteria or practice places a disabled person at a substantial disadvantage compared with persons who are not disabled and where it is reasonable for the employer to take steps to prevent such effect. Where a failure to provide an auxiliary aid would place a disabled person at a substantial disadvantage, there is also a duty to take such steps as is reasonable to provide the aid.

The EHRC Code of Practice provides examples of possible reasonable adjustments including[44]:

- making adjustments to premises;
- allocating duties to others;

---

[39] As for what can amount to "belief" see *Grainger Plc v Nicholson* [2010] I.R.L.R. 4 (belief in man-made climate change amounted to protected belief).

[40] Equality Act 2010 s.6.

[41] Office of Disability Issues, *Guidance on matters to be taken into account in determining questions relating to the definition of disability*, available at *https://www.gov.uk/government/organisations/office-for-disability-issues* [Accessed May 15, 2015].

[42] Equality Act 2010 Sch.1 para.6(1).

[43] Equality Act 2010 s.15(1).

[44] EHRC *Code of Practice on employment*, para.6.33.

- transferring to an existing vacancy;
- altering hours of work;
- allowing absence from the workplace for assessment, treatment or rehabilitation;
- giving or arranging training or mentoring;
- acquiring or modifying equipment;
- modifying procedures for testing or assessment;
- providing a reader or interpreter;
- providing supervision or other support;
- allowing a period of disability leave; or
- adjusting redundancy selection criteria.

Equally, it outlines a variety of factors which might be taken into account in determining whether it is reasonable for adjustments to be made, including the extent to which doing so would prevent the effect, the practicability of the measure, the financial and other costs involved and resources of the employer, the nature of the employer's activities, size of the undertaking and the availability of financial assistance.[45]

Direct discrimination

Direct discrimination arises where because of a protected characteristic A **8–35** treats B less favourably than A treats or would treat others.[46] Generally, an employee has to establish a comparator, real or hypothetical, whose circumstances are not materially different for the purpose of bringing such a claim. Thus, where a female probationer police officer was not offered a permanent role, in circumstances where the evidence established that a hypothetical male in similar circumstances would have been, direct discrimination was found to have taken place.[47] An exception exists in relation to pregnancy and maternity discrimination, where no comparator is required.[48]

The definition is deliberately wide so as to encompass discrimination against an employee because of the employee's association with a person who has a protected characteristic (sometimes known as "associative discrimination") as well as cases of discrimination by "perception" where the employer treats an employee less favourably because the employer mistakenly believes the employee has a protected characteristic.[49]

It is not possible to justify direct discrimination, with the exception of direct age discrimination, where an employer can argue that the less favourable treatment can be justified as a proportionate means of achieving a legitimate aim.[50] Aside from this exception, it matters not

---

[45] EHRC *Code of Practice on employment*, para.6.28.
[46] Equality Act 2010 s.13.
[47] *Chief Constable of West Yorkshire v Vento* [2001] I.R.L.R. 124, EAT. For the appeal as to remedy see the decision of the Court of Appeal at [2003] I.R.L.R. 102.
[48] Equality Act 2010 s.18.
[49] Direct discrimination by association or perception, however, does not apply to the protected characteristics of marriage and civil partnership or pregnancy and maternity.
[50] Equality Act 2010 s.13(2).

what the employer's motive or intention was or whether the less favourable treatment was conscious or unconscious.

However, in certain circumstances, the Act permits an employer to require a job applicant or an employee to have a particular protected characteristic where an "occupational requirement" exists.[51] So, for example, a role might be limited to one gender for reasons of "decency or privacy" where a job is likely to involve physical contact where objection might reasonably be taken (e.g. a bra-fitting service), or where the holder of a job provides personal welfare or education services which can most effectively be provided by one gender (e.g. a rape counselling service).

Combined discrimination

8–36 The Act also provides for protection against "combined" discrimination although as at the time of writing, these provisions have not yet been brought into force and the Government has indicated no present intention to do so.[52] Such claims, if the provisions are introduced in the future, will arise where a person A treats B less favourably because of a combination of two "relevant" protected characteristics (being age, disability, gender reassignment, race, religion or belief, sex or sexual orientation) than A treats or would treat a person who does not share either of those characteristics.[53]

Indirect discrimination

8–37 Indirect discrimination arises where a person A applies to B a provision, criterion or practice which is discriminatory in relation to a relevant protected characteristic of B's (being age, disability, gender reassignment, marriage and civil partnership, race, religion or belief, sex, or sexual orientation). It will be discriminatory where:

- A applies or would apply the provision, criterion or practice to persons with whom B does not share the protected characteristic.
- It puts or would put persons with whom B shares the characteristic at a particular disadvantage when compared with persons with whom B does not share it.
- It puts or would put B at that disadvantage.
- A cannot show it to be a proportionate means of achieving a legitimate aim.[54]

Typically, this arises where an apparently "neutral" requirement is applied across the board but which disadvantages persons with a protected characteristic, including the individual in question, and which cannot be objectively justified.

---

[51] Equality Act 2010 Sch.9 para.1.
[52] Department for Business, Innovation and Skills, *Plan for Growth* (The Stationery Office, 2011).
[53] Equality Act 2010 s.14.
[54] Equality Act 2010 s.19.

An example of such discrimination involving gender can be seen in a case involving a female airline pilot, employed by British Airways, who refused her request to reduce her flying hours by 50 per cent and would allow only a reduction of 25 per cent. There was sufficient evidence to establish that a provision requiring those requesting to work part-time to move only to 75 per cent of normal hours would be to the detriment of a considerably larger proportion of women than men. The reasons put forward by the employer in this case were held to be insufficient to objectively justify the provision as being a proportionate means of achieving a legitimate aim.[55]

Harassment

Harassment encompasses three types of unlawful conduct[56]: **8–38**

- Harassment related to a "relevant" protected characteristic.
- Sexual harassment.
- Less favourable treatment because a person submits to, or rejects, sexual harassment or harassment related to sex or gender reassignment.

Again, for the purposes of harassment "relevant" protected characteristics are age, disability, gender reassignment, race, religion or belief, sex or sexual orientation.

The first category of harassment takes place where a person engages in unwanted conduct related to the relevant protected characteristic which has the purpose or effect of: (a) violating the person's dignity; or (b) creating an intimidating, hostile, degrading, humiliating or offensive environment for them. It is important to note that it is sufficient that the conduct in question has brought about this effect, regardless of purpose. In deciding the question of whether such effect has occurred, tribunals are required to take into account the perception of the claimant, the other circumstances of the case and whether it is reasonable for the conduct to have that effect.[57]

For example, in one case where a senior manager told a British employee of Indian ethnic origin who had handed in her notice "*We will probably bump into each other in future unless you are married off in India*" this was found to amount to unlawful harassment related to race. It did not matter that marriage plans had previously been discussed between the parties, who had to that time enjoyed a good working relationship. It was sufficient that the remark evoked a stereotype of forced marriages which the claimant reasonably found offensive.[58]

It should again be noted that protection is broad insofar as the claimant need not hold the relevant protected characteristic provided the

---

[55] *British Airways Plc v Starmer* [2005] I.R.L.R. 863.
[56] Equality Act 2010 s.26.
[57] Equality Act 2010 s.26(4).
[58] *Richmond Pharmacology v Dhaliwal* [2009] I.R.L.R. 336.

harassment is "related to" the same. As such, it has been held that a man could bring a claim arising from homophobic remarks directed towards him, in circumstances where he was a married heterosexual man and where those making remarks did not perceive him to be homosexual. It was sufficient that he was subjected to unwanted conduct related to sexual orientation.[59]

As for the other two types of harassment, "sexual harassment" will arise where there is unwanted conduct with the same purpose or effect as above, but which is of a sexual nature. This might encompass verbal, non-verbal or physical conduct included unwanted advances, touching, sexual jokes, displaying pornography, or sending emails of a sexual nature.

The last type of harassment is designed to give protection where a person suffers less favourable treatment because they submit to or reject unwanted conduct of a sexual nature, or which is related to sex or gender reassignment and which has the above purpose or effect.

Victimisation

8–39 The Act also makes it unlawful to subject a person to a detriment for having carried out a "protected act" or in the belief that a person may do so in the future.[60]

A "protected act" includes:

- bringing proceedings under the Act;
- giving evidence or information in connection with proceedings brought under the Act;
- doing anything which is related to the provisions of the Act; or
- making an allegation (whether or not express) that another person has done something in breach of the Act.

Victimisation will arise where the protected act is one of the reasons for the treatment, even if it is not the only reason.

Obligations and liability

8–40 In relation to job applicants, it is unlawful for an employer to discriminate in relation to arrangements made for determining who should be offered employment, in the terms on which employment is offered, or by refusing or deliberately omitting to offer employment.[61]

Similarly, in relation to employment, it is unlawful to discriminate in relation to access to opportunities for promotion, transfer or training, or any other benefits, facilities, services or by subjecting to any detriment, or dismissal from employment.[62] There is also protection from post-

---

[59] *English v Thomas Sanderson Blinds Ltd* [2009] I.R.L.R. 206.
[60] Equality Act 2010 s.27.
[61] Equality Act 2010 s.39(1).
[62] Equality Act 2010 s.39(2).

employment detriment, which may include, for example, the provision of a reference.

For liability purposes, anything done by a person in the course of their employment is treated by the Act as being done by the employer, unless the employer can establish having taken all such steps as were reasonably practicable to prevent the employee doing the relevant act or acts in question.[63] As indicated earlier in the chapter, the scope of discrimination law generally extends beyond "employees" in the narrow sense and protects most workers and certain other persons.

Complaint

A complaint lies to an employment tribunal, within three months of an **8–41** unlawful act (or where the act extends over a period, the end of the period).[64] A tribunal that finds a complaint to be well-founded has power to make an order upholding the claim and can award compensation.[65] There is no upper limit on discrimination awards, which can include sums in relation to financial loss, injury to feelings, personal injury, and interest. In addition, a tribunal can make a recommendation that the employer take certain action to avoid or reduce the adverse effect of any act of discrimination to which the complaint relates. The tribunal also has power to increase or reduce awards by up to 25 per cent where either party has unreasonably failed to follow the Acas *Code of practice on disciplinary and grievance procedures.*

Employment tribunal fees and Acas pre-claim conciliation

With effect from July 29, 2013, the Government introduced a system of **8–42** fees which are payable by claimants or groups of claimants wishing to pursue employment tribunal claims. At the time of writing, a single claimant must pay an issue fee of either £160 or £250 at the time of raising an employment tribunal claim. The fee depends on the nature of claim brought with more straightforward "type A" claims attracting the lower charge. Unfair dismissal and discrimination claims both fall into "type B" claims with the higher fee payable. In addition, before an employment tribunal hearing takes place, a single claimant must pay a further hearing fee of £230 or £950. This is again determined by the category – A or B— that the claim falls within. There is a separate sliding scale of fees which applies to a claim brought by more than one claimant. Although there is a limited fee remission scheme based on gross income and disposable capital, the introduction of fees has proved controversial although so far judicial review attempts to challenge them have been unsuccessful. In addition, from April 6, 2014, individuals wishing to bring an employment tribunal claim must first participate in a mandatory Acas pre-claim

---

[63] Equality Act 2010 s.109(4).
[64] Equality Act 2010 s.123.
[65] Equality Act 2010 s.124.

conciliation process. Further details can be obtained from the Acas
website.[66]

▼ CHAPTER SUMMARY

THE CONTRACT OF EMPLOYMENT

8–42 It is important to be able to identify a contract of employment as certain rights
are restricted to employees only.

(1) A minimum level of obligation needs to exist between the parties before
a contract of service will arise. This will include mutual obligations to
provide and perform work.
(2) An obligation to perform the work personally will usually also have to
exist and there has to be sufficient control.
(3) Other provisions within the contract should be consistent with that of
employment.
(4) Workers may also qualify for certain rights arising under employment
law, including in relation to the Working Time Regulations 1998.

TERMS AND CONDITIONS OF EMPLOYMENT

(1) Contracts of employment do not require to be in writing—terms can be
written or oral and express or implied.
(2) An employer is required to give an employee a written statement of
terms and conditions within two months of employment commencing—
this is not contractual but can evidence what the contractual terms are:

➤ ERA s.1.

(3) Collective agreements may also be a source of terms and conditions
through becoming incorporated in contracts of employment.
(4) Employees have a right not to be subjected to unlawful deductions from
wages:

➤ ERA s.13.

(5) Minimum rights exist in relation to wages and working hours/rest
periods:

➤ National Minimum Wage Act 1998 & Working Time Regulations
1998.

(6) Important terms are implied in all contracts of employment, including
the duty of the employer not to engage in conduct likely to undermine
trust and confidence without reasonable or proper cause:

➤ *United Bank v Akhtar* [1989] I.R.L.R. 507; *Malik v Bank of Credit
and Commerce International SA* [1997] I.R.L.R. 462, HL.

---

[66] *http://www.acas.org.uk* [Accessed May 15, 2015].

TERMINATION OF EMPLOYMENT AND WRONGFUL DISMISSAL

(1) Statutory minimum notice rights exist for employers and employees:

> ➤ ERA s.86.

(2) A fundamental or material breach of contract will generally permit the party not in default to terminate the contract.

(3) If an employer dismisses in breach of contract, an employee will be able to bring a claim of wrongful dismissal seeking damages. An employer may also bring a similar breach of contract claim against an employee who resigns and fails to give notice, in circumstances not involving a fundamental or material breach of contract.

(4) A contract of employment can also terminate by operation of law where an unforeseen event or circumstances renders all future performance of the contract impossible. This is known as "frustration".

UNFAIR DISMISSAL

(1) The right to claim unfair dismissal is generally restricted to employees with at least two years continuous service:

> ➤ ERA s.108.

(2) Exceptions apply to this general rule in relation to certain dismissals which are also automatically unfair, for example, dismissals on grounds of pregnancy, childbirth, maternity or certain health and safety grounds.

(3) Dismissal is a statutory concept and includes termination of a fixed-term contract which is not renewed and also termination of the contract by an employee in circumstances where they are entitled to do so because of the employer's conduct (constructive dismissal):

> ➤ ERA s.95.

(4) An Acas statutory code of practice applies to situations involving misconduct and/or poor performance. A failure to follow the Code will be taken into account by an employment tribunal who may increase any award made by up to 25 per cent where an employer has unreasonably failed to comply.

(5) There are five potentially fair reasons for dismissal: capability/qualifications, conduct, redundancy, inability to work without contravening an enactment, and some other substantial reason:

> ➤ ERA s.98(2).

(6) Once a potentially fair reason is established, a tribunal must determine whether the employer acted reasonably or unreasonably in treating that reason as sufficient to dismiss the employee in the circumstances:

> ➤ ERA s.98(4).

(7) A complaint of unfair dismissal requires to be raised to an employment within three months of the effective date of termination.

(8) Remedies for unfair dismissal include compensation, reinstatement and re-engagement. A cap on compensation exists, unless the dismissal is on

the ground of certain health and safety reasons or a protected disclosure (whistle-blowing).

REDUNDANCY PAYMENTS

(1) An employee requires two years service to be eligible for a redundancy payment:

> ➤ ERA s.155.

(2) Redundancy arises where there is a disappearing role, workplace or a cessation or diminution of work.
(3) A redundancy payment is calculated by reference to weekly pay, age and length of service. A limit on "weekly pay" is applied for this purpose.
(4) An employee is entitled to a four-week trial period if alternative employment is offered, without losing a right to a redundancy payment.
(5) A redundancy payment may be lost if an employee unreasonably refuses suitable alternative employment.
(6) Employees may also be entitled under their contracts of employment to enhanced redundancy terms.
(7) Detailed requirements in relation to collective consultation apply where an employer is proposing to dismiss as redundant 20 or more employees "at one establishment" within a period of 90 days:

> ➤ TULR(C)A s.188.

DISCRIMINATION

(1) Discrimination is unlawful on grounds of age, disability, gender reassignment, marriage and civil partnership, pregnancy and maternity, race, religion or belief, sex or sexual orientation. There are also specific equal pay provisions and separate legislation relating to discrimination relating to part-time or fixed-term status:

> ➤ Equality Act 2010.
> ➤ Part-time Workers (Prevention of Less Favourable Treatment) Regulations 2000.
> ➤ Fixed-term Employees (Prevention of Less Favourable Treatment) Regulations 2002.

(2) Much discrimination law now focuses on three main types of discrimination: direct, indirect and harassment.
(3) Direct discrimination will generally arise where an employer subjects a person to less favourable treatment because of a protected characteristic.
(4) Indirect discrimination will generally arise where an employer applies an apparently "neutral" provision, criteria or practice to everyone, but which is one that places one group (including the individual) at a particular disadvantage and which cannot be shown to be proportionate means of achieving a legitimate aim.
(5) Harassment will generally arise where a person is subjected to unwanted conduct related to a protected characteristic which has the purpose or

effect of violating dignity or creating an intimidating, hostile, degrading, humiliating or offensive environment. The perception of the person is taken into account in considering whether or not it is reasonable to consider that harassment has taken place in the circumstances.

(6) A complaint in relation to unlawful discrimination can be brought to an employment tribunal within three months, which has power to award compensation, including for injury to feelings. There is no limit on the compensation that may be awarded.

(7) The disability discrimination provisions within the Equality Act 2010 apply to disabled persons—this generally requires a claimant to establish a physical or mental impairment which has a long-term substantial adverse effect on normal day-to-day activities.

(8) These provisions also prohibit additional types of discrimination: less favourable treatment because of something arising in consequence of disability and a failure to make reasonable adjustments.

? QUICK QUIZ

- What are the key ingredients for a contract of service?
- Can a director who is a controlling shareholder also be an employee?
- When does a written statement of employment particulars have to be provided by an employer?
- What is a collective agreement? How can such agreements be sources of terms and conditions of employment?
- What limit does the Working Time Regulations 1998 place on maximum weekly working hours? Can employees waive their rights to this limit?
- What is wrongful dismissal and how is this different from unfair dismissal?
- What are the five potentially fair reasons for dismissal in unfair dismissal law?
- How much continuous service is required to be eligible to claim a redundancy payment?
- Can direct sex discrimination ever be justified?
- What is the general test for "disability" under the Equality Act 2010?

FURTHER READING

➢ *Harvey on Industrial Relations and Employment Law* (London: Butterworths)—authoritative commentary designed for the practitioner.

➢ Professor Gwyneth Pitt, *Employment Law*, 9th edn (London: Sweet & Maxwell, 2014)—leading textbook.

🖱 RELEVANT WEBLINKS

➤ Acas: *http://www.acas.org.uk* [Accessed May 15, 2015].
➤ Department for Business, Innovation and Skills: *https:// www.gov.uk/government/organisations/department-for-business-innovation-skills* [Accessed May 15, 2015].
➤ Equality and Human Rights Commission: *http://www.equality-humanrights.com* [Accessed May 15, 2015].

Chapter 9   Agency

STUART CROSS[1]

▶ CHAPTER OVERVIEW

This chapter is concerned with the law of agency. It starts by looking at **9–01**
what is meant by agency and the key features or characteristics of an
agency relationship. Different kinds of agency relationships and examples
of common types of agency are examined which demonstrate how
important agency is to the effective operation of business and in commercial law generally. The ways of creating agency relationships are
discussed along with the legal consequences for each of the parties to the
agency. The chapter goes on to consider how third parties are affected by
an agency situation and how agency may be brought to an end. The
chapter concludes by looking at commercial agents and the impact of the
Commercial Agents (Council Directive) Regulations 1993[2] on the Scots
law of agency.

✓ OUTCOMES

At the end of this chapter you should be able to: **9–02**

- ✓   identify an agency relationship;
- ✓   recognise differing types and forms of agency;
- ✓   recognise and understand the various ways in which agency can
  be brought into existence;
- ✓   recognise the different parties involved in agency and understand
  the nature and extent of their legal relationship with each other;
- ✓   understand the duties owed by an agent to their principal;
- ✓   understand the duties owed by a principal to their agent;
- ✓   appreciate the impact agency can have on third parties and
  understand the rights third parties may have against agents and
  principals;
- ✓   understand how agency may be brought to an end; and
- ✓   identify commercial agents and understand how they are protected by the Commercial Agents (Council Directive) Regulations 1993.

---

[1] Professor of Law, University of Dundee.
[2] SI 1993/3053.

MEANING AND KEY FEATURES OF AGENCY

9–03 In the commercial world it is common to encounter situations where business and transactions are entered into or concluded via intermediaries. This may come about because the main parties to the transaction are too busy, do not have the necessary expertise or simply prefer that someone else concludes their commercial arrangements on their behalf. Whatever the reason for using someone else to act on your behalf, the relationship that is being created and relied upon is known as agency. Legally, agency is the relationship which exists when one person instructs or allows another person to act for them in what will be a binding legal arrangement with a third party. This means that there are three parties involved in an agency relationship and two contracts. The three parties are the agent, the principal and the third party. The agent acts on behalf of the principal and brings the principal into a binding relationship with the third party and normally the agent will have no involvement in that contract. The two contracts are, therefore, the relationship between the principal and the agent in the first instance and the relationship between the principal and the third party that results from the agent's actions. Agency can be seen as a triangle which links all three parties:

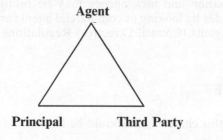

Agent

Principal   **Third Party**

There is no single or precise definition of agency in Scots law and the courts are more concerned with the consequences of a commercial relationship and the effect on the parties rather than the description given to a particular relationship. Agency is a vital tool in business and it has been commented that:

> "Commerce would literally come to a standstill if businessmen and merchants could not employ the services of factors, brokers, estate agents and the like and were expected to do everything themselves."[3]

---

[3] B.S. Markesinis and R.J.C. Munday, *An Outline of the Law of Agency*, 3rd edn (London: Butterworths, 1992), p.3.

> **Key Concept**
>
> There are three parties involved in an agency relationship; the agent, the principal and the third party. The agent acts on behalf of the principal and binds the principal to the third party in a contractual relationship without himself necessarily becoming a legal part of that relationship.

DIFFERENT KINDS AND EXAMPLES OF AGENCY

Kinds of agents

There are many different types of agents and many differing names and **9–04** labels are used to describe agency relationships. The use of a particular name or description to describe a relationship is not always a conclusive guide as to what the actual legal relationship is between the parties involved. What all the varying descriptions and categories have in common is usefulness in showing what the intentions of the parties involved may have been in creating the relationship in question and what is the actual legal nature of the relationship. There are a number of relatively well understood and long established broad categories or kinds of agency in Scots law. These are:

(a) general and special agents;
(b) mercantile agents; and
(c) *del credere* agents.

A further more recent category, commercial agents, is looked at later in this chapter.

General and special agents

A general agent is an agent who has been engaged to conduct all of the **9–05** business for a particular principal or, at a minimum, all of the business of the principal of a particular sort. A special agent has a different kind of relationship with the principal and is only engaged by the principal to carry out a particular transaction or piece of business. The differing relationship between the principal and a general or special agent will shape the type and extent of authority which the agent has to act on behalf of the principal and bind the principal to third parties. Normally, third parties will be able to assume that a general agent has all the powers that an agent of that kind would normally have whereas a special agent would only have the powers and authority needed to carry out the particular transaction. A family solicitor who looks after all the legal affairs for a family would usually be treated as a general agent[4] while a solicitor

---

[4] See *Morrison v Statter* (1885) 12 R. 1152.

appointed by a new client to look after a single transaction could be considered to be acting as a special agent.[5]

Mercantile agents

9–06 A mercantile agent is a very particular kind of agent and the agency relationship is defined in the Factors Acts of 1889 and 1890. A mercantile agent is defined as someone who, "in the customary course of business as such agent" has "authority either to sell goods or consign goods for the purpose of sale, or to buy goods, or to raise money on the security of goods".[6] So, in establishing whether mercantile agency exists it is important to consider all the facts surrounding the type of business and relationship in assessing the "customary course of business" of the particular agent. The crucial feature of the relationship between a mercantile agent and the principal is that because of the Factors Acts the agent has the authority and ability to transfer title to the principal's goods where the principal has not given consent to the transfer and where the principal would not have given permission for the transaction entered into by the agent. This means that a third party transacting with a mercantile agent can transact with the agent with few concerns over the extent of the agent's authority provided the third party enters into the transaction in good faith and doesn't know of any restriction on the agent's authority relating to the transaction.[7]

Del credere agency

9–07 This is a long established but not very common and fairly specialised form of agency. When an agent acts on behalf of a principal it is not normal or common practice for the agent to give any form of guarantee or indemnity to the principal as to the solvency or ability to pay of the third party the agent has introduced to the principal. When the agent does provide a guarantee or indemnity to the principal then the agent is described to be acting as a *del credere* agent.[8] The agent would charge a fee for this additional service to the principal but in all other aspects the agency relationship between the agent and principal is like other forms of agency. The *del credere* agency is usually a mercantile agent and this type of relationship was often used where goods were being sold abroad and the principal wished to minimise any risk of not being paid for the goods. This type of agency arrangement is far less common now as far more sophisticated mechanisms such as credit guarantee schemes are available. These schemes are often state or government supported.

---

[5] See the position outlined in Bell, *Principles* s.219(7) where a solicitor is treated as a special agent.
[6] Section 1(1) Factors Act 1889 as applied in Scotland by the Factors Act 1890.
[7] Factors Act 1889 s.2(1).
[8] *Lloyd's Executors v Wright* (1870) 7 S.L.R. 216.

Examples of agency

Looking at different examples of agency relationships can be a useful way **9–08** to identify not only the parties to the agency but also the types of authority which can be given to an agent or deemed to have been given to an agent by a principal. Many commonly encountered business relationships are simple examples of agency. The relationship between a client (principal) and an estate agent, accountant, surveyor or stock-broker (all agents) is a simple agency relationship. Other common examples of agency relationships are as follows:

Solicitors

A solicitor can be both a general and a special agent, and the true nature **9–09** of the relationship will depend on the facts and circumstances of each case. Traditionally, the "law agent" was engaged in Scotland on a broad basis, looking after the general interests of clients. There is now much more variety in the manner in which solicitors are engaged, with specialist practitioners often now engaged by clients solely for a particular piece of work. Whether the relationship is special or general it is in all respects fiduciary in nature[9] and, as such, the solicitor must carry out the instructions given by the client (principal). The other elements of the fiduciary relationship between a solicitor and client mean that a solicitor should not make a secret profit from his client as a result of a transaction in which the solicitor is a party.[10] Various other features apply in relation to a solicitor/client relationship which mainly relate to the type of authority a solicitor has to act on behalf of the client. For example, a solicitor engaged in a court matter has authority to take all necessary steps to pursue the court process including the instruction of a local solicitor[11] and the implied authority to instruct counsel (an advocate).[12] In Scotland the Law Society of Scotland is the professional body for solicitors and it regulates the activities of solicitors. Law Society rules reflect the fiduciary nature of the solicitor/client relationship and solicitors would not be expected to act for more than one principal where their interests conflict.

Partners

An important and very clear example of a commonly used business **9–10** structure which involves an agency relationship is partnership.[13] In Scotland partnership is regulated by the Partnership Act 1890 and s.5 of that Act says that:

> "Every partner is an agent of the firm and his other partners for the purpose of the business of the partnership."

---

[9] *Brown v Inland Revenue Commissioners*, 1964 S.C. (H.L.) 180.
[10] See *Brown v Inland Revenue Commissioners* at 197.
[11] *Bannatyne, Kirkwood, France & Co*, 1907 S.C. 705.
[12] *Torbat v Torbat's Trustees*, 1906 14 S.L.T. 830.
[13] For further details on partnership, see Ch.15, "The Law of Partnership".

This means that the partnership (the firm) and the fellow partners are bound by actions taken by any of their other partners. There are restrictions on what partners can do which will bind their fellow partners and the firm and the main condition is that the action taken must have been carried out in the course of the partnership's normal business.[14] The type of authority that individual partners can have may also vary. In some situations their authority will be implied but in others (as will be seen later in the chapter) it will be actual.

Members of a limited liability partnership[15]

9–11 The limited liability partnership ("LLP") has now become almost the default organisational structure for professionals such as solicitors and accountants. The LLP is a hybrid organisation which draws on features and principles of company and partnership law. The key legal personae involved in ownership and control of an LLP are its members[16] and every member of a LLP is the agent of the LLP.[17]

Company directors

9–12 In the UK, registered companies, of which the limited company is by far the most common, are treated by the law as having a separate legal personality from those who are the shareholders and directors of the company.[18] This means that registered companies are recognised as legal persons in their own right but that personality is entirely artificial. Companies need human beings to act on their behalf. The responsibility for acting on behalf of companies is normally delegated to the directors of the company. The internal rules of a company are to be found in its articles of association and these deal with the delegation of authority from the company to directors. That delegation of authority to the directors to act on the company's behalf places the directors in the role of agents for the company. The power and authority granted to directors is normally extensive.

CREATING AGENCY

9–13 Agency is a contractual relationship and in similar fashion to most other types of contract an agency relationship can be brought into existence in a variety of ways. The main ways that agency can be created are:

- Express creation.

---

[14] Partnership Act 1890 s.5.
[15] For further details on limited liability partnerships see Ch.17, "Limited Liability Partnerships".
[16] See s.4 of the Limited Liability Partnerships Act 2000.
[17] See s.6(1) of the Limited Liability partnerships Act 2000.
[18] See the case of *Salomon v Salomon* [1897] A.C. 22.

- Implied creation.
- Creation by ratification.
- Creation by necessity.
- Creation by holding out.

Express creation of agency

The express creation of agency simply means that there has been a **9–14** deliberate and conscious act on the part of the principal to appoint someone as their agent. There is no special form or process required for express creation and it can be done either orally or in writing.[19] Differing types of documents may be used to create agency and the extent of the formality involved can vary. In a commercial agency relationship both the agent and principal are entitled to request a signed written document setting out the terms of the agency arrangement.[20] Sometimes where the agency relationship is of particular importance the document creating the agency will itself be formal and the nature and extent of the agency clearly stated. A good example of such an arrangement is where one party (the principal) grants a power of attorney in favour of another (the agent) which permits the principal's affairs to be looked after by the agent.

In the majority of instances agency will be created by less formal means. This may be orally, or by other informal means. Agency may simply come about by virtue of the agent acting on behalf of the principal and with the principal's agreement.[21] Provided issues of proof can be dealt with satisfactorily there is no reason why agency cannot be created by more modern means of communication such as email or text messages.

Implied creation of agency

An agency relationship can be brought into existence because the actions **9–15** of the parties involved imply that this is what they actually intended to happen even though there is no express appointment of the agent by the principal.[22] In many cases this will be obvious from the circumstances involved. This might simply involve looking at the facts and the actions of the various parties involved.[23] It is also possible that agency will be implied as a result of a particular rule of law. A good example arises in partnerships. In the case of a partnership s.5 of the Partnership Act 1890 says that every partner is "deemed or implied" to be an agent of the firm and the other partners. Combining the factual position that someone is a partner with the rule of law in s.5 gives rise to an implied agency relationship. In other factual situations such as employment the seniority of

---

[19] *Robert Barry & Co v Doyle*, 1998 S.L.T. 1238.
[20] Commercial Agents (Council Directive) Regulations 1993 (SI 1993/3053) reg.13.
[21] *Gilmour v Clark* (1853) 15 D. 478.
[22] *Royal Bank of Scotland Plc v Shanks*, 1998 S.L.T. 355, per Lord Penrose at 360.
[23] See the comments of Lord Reed in *Ben Cleuch Estates Ltd v Scottish Enterprise* [2006] CSOH 35 at 143.

an employee or manager or the circumstances of employment may imply an agency relationship.[24]

Creation by ratification

9–16 It will normally be the case that an agency agreement or relationship is brought into existence between the agent and the principal before the agent takes any action on the principal's behalf. In some situations this may not happen and may not even be possible and "an agent" takes action on behalf of "a principal" when the principal may be completely unaware of the agent's actions. This does not mean that agency cannot exist or be brought into existence. The critical issue is what happens when the "principal" becomes aware of the action taken by the "agent". At that stage it is possible for the principal to "ratify" (or adopt) the actions that have already been taken by the agent. The principal can ratify the agent's actions either expressly (i.e. by taking some form of positive action) or by implication (e.g. by some form of action or course of conduct). In working out whether ratification has taken place the factual position is crucial and any act, behaviour or statement by the principal which is clear enough to show an intention to ratify will be enough. Before it can be shown that ratification has been effective and taken place a number of conditions have to be met:

- The agent must have been acting in the capacity of an agent and disclosed this to the third party.[25]
- The principal must have been in existence at the time of the "agent's" actions.[26]

Tinnevelly Sugar Refining Co Ltd v Mirrlees Watson and Yaryan Co Ltd
(1894) 21 R. 1009; (1894) 2 S.L.T. 103, IH (1 Div)

Two men bought machinery from Mirrlees Watson, saying that they were acting on behalf of the Tinnevelly company. In fact the company wasn't formed until two weeks later. The machinery supplied turned out to be defective and the Tinnevelly company (which had by now been registered) attempted to sue on the basis of the defects. It was held that Tinnevelly had no rights under the original "contract" because it could not be a party to that contract. It had not existed at the time the original "contract" was entered into and it could, therefore, not subsequently ratify the actions of the two "agents".

---

[24] See *Neville v C and A Modes*, 1945 S.C. 175 and *Mackenzie v Cluny Hill Hydro*, 1908 S.C. 200.
[25] *Keighley, Maxsted & Co v Durant* [1901] A.C. 240 H.L.
[26] *Tinnevelly Sugar Refining Co Ltd v Mirrlees Watson and Yaryan Co Ltd* (1894) 21 R. 1009; *Kelner v Baxter* (1866) L.R. C.P. 174.

- The principal must have had the necessary legal capacity to take the action in question.[27]
- The principal must have been informed of or known of all the relevant facts behind the agent's actions at the stage the principal elects to ratify unless it can be shown that the principal was willing to ratify whatever the circumstances.[28]
- The ratification by the principal must take place within any relevant timescales, so that any action taken by a principal which is outwith, for example, the statutory time limit for the lodging of an appeal will not amount to valid ratification even though the appeal may have been successfully lodged on time by the "agent".[29]
- The action being ratified must itself have been legal.[30]

The overall effect of ratification is to put the agent and principal in the same position they would have been in had agency been agreed in the conventional way before anything was done by the agent. If the "principal" opts not to take any action to ratify the action that has already been taken by the "agent" then the "agent" will be personally liable to the third party for the action they have taken.

Creation by necessity

Agency can be created in situations of necessity where in an emergency or **9–17** critical situation an agent carries out essential actions for a principal without having been instructed to do so. In Scots law this notion of agency of necessity sits within the doctrine of *negotiorum gestio*.[31] All of this takes place in circumstances where it is impossible to communicate with the person on whose behalf action is being taken. The situations in which this is likely to occur are now far less common with the advent of modern means of instantaneous communication such as mobile and satellite telephones and computer based communication such as email, but unforeseen and uncontrollable circumstances involving civil disturbance, war or extreme weather events could still provide opportunities for the effective operation of agency by necessity. Situations of ill-health leading to an inability to give instructions which forces someone to act on behalf of the infirm person can also trigger agency by necessity.[32] When agency of necessity is relied upon the actions taken should be taken in

---

[27] *Boston Deep Sea Fishing and Ice Co Ltd v Farnham* [1957] 3 All E.R. 204.
[28] *Suncorp Insurance and Finance v Milano Assecurazioni SpA* [1992] 2 Lloyd's Rep. 225, QBD (Comm).
[29] *Goodall v Bilsland*, 1909 S.C. 1152; 1 S.L.T. 376 IH (1 Div).
[30] *Bedford Insurance Co Ltd v Instituto de Resseguros do Brasil* [1985] Q.B. 966.
[31] *Negotiorum gestio* is the doctrine which protects an unappointed agent (the gestor) who acts for the benefit of the principal and in doing so, helps the principal make a saving or avoid a loss, where the principal is absent or incapacitated. A typical example is where the gestor saves the principal's property from destruction, while the principal is on holiday, for example. The gestor is entitled to reimbursement of expenses.
[32] *Fernie v Robertson* (1871) 9 M. 437.

good faith, should be reasonable and should be in the best interests of the person on whose behalf they are taken.

Creation by holding out

9–18 This type of agency arises when a third party receives the impression that someone is an agent or acting as an agent because of either positive encouragement of that impression by the principal or the fact that the principal takes no action to contradict the impression that agency actually exists. In this situation the action or inaction of the principal results in someone being "held out" or represented as being an agent. Agency by holding out often arises from situations where agency proper did in fact exist at some stage between the principal and the agent but the agent's earlier authority to act has been withdrawn and third parties have not been told.

Key Concept

Agency can be brought into existence in a whole variety of ways. Whatever the route to agency, provided the required conditions in each instance have been met the contractual relationship in each instance will be binding on the principal and agent.

THE AGENCY RELATIONSHIP

9–19 The nature of the relationship between a principal and an agent will largely be shaped by the following:

- The nature and extent of the agent's authority.
- The agent's duties and the principal's rights.
- The agent's rights and the principal's duties.

Each of these is now considered in turn.

The agent's authority

9–20 The extent of an agent's authority is a critical part of the relationship between an agent and a principal. Normally an agent will act within the limits of the authority given by the principal and in those situations the principal will be bound to third parties by the agent's actions. More problematic issues arise when an agent is unclear as to the nature and extent of authority given by a principal. Authority is, therefore, crucial to the successful operation of agency. There are three broadly recognised categories used to identify types of authority given to an agent. These are:

- Express.
- Implied.
- Apparent or ostensible.

The first two categories can be regarded as together being examples of actual or real authority and can be contrasted with apparent or ostensible authority which should more properly be considered as an example of the operation of the quite separate legal concept of personal bar against the principal.

Express authority

In an ideal situation the extent of the authority given to an agent will be **9–21** set out in the agreement between the agent and the principal. If an agent exceeds the extent of the authority given by the principal then that can jeopardise the validity of the contract that the agent has tried to enter into. If there is no other type of authority open to an agent and the principal opts not to ratify an action by an agent which exceeds the express authority the agent has then the principal will normally not be liable to the third party.

Implied authority

For a variety of reasons it is common to find that the exact boundaries of **9–22** an agent's authority have not been clearly recorded as part of the agreement between the agent and the principal. This absence of express authority does not mean that the agent has no authority to act. Commonly, an agent's authority is implied. This may be because of the particular facts and circumstances surrounding the relationship between the agent and the principal, or because of the particular type of transaction or because the agent is a member of a particular profession and a particular level or type of authority is afforded to members of that profession when acting as an agent. A good example of the professional situation is an accountant who has implied powers to take certain actions without the express authority of his or her principal. In other situations the nature of the relationship between the agent and the principal will imply a certain type and level of authority. For example, a member of staff responsible for sales will have implied authority to take an order. In *Barry, Ostlere & Shepherd Ltd v Edinburgh Cork Importing Co*[33] an order was placed by Barry, Ostlere and Shepherd with Edinburgh Cork for a supply of cork shavings. The order was placed via one of Edinburgh Cork's salesmen. The order wasn't fulfilled and B, O and S brought an action against Edinburgh Cork for breach of contract. The defence was to the effect that the salesman had no authority to conclude the contract. It was held that B, O and S were entitled to assume that the salesman did have the necessary authority to accept the order.

---

[33] 1909 S.C. 1113.

Apparent or ostensible authority[34]

9–23 This type of authority arises in situations where the behaviour of the principal gives rise to an impression that the agent has been given authority to act. These instances tend to arise because of the way the principal has acted or because the principal has allowed a particular set of circumstances to continue which gave the impression to a third party that the principal has, in fact, granted authority to an agent to act on the principal's behalf. There must be a clear linkage between the various elements. First, the principal must have created a particular impression, usually by means of some form of direct representation or allowing a set of circumstances to continue. Secondly, the third party has to believe that the agent was authorised to act on the basis of the principal's behaviour or representation. Finally, the third party has to have placed some form of reliance on the principal's behaviour or representation and suffered a loss as a result. This type of authority can operate to render a transaction valid even where the agent did not in fact have the necessary authority from the principal at the outset to carry out the transaction. There are two common situations where this type of authority can operate to validate an otherwise unauthorised transaction. The first example is when a principal has given authority to an agent at some stage but has, at a later date, withdrawn that authority without having told third parties. To make the later withdrawal of authority effective the principal should have told the third parties of the change in the agent's authority. The second example of a situation when this type of authority comes about is when the principal has an agreement with the agent which places a limit on the extent of the agent's authority but the agent exceeds that authority when dealing with third parties. If the third parties dealing with the agent continue to believe that the agent has the original level of authority they experienced in their previous dealings with the agent then that level of "apparent" authority will continue to exist until they are properly told otherwise by the principal. In the case of:

> **International Sponge Importers Ltd v Andrew Watt & Sons**
> **[1911] A.C. 279 and 1911 S.C (H.L.) 57**
>
> Cohen, a commercial travelling salesman was authorised to sell sponges on behalf of International Sponge Importers Ltd. Cohen was a regular caller to Watt & Sons and he had sold them sponges on a number of occasions in the past. Normally Watt & Sons made payment directly to International Sponge Importers ("ISI") by sending them a cheque. On a few occasions Cohen had collected cheques from Watt which were payable to ISI and that Cohen had then passed on to ISI. On four instances Cohen had also

---

[34] For a useful discussion of apparent authority see D. Busch and L. Macgregor, "Apparent authority in Scots law: Some international perspectives", 2007 Edin. L.R. 349. See also Lord Diplock's definition of apparent authority in *Freeman and Lockyer v Buckhurst Park Properties (Mangal) Ltd* [1964] 2 Q.B. 480, 502–503.

persuaded Watt & Sons to pay with cheques made out to Cohen or by means of cash. Cohen eventually absconded with money owing to ISI. Both the Court of Session and the House of Lords held that ISI could not recover the missing money from the customers who had paid Cohen. They were entitled to conclude from the earlier course of dealings that Cohen did have authority to accept payment personally.

The whole concept of apparent or ostensible authority is closely linked to the principle of personal bar and the net effect of apparent or ostensible authority is to place the principal in a position where the principal cannot deny that the agent has authority to act.[35]

Key Concept

An agent's authority is critical in determining whether his principal will be bound to a third party by the agent's actions and to what extent. If the agent has acted within the boundaries of the authority given by the principal then the principal will be liable for all the agent's actions. In the same way, if the principal ratifies the agent's actions the principal is liable in exactly the same way as if the agent had full authority in the first place.

The agent's duties/principal's rights

In an ideal situation there will be a contract between the principal and **9–24** agent which deals not only with the obvious issue of the agent's authority but also sets out the duties the agent has to the principal and the rights the principal enjoys in the agency relationship. Unfortunately, it is surprisingly common to encounter agency arrangements when no clear agreement exists setting out the terms of the agency relationship or if it does exist it is silent about the some or all of the agent's duties and principal's rights. In such situations the law will imply a number of duties to apply between the principal and agent. These are as follows:

- The duty to perform instructions.
- Good faith/fiduciary duty.
- The duty to exercise skill and care.
- The duty to keep accounts.

These are each considered in turn.

---

[35] *British Bata Shoe Co Ltd v Double M Shah Ltd*, 1980 S.C 311; *Armagus Ltd v Mundogas* [1986] 1 A.C. 717.

To perform instructions

9–25 An agent is obliged to do what he or she has been asked to do by the principal in terms of the agency agreement. In a situation where the agent has only been given general instructions by the principal or there are no instructions then the agent is expected to act in a way which reflects their best judgement and the generally accepted customs of their profession.[36] If the principal's instructions are not clear then the principal cannot hold the agent responsible for any loss flowing from the poor instructions.[37]

When an agent does not comply with the principal's clear instructions then the agent will be personally liable to the principal for any losses arising as a consequence of the non-compliance.

Gilmour v Clark
(1853) 15 D. 478

Gilmour, an Edinburgh merchant, gave instructions to a local carrier to take a consignment of goods to Leith docks to be loaded onto a specifically identified ship, the *Earl of Zetland*. For apparently legitimate reasons the goods were loaded onto another ship, the *Magnet*. This ship sank en route and Gilmour's cargo was lost. It was held that Clark was liable to Gilmour for the loss of the goods even though the change in ship was well intentioned.

An agent who does not follow instructions also loses the right to claim any payment or commission so long as the non-compliance continues.[38]

Good faith/fiduciary duty

9–26 A key element of the relationship between an agent and a principal is the fiduciary duty which is owed by the agent to the principal. An agent is bound to act in good faith and in the best interests of the principal.[39] This duty stands as a clear duty in its own right but it is often seen more clearly in operation in the range of other duties to be observed by an agent which are influenced by the good faith obligation but which should not be seen as fiduciary duties in their own right. These duties are:

(1) The duty to act personally.
(2) The duty to account.
(3) The duty not to disclose confidential information.
(4) The duty to avoid conflicts of interest.

Each of these duties is considered in turn.

---

[36] Bell, *Commentaries*, I, 517; *Fearn v Gordon and Craig* (1893) 20 R. 352.
[37] *Ireland v Livingston* (1872) L.R. 5 H.L. 395.
[38] *Alexander Graham & Co v United Turkey Red Co Ltd*, 1922 S.C. 533.
[39] Bell, *Principles* s.222.

(1) The duty to act personally

The starting assumption in an agency relationship is that because the **9–27** principal has selected the agent to act the agent must not delegate the work to anyone else.[40] While this is the generally accepted rule it is also recognised and accepted that there are many situations where there can be exceptions to the rule and delegation can take place. Delegation may be expressly permitted by the agency agreement itself. It is also possible that delegation may be implied from the particular facts and circumstances of the particular agency situation or because it may be common or accepted practice in particular industries, trades and professions. It is accepted practice that architects can delegate certain types of work to a surveyor[41] and that solicitors can instruct a local solicitor to act when the original case is being heard in another part of the country.[42] When delegation is allowed then the sub-agent will also owe duties to the principal. In the case of *De Bussche v Alt*[43] De Bussche had been appointed as an agent to sell a ship for a particular price. Permission had been given for the appointment of a sub-agent and Alt had been given that appointment and was instructed to sell the ship in Japan. In a dispute over the sale and appointment of the sub-agent it was held that Alt's appointment was valid and there was a contractual relationship between the principal and Alt. However, even when delegation is allowed the original agent may remain liable for acts and omissions of the sub-agent. In instances where delegation is not permissible but the agent has purported to delegate the agent will be liable to the principal for breach of the agency agreement.

(2) The duty to account

An agent must account to the principal for all benefits received by the **9–28** agent during the period of the agency.[44] This duty is concerned with potential secret profits or benefits earned or retained by an agent and should not be confused with the quite separate obligation on an agent to keep accounts of the transactions occurring during the agency. The duty to account does not stop an agent from acting for another principal at the same time, even if the two or more principals are in competition.[45]

---

[40] Two Latin phrases are often used in this connection. The first is *delectus personae*, which simply refers to the fact that the agent has been chosen by the principal on the basis of special skills or attributes. The second phrase, *delegatus non potest delegare*, is more direct and simply translates as meaning that an agent cannot delegate.

[41] *Cornelius v Black* (1879) 6 R. 581.

[42] *Robertson v Foulds* (1860) 22 D. 714.

[43] (1878) 8 Ch. D. 286.

[44] *Neilson v Skinner & Co* (1890) 17 R. 1243; *Trans Barvil Agencies (UK) Ltd v John S. Baird & Co Ltd*, 1988 S.C. 222.

[45] *Lothian v Jenolite Ltd*, 1969 S.C. 111.

(3) The duty not to disclose confidential information

9–29 It is commonly the case that an agent will receive confidential or sensitive information from a principal during an agency relationship. In such situations the agent is under a duty not to disclose or to make use of that information.

> ### Liverpool Victoria Friendly Society v Houston
> ### (1900) 3 F. 42
>
> For four years Houston was an insurance agent for Liverpool Victoria. Over that time he saw detailed lists of people insured by the company. After being dismissed by the company Houston offered the customer lists to a competing society which then made approaches to the people on the lists. It was held that Houston had a duty to treat the customer information as confidential and was liable in damages for the loss of business suffered by Liverpool Victoria.

(4) The duty to avoid conflicts of interest

9–30 The general position is that an agent should avoid situations where the agent's interests conflict with the principal's interests.[46] This does not mean that an agent cannot act at the same time for more than one principal who may have directly competing interest. In *Lothian v Jenolite Ltd*[47] Lothian agreed to sell some of Jenolite's products in Scotland and to be paid on commission. The initial agreement covered a four year period but it was ended by Jenolite after just over a year. Lothian claimed damages for breach of contract. Lothian counterclaimed and argued that as Lothian had bought and sold products from competitors that was itself a breach of contract. It has held that because the original contract had not said that Lothian could only sell Jenolite's products then he was permitted to sell other products.

If an agent does not avoid potentially conflicting situations then the risk is that anything the agent does which creates a benefit for the agent may be seen as the agent generating what is often referred to as a secret profit and being liable to account to the principle for that profit. A conflict of interest will not always generate a secret profit but it is the most commonly encountered example of how a conflict of interest can affect the relationship between a principal and agent.

---

[46] *Huntingdon Copper and Sulphur Co Ltd v Henderson* (1877) 4 R. 294.
[47] 1969 S.C. 111.

McPherson's Trustees v Watt
(1877) 5 R. (H.L.) 9

Watt was a solicitor who acted on behalf of the trustees in relation to the sale of four houses. Without telling the trustees he had arranged for his brother to be the purchaser of the houses and Watt intended to buy the other two for himself by paying half the purchase price to his brother. The transaction was set aside by the court. The court also pointed out that it was of no consequence that the transaction might have been a good bargain; the sale could be set aside even if the price was a fair one.

While it is possible that if the agent tells the principal about any additional benefit and the principal agrees to the benefit being retained the agent may be able to retain the benefit it is still possible, especially in situations such as a solicitor/client relationship, that even with disclosure of a conflict this may still amount to a breach of the duty.[48] If the principal discovers a secret profit which the agent has not disclosed then the principal is entitled to terminate the contract[49] and the agent will lose any entitlement to be paid for the period of the contract during which the breach continues.

The duty to exercise skill and care

An agent must perform the agency arrangement with skill and care. The **9–31** nature and extent of that duty may vary. If the agent is not a member of a particular profession then the level of skill and care that can be expected is that which is associated with an ordinary prudent man managing his own affairs.[50] If the agent is a member of a particular profession or trade then the level of skill and care to be expected is that of a reasonably competent member of that trade or profession.[51] An agent from a particular trade or profession who makes an error of judgement will not be held to have breached the duty of skill and care if they can establish that they acted in a way which showed reasonable knowledge, skill and care.[52]

In cases where the agent is not receiving any payment the agent is still expected to act with due care and skill.[53] An agent will be liable to the principal for damages for breach of contract if the agent breaches the duty of skill and care.[54] The agent will not be liable where an action taken

---

[48] *Cleland v Morrison* (1876) 6 R. 156.
[49] *Boston Deep Sea Fishing Co Ltd v Ansell* (1888) L.R. 39 Ch. D. 339.
[50] Bell, *Commentaries*, I, 516.
[51] *Cooke v Falconer's Representatives* (1850) 13 D. 157.
[52] *Simpson v Kidstons, Watson, Turnbull & Co*, 1913 S.L.T. 74.
[53] *Copland v Brogan*, 1916 S.C. 277.
[54] *Salvesen & Co v Rederi Aktiebolaget Nordstjernan* (1905) 7 F. (H.L.) 101.

turns out not to be in the interests of the principal but it was taken on the basis of instructions issued by the principal.

The duty to keep accounts

9–32 The agent must keep accounts. Although there is no fundamental requirement that these be written most agency agreements require that they are in fact in writing. If there is any discrepancy which the agent is unable to explain then this has to be made good by the agent even in the absence of any suggestion of dishonesty. In *Tyler v Logan*[55] there was a shortfall of £62 when stocktaking was taken in a Dundee shoe shop. Logan was the manager of the shop and he was held liable to pay the shortfall even though there was no suggestion of dishonesty.

Key Concept

The concept of good faith lies at the heart of the agency relationship and shapes the main duty owed by an agent to a principal. The good faith duty to act in the best interest of the principal shapes and informs other duties owed by an agent.

The agent's rights/principal's duties

9–33 The main rights an agent can expect to flow from agency and which the agent will expect the principal to observe centre on ensuring that the agent is properly rewarded and not out of pocket and is in a position to secure those entitlements. This can be seen in each of the main rights, which are:

- To be remunerated and reimbursed.
- To be relieved of liabilities.
- To enjoy rights of lien and security.

These are considered in turn:

Remuneration and reimbursement

9–34 Hopefully the agency agreement will set out that the agent is entitled to remuneration and the basis upon which the agent is to be remunerated by the principal. If the agreement says nothing or it is not clear then there is a rebuttable presumption that an agent is entitled to be remunerated if the work the agent has done forms part of the agent's livelihood.[56] If the agreement is silent or unclear about the level of remuneration then the normal practice is for the courts to consider what is customary in the particular trade or profession and attempt to set a level of payment on

---

[55] (1904) 12 S.L.T. 466.
[56] *Mackersy's Executors v St Giles Cathedral Managing Board* (1904) 12 S.L.T. 391.

this basis. If this cannot be done or the agent is not part of a recognised trade or profession then the remuneration will be worked out on the basis of the work done and the amount the agent has actually earned.[57] An agent also has a right to be reimbursed by the principal for expenses which the agent has incurred in properly carrying out the work of the agency contract.[58]

To be relieved of liabilities

An agent has the right to be relieved by the principal of all liabilities **9–35** which have been incurred by the agent because of the proper performance of the agency contract.[59] The principal will not be obliged to provide relief to the principal when the agent has not acted in accordance with the agency agreement or has acted in a way which is illegal or negligent.[60]

To enjoy rights of lien and security

If an agent is not paid or is not reimbursed for expenses when they are **9–36** entitled to payment then the agent is entitled to exercise certain rights in relation to the principal's assets. These rights are by way of security and are referred to as rights of lien or security. There are two types of lien: general and special. General lien allows an agent to retain the principal's goods or assets in relation to a particular agency transaction even though the retained goods may not have been involved in that particular transaction. Certain professions such as solicitors and bankers[61] and stockbrokers[62] and particular types of agents such as mercantile agents[63] are recognised as being able to exercise a general lien. The right to use a general lien isn't automatic in all cases of agency and where it does not exist the type of lien is known as a special lien. This right only allows the agent to retain assets which are involved in the transaction which has given rise to the agent's entitlement to be paid. Accountants are only entitled to use the special lien.[64]

The right of lien is only a security right. Unless there has been agreement with the principal the right of lien does not allow the agent to sell the assets belonging to the principal which have been retained.

---

[57] This way of calculating the payment is referred to as being *quantum meruit*, i.e. the amount which has been earned. See *Kennedy v Glass* (1890) 17 R. 1085.
[58] *Marshall Wilson Dean and Turnbull v Feymac Properties Ltd*, 1996 G.W.D. 22-1247.
[59] *Stevenson & Sons v Duncan* (1842) 5 D. 167.
[60] *Thacker v Hardy* (1878) L.R. Q.B.D. 685.
[61] *Drummond v Muirhead and Guthrie Smith* (1900) 2 F. 585.
[62] *Glendinning v John D. Hope & Co*, 1911 S.C. (H.L.) 73.
[63] *Powdrill v Murrayhead* 1996 G.W.D. 34-2011.
[64] *Findlay (Liquidator of Scottish Workmen's Assurance Co Ltd) v Waddell*, 1910 S.C. 670.

THIRD PARTIES

9–37 The aim of agency is to provide a way for agents to enter into transactions which contractually bind the principal and third party together but does not create any liability for the agent. Whether this situation comes about will depend on a range of factors but the most significant of these is the way the agent has behaved during the course of the agency transactions. There are two main ways in which an agent can act. These are as follows:

- The agent acts as agent.
- The agent exceeds his/her authority.

Each of these is now considered:

The agent acts as an agent

9–38 In this situation the information that the agent has disclosed to the third party is of particular importance. The three types of situations which are likely to occur are:

(1) The agent acts discloses that there is a principal and names the principal.
(2) The agent discloses that there is a principal but does not name the principal.
(3) The agent does not disclose that there is a principal.

Each of these situations is now considered:

(1) The principal is disclosed and named

9–39 The general rule is that when the agent discloses that there is agency involved and names the principal the contract is between the third party and the principal and the agent has no part in the contract and incurs no personal liability.[65] There will be the same outcome where the principal's actual name has not been disclosed but the principal can be easily identified by the third party.[66] There can be exceptions to this general rule and an agent can be held liable to third parties if the parties to the agency intend that this should happen or the agreement makes it clear that is what was intended. In some trades and professions the agent will still be personally liable to third parties even though clearly acting as an agent for a named and disclosed principal. One of the clearest examples of this practice is solicitors, who can be held personally liable for obligations they grant during the course of a transaction.[67]

---

[65] *Stone and Rolfe Ltd v Kimber Coal Co Ltd*, 1926 S.C. (H.L.) 45.
[66] *Armour v T.L. Duff & Co*, 192 S.C. 120.
[67] *Digby Brown & Co v Lyall*, 1995 S.L.T. 932.

(2) The principal is disclosed but not named

In this situation the fact there is a principal involved is known to the third **9–40** party but the name of the principal is not disclosed. There is very little clear authority on this situation in Scots law. If it is possible by other means to identify the principal then the outcome will be similar to that when the principal is named and the agent has no liability to the third party.[68] If easy identification is not possible then the third party may have to choose or elect whether to hold the principal or the agent liable under the contract.[69] The position is simpler when the agent refuses to identify the undisclosed principal. To do this is to deny the third party any remedy against the principal and the agent can be held personally liable.[70]

(3) The agent does not disclose that there is a principal

If an agent acts without disclosing that the actions are on behalf of a **9–41** principal then the likelihood is that third parties will believe that the agent is in fact acting as a principal. There is nothing to suggest agency even exists as far as the third party is concerned. In such situations the agent runs the risk that the third party will consider that they have entered into a contract with the agent and hold the agent liable under the contract. The normal position is that in situations where the existence of a principal remains undisclosed then the agent may be sued by the third party. Once a contract has been concluded by the agent it is open to the principal to disclose his/her identity. Provided the agent has acted within the limits of his/her authority then the principal may sue the third party.[71] Once the identity of the principal has been disclosed then the third party also has the option to sue the principal. This is an optional process. The third party must elect to sue the principal or the agent and cannot pursue both.

> ### Bennett v Inveresk Paper Co
> ### (1891) 18 R. 975
>
> Bennett owned an Australian newspaper and instructed his agent in London to make arrangements for the supply of paper for the newspaper. The agent contracted with Inveresk to supply the paper and transport it to Australia. Inveresk knew nothing about Bennett's existence at this stage. The paper arrived in Australia but was damaged. Bennett raised an action against Inveresk for breach of contract. It was held that he had title to sue.

Once an agent has elected who to sue then the choice is final.[72] There can

---

[68] *Matthews v Auld & Guild* (1873) 1 R. 1224.
[69] See *Lamont Nisbet & Co v Hamilton*, 1907 S.C. 628 and *Ferrier v Dods* (1865) 3 M. 561.
[70] *Gibb v Cunningham and Robertson*, 1925 S.L.T. 608.
[71] *Hutton v Bulloch* (1874) L.R. 9 Q.B. 572.
[72] *Ferrier v Dods* (1865) 3 M. 561.

be confusion as to whether or not a clear election has been made by the third party. This can be evidenced in a variety of ways but the common element is that the choice must have been clear. Raising a court action alone will not be enough to establish that a clear election has taken place.[73]

The agent exceeds his/her authority

9–42 If an agent acts in a way that exceeds the authority given by the principal then there will be no binding contract between the principal and the third party unless the principal chooses to ratify the agent's actions or the doctrine of apparent/ostensible authority can be relied on. While there is no absolute rule that an agent acting outside the authority given by a principal will be bound into a contract with the third party the agent will almost certainly have some sort of personal liability to the third party. So, in situations where the agent has acted fraudulently or has negligently misrepresented the extent of the authority given by the principal the third party will have a right of action in delict. Even if the agent's actions are innocent the third party may still have a right of action and the agent may still be liable for damages. This type of liability arises because the agent is considered, as a matter of law, as having given an implied warranty to the third party that the agent had the authority needed to contract when in fact that was not the case. The agent can be held liable for having breached that authority.[74]

Key Concept

Agency will operate in such a way as to bind the third party to the principal in a valid contract when the agent acts within the level of authority given by the principal. When the agent acts outwith the authority given by the principal or does not properly disclose the existence or identity of the principal to the third party then the agent runs the risk of incurring some form of personal liability.

ENDING AGENCY

9–43 Agency can be brought to an end in a variety of differing ways. Many of the ways relied upon to bring agency to an end simply rely on principles of common law. The most common ways that an agency arrangement may be ended are as follows:

- Termination by the agent or principal.
- Termination under the agency contract.
- Termination by frustration.

---

[73] *Meier & Co v Kuchenmeister* (1881) 8 R. 642.
[74] *Anderson v Croall & Sons* (1903) 6 F. 153.

Each of these methods is now considered.

Termination by the agent or principal

Both the agent and the principal can agree together that the agency **9–44** relationship should be terminated. In some situations, such as partnership, even an agreed termination will not be effective unless notice is given to third parties who may be affected by the termination.[75] The principal may also attempt to unilaterally terminate the agency without the agent's consent. If this is possible within the terms of the agency agreement then the principal must give notice to third parties to ensure that there is no potential for ongoing liability on the basis of apparent/ostensible authority. When a principal attempts to unilaterally end an agency when that is not permitted then the principal may be liable to the agent for damages.[76] An agent may also be permitted to unilaterally terminate within the terms of the agency arrangement. An agent may also be liable to the principal for any delays in telling the principal that the agency is being terminated or for terminating the agency at a critical moment.[77]

Termination under contract

If the agency contract itself has provisions on termination then these will **9–45** bring the agency relationship to an end. The simplest situation which will bring about termination is the end of a fixed period of time which is set out in the contract as the duration of the agency relationship.[78] Agency will also come to an end if a specified purpose for which the agency was established has been fulfilled or come to an end.[79]

Termination by frustration

As with any other contract, agency can be brought to an end through **9–46** frustration. This simply refers to the occurrence of unexpected events which are outwith the control of the parties to the agency. Once the relationship is terminated on the basis of frustration then the agent and principal have no further or ongoing obligations under the contract.

Subject to very limited exceptions the death of the principal or agent will terminate the agency relationship. The personal bankruptcy (sequestration) or insolvency (for corporate bodies) of either the principal will normally also bring the agency to an end. An agent's insanity will bring the agency to an end and the principal's insanity will also bring the agency to an end if the insanity is permanent.[80] If the principal's business is discontinued then the agency relationship is also terminated.[81]

---

[75] See s.36(1) of the Partnership Act 1890.
[76] *Galbraith and Moorhead v Arethusa Ship Co Ltd* (1896) 23 R. 1011.
[77] Erskine, *Institute*, III, 3, 40.
[78] *Brenan v Campbell's Trustees* (1898) 25 R. 423.
[79] *Black v Cullen* (1853) 15 D. 646.
[80] *Daily Telegraph Co v McLaughlin* [1904] A.C. 776.
[81] *SS State of California Co Ltd v Moore* (1895) 22 R. 562.

> **Key Concepts**
>
> Agency can be brought to an end in a variety of ways. This can be on the basis of terms in the contract of agency or as a matter of law, which can include termination by mutual agreement, termination by revocation or frustration.

COMMERCIAL AGENTS/THE COMMERCIAL AGENTS (COUNCIL DIRECTIVE) REGULATIONS 1993

9–47 The Commercial Agents (Council Directive) Regulations 1993[82] ("the Regulations") implemented the Commercial Agents Directive 1986. They defined a new class of commercial agents who are bound by a set of special rules which are in many respects different from the normal rules of agency in Scots and English law. One of the key aims of the Directive was to harmonise the conditions for commercial agents across Europe and to provide standard levels of protection for commercial agents. While there is some scope for agents and principals to negotiate and agree changes to the application of the Regulations, most of the Regulations cannot be changed or excluded and they will operate in priority to common law rules of agency.[83]

Meaning of commercial agents

9–48 The Regulations define a commercial agent as:

> "A self-employed intermediary who has continuing authority to negotiate the sale or purchase of goods on behalf of another person (the 'principal'), or to negotiate and conclude the sale or purchase of goods on behalf of and in the name of that principal."[84]

This definition is important in that it creates a classification of agency which includes certain people who would not normally be treated by Scots law as being agents but also excludes others who would normally have been recognised as agents in Scots law. Being an employee is an express exclusion so anyone acting in that capacity is excluded from the application of the Regulations. Anyone who is a partner in a firm or a company director is excluded[85] and also excluded are insolvency practitioners,[86] commercial agents who are unpaid[87] and a range of specialist agents involved in commodity exchanges and markets.[88] However it is

---

[82] SI 1993/3053 (as amended in 1993 and 1998 by SI 1993/3173 and SI 1998/2868).
[83] *Roy v M.R. Pearlman*, 1999 S.C. 459.
[84] See Commercial Agents (Council Directive) Regulations 1993 reg.2(1).
[85] Commercial Agents (Council Directive) Regulations 1993 reg.2(1)(i) and 2(1)(ii).
[86] Commercial Agents (Council Directive) Regulations 1993 reg.2(1)(iii).
[87] Commercial Agents (Council Directive) Regulations 1993 reg.2(2)(a).
[88] Commercial Agents (Council Directive) Regulations 1993 reg.2(2)(b).

possible that a partnership or a company can be a commercial agent.[89] The Regulations will not apply where there is only a single transaction involved which is not repeated or where the agent is acting for an undisclosed principal. The Regulations only apply where the agent sells goods, so they will also not apply where the transactions involve services.

Duties owed by commercial agents

Commercial agents owe their principals a general duty to act dutifully **9–49** and in good faith and to look after the interests of the principal.[90] The Regulations elaborate on this and give further non-exhaustive indications of what a commercial agent must do. This includes:

- making proper efforts to negotiate and, if appropriate, conclude transactions which the agent has been instructed to take care of[91];
- communicating to the principal all the necessary information available to the agent[92]; and
- complying with all reasonable instructions given by the principal.[93]

Duties owed by principals to commercial agents

The principal in a relationship governed by the Regulations must also act **9–50** dutifully and in good faith towards the commercial agent. The Regulations approach this duty in the same way as the agent's duties are treated and a series of non-exhaustive "good faith" duties are listed. These include:

- obliging the principal to provide the agent with all necessary documentation relating to the goods involved[94];
- obtaining for the agent any information which is needed to perform the contract[95];
- notifying the agent within a reasonable time if it is anticipated that the volume of transactions will be significantly lower than the agent could reasonably have expected[96]; and
- informing the agent within a reasonable time of the principal's acceptance or refusal or non-performance of a transaction which the agent has arranged.[97]

---

[89] *AMB Imballaggi Plastici Srl v Pacflex Ltd* [1999] 2 All E.R. (Comm) 249, CA.
[90] Commercial Agents (Council Directive) Regulations 1993 reg.3(1).
[91] Commercial Agents (Council Directive) Regulations 1993 reg.3(2)(a).
[92] Commercial Agents (Council Directive) Regulations 1993 reg.3(2)(b).
[93] Commercial Agents (Council Directive) Regulations 1993 reg.3(2)(c).
[94] Commercial Agents (Council Directive) Regulations 1993 reg.4(2).
[95] Commercial Agents (Council Directive) Regulations 1993 reg.4(2)(b).
[96] Commercial Agents (Council Directive) Regulations 1993 reg.4(2)(b).
[97] Commercial Agents (Council Directive) Regulations 1993 reg.4(3).

Remuneration and commission

9–51 As with conventional agency arrangements it is open to the agent and principal to agree levels of payment. If there is no provision for remuneration then the agent is entitled to be paid what is customarily paid to agents who are appointed in relation to the type of goods involved in the agency. If there is no such customary practice then the agent is entitled to a reasonable level of remuneration which takes into account all elements of the transaction.[98]

An agent will be entitled to commission when:

- the transaction has taken place because of the agent's actions[99]; or
- the transaction has been concluded with a third party who the agent had previously acquired as a customer for similar transactions.[100]

The agent is given a degree of protection in relation to the payment of commission. Commission must be paid to the agent at the very latest when the third party has completed his part of the transaction or would have completed the transaction had the principal also completed his part of the transaction.[101] The agent's entitlement to commission ends if it can be shown that the contract between the principal and the third party will not be completed because of circumstances for which the principal is not to blame.[102]

Termination of agency

9–52 The Regulations contain detailed provisions about the termination of agency arrangements which are covered by the Regulations. The key provisions on termination relate to the period of notice that has to be given. When the contract is for an indefinite period then either the agent or principal can terminate the contract. The notice periods that they must give are:

- one month during the first year of the contract;
- two months in the second year; and
- three months in the third and any subsequent years.[103]

The agent and principal cannot opt out of these minimum periods but they can agree on longer notice periods. If longer notice periods are agreed then the principal has to give at least the same notice to the agent as the agent has to give to the principal.[104]

---

[98] Commercial Agents (Council Directive) Regulations 1993 reg.6(1).
[99] Commercial Agents (Council Directive) Regulations 1993 reg.7(1)(a).
[100] Commercial Agents (Council Directive) Regulations 1993 reg.7(1)(b).
[101] Commercial Agents (Council Directive) Regulations 1993 reg.10(2).
[102] Commercial Agents (Council Directive) Regulations 1993 reg.11(1).
[103] Commercial Agents (Council Directive) Regulations 1993 reg.15(2)(a)–(2)(c).
[104] Commercial Agents (Council Directive) Regulations 1993 reg.15(3).

Compensation and indemnity

The Regulations set out the circumstances in which compensation may be **9–53** payable to the agent on termination and when an indemnity may be available to the agent. The starting position is that the agent and principal cannot agree to opt out of payment of compensation or the grant of an indemnity.[105] If the agreement says nothing then compensation is the option that is available to the agent and an indemnity is not available. Compensation is intended to compensate the agent for damage suffered as a result of the termination of the contract. The most difficult part of the compensation mechanism as applied in the UK has been the way the compensation is calculated. Until 2007 the position was that the Scottish courts calculated levels of compensation on the basis of French principles which had informed the 1986 Directive on which the Regulations are based.[106] The House of Lords case of *Lonsdale v Howard and Hallam Ltd*[107] has now made it clear that the agent is entitled to compensation for loss, which is calculated by valuing the level of income which the agency would have generated.

The right to an indemnity is intended to give the agent the benefit of any work the agent has done before the agency is ended, the benefit of which would go to the principal. The right to indemnity comes about when the agent has:

- brought the principal new customers or has significantly increased the level of business with current customers and the principal continues to enjoy the benefit of those customers; and
- the payment of an indemnity is seen as equitable taking into account of all the circumstances, especially any commission lost by the agent on business with these customers.[108]

There is a maximum level of indemnity which amounts to the equivalent of one year's commission, which is worked out on the basis of an average of the last five years or if the agency has been less than that, the average of the period of the agency.[109]

---

[105] Commercial Agents (Council Directive) Regulations 1993 reg.17(2).
[106] See *King v Tunnock Ltd*, 2000 S.C. 424, as discussed in *Barrett McKenzie v Escada (UK) Ltd* [2001] All E.R. (D) 78; *Ingmar GB Ltd v Eaton Leonard Inc* [2001] C.L.C. 1825; and *Tigana Ltd v Decoro Ltd* [2003] EWHC 23 (Q.B.).
[107] [2007] UKHL 32; [2007] 4 All E.R. 1.
[108] Commercial Agents (Council Directive) Regulations 1993 reg.17(3).
[109] Commercial Agents (Council Directive) Regulations 1993 reg.17(4).

> **Key Concepts**
>
> The Commercial Agents (Council Directive) Regulations 1993 regulate the very particular form of agency involved when a self employed agent is involved in negotiating the sale and/or purchase of goods for a principal. The Regulations provide particular rules to deal with such matters as reciprocal duties, remuneration, commission and termination.

▼ CHAPTER SUMMARY

MEANING AND KEY FEATURES OF AGENCY

9–54
(1) Agency is a three-way relationship by which an agent acts on behalf of a principal and legally binds the principal to the third party involved in the relationship.

(2) There are many differing names and labels given to differing types of agency. What the courts are concerned with is establishing whether agency in fact exists and who the parties are.

(3) Agency can be created in a variety of ways:

- Express (i.e. deliberate or conscious) creation.
- Implied creation.
- Creation by ratification.
- Creation by necessity.
- Creation by holding out.

(4) Express creation of agency means that there has been a conscious or deliberate set of actions involving the principal and agent which shows their intention to set up an agency relationship. There is no set or special form or process required:

➢ *Robert Barry & Co v Doyle* (1998).

(5) Implied agency arises because the actions of the parties imply that agency was intended even though the principal has not made an express appointment.

(6) Agency is created by ratification when the principal ratifies action taken by an "agent" after the actions have already been taken. The principal has to have existed at the time the ratified actions took place, know all the relevant facts and satisfy a number of other conditions:

➢ *Tinnevelly Sugar Refining Co Ltd v Mirrlees Watson and Yaryan Co Ltd* (1894).

(7) Agency by necessity is created when it is impossible to communicate with the principal.

(8) Agency by holding out is created when the principal's actions create the impression that the agent has been appointed and given authority to act even though that has not actually happened.

THE AGENCY RELATIONSHIP

(1) The nature and extent of the authority given to an agent by a principal is a crucial element of the relationship between the agent and principal. There are three broad categories of authority:

- Express authority.
- Implied authority.
- Apparent or ostensible authority.

The principal will normally be liable for the actions of an agent who acts within their authority.

(2) Express authority will be clearly agreed between the agent and principal and, ideally, will appear in the agreement between them.

(3) Implied authority often exists in the absence of express authority and arises because the facts and circumstances of the transaction or relationship imply that the principal has given a level of authority to the agent:

➢ *Barry, Ostlere & Shepherd Ltd v Edinburgh Cork Importing Co* (1909).

(4) Apparent or ostensible arises where the principal's behaviour gives the impression that the agent has been given authority to act:

➢ *International Sponge Importers Ltd v Andrew Watt & Sons* [1911] A.C. 279.

(5) An agent owes various duties to the principal. The key duties are:

-
- to perform instructions;
- to act in good faith (the fiduciary duty);
- to exercise skill and care; and
- to keep accounts.

(6) An agent who does not follow instructions will be personally liable for losses flowing from the actions taken:

➢ *Gilmour v Clark* (1853).

(7) The fiduciary duty can be seen in a range of specific examples, which include:

- the duty to act personally:

  ➢ *De Bussche v Alt* (1878).

- the duty to account;
- the duty not to disclose confidential information:

  ➢ *Liverpool Victoria Friendly Society v Houston* (1903).

- the duty to avoid conflicts of interest:

  ➢ *McPherson's Trustees v Watt* (1877).

(8) An agent is owed certain duties by the principal and enjoys a number of rights. The main rights are:

- to be remunerated and reimbursed;

- to be relieved of liabilities; and
- to enjoy rights of lien and security.

(9) If agency works properly then normally third parties will be legally bound to the principal and there will be no rights or liabilities in place between the agent and the third party. When the agent acts as agent the key issue which affect potential rights and liabilities with third parties is disclosure of the agency relationship.

(10) If the agent discloses the existence and name of the principal then the principal is bound to the third party.

(11) If the existence of the principal is disclosed but not the name then normally the principal will be bound to the third party.

(12) When the very existence of the principal is not disclosed then the agent will normally be bound to and liable to the third party. Once the identity of the principal has been revealed then the third party has the option to sue the principal or the agent:

➢ *Bennett v Inveresk Paper Co* (1891).

(13) If an agent exceeds their authority then the agent will be liable and there will be no binding contract with the principal unless the principal opts to ratify.

ENDING AGENCY

(1) Agency can be ended in a variety of ways, many of which are based on common law principles. The most common ways are:

- Termination by the agent or principal.
- Termination in terms of the agency agreement.
- Termination by frustration.

COMMERCIAL AGENTS

(1) The Commercial Agents (Council Directive) Regulations 1993 provide a range of rights and safeguards for "commercial agents" which are not subject to change or exclusion by common law.

(2) A commercial agent is someone who is self employed and acts for a principal in buying or selling goods.

(3) A commercial agent must act dutifully for the principal and act in good faith and look after the principal's interests.

(4) A principal must also act dutifully and in good faith towards a commercial agent and observe the particular good faith duties contained in the regulations.

(5) If remuneration levels are not agreed between the principal and agent then the agent is entitled to what is customary, failing which, what is reasonable for the work done.

(6) Agents are entitled to minimum periods of notice of termination of their agency arrangement and to potential compensation on termination.

? QUICK QUIZ

- What is the purpose of agency?
- What are the main categories and types of agency?
- What are the main ways that agency can be created?
- Give an example of agency created by implication
- What are the conditions needed to establish agency by ratification?
- What is needed for agency to exist on the basis of holding out?
- What are the main types of authority an agent may have?
- How does apparent or ostensible authority differ from implied authority?
- What are the duties owed by an agent to a principal?
- What rights does an agent enjoy?
- When might an agent become liable to a third party?
- What happens if an agent exceeds the authority given by a principal?
- What is a commercial agent?
- What rights do the Commercial Agents (Council Directive) Regulations give to a commercial agent?
- What duties are owed to a principal by a commercial agent?
- How can commercial agency be terminated?

? FURTHER READING

➤ L.J. Macgregor, *The Law of Agency in Scotland* (Edinburgh: W. Green, 2013).
➤ M.F. Davidson and L.J. Macgregor, *Commercial Law in Scotland*, 3rd edn (Edinburgh: W. Green, 2014), Ch.2.
➤ Gloag and Henderson, *The Law of Scotland*, 13th edn (Edinburgh: W. Green, 2012), Ch.19.

Chapter 10   Delict

FRANKIE MCCARTHY[1]

▶ CHAPTER OVERVIEW

10–01 A delict is a civil wrong. The law of delict details when a person will be legally responsible for a wrong they have committed, whether intentionally or accidentally. The chapter looks first at how to define and remedy intentional delicts. It then considers negligent or unintentional delicts, and details the five steps that must be taken in order to establish liability for unintentional harm. The chapter goes on to look at examples of delict in specific contexts such as between employee and employer, for professionals and where the rules are regulated by statute. Finally, the remedies available in respect of a delict once proved are explained and evaluated.

✓ OUTCOMES

10–02 At the conclusion of this chapter, you should be able to:

- ✓ explain the overarching principle of the law of delict using the maxim *damnum injuria datum*;
- ✓ identify and explain intentional delicts including assault, trespass, harassment, the economic delicts, fraud and passing off;
- ✓ list the five key steps in establishing a case of liability for unintentional harm;
- ✓ explain and apply the tripartite test of duty of care;
- ✓ explain and apply the calculus of risk used to determine whether a duty of care has been breached;
- ✓ discuss the different types of loss that will give rise to a remedy in delict;
- ✓ understand and apply the tests of causation and remoteness of injury;
- ✓ outline the specific rules of delict that apply in the employment context, for professional liability, for breach of statutory duty and for nuisance; and
- ✓ explain the different remedies available for delictual claims and evaluate which is most appropriate in different situations.

---

[1] Senior Lecturer in Private Law, University of Glasgow.

WHAT IS DELICT?

Delict is the area of law which details when a person will be responsible **10–03** for their intentional or negligent acts which cause loss to others. In England, this is known as the law of tort. Unlike contractual obligations, delictual responsibilities have not been voluntarily assumed, but rather are imposed on every person by the law itself. Unlike criminal law, delict does not define offences which are punishable by the state on behalf of society, but rather regulates the relationship between individuals, often awarding damages (financial compensation) to make up for a loss suffered by one individual as a result of the negligence of another. For example, if Tony has an accident whilst driving and bumps Gina's car, he will have to pay the cost of repairing her car. This is not because he signed a contract beforehand agreeing that he would pay for Gina's car if he damaged it, but because the law says he must take responsibility for his actions, even though they were accidental.

Delict can be summed up by the Latin maxim *damnum injuria datum*. *Damnum* means a loss, which could be a physical injury, damage to property or a financial loss. *Injuria* means a legal wrong, the intentional or accidental act of one party which has caused loss to another. *Datum* means a connection between these two elements—in other words, a loss caused by a legal wrong.

A delict can be intentional, where harm is deliberately caused, such as when an individual is assaulted. It can also be unintentional, as in the example of Tony hitting Gina's car; Tony did not intend to cause any damage, but the law says he must be responsible nonetheless.

TERMINOLOGY

The person who has suffered harm at the hands of another can seek a **10–04** legal remedy (discussed below) for his loss. This person is called the pursuer. The other party, who is allegedly responsible for the loss, is called the defender. In English legal terminology, the pursuer is known as the claimant and the defender as the defendant.

INTENTIONAL DELICTS

Where one person deliberately causes harm to another, they will be **10–05** responsible for that loss in delict. Five key intentional delicts are outlined below.

Assault

Imagine Phil and Grant have a disagreement, and then Phil punches **10–06** Grant in the face. A physical attack of this kind will constitute an assault, and is likely to lead to Phil being charged with a criminal offence. However, the attack may also have civil consequences. Grant may wish to seek damages as recompense for the injury he has suffered, which he would do by making a civil claim for the delict of assault.

In addition to a physical attack, assault can also take the form of threats or verbal abuse. Delictual liability will arise if the victim has suffered physical or psychiatric harm as a result of the attack.

In order to qualify as assault, the invasion of the pursuer's bodily integrity must be non-consensual. So, if Phil had tackled Grant to the ground in a game of rugby, there is unlikely to be any claim in delict, since tackles of this kind are part and parcel of the game Grant has consented to play. This principle is important in medical situations, where a patient must give consent before treatment can be carried out. In *Montgomery v Lanarkshire Health Board*,[2] the court ruled that a patient must be advised of all the risks of the procedure or else the patient's consent will not be valid.

A defence to a claim of assault can be established if the assault was carried out in self-defence,[3] or where the actions comprising the assault are authorised by statute, for example where a parent subjects a child to reasonable chastisement.[4]

The remedy for assault will usually be damages, although interdict can also be granted if the conduct is likely to be repeated.[5]

Trespass

10-07 The delict of trespass occurs when a person temporarily intrudes onto another person's property without any legal right of access or the appropriate consent from the property's owner.[6] Land in Scotland is owned from the heavens to the centre of the earth, so trespass can include not only, for example, an individual walking across land, but also an intrusion under a person's land or through their airspace. In *Brown v Lee Construction*,[7] the defenders were building developers who had set up a crane which passed above the pursuer's property. The court was satisfied that this constituted trespass.

One remedy for trespass is interdict, to prevent the behaviour being repeated. It is important that the conduct appear *likely* to recur before this order will be granted, however. In *Winans v Macrae*,[8] the pursuer sought an interdict in respect of the defender's pet lamb, which kept straying into his fields and eating grass. By the time of the case, the defender no longer owned the lamb, and no interdict was granted. If the

---

[2] [2015] UKSC 11.
[3] *Ashley v Chief Constable of Sussex Police* [2008] UKHL 25.
[4] Criminal Justice (Scotland) Act 2003 s.51; see *Tolmie v Scottish Ministers*, 2003 S.L.T. 215 for an alternative example.
[5] See the discussion of remedies at paras 10—44—10—45.
[6] In Scotland, extensive rights of access to land are available. See the Scottish Outdoor Access Code at *http://www.outdooraccess-scotland.com* [Accessed May 15, 2015]. See also the relevant section on trespass in Ch.11, "Property".
[7] 1977 S.L.T. (Notes) 61.
[8] (1885) 12 R. 1051.

trespasser has damaged the property in some way, compensation in the form of damages can also be sought.

As a side note, it is important to differentiate trespass from encroachment, which is the name for a permanent intrusion, such as extending a building onto another person's land. Encroachment is dealt with under the rules of property law.

Harassment

Legislation provides that every individual has a right to be free from **10–08** harassment.[9] There is no statutory definition of harassment, but it includes behaviour which caused the pursuer alarm or distress.[10] The behaviour must have happened on at least two occasions,[11] and "behaviour" can simply mean speech.[12]

The most common example of harassment to be found in the reported legal cases is workplace bullying, where one employee harasses another.[13] It has also been suggested that celebrities could be subject to harassment when they are repeatedly photographed by paparazzi. A bank was found to have harassed its customer after making hundreds of telephone calls in order to discuss the state of her accounts.[14]

Economic delicts

As a general rule, the law will not interfere in the conduct of business. **10–09** The market operates in such a way that some businesses succeed while others fail. However, in certain very specific situations, the law will regard use of extreme forms of economic duress as amounting to a delictual act. The three principal examples of this doctrine are induced breach of contract, infliction of harm or loss by unlawful means and conspiracy.

Induced breach of contract

Imagine that Phil runs a pub and Ian supplies him with barrels of beer. **10–10** Grant, who is opening a rival bar, tells Ian he'll give him £1,000 if he "forgets" to make the barrel delivery to Phil on the day Grant's bar is opening for the first time. Ian, desperate for the money, fails to deliver that day, and therefore breaches his contract with Phil. Phil could sue Ian for straightforward breach of contract. However, the law says Phil can also sue Grant in delict, since Grant induced Ian to break the contract.

The various elements required to make a successful claim under this head are now set out in *OBG Ltd v Allan*.[15] First, the contract between the pursuer (Phil, in our example) and the third party (Ian) must actually be breached. The defender (Grant) must know his actions will have the effect

---

[9] Protection from Harassment Act 1997 s.8(1).
[10] Protection from Harassment Act 1997 s.8(3).
[11] Protection from Harassment Act 1997 s.8(3).
[12] Protection from Harassment Act 1997 s.8(3).
[13] A recent example is *Marinello v Edinburgh City Council*, 2011 S.L.T. 615.
[14] *Roberts v Bank of Scotland plc* [2013] EWCA Civ 882.
[15] [2007] UKHL 21; [2008] 1 A.C. 1.

of inducing breach, and must intend that outcome. The breach must be induced by the defender's persuasion, encouragement or assistance, and his actions can have no objective justification, for example, that they were necessary to enforce a right of the defender's own. If all these elements are present, the defender will be liable in damages to the pursuer for the loss suffered.

Infliction of harm or loss by unlawful means

10–11 The second economic delict is intentional infliction of harm or loss by unlawful means. This arises where the defender wrongfully interferes with the actions of a third party in which the pursuer has an economic interest, with the intention of causing the pursuer harm or loss.

In this case, there is no need for a contract to exist between the pursuer and the third party. For example, Ian may simply be a regular customer at Phil's pub, rather than a supplier. Imagine Grant threatens to assault Ian unless he stops going to the pub. If Ian complies, Phil will have lost income despite the fact there is no contract between Phil and Ian. Provided Grant's intention in threatening Ian was to cause economic harm to Phil, Grant will be liable in delict for Phil's losses. This delict will also be relevant where a contract exists between the pursuer and the third party, and the actions of the defender do not go so far as to induce breach of that contract, but nevertheless cause the pursuer loss.

The defender's actions here will be considered unlawful if they amount to a civil wrong against the third party. In our case, Grant's threat of assault is in itself a delict against Ian, and therefore amounts to a civil wrong.

Conspiracy

10–12 The third economic delict is conspiracy, first recognised in *Quinn v Leathem*.[16] This occurs where two parties join together in order to harm the economic interests of a third. Grant and Ian, for example, might agree to drop their beer prices in order to cut Phil out of the market. The mechanism used to harm the third party is important. If the conspired conduct is legal, such as Grant and Ian's agreement to cut prices, the aim of damaging the third party must be the primary motive of the conspiracy before a delict will be found to exist. If the conspired conduct is unlawful, for example if Grant and Ian kidnap Phil's bar staff so that the pub cannot open, the intention to harm Phil as a result of their actions need only be a secondary motivation for a delict to be shown. The definition of unlawful conduct here seems to include both civil wrongs and criminal offences, even where that criminal offence would not in itself give rise to a civil claim.[17]

---

[16] [1901] A.C. 495.
[17] *Commissioners of Customs & Excise v Total Network SL* [2008] UKHL 19; [2008] 1 A.C. 1174.

Remedies

The remedy for any economic delict will usually be damages in recom- **10–13** pense for the economic harm suffered. Interdict may also be appropriate if the conduct is likely to be repeated.

Fraud

The classic definition of fraud is "a machination or contrivance to **10–14** deceive".[18] One party makes a statement or takes some other action to represent something as a fact. The party is telling a straightforward lie, or at least does not believe what he is saying is true.[19] The intention of making this representation is to cause a loss to another party. For example, Grant might tell Phil that Ian is selling very high quality champagne at a very cheap price with the aim of convincing Phil to waste a lot of money buying bottles. If Grant knows the so-called champagne is actually supermarket cava relabelled, or else suspects it must be based on dodgy dealings he has had with Ian in the past, Grant has committed the delict of fraud. If Grant honestly believes the champagne is excellent and at a cheap price, even though his belief might be inaccurate, there is no intentional delict.

The remedy for fraud will usually be damages for any losses suffered as a result.[20]

Passing off

The delict of passing off is concerned with protecting the "goodwill" of a **10–15** business. Goodwill is the term given to what might be considered the good name of a business, its reputation, the marketability of the brand. Imagine that Grant opens a coffee shop in the east end of Glasgow. He furnishes it with comfortable armchairs and pine furniture, plays jazz music and sells muffins and panini. He calls the shop Starstrucks, and writes the sign in a white font on a green background. Customers may well become confused by the similarities and think that Grant's shop is, in fact, a branch of Starbucks. This confusion is the essence of the delict of passing off; Grant is attempting to pass off his coffee shop as being a Starbucks in order to take advantage of their popularity.

The criteria for this delict are set out in the case of *Erven Warnink BV v J. Townend & Sons (Hull) Ltd (No.1)*.[21] The five criteria are:

    (i) a misrepresentation (in our example, the way in which Grant has set up his shop and the name are likely to amount to misrepresentations);

   (ii) made by a trader in the course of a trade (if Grant had simply set up his living room like a coffee shop, there would be no delict);

---

[18] Erskine *Institute* III, 1, 16.
[19] *Derry v Peek* (1889) L.R. 14 App. Cas. 337.
[20] However, see the discussion regarding liability for pure economic loss resulting from misrepresentation at para.10–28.
[21] [1979] A.C. 731.

     (iii) to prospective customers or to the ultimate consumers of the good or services;
     (iv) which is calculated to injure the goodwill of another; and
     (v) which caused actual damage to the business or goodwill of the trader by whom the action is brought. This is likely to be the most difficult aspect to prove in our example. (Starbucks would have to show they had lost profit as a result of the confusion caused by Grant's café.)

The usual remedy for passing off will be interdict, although a damages claim may also be possible if losses can be proved and accurately quantified.

Unintentional Delicts

10–16 The concept of liability for intentional harm is easy to understand; a person who deliberately hurts another should be responsible for repairing that damage. However, the law does not restrict liability in delict to situations where the harm has been caused deliberately. Damage caused accidentally still requires repair; personal injury suffered at the hands of another is incapacitating whether that person intended it to be so or not. The law says that, where a person causes harm as a result of not taking enough care, they will be responsible for that harm, even though it was accidental. In other words, where an individual has been negligent, they will be liable for any unintentional delicts which occur as a result.

    When is a person responsible for an act of unintentional harm? The law answers this question as follows:

- There must be a duty of care between the pursuer and defender.
- The defender must have breached this duty of care, by falling below the standard of care exercised by the reasonable man.
- The pursuer must have sustained a loss.
- The breach of duty of care must have been the factual and legal cause of the loss to the pursuer.
- The loss must not be too remote.

In any situation where one person has accidentally suffered harm as a result of the actions of another, these five criteria must be fulfilled for a case in delict to be made out.

There must be a duty of care

What is a duty of care?

10–17 Each person has a responsibility to take care in their acts (and omissions to act) so as to avoid causing harm to others. That is the essence of the duty of care.

    Imagine that Tony decides to park his car at the top of a hill while he goes into a shop to buy a newspaper. He forgets to put on his handbrake.

While he is in the shop, the car is disturbed by passing traffic and rolls down the hill until it collides with Gina's car. Obviously the damage here is accidental. Tony did not want to damage Gina's car, and he will have damaged his own vehicle in the process. However, the accident is still Tony's fault, since it was he who forgot to put on the handbrake. His thoughtlessness—or lack of care—is the reason for the accident. Tony had a duty to take care to apply his handbrake when parking his car.

This idea of duty of care was first described in the case of *Donoghue v Stevenson*,[22] often called the "snail in the bottle" case.

Donoghue v Stevenson
1932 S.C. (H.L.) 31

Mrs Donoghue went to a café with a friend. The friend bought her a bottle of ginger beer, and poured half the bottle into a glass, which Mrs Donoghue then drank. When she poured the rest of the drink into the glass, the remainder of a decomposing snail appeared along with it. Mrs Donoghue became ill as a result, and wished to make a claim against the manufacturers of the drink. However, she had no contract on which to base such a legal claim; it had been her friend who had bought the drink, and therefore her friend who had a contract with the café owner. The court decided that, even in the absence of a contractual relationship, there was still a legal basis on which Mrs Donoghue could make a claim. The drink manufacturers should have been able to foresee that someone other than the person who bought the drink might ultimately be the consumer of the drink. They should also have been able to foresee that finding half a snail in the bottle would make the consumer of the drink fall ill. The court was of the view that the drink manufacturer therefore had a duty towards the eventual consumer of the drink to take reasonable care to prevent snails falling into their bottles. Mrs Donoghue was, on that basis of that delictual duty, entitled to make a claim against the drink manufacturer.

In *Donoghue*, Lord Atkin explained the idea of duty of care using what has become known as the "neighbourhood principle".

> "The rule that you are to love your neighbour becomes in law that you must not injure your neighbour. Who, then in law is my neighbour? The answer seems to be—persons who are so closely and directly affected by my act that I ought reasonably to have them in contemplation as being so affected when I am directing my mind to the acts or omissions which are called into question."[23]

---

[22] 1932 S.C. (H.L.) 31.
[23] 1932 S.C. (H.L.) 31 at 44.

Essentially, Lord Atkin is saying that we owe a duty of care to anyone who we can reasonably foresee might be affected by the way we act.

This principle has been refined and extended over time, most importantly in *Caparo Industries Plc v Dickman*.[24]

Caparo Industries Plc v Dickman
[1990] 2 A.C. 605

In this case an auditor produced a set of figures suggesting a company was in a stronger financial position than it actually was. Investors bought shares in the company as a result, and then lost money. The auditor had no contract with the investors; his contract was with the company. However, the court was satisfied that he owed a duty of care to the investors. The court set out three criteria that had to be fulfilled before a duty of care could exist in a given situation. In the first place, the harm suffered by the pursuer must be foreseeable. In the second place, there must be proximity between the pursuer and the defender. Finally, it must be fair, just and reasonable to impose a duty in the particular circumstances of the case. This is now known as the "tripartite test" of duty of care, and has been adopted in a number of subsequent cases.[25]

Foreseeability of harm

10–18 A duty of care will be owed by one person to another when it is reasonably foreseeable that the actions of the first will cause harm to the second. So when is harm reasonably foreseeable? The answer to this is largely a matter of common sense. Take the example of our motorist, Tony. If, whilst driving, he decides to make a right turn, but does not use his indicator to show he intends to do so, what might happen? The car travelling behind him might run into him, since the driver is not expecting Tony to slow down for the turn. A car travelling in the lane of traffic Tony must cross to make his turn might collide with Tony, since the driver of that car is not anticipating Tony's manoeuvre across the lane. Tony might hit a pedestrian crossing the road he is turning into, since the pedestrian may not be alerted to Tony's intention to enter the road. The possibility that these things may happen is obvious. They are foreseeable consequences of Tony's failure to use his indicator.

Not every possible consequence will be foreseeable, however. If a parachutist descended on to the road in front of Tony as he made his right turn, Tony would hit the parachutist. This is a possible consequence of Tony's failure to indicate, but it is not a foreseeable one. Foreseeable consequences have to be the reasonable and probable outcome of the pursuer's conduct.

---

[24] [1990] 2 A.C. 605.
[25] *Gibson v Orr*, 1999 S.C. 420 and *Mitchell v Glasgow City Council*, 2009 S.L.T. 247 are the most important examples.

This distinction is illustrated by two similar cases involving sporting accidents. In *Bolton v Stone*,[26] a cricket ball was struck right out of a cricket ground where it injured a person around 100 yards from the wicket. Balls had been struck out of the ground on only six occasions in the previous 30 years. The harm to the pursuer was not considered foreseeable, as the risk of injury was so unlikely it could not be considered a reasonable and probable consequence of hitting the ball. Conversely, in *Lamond v Glasgow Corporation*,[27] a golf ball was struck out into a footpath which ran alongside the golf course, where it hit the pursuer in the head. On average, 6,000 golf balls were played onto the footpath every year, although there was no evidence of anyone having been struck before. Given the frequency with which balls entered the footpath, it was considered to be reasonable and probable that a passer-by would be struck eventually, and the harm was therefore foreseeable.

Where a certain type of loss is a reasonable and probable outcome of the pursuer's actions, the exact chain of circumstances leading to that loss may not have to be foreseeable. *Hughes v Lord Advocate*[28] concerned two young boys who were burned following an explosion of paraffin. They had been investigating a work site, where employees of the Post Office had uncovered a manhole and left it unattended, with a canvas tent protecting the manhole and two paraffin lamps set outside as a warning. The boys took the lamps inside the tent, at which point one was knocked over and exploded on contact with air. The court found it to be foreseeable that leaving paraffin lamps unattended would lead to burning injuries. The fact the burns had been caused by an explosion rather than by straightforward contact with the flames in the lamp was irrelevant. The nature of the harm was foreseeable.

Proximity

This criterion is concerned with the identity of the persons who may be **10–19** affected by the conduct of another. It is not enough to say that the pursuer's actions may reasonably and probably cause harm to somebody, somewhere. A particular class or category of people must be in mind.

Return to our example of Tony with his careless car parking at the top of the hill. It is clear that other road users, such as Gina, may be affected by his carelessness. It is also possible that Chet, watching CCTV footage of the accident over the internet in California, might laugh so much at the Tony's car rolling down the hill that he ruptures his spleen. Chet's injury is possible, but it is not reasonably foreseeable. It is not within the normal range of consequences of Tony's actions. Chet is not proximate to Tony, so he is not Tony's neighbour in law.

A useful illustration of this concept comes in the case of *Bourhill v Young*.[29] A motorcyclist, Young, crashed into a car and died as a result of

---

[26] [1951] A.C. 850.
[27] 1968 S.L.T. 291.
[28] 1963 S.C. (H.L.) 31.
[29] 1942 S.C. (H.L.) 78.

his own negligence. Mrs Bourhill was a pedestrian who happened to be in the vicinity at the time. She did not see the accident, but heard the noise of the collision and witnessed blood on the road. She claimed to have suffered "nervous shock" as a result which lead to a miscarriage. The court was satisfied that the defender owed a duty of care to nearby road users. However, Mrs Bourhill had not been at risk of physical injury from the accident, and had not even seen it happening. Although it was possible she could be affected by the defender's negligence, it was not probable. She was not proximate to the defender, and so no duty of care could arise.

A very different example of this doctrine is shown in *Hill v Chief Constable of West Yorkshire*.[30]

Hill v Chief Constable of West Yorkshire
[1989] A.C. 53

The mother of the final victim of Peter Sutcliffe, the Yorkshire Ripper, sued the police. She argued the police were negligent in failing to find Sutcliffe sooner, and it was reasonably foreseeable that because they had not found him, he would murder again. The case failed for lack of proximity. All of Sutcliffe's victims had been women in the Leeds area, and the argument was that the police owed a duty of care to this limited class of people—the women of Leeds—to catch Sutcliffe. However, the court was of the view that, although this category was limited, it was still too wide for a relationship of proximity to exist between the police and this group of women. No duty of care could be said to exist.

"Fair, just and reasonable"

10–20 A duty of care can only be found to exist where it is fair, just and reasonable in the circumstances of the case. This is a type of catch-all provision which allows the court to take into account broader economic or policy arguments when determining if a duty of care should be imposed.

Again, *Hill*[31] provides assistance. If the police were under a duty of care to every victim of crime, even if limited to every victim of a recidivist, this could give rise to an enormous number of claims in delict. Defending such claims and paying damages would cost a huge amount of money, which in turn would make police funding an impossible issue for government. Additionally, it would be extremely difficult for the police to investigate reported crimes with the threat of legal action looming at all times. Ultimately, recognising a duty of care in situations of this type would impact negatively on society as a whole. These are the types of

---

[30] [1989] A.C. 53.
[31] [1989] A.C. 53.

considerations the court may take into account under this head of the tripartite test.

In many cases, it is settled law that a duty of care exists. There is no real question that a motorist owes a duty of care to pedestrians and other road users, for example, or that an employer owes a duty of care to his employees. The tripartite test is particularly useful for establishing the existence of a duty of care (or otherwise) in novel situations.

Key Concept

A duty of care is owed to anyone who it can be reasonably foreseen will be affected by the defender's conduct. This is assessed using the tripartite test:

- Is the harm of a type that was reasonably foreseeable?
- Is the pursuer proximate to the defender?
- Is it fair, just & reasonable to impose a duty of care in this situation?

The defender must have breached his duty of care

We have seen that every person has a duty to take care in the way they act **10–21** so as to avoid causing harm to others. This duty is breached when a person fails to take the requisite amount of care, or, in other words, when a person is negligent.

In the first place, for a breach of duty to occur, the defender must have been acting voluntarily. Imagine Kerry is standing on a bus which lurches suddenly, causing her to lose her footing and fall into Karim, bruising his arm. In a technical sense, Kerry is the cause of Karim's injury. However, she could not have taken care to avoid the accident; it was beyond her control. In *Waugh v James K Allan Ltd*,[32] a lorry driver suffered the onset of coronary thrombosis at the wheel and died. In so doing, the lorry swerved and hit a pedestrian, causing serious injury. The court held that the lorry driver had not breached his duty of care, since the onset of illness was beyond his control, and he could not have known it was about to happen.

For a voluntary act, then, how much care is enough? In law, we call this the standard of care. A person is expected to display the standard of care a reasonable man would display in the same situation. If a heart surgeon is carrying out heart surgery, they will be expected to take the same amount of care as a reasonable heart surgeon performing the same operation. This is discussed in *Muir v Glasgow Corporation (No.2)*,[33] in which some schoolchildren, having lunch in a tea shop operated by the defenders, were scalded when a tea urn being carried by employees of the

---

[32] 1964 S.C. (H.L.) 102.
[33] 1943 S.C. (H.L.) 3.

defenders was upset. The court held that the defenders had demonstrated the standard of care to be expected of reasonable café owners. The urn required to be transported through the café, and was being carried by competent members of staff. It is impossible to prevent every accident from happening, and the defenders had done everything they could reasonably be expected to do in the circumstances.

In ascertaining the standard of care expected of a reasonable man in a given situation, and deciding whether this standard has been met, the court will give weight to a number of factors known as the calculus of risk. This is made up of four main questions.

How likely was it that the defender's conduct would cause an injury?

10–22 If the defender's act or omission was very likely to cause harm, then it is more likely that he will be found to fall below the standard of care expected. In *St George v Home Office*,[34] a prisoner was allocated a top bunk on his arrival to prison, despite explaining that he was addicted to heroin and had suffered with seizures when withdrawing from the drug previously. He fell from the bunk during a seizure a few nights later and suffered a head injury leading to brain damage. The prison authority was found to be negligent, in part because the risk of placing the claimant in a top bunk had been clearly indicated.

How serious was the injury likely to be?

10–23 The risk of a serious injury or major property damage is more likely to lead the court to the conclusion that the appropriate standard of care has not been reached. The severity of any injury will be looked at in the circumstances of the case in question. For example, *Paris v Stepney Borough Council*[35] concerned an accident in a garage where a mechanic was struck in the eye by a chip of metal from a car he had been working on. The mechanic was blind in one eye, and the metal chip hit his remaining good eye, resulting in total blindness. Safety goggles had not been supplied. The standard of care expected of the mechanic's employers was higher than it would have been for a fully sighted mechanic, precisely because the result of the accident was so serious for the pursuer.

How difficult/expensive would it have been to take precautions against the accident?

10–24 Again, if a cheap and easy precaution which would have prevented the accident was not taken, it is more likely that the necessary standard of care will not have been reached. In *Paris*, the defenders could have supplied safety goggles to their employees cheaply and easily, but failed to do so. Conversely, in *Latimer v AEC Ltd*,[36] an employee who slipped on a flooded factory floor argued that the factory should have been

---

[34] [2009] 1 W.L.R. 1670.
[35] [1951] A.C. 367.
[36] [1953] A.C. 643.

closed down. The court thought such an inconvenient and expensive precaution was unnecessary in the circumstances, and considered that the defenders had successfully met the required standard of care by spreading sawdust on the floor.

What was the purpose of the defender's conduct?

The basic idea behind this question is that, if the defender was doing **10–25** something particularly important which perhaps required him to act quickly, a lower standard of care could reasonably be expected. A helpful example is *Watt v Hertfordshire County Council*,[37] in which a fireman was injured by a heavy jack which fell into him as the fire engine was rushing to the scene of an accident. The fire engine was not adapted to carry the particular jack, but the fire crew had taken it from the station because they knew it was needed urgently to rescue a woman trapped under a car. The court was of the view that the risk to the plaintiff had to be weighed against the cost of the woman's life. In the circumstances, the requisite standard of care had been displayed.

In addition to the four questions set out above, the court will also consider anything else relevant in deciding whether the standard of care has been breached, including previous case law which may be in point. Ultimately, the decision should be largely a matter of common sense.

Key Concept

- Only a voluntary act can breach the duty of care.
- The standard of care expected is that of a reasonable man in the same situation.
- Whether the standard of care has been reached will be assessed using the calculus of risk.

The pursuer must have sustained a loss

In order for a claim to be made in delict, the pursuer must have suffered **10–26** some loss. Consider again Tony's car, parked at the top of the hill without application of the handbrake. Say his car rolls down the hill, but bypasses Gina's car, and instead comes to a rest harmlessly at the bottom of the hill, out of the way of traffic. Tony still owes Gina a duty of care, and he has still breached this duty by failing to meet the requisite standard of care. But Gina has not suffered any loss as a result of the breach. She cannot make a claim, and no successful action in delict could be established.

Many different types of loss can give rise to a delictual claim. Most obviously, a person suffering a physical injury can claim for the pain and suffering they have endured, known as solatium. They may also claim for any losses following on that injury, such as loss of income if they have

---

[37] [1954] 1 W.L.R. 835.

been unable to work. Damage to property, such as the dent in Gina's car, can also be recovered.

Not all forms of loss are so straightforward, however. We will consider two types of loss which have additional complications: psychiatric injury and pure economic loss.

Psychiatric injury

10–27 A psychiatric injury will constitute a loss for the purposes of an action in delict, provided that it is a diagnosable condition, and not simply ordinary distress or upset.

A person suffering from a psychiatric illness caused by negligence will be categorised by the law as either a primary or a secondary victim, following *Page v Smith*.[38] A primary victim is defined as someone who was at risk of physical injury as a result of the breach, whether they actually suffered physical injury or not. A primary victim is always entitled to claim for psychiatric harm.

The position of a secondary victim is more complex. Secondary victims are those who suffer psychiatric harm as a result of witnessing another person suffering injury in an accident caused through negligence. The rules on secondary victims were first established in *Bourhill v Young*,[39] discussed above,[40] in which the pursuer was categorised as a secondary victim, having been at no risk of physical harm herself.

The doctrine was developed in *Alcock v Chief Constable of South Yorkshire Police*.[41]

Alcock v Chief Constable of South Yorkshire Police
[1992] 1 A.C. 310

This case arose from the tragedy at Hillsborough football stadium in which dozens of supporters were killed in a crush caused by overcrowding. Friends and relatives of the victims sought damages for psychiatric harm caused by viewing television footage of the incident. The court set out three criteria which had to be fulfilled before a secondary victim would be entitled to recover damages:
(i)   There must have been a close tie of love and affection between the primary and secondary victims.
(ii) The secondary victim must have been present at the accident or its immediate aftermath.
(iii) The secondary victim must have had direct perception of the accident with his unaided senses.

---

[38] [1996] A.C. 155.
[39] 1942 S.C. (H.L.) 78.
[40] See para.10–19.
[41] [1992] 1 A.C. 310.

So, for example, if a mother is advised by telephone that her daughter has been in an accident, and attends the scene of the accident, witnessing her child in distress, it is likely she will be entitled to recover for any psychiatric injury which results. However, if she was simply advised by telephone that her child had died, and did not attend the scene, she will be unlikely to have a claim.

Pure economic loss

As mentioned above, economic loss which is consequent on a physical **10–28** injury (such as loss of earnings) or property damage can usually be recovered in delict. However, a loss which is purely financial—in other words, does not result from some other direct damage to a person or property—is not usually recoverable. The reason for this is simple practicality. If Tony's car hits Gina's, there is likely to be a hold-up in the traffic on the road. Many cars will be stuck, and every one of those drivers will have to pay for petrol they have burned whilst sitting in a traffic jam which could have been avoided. If Tony were liable for the costs of all that extra petrol, it would be a heavy burden—too heavy, in the eyes of the law.

A useful illustration is provided by the contrast of two cases involving power cuts. In *Dynamco Ltd v Holland & Hannen & Cubitts (Scotland) Ltd*,[42] the defenders negligently severed an electricity cable, with the result that the pursuer's factory was out of operation for a period of time since its machinery could not operate without power. The court held that no recovery was possible. The physical damage had been done to the power cable, owned by the electricity company. The pursuer's loss was purely financial. In *SCM (UK) Ltd v WJ Whittall & Son Ltd*,[43] a power cable was again cut, causing molten metal in the plaintiff's mixing machines to solidify, effectively destroying the machines. The plaintiff was entitled to recover the cost of replacing the machines, since the property had been damaged directly by the power cut.

There is, however, an exception to this principle regarding pure economic loss in the situation where the loss has resulted from a negligent misrepresentation on the part of the defender. If a person makes a negligent statement which is false, but which they reasonably believed to be true, and a second person acts on that statement to their economic loss, the first may be liable in damages.[44] This was first established in the case of *Hedley Byrne & Co Ltd v Heller & Partners Ltd*.[45]

---

[42] 1971 S.C. 257.
[43] [1971] 1 Q.B. 337.
[44] A deliberate false statement will be the intentional delict of fraud, as discussed above.
[45] [1964] A.C. 465.

Hedley Byrne & Co Ltd v Heller & Partners Ltd
[1964] 2 A.C. 465

The plaintiff was an advertising agency. When considering whether to take on a company, E, as a client, it sought the advice of E's bankers, Heller & Partners, who advised that E was reliable. The plaintiff engaged E on that basis. E went into liquidation shortly afterwards, leaving the plaintiff with a substantial financial loss. The court held that the defendants should have known that the plaintiff would rely on their statement as to E's reliability, and on that basis a "special duty of care" arose between the parties which allowed recovery for pure economic loss.

This "special" duty of care will only arise in relationships where there are additional proximity factors between the parties, a situation which most often arises where one party is offering advice in a professional capacity and should know the other will rely on that advice. One example in case law is that of a surveyor who made critical errors in a survey instructed by the mortgage lender. The surveyor was held liable to the house buyer who relied on that survey when purchasing the house.[46]

In *Henderson v Merrett Syndicates Ltd*,[47] this proposition was expanded to include not only negligent statements, but any type of negligent action or omission on the part of the defender, provided that the defender has voluntarily assumed responsibility for the economic interests of the pursuer.

Whether responsibility has been voluntarily assumed will depend on the facts of the case. An employer agreeing to write a reference for an employee has been held to have voluntarily assumed responsibility for his economic interests, since the employee is relying on the reference being accurate and timeously provided.[48] However, an exemption clause was enough to demonstrate no responsibility had been assumed by the defenders in *Bank of Scotland v Fuller Peiser*,[49] where the defenders, a firm of surveyors, stated on the valuation report that they took no responsibility for anyone other than the purchaser. The mortgage lender later tried to make a claim against them, but the court held that the disclaimer prevented the *Henderson v Merrett Syndicates Ltd* test from being satisfied. A focus on the exact circumstances of every case has been affirmed by the court as the correct approach to determining the existence of a duty of care in these situations.[50]

[46] *Martin v Bell-Ingram*, 1986 S.C. 208.
[47] [1995] 2 A.C. 145.
[48] *Spring v Guardian Assurance Plc* [1995] 2 A.C. 296.
[49] 2002 S.L.T. 574.
[50] *Customs and Excise Commissioners v Barclays Bank Plc* [2007] 1 A.C. 181.

The pursuer's loss must have been caused by the defender's breach of duty of care

This is the crucial link between the pursuer and the defender. The pursuer's loss must have been caused by the defender's breach of duty of care. In law, this is often described as the "but for" test. But for the defender's breach, the pursuer would not have suffered a loss.

There are two different types of causation. Factual causation deals with whether, as a matter of simple fact, the defender's breach caused the pursuer's loss. Of course, there could be several factual causes for one accident. Think again of Tony's parked car. Imagine the road was icy at the time, and that Gina had parked her own car dangerously far out from the kerb. All the elements have combined to cause the accident. All that matters, for the test of factual causation to be satisfied, is that the defender's breach was *one* such factor. In law, we say that it was a *causa sine qua non* of the pursuer's loss.

Legal causation deals with the effective, dominant or immediate cause of the loss. What was the primary cause, or *causa causans*, of the pursuer's injury? If the answer to that question is the defender's breach of duty, only then is the test of legal causation satisfied, and the defender will be liable for the pursuer's losses.

The concept of causation is usefully illustrated by *McWilliams v Sir William Arrol & Co, Lithgows, Ltd,*[51] in which a steel erector fell to his death. The defenders, his employers, were held to be in breach of duty of care by failing to provide him with a safety belt. However, the evidence was that, even if the belt had been provided, the pursuer would not have worn it. Provision of the belt would not have stopped the accident, and so the test of causation was not satisfied. More dramatically, in *Barnett v Chelsea and Kensington Hospital Management Committee,*[52] a man attended the casualty department of the defendant's hospital complaining of sickness and vomiting. This should have marked him as a priority patient, but in fact he was not seen by a doctor, and instead he was sent home, where he died later that night. The defendant had clearly breached its duty of care. However, the evidence was that the man's death was the result of arsenic poisoning. Even if he had been seen by a doctor as soon as he arrived at casualty, there would have been nothing the doctor could have done to help him. He would have died anyway. The breach of duty was therefore not the legal cause of his death.

In limited circumstances, the test of causation can be satisfied provided the defender's breach of duty made a material contribution to the pursuer's loss, or else materially increased the risk of the pursuer's loss. This doctrine has so far only been used in cases in which the harm to the pursuer was the contraction of a disease, and the courts have said that material increase in risk can only satisfy the causation test where science is unable to identify the exact cause of an illness. These rules were

---

[51] 1962 S.C. (H.L.) 70.
[52] [1969] 1 Q.B. 428.

reviewed in *Fairchild v Glenhaven Funeral Services Ltd*,[53] in which the pursuer contracted terminal lung cancer as a result of exposure to asbestos. Scientific evidence suggested that the cancer could be caused by inhalation of one single fibre of asbestos dust. The pursuer had been negligently exposed by two different employers, and it was impossible to say during which of these employments he might have inhaled the particular fibre. The court held that, since both employers had materially increased his risk of contracting the disease, and since there was no other possible way the disease could have developed, the test of causation was satisfied. Both employers were held to be at fault.

The chain of causation leading from the defender's breach to the pursuer's loss can be broken by a natural event, the actions of other people, or by the actions of the pursuer himself. Any action or event which causes a break in the chain is known as a novus actus interveniens, which means "new act intervening". In *McKew v Holland & Hannen & Cubitts (Scotland) Ltd*,[54] the pursuer had injured his ankle in consequence of the defender's negligence, with the result that his leg was liable to give way on occasion. Shortly afterwards, the pursuer was descending a steep staircase with no handrail. His leg gave way, and he panicked and jumped down 10 steps, causing further injury to his leg. The court said that the original injury was a *causa sine qua non* of the second injury, but not the *causa causans*. The pursuer's own act, in panicking and jumping down the steps, constituted a novus actus interveniens. The second injury was the pursuer's own fault.

It is important to note, however, that conduct on the part of the pursuer which might reasonably be foreseen as a result of the initial breach will not break the causal chain. In *Sayers v Harlow Urban District Council*,[55] the pursuer found herself locked in a public toilet as the result of a faulty lock. Panicking, she attempted to escape over the top of the cubicle wall and put her foot on the toilet roll holder, which snapped, causing her to fall to her injury. The court was not satisfied that her actions in trying to escape constituted a novus actus interveniens, since it was foreseeable that a person, on becoming trapped, would try to escape.

Key Concept

- The pursuer's loss must have been caused by the defender's breach of duty of care.
- The "but for" test must be satisfied to show that the defender's breach was the effective, dominant or immediate cause of the loss.
- The chain of causation can be broken by a novus actus interveniens.

---

[53] [2003] 1 A.C. 32.
[54] 1970 S.C. (H.L.) 20.
[55] [1958] 1 W.L.R. 623.

The loss must not be too remote

Accidents can have far-reaching consequences. Think of Tony's car, **10–30** which has collided with Gina's car, damaging it so that it cannot be driven. Gina calls the AA, but by the time they have arrived to deal with the problem, she has missed the job interview she was going to, and does not get the job she really wanted. Bitter about missing out, she goes home and has a fight with her husband, which turns into a series of fights and eventually they divorce. In one way this all leads back to the accident. Should Tony have to pay compensation for all of it?

The law says you have to draw the line somewhere. This is where the concept of remoteness of damage comes in. The concept of foreseeability is again important; if the losses are not foreseeable, the defender should not be held liable for them.

What is the test of foreseeability in this context? The law is not entirely clear. Two leading cases offer conflicting viewpoints. The first of these is the "direct consequences" test, set out in *Re Polemis, Furness Withy & Co Ltd.*[56] A ship was destroyed in a fire caused when a stevedore negligently knocked a timber board into the hold of a ship. The board collided with another object, causing a spark which ignited petrol vapour in the hold. The court admitted that the fire itself was not foreseeable. However, it was foreseeable that some type of harm to the ship would result from the negligence of the stevedore, and so the loss was recoverable on the basis that the fire was a direct consequence of a foreseeable harm. In other words, if it can be foreseen that something bad will happen, the defender will be liable for anything bad which actually happens as a direct consequence of the breach.

The *Polemis* test was rejected by the Privy Council in *Overseas Tankship (UK) Ltd v Morts Dock & Engineering Co Ltd (The Wagon Mound)*,[57] another case involving an unusual fire. The *Wagon Mound*, a ship, was docked and being refuelled when some of the fuel oil was negligently allowed to leak into the water in the bay. The leaked oil travelled on the water to a wharf, where repair work was being carried out on another vessel. A piece of molten metal fell from the repair works onto cotton waste floating on top of the oil, setting the cotton alight. This, in turn, led to the oil catching light and a huge fire taking place. The Privy Council said "direct consequences" was not the proper test of remoteness, and the loss should rather be a reasonably foreseeable consequence of the breach. Here, it was foreseeable that the wharf might be fouled by the oil, but damage by fire was not foreseeable, because oil on water would not usually ignite.

Which of these two approaches is the correct test in Scots law is not certain. The courts have vacillated between the two, and on occasion have used what appears to be a combination of both. Recent authority, however, seems to come down more strongly in favour of the *Wagon*

---

[56] [1921] 3 K.B. 560.
[57] [1961] A.C. 388.

Mound test of reasonable foreseeability. In *Simmons v British Steel Plc*,[58] it was held that the defender should be liable for harm of a kind that was reasonably foreseeable, even though the harm was greater than could have been foreseen, or where it was caused in a way that could not have been foreseen.

What is clear from the case law is that, where the harm is foreseeable, the defender must "take his victim as he finds him". This is known as the "eggshell skull" rule. If the defender accidentally trips the pursuer, and the pursuer suffers from osteoporosis and breaks several bones as a result of a fall which would, for most people, have no serious consequences, that is simply the defender's bad luck. Liability persists. This rule was first established in *McKillen v Barclay Curle & Co Ltd*,[59] in which the pursuer's rib was broken in an accident causing a reactivation of dormant tuberculosis.

DEFENCES

10–31   If a pursuer is able to successfully negotiate the five steps of liability for unintentional harm, he will have proved his case. The defender may, however, have a defence to the claim that will defeat or reduce the pursuer's right to damages.

Volenti

10–32   One potential line of defence is volenti non fit injuria, which translates to mean that no harm can be done to someone who consents. Volenti will be a defence where the defender can prove the pursuer consented to the risk inherent in the defender's behaviour. If volenti can be established, it will relieve the defender of all liability for the harm. For example, say Gina is out drinking with Tony, and then agrees to let Tony drive her home despite the fact she is aware that Tony is several drinks over the limit. Tony will not be liable to her for crashing his car and killing her.

The classic example of volenti is *Titchener v British Railways Board*.[60]

---

[58] [2004] S.C. (H.L.) 94.
[59] 1967 S.L.T. 41.
[60] 1984 S.C. (H.L.) 34.

> ### Titchener v British Railways Board
> #### 1984 S.C. (H.L.) 34
>
> A girl climbed through the hole in a protective fence in order to cross a railway line and was hit by a train. No duty of care was found to exist, but the court also commented that, in any event, the pursuer was *volens* to the risks of being on the train line. The fence was there to prevent passers-by straying on to the track. The pursuer had deliberately ignored that protection, demonstrating her willingness to accept the risk of injury inherent in being on a train line.

Contributory negligence

10–33 In some cases, the accident may have been partly caused or exacerbated by the pursuer's own actions. In this case, the defender can argue that the pursuer was contributorily negligent, based on the Law Reform (Contributory Negligence) (Scotland) Act 1945. For example, if Tony (sober this time) is driving Gina home and negligently crashes his car, he will be responsible for her injuries. But if her injuries are exacerbated by the fact she did not bother to put on her seatbelt when she got into the car, she will have contributed to the loss through her own failure to take reasonable care of herself.

If the defender can successfully argue for contributory negligence, this will not relieve him of all liability for the accident, but will reduce the amount of damages he has to pay by the percentage of liability the courts attribute to the pursuer. The percentage will depend entirely on the facts and circumstances of the case. For example, a deduction of 25 per cent is often applied for failure to wear a seatbelt. In S*ayers v Harlow Urban District Council*, discussed above,[61] the pursuer's dangerous escape route from the toilet cubicle was considered to have contributed to the accident and her damages were reduced by 25 per cent.

Sole fault/joint fault

10–34 Where a loss is the result of breaches of duty of care by two different persons, the responsibility for the accident will be attributed between them in the appropriate percentages. Equally, the pursuer can be considered the sole cause of the loss, or the author of his own misfortune. This may be the case where his actions constitute a novus actus interveniens between his loss and the defender's breach of duty of care.

---

[61] See para.10–29.

Delict in the Employment Context[62]

Employers' liability

10-35 Every employer owes his employee a duty to take reasonable care for the employee's safety. This will include more specific duties to provide the employee with a safe workplace, to devise a safe system of working and to provide appropriate plant and equipment for the employee's tasks. At common law, the employer's duty is to take reasonable care, and the usual calculus of risk will be applied in determining whether that standard of care has been reached in a particular case. However, the law in this area is heavily regulated by a statutory regime implementing a range of EU Directives which tend to impose a much higher standard of care on the employer. A full examination of the statutory scheme is beyond the scope of this book.[63]

Vicarious liability

10-36 Vicarious liability is the doctrine by which one person can be held responsible for the actions of another. An employer will be vicariously liable for the actions of his employee during the course of employment. In simple terms, this means that if Ewan's car is damaged by Jasmine whilst she is out driving on a business errand for her employers, Nowhere City Council, Ewan is entitled to make a claim against Jasmine's employers rather than against Jasmine personally. Often this will make sound economic sense, since Jasmine's employers are likely to have more money than Jasmine.

For an employer to be vicariously liable, two conditions must be fulfilled:

(1) a contract of employment must exist between the two parties;
(2) the employee must have been acting in the course of his employment at the time the delictual act took place.

In some situations, the fact of employment will be easy to ascertain, but the modern working environment has resulted in employment relationships growing increasingly complex. The court will not place too much reliance on how the parties describe their relationship, but rather will look at the circumstances in order to ascertain whether one party was employed, or was merely providing services to the other. One concept which has traditionally been important is that of control; if the purported employer is able to direct specifically how the other party carries out his duties, that tends to suggest the contract is one of employment. For example, if Jasmine employs someone to cook her meals at home, she can specify what she wants to eat and how she wants it to be cooked, and can

---

[62] For a more detailed review of different aspects of employment law, see Ch.8, "Employment Law".
[63] Further information is available at the website of the Health and Safety Executive: *http://www.hse.gov.uk* [Accessed May 15, 2015].

stand over the chef in the kitchen if she so wishes; that is a contract of employment. However, if Jasmine goes to a restaurant, she will usually be limited in her choice to what appears on the menu and will have very little say in how exactly her meal is prepared; that is merely a contract for services. The court will also look at factors such as the role the employee plays in a large organisation, who paid for the tools required to carry out the work (be they tools in the traditional sense or, for example, IT facilities) and whether the "employee" requires to take an economic risk in the course of carrying out the duties assigned, which will tend to suggest he is independent. This multiple factor approach, first discussed in the English case of *Ready Mixed Concrete (South East) Ltd v Minister of Pensions and National Insurance*,[64] has been affirmed as the correct approach in Scotland in cases including *United Wholesale Grocers Ltd v Sher*.[65]

Similarly, the question of whether an employee was acting in the course of his employment, or was "off on a frolic of his own", must be decided with reference to all the circumstances of the case. In *Kirby v National Coal Board*,[66] the Court stated that if an employee was carrying out his master's work, even in a way in which the employer may not have envisaged that work being carried out, the employer will be vicariously liable. For example, in *Williams v A&W Hemphill Ltd*,[67] a bus driver was persuaded by his passengers to drive his bus from Argyll back to Glasgow taking a circuitous route through Stirling so that they could be dropped off nearer home. The bus was then involved in an accident. The court was of the view that, although the driver had taken a different route to that authorised by his employer, he was still performing the task he was employed to do, and so his employer was vicariously liable. More recently, a trainee fireman participating in a football game traditionally staged at the end of the 16-week residential induction course for new recruits was held to be acting in the course of his employment, since the game was one of the activities associated with the course in which recruits were expected to participate.[68]

On the other hand, if an employee acts outwith the scope of his employment, or uses his employer's tools and time to embark on a project of his own, his employer has no liability. This was the situation in *Kirby v National Coal Board*,[69] where a coal miner caused an explosion whilst smoking a cigarette on his break in an area where smoking was expressly prohibited. His employer was not considered vicariously liable, since this action could not be said to have been carried out in the scope of his employment. Similarly, where a supermarket employee murdered his co-worker during a shift, no vicarious liability was found to exist.[70]

---

[64] [1968] 2 Q.B. 497.
[65] 1993 S.L.T. 284.
[66] 1958 S.C. 514.
[67] 1966 S.C. (H.L.) 31.
[68] *Sharp v Highland and Islands Fire Board*, 2005 S.L.T. 855.
[69] 1958 S.C. 514.
[70] *Vaickuviene v J Sainsbury plc* [2013] CSIH 67; 2013 S.L.T. 1032.

Difficult cases often arise. One example is *Lister v Hesley Hall Ltd*,[71] in which the warden of a residential care home was found to have been abusing children in his care during the course of his night time duties. The defender argued that this could not possibly be said to be an unauthorised mode of the employee carrying out his work; his actions were in fact contrary to the whole purpose of his employment. However, the court was of the view that his actions were so closely connected with the nature of his employment that imposition of vicarious liability was justified. In a similar factual context, the court has also deemed it relevant to consider the risk to third parties created by the employer in entrusting duties to an employee.[72] In *Brink's Global Services Inc v Igrox*,[73] the theft of silver bars from a shipping container by an employee instructed to fumigate the container was considered a risk sufficiently incidental to the assigned task for vicarious liability to exist. It is unclear at present whether the "close connection" test only applies where the employee has committed an intentional wrong, or whether it has a more general application.

PROFESSIONAL LIABILITY

10–37 On most occasions where a person provides a service in a professional capacity (e.g. as a doctor, lawyer, accountant or surveyor) there will be a contract between the professional and their client. Any loss which results can be remedied under contract in the usual way. However, this does not prevent a separate liability in delict arising, as seen in cases such as *Henderson v Merrett Syndicates Ltd*.[74]

The test for breach of professional duty is set very high. A pursuer seeking to prove that a professional has breached his duty of care must show that the professional took a course of action that no reasonable professional person in the same circumstances would have taken. This rule was first elaborated in the case of *Hunter v Hanley*,[75] in which a patient sued his doctor for using a needle which the patient alleged was not strong enough for the injection for which it was being used. Although there was a body of medical opinion that regarded the doctor's treatment as wrong, there was also a body of opinion which considered it reasonable in the circumstances. The court considered the doctor's duty of care had been fulfilled. The court's approach was affirmed in *Kay v Ayrshire and Arran Health Board*.[76]

Any situation in which a professional is required to exercise professional judgment will share this high standard of proof.

In the case of solicitors, there can be an additional complication. The

---

[71] [2002] 1 A.C. 215. This approach was confirmed as correct in *Majrowski v Guy's and St Thomas's NHS Trust* [2007] 1 A.C. 224.
[72] *Various Claimants v Catholic Child Welfare Society* [2012] UKSC 56; [2013] 2 A.C. 1.
[73] [2010] EWCA Civ 1207.
[74] [1995] 2 A.C. 145.
[75] 1955 S.C. 200.
[76] S.C. (H.L.) 145.

solicitor obviously has a duty of care towards his client in contract, and in delict as outlined above. However, the solicitor's negligence may not impact only on his client. Say a client instructs his solicitor to change his will, so that all his money rather than being left to Jasmine is now to be left to Ewan. The solicitor does not carry out the instructions in good time. The client then dies. It is Ewan who has lost out here, since the solicitor's failure to act will result in the inheritance going to Jasmine. Ewan is known in this situation as the "disappointed legatee". *White v Jones*[77] is authority for the premise that, in this situation, the solicitor owes a duty of care to the disappointed legatee to carry out the alterations to the will timeously.

BREACH OF STATUTORY DUTY

Certain pieces of legislation impose their own duty of care in respect of **10–38** acts which result in loss to other people. The steps for proving liability as a result of breach of a statutory duty are essentially the same as for proof of liability through negligence; it must be shown that the pursuer has breached a duty of care towards the defender causing a loss. The difference is that the content of the duty will be defined by the statute rather than by the usual rules on foreseeability, and the exact definition of the duty set out in a given statute, or what is required to satisfy the duty, can be a matter of considerable debate in practice. Statutory duties often import strict liability, which means the element of "reasonableness" is removed from any discussion. If the duty has been breached, the pursuer is automatically liable, no matter how unexpected the result. This is commonplace in the Regulations on workplace safety, for example.[78] A statute will often expressly provide whether breach of its terms will give rise to civil liability or otherwise. If it is silent on the matter, it will be left to the courts to interpret the intention of Parliament as regards liability.

We will now look at three specific instances of statutory liability: product liability, liability for animals and occupiers' liability.

Product liability

At common law, producers obviously have a liability to their ultimate **10–39** consumer in terms of *Donoghue v Stevenson*.[79] This common law duty is backed up by the Consumer Protection Act 1987, which is significantly more exacting on the producer.[80] Under s.2(1) of the Act, the producer of a defective product *will* be liable for any damage caused wholly or partly by the defect. This means that, where personal injury or damage to property is caused, the producer of the product will be required to make

---

[77] [1995] 2 A.C. 207.
[78] See the Workplace (Health, Safety and Welfare) Regulations 1992 (SI 1992/3004), Provision and Use of Work Equipment Regulations 1998 (SI 1998/2306) and the Personal Equipment at Work Regulations 1992 (SI 1992/2966) for examples.
[79] 1932 S.C. (H.L.) 31.
[80] For other statutory consumer protection measures, see Chs 5, 6 and 7.

payment of damages even though there may have been no fault on his part. This is known as "strict liability", since there is no available defence based on lack of fault: liability will be imposed regardless. The Act does not apply to damage to the product itself,[81] or to losses under £275.[82] The product must also be a "consumer" product, loosely defined to mean something you would use in the home rather than a product designed for business use.[83] "Producer" is given a wide meaning, to include not only the manufacturer of the product, but anyone in the supply chain, including wholesalers, retailers and any person who markets the item as their "own brand" (such as a supermarket).[84] "Product" is also widely defined to include any goods or electricity, in addition to components or materials which make up a larger product.[85]

So what is considered a "defect" for the purposes of the Act? Essentially anything that falls below the standard the consumer is entitled to expect[86]: a much higher standard than that of negligence at common law. It also includes products which are inherently dangerous, such as drugs, if they are not labelled appropriately with adequate warnings as to their risks.[87]

Certain defences are available to producers under s.4 of the 1987 Act, the most problematic of which is that there will be no liability if the defect did not exist at the "relevant time" (broadly speaking, the time at which the producer in question had control of the product). This defence should be based on straightforward factual evidence of when the defect came into being. However, often clear evidence is not available, and the court is left trying to ascertain the existence of a defect at a given time on a balance of probabilities. In the case of *Piper v JRI (Manufacturing) Ltd*,[88] where a prosthetic hip had split inside the patient only 18 months after the replacement operation, the court used evidence of the producer's inspection procedures to draw the conclusion that the defect most probably had not existed at the time the prosthesis left the factory. This decision harks back to common law negligence with the idea of whether everything "reasonable" had been done to prevent a defect arising. In some senses, this could be said to undermine the point of the legislation altogether.

Liability for animals

10–40 The Animals (Scotland) Act 1987 provides that the keeper of an animal shall be liable for any injury or damage caused by that animal.[89] Again, the statutory regime imposes strict liability, so there is no need to show

---

[81] Consumer Protection Act 1987 s.5(2).
[82] Consumer Protection Act 1987 s.5(4).
[83] Consumer Protection Act 1987 s.5(3).
[84] Consumer Protection Act 1987 s.1(2).
[85] Consumer Protection Act 1987 s.1(2).
[86] Consumer Protection Act 1987 s.3(1).
[87] *X v Schering Health Care Ltd* [2002] EWHC 1420.
[88] (2006) 92 B.M.L.R. 141.
[89] Animals (Scotland) Act 1987 s.1(1).

negligence on the part of the defender. "Keeper" is defined in s.5 of the Act and will normally mean the owner or person in possession of the animal. Liability is imposed on two different groups of animals: first, dogs and dangerous wild animals[90] who are likely to kill or severely injure persons or other animals or damage property; and secondly, animals listed in s.1(3)(b) (principally farmyard animals) who are likely to cause property damage by foraging.

In relation to the first category, the keeper will be liable only if the harm is caused by the animal attacking a person or another animal in some way. The fact of the animal's mere presence, for example in the middle of the road, will not be enough. However, there could be ordinary negligence-based common law liability in a situation of that kind. In *Fairlie v Carruthers*,[91] the elderly pursuer was knocked over by the defender's over-enthusiastic retriever. The court did not find liability under the Act to be established, since the dog had not attacked, chased or harried the pursuer.

Defences to liability are set out in s.2 of the Act. These focus on the pursuer's own responsibility towards the animal. If the accident was caused by the pursuer, or the pursuer was *volens* to the risk, there will be no liability. Equally, trespassers will not be protected by the Act.

Occupiers' liability

Unlike the other statutory schemes we have considered, liability for **10–41** occupiers is not strict. Section 2 of the Occupiers' Liability (Scotland) Act 1960 provides that the occupiers of land or premises should take reasonable care to avoid damage to persons entering onto the property as a result of the state of the property, or anything done or omitted to be done there. This will include temporary hazards, such as a spilled drink on the floor which has not been cleaned up, or more permanent dangers such as a hole in the ground.

The occupier will be the person who is in possession of the premises at the time of the accident. Their duty is to take positive steps to ensure the premises are kept safe. However, it is for the pursuer to show that not all reasonable steps have been taken, for example, that the defender did not have in place a system for cleaning up spilled drinks. Whether or not reasonable care has been taken will be a matter for the court to decide in applying the calculus of risk, in the same way as it would do in a regular case of liability for unintentional harm. In *McGlone v British Railways Board*,[92] a 12-year-old boy was burned on a transformer with live wires at 2,500 volts after climbing through the defender's ill-maintained fence. The pursuer argued that the defender had not taken reasonable care to protect the boy from the transformer by allowing the fence to fall into disrepair. The court disagreed. The boy was aware the fence was there to keep him from the transformer, which was dangerous, and had climbed

---

[90] As defined by the Dangerous Wild Animals Act 1976.
[91] 1996 S.L.T. (Sh Ct) 56.
[92] 1966 S.C. 1.

through it anyway. It would not be reasonable to expect the defenders to erect an impenetrable fence. *Tomlinson v Congleton BC*[93] is authority for the proposition that a defender is not under a duty to protect against a danger arising from a natural feature of his property, such a steep hill or a lake.

Various defences are also set out in s.2. The defence of volenti will apply, and it is also possible for a pursuer's damages to be reduced on grounds of contributory negligence.

NUISANCE

10–42 A general principle of Scots law is that an owner of property is entitled to do whatever he wants on that property.[94] However, in reality, the actions of one property owner can impact on his neighbours. If Ewan plays loud music all through the night, or allows his rubbish to build up so that noxious odours permeate the atmosphere and vermin are attracted, these actions will obviously have a negative effect on those living next to him. This negative impact on his neighbours is the focus of the delict of nuisance.

Nuisance was defined by Lord President Cooper in *Watt v Jamieson*[95]:

> "If any person so uses his property as to occasion serious disturbance or substantial inconvenience to his neighbour or material damage to his neighbour's property, it is in the general case irrelevant to plead merely that he was making a normal and familiar use of his own property The critical question is whether what he was exposed to was *plus quam tolerabile* [more than is tolerable] when due weight has been given to all the surrounding circumstances of the offensive conduct and its effects."

An important balancing exercise has to be carried out: the owner's right to enjoy his property must be balanced against the neighbour's right to enjoy *his* property. Is the neighbour being asked to put up with more than is reasonable? There is no clear and simple line to be drawn here. What is reasonable in a large house in the countryside is likely to be different to what is reasonable in a tenement flat in Glasgow city centre. The conduct must be beyond tolerance for an action of nuisance to apply; conduct which is simply annoying will not be enough.[96] The court will consider what would be tolerable for a reasonable person. In *Simpson v Miller*,[97] the pursuer complained that the noise of bread mixing machines in the basement of her building was intolerable, but several witnesses gave evidence to the effect the noise and vibrations were virtually

---

[93] [2004] 1 A.C. 46.
[94] See also the relevant section in Ch.11, "Property".
[95] 1954 S.C. 56.
[96] *Anderson v Dundee City Council*, 2000 S.L.T. (Sh Ct) 134.
[97] (1923) 39 Sh. Ct. Rep. 182.

imperceptible in the pursuer's premises. The court held that the pursuer was unusually sensitive, and no finding of nuisance could be made in those circumstances. The court will also take account of the purpose of the disturbance. Even if the disturbance is caused for the public benefit, that will not amount to a defence to nuisance. In *Webster v Lord Advocate* a resident of Ramsay Garden in Edinburgh, adjacent to the Castle, was inconvenienced by the "metallic construction noise" of erecting the stands for the Edinburgh Military Tattoo. She was entitled to an interdict to prevent the nuisance, so that the stands thereafter had to be erected in a quieter manner.[98]

Liability for nuisance is usually strict, so that no fault has to be shown on the part of the defender for a finding in delict to be made. The remedy will usually be interdict, obliging the defender to cease the conduct causing the nuisance. However, if the conduct has actually caused damage to the pursuer's property such that damages are sought, in that case fault must be shown. This was decided by the case of *RHM Bakeries (Scotland) Ltd v Strathclyde Regional Council*,[99] in which the pursuer's premises and goods were damaged when a sewer collapsed. Although it was admitted that maintenance of the sewer was the responsibility of the defenders, the pursuer had not made any argument that the defenders had, in fact, failed to maintain it, or to show that this failure was the reason for the collapse. In the absence of any proof of fault, no finding of nuisance could be made.

PRESCRIPTION AND LIMITATION

A pursuer who has suffered must make his claim within a specified time **10–43** limit or he will lose the right to do so. In general, a case in delict must be brought within five years of the date of the loss, or the pursuer's right to action will prescribe.[100] If the claim is for personal injury, the pursuer cannot enforce his claim more than three years after the loss date.[101] The rationale behind these time limits is that, as time passes, it becomes increasingly difficult to obtain clear evidence of what happened and who may have been responsible. It is in the interests of justice to have cases come before the court before they become stale.

---

[98] 1985 S.C. 173. Note that the separate claim that the noise of the Tattoo itself constituted a nuisance was not pursued in the final appeal.
[99] 1985 S.C. (H.L.) 17.
[100] Prescription and Limitation (Scotland) Act 1973 s.6.
[101] Prescription and Limitation (Scotland) Act 1973 ss.17 and 18.

REMEDIES

Interdict

10–44 An interdict is a court decree ordering a person to cease a particular type of conduct, for example trespassing on another person's land. In English legal terminology, this type of order is known as an injunction.

Interdict can be sought to bring ongoing conduct to an end, or to prevent an anticipated wrong before it occurs. It is important that any order for interdict is framed in very clear and specific terms so that there is no question of the order being breached accidentally. If a person continues the conduct in breach of interdict, they could be liable to a fine or imprisonment.

Damages

10–45 Damages is the legal term for financial compensation awarded to a pursuer who has successfully established a claim. The key principle underlying delictual damages is that they should put the pursuer in the position he would have been in had the accident never happened. If the loss in the case is a straightforward matter of damage to property, the damages awarded by the court will simply be the cost of the repair. In personal injury cases, the pursuer will be awarded damages for *solatium*—the pain and suffering they have endured—in addition to financial losses following on from the injury, such as lost wages, the price of a cancelled holiday or childcare expenses. If the injury is likely to have long-term consequences, future damages will be calculated to take account of further losses likely to be incurred.

Damages can also be awarded on either a provisional or interim basis. Provisional damages are awarded in personal injury cases where there is a possibility that the pursuer's condition may substantially deteriorate in the future. An assessment of damages will be made on the basis of the pursuer's condition at the time of proof, and the option will be left open for the pursuer to return for a second payment if they deteriorate. For example, if a child is injured in an accident and suffers brain damage, it may be impossible for doctors to ascertain the full extent of the injury until the child is closer to adulthood. Provisional damages could be awarded after the accident, and the child could return to the court at a later stage when their condition was fully known. Provisional damages are regulated by s.12 of the Administration of Justice Act 1982.

Interim damages may be awarded prior to proof in a case where the defender has admitted that he was liable in delict for the harm. In some cases, although there is clear evidence of negligence, it may still take some time to resolve matters while the necessary evidence is gathered to fully quantify the claim. However, the pursuer may be in financial hardship in the meantime. For example, if a pursuer is seriously injured in a car crash caused by a drunk driver, it is likely that the defender will have admitted his liability for the accident. It may take months or even years for the solicitors acting for each party to obtain the necessary medical reports and other evidence to allow a full quantification of the financial loss to the pursuer for the rest of his life. In the meantime, however, the pursuer must still pay his bills and may be incapable of working. In such a situation, the pursuer may apply for an award of interim damages to "tide him over" until the case is finally resolved. Interim damages will be a lump sum paid immediately by the defender, which will then be deducted from the total damages awarded to the pursuer on the conclusion of the case.

Key Concept

- The primary remedies in delict are interdict and damages.
- An interdict can be granted only in respect of clear and specific conduct.
- Damages can be awarded for *solatium* and patrimonial loss, and can be assessed on a provisional or interim basis where appropriate.

MODES OF LIABILITY

A loss may be caused by more than one person. In such cases, the courts **10–46** will often find all the defenders "jointly and severally liable".[102] What this means is that each defender is liable to the pursuer for the whole amount of damages awarded. The pursuer, if they so choose, can recover the full amount from one defender, and that defender is left with a "right of recovery", meaning they are then entitled to recover the appropriate share of the damages from each of the other defenders.

▼ CHAPTER SUMMARY

WHAT IS DELICT?

(1) A delict is a civil wrong. The law of delict determines when a remedy **10–47** will be available for a loss caused by one person to another.
(2) The basic principle of delict can be summed up by the maxim *damnum injuria datum*: a loss caused by a legal wrong.

INTENTIONAL DELICTS

(1) An intentional delict is a deliberate act causing harm to another.
(2) An assault, whether physical or verbal, which causes loss will give rise to liability in delict.
(3) An assault must be non-consensual.

---

[102] Law Reform (Miscellaneous Provisions) (Scotland) Act 1940 s.3(1).

> ➤ *Sidaway v Board of Governors of Bethlehem Royal Hospital*: a patient must be advised of all the risks of a treatment to give valid consent.

(4) Trespass is the temporary intrusion onto, over or under another person's property.
(5) The remedy for trespass will be interdict, provided the trespass is likely to be repeated.
(6) Harassment is conduct, repeated on at least two occasions, which causes the pursuer alarm or distress.
(7) Extreme forms of economic duress will give rise to a claim in delict.
(8) The principal economic delicts are induced breach of contract, infliction of harm or loss by unlawful means and conspiracy.
(9) Fraud is a misrepresentation made with the intention of causing a loss to another person.
(10) Passing off is the delict of taking advantage of the goodwill in another person's business.

> ➤ *Erven Warnink BV v J Townend & Sons (Hull) Ltd (No.1)*: sets out the five criteria which must be fulfilled to establish a case of passing off.

UNINTENTIONAL DELICTS

(1) Where a person causes a loss to another through a lack of care, or negligence, this will give rise to liability in delict.
(2) A duty of care must exist between pursuer and defender.

> ➤ *Donoghue v Stevenson:* the "snail in a bottle case" which established the "neighbourhood principle".

(3) The existence of a duty can be established through the tripartite test of foreseeability of harm, proximity and the requirement that a duty be "fair, just and reasonable".

> ➤ *Caparo Industries Plc v Dickman*: authority for the tripartite test.
> ➤ *Hill v Chief Constable of West Yorkshire*: the Yorkshire Ripper case in which it was not considered fair, just and reasonable to impose a duty of care.

(4) The defender must have breached his duty of care.
(5) To breach his duty, the defender's conduct must have been voluntary.

> ➤ *Waugh v James K Allan*: a driver who suffered the onset of thrombosis at the wheel did not voluntarily cause an accident.

(6) A duty will be breached if the defender's conduct falls below the standard of care expected of a reasonable man in the same situation.

> ➤ *Muir v Glasgow Corporation (No.2)*: it is impossible to prevent every accident from happening, and a defender can only do what is reasonable in the circumstances.

(7) Whether the standard of care has been reached will be assessed by applying the calculus of risk.
(8) The pursuer must have sustained a loss to their person or property.

(9) Psychiatric loss will give rise to recovery for primary victims, and for secondary victims only where they satisfy the test set out in Alcock v Chief Constable of South Yorkshire Police.

(10) Pure economic loss cannot generally be recovered. However, recovery will be available where the loss results from a negligent act or omission where the defender has voluntarily assumed responsibility for the economic interests of the pursuer and sufficient proximity exists between the parties.

(11) The defender's breach of duty must have been the *causa causans* of the pursuer's loss.

> ➤ *Barnett v Chelsea & Kensington Hospital Management Committee*: set out the "but for" test of causation.

(12) The chain of causation can be broken by a novus actus interveniens.

(13) The pursuer's loss must not be too remote from the defender's conduct for recovery to be allowed.

> ➤ *Simmons v British Steel*: the type of losses sustained must be a reasonably foreseeable consequence of the breach of duty.

(14) The loss will not be too remote where the harm is of a kind that was reasonably foreseeable, even though the harm was greater than could have been foreseen, or was caused in a way that could not have been foreseen.

(15) The defender can defend a claim for liability for unintentional harm using the plea of volenti non fit injuria if the pursuer was or should have been aware of the risks of the activity.

(16) The pursuer's damages may be reduced if he was contributorily negligent.

Delict in the Employment Context

(1) Employers owe a duty to their employees to take reasonable care for their safety in the workplace.

(2) An employer will be vicariously liable for the actions of his employee during the course of his employment.

(3) For vicarious liability to arise, a contract of employment must exist between the two parties, and the employee must have been acting in the course of his duties at the time the delictual conduct occurred.

> ➤ *Kirby v National Coal Board*: an employee smoking a cigarette during his break in a designated no-smoking zone was not acting in the course of his employment.

Professional Liability

(1) A person providing a service in a professional capacity will owe a delictual as well as a contractual duty to his client.

(2) The test for breach of professional duty is that no other reasonable professional in the same circumstances would have acted in the way the defender acted, established in *Hunter v Hanley*.

(3) A solicitor will also owe a duty of care to a disappointed beneficiary, set out in *White v Jones*.

BREACH OF STATUTORY DUTY

(1) Where a duty of care is imposed in a particular situation by a statute, the content of that duty will be defined by the wording of the statute and not by the usual tripartite test.

(2) Where a statute imposes strict liability, there will be no need to prove negligence.

(3) Product liability is regulated by the Consumer Protection Act 1987. Section 2 of the Act provides that a producer of a defective product will be strictly liable for any damage caused by the defect.

(4) A "defect" is defined as anything that falls below the standard the consumer is entitled to expect.

(5) Certain remedies are available to producers under s.4 of the Act, particularly that there is no remedy if the defect did not exist at the "relevant time", meaning at the time when the product was within the producer's control.

(6) Liability for animals is regulated by the Animals (Scotland) Act 1987. Section 1 provides that the keeper of an animal will be strictly liable for injury or damage caused by that animal.

(7) Liability is imposed on wild animals which are likely to kill or severely injure persons, animals or property, and on farmyard animals which are likely to cause damage by foraging.

(8) Defences are set out in s.2 of the Act.

(9) Occupiers' liability is regulated by the Occupiers' Liability (Scotland) Act 1960. Liability under this statute is not strict, but requires owners or occupiers of premises to take reasonable care for the safety of people in or on their property.

(10) It is for the pursuer to show that the occupier has failed to take all reasonable steps.

(11) Defences are set out in s.2 of the Act. In particular, the defence of volenti can be used.

NUISANCE

(1) Where one person uses his property in such a way that it negatively impacts on his neighbours to an intolerable extent, this will constitute the delict of nuisance.

(2) Liability for nuisance is strict, unless damages are sought, in which case fault must be shown.

PRESCRIPTION AND LIMITATION

(1) An action for personal injury must be brought within three years.

(2) An action for property damage must be brought within five years.

REMEDIES

(1) Interdict is a court order prohibiting a certain type of conduct from continuing.
(2) Breach of interdict can result in a fine or prison sentence.
(3) Damages are financial compensation for loss designed to put the pursuer in the position he would have been in if the delict had not occurred.
(4) Damages can be claimed for *solatium* and financial loss.
(5) Damages may be awarded on a provisional basis, if the pursuer's condition is likely to deteriorate, or on an interim basis where liability on the part of the defender has been admitted and the pursuer is likely to suffer financial hardship while agreement on final damages is reached.

? QUICK QUIZ

- Explain what is meant by *damnum injuria datum*.
- Which case set out the criteria for the delict of passing off?
- State the five steps used to establish a case of liability for unintentional harm?
- What is a duty of care and what is the test for identifying whether a duty exists?
- How will the court determine whether a duty of care has been breached?
- What types of loss will give rise to recovery in delict?
- Explain the meaning of the term *causa causans*?
- What is the correct test for remoteness of damage?
- What will be the effect of a finding of contributory negligence in a case of liability for unintentional harm?
- Name the two conditions which must be satisfied before an employer will be found vicariously liable for the actions of his employee?
- What rule was set out by the case of *Hunter v Hanley*?
- What is an interdict?

? FURTHER READING

➤ J. Thomson, *Delictual Liability*, 5th edn (Edinburgh: Bloomsbury Professional, 2014).
➤ G. Cameron, *Law Basics: Delict*, 4th edn (Edinburgh: W. Green, 2011).
➤ B. Pillans, *Delict: Law & Policy*, 5th edn (Edinburgh: W. Green, 2014).

Chapter 11   Property

Angus McAllister[1]

▶ CHAPTER OVERVIEW

11–01 This chapter describes the main concepts relating to heritable and moveable property, though the main emphasis will be upon heritable property. Consideration will be given to the abolition of feudal tenure, land registration, rights of ownership and restrictions upon property rights. An overview will be given of the law of leases and the chapter will end with a brief outline of the procedure for the transfer of ownership of heritable property.

✓ OUTCOMES

11–02 At the end of this chapter you should be able to:

    ✓ understand some basic concepts of property law;
    ✓ have some appreciation of the historical background to land ownership;
    ✓ understand the function of the Land Register;
    ✓ know what the main rights are attaching to the ownership of property;
    ✓ appreciate the main restrictions upon property ownership, whether these are undertaken voluntarily or imposed by law;
    ✓ understand the main principles of the law of leases, including commercial leases; and
    ✓ have an overview of how ownership in heritable property is transferred.

INTRODUCTION: BASIC CONCEPTS

Nature of property

11–03 The word "property" is somewhat ambiguous. It is regularly used in several senses, both legal and colloquial. It is therefore desirable to be clear at the outset about these various meanings.

In the first place, "property" is commonly used to mean anything that

---

[1] Solicitor, Emeritus Professor of Law at the University of the West of Scotland.

can be owned. A TV set, a car, company shares, a house are all property in this sense. However, the term is also understood in other, slightly different ways. We talk about property rights to describe the various legal interests that a person may have in a piece of property, such as the right of an owner or of a tenant. We also use the word "property" to denote ownership itself, the legal right enjoyed by a property owner. The word will be used in all of these senses at various points in this chapter.

"Property" in the first sense is also commonly used in a much narrower sense, to refer to land and buildings (or, in England or the US, "real property" or "real estate"). In Scotland the correct term is "heritable property". In a strict legal sense, this is only one type of property, and the general term "property" also includes other things that can be owned, such as moveable or intellectual property. These other aspects will briefly be discussed in this chapter, though the main emphasis will be upon heritable property.

Classification of property

Heritable and moveable property

This is by far the most important way in which different types of property **11–04** may be classified. The most convenient way to formulate the distinction is that heritable property consists of land and anything (including buildings) permanently attached to the land. Heritable property also includes rights over, or connected with, land and buildings, such as the right of a tenant, or a right in security; the latter is colloquially known as a "mortgage", though in Scotland the correct legal term is "heritable security".

Moveable property, on the other hand, is simply every kind of property other than heritable property, such as a book, a car or a TV set.

Unfortunately, this formulation is not completely accurate. The word "heritable" does not simply mean "immoveable". Historically, the term derives from the law of succession as it used to be before radical reforms were made to the system in 1964.[2] Under the old system of succession, heritable property was the property which, after a person's death, passed entirely to the heir, usually the eldest son. This mainly included land and buildings. However, in strict law, the scope of the term heritable property extends a little wider than this to include, for example, pensions, annuities, interest-bearing bonds and titles of honour.

Corporeal and incorporeal property

Another way in which property can be classified is into corporeal and **11–05** incorporeal property. Corporeal property consists of things that exist in the physical world and can be seen or touched, such as a car or a house. Incorporeal property, on the other hand, consists of rights, such as company shares, or intellectual property such as patents, copyright, etc.

---

[2] By the Succession (Scotland) Act 1964.

Ownership

11–06 We saw above that "ownership" is one of the common meanings of the word "property". One of the best definitions of this is by the institutional writer Erskine, one of several historical figures who made a key contribution to the development of Scots law. Erskine defined ownership (or property) as, "the right of using and disposing of a subject as our own, except in so far as we are restrained by law or paction".[3] "Paction" means "agreement" or "contract". In other words, there are restrictions imposed upon the absolute rights of an owner, which may be imposed upon the owner by the law or may be incurred voluntarily.

Erskine's definition is useful because, as well as being concise, it draws to our attention two fundamental aspects of ownership. It recognises that, although ownership is still the largest right a person can have in a thing, there are many ways in which the rights of an owner are qualified by the law. Some of these, mainly those which apply to heritable property, are considered briefly below.

Owners may also, of their own free will, further restrict their right of ownership by granting subsidiary property rights to others, such as servitude rights (like a right of way) or a lease. These will also be discussed later in the chapter.[4]

Real and personal rights

11–07 This distinction has a general significance within the law of obligations, but has particular importance within the law of property. A real right is one that can be enforced against anyone in the world, whereas a personal right can only be enforced against a particular person, the one who owes the corresponding obligation. A real right is typically (though not exclusively) completed by some kind of formality, such as the registration of a document in the Land Register.

The most obvious, and most easily understood, real right is that of ownership. If I own a piece of property I may defend my right against anyone at all, not just against a particular person. Some subsidiary property rights are also real rights, such as the right of a tenant or the rights of a creditor (such as a bank or building society) under a heritable security. An important feature of such real rights is that they "run with the land". This means that they attach to a property right rather than to the person who has that right at a particular time. For example, if a property owner enjoys a servitude right of way over another property, that right will transfer to the new owner when the property is sold.

---

[3] Erskine, *An Institute of the Law of Scotland*, 8th edn (Edinburgh: Bell & Bradfute, 1871), II, 1, 1.

[4] See paras 11–44—11–63.

Prescription

Prescription is a process whereby rights (including rights of ownership) **11–08** may either be acquired or lost as a result of the passage of time. The period of time required varies depending upon the type of right involved. A right (e.g. a right to claim damages, or a servitude right) is lost by negative prescription if it is not exercised within the relevant time period. Certain rights may be acquired by positive prescription, such as servitude rights (if exercised for 20 years) and even ownership (10 years). However, for the 10-year prescription to operate, a registered title deed will also be required.

Positive prescription used to be very important in relation to the acquisition of heritable property, as it operated to cure defects in older title deeds. It is less important now that there is a system of registration of title backed by a warranty from the Keeper of the Registers. However, prescription may still be important in eventually curing defects in a title where the Keeper has initially withheld the warranty. This is discussed further below in the section relating to land registration.[5]

The law relating to prescription, which is somewhat complex, is governed by the Prescription and Limitation (Scotland) Act 1973.

MOVEABLE AND INTELLECTUAL PROPERTY

Corporeal moveable property

Ownership of corporeal moveable property can be acquired by acquisi- **11–09** tion (where it has not been owned before) or by transfer from another owner. The existing owner must intend to transfer ownership, with the result that a thief (for example) will not acquire ownership. Evidence of an owner's intention to transfer may be contained in some kind of written agreement. Transfer of ownership will be completed (and a real right of ownership acquired by the new owner) when the property has been delivered. This may involve a physical transfer, but not necessarily so.

The sale of goods is governed by the Sale of Goods Act 1979.[6] Where that act applies, it is sometimes possible for ownership to pass without delivery.

Incorporeal moveable property

Incorporeal moveable property effectively means the ownership of a **11–10** right, as opposed to something tangible. Examples include company shares and insurance policies. Another example is intellectual property, which concerns rights in original and creative works, such as patents, copyright, trademarks and designs. This important category is dealt with in Ch.12, "Intellectual Property".

Incorporeal moveable property is transferred by assignation, which

---

[5] See paras 11–14—11–21.
[6] See Ch.5, "Commercial Sale and Supply of Goods".

may or may not be in writing. However, the new owner will not acquire a real right unless the assignation has been intimated. This means that the person against whom the right can be enforced must be informed of the transfer. For example, the assignation of an insurance policy will only become effective when the insurance company has been notified of the change.

Key Concepts

- The most fundamental distinction is between heritable property (land and buildings) and moveable property (everything else).
- Moveable property can be divided between corporeal moveable property (things that can be seen or touched) and incorporeal property (rights).
- There are restrictions upon the absolute right of ownership, which may be imposed upon an owner by law or be incurred voluntarily.
- A real right (such as ownership) can be defended against anyone in the world, whereas a personal right (such as a contractual right) can only be enforced against a particular person.
- Property rights (and other rights) can either be acquired or lost by the passage of time by the processes of positive and negative prescription.

HERITABLE PROPERTY: HISTORICAL BACKGROUND AND MODERN REFORMS

The feudal system

11-11 Until fairly recently the system of landholding in Scotland was based upon the feudal system, though it survived in a form that had been greatly modified over the centuries. Although the feudal system of landholding is no longer with us, its demise is still recent enough to require something to be said about it, in order to explain the references to it that still crop up in legal documents and elsewhere.

The feudal system was a pyramid-like structure, at the top of which was the king, the ultimate feudal superior. Grants of land were made to subjects (or "vassals") in return for military service or other favours. These vassals had the power to make subgrants (to subfeu) and there was, in theory, no limit to the number of times this process could be repeated.

The modern version of this was that in Scotland land was not owned outright, but there were different layers of ownership. Above the vassal, who actually occupied the land, there would be one or more feudal superiors. The superior had no right to occupy the land, but enjoyed a number of powers that could be exercised over the vassal. These included the right to charge the vassal an annual sum (known as "feu-duty") and the right to impose and enforce conditions upon the vassal's title. These feuing conditions would not normally be arbitrary exercises of power, but typically would regulate the amenity of the area by placing restrictions upon the way the vassal could build upon and use the land.

Even in its evolved form, the feudal system was difficult to defend in modern times. Regulation of land use had properly become the function of the town and country planning system.[7] There was a case for title conditions that protected amenity being enforced by neighbouring proprietors against one another, but not by a superior. The imposition of feu-duty was difficult to justify at all.

Reform and abolition

In the second half of the twentieth century a number of reforms were **11–12** made to the system. These included machinery for the gradual redemption of feuduties, usually when a property was sold. Finally, in the early years of the present century, a series of statutes passed by the Scottish Parliament completed a virtual revolution in Scottish land law.[8] The effect of these various statutes will be noted at various points in this chapter. Notably, the feudal system was abolished entirely, as from November 28, 2004 (referred to in the statutes as "the appointed day"). The last feuduties were redeemed and superiors were stripped entirely of their powers, though they were entitled to compensation. Feudal layers of ownership were swept away and all land in Scotland was now owned outright. Title conditions survived in a modified form, but could now only be enforced by neighbouring owners against each other, when they could demonstrate a title and interest to do so.

Key Concept

Land ownership in Scotland was formerly based upon the feudal system, but feudal tenure was abolished as from November 28, 2004.

HERITABLE PROPERTY: LAND REGISTRATION

The General Register of Sasines

For many centuries there has been a public register of deeds relating to **11–13** heritable property. The General Register of Sasines was established in 1617. In it could be recorded all types of legal document relating to heritable property, including those creating feudal rights, transferring ownership, creating security rights, etc. By preserving transcripts of these deeds and making them accessible to the public, the legal rights of the parties involved (owners, creditors, etc.) were protected. The title deeds of

---

[7] See para.11–53.
[8] Abolition of Feudal Tenure etc. (Scotland) Act 2000; Title Conditions (Scotland) Act 2003; Land Reform (Scotland) Act 2003; Tenements (Scotland) Act 2004; Land Registration etc. (Scotland) Act 2012.

a property, which provided legal evidence of ownership, comprised all of the deeds relating to that property to have been recorded in the Register.

The registration of title deeds in the General Register of Sasines was an effective system, but had a number of disadvantages. In particular:

- Transfer of ownership was cumbersome. The purchaser's solicitor had to examine the title deeds for validity. The process of positive prescription (see above) reduced the number of deeds that had to be examined by making flaws in older deeds irrelevant, but it was still a considerable task. This process had to be repeated every time the property changed hands.
- The description of the relevant property contained in the title deeds was often vague or inaccurate, mainly due to the passage of time, sometimes making it difficult to identify the property precisely. This made disputes over ownership or boundaries more likely.

The Land Register

11–14 The Land Register for Scotland was originally set up and governed by the Land Registration (Scotland) Act 1979, though it has now been revised and substantially replaced by the Land Registration etc. (Scotland) Act 2012. Since the passing of the 1979 Act, the Land Register has gradually been superseding the General Register of Sasines. The Land Register built upon the system created by the sasine register, but took it much further by creating a system of registration of title. Effectively, this dealt with the above criticisms in the following ways:

- The Land Register records, not individual documents, but the title as a whole. All the information relevant to ownership is now contained in a computer file (the title sheet). The title sheet is amended after every sale of the property, or other transaction (such as the creation of a security) that may affect it. The validity of the title is backed by a warranty from the Keeper of the Registers of Scotland, which makes repeated examination of the title deeds unnecessary.[9]
- Each property is mapped on to a master plan,[10] based upon Ordnance Survey plans, thereby enabling it to be precisely identified.

First registration

11–15 The changeover to the new system could not happen overnight. Each individual property in Scotland had first of all to undergo a process of first registration. This involves the Keeper of the Registers (or a member of the Keeper's staff) performing the task formerly undertaken by a

---

[9] Land Registration etc. (Scotland) Act 2012 ss.73–79.
[10] Defined in the legislation as "the cadastral map"—see the Land Registration etc. (Scotland) Act 2012 s.11(1).

purchaser's solicitor. In other words, the title deeds of the property have to be examined for one last time, so as to ensure that the title is valid and a warranty can be given. At the same time, the boundaries of the property have to be mapped on to the master plan, using the description in the title deeds. If the title contains any flaws or uncertainties, the Keeper can proceed to registration, but withhold, or partially withhold, the warranty. However, the Keeper may grant or vary the warranty at a later date if any of the objections to the title's validity have subsequently been overcome, for example if the process of positive prescription has cured any defects.

The divisions of the General Register of Sasines were based upon the old Scottish counties. The process of first registration was introduced piecemeal, one or two counties at a time. The first operational county was the county of Renfrew, which became open for registration in 1981, and other counties gradually followed. First registration took place whenever a property in an operational division was sold. Once its title had been registered, future sales or other transactions relating to that property became much more straightforward.

The Land Register became operational across the whole of Scotland in 2003. However, many properties remained on the sasine register due to the fact that they had not been sold since their county had become operational for registration. The 2012 Act introduced certain measures designed to speed up the process of transfer from the sasine to the land register:

(a) In addition to sale of the property, first registration may now be triggered by other transactions which affect it (for example, if it is gifted, inherited, a security is granted over it, or a lease of it is registered)[11]; and

(b) Even where there is no such transaction, it may be triggered by a voluntary application for registration (which the Keeper is obliged to accept) or under a new power given to the Keeper to compel registration.[12]

The latter provisions should enable the transfer of properties that have remained on the sasine register because none of the relevant transactions have occurred, for example many properties owned by the public sector, such as local authorities or central government.

The title sheet

When a person becomes the owner of heritable property, their title **11–16** documentation no longer consists of a bundle of legal deeds, but is contained in the title sheet relating to that property. Originally the purchaser was issued with a land certificate, an updated printout of the relevant title sheet, but now he or she is merely issued with an electronic copy of the title sheet, in PDF form.

---

[11] Land Registration etc. (Scotland) Act 2012 s.48.
[12] Land Registration etc. (Scotland) Act 2012 ss.27–29.

The title sheet has four sections, outlined below.

(1) Property section

11–17 This states briefly the property interest being registered, e.g. that of owner, or perhaps tenant. It also identifies the property very briefly by its address and a reference to the Keeper's master plan. An extract from the plan will also be included, on which the boundaries of the property will be marked.

(2) Proprietorship section

11–18 This will include the name of the person whose interest is being recorded, the date of registration, the price and the date of entry.

(3) Securities section (formerly the charges section)

11–19 This will specify any heritable securities over the property, e.g. in favour of a bank that granted a loan over it.

(4) Burdens section

11–20 This is the only section that normally extends to any length. In it are gathered together the conditions from all of the deeds that contained burdens over the property.

Automated registration of title to land ("ARTL")

11–21 Automated registration of title to land ("ARTL") is a system which can replace paper-based documentation relating to certain transactions on the Land Register with documents that have been electronically created and communicated. Its purpose is to simplify and considerably speed up the process of registration.

It is only available to authorised users who have applied for and been granted a licence to use ARTL. These may be solicitors, licensed conveyancers, mortgage lenders or local authorities, but not private individuals conducting their own conveyancing.

ARTL can only be used for straightforward transactions involving properties that have already been registered, and paper-based documentation is still required for first registrations and transactions where a property is split off from a larger title.

Key Concepts

- Real rights in heritable property (including ownership) are completed by registration in the Land Register for Scotland.
- When a title has been registered, the property is identified upon a master plan and the title is backed by a warranty from the Keeper of the Registers of Scotland.
- Records in the register are held electronically, and a new system has been introduced which allows certain transactions to take place electronically also.

OWNERSHIP RIGHTS

In our definition of "ownership" above, we emphasised the restrictions **11–22** upon the absolute right of ownership. However, before looking at a few of these restrictions in a little more detail, we will consider some of the rights that go along with ownership. In other words, we will consider what is involved in the right "to use a subject as our own". These rights are mainly relevant to the ownership of heritable rather than moveable property.

It should be noted that "trespass" and "nuisance" which are discussed below, as well as being aspects of the law of property, are also civil wrongs and have been separately considered under "delict" in Ch.10.

Right to exclusive possession

Owners normally have the sole right to occupy their property and have **11–23** the legal right to defend themselves against anyone who encroaches upon this right in any way.

Within the boundaries of their land, the right of owners to exclusive possession is, in theory, without limit. Traditionally it is said to extend *a coelo usque ad centrum* (from the sky to the centre of the earth). For practical purposes, there are a number of qualifications to this right, notably by the Civil Aviation Act 1982,[13] which permits flights over another person's property at a reasonable height. Without this, airline companies would be guilty of multiple trespasses on a daily basis.

Another common exception relates to mineral rights. Under the feudal system, these were normally reserved to the superior in feudal grants, and are likely to have survived the abolition of that system in separate ownership

Trespass

This is where an owner's right to exclusive possession has been encroa- **11–24** ched upon by the temporary presence of a person or persons who have no right to be there. Despite the prevalence of notices threatening

---

[13] Civil Aviation Act 1982 s.76(1).

prosecution for trespassers, trespass as such is not a crime (unless some crime is committed in the process, such as breaking and entering upon a dwellinghouse or other building).

However, an owner is entitled to ask a trespasser to leave the property. Also, if the trespass is a regular occurrence, or if there is any other good reason to believe that it might be repeated, the owner may obtain an interdict from the court to prevent a recurrence. An interdict is a court order forbidding a person from carrying out an illegal act that has been occurring on a regular basis. It is the Scottish equivalent of the English remedy known as an injunction.

Access rights

11–25 The law of trespass was modified by Pt I of the Land Reform (Scotland) Act 2003 ("2003 Act"), which came into force on February 9, 2005. This gives everyone a right of access to land for recreational, educational and, in some cases, commercial purposes. It also confers a right to cross land. A person has such rights only if they are exercised responsibly. There is a reciprocal obligation upon every owner of land to use and manage the land and otherwise conduct the ownership of it in a responsible way in relation to those rights.

There are certain types of property to which the access rights do not apply. These include buildings and their surroundings, building sites and sites of mineral workings, sports grounds and schools, and land where there are crops.

Guidance about the responsible exercise of access rights and the responsible management of ownership can be found in the *Scottish Outdoor Access Code* drawn up by Scottish Natural Heritage,[14] under powers granted by the 2003 Act.

Unlawful possession

11–26 This is where the encroachment is not temporary, but the property has in fact been occupied by someone having no right to do so. In such a case the owner may take a civil court action to evict the occupant. There are several variants of this court action, which are known collectively as possessory remedies.

Right to freedom from interference by neighbours

11–27 There are several categories of harmful action by a neighbour to which a property owner may take legal exception. Here we will focus upon the one known as nuisance. Others include malicious action and non-natural use of property.

---

[14] Scottish Natural Heritage, *Scottish Outdoor Access Code* (2005), available at *http://www.outdooraccess-scotland.com* [Accessed May 15, 2015].

Nuisance

The most common types of nuisance are noise, vibration, smoke, fumes, **11–28** etc. though the categories of nuisance are in theory unlimited. The most common (though not all) cases of nuisance arise between neighbours, not necessarily owners, where the activities of one neighbour interfere with the other's peaceful enjoyment of his or her property. For this reason, nuisance is also often known as the law of the neighbourhood.

A nuisance is something that happens on a regular basis, and there can be no liability for a one-off occurrence. It must be substantial and not of a trivial nature. Also, it is irrelevant that the nuisance may have predated the arrival of the complaining owner, and it is no defence for the perpetrator to say that the party complaining willingly moved into the area where the nuisance already existed. However, failure to object over a period of time may bar an owner from taking action under the principle of acquiescence, and any right of action (including that of future owners of the property) will be extinguished by the long negative prescription if the nuisance has continued unchallenged for 20 years or more.[15] The main legal remedy for nuisance is a court action of interdict, to restrain the offending party from carrying on the nuisance in future. Damages may also be claimed if the nuisance has had a detrimental effect upon the pursuer's health or upon the value of the pursuer's property. However, unlike interdict (which automatically becomes available if the nuisance occurs) damages can only be claimed where the pursuer can establish negligence or other form of *culpa* (blame) on the part of the defender.

Webster v Lord Advocate
1985 S.C. 173

The owner of a flat adjoining the esplanade of Edinburgh Castle raised an action of nuisance in respect of the annual military tattoo and, more particularly, the noise caused by the erection and dismantling of the scaffolding for the seating, a process which continued throughout a considerable portion of the year.

It was held that the neither the tattoo itself nor the rehearsals for it amounted to a nuisance, since they only occurred for a brief period during the year. However, the noise caused by the erection and dismantling of the scaffolding did amount to a nuisance. It made no difference that the tattoo had existed for many years prior to the date when the pursuer bought her flat. Nor did it matter that the tattoo might be considered to be in the public interest.

The court granted an interdict. However, its effect was suspended for a period of six months in order to allow that year's tattoo to go ahead and to allow the organisers the opportunity to devise quieter ways of carrying out the work.

---

[15] Prescription and Limitation (Scotland) Act 1973 ss.7 and 8.

Statutory nuisance

11–29 The above discussion relates to the traditional law of nuisance under the common law. A number of activities are also categorised as nuisances by the Environmental Protection Act 1990.[16] These place a particular emphasis on activities that are prejudicial to health. They duplicate the main types of common law nuisance, but also extend much further to include, for example, nuisances arising from accumulations or deposits, or the keeping of animals. The main responsibility for dealing with statutory nuisances lies with local authorities, who are under a duty to detect statutory nuisances and investigate complaints about them.

The most convenient way for a member of the public to take action against a statutory nuisance will normally be to complain to the local authority. However, it is also possible for a member of the public to apply directly to the sheriff court in order to bring about the abatement of a statutory nuisance.

Right of support

11–30 There is an automatic right of support for land that is in its natural state and, in the vast majority of cases, a right of support is also implied where there are buildings on the ground. This gives property owners a right to claim damages from the person responsible in respect of damage caused by subsidence.

Most disputes regarding support arise as a result of mineral workings, where the minerals are in separate ownership. Under the Coal Mining Subsidence Act 1991 the licensed operator or the Coal Authority are required to carry out remedial work (or in some cases pay compensation instead) in respect of damage caused to land or buildings from lawful coal-mining operations.

Questions of support can also arise between the owners of buildings in multiple ownership. This is dealt with below under the law of the tenement.[17]

Fixtures

11–31 When talking of heritable property, it is natural to think mainly of buildings rather than the land on which they are built. This is because, unless we are talking about substantial tracts of land, buildings are likely to be the most valuable element in the property. In strict law, however, what is owned is the land and anything attached to the land.

Anything, including a building, that is attached to the land in a suffi-ciently permanent way is known as a heritable fixture and becomes part of the heritable property by a process known as "accession". However, questions relating to fixtures may arise when there is some dubiety about the status of an article on the land. Has it become so attached that it has become part of the heritable property, or is it still a moveable item?

---

[16] Environmental Protection Act 1990 ss.79–82.
[17] See para.11–42; see also para.11–46 (servitude right of support).

There are a number of situations where disputes about fixtures may arise, but not all of them can be discussed here. Disputes may arise, for example, between a seller and purchaser. A prospective purchaser of a house is likely to view it while the seller is still living there. It will contain items such as curtains, fitted carpets, light bulbs, fitted cupboards and shelves, a central heating system, etc. Which of these are moveable items, that can be removed by the seller, and which have become part of the heritable property and will pass to the purchaser? Another example is a tenant who spends money improving a property. To what extent will these improvements pass to the landlord as a windfall at the end of the lease?

Determination of fixtures

There is no hard-and-fast rule determining what is and what is not a **11–32** fixture, but a number of guidelines have been established. In any particular case, one or more of them may be enough to decide the matter:

- An article may not be a fixture if it can be removed either without destroying itself as a separate entity or damaging the soil or building to which it is attached.
- If an article was intended to be a permanent attachment, it is more likely to be a fixture.
- If the building or land has been specially adapted to the use of the article, it is probably a fixture.
- The extent to which the use and enjoyment of the building or land would be affected by the article's removal will help to determine whether or not it is a fixture.
- A particularly heavy article may be a fixture, even if it is not physically attached.

Christie v Smith's Executrix
1949 S.C. 572

A two-ton summerhouse, which rested on its own weight on a prepared site, was removed by a seller. Its removal left a gap in the garden wall.

It was held that the summerhouse was a fixture and should have been left: (a) because of its weight; and (b) because the property had been specially adapted to it.

Examples of fixtures

Things growing in the soil, e.g. trees, shrubs, turf, crops, etc. are generally **11–33** fixtures.

Articles in a house which are generally considered to be fixtures include doors and windows, tiles, fireplaces, grates, chandeliers, picture rods, built-in cupboards and wardrobes, built-in kitchen units and electric light flexes down to the bulb holder. Carpets (even though fitted), lino, pictures and mirrors (even if screwed to the wall) are generally considered *not* to be fixtures.

Constructive fixtures

11–34 Certain items, which are not physically annexed, qualify as fixtures because they are necessary accessories to the heritable property. Examples include the keys of a house, and the loose parts which are necessary for the operation of fixed machinery.

Contracting out

11–35 There are many cases where it will be convenient for the parties involved to contract out of the law of fixtures. For example, when parties conclude missives for the sale of a house or other property,[18] it is common to override the law of fixtures by specifying which items should be included in the sale. Thus, things like fitted carpets or curtains, although they are moveable, will often be left as part of the deal.

Similarly, a lease document may allow certain fixtures to be removed by the tenant when the lease comes to an end.

Trade fixtures

11–36 A tenant may remove fixtures (such as heavy machinery) at the end of the lease, provided that they have been annexed for the purpose of the tenant's trade or business. This only applies if the articles can be removed without material injury to the heritable property and without themselves being destroyed in the process, or losing their essential character or value.

COMMON RIGHTS

11–37 Under this heading we will look at several situations where two or more people may have some sort of legal interest in the same property:

Common property

11–38 Where there is common property (or co-ownership) a single piece of heritable property has more than one owner. Each co-owner has a separate title to a share of the property. All co-owners have a right to an equal say in the management or control of the common property.

We will consider examples of common property below in relation to the law of the tenement.

---

[18] See para.11–64.

Joint property

This is also a situation where a single piece of heritable property has more **11–39** than one owner. The difference is that, unlike a co-owner, a joint owner cannot sell his or her share separately or will it to a third party. A common example of joint property is the property of a club. A member automatically becomes a joint owner of the club property when joining, and ceases in that ownership on resignation. The same is true of trustees in relation to trust property.

Law of the tenement

This applies mainly to blocks of flats, but may also apply to other **11–40** properties (such as office blocks) where there is multiple occupation within one building. In the vast majority of cases, the situation will be governed contractually, by means of real burdens[19] within the titles of the various owners, and the relevant information will be found in their title sheets.[20] In the case of blocks of flats, the close, stairs, landings, division walls, roof, *solum* (the land beneath the building), garden ground, etc. will all be common property. Maintenance will be equal, or perhaps in proportion to the size of each property. There will be provision for the appointment of a common factor to manage the building.

If the titles do not contain such provisions, or there is an insufficient provision, it was formerly the case that the gap or gaps would be filled in by the common law of the tenement. However, this old law was generally thought to operate unfairly in modern times (e.g. by making top-floor owners entirely responsible for the maintenance of the roof). The new law of the tenement (which still operates only in default of a sufficient title provision) can be found in the Tenements (Scotland) Act 2004 ("2004 Act").

Ownership

The following are the main default provisions regarding ownership:[21] **11–41**

- The boundary between adjacent flats, between flats and the close, and between a lower and upper flat, is the midpoint.
- A door or window serving one flat only is the sole property of that flat's owner.
- A top flat includes the roof over that flat and the air space up to the roof's highest point.
- A bottom flat includes the *solum* (the site) under the flat.
- The close, stair and landings are common property.
- A lift is common property, unless it serves one flat only.
- Ground is owned by the owner of the immediately adjacent bottom flat.

---

[19] See para.11–48.
[20] See paras 11–14—11–21.
[21] Tenements (Scotland) Act 2004 ss.1–3.

- Chimney stacks are common property.

Any parts not listed will be common property if they serve more than one flat, but otherwise will be owned exclusively by the individual owners whose flats they serve.

Support, etc.

11–42 The owner of each flat is obliged to provide shelter for any flat below it and support for any flat above.[22] Within reason, each owner is prohibited from doing anything that would interfere substantially with the support, shelter or natural light of another flat or flats, and obliged to carry out any necessary maintenance in order to fulfil these obligations.

Management and maintenance

11–43 The 2004 Act sets out a tenement management scheme, which also operates in default of relevant title provisions.[23] However, since the scheme is more comprehensive than many title provisions are likely to be, particularly in the case of older properties, the scheme will very often apply, in part at least, to plug any gaps in the title provision.

Strategic parts of the tenement are to be maintained by everyone on an equitable basis, whether they are common property or not. Strategic parts include the *solum* (site), foundations, external walls, the roof, mutual gables, mutual gable walls to the mid-point, and load-bearing walls, beams or columns.

Thus (for example), parts of the roof and *solum*, while individually owned, will have to be maintained by everyone. Any parts not included in the list but which are common property (e.g. the close and stairs) will of course be maintainable by the co-owners.

Key Concepts

- In principle, a landowner has a right to exclusive possession from the sky to the centre of the earth.
- An owner's right to exclusive possession is protected by the law of trespass.
- The law of trespass has been modified by certain access rights of the public to private land, guidance about which can be found in the *Scottish Outdoor Access Code.*
- A property owner's right to peaceful enjoyment of his or her property and to freedom from interference by neighbours is protected by the law of nuisance, both under the common law and by statute.
- Property owners enjoy certain rights of support, and often may be entitled to compensation for damage caused by subsidence.

---

[22] Tenements (Scotland) Act 2004 ss.7–10.
[23] Tenements (Scotland) Act 2004 s.4 and Sch.1.

> - A heritable fixture is an item which has become attached to land or a building in a sufficiently permanent way to become part of the heritable property.
> - When a building is in multiple ownership, the rights and obligations of the various owners are generally set out in the titles of the various properties, but any gaps in this provision are filled in by a statutory law of the tenement.

RESTRICTIONS ON PROPERTY RIGHTS

The following are some of the ways in which the rights of an owner may **11–44** be qualified "by law or paction". In some cases (such as servitudes or real burdens, where the obligation runs with the land) the current owner may be bound by the agreement of a previous owner. Most of these refer to heritable property, but securities over moveable property are also briefly considered.

Servitudes

A servitude is a right (such as a right of way) which an owner of heritable **11–45** property has over another property. Servitude rights are not personal to the respective owners of the properties in question, but they run with the land. They are therefore real rights. In other words, they can be exercised, or must be suffered, not only by the current owners of the properties in question, but also by any future owners who may succeed them. Servitude rights cannot therefore be separated from the ownership of the properties in question. In this way they resemble real burdens (see below) though there are important differences between the two. The owner of a property which benefits from a servitude right was traditionally known as the "dominant owner", and the property was known as the "dominant tenement". In the case of the property subject to the servitude right, the traditional terms were "servient owner" and "servient tenement". In modern times the terms "benefited" or "burdened owner" or "benefited" or "burdened property" are more commonly used. The word "tenement" is not used in its colloquial sense of a block of flats, but in a technical legal sense. It simply means a piece of heritable property that may be separately owned, or be the subject of some other property right.

Types of servitude

Recognised servitude rights include: **11–46**

- **Support**: the right for a building to be supported, in certain respects, by an adjoining building.[24]

---

[24] See also "right of support" at para.11–30 above and support within tenement buildings at para.11–42 above.

- **Access (or "way")**: the benefited owner is allowed to pass over the burdened property. Traditionally, a right of way can be either a footpath, a horse road or a carriage road (in modern times, a road for motor vehicles). The last of these now includes the right to park a vehicle.
- **Aqueduct**: The right to convey water through the burdened property by means of a pipe or canal.

Creation of servitudes

11–47 Servitudes may be created between two properties that already exist, and also when a single property is being divided in two for the first time. For example, when a property is subdivided, it may be necessary or convenient for one of the owners to have a servitude (such as a right of way) over the other property. The servitude requires to be registered in the Land Register in the titles of both the benefited and the burdened property, unless it has been created by prescription.

Real burdens

11–48 The law relating to real burdens is contained in the Title Conditions (Scotland) Act 2003.

Real burdens are obligations that appear in a property title and bind the owner for the time being of that property. They are there for the benefit of a neighbouring property or properties.

Like servitudes, real burdens run with the land and they must appear on the Land Register, registered against both the benefited and the burdened property.[25] Unlike servitudes, however, they cannot also be created by prescription, and also unlike servitudes, they may require the owner of the burdened property to carry out some kind of positive action.

Before the abolition of the feudal system, real burdens were regularly inserted by superiors in feudal titles and would be enforceable by superiors. Now the only people who can enforce real burdens are persons who can demonstrate both a title and an interest to enforce the burden.[26] Those with a title to enforce the burden include, not only the owner of the benefited property, but also others, such as a tenant, who have a legal right to occupy it. In order to have an interest to enforce it, the rights of the person concerned must either be detrimentally affected to a material extent by the failure to comply with the burden, or else have the right to recover a financial outlay (such as the burdened owner's share of a common repair).

Real burdens may be affirmative, which means that the burdened owner is bound to carry out a positive action or actions, such as maintaining a boundary wall. Real burdens may also be negative. This means that the burdened owner is obliged to refrain from doing something, such as using a residential property for commercial purposes.

---

[25] Title Conditions (Scotland) Act 2003 s.4.
[26] Title Conditions (Scotland) Act 2003 s.8.

Real burdens are used for such purposes as regulating the amenity of an area, or for setting out the mutual rights and obligations of the proprietors of a building (such as a tenement) that is in multiple ownership.

Securities[27]

A security is a right over a piece of property which is granted to a creditor **11–49** in order to safeguard the repayment of a loan. The creation of a security gives a creditor certain legal rights, including the right to recover the debt by selling the property if the debtor should default.

A common type of security over moveable property is "pledge", which takes effect by the delivery of the security property to the creditor, probably a pawnbroker.

A security over heritable property (colloquially known as a mortgage) **11–50** is known in Scotland as a "standard security". It is a formal document signed by the debtor and delivered to the creditor (probably a bank or building society). It takes effect by registration in the Land Register.[28]

A "floating charge" is a security that can only be granted by limited **11–51** companies and a limited number of other commercial organisations. It covers all the property, heritable and moveable, which the debtor organisation owns at any particular time. It takes effect on the occurrence of a particular event, such as the winding up of a company. At that time it is said to crystallise, which means that it attaches to all the property then owned by the debtor organisation, thereby conferring a preference upon the creditor. A floating charge may be granted, for example, by a company to a bank, in order to secure an overdraft.

Statutory controls

There are a wide variety of statutory controls over heritable property, **11–52** including legislation relating to health and safety at work, environmental protection, local authority housing controls, compulsory purchase and many others. Two of them, outlined below, perhaps merit particular mention.

Planning control

Local authorities regulate land use and development under a statutory **11–53** framework laid down by central government. Planning permission is required for material changes of use and new building projects of a substantial nature. Councils also have enforcement powers in relation to unauthorised development. There are special, more stringent controls in relation to (among others) listed buildings (buildings of special architectural or historical interest), conservation areas, tree preservation, advertisements, hazardous substances and projects of an environmentally sensitive nature (which may require an environmental assessment).

The current planning legislation is mainly embodied in the Town and

---

[27] For a fuller account of rights in security see Ch.21.
[28] See paras 11–14—11–21.

Country Planning (Scotland) Act 1997 (as amended), the Planning (Listed Buildings and Conservation Areas) (Scotland) Act 1997 and the Planning (Hazardous Substances) (Scotland) Act 1997.

Building control

11–54 Building control is also a function of local authorities. Unlike planning controls (which are concerned with the way in which property is used), building control relates to the technical standards in relation to health, safety, etc. to which buildings must conform, in accordance with building standards regulations. Building permission is required for new buildings or for substantial alterations to existing ones.

The current building control legislation is embodied in the Building (Scotland) Act 2003 and the building regulations made under that act.

Key Concepts

- A servitude is a right (such as a right of way) which an owner of heritable property has over another property.
- Real burdens are obligations which appear in a property title and bind the owner for the time being of that property.
- A security is a right over a piece of property which is granted to a creditor in order to safeguard the repayment of a loan.
- Land use and development is regulated by local authorities under powers granted by the legislation on town and country planning.
- Building control in relation to the health and safety aspects of buildings is also regulated by local authorities under statutory powers.

LEASES

Nature of leases

11–55 A lease is a contract by which a person (a tenant) is allowed to occupy someone else's heritable property for a finite period. In return the tenant pays the owner (the landlord) a periodical sum of money as rent. The equivalent contract in relation to moveable property is that of hire.

In one sense, a lease may be regarded as a restriction upon ownership, which the property owner (the landlord) has granted voluntarily. However, a tenant's right is itself a right of property and it is more convenient to classify it in this way.

Since a lease is a contract, the general law of contract applies to leases in the same way as it applies to any other contract.[29] However, in several respects the rights of a tenant transcend those normally conferred by a contract, with the result that a tenant also acquires a right of property:

---

[29] For the law of contract, see Ch.4.

- **A lease confers a real right**. Under a very old statute (the Leases Act 1449) a tenant's right is protected if the landlord sells the property to a new owner. Even though the new owner did not have a contract with the tenant, he or she will normally have to recognise the lease and allow the tenant to continue in occupation at the same rent until the lease is due to end. This only applies if the lease is for 20 years or less. For longer leases, the tenant acquires a real right by registration of the lease in the Land Register.
- **Length of tenure**. If a lease is for a sufficiently long period, a tenant's legal interest will acquire a capital value and become a marketable asset. If the lease is sufficiently long (e.g. 99 years), the market price payable on transfer (assignation) may be as high as that obtainable by an outright sale of the property. One common type of long lease is a "ground lease" under which the landlord leases the ground only, at a comparatively modest rent, and the tenant erects (or pays for) the building. As the building is a fixture and will revert to the landlord at the end of the lease,[30] a tenant is unlikely to take on such a lease without a substantial period of tenure. However, where a ground lease has a long unexpired term the tenant's interest can be sold for a substantial capital sum.
- **Registration**. A lease of more than 20 years may be registered in the Land Register. This strengthens a tenant's rights considerably. In particular, it allows the lease to be used as security for a loan.
- **Statutory protection**. In relation to certain types of lease (e.g. residential leases or farm leases) a lease may be extended by statute beyond the period contracted for.[31] However, such leases are now much fewer in number than was formerly the case.[32]

Essential elements in leases

Lease documents (particularly commercial leases) may be long and **11–56** complex and contain many provisions, but only four elements are essential for a valid lease at common law:

- **Parties**. The landlord and tenant must be named and properly identified (usually by the inclusion of an address).
- **Subjects**. The property being leased must be accurately described. Sometimes an address will be sufficient, but often a longer description and/or a plan will be used.
- **Rent**. There must be a rent. Usually the lease document will also specify how it should be paid (e.g. weekly, monthly or quarterly, or whether it is payable in advance or in arrear).
- **Duration**. A lease must have a definite duration, though if this is accidentally omitted, a period of one year will be implied.

---

[30] See para.11–31.
[31] See paras 11–60 and 11–61.
[32] See paras 11–60 and 11–61.

The maximum duration of a residential lease is 20 years.[33] For all other leases, it is 175 years.[34]

Leases of more than one year must be in writing.[35] A lease for one year or less may be entered orally, though this is not recommended.

Rights and obligations of the parties

11–57 The contractual rights and obligations of the landlord and tenant will be set out in the lease document. In relation to residential leases and farm leases, certain rights and obligations are also conferred by statute (e.g. a residential landlord's obligation to carry out repairs).

A number of rights and obligations also apply automatically at common law, unless the lease document provides otherwise:

- The tenant must enter into possession, and continue to occupy and use the property.
- The tenant must pay the rent when it is due.
- The tenant must use the property only for the purpose for which it is let.
- The tenant must take reasonable care of the property.
- The tenant must plenish the property, i.e. keep enough moveable property there to provide security for the rent.
- The landlord must give the tenant full possession of the property, and thereafter maintain the tenant in full possession, without encroaching upon it in any way.
- The landlord warrants that the property will be in a tenantable or habitable condition at entry, i.e. it should be wind and watertight, free from damp and in a safe condition.
- The landlord will maintain the property in a tenantable or habitable condition throughout the duration of the lease, though only after notification by the tenant that a repair is necessary. In commercial leases (though *not* residential leases) this obligation is normally contracted out of in the lease document and all repairing obligations transferred to the tenant.

Legal remedies of the parties

11–58 If either the landlord or tenant is in breach of a lease obligation, the other party has a number of legal remedies. These include the normal remedies for breach of contract,[36] with certain additional remedies being available to the landlord. The following are the main ones:

- **Implement.** Either the landlord or tenant may force compliance with a lease term by means of court action. If the obligation is a positive one (e.g. to carry out repairs) the appropriate action is

---

[33] Land Tenure Reform (Scotland) Act 1974 s.8.
[34] Abolition of Feudal Tenure etc. (Scotland) Act 2000 s.67.
[35] Requirements of Writing (Scotland) Act 1995 s.1.
[36] See Ch.4, "The Law of Contract".

called specific implement. If the obligation is a negative one (e.g. not to use the property for an unauthorised use) the action is known as an interdict (the Scottish equivalent of the English injunction). In the case of residential leases let by a private landlord (but *not* in the case of social tenancies)[37] the tenant may seek a repairing standard enforcement order ("RSEO") by applying to the Private Rented Housing Panel.[38] An RSEO is effectively a statutory form of specific implement.

- **Court action for debt.** This is appropriate where the obligation is to pay money (e.g. rent).
- **Rescission.** If the breach is material, the injured party may withdraw from the lease.
- **Damages.** The injured party is entitled to claim compensation for any loss caused by the breach.
- **Rent retention.** If the landlord is in breach, the tenant may withhold rent until such time as the breach has been remedied. This right may be contracted out of by a lease provision.
- **Landlord's hypothec.** Commercial landlords have a right in security over moveable property on the leased premises in order to recover the rent. This gives the landlord a preferential claim if the tenant should go bankrupt or (if the tenant is a limited company) go into receivership or liquidation.[39]
- **Irritancy.** In commercial leases there is normally a provision entitling the landlord to terminate the lease for non-payment of rent and for other specified breaches. This right may only be exercised (for non-payment of rent) after the tenant has been given 14 days' notice to pay and (for other breaches) where the court considers the landlord to be acting fairly and reasonably.[40] This remedy has been controversial in modern times, as it may seem disproportionately severe in relation to the tenant's breach, particularly in the case of long leases where the tenant's interest may be a valuable one.

Retail Parks Investments Ltd v Royal Bank of Scotland (No.2)
1996 S.L.T. 669

The Royal Bank proposed to close their branch in the Sauchiehall Centre in Glasgow on economic grounds. As the landlords would not release them from the lease, they wanted to minimise their overheads, while continuing to pay rent.

The court granted an order of specific implement, requiring the tenants to use the premises as bank offices during all normal business hours for the remaining seven years of the lease.

---

[37] See para.11–60.
[38] Housing (Scotland) Act 2006 s.24.
[39] Bankruptcy and Diligence etc. (Scotland) Act 2007 s.208.
[40] Law Reform (Miscellaneous Provisions) (Scotland) Act 1985 ss.4–7.

> ## CIN Properties Ltd v Dollar Land (Cumbernauld) Ltd
> ### 1992 S.L.T. 669
>
> This concerned a 99-year ground lease of 6.73 acres, comprising a substantial proportion of Cumbernauld Town Centre. The tenants had purchased the lease from the former tenants at a price of £2.2 million. The tenants failed to pay the quarter's rent due on November 11, 1988. The landlords sent a notice on December 15 requiring the rent to be paid by January 4, which the tenants failed to do by that date.
>
> The House of Lords held that the landlords were entitled to irritate the lease. The tenants lost a valuable property interest and the landlords received a considerable windfall.

Termination of leases

11–59 A lease may be terminated prematurely if it contains a break clause, or otherwise by the mutual agreement of the parties. It may also be terminated by rescission, irritancy, accidental damage or destruction of the premises or (in certain circumstances) by the death or insolvency of the tenant.

When a lease is due to terminate it does not end automatically. It will only end if either the landlord or tenant sends the other a notice to quit. The minimum period of notice for commercial leases is normally 40 days, and for residential leases there is a statutory minimum period of 28 days.[41]

If no notice to quit is sent, the lease will continue automatically on the same terms by a process known as *tacit relocation* (silent renewal). For leases of up to one year, it will be renewed for the same period as before. For leases of a year or more, it will be continued for one year. The same will apply at the end of the renewed period, and this process can continue indefinitely until such time as a notice to quit is sent.

Types of lease

Residential leases

11–60 Leases of houses and flats are heavily regulated by statute, mainly designed to protect the rights of tenants. The overall situation is complex, but residential leases can be very broadly divided into two categories:

- **Private sector lets**. These are lets by private landlords. The most common categories are Assured Tenancies and Short Assured Tenancies. The main relevant statutes are the Housing (Scotland) Acts 1988 and 2006.

---

[41] Sheriff Courts (Scotland) Act 1907 ss.34–38; Rent (Scotland) Act 1984 s.112.

- **Social tenancies**. These are lets by social landlords such as housing associations or councils. The main category is the Scottish Secure Tenancy and the main relevant statute is the Housing (Scotland) Act 2001.[42]

There are provisions in relation to matters like rents, repairs and other tenancy conditions. Assured tenants (but not short assured tenants) and Scottish secure tenants generally have security of tenure. This means that they can only be evicted on certain specified grounds, whether or not the contractual term of the lease is due to come to an end. However, the great majority of private sector tenancies are short assured tenancies, where the security of tenure provisions do not apply.

For several decades, many social tenants had the right to buy their dwellinghouse, often at a considerable discount. However, the right to buy has now been severely restricted and will be completely abolished as from August 1, 1916.[43]

Agricultural leases

For well over 100 years farm leases have been regulated by a series of **11–61** statutes, the most recent being the Agricultural Holdings (Scotland) Acts 1991 and 2003. In some cases (mostly older leases), farm tenants enjoy security of tenure beyond the contractual terms of their leases. Alternatively, if evicted, they may be entitled to compensation for improvements, etc.

There is separate legislation relating to crofts and small landholdings.

Commercial leases

This is the title normally given to leases of shops, offices, factories and **11–62** other business premises. Unlike other types of lease, commercial leases are largely unaffected by statute, and the terms of the lease will be governed by the lease document, with the common law filling in any gaps. There is a minor exception that only applies to shops. Under the Tenancy of Shops (Scotland) Act 1949, a shop tenant whose lease is about to expire may apply to the sheriff court for an extension of up to one year.

The situation is different in England, where there is more statutory regulation. In particular, the purely English Landlord and Tenant Act 1954 gives the courts power to extend business leases for up to 15 years.

Commercial landlords are often financial institutions (such as banks, insurance companies or pension funds) which purchase commercial properties as an investment. Business concerns generally prefer to rent rather than buy their premises in order to minimise their capital investment. The traditional investment lease was for 25 years, though market pressure from tenants in recent years has led to much shorter commercial leases.

---

[42] See also the Housing (Scotland) Acts 2010 and 2014.
[43] Housing (Scotland) Act 2010 Pt 14; Housing (Scotland) Act 2014 s.1.

Lease provisions

11–63 Commercial lease documents tend to be long and complex, but the following are a few of the provisions likely to be encountered:

- **Alienation**. The tenant will not normally be entitled to assign (transfer the tenancy to another tenant) or sublet without the landlord's consent. Often it is stated that the landlord's consent will not be unreasonably withheld.
- **Rent**. This will generally be payable quarterly in advance.
- **Use**. The lease will state how the property should be used. This will often limit the tenant to a specific business, particularly in shopping centres, where the landlord will want to control the trade mix.
- **Insurance**. The tenant will normally have to meet the cost of insurance.
- **Repairs**. The most common type of commercial lease is the tenant's full repairing and insuring ("FRI") lease. This means that the tenant will normally have to carry out all repairs as well as pay for the insurance. This contracts out of the landlord's common law repairing obligation.[44]
- **Service charges**. Where there is a building in multiple occupation (such as a shopping centre or office block) the landlord will normally take responsibility for repairs to the common parts, as well as insurance and common services such as heating, car parking, toilets, cleaning, etc. The cost will then be recovered from each tenant in proportion to the size of their premises, in the form of a periodic service charge.
- **Rent reviews**. The landlord will require the rent to be reviewed at regular intervals, most often every five years. Rent review clauses are often complex and have been subject to much litigation.

Key Concepts

- A lease is a contract, but also confers rights of property upon the tenant.
- The four essential elements in a lease are the parties, the subjects, the rent and the duration.
- A lease for more than one year must be in writing.
- The legal rights and obligations of the landlord and tenant are set out in the common law, in the lease document and (in some cases) imposed by statute.
- Both parties under a lease are entitled to the usual remedies for breach of contract, but commercial landlords also enjoy some additional rights, such as the right to terminate the lease by irritancy.

---

[44] See para.11–57.

- The main types of lease are residential leases (houses and flats), agricultural leases (farms) and commercial leases (business premises).
- Leases may terminate prematurely in a number of circumstances, and also at the end of the lease.
- Leases do not end automatically at their termination date, but only if either party sends the other a notice to quit. Otherwise the lease will be renewed for up to one year on the same terms and conditions, by a process known as tacit relocation (silent renewal).
- Residential and agricultural leases are largely regulated by statute, but commercial leases in Scotland are mainly free from statutory control.
- Shop tenants may apply to the sheriff court at the end of their lease for an extension of up to one year.

TRANSFER OF HERITABLE PROPERTY

The first stage of this procedure is the completion of a contract (or **11–64** missives). This gives the purchaser a personal right against the seller, which confers the right to claim breach of contract remedies if the seller fails in any contractual obligations; these remedies include damages and, in extreme cases, the right to withdraw from the contract entirely (i.e. to rescind). However, such a personal right does not safeguard the purchaser's entitlement to the actual property in the face of, for example, the rights of a competing owner. Nor does it correct any flaws there may be in the seller's title.

The second stage is for the seller to fulfil this personal obligation by taking the necessary steps to transfer ownership to the purchaser. This includes signing and handing over a formal document of transfer (a disposition), which the purchaser will register in the Land Register. At the end of this process the purchaser's personal right will be converted into a real right of ownership.

A purchaser of heritable property will not normally have the funds to purchase the property outright, but will need to obtain a loan from a bank, building society or other lender. The lender will require to have the loan secured by a standard security, which will be registered in the Land Register at the same time as the disposition transferring ownership.[45]

In some cases dispositions and standard securities may be created and signed electronically under a system of Automated Registration of Title to Land ("ARTL").[46]

It is normal for both purchaser and seller to be represented by a solicitor or other agent.

---

[45] See para.11–50.
[46] See para.11–21.

Key Concepts

- Personal rights of contract between the purchaser and seller are created by completion of missives of sale.
- A purchaser obtains a real right of ownership by registration of a disposition in the Land Register.
- A creditor obtains a real right in security by the registration in the Land Register of a standard security, signed by the debtor.

▼ CHAPTER SUMMARY

INTRODUCTION: BASIC CONCEPTS

11–65
(1) The word "property" has several meanings. It can mean anything that is owned, the rights a person can have in a piece of property, and it can mean "ownership".

(2) Property can be classified as:

    (a) Heritable (land and buildings) and moveable (everything else).

    (b) Corporeal (things in the physical world) and incorporeal (rights).

(3) Property in the sense of ownership may be defined as "the right of using and disposing of a subject as our own, except in so far as we are restrained by law or paction":

    ➢ Erskine *An Institute of the Law of Scotland*, 8th edn (1871), II, 2, 1.

(4) Prescription is a process by which rights may be acquired (positive prescription) or lost (negative prescription) as a result of the passage of time:

    ➢ Prescription and Limitation (Scotland) Act 1973.

MOVEABLE AND INTELLECTUAL PROPERTY

(1) Ownership of corporeal moveable property can be acquired by acquisition (where it has not been owned before) or by transfer from another owner.

(2) The sale of goods is governed by statute:

    ➢ Sale of Goods Act 1979.

(3) Incorporeal moveable property (e.g. company shares or insurance policies) is transferred by an assignation, which must be intimated.

HERITABLE PROPERTY: HISTORICAL BACKGROUND AND MODERN REFORMS

(1) The system of landholding in Scotland was formerly based upon the feudal system, which was abolished as from November 28, 2004:

➢ Abolition of Feudal Tenure etc. (Scotland) Act 2000.

HERITABLE PROPERTY: LAND REGISTRATION

(1) Real rights in heritable property were formerly acquired by the registration of the relevant deed in the Register of Sasines.
(2) The Register of Sasines is now being replaced by the Land Register for Scotland, in which the title to a property is registered as an entity:

➢ Land Registration etc. (Scotland) Act 2012.

(3) When a title has been registered, it is identified on a master plan and backed by a warranty from the Keeper of the Registers of Scotland.
(4) An owner's title documentation is contained in the title sheet to the property contained in the land register.
(5) Some paper-based transactions on the Land Register can be replaced by an electronic system known as Automated Registration of Title to Land ("ARTL").

OWNERSHIP RIGHTS

(1) Owners normally have a right of exclusive possession to their property, which is protected by the law of trespass.
(2) The law of trespass has been modified by public access rights to private land:

➢ Land Reform (Scotland) Act 2003.
➢ *Scottish Outdoor Access Code* (2005).

(3) The rights of an owner (or other occupier) to freedom from interference by neighbours is protected by the law of nuisance, under both common law and statute:

➢ *Webster v Lord Advocate* (1985).
➢ Environmental Protection Act 1990.

(4) Landowners normally have a right of support to their property and can claim compensation for subsidence damage:

➢ Coal Mining Subsidence Act 1991.

(5) A heritable fixture is an item which has become attached to land or a building in a sufficiently permanent way to become part of the heritable property.

➢ *Christie v Smith's Executrix* (1949).

(6) When heritable property is sold, the law of fixtures is generally modified by contract under the missives of sale.

(7) A tenant may remove trade fixtures at the end of the lease.
(8) The main distinction between common property and joint property is that a co-owner can sell his or her share of the property separately, whereas a joint owner cannot.
(9) When a building is in multiple ownership, the rights and obligations of the various owners are generally contained in the titles to the property.
(10) Any necessary provisions not covered in the titles can be found in a statutory law of the tenement:

> ➤ Tenements (Scotland) Act 2004.

RESTRICTIONS ON PROPERTY RIGHTS

(1) A servitude is a right which an owner of heritable property has over another property.
(2) Servitude rights include rights of support, rights of way and rights of aqueduct (the right to convey water across another property by a pipe or canal).
(3) Real burdens are obligations which appear in a property title and bind the owner for the time being of that property:

> ➤ Title Conditions (Scotland) Act 2003.

(4) A security is a right over a piece of property which is granted to a creditor in order to safeguard the repayment of a loan.
(5) Three common types of security are pledge, standard securities and floating charges.
(6) There are many statutory controls over heritable property, including planning control and building control:

> ➤ Town and Country Planning (Scotland) Act 1997.
> ➤ Planning (Listed Buildings and Conservation Areas) (Scotland) Act 1997.
> ➤ Planning (Hazardous Substances) (Scotland) Act 1997.
> ➤ Building (Scotland) Act 2003.

LEASES

(1) A lease is a contract, but it also confers a right of property upon a tenant.
(2) An important element in a tenant's property right is that a tenant enjoys a real right. This means that, should the landlord sell the property, the lease can be enforced against the new owner:

> ➤ Leases Act 1449.

(3) The four essential elements in a lease are the parties, the subjects, the rent and the duration.
(4) A lease for more than one year must be in writing:

> ➤ Requirements of Writing (Scotland) Act 1995.

(5) The maximum duration of a residential lease is 20 years. For all other leases it is 175 years:

> ➤ Land Tenure Reform (Scotland) Act 1974.
> ➤ Abolition of Feudal Tenure etc. (Scotland) Act 2000.

(6) The legal rights and obligations of the landlord and tenant are set out in the common law, in the lease document and (in some cases) imposed by statute.

(7) The common law obligations of a landlord include the obligation to carry out repairs. This is normally contracted out of in commercial, but not in residential, leases.

(8) Both parties under a lease are entitled to the usual remedies for breach of contract. These are implement, court action for debt, rescission, damages and rent retention:

> ➤ *Retail Parks Investments Ltd v Royal Bank of Scotland (No.2)* (1996).

(9) Commercial landlords also enjoy important additional rights. These include the landlord's right of hypothec and the right to terminate the lease by irritancy:

> ➤ *CIN Properties Ltd v Dollar Land (Cumbernauld) Ltd* (1992).

(10) Leases may terminate prematurely in a number of circumstances, and also at the end of the lease.

(11) Leases do not end automatically at their termination date, but only if either party sends the other a notice to quit. Otherwise the lease will be renewed for up to one year on the same terms and conditions by a process known as tacit relocation (silent renewal).

(12) The main types of lease are residential leases (houses and flats), agricultural leases (farms) and commercial leases (business premises).

(13) The main types of residential lease are assured and short assured tenancies (private sector) and Scottish secure tenancies (social tenancies):

> ➤ Housing (Scotland) Act 1988.
> ➤ Housing (Scotland) Act 2006.
> ➤ Housing (Scotland) Act 2001.

(14) Agricultural leases are extensively regulated by statute:

> ➤ Agricultural Holdings (Scotland) Act 1991.
> ➤ Agricultural Holdings (Scotland) Act 2003.

(15) Commercial leases in Scotland are largely free from statutory control.

(16) Commercial lease documents tend to be long and complex, but generally include provisions relating to alienation (assignation and subletting), rental payment dates, the use of the premises, insurance, repairs, service charges (if the property is in multiple occupation) and rent review.

(17) Shop tenants may apply to the Sheriff Court at the end of their lease for an extension of up to one year:

> ➤ Tenancy of Shops (Scotland) Act 1949.

TRANSFER OF HERITABLE PROPERTY

(1) Personal rights of contract between the purchaser and seller are created by completion of missives of sale.

(2) A purchaser obtains a real right of ownership by registration of a disposition in the Land Register.

(3) A creditor obtains a real right in security by the registration in the Land Register of a Standard Security, signed by the debtor.

(4) In some cases dispositions and standard securities may be created and signed electronically under a system of Automated Registration of Title to Land ("ARTL").

? QUICK QUIZ

- What are the main ways in which property can be classified?
- What is the difference between real rights and personal rights?
- What are the main characteristics of registration of title?
- What are the main rights of ownership?
- In what circumstances can a person raise an action under the common law of nuisance and what remedies may be available to him or her?
- In what respects has the law of trespass been modified by the Land Reform (Scotland) Act 2003?
- What are the rules for determining whether or not an item is a heritable fixture?
- What are the main rules of the law of the tenement?
- What are the main legal restrictions upon ownership?
- What is meant by saying that a lease confers a real right upon a tenant?
- What are the main legal remedies of the parties to a lease in the event of a breach of the lease contract?
- What are the main categories of lease and the statutes regulating them?

📖 FURTHER READING

➤ Daniel J. Carr, *Property*, 2nd edn (Edinburgh: W. Green, 2014).
➤ Gretton & Steven, *Property, Trusts & Succession*, 2nd edn (Bloomsbury Professional, 2013).
➤ Gloag and Henderson, *The Law of Scotland*, 13th edn (Edinburgh: W. Green, 2012), Pt III.
➤ McAllister, *Scottish Law of Leases*, 4th edn (Bloomsbury Professional, 2013).

🖱 RELEVANT WEBLINKS

➤ Scottish Courts: *www.scotcourts.gov.uk* [Accessed May 15, 2015].

➤ Scottish Government: *www.gov.scot* [Accessed May 15. 2015].
➤ Scottish Law Online: *www.scottishlaw.org.uk* [Accessed May 15, 2015].
➤ Scottish Outdoor Access Code: *www.outdooraccess-scotland.com* [Accessed May 15, 2015].
➤ Scottish Parliament: *www.scottish.parliament.uk* [Accessed May 15, 2015].
➤ Registers of Scotland: *www.ros.gov.uk* [Accessed May 15, 2015]. Includes information about the Land Register.
➤ UK legislation: *www.legislation.gov.uk* [Accessed May 15, 2015]. Includes full text of Scottish and UK statutes and statutory instruments.

Chapter 12   Intellectual Property

JANE CORNWELL[1]

▶ CHAPTER OVERVIEW

12–01 Intellectual property is an important business asset. The four major pillars of intellectual property law are trade marks (including registered trade marks and passing off), copyright, designs, and patents. These intellectual property rights are discussed in this chapter. Intellectual property also includes other rights, such as geographical indications, confidential information and plant varieties, which are beyond the scope of this chapter. The focus in this chapter is on UK law.

This chapter will begin with an overview of some basic common characteristics of intellectual property rights and will then outline the law relating to passing off, registered trade marks, copyright, designs and patents. Throughout, it is important to differentiate between common law and statutory rights and between registered and unregistered rights:

(1) **The right against passing off** is an unregistered form of intellectual property which serves to protect against certain types of misrepresentation. Passing off is a common law remedy and is typically relied upon as an addition or alternative to claims of registered trade mark infringement.

(2) **Registered trade marks as set out in the Trade Marks Act 1994 ("TMA")** protect trade marks as the "badge of origin" by which consumers differentiate between different traders' goods and services.

(3) **Copyright as set out in the Copyright, Designs and Patents Act 1988 ("CDPA")** protects economic rights and moral rights in creative works. For example, each chapter of this book is a "literary work" under the CDPA. Copyright is an unregistered intellectual property right.

(4) **Unregistered and registered design rights as set out respectively in the CDPA and Registered Designs Act 1949 ("RDA")** relate to the design of the appearance of an object. This could include objects as wide-ranging as car parts, household utensils or fashion items. Unregistered design rights are covered by the CDPA; registered design rights are covered by the RDA.

---

[1] Lecturer in Intellectual Property Law, University of Edinburgh. The work of the previous author of this chapter, Dr Catherine Ng, is gratefully acknowledged.

(5) **Patents as set out in the Patents Act 1977 ("PA")** relate to technical inventions, such as mechanical devices and pharmaceuticals. All patents must be registered.

Intellectual property rights are negative rights, in that they entitle the **12–02** right holder to prevent third parties from carrying out certain activities (for example, from using a patented invention without permission). Each of the main intellectual property rights can be best understood in terms of the following elements:

(1) Protection:

    (a) the subject matter protected by the right, as defined by:

        (i) the *type* of subject matter protected (for example, in the case of a registered trade mark, a sign capable of graphical representation); and

        (ii) the *characteristics* of the subject matter required to attract protection (for example, in the case of a registered trade mark, its ability to distinguish the goods or services of one undertaking from those of other undertakings);

    (b) the nature and scope of the rights conferred; and

    (c) the duration of those rights.

(2) Registration: for registered trade marks, registered designs, and all patents:

    (a) the statutory requirements for registration; and

    (b) the conditions for revoking and/or invalidating the registration.

(3) Infringement: the third party acts which, if unauthorised, would constitute an infringement of the intellectual property right; and the permitted third party acts which would not constitute such an infringement.

(4) Defences: if infringement is established, the defences available to an otherwise infringing third party.

✓ OUTCOMES

At the end of this chapter, you should be able to: **12–03**

    ✓ identify some key common characteristics among intellectual property rights;
    ✓ understand the principles relating to the law of passing off;
    ✓ understand registered trade marks;
    ✓ understand copyright, including moral rights;
    ✓ understand unregistered and registered design rights; and
    ✓ understand patents.

INTELLECTUAL PROPERTY RIGHTS

12–04 Trade marks, copyright, design rights and patents share some basic characteristics which are useful in conceptualising them in a business context:

(1) Registered trade marks and applications for trade mark registration,[2] registered designs and applications for design registration,[3] patents and applications for patent registration[4] are all incorporeal moveable properties.[5] Copyright and unregistered design right under the CDPA are property rights.[6] These properties and rights can be licensed, assigned and made the subject of a security interest.[7]

(2) Each intellectual property right has its own discrete legal existence. For example, while a student may own this book as corporeal moveable property, the copyright in the book is held by the publisher, and the moral rights to this chapter remain with the author unless those rights are waived.

(3) Intellectual property rights may be exploited by several parties at any one time. For example, the copyright in a painting may be licensed to a trader for printing posters and to another trader for printing postcards. It may also be licensed to different traders for printing the same postcards in different parts of the world.

(4) International conventions, treaties, and EU Directives, among other international instruments, influence the domestic UK laws which govern intellectual property rights. There are also certain forms of intellectual property right, most notably the Community trade mark and the Community design, which exist at a pan-EU level in addition to the UK intellectual property rights discussed in this chapter. These EU-level rights (the detail of which is outwith the scope of this chapter) were created by EU Regulations which have direct effect in the UK and other EU Member States. Within the UK, intellectual property law is a matter specifically reserved to the Westminster Parliament under the Scotland Act 1998.[8]

(5) Public interests are often at stake. For example, a patentee can determine when and how his patented medicines may be made available to the public.

(6) A breach of intellectual property rights may cause serious damage for the right holder. The primary remedy often sought by right holders is an interdict, to order the offending activity to

---

[2] TMA ss.22, 27(1).
[3] RDA s.15A.
[4] PA s.31(2).
[5] For a discussion of property rights, see Ch.11, "Property".
[6] Copyright: CDPA s.1(1); designs: CDPA s.213(1).
[7] Trade marks: TMA ss.24 and 28–31; copyright: CDPA s.90; unregistered design right: CDPA ss.222–225; registered designs: RDA 1949 ss.15B–19; patents: PA ss.30–31.
[8] Scotland Act 1998 Sch.5.

cease. Right holders may also have the offending materials delivered or destroyed, and have the right to elect between recovering damages for loss caused or to have the defender's profits from the infringing activity accounted and paid. Statutory remedies are available against the making of certain unjustified threats of infringement proceedings.[9] Criminal sanctions against infringement are also available in respect of certain infringements of intellectual property rights.

The Law of Passing Off

The basic principle of the law of passing off is to protect against the use of **12–05** trade marks and other distinctive indicators of the origin of goods and services to mislead the public into confusing one trader's goods or services for those of another trader. Passing off is a common law remedy and the law is established through judicial decisions.

Reckitt & Colman Products Ltd v Borden Inc
[1990] 1 W.L.R. 491, HL

The defendant proposed to supply lemon juice in packaging similar to the packaging in which the plaintiff's lemon juice product had been marketed for many years: plastic containers in the shape and size of a lemon. The court established that to succeed in an action of passing off, three elements must be proven:

(1) a goodwill or reputation connected with the plaintiff's goods or services in the mind of the purchasing public and identified with the plaintiff by some distinctive get-up or other identifying feature used by the plaintiff for its goods or services;
(2) misrepresentation by the defendant (whether or not intentional) which would lead or be likely to lead the public to believe that his goods or services were those of the plaintiff; and
(3) damage or likelihood of damage as a result of the misrepresentation.

The Inner House, Court of Session, has applied these elements in a Scots law context.[10]

---

[9] Trade marks: TMA s.21; patents: PA s.70; unregistered design right: CDPA s.253; registered designs: RDA s.26.
[10] For a recent example of a Scottish interim interdict decision on passing off, see *Wise Property Care Limited v White Thomson Preservation Ltd* [2008] CSIH 44.

Goodwill

12–06 The pursuer must establish at trial that some form of identifying feature, be it a word mark, logo, overall product get-up, or some other indicator of origin, has been so used in connection with the pursuer's goods or services in the market place that it has come to be distinctive of the pursuer's goods or services. For example, the publisher W. Green has developed goodwill in its name in association with law books such that by that name, the relevant public can distinguish books published by W. Green from books by other publishers. The more distinctive the relevant indicator of origin is as an identifier, and the less descriptive it is of its underlying goods or services (for example, the distinctive identifier "W. GREEN", rather than the descriptive brand "LEGAL PUBLISH-ING"—a generic and descriptive term for legal publishing generally), the easier it is for the trader to establish that this goodwill exists. Nevertheless, where a trader has used a generic or descriptive word or device to such a degree and to such an extent that it becomes exclusively identified with that particular trader, goodwill may also be established. The otherwise non-distinctive word or device would have acquired a "secondary meaning" to denote the goods and services of that particular trader. The relevant public need not know the exact identity of the trader represented by a distinctive word or device, provided that it is understood that all goods and services bearing that word or device originate from one source.

The scope of protection against passing off is limited by the scope of goodwill. Protection in passing off will extend geographically only so far as the pursuer has established goodwill. Protection in passing off will expire if the pursuer's goodwill expires. Businesses must therefore be vigilant in using and keeping their identifying words and devices present in the mind of their relevant public.

Misrepresentation

12–07 The second element in a passing off claim is misrepresentation. The pursuer must establish that, intentionally or otherwise, the defender is making a misrepresentation which is misleading or likely to mislead the public into believing that the goods or services offered by the defender are those of the pursuer. This element has been extended to include certain misrepresentations that the defender's goods or services share the same distinctive characteristics as those of the pursuer or group of pursuers— for example, to protect against the use of the name "Advocaat" for a product not made to the traditional Advocaat recipe, to prevent the use of the term "Elderflower champagne" and, most recently, in the "Vodkat" case to prevent use of that name on a product which was not vodka.[11] This element of the law has also been further extended to include

---

[11] *Erven Warnink Besloten Vennootschap v J Townend & Sons (Hull) Ltd* [1979] A.C. 731, HL ("Advocaat"); *Taittinger SA v Allbev Ltd* [1993] F.S.R. 641 CA ("Elderflower champagne"); *Diageo North America Inc v Intercontinental Brands (UCB) Ltd* [2011] R.P.C. 2 CA ("Vodkat").

misrepresentations that the defender or the defender's goods or services are in some way endorsed by the pursuer, which may include false claims of celebrity endorsement.[12]

Damage

The third element is damage or a likelihood of damage suffered by the **12–08** pursuer as a result of the erroneous belief engendered by the defender's misrepresentation. The damage that usually results is a diversion of custom from the pursuer to the defender. The pursuer may also suffer from damage to its reputation as a result of public confusion between the pursuer's and defender's goods or services or because of a false impression that the pursuer has endorsed the defender's goods or services.

Key Concepts

Passing off: The basic principle set out in *Reckitt & Colman Products Ltd v Borden Inc* (1990) is that no one may pass off one person's goods or services as those of another. The pursuer must establish three elements:

- Goodwill attaching to the distinctive identifying word or device by which his goods and services are known to the relevant public.
- Misrepresentation by the defender leading or likely lead the public into believing the defender's goods or services are the pursuer's.
- Damage or likelihood of damage as a result of that misrepresentation.

REGISTERED TRADE MARKS

Traders may register their marks to gain statutory protection.[13] The **12–09** protection conferred by trade mark registration may be wider than the protection available in passing off. Trade mark registration will also avoid the cost and uncertainty of having to establish the elements required to prove passing off against an infringer. Trade marks can be protected UK-wide through registration with the UK Intellectual Property Office under the Trade Marks Act 1994 ("TMA"). Trade marks can also be registered EU-wide, as Community trade marks effective in all EU Member States, at OHIM.[14] In addition, international applications can

---

[12] *Irvine v Talksport Ltd* [2002] 2 All E.R. 414, and most recently in a claim by the pop star, Rihanna, *Fenty v Arcadia Group Brands Ltd* [2015] EWCA Civ 3, CA.

[13] Only standard registered trade marks are considered here. For collective or certification marks, see TMA ss.49, 50 respectively.

[14] OHIM is the Office for Harmonization in the Internal Market. It is the body charged with administering the Community trade mark and is based in Alicante, Spain. The law governing Community trade marks can be found in Council Regulation 207/2009/EC of 26 February 2009 on the Community trade mark.

be filed at the World Intellectual Property Organisation; this is an administrative procedure which will result in a bundle of national marks in the different states designated by the applicant.[15] This chapter will focus on UK domestic trade mark registrations under the TMA. Under the TMA, the registered trade mark owner's rights under the law of passing off remain unaffected[16]; as a result, registered trade marks and protection in passing off can, and often do, co-exist.

Protection

12–10 A registered mark is protected from later conflicting trade mark applications and infringements.[17] An actionable conflict with a later trade mark application or infringement will arise:

(1) Where a third party mark is identical to an earlier registered mark, and the goods or services which the later mark has been applied for, or for which it is being used, are identical to the goods or services for which the earlier mark has been registered.[18] A classic example of this form of trade mark infringement would be luxury goods counterfeiting, where the infringer produces goods which are the same as those covered by the luxury brand's trade mark registration and which bear a name or logo identical to the registered mark.

(2) Where a third party mark is identical to an earlier registered mark and has been applied for or is being used for goods or services similar to those for which the earlier mark is registered, or where a third party mark is similar to an earlier registered mark and has been applied for or is being used for goods or services identical or similar to those for which the earlier trade mark is registered. In both cases, there must be a likelihood of confusion on the part of the public.[19] This form of infringement might arise, for example, where two businesses sell the same or similar goods under marks which are not identical but which are confusingly similar.

(3) Where a third party mark is identical or similar to an earlier registered mark and where the earlier registered mark has a reputation in the UK and the use of the later mark would, without due cause, take unfair advantage of, or be detrimental to, the distinctive character or repute of the earlier mark.[20] This form of infringement may arise when the third party's goods and services are the same as, similar to or even dissimilar to those

---

[15] See the Madrid Agreement Concerning the International Registration of Marks (adopted April 14, 1891) and the Protocol Relating to the Madrid Agreement Concerning the International Registration of Marks (adopted June 27, 1989).

[16] TMA s.2(2).

[17] Conflicting later trade mark applications: TMA s.5; infringements: TMA ss.9, 10.

[18] Conflicting later trade mark applications: TMA s.5(1); infringements: TMA s.10(1).

[19] Conflicting later trade mark applications: TMA s.5(2); infringements: TMA s.10(2).

[20] Conflicting later trade mark applications: TMA s.5(3); infringements: TMA s.10(3).

covered by the earlier trade mark registration. A recent high-profile dispute involving this form of trade mark infringement related to the sale of low-cost "smell-alike" perfumes in packaging which was similar to styles of perfume packaging which had been registered as trade marks by a major luxury brand owner; although there was no likelihood of confusion between the right holder's and defender's packaging styles, the defender's packaging was nonetheless ultimately held to infringe the right holder's registered trade marks because the packaging style was sufficiently close to take unfair advantage of the reputation attaching to the registered marks.[21]

Registration

To qualify for registration, a trade mark must be a "sign capable of being **12–11** represented graphically which is capable of distinguishing goods or services of one undertaking from those of other undertakings".[22] A trade mark may consist of words, logos, numerals or the shape of goods or their packaging.[23] Further types of mark including colours, sounds and holograms have also been registered. Looking at this book, the mark:

is a registered mark for books and other goods and services.[24] The name THOMSON REUTERS itself is also a registered mark for books and other goods and services.[25]

To be registered, a mark must not meet with any absolute grounds for refusal.[26] Absolute grounds for refusal are concerned with the inherent characteristics of a trade mark. Marks which are non-distinctive, descriptive of their underlying goods or services, or which are customary expressions in the relevant trade cannot be registered. For example, the word APPLE could not be registered as a trade mark for apples because it is descriptive and non-distinctive for these goods, although it could be registered for computers.[27] Where marks which would otherwise fail on

---

[21] *L'Oreal SA v Bellure NV* [2008] E.T.M.R. 1 and [2010] E.T.M.R. 47.
[22] TMA s.1(1).
[23] TMA s.1(2).
[24] Community trade mark no.6680987 in the name of Thomson Reuters Global Resources. See *https://www.gov.uk/government/organisations/intellectual-property-office* [Accessed May 15, 2015].
[25] Community trade mark no.6474341 in the name of Thomson Reuters Global Resources. See *https://www.gov.uk/government/organisations/intellectual-property-office* [Accessed May 15, 2015].
[26] TMA s.3.
[27] See, e.g. UK registered trade mark no.1246443, and Community trade mark no.6313316 in the name of Apple Inc. See *https://www.gov.uk/government/organisations/intellectual-property-office* [Accessed May 15, 2015].

these grounds have acquired a distinctive character through use in the relevant market, they can overcome these objections.[28] Other absolute grounds for refusal (which cannot be overcome by proof of acquired distinctiveness) include marks which consist exclusively of shapes which result from the nature of the goods themselves, which are necessary to obtain a technical result, or which give substantial value to the goods,[29] and marks which are deceptive or contrary to public policy or morality.[30]

To gain registration, a mark must also not encounter any relative grounds for refusal.[31] Relative grounds for refusal are concerned with conflict with earlier rights. For this purpose, earlier trade marks include earlier registered trade marks, earlier-filed pending trade mark applications and trade mark registrations or applications with an earlier "priority date".[32] In terms of conflict with earlier trade marks, the relative grounds for refusal have been set out at para.12–10 above.[33] A trade mark can also be refused where use of the mark would be prevented by any rule of law (such as the law of passing off) or by reason of another earlier intellectual property right (for example, a conflicting earlier right in copyright, UK unregistered design right or registered designs).

Upon an application for registration, the UK Intellectual Property Office will examine the application for any objections on absolute grounds. If there are any such objections, the applicant will be given an opportunity to respond. If those objections can be overcome, the application will be published and will become open, for a defined period of time, for public opposition on the grounds above. If an opposition is filed and succeeds, the application will fail. Otherwise, or if there is no successful opposition, the application will proceed to registration.

Infringement and defences

12–12 Once registered, a trade mark is protected against infringing use in the course of trade for a period of 10 years backdated to its filing date, renewable indefinitely for further periods of 10 years.[34] The different forms of registered trade mark infringement are outlined at para.12–10 above. Infringing use includes affixing a mark to goods or their packaging, offering for sale or supplying goods or services under a mark, stocking goods bearing a mark for such purposes, importing or exporting

---

[28] TMA s.3(1).
[29] TMA s.3(2).
[30] TMA s.3(3).
[31] TMA s.5.
[32] TMA s.6. The "priority date" of a trade mark application or registration may be up to six months earlier than the date of filing of that application or registration if "priority" has been claimed from an earlier identical application or registration in another jurisdiction covered by the Paris Convention.
[33] The protection conferred on earlier trade mark registrations described at para.12–10 above is, for these purposes, also available for earlier trade mark applications which have not yet been registered.
[34] TMA ss.42, 43.

goods under a mark or using a mark on business papers or in advertising.[35]

No infringement will be found where a person uses his own name or address, uses an indication of the kind, quality, quantity, intended purpose, value, geographical origin, or other characteristics of goods or services, or uses a mark where it is necessary to indicate the intended purpose of a product or service (for example, as accessories or spare parts), provided that these activities are in accordance with honest practices in industrial or commercial matters.[36] It is accordingly not an infringement to use another's registered mark to indicate the compatibility of one's own product or service with the trade mark owner's goods or services.

Revocation and invalidity

A trade mark registration may be revoked if the mark has not been in **12–13** genuine use in the UK for a period of five years without a proper reason for non-use, where, as a result of action or inaction by the trade mark owner, the mark has become a common name in trade for its underlying goods or services or if it has become liable to mislead the public as a result of any use made of the mark by the owner or with his consent.[37] The registration may also be declared invalid where the mark has been registered in breach of the absolute or relative grounds for refusal of registration.[38] Given the public interest in ensuring that invalid or revocable marks do not stay on the trade mark register indefinitely, anyone may challenge a trade mark registration in these ways.

Key Concepts

Trade marks: Under the Trade Marks Act 1994, to gain registration, a trade mark must be:

- a sign (word, logo or shape, among other possibilities);
- capable of being represented graphically; and
- capable of distinguishing the goods or services of one undertaking from those of other undertakings.

Registered marks are entitled to:

- protection against the conflicting registration or infringing use of a later mark:
  —where the marks are identical, and their goods and services are identical;

---

[35] TMA s.10(4).
[36] TMA s.11(2).
[37] TMA s.46(1).
[38] TMA s.47.

—where the marks are identical and their goods and services are similar, or where the marks are similar and their goods and services are identical or similar, in both cases if there is a likelihood of confusion on the part of the relevant public; and

—where the marks are identical or similar, the earlier registered mark has a reputation in the UK and the use of the later mark would, without due cause, take unfair advantage of or be detrimental to the distinctiveness or repute of the earlier mark;

● protection for initial period of 10 years, renewable indefinitely for further periods of 10 years.

COPYRIGHT

12–14 Copyright consists of two aspects: economic rights and moral rights. These are unregistered rights. Both are set out in the Copyright, Designs and Patents Act 1988 ("CDPA").[39] Economic rights, the generally more commonly recognised aspect of copyright, are intended to encourage and to reward creativity by permitting the copyright holder (not necessarily the creator) to exploit a work for gain for a limited period. Moral rights seek to protect the creator's interests in the work. Moral rights are discussed in a separate section below.

Protection

12–15 Copyright subsists in a wide range of works[40]:

● original literary, dramatic, musical or artistic works[41];
● sound recordings, films and broadcasts[42]; and
● typographical arrangements of published editions.[43]

Literary works include computer programs and databases, as set out in the legislation.[44]

Copyright protection is conferred automatically when the requirements of the CDPA are fulfilled. Literary, dramatic, musical or artistic works need to be original.[45] In UK law, the threshold for this requirement has traditionally been low, requiring not that the work in question be unique or meritorious, but simply that it not be a copy of an earlier work and should originate from the author. The UK courts have traditionally applied a test for originality focussed on whether a sufficient (although not high) level of "skill, labour and judgment" had been expended by the author, although EU law has now had an impact on the current test for

---

[39] CDPA s.2.
[40] CDPA s.1. See CDPA s.180 in respect of rights in performances.
[41] CDPA ss.3–4.
[42] CDPA ss.5A–6A.
[43] CDPA s.8.
[44] CDPA ss.3(1)(b)–(d), 3A.
[45] CDPA s.1(1)(a).

originality in UK law, as noted below. Literary, dramatic, musical or artistic works must also be recorded, in writing or otherwise, to be entitled to copyright protection.[46] Finally, with some exceptions, the work must have sufficient connection with the UK and/or specified countries and territories. This connection may be established either by reference to the author of the work or by reference to the country of first publication or broadcast.[47] As an example, this book attracts copyright under the CDPA because it is a literary work, original to the authors, written (and thus recorded) by them, and first published in the UK.

Temple Island Collections Ltd v New English Teas Ltd
[2012] F.S.R. 9

This dispute concerned infringement of copyright in a photograph showing a Routemaster bus crossing Westminster Bridge. The photograph was almost entirely in black and white, with the Houses of Parliament and bridge shown in grey but with the Routemaster bus shown in red. The photograph had been taken from a position on Westminster Bridge where many tourists take photographs of the view of the Houses of Parliament. The photograph had been digitally manipulated to achieve the desired overall effect. Following EU case law on the concept of originality, it was held that the test for correct test for originality in the photograph under UK law was now whether the work constituted "the author's own intellectual creation". Although the photograph had been taken from a viewpoint from which many other photographs had been taken, there was room for originality in a photograph arising from matters such as the choice of angle of shot, light and shade, exposure, effects of using different filters, creation of the scene and digital manipulation. It was therefore held that the photograph could be the product of, using the old UK law test, sufficient skill and labour or, using the newer originality test developed in EU law, the "intellectual creation" of the photographer.

Generally the creator of the work is the first owner of the copyright. However, where a literary, dramatic, musical or artistic work or a film is made by an employee in the course of employment, the employer is the first owner of the right subject to any agreement to the contrary.[48]

The duration of copyright varies depending on the type of work under protection. For a literary, dramatic, musical or artistic work, copyright lasts a maximum of 70 years from the end of the calendar year in which the known author (or the last of the known authors) dies. The same period holds for copyright in films, but is calculated from the last to die

---

[46] CDPA s.3(2), (3).
[47] CDPA ss.153–156.
[48] CDPA ss.9–11.

among the known principal director, the author of the screenplay, the author of the dialogue, or the composer of music specially created for and used in the film. Copyright in sound recordings has a shorter duration, lasting a maximum of 50 years from the end of the calendar year in which the recording was made or first published, or, if no authorised publication of the recording has been published, 50 years from the end of the calendar year in which the work was first played in public or communicated to the public. Copyright in broadcasts generally lasts a maximum of 50 years from the end of the calendar year of the initial broadcast.[49]

Infringement and defences

12–16 It is a primary infringement of copyright to perform or to authorise another to perform the following restricted acts within the UK[50]:

>   (1) to copy the work (including, for an artistic work, to make a copy in three dimensions of a two-dimensional work, and to make a copy in two dimensions of a three-dimensional work);
>   (2) to issue copies of the work to the public;
>   (3) to rent or lend the work to the public;
>   (4) to perform, show, or play the work in public;
>   (5) to communicate the work to the public; or
>   (6) to make an adaptation of the work or do any of the above in relation to an adaptation.

Copyright is infringed by anyone who commits, or authorises another to commit, any of these restricted acts.[51] There will be infringement if a restricted act is done in relation to the whole or a substantial part of a copyright work and if the restricted act is committed directly or indirectly (for example, by copying a copy of a copyright work).[52]

In practice, copyright holders often license a collecting society such as the Copyright Licensing Agency or PRS for Music to collect royalties from the public on behalf of the copyright holders. For example, the Copyright Licensing Agency's licence permits an organisation such as an educational institution to copy articles from certain publications without having to seek permission from each copyright holder each time a copy is made. In exchange, the Agency collects from the organisation a single annual payment. The Agency then undertakes surveys and audits to determine how the royalties should be distributed among the copyright holders.

Secondary infringement of copyright occurs where a person, without the licence of the copyright owner[53]:

[49] CDPA ss.12–15A.
[50] CDPA ss.16–21.
[51] CDPA ss.16(2).
[52] CDPA ss.16(3).
[53] CDPA ss.22–27.

(1) imports an infringing copy of a copyright work into the UK other than for his private and domestic use, knowing or with reason to believe that he is dealing with an infringing copy;

(2) sells or lets for hire, offers or exposes for sale or hire, or in the course of a business possesses, exhibits in public or distributes an infringing copy, or otherwise than in the course of a business distributes an infringing copy to such an extent as to prejudicially affect the copyright owner, all knowing or with reason to believe that he is dealing with an infringing copy;

(3) makes, imports into the UK, possesses in the course of a business, or sells or lets for hire, or offers or exposes for sale or hire an article specifically designed or adapted for making infringing copies of a copyright work, knowing or with reason to believe that it is used to make infringing copies;

(4) permits the use of a place of public entertainment for the performance of a literary, dramatic or musical work; or

(5) commits various further acts relating to the supply of a copyright work or apparatus used for the performance, playing or showing of the work in public.

However, a number of permitted uses by non-copyright holders are set out in the legislation. They include (of particular importance to students): (1) fair dealing with a literary, dramatic, musical or artistic work for private study or for non-commercial research, if such use is accompanied by sufficient acknowledgement; and (2) fair dealing with a work already available to the public for the purpose of criticism or review or for reporting current events, again with a requirement of sufficient acknowledgment.[54]

Moral rights

Moral rights specifically seek to protect the creators of certain copyright **12–17** works. Four types of moral rights are recognised under the CDPA.[55]

First is the right to be identified as the author of a copyright literary, dramatic, musical, or artistic work, or the director of a copyright film. This right is not infringed unless it has been asserted in accordance with the statute, for example, by printing on the opening page of a book: "The moral rights of the authors have been asserted". Second is the right to object to the derogatory treatment of a copyright literary, dramatic, musical or artistic work or a copyright film. The treatment of a work is derogatory if it distorts or mutilates the work or otherwise prejudices the honour or reputation of the author or director of the work. Third is the right against the false attribution to a person other than the true author or director of a copyright literary, dramatic, musical or artistic work or a film. Fourth is the right of the commissioner of copyright photographs or films taken or made for private and domestic purposes, where copyright

---

[54] CDPA ss.29, 30.
[55] CDPA ss.77–85.

subsists in those works, not to have copies of the work issued, exhibited, shown, or communicated to the public.

Unlike economic rights, moral rights cannot be transferred.[56] Moral rights may, however, be waived.[57] All moral rights other than the right against false attribution last for the same duration as the economic rights. The right against false attribution lasts for 20 years after the author's or the director's death.[58] A person entitled to a moral right can take action against any infringement of that right as a breach of a statutory duty and, in the case of the right to object to derogatory treatment of a work, the court may grant an interdict to prohibit the infringing act unless a satisfactory disclaimer is made to dissociate the author or director from the treatment of the work.[59]

Key Concepts

Copyright: Under the CDPA, copyright consists of economic rights and moral rights. These rights are unregistered. Copyright automatically subsists in:

- original literary, dramatic, musical or artistic works, once recorded;
- sound recordings, films or broadcasts; and
- typographical arrangements of published editions,

where the creator or the work has sufficient connection with the UK or a specified country or territory. The duration of the rights varies based on the type of work and the type of right at issue.

During the period of protection, the economic right holder is entitled to:

- protection of qualifying work from being:
  —copied;
  —issued to the public;
  —rented or lent to the public;
  —performed, shown, or played in public;
  —communicated to the public; or
  —adapted,
- protection against third-party authorisation of the foregoing acts.

However, certain acts are permitted where applicable conditions are met, such as the fair dealing with a literary, dramatic, musical or artistic work for non-commercial research or private study or for the purpose of criticism or review of a work already available to the public.

---

[56] CDPA s.94.
[57] CDPA s.87.
[58] CDPA s.86.
[59] CDPA s.103.

> In addition, four types of moral rights are recognised under the CDPA:
>
> • the right to be identified as the author or director of a copyright work;
> • the right to object to any derogatory treatment of the copyright work;
> • the right against false attribution; and
> • the right to privacy of certain photographs and films.
>
> Moral right holders are entitled to:
>
> • protection against infringement as a breach of statutory duty.
>
> Moral rights can be waived, but not transferred.

DESIGNS

Design, in intellectual property terms, refers to the appearance of an **12–18** object or a part of it. In UK law, unregistered design right may arise under the CDPA. Designs also be protected by registration under the Registered Designs Act 1949 ("RDA"). These two types of design protection have different requirements. Designs may also be protected in unregistered and registered form at the EU-level, via the Community design.[60] However, this chapter will again focus just on the protection of designs under UK domestic legislation.

CDPA unregistered design rights

Protection

In the UK, design rights may arise without registration under the pro- **12–19** visions at Pt III of the CDPA.[61] UK unregistered design right—commonly referred to as "UK UDR"—protects "designs" consisting of the design of any aspect of the shape or configuration (internal or external) of the whole or a part of an article. The design must be original and not commonplace. For UK UDR to subsist, the design must have been recorded in a design document or an article must have been made to the design. The design must also meet certain qualifying requirements in terms of connection with the UK.[62]

UK UDR will protect purely functional designs as well as designs which have aesthetic aspects. UK UDR does not subsist in surface decoration or methods or principles of construction. UK UDR also does not subsist in features of shape or configuration of an article which enable the article to

---

[60] See Regulation 6/2002/EC on the Community design.
[61] CDPA ss.213–264.
[62] CDPA ss.217–221.

fit with another article so that either may perform its function, or which are dependent on the appearance of another article of which the article is intended to form an integral part.[63] These two so-called "must fit" and "must match" exclusions may permit third parties to manufacture spare parts or accessories for a protected article or portion of an article.

UK UDR lasts 15 years from the end of the calendar year in which the design is first recorded or an article is first made to the design, whichever is earlier. However, where articles made to the design are made available for sale or hire within five years from the end of that calendar year, the rights expire 10 years from the end of the calendar year in which that availability first occurs.[64] Furthermore, any person may be entitled to a licence of right for a design protected by UK UDR within the last five years of the subsistence of the right.[65] So, in effect, it is possible that a UK UDR right holder may only enjoy five years of exclusivity from the commencement of his exploitation of the design right.

The designer is generally the first owner of UK UDR, unless the design is created by an employee in the course of employment.[66] An owner of UK UDR has the exclusive right to reproduce the design for commercial purposes by making articles to that design or by making a design document recording the design for the purpose of enabling such articles to be made.[67]

Infringement and defences

12–20 Any person without a licence will infringe UK UDR by doing any of the acts that are exclusively reserved to the holder of the design right. This includes copying the protected design so as to produce articles exactly or substantially to that design.[68] It is also a secondary infringement of UK UDR to import an infringing article into the UK for commercial purposes, to possess such an article for commercial purposes, or to sell, let for hire, or offer for sale or hire in the course of a business such an article where a person knows or has reason to know that the article is infringing.[69]

Unlike copyright, the protection conferred by UK UDR under Pt III of the CDPA is limited to commercial use of the design. Where a work attracts copyright as well as design right (for example, because the design is for an object which is a work of sculpture or artistic craftsmanship), it is not an infringement of design right to do anything which is an infringement of the copyright in that work.[70] In that case, only an action in copyright would lie. The CDPA also stipulates that it is not an infringement of copyright in design documents for anything other than an artistic work or typeface, or of copyright in a model recording or

---

[63] CDPA s.213(3)(b).
[64] CDPA s.216.
[65] CDPA s.237.
[66] CDPA s.215.
[67] CDPA s.226(1).
[68] CDPA s.226(2).
[69] CDPA s.227.
[70] CDPA s.236.

embodying such a design, to make an article to a design or to copy an article made to a design.[71] In effect this means that it is not possible to bring a copyright infringement claim based on copyright in design drawings for utilitarian or functional items; if the design of such an item is copied, the only remedy will be in design right. So, for example, the production of an exhaust pipe from copying a rightholder's blueprint would not infringe the copyright in the blueprint because it is a design document recording a design for an item which, in itself, is not protected in copyright as an artistic work. The basic purpose of this provision is to prevent copyright in design drawings being used to reduce competition in the market for spare parts.

Registered designs

While design protection under the CDPA and the RDA may overlap, **12–21** they do not protect the same subject matter nor do they confer the same rights. Designs which are registered under the RDA are protected for longer and enjoy stronger protection.

Protection

Design registration under the RDA protects the appearance of the whole **12–22** or a part of an product (being any kind of industrial or handicraft item) resulting from the features of, in particular, the lines, contours, colours, shape, texture or materials of the product or its ornamentation.[72] To be registered, the design must be new (or "novel"), such that no identical design or design which varies only in immaterial detail has been made available to the public before the date of application for the design registration or priority date, if earlier. To be registered, the design must also have "individual character", meaning that it must produce on the informed user a different overall impression from the overall impression produced by any earlier design.[73] Designs which are solely dictated by technical function cannot be registered under the RDA. No registered design protection subsists in features of appearance of a product which must necessarily be reproduced in their exact form and dimensions so as to permit the product to fit another product so that either may perform its function.[74] Designs which are contrary to public policy or morality also cannot be registered.[75]

Registration

The creator is the original proprietor of the design save where a design is **12–23** created by an employee in the course of employment.[76]

---

[71] CDPA s.51.
[72] RDA s.1.
[73] RDA s.1B.
[74] RDA s.1C.
[75] RDA s.1D.
[76] RDA s.2.

Infringement and defences

12–24 Once registered, the proprietor has the exclusive right to use the design and any other design which does not produce on the informed user a different overall impression.[77] Such use includes the making, offering, putting on the market, importing, exporting or using of a product in which the design is incorporated or to which it is applied, or stocking such a product for these purposes. It is infringement of a registered design to do anything falling within this exclusive right without the right holder's consent. There is no need to prove copying. However, the use of a design for private and non-commercial purposes, or teaching or experimental purposes is not an infringement where the source is mentioned and the use is compatible with fair trade practice and does not unduly prejudice the normal exploitation of the design.[78] To allow competition in the sale of spare parts, registered designs are not infringed where the design of a component part is used for the purpose of the repair of a complex product to restore the complex product to its original appearance.[79] Registered designs last for an initial period of five years, and are renewable for up to four additional periods of five years each, through to a maximum of 25 years in total.[80]

> **Samsung Electronics (UK) Ltd v Apple Inc**
> **[2013] E.C.D.R. 1, HC; [2013] E.C.D.R. 2, CA**
>
> This dispute concerned whether various tablet computing devices produced by Samsung infringed a Community registered design belonging to Apple for the design of its iPad device. Apple argued that Samsung's tablet devices produced the same overall impression as its registered design. It was held at first instance that, although the registered design and Samsung devices were very similar when viewed from the front, the effect of that similarity in the eyes of the informed user was much reduced when the disputed designs were considered in light of other, prior designs constituting a wider "family" of which the Apple and Samsung designs were part. There were differences between the disputed designs, particularly when viewed from the side and rear. The informed user would pay close attention to those differences and, given their significance in the informed user's eyes, the designs produced different overall impressions. There was therefore no infringement. This ruling was upheld on appeal.

---

[77] RDA s.7.
[78] RDA s.7A.
[79] RDA s.7A(5).
[80] RDA s.8.

Revocation and invalidity

As with other registered intellectual property rights, registered designs **12–25** may be declared invalid if they have been wrongly granted.[81] Where the design constitutes an unauthorised use of a work protected by UK copyright law, the registration may also be invalidated based on an objection by the owner of the copyright.[82] Where the design constitutes a distinctive sign, it may also be invalidated by a prior right holder of a distinctive sign who has the right to object to the use of the design in the UK.[83]

Key Concepts

Design Rights: The CDPA and RDA both provide forms of protection for designs.

Designs may be protected under Part III (Design Right) of the CDPA. This provides that unregistered design rights subsist in:

- the shape or configuration (internal or external) of the whole or part of an article;
- which is original and not commonplace;
- which is recorded or made into an article; and
- which meets the relevant qualifying requirements,

but do not subsist:

- in surface decoration;
- in methods or principles of construction;
- in features of shape or configuration which "must fit" another for either to function, or "must match" another in appearance.

CDPA unregistered design right holders are entitled to:

- The exclusive right to reproduce the design for commercial purposes by making articles to that design or by making a design document recording the design for the purpose of enabling such articles to be made.
- Protection for up to 15 years from the year the design is first recorded or made, or 10 years from the year the recorded design is first made available for sale or hire, whichever expires earlier. In any event, anyone may take a licence of right of the design during the last 5 years of protection.

---

[81] RDA s.11ZA.
[82] RDA s.11ZA(4).
[83] RDA s.11ZA(3).

RDA registered design rights subsist:

- in the appearance of the whole or a part of a product;
- where the design is new; and
- where the design has individual character,

but do not subsist:

- to the extent that the design is dictated solely by function;
- where the design "must fit" another product so that either product may function; or
- where the design is contrary to public policy or morality.

Registered design right holders are entitled to:

- The exclusive use of the design and any design which does not produce on the informed user a different overall impression. Certain uses of a product bearing or incorporating the registered design for private and non-commercial, teaching, experimental, or "must match" purposes are not infringements.
- Protection is available for an initial period of 5 years, renewable every 5 years, up to 25 years in total.

PATENTS

12–26 Patents are granted for technical inventions. Patents can be granted for inventions as wide-ranging in subject matter as life-saving medicines or innovative toys. An example of the latter (for which the patent has now expired) is the Lego brick[84]:

Abstract of **GB1065932**

1,065,932. Toy building elements. LEGO SYSTEMS A.S. Feb. 14, 1966 [March 1, 1965], No. 6453/66. Heading A6S. Toy building elements comprise hollow parallel sided blocks adapted to be interconnected by uniformly spaced projections P by axial distances constituting a module q, and cog-wheel elements having teeth in accordance with the formula $r=cq$, where c is an integer and r is half the pitch diameter D.

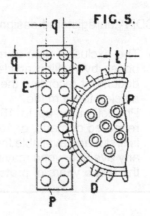

FIG. 5.

---

[84] © 2015 The LEGO Group, used with permission.

The UK Patents Act 1977 ("PA"), as amended, incorporates the requirements of the European Patent Convention 1973 as amended ("EPC"). The EPC is an international treaty, separate from the EU, which sought to harmonise important aspects of patent law between signatory states, as well as setting up the European Patent Office and creating the concept of the "European Patent", a single patent filing which can be applied for at the EPO and which acts as a national patent in all designated signatory states. The EU is in the process of also creating a "unitary patent" which will be a single unitary patent right effective across EU Member States. For the purposes of this chapter, however, we will again focus only on UK domestic law, looking at patents granted by the UK Intellectual Property Office under the PA.

Protection

Patents may only be granted for inventions: that are (i) new ("novel"); (ii) **12–27** involve an inventive step; (iii) are capable of industrial application; and (iv) are not excluded on various grounds, for example where their commercial exploitation would be contrary to public policy or morality.[85] An invention is novel if, at the patent's priority date,[86] the invention is not yet part of the "state of the art", which comprises all matters in the public domain whether by use, a publicly-available product, a publicly-known process, information published in a book, journal article or anything else.[87] It is essential to file a patent application before anyone, including the inventor, discloses the invention or the novelty of the invention will be lost. An invention must also involve an "inventive step", such that the invention is not obvious to a person skilled in the relevant art, having regard to the state of the art and common general knowledge in the field.[88] Finally, the invention must be capable of industrial application such that it can be made or used in any kind of industry, including agriculture,[89] and must not fall within any exclusions from patentability.

Under the PA, an invention cannot be patented if it consists of a discovery, scientific theory or mathematical method, a literary, dramatic, musical or artistic work or any other aesthetic creation (such work or creation may attract copyright under the CDPA as discussed above) or any scheme, rule or method for performing a mental act, playing a game or doing business, or a computer program, or the presentation of information.[90] Inventions which consist of a method of human or animal diagnosis practised upon the body or treatment by surgery or therapy are

---

[85] PA s.1.
[86] PA s.5.
[87] PA s.2. There are certain very limited categories of disclosure which do not form part of the "state of the art".
[88] PA s.3.
[89] PA s.4.
[90] PA s.1(2). Some business methods and computer programs will be patentable, but the detail of this is outwith the scope of this chapter.

also not patentable. A substance or composition invented for use in such method may nevertheless be patentable.[91]

Registration

12–28 A patent application must contain: (1) a request for the grant of a patent; (2) an abstract; and (3) a specification which contains a description of the invention, a claim or claims defining the monopoly sought and any drawings referred to in the description or claims.[92] The specification must disclose the invention in a manner clear and complete enough for a person skilled in the art to work the invention. The claims will define the essence of the invention and will set the parameters of the monopoly claimed. The scope of this monopoly should correspond with the technical contribution made through the invention.

Anyone may apply for a patent, which is primarily granted to the inventor or anyone entitled by law or agreement to the property in the invention in the UK at the time.[93] There are detailed rules relating to the ownership of patents created by employees.[94] Once filed at the UK Intellectual Property Office, the patent application is first subject to a preliminary examination to ensure that the application requirements are fulfilled and, through a search of prior art, that the application is indeed for a new, inventive, and patentable technology. The application will then be published and a full substantive examination of it made by a skilled examiner before the patent is granted and published in its final form.[95] Once granted, a patent will be effective for a period of up to 20 years from the date of filing of the patent application.[96]

Infringement and defences

12–29 There is no need to prove copying as part of a patent infringement claim. A *product* patent grants a patentee an exclusive right to make, dispose of, offer to dispose of, use or import the product or keep the product. Engaging in these acts without consent in respect of a patented product will infringe the patent. The exclusive right in a *process* patent lies in using the process or offering it for use in the UK. Anyone who uses the patented process or offers it for use in the UK will infringe the patent when he knows or it is obvious to a reasonable person that such use without the consent of the patent owner would infringe the patent. Anyone who disposes of, offers to dispose of, uses or imports any product obtained directly through the patented process or keeps any such product will also infringe the patent. Infringement may also occur by supplying or offering to supply, without authorisation, means (other than a staple commercial product) that are essential to work the invention when the

---

91 PA s.4A.
92 PA s.14.
93 PA s.7.
94 PA s.39.
95 PA ss.14–24.
96 PA s.25.

supplier knows or ought to know that the means are suitable and intended for working the invention in the UK. Exceptions to infringement include the private and non-commercial use of an invention, and experimental use relating to the subject matter of the invention.[97]

To prove infringement, the patentee's claims are compared with the defender's product or process. The defender's product or process need not be identical to the patentee's claims; the determination of infringement will depend on how the claims are construed by the courts and, in particular, how far the protection conferred by the patent extends to capture variants on the patented invention itself.

Pozzoli SPA v BDMO SA
[2007] EWCA Civ 588

The Court of Appeal reformulated the steps for determining inventiveness established in the earlier leading case of *Windsurfing International v Tabor Marine* [1985] R.P.C. 59. The reformulation of the test for inventiveness in *Pozzoli* is as follows:

(1) (a) Identify the notional "person skilled in the art";
    (b) Identify the relevant common general knowledge of that person;
(2) Identify the inventive concept of the patent claim in question or if that cannot readily be done, construe it;
(3) Identify what, if any, differences exist between the matter cited as forming part of the "state of the art" and the inventive concept of the claim or the claim as construed;
(4) Viewed without any knowledge of the alleged invention as claimed, assess whether those differences constitute steps which would have been obvious to the person skilled in the art or whether they require any degree of invention.

Revocation and invalidity

The validity of a patent may be challenged on various grounds, including **12–30** on the basis that the requirements for patentability have not been met.[98] Where a patent is too broad, it may also be revoked for failing to disclose the full scope of the invention claimed. A challenge to the validity of a patent may arise by way of a defence in an infringement proceeding, as well as being brought directly in the form of revocation proceedings.[99] In an infringement or revocation proceeding, the patentee may be allowed to amend the specification, but only to narrow (not to extend) the scope of the patent.[100]

---

[97] PA s.60.
[98] PA ss.72.
[99] PA s.74.
[100] PA ss.75, 76.

Key Concepts

Patents: To be patentable an invention, which may be a product or a process, must:

- be novel;
- involve an inventive step;
- be capable of industrial application; and
- not be excluded from patentability on any relevant grounds.

A patentee is entitled to:

- protection in respect of:
  —product patents: an exclusive right to make, dispose of, offer to dispose of, use or import the product or keep the product;
  —process patents: an exclusive right to use the process or offer it for use in the UK, and an exclusive right to dispose of, offer to dispose of, use or import any product obtained directly through the patented process or to keep any such product.
- protection against unauthorised supply or offer to supply in the UK of means relating to an essential element of the invention (other than a staple commercial product) when the supplier knows or ought to know that the means are suitable and intended for working the invention in the UK;
- protection up to 20 years.

Exceptions to infringement include the private and non-commercial use of a patented invention, and experimental use relating to the subject matter of the invention.

▼ CHAPTER SUMMARY

12–31
(1) Intellectual property rights protect certain products of the human mind.
(2) A breach of intellectual property rights may be remedied by the grant of an interdict, having the offending materials delivered up or destroyed, and recovering damages for loss suffered or having the defender's profits from the activity accounted and paid. Criminal sanctions are also available for certain intellectual property infringements.
(3) Intellectual property rights may be registered or unregistered. Save for the law of passing off, the four other major types of intellectual property rights—trade marks, copyright, designs, and patents—are statutory rights.

PASSING OFF

(1) The basic principle for the law of passing off is that no one may pass off one person's goods as those of another. Passing off is often relied upon as an addition or alternative to registered trade mark infringement.

> ➤ *Reckitt & Colman Products Ltd v Borden Inc* (1990): three basic elements must be proven to constitute passing off—goodwill, misrepresentation, and damage.

REGISTERED TRADE MARKS

> ➤ Trade Marks Act 1994.

(1) To gain registration, a trade mark must be a sign capable of being represented graphically and capable of distinguishing the goods and services of one undertaking from those of other undertakings.
(2) A registered mark is protected from later conflicting registration or infringing use where: an identical mark is applied for or used for identical goods and services; where an identical mark is applied for or used for similar goods and services or where a similar mark is applied for or used for identical or similar goods and services, and in both cases there is a likelihood of confusion; or where an identical or similar mark is applied for or used and the earlier registered mark has a reputation and the use of the later mark would, without due cause, take unfair advantage of or be detrimental to the distinctive character or repute of that earlier mark.
(3) A trade mark registration lasts 10 years, renewable indefinitely for periods of 10 years. The registration may be revoked or invalidated on various grounds.

COPYRIGHT

> ➤ Copyright, Designs and Patents Act 1988.

(1) Copyright is an unregistered right which is automatically conferred on original literary, dramatic, musical or artistic works, sound recordings, films or broadcasts, and typographical arrangements of published editions. In all cases, the creator or the work must have sufficient connection with the UK or a specified country or territory.
(2) The copyright holder can protect a qualifying work from being copied, issued to the public, rented or lent to the public, performed, shown or played in the public, communicated to the public, or adapted. The copyright holder may also take action against third parties who authorise these activities. Infringement will occur if the work is copied in whole or in substantial part, directly or indirectly. Exceptions include certain types of fair dealing with a copyright work.
(3) In addition to economic rights, four types of moral rights are recognised under the CDPA—the right to be identified as the author or director of the copyright work, the right to object to any derogatory treatment of the copyright work, the right against false attribution, and the right to privacy of certain copyright photographs and films. These rights can be waived but not transferred during the life of the creator.
(4) The duration of copyright protection varies depending on the type of protected work and the right at issue.

DESIGNS

(1) The two major pieces of UK legislation governing design rights are the CDPA and RDA.

> ➢ Copyright, Designs and Patents Act 1988.

(2) CDPA design rights are unregistered and arise automatically under the statute.

(3) CDPA unregistered design rights subsist in aspects of shape or configuration of an article which are original and not commonplace, which have been recorded or made into an article and which meet the relevant qualifying requirements.

(4) CDPA unregistered design rights can subsist in purely functional designs, but do not subsist in surface decoration, methods or principles of construction, or where the design must fit or must match with another article.

(5) CDPA unregistered design right holders are protected from the exact or substantial making or copying of articles to the protected design, or the making of a design document recording the protected design to enable such article to be made. Their rights last for up to 15 years. Other provisions apply to vary the period of exclusive rights.

> ➢ Registered Designs Act 1949.

(6) Registered design rights are set out in legislation.

(7) Registered design rights subsist in the appearance of the whole or a part of a product, being any industrial or handicraft item, where the design is new, and where the design has an individual character.

(8) Registered design rights do not subsist where the designs are dictated solely by function (including those which "must fit") or where the designs are contrary to public policy or morality.

(9) Registered design right holders are entitled to the exclusive use of the design and any design which does not produce on the informed user a different overall impression. However, certain uses of a product bearing or incorporating the registered design for private and non-commercial, teaching, experimental, or certain specific "must match" purposes are not infringements.

(10) Design registrations initially last for 5 years, and are renewable every 5 years, up to 25 years in total.

PATENTS

> ➢ Patents Act 1977.

(1) To be registered as a patent an invention, which may be for a product or a process, must be new, involve an inventive step, be capable of industrial application and not be subject to any relevant exclusions.

(2) Patentees have an exclusive right to make, dispose of, offer to dispose of, use or import the patented product or keep the product, and an exclusive right to use the patented process or offer it for use in the UK, and an exclusive right to dispose of, offer to dispose of, use or import any product obtained directly through the patented process or to keep any such product. Infringement may also occur by unauthorised supply

of essential means to work the invention knowing that the means would be so used. Exceptions include the private and non-commercial use of an invention, and experimental use relating to the subject matter of the invention.

(3) Patent protection lasts up to 20 years.

? QUICK QUIZ

- What are the elements that a pursuer must establish to constitute the action of passing off?
- What are some advantages of registering trade marks?
- Are written responses to this quick quiz protected by copyright? How?
- What intellectual property rights may exist in the THOMSON REUTERS logo?
- What are the advantages to registering design rights?
- What are the basic criteria in determining the patentability of an invention?

☐ FURTHER READING

➤ Christie and S. Gare, *Blackstone's Statutes on Intellectual Property*, 12th edn (Oxford: Oxford University Press, 2012).

➤ D.I. Bainbridge, *Intellectual Property*, 9th edn (Harlow: Pearson Education Ltd, 2012).

➤ C. Waelde, G. Laurie, A. Brown, S. Kheria and J. Cornwell, *Contemporary Intellectual Property: law and policy*, 3rd edn (Oxford: Oxford University Press, 2013).

➤ L. Bently and B. Sherman, *Intellectual Property Law*, 4th edn (Oxford: Oxford University Press, 2014).

➤ P.L. Torremans, *Intellectual Property Law*, 7th edn (Oxford: Oxford University Press, 2013).

➤ W. Cornish, D. Llewelyn, T. Aplin, *Intellectual Property: Patents, Copyright, Trade Marks and Allied Rights*, 8th edn (London: Sweet & Maxwell, 2013).

⌗ RELEVANT WEBLINKS

➤ Office for Harmonisation in the Internal Market: *https://oami.europa.eu* [Accessed May 15, 2015].

➤ UK Intellectual Property Office: *https://www.gov.uk/government/organisations/intellectual-property-office* [Accessed May 15, 2015].

➤ World Intellectual Property Organisation: *http://www.wipo.int* [Accessed May 15, 2015].

Chapter 13   Trusts

JAMES CHALMERS[1]

▶ CHAPTER OVERVIEW

13–01 This chapter is concerned with the law of trusts. It starts by explaining the concept of the trust as it is recognised in Scots law. The chapter goes on to explain how trusts are created and administered, and sets out the duties, powers and potential liabilities of trustees. It then considers how trust purposes may be varied and how trusts may be brought to an end (terminated).

✓ OUTCOMES

13–02 At the end of the chapter, you should be able to explain and apply the following:

- ✓ what a trust is and how one can be created;
- ✓ how trusts are administered;
- ✓ the general duties and powers of trustees;
- ✓ the rule against auctor in rem suam (conflict of interest);
- ✓ the potential liabilities of trustees to beneficiaries and third parties;
- ✓ the rules and procedures for varying trust purposes; and
- ✓ the means by which a trust may be terminated.

THE TRUST CONCEPT

13–03 A trust may be most easily understood as a tripartite relationship, involving three roles:

- the truster (the person who creates the trust and is the owner of the trust property before its creation);
- the trustee (who is the owner of the trust property after the trust is created and is responsible for administering the trust); and
- the beneficiary (the person for whose benefit the trust property is held by the trustee).

---

[1] Regius Professor of Law, University of Glasgow.

In other words, a trust is created when one person (the truster) transfers property to a second person (the trustee) who is then under an obligation to apply the property for the benefit of a third person (the beneficiary).

It is possible for there to be more than one truster, trustee or beneficiary, and it is possible for one person to hold more than one of those roles (except that a sole trustee cannot be a sole beneficiary).

Trust property is owned by the trustee.[2] However, if the trustee becomes insolvent, the trust property is not available to satisfy the claims of his creditors.[3] Nor is it available to satisfy the claims of the truster's creditors. This "insolvency effect" is the most important—and often the most useful—feature of the trust. The trust can *itself* become insolvent and be sequestrated, however.[4]

Consequences of a trust

The trust is a versatile device and its use is not restricted to any one **13–04** particular context. Six useful features of the trust may be noted:

- it can divorce the right to benefit from property from the right of ownership—and the control and administration—of that property;
- it can split the right to benefit from property between two or more individuals;
- it can place restrictions on the right to benefit from trust property, or lay down conditions which must be fulfilled before an individual is entitled to become owner of that property;
- it can be used to postpone a decision on who is to benefit from that property;
- it can be used to place property in the hands of persons who are regarded as more appropriate to administer it than the truster—perhaps because they are better qualified to do so, or are able to devote more time to the role; and
- as noted earlier, trust property is protected from the insolvency of either the truster or the trustee.

Why create a trust?

Trusts may be created for any number of reasons. Some of the more **13–05** common are as follows:

- *Protection of the incompetent or the vulnerable.* A truster may wish to set up a trust for a beneficiary who is legally incapable of managing property, or whom the truster believes would not manage the property sensibly.
- *Trusts for the benefit of the public.* A truster may set up a trust fund to be applied to specified public purposes.

---

[2] See *Sharp v Thomson*, 1995 S.C. 455, per the Lord President (Hope) at 474–475.
[3] *Heritable Reversionary Co Ltd v Millar* (1892) 19 R. (H.L.) 43.
[4] *Bain, Petitioner* (1901) 9 S.L.T. 14.

- *Collective investment purposes.* Trusts provide a convenient means of administering collective investment schemes (such as pension funds), which allow for professional management and diversification of investment to a degree which would not normally be available to individual investors.
- *Tax efficiency.* Manipulation of ownership and control by means of the trust device may be used by a truster in order to minimise liability to taxation.

Classifications of trusts

13–06 Trusts are frequently classified in various ways. The following are the two most important classifications:

Public and private trusts

13–07 Public trusts are those set up for the benefit of the public in general, or a specified class of the public. Private trusts are those set up for a specified individual or group of individuals.[5] The most important consequence of this distinction is the procedure for varying trust purposes, as the relevant law differs for the two types of trust.[6]

Inter vivos and mortis causa trusts

13–08 An *inter vivos* trust takes effect during the truster's lifetime; a *mortis causa* (or "testamentary") trust takes effect on the truster's death.

Key Concepts

A **trust** is created when one person (the truster) transfers property to a second person (the trustee) who is then under an obligation to apply the property for the benefit of a third person (the beneficiary).

It is possible for there to be more than one truster, trustee or beneficiary.

The trustee is the owner of trust property.

Trust property is protected from the insolvency of either the truster or the trustee.

Trusts may be either **private trusts** (for the benefit of individuals or a specified group of individuals) or **public trusts** (for the benefit of the general public or a specified class of the public).

Trusts may be also be either *inter vivos* (taking effect during the truster's lifetime) or *mortis causa* (taking effect on the death of the truster).

---

[5] K.McK. Norrie and E.M. Scobbie, *Trusts* (Edinburgh: W. Green, 1991), pp.17–18.
[6] See below, paras 13–54—13–59.

CREATION OF A TRUST

The law does not place any specific restrictions on the type of person who **13–09** may create a trust. The general rules of legal capacity apply, and therefore children under 16—who normally have no legal capacity to enter into any transaction—cannot normally be trusters.[7] Nor are there any legal restrictions on the type of property which can be subject to a trust.

Trusts may be divided into two types—those created voluntarily and those created by legal implication. There are different rules governing the creation of each type of trust.

How to create a trust: voluntarily created trusts

Two requirements must be satisfied for the creation of a voluntary trust. **13–10** There must be: (a) a declaration of trust; and (b) a transfer of property from the truster to the trustee.

Declaration of trust

In order to create a trust, A must transfer property to B accompanied by **13–11** a declaration that B is to apply the property for specified purposes.

The crucial question is this. Did A: (i) intend to make an outright gift of the property to B coupled with a recommendation as to how the property should be applied, but ultimately leaving it up to B as to what he chose to do with the property—in which case no trust is created?; or, did A (ii) intend to bind B to apply the property to specified purposes, thus creating a trust?

For example, in one case a woman left money in her will "to Katherine Alexandrina Macpherson, for the benefit of herself and her sister Jane Macpherson". The court held that this was a trust and that Katherine had to administer the money as a trust for herself and Jane (who was mentally incapable).[8] One judge remarked that no "special or technical" form of words was required to create a trust.[9]

The declaration may be verbal—except in the following three cases, where a written document subscribed by the truster is required[10]:

- a trust whereby a person declares himself to be sole trustee of his own property or any property which he may require;
- a trust of an interest in land (except where created by court decree, statute or rule of law); and
- a *mortis causa* trust (i.e. one created by a will).

---

[7] Age of Legal Capacity (Scotland) Act 1991 ss.1(1)(a) and 2(1).
[8] *Macpherson v Macpherson's CB* (1894) 21 R. 386.
[9] *Macpherson v Macpherson's CB* (1894) 21 R. 386, per Lord McLaren at 387.
[10] See Requirements of Writing (Scotland) Act 1995 s.2.

Transfer of property

13–12 A trust will not be effective until the trust property is transferred to the trustee. The requirement of a transfer of property is necessary to prevent fraudulent misuse of the trust device:

> **Allan's Trustees v Inland Revenue**
> 1971 S.L.T. 62
>
> Lord Reid: "I reject the argument that a mere proved intention to make a trust coupled with the execution of a declaration of trust can suffice. If that were so it would be easy to execute such a declaration, keep it in reserve, use it in case of bankruptcy to defeat the claims of creditors, but if all went well and the trustee desired to regain control of the fund simply suppress the declaration of trust."

Problem of the truster as trustee

13–13 It is possible for a truster to declare himself to be sole trustee of his own property. In such a case, it is impossible to transfer property from the truster and the trustee. The recognised alternative is intimation to the beneficiaries (or their representatives) of their rights under the trust.[11]

The intimation must take place simultaneously with, or subsequent to, the execution of the declaration of trust.[12] If it takes place before the declaration of trust, it is merely an expression of an intention to create a trust and is not legally effective. Furthermore, a declaration of trust cannot be made unless there is actually a trust fund in existence. In other words, a person cannot declare themselves trustee of property they intend to acquire in the future.[13]

Validity of the trust purposes

13–14 The declaration of trust must specify the purposes of the trust in order to be effective. Trust purposes may be invalid for three reasons. First, they may be void from uncertainty. Secondly, they may be overly wide and therefore ineffective. Thirdly, they may be illegal.

Purposes void from uncertainty

13–15 Purposes will be void from uncertainty if it is impossible to establish their meaning. For example, in one case the purpose of establishing "a shop in which one of the objects is the sale of books dealing with the subject of free thought" was held to be too vague, because the term "free thought" had no "recognised or determinate meaning".[14]

---

[11] *Allan's Trustees v Inland Revenue*, 1971 S.L.T. 62.
[12] *Kerr's Trustees v Inland Revenue*, 1974 S.L.T. 193.
[13] *Clark Taylor & Co Ltd v Quality Site Development (Edinburgh) Ltd*, 1981 S.C. 111.
[14] *Hardie v Morison* (1899) 7 S.L.T. 42.

Overly wide purposes

It is not essential for a truster to specify down to the last detail how his **13–16**
trustees should distribute or apply his property. He can choose a "particular class" of individuals or purposes and give his trustees discretion to
select between them.[15]

Two things are required for this to work. First, there must be a
selection of a "particular individual" (or individuals) as trustee(s). Secondly, the truster must select a "particular class" of individuals and
objects.

The selection of a "particular individual" may be problematic in *mortis
causa* trusts (those created by a will). In such cases, the trustees named in
the testator's will may have died before the testator or may decline
office—or the testator may simply fail to name an executor in his will. In
such cases, although a person can be appointed to administer the estate
for other purposes, the trust purposes will be invalid as being overly wide,
and the trust will fail.[16]

Secondly, the "particular class", which should not be so wide as to
prevent a reasonable man from knowing who the truster meant to benefit,
must be specified by the trustee. It is not enough for a testator to say, for
example, that his property should be disposed of "in such way or ways as
my trustees shall deem best".[17]

Illegal purposes

There are four types of purpose which will be held invalid due to illeg- **13–17**
ality, which are as follows[18]:

- criminal purposes;
- directly prohibited purposes;
- purposes which are *contra bonos mores*; and
- purposes which are contrary to public policy.

Each of these will be dealt with in turn.

(i) Criminal purposes

There is an almost total absence of authority on this issue, and it is **13–18**
doubtful that it is of much practical importance. It is clear, however, that
a trust for criminal purposes is void.[19]

(ii) Directly prohibited purposes

There are three forms of trust purpose which are directly prohibited by **13–19**
statute, as follows:

---

[15] See *Crichton v Grierson* (1828) 3 W. & S. 329.
[16] *Angus's Executrix v Batchan's Trustees*, 1949 S.C. 335.
[17] *Allan (Shaw's Trustees)* (1893) 1 S.L.T. 308.
[18] *Bowman v Secular Society Ltd* [1917] A.C. 406, per Lord Dunedin at 434.
[19] This was accepted in *Bowman v Secular Society Ltd* [1917] A.C. 406.

(a) *Entails.* An entail is a device which was historically used to keep heritable property in the same family indefinitely. The owner would normally be obliged to pass the property to his eldest son on his death, and the son on to his eldest son, and so on. It has not been possible to create entails since 1914,[20] and any entails which continued to exist until recently were finally brought to an end by the Abolition of Feudal Tenure etc. (Scotland) Act 2000.[21]

(b) *Successive liferents.* Successive liferents are similar to entails but can be used in relation to moveable property. A truster might, for example, direct that the trustee is to receive a liferent of the property and hold the fee in trust for his (the trustee's) eldest son, who is then to receive a liferent of the property and hold the fee in trust for his eldest son, and so on. While successive liferents can still be created, their duration can no longer be indefinite thanks to statutory restrictions.[22]

(c) *Excessive accumulations of income.* A truster may not create a trust where the trust income is simply added to the trust fund and not spent for longer than certain periods of time. The applicable period of time is generally 21 years, but there are a number of other possibilities depending on the applicability of certain rather complex statutory provisions.[23]

(iii) Purposes which are contra bonos mores

13–20 Trust purposes may be invalid as being *contra bonos mores* (an "offence against what may be termed the natural moral sense"[24]). This head of invalidity has most commonly been used to hold that conditions attached to bequests in wills are invalid. The cases may be divided into three categories, as follows:

(a) *Conditions relating to living arrangements.* In *Fraser v Rose,*[25] a testator left money to his (adult) daughter on the condition that she should leave her mother within four weeks of his death and never live with her again. It was held that the condition was invalid.

(b) *Conditions relating to marriage.* A condition that a person may only take a benefit under a trust if they remain unmarried is generally thought to be invalid.[26] However, it is competent to

---

[20] Entail (Scotland) Act 1914.
[21] Abolition of Feudal Tenure etc. (Scotland) Act 2000 ss.50–52.
[22] For the relevant rules, see the Law Reform (Miscellaneous Provisions) (Scotland) Act 1968 s.18.
[23] Trusts (Scotland) Act 1961 s.5 and the Law Reform (Miscellaneous Provisions) (Scotland) Act 1966 s.6.
[24] *Bowman v Secular Society Ltd* [1917] A.C. 406, per Lord Dunedin at 434.
[25] (1849) 11 D. 1466. See also *Grant's Trustees v Grant* (1898) 25 R. 929.
[26] *Aird's Executors v Aird*, 1949 S.C. 154.

establish a trust to provide financial support for a person for as long as they remain unmarried.[27]

(c) *Conditions relating to religion.* Although there has been some debate on the point, a truster may provide that a person may only benefit under a trust if he adheres (or refrains from adhering) to a particular religion.[28]

Where a condition is held invalid, the beneficiary will normally take the benefit without being required to comply with the condition.

(iv) Purposes which are contrary to public policy

The term "public policy" refers here to a very narrow doctrine, which is **13–21** that if trust purposes "are unreasonable as conferring neither a patrimonial benefit upon anybody nor a benefit upon the public or any section thereof, the directions are invalid".[29]

McCaig's Trustees v Kirk-Session of United Free Church of Lismore
1915 S.C. 426

In her will, Catherine McCaig directed that her trustees should convert the McCaig Tower in Oban into a private enclosure, and should, within the tower, erect bronze statues of members of her family, each of which was to cost not less than £1,000. The trustees were to be bound for all time coming not to sell the tower and statues. It was held that these purposes were invalid as conferring no benefit on any person: the incidental benefit which might be received by workmen in constructing the enclosure was insufficient.

There are two exceptional cases, however, where trust purposes may be valid despite the fact that they do not confer any benefit upon particular individuals or the general public. These are trusts for memorials,[30] and trusts for the maintenance of particular animals.[31] Trusts for the benefit of a class of animals or the prevention of cruelty to animals are regarded as conferring a benefit upon the general public.[32]

---

[27] See, e.g. *Sturrock v Rankin's Trustees* (1875) 2 R. 850.
[28] *Blathwayt v Baron Cawley* [1976] A.C. 397.
[29] *Aitken's Trustees v Aitken*, 1927 S.C. 374, per Lord Sands at 381.
[30] *Lindsay's Executor v Forsyth*, 1940 S.C. 568, per the Lord Justice-Clerk (Aitchison) at 572.
[31] See, e.g. *Flockhart's Trustees v Bourlet*, 1934 S.N. 23.
[32] *Aitken's Trustees v Aitken*, 1927 S.C. 374, per Lord Sands at 381.

How to create a trust: legally implied trusts

Resulting trusts

13–22 A resulting trust will arise where the purposes of an existing trust fail to dispose of all the trust property. In such a case, the trustees will hold the trust property in a resulting trust for the benefit of the truster or his representatives.

A resulting trust may arise in two principal types of case. First, the trust purposes may be void or impossible to fulfil.[33] Secondly, the trust purposes may not exhaust the full trust estate, as in *Anderson v Smoke*[34] where a trust was created for the benefit of Mr Anderson's son, who died before the fund had been spent.

Constructive trusts

13–23 Scots law only recognises "constructive trusts" to a very limited extent. It is commonly thought that such trusts will be created in two situations[35]:

(a) *Where a person in a fiduciary position gains an advantage by virtue of that position.* That is, a trustee who in some way profits from his position will be obliged to return any benefit obtained to the trust.[36]

(b) *Where a person who is a stranger to an existing trust is to his knowledge in possession of property belonging to the trust.*[37]

Key Concepts

There are no specific restrictions on the persons who may create a trust or the type of property which may be subject to a trust. The general rules of property and legal capacity apply.

A **voluntarily created trust** is created by: (a) a **declaration of trust;** accompanied by (b) a **transfer of property** from the truster to the trustee.

Where the truster and the trustee are the same person, there can be no transfer of property. In such cases, **intimation to the beneficiaries** of their rights under the trust is required for the creation of the trust.

Trust purposes may be **invalid** for the following reasons:

---

[33] See, e.g. *Templeton v Burgh of Ayr*, 1910 2 S.L.T. 12.

[34] *Anderson v Smoke* (1898) 25 R. 493.

[35] See W.A. Wilson and A.G.M. Duncan, *Trusts, Trustees and Executors*, 2nd edn (Edinburgh: W. Green, 1995), para.6–61. This is the orthodox view, but there is considerable debate as to whether "constructive trusts" really exist in Scots law at all: see G.L. Gretton, "Constructive Trusts" (1997) 1 Edin. L.R. 281.

[36] See, e.g. *Cherry's Trustees v Patrick*, 1911 2 S.L.T. 313.

[37] One case is *Huisman v Soepboer*, 1994 S.L.T. 682.

- they may be too uncertain (i.e. the truster's meaning cannot be ascertained);
- they may be overly wide;
- they may be illegal as being:
  - —contrary to the criminal law;
  - —directly prohibited (entails, accumulations of income and successive liferents);
  - —*contra bonos mores* (an offence against the "natural moral sense"); or
  - —contrary to public policy (if they confer no benefit upon any person).

A **resulting trust** is a type of legally implied trust. It will arise where the purposes of an existing trust fail to dispose of all the trust property. In such a case, the trustees will hold the remaining property in trust for the original truster or his representatives.

A **constructive trust** will be created where:

- a person in a fiduciary position gains an advantage by virtue of that position; or
- a person who is a stranger to a trust is to his knowledge in possession of property belonging to the trust.

In such cases, the constructive trustee will be required to communicate the relevant property to the trust estate.

OFFICE OF TRUSTEE

Who can be a trustee?

The law does not generally place any specific restrictions on the type of **13–24** person who may act as trustees. The general rules of legal capacity apply and, therefore, children under 16—who, as noted earlier, normally have no legal capacity to enter into any transaction—cannot normally be trustees.[38] Bankruptcy or insolvency is not normally a barrier. There are, however, specific statutory restrictions regarding certain types of trust, particularly charitable trusts.[39]

---

[38] Age of Legal Capacity (Scotland) Act 1991 s.9(f).
[39] Charities and Trustee Investment (Scotland) Act 2005 s.69. See also Pensions Act 1995 ss.3–6 and 29–30 (pension trusts); Finance Act 1989 Sch.5 para.3(3)(c) (employee share ownership trusts) and the Inheritance Tax Act 1984 Sch.4 para.2(b).

Appointment, assumption, acceptance and resignation of trustees

13–25 Trustees will generally be appointed in the trust deed. They may be named as individuals, or identified *ex officio* (as the holder of an office). Essentially, any description which is sufficient to identify the relevant individual is enough.[40]

The trustee must accept office. No trustee can be forced to accept office against his will.[41] Acceptance need not necessarily be express but can be inferred from actions.[42]

Trustees always have a power to assume additional trustees unless this is excluded by the terms of the trust deed.[43]

The court has a statutory power to appoint trustees where there is no power to assume additional trustees under the trust deed, or where a sole trustee is or has become insane or incapable, or has been absent from the UK for six months or has disappeared for that period.[44] The court may also appoint new trustees at common law in exceptional cases. This power has been used where two trustees were unable to work together and the appointment of a third was required to resolve the deadlock.[45]

Trustees normally have a power to resign office unless the trust deed provides otherwise,[46] although a sole trustee is not entitled to resign unless new trustees are appointed.[47]

Removal and death of trustees

13–26 The court has a statutory power to remove a trustee who is insane: "incapable of acting by reason of physical or mental disability"; has been absent from the UK continuously for at least six months; or who has disappeared for at least six months.[48] The court also has a common law power to remove a trustee for misconduct in office,[49] but this will only be exercised in exceptional circumstances.[50] Where one of several trustees dies, his share in the trust property passes automatically to the other trustees.[51] The position is more complex where a sole trustee dies. In such cases, the title remains with the sole trustee "and has to be taken out of him by process of conveyancing".[52]

---

[40] See, e.g. *Martin v Ferguson's Trustees* (1892) 19 R. 474.
[41] *Vestry of St Silas Church v Trustees of St Silas Church*, 1945 S.C. 110, per the Lord Justice-Clerk (Cooper) at 121.
[42] *Ker v City of Glasgow Bank* (1879) 6 R. (H.L.) 52.
[43] Trusts (Scotland) Act 1921 s.3.
[44] Trusts (Scotland) Act 1921 s.22.
[45] *Aikman, Petitioner* (1881) 9 R. 213; *Taylor, Petitioner*, 1932 S.C. 1.
[46] Trusts (Scotland) Act 1921 s.3(a).
[47] Trusts (Scotland) Act 1921 s.3.
[48] Trusts (Scotland) Act 1921 s.23.
[49] *Stewart v Chalmers* (1904) 7 F. 163.
[50] *Earl of Cawdor, Petitioner*, 2006 S.L.T. 1070.
[51] *Gordon's Trustees v Eglinton* (1851) 13 D. 1381.
[52] A.J.P. Menzies, *The Law of Scotland Affecting Trustees*, 2nd edn (Edinburgh: W. Green, 1913), Vol.1 para.153.

Key Concepts

Trustees may be **appointed** by any description which is sufficient to identify the relevant individual. They must **accept** office; they cannot be forced to do so. Acceptance may be either express or implied.

Trustees always have the power to **assume additional trustees** unless this is excluded by the terms of the trust deed. The court has the power to **appoint additional trustees** in certain cases.

Trustees always have a power to **resign office** unless the trust deed provides otherwise.

The court has the power to **remove** trustees who are insane, incapable, have been absent from the UK or who have disappeared for at least six months, or who have been guilty of misconduct in office.

DECISION-MAKING BY TRUSTEES

As a general rule, trust decisions may validly be made by a majority of **13–27** trustees.[53]

Importance of a quorum

A "quorum" is the minimum number of trustees who must participate in **13–28** trust decision-making for any decisions taken to be valid. Unless the trust deed provides otherwise, the quorum is a "majority of the trustees accepting and surviving".[54]

All trustees have a right to be consulted in trust decision-making. A failure to consult a trustee will render a decision taken by the remaining trustees void.[55] Third parties are, however, protected in such a situation by two factors: (a) the personal liability of trustees who make contracts on behalf of the trust[56]; and (b) s.7 of the Trusts (Scotland) Act 1921 ("the 1921 Act"), which states that a deed which bears to be granted by trustees but is "in fact executed by a quorum of such trustees in favour of any person other than a beneficiary or co-trustee" shall not normally be challengeable for lack of consultation or other irregularity of procedure.

---

[53] *McCulloch v Wallace* (1846) 9 D. 32. One-half of the body of trustees is insufficient: *Neilson v Mossend Iron Co* (1885) 12 R. 499.

[54] Trusts (Scotland) Act 1921 s.3(c).

[55] *Wyse v Abbott* (1881) 8 R. 983.

[56] See below, para.13–52.

Can the courts interfere in the trustees' exercise of discretion?

13–29 The courts will not normally interfere with decisions taken by trustees except in very limited circumstances, such as where trustees considered the wrong question or acted in bad faith.[57] Trustees are not obliged to give reasons for their decisions.[58]

Key Concepts

Trust decisions may validly be made by a **majority** of trustees.

A **quorum** is a majority of the trustees unless the trust deed provides otherwise. This is the minimum number of trustees who must participate in decision-making for any decisions taken to be valid.

All trustees have a **right to be consulted** in trust decision-making.

The courts will not **interfere with decisions taken by trustees** unless it can be shown that they have considered the wrong question or have acted in bad faith.

Duties of a Trustee

General duty of care

13–30 Trustees must, in all cases, exercise due care in their dealings with the trust estate. The standard of care required is that of the "ordinary prudent man".[59] A trustee who fails to live up to this standard will be liable for any loss caused thereby even if he has acted in good faith and to the best of his abilities.

Duty not to delegate the trust

13–31 Trustees must take responsibility for trust decision-making themselves and cannot delegate this responsibility to a third party.[60] They are, however, entitled to employ agents when a person of reasonable prudence would do so.[61]

Duty to secure trust property

13–32 A trustee is responsible for ingathering and securing trust property.[62]

---

[57] *Dundee General Hospital Board of Management v Bell's Trustees*, 1952 S.C. (H.L.) 78.
[58] *Scott v National Trust* [1998] 2 All E.R. 705.
[59] *Raes v Meek* (1889) 16 R. (H.L.) 31.
[60] *Scott v Occidental Petroleum (Caledonia) Ltd*, 1990 S.L.T. 882.
[61] *Hay v Binny* (1861) 23 D. 594. See also Trusts (Scotland) Act 1921 s.4(1)(f).
[62] *Forman v Burns* (1853) 15 D. 362.

Investment duties

When trustees hold the trust estate for any period of time, they must **13–33** consider investing the estate to protect its value.

> ### Melville v Noble's Trustees
> ### (1896) 24 R. 243
>
> Trustees left a substantial trust fund on deposit-receipt with a bank for 19 years without considering the question of investment. If it had been invested properly, a return of 3 per cent per annum could have been received. It was held that they were liable to make up this 3 per cent return personally.

Trustee investment was until recently subject to restrictive statutory rules. Trustees now have a general power to "make any kind of investment of the trust estate".[63] They must consider whether the investment is a suitable one and consider the need for diversification of the trust investments. They must also obtain and consider proper advice, except where they reasonably consider that such advice is unnecessary or inappropriate.[64]

The problem of "ethical" investment

In taking investment decisions, trustees must act in the best interests of **13–34** the trust beneficiaries. They are not entitled to disregard those interests in favour of other considerations, as the following case demonstrates:

> ### Cowan v Scargill
> ### [1985] Ch. 270
>
> A mineworkers' pension scheme was established under statute. There were 10 trustees, five of whom were appointed by the National Union of Mineworkers ("NUM"). The NUM trustees objected to the investment plan on the basis that it involved investment overseas and investment in energies in competition with coal, both of which conflicted with NUM policy. The other trustees sought a declaration that the NUM trustees were in breach of their duties as trustees by demanding that investment decisions be made in accordance with NUM policy. The declaration was granted.

---

[63] Trusts (Scotland) Act 1921 s.4(1)(ea), as inserted by the Charities and Trustee Investment (Scotland) Act 2005 s.93(2).

[64] Trusts (Scotland) Act 1921 s.4A, as inserted by the Charities and Trustee Investment (Scotland) Act 2005 s.94. There is also a common law duty to take advice: see below, para.13–35.

This decision does not necessarily prevent trustees from taking into account what might be termed "ethical" considerations in making investment decisions. If two investments are equally attractive, there is nothing to stop trustees choosing the one which they consider to be most "ethical".[65] But what they cannot do is choose a *less* attractive investment on the basis of "ethical" factors.

Duty to take advice

13–35 It was noted earlier that trustees must administer the trust-estate to the standard that a man of ordinary prudence would exercise in the management of his own affairs. The man of ordinary prudence, of course, recognises that he is not an expert in all matters and must seek professional advice in appropriate cases. A failure to seek such advice may leave the decision open to challenge.[66]

Duties regarding existing debts and obligations

13–36 While it is unusual for an *inter vivos* trust to have existing debts and obligations, these will exist as a matter of course in *mortis causa* trusts. In such cases, trustees are required to pay off the debts of the deceased, but are not personally liable for those debts.[67]

Duties regarding new debts and obligations

13–37 In most cases, in order to discharge their duties, trustees will have to enter into contracts with third parties. The general rule is that they incur personal liability in respect of any such contracts, unless they explicitly contract out of such liability.[68] They are, of course, entitled to be reimbursed from the trust-estate.[69]

Duty to keep accounts

13–38 Trustees must keep accounts which detail their dealings with the trust estate.[70] A beneficiary has a right to see the trust accounts and supporting documentation.[71] Exceptionally, the truster may be regarded as having excluded any duty to keep accounts.[72]

---

[65] See *Harries v Church Commissioners for England* [1992] 1 W.L.R. 1241, per Nicholls V.C. at 1247–1248.

[66] *Martin v City of Edinburgh District Council*, 1988 S.L.T. 329.

[67] Bankruptcy (Scotland) Act 1985 s.5.

[68] See below, para.13–52.

[69] See below, para.13–41.

[70] *Ross v Ross* (1896) 23 R. (H.L.) 67.

[71] *Murray v Cameron*, 1969 S.L.T. (Notes) 76; *Nouillan v Nouillan's Executors*, 1991 S.L.T. 270.

[72] *Leitch v Leitch*, 1927 S.C. 823.

Duty to pay the correct beneficiaries

A trustee must pay out funds to the correct beneficiaries. If a trustee pays **13–39** out funds to the wrong beneficiaries, he is obliged to make payment to the correct beneficiary out of his own funds.

Key Concepts

Trustees have the following duties:

- The duty to **exercise due care** in their dealings with the trust estate. The standard of care required is that of the "ordinary prudent man".
- The duty **not to delegate the trust** and to take responsibility for trust decision-making themselves.
- The duty to **secure trust property**.
- The duty to **invest the trust estate** if they hold it for any period of time.
- The duty to **take advice** where it is prudent to do so, particularly in relation to investment matters.
- The duty to **meet trust debts and obligations**.
- The duty to **keep accounts**.
- The duty to **pay the correct beneficiaries**.

RULE AGAINST AUCTOR IN REM SUAM

Auctor in rem suam may be translated as "actor in his own cause". This **13–40** rule prohibits a trustee from placing himself in a position where his position as trustee conflicts with his interests as an individual.

If a trustee enters into a transaction in breach of the rule, the transaction is voidable regardless of whether he was acting in good faith or whether or not the transaction was a fair one.[73] If he profits from a breach of the rule, he must hand over those profits to the trust-estate regardless of whether the trust-estate has in fact suffered any loss.[74]

The rule has three main consequences:

- Trustees may not enter into transactions with the trust estate.[75]
- Trustees may not use their position to obtain a personal advantage (e.g. if a trustee is given a discretion, he may not exercise it in his favour).[76]
- Trustees may not charge fees for work done for the trust.[77]

---

[73] *Aberdeen Railway Co v Blaikie Bros* (1854) 1 Macq. 461.
[74] *Hamilton v Wright* (1842) 1 Bell 574.
[75] *University of Aberdeen v Town Council of Aberdeen* (1876) 3 R. 1087.
[76] *Inglis v Inglis*, 1983 S.C. 8.
[77] *Home v Pringle* (1841) 2 Rob. 384.

A trustee may, however, be *auctor in rem suam* where this is permitted by the trust deed. The sanction should normally be express, but may be implied.[78] A trustee may also be *auctor in rem suam* if this is permitted by the beneficiaries.[79]

Key Concepts

A trustee may not be *auctor in rem suam*. This means that he may not place himself in a position where his interests as trustee conflicts with his interests as an individual.

The rule has three main consequences:

● trustees may not enter into transactions with the trust estate;
● trustees may not use their position to obtain a personal advantage; and
● trustees may not charge fees for work done for the trust.

A trustee may, however, be *auctor in rem suam* if this is **sanctioned** in the trust deed or by the beneficiaries.

TRUSTEE'S RIGHT TO REIMBURSEMENT

13–41 Trustees are entitled to be reimbursed for monies legitimately spent on trust business. They can, of course, apply the trust funds directly to payments which are necessary for the trust—they are not required to pay such expenses themselves and claim reimbursement later.[80]

Key Concept

A trustee is entitled to be **reimbursed** for any expenses properly incurred in administering the trust.

POWERS OF A TRUSTEE

13–42 Trustees may not do any act in furtherance of the trust purposes unless they have the power to perform such an act (e.g. a power to sell the trust estate; a power to pay debts, etc.) Trustees' powers may be divided into three categories, as follows:

● powers granted in the trust deed;
● powers conferred by statutory provisions; and

---

[78] *Sarris v Clark*, 1995 S.L.T. 44.
[79] *Bruckner v Jopp's Trustees* (1887) 14 R. 1006.
[80] *Cunningham v Montgomerie* (1879) 6 R. 1333.

- common law powers which may be granted upon an application to the court.

The trust deed must be examined in all instances to establish any other powers it confers upon trustees (and also whether it excludes any of the powers which are otherwise conferred by s.4 of the 1921 Act).

Powers conferred by statutory provisions

Section 4 of the 1921 Act, as amended by later legislation, contains a list **13–43** of general powers which all trustees have unless to so act would be "at variance with the terms or purposes of the trust". The principal powers conferred by this section are as follows:

- to sell the trust estate or any part thereof;
- to grant leases of the trust estate or any part thereof;
- to acquire or invest in heritable property;
- to appoint factors and law agents and pay them suitable remuneration;
- to uplift, discharge or assign debts due to the trust estate;
- to grant all deeds necessary for carrying into effect the powers vested in the trustees; and
- to pay trust debts without requiring the creditors to constitute such debts.

Trustees may, of course, only exercise these powers if to do so would further the purposes of the trust.

Occasionally, some of these powers may be specifically excluded by the trust deed. In such cases, the trustees may petition the court under s.5 of the 1921 Act for power to do the relevant act. The court may grant the power if it is "satisfied that such act is in all the circumstances expedient for the execution of the trust".[81]

Common law powers with court application

Aside from s.5 of the 1921 Act, the court cannot normally grant addi- **13–44** tional powers to trustees.[82] In exceptional cases, however, where it would be impossible to fulfil the trust purposes without additional powers being granted, the court may be able to intervene.[83]

---

[81] For an example, see *Tods Trustees, Petitioners*, 1999 S.L.T. 308.
[82] *Scott's Hospital Trustees*, 1913 S.C. 289, per the Lord Justice Clerk (Macdonald) at 290–291.
[83] *Anderson's Trustees*, 1921 S.C. 315.

Key Concepts

The trust deed is the principal source of trustees' powers, although **there are a number of powers which are conferred by statute upon all trustees** unless they are "at variance with the terms or purposes of the trust". The principal statutory powers are as follows:

- to sell the trust estate or any part thereof;
- to grant leases of the trust estate or any part thereof;
- to acquire with trust funds any interest in residential accommodation "reasonably required to enable the trustees to provide a suitable residence for occupation by any of the beneficiaries";
- to appoint factors and law agents and pay them suitable remuneration;
- to uplift, discharge or assign debts due to the trust estate;
- to grant all deeds necessary for carrying into effect the powers vested in the trustees; and
- to pay trust debts without requiring the creditors to constitute such debts.

If one of these powers is excluded by the trust deed, the trustees may **petition the court** for authority to exercise it.

LIABILITIES OF A TRUSTEE

Liability to beneficiaries

13–45 Where a trustee has committed or appears likely to commit a breach of trust, various remedies may be open to the beneficiary. The principal remedies for breach of trust are as follows:

(a) Interdict

13–46 Where a trustee proposes to do something which a beneficiary believes to be a breach of trust, the beneficiary is entitled to seek an interdict. An interdict is a court order prohibiting a person from doing a specified act. If the breach of trust has already taken place, interdict is useless and will not be granted.

(b) Damages

13–47 Where a breach of trust has caused a loss to the trust estate, a beneficiary may take a court action to require the offending trustee to make up the loss in damages. It is a defence for the trustee(s) to show that the loss would have occurred even if the breach had not taken place.[84]

---

[84] See, e.g. *Millar's Trustees v Polson* (1897) 24 R. 1038.

(c) Accounting (count, reckoning and payment)

A beneficiary may also bring an action of "count, reckoning and pay- **13–48** ment" (commonly referred to as an action for accounting), calling upon the trustee to produce trust accounts and to make up any shortfall.[85] This should generally have the same practical result as an action for damages, but it may provide a means of ascertaining the amount of any loss where this cannot be otherwise done.

Protecting trustees from liability

Trustees may receive some protection from liability for breach of trust **13–49** through an immunity clause in the trust deed or under statute, as follows.

(a) Immunity clauses

An attempt is sometimes made to protect trustees from liability for **13–50** breach of trust by inserting an immunity clause into the trust deed stating that they will not be liable for errors or neglect of management. It is thought that such clauses will protect trustees from liability for negligence, but not from liability from gross negligence.[86]

(b) Statutory protections

There are two principal statutory protections from liability under the **13–51** 1921 Act.

>   (i) **Trustees who have acted "honestly and reasonably".** Section 32 of the 1921 Act gives the court a discretion to relieve a trustee from personal liability for a breach of trust if he "has acted honestly and reasonably" and "ought fairly to be excused". Where a trustee has acted honestly and reasonably, it will normally be assumed that it is fair to grant relief.[87]
>   (ii) **Trustees who have committed a breach of trust with the beneficiary's consent.** Under s.31 of the 1921 Act, if a trustee has committed a breach of trust at the instigation or request or with the written consent of a beneficiary, the court is entitled to apply or of any part of that beneficiary's interest in the trust estate to indemnify the trustee. For s.31 to operate, the beneficiary must have been aware of the facts which made the proposed action a breach of trust.[88]

---

[85] On the duty to keep accounts, see above, para.13–38.
[86] *Lutea Trustees Ltd v Orbis Trustees Guernsey Ltd*, 1997 S.C.L.R. 735.
[87] *Perrins v Bellamy* [1898] 2 Ch. 521, per Kekewich J. at 528.
[88] See *Cathcart's Trustees v Cathcart* (1907) 15 S.L.T. 646; *Henderson v Henderson's Trustees* (1900) 2 F. 1295.

Liability to third parties

13–52 Trustees will commonly, in order to discharge their responsibilities as trustees, enter into contracts with third parties. As a general rule, they are personally liable on such contracts unless there is an agreement to exclude such liability.[89] Where a person signs a contract "as trustee", this will generally be taken as indicating such an agreement.[90] The mere use of the word "trustee" is not sufficient, as this may be intended only to describe or identify the signatory.[91] Personal liability is generally only of importance if the trust fund is or becomes insolvent.

Third parties who acquire trust property

13–53 Where a trustee, acting in breach of trust, sells trust property to a third party, that third party will acquire a good title to the property provided that he purchased the property in good faith and for value.[92]

Key Concepts

Where a trustee has committed or appears likely to commit a breach of trust, the following remedies may be open to the beneficiaries:

- interdict (a court order preventing the trustee from doing a particular act);
- an action for damages; and
- an action for accounting (a combination of an action to produce accounts and for payment of any shortfall in the trust funds).

Trustees may be protected from liability by **immunity clauses** in the trust deed providing that they are not to be liable for negligence.

Trustees who commit a breach of trust but who have acted **honestly and reasonably** may apply to the court to be relieved from the consequences of their breach of trust.

Trustees who commit a breach of trust at the request of or with the consent of a beneficiary may apply to the court to be **indemnified** by that beneficiary's interest in the trust estate.

Trustees will be **personally liable to third parties** on contracts which they make on behalf of the trust unless they have contracted out of such liability.

Third parties who acquire trust property **in good faith and for value** will receive a good title to the property even if the trustee was acting in breach of trust.

---

[89] *Brown v Sutherland* (1875) 2 R. 615.
[90] *Gordon v Campbell* (1842) 1 Bell App 428.
[91] *Thomson v McLachlan's Trustees* (1829) 7 S. 787; *Lumsden v Buchanan* (1865) 3 M. (H.L.) 89.
[92] Hume, *Lectures* (1821–1822) in G.C.H. Paton (ed.) Vol.17, *Stair Society*, 1952), Vol. IV, 315; Trusts (Scotland) Act 1961 s.2.

VARIATION OF TRUST PURPOSES

A trust, by its very nature, severely limits the manner in which the **13–54** property that is subject to it may be held and applied. Circumstances change, and what appears appropriate when the trust is established may cease to be appropriate with the passage of time. The scope which exists for varying the terms of the trust differs according to whether the trust is private or public.[93]

Private trusts

At common law, variation of the terms of a private trust is competent if **13–55** all the beneficiaries consented to the variation. However, not all the beneficiaries may be capable of consenting. For example, the beneficiaries may include children, or the trust deed may even make provision for persons who have not yet been born (and who may never be).

The matter is now dealt with by the Trusts (Scotland) Act 1961. Section 1 of the Trusts (Scotland) Act 1961 enables the court to give consent to a variation on behalf of:

> (a) any person who is incapable of consenting by reason of non-age or other disability;
> (b) any person who is not currently a beneficiary but may become one on the happening of a future event or on a particular date, unless that person is currently ascertained and is capable of assenting; or
> (c) any unborn person.

The court is not entitled to approve the arrangement on behalf of any person "unless it is of the opinion that the carrying out thereof would not be prejudicial to that person".[94]

The court is not obliged to grant approval simply because a proposed variation is shown not to be prejudicial.[95] The court has a discretion and will take into account all relevant circumstances including the relative benefits which the various parties would gain from the variation.[96]

Public trusts

There are two mechanisms available for varying the terms of a public **13–56** trust. These are, first, the common law "cy-prés" jurisdiction, and secondly, variation under s.9(1) of the Law Reform (Miscellaneous Provisions) (Scotland) Act 1990. Variation under the 1990 Act is only possible where the trust has already taken effect in some form. It is not permitted where it is impossible to give any effect to the terms of the trust. Cy-prés

---

[93] On this distinction generally, see above, para.13–07.
[94] Trusts (Scotland) Act 1961 s.1(1). For an application of this rule, see *Pollok-Morris, Petitioners*, 1969 S.L.T. (Notes) 60.
[95] *Lobnitz, Petitioner*, 1966 S.L.T. (Notes) 81.
[96] *Goulding v James* [1997] 2 All E.R. 239; *Lobnitz, Petitioner*, 1966 S.L.T. (Notes) 81.

is available in both cases, but much stricter criteria must be met for this power to be available.

The criteria which must be satisfied in order for the court to sanction variation are therefore different depending on whether the case involves "initial failure" (where it was never possible to give effect to the trust) or "subsequent failure" (where the trust was initially given effect to but later failed).

Initial failure

13–57 Variation in such cases must be under the cy-prés jurisdiction. In such cases, two factors must be established for variation to be permissible:

- a "general charitable intention" on the part of the truster; and
- failure of the trust purposes (impossibility).

In determining whether the truster had a "general charitable intention", the court must ask whether his object was "to establish a charity for the benefit of a certain class with a particular mode of doing it? Or was the mode of application such an essential part of the gift that it is not possible to distinguish any general purpose of charity?".[97] The distinction is illustrated by the following case:

> ### Hay's J.F. v Hay's Trustees
> #### 1952 S.C. (H.L.) 29
>
> A testatrix directed in her will that her trustees should maintain a mansion-house "under the style and designation of 'The Hay Memorial'" as a hospital on Shetland. The funds available under the trust-deed were insufficient to maintain the house for this purpose. The trustees applied to the court for a variation of the trust purposes under the cy-prés jurisdiction. Held, that cy-prés was not available as no general charitable intention existed. It was clear that the use of the house as the "Hay Memorial" was an essential part of the testatrix's intention. If this was not possible, there was no general purpose of charity to fall back on.

Subsequent failure

13–58 In cases of subsequent failure, it is not necessary to establish a general charitable intention. It is only necessary to establish impossibility (in which case cy-prés may be invoked)[98] or one of the statutory grounds

---

[97] *Burgess' Trustees v Crawford*, 1912 S.C. 387, per Lord Mackenzie at 398.
[98] In *RS Macdonald Charitable Trust Trustees v Scottish Society for the Prevention of Cruelty to Animals*, 2009 S.C. 6, the court went further, permitting cy-prés to be invoked on the basis of "strong or compelling expediency". It is not clear why the application in that case was not made under the statutory grounds discussed here.

under s.9(1) of the Law Reform (Miscellaneous Provisions) (Scotland) Act 1990, which are:

"(a) that the purposes of the trust, whether in whole or in part—

    (i) have been fulfilled as far as it is possible to do so; or

    (ii) can no longer be given effect to, whether in accordance with the directions or spirit of the trust deed or other document constituting the trust or otherwise;

(b) that the purposes of the trust provide a use for only part of the property available under the trust;

(c) that the purposes of the trust were expressed by reference to—

    (i) an area which has, since the trust was constituted, ceased to have effect for the purpose described expressly or by implication in the trust deed or other document constituting the trust;

    (ii) a class of persons or area which has ceased to be suitable or appropriate, having regard to the spirit of the trust deed or other document constituting the trust, or as regards which it has ceased to be practicable to administer the property available under the trust; or

(d) that the purpose of the trust, whether in whole or in part, have, since the trust was constituted—

    (i) been adequately provided for by other means;

    (ii) ceased to be such as would enable the trust to become a recognised body [a charity]; or

    (iii) ceased in any other way to provide a suitable and effective method of using the property available under the trust, having regard to the spirit of the trust deed or other document constituting the trust."

In cases involving small public trusts (those having an annual income not exceeding £5,000) where one of these conditions is satisfied, the trustees may vary the purposes of such a trust, transfer its assets to another public trust, or amalgamate it with one or more public trusts without the necessity of court application, provided that the Lord Advocate does not object.[99]

What can the court do once the variation jurisdiction is triggered?

Once the criteria for variation have been met, the court may approve a **13–59** scheme for the variation of the trust. In doing so, the court will adhere to the "principle of approximation". This means that the objects of the varied trust must "approximate as closely as may be" to those which were

---

[99] Law Reform (Miscellaneous Provisions) (Scotland) Act 1990 s.10; Public Trusts (Reorganisation) (Scotland) (No.2) Regulations 1993 (SI 1993/2254).

originally selected by the truster.[100] As part of variation, the court may transfer trust funds to another body,[101] widen the class of persons who are entitled to benefit from the trust,[102] or extend the powers of the trustees.[103]

Key Concepts

In some cases, it may be desirable to **vary the purposes** of a trust.

In **private trusts**, the basic principle is that variation is possible with the consent of all the beneficiaries. Where a person who is or may be a beneficiary is unable to consent to a variation, the court may consent on their behalf provided that it is satisfied the variation would not be **prejudicial** to that person.

Where it has never been possible to give effect to the terms of a **public trust** (**initial failure**), the court may apply **cy-prés** to vary the terms of the trust provided that a **general charitable intention** on the part of the truster can be shown and that it is **impossible** to give effect to the trust purposes.

Where it has been possible initially to give effect to the terms of a public trust (cases of **subsequent failure**), **cy-prés** may be applied if it has become **impossible** to give effect to the trust purposes. It is not necessary to show a general charitable intention in such cases. Variation may also be possible under s.9 of the Law Reform (Miscellaneous Provisions) (Scotland) Act 1990 if the trust purposes have become in some way inappropriate—s.9 lays down criteria which must be satisfied for variation under this section.

Where grounds for variation of a public trust have been established, the court may **vary the purposes** of the trust, **transfer trust funds** to another body, or **extend the powers** of the trustees.

TERMINATION OF A TRUST

13–60 This section considers the circumstances in which a trust may be brought to an end.

Revocation by the truster

13–61 Because a *mortis causa* trust is not effective until the testator's death, it is open to the testator to revoke his will and prevent the trust from even taking effect.

An *inter vivos* trust is only irrevocable if the following conditions are satisfied:

---

[100] *Stranraer Original Secession Corporation*, 1923 S.C. 722, per the Lord President (Clyde) at 725.

[101] See, e.g. *Clyde Industrial Training Ship Association*, 1925 S.C. 676.

[102] See, e.g. *Trustees of Carnegie Park Orphanage* (1892) 19 R. 605.

[103] *McCrie's Trustees*, 1927 S.C. 556.

- there must be an ascertained beneficiary (if the only ascertained beneficiary is the truster himself, the trust remains revocable)[104]; and
- the beneficiary must have an "immediate beneficial interest" (called a *jus quaesitium*). If the beneficiary's interest depends on a particular event taking place, then the trust is revocable,[105] unless all that is required is that the beneficiary survive to a specified date.[106]

If these conditions are not satisfied, the truster is entitled to revoke the trust.

Termination by the trustees

The trustees may bring the trust to an end by fulfilling the trust purposes **13–62** and distributing the trust estate.

Termination by the beneficiaries

There are two relevant principles here. First, if all the beneficiaries in a **13–63** private trust consent to the termination of a trust, the trustees must normally comply, except where termination would prejudice the proper administration of the trust.[107] Secondly, according to the case of *Miller's Trustees v Miller*,[108] a beneficiary who has acquired a right in fee to property is entitled to insist that the trustees transfer the property to him absolutely, even if they have instructions to the contrary.

Key Concepts

Trusts may be **terminated** in a number of ways.
By the **truster**:

- Because a ***mortis causa*** trust does not take effect until the testator's death, it is normally open to the testator to revoke his will at any time before his death and prevent the trust ever taking effect.
- An ***inter vivos*** trust may be revoked by the truster unless: (a) there is an ascertained beneficiary (other than the truster himself); and (b) that beneficiary has an "immediate beneficial interest".

---

[104] *Bertram's Trustees v Bertram*, 1909 S.C. 1238.
[105] *Bulkeley-Gavin's Trustees v Bulkeley-Gavin's Trustees*, 1971 S.C. 209 (benefit contingent on the wholesale nationalisation of land).
[106] *Robertson v Robertson's Trustees* (1892) 19 R. 849.
[107] See, e.g. *De Robeck v Inland Revenue*, 1928 S.C. (H.L.) 34 (termination would have prejudiced taxation arrangements).
[108] (1890) 18 R. 301.

By the **trustees**: the **trustees** may terminate a trust by fulfilling the trust purposes and distributing the trust estate.
By the **beneficiaries**:

- In a private trust, all the beneficiaries acting together may compel the termination of a trust.
- A beneficiary who has acquired a right in fee to property is normally entitled to insist that the trustees pass the property to him absolutely.

▼ CHAPTER SUMMARY

THE TRUST CONCEPT

13–64
(1) A trust involves three roles: a truster, trustee and a beneficiary.
(2) The truster is the person who sets up the trust; the trustee is the person who owns and administers the property; the beneficiary is the person for whose benefit the property is administered.
(3) These are roles rather than persons: the same person can hold more than one of these roles, and there can be more than one person in each role.
(4) There are various practical advantages to the trust device, mainly because it allows a separation of benefit from property from the control of that property. Some of these advantages could be achieved by other legal devices, but the one unique advantage of the trust is that it protects against insolvency: if the trustee is made bankrupt, the trust property cannot be used to pay off his debts.
(5) A trust may be *mortis causa*, and the effect on the truster's death, or *inter vivos*, and take effect during the trusters lifetime.

PUBLIC AND PRIVATE TRUSTS

(1) Trusts may be either public or private: that is, for the benefit of the public as whole (or a specific section of the public), or for a defined group of individuals.

CREATING A TRUST

(1) A trust is created by: (a) declaring the trust; and (b) transferring property from the truster to the trustee. Trusts can also be created by "legal implication" in some circumstances.

> ➢ *Allan's Trustees v Inland Revenue* (1971): to create a trust, delivery of the property, or some equivalent to delivery, is essential.

(2) Where the truster and trustee are the same person, there must be some "equivalent of delivery" to create the trust. This will normally take the form of intimating the rights created by the trust to the beneficiaries.

(3) In order to be valid, trust purposes must not be: (a) too uncertain; (b) too wide; or (c) illegal.

> ➢ *McCaig's Trustees v Kirk-Session of United Free Church of Lismore* (1915): a trust to create a private enclosure with inordinately expensive statues was invalid because it conferred no benefit on anyone.

TRUST ADMINISTRATION

(1) Trust decision-making is by a majority of trustees, unless the trust deed provides otherwise.

DUTIES AND POWERS OF TRUSTEES

(1) Trustees have a number of general duties which are implied by law. The most important of these is to exercise due care in their dealings with the trust estate.
(2) Trustees are also under a duty not to delegate the trust (that is, to take responsibility for decision-making themselves); to secure trust property; to invest trust property; to take advice where appropriate; to meet trust debts and obligations; to keep accounts; and to pay the correct beneficiaries.

> ➢ *Melville v Noble's Trustees* (1896): trustees who failed to invest trust property were liable personally to pay the money that could have been earned if it had been invested.

(3) Trustees must not be *auctor in rem suam* (actors in their own cause). This means they must not put themselves in a position where their personal interests are in conflict with their position as trustee. Specifically, this means they: (a) cannot contract with the trust estate; (b) cannot obtain a personal advantage from their position as trustee; and (c) cannot charge for work done for the trust.

> ➢ *Cowan v Scargill* (1985): pension fund trustees could not use their position to further the aims of the National Union of Mineworkers, but had to restrict their considerations to the best interests of the beneficiaries.

(4) A trustee may be *auctor in rem suam* if this is sanctioned in the trust deed or by the beneficiaries.
(5) The powers of a trustee may be set out in the trust deed, or the trustee may rely on general powers which are set out in s.4 of the 1921 Act. These general powers may, however, be excluded by the terms of the trust deed.

> ➢ The 1921 Act s.4: sets out various general powers which all trustees have unless they would be "at variance with the terms and purposes of the trust".

REMEDIES FOR BREACH OF TRUST

(1) Where trustees are in breach of trust or plan to do something which would be a breach, the principal remedies open to the beneficiaries are: (a) interdict (a court order which prohibits a person from a specific act); (b) an action for damages; or (c) an action for "accounting".

TRUSTEES' LIABILITY TO THIRD PARTIES

(1) If trustees enter into contracts on behalf of the trust, they are personally liable on these contracts unless there is an agreement to the contrary. Signing contracts "as trustee" is enough to imply such an agreement.

VARIATION OF TRUSTS

(1) The purposes of a private trust may be varied by consent of all the beneficiaries. Where a beneficiary is unable to consent, the court may be asked to consent on their behalf. The court cannot do this unless satisfied that the variation would not be "prejudicial" to that person.

> ➤ Trusts (Scotland) Act 1961 s.1: where a beneficiary (or potential beneficiary) is unable to consent to a proposed variation of a private trust, this section gives the court a discretionary power to consent on their behalf.

(2) The purposes of a public trust may be varied by way of a court application. Where the trust is a small one, it may be possible to avoid the need for a court application by following alternative statutory procedures.

(3) Where it has never been possible to give effect to the purposes of a public trust, an application for variation must be under the cy-près jurisdiction. It must be shown that: (a) the truster had a "general charitable intention"; and (b) that the purposes set out in the trust are impossible.

> ➤ *Hay's J.F. v Hay's Trustees* (1952): where Ms Hay wished her trustees to maintain a mansion-house as a hospital named the "Hay Memorial", but there were insufficient funds to do this, there was no "general charitable intention". This is because it was clear that the use of the house as the "Hay Memorial" was an essential part of her intention.

(4) Where it has been possible to give effect to the purposes of a public trust, an application for variation may be made under the broader grounds set out in the statute.

> ➤ Law Reform (Miscellaneous Provisions) (Scotland) Act 1990 s.9: makes statutory provision for the variation of the purposes of a public trust.

TERMINATION OF TRUSTS

(1) A trust may be terminated primarily by: (a) the trustees fulfilling the trust purposes and bringing the trust to an end; or (b) by the beneficiaries acting together to compel its termination.

? QUICK QUIZ

BASIC CONCEPTS AND THE CREATION OF A TRUST

- What is a trust?
- Who owns trust property?
- How is a voluntary trust created?
- What restrictions does Scots law place on the validity of trust purposes?

TRUSTEES AND TRUST MANAGEMENT

- Must trust decisions be taken unanimously?
- What general duties does the law impose on trustees?

WHAT IS MEANT BY THE RULE AGAINST *AUCTOR IN REM SUAM*?

- What are the sources of trustees' powers?

TRUSTEES' LIABILITIES

- When a trustee has been in breach of trust, what remedies are open to the beneficiaries?
- How may trustees be protected from liability for breach of trust?
- Are trustees personally liable on trust contracts?

VARIATION OF TRUST PURPOSES

- What requirements must be satisfied before the terms of a private trust can be varied? To what extent is the court involved in this process?

📖 FURTHER READING

➢ The leading textbook on the Scottish law of trusts is W.A. Wilson and A.G.M. Duncan, *Trusts, Trustees and Executors,* 2nd edn (Edinburgh: W. Green, 1995). It is a detailed reference work but is generally unsuitable for someone who is approaching the subject for the first time.

➢ There are relatively few student textbooks which deal only with the law of trusts, although substantial coverage can be found in G.L. Gretton and A.J.M. Steven, *Property, Trusts and Succession*, 2nd edn (Edinburgh: Tottel Publishing, 2014).

➢ The most recent book on trusts alone is a cases and materials book: J. Chalmers, *Trusts: Cases and Materials* (Edinburgh: W. Green, 2002), and there is one textbook: K.McK. Norrie and E.M. Scobbie, *Trusts* (Edinburgh: W. Green, 1991). R.R.M. Paisley, *Trusts LawBasics* (Edinburgh: W. Green, 1999) is a very brief introduction to the subject.

⌨ RELEVANT WEBLINKS

➢ The Scottish Law Commission (*http://www.scotlawcom.gov.uk* [Accessed May 15, 2015]) has carried out a long-term project reviewing the law of trusts in recent years, publishing a series of discussion papers and reports culminating in a general *Report on Trust Law* in 2014. That report makes extensive proposals for reform of the law in this area.

Chapter 14   Choice of Business Medium

Dᴀᴠɪᴅ Cᴀʙʀᴇʟʟɪ[1]

▶ CHAPTER OVERVIEW

This chapter concentrates on the legal forms that are available to a **14–01** person seeking to carry on a business. First, we consider the concept of the sole trader and the implications of running a business through this medium. The chapter goes on to explore the principal characteristics of business forms provided by the law which enable more than one person to come together to carry on a business, e.g. the partnership or "firm", the registered company and the limited liability partnership ("LLP"). Finally, the chapter examines the advantages and disadvantages of each of these business forms and offers insights into the approach a person or persons should take when deciding which form to select.

✓ OUTCOMES

At the end of this chapter you should be able to understand: **14–02**

- ✓ the implications of conducting business as, and the principal characteristics of, a sole trader;
- ✓ the implications of conducting business as, and the principal characteristics of, a partnership or LLP;
- ✓ the implications of conducting business as, and the principal characteristics of, a registered company;
- ✓ the differences between conducting business as a sole trader, partnership, LLP and registered company;
- ✓ the merits and demerits of conducting business as a sole trader, partnership or registered company; and
- ✓ the meaning and importance of concepts such as personal liability, limited liability, separate legal personality, the division between ownership and control, and perpetual succession.

---

[1] Senior Lecturer in Commercial Law, University of Edinburgh.

THE SOLE TRADER

14–03 An individual who wishes to carry on a business may choose to run his/ her business as a sole trader. By definition, it is only that individual person who is involved in the management and control of the business. Thus, the sole trader business form is not suitable where a group of persons wish to come together to carry on a business and, by definition, a sole trader will be a small business. Only the sole trader has the right to manage the business and only he or she is the owner of the capital of the business. So there is no separation between the ownership and the control of the business of the sole trader. Thus, if the business is valued by the sole trader's accountant at £50,000, it is only the sole trader who will have the right to receive that sum in the event that the business of the sole trader is sold at that price to a third party on the open market. The sole trader also has the sole right to participate in the profits of the business. However, if the business makes a loss in a particular financial year, it is the sole trader who will require to bear those losses—no one else. The debts of the business are not separated from the sole trader's own personal debts and income. That is because the individual can in no way be separated from the business: the two are indissoluble and the sole trader business form possesses no separate legal personality. This means that the sole trader is personally liable for the debts of the business. So if the business has debts of £50,000 owing to its creditors, the sole trader is personally liable for those debts. For example, if the business has only £10,000 of funds and assets, the sole trader will be required to meet the shortfall of £40,000 from his own personal funds. If the sole trader refuses or is unable to meet that shortfall, the creditors of the sole trader's business have the power to petition the court for the sequestration of the sole trader, i.e. to make him personally bankrupt. In such circumstances, the personal assets of the sole trader can be secured and sold by the trustee in sequestration (appointed to the estate of the sole trader) in order to meet the debts of the business.

The sole trader business form is characterised by a large degree of informality and privacy. There are no initial or continuing registration requirements or other formalities involved in operating as a sole trader. Moreover, there is no legal requirement for a sole trader to produce or publish accounts and financial records. Depending on the size of the sole trader's annual turnover (i.e. its annual total sales), it may or may not require to keep records for the purposes of VAT. Finally, when the individual sole trader dies, the assets of the business are distributed alongside the personal assets of the individual in accordance with the law of succession contained in the Succession (Scotland) Act 1964. The death of the sole trader heralds the automatic cessation of the business.

One area where formalities are imposed on sole traders by law is in the area of business names. Part 41 of the Companies Act 2006 ("CA 2006") applies to all sole traders. Under ss.1201 and 1202 of the CA 2006, traders must specify their name and address on all business letters, written orders for goods or services to be supplied to the business, invoices and receipts issued in the course of the business and written demands for payment of debts arising in the course of the business. Both civil and criminal liability attaches to those sole traders who fail to comply in terms of ss.1205 and 1206 of the CA 2006. The purpose of ss.1201 and 1202 of the CA 2006 is to enable the creditors, suppliers and contractors of the sole trader to identify the "owners" of the business. It is worth noting that the business name requirements of ss.1200–1208 of the CA 2006 also apply to partnerships.

> **Key Concepts**
>
> A sole trader is an individual who carries on a business on an individual basis in his own name or some other name. The sole trader owns and manages the business, enjoys the profits of the business and bears the losses of the business. The sole trader is personally liable for the debts of the business.

THE PARTNERSHIP: AN INTRODUCTION

Unlike the sole trader, the partnership vehicle is well-suited towards the **14–04** joining together of a number of persons for the purposes of carrying on a business. In the case of a partnership, a number of individuals, namely the partners, voluntarily agree to combine for a common purpose and, thus, form a partnership business. Each of those individuals will contribute capital investment, skills, know-how, expertise and contacts and pool those resources as a means of selling products or services. Each partner has the right to participate in the business of the partnership and is an agent of the partnership firm, with the ability to bind the firm in law. Partnership businesses range from very small organisations, such as two partners running a local store, to large international firms of solicitors and accountants.

SEPARATE LEGAL PERSONALITY AND CONTINUITY

For the purposes of Scots law, s.4(2) of the Partnership Act 1890 provides **14–05** that a partnership firm possesses separate legal personality, i.e. that it is a legal body distinct from its constituent partners.[2] Since the firm enjoys separate legal personality, it can enter into binding contracts in its own name and it has the power to sue and be sued in its own name. It can commit delicts and own property by taking title to heritable property in its own name in terms of s.70 of the Abolition of Feudal Tenure (Scotland) Act 2000. Since the partnership is a separate legal personality, one might assume that it would survive the death or bankruptcy of any of its constituent partners. However, this is not the case. Section 33(1) of the Partnership Act 1890 provides that the death or bankruptcy of a partner

---

[2] The position in English law is different.

automatically dissolves the partnership.[3] Moreover, whether the partnership continues to exist on a change in the membership of its partners, e.g. the assumption of a new partner or the retiral or resignation of an existing partner, is not altogether wholly clear.[4]

THE PARTNERSHIP ACT 1890

14–06 The partnership is regulated by the Partnership Act 1890 ("the Act"). The Act provides a definition of a partnership and provides for various legal relationships and scenarios which, while resembling a partnership, are excluded from the definition. The basic definition of a partnership is contained in s.1(1) of the Act which provides that a partnership, "is the relation which subsists between persons carrying on a business in common with a view of profit". The implication of that definition is that the parties must have the objective of realising a profit in coming together to form a business. However, the Act includes certain exceptions which will be analysed in more detail in Ch.15, "The Law of Partnership". The Act contains rules which govern and regulate partnerships. Those rules can be divided into the following broad categories:

- the nature of a partnership—ss.1–4;
- the relationship between the partnership and third parties and the liability of the partners to third parties—ss.5–18;
- property owned by the partnership—s.20;
- the duties of partners, the relations of partners to one another and the regulation of the internal affairs of the partnership—ss.19–31; and
- the dissolution of the partnership and the distribution of its assets on dissolution—ss.32–44.

THE ADVANTAGES OF THE PARTNERSHIP

14–07 One of the advantages of running a business through the medium of a partnership is that there are very few formalities or administrative requirements involved in its creation or continuing operation. For example, there is no requirement for a partnership to be constituted in writing. Moreover, there is no need to notify any public registry of any changes in the composition of the membership of a partnership. A partnership does not require to file accounts or details of its financial affairs on a continuing basis. However, there is one exception. That is to

---

[3] However, this is subject to agreement to the contrary in the partnership agreement. See the terms of s.33(1) of the Partnership Act 1890.

[4] See F. Davidson and L. Macgregor, *Commercial Law in Scotland*, 3rd edn (Edinburgh: W. Green, 2014), Ch.8 and Joint Law Commission and Scottish Law Commission Report, *Partnership Law* (2003), Law Com. No.283, Cm.6015 and Scot. Law Com. No.192, Cm.6015 at para.8.7, p.107.

say that a partnership must comply with the provisions of ss.1201 and 1202 of the CA 2006 where the partnership is trading under a name other than the personal names of the partners. Thus, the names and addresses of all partners of the partnership must be stated in legible characters on all business letters, written orders for goods or services to be supplied to the business, invoices and receipts issued in the course of the business and written demands for payment of debts arising in the course of the business. If a partner fails to comply with the provisions of ss.1201 and 1202 of the CA 2006, they are subject to civil and criminal sanctions if found liable.

Allied to the lack of formalities and administration is the advantage of privacy. There is no requirement for a partnership to publicise the management of its internal affairs, e.g. how the votes of partners on partnership matters are to be weighted, how profits are shared by the partners (e.g. the profit percentages per partner), etc. A partnership is not obliged to disclose its financial affairs. One of the causes of the advantage of privacy is the lack of complexity of partnership law. In comparison with the limited liability company incorporated under the Companies Acts, the partnership is regulated very loosely. The light touch regulation of the Act is complemented by the fact that a partnership may disapply all or some of the provisions of that Act by agreement. The lack of complexity leads to low compliance costs and expenses which is another advantage over the incorporated company. It also ensures that the partnership model benefits from the advantage of flexibility. In other words, given the absence of formalities, the partnership vehicle is more responsive to changes in underlying economic or market conditions.

THE DISADVANTAGES OF THE PARTNERSHIP

Of course, the benefits associated with the partnership model are offset, **14–08** and one might argue overshadowed, by certain disadvantages. The first disadvantage is the absence of any division between its ownership and control. The provisions of the Act countenance little scope for such an innovation. The chief culprit is s.24(5) of the Act which states that every partner is entitled to take part in the management of the partnership. Thus, a partner who contributes capital to the firm has a prima facie entitlement to participate in management. The effect is that the introduction of a passive investor who does not intend to involve himself in the day-to-day affairs of the partnership requires the partnership to oust the terms of s.24(5) of the Act at cost. This can be contrasted with a limited liability company where there is a natural division between ownership, i.e. investors, and control, i.e. management. Companies can offer shares in return for capital investment with no requirement for the investor to take part in the management of the company. This is difficult to achieve in the case of a partnership as a result of: (i) the provisions of s.24(5) of the Act; and (ii) the inability of partnerships to issue transferable shares to investors. Transferable shares make a company attractive to investors since they can purchase shares and sell them to third parties at market value as and when they please. Another consequence of the absence of a division between ownership and control in the case of a partnership is that it is more difficult for a partnership to introduce specialised outside management to control its affairs. This is the case since partners can only be introduced to manage a partnership in return for a contribution to the capital of the firm. In the case of a company, it is not necessary for new management to make a capital contribution.

A second disadvantage of the partnership is the absence of limited liability of the partners for the debts of the partnership. Sections 9–12 of the Act provide that the partners are jointly and severally liable for the debts of the partnership. In practice, what this means is that a creditor who is owed £100,000 from the partnership in the following scenario can sue all of the partners or some or one of the partners (of the creditor's own choice) to recover the shortfall of £90,000:

- Partnership assets—worth £10,000;
- Partner 1—personal assets worth £40,000;
- Partner 2—personal assets worth £50,000; and
- Partner 3—personal assets worth £230,000.

Meanwhile, the members of a company incorporated under the Companies Acts would have limited liability in the above scenario to the extent that their liability would be limited to the value of: (i) any sum remaining unpaid on their shares (in an incorporated company limited by shares); or (ii) any sum guaranteed (in the case of an incorporated company limited by guarantee). A consequence of the lack of limited liability in the case of the partnership is that partners and their personal assets are left exposed to attack from the creditors of the partnership, whereas in the case of a company, the members do not have such concerns.[5]

14–09   Another disadvantage of the partnership is that it does not possess the benefit of perpetual succession. Whenever a partner dies or becomes bankrupt, the partnership ceases to exist, as per s.33(1) of the Act. If the remaining partners continue to trade, the law treats a new partnership as having been created. This can be distinguished from the position in the case of an incorporated company. The incorporated company continues to exist notwithstanding any change in the composition of its membership or management (i.e. the identity of its shareholders or directors). On the face of it, the cessation of a partnership and the constitution of a new partnership on the death or bankruptcy of a partner may seem inconsequential. However, this overlooks the significance of such an event. Of most importance is the accounting and taxation treatment of the old and new partnership and, in turn, the financial and tax position of the partners. The interruption of continuity in the affairs of the partnership results in extra costs and complications from an accountancy and

---

[5] Although, in practice, more sophisticated creditors of a company (such as banks and other lenders) will demand and obtain personal guarantees from certain members of the company in respect of the company's indebtedness towards them.

taxation perspective which would not have arisen in the case of a change of membership or management in a company.

The final disadvantage of the partnership is its inability to grant a floating charge.[6] A company can grant a floating charge to a creditor as a security for loans advanced to it by creditors and debts owed by it to creditors. Essentially, a floating charge is a security which is granted over the whole assets and undertaking of the company. When it is created, the charge "hovers" over those assets and the company can sell its assets in the ordinary course of business without requiring the prior consent of the creditor/chargeholder. It is only when a liquidator or receiver is appointed over the assets and undertaking of the company that the charge is said to "crystallise". When the charge crystallises, the charge becomes fixed and the liquidator or receiver is entitled to ingather and sell the assets in order to meet the debts which the company owes to the creditor/chargeholder. Since partnerships are not permitted to grant a floating charge, there is the possibility that a creditor may decide not to advance funding to a partnership on the same terms and conditions as a company, duly rendering the cost of borrowing more expensive.

Key Concepts

Advantages of the partnership: (1) the lack of formalities in constituting and operating a partnership; (2) no requirement to make public the internal affairs and financial performance of the partnership; (3) lack of complexity in managing the partnership; (4) low costs of compliance with law; and (5) flexibility in the affairs and management of the partnership.

Disadvantages of the partnership: (1) the lack of a separation between ownership and control in the partnership; (2) the absence of transferable shares which can be issued to investors; (3) the difficulty in removing existing management and introducing specialised management to run the partnership; (4) the joint and several liability of the partners for the debts of the partnership; (5) the lack of perpetual succession; and (6) the inability of a partnership to grant a floating charge.

THE COMPANY: AN INTRODUCTION

Like a partnership governed by the Partnership Act 1890, a company is **14–10** well-suited towards the joining together of a number of persons for the purposes of carrying on a business. In the case of a company, a number of individuals, namely the members, voluntarily agree to combine for a common purpose and thus form a company as a means of carrying on business. Each of those individuals will contribute capital investment, skills, know-how, expertise and contacts and pool those resources as a

---

[6] For further details on floating charges, see Ch.21, "Rights in Security".

means of selling products or services. In terms of ss.7–16 of the CA 2006, a company is formed by registration with the Registrar of Companies and is incorporated when the Registrar has issued a document to the company called a certificate of incorporation. Section 16 of the CA 2006 also provides that a company is a body corporate. This can be contrasted with sole traders and partnerships which are not bodies corporate.

There are many types of company. By far the most common form of company is the company incorporated under the Companies Acts with limited liability. All references in this chapter are to such limited liability companies.[7] Limited liability companies can be divided in terms of two distinctions, namely: (i) the limited liability company by shares or guarantee; and (ii) the private limited liability company and the public limited liability company. In the case of a limited liability company by shares, the members are referred to as "shareholders" and in terms of s.3(2) of the CA 2006 the extent of their liability for the debts of the company is limited to any value which remains unpaid on their shares. Thus, if their shareholding is 100 ordinary shares of £1 each, the full extent of their liability to the company for its debts is £100. If a shareholder has paid £30 to the company towards their liability of £100, their liability would be limited to £70 for the company's debts. Meanwhile, if the shareholder has paid £100, their residual liability to the company and its creditors for the company's debts would be zero.

Shareholders can be distinguished from the members of limited liability companies by guarantee. Here, the liability of the members for the debts of the company is not limited to the value of any shares in the company (since a company limited by guarantee will not usually have any shares) but to the value of the contribution which they have agreed to make towards the assets of the company on its winding up.[8] The company and the members agree the extent of the guarantee in the memorandum of association of the company[9] and the specified amount must be outlined in the company's application for registration when it applies to the Registrar of Companies to be incorporated.[10] The effect of the above is that if a company owes £100,000 to a creditor when it is wound up, the member can only be called upon to pay the value of his/her agreed contribution towards the debts of the company.

Companies can also be divided into the private limited liability company and the public limited liability company ("Plc"). Section 4 of the CA 2006 provides that a private company is a company which is not a public company and that a Plc is a company: (i) limited by shares; or (ii) limited by guarantee whose certificate of incorporation states that it is a Plc. Although s.4 of the CA 2006 is not particularly illuminating regarding the nature of the principal differences between a private company and a Plc, the other provisions of the CA 2006 serve to underline them. For example, ss.755–760 of the CA 2006 prohibit a private limited

---

[7] As explored in Ch.16, there are also unlimited liability companies, but these are rare.
[8] CA 2006 s.3(3).
[9] In practice, it is common for the contribution to be limited to £5.
[10] CA 2006 ss.9(4)(b) and 11(3).

company from offering its shares or debentures to the public. In contrast, a Plc is permitted to do so. Another distinction is that s.271 of the CA 2006 requires every public limited company to have a company secretary, whereas s.270 of the CA 2006 gives a private limited company the choice whether to appoint a company secretary. A third distinction is that s.154 of the CA 2006 provides that a private company must have a minimum of one director, whereas a public company must have at least two directors. Public companies must also comply with the minimum authorised share capital requirements in terms of ss.761–767 of the CA 2006. These provisions provide that every public company is not permitted to do business or borrow money unless it has a trading certificate and it can only obtain a trading certificate from the Registrar of Companies if the nominal value of the company's allotted share capital is not less than the authorised minimum of £50,000. Meanwhile, there are no such restrictions on private companies. Another difference between private and public companies is apparent from the terms of ss.58–60 of the CA 2006. The name of every public limited company must end with the words "public limited company" or the abbreviation "Plc", whereas the name of every private limited company must end with the word "limited" or the abbreviation "ltd".

THE ADVANTAGES OF THE CORPORATE FORM

The case of *Salomon v A. Salomon & Co Ltd*[11] is the most important of all **14–11** company law cases. It settled once and for all that the shareholders of limited liability companies enjoy limited liability for the debts of the company. It also established that a company is a body corporate having separate legal personality distinct from its constituent members. The effect of the rule that a company is a separate legal person is that it can be sued, sue third parties in its own name, enter into contracts, own property in its own name, etc.

Salomon v A. Salomon & Co Ltd
[1897] A.C. 22

Concerning: The liability of the members of a private limited liability company for the debts of the company and the separate legal personality of a company.

Facts: Mr Salomon was a merchant running a wholesale leather boot manufacturing business as a sole trader. He decided to convert his business from a sole trader to a limited liability company. Mr Salomon took 20,001 shares of £1 each in the share capital of the company with his wife and five children each taking one share of £1 each. Mr Salomon's business was transferred to the company in exchange for those 20,001 shares. Mr Salomon

---

[11] [1897] A.C. 22.

also received £1,000 in cash and £10,000 worth of debentures (debt instruments issued by the company) from the company in return for the transfer of his business to the company. In essence, Mr Salomon controlled the company and it was a "one-man" company despite the fact that it had seven shareholders. Subsequent to the transfer, the company continued the leather manufacturing trade, but eventually fell on hard times. Mr Salomon cancelled his debentures and reissued them to a Mr Broderip in return for an advance of £5,000 which Mr Salomon then applied towards the company's debts. Unfortunately, this did not resolve the financial difficulties of the company. A liquidator was appointed over the company, who realised the company's assets and held the proceeds of sale. When the proceeds of sale were distributed amongst the company's creditors, the effect was that there was enough money to repay only part of the debt due to Mr Broderip, but the company's unsecured trade creditors received nothing. Mr Broderip challenged the distribution of the proceeds of sale on a number of grounds, ultimately seeking recovery of funds from Mr Salomon in respect of the shortfall on his debentures. The trial judge held that Mr Broderip had a right to be indemnified from Mr Salomon who was an agent of the company. The case was appealed all the way to the House of Lords.

Decision: The House of Lords held that Mr Salomon did not require to indemnify the company or its creditors in respect of the debts of the company. The requirements of the Companies Act 1862 had been complied with in full and the effect of that Act was clear, namely that members have limited liability for the debts of the company and that the company has its own legal personality which is distinct from its members. So the decision of the trial judge was set aside and the Law Lords ruled that Mr Broderip could not recover from Mr Salomon.

14-12 As the case of *Salomon* demonstrates, separate legal personality and the limited liability of the membership of the company are major benefits of the corporate form. Another advantage which limited liability companies have over other business forms (such as partnerships, sole traders, etc.) is the ability to issue transferable shares as investments to shareholders/investors.[12] This enables the company to raise finance from investors/shareholders in return for the allotment and issue of its own shares to the investor/shareholder. Only limited liability companies by shares can raise this form of finance, which is referred to as "equity finance". Companies limited by guarantee do not have the facility to offer shares to investors, since generally they are not permitted to issue such shares. Moreover, other business vehicles such as sole traders and partnerships do not have

---

[12] Of course, this advantage applies only to share companies and not to companies limited by guarantee.

the ability to raise money by issuing shares and if such organisations wish to raise finance from outside third parties, debt finance (i.e. a loan-based arrangement) is the only available option. When shares are allotted and issued to investors in return for finance, the shares are treated as property owned by the investors. Section 541 of the CA 2006 provides that shares are moveable property owned by and belonging to the investor in terms of Scots law. Shares represent a measure of the shareholder's liability and interest in the company, consisting of a bundle of rights in favour of them and obligations imposed on them. In other words, they have an open market value, representing a percentage of the overall value of the company.[13] A great benefit of shares is the ease with which they may be transferred to third parties or offered to a lender as a security in return for borrowing.

A related benefit of the corporate form is the distinction between ownership of the company and its control. If an individual owns shares in a company, they have no obligation or right to manage the affairs of the company. In other words, simply because a person owns shares does not mean that they are required to participate in management. This enables a company to introduce passive investors who have no intention of administering the day-to-day affairs of the company. On the other hand, if an individual wishes to enter into the management of a company or is identified by the company as someone suitable for appointment as a director, it is not a prerequisite of acting as a director that the individual must invest money in the company in return for shares and become a shareholder. Since shareholders do not require to be directors of a company, the company can introduce specialised management to run the business of the company without offering them shares in the company. The company can thus seek out the best managers for their business on the open market. The contrast with the partnership where no division exists between control and ownership of the company is abundantly stark. By the same token that management can be readily introduced to a company, ss.168 and 169 of the CA 2006 also provide for a readily accessible means of removing the management of a company. A director can be removed by the shareholders passing an ordinary resolution, namely a simple majority of the members who vote in person or by proxy on a show of hands or on a poll at a general meeting or by written resolution procedure (if the company is private). This can be contrasted with a partnership where the general rule (subject to contrary agreement) is that unanimity of the partners is required to expel a partner in terms of s.25 of the Partnership Act 1890.

Companies are also advantageous in the sense that they outlive their constituent members and directors. In other words, one of their attributes is perpetual succession. The "life" of a company can only be terminated

---

[13] However, for the purposes of the valuation of shareholdings, accounting conventions and practices do not adopt the practice whereby a 15% shareholding in a company is automatically valued at 15% of the overall value of the company. Discounts are commonly applied for minority shareholdings and premiums applied in respect of majority shareholdings.

by the process of liquidation in terms of the Insolvency Act 1986. Until liquidation, the company will continue to subsist, regardless of any changes in the composition of its members or directors.

A final advantage is the power of a company to grant a floating charge. As mentioned in the context of the discussion of partnerships, a floating charge is a form of "enterprise" security that can be granted over the entirety of the assets and undertaking of a company to a lender in exchange for debt funding. Sole traders and partnerships cannot grant floating charges and so there is the potential that the borrowing costs of such business organisations will be higher.

THE DISADVANTAGES OF THE CORPORATE FORM

14–13 One of the dominant features of the CA 2006 is the requirement for companies to comply with a number of initial and continuing administrative and filing obligations. For example, there are various formalities which must be fulfilled before a company can be formed. In terms of ss.7–13 of the CA 2006, a company must submit a memorandum of association, articles of association and an application for registration (which includes a statement of compliance) on a Form IN01 to the Registrar of Companies. In return for such documents and a cheque in respect of registration dues, the Registrar of Companies will issue the company with a certificate of incorporation which amounts to conclusive evidence that the formalities of the CA 2006 as regards formation have been complied with and that the company is registered under the CA 2006 as a body corporate. Once the company is incorporated, there are various continuing obligations which are imposed on companies. For example, in terms of ss.394 and 441 of the CA 2006, companies must prepare individual accounts and file their annual accounts with the Registrar of Companies. Likewise, every year, a company must prepare and file a document containing information about the company called a confirmation statement in terms of s.853A of the CA 2006. A common feature of most of these formalities is that they are generally administrative. Furthermore, the formalities and registration requirements are imposed in the public interest. The public interest is served by casting the light of publicity on certain aspects of the organisation of the company. Any member of the public can consult and review details about a particular company from the website of the Registrar of Companies. Of course, whilst such publicity is necessary given the limited liability enjoyed by the members of the company and the economic and social power wielded by companies, it does result in disadvantages for the company and its directors and members. It is impossible for the company to keep certain matters secret and, for obvious reasons, this may sometimes be undesirable from a commercial perspective.

Another downside of running a business as a company is that companies, their directors and members must grapple with the complexities of the CA 2006, the Insolvency Act 1986, the Company Directors Disqualification Act 1986 and other legislation. It is common for companies to seek out external professional advice to assist them in navigating around the intricacies of the legislation and regulatory requirements. An outcome of the complexity of company law is the fourth disadvantage of adopting the corporate form, namely the costs and expenses which must be borne in order to ensure compliance with the statutory requirements. Finally, a large chunk of the legislation is prescriptive to the extent that it erodes some of the flexibility which lies at the heart of the corporation. That is not to say that the internal organisation of companies is completely inflexible, but that the freedom of autonomy of the corporate actors, namely the company, the directors and the members to contract and agree amongst themselves is circumscribed and controlled by the provisions of the legislation. This can be contrasted with the partnership form where the rules contained in the Partnership Act 1890 are mainly default rules. In other words, the partnership and the partners can choose to disapply or adopt the rules contained in the Partnership Act 1890 as they wish in terms of a partnership agreement—not so in the case of the company.

Key Concepts

Advantages of the company: (1) separate legal personality; (2) limited liability of members for the debts of the company; (3) the separation between ownership and control in the company; (4) the ease with which a company can issue transferable shares to investors; (5) the ease with which existing management may be removed and specialised management introduced to run the company; (6) perpetual succession; and (7) the ability of the company to grant a floating charge.

Disadvantages of the company: (1) the formalities which must be complied with in order to form a company and in respect of the continuing management of the company; (2) the requirement to make public the internal affairs and financial performance of the company; (3) the complexity of company rules in relation to the management and ownership structure of the company; (4) the costs of legal compliance; and (5) the lack of flexibility in the affairs and management of the company, which are conditioned by the terms of the CA 2006.

THE LIMITED LIABILITY PARTNERSHIP: AN INTRODUCTION

Another vehicle which a collection of persons can adopt for the purposes **14–14** of running a business is the limited liability partnership. The limited liability partnership ("LLP") is addressed in comprehensive detail in Chapter 17. In this chapter, we are seeking to provide guidance as to why businesspersons may decide to incorporate an LLP, rather than run their business through an ordinary partnership arrangement or a company registered under the Companies Act 20006. The LLP is governed by the

Limited Liability Partnerships Act 2000, the Limited Liability Partnerships Regulations 2001,[14] the Limited Liability Partnerships (Scotland) Regulations 2001[15] and the Limited Liability Partnerships (Application of Companies Act 2006) Regulations 2009.[16] The limited liability partnership is a hybrid form of business vehicle, representing a cross between a partnership and a company registered under the CA 2006. Like the partnership form, the limited liability partnership enables more than two persons to come together for the purposes of carrying on a lawful business with a view to profit. Section 1(2) of the Limited Liability Partnerships Act 2000 makes it abundantly clear that the LLP is a body corporate with separate legal personality distinct from its constituent members. Moreover, the members of the LLP enjoy limited liability for the debts of the LLP in terms of ss.1(4) of the Limited Liability Partnerships Act 2000. The members are liable to contribute towards the assets of the LLP on its winding up to the extent stipulated in the limited liability partnership agreement. It is the corporate nature of the LLP and the limited liability of the members of an LLP for the debts of the LLP which signal it as a radical departure from partnership law.

The LLP is similar to the partnership in that there must be two members or more which combine to form the LLP. Moreover, their objective in forming the LLP must be to achieve a profit. Another similarity between the LLP and the partnership arises in connection with the ability of members of an LLP to bind the LLP in contract. Thus, in terms of s.6 of the Limited Liability Partnerships Act 2000, members are deemed to be the agents of the LLP and can bind it in contract. However, there is an exception which is more or less identical to the exception contained in the Partnership Act 1890. That is to say that the LLP is not bound by a contract concluded with a third party on its behalf by a member, where the member is exceeding their authority to bind the LLP and the third party knows that he has no authority or does not know or believe him to be a member of the LLP. Thus, s.6 of the Limited Liability Partnerships Act 2000 reflects the terms of s.5 of the Partnership Act 1890. LLPs also resemble partnerships in relation to the manner in which the profits of the LLP are taxed. Thus the taxation rules which apply to partnerships are deemed to apply to LLPs in terms of s.10(3) of the Limited Liability Partnerships Act 2000. Finally, the Partnership Act 1890 and the Limited Liability Partnerships Act 2000 apply the same techniques to regulate the internal affairs of the partnership and the LLP. Therefore, we find that ss.24 and 25 of the Partnership Act 1890 and regs 7 and 8 of the Limited Liability Partnerships Regulations 2001[17] mirror each other to the effect that they both provide that the internal affairs of the partnership and the LLP are to be regulated by the partnership agreement. In the absence of any provision in the partnership agreement,

---

[14] SI 2001/1090.
[15] SSI 2001/128.
[16] SI 2009/1804.
[17] SI 2001/1090.

the relevant default rules in the Partnership Act 1890 or the Limited Liability Partnerships Regulations 2001[18] will apply.

Nevertheless, there are crucial differences between the partnership and the LLP. First, in terms of s.2(1) of the Limited Liability Partnerships Act 2000, every LLP must have at least two members in order to be incorporated by the Registrar of Companies. There is no minimum number of designated members. However, if there would appear to be no designated members or only one designated member, s.8(2) of the Limited Liability Partnerships Act 2000 provides that every member is deemed to be a designated member and there is a requirement to give notice to the Registrar of Companies of the identity of designated members. Of course, partnerships do not require to have designated members. The second difference between the LLP and the partnership is the demands which the Limited Liability Partnerships Act 2000 imposes on LLPs by way of formalities, publicity and the registration of particulars. For example, in terms of ss.2 and 3 of the Limited Liability Partnerships Act 2000, there are various registration requirements which must be complied with before an LLP can be formed: not so in the case of a partnership. Thirdly, unlike the partnership, by virtue of ss.8 and 9 of the Limited Liability Partnerships Act 2000, notices of the identity of designated members and changes in composition of designated members must be notified to the Registrar of Companies by the filing of appropriate documentation. On a similar note, s.9 of the Limited Liability Partnerships Act 2000 requires the registration of changes in the composition of the membership of an LLP to be notified to the Registrar of Companies. Finally, regs 4 and 5 of the Limited Liability Partnerships Regulations 2001[19] and the Limited Liability Partnerships (Application of Companies Act 2006) Regulations 2009[20] incorporate many provisions from the CA 2006 and the Insolvency Act 1986 into the Limited Liability Partnerships Act 2000. Therefore, for example, it is possible for an LLP to grant a floating charge to a lender in return for funding in the same manner as a company registered under the Companies Acts and an LLP must file a confirmation statement and annual accounts with the Registrar of Companies.[21]

THE LIMITED LIABILITY PARTNERSHIP: ADVANTAGES AND DISADVANTAGES

The following statement is perhaps simplistic but it is nevertheless true: **14–15** that is to say that the advantages and disadvantages of the LLP closely mirror the benefits and demerits of a company registered under the

---

[18] SI 2001/1090.
[19] SI 2001/1090.
[20] SI 2009/1804.
[21] However, when s.92 of the Small Business, Enterprise and Employment Act 2015 comes into force, there will no longer by any legal requirement for an LLP to lodge a confirmation statement with the Registrar of Companies. Instead, the LLP will be required to provide annual confirmation of the accuracy of the information held about it on the Registrar of Companies.

Companies Acts. Thus, the LLP enjoys separate legal personality and the liability of members for the debts of the LLP is limited to the making of a contribution towards the assets of the LLP on winding up to the extent stipulated in the limited liability partnership agreement. Moreover, since an LLP possesses separate legal personality, it has the benefit of perpetual succession. The LLP also has the advantage that it is able to grant a floating charge over the whole of its assets and undertaking with the potential for lower costs of borrowing. Moreover, in the case of an LLP, the members are able to keep secret the details regarding the internal affairs of the LLP. There is no requirement under the Limited Liability Partnerships Act 2000 to publicise the limited liability partnership agreement—only details of the financial performance of the LLP, namely the financial accounts and reports (e.g. profit and loss account and balance sheet) need be registered in a public register.

However, a disadvantage of the LLP is that there is no separation between ownership and control. Here, the LLP resembles the partnership in that it is difficult for outside investors to contribute capital towards the company without taking a management position. The relevant regulation is reg.7(3) of the Limited Liability Partnerships Regulations 2001 which provides that every member of an LLP is entitled to participate in its management.[22] Although it is possible to disapply reg.7(3) in terms of the limited liability partnership agreement, the inherent structure of the LLP is nevertheless geared towards the absence of a division between ownership and control. Another difficulty with the LLP is that it is impossible for an LLP to issue transferable shares as a means of attracting outside capital investment. Moreover, there are also various formalities which must be complied with in exactly the same mould as the incorporated company, e.g. the initial and continuing registration requirements which were outlined above. Like the company, the LLP has the disadvantage that various matters concerning its affairs must be made public. However, the publicity is more limited than in the case of the company, since it is only the accounts of the LLP that must be disclosed —the limited liability partnership agreement which specifies the details of the internal control and management of the LLP does not require to be registered. This can be contrasted with the company where the articles of association of the company (which are the equivalent of the limited liability partnership agreement), do indeed require to be registered. Another disadvantage of the LLP is the complexity surrounding its management and administration. The regulation of the LLP closely resembles the regulation of the company. This is the case since the Limited Liability Partnerships Act 2000, the Limited Liability Partnerships Regulations 2001,[23] the Limited Liability Partnerships (Scotland) Regulations 2001[24] and the Limited Liability Partnerships (Application of Companies Act 2006) Regulations

---

[22] SI 2001/1090.
[23] SI 2001/1090.
[24] SSI 2001/128.

2009[25] incorporate by reference the majority of the CA 2006, the Insolvency Act 1986 and other company legislation into the management and administration of the LLP. This means that the complexity of company law and insolvency law is incorporated into the regulation of the LLP form by implication, with all of the costs and expenses of compliance which that entails. The lack of flexibility inherent in the structure of the LLP is another drawback of this business form. Moreover, another difficulty with the LLP is that unanimity is required to expel a member, unless the limited liability partnership agreement provides otherwise. Therefore, it is not always straightforward to remove management and replace them with specialised management.

Key Concepts

Advantages of the LLP: (1) separate legal personality; (2) limited liability of members for the debts of the LLP; (3) perpetual succession; (4) the ability to keep secret the details regarding the internal affairs of the LLP, namely the voting rights of the members of the LLP and the profit sharing (and loss-bearing) rights of the members of the LLP; and (5) the ability of the LLP to grant a floating charge.

Disadvantages of the LLP: (1) the lack of any separation between ownership and control of the LLP; (2) the inability of the LLP to issue transferable shares to shareholders in return for outside capital investment; (3) the formalities which must be complied with in order to form an LLP and in respect of the continued management of the LLP; (4) the requirement to make public the accounts and details of the financial performance of the LLP, namely the financial accounts and reports, e.g. profit-and-loss account and balance sheet; (5) the complexity of the company law and insolvency law rules in relation to the management and ownership structure of the LLP which are specifically applied to the LLP; (6) the costs of legal compliance; (7) the lack of flexibility in the affairs and management of the LLP, which are conditioned by the terms of the Limited Liability Partnerships Act 2000, the Limited Liability Partnerships Regulations 2001, the Limited Liability Partnerships (Scotland) Regulations 2001 and the Limited Liability Partnerships (Application of Companies Act 2006) Regulations 2009[26]; and (8) the difficulties involved in (i) removing the existing management of the LLP and (ii) introducing specialised management to run the LLP.

---

[25] SI 2009/1804.
[26] SI 2009/1804.

▼ CHAPTER SUMMARY

SOLE TRADERS

14–16
(1) A sole trader is an individual involved in the management and control of his/her own business.
(2) There is no separation between the ownership and the control of the business of the sole trader and only the sole trader has the sole right to participate in the profits of the business or bear the losses of that business.
(3) The sole trader business form possesses no separate legal personality and the sole trader is personally liable for the debts of the business.

PARTNERSHIP

(1) A partnership is the relation which subsists between persons carrying on a business in common with a view of profit—s.1(1) of the Partnership Act 1890.
(2) It is a vehicle which is well-suited towards the joining together of a number of persons for the purposes of carrying on a business.
(3) Each partner of the partnership contributes capital investment, skills, know-how, expertise and contacts and pools those resources.
(4) Each partner in the partnership has the right to participate in the business of the partnership and is an agent of the partnership firm, with the ability to bind the firm in law—ss.5 and 24(5) of the Partnership Act 1890.

Advantages and disadvantages of partnership

(1) Advantages of the partnership:
- the lack of formalities in constituting and operating a partnership;
- lack of publicity in respect of the internal affairs and financial performance of the partnership;
- lack of complexity involved in the management of the partnership;
- low costs of compliance of partnership law; and
- large degree of flexibility in connection with the affairs and management of the partnership.

(2) Disadvantages of the partnership:
- the lack of a separation between ownership and control in the partnership;
- the absence of transferable shares which can be issued to shareholders in return for capital investment;
- difficulties involved in removing existing management and introducing specialised management to run the partnership;
- the partners are jointly and severally liable for the debts of the partnership—ss.9 and 12 of the Partnership Act 1890;
- the lack of perpetual succession; and
- the inability of a partnership to grant a floating charge.

INCORPORATED COMPANIES

(1) A company has separate legal personality distinct from its members or directors:

> ➤ *Salomon v A. Salomon & Co Ltd* [1897] A.C. 22.

(2) A company consists of a number of individuals, namely the members, who voluntarily agree to combine for a common purpose and thus, form a company as a means of carrying on business.

(3) Each member will contribute capital investment, skills, know-how, expertise and contacts to the company and pool those resources.

(4) A company is formed when it has been registered with the Registrar of Companies and the Registrar has issued a document called a certificate of incorporation—ss.7–16 of the CA 2006.

(5) In the case of a limited liability company, the liability of the members for the debts of the company is limited to: (i) (in the case of a company limited by shares) the value remaining unpaid on their shares; or (ii) (in the case of a company limited by guarantee) the contribution which they have agreed to make towards the assets of the company on its winding up in terms of the memorandum of association of the company—s.3(2) and (3) of the CA 2006.

Advantages and disadvantages of company

(1) Advantages of the company:

- a company has separate legal personality;
- the members have limited liability for the debts of the company;
- there is a clear separation between ownership and control in the company;
- companies can issue transferable shares to shareholders in return for capital investment;
- the ease with which existing management may be removed and specialised management introduced to run the company;
- perpetual succession of the company; and
- the ability of the company to grant a floating charge.

(2) Disadvantages of the company:

- the formalities which must be complied with in order to form a company and in respect of the continued management of the company;
- the requirement to make public the internal affairs and financial performance of the company;
- the complexity of company rules in relation to the management and ownership structure of the company;
- the costs of legal compliance in relation to the CA 2006 and other legislation; and
- the lack of flexibility in the affairs and management of the company, which are conditioned by the terms of the CA 2006.

DISTINCTION BETWEEN SOLE TRADERS, PARTNERSHIPS, LLPS AND INCORPORATED COMPANIES

(1) Companies and LLPs are both bodies corporate (s.16 of the CA 2006 and s.1(2) of the Limited Liability Partnerships Act 2000) whereas sole traders and partnerships are not. Partnerships, LLPs and companies possess legal personality and are legally distinct from their partners, members and managers/directors. This can be contrasted with the sole trader which has no separate legal personality.

Advantages and disadvantages of conducting business as a sole trader, partnership, LLP or incorporated company

1. See the table.

Advantage/ Disadvantage	Sole Trader	Partnership	LLP	Company
Advantages				
Separate legal personality	x	✓	✓	✓
Body corporate	x	x	✓	✓
Limited liability of members/ partners/owners	x	x	✓	✓
Perpetual succession	x	x	✓	✓
Division between ownership and control	x	x	x	✓
Can issue transferable shares in return for capital investment	x	x	x	✓
Ease of removal of management and introduction of outside specialised management	x	x	x	✓
Ability to grant floating charge	x	x	✓	✓

Disadvantages				
Publicity	x	x	x – but no need to disclose LLP agreement	✓
Formalities	x	x	✓	✓
Expense	x	x	✓	✓
Complexity	x	x	Some	✓
Lack of flexibility	x	x	Some	✓
Personal liability of owners or joint and several liability of owners/partners/ members	✓	✓	x	x

PERSONAL LIABILITY

(1) Personal liability means that the owners or members of an organisation are fully liable for the debts of that organisation.

LIMITED LIABILITY

(1) Limited liability means that the owners or members of an organisation enjoy limited liability for the debts of that organisation. The extent of the limitation is regulated by the limited liability partnership agreement in the case of an LLP and in the case of an incorporated company limited by shares, the shareholder's liability is limited to the value which remains unpaid on their shares. In the case of an incorporated company limited by guarantee, the extent of a member's liability is limited to the monetary value which they have agreed to contribute towards the debts of the company on a winding up in terms of the memorandum of association.

SEPARATE LEGAL PERSONALITY

(1) An organisation has separate legal personality when it is an organisation which is distinct from its members, partners or owners. It can sue, be sued, enter into contractual relations and own property in its own name.

PERPETUAL SUCCESSION

(1) If an organisation possesses perpetual succession, this means that it is
    not dissolved or terminated by a change in the composition of its
    membership or management. In other words, it continues to exist not-
    withstanding such changes.

DIVISION OF OWNERSHIP AND CONTROL

(1) If an organisation exhibits a separation between ownership and control,
    this means that a manager of the organisation does not require to be an
    owner or vice versa and thus it is easier to obtain outside capital
    investment since investors know that they do not necessarily need to
    participate in the management of the business.

? QUICK QUIZ

- What is a sole trader?
- What is a partnership?
- How are the sole trader, partnership, LLP and incorporated
  company distinct?
- What is meant by personal liability in this context?
- What is meant by limited liability?
- What does separate legal personality mean?
- What is perpetual succession?
- What is meant by a division of ownership and control?

FURTHER READING

➢ Forte, *Scots Commercial Law* (Edinburgh: LexisNexis / Butter-
  worths, 1997), Ch.9.
➢ F. Davidson and L. Macgregor, *Commercial Law in Scotland*,
  3rd edn (Edinburgh: W Green, 2014), Ch.8.
➢ Gloag and Henderson, *The Law of Scotland*, 13th edn (Edin-
  burgh, W. Green, 2012), Chs 46–47.
➢ S. Mayson, D. French and C. Ryan, *Company Law*, 31st edn
  (Oxford: OUP, 2014), Ch.1.

RELEVANT WEBLINKS

➢ Business Gateway: *http://www.bgateway.com* [Accessed May 15,
  2015].
➢ Business Link: *http://www.businesslink.gov.uk/*.

Chapter 15   The Law of Partnership

Dᴀᴠɪᴅ Cᴀʙʀᴇʟʟɪ[1]

► CHAPTER OVERVIEW

This chapter concentrates on the law and regulation of partnerships. As **15–01**
stated in Ch.14, "Choice of Business Medium", a partnership[2] is a legal
form which is available to persons who are seeking to come together to
carry on a business. In Ch.14, the main characteristics of the partnership as
a business vehicle were explored, together with the advantages and disadvantages of the partnership over other business forms. In this chapter,
the partnership will be analysed in much more detail. For this purpose, the
chapter is divided into the following five categories which closely follow
the architecture and flow of the Partnership Act 1890 ("1890 Act"):

- the nature of a partnership (dealt with by ss.1–4 of the 1890 Act);
- the relationship between the partnership and third parties and the
  liability of the partners to third parties (considered by ss.5–18 of
  the 1890 Act);
- property owned by the partnership (dealt with by s.20 of the 1890
  Act);
- the duties of the partners, their relations to one another and the
  regulation of the internal affairs of the partnership (dealt with by
  ss.19–31 of the 1890 Act); and
- the dissolution of the partnership and the distribution of its assets
  on dissolution (considered in detail in ss.32–44 of the 1890 Act).

✓ OUTCOMES

At the end of this chapter you should be able to understand: **15–02**

- ✓   that a partnership in Scots law is a separate legal person distinct
      from its partners;
- ✓   the rules for determining whether the relationship which arises
      between individuals amounts to a partnership;
- ✓   the relevant rules which determine whether a partner has bound
      the partnership in contract with a third party;

---

[1] Senior Lecturer in Commercial Law, University of Edinburgh.
[2] References in this chapter to a "firm" are synonymous with references to a
"partnership".

✓ the relevant rules which ascertain whether the partnership or other partners are liable for wrongs, delicts or omissions of a partner which have caused injury or loss to a third party;
✓ how partnership property is regulated;
✓ the principles which regulate the internal affairs of the partnership, e.g. the duties of the partners towards each other and the partnership and the co-relative rights which they enjoy against each other and the partnership itself; and
✓ how a partnership may come to be terminated or expire and the principles which must be applied towards the distribution of the assets of the partnership on its dissolution and winding up.

THE PARTNERSHIP: AN INTRODUCTION

15–03 As explored in Ch.14, "Choice of Business Medium", the partnership vehicle is well-suited towards the joining together of a number of persons for the purposes of carrying on a business. Partnerships range from large accountancy firms to small businesses. The partnership is regulated by the 1890 Act and, in connection with the control of the trading name of a partnership, Pt 41 of the Companies Act 2006 applies. It is crucial to stress that the 1890 Act provides default rules for the regulation of the partnership. This is significant since it means that the partners can oust or modify the rules of partnership law contained in the 1890 Act by providing for alternative rules in a partnership agreement. Thus, the 1890 Act is subject to the terms of the partnership agreement entered into between the partners and/or the partnership.

One of the most important issues which the law must decide is how the relationship between individuals in business can be classified. In other words, how is a partnership defined and what relationships are excluded which are similar to partnerships?

THE NATURE OF A PARTNERSHIP

15–04 In this first section of this chapter, the rules for the constitution of the partnership, its legal nature, the duties of the partners on the constitution of the partnership and, most importantly, the statutory definition of a partnership in the 1890 Act, will be explored each in turn. First, a partnership can be constituted in writing or orally. It may also be inferred from the actions of the parties and in particular the nature of their relationship towards each other. The important issue is to ascertain the intention of the parties from all of the circumstances of the case. Secondly, for the purposes of Scots law, s.4(2) of the 1890 Act provides that a partnership firm possesses separate legal personality, i.e. that it is a legal body distinct from its constituent partners.[3] Since the firm enjoys separate

---

[3] The position in English law is different.

legal personality, it can enter into binding contracts in its own name and it has the power to sue and be sued in its own name. It can commit delicts and own property. The separate legal personality of the partnership is important in relation to matters such as the prescription of rights of the partnership, diligence and ranking in sequestration.

When persons combine to form a partnership, they owe certain duties towards each other which cannot be displaced. As will become evident later in this chapter, the partners are in a fiduciary relationship to each other and the partnership itself and thus owe a duty of good faith towards each other during the course of the partnership.[4] However, the duty of good faith also exists at the inception of their relationship when they are about to form the partnership. A good example of this premise is provided by the case of *Conlon v Simms*.

Conlon v Simms
[2007] 3 All E.R. 802

Concerning: The duties which partners owe towards each other when they initially come together to form a partnership.

Facts: Conlon was a partner and Simms was the senior partner in a firm of solicitors which was composed of eight partners. Six of the partners joined another firm and all of the partners entered into a deed of dissolution which dissolved the original partnership. Conlon and Simms decided to enter into a new partnership and some months later a Mr Harris joined this new partnership. The Law Society of England and Wales commenced disciplinary proceedings against Mr Simms on the grounds of suspected dishonesty, the outcome of which was a conclusion that Mr Simms should be struck off from the roll of solicitors. Conlon, Harris and Simms entered into an agreement to deal with the position of Simms' suspension from practice and Conlon and Harris raised court proceedings against Simms claiming damages for negligence and misrepresentation. Conlon and Harris claimed that Simms owed them a duty to disclose anything which might affect his status as a solicitor and his ability to enter into partnership agreements. Simms had failed to do so and, if he had, Conlon and Harris claimed that they would not have entered into the partnership agreement. Simms argued that there was no such duty of disclosure and no dishonesty on his part and that Conlon and Harris had believed in his innocence.

Decision: The Court of Appeal held that in negotiating a partnership agreement, a prospective partner owed a duty to the other negotiating partners to disclose all material facts of which he had knowledge and in respect of which the other negotiating partners might not be aware. Thus, prospective partners had a duty to

---

[4] Gloag and Henderson, *The Law of Scotland*, 13th edn (Edinburgh: W. Green, 2012), para.45.18.

disclose material facts to each other and in the event of a fraudulent breach of such duty, the innocent partners who suffered loss as a result of the breach would be able to recover damages in respect of such loss.

15–05 *Conlon v Simms* demonstrates the nature of the duties which partners owe towards each other when a partnership is formed. But it is not always straightforward to ascertain whether a partnership exists and, to this end, it is critical to consider the definition of a partnership which is contained in s.1 of the 1890 Act. So s.1(1) of the 1890 Act provides that a partnership "is the relation which subsists between persons carrying on a business in common with a view of profit". The effect of this definition is that the parties must have the objective of realising a profit when they come together to form a business. The fact that the relevant persons realise a loss is irrelevant, provided that their aim is to be profitable.

The 1890 Act also provides for various organisations, legal relationships and scenarios which, while resembling a partnership, are excluded from the definition. First, s.1(2) of the 1890 Act provides that the relationship between members of a company or association which is an incorporated company or company formed by Act of Parliament or Royal Charter is deemed not to be a partnership under the 1890 Act. Secondly, s.2(1) of the 1890 Act states that the owners of joint property or common property are not to be considered partners without more, regardless of the profit sharing arrangements which exist between them. Thirdly, s.2(2) of the 1890 Act prescribes that where persons share in gross returns, this does not of itself constitute a partnership. A good example of this point is provided by the case of *Cox v Coulson*.

Cox v Coulson
[1916] 2 K.B. 177

Concerning: The nature of the relationship between the manager of a theatrical company and the lessee and manager of a theatre and whether they were partners.

Facts: Coulson was the lessee and manager of a theatre. The manager of a touring theatrical company named Mill provided actors and scenery for a theatrical production and Coulson provided the theatre, the lighting and the playbills. Coulson and Mill agreed to share in the gross receipts taken from the box office on a 60/40 basis. Cox attended the play at the theatre one night. During the performance, one of the actors fired a pistol which ought to have contained a blank cartridge. However, for some reason, the barrel of the pistol was loaded with a live cartridge that night and when it was fired it struck Cox on the wrist and as a result he was wounded. Cox sued Coulson and, during the proceedings, a question was raised as to the relationship between Coulson and Mill.

Decision: In the Court of Appeal, two of the judges specifically stated that the sharing of gross receipts by individuals does not constitute a partnership between them. Therefore, Coulson and Mill were not partners in a partnership.

So *Cox v Coulson* is a case which exemplifies the rule in s.2(2) of the 1890 Act that the sharing of a proportion of gross returns does not of itself create a partnership between individuals. This makes sense since it will be recalled that s.1(1) of the 1890 Act enunciates the principle that individuals must be involved in a relationship whose purpose is the achievement of a profit.

Nevertheless, it should be stressed that the sharing of profits by two or more persons is only prima facie evidence of a partnership. Section 2(3) of the 1890 Act goes on to provide for five scenarios where the mere objective of attaining a profit will not of itself amount to a presumption of a relationship of partnership. Thus, in certain circumstances, the 1890 Act provides that persons who are sharing in profits will be deemed not to be partners. For example, s.2(3)(a) states that the receipt by a person of a debt or other liquidated amount by instalments or otherwise out of the accruing profits of a business does not of itself make him a partner in the business or liable as such. This provision seeks to ensure that a creditor who is paid a debt by a debtor in instalments out of the profits of the business of the debtor does not qualify the creditor as a partner of the debtor. Section 2(3)(b) of the 1890 Act states that employees or agents who are remunerated out of the profits of the business of their employers or principals are not partners of the latter. Section 2(3)(c) of the 1890 Act creates the presumption that widows, widowers, children and surviving civil partners who receive a share of the profits of the business in which the deceased was a partner prior to their death are deemed not to be partners of that business without further factors present. Likewise, s.2(3)(d) of the 1890 Act seeks to ensure that creditors are deemed not to be partners of their debtors where: (i) the capital or interest which they receive from debtors is paid out of, or varies with, the profits of the business of the debtor; or (ii) the creditors receive a share of the profits of the business of the debtor. Finally, where a person sells their goodwill in a business and receives an annuity or share in the profits of that business as the consideration for the sale, s.2(3)(e) of the 1890 Act states that the seller will be deemed not to be a partner. Therefore, in ascertaining whether persons are engaged in a partnership, care must be taken to ensure that the principles in s.2(3) are considered, since the mere aim of realising a profit on the part of the parties will not always be a factor which tips the balance in favour of a conclusion tending towards a partnership relationship.

> **Key Concepts**
>
> A partnership is defined as "the relation which subsists between persons carrying on a business in common with a view of profit" and it may be constituted orally or in writing or may be inferred from the conduct of the parties. A partnership possesses separate legal personality distinct from its partners in terms of Scots law. On the constitution of a partnership, the partners owe each other duties of good faith and in particular duties to disclose any material facts of which they have knowledge and in respect of which the other partners might not be aware.

THE RELATIONSHIP BETWEEN THE PARTNERS, THE PARTNERSHIP AND THIRD PARTIES

15–06 The relevant provisions of the 1890 Act which deal with the relationship of the partnership and the partners to the outside world are contained in ss.5–18 of the 1890 Act. In analysing ss.5–18 of the 1890 Act, matters are divided into three portions. First, we will deal with ss.5–9. Secondly, consideration will be given to ss.10–13 and, finally, ss.14–18 will be reviewed.

Sections 5–9 of the 1890 Act deal with the liability of the partnership and the partners to third parties in contract. Section 5 of the 1890 Act states that every partner is deemed to be an agent of the partnership and of the other partners. In this context, it is worth setting out the terms of s.5 of the 1890 Act in full:

> "Every partner is an agent of the firm and his other partners for the purpose of the business of the partnership; and the acts of every partner who does any act for carrying on in the usual way business of the kind carried on by the firm of which he is a member bind the firm and the partners, unless the partner so acting has in fact no authority to act for the firm in the particular matter, and the person with whom he is dealing either knows that he has no authority, or does not know or believe him to be a partner."

Thus, a partner has the power to bind the partnership in contract with third parties where the partner engages in acts "for carrying on in the usual way business of the kind carried on by the" partnership. For example, where the partner enters into a contract with a third party which falls in the ordinary course of business of the partnership, the partnership will be bound by that contract. However, s.5 of the 1890 Act provides for two situations where the partnership will not be liable under such a contract. First, where the partner has no authority to bind the partnership and the third party knows that the partner has no such authority, the partnership will not be bound. Secondly, the partnership will have no liability under a contract with a third party where the partner has no authority to bind the partnership and the third party does not know or believe him to be a partner.

The authority of the partners to bind the partnership is commonly controlled by a partnership agreement. For example, where a partnership agreement directs that a partner has the power to enter into contracts with third parties having a value of no more than £500,000, the partner who acts in contravention of such express authority is said to have "exceeded their authority". Nevertheless, even in those circumstances where the partnership agreement is silent regarding the authority of the partners, or there is no partnership agreement at all, the common law doctrines of implied authority and ostensible authority may apply to bind the partnership where a partner purports to enter into a contract with a third party in the name of that partnership. A partner, being a manager and owner of a partnership, will enjoy a broad canvass to bind the partnership in contract by virtue of the doctrine of implied authority. However, where it is arguable that the partner does not possess such implicit authority, there may be circumstances in which the partnership has represented to third parties, by their own words or conduct that the partner has authority to act on their behalf. In the latter circumstance, the partner is said to have ostensible authority to bind the partnership. The effect of s.5 of the 1890 Act is that the partnership will be bound by the actions of a partner where that partner possesses express, implied or ostensible authority, subject to the two exceptions outlined above.

One of the difficulties with s.5 of the 1890 Act is that it is not clear **15–07** when the actions of the partners are such that they are, "carrying on in the usual way business of the kind carried on by the" partnership. A useful case is *Mann v D'Arcy* which provides an example of a situation where a partner was held by a court to be engaged in carrying on in the usual way business of the kind carried on by the partnership.

Mann v D'Arcy
[1968] 1 W.L.R. 893

Concerning: Whether a partnership was bound by a single venture with Mr Mann as a result of the actions of a partner of the partnership.

Facts: An oral agreement was entered into between Mann and D'Arcy whereby D'Arcy would go on "joint account" with Mann on the purchase and re-sale of approximately 350 tons of potatoes which formed part of the cargo of a vessel. D'Arcy was the active partner in a partnership of produce merchants carried on under the name of D'Arcy & Co and the arrangement between Mann and D'Arcy envisaged a partnership between D'Arcy & Co and Mann. In other words, D'Arcy had purported to bind the partnership in contract with Mann for a single venture. The question arose whether D'Arcy had implied authority to bind the partnership, D'Arcy & Co, to a partnership with Mann for the joint venture. This depended on whether D'Arcy had acted, "for carrying on in the usual way business of the kind carried on by the firm of which the partner is a member" in accordance with s.5 of the 1890 Act.

Decision: The High Court ruled that the arrangement entered into between Mann and D'Arcy, being an arrangement for sharing profit and loss on a transaction of purchase and re-sale of potatoes, was something done for carrying on "in the usual way business of the kind carried on by" the partnership. D'Arcy & Co were produce merchants and a significant part of such a business was the purchase and re-sale of potatoes. Thus, even though a partner has no implied authority to make his co-partners partners with another person in another business, D'Arcy had authority to bind, and did bind, the partnership D'Arcy & Co to a partnership with Mann for the single venture.

If the court had held that the actions of D'Arcy did not fall within the ordinary course of business of the partnership, the result would have been very different. First, the partnership would not have been liable on the contract to Mann. Secondly, and most importantly, D'Arcy would have been personally liable on the contract to Mann. Thus, if there was a breach of the contract which caused loss to Mann, D'Arcy would have been liable to Mann. As Lord Justice-Clerk Scott Dickson stated in the case of *Fortune v Young*[5]:

> "A partner who signs an obligatory document outwith the scope of his copartnery does not bind the firm, but he undoubtedly binds himself. Therefore in this case I think it is quite clear in law that the [partner], while he did not bind his copartnery, did bind himself by signing this document."[6]

Section 6 of the 1890 Act enunciates another rule which deals with the partners, the partnership and third parties. It provides that any act or instrument executed by a partner or authorised person relating to the business of the partnership which is done or executed in the name of the partnership, or in any other manner showing an intention to bind the partnership, is deemed to be duly binding on the partnership and all the partners. Moreover, s.8 of the 1890 Act supplements s.6 by detailing the legal position where the partners agree that a restriction is to be placed on the power of any one or more of them to bind the partnership. In such circumstances, any act done in contravention of the agreement is not binding on the partnership with respect to any persons having notice of the agreement. Most importantly, s.9 of the 1890 Act provides that persons are jointly and severally liable for the debts of the partnership which are incurred by the partnership whilst such persons are partners of

---

[5] 1918 S.C. 1.
[6] 1918 S.C. 1 at 6, per Lord Justice-Clerk Scott Dickson. Writer's annotations are shown in square brackets throughout this chapter.

the partnership. Moreover, s.9 of the 1890 Act provides that the estate of a deceased partner is also jointly and severally liable for the partnership's debts and s.17(2) of the 1890 Act sets out the position regarding a partner who has retired whereby they do not cease to be liable for the debts or obligations of the partnership which were incurred when he/she was a partner. The joint and several liability rule is significant since it means that a creditor of the partnership can choose to sue one partner, some partners or all of the partners for the recovery of debts due to them by the partnership. The creditor can also choose to sue such partners for different amounts. If the creditor does seek to call the partners to account for the debt due to them by the partnership in differing amounts, s.4(2) of the 1890 Act imparts the rule that the partner who has paid the debt of the partnership to the third party is entitled to pro rata relief from the remaining partners. For example, if the debt due by the partnership to the third party is £26,000 and the third party recovers £20,000 from partner 1 and £6,000 from partner 2, partner 1 has the right to be reimbursed £7,000 from partner 2.

Sections 10–13 of the 1890 Act cover the liability of the partnership **15–08** and partners for wrongs committed against third parties. Section 10 provides as follows:

> "Where, by any wrongful act or omission of any partner acting in the ordinary course of the business of the firm, or with the authority of his co-partners, loss or injury is caused to any person not being a partner in the firm, or any penalty is incurred, the firm is liable therefor to the same extent as the partner so acting or omitting to act."

For the purposes of the above, it is beneficial to make a distinction between two different scenarios:

(1) where a partner acts in the ordinary course of business; and
(2) where a partner acts with the authority of his co-partners.

In the case of (1), the partnership will be liable for delicts and defaults to the same degree as the partner who has committed the wrongful act or omission. However, the partner may also be liable to the partnership as witnessed by the case of *Ross, Harper & Murphy v Banks*.[7] With regard to (2), again, the partnership will be liable for wrongs committed by a partner where the partner has acted with the authority of his fellow partners. This rule applies regardless of whether the partner is acting in the ordinary course of business or not. However, an exception applies where a wrong committed by a partner acting on behalf of the partnership results in a negligent injury to another partner. Here, the case of

---

[7] 2000 S.C. 500.

Mair v Wood[8] ruled that the partnership will not be liable for the negligence of the partner.

As in the case of s.5 of the 1890 Act, in the case of (1) above, difficulties arise in ascertaining whether the partner is actually acting in the ordinary course of business of the partnership. The case of *Dubai Aluminium v Salaam*[9] establishes how the courts will tackle this issue.

Dubai Aluminium v Salaam
[2003] 2 A.C. 366

Concerning: Whether a partnership was liable to third parties as a result of the activities of a partner who dishonestly assisted one of his clients in perpetrating a fraud.

Facts: A senior partner in a firm of solicitors dishonestly assisted a client in perpetrating a fraud against Dubai Aluminium which resulted in the latter paying out $US50m in terms of a fake consultancy agreement. Dubai Aluminium sued the partnership on the basis that the senior partner was acting in his capacity as a partner when he assisted his client in perpetrating the fraud by drafting certain contracts and agreements. The question was whether the senior partner was acting in the ordinary course of business of the partnership in drafting the agreements. The Court of Appeal held that the activities of the senior partner had been performed outwith the ordinary course of business of the partnership, since it was not in the business of committing fraudulent activities.

Decision: The House of Lords ruled that the Court of Appeal had erred in holding that the senior partner's acts had not been done in the ordinary course of business of the partnership. For the wrongful activities of a partner to have been conducted in the ordinary course of a partnership's business, they must be so closely connected with acts he or she was authorised to do that, for the purpose of the liability of the firm to third parties, it might fairly and properly be considered as done by the partner whilst acting in the ordinary course of the firm's business. In this particular case, it was ruled that the drafting of agreements and contracts for clients was part and portion of the role of a firm of solicitors practising law. As such, the partner's wrongful conduct in assisting in the perpetration of the fraud was such that it amounted to actions conducted in the ordinary course of the business of the partnership and so the partnership was liable to Dubai Aluminium. Thus, the courts will apply a "sufficiently close connection" test.

Section 10 of the 1890 Act is complemented by s.11 which applies to a

---

[8] 1948 S.C. 83.
[9] [2003] 2 A.C. 366.

fact-specific situation. That is to say that the partnership will be liable for financial losses suffered by third parties where a partner misapplies money or property received from such third party which is held in the custody of the firm. Section 12 of the 1890 Act mirrors the terms of s.9 of the same Act. That is to say that all of the partners are jointly and severally liable to the extent that the partnership is liable to third parties who suffer injury or loss as a result of the wrongful actions or omissions of one of the partners. Again, what this means is that an injured third party may sue one partner, some partners or all of the partners to recover damages or compensation which is due to them by the partnership. The injured third party also has the right to sue such partners for different amounts and, if they do so, s.4(2) of the 1890 Act applies to settle matters amongst the partners. Thus, a partner who has paid sums to the third party on behalf of the partnership in damages or compensation is entitled to pro rata relief from the remaining partners.

Finally, we turn to ss.14–18 of the 1890 Act which deal with various miscellaneous matters which arise where the partners and/or the partnership interact with third parties. First, s.14(1) of the 1890 Act ascertains the legal position where an individual who is not legally a partner holds himself/herself out as a partner to a third party. It is provided that any person who represents himself/herself as a partner is liable as a partner to a third party who has on the faith of such representation given credit to the firm. This rule applies regardless of whether the representation has or has not been made or communicated to the third party who gives credit by or with the knowledge of the apparent partner making the representation. The 1890 Act makes specific provision for the situation where after a partner's death the business of the partnership is continued in the name of the old partnership. Hence, by virtue of s.14(2) of the 1890 Act, the continued use of that name or of the deceased partner's name as part thereof does not of itself make his executors or his estate or effects liable for any partnership debts contracted after his death. Thus, in such circumstances, the executors and/or estate of the deceased partner are not held out as being a partner of the partnership and the general rule in s.14(1) does not apply.

Another rule of partnership law is contained in s.15 of the 1890 Act whereby an admission or representation made by any partner concerning the partnership affairs, and in the ordinary course of its business, is evidence against the firm. Moreover, notice to any partner who habitually acts in the partnership business of any matter relating to partnership affairs operates as notice to the firm. However, an exception applies in the case of a fraud on the firm committed by or with the consent of that partner.

In terms of s.17 of the 1890 Act, there are essentially two circumstances **15–09** in which the partners of the partnership may change. First, where a new partner is admitted to the partnership. Here, s.17(1) of the 1890 Act sets out the position regarding the liability of such new partner for the debts of the partnership which were incurred prior to that new partner's assumption. It is provided that such a new partner does not become liable to the creditors of the firm for anything done before he became a partner.

Secondly, the composition of a partnership will change when a partner retires from the partnership. On retiral, s.17(2) of the 1890 Act stipulates that a partner does not automatically cease to be liable for the debts or obligations of the partnership which were incurred before his retirement. If the partnership wishes to relieve the retiring partner of such liability, s.17(3) of the 1890 Act narrates that this must be specified in an agreement entered into between the retiring partner, the remaining partners of the partnership as newly constituted and the creditors of the partnership. Such agreement may be either constituted orally or in writing or inferred as a fact from the course of dealing between the creditors and the partnership as newly constituted. The liability of retiring partners is also considered by s.36 of the 1890 Act. Here, it is stated that a retiring partner who has not provided creditors of the partnership with notice of his retiral may be liable for debts incurred by the partnership after his retirement. However, a partner who has not given notice of his retirement will not be liable for partnership debts incurred after the date of his retirement if he was not known to be a partner by the third party dealing with the firm. Section 36(2) of the 1890 Act clarifies the position regarding notice to parties who had not dealt with the partnership whereby an advertisement in the *Edinburgh Gazette* will be deemed to be proper notice of a partner's retirement to all such persons who had no prior dealings with the partnership. However, in the case of third parties who have had such dealings with the partnership, the publication of an advertisement in the *Edinburgh Gazette* will not amount to sufficient notice. Unless there has been an amendment to the name of the partnership or specific notice has been given to the third party, the retiring partner will continue to be liable post-retirement.

Key Concepts

Every partner is deemed to be an agent of the partnership and of the other partners.

The acts of every partner who does any act for carrying on in the usual way business of the kind carried on by the firm will bind the firm and the partners. However, the partnership will not be liable on such a third party contract where: (i) the partner has in fact no authority to act for the firm in the particular matter, and the person with whom he is dealing knows that he has no authority; or (ii) or the partner has no authority to bind the partnership and the third party does not know or believe him to be a partner.

If the partnership is not liable on a contract entered into with a third party, the partner will be personally liable. But, if the partnership is liable, the partners are jointly and severally liable to the third party for the debts of the partnership.

If a partner commits a wrongful act or omission when acting in the ordinary course of business of the partnership, or with the authority of his co-partners, the firm is liable to a third party who has suffered injury or loss as a result of such a wrongful act or omission. In such circumstances, the partners are jointly and severally liable for any debt incurred by the partnership pursuant to the partnership's liability to third parties to make good the injury or loss which the latter has suffered. However, if the third party who has sustained an injury or loss is a partner, the partnership is not liable and it is only the partner who has committed the wrongful act who is liable.

An individual who is not a partner but holds himself out to a third party as a partner is personally liable on that contract.

PARTNERSHIP PROPERTY

If property is purchased with the money of the partnership or on account **15–10** of the partnership in the ordinary course of the business of the partnership, such property is deemed to be partnership property. In terms of s.20(1) of the 1890 Act, partnership property must be held by the partners exclusively for the purposes of the partnership and in accordance with the partnership agreement. Section 21 of the 1890 Act creates a presumption of law whereby unless the contrary intention appears, property bought with money belonging to a partnership is deemed to have been bought on account of the firm. The practice used to be that a partnership would take title to heritable property in the name of the partners in trust for the firm. However, since the coming into force of s.70 of the Abolition of Feudal Tenure (Scotland) Act 2000, it is now competent for title to partnership property to be taken in the name of the partnership, rather in the name of the partners in trust. The effect of ss.20 and 21 of the 1890 Act is that the rights of each partner in partnership property amounts to a right to a *pro indiviso* share of the assets of the partnership.

PARTNERS' DUTIES, THE RELATIONS OF PARTNERS TO ONE ANOTHER AND THE REGULATION OF THE INTERNAL AFFAIRS OF THE PARTNERSHIP

At the beginning of this chapter, it was stated that the partners may **15–11** depart from the rules of partnership law contained in the 1890 Act by providing for their own set of tailor-made rules in a partnership agreement. Regardless of whether those rules which govern the partnership are adopted from the 1890 Act or ousted by virtue of the terms of a partnership agreement, by virtue of s.19 of the 1890 Act, the partners have the power to vary the terms and conditions which regulate the partnership either orally or in writing or such variation may be inferred from a course of dealing.

Partners are fiduciaries and owe each other fiduciary duties. This means that the partners owe each other duties of good faith in their accounts with each other and third parties. Since partners owe fiduciary duties of good faith to one another, we find sections of the 1890 Act such as s.28 which provides that the partners are bound to render true accounts and full information of all things affecting the partnership to the other partners or their legal representatives. Moreover, s.29 states that every partner must account to the partnership for any benefit he/she derives without the consent of the other partners from any transaction concerning the partnership, or from any use by him of the partnership property name or business connection. In other words, partners must not make a personal profit. If they do, they must account to the partnership for that private profit. Another aspect of the duty of good faith is detailed in s.30 of the 1890 Act to the effect that if a partner, without the consent of the other partners, carries on any business of the same nature as and competing with that of the firm, he must account for and pay over to the firm all profits made by him in that business.

Sections 24–26 of the 1890 Act provide for a number of default rules which regulate the interests, duties and rights of the partners in the partnership. Thus, these rules may be disapplied by the partners by express or implied agreement. The rules are as follows:

- All the partners are entitled to share equally in the capital and profits of the business, and must contribute equally towards the losses whether of capital or otherwise sustained by the firm.[10]
- The firm must indemnify every partner in respect of payments made and personal liabilities incurred by him:
  - in the ordinary and proper conduct of the business of the firm; or
  - in or about anything necessarily done for the preservation of the business or property of the firm.

- A partner making, for the purpose of the partnership, any actual payment or advance beyond the amount of capital which he has agreed to subscribe, is entitled to interest at the rate of 5 per cent per annum from the date of the payment or advance.
- A partner is not entitled, before the ascertainment of profits, to interest on the capital subscribed by him.
- Every partner may take part in the management of the partnership business.[11]
- No partner shall be entitled to remuneration for acting in the partnership business.[12]
- No person may be introduced as a partner without the consent of all existing partners.
- Any difference arising as to ordinary matters connected with the partnership business may be decided by a majority of the

---

[10] This rule is commonly displaced by the partners in the partnership agreement.
[11] In the case of "silent" partners, this rule will be disapplied.
[12] For obvious reasons, this default rule will be removed to ensure that the partners are entitled to remuneration.

partners, but no change may be made in the nature of the partnership business without the consent of all existing partners.[13]

- The partnership books are to be kept at the place of business of
  the partnership (or the principal place, if there is more than one),
  and every partner may, when he thinks fit, have access to and
  inspect and copy any of them.

Section 25 of the 1890 Act goes on to impose a default rule to the effect
that no majority of the partners has the power to expel any partner unless
a power to do so has been conferred by express agreement between the
partners. If the partnership does include such a power of majority
expulsion in terms of the partnership agreement, the courts have
demonstrated that they will police such a power very rigorously and will
on occasion refuse the partners the power to insist on such a power.
Moreover, in terms of s.44 of the Equality Act 2010, it is unlawful for the
partners to remove a partner on the basis of any of the protected characteristics in that Act, such as the partner's sex, race, disability, religious
belief, philosophical belief, sexual orientation, marital status, pregnancy,
maternity and/or age.

In the case of a partnership of an indefinite duration, s.26 sets out the
rule that any partner may determine the partnership at any time on giving
notice of his intention so to do to all the other partners. In such a case,
where the retiring partner intimates his intention to dissolve the partnership, this will be effective in terms of s.32(c) of the 1890 Act. Where
the partnership has originally been constituted by deed, a notice in
writing, signed by the partner giving it, shall be sufficient for this purpose.
However, it is common for a partnership agreement to state that the
partnership will not be terminated without the consent of all of the
partners. As regards the partners, this will be valid in law. As regards
third parties, Scots common law is to the effect that the partnership will
not be determined provided notice is given to them.[14] In such circumstances, third parties will be bound by such a notice.[15]

Meanwhile, in terms of s.27 of the 1890 Act, if a partnership for a fixed
duration is continued after the term has expired, and without any express
new agreement, the rights and duties of the partners remain the same as
they were at the expiry of the term, so far as is consistent with the
incidents of a partnership at will. The precise legal terminology for such
continuation of the partnership is "tacit relocation". If the business of the
partnership is continued by the partners or such of them as habitually
acted therein during the term, without any settlement or liquidation of
the partnership affairs, a presumption duly applies that the partnership is

---

[13] This rule introduces what amounts to a distinction between ordinary and significant
matters of partnership business and for the reason that it is not always straightforward to
distinguish between the two, it is a rule which is routinely modified or ousted in the
partnership agreement.

[14] This is despite what may be stipulated in the partnership deed, e.g. a provision to the
effect that the partnership is dissolved after the passage of a fixed term.

[15] Bell, *Commentaries*, II, 530.

continued. However, there must remain at least two partners at the date of expiry. Otherwise, the presumption in s.27 will not apply and the partnership will terminate on expiry with a new partnership coming into being.

Key Concepts

The rules of partnership law contained in the 1890 Act are subject to the terms and conditions expressly agreed upon by the parties.

Partners are fiduciaries and owe each other fiduciary duties. They owe each other duties of good faith in their accounts with each other and third parties. Partners must account to the partnership for any benefit which they have derived without the consent of the other partners from any partnership transaction, or from any use of the partnership property name or business connection. A partner who competes with the partnership must account for and pay over to the firm all profits made by him in that business.

Sections 24–26 of the 1890 Act provide for a number of default rules which regulate the interests, duties and rights of the partners in the partnership. So, all the partners are entitled to share equally in the capital and profits of the business, and must contribute equally towards the losses whether of capital or otherwise sustained by the firm. Every partner may take part in the management of the partnership business and no partner is entitled to remuneration for acting in the partnership business. Moreover, no majority of the partners has the power to expel any partner unless a power to do so has been conferred by express agreement between the partners.

In the case of a partnership of unlimited duration, any partner may determine the partnership at any time on giving notice of his intention so to do to all the other partners. However, it is common for a partnership agreement to state that the partnership will not be terminated without the consent of all of the partners and as regards the partners and third parties, this will be valid in law. If a partnership for a fixed duration is continued after the term has expired, and without any express new agreement, the doctrine of "tacit relocation" applies, to the effect that the partnership continues.

THE DISSOLUTION OF THE PARTNERSHIP AND THE DISTRIBUTION OF ITS ASSETS ON DISSOLUTION

15–12 The principles which apply in the case of the determination and dissolution of a partnership will now be considered. Essentially, there are two mechanisms by which the partnership may be dissolved. First, it may be dissolved without the intervention of the courts. Secondly, it may be dissolved under the superintendence and approval of the courts. Each of these methods for dissolution will be considered in turn.

First, in connection with the dissolution of the partnership without court approval, the first way in which this may be achieved is by agreement of all the partners. A second method is specified in s.32(a) of the 1890 Act. This states that subject to: (i) what is provided in the partnership agreement; and (ii) what was stated above in connection with the tacit relocation of a fixed-term partnership in terms of s.27 of the 1890 Act, the general rule is that a fixed-term partnership is dissolved by expiration of that term. Meanwhile, s.32(c) of the 1890 Act covers the position as regards determination in the context of a partnership of unlimited duration. Here, it is stated that any partner can dissolve the partnership by providing notice to the other partners of his intention to do so. Moreover, in terms of s.33(1) of the 1890 Act, the death or bankruptcy of a partner automatically dissolves the partnership. However, this is subject to agreement to the contrary in the partnership agreement. The case of *WS Gordon & Co Ltd v Thomson Partnership* is a case in point.[16]

WS Gordon & Co Ltd v Thomson Partnership
1985 S.L.T. 122

Concerning: Whether a partnership dissolves on the death or bankruptcy of one of the partners where the partnership agreement specifically provides that it does not.

Facts: A partnership agreement stated that in the event of the death or incapacity of any of the partners, the remaining partners were required to decide within two months of such date either: (i) to wind up the business of the partnership; or (ii) to assume the estate and assets of the business of the partnership and to carry on the business of the partnership to the exclusion of the representatives of the deceased or incapacitated partner with exclusive right to the goodwill and use of the partnership name. When one of the partners died, the owners of a farm leased to the partnership raised proceedings to eject the remaining partners on the basis that the partnership had dissolved when the partner died.

Decision: The Inner House of the Court of Session ruled that the partnership agreement incorporated tailor-made provisions into the relationship of the parties to the effect that the death of a partner did not function so as to dissolve the partnership.

As well as the dissolution of the partnership on the death or bankruptcy of one of the partners, s.33(2) of the 1890 Act provides that a partnership may, at the option of the other partners, be dissolved if any partner arranges for his share of the partnership property to be charged under the 1890 Act for his own personal debts. A partnership may also be dissolved by the occurrence of an event which makes it unlawful for the business of the partnership to be continued, e.g. for reasons of illegality. In the case

---

[16] 1985 S.L.T. 122.

of *Hugh Stevenson & Sons v AG Fur Cartonnagen-Industrie*,[17] the House of Lords ruled that the outbreak of war between the UK and Germany dissolved a partnership between a UK company and German company on the basis that it was illegal to trade with the enemy in terms of UK legislation. Finally, a partnership may be dissolved outwith the super-intendence of the courts by rescission of the partnership agreement. A partner may rescind the partnership on the basis that one of the partners has perpetrated a fraud or has misrepresented the position. In terms of s.41 of the 1890 Act, it is provided that the partner who seeks to rescind on the basis of fraud or misrepresentation is entitled to a lien on the surplus of the partnership assets, to stand in the place of the creditors of the firm for any payments made by him in respect of the liabilities of the partnership and to be indemnified by the person guilty of fraud or making the misrepresentation against all debts and liabilities of the partnership.

As mentioned above, the partnership may be dissolved with the authority of the court. Section 35 of the 1890 Act sets out the grounds on which the court may sanction the dissolution of the partnership. First, s.35(b) specifies that the court may dissolve the partnership when one of the partners is permanently incapable of performing his part of the partnership contract. Moreover, conduct by one of the partners which is prejudicial to the carrying on of the partnership's business will give the court the authority to dissolve the partnership in terms of s.35(c) of the 1890 Act. An example of prejudicial conduct is provided by the case of *Carmichael v Evans*.[18]

Carmichael v Evans
[1904] 1 Ch. 486

Concerning: Whether the conduct of a partner in being convicted of travelling on a train without a ticket amounted to conduct prejudicial to the business of the partnership.

Facts: A partnership agreement provided that where a junior partner had been, "addicted to scandalous conduct detrimental to the partnership business", or had been found guilty of "any flagrant breach of the duties of a partner", the senior partner might give the offending partner six days' notice of expulsion from the partnership. One of the junior partners was convicted of travelling on a train without a ticket with intent to avoid payment, and fined the full penalty. The senior partner served the offending partner with notice of expulsion.

Decision: The court held that the junior partner had been found guilty of a crime of dishonesty. Accordingly it was valid for him to be expelled and for the partnership to be dissolved.

---

[17] [1918] A.C. 239 HL.
[18] [1904] 1 Ch. 486.

Where a partner is in breach of contract or conducts himself in a manner **15–13**
which renders it not reasonably practicable for the other partners to carry
on the business in partnership with him, it is lawful for the other partners
to dissolve the partnership. This is provided for in s.35(d) of the 1890 Act.
Moreover, in terms of s.35(e) of the Act, the partnership may be dissolved
by the court where the business of the partnership can only be carried on
at a loss. Finally, the court has the power to dissolve a partnership where
it is just and equitable to do so in terms of s.35(f) of the 1890 Act. The
"just and equitable" ground is very wide in scope and a case such as
Sutherland v Barnes exemplifies the circumstances in which the court will
be prepared to dissolve a partnership on this particular basis.[19]

Sutherland v Barnes
Unreported October 8, 1997 Vinelott J. (CA)

Concerning: Whether it was just and equitable that a partnership be
dissolved by the court.

Facts: The case concerned a general medical practice. One of
the partners of the partnership, namely a Dr Barnes, consistently
refused to: (i) take part in necessary discussions concerning the
future of the partnership, in particular the acquisition of new and
more commodious premises; and (ii) consider the terms of a new
partnership agreement.

Decision: The Court of Appeal in England ruled that Dr Barnes'
refusal to take part in discussions regarding the partnership's future
had been intransigent and unreasonable. His failure to take part in
discussions concerning the terms of a new partnership agreement
in the face of a deed which was no longer appropriate, having
regard to the changes in the structure and membership of the
partnership and in the nature of the practice since 1973, was
equally unreasonable. In light of such factors, the court held that
the relationship of trust and confidence between Dr Barnes and his
co-partners had irrevocably broken down. Consequently, it was just
and equitable that the partnership be dissolved.

In connection with the dissolution of a partnership by the court or
otherwise, issues concerning notification of the dissolution are covered by
the 1890 Act. In this context, it is important to distinguish between two
different scenarios. First, there is the situation where the partnership is
dissolved and the partners cease to trade. Secondly, consider the case
where the partnership is dissolved and the remaining partners continue to
trade as a new partnership after dissolution in the old name. As regards
third parties who trade with the partnership, they will obviously be
anxious to know of the composition of the partners after dissolution in
the latter case, since the partnership will continue to trade and the

---

[19] Unreported October 8, 1997 Vinelott J. (CA).

creditworthiness of the partners will be a paramount concern. However, in the first case, the creditors will be less concerned since there will be an accounting, winding up and distribution of assets in accordance with the 1890 Act and the creditworthiness of the partners going forward is less of an issue. The general rule regarding notification contained in s.36 of the 1890 Act is that there is a requirement for notice to be given in order to extinguish the liability of partners following dissolution of the firm where the business is carried on in the old name. Having said that, there are three exceptions which apply. First, the estate of a partner who dies is not liable for partnership debts contracted after the date of his/her death. Secondly, the same rule applies in the case of the estate of a partner who is made bankrupt, i.e. a partner who enters into sequestration. Finally, as outlined above, the estate of a dormant partner is not liable on his retiral from the firm for partnership debts which are incurred after the date of his retirement.

Once it has been clarified that the partnership is to be dissolved with or without the intervention of the court, there are various consequences which follow. First, under s.37 of the 1890 Act, the partners may intimate publicly the fact of dissolution of the partnership or the retirement of a partner from the partnership. The partners making such notification may require the other partner or partners to participate for that purpose in all necessary or proper acts, if any, which cannot be done without his or their participation. Section 37 is intended to allow the partners to protect themselves by ensuring that notice is given of dissolution or retirement of a partner. Once the partnership has been dissolved, the general authority of the partners to bind the partnership in terms of s.5 of the 1890 Act ceases to be effective. However, s.38 of the 1890 Act clarifies that the authority of each partner to bind the firm, and the other rights and obligations of the partners, both continue for certain purposes notwithstanding its dissolution. Such authority is however restricted. It continues so far as may be necessary to wind up the affairs of the partnership, and to complete transactions begun but unfinished at the time of the dissolution, but not otherwise. Nevertheless, the partnership will not be bound by the acts of a partner who has become bankrupt. But this exception does not affect the liability of any person who has after the bankruptcy represented himself or knowingly suffered himself to be represented as a partner of the bankrupt in terms of s.47 of the 1890 Act.

Once the partnership has been dissolved, s.39 (which is set out in full below) of the 1890 Act provides that every partner or representative has the right to apply to the court to have the business and affairs of the partnership wound up:

> "On the dissolution of a partnership every partner is entitled, as against the other partners in the firm, and all persons claiming through them in respect of their interests as partners, to have the property of the partnership applied in payment of the debts and liabilities of the firm, and to have the surplus assets after such payment applied in payment of what may be due to the partners respectively after deducting what may be due from them as partners

to the firm; and for that purpose any partner or his representatives may on the termination of the partnership apply to the Court to wind up the business and affairs of the firm."

In terms of the common law, it was and continues to be the practice for **15–14** the surviving partners to take charge of the winding up of the affairs of the partnership. However, on application to the court, the court has the discretion to appoint a judicial factor to the estate of the partnership to organise and arrange for the winding up of the partnership. The appointment of a judicial factor may be desirable where a partner or partners die, partners are made bankrupt or a partner is seeking an impartial agent to administer the winding up of the partnership in order to protect himself/herself from the influence and interests of the remaining surviving partners. In such circumstances, rather than apply personally to the court for the business and affairs of the partnership to be wound up, the partner may prefer to apply to the court for the appointment of an independent judicial factor to oversee the winding up of the partnership.

Section 40 of the 1890 Act governs the situation where a partner has paid a premium on entering a fixed-term partnership and the partnership has been dissolved before the expiration of the fixed term otherwise than by the death of a partner. It is provided that the court may order the whole or any part of the repayment of the premium to the partner as it thinks is just. The court must take into account the terms and conditions of the partnership agreement and have regard to the length of time during which the partnership has continued. However, the court may refuse an order to repay the premium where the dissolution of the partnership was wholly due to the misconduct of the partner who paid the premium or the partnership was dissolved by an agreement containing no provision for a return of any part of the premium.

Where a partner has died or otherwise ceased to be a partner, and the surviving or continuing partners carry on the partnership's business with its capital or assets without any final settlement of accounts as between the partnership and the outgoing partner or his estate, unless there is any agreement to the contrary, or an option to purchase the share of the deceased or outgoing partner has been exercised in terms of the partnership agreement or otherwise, s.42 of the 1890 Act will apply. Section 42 of the 1890 Act states that the outgoing partner or his estate is entitled to receive either a share of any profits made after dissolution from use of that partner's share in the partnership assets, or, at the option of the outgoing partner or his representatives, interest at the rate of 5 per cent per annum on the amount of his share in the partnership assets. So where a partner dies and the surviving partners continue the business of the partnership without accounting for the share of the deceased, s.42 of the 1890 Act will apply. Section 42 of the 1890 Act will also be applicable where a partner becomes bankrupt and the remaining solvent partners carry on the business without paying out the bankrupt partner's share. Section 43 of the 1890 Act stipulates that the amount due from surviving or continuing partners to an outgoing partner or the representatives of a deceased partner in respect of the outgoing or deceased partner's share is a debt accruing at the date of the dissolution or death. However, the case of *Duncan v The MFV Marigold PD145*[20] ruled that cessation accounts drawn up as at the date of dissolution by a partnership's accountants which purported to represent a deceased's share of the capital in the partnership did not represent, unless otherwise agreed, the measure of the amount due to the estate of a deceased partner. Instead, the balance due must be ascertained by winding up the affairs of the partnership and following the specific rules described in s.44 of the 1890 Act.

Turning now to s.44 of the 1890 Act, this sets out the rules to be applied in settling accounts between the partners after the dissolution of a partnership:

- Losses, including losses and deficiencies of capital, are to be paid first out of profits, next out of capital, and lastly, if necessary, by the partners individually in the proportion in which they are entitled to share profits.
- The assets of the firm including the sums, if any, contributed by the partners to make up losses or deficiencies of capital, are applied in the following manner and order:

  — in paying the debts and liabilities of the firm to persons who are not partners therein;
  — in paying to each partner rateably what is due from the firm to him for advances as distinguished from capital;
  — in paying to each partner rateably what is due from the firm to him in respect of capital; and
  — the ultimate residue, if any, is to be divided among the partners in the proportion in which profits are divisible. With regard to rights in capital which require to be ascertained pursuant to valuations in accounts or balance sheets, a fair market valuation of the assets should be entered.

It is worth stressing that the above rules are inapplicable where the partnership agreement provides otherwise. An example is provided by the case of *Thom's Executrix v Russel & Aitken*.[21]

Thom's Executrix v Russel and Aitken
1983 S.L.T. 335 OH

Concerning: How the share of a deceased partner in the assets of a partnership should be valued pursuant to a partnership agreement.

Facts: A partnership agreement provided that on the death of a partner no accounts up to the date of death were to be made up but

---

[20] 2006 S.L.T. 975.
[21] 1983 S.L.T. 335 OH.

that his representatives were to be entitled to receive "(one) the share standing at his credit in the capital of the firm as the amount thereof may be determined by the partnership's auditors and (two) the share of profits up to the date of his death" calculated by applying the share to which the partner had been entitled to the proportion of annual profits represented by the period up to his death. The representatives of the deceased partner argued that there should be a revaluation of assets. The remaining partners argued that the share of capital was restricted to the book value.

Decision: The court ruled that the partnership deed provided that payment of a deceased partner's share was restricted to book value of capital and that the actings of the parties demonstrated that they had agreed that a retiring partner or the representatives of a deceased partner would receive only a share calculated by reference to book value.

Partnership Law Reform

The Law Commission and the Scottish Law Commission published a **15–15** joint paper on partnership law on November 18, 2003.[22] It was recommended that legislation be introduced to reform the Scots and English law of partnership. Essentially, the proposals were that the English law of partnership ought to be re-aligned so that it was more in line with the Scots law of partnership, e.g. that a partnership constituted under English law should have separate legal personality and be able to enter into contracts and hold property in its own name, etc. Moreover, the joint proposals envisaged the implementation of a new Partnership Act with an emphasis on flexible default rules which could be adopted or displaced by a partnership in a partnership agreement. Moreover, partnership law would be altered so that its default rules were geared more towards small firms and the rules for the determination and winding up of a solvent partnership would be made simpler, fairer, quicker and more cost effective.

However, in 2006 the Government announced that it did not intend to take forward the proposed reforms for general partnership law at that particular point in time.

The Limited Partnership

As noted earlier in this chapter, one of the defining characteristics of a **15–16** partnership is that the partners are jointly and severally liable for the debts of the partnership. However, it is open to businesspersons to form a

---

[22] Joint Law Commission and Scottish Law Commission Report, *Partnership Law* (2003), Law Com. No.283 and Scot. Law Com. No.192, Cm.6015 (available at *http://www.scotlawcom.gov.uk/files/3812/7989/6640/rep192.pdf* [Accessed May 15, 2015]).

limited partnership under the Limited Partnerships Act 1907 ("1907 Act"). A limited partnership is a different creature from the limited liability partnership incorporated under the Limited Liability Partnerships Act 2000 which we explored in Ch.14, "Choice of Business Medium", and is covered in detail in Ch.17, "Limited Liability Partnerships". In the case of a limited partnership, one or more persons are referred to as "general partners" and one or more persons are called "limited partners". A general partner in a limited partnership is personally liable to contribute towards the debts and obligations of the limited partnership. However, a limited partner will contribute capital towards the limited partnership when he or she enters the limited partnership but will not be personally liable for the debts or obligations of the limited partnership in terms of s.4(2) of the 1907 Act. If the limited partnership is not registered with the Registrar of Companies, the limited partner will be deemed to be a general partner and will not enjoy limited liability in terms of ss.5 and 15 of the 1907 Act. Moreover, a limited partner has no power to bind the limited partnership.[23] So a general partner is responsible for the day-to-day management of the limited partnership and the limited partners are essentially anonymous in the sense that their names do not require to be included in the firm name. Like a partnership, there will be a (limited) partnership agreement which sets out the rights and obligations of the general and limited partners. However, there are very few limited partnerships registered in the UK. Where they exist, they tend to be formed and used to take the benefit of tax advantages. They are encountered particularly in the fund management area of the financial services sector. A final point to make is that the general law of partnership in terms of the Partnership Act 1890 applies to the limited partnership save where the 1907 Act provides otherwise.

▼ CHAPTER SUMMARY

MAIN ATTRIBUTES OF A PARTNERSHIP

15–17   (1) A partnership is a separate legal person distinct from its partners in terms of Scots law—s.4(2) of the 1890 Act. A partnership can be constituted orally or in writing. It may also be inferred from the actions of the parties and in particular the nature of their relationship towards each other. Where the relationship between partners amounts to a partnership, they are deemed to be fiduciaries.

   (2) The rules that determine whether the relationship which arises between individuals amounts to a partnership are as follows:

   ● A partnership is the relation which subsists between persons carrying on a business in common with a view of profit—s.1(1) of the 1890 Act.

---

[23] 1907 Act s.6.

- But the owners of joint property or common property are not to be considered partners without more, regardless of the profit sharing arrangements which exist between them—s.2(1) of the 1890 Act.
- The sharing of gross returns by parties does not of itself create a partnership—s.2(2) of the 1890 Act and *Cox v Coulson*.[24]
- If a person receives a share of the profits of a business, this is prima facie evidence that he is a partner in the business—s.2(3) of the 1890 Act. However, there are exceptions where profit-sharing does not necessarily amount to a partnership:

    (a) The receipt by a person of a debt or other liquidated amount by instalments or otherwise out of the accruing profits of a business does not of itself make him a partner in the business, e.g. a creditor who is paid a debt by a debtor in instalments out of the profits of the business of the debtor does not qualify the creditor as a partner of the debtor—s.2(3)(a) of the 1890 Act.

    (b) Where an employee or agent is remunerated out of the profits of the business of his employer or principal, he is not a partner of either of the latter—s.2(3)(b) of the 1890 Act.

    (c) Widows, widowers, children and surviving civil partners who receive a share of the profits of the business in which the deceased was a partner prior to his/her death are deemed not to be partners of that business without more—s.2(3)(c) of the 1890 Act.

    (d) Creditors are deemed not to be partners of their debtors where: (i) the capital or interest which they receive from their debtors is paid out of, or varies with, the profits of the business of the debtor; or (ii) the creditors receive a share of the profits of the business of the debtor—s.2(3)(d) of the 1890 Act.

    (e) Where a person sells his/her goodwill in a business and receives an annuity or share in the profits of that business as the consideration for the sale, s.2(3)(e) of the 1890 Act states that the seller will not necessarily be a partner.

(3) The following rules determine whether a partner has bound the partnership in contract with a third party:

- Where a partner engages in acts "for carrying on in the usual way business of the kind carried on by the" partnership, the partnership will be bound in contract with a third party as a result of the actions of the partner—s.5 of the 1890 Act.
- However, the partnership will not be liable under such a contract with a third party where:

    (a) the partner has no authority to bind the partnership and the third party knows that the partner has no such authority, or

    (b) the partner has no authority to bind the partnership and the third party does not know or believe him to be a partner.

(4) The rules for determining whether the partnership or other partners are liable for wrongs, delicts or omissions of a partner which have caused injury or loss to a third party are as follows:

---

[24] [1916] 2 K.B. 177.

- Where a partner commits a wrongful act or omits to act in the ordinary course of the business of the partnership, or with the authority of his co-partners, loss or injury is caused to a third party, or any penalty is incurred, the partnership is liable to the same extent as the partner so acting or omitting to act.
- Where a partner in a firm of solicitors dishonestly assists a client in perpetrating a fraud by drafting bogus agreements, this will amount to the ordinary course of the business of the partnership, since drafting and advising on agreements is part and portion of the business of a firm of solicitors: *Dubai Aluminium v Salaam*.[25]

(5) The following rules in the 1890 Act regulate partnership property:

- Property purchased with the money of the partnership or on account of the partnership in the ordinary course of the business of the partnership, is deemed to be partnership property. Such property must be held by the partners exclusively for the purposes of the partnership and in accordance with the partnership agreement— s.20(1) of the 1890 Act.

(6) The principles which regulate the internal affairs of the partnership are as follows:

- The partners are bound to render true accounts and full information of all things affecting the partnership to the other partners or their legal representatives—s.28 of the 1890 Act.
- Every partner must account to the partnership for any benefit derived by him without the consent of the other partners from any transaction concerning the partnership, or from any use by him of the partnership property name or business connection. In other words, partners must not make a personal profit and any breach of this duty will result in the partnership accounting for the profit— s.29 of the 1890 Act.
- If a partner engages in business of the same nature as and competing with that of the firm, he must account for and pay over to the firm all profits made by him in that business—s.30 of the 1890 Act.
- A number of default rules regulate the interests, duties and rights of the partners in the partnership, some of which are as follows:
  —all the partners are entitled to share equally in the capital and profits of the business, and must contribute equally towards the losses whether of capital or otherwise sustained by the firm;
  —a partner is not entitled, before the ascertainment of profits, to interest on the capital subscribed by him;
  —every partner may take part in the management of the partnership business;
  —no partner shall be entitled to remuneration for acting in the partnership business;
  —no person may be introduced as a partner without the consent of all existing partners;
  —no majority of the partners has the power to expel any partner unless a power to do so has been conferred by express agreement between the partners;

---

[25] [2003] 2 A.C. 366.

—in the case of a partnership of an indefinite duration, any partner may determine the partnership at any time on giving notice of his intention so to do to all the other partners; and

—if a partnership for a fixed duration is continued after the term has expired, and without any express new agreement, the rights and duties of the partners remain the same as they were at the expiration of the term, so far as is consistent with the incidents of a partnership at will, i.e. "tacit relocation" applies—see ss.24–27 of the 1890 Act.

(7) There are several ways in which a partnership may come to be terminated or expire:

A partnership may be dissolved with or without the intervention of the courts on different grounds.

First, dissolution may be effected on the following grounds without court approval:

- by agreement of all the partners;
- in the case of a partnership for a fixed duration, by expiration of that term—s.32(a) of the 1890 Act;
- for a partnership of unlimited duration, by a partner providing notice to the other partners of his intention to do so—s.32(c) of the 1890 Act;
- subject to contrary agreement, the death or bankruptcy of a partner—s.33(1) of the 1890 Act;
- if a partner arranges for his share of the partnership property to be charged under the 1890 Act for his own personal debts—s.33(2) of the 1890 Act.
- if an event occurs which makes it unlawful for the business of the partnership to be continued, e.g. for reasons of illegality—s.34 of the 1890 Act; or
- where the partnership agreement is rescinded by a partner on the basis that one of the partners has perpetrated a fraud or has misrepresented the position—s.41 of the 1890 Act.

Secondly, the partnership may be dissolved with the authority of the court in the following circumstances:

- when one of the partners is permanently incapable of performing his part of the partnership contract—s.35(b) of the 1890 Act;
- where a partner is guilty of conduct which is prejudicial to the carrying on of the partnership's business—s.35(c) of the 1890 Act;
- if a partner is in breach of contract or conducts himself in a manner which renders it not reasonably practicable for the other partners to carry on the business in partnership with him—s.35(d) of the 1890 Act;
- if the business of the partnership can only be carried on at a loss—s.35(e) of the 1890 Act; or
- if it is just and equitable to dissolve the partnership—s.35(f) of the 1890 Act.

(8) The following principles are applied towards the distribution of the assets of the partnership on its dissolution and winding up:

- Once a partnership has been dissolved, every partner or representative has the right to apply to the court to have the business and affairs of the partnership wound up—s.39 of the 1890 Act.
- Where a partner has died or otherwise ceased to be a partner, and the surviving or continuing partners carry on the partnership's business with its capital or assets without any final settlement between the partnership and the outgoing partner or his estate, unless there is any agreement to the contrary, or an option to purchase the share of the deceased or outgoing partner has been exercised in terms of the partnership agreement or otherwise, then the outgoing partner or his estate is entitled to receive either a share of any profits made after dissolution from use of that partner's share in the partnership assets, or, at the option of the outgoing partner or his representatives, interest at the rate of 5 per cent per annum on the amount of his share in the partnership assets—s.42 of the 1890 Act.
- The rules for settling accounts between the partners after the dissolution of a partnership are as follows:
  (a) Losses, including losses and deficiencies of capital, are paid first out of profits, next out of capital, and lastly, if necessary, by the partners individually in the proportion in which they were entitled to share profits.
  (b) The assets of the firm including the sums, if any, contributed by the partners to make up losses or deficiencies of capital, are applied in the following manner and order:
    (i) In paying the debts and liabilities of the firm to persons who are not partners therein.
    (ii) In paying to each partner rateably what is due from the firm to him for advances as distinguished from capital.
    (iii) In paying to each partner rateably what is due from the firm to him in respect of capital.
    (iv) The ultimate residue, if any, is divided among the partners in the proportion in which profits are divisible. With regard to rights in capital which require to be ascertained pursuant to valuations in accounts or balance sheets, a fair market valuation of the assets should be entered—s.44 of the 1890 Act.

? QUICK QUIZ

- What is a partnership and what are its main attributes?
- What are the rules for determining whether the partnership or other partners are liable for wrongs, delicts or omissions of a partner which have caused injury or loss to a third party?
- Which rules in the 1890 Act regulate partnership property?
- Can the partners dismiss a partner by majority vote?
- Is a partnership legally bound where a third party enters into a contract with the partnership knowing that the partner has no authority to bind the partnership?
- Is a partner entitled to retain a personal profit?

- Is a provision in the partnership agreement which provides that the partnership will continue notwithstanding the death of a partner a lawful provision which will be upheld by the courts?
- Section 35(f) of the 1890 Act stipulates that a partnership can be dissolved by the court where it is "just and equitable". What does this mean?
- I don't understand the case of *Dubai Aluminium v Salaam*.[26] How can it be logical that a partnership is liable to third parties under s.10 of the 1890 Act for the fraudulent activities of a partner?
- What is joint and several liability?

FURTHER READING

> A.D.M. Forte, *Scots Commercial Law* (LexisNexis / Butterworths, 1997), Ch.9.
> D. Bennett, *An Introduction to the Law of Partnership in Scotland* (Edinburgh: W. Green, 1995).
> F. Davidson and L. Macgregor, *Commercial Law in Scotland*, 3rd edn (Edinburgh: W. Green, 2014), Ch.8.
> G. Brough, *Miller on Partnership in Scotland*, 2nd edn (Edinburgh: W. Green, 1994).
> Gloag and Henderson, *The Law of Scotland*, 13th edn (Edinburgh: W. Green, 2012), Ch.45.

RELEVANT WEBLINKS

> Business Gateway: *http://www.bgateway.com* [Accessed May 15, 2015].
> Joint Law Commission and Scottish Law Commission Report, *Partnership Law* (2003), Law Com. No.283 and Scot. Law Com. No.192, Cm.6015: *http://www.scotlawcom.gov.uk/files/3812/7989/6640/rep192.pdf* [Accessed May 15, 2015].

---

[26] [2003] 2 A.C. 366.

Chapter 16   Company Law

Chapter 16   Company Law

DAVID CABRELLI[1]

► CHAPTER OVERVIEW

16–01 This chapter is designed to introduce students to the law which governs the creation and operation of companies registered under the Companies Acts. Like a partnership, a registered company is a vehicle which persons can deploy as a means of combining together to carry on a business. The main attributes of the company as a business vehicle were explored in Ch.14, "Choice of Business Medium", together with the advantages and disadvantages of the company over other business forms. In this chapter, the company and company law will be analysed in much more detail. The general principles (including case law and statutory material) relating to the following aspects of company law will be considered:

- the sources, purposes and core features of company law and the consequences of incorporation;
- the types of company, the regulation of company names and administrative requirements in connection with the incorporation of a company;
- the basic constitutional documents of a company, the memorandum and articles of association, and the legal effect and significance of these;
- the continuing regulation of companies, the reason for, the nature of, and the formal requirements for accounts, audits and auditors;
- corporate decision-making and corporate governance: (i) officers and directors. The appointment, eligibility, powers, types, removal, disqualification and duties of directors and their position vis-a-vis the company and shareholders;
- corporate decision-making and corporate governance: (ii) company meetings and resolutions. The nature and purpose of company meetings, and how they are called and run. The types of resolutions and how they are passed;
- the nature and types of shares; how shares can be allotted, issued and transferred; the rights that ownership of a share confers on the member of the company; how a company can raise capital, "offers to the public" via a prospectus and the law of prospectuses;

---

[1] Senior Lecturer in Commercial Law, University of Edinburgh.

- the issuance of debt instruments by the company as a means of raising loan capital;
- the legal requirement of a company to maintain its capital and what this means in terms of company law, including the rules governing the repurchase by a company of its own shares, the rules prohibiting "financial assistance" by a company for the purchase of its shares, and the distribution of dividends; and
- the position of a minority shareholder, and the protection that a minority shareholder may seek in the event of "unfairness".

✓ OUTCOMES

At the end of this chapter you should be able to understand: **16–02**

- ✓ the legislation which governs company law;
- ✓ the importance of the concepts of separate legal personality, limited liability and the corporate veil;
- ✓ the different types of registered company which exist under company legislation, how company names are regulated and the requirements for incorporating companies;
- ✓ the law governing the constitutional documentation of the company and the rules which govern the amendment of the articles of association of a company;
- ✓ the nature of the continuing disclosure and administrative requirements in terms of company law and the rationales for these rules;
- ✓ that decision-making on behalf of a company is divided between the board of directors and the shareholders in general meeting under company law;
- ✓ how directors are appointed, their powers and duties and the applicable rules for their disqualification and removal;
- ✓ the law relating to company meetings and resolutions, including how and why company meetings are called and run and the types of resolutions and how they are passed;
- ✓ issues relating to corporate finance, and in particular the nature of shares and share capital, including how companies raise equity finance, the rules for raising finance and the requirement for a prospectus;
- ✓ what is meant by "debentures" and how these can be used by companies as an alternative to equity finance to raise capital to finance the strategy and objectives of the company;
- ✓ how the share capital of a company can be altered or reduced and the rules on the maintenance of a company's capital; and
- ✓ what routes are available for a shareholder to seek redress against: (i) directors who are in breach of duty, breach of trust or are negligent; or (ii) majority shareholders and the nature of the redress which is available to a shareholder in such circumstances.

AN INTRODUCTION TO COMPANY LAW

Sources of company law

16–03 Company law has recently undergone a degree of material change. The Companies Act 2006 ("CA 2006" or "the Act") was the vehicle for that reform and replaced the Companies Act 1985. The CA 2006 applies to England, Wales, Scotland and Northern Ireland, but there is little company law which can be referred to as "Scottish". Most company law is national in scope and so company law is a classic example of "British law".

Companies are also regulated by the Insolvency Act 1986. The Insolvency Act 1986 applies to govern the affairs of companies in financial difficulty when they have entered into administration, liquidation, receivership or a company voluntary arrangement. Other legislation of the UK Parliament will be referred to from time-to-time in this chapter including in particular the Company Directors Disqualification Act 1986 ("CDDA") and the Financial Services and Markets Act 2000 ("FSMA"). Both of these Acts contain concepts and principles that are largely incidental to company law and so will be routinely mentioned in passing, rather than in any specific detail. The former Act of Parliament controls the disqualification of directors. The latter Act of Parliament is primarily concerned with the regulation of firms engaged in the business of providing financial services. However, certain parts of the FSMA are extremely important for the purposes of company law.

Together with the legislation mentioned above, there is much subordinate legislation, e.g. statutory instruments, regulations and orders in council, which regulate companies and company law. Although company law is heavily controlled by statute and subordinate legislation, this does not by any means signify the absence of a role for the common law. For example, the rules which concern the duties of shareholders in applying their mind to a vote on a special resolution purporting to alter the company's articles of association lie within the territory of the common law.

The purposes of company law

16–04 Company law is concerned with the regulation of the powers, rights, duties and liabilities of companies and constituencies which are closely connected with the company. In Ch.14, "Choice of Business Medium", we were introduced to one of the fundamental features of the company. That is to say, that the company, once properly incorporated and registered in terms of the Act, possesses a separate legal personality which is distinct from its owners, managers and other third parties. Much of company law is about regulating the relationship between:

- the company and its managers, namely the board of directors. The company is an artificial person and so cannot act of its own accord and must act through certain designated persons. The articles of association of companies commonly provide that the board of directors are agents of the company, may exercise all of the powers of the company and take the majority of the decisions on behalf of the company.[2] Since the board of directors may act in the name of the company, company law promulgates principles and rules that seek to harness the freedom of action of the board, whilst ensuring that the company is not prejudiced at the hands of the same directors;

- the company and its owners, namely the members or the shareholders (in the case of a company limited by shares). The principles of company law seek to ensure that members are protected from the activities of the majority shareholders of the company and conversely, that the company is not held to ransom by the actions or decisions of the minority shareholders;

- the owners (i.e. the members or the shareholders) and the managers (i.e. the board of directors). As expressed above, the lion's share of decisions are taken for the company by the board of directors. However, company law proscribes the directors from taking certain decisions unless they have obtained the approval of the owners by members' resolution. Such decisions are deemed so important that the shareholders must be consulted and vote on them beforehand. Moreover, a number of principles of company law are designed to protect owners from self-serving directors, e.g. directors who breach their duties towards the company, or directors who put their own interests before that of the company which they represent; and

- the protection of creditors of the company. Creditors are affected by the actions or omissions of the company and its directors and members. Whilst the law of corporate insolvency is principally concerned with the fair treatment of the creditors of a company when the latter enters into some form of insolvency procedure (e.g. liquidation, administration, receivership, etc.), company law also performs a residual role for the protection of creditors. Some rules of company law seek to safeguard creditors' interests, amounting to pre-insolvency or preventive regulation. This can be contrasted with corporate insolvency laws which represent post-insolvency, protective regulation of creditors, whereby the interests of creditors are upheld once the company has entered into financial difficulties.

---

[2] For example, see art.3 of the model articles for: (i) private companies limited by shares; (ii) private companies limited by guarantee; and (iii) public companies in Schs 1, 2 and 3 to the Companies (Model Articles) Regulations 2008 (SI 2008/3229)—see *http://www.legislation.gov.uk/uksi/2008/3229/contents/made* [Accessed May 15, 2015].

Seven core features of company law

16–05 In Ch.14, "Choice of Business Medium", the significant case of *Salomon v A. Salomon & Co Ltd*[3] was analysed in detail. In this case, the House of Lords ruled that: (i) the shareholders of limited liability companies enjoy limited liability for the debts of the company; and (ii) a company is a body corporate having separate legal personality distinct from its constituent members.[4] It was stated that the effect of this rule is that a company can be sued, sue third parties in its own name, enter into contracts, own property in its own name, etc. The separate legal personality of the company is otherwise known as the "corporate veil", whereby the creditors of the company are unable to obtain redress from its members, managers, directors, employees or other third parties in respect of the debts, obligations and/or liabilities of the company.

Another core characteristic of limited liability companies is that they have the power to issue transferable shares as investments to shareholders/investors.[5] So a company can raise corporate finance known as equity finance from investors/shareholders in return for the allotment and issue of its own shares to the investor/shareholder. Shareholders can alienate their shares like any other piece of property that they own and, thus, realise their equity stake in the company, which will equate to a proportion (broadly equivalent to the percentage their shares bear to the overall issued share capital of the company) of: (i) the overall market capitalisation of the company in the case of a public limited company whose shares are admitted to trading on the official list maintained by the Financial Conduct Authority ("FCA") as the UK listing authority[6]; or (ii) the open market value of the company (taking into account factors such as marketability, liquidity and transferability which will be governed by the articles of association of the company and the market) in the case of a private company.

Another principal feature of company law is the manner in which it naturally distinguishes between ownership of the company and its control. One of the consequences of such a division is that a company may: (i) with significant ease introduce passive investors as shareholders who have no intention of administering the day-to-day affairs of the company; and/or (ii) introduce specialised management to run the business of the company without any prerequisite that they be offered or take up shares in the company or invest money in the company in return for shares. The company can thus seek out the best managers for their business on the

---

[3] [1897] A.C. 22.
[4] In addition, see s.16(2) of the Act (unless otherwise stated, all references to sections of an Act in the footnotes to this chapter are to the CA 2006).
[5] Of course, this applies only to share companies and not to companies limited by guarantee.
[6] FSMA s.74(1).

open market and (in theory, at least) readily remove incumbent management from the company.[7]

Moreover, since company law dictates that the company is a legal person which is separate from its members or managers, another characteristic which defines it is perpetual succession. Only the application of the liquidation processes in terms of the Insolvency Act 1986 can bring the company to an end. Finally, the company is characterised by the power which it has to grant a floating charge. The floating charge is a form of security which can be granted over the entirety of the assets and undertaking of a company to a lender in exchange for debt funding.

Consequences of incorporation: the corporate veil

The fundamental premise of company law that a company is a distinct **16–06** legal person has the effect of erecting a natural barrier between the managers and owners of a company and the company itself. The metaphorical legal term for this barrier or cloak is the "corporate veil". It is rare for the corporate veil to be lifted. For example in the case of *Macaura v Northern Assurance Ltd*,[8] Macaura was the owner of a timber estate and he sold the whole of the timber on the estate to a company of which he was the sole shareholder and a substantial creditor. He insured the timber against fire in his own name with several insurance companies. When the majority of the timber was destroyed by fire, he sued the insurance companies to recover the loss. The House of Lords ruled that Macaura stood in no "legal or equitable relation to" the timber at all, that he had no "concern in" the timber insured since it was owned by the company and that the insurance company was legally entitled to refuse to indemnify him in respect of the loss. The House of Lords were not prepared to pierce the corporate veil between Macaura and the company to enable him to recover.

Since it is evident that the courts will lift the veil sparingly, it is crucial to understand the general common law tests which apply. What emerges from the cases is that the courts will only lift the veil where:

- the laws concerning trading with the enemy in times of war apply, i.e. the company's shareholders are foreign nationals of an enemy state;
- special circumstances exist which demonstrate that the company is a mere facade or sham concealing the true facts, i.e. where a company or several companies are incorporated to conceal the real actors lying behind the company or those companies: this is known as the "concealment principle".[9] However, where a corporate group structure has been used or exploited whereby a new company within the group has been specifically incorporated

---

[7] A director can be removed by the shareholders passing an ordinary resolution, namely a simple majority of the members who vote in person or by proxy on a show of hands or on a poll in terms of s.168 of CA 2006.

[8] [1925] A.C. 619.

[9] *Prest v Petrodel Resources Ltd.* [2013] 2 A.C. 415.

("specific company") as a means of ensuring that the legal liability (if any) in respect of particular future activities of the group (and correspondingly the risk of enforcement of that liability) will fall on the specific company rather than other companies within the group, this is perfectly legitimate and the court will not be entitled to lift the corporate veil as against the other companies in the group or the group itself[10]; or

- the company has been incorporated with the specific objective of facilitating fraud or evading its existing legal obligations or liabilities: this is known as the "evasion principle".[11] A good example is provided by *Gilford Motor C. v Horne.*

Gilford Motor Co v Horne
[1933] Ch. 935

Concerning: Whether the court was entitled to lift the corporate veil where an individual incorporated a company purely as a means of defeating the terms and enforceability of a legally binding restrictive covenant.

Facts: Mr Horne entered into a restrictive covenant which restricted him from soliciting or dealing with customers of his former employer for a period of five years subsequent to the termination of a contract appointing him as a managing director. When his employment terminated, he solicited and entered into contracts with third parties, but channelled such contracts through a company of which his wife and an employee called Howard were the only shareholders and directors. That company had been incorporated only six months after the termination of Mr Horne's contract of employment. The reason he channelled the third party contracts through the company was that he recognised that he would be in patent breach of the restrictive covenants in his contract of appointment if he entered into the contracts with the third parties on a personal basis.

Decision: Lord Hanworth M.R. ruled that the company was formed as a device, a stratagem, in order to mask the effective carrying on of a business of Horne and to avoid a perfectly valid, *existing* personal legal obligation incumbent on Horne. The purpose of it was to try to enable him to avoid the application of the restrictive covenant. So the court was prepared to pierce the corporate veil to make both Horne and the company liable on the covenants to the former employer.

Whilst the common law demonstrates that the courts are far from enthusiastic about piercing the corporate veil to enable creditors or other

---

[10] *Adams v Cape Industries Plc* [1990] Ch. 433, per Slade L.J at 544.
[11] *Prest v Petrodel Resources Ltd* [2013] 2 A.C. 415, per Lord Sumption at 484.

third parties to obtain a remedy against the members or directors, the corporate veil is not impregnable. Provisions in the CA 2006 and the Insolvency Act 1986 impose liability on the directors and the members of a company in certain circumstances for the debts, obligations or liabilities of the company. Section 767(3) and 767(4) of the CA 2006 stipulates that every director or officer of a public company that does business or exercises borrowing powers without having been issued a trading certificate from the Registrar of Companies is jointly and severally liable to indemnify any third party who has suffered loss or damage as a result of such a failure. Likewise, s.563(2) of the CA 2006 provides that any officer of a company who knowingly authorises or permits the contravention of the rules in ss.561 and 562 of the Act (which concern the rights of pre-emption of existing shareholders on an allotment of shares) is jointly and severally liable to compensate any third party to whom an offer of shares ought to have been made in respect of any loss, damage or expenses that third party might have incurred as a result of that contravention. Personal liability is also imposed on members of a company in terms of ss.76 and 213 of the Insolvency Act 1986. For example, in terms of s.213(2), the court may declare any person to be liable to make a contribution to the assets of a company, including the members or the directors, where the company is guilty of fraudulent trading. Furthermore, s.76(3) of the Insolvency Act 1986 provides for circumstances in which past members of a company may be liable to make a personal contribution to the assets of the company. The CA 2006 and other statutes also provide for circumstances in which directors will be made criminally liable.

Key Concept

A core feature of company law is the separate legal personality of the company. A company is a person distinct from its directors, members and creditors. This barrier is referred to as the "corporate veil". In limited circumstances, the common law and statute can be used to enjoin the courts to pierce the "corporate veil" and thus enable third parties to seek redress personally against the directors or members for the debts of the company.

Key Concept

In the case of a limited liability company, the members of that company know in advance that their liability for the debts of the company are restricted to the amount they have invested in the company or the amount which they are prepared to so invest. The worst case scenario is that they will lose their investment, but their personal assets are not at risk.

THE TYPES OF COMPANY, COMPANY NAMES AND INCORPORATING A COMPANY

Types of company

16–07 By virtue of the CA 2006, companies come in many shapes and sizes. Leaving aside the obvious distinction between companies which can be described as small businesses and those which are so large that they display a not insignificant degree of economic power, companies can be classified according to three particular categories as follows:

- limited liability companies v unlimited companies;
- companies limited by shares v companies limited by guarantee; and
- private companies v public companies.

The distinction between each of the above will be considered in turn.

First, a company can be one in which the liability of the members for the debts of the company is: (i) limited; or (ii) unlimited. By far the most common form of company is the company incorporated under the Companies Acts with limited liability. The reasons for such a factual phenomenon are obvious. Members of a limited liability company can go into business safe in the knowledge that their personal assets are not subject to attack if the company gets into financial difficulties and folds with debts remaining to be paid to creditors. Notwithstanding this, that is not to say that all companies are incorporated with limited liability status. In certain circumstances, members may be more attracted to the unlimited liability form of company. Whilst such members are personally liable for the debts of the company, the unlimited company possesses the potentially attractive characteristic that the affairs of the company do not require to be publicised, e.g. there is no requirement to disclose: (i) the internal affairs of the company, such as allocation of voting rights, entitlements to profits and a return of capital on winding up; (ii) the composition of its management and membership; and (iii) its financial performance.

Secondly, limited liability companies can be divided into two camps, namely: (i) the limited liability company by shares; and (ii) the limited liability company by guarantee. In Ch.14, "Choice of Business Medium", the distinction between these two categories was explored. To recap, in terms of s.3(2) of the CA 2006, the extent of a shareholder's liability for the debts of a company limited by shares is limited to any value which remains unpaid on his shares. Meanwhile, the liability of the members of a company limited by guarantee is limited to the value of the contribution which they have agreed to make towards the assets of the company on its winding up in terms of the memorandum of association of the company.[12]

Thirdly, companies can also be divided between the private limited liability company and public limited liability company categories. The

---

[12] CA 2006 s.3(3).

major differences between these classifications were considered in detail in Ch.14, "Choice of Business Medium", and suffice to say at this juncture that public limited companies are entitled to offer shares and seek membership from the public whereas private limited companies are prohibited in the CA 2006 from doing so.[13] Public companies have the benefit of access to the capital markets such as the London Stock Exchange ("LSE") or the Alternative Investment Market ("AIM") to finance their activities and so are more heavily regulated under the Act, the common law, subordinate legislation and extra-legal regulation (such as the FCA's Handbook, the UK Corporate Governance Code and the Takeover Code) than private limited companies. The CA 2006 represents a further piece of legislation which has perpetuated the increasing trend in recent years towards the de-regulation of private companies.

Figure 17.1: Overview of the different types of company

	Limited by shares	*Limited by guarantee*	*Unlimited*
Public	Yes	Yes (new innovation—see s.4(2) of CA 2006)	No
Private	Yes	Yes	Yes

The regulation of company names and the registered office

Every company must choose a name and there are controls in the CA **16–08** 2006 on the words that can be used as part of a company's name. The restrictions on company names can be divided into the following four camps:

- prohibited names;
- sensitive words or expressions;
- required indications for limited companies; and
- similar names and the company names adjudicator.

Section 53 of the CA 2006 provides that a company cannot be registered with a name which, in the opinion of the Secretary of State, is offensive or its use would constitute an offence. Meanwhile, ss.54 and 55 of the CA 2006 state that the approval of the Secretary of State is required for a company to use certain words or phrases which: (i) are likely to give the impression that the company is connected with the Government, the Scottish Government, the Welsh Assembly Government, HM's Government in Northern Ireland, a local authority or any of the organisations specified in Sch.4 to the Companies, Limited Liability Partnerships and Business (Names and Trading Disclosures) Regulations 2015[14]; or (ii)

---

[13] CA 2006 s.755.
[14] SI 2015/17.

are deemed by subordinate legislation to be "sensitive".[15] The types of words and phrases which are considered "sensitive" is provided by the Company, Limited Liability Partnership and Business Names (Sensitive Words and Expressions) Regulations 2014.[16] Some examples of words or phrases which are deemed to be sensitive are "accredit", "association", "assurance", "assurer", "Britain" and "Charter".

Sections 58–59 of the Act narrate the fact that the names of public limited companies must end with the words "public limited company" or the abbreviation "Plc" and that private limited companies must end with the word "limited" or "ltd". However, private companies which are charities are exempt from using the word "limited" or "ltd" in terms of s.60(1)(a) of the CA 2006.[17] When a company applies for registration with a name which is the same as another name appearing in the index of names of companies maintained by the Registrar of Companies, s.66 of the CA 2006 states that the application must be refused. If the name is not identical to an existing name and is duly registered by the Registrar of Companies, the Secretary of State has power under s.67 of the CA 2006 to direct a company to change its name if, in his opinion, it is the same or too like the name of an existing company appearing in the index of names of companies. Moreover, s.69 provides that a person may make an objection to a company names adjudicator if that person believes that the name of a company is: (i) the same as; or (ii) sufficiently similar, to a name associated with him/her in which he/she has goodwill. So this provision enables an individual having an association with a company to object to another company's name which is the same as, or very similar to, the former. For example, if an individual is associated with a company with the name "Clothes For You Ltd" and has goodwill in such a name, they may seek to object to another company subsequently listed in the Registrar of Companies' index of names that has the name "Clothes 4 U Ltd". The key issue which the company names adjudicator must take into account in making a decision is whether the registration of a name that is the same or sufficiently similar as another is likely to mislead. Further guidance is contained in the Company Names Adjudicator Rules 2008.[18] If the company names adjudicator upholds the applicant's objection, he has the power to make an order requiring the name of the respondent company to be changed to one that is no longer offending.[19]

The CA 2006 confers a power in favour of the company to change its

---

[15] The list of "sensitive" words and expressions is set out in Parts I and II of Schedule I to the Companies, Limited Liability Partnerships and Business Names (Sensitive Words and Expressions) Regulations 2014 (SI 2014/3140).

[16] SI 2014/3140.

[17] Other grounds for exemption are set out in reg.3 of the Companies, Limited Liability Partnerships and Business (Names and Trading Disclosures) Regulations 2015 (SI 2015/17).

[18] Company Names Adjudicator Rules 2008 (SI 2008/1738).

[19] CA 2006 s.73.

name. Section 77(1) of the CA 2006 provides that a special resolution of the shareholders is required to effect such a name change.[20] Another option specified in s.77(2) of the CA 2006 is for the company to change its name in conformity with a procedure already provided for in the company's articles. However, by definition, this option is available only where the company already has a change of name procedure narrated in its articles of association. So if there is no such procedure in the company's articles, the change of name will require to be effected by the shareholders passing a special resolution. When a company changes its name, notice of that fact must be given to the Registrar of Companies under s.80 of the Act, together with a copy of the special resolution under s.30 of the Act. In return, the Registrar of Companies will issue a certificate of incorporation on change of name if it is convinced that the new name complies with the requirements of the CA 2006 and the company's articles of association.[21] The change of name has effect from the date on which the certificate of incorporation on change of name is issued by the Registrar of Companies.[22]

In addition to a name, every company must have a registered office.[23] The location of the registered office must be detailed on the initial application for registration in terms of s.9 of the CA 2006. If a company wishes to change its registered office, this is a decision for the board of directors and not the shareholders of the company. Section 87 states that a company may change the address of its registered office by giving notice to the Registrar of Companies.

Incorporating a company and the necessary documentation

All companies in the UK are registered with the Registrar of Companies **16–09** at Companies House. There are three offices. The principal office for companies incorporated in England and Wales is based in Cardiff. The second office which deals with companies incorporated in Scotland is located in Edinburgh. The Northern Ireland office of Companies House is in Belfast. A number of documents are required to incorporate a company, which must be submitted to Companies House. First, a company must prepare and submit its memorandum of association and articles of association in terms of s.9(1) and (5) of the Act. However, s.9(5)(b) of the Act narrates that the articles do not require to be delivered to the Registrar where the company is proposing to adopt the model articles of association referred to in s.20.[24] A statement of compliance and

---

[20] A special resolution is a resolution passed by a majority of not less than 75% of the shareholders: (i) in general meeting in the case of a Plc; or (ii) by written resolution procedure or in general meeting in the case of a private company.

[21] CA 2006 s.80.

[22] CA 2006 s.81.

[23] CA 2006 s.86.

[24] See the model articles for: (i) private companies limited by shares; (ii) private companies limited by guarantee; and (iii) public companies in Schs 1, 2 and 3 to the Companies (Model Articles) Regulations 2008 (SI 2008/3229)—see *http://www.legislation.gov.uk/uksi/2008/3229/contents/made* [Accessed May 15, 2015].

an application for registration must also be submitted to the Registrar of Companies under the terms of s.9 and this is effected by completing a Companies House Form IN01. Section 13 explains the nature of the statement of compliance in that it is a statement to the effect that the requirements of the CA 2006 as to registration have been observed. The contents of the application for registration contained in the Companies House Form IN01 are dictated by ss.9, 10, 11 and 12 of the CA 2006 and are as follows:

(1) a statement of the company's proposed name.
(2) confirmation whether the company's registered office is to be situated in England and Wales, in Scotland or in Northern Ireland.
(3) confirmation as to whether the liability of the members is to be limited and if so, whether it is limited by shares or guarantee.
(4) confirmation as to whether the company is private or public.
(5) a statement of the name and address of the agent of the company in the incorporation.
(6) a statement of capital and initial shareholdings *if the company is to be formed as a company limited by shares* which itself will contain:

- a note of the total number of shares of the company to be taken on formation by the subscribers to the memorandum of association;
- a note of the aggregate nominal value of those shares;
- a note of the aggregate amount (if any) to be unpaid on those shares (whether on account of their nominal value or by way of premium); and
- for each class of shares:

—"prescribed particulars" of the rights attached to those shares;
—the total number of shares of that class; and
—the aggregate nominal value of shares of that class;

- such information as may be prescribed for the purpose of identifying the subscribers to the memorandum of association;
- a statement, with respect to each subscriber to the memorandum providing details of the: (a) number, nominal value (of each share) and class of shares to be taken by him on formation; and (b) amount to be paid up and the amount (if any) unpaid on each share (whether on account of the nominal value of the share or by way of premium); and/or

(7) a statement of guarantee *if the company is to be formed as a company limited by guarantee* containing the following information:

- such information as may be prescribed for the purpose of identifying the subscribers to the memorandum of association;
- a statement that each member undertakes that, if the company is wound up while he is a member, or within one year after he ceases to be a member, he will contribute to the assets of the company such amount as may be required for: (i) payment of the debts and liabilities of the company contracted before he ceases to be a member; (ii) payment of the costs, charges and expenses of winding up; and (iii) adjustment of the rights of the contributories among themselves, not exceeding a specified amount; and

(8) a statement of the company's proposed officers which will contain the following:

- particulars of the person who is, or persons who are, to be the first director or directors of the company; and
- in the case of a company that is to be a private company, particulars of the person who is, or persons who are, to be the first secretary (or joint secretaries) of the company[25]; and
- in the case of a company that is to be a Plc, particulars of the person who is or the persons who are to be the first secretary (or joint secretaries) of the company; and
- a statement by the subscribers to the memorandum of association that each of the persons named as a director of as a secretary has consented to act as a director or secretary; and

(9) a statement of the intended address of the registered office of the company.

Provided that the Registrar of Companies is satisfied that the requirements of ss.7–13 of the Act have been followed, then in return for such documents, the Registrar will issue a certificate of incorporation, which will look something like the following:

---

[25] That is, if the private company chooses to have a company secretary, since there is no legal requirement for a company to do so—see s.270 of the CA 2006.

CERTIFICATE OF INCORPORATION

No. 8888888

I hereby certify that

RAZORS 'R' US LIMITED

is this day incorporated under the Companies Act 2006 and that the company is a [private] OR [public] company limited [by shares] OR [by guarantee] with a registered office situated in [Scotland] OR [England and Wales] OR [Northern Ireland].

Given under my hand at [Cardiff] OR [Edinburgh] OR [Belfast] on the 23rd day of November, 2016

Donald Mambo Smith Registrar of Companies

In terms of s.16 of the CA 2006, the effect of the issuance of the certificate of incorporation is that the subscribers to the memorandum, together with future members of the company, are deemed to be a body corporate by the name stated in the certificate and with effect from the date of incorporation (also specified on the certificate).

It is worthwhile clarifying that although the CA 2006 envisages that companies will be incorporated specifically by individuals coming together for the purposes of setting up a business who have drawn up the initial documentation with their own specific requirements in mind, in practical reality, this is a rare occurrence indeed. Sealy and Worthington estimate that approximately 60 per cent of all companies incorporated in the UK are initially formed as what are called "shelf companies" by company formation agents, law firms or accountancy firms.[26] Such agents and firms form a number of these shelf companies at the same time, with the subscribers and officers of such companies being employees of the agents or firms. The office of the agent or firm is commonly narrated as the registered office of the shelf company, with the company name picked at random. The shelf companies do not trade, thus lie dormant until one of the clients of the agent or firm makes an "order" for a company. At this point, the members, officers, name, registered office and share capital of the company are altered, with the memorandum of association and articles of association being tailored to the needs of the client in accordance with their instructions. The documentation effecting such changes are signed and registered and the client can then use the company to trade.

---

[26] L. Sealy and S. Worthington, *Cases and Materials in Company Law*, 10th edn (Oxford: Oxford University Press, 2013), p.134.

THE CONSTITUTION: THE MEMORANDUM AND ARTICLES OF ASSOCIATION

Introduction

The most important legal documents which describe the powers, rights, **16–10** duties, and liabilities of the company, its directors and members are:

- the memorandum of association; and
- the articles of association.

In s.8 of the CA 2006, the memorandum of association of a company is described as a document which states that the subscribers: (i) wish to form a company under the Act; and (ii) agree to become members of the company and, in the case of a company that is to have a share capital, to take at least one share each. It must be subscribed by each member on incorporation of the company. To that extent, s.8 clarifies that the memorandum states very little. The form of Memorandum of Association of a company is governed by Schs 1 and 2 to the Companies (Registration) Regulations 2008[27] and looks something like the following:

Memorandum of Association of Razors 'R' Us Limited

We, the subscribers to this memorandum of association, wish to form a company under the Companies Act 2006 and agree to become members of the company and to take at least one share each.

(1) *H. Brocklebank*
Hector Brocklebank
2 Marchmont Terrace
Edinburgh

(2) *H.B. Fash*
Harriet Birchard Fash
5 Strathearn Place
Edinburgh

Dated November 31, 2016

Witness to the above signatures
Jenny McLeod
Jenny McLeod
22 Earl Street
Edinburgh

---

[27] Companies (Registration) Regulations 2008 (SI 2008/3014).

In the Companies Acts enacted prior to the CA 2006, the purpose of the memorandum of association was clear. It functioned to inform the general public of the nature of the objectives and purposes of the company, e.g. whether it was a property letting company, a manufacturing company, distribution company, mining company, etc.[28] A particular portion of the memorandum provided notice to the public of the company's objectives. This particular section of the memorandum of association was referred to as its "objects" clause. In addition, the memorandum of association would include the powers which the company enjoyed in order to achieve those "objects". For example, there would be a statement that the company would have the power to borrow money, purchase property, sell property, etc. all of which powers would be exercised by the directors. In strict company law, if a company entered into transactions which fell outwith the activities specified in the objects clause, then they would be deemed to be acting "ultra vires", that is to say beyond their capacity to contract. Where a company entered into a transaction on the basis of activities which were ultra vires, the general law was that the contract would be invalid and neither the third party nor the company would be bound.[29] Moreover, the contract could not be ratified by the company's shareholders.

Under existing law, it is crucial to draw a distinction between contracts which are entered into between third parties and the company in circumstances where: (i) the directors or the company have exceeded or abused the *company's* constitutional powers, e.g. have entered into a transaction or done something which is beyond the objects clause; and (ii) the directors have exceeded or abused *their own* powers (in terms of the company's constitution). With regard to the capacity of the company, i.e. (i) above, it is now provided in s.39 of the CA 2006 that the company has the capacity to enter into a contract or that such capacity can be assumed. So as regards third parties and the company, a contract is binding whether it involves the corporate powers being exceeded or abused or not. However, for internal purposes, where the directors have abused the powers of the company, whether: (a) the actions of the director may be ratified by the company by resolution; or (b) a director may be relieved from liability by resolution of the shareholders,[30] are two issues which are not wholly clear.

With regard to the situation where the directors exceed or abuse the powers afforded to them to act on behalf of the company in terms of the company's constitution, the position is different. First, in so far as a third party deals with a company in good faith, the power of the directors to bind the company (i.e. (ii) above) is deemed to be free of any limitation under the company's constitution, which will include any objects clause.[31] In such circumstances, the company and the third party will be bound by

---

[28] See Companies Act 1985 s.2.
[29] See *Ashbury Railway Carriage and Iron Co Ltd v Riche* (1875) L.R. H.L. 653.
[30] In terms of the Companies Act 1985 s.35(3), the shareholders could so ratify by passing a special resolution.
[31] CA 2006 s.40(1).

the contract where the directors have exceeded their powers. Internally, the shareholders may ratify the director's abuse of his/her constitutional powers by ordinary resolution.[32] The director will be in breach of his/her statutory duty to observe the company's constitution[33] and only an ordinary resolution of the shareholders can absolve the director of such a breach.[34] Where such an ordinary resolution is passed, the court must refuse an aggrieved shareholder leave to raise derivative proceedings against a director that the director's breach of the constitution: (i) has caused the company loss; or (ii) has resulted in a gain in the hands of the director which should be restored to the company.[35]

In terms of s.8, the memorandum of association of a company incorporated under the CA 2006 no longer contains objects clauses or details concerning the powers of the company or its capacity to contract. However, that is not to say that ss.39 and 40 of the CA 2006 and the rules regarding shareholder ratification are irrelevant. There are two reasons for this. First, the memoranda of association of many companies incorporated under the Companies Acts prior to the coming into force of the CA 2006 will continue to have objects clauses and provisions regulating the powers and capacity of the company. Section 28 states that these provisions are deemed to be provisions of the company's articles of association and will be regulated by ss.39 and 40 CA 2006 (and the rules on ratification). Moreover, if a company (an existing company incorporated under the Companies Acts in force prior to the CA 2006, or in circumstances where a company is incorporated under the Act with an objects clause) has an objects clause in its articles of association, its objects are deemed to be unrestricted. Secondly, although no such provisions are permitted in the memoranda of association of companies formed under the Act, such companies may include identical or broadly similar provisions in their articles of association. Where this is done, ss.39 and 40 of the CA 2006 will have a bearing on matters.

Key Concept

A company's memorandum of association is a public document which states that the subscribers: (i) wish to form a company under the Act; and (ii) agree to become members of the company and, in the case of a company that is to have a share capital, to take at least one share each.

---

[32] *Bamford v Bamford* [1970] Ch. 212 and CA 2006 s.239. An ordinary resolution is a resolution of the shareholders passed by a simple majority, i.e. more than 50% of the shareholders (s.282(1)): (i) in general meeting in the case of a public limited company; or (ii) by written resolution procedure or in general meeting in the case of a private limited company.
[33] CA 2006 s.171(1)(a).
[34] CA 2006 s.239(1).
[35] CA 2006 s.268(1)(c)(ii).

16–11 Whilst the memorandum of association was a document which traditionally intimated to the world the nature of the activities undertaken by the company, the articles of association would regulate the internal affairs of the company, its directors and members. The articles of association continue to perform that role. In s.17(a) of the CA 2006, the articles are referred to as the "constitution of the company" and s.33 provides that the articles represent a "contract" entered into between the members and the company and the members inter se:

> "The provisions of a company's constitution bind the company and its members to the same extent as if there were covenants on the part of the company and of each member to observe these provisions."

Accordingly, the members of the company can enforce the articles as a "contract" against the company and the company can enforce the articles against the members.

Hickman v Kent or Romney March Sheep Breeders Association
[1915] 1 Ch. 881

Concerning: Whether a member was contractually bound by an article in the articles of association of the company which provided that any disputes or differences between the members and the company regarding the "true intent or construction or the incidents or consequences" of the articles of association or the Companies (Consolidation) Act 1908 (8 Edw. 7, c.69) would be referred to arbitration.

Facts: A company was formed with articles of association which contained an article providing that any disputes or differences between the members and the company regarding the, "true intent or construction or the incidents or consequences" of the articles of association or the Companies (Consolidation) Act 1908 (8 Edw. 7, c.69) required to be referred to arbitration. A dispute emerged between Hickman, the company and its company secretary. Hickman raised court proceedings seeking (amongst other orders): (i) an interdict to restrain the company from taking any steps to expel him from the company; and (ii) a declaration that Hickman was entitled to have the resolutions and proceedings of the company and of any committee thereof truly and accurately entered in its minutes. The company issued a summons requesting that all further proceedings in the action be stopped and that the matters in question in the proceedings be referred to arbitration in accordance with the provisions of the relevant article.

Decision: Astbury J. held that the proceedings should be stopped and that the matters at issue ought to proceed to arbitration in terms of the relevant article. The articles constituted a contract between the company and the members, creating rights and obligations between them and the company respectively. He also held that no article can constitute a contract between the company and a third party and that no right purporting to be given by an article to a person, whether a member or not, in a capacity other than that of a member, as, for instance, as solicitor, promoter, director, can be enforced against the company.

The articles of association must be contained in a single document and divided into paragraphs numbered consecutively.[36] The Companies Act 1985 prescribed a form of model articles of association for use by companies which were known as "Table A".[37] When they were formed, companies would base their articles of association on Table A by adopting it in full, or adopting it subject to amendments. The CA 2006 provides for an equivalent set of model articles of association.[38] The model articles contain provisions on shares and distributions, the organisation of, and voting at, general meetings and the regulation of: (i) directors' powers and responsibilities; (ii) decision-making by directors; and (iii) the appointment of directors. For public companies limited by shares, a greater number of matters are catered for in the model articles given the more complex nature of that form of company and the fact that certain issues apply to them which are irrelevant to private companies, e.g. Annual General Meetings.

When the subscribers to the memorandum of association apply to the Registrar of Companies to form a company, they must register the articles of association of the company. However, there is an exception if the subscribers are adopting the model articles of association without any amendment. In such circumstances, there is no need to register a copy of the company's articles.[39]

Section 21 of the CA 2006 stipulates that a company may amend its articles of association by special resolution, that is to say a resolution passed by a majority of not less than 75 per cent of the members of the company: (i) in general meeting in the case of a public limited company; or (ii) by written resolution procedure or in general meeting in the case of a private limited company.[40] Once passed by special resolution, the alteration takes immediate effect. But if the alteration to the articles is such that it is adding, removing or altering a statement of the company's objects, notice of such an alteration must be given to the Registrar of Companies and the amendment of the company's objects is not effective

---

[36] CA 2006 s.18(3).
[37] Companies (Tables A to F) Regulations 1985 (SI 1985/805).
[38] See the model articles for: (i) private companies limited by shares; (ii) private companies limited by guarantee; and (iii) public companies in Schs 1, 2 and 3 to the Companies (Model Articles) Regulations 2008 (SI 2008/3229) ("the Model Articles")—see *http:// www.legislation.gov.uk/uksi/2008/3229/contents/made* [Accessed May 15, 2015].
[39] CA 2006 s.18(4).
[40] CA 2006 s.283(1).

until the notice is entered on the register.[41] Moreover, if the alteration of the articles of association: (i) purports to require a member to take or subscribe for more shares than the number held by him at the date on which the alteration was made; or (ii) in any way increases a members' liability as at the date of the alteration to contribute to the company's share capital or otherwise to pay money to the company, then the member is not bound by the alteration.[42] Once the special resolution amending the articles of association has been passed, the company has 15 days from the amendment taking effect to lodge with the Registrar of Companies: (i) a copy of the special resolution or a written memorandum of its terms; and (ii) a new copy of the articles of association incorporating the amendments.[43] The Registrar of Companies may take action against a company if the company fails to lodge the necessary documentation.

16–12   An important control exerted by company law arises where the members of a company pass a special resolution to alter the articles of association and the amendment introduced is likely to result in harm or loss to the company. In such circumstances, the question is whether company law should develop rules to enable an aggrieved shareholder (e.g. a minority shareholder) to take action against the company or the 75 per cent or more of the shareholders who voted in favour of the amendment on the premise that it is not in the best interests of the company? Another way of looking at this issue is to contemplate whether shareholders should have the right to freely cast their votes as they wish when voting on a resolution of the company. It may be that company law might reject any notion that it ought to evolve rules to enable aggrieved shareholders to take action against the company in such circumstances on the basis that this would amount to an unwarranted curtailment of the individual freedom, liberty and autonomy of shareholders to vote their shares as they please. Indeed, the general rule of company law is that a share is a property right[44] and that members have the right to cast their votes in any way they please.[45] In doing so, the member can vote in a way which advances his own personal interests and he is not bound to consider the effect of the vote on the interests of the company or any third party for that matter.

Company law responds to the matters raised by this issue by forging a common law principle that on a special resolution to alter the articles of association there is an exception to the general rule that members can exercise their vote in any way they think fit. So when a member is confronted with such a special resolution, the wide scope of manoeuvre afforded to him by the general rule is curtailed to the effect that he must exercise his vote in a way which is "bona fide" for the benefit of the

---

[41] CA 2006 s.31(2).
[42] CA 2006 s.25(1).
[43] CA 2006 ss.30(1) and 26(1).
[44] CA 2006 s.541.
[45] *North-West Transportation Co Ltd v Beatty* (1887) 12 L.R. App. Cas. 589 (Privy Council) and *Northern Counties Securities Ltd v Jackson & Steeple Ltd* [1974] 1 W.L.R. 1133.

company as a whole. The key case enunciating this principle is *Allen v Gold Reefs of West Africa Ltd.*[46]

Allen v Gold Reefs of West Africa Ltd
[1900] 1 Ch. 656

Concerning: Whether an amendment to the articles of association of a company authorised by the members by special resolution was lawful.

Facts: A company amended its articles of association by removing the words "(not being fully paid)" from a provision in a company's articles which provided that a company had a lien "upon all shares (not being fully paid) held by such members". So the effect of the original provision was that the company had a lien over shares which were not fully paid up, whereas the effect of the amendment was to give the company a lien over all shares whether they were fully paid or not. Only one member had fully paid up shares in the company and when he died his executors challenged the company when they sought to claim a lien on his shares pursuant to the amended articles.

Decision: Lindley M.R. in the Court of Appeal ruled that the company had the power to exercise the lien over the deceased member's shares. The special resolution which amended the articles of association of the company was valid. However, in coming to this view, Lindley M.R. introduced the principle that the members must exercise their vote in a way which is likely to be "bona fide" for the benefit of the company as a whole. So if the members vote against the proposed alteration, they must do so on the basis that they are of the view that the proposed alteration is not for the benefit of the company. Conversely, if they vote in favour, they must be satisfied that the proposed alteration is for the good of the company.

The difficulty with the "'bona fide' for the benefit of the company as a whole" test is that it is a concept which is inherently subjective and vague. What is the content of such a rule? In the case of *Citco Banking Corporation NV v Pusser's Ltd*,[47] Lord Hoffmann held in the Privy Council that whether a proposed or actual alteration of the articles is "bona fide" for the benefit of the company as a whole ought to be assessed on a subjective basis, i.e. from the perspective of the shareholders who sought to amend or voted in favour of the amendment and subjecting their motivations to scrutiny. Therefore, the court will be disentitled from adopting an objective test of what the hypothetical reasonable person might think of the proposed or actual alteration. Another vexed issue is

16–13

---

[46] [1900] 1 Ch. 656.
[47] [2007] UKPC 13; [2007] 2 B.C.L.C. 483.

how the court ought to approach a case where the proposed amendment
to the articles of association is such that it enables one section of the
membership of the company or the directors to expropriate the shares of
another section of the membership of the company. In such circumstances, is the proposal necessarily disadvantageous to the company?
Here the argument is that the amendment is nothing but an attempt by
those members who vote in favour to compel those who vote against to
forfeit their shares. The principal concern of the court is to ensure that
the implementation of the amendment will not serve to tear a rupture in
the established constitutional balance of power in the company. A prime
example is where the majority shareholders pass a special resolution
which amends the articles to insert a provision forcing the minority
shareholders or a particular body of shareholders to sell their shares to
the majority shareholders on the occurrence of a particular event, e.g. a
takeover bid for the company, the minority shareholders proposing to
sell to an outsider, etc.[48] A prime example is the case of *Sidebotham v
Kershaw Leese & Co Ltd*.[49] In such circumstances, the difficulty facing a
court is how they are to ascertain whether the amendments which
introduce the power of expropriation or forfeiture are nevertheless
"'bona fide' for the benefit of the company as a whole".

Sidebotham v Kershaw Leese & Co Ltd
[1920] 1 Ch. 154

Concerning: Whether an amendment to the articles of association
of a company authorised by the members by special resolution was
lawful.

Facts: A company's articles of association were amended to
provide that the directors would be given the power to purchase the
shares of any members at a fair price who had been found to be
competing with the business of the company. Minority shareholders
in the company who ran a business which competed with the
company sought to challenge the amendment on the basis that it
was not "'bona fide' for the benefit of the company as a whole".
They argued that the amendment was nothing more than an
attempt by the majority shareholders and the directors to expropriate their shares.

Decision: Lord Sterndale M.R. in the Court of Appeal held that
the amendment was clearly "'bona fide' for the benefit of the
company as a whole". He stated that it was:

"[V]ery much to the benefit of the company to get rid of
members who are in competing businesses. I think there can
be no doubt that a member of a competing business or an
owner of a competing business who is a member of the

---

[48] Such clauses are generally known as "compulsory transfer" provisions.
[49] [1920] 1 Ch. 154.

> company has a much better chance of knowing what is going on in the business of the company, and of thereby helping his own competition with it, than if he were a non-member. I think, looking at the alteration broadly, that it is for the benefit of the company that they should not be obliged to have amongst them as members persons who are competing with them in business, and who may get knowledge from their membership which would enable them to compete better."

Key Concept

A company's articles of association represent its internal constitution, detailing how shares may be transferred, directors appointed, meetings of directors held, etc. If a company proposes to alter its articles of association, it must obtain the approval of its members by special resolution. Where an alteration is authorised by special resolution, it may nevertheless be challenged in terms of the common law if it is not "bona fide" for the benefit of the company as a whole.

ONGOING ADMINISTRATIVE MATTERS

Introduction to disclosure and administration

As earlier sections of this chapter have shown, a number of formal steps **16–14** are required to form a limited liability company which involve registration of documents and the disclosure of information about the company at the point in time at which it is formed. However, such formal requirements are not restricted to the formation stage. Hence, the Act imposes a number of ongoing administrative requirements on companies subsequent to their incorporation. The rationale for such requirements—which generally involve registration and disclosure of information about the company with the Registrar of Companies—is that the members of limited liability companies enjoy the privilege of limited liability for the debts of the company.[50] To the extent that the members are protected by limited liability, the creditors are prejudiced. In return for such a privilege, members must make ongoing disclosure of information about the company. Disclosure offsets (to some extent) the dangers faced by creditors, since the quality of the information about the company which the company is compelled by the CA 2006 to introduce into the public domain enables creditors to assess the: (i) competency of the management team at the helm of the company; and (ii) the capital position and so the

---

[50] That this is the relevant principle is supported by s.448 which provides that unlimited liability companies are exempt from publishing their accounts provided certain conditions are met.

relative financial health of the company. Therefore, limited liability comes hand in hand with disclosure and the registration of information.

Ongoing disclosure is effected under the CA 2006 by four mechanisms, namely: (i) the provision of information about the company on business correspondence and other media (generally referred to as "trading disclosures"); (ii) the provision of information about the company at its registered office; (iii) publication of information about the company on its website, electronically and in newspapers such as the *London Gazette*, the *Edinburgh Gazette* and the *Belfast Gazette*[51]; and (iv) the submission of certain information about the company to the Registrar of Companies.[52] In this section, consideration will be limited to (i), (ii) and (iv) in particular. Information published in the respective Gazettes is commonly encountered in the CA 2006 in the case of topic-specific contexts, e.g. alterations in the share capital position of the company[53] or in the context of the dissolution or striking off[54] of companies. Reference will be made to such disclosure throughout this chapter when such topics are being considered in more detail.

Trading disclosures

16–15   The first ongoing administrative requirements which will be analysed are the provisions in the CA 2006 and subordinate legislation which oblige companies to make certain trading disclosures. Therefore, s.82 of the Act states that the Secretary of State may pass subordinate legislation obliging a company to display, state and provide information about itself in certain locations and communications, including its name and registered office. There are civil and criminal consequences for a company where they fail to comply with such requirements. To discover the nature of such obligations, consideration must be given to the subordinate legislation promulgated by the Secretary of State, namely the Companies, Limited Liability Partnerships and Business (Names and Trading Disclosures) Regulations 2015.[55] Regulation 21 provides that a company must display its registered name at (i) its registered office, (ii) any location at which the company keeps available for inspection any company record which it is required under the Companies Acts to keep available for inspection ("inspection place"), or (iii) any other location at which the company carries on its business. Regulation 24 goes on to impose obligations on a company to disclose its registered name on all business letters, notices and other official publications, bills of exchange, promissory notes, endorsements, order forms, cheques signed by or on behalf of the company, invoices, other demands for payment, receipts, letters of credit, licences, business correspondence, business documentation, and

---

[51]   See CA 2006 s.1173(1).

[52]   The Registrar of Companies is the relevant authority to which disclosure should be made for the purposes of the CA 2006, see s.1061.

[53]   See ss.562(3)(b) (pre-emption rights on the allotment of ordinary shares) and 719(1) (redemption or repurchase of shares out of capital).

[54]   See CA 2006 ss.1000(6) and 1003(3).

[55]   SI 2015/17.

websites. Regulation 25 is crafted in similar terms to the effect that every company must disclose information regarding the part of the UK in which it is registered, its registered number and the address of its registered office on its website and all business letters and order forms. If a company discloses its share capital on its business letters, order forms or website, that reference must be to the paid up share capital of the company. A company may also disclose the identity of a director on its business letters, but if it does so, reg.26 enjoins the company to disclose the names of all directors—not just one. Finally, a person who deals with the company in the course of its business has the right to request details from the company regarding the address of its registered office, any inspection place and the nature of the records kept at the registered office or inspection place.[56] The company has five working days of the receipt of the request to provide such information.[57] If a company fails to comply with the above requirements in the absence of a reasonable excuse, the company and every officer of the company in default will be deemed to have committed a criminal offence.[58]

Maintenance of statutory registers

Trading disclosures are only one of the ongoing administrative require- **16–16** ments imposed on companies. In terms of ss.162–167 of the CA 2006, every company must keep a register of directors at its registered office, or some other place notified to the Registrar of Companies, unless it is a private company and opts to have such information kept on the central register maintained by the Registrar of Companies in terms of the right of election in ss.167A–167E of the CA 2006: the power conferred on private companies to make such an election will be available with effect from April 2016. This register must be kept available for inspection.[59] If the company does not keep the register of directors at their registered office, it must intimate that fact to the Registrar of Companies.[60] Any changes to this register must be notified to the Registrar of Companies within 14 days,[61] or if the company has elected to keep such information centrally on the Registrar of Companies, such changes must be notified as soon as reasonably practicable after the company becomes aware of them. A company must take minutes of any proceedings of the board of directors and keep them for a period of at least 10 years from the date of that meeting.[62] Otherwise, a criminal offence will have been committed.[63] Such minutes are important for evidential purposes, i.e. as evidence of

---

[56] Companies, Limited Liability Partnerships and Business (Names and Trading Disclosures) Regulations 2015 reg.27(1).
[57] Companies, Limited Liability Partnerships and Business (Names and Trading Disclosures) Regulations 2015 reg.27(2).
[58] Companies, Limited Liability Partnerships and Business (Names and Trading Disclosures) Regulations 2015 reg.28(1).
[59] CA 2006 s.162(3).
[60] CA 2006 s.162(4).
[61] CA 2006 s.167(1).
[62] CA 2006 s.248(1).
[63] CA 2006 s.248(3).

decisions taken by the board.[64] Sections 275–280 of the CA 2006 provide that every public limited company must keep a register of company secretaries available for inspection at its registered office or some other place notified to the Registrar of Companies, and any changes to this register must be notified to the Registrar of Companies within 14 days.[65] There is no requirement for a private company to have a company secretary,[66] and thus, no requirement to keep a register of secretaries. However, if a private company does choose to have a company secretary, it is under a legal duty to keep a register of secretaries in terms of s.275 of the Act. Alternatively, with effect from April 2016, a private company may elect to have such information regarding its secretary or secretaries kept on the central register maintained by the Registrar of Companies in terms of the right of election set out in ss.279A–279F of the CA 2006. Companies must also keep a register of members.[67] Every company must keep its register of members available for inspection at its registered office or some other place notified to the Registrar of Companies.[68] However, if the company is a private company, with effect from April 2016, it will be possible for that company to choose to keep such information about its members held centrally by the Registrar of Companies in terms of ss.128A–128K of the CA 2006. If the company does not keep the register of members at its registered office, they must intimate that fact to the Registrar of Companies.[69] In the case of a single member company, a statement must be provided in the register of members to the effect that there is only one member of the company, together with the name and address of that sole member.[70] A register of charges containing details about charges and floating charges granted by a limited company must be maintained by that company in terms of s.876 of the Act and kept available at its registered office or some other place notified to the Registrar of Companies.[71] A copy of the instrument creating the charge must be also kept available for inspection at its registered office or some other place notified to the Registrar of Companies.[72] Finally, in relation to the maintenance of a register of debenture holders, a close inspection of the language of s.743 of the CA 2006 reveals that there is no equivalent of s.190 of the Companies Act 1985 which compelled a company to maintain a register of debenture holders. Section 743(1) of the CA 2006 stipulates that a company has a choice whether to keep such a register of debenture holders. If the company chooses to keep such a register, then it must be kept available for inspection: (i) at its registered office; or (ii)

---

[64] CA 2006 s.249(1).
[65] CA 2006 s.276(1).
[66] CA 2006 s.270(1).
[67] CA 2006 s.113(1).
[68] CA 2006 s.114(1).
[69] CA 2006 s.114(2) and (3).
[70] CA 2006 s.123(1).
[71] CA 2006 s.877(2) and (3).
[72] CA 2006 ss.875(1) and 877(2) and (3).

some other place.[73] If the company does not keep the register of debenture holders at its registered office, it must intimate that fact to the Register of Companies in terms of s.743(2) of the Act. Section 743(4) states that, if a company makes default for 14 days in complying with its duty to provide notice to the Registrar, an offence is committed by the company and every officer in default.

The annual confirmation statement

Coupled with trading disclosures and the requirement to make certain **16–17** information available at its registered office, with effect from April 2016, companies must submit a confirmation statement to the Registrar of Companies in compliance with their obligations contained in s.853A of the CA 2006. The confirmation statement amounts to a "snapshot" of the company taken annually on a specific date. The information which must be provided includes changes in the registered office address of the company, changes in the nature of the company, e.g. whether it is private or public, its principal business activities, details of the directors and company secretary of the company, details of any changes in the members of the company and the share capital of the company (including details of transfers of shares in the company) since the last confirmation statement date.[74] Information must also be provided regarding classes of shares, e.g. the rights attached to those shares, the total number of shares of that class, the aggregate nominal value of shares of that class and a note of the paid and unpaid amount on the shares.[75]

Annual accounts: introduction

The fourth and most important administrative requirement that is **16–18** imposed on companies on an ongoing basis is contained in Pts 15 and 16 of the CA 2006 which deal with the accounts of companies and their audit. Part 15 deals with the regulation of annual accounts which must be submitted by companies to the Registrar of Companies. Section 386 of the CA 2006 obliges companies to keep adequate accounting records. Such records are defined as records which are sufficient: (i) to show and explain the company's transactions; (ii) to disclose with reasonable accuracy, at any time, the financial position of the company at that time; and (iii) to enable the directors to ensure that any accounts required to be prepared comply with the requirements of the CA 2006. Section 394 compels the directors of a company to prepare individual accounts in respect of each of its financial years. Once compiled, the company's annual accounts must be approved by the board of directors and signed on behalf of the board by a director of the company on the balance sheet. A director is under a duty to produce a directors' report for each financial year in terms of s.415 of the CA 2006. It must narrate the names of each person who was a director of the company during the relevant financial

---

[73] CA 2006 s.743(1) and (2).
[74] CA 2006 ss.853B–853I.
[75] CA 2006 s.856.

year and the principal activities of the company in that financial year.[76]
Finally, the directors' report must be approved by the board of directors
and signed on behalf of the board by a director or the secretary of the
company.

Annual accounts: submission and laying of accounts

16–19 In terms of s.423 of the CA 2006, every company must send a copy of its
annual accounts and reports for each financial year to every member of
the company, every holder of debentures of the company and to every
person who is entitled to receive notice of general meetings of the company. A private company has until the date for filing its annual accounts
with the Registrar of Companies to send out copies of its annual accounts
and reports to its members, debenture-holders, etc.[77] In the case of a
public company, the period for sending the annual accounts and reports
is before 21 days of the date of the general meeting of the company at
which the accounts are to be laid.[78] A failure to comply with such
requirements to send out copies of the annual accounts in accordance
with s.423 of the CA 2006 is a criminal offence and the company and its
officers are liable to criminal penalties.[79] Once the annual accounts and
reports have been prepared and duly signed by the directors or company
secretary they must be filed with the Registrar of Companies.[80] A private
company has a period of nine months from the end of the relevant
financial year to file the accounts.[81] In the case of a public limited company, the period is six months from the financial year end.[82] If the
directors fail to file the annual accounts and reports with the Registrar,
the directors are deemed to have committed a criminal offence.[83]

Annual accounts: audit and auditors

16–20 Every company must ensure that its annual accounts for a financial year
are audited.[84] In terms of ss.485 and 489 of the CA 2006, all companies
must appoint an auditor by ordinary resolution of the members.[85]
However, in the case of private limited companies, the directors may
resolve not to appoint auditors, "on the ground that audited accounts are
unlikely to be required".[86] The same rules apply in respect of public
limited companies.[87] There can only be one auditor of a private company

---

[76] CA 2006 s.416(1).
[77] CA 2006 s.424(2).
[78] CA 2006 s.424(3).
[79] CA 2006 s.425.
[80] CA 2006 s.441(1).
[81] CA 2006 s.442(2)(a).
[82] CA 2006 s.442(2)(b).
[83] CA 2006 s.451(1).
[84] CA 2006 s.475(1).
[85] CA 2006 s.485(1) and (4) and s.489(1) and (4).
[86] CA 2006 s.485(1).
[87] CA 2006 s.489(1) and (4).

or public company at any one point in time.[88] In the case of a private company, subject to certain exceptions, where an auditor has not been re-appointed in respect of the next financial year, the auditor in office in the previous financial year is deemed to be re-appointed.[89]

The duties of the auditor are spelt out in ss.495, 496, 497 and 498 of the CA 2006. This requires the auditor to investigate matters in order to form an opinion on the adequacy of the company's accounting records and whether the company's individual accounts agree with those accounting records. The auditor must compile an auditor's report which will state whether the annual accounts give a true and fair view of the state of affairs of the company as represented in the balance sheet and the profit and loss of the company. Moreover, the auditor must state in the auditor's report whether the information provided by the directors in the directors' report is consistent with the details in the annual accounts. An auditor has the right to: (i) receive all notices and communications relating to a general meeting of the company; (ii) attend any general meeting of the company; and (iii) be heard at any general meeting which he attends on any part of the business of the meeting which concerns him as an auditor.[90] The auditor's report must state the name of the auditor and be signed and dated.[91] A final point to make is that the auditor may be removed by ordinary resolution of the members by special notice procedure in accordance with ss.510–511 of the CA 2006. At any meeting proposing to remove him or her as an auditor, the auditor has the right to be heard.[92] An auditor cannot be removed by the members of a private company by written resolution procedure.[93]

CORPORATE DECISION-MAKING AND CORPORATE GOVERNANCE: (I) OFFICERS AND DIRECTORS

Introduction: the constitutional balance of power between the directors and members

Since a company is an artificial person, it can only act and take decisions **16–21** through its human actors. The two organs which take decisions for the company and steer the direction of a company are: (i) the board of directors; and (ii) the members: (a) in general meeting; or (b) by written resolution procedure under the CA 2006. The regulation of the board of directors and directors generally are to be found in ss.154–259 of the Act and regs 3–20 and 52–53 of the Model Articles in the case of a private limited company by shares, regs 3–20 and 38–39 of the Model Articles in the case of a private company limited by guarantee and regs 3–27 and 85–

---

[88] CA 2006 ss.487(1) and 491(1).
[89] CA 2006 s.487(2).
[90] CA 2006 s.502(2).
[91] CA 2006 s.503(1).
[92] CA 2006 s.513(2).
[93] CA 2006 s.288(2)(b).

86 of the Model Articles in respect of public limited companies.[94]
Meanwhile, the rules regarding general meetings and the written resolution procedure in the case of private companies are detailed in ss.281–361 of the CA 2006 and regs 37–47 of the Model Articles in the case of a private limited company by shares, regs 23–33 of the Model Articles in the case of a private company limited by guarantee and regs 28–42 of the Model Articles in respect of public limited companies. The Model Articles set out the division of responsibility for decision-making between the board of directors and the members. The principal articles which embody such a distribution of decision-making authority are regs 3 and 4 of the Model Articles in the case of private limited companies by shares, private companies limited by guarantee and public limited companies. Regulation 3 gives wide powers to the board of directors in the following terms:

> "Subject to the articles, the directors are responsible for the management of the company's business, for which purpose they may exercise all the powers of the company."

As such, the board of directors has the full power to manage and take decisions for the company. Regulations 5 and 6 of the Model Articles give the directors the authority to delegate to managers or committees as they think fit. For example, certain decisions may be allocated to managing directors or the chairman.

However, reg.4 of the Model Articles reserves certain powers of instruction and initiation in favour of the members as follows:

> "The shareholders/members may, by special resolution, direct the directors to take, or refrain from taking, specified action."

This provision demonstrates that the originating power of company law is vested in the members rather than the directors by virtue of the articles of association. Since s.21 of the CA 2006 empowers the members to alter the articles of association, the Act entrenches the right of members to remove reg.3 of the Model Articles and, thus, repatriate decision-making powers from the directors to the members.

Moreover, the CA 2006 provides that certain corporate decisions are so important or influential that only the members may sanction them. The board has no authority in such circumstances to proceed to take these decisions without the approval of the members. For example, s.21 of the Act narrates the fact that only the members can alter the articles of the company by special resolution. The directors have no such power of their own to change the company's articles. So whenever the CA 2006 provides that an ordinary resolution or special resolution is required before a company can take a certain course of action or decision, the directors are disempowered in such contexts.

The above discourse presents an abridged exposition of the constitutional

---

[94] Companies (Model Articles) Regulations 2008 (SI 2008/3229).

balance of power in the company. What is clear is that the board of directors generally has a free hand to guide the course which a company takes. However, the members have residual "step in" rights. Provided that the members can meet the relevant 75 per cent threshold attached to a special resolution, they can instruct the directors how to act. Moreover, there are certain decisions which the directors are disqualified from making. Here, the Act draws the contours of the constitutional settlement between the directors and members. It does so by stipulating that certain decisions or actions must not be taken forward without the requisite degree of shareholder approval. The degree of shareholder approval required varies, depending on the decision at hand.

The company secretary

Prior to any detailed consideration of the role of the directors in the **16–22** governance of the company, it is important not to lose sight of the pivotal role played by the company secretary. The company secretary performs an administrative role, dealing with official correspondence on behalf of the company, maintaining the statutory registers and ensuring that the filing and other administrative obligations imposed on the company are complied with in accordance with the terms of the CA 2006. So it will commonly be the company secretary who arranges for all notifications to be made to the Registrar of Companies in accordance with the CA 2006 or by law generally. Company secretaries commonly sit in on meetings of the board of directors and take the minutes of the deliberations. They will also produce draft board minutes,[95] briefing papers, draft resolutions and other documents for approval or consideration by the directors. Company secretaries have the power to sign contracts and documents on behalf of the company in terms of the Requirements of Writing (Scotland) Act 1995.[96] So they have the power to bind the company.

Section 270(1) of the CA 2006 states that a private company does not require to have a company secretary. Nevertheless, many private companies have and will continue to have company secretaries, since the administrative requirements imposed by the Act and the law generally will continue to be required to be fulfilled. In contrast, a public company must have a secretary at all times.[97] So it is unlawful for a public company not to have a company secretary in office at any particular point in time. A director may be a company secretary. In terms of the Companies Act 1985, where a company had only one director, that individual could not also be the secretary of the company.[98] Thus, it was not possible to have one director and secretary, the identities of which were the same. However, there is no equivalent provision in the CA 2006. Therefore, where a private company has a sole director and opts to appoint a company secretary (which it is not required to do in terms of s.270 of the CA 2006),

---

[95] In other words, minutes prepared and kept in conformance with the company's obligation in terms of s.248(1).
[96] Requirements of Writing (Scotland) Act 1995 Sch.2 para.3(1).
[97] CA 2006 s.271.
[98] Companies Act 1985 s.283(2).

there is no legal impediment to that director also acting as the company secretary.

There are various eligibility requirements regarding the qualifications of the company secretaries of public companies which must be satisfied before someone can be appointed a secretary of a public company in terms of CA 2006 s.273. The company must keep a register of secretaries at its registered office or some other place notified to the Registrar of Companies. The details about company secretaries which must be kept in the register are his/her name, former name and address. Any change in: (i) the identity of the company secretary; or (ii) the particulars contained in the company's register of secretaries, must be intimated to the Registrar of Companies within 14 days of the alteration. However, ss.279A to 279E of the CA 2006 enable private companies to elect to have the Registrar of Companies maintain such a register, in which case, the private company is relieved of the obligation of keeping such a register of secretaries at its registered office or other place notified to the Registrar. Where such an election is made by the private company, s.279D imposes a duty on the private company to deliver any information of which it would have been obliged to give notice to the Registrar had the election not been in force, together with any statement that would have had to accompany such notice.

The directors: general

16–23 This section of the chapter considers the appointment, eligibility, powers, types, removal, disqualification and duties of directors and their position vis-a-vis the company and its members. Directors are the agents of the company.[99] They are not the agents of the members of the company. In terms of s.250 of the CA 2006, a director is defined as a, "person occupying the position of director, by whatever name called". This definition includes a "shadow director", which is someone who has not been officially appointed as a director, but is a person in accordance with whose instructions the board of directors is accustomed to act.[100] Every private company must have at least one director,[101] and a public company must have no less than two directors.[102] In all cases, with effect from October 2015, every director must be a natural person.[103] The CA 2006 contains various restrictions on the eligibility of persons to be a director. For example, persons under 16 years of age are not eligible for appointment as a director.[104] Moreover, s.11 of the CDDA states that an "undischarged bankrupt" cannot be appointed as a director of a company without the prior leave of the court.

---

[99] *Meridian Global Funds Management Asia Ltd v Securities Commission* [1995] 2 A.C. 500 (Privy Council).
[100] CA 2006 s.251.
[101] CA 2006 s.154(1).
[102] CA 2006 s.154(2).
[103] CA 2006 s.156A.
[104] CA 2006 s.157(1).

The directors: appointment

Regulation 17 of the Model Articles in the case of a private company **16–24** limited by shares states that a director may be appointed to the board by ordinary resolution of the members or by co-option by the directors. A person will cease to be a director where he/she is made bankrupt, is prohibited from being a director by law, e.g. where he/she is disqualified from being a director, or is declared to be physically or mentally incapable of acting as a director by a registered medical practitioner.[105]

The directors: types of director

There are essentially two types of directors. First, there are executive **16–25** directors. Executive directors are involved in the "day-to-day" management of the business, take executive decisions on behalf of the company and usually have a service contract with the company which details their terms and conditions of service, including their contractual duties, obligations and powers. Meanwhile, non-executive directors do not directly run or manage the business of the company on a full-time basis. They attend meetings of the board of directors and act as a check on the executive directors, principally performing a supervisory function over the executive members of the board. Decisions of the directors may be taken by unanimity in terms of a written resolution or by a majority decision at a board meeting.[106] However, this rule does not apply in the case where the company has a sole director.[107]

The directors: removal

Directors may be removed in terms of s.168(1) of the CA 2006 by an **16–26** ordinary resolution of the members of the company. The power of the members to remove a director arises, "notwithstanding anything in any agreement between [the company] and [the director]". A member proposing to remove a director must proceed by special notice procedure in terms of s.312 of the CA 2006. The special notice procedure envisages the member providing notice to the company of their intention to remove a director at least 28 days before the general meeting at which the resolution is moved.[108] The company is then under an obligation to give notice to the members of any such ordinary resolution in the same manner and at the same time as it gives notice of the meeting.[109] If it is impracticable for the company to give notice within the said 28-day timescale, the company must give its members notice at least 14 days before the meeting by advertisement in a newspaper having an appropriate circulation or in any other manner permitted by the company's articles of association.[110] Moreover, when the company receives notice from a member intending

---

[105] reg.18 of the Model Articles.
[106] regs 7(1) and 8 of the Model Articles.
[107] reg.7(2) of the Model Articles.
[108] CA 2006 s.312(1).
[109] CA 2006 s.312(2).
[110] CA 2006 s.312(3).

to remove a director, the company must forthwith send a copy of that notice to the director concerned.[111] At the meeting, the director has the right to protest his or her removal and has a right to be heard.[112] If the director provides the company with representations in writing regarding his proposed removal, if time will allow, the company must send a copy of those representations to each of the members with the notice of the resolution given to the members of the company.[113]

The directors: disqualification

16–27 Notwithstanding the rules in the CA 2006 concerning the removal of directors, individuals may be disqualified from acting as a director. The relevant legislation is the CDDA. The CDDA outlines a number of grounds on which a natural person may be disqualified from taking up a directorship or shadow directorship without judicial consent. The intervention of the court is required and where any of the statutory grounds are satisfied, the court may, and in certain circumstances must, grant what is called a disqualification order. The CDDA states that the court may make a disqualification order against a person where any of the following grounds have been fulfilled:

- he/she is convicted of an indictable offence in connection with the promotion, formation, management, liquidation or striking off of a company[114];
- he/she is found to be in persistent breach of his/her obligations under company law[115];
- he/she has been found guilty of fraudulent trading in terms of s.993 of the CA 2006 which manifested itself in the context of a winding up, that is to say that the directors have traded in a manner which demonstrates an intention on their part to defraud creditors of the company or creditors of any other person[116];
- he/she is convicted of a summary offence in consequence of a contravention of, or a failure to comply with, any provision of the companies legislation requiring a return, account or other document to be filed with the Registrar of Companies[117];
- a court has made a declaration finding an individual to have participated in fraudulent trading or wrongful trading in contravention of s.213 or s.214 of the Insolvency Act 1986.[118]

Where a company has gone into insolvent liquidation and a director is ruled to be unfit to be concerned in the management of a company, the

---

[111] CA 2006 s.169(1).
[112] CA 2006 s.169(2).
[113] CA 2006 s.169(3).
[114] CDDA s.2(1).
[115] CDDA s.3(1).
[116] CDDA s.4(1).
[117] CDDA s.5(1).
[118] CDDA s.10(1).

court must make a disqualification order in respect of that individual.[119] Sch.1 to the CDDA provide a non-exhaustive list of the circumstances in which an individual will be deemed to be unfit. The director may be disqualified for a period of up to 15 years for serious misconduct and up to two years in cases of a less serious nature.[120]

The directors: powers and duties

Turning to the powers of directors, as mentioned above, the default rule **16–28** in terms of reg.3 of the Model Articles is that the directors have the right to exercise all of the powers of the company. Thus decision-making authority and responsibility for steering the company in a particular direction is conferred upon the directors. Given the wide potential for directors to self-deal at the company's expense or to apply the funds and resources of the company for their own personal benefit, company law has developed rules over the years to inhibit such conduct. Such rules which are designed to stymie the potential for directors to abuse their powers are derived from the law of trusts and so historically, in developing the law here, an analogy was made by the English courts of Chancery between a trustee and a director. In the case of the law of trusts, the courts imposed duties on trustees as regards the property of the trust. Likewise, in the case of the company, the common law courts imposed duties on directors as regards the direction of the company, corporate decision-making and the application of the company's assets. The common law duties established by the courts can be broadly divided into two categories. First, a director owes a fiduciary duty of loyalty towards the company, that is to say that the large degree of trust and confidence inherent within the relationship between the company and the director is such that the director must not use corporate assets, or deal with the company, as to benefit himself at the expense of the company and its shareholders. Secondly, the directors owe a duty of care and skill to the company in respect of their actions and decision-making. The duty of loyalty is the basis upon which the courts test the impartiality of a decision taken by the director and the duty of care and skill is the means by which the law lays down its expectations about the degree of competence and care which directors should exercise in taking a decision.

The common law duties of loyalty and care owed by directors now find their expression in statutory form and have been superseded by the terms of ss.170–178 of the CA 2006. Section 170(3) clarifies that the statutory duties "have effect in place of" the common law rules as regards the duties owed to a company by a director. However, the common law rules have not simply "gone away". The statutory statement of director's duties in the CA 2006 does not offer a complete codification of the existing common law rules. This is partly due to simple gaps, such as the common law duty of directors to consider the interests of creditors when insolvency is threatened, which are expressed in s.172(3) of the Act to be

---

[119] CDDA s.6(1).
[120] CDDA s.6(4) and see *Re Sevenoaks Stationers (Retail) Ltd* [1991] Ch. 164.

found in the common law. Likewise, it is not clear whether a director has a duty to disclose his own misconduct to the company and whether this is codified in the Act.[121] The partial nature of the codification exercise is also evident from the terms of s.170(4) of the CA 2006. This provision states that the statutory duties must be interpreted and applied in the same way as the common rules that they replace and regard must be had to the corresponding common law rules in interpreting and applying the statutory duties. What this means is that the case law which was relevant prior to the coming into force of the CA 2006 will continue to command importance for the purposes of construing the meaning and application of the statutory duties. For that reason, recourse will be made to case law from time to time during the ensuing discussion to enhance understanding of the relevant statutory duty to which that case law corresponds. Another point to stress is that there is more than one duty. Thus, in a particular case, more than one duty may apply and this is recognised by s.179 of the CA 2006. To that extent, there may be an overlap between the duties in any given case.

The directors: to whom are the duties owed?

16–29 Prior to initiating a discussion of the content of the duties, it is beneficial to clarify to whom a director owes those duties. Section 170(1) of the CA 2006 answers this question in terms that the duties are owed by a director to the company. But to what extent and in what circumstances does a director owe duties to an individual shareholder? As is clear from the case of *Peskin v Anderson*,[122] it will only be in special factual circumstances that third parties will be able to demonstrate to a court that a director owes them duties of the nature enumerated in ss.171–177 of the CA 2006.

Peskin v Anderson
[2001] 1 B.C.L.C. 372

Concerning: Whether the directors of a company owed duties to a particular shareholder of the company.

Facts: In terms of a company's articles of association, profits generated by the commercial activities of the company could not be distributed to its members. The company entered into negotiations with, and agreed to sell its business to, a third party. The sale and purchase arrangements involved the alteration of the company's articles to permit the distribution of some of the sale proceeds to the members. Members who had resigned their membership

---

[121] In other words, the English law rule in *Item Software (UK) Ltd v Fassihi* [2005] 2 B.C.L.C. 91 which Lord President Hamilton doubted formed part of Scots law in *Commonwealth Oil & Gas Ltd v Baxter*, 2009 S.C. 156, 162 at [14].
[122] [2001] 1 B.C.L.C. 372.

approximately three years prior to the announcement of the sale of the company's business to the third party sued the directors for breach of their duties as directors. The former members' claim against the directors was formulated on the basis that had the directors disclosed to them that the company was in negotiations to sell its business to the third party, those members would not have decided to resign as members when they did. So the members claimed that the directors breached a duty which the directors owed to them as members.

Decision: The Court of Appeal recognised that there are circumstances in which the directors of a company will owe fiduciary duties to members, e.g. where the directors make direct approaches to, and deal with, the shareholders in relation to a specific transaction and hold themselves out as agents for them in connection with the acquisition or disposal of shares.[123] Likewise, the directors may owe duties to members where the former make material representations to the latter, where the former fail to make material disclosure to the latter of insider information in the context of negotiations for a take-over of the company's business or where the former supply to the latter specific information and advice on which the latter have relied. But absent such circumstances, generally, directors will owe their duties to the company only. In this particular case, the Court of Appeal ruled that there was nothing special in the factual relationship between the directors and the members to give rise to a fiduciary duty of disclosure. In particular there were no relevant dealings, negotiations, communications or other contact directly between the directors and the members. The actions of the directors had not caused the members to sell their shares when they did and, probably most important of all, at the beginning of the year in which the business of the company was sold, there was nothing sufficiently concrete and specific, either in existence or in contemplation, for the directors to disclose to the members.

The directors: duty to obey the constitution and act for a proper purpose

The first duty of a director to consider is the duty in s.171 which provides **16–30** that directors must act in accordance with a company's constitution and that they must only exercise the powers which they are conferred under the constitution for the purposes for which they were conferred. The duty to obey the constitution means that the directors must not attempt to do something which it is not in the power of the company to undertake. As for the duty that a director must not use their powers for an improper

---

[123] A good example of a director holding himself out as an agent of the shareholders is provided by the case of *Park's of Hamilton's (Holdings) Ltd v Campbell* [2011] CSOH 38; 2011 G.W.D. 8-196.

purpose which is set out in s.171(b) of the CA 2006, examples of what are meant by this duty are provided by the case law.

Howard Smith Ltd v Ampol Petroleum Ltd
[1974] A.C. 821 (Privy Council)

Concerning: Whether the directors of a company had breached their duty not to exercise their powers for an improper purpose where they used their constitutional power to issue shares in the company to one preferred bidder over another in the context of a takeover battle for the company.

Facts: Two companies, Ampol and Bulkships, held 30 per cent and 25 per cent respectively of the issued shares of RW Miller (Holdings) Ltd ("Millers"), which required more capital. Ampol made an offer for all the issued shares of Millers, and another company, Howard Smith, announced an intention to make a higher offer for those shares. Millers' directors considered Ampol's offer to be too low and decided to recommend that the offer be rejected. Ampol and Bulkships then stated that they intended to act jointly in the future operations of Millers and would reject any offer for their shares. Howard Smith then applied to Millers for an allotment of 4 million ordinary shares. Millers' directors decided by a majority to make the allotment and immediately issued the shares. The effect of that issue was that Millers secured the much needed capital, Ampol and Bulkship's respective shareholdings were reduced to 36.6 per cent of the issued shares and Howard Smith was in a position to make an effective takeover offer. Ampol challenged the validity of the issue of the shares to Howard Smith and sought an order for the rectification of Millers' share register by the removal of Howard Smith as a member of Millers in respect of the allotted shares. Millers' directors contended that the primary reason for the issue of the shares to Howard Smith was to obtain more capital. Ampol argued that the reason for the issue of the shares was to destroy their majority shareholding, which was an improper purpose.

Decision: The Privy Council ruled that it is unconstitutional and a breach of duty for a director to use his fiduciary powers over the shares in the company purely for the purpose of destroying an existing majority shareholding, or creating a new majority which did not previously exist. To do so is to disturb that element of the company's constitution which is separate from and set against their powers. If there is added to this immediate purpose an ulterior purpose to enable an offer for shares to proceed which the existing majority was in a position to block, the departure from the legitimate use of the fiduciary power becomes not less, but all the greater. The right to dispose of shares at a given price is essentially an individual right to be exercised on individual decision and on which a majority, in the absence of oppression or similar impropriety, is

> entitled to prevail. So for directors to use their fiduciary powers solely for the purpose of upsetting the balance of power to decide to whom and at what price shares are to be sold cannot be related to any purpose for which the power over the share capital was conferred upon them.

So, in the case of *Howard Smith*, where the directors issue shares in order to raise capital, that should not be undertaken in a manner which is designed to upset the existing constitutional balance of shareholder power. Moreover, in order to ascertain whether the director is applying a power for an improper purpose, the court must focus on the purpose or purposes for which the director was exercising his/her powers, i.e. his/her motivation. If an improper motivation can be shown, if only by inference from an objective assessment of all the surrounding circumstances, the basis for a case of breach of s.171(b) of the CA 2006 might be established.[124]

The directors: duty to promote the success of the company

The second statutory duty to examine is the duty of a director to promote **16–31** the success of the company. Section 172(1) of the CA 2006 is as follows:

> "A director of a company must act in the way he considers, in good faith, would be most likely to promote the success of the company for the benefit of its members as a whole, and in doing so have regard (amongst other matters) to—
>
> (a) the likely consequences of any decision in the long term,
> (b) the interests of the company's employees,
> (c) the need to foster the company's business relationships with suppliers, customers and others,
> (d) the impact of the company's operations on the community and the environment,
> (e) the desirability of the company maintaining a reputation for high standards of business conduct, and
> (f) the need to act fairly as between members of the company."

This is the overarching fiduciary duty owed by directors by virtue of the CA 2006. What is clear from s.172(1) is that a subjective test is applied to the director's decision.[125] So provided the director acts in good faith and genuinely believes the decision he takes will promote the success of the company, what only matters is that director's view, not that of the court—and the court will be unable to substitute its own judgment for that of the director. Moreover, the duty of the director is, "to promote

---

[124] *West Coast Capital (Lios) Ltd, Petitioner* [2008] CSOH 72, per Lord Glennie at [21].
[125] *Madoff Securities International v Raven* [2013] EWHC 3147 (Comm), per the Hon. Mr Justice Popplewell at [190].

the success of the company for the benefit of its members as a whole". In practice, this will enjoin the director to take decisions which realise the objectives for which the company has been established and in the case of commercial non-charitable companies, this will be a decision which results in a long-term increase in value for the company.[126] From s.172(1) of the CA 2006, it is clear that the primary obligation of the director is to promote the success of the company. So the interests of the company and its members are paramount and the other six constituencies and factors listed in subs.(1)(a)–(f),[127] e.g. the interests of employees, suppliers, customers, the community, the environment, etc. which the directors must have regard to in taking a decision,[128] are subordinate. Hence, if a director takes a decision which is in the interests of the company, but contrary to the interests of one of the other constituencies, the director will not be in breach of duty. So long as a director can show that he did actually consider these statutory factors, even if he ultimately decided that they were less important than other factors, he will probably have discharged his duty. A further important point to make is that s.172(1)(a) imposes a requirement on the directors to consider the likely long-term consequences of their decision. This represents a departure from the common law. However, the concern is that the CA 2006 does not provide the directors with any particular direction as to how they are supposed to reconcile long-term and short-term interests where they are clearly incompatible with each other. In certain cases, it may be commercially sensible for a director to accept a loan from a lender which resolves the short-term financial difficulties of the company. However, in the long term, that decision may be disadvantageous to the company. So in such a situation is the director bound to forgo the offer of the loan? It is not particularly clear how the director ought to proceed in such a case and the courts may be asked to adjudicate on such a matter in the future.

The directors: duty to exercise independent judgment

16–32 Turning to the third duty of directors, the duty in s.173(1) of the CA 2006 imposes a requirement on directors to exercise independent judgment. This is particularly relevant in the context of the exercise of their decision-making powers. This duty compels a director to approach matters with an open mind and without bias when exercising discretionary decision-making powers. Therefore, in circumstances where directors have legally bound themselves in advance to take a certain course of

---

[126] See the statement of Lord Goldsmith, Lords Grand Committee, February 6, 2006, cols 255–258, *Hansard*, available at *http://webarchive.nationalarchives.gov.uk/20121212135622/http://www.bis.gov.uk/files/file40139.pdf* [Accessed May 15, 2015].

[127] Which list is not intended to be exhaustive of the matters which the directors "must have regard to" in forming their decision.

[128] In the view of Margaret Hodge MP, Minister of State for Industry and the Regions at the time of the passage of the Companies Bill, "have regard to" will mean "think about" or "give proper consideration to", see Commons Report, October 17, 2006, col.789, *Hansard*, available at *http://webarchive.nationalarchives.gov.uk/20121212135622/http://www.bis.gov.uk/files/file40139.pdf* [Accessed May 15, 2015].

action, they will be ostensibly in breach of such a duty. However, s.173(2) provides two exceptions to the general rule. First, where a director has entered into a contractual agreement which restricts the future exercise of their discretionary powers of decision-making, they will not be in breach of such duty. So the Act recognises that there may be circumstances in which the company has bound itself in contract to a course of action which may fetter the discretion of the directors in the future and that this will not be unlawful. Secondly, a director will not be in breach of duty where the company's articles of association enable directors to restrict their independent judgment. Hence, a director will not be prevented from exercising a power to delegate conferred by the company's articles provided that its exercise is in accordance with the company's articles.

The directors: duty to avoid conflicts of interest

One of the principal ramifications of the loyalty obligation is that a **16–33** director must avoid conflicts between his/her interests and the company's interests. Section 175(1) of the CA 2006 provides as follows:

"A director of a company must avoid a situation in which he has, or can have, a direct or indirect interest that conflicts, or possibly may conflict, with the interests of the company."

In terms of s.175(7), the scope of s.175(1) covers both conflicts of interest and duty and conflicts of duties. The conflicting interest of the director may be direct or indirect, e.g. the conflicting interest of a director may be indirect where the director has been appointed by a major shareholder to serve his/her interests and those interests are contrary to the interests of the company. Section 175(2) provides in particular that the duty applies to the exploitation of property, information or opportunities by the director. So if a director comes across information in the capacity of director and then seeks to use that information for his own personal advantage, the director will be in breach. Most importantly, s.175(2) states that it is immaterial that the company could not itself take advantage of the information, opportunity or property. That is to say, that a director will not be able to defend a claim of breach of duty by arguing that the property, information or opportunity which the director sought to exploit was one which the company could not take advantage for itself.[129]

Section 175(4) of the CA 2006 makes it clear that the duty to avoid conflicts of interest in s.175(1) will not be breached if the situation cannot reasonably be regarded as likely to give rise to a conflict of interest. Furthermore, a director will not be in breach of duty in circumstances where the breach has been authorised in advance. Section 175(5)(a) of the CA 2006 states that the conflict of interest may be authorised in advance by the directors. For such prior authorisation by the directors to be valid,

---

[129] A point discussed by Lord Hodge in *Park's of Hamilton's (Holdings) Ltd v Campbell* [2011] CSOH 38; 2011 G.W.D. 8-196.

in the case of a private company there must be nothing in the company's articles which invalidates such authorisation, and in the case of a public company there must be specific provision in the company's articles which entitles the directors to authorise conflicts and the directors must follow that particular procedure for authorising conflicts. If the directors do not authorise the conflict in advance, it is open to the members of the company to ratify any infringement of the duty in accordance with ss.180 and 239 of the Act.

An important exception to the duty to avoid conflicts of interest and duty is spelled out in CA 2006 s.175(3). Here, it is provided that s.175 does not apply to a conflict of interest arising in relation to a transaction or arrangement with the company. Sections 177 and 182–187 of the CA 2006 apply where such a conflict of interest arises and consideration will be given to the specific rules which apply shortly. Moreover, the duty to avoid conflicts of interest applies to a limited extent in relation to directors who have resigned and thus ceased to be a director and are no longer in office by virtue of the terms of s.170(2). There have been a number of cases in which the common law considered the culpability of directors for breach of the duty to avoid conflicts of interest in circumstances where they had resigned from office. One such case is *Industrial Development Consultants Ltd v Cooley*.

Industrial Development Consultants Ltd v Cooley
[1972] 1 W.L.R. 443

Concerning: Whether a director who had resigned from office and had taken advantage of an opportunity presented to him in his capacity as a director was in breach of duty to avoid conflicts of interest.

Facts: Cooley was an architect and managing director of a building and development consultancy company. In his capacity as a director, he entered into negotiations with the Eastern Gas Board ("EGB"). His remit was to secure contracts for the company from EGB. However, EGB refused to enter into contracts with consultants and so the company could not take advantage of the opportunity. However, EGB were happy to offer the work to private architects and so offered contracts to Cooley in a private capacity. Cooley was released from office as a director on the false basis of ill-health and then took advantage of the contract offered by EGB. When the company sued Cooley for recovery of the benefits which he had personally derived from the contract with EGB, he sought to defend his conduct by arguing that: (i) he was no longer a director of the company when he had taken the contractual opportunity; and (ii) the opportunity was one which the company could not take advantage of itself.

Decision: Roskill J. in the High Court held that while Cooley was a managing director of the company, a fiduciary relationship existed between him and the company. Accordingly, information that came to him while he was managing director and was of concern to the company, was information which it was his duty to disclose to the company. He was under a duty, therefore, to disclose all information which he received in the course of his dealings with EGB. Instead he had embarked on a deliberate course of conduct which had put his personal interests as a potential contracting party with EGB in direct conflict with his pre-existing and continuing duty as managing director to the company. He was therefore in breach of his fiduciary duty to the company in failing to pass on to them all the relevant information received in the course of his dealings with EGB and in guarding it for his own personal purposes and profit. Moreover, it was irrelevant that he was no longer a director when he had exploited the contractual opportunity with EGB and the question whether the benefit of the contract would have been obtained for the company but for Cooley's breach of fiduciary duty was irrelevant.

The directors: duty not to accept benefits from third parties

Coupled with the duty of a director to avoid conflicts of interest, s.176 of **16–34** the CA 2006 provides that a director must not accept benefits from third parties. So it stands to reason that directors must not accept bribes or commissions from clients or potential clients. The duty not to accept benefits is not breached if the acceptance of the benefit cannot reasonably be regarded as likely to give rise to a conflict of interest. So this provision covers minor gifts and benefits received by directors which are of a trivial nature. However, unlike s.175(4)(b) and (5), there is no specific provision empowering the directors to authorise a director's breach of the duty not to accept benefits from third parties. Having said that, ss.180 and 239 enable the members to authorise or ratify breaches of this duty.

The directors: duty to declare interest in proposed or existing transaction or arrangement with the company

As mentioned above, where the conflict of interest concerns a transaction **16–35** or arrangement arising between the director and the company, ss.177 and 182–187 of the CA 2006 will apply. Section 177 applies in the case of a proposed transaction or arrangement between the director and the company, while ss.182–187 are the relevant provisions in the context of an existing transaction or arrangement. First, s.177 recognises that directors may be directly or indirectly interested in a proposed transaction or arrangement with the company. Rather than prohibit the entering into of such conflicted transactions, s.177(1), (2) and (4) of the CA 2006 provides that a director has an obligation to declare that interest to the directors at a board meeting or by notice in advance of the transaction or arrangement being concluded or entered into. If the director fails to comply with the duty in s.177, the contract, transaction or arrangement is voidable if it is entered into. That is to say that it is not invalidated, but that it may be set aside at the insistence or option of the company. Moreover, there are other remedies available, which are narrated in s.178 of the CA 2006. It is stipulated in s.177(5) and (6) that a director need not declare an interest in a proposed transaction if he could not reasonably be aware of it, or it could not be reasonably regarded as likely to give rise to a conflict of interest. A director is also relieved from making disclosure where the other directors are already aware of the transaction. Section 180 of the CA 2006 provides that, subject to the company's articles of association, if the directors observe their duty to declare their interest in accordance with s.177, the transaction is not liable to be set aside on the basis of the common law rule that the consent of the members is also required.

Section 182 of the CA 2006 states that where a director is directly or indirectly interested in an existing (rather than proposed) transaction or arrangement that has been entered into by a company, the director must declare that interest to the other directors as soon as reasonably practicable at a board meeting, by written notice in terms of s.184 or by general notice in accordance with s.185 of the CA 2006. Moreover, where a director fails to comply with his duty to declare his interest in a proposed transaction or arrangement with the company of which he ought reasonably to have been aware in accordance with s.177 and subsequently enters into the transaction with the company, not only will he be in breach of his duty to disclose under s.177, but he must make separate disclosure in accordance with the terms of s.182 of the Act. Breach of the duty in s.182 of the CA 2006 to disclose an interest in an existing transaction or arrangement is a criminal offence in terms of s.183 of the CA 2006. Again, it is narrated in s.182(5) and (6) that a director need not declare an interest in an existing transaction if he could not reasonably be aware of it, or it could not be reasonably regarded as likely to give rise to a conflict of interest. A director is also relieved from making disclosure where the other directors are already aware of the transaction.

The directors: duty of care, skill and diligence

16–36 It should be stressed that each of the duties of directors which have been considered so far are statutorily imposed fiduciary duties; that is to say, the duty to obey the constitution and not to act for an improper purpose,[130] the duty to promote the success of the company,[131] the duty to exercise independent judgment,[132] the duty to avoid conflicts of interest,[133] the duty not to accept benefits from third parties,[134] and the duties of disclosure in respect of proposed or existing transactions or arrangements entered into between the director and the company.[135] This is important since it explains the loyalty obligation which underpins those particular

---

[130] CA 2006 s.171.
[131] CA 2006 s.172.
[132] CA 2006 s.173.
[133] CA 2006 s.175.
[134] CA 2006 s.176.
[135] CA 2006 ss.177, 180 and 182 to 187.

duties and, as will become apparent in the ensuing discussion of s.178 of the CA 2006, it is important to make the classification between statutorily imposed fiduciary duties and non-fiduciary duties for the purposes of ascertaining the nature of the remedies open to parties seeking to challenge a director for breach of duty. One duty which is non-fiduciary in nature is the duty in s.174.[136] Section 174(1) states that a director must exercise reasonable care, skill and diligence. An exploration of the content of such a duty is made in s.174(2) where the duty is taken to signify the care, skill and diligence that would be exercised by a reasonably diligent person with: (a) the general knowledge, skill and experience that may reasonably be expected of a person carrying out the functions carried out by the director in relation to the company; and (b) the general knowledge, skill and experience that the director has. Thus, in determining whether a director has breached his duty of care and skill in terms of s.174, the court must apply a mixture of an objective and subjective test. Therefore, what the reasonable person would regard as the knowledge, skill and experience to be expected of the hypothetical director sets the lowest acceptable standard (this is the objective assessment), with the actual director's knowledge, skill and experience operating to lift that threshold where it is clear that the attributes of the actual director are higher than the reasonable, hypothetical standard (this is the subjective assessment). In deciding whether directors have fallen short of their duty of skill and care, particularly where the breach of duty concerns the way in which the business is run, evidence of what is normal in the field of commerce in which the company operates is of considerable relevance.[137] Section 174 codifies the existing common law, a good example of which is provided by the case of *Re D'Jan of London Ltd*.

Re D'Jan of London Ltd
[1994] 1 B.C.L.C. 561

Concerning: Whether a director who had failed to read an insurance policy proposal form before signing it was in breach of his duty of care, skill and diligence.

Facts: Mr D'Jan was a director. He failed to read an insurance policy proposal form in taking out insurance on behalf of the company of which he was a director. The effect of his signature was that certain questions which had been answered in the negative by his insurance broker were in fact true. When the company's premises and stock to the value of £174,000 were destroyed by fire, the insurance company avoided the insurance policy on the basis of breach of warranty. The result was that the company became insolvent and the liquidator of the company brought proceedings for the benefit of the unsecured creditors on

---

[136] Lord Goldsmith, Lords Grand Committee, February 9, 2006, col.334, *Hansard*.
[137] *Abbey Forwarding Ltd v Hone* [2010] EWHC 2029 (Ch.), per Mr Justice Lewison at [196]–[207].

the basis of a breach of the director's duty of care, skill and diligence.

Decision: The High Court in England ruled that Mr D'Jan had been negligent. In failing to read the insurance policy proposal form before signing it on behalf of the company, he had failed to discharge the duty of care, skill and diligence which he owed to the company on an objective assessment (i.e. the standard which the reasonable person would regard as the knowledge, skill and experience to be expected of the hypothetical director) and a subjective assessment (i.e. the standard of knowledge, skill and experience which the actual director possessed). So he was in breach of duty.

Moreover, in *Lexi Holdings (In Administration) v Luqman*,[138] it was held that the s.174 duty also applies to non-executive directors. The Court of Appeal ruled that non-executive directors could be liable for a breach of the s.174 duty of care, skill and diligence if they failed to actively monitor, and report to the company's professional directors and auditors, the criminal actions of a rogue executive director who had dishonestly misapplied the funds of the company causing resulting loss to the company. The relevance of the duty of care, skill and diligence lies in the fact that it must be observed by a director in applying his mind to his fiduciary duties in the context of decision-making. So this duty will apply in connection with the duty to promote the success of the company under s.172 of the Act, i.e. to any good faith assessment as to which of the factors are relevant to a business decision and to what extent they need to be taken into account. If the good faith assessment turns out to be wrong, the decision could be open to challenge if the directors fail either the subjective or the objective test in s.174 of the CA 2006, which underscores the importance of directors taking care and exercising the appropriate standard of diligence in undertaking a consideration of the list of statutory factors enumerated in s.172 of the CA 2006.

The directors: remedies for breach of duty

16–37 The consequences of a director breaching the duties in ss.171–177 of the CA 2006 are set out in s.178 of the CA 2006 which provides as follows:

"(1) The consequences of breach (or threatened breach) of sections 171 to 177 are the same as would apply if the corresponding common law rule or equitable principle applied.

(2) The duties in those sections (with the exception of section 174 (duty to exercise reasonable care, skill and diligence)) are, accordingly, enforceable in the same way as any other fiduciary duty owed to a company by its directors."

---

[138] [2009] EWCA Civ 117; [2009] 2 B.C.L.C. 1.

Therefore, in the case of fiduciary duties (i.e. all of the statutory duties with the exception of s.174), the consequences of breach may include:

- damages or compensation where the company has suffered loss;
- restoration of the company's property;
- an account of profits made by the director; and/or
- rescission of a contract entered into between the company and a third party where the director failed to disclose an interest.

In the case of a breach of s.174, i.e. the non-fiduciary duty of care, skill and diligence, only the damages remedy from the above list will be available and the other remedies in the bullet points above will be irrelevant.

However, the company may wish to ratify a director's conduct which amounts to a breach of the duties in ss.171–177. Section 239 of the CA 2006 permits this and so, the members may pass an ordinary resolution in general meeting. There are certain anti-avoidance provisions which apply whereby any votes held by a director in breach, or any member connected with him, are not to be taken into account. Bodies corporate in which the director and any persons connected with him together have broadly a 20 per cent interest in the equity or the voting rights are connected with a director for this purpose. Ratification may not be possible where a holding company is asked to ratify the acts of a director of its subsidiary company and the director has a material interest in the holding company. Finally, if a director is found to be in breach of duty by a court, the court has a discretion to grant relief to that director under s.1157 of the CA 2006, if they are satisfied that the director acted, "honestly and reasonably and having regard to all the circumstances of the case he ought fairly to be excused". In the case of *Gillespie Investments Ltd v Gillespie*,[139] it was held that it would be unreasonable to excuse a director where there had been a failure to keep proper records to verify various transactions entered into by the company which resulted in third parties benefitting from the irregular appropriation of the company's funds.

The directors: statutory obligations

Notwithstanding the statutory statement of general duties owed by the directors to the company expressed in ss.171–177 of the CA 2006, there are further statutory restrictions contained in the Act in respect of contracts, transactions and arrangements entered into between the company and a director. The restrictions are imposed in connection with: **16–38**

- long-term service contracts entered into between the company and a director[140];

---

[139] [2010] CSOH 113; 2011 G.W.D. 1-10, per Lord Hodge at [55].
[140] CA 2006 ss.188–189.

- transactions where the company sells or buys a substantial non-cash asset to or from a director of the company[141];
- loan and similar type transactions by companies to their directors[142]; and
- payments by companies to directors for loss of office.[143]

Each of the above transactions or payments must be approved by an ordinary resolution of the members to be effective.

Key Concept

A director is an officer of the company who is responsible for the day-to-day management of the company. The law imposes duties on directors in an effort to control self-dealing and opportunistic behaviour on the part of directors. Such duties can be divided into statutorily imposed fiduciary duties, embodying a director's: (i) duty of loyalty and fidelity towards the company, and non-fiduciary duties; namely the (ii) duty of care, skill and diligence in decision-making.

CORPORATE DECISION-MAKING AND CORPORATE GOVERNANCE: (II) COMPANY MEETINGS AND RESOLUTIONS

Introduction

16–39 The general meeting is the forum at which the members of the company can come together to consider the performance of the directors of the company and vote on matters which the CA 2006 and the articles of association of the company specify must be passed by resolution of the members. For example, in terms of s.188(2) of the CA 2006, it is at the general meeting that the members can consider whether to pass an ordinary resolution (or not as the case may be) to approve a long-term service contract entered into between the company and a director. Likewise, a decision to amend the company's articles of association by special resolution in terms of s.21(1) of the CA 2006 will be considered at a general meeting. As will be explored shortly, there are three types of resolutions, each with different consequences and each required in differing contexts as prescribed by the Act or the company's articles of association.

General meetings: general

16–40 In undertaking any examination of the rules in the CA 2006 concerning general meetings, it is salutary to keep in mind the distinction between private companies and public companies. This is so, since there is no legal

---

[141] CA 2006 ss.190–196.
[142] CA 2006 ss.197–214.
[143] CA 2006 ss.215–222.

requirement for a private limited company to hold a general meeting as a matter of course. By contrast, Plcs (whether quoted or not) are under a statutory obligation to hold an annual general meeting ("AGM") in terms of s.336 of the CA 2006, that is to say a general meeting which takes place once a year. The AGM of the public company must be held within six months of its financial year end.[144] However, public companies may call and hold general meetings other than AGMs where there is a requirement to undertake and complete business which is so pressing or urgent that it is impracticable to wait until the next AGM.

General meetings: power to call general meetings

If a public company wishes to hold a general meeting (other than an **16–41** AGM) or a private company proposes to call and hold a general meeting,[145] the company must opt in to the holding of general meetings through the relevant procedures in the CA 2006.[146] Section 302 enables the directors of a private company or public company to call a general meeting. Section 303 contains a separate members' requisition procedure. Where a member or members holding:

- at least 5 per cent of the paid up capital of the company as carries the right of voting at general meetings; or
- in the case of a non-share company, at least 5 per cent[147] of the total voting rights of all the members having a right to vote at general meetings,

request a general meeting, the directors are required to call such a meeting:

- within 21 days from the date on which they become subject to the requirement; and
- to be held on a date not more than 28 days after the date of the notice convening the meeting.[148]

The member(s)' request under s.303(2) of the CA 2006 may be in hard copy or electronic form and must be authenticated by the member or members and state the general nature of the business to be dealt with at the general meeting.[149] It may also include the text of a resolution that may be properly moved and is intended to be moved at the meeting.[150] As regards the proposed resolution, any resolution may be moved by a member or members unless:

---

[144] CA 2006 s.336.
[145] There is no such thing as an AGM in the case of a private company.
[146] For example, by following the procedure in ss.302 or 303 of the CA 2006.
[147] CA 2006 ss.302 or 303.
[148] CA 2006 ss.303(2) and 304(1).
[149] CA 2006 s.303(4)(a).
[150] CA 2006 s.303(4)(b).

- it would, if passed, be ineffective—whether by reason of inconsistency with any enactment or the company's constitution or otherwise;
- it is defamatory of any person; or
- it is frivolous or vexatious.[151]

As a complete stop gap, the court has the power to order a general meeting where it is impracticable to call the meeting of a company in any manner in which meetings of that company may be called or to conduct the meeting in the manner prescribed by the company's articles or the Act.[152] This is on the application of a director or any member who would be entitled to vote at the meeting. The intervention of the court to order the calling of a meeting will be appropriate in circumstances where there has been an irretrievable breakdown in relations between the members and there is a clear deadlock.

Union Music Ltd v Watson
[2003] EWCA Civ 180; [2004] B.C.C. 37

Concerning: The circumstances in which the court should exercise its discretion under s.306(1) of the CA 2006 to order the calling of a general meeting.

Facts: Union Music Ltd ("UML") was the majority shareholder of the company and Russell Watson, the opera singer, was the minority shareholder. A shareholders' agreement entered into between UML and Watson provided that both shareholders' prior written consent was required for the holding of a general meeting of the members of the company. There was a breakdown in the relationship between the two members. UML refused to attend meetings of the company and one of the directors of the company resigned. UML applied to the court seeking an order for the calling of a general meeting in order to appoint a new director. At first instance, it was ruled that the court had no authority to exercise its discretion to call a meeting where a shareholders' agreement provided expressly that the consent of both members was required for any general meeting. UML appealed to the Court of Appeal.

Decision: The Court of Appeal granted the appeal. The identical statutory predecessor of s.306 of the CA 2006 was a procedural section intended to enable company business that needed to be conducted at a meeting of the company to be so conducted, and to allow a company not to be frustrated in its affairs by the impracticability of calling a meeting in the manner prescribed by its articles. Where, as in the instant case, there were unequal shareholdings the court was under no obligation to assume that the parties had intended that a veto had been intended on the part of

---

[151] CA 2006 s.303(5).
[152] CA 2006 s.306(1).

either shareholder, much less the minority shareholder. The shareholders' agreement had to be read against that situation, and it was not to be viewed as giving one party a veto over another from calling any meeting at all. Instead, it should be viewed as a provision relating to a quorum. In those circumstances, it was plain that the court should exercise its discretion to make an order for a meeting under the Act.

General meetings: AGMs of public companies

Every Plc must hold an AGM in the period of six months beginning with **16–42** the day following its accounting reference date each year.[153] The procedures for holding an AGM of a public company are distinct from the conventions in the CA 2006 which apply in the context of a general meeting of a Plc (which were considered above). The effect of a failure to hold such an AGM is that each officer of the public company is deemed to have committed a criminal offence. In practice, it is commonly the directors who will take the necessary steps to arrange the AGM and the business and resolutions to be considered. The members have a separate power under s.338 of the Act to require the company to circulate resolutions for AGMs—over and above the right they have under s.303(4) and (5) of the CA 2006 to propose certain items of business and resolutions for consideration at the meeting. However, there are crucial differences. Under s.303 of the CA 2006, the threshold is 5 per cent of the paid-up members for the calling of a general meeting which is not an AGM, whereas under s.338(3), the threshold is:

- 5 per cent of the total voting rights of all of the members of the Plc who have a right to vote on the resolution at the AGM to which the requests relate (excluding voting rights attached to any shares in the company which are held as treasury shares); or
- at least 100 members who have a right to vote on the resolution at the AGM to which the requests relate and hold shares in the company on which there has been paid up an average sum, per member, of at least £100.

Any resolution may be moved by a member at an AGM unless:

- it would, if passed, be ineffective—whether by reason of inconsistency with any enactment or the company's constitution or otherwise;
- it is defamatory of any person; or
- it is frivolous or vexatious.

Additional requirements are imposed on quoted companies as follows:

---

[153] CA 2006 s.336(1).

- there is a requirement to publish poll results online[154]; and
- shareholders (100 in number or representing 5 per cent of more of the voting rights) have the power to require a report on a poll to be procured from an independent assessor.[155]

General meetings: notice of general meetings

16–43 Subject to any longer period of notice stipulated in the articles,[156] a general meeting of a private company requires 14 days' prior notice to the members.[157] In the case of a Plc, a general meeting must be called by 21 days' prior notice to the members in the case of an AGM[158] or 14 days' prior notice to the members in the case of any other general meeting.[159] However, there are separate rules for companies which are traded companies, i.e. companies whose shares are admitted to trading on a regulated market such as the main market of the London Stock Exchange.[160] In the case of an AGM of a public company or a traded company, it is a legal requirement for the Plc to specify in the notice that the meeting is an annual general meeting.[161]

Notwithstanding the periods for the provision of notice, there is a procedure in the CA 2006 whereby a general meeting may be held on short notice. The threshold for members' consent to short notice in the case of a private company limited by shares is 90 per cent in nominal value of the shares of the company which give a right to attend and vote at the meeting—subject to the right of the company in its articles to increase this threshold to a maximum of 95 per cent.[162] In the case of a private company limited by guarantee, the requisite percentage of the members requiring to give consent to short notice is 90 per cent of the total voting rights at a meeting of all the members—subject to the right of the company in its articles to increase this threshold to a maximum of 95 per cent. In the case of a Plc, the consent to short notice procedure is slightly more complicated. First, one must make a distinction between a general meeting and an AGM. In the case of a general meeting, the requisite percentage of the members of a Plc limited by shares requiring to give consent to short notice is 95 per cent in nominal value of the shares of the company which give a right to attend and vote at the meeting.[163] Meanwhile, in the case of a general meeting of a Plc limited by guarantee the requisite percentage of the members requiring to give consent to short notice is 95 per cent of the total voting rights at a

---

[154] CA 2006 s.341.
[155] CA 2006 s.342.
[156] CA 2006 s.307(3).
[157] CA 2006 s.307(1).
[158] CA 2006 s.307(2)(a).
[159] CA 2006 s.307(2)(b). This is subject to any longer period of notice stipulated in the articles.
[160] CA 2006 s.360C.
[161] CA 2006 s.337(1).
[162] CA 2006 s.307(5)(a) and (6)(a).
[163] CA 2006 s.307(5)(a) and (6)(b).

meeting of all the members.[164] As for the AGMs of a Plc, the regime is different. Section 337(2) of the CA 2006 provides that an AGM of a public company which is not a traded company may be called by short notice if all the members entitled to attend and vote at the meeting agree to the shorter notice.

Sections 308 and 309 of the CA 2006 dictate the manner in which the notice of a general meeting must be given, namely hard copy form, electronic form or by means of a website. The notice must be served on every member and every director of the company.[165] However, the company's articles may validly provide otherwise.[166] It is a requirement for the notice of a general meeting to provide the following information:

- the time and date of the meeting; and
- the place of the meeting.[167]

The notice must also state the general nature of the business to be dealt with at the meeting, but this is subject to any provision in the company's articles where the company is not a traded company.[168]

Where the CA 2006 requires special notice of a resolution,[169] the resolution will not be effective unless notice of the intention to move it has been given to the company at least 28 days before the meeting at which it is to be moved.[170] The company must, where practicable, give its members notice of any such resolution in the same manner and at the same time as it gives notice of the meeting.[171] Where that is not practicable, the company must give its members notice at least 14 days before the meeting:

- by advertisement in a newspaper having an appropriate circulation; or
- in any other manner allowed by the company's articles.[172]

General meetings: procedure at general meetings

If a general meeting is not quorate, any business or resolutions conducted **16–44** or passed at that meeting are invalid.[173] A quorum for a single member private company is one member[174] and, as a default, a quorum are two

---

[164] CA 2006 s.307(5)(b) and (6)(b).
[165] CA 2006 s.310(1).
[166] CA 2006 s.310(4)(b).
[167] CA 2006 s.311(1).
[168] CA 2006 s.311(2).
[169] For example, in the context of an ordinary resolution to remove a director in terms of CA 2006 s.168(1).
[170] CA 2006 s.312(1).
[171] CA 2006 s.312(2).
[172] CA 2006 s.312(3).
[173] *Prain & Sons Ltd, Petitioners*, 1947 S.C. 325.
[174] CA 2006 s.318(1).

"qualifying persons" in any other case.[175] A member, corporate representative or proxy present at the meeting may all be "qualifying persons". As for the election of a chairman to a meeting, s.319 of the CA 2006 provides that where the articles are silent, a member may be elected to be the chairman of a general meeting by an ordinary resolution of the company passed at the meeting.[176] When the members vote on a resolution tabled at a general meeting, their votes may be counted on: (i) a show of hands; or (ii) a poll. As will become apparent, on a show of hands each member has one vote, whereas on a poll, each member has one vote for each share which they hold. The chairman's declaration of a vote taken on a show hands is conclusive evidence of the resolution being passed or lost without further proof being provided, unless a poll is demanded on the resolution.[177] The minutes of the meeting also provide conclusive evidence of the chairman's declaration.[178] These provisions are designed to provide certainty by preventing members from challenging a declaration of the chairman as to the votes cast on a resolution at a meeting otherwise than by calling a poll. In relation to voting on a poll, s.321 of the CA 2006 states that any provision in a company's articles that restricts the right of a member to demand a poll at a general meeting is void other than a question regarding: (i) the election of the chairman of the meeting; or (ii) the adjournment of the meeting.[179] On a poll, a member entitled to more than one vote need not, if he votes, use all his votes or cast all the votes he uses in the same way.[180] Therefore, this provision recognises that a member may hold shares on behalf of third parties and allows that member to cast votes in different ways according to instructions from third party clients. A poll may be demanded by the chairman of the meeting, a proxy, any director of the company, at least two shareholders having the right to vote or a person or persons representing not less than one-tenth of the total voting rights of all the shareholders having the right to vote on the resolution.[181]

General meetings: proxies

16–45 A proxy is a person who attends a general meeting on behalf of a member. Proxies are commonly appointed where a member is unable to attend a meeting due to illness or other commitments and must vote in accordance with the instructions of the members who appointed them.[182] Members of both private companies and Plcs have the right to appoint more than one proxy, provided that each proxy is appointed to exercise

---

[175] CA 2006 s.318(2).
[176] CA 2006 s.319(1).
[177] CA 2006 s.320(1) and 320(3).
[178] CA 2006 s.320(2).
[179] CA 2006 s.321(1).
[180] CA 2006 s.322.
[181] See CA 2006 s.329(1) and reg.44(2) of the Model Articles in the case of a private limited company by shares, reg.30(2) of the Model Articles in the case of a private company limited by guarantee and reg.36(2) of the Model Articles in respect of public limited companies.
[182] CA 2006 s.324A.

the rights attached to a different share or shares held by him.[183] All proxies are able to attend, to speak and to vote at a general meeting on behalf of their appointing member on a show of hands or on a poll.[184] A proxy also has the right to demand a vote on a poll.[185] The effect of all of the provisions relating to proxies is that, where a member appoints more than one proxy, each proxy will have a vote. The articles may restrict the number of votes of the proxies, provided that they still have at least one vote between them.

Every notice calling a meeting must contain a statement informing the member of his right to appoint one or more proxies and any more extensive rights conferred upon that member by the articles of association of the company.[186] Failure to include such a statement will not invalidate the meeting, but is an offence attracting a fine for every officer of the company found in default.[187] The minimum period for notice to the company of the appointment of a proxy is 48 hours.[188] A proxy may be appointed chairman of a general meeting,[189] but this is subject to the terms of the company's articles. The CA 2006 also provides that an appointed proxy's actions at a meeting are valid unless notice of termination of the proxy's authority is given before the meeting starts.[190] Finally, the CA 2006 makes it clear that the company's articles may confer more extensive rights than are provided for under the provisions in the Act on members and their proxies.[191]

Resolutions: general

As has been stipulated elsewhere in this chapter, the power of the com- **16–46** pany to take decisions is divided amongst the board of directors of the company and the members of the company. The members exercise their decision-making prerogative by voting on resolutions. Section 281(1) of the CA 2006 empowers a private company to pass a resolution of its members either as a written resolution or at a general meeting of the members. Section 282(1) provides that a Plc will only be entitled to pass a resolution at a meeting of the members. The unanimous consent rule of the common law, i.e. the rule in *Re Duomatic*[192] is preserved by s.281(4), which provides that the rules on resolutions in the CA 2006 do not affect any enactment or rule of law as to the circumstances in which a resolution is or is not treated as having been passed or cases in which a person is precluded from alleging that a resolution has not been duly passed. The unanimous consent rule confers a discretion on the court to rule that

---

[183] CA 2006 s.324(2).
[184] CA 2006 s.324(1).
[185] CA 2006 s.329(1).
[186] CA 2006 s.325(1).
[187] CA 2006 s.325(2) and (3).
[188] CA 2006 s.327(2).
[189] CA 2006 s.328(1).
[190] CA 2006 s.330(2).
[191] CA 2006 s.331.
[192] [1969] 1 All E.R. 161.

where it is clear that a decision taken by the company commanded the unanimous approval of the members, it is binding on a company notwithstanding the fact that the members of the company failed to pass any resolution required in accordance with the Act or the company's articles. So the unanimous consent rule disentitles a person from seeking to challenge the validity of the decision for want of a resolution.

Section 281(3) states that any reference to a resolution in the CA 2006 is taken to be a reference to an ordinary resolution, unless the company's articles specify a higher majority. There are only three types of resolution valid under the CA 2006, as follows:

- ordinary resolutions;
- special resolutions; and
- written resolutions.[193]

An ordinary resolution or a special resolution may be passed at a general meeting of the company.[194] In the case of a private company only, an ordinary resolution or a special resolution may be also passed as a written resolution in terms of the written resolution procedure under the CA 2006.[195] Sections 29 and 30 of the CA 2006 make it clear that copies of resolutions duly passed by the members of the company must be filed with the Registrar of Companies within 15 days of them having been passed or made. The CA 2006 provides that anything that may be done by ordinary resolution may also be done by special resolution.[196]

Resolutions: ordinary resolutions

16–47 Section 282(1) of the CA 2006 provides that an ordinary resolution of the members of a company or of a class of members of a company means a resolution that is passed by a simple majority of the members. Section 282(2) states that if an ordinary resolution is passed as a written resolution it will be passed by the members of the company representing a simple majority of the total voting rights of eligible members. Moreover, s.282(3) goes on to provide that a resolution passed at a meeting on a show of hands is passed by a simple majority if it is passed by a simple majority of the members who, being entitled to do so, vote in person on the resolution or their appointed proxies. A resolution passed on a poll taken at a meeting is passed by a simple majority in terms of s.282(4) if it is passed by members representing a simple majority of the total voting rights of members who (being entitled to do so) vote in person or by proxy on the resolution. The CA 2006 specifies a number of decisions which require an ordinary resolution to be passed validly, e.g. an ordinary resolution is required to remove the auditors of the company,[197]

---

[193] CA 2006 ss.282, 283 and 288.
[194] CA 2006 s.281(1)(b) and 281(2).
[195] CA 2006 ss.281(1)(a), 288(1) and 288(5).
[196] CA 2006 s.282(5).
[197] CA 2006 s.510(2)(a).

to remove a director[198] or to approve a substantial property transaction entered into between the director and the company.[199]

Resolutions: special resolutions

In terms of s.283(1) of the CA 2006, a special resolution of the members **16–48** of a company or of a class of members of a company means a resolution that is passed by a majority of not less than 75 per cent. Section 283(2) is to the effect that a special resolution is passed validly as a written resolution if it is passed by a majority of the members of the company representing not less than 75 per cent of the total voting rights of eligible members. Moreover, s.283(3) states that where a resolution of a private company is passed as a written resolution: (a) the resolution is not a special resolution unless it states that it was proposed as a special resolution; and (b) if the resolution is so framed, it may only be passed as a special resolution.

The effect of s.283(4) is that a special resolution passed at a meeting on a show of hands is passed by a majority of not less than 75 per cent if it is passed by not less than 75 per cent of the members who, being entitled to do so, vote in person on the resolution or by proxy. A special resolution passed on a poll taken at a meeting is passed by a majority of not less than 75 per cent in terms of s.283(5) if it is passed by members representing a majority of not less than 75 per cent of the total voting rights of members who (being entitled to do so) vote in person or by proxy on the resolution. Finally, s.283(6) states that where a resolution is passed at a meeting: (i) the resolution is not a special resolution unless the notice of the meeting includes the text of the resolution and specifies the intention to propose the resolution as a special resolution; and (ii) if the notice of the meeting so specifies, the resolution may only be passed as a special resolution. Some of the decisions which the Act specifies must be passed by special resolution in order to be valid are as follows:

- the alteration of the articles of association of the company[200];
- to change the company's name[201]; and
- to disapply the statutory pre-emption rights on the allotment of shares.[202]

Resolutions: voting of members on resolutions

Where the members are voting on a written resolution: **16–49**

- in the case of a company having a share capital, every member has one vote in respect of each share which they own or each £10 of stock held by them; and

---

[198] CA 2006 s.168(1).
[199] CA 2006 s.190(1).
[200] CA 2006 s.22(1).
[201] CA 2006 s.77(2)(a).
[202] CA 2006 ss.570 and 571.

- in any other case, every member has one vote.[203]

Where the members are voting on a show of hands at a general meeting:

- every member present has one vote; and
- every proxy present who has been duly appointed by a member entitled to vote on the resolution has one vote.[204]

Where the members are voting on a poll at a general meeting:

- in the case of a company having a share capital, every member has one vote in respect of each share which they own or each £10 of stock held by them; and
- in any other case, every member has one vote.[205]

However, s.284(4) of the CA 2006 clarifies that all of the above is subject to any provisions to the contrary contained in the articles of association of the company. So the Act expressly recognises that the articles of association may alter the voting rights attaching to shares. A prime example is the case of *Bushell v Faith*.

Bushell v Faith
[1970] A.C. 1099

Concerning: Whether it is competent for a member to have "weighted" voting rights in terms of the articles of association of a company.

Facts: Mr Bushell was a director of Bush Court (Southgate) Ltd and held one-third in total of the shares of the company. His two sisters owned the remaining two-thirds of the shares. Article 9 of the articles of association of the company provided that any director would have three votes per share on a poll at a general meeting in respect of a resolution to remove him/her as a director of the company. His two sisters proposed a resolution to remove him as a director and Mr Bushell demanded a poll on the resolution at the general meeting. When a vote was taken on a poll, he was able to defeat the resolution since he had three votes per share. The sisters challenged art.9 of the articles of association which purported to give Mr Bushell weighted voting rights on the basis that s.184 of the Companies Act 1948 (the equivalent of what is now s.168(1) of the CA 2006) provided that every director may be removed by passing an ordinary resolution of the members, i.e. 50 per cent of the members having the right to vote on the resolution.

Decision: The House of Lords decided that there was nothing in

---

[203] CA 2006 s.284(1).
[204] CA 2006 s.284(2) and 285(1).
[205] CA 2006 s.284(3).

> the Companies Act 1948 that precluded the company from providing for weighted voting rights in its articles of association. Parliament could easily have provided that weighted voting rights were prohibited in the case of a resolution to remove a director, but they didn't. Thus, the vote that defeated the resolution to remove Mr Bushell as a director could not be set aside and was valid.

Resolutions: written resolutions

The CA 2006 contains a procedure called the written resolution procedure which enables ordinary resolutions and special resolutions to be passed otherwise than at a general meeting of the company. The CA 2006 includes specific provisions dealing with the competence, circulation and effect of written resolutions. However, s.288(2) specifies certain resolutions which may not be proposed and passed as a written resolution, e.g.: **16–50**

- a resolution removing a director from office prior to the expiration of his period of office in terms of s.168 of the Act; and
- a resolution removing an auditor from office prior to the expiration of his term of office in terms of s.510 of the CA 2006.

It is competent for the directors or the members of a private company to propose and pass a written resolution.[206] A written resolution has effect as if passed by the company in general meeting or by a meeting of a class of members of the company. However, written resolutions can only be passed under the Act. It is no longer competent to pass written resolutions pursuant to a company's articles.[207] Since the Act prohibits public limited companies from passing written resolutions, the effect is that any attempt by a public company to pass a written resolution after October 1, 2007 will be ineffective.

Section 289 of the CA 2006 identities the members who are eligible to vote on written resolutions. The eligible members are the members who would have been entitled to vote on the resolution on the *circulation date* of the resolution.[208] The circulation date of the written resolution is the date on which copies of it are sent or submitted to members. If copies are sent or submitted to members on different days, then the first of those days is deemed to be the relevant circulation date.

As outlined above, a written resolution may be proposed by the directors or the members. As regards the director-initiated procedure, it is stated that the company must send or submit a copy of the resolution to **16–51**

---

[206] CA 2006 s.288(3). The procedures differ depending on whether the written resolution is initiated by the directors or the members—see para.16–51 below.
[207] Regulation 53 of the Model Articles of Association for a company incorporated under the Companies Act 1985 in Table A (the Schedule to the Companies (Tables A–F) Regulations 1985 (SI 1985/805)) purported to enable companies to pass written resolutions.
[208] CA 2006 s.289(1).

every eligible member.[209] When the company sends the copy of the written resolution to the eligible members it must be accompanied by a statement informing the member:

- how to signify agreement to the resolution; and
- as to the date by which the resolution must be passed if it is not to lapse.[210]

A failure to follow the above procedure is a criminal offence.[211] However, somewhat interestingly, the CA 2006 provides that the validity of a resolution which fails to comply with the above is not to be questioned where it is passed.[212]

The written resolution procedure also enables members (rather than the directors) to propose and move a written resolution.[213] Any written resolution may be proposed and moved by the members, unless:

- it would, if passed, be ineffective (whether by reason of inconsistency with any enactment or the company's constitution or otherwise);
- it is defamatory of any person; or
- it is frivolous or vexatious.[214]

The percentage of members required to compel the company to propose and circulate the written resolution is 5 per cent of the total voting rights of all members entitled to vote on the resolution.[215] Where the requisite percentage of members have proposed the written resolution, the company is bound to send or submit a copy of the written resolution to every eligible member.[216]

The company has no more than 21 days from the date of the requisite percentage member(s)' request (proposing the written resolution and requiring the company to circulate it in accordance with s.292 of the CA 2006) to send or submit the copies of the written resolution to the eligible members.[217] When the company sends the copy of the written resolution to an eligible member it must be accompanied by guidance informing the member:

- how he must signify his agreement to the resolution; and
- the date by which the resolution must be passed if it is not to lapse—which is 28 days beginning with the circulation date of the written resolution (i.e. the date on which copies of it were sent or

---

[209] CA 2006 s.291(2).
[210] CA 2006 s.291(4).
[211] CA 2006 s.291(5).
[212] CA 2006 s.291(7).
[213] CA 2006 s.292(1).
[214] CA 2006 s.292(2).
[215] CA 2006 s.292(5). The company's articles of association may specify a lower percentage.
[216] CA 2006 s.293(1).
[217] CA 2006 s.293(3).

submitted to members), or some other period specified in the company's articles.[218]

Any failure to follow the above procedure is a criminal offence.[219] However, again, the CA 2006 provides that the validity of a resolution which fails to comply with the above is not to be questioned where it is passed.[220]

Another point to make is that s.295 contains an objection procedure where the requisite percentage of members utilise their power to propose and move a written resolution.[221] Section 295 provides that a company is not required to circulate a members' statement under s.293 if, on the application by the company or another person who claims to be aggrieved, the court is satisfied that the right of the members to propose a written resolution is being abused.

It is provided in the CA 2006 that a written resolution is passed when the required majority of eligible members have signified their agreement to it.[222] A member's agreement is irrevocable once he has signified his agreement to it.[223] A written resolution automatically lapses if it has not been passed by the period stipulated in the written resolution or 28 days beginning with the circulation date if no particular period is stipulated.[224] The agreement of a member to a written resolution is ineffective if signified after the expiry of the period for agreeing to the written resolution.[225] A final point to make is that the articles of association of a company cannot remove the ability of a private company and its members to propose and pass a resolution using the statutory written resolution procedures.[226]

CORPORATE FINANCE: (I) SHARE CAPITAL

Share capital: general

In return for "risk" investment or "risk" capital, a company limited by **16–52** shares has the power to issue shares to investors. On investing in the company and obtaining such shares from the company, the investors become members of the company. As noted earlier in this chapter, the effect of a person becoming a member is that they are bound by the articles of association of the company which form a contract between the company and the members inter se.[227] When shares are issued to investors

---

[218] CA 2006 ss.293(4) and 297(1).
[219] CA 2006 s.293(5).
[220] CA 2006 s.293(7).
[221] CA 2006 s.295(1).
[222] CA 2006 s.296(4).
[223] CA 2006 s.296(3).
[224] CA 2006 s.297(1).
[225] CA 2006 s.297(2).
[226] CA 2006 s.300.
[227] CA 2006 s.33.

in return for the introduction of finance into the company, the shares are treated as property owned by the investors. Section 541 of the CA 2006 provides that shares are moveable property belonging to the investor in terms of Scots law. The relevant statutory provisions governing the share capital of companies are contained in ss.540–657 inclusive. In this section of the chapter, consideration will be given to the central areas surrounding shares and share capital which require particular attention.

Share capital: definition of the nature of a share

16–53 What is the juridical nature of a "share"? Section 540(1) of the CA 2006 defines a "share" as a "share in the company's share capital". Such a statutory definition is not particularly helpful as it fails to craft the precise contours of a share and so it is worthwhile looking to case law for some further guidance. What is clear from the case law is that a share does not confer a member with real rights or other property rights in the assets of the company. Nor does a member have any rights as a beneficiary in the assets of the company in the sense of the company owning the underlying assets but holding them in trust for the members.[228] This must be accurate since the company has a separate legal personality and so owns its own assets. In the case of *Borland's Trustee v Steel Bros & Co Ltd*,[229] Farwell J. gave the following description of a share, which is generally considered to be the most revealing exposition of the nature of a share in a company:

> "A share is the interest of a shareholder in the company measured by a sum of money, for the purpose of liability in the first place, and of interest in the second, but also consisting of a series of mutual covenants entered into by all the shareholders inter se in accordance with s.16 of the Companies Act, 1862 [now s.33 of the CA 2006].[230] The contract contained in the articles of association is one of the original incidents of the share. A share is not a sum of money settled in the way suggested, but is an interest measured by a sum of money and made up of various rights contained in the contract, including the right to a sum of money of a more or less amount."[231]

In terms of the excerpt above from Farwell J.'s judgment, shares represent a measure of a shareholder's liability to contribute monies on a call in the winding up of the company and his interest in the company, such interest consisting of a bundle of rights in favour of him and imposing concomitant obligations upon him. A share also conceives of the rights of a member as the owner of a type of property and in terms of s.541 of the CA 2006, it is clear that the share falls within the incorporeal moveable classification of property in Scots law. So shares have an open market value, representing a percentage of the overall value of the company.

---

[228] See *Commissioners of Inland Revenue v Crossman* [1937] A.C. 26 and *Short v Treasury Commissioners* [1948] 1 K.B. 116, affirmed [1948] A.C. 534 H.L.
[229] [1901] 1 Ch. 279.
[230] Writer's annotation in square brackets.
[231] [1901] 1 Ch. 279, 288.

Share capital: nominal value, "paid-up" and "called up" share capital

Section 542 of the CA 2006 stipulates that every share must have a **16–54** nominal value and have a number attached to it, that is to say that it must have a particular monetary value attached to it and be numbered.[232] Thus, it is incompetent for a company to issue 100 ordinary shares. Such shares must be issued as 100 ordinary shares of so many pounds sterling or pence each (e.g. 100 ordinary shares of £1 each or 100 ordinary shares of 10p each). The same point applies regardless of the class of shares involved.

A distinction is made in the CA 2006 between paid up capital, called up capital and unpaid/uncalled capital.[233] To explain these concepts, some examples might be of assistance. Let us imagine that X subscribes for 100 shares in a company at £1 each. In such circumstances, X's total stake is worth £100, i.e. 100 shares at a nominal value of £1 each. X's total liability is, thus, £100. If X has paid £100 to the company, then X has no further liability and so the shares are fully paid-up and fully called up. Since X's share capital is fully paid up, no further calls may be made on X by the company for a capital contribution and so X cannot be asked to pay any more, even if the company has debts of £1 million. However, if X has not paid for all his shares, the shares are partly paid-up and the company may seek the outstanding balance from him to pay creditors. Thus, if X has only paid 60p for each share, making a stake of £60, £60 of the share capital is paid up and the company may seek the remaining £40 from X to help pay its debts by making a "call". The £60 that has been paid is X's paid up/called up share capital, while the outstanding £40 is uncalled capital. However, the overall sum of £100 is the total extent of X's liability. X cannot be asked to contribute a further sum, even if the company has debts of £1 million. If X transfers his shares to Y, then Y is liable for the remaining 40p per share (£40), but nothing more. So £40 is the total extent of Y's liability to the company for the debts of the company. The sale price of the shares is irrelevant to Y's liability. X "pockets" the sale price, with Y now assuming whatever liabilities X had (if any) concerning the nominal value of the shares.

Share capital: classes of shares

In the above extract from the judgment of Farwell J. in the case of **16–55** *Borland's Trustee v Steel Bros & Co Ltd*,[234] it was remarked that a share represents an interest measured by a sum of money and made up of various rights contained in the articles of association. Hence, company law and the CA 2006 enables the members to attach various rights to shares in the articles of association and this is commonly achieved by creating different classes of shares with different rights. Section 629(1) of

---

[232] If a share is allotted without a nominal value, the allotment is void and every officer of the company has committed a criminal offence—see CA 2006 s.542(2) and (4).

[233] See CA 2006 s.547.

[234] [1901] 1 Ch. 279.

the CA 2006 provides that shares are to be treated as being of one class if the rights attached to them are uniform. There are no restrictions on the kinds of classes of shares which may be created and so there is no such thing as a "closed list" of classes of shares, but it is common to find certain classes of shares in practice which are as follows:

- ordinary shares;
- preference shares;
- redeemable shares;
- convertible shares; and
- cumulative shares.[235]

The above classes of shares can be analysed by concentrating on the nature of the rights which attach to them. The most important rights which a member will have as an incident of their shareholding are the rights to: (i) vote on a resolution, (a) in general meeting, and/or (b) by written resolution procedure; (ii) be paid a dividend out of the annual profits of the company; and (iii) a return of capital on a winding-up of the company. An examination of the above classes of shares, duly mapped against such rights and other important rights would reveal the following table:

Class	Right to Vote	Right to be paid a dividend	Right to a return of capital	Right to have shares bought back	Right to convert shares into debentures/ debt instruments
Ordinary share	✓	✓	✓	x	x
Preference share	x	✓ Preferential over all other classes	✓ Preferential over all other classes	x	x
Redeemable share	Possibly	✓	✓	✓	x
Convertible share	Possibly	✓	✓	x	✓
Cumulative share	Possibly	✓ (if the dividend is not paid in a particular year, it becomes a debt payable in the following year.)	✓	x	x

---

[235] This list is not intended to be exhaustive.

Ordinary shares are by far the most common class of shares, which entitle the member to vote on resolutions, the right to be paid a dividend and to a return of capital on a winding up. Preferential shareholders do not usually have the right to vote. In return for relinquishing the right to vote, preferential shareholders have a preferential right to: (i) be paid a dividend; and (ii) a return of capital on a winding up, in priority to other classes of shareholders, e.g. ordinary shareholders. Redeemable shareholders may have the right to vote and are usually given the right to be paid a dividend and a return of capital on a winding up on an equal par with the ordinary shareholders. By virtue of the nature of the class, the redeemable shareholders are entitled to have their shares bought back by the company. The articles of association and ss.684–689 of the CA 2006 will govern the terms, conditions and the manner of the redemption of the shares by the company. It is open to the company to stipulate that the convertible shareholders will have a right to vote on resolutions. Convertible shareholders may also be given a right to be paid a dividend and a return of capital on a winding up and by definition will be given a right to convert their shares into a debenture or other debt instrument issued by the company, thereby converting their equity stake into a debt stake. Cumulative shares share many of the affinities of preference shares. The main difference is that cumulative shares confer a right to be paid a dividend as a debt, whereby if the company is unable to declare a dividend in a particular year, it is nevertheless cumulative and must be paid in the following year. Finally, since the nature of the rights attaching to different classes of shares are governed by the principle of freedom of contract, it is possible by appropriate drafting of the articles of association to "mix and match" the above rights and indeed the classes of shares. So it is not uncommon to find that a company has issued preference redeemable convertible cumulative shares. Alternatively, the articles of association may create an ordinary redeemable share or ordinary convertible share.

The rules on the variation of the rights attaching to classes of shares are found in ss.629–640 of the CA 2006. The general rule is that class rights may be varied in only one of two ways, namely: (i) in accordance with any procedures and provisions specified in the company's articles; or by (ii) (a) the written consent of holders of at least three-quarters in nominal value of the issued shares of that class, or (b) a special resolution passed by holders of issued shares of that class at a separate class meeting.[236] However, notwithstanding the fact that the variation has been approved, it is open to holders of no less than 15 per cent in nominal value of the issued shares of that class to apply to the court to have the variation cancelled on the basis that it is unfairly prejudicial to them.[237] If satisfied that unfair prejudice has been caused, the court has the power to uphold the applicant's objection and disallow the variation.[238]

---

[236] CA 2006 s.630(2) and (4).
[237] CA 2006 s.633(2) and (5).
[238] CA 2006 s.633(5).

Share capital: acquisition of shares

16–56 Shares may be acquired by original acquisition or derivative acquisition. Original acquisition occurs when fresh shares are newly issued by a company, referred to as an allotment and issue of shares in terms of the CA 2006. Meanwhile derivative acquisition takes place where issued shares are acquired from an existing shareholder by another person, e.g. by a transfer of shares in terms of the CA 2006 or a transmission in terms of the Model Articles.[239] First, in this section, consideration will be given to the mechanics of original acquisition, namely the allotment and issue of shares. Secondly, the rules on derivative acquisition and in particular the transfer of shares from an existing shareholder to a transferee will be examined.

Sections 549–616 of the CA 2006 cover the rules on the allotment and issue of shares. Shares may be issued by a rights issue or pursuant to a bonus issue. A rights issue describes the situation where the company issues shares in return for cash or kind as a means of raising corporate finance. This can be contrasted with a bonus issue. Where a company issues shares to persons without payment in cash or in kind in lieu of a distribution of annual profits by way of dividend, this is referred to as a bonus issue. The power to allot shares resides in the company. However, the CA 2006 provides that such power may be devolved to directors. Thus, prior to an allotment of shares, the directors must have the authority from the company to allot such shares in terms of ss.549–551 of the CA 2006. However, if the company is a private company with only one class of shares, the directors may allot shares without first seeking the authority of the members of the company.[240] The general rule is that the authority to allot may be conferred on directors in the articles of association or by ordinary resolution of the members.[241] Such authority may be generally conferred on the directors or granted for a specific exercise of the power only and it is possible for conditions to be attached.[242] The terms of the authorisation must state: (i) the maximum amount of shares that may be allotted under it; and (ii) the duration of the authority which cannot be for more than five years.[243] In terms of s.561, existing shareholders have a right of pre-emption on allotment, that is to say that any shares to be allotted must first be offered to the existing shareholders in proportion to their holdings at the time of the proposed allotment.[244] The purpose of such a provision is to protect existing shareholders from the dilution of their shares. Nevertheless, there are a number of exceptions which apply to the general pre-emption rights of members[245] and it is

---

[239] For transmissions of shares on the death of a shareholder, see regs 27–29 of the Model Articles in the case of a private limited company by shares and regs 65–68 of the Model Articles in respect of public limited companies.
[240] CA 2006 s.550. This is subject to any prohibition in the articles of association.
[241] CA 2006 s.551(1).
[242] CA 2006 s.551(2).
[243] CA 2006 s.551(3).
[244] The procedure is outlined in CA 2006 s.562.
[245] See CA 2006 ss.564–566.

possible to disapply pre-emption rights in the articles of association or by special resolution, depending on the nature of the authority to allot conferred upon the directors and whether the company is a private or public company.[246]

The mechanics of an allotment are, first, that the directors will publicise their intention to have a rights issue. Pre-printed letters of application for the allotment of shares are sent by the company to potentially interested parties (which may include existing shareholders of the company, depending on whether the statutory pre-exemption rights on allotment have been disapplied or not as the case may be). When a person signs a letter of application for the allotment of shares and transfers cash to the company, the company and that person enter into a contractual relationship. Section 558 of the Act explains the nature and effect of an allotment. It is provided that a share is allotted when a person acquires an unconditional right to be entered into the register of members of the company, i.e. at the point when a person has a contractual right to be issued with shares in the capital of the company. Within one month of the shares having been allotted, the company is under an obligation to make a return of allotment to the Registrar of Companies in terms of s.555 of the CA 2006. The difference between an allotment and an issue of shares is revealed by s.113 of the CA 2006, which states that a share is only issued when the name of the person to whom shares have been allotted has been entered into the company's register of members. It is only at that point that the person becomes a shareholder of the company and the owner of shares in the company is duly entitled to a share certificate.[247]

One of the great benefits of shares is the ease with which they may be transferred to third parties for value or offered to a lender as security in return for borrowing. Where shares are transferred from an existing shareholder to a third party, this is the most common form of derivative acquisition. Another form of derivative acquisition is the situation where the shares of a member are involuntarily assigned to another person, which is otherwise known as the transmission of shares. Transmission occurs where a member dies or is made bankrupt and their shares are transmitted to their personal representatives (such as an executor or a trustee in sequestration) in accordance with the articles of association of the company.

Very few restrictions on the transferability of shares are contained in the Act. For example, ss.770–771 of the CA 2006 provide that the company may not register a transfer of shares in the register of members of the company unless it has received a properly completed and executed stock transfer form in accordance with the Stock Transfer Act 1982. A person becomes a member of the company when the stock transfer form is forwarded to the directors of the company and their name is entered by the directors into the company's register of members. But there are some restrictions on share transfers. For example, reg.26(5) of the Model

---

[246] See CA 2006 ss.567–573.
[247] See *National Westminster Bank Plc v Inland Revenue Commissioners* [1995] 1 A.C. 119.

Articles of association in the case of a private limited company by shares[248] provides the directors with a discretion to refuse to register a transfer of shares. If the directors refuse to register, s.771 of the CA 2006 stipulates that the company must specify the reasons for the decision to refuse to register. The notification of the reasons for the refusal will have to be given as soon as practicable, and s.771(1) sets a final deadline of two months from the date that the stock transfer form was lodged with the company. The transferee is entitled to receive such information as he may reasonably require regarding the reasons for the directors' refusal to register the transfer, but such information does not extend to minutes of meetings with directors. Moreover, the articles of association of private limited companies commonly include pre-emption rights in favour of existing shareholders which are applicable to a proposed transfer of shares, which like pre-emption rights on allotment, operate as an anti-dilution protection. Sections 783–790 of the CA 2006 enable the transfer of shares without a written instrument of transfer, i.e. a stock transfer form.

Share capital: minimum capital requirements

16–57 Minimum capital requirements apply in the case of public companies. Such rules are premised on the need to protect creditors and stem from the obligations imposed on the UK by art.6 of the Second EU Company Law Directive.[249] Hence, s.761 of the CA 2006 narrates that a public company must not do business or exercise any borrowing powers unless the Registrar of Companies has issued it with a trading certificate.[250] A trading certificate will be issued by the Registrar of Companies if it is satisfied that the nominal value of the company's allotted share capital is not less than £50,000. However, only one-quarter of the minimum capital requires to be paid up. Thus, a public company will be able to obtain the trading certificate which it requires if it is able to confirm that it has procured £12,500 of capital investment.[251]

Prospectuses

16–58 Various requirements are imposed on public companies which seek finance from the public in return for the issue of shares in the context of: (i) an initial public offering of shares, i.e. the situation where shares of a public company are admitted to listing on a regulated market such as the LSE or the AIM; and/or (ii) a rights issue. These requirements stem from the Prospectus Directive.[252] The UK implemented its obligations in terms of ss.84–87Q and 102A–103 of, and Sch.11A to, the FSMA. Moreover, the terms of the Financial Conduct Authority Handbook issued by the FCA were amended to ensure compliance with the Prospectus Directive.

---

[248] See reg.63(5) of the Model Articles in respect of public limited companies.
[249] Second Company Law Directive 2012/30/EU.
[250] CA 2006 s.761(1).
[251] CA 2006 s.586.
[252] 2003/71/EC.

The relevant section of the FCA's Handbook is the detailed Prospectus Rules which must be observed by public companies.[253]

The Prospectus Directive requires disclosure of information: (i) regarding the issuer, i.e. the company; and (ii) the transferable securities of the issuer with annual updating of information regarding the issuer, i.e. (i). The prospectus may be divided into two documents, namely (a) the registration document, which contains information about the issuer and is valid for a period of 12 months; and (b) the securities note, which contains information about the securities to be issued. It applies to an "offer of securities to the public", i.e. a, "communication to persons in any form and by any means, presenting sufficient information on the terms of the offer and the securities to be offered so as to enable an investor to decide to purchase or subscribe to the securities".[254]

The principal obligation of the public company seeking to offer its shares to the public is to issue a document called a "prospectus". The main rules as regards the content and presentation of prospectuses are contained in the Prospectus Rules, which are given the force of legal recognition by s.84 of the FSMA. It is a criminal offence for a company to offer transferable securities, i.e. shares and other instruments issued by companies to the public unless a prospectus approved by the FCA[255] has been made available to the public before the offer is made.[256] It is also an offence for a company to request the admission of transferable securities to trading on a regulated market in the UK, e.g. the LSE or AIM, unless an approved prospectus has been made available to the public before the offer is made.[257] Thus, the terms of the relevant sections of the FSMA above and the Prospectus Rules must be followed by a company where it seeks to: (i) admit its shares/securities to listing; and (ii) make an offer of shares/securities to the public (e.g. non-admission arrangements such as rights issues).

The relevant sections of the FSMA and the Prospectus Rules regulate the content and presentation of prospectuses which are made available to the public[258] and impose a requirement for regulatory approval of prospectuses by the FSA. For example, s.87A(1) of the FSMA provides that the FCA must not approve a prospectus unless it is satisfied that the UK is the home state in relation to the issuer of transferable shares/securities to which it relates, the prospectus contains the necessary information and the requirements of the Prospectus Directive have been complied with.[259]

---

[253] See Prospective Rules, *https://fshandbook.info/FS/html/FCA/PR* [Accessed May 15, 2015].

[254] art.2.1(d).

[255] See s.85(7) of and Sch.11A to the FSMA for a list of transferable securities subject to the CA 2006.

[256] FSMA s.85(1). However, there are exceptions to these requirements which may apply in terms of s.86 of the FSMA, e.g. (a) "qualifying investors" such as banks, insurance companies, collective investment schemes; and (b) where the offer is being made to less than 150 persons.

[257] FSMA s.85(2).

[258] FSMA ss.84 and 87A and Prospectus Rules rr.2.1–2.5.

[259] Prospectus Rule r.3.1 is also important here.

Section 87A of the FSMA goes on to state that the "necessary information" is the information necessary to enable investors to make an informed assessment of the assets and liabilities, financial position, profits and losses and prospects of the issuer of the transferable securities and the rights attaching to those shares/securities.[260] The prospectus must contain a summary which in a brief manner and non-technical language conveys the essential characteristics and risks associated with the issuer and the securities. The FSMA and the Prospectus Rules also deal with the filing and the actual publication of the prospectus,[261] advertising in connection with the prospectus,[262] administrative sanctions for non-compliance[263] and liability for misstatements in the prospectus. The relevant provisions of the FSMA and the Prospectus Rules do not impose continuing obligations on the disclosure of information. Instead, continuing obligations are governed by the Market Abuse Directive,[264] the Transparency Directive[265] and other EU Directives.

CORPORATE FINANCE: (II) DEBENTURES/LOAN STOCK

Introduction

16–59 As explored above, one particular route open to a company to raise money is to issue shares in return for capital investment. Such capital is risk capital and so an investor stands to gain on their investment through capital growth or to lose the entirety of their original investment. That is the risk which they take. When they invest in the company, they become shareholders. An alternative source of finance available to a company is to raise loan finance by issuing debt instruments to investors. Such investment is loan capital and the investor is not a shareholder. Instead, they are a creditor of the company. In the capital markets, such loan capital comes in a variety of shapes, sizes and names. For example, a company may issue tradable debt instruments, sometimes known as bonds, loan stock, loan notes, etc. Section 738 of the CA 2006 collectively refers to such debt instruments as "debentures" and the common law treats any document evidencing a debt of any kind as a debenture.[266] By their very nature, these debt instruments are tradable, that is to say that they may be transferred or traded on or off a recognised exchange, such as a public bond market. Debt may also be non-tradable, that is to say it

---

[260] FSMA s.87A(2).

[261] Prospectus Rule r.3.2.

[262] Prospectus Rule r.3.3.

[263] FSMA ss.87K, 87L and 87M.

[264] Directive 2003/6/EC of the European Parliament and of the Council on insider dealing and market manipulation (market abuse).

[265] Directive 2004/109/EC of the European Parliament and of the Council on the harmonisation of transparency requirements in relation to information about issuers whose securities are admitted to trading on a regulated market.

[266] *Levy v Abercorris Slate and Slab Co* (1887) 37 Ch. D 260.

amounts to debt which cannot be transferred on or off a recognised exchange or market.

One of the advantages of issuing debentures as opposed to shares in return for capital investment is that a company does not require to comply with the capital maintenance requirements in the CA 2006, which are considered in the next section of this chapter. Thus, debentures may be issued at a discount to their nominal value and may be bought back from investors without requiring to comply with company laws. Another benefit of issuing debentures is that such financing exercises are generally considered to be cheaper than issuing shares through a rights issue or a public offer. Another difference between equity share capital and debt capital is that the owners of the latter are creditors and thus rank before shareholders on the distribution of assets of the company on a winding up in terms of the Insolvency Act 1986, i.e. the claims of creditors are paid out in priority to the claims of shareholders. Moreover, whilst shareholders have a right to vote, a right to income and a right to the return of their capital on a winding up (and sometimes a trade sale, depending on the terms of the articles of association and/or investment agreement entered into with the company), debenture holders enjoy no such rights in terms of company law and any rights they have will be narrated in the written instrument which creates the debenture. The taxation position also differs, depending on whether the investor's stake in the company is a share or a debenture.

A debenture-holder will enter into a debenture instrument with the company. The terms of the debenture are settled by negotiation and are subject to freedom of contract and the general tenets of contract law. A well-framed debenture instrument will settle the level of the debt, i.e. the outstanding capital sum. The terms and conditions and manner of payment of interest will be outlined in detail, together with the applicable interest rate. Provision will usually be made for the levy of penalty interest in the event that an interest and/or capital repayment is missed by the company. Moreover, various financial covenants and "events of default" will be set out in the debenture. Where an "event of default" occurs, the debenture will stipulate that the investor/debenture-holder will have the right to call for the full repayment of the outstanding capital and interest, i.e. an accelerated payment provision.

Register of debenture-holders

Where debentures are allotted to investors in return for debt finance, the **16–60** company must lodge an allotment of debentures as soon as reasonably practicable and in any event within two months after the date of allotment.[267] Thus, notification must be made of the allotment on the company's public register maintained by the Registrar of Companies at Companies House. The CA 2006 provides that the company may maintain a register of debenture-holders. If the company chooses to keep a register, it must keep it available for inspection. The register must be

---

[267] CA 2006 s.741(1).

kept at the registered office of the company or some other place notified to the Registrar of Companies.[268] Debenture holders and the public have a right to inspect the register in accordance with the requirements in the Act and to request copies of the register from the company.[269]

Secured debentures

16–61 Debentures may be secured or unsecured by the assets, property and/or undertaking of the company. It is extremely common for debentures to be secured since if the company defaults in discharging its monetary or non-monetary obligations stipulated in the debenture, the debenture-holder may "call up" his security and sell the secured assets and property of the company as a means of realising the outstanding indebtedness owed. For example, if there is £340,000 of debt capital outstanding in terms of the debenture and the company defaults on the interest and capital payments which it is obliged to make to the investor in accordance with the terms of the debenture, the investor may choose to exercise the powers of sale and entry conferred upon him under the rights in security granted by the company at the time the debenture was granted. This enables the investor to sell the assets of the company and realise the outstanding indebtedness of the £340,000 owed to him.

In terms of Scots law, the rights in security which may be granted by the company include standard securities over heritage, floating charges over part or the entirety of the company's assets, property and undertaking, together with assignations of debts/receivables, life assurance policies and other incorporeal moveables owned by the company in security. Where more than one security has been granted by the company to various security-holders, a ranking agreement will commonly be concluded between the security-holders and the company which settles the priority of payment in the event that the securities are called up in an effort to realise the outstanding indebtedness owed to the security-holders. In the case of most rights in security, various registration requirements must be followed. Otherwise, the failure to register may invalidate the security. For a more detailed treatment of rights in security, Ch.21 should be consulted.

Key Concept

A "debenture" is a document issued by a company evidencing a debt of any kind which is owed by the company to an "investor".

---

[268] CA 2006 s.743(1).
[269] CA 2006 ss.744–749.

MAINTENANCE OF SHARE CAPITAL AND PURCHASE OF OWN SHARES

Capital maintenance: general

It is a fundamental premise of company law that once capital has been **16–62** advanced to a company, it should be maintained—the so-called capital maintenance principle. Thus, capital, assets or funds must not be returned to shareholders and should be maintained by the company. A number of rules of company law stem from this principle. For example, a company is generally prohibited from repurchasing its shares, reducing its capital and granting financial assistance to a third party for the acquisition of its own shares. Each of these rules are concerned with ensuring that capital is not given back to the members by direct or indirect means. Nevertheless, as company law has developed over time, a number of innovations have been introduced to relax the strict effect of the principle.

Capital maintenance: general restrictions

First, s.552 of the CA 2006 provides that a company may not issue shares **16–63** at a discount.[270] Shares are issued at a discount when they are issued at less than their nominal value. So if 100 ordinary shares of £1 each have been issued at 50p each in return for £50 of investment, this is a contravention of s.552 of the CA 2006. However, there is a distinction between issuing shares at a discount and issuing shares which are partly paid up. In the previous example, it is competent for the company to issue 100 ordinary shares of £1 each partly paid up 50 per cent to £50. In such a case, the shares have not been issued at a discount, but are half paid up: The company has the option to call on the shareholders to pay up the remaining £50 on their shares.

Another rule which emerges from the capital maintenance principle is that dividends can only be paid to shareholders out of the company's annual distributable profits.[271] A company's distributable profits are its accumulated, realised profits, so far as not previously utilised by distribution or capitalisation, less its accumulated, realised losses, so far as not previously written off in a reduction or reorganisation of capital duly made.[272] Dividends are payments which are made to members on an annual basis based on a percentage of the nominal value of their shares. So if a company achieves no profits in a financial year, it will be unable to declare a dividend and issue a payment to the shareholders. Since the rule in s.830(2) of the CA 2006 is that losses accumulated from previous years are taken into account and brought forward to the following years, in the

---

[270] Shares may be issued at a premium, that is to say that shares are issued at more than their nominal value, e.g. to issue 100 ordinary shares of £1 each at £5 each. In such an example, the excess over the nominal value of £4 is referred to as a "premium", £5 representing the market value of the share. However, if shares are issued at a premium, the premium must be shown in the company's balance sheet as a share premium account in terms of CA 2006 s.610(1).

[271] CA 2006 s.830(1).

[272] CA 2006 s.830(2).

following examples, the company would not be able to pay a dividend to its members in financial years one to five inclusive.

Financial Year	Profit
1	(£200,000)
2	(£100,000)
3	£0
4	£55,000
5	£185,000

Capital maintenance: acquisition of own shares

16–64 In the case of *Trevor v Whitworth*,[273] the common law enunciated a principle that a company could not buy back its own shares whether by purchase, subscription or otherwise, since this would represent a return of capital to shareholders which was contrary to the capital maintenance principle. Parliament codified this rule in subsequent Companies Acts. In the CA 2006, the rule is now found in s.658 which states that a failure to observe the prohibition on the acquisition of shares constitutes a criminal offence.

However, over time, the Companies Acts progressively relaxed the rule against a company acquiring its own shares. Thus, it is now possible for a company to issue shares which, by definition, may be repurchased by the company. Such shares represent a particular class of shares and are known as "redeemable" shares. Section 684(1) and (2) of the CA 2006 empowers every company to issue redeemable shares unless the articles of association of the company prohibit or restrict the same. The shares may be redeemed at the option of the shareholder or the company. A public company may only issue redeemable shares if it is authorised to do so in terms of its articles of association.[274] No redeemable shares may be issued at a time when there are no issued shares of the company that are not redeemable.[275] The terms, conditions and manner of redemption may be: (i) contained in the articles of association of the company; or (ii) determined by the directors if they are authorised to do so by the articles or an ordinary resolution of the members.[276] The redeemable shares must be fully paid when the company repurchases them.[277] Payment for the redemption of the redeemable shares may be made by the company on a date later than the redemption date if the terms and conditions of redemption permit this.[278] Redemption of redeemable shares may be

---

[273] (1887) 12 App. Cas. 409.
[274] CA 2006 s.684(3).
[275] CA 2006 s.684(4).
[276] CA 2006 s.685(1) and (4).
[277] CA 2006 s.686(1).
[278] CA 2006 s.686(2).

made out of: (i) distributable profits; and/or (ii) a fresh issue of shares.[279] Private companies also have the option to repurchase redeemable shares out of capital (but only if the strict requirements narrated in Ch.5 of Pt 18 of the CA 2006 are complied with).[280] Once the company has purchased the redeemed shares, the redeemed shares must be cancelled and notice of the redemption must be given to the Registrar of Companies.[281]

A company also has the power to repurchase shares other than redeemable shares in terms of the CA 2006. Section 690 provides that every company may buy back its own shares unless the articles of association of the company prohibit or restrict this. A resolution of the members approving the purchase is required and the nature of the resolution depends on whether the repurchase is "off-market" or on the market. If it is "off-market", then the contract embodying the repurchase must be authorised by a special resolution[282] and if it is on market (i.e. a trade on a recognised investment exchange such as the LSE, AIM, etc.), then an ordinary resolution is required.[283] When a company repurchases shares, those shares must be fully paid up.[284] Shares may be repurchased out of: (i) distributable profits; and/or (ii) a fresh issue of shares.[285] Private companies may also repurchase their shares out of capital (but only if the strict requirements narrated in Ch.5 of Pt 18 of the CA 2006 are complied with).[286] Unlike the repurchase of redeemable shares, the company must make payment for the repurchase of the shares on the repurchase date—and not later.[287] The repurchased shares must be cancelled or held by the company in treasury.[288] If the company chooses to cancel the shares, notice must be given to the Registrar of Companies to that effect.[289] Whether the shares are cancelled or not, the company must give notice of the repurchase within 28 days of it being effected to the Registrar of Companies.[290]

Capital maintenance: prohibition against financial assistance

A public company is prohibited from providing financial assistance to a third party to enable that third party to purchase the company's shares.[291] However, a private company is not precluded from giving such financial assistance. So it is unlawful for public company A to provide cash or exchange value to party B to enable party B to acquire the shares of company A. Such a rule is a manifestation of the capital maintenance **16–65**

---

[279] CA 2006 s.687(2).
[280] CA 2006 s.687(1).
[281] CA 2006 ss.688 and 689.
[282] CA 2006 s.694(2).
[283] CA 2006 s.701(1).
[284] CA 2006 s.691(1).
[285] CA 2006 s.692(2).
[286] CA 2006 s.692(1).
[287] CA 2006 s.691(2).
[288] CA 2006 s.706.
[289] CA 2006 s.708(1).
[290] CA 2006 s.707(1).
[291] CA 2006 s.678(1).

principle and complements the general rule which precludes a company from repurchasing its shares otherwise than in accordance with the CA 2006. The prohibition against financial assistance is paramount since in its absence a company could easily circumvent the "no-repurchase of shares" rule by effecting a return of capital to shareholders indirectly by routing the capital into the hands of a third party who subsequently becomes a shareholder. This rule in effect seeks to counter what is known as "asset-stripping".

The definition of "financial assistance" is wide-ranging and covers more than the simple transfer of cash or property. For example, a gift or loan may amount to financial assistance.[292] Furthermore, the grant of a guarantee, security, indemnity, release, waiver or novation may fall within the scope of the definition of financial assistance.[293] So if a company grants a security such as a standard security or a floating charge to a bank over its heritage and/or assets generally to enable a third party to obtain finance from that bank to acquire the shares of the company, the standard security and floating charge will amount to unlawful financial assistance, since the assistance will be given for the purpose of the acquisition.

Capital maintenance: reduction of capital

16–66 Sections 641–651 of the CA 2006 enable a company to reduce its capital in accordance with certain procedures. A company does not need to have the power in its articles to reduce its capital—the CA 2006 stipulates that the company will have this power, unless the company's articles themselves prohibit or restrict the reduction of the company's share capital.[294] A private company may reduce its capital by passing a special resolution of its shareholders and the directors making a solvency statement not more than 15 days before the date on which the special resolution is passed.[295] A solvency statement is a declaration by each of the directors of the private company to the effect that each of them has formed the opinion:

    (i) as regards the company's situation at the date of the statement, that there is no ground on which the company could then be found to be unable to pay (or otherwise discharge) its debts;

    (ii) if it is intended to commence the winding up of the company within 12 months of that date, that the company will be able to pay (or otherwise discharge) its debts in full within 12 months of the commencement of the winding up; or

    (iii) in any other case, that the company will be able to pay (or otherwise discharge) its debts as they fall due during the year immediately following that date.[296]

---

292 CA 2006 s.677(1)(a) and (c)(i).
293 CA 2006 s.677(1)(b)(i), (b)(ii) and (c)(ii).
294 CA 2006 s.641(6).
295 CA 2006 ss.641(1)(a) and 642(1)(a).
296 CA 2006 s.643(1).

In forming these opinions, the directors must take into account all of the company's liabilities (including any contingent or prospective liabilities).[297] If the directors make a solvency statement without having reasonable grounds for the opinions expressed in it, and the statement is delivered to the Registrar, an offence is committed by every director who is in default.[298] Within 15 days of the special resolution having been passed, a copy of the resolution, the solvency statement and a statement of capital must be lodged with the Registrar of Companies.[299]

A public company, or a private company for that matter, may apply to the court for an order confirming a reduction of capital where the company has passed a special resolution to reduce its share capital.[300] Every creditor of the company who at the date fixed by the court is entitled to any debt or claim that, if that date were the commencement of the winding up of the company would be admissible in proof against the company, is entitled to object to the reduction of capital.[301] The court has the power to make an order confirming the reduction of capital on such terms and conditions as it thinks fit.[302] Before confirming the reduction, the court must be satisfied, with respect to every creditor of the company who is entitled to object to the reduction of capital that either his consent to the reduction has been obtained, or his debt or claim has been discharged, or has determined or has been secured.[303] Where the court confirms the reduction, it may order the company to publish (as the court directs) the reasons for reduction of capital, or such other information in regard to it as the court thinks expedient with a view to giving proper information to the public, and (if the court thinks fit) the causes that led to the reduction.[304] On the production of an order of the court confirming the reduction of a company's share capital and the delivery of a copy of the order and of a statement of capital (approved by the court), the Registrar of Companies must register the order and statement.[305]

MINORITY SHAREHOLDER PROTECTION

Introduction

As noted in prior sections of this chapter, the general rule is that each **16–67** shareholder is entitled to one vote per share on a vote on: (i) a poll in a general meeting; or (ii) a written resolution (in the case of a private company).[306] Since a poll may be demanded by the chairman of the

---

[297] CA 2006 s.643(2).
[298] CA 2006 s.643(4).
[299] CA 2006 s.644(1).
[300] CA 2006 s.645(1).
[301] CA 2006 s.646(1).
[302] CA 2006 s.648(1).
[303] CA 2006 s.648(2).
[304] CA 2006 s.648(3).
[305] CA 2006 s.649(1).
[306] CA 2006 s.284(1) and (3).

meeting, a proxy, any director of the company, at least two shareholders having the right to vote, or a person or persons representing not less than one-tenth of the total voting rights of all the shareholders having the right to vote on the resolution,[307] and there is no restriction on the number of shareholders which a company may have, it is inevitable that some members will be in the majority and others in the minority. Minority shareholders are essentially shareholders or a body of shareholders who are unable to exert sufficient influence over the direction of the affairs of the company by virtue of the voting rights attached to their shares. Since company law provides that the general authority to direct the affairs of the company is vested in the: (i) directors; and (ii) shareholders who are able to command sufficient votes to pass ordinary and special resolutions, the effect is that shareholders or groupings of shareholders possessing less than 25 per cent of the voting base of the company will be minority shareholders. Whilst it is accurate to say that shareholders may: (i) request that the company hold a general meeting; and (ii) table a resolution to be considered at such general meeting, with 5 per cent of the voting shares,[308] unless the minority shareholders are able to rally support for the resolution amongst the other shareholders of the company, it is unlikely that the resolution will be carried, since 5 per cent alone will be insufficient.

On the face of matters, one might assume that minority shareholders have no influence or control over the affairs of the company since they are susceptible to being outvoted at every turn. However, such an assumption would be mistaken. For example, minority shareholders may protect themselves by bargaining with the company for specific rights in order to safeguard their interests. Such contractual protections are commonly inserted into the articles of association of the company or a shareholders' agreement concluded between the members and the company. For example, specific voting rights, such as weighted voting rights may be included in the articles in favour of a particular minority shareholder. Alternatively, a minority shareholder may insist on the inclusion of a provision in a shareholders' agreement to the effect that certain decisions cannot be taken by the directors or the majority shareholders without the approval or consent of the minority shareholder. Whilst such contractual mechanisms are an extremely effective means of protection, for obvious reasons, not all minority shareholders will be in a position of sufficient bargaining strength to secure such concessions from the company. Thus, these forms of protection will not usually be available to the vast majority of minority shareholders. So, in most cases, minority shareholders will be required to rely on the principles and techniques of company law which are specifically designed to safeguard their interests.

---

[307] See s.329(1) of the CA 2006 and reg.44(2) of the Model Articles in the case of a private limited company by shares, reg.30(2) of the Model Articles in the case of a private company limited by guarantee and reg.36(2) of the Model Articles in respect of public limited companies.

[308] s.303 of the CA 2006.

Common law derivative proceedings

In the nineteenth century, the courts in England recognised the need to **16–68** introduce certain rules to tackle subversive action taken by directors or majority shareholders which may have damaging consequences for the interests of minority shareholders. A distinction should be made at this point between actions taken by third parties which result in loss, prejudice or damage to: (i) the minority shareholder himself or herself; and (ii) the company. Traditionally, absent any tailored rights in favour of the minority shareholder in the articles of association or a contract such as a shareholders' agreement, there was no means of recovering for loss in respect of (i) under the principles or rules of company law. However, loss of the kind described in (ii) is an altogether different proposition and was and is something which the common law considered. Consideration of (ii) takes us to the classic rule in the case of *Foss v Harbottle*[309] which provided that where a wrong has been done to the company, only the company itself may initiate an action to recover any loss which it has sustained as a result of that wrong. This is the so-called "proper plaintiff" principle. However, a company is an artificial person and can only act through its organs, namely the board of directors or the shareholders in general meeting. So, if a majority of the shareholders of the company voted on an ordinary resolution not to take action against a third party who has perpetrated a wrong on the company, a minority shareholder who is aggrieved at that decision is precluded from raising a "derivative" action of his/her own initiative. A "derivative" action is said to "derive" from the company since it represents an action taken by the minority shareholder in his/her own personal name on behalf of the company to recover loss suffered by the company as a result of the occurrence of the particular wrong. The "proper plaintiff" principle (to which the derivative action is an exception) recognises the force of "majority rule" and where the majority have spoken, no minority has any standing to seek recovery. Generally, a court will not interfere in matters of internal management which have been sanctioned by a majority of the members.

However, the courts recognised that such a principle, while sensible, may result in prejudice. It may be harsh on minority shareholders, especially in a situation where a director has perpetrated a wrong on the company and the majority shareholders, in the throng of the directors, have voted to protect that director by denying the company the ability to sue the director to effect a recovery. Thus, in the case of *Edwards v Halliwell*,[310] the court established four exceptions to the "proper plaintiff" and "majority rule" principles, which established circumstances in which derivative proceedings may be raised, as follows:

(1) where the personal rights of a member have been infringed, then that member can sue to seek recovery of any loss suffered;

---

[309] (1843) 2 Hare 461.
[310] [1950] 2 All E.R. 1064.

(2) where a company proposes to do something which is ultra vires, i.e. beyond its constitutional powers or purpose, then a shareholder can raise an action to prevent the ultra vires act. Since the abolition of the ultra vires rule,[311] for obvious reasons, this particular exception is now of little relevance;

(3) where a resolution required to be passed by special majority and it was not so passed then a member can object; and

(4) where the majority shareholders perpetrate a fraud on the minority.

The fourth exception was the most important exception in practice. Derivative proceedings were raised to seek recovery of assets, funds and property where there had been a "fraud on the minority". However, the difficulty with this common law exception was that it was never clear what was meant by "fraud on the minority". The common law was clear that the majority shareholders or a director would have committed a fraud on the minority where either of the former had committed a fraud,[312] misappropriated or misapplied the assets or funds of the company for their own personal benefit[313] or engaged in self-serving negligence, i.e. the negligent sale of an asset at undervalue which indirectly benefits the majority shareholder or director who committed the company to the transaction.[314] However, beyond these particular circumstances, it was not particularly easy to understand the nature and content of the fraud on the minority exception. Another difficulty with the fraud on the minority exception was the potential for the shareholders to ratify the conduct after the event. Another requirement was imposed on minority shareholders to demonstrate to a court that the "wrongdoers" were in control of the company, i.e. that the wrongdoers had command of the majority of votes and had exercised such votes to stifle the opportunity to initiate proceedings for recovery.[315] Even where there was evidence of wrongdoer control, a minority shareholder would not succeed in their derivative action where the evidence demonstrated that the remaining shareholders, independent of the wrongdoers, were opposed to the raising of proceedings.[316] Other hurdles placed before the minority shareholder were that he/she was bound to demonstrate that: (i) the derivative action was being raised for a proper purpose; and (ii) he/she had no other remedy available.[317] In short, the common law "fraud on the minority"

---

[311] See CA 2006 s.39 and above for a wider discussion.

[312] *Atwool v Merryweather* (1867) L.R. 5 Eq. 464n.

[313] *Cook v Deeks* [1916] 1 A.C. 554 (P.C.); and *Burland v Earle* [1902] A.C. 83 (P.C.).

[314] See *Daniels v Daniels* [1978] Ch. 406.

[315] See *Prudential Assurance Co Ltd v Newman Industries Ltd (No.2)* [1981] Ch. 257. However, whether the Court of Appeal in *Prudential Assurance Co Ltd v Newman Industries Ltd (No.2)* [1982] Ch. 204 endorsed the requirement to show wrongdoer control outlined by Vinelott J. in the High Court is not altogether clear.

[316] *Smith v Croft (No.2)* [1988] Ch. 114.

[317] *Barrett v Duckett* [1995] 1 B.C.L.C. 243. However, (ii) may not be a rule forming part of Scots law, see *Anderson v Hogg*, 2002 S.L.T. 354 and *Wilson v Inverness Retail and Business Park Ltd*, 2003 S.L.T. 301.

exception was so difficult to enforce that the likelihood of a minority shareholder being successful was extremely slim.

Statutory intervention

Since the common law avenues to obtain relief were restricted, Parlia- **16–69** ment intervened to protect minority shareholders. First, ss.265–269 of the CA 2006 enable shareholders to raise statutory derivative proceedings to recover losses sustained by the company in certain circumstances. Secondly, ss.994–999 of the CA 2006 provide that a shareholder may present a petition to the court to obtain certain remedies where the affairs of the company are being conducted in a manner which is unfairly prejudicial to their interests. Each of these statutory innovations will be considered in turn.

Statutory derivative proceedings

Sections 265–269 of the CA 2006 introduce a right to raise derivative **16–70** proceedings in Scots law and abolish the common law "derivative action" discussed above. This statutory process enables a minority shareholder to seek redress against a director or a third party where the conduct of the director results in the company sustaining a loss. So, if the statutory claim is successful, the damages awarded flow to the company. Section 265 provides that a member[318] of a company may raise an action in respect of certain acts or omissions in order to protect the interests of the company and obtain a remedy on its behalf. The specified actions or omissions may be actual or proposed[319] and are as follows: negligence, default, breach of duty or breach of trust by a director[320] of the company.

The statutory provisions enable a minority shareholder to raise proceedings against a director or "another person".[321] The import is that derivative proceedings can be taken against persons who are implicated in a director's breach of duty. For example, in proceedings concerning the transfer of funds by a director in breach of trust, the proceedings may also be brought against the recipient who has colluded with the director and has knowledge of their source or nature.

Members may only raise derivative proceedings if they have obtained the leave of the court, i.e. prior permission from the court. The applicant minority shareholder must specify the cause of action in the application for leave via the petition procedure of the Court of Session and summarise the facts on which the derivative proceedings are to be based in the application.[322] It is only if the court grants the application for leave that the applicant will then have the green light to go on to raise substantive derivative proceedings against a director and/or third party. The purpose

---

[318] "Member of a company" in this context includes a person who is not a member but to whom shares in the company have been transferred or transmitted by operation of law.
[319] The actions or omissions are defined in the CA 2006 as the "cause of action".
[320] "Director" includes former directors or shadow directors.
[321] CA 2006 s.265(4)(b).
[322] CA 2006 s.266(2).

of the application for leave process is to enable the court to weed out baseless, vexatious or unsubstantiated claims at an early stage. The CA 2006 divides the application for leave process into two stages. The first stage is an ex facie stage where the court considers the application for leave without hearing from the parties, i.e. the applicant minority shareholder, the company or the director. The court must refuse the application for leave to raise derivative proceedings at this initial ex facie stage if it is satisfied that the application and the evidence produced by the applicant in its support do not disclose a prima facie case for granting it. In assessing whether the application should be refused on these grounds at the ex facie stage, the court must consider the non-exhaustive criteria referred to in s.268(1)–(3) of the CA 2006 which are discussed below.[323] If the application for leave is not refused at the ex facie stage, the court must serve the application on the company and it may make an order requiring evidence to be produced by the company and/or adjourn proceedings on the application to enable the evidence to be obtained. The court may also permit the company to take part in further proceedings on the application.[324] The second stage of the application for leave process entails an inter partes hearing, i.e. the court considers the application for leave having heard from the applicant minority shareholder and the company. However, the prospective defender director(s) and third parties against whom any subsequent substantive derivative proceedings would be directed will ordinarily be disentitled from involvement in the inter partes hearing.[325]

16–71   At the inter partes stage, the court may:

- grant the application for leave on such terms as it thinks fit;
- refuse the application; or
- adjourn the proceedings on the application and make such order as to further procedure as it thinks fit.[326]

The CA 2006 provides that the court must refuse leave to raise derivative proceedings if it is satisfied that:

- a person acting in accordance with the director's duty to promote the success of the company for the benefit of its members as a whole, would not seek to raise or continue the claim;
- where the cause of action is an act or omission that is yet to occur, that the act or omission has been authorised by the company; or
- where the cause of action is an act or omission that has already occurred, that the act or omission: (i) was authorised by the company before it occurred; or (ii) has been ratified by the company since it occurred.[327]

---

[323] *Wishart v Castlecroft Securities Ltd*, 2010 S.C. 16, per Lord Reed at [36]–[38].
[324] CA 2006 s.266(4).
[325] *Wishart v Castlecroft Securities Ltd*, 2010 S.C. 16, per Lord Reed at [18]–[26].
[326] CA 2006 s.266(5).
[327] CA 2006 s.268(1).

The effect of the above criteria is that an application for leave must be refused if the company has authorised or ratified the director or third party's alleged breach of duty. In considering whether to grant leave to raise derivative proceedings, the court must also take into account the following criteria:

- whether the member is acting in good faith in seeking to raise the proceedings;
- the importance that a person acting in good faith in accordance with the director's duty to promote the success of the company for the benefit of its members as a whole, would attach to raising or continuing it;
- where the cause of action is an act or omission that is yet to occur, whether the act or omission could be, and in the circumstances would likely to be: (i) authorised by the company before it occurs; or (ii) ratified by the company after it occurs;
- where the cause of action is an act or omission that has already occurred, whether the act or omission could be, and in the circumstances would be likely to be, ratified by the company;
- whether the company has decided not to raise proceedings in respect of the same cause of action or to persist in the proceedings (as the case may be); and
- whether the cause of action is one in respect of which the member could raise an action in his own right rather than on behalf of the company.[328]

Finally, in considering whether to grant leave to raise derivative proceedings, the court must have regard to any evidence before it as to the views of members of the company who have no personal interest, direct or indirect, in the matter (i.e. the passive members).[329] It is important to stress that the courts are keen to avoid a situation whereby the inter partes application for leave turns into a dress rehearsal of the full merits of the case.[330] In the only case to have been considered in Scotland so far, an applicant shareholder was successful in persuading the Inner House of the Court of Session that the application for leave to raise substantive derivative proceedings should be granted. In *Wishart v Castlecroft Securities Ltd*,[331] the applicant, a 40 per cent shareholder of a company, alleged that one of its directors was in breach of his duty not to divert a business opportunity of the company to a third party. Having taken into account the evidence and the productions lodged in court in light of the criteria discussed above, the Inner House of the Court of Session was satisfied that the proposed derivative proceedings ought to proceed.

---

[328] CA 2006 s.268(2).
[329] CA 2006 s.268(3).
[330] *Wishart v Castlecroft Securities Ltd*, 2010 S.C. 16, per Lord Reed at [27]–[28] and [39].
[331] 2010 S.C. 16.

The statutory "unfair prejudice" remedy

16–72 Section 994(1) of the CA 2006 enables a member to petition the court to declare that the company's affairs are being or have been conducted in an unfairly prejudicial manner to the members generally or to particular members. Section 994 of the CA 2006 differs from the statutory derivative proceedings in that: (i) the remedies available are wider; (ii) the remedies may be awarded to the successful petitioner rather than the company; and (iii) unlike the statutory derivative proceedings, the wrongdoing may have been perpetrated by persons other than the directors, e.g. the majority shareholders. The precise terms of s.994 are as follows:

> "A member of a company may apply to the court by petition for an order on the ground—
>
> > (a) that the company's affairs are being or have been conducted in a manner that is unfairly prejudicial to the interests of members generally or of some part of its members (including at least himself), or
> >
> > (b) that an actual or proposed act or omission of the company (including an act or omission on its behalf) is or would be so prejudicial."

If the petition is successful, the court has the power to:

- order the company to carry out certain acts or refrain from doing or continuing an act—including ordering the company to sue for a wrong done;
- prevent the company from carrying out certain acts;
- order members of the company to buy the shares of the pre-judiced members, at a fair price; or
- make any order which it sees fit.[332]

In practice, the lion's share of minority shareholders presenting a petition before the court will be seeking an exit from the company by obtaining an order from the court for their shares to be bought by the majority shareholders or the company at a fair price. In the case law, the courts have provided a number of examples of unfair prejudice, e.g. the non-payment of dividends, the exclusion of a shareholder from the management of the company without offering a reasonable fair value for his/her shares, the payment of excessive remuneration to directors and the sanctioning of a rights issue which the minority were unable to afford.[333] The most important case on the width of the court's jurisdiction is the decision of the House of Lords in *O'Neill v Phillips*.[334]

---

[332] CA 2006 s.996.
[333] See *Grace v Biagoli* [2005] EWCA Civ 122; [2006] 2 B.C.L.C. 70; *O'Neill v Phillips* [1999] 1 W.L.R. 1092 and *Re Cumana Ltd* [1986] B.C.L.C. 430.
[334] [1999] 1 W.L.R. 1092.

O'Neill v Phillips
[1999] 1 W.L.R. 1092

Concerning: The kinds of conduct which amount to "unfair prejudice".

Facts: Phillips owned the entire issued share capital of Pectel Ltd, namely 100 ordinary shares of £1 each. O'Neill was employed by the company as a manual worker and, after two years, Phillips gave O'Neill 25 shares in the company and appointed him as a director. At the same time, Phillips resigned as a director. Pectel Ltd performed well under O'Neill's stewardship and he was credited with half the profits of the business. This was drawn as salary and dividends and some money was left in the company. As regards Phillip's dividend, he decided to waive a third of his 75 per cent entitlement in favour of O'Neill in order to produce equality. In one particular year, the retained profits which amounted to O'Neill's undrawn entitlement were capitalised as bonus shares to increase the issued share capital of the company to £50,000. The bonus shares were allotted in the same proportions as their existing shareholdings. Various discussions ensued with regard to O'Neill obtaining a 50 per cent shareholding. However, negotiations were never concluded. The onset of an economic recession had a detrimental impact upon the fortunes of the company. Phillips became concerned about the financial performance of the company and O'Neill's management. Finally, he decided to resume personal command of the company and gave O'Neill the option of managing the UK or German branches of the business under his overall stewardship. O'Neill chose to manage the German side of the business and remain on the board as a director under the overall command of Phillips. Phillips determined that O'Neill would be paid only his salary and any dividends payable upon his 25 per cent shareholding. This was the final straw for O'Neill who decided to cut all ties with the company. He presented a petition to the court seeking an order that the company's affairs were being conducted in a manner which was unfairly prejudicial to his interests. The Court of Appeal ruled that unfair prejudice had been established and ordered Phillips to purchase O'Neill's shares. Phillips appealed to the House of Lords.

Decision: The House of Lords ruled that Phillips' appeal would be allowed and the petition dismissed. In s.994 of the CA 2006 Parliament had chosen fairness as the criterion by which the court had to decide whether it had jurisdiction to grant relief. For the purposes of that section, a member of a company would not ordinarily be entitled to complain of unfairness unless there had been some breach of the terms on which he had agreed that the company should be conducted. Although the answer would normally be found in the understandings between the members at the time they entered into association, there might be later promises, by words or conduct, which it would be unfair to allow a member to ignore, and it was not necessary that such promises should be independently enforceable as a matter of contract. In addition, unfairness might arise not from what the parties had positively agreed but from a majority using its legal powers to maintain the association in circumstances to which the minority could reasonably say it did not agree. In the instant case, the real question was whether in fairness or in equity O'Neill had a right to the shares or to 50 per cent of the profits. Since the judge had found that Phillips had made no promises, there was no basis, consistent with the principles of equity, for a court to hold that Phillips was behaving unfairly in withdrawing from negotiations.

One final point to make is that the right to raise proceedings under s.994 of the CA 2006 is not restricted to minority shareholders. For example, in a two-member company, one of the 50 per cent shareholders was entitled to do so in the decision of the Court of Session in *Robertson, Petitioner*.[335] There it was held that he should be entitled to buy out the shares of the other 50 per cent shareholder.

▼ CHAPTER SUMMARY

16–73
(1) Companies are regulated by the CA 2006 and the common law.
(2) The main features of company law are that limited companies have their own legal personality and the members are not responsible for their companies' debts, except to the extent of the capital they have contributed or have agreed to contribute.
(3) The main case authorities for the separate legal personality of the company are:

> ➢ *Salomon v A Salomon & Co Ltd* (1897).
> ➢ *Macaura v Northern Assurance Co Ltd* (1925).

(4) Where the company is incorporated to conceal the real actors lying behind the company (the "concealment principle), to evade existing legal obligations or liabilities, or statute empowers the courts to intervene, the courts may lift the "corporate veil" to enable a creditor to sue the directors or members:

> ➢ *Gilford Motor Co v Horne* [1933] Ch. 935
> ➢ *Prest v Petrodel Resources Ltd.* [2013] 2 A.C. 415.

(5) Companies can be classified according to three particular categories as follows:

> ➢ limited liability companies v unlimited companies;
> ➢ companies limited by shares v companies limited by guarantee; and

---

[335] *Robertson, Petitioner* [2009] CSOH 23; 2009 G.W.D. 16-249.

> private companies v public companies.

(6) To incorporate a company, an application for registration including a statement of compliance on a Form IN01 must be completed and sent to the Registrar of Companies together with the company's memorandum and articles of association.

(7) A company's memorandum of association is a public document which states that the subscribers: (i) wish to form a company under the CA 2006; and (ii) agree to become members of the company and, in the case of a company that is to have a share capital, to take at least one share each:

> s.8 of the CA 2006.

(8) A company's articles of association are its internal constitution, detailing how shares may be transferred, directors appointed, meetings of directors held, etc. The articles represent a "contract" entered into between the members and the company and the members inter se. If a company proposes to alter its articles of association, it must obtain the approval of its members by special resolution. Where an alteration is authorised by special resolution, it may nevertheless be challenged in terms of the common law if it is not "bona fide" for the benefit of the company as a whole:

> ss.17(a), 21 and 33 of the CA 2006.
> *Allen v Gold Reefs of West Africa Ltd* [1900] 1 Ch. 656.
> *Sidebotham v Kershaw Leese & Co Ltd* [1920] 1 Ch. 154.

(9) Directors manage the company, but are still subject to certain restraints imposed by the law, the company's articles and contracts with shareholders.

(10) (a) Directors owe various duties to their company, the most important being the statutory duties which are fiduciary in nature:

> ss.170–173 and 175–177 of the CA 2006.

(b) The duty of care, skill and diligence:

> s.174 of the CA 2006.

(c) and various statutory duties:

> ss.182–222 of the CA 2006.

(11) There are three types of resolutions which the members may pass:

- ordinary resolutions;
- special resolutions; and
- written resolutions—see ss.282, 283 and 288 of the CA 2006.

(12) Shareholders of public limited companies may meet to review the directors' performance at annual general meetings. A director, the court or members representing at least 5 per cent of the paid up capital of the company as carries the right of voting at general meetings may request a general meeting to be held:

> ss.302, 303 and 306 of the CA 2006.

(13) A share is a unit of ownership in a company, measured by a sum of money, for the purpose of liability in the first place, and of interest in

the second, but also consisting of a series of mutual covenants entered into by all the shareholders *inter se* in accordance with the Act:

> ➤ *Borland's Trustee v Steel Bros & Co Ltd* [1901] 1 Ch. 279.

(14) Shares may be acquired by members by original acquisition or derivative acquisition. The original acquisition of shares is referred to as an allotment and issue of shares. The derivative acquisition of shares may take place by transfer or transmission.

(15) Once capital has been advanced to a company, it should be maintained: the so-called capital maintenance principle. Thus, capital, assets or funds must not be returned to shareholders and should be maintained by the company.

(16) If a shareholder receives the leave of the court to do so, a shareholder may raise derivative proceedings against directors or other persons to recover losses sustained by the company as a result of the negligence, default, breach of duty or breach of trust of a director or directors of the company:

> ➤ ss.265–269 of the CA 2006.

(17) A shareholder has the right to present a petition to the court alleging that the affairs of the company are being or have been conducted in a manner which is unfairly prejudicial to the interests of the shareholders generally or some particular shareholder or shareholders:

> ➤ s.994 of the CA 2006.

? QUICK QUIZ

- What are the sources of company law?
- What are the objectives and purposes of company law?
- What are the core features of companies?
- What are the main types of company?
- What documentation is required to incorporate a company?
- What are the constitutional documents of the company?
- What is the memorandum of association?
- What are the articles of association of the company?
- What is the legal effect of the articles of association?
- What are trading disclosures?
- Through which organs can a company act?
- Explain the role of the company secretary.
- What is the role of a company director?
- How many directors must a company have?
- Are there any restrictions on who can be a director?
- List the different types of directors.
- Explain how directors can be removed in terms of the law.
- To whom do directors owe their duties?
- What is the general meeting and what is its purpose?
- Who has the power to call general meetings?
- How much notice must be given of general meetings?

- What information must be included in a notice of a general meeting?
- What is a proxy?
- What is an ordinary resolution?
- What is a special resolution?
- What is a written resolution?
- What is a share?
- What is meant by different classes of shares?
- How can shares be acquired?
- What is a prospectus?
- What is a debenture?
- What protections are available to minority shareholders?

📖 FURTHER READING

- ➤ D. French, S. Mayson and C. Ryan, *Mayson, French & Ryan on Company Law*, 32nd edn (Oxford: OUP, 2015).
- ➤ D. Kershaw, *Company Law in Context—Text and Materials*, 2nd edn (Oxford: OUP, 2012).
- ➤ L.S. Sealy and S. Worthington, *Cases and Materials in Company Law*, 10th edn (Oxford: OUP, 2013).
- ➤ P. Davies, *Introduction to Company Law*, 2nd edn (Oxford: OUP, 2010).

🖱 RELEVANT WEBLINKS

- ➤ Business Gateway: *http://www.bgateway.com* [Accessed May 15, 2015].
- ➤ Department for Business, Innovation and Skills site on CA 2006: *https://www.gov.uk/company-and-partnership-law–2* [Accessed May 15, 2015].

Chapter 17   Limited Liability Partnerships

DOMINIC SCULLION[1]

▶ CHAPTER OVERVIEW

17–01 This chapter is concerned with Limited Liability Partnerships ("LLP"). The LLP is a unique business medium to which large numbers of traditional partnerships converted in the years following the passing of the Limited Liability Partnerships Act 2000. An LLP is often described as a hybrid of a traditional partnership and a limited company. The purpose of this chapter is to introduce the reader to the concept of the LLP; it does not seek to act as a guide or a handbook for current members[2] of LLPs. It is not intended to deal in detail with the administrative obligations incumbent upon designated members nor to examine the plethora of regulations applicable to LLPs in great depth. Instead, it is hoped that this chapter will allow the reader to have an appreciation of the advantages and disadvantages of the LLP business model, and highlight some of what must be considered when converting a traditional partnership to an LLP.

✓ OUTCOMES

By the end of this chapter you should:

- ✓ understand the differences between LLPs and traditional partnerships;
- ✓ have an appreciation of the reasons why LLPs were introduced in the UK;
- ✓ be aware of the importance of the 2000 Act and the regulations and the importance of these enactments;
- ✓ understand the extent to which members' liability is limited;
- ✓ be comfortable with the default rules found in the 2001 Regulations and have an understanding of why having a written LLP agreement is desirable; and
- ✓ appreciate what needs to be considered prior to converting a traditional partnership to an LLP.

---

[1] Senior Solicitor, Anderson Strathern LLP, Edinburgh; former Lecturer in Scots Law at the University of Dundee.
[2] As "partners" in LLPs are known.

HISTORICAL BACKGROUND TO THE LLP

The LLP is the newest form of business medium to be introduced in the **17–02**
UK. Prior to its introduction, those wishing to go into business with
others could form a traditional partnership, a limited partnership or a
company. However, partners in traditional partnerships had (and still
have) unlimited personal liability for the debts and obligations of the
business and the limited partnership vehicle offered protection only to
those partners who did not take part in the management of the firm.[3]
Whilst incorporating as a limited company would have limited the liability of those running the business, it was not always an attractive option
to those who did not wish either to separate ownership from control or to
be subject to the tax regimes of companies. The traditional partnership
therefore remained popular with those who wished both to own their
business and take part in its management, while at the same time taking
advantage of the organisational flexibility and financial secrecy that the
traditional partnership offered.

The twentieth century, however, saw a significant increase in the size of
partnerships[4] which led to concerns about the appropriateness of
unlimited liability of partners in many hundred partner firms. In firms
with offices around the globe, there was a high chance that not all of the
partners had met each other, let alone could vouch for each other's
professional integrity and competence, but who could nonetheless face
bankruptcy as a result of a negligence action raised against one of their
number.[5] In addition, LLPs had already been introduced in the USA and
in Jersey[6] and the large professional services and accountancy firms were
pressing for the introduction of LLPs in the UK. The Department for
Trade and Industry published its first consultation paper on LLPs[7] in
February 1997. The Department's stated aims were to:

---

[3] s.6(1) of the Limited Partnerships Act 1907.

[4] Partnerships used to be subject to an upper limit of 20 partners, but that restriction was
removed for those partnerships carrying on the business of certain professions by a series
of statutory instruments in the late twentieth century, and was subsequently removed for
all types of partnerships by the Regulatory Reform (Reform of 20 Member Limit in
Partnerships etc) Order 2002 (SI 2002/3203).

[5] The case often cited as an example of the impact which negligence actions can have on
traditional partnerships is *ADT Ltd v BDO Binder Hamlyn* [1996] B.C.C. 808. Here, the
defendant auditors were liable to the plaintiffs for £65 million in damages as a result of a
negligent audit. However the defendant's professional indemnity insurance was capped
and there was a significant (reportedly eight figure) shortfall.

[6] It is clear that there was a fear that large partnerships would register as a Jersey LLP. See
the report by the Commons Select Committee on Trade and Industry, *Fourth Report:
Draft Limited Liability Partnership Bill* (Feb 1999), HC Paper No.69, para.26.

[7] Department for Trade and Industry, *Limited Liability Partnership—A New Form of
Business Association for Professions* (Department for Trade and Industry, 1997, URN
97/597).

"make available a business vehicle with **limited liability**, thus limiting the members' exposure to the extent of their stake in the business ... preserve valued aspects of **partnership**; and provide a package of **safeguards** for those dealing with the firm ...".[8]

Following a lengthy consultation process, the Limited Liability Partnerships Act 2000 ("the 2000 Act"), the Limited Liability Partnerships Regulations 2001 ("the 2001 Regulations")[9] and the Limited Liability Partnerships (Scotland) Regulations 2001 ("the 2001 Scottish Regulations")[10] came into force on April 6, 2001.[11]

WHAT IS AN LLP?

Statutory framework

17–03 The 2000 Act contains only 19 sections and one Schedule. There are provisions concerning the existence and nature of an LLP, the incorporation of an LLP, details as to its membership (including an introduction to the new concept of "designated member") and taxation. Sections 14 to 17 give the Secretary of State powers to introduce subordinate legislation which will provide the vast majority of the substantive law relating to LLPs. There was considerable opposition to legislating by statutory instrument,[12] and to the piecemeal application, disapplication and modification of numerous other statutes by way of the Schedules to the 2000 Act and through regulations,[13] but the Government proceeded regardless. As a result, much of the detail of the LLP regime is provided for by the 2001 Regulations (which, among other things, provide for a default partnership agreement unless contracted out of, and also apply various provisions of the Companies Act 1985, the Company Directors Disqualification Act 1986)[14] and the 2001 Scottish Regulations

---

[8] Department for Trade and Industry, *Limited Liability Partnership—A New Form of Business Association for Professions* (Department for Trade and Industry, 1997, URN 97/597), p.3 (emphases in original).

[9] SI 2001/1090.

[10] SI 2001/128.

[11] For a detailed account of the "somewhat tortuous consultation process", see G. Morse (ed.), *Palmer's Limited Liability Partnership Law* (London: Sweet & Maxwell, 2002), pp.5–10.

[12] At the time of writing, 20 statutory instruments have been made under the 2000 Act.

[13] Notably provisions of the Companies Act 1985, the Insolvency Act 1986 and the Company Directors Disqualification Act 1986.

[14] On this point regard now must be had to: the Limited Liability Partnerships (Amendment) Regulations 2005 (SI 2005/1989); the Limited Liability Partnerships (Accounts and Audit) (Application of Companies Act 2006) Regulations 2008 (SI 2008/1911); the Limited Liability Partnerships (Application of Companies Act 2006) Regulations 2009 (SI 2009/1804), the Limited Liability Partnerships (Application of Companies Act 2006) (Amendment) Regulations 2013 (SI 2013/618).

(which modify inter alia those provisions of the Companies Act 1985 and the Insolvency Act 1986 which apply specifically to Scotland).[15]

The Limited Liability Partnership

Definition

Whilst a limited liability partnership has some of the characteristics of a **17–04** partnership and a limited company, it is a "new form of legal entity"[16] and must therefore be viewed as a unique form of business vehicle. It is defined as "a body corporate (with legal personality separate from that of its members) which is formed by being incorporated under [the] Act".[17] The separate legal personality, although not a new concept for the Scottish partnership,[18] allows it to own property in its own name, sue and be sued, grant floating charges[19] and become a partner, shareholder or member in other businesses. An LLP has unlimited capacity[20] and therefore it cannot act ultra vires.

Partners in an LLP are known as members, although in practice members of an LLP are often styled as partners,[21] and, confusingly, the 2001 Regulations term an agreement between the members as to their rights and duties as a limited liability *partnership* agreement.[22] The members of the LLP must be carrying on a lawful business with a view to profit,[23] thus precluding charities, Scottish Charitable Incorporated Organisations or non-profit making associations from incorporating as LLPs.

---

[15] And apply the Insolvency (Scotland) Rules 1986 (SI 1986/1915). The need for separate Scottish regulations is also due to those parts of insolvency law which are devolved to Holyrood. See also the Limited Liability Partnerships (Scotland) Amendment Regulations 2009 (SSI 2009/310).

[16] s.1(1) of the Limited Liability Partnerships Act 2000 ("2000 Act").

[17] s.1(2) of the 2000 Act.

[18] See Ch.15, "The Law of Partnership".

[19] Which a traditional partnership in Scotland cannot do.

[20] s.1(2) of the 2000 Act.

[21] It would be wise for LLPs which use the term "partner" to make it known to the outside world on letterheads and email footers that the term denotes a "member" of the LLP. This would be particularly important for traditional partnerships which incorporate as LLPs so that third parties are not under any illusion as to which firm they are dealing with.

[22] reg.7 of the Limited Liability Partnerships Regulations 2001 (SI 2001/109 ("2001 Regulations")), (emphasis added).

[23] s.2(1) of the 2000 Act.

Key Concept

An LLP is a unique business entity. It is neither a partnership nor a company. LLPs are governed by the Limited Liability Partnerships Act 2000 and a number of statutory instruments. The LLP has separate legal personality from its members, can own property in its own name, can sue and be sued, grant floating charges[24] and become a partner, shareholder or member in other businesses. Non-profit making organisations cannot be LLPs.

Incorporation

17–05 To form an LLP, a minimum of two persons must subscribe their names to an incorporation document.[25] The document must state the name of the LLP,[26] the country in which the registered office is to be based and the address of that registered office,[27] the names and addresses of those who will become the members of the LLP upon incorporation,[28] and which of the members are to be the designated members.[29] The incorporation document must then be delivered to the registrar[30] who, upon being satisfied that the application has been completed properly, that the proposed name is acceptable and that the fee has been paid, will issue a certificate of incorporation.

Unlike a traditional partnership, an LLP can neither begin to exist nor be deemed retrospectively to have existed simply by the commencement of the trade or adventure. The certificate of incorporation is essential, and the LLP cannot trade until the registrar has issued a valid certificate of incorporation.[31]

---

[24] Which a traditional partnership in Scotland cannot do.
[25] As above.
[26] s.2(2)(b) of the 2000 Act. The Limited Liability Partnerships (Application of Companies Act 2006) Regulations 2009 (SI 2009/1804) apply the restrictions on names of companies, as stated in the Companies Act 2006, to LLPs.
[27] s.2(2)(c)–(d) of the 2000 Act.
[28] s.2(2)(e) of the 2000 Act. The "persons" who can be members includes all legal persons and not just natural persons.
[29] s.2(2)(f) of the 2000 Act. Note that there must be a minimum of two designated members at any time and that it is also possible for all members to be designated members. If at any time there are no designated members or if there becomes only one designated member, all members will become designated members (s.8(2) of the 2000 Act). For more on designated members, see para.17–06.
[30] s.2(1)(b) of the 2000 Act. The incorporation document can be filed electronically or by paper. There is a registration fee which varies depending on whether electronically or paper filing has been selected and depending on whether same day incorporation is requested. A statement that the requirements of s.2(1)(a) have been complied with must also be provided to the registrar (s.2(1)(c)).
[31] There is useful guidance available on the Companies House website: *https://www.gov.uk/ government/publications/limited-liability-partnership-incorporation-and-names* [Accessed May 15, 2015].

The designated member

The 2000 Act introduces the concept of the designated member. This **17–06** concept is unique to the LLP regime. A designated member of an LLP is one who has additional administrative responsibilities to those imposed on other members. Among the designated members' duties is a responsibility to ensure that the LLP complies with the statutory regime; the duty to inform the registrar of any changes to the membership of the LLP; the duty to prepare the annual return, sign the annual accounts and deliver them to the registrar; and the duty to act on the LLP's behalf during winding up or dissolution. The designated member therefore has similar duties to the company director but without the corresponding management responsibilities.[32] A failure by a designated member to carry out his/her duties could result in that member and the LLP being convicted of an offence. The designated member risks disqualification under s.3 of the Company Directors Disqualification Act 1986.

The applicable law

The LLP was not intended to be seen as a type of partnership; it is clear **17–07** from the terms of s.1(5) that it was to be a new and unique business medium:

> "...except as far as other provided by this Act or any other enactment, the law relating to partnerships does not apply to a limited liability partnership".

This provision appears to preclude any provision of the Partnership Act 1890, or any principle derived from case law relating to traditional or limited partnerships, from being applicable to LLPs unless parliament expressly states otherwise. However, regard must be had to the 2001 Regulations made under s.15(c) of the 2000 Act. While incorporating significant elements of UK company and insolvency law, the 2001 Regulations also establish default rules to regulate the rights and duties of members in the absence of an LLP agreement.[33] These default provisions are in many respects similar to those found in the 1890 Act and thus it may appear curious that the law relating to partnerships does not apply to the interpretation of these default provisions. It is not entirely clear, however, that this is the case, as reg.7 specifies that "the mutual rights and duties of the members and the mutual rights and duties of the [LLP] shall be determined, subject to the provisions of the general law...".[34] The question therefore is whether the courts can consider case law decided in

---

[32] There is nothing to stop the members of an LLP from deciding by agreement that the designated members are also those with day-to-day management duties.

[33] reg.7 of the 2001 Regulations.

[34] As above.

terms of the 1890 Act in a dispute on the interpretation of these default provisions. While this question has not been specifically put to the courts,[35] it is suggested that the answer is yes, and that "the general law" includes partnership law.[36]

THE MEMBERS OF THE LLP

17–08 The persons who would have been known as partners in traditional partnerships are known as members in LLPs.[37] Presumably this term was chosen to reinforce the proposition that the LLP is a unique type of business organisation and to ensure a distinction is drawn between members of an LLP and those other business actors: partners, directors and shareholders.

Becoming a member

17–09 The 2000 Act provides two routes to membership. Membership is automatically conferred on founding members: a subscriber member.[38] The subscriber members are those who have subscribed their names to the incorporation document; the mere status of subscriber membership does not confer any additional rights or obligations on subscriber members compared to the members who join the LLP at a later date.[39] The second way to become member of an LLP is by the other members agreeing to admit a new member.[40] In the absence of a provision in an LLP agreement regulating the admission of new members, the default provision of reg.7(5) will apply. This regulation provides that a new member can only be admitted with the consent of all existing members. It is suggested that for many larger LLPs, the default provision provided for in reg.7(5) will not prove attractive and that consideration should be given to how new members ought to be admitted. In the larger LLPs, it may well be that the members who sit on an elected board or management group are given the authority to decide who can be admitted to the LLP. As long as the LLP agreement is clear, each LLP can admit new members in the manner which best suits its business.[41]

---

[35] In *Eaton v Caulfield* [2011] EWHC 173 (Ch); [2011] B.C.C. 386, Proudman J. referred to *Blisset v Daniel* (1853) 10 Hare 493; 68 E.R. 1022 when interpreting reg.8 of the 2001 Regulations on the expulsions of members.

[36] For comments on this point, and on LLPs in general, see S.R. Cross, "Limited Liability Partnerships Act 2000: problems ahead?" (2003) (May) J.B.L. 268.

[37] See para.17–04.

[38] s.4(1) of the 2000 Act.

[39] Although it is of course possible to differentiate between the subscriber members and those who join later by express provision in an LLP agreement.

[40] s.4(2) of the 2000 Act.

[41] See paras 17–18 to 17–29 below for information on the management of LLPs.

Key Concept

To incorporate as an LLP, a minimum of two persons must subscribe their names to an incorporation document which is sent to the registrar who will issue a certificate of incorporation. There must be designated members who have additional administrative obligations than those imposed on other members. Provided that it is set out clearly in an LLP agreement, each LLP can admit new members in a manner which suits its business.

The agency relationship and the members' authority to bind the firm

Section 6(1) of the 2000 Act provides that every member of an LLP is an **17–10** agent of the LLP. Members are not agents of each other. This is in contrast to traditional partnerships where the partners are agents of both the firm and every other partner.[42] However the scope of the agency relationship (found in s.6(2) of the 2000 Act) is nearly identical to that found in s.5 of the Partnership Act 1890, namely that the LLP is bound by the actions of the member unless the member had no authority to act *and* the person with whom he was dealing either knew him or her not to have authority or did not believe him or her to be a member at all.[43] These provisions merit further comment.

For an LLP to avoid being bound by the act of the member in question, both parts of s.6(2) must be satisfied. The first requirement is that the member *in fact* has no authority to act for the LLP in relation to the particular act in question. However, the default position under s.6 is that each member of an LLP is presumed to have authority to act on its behalf.[44] An LLP wishing to displace that presumption will require to produce evidence. The easiest way to do so would be for the authority of members to be set out fully in the LLP agreement. While there is no requirement for the LLP agreement to be in writing, the advantages of having it in writing will be obvious in resolving potential disputes.

The second requirement in s.6(2) is that the third party with whom the member acting out with his authority was dealing must know that the member had no such authority, or must not know or believe him or her to be a member of the LLP at all. The first part of the conjunctive test, it is suggested, is unlikely to be satisfied and indeed a third party would be able to rely upon the presumption that every member has the authority to bind the LLP. The second branch[45] also seems unlikely to occur, and as

---

[42] s.5 of the Partnership Act 1890.
[43] s.6(2) of the 2000 Act.
[44] Note that, unlike in s.5 of the Partnership Act 1890, there is no equivalent requirement that the member's act be done "for carrying on in the usual way business of the kind carried on by the firm".
[45] Note that there is no requirement for the third party to check the position with Companies House.

long as the third party has *some* reason to believe that he or she *is* dealing with a member, then the LLP will be bound by the act.

Ability of former members to bind the firm

17–11 Section 6(3) of the 2000 Act provides that the LLP is not bound by an act of a former member if the third party with whom the LLP is dealing has had notice that the former member is indeed a former member, *or* if notice of the cessation of membership in question has been delivered to the registrar. Therefore, delivery to the registrar of the cessation of membership is deemed to be implied notice to the world of the cessation. Those dealing with an LLP might therefore be wise to confirm that the person with whom they are dealing is still a member of the LLP by checking with Companies House.

Key Concept

For an LLP to avoid being bound by the act of a member acting outwith the scope of his or her authority, both parts of s.6(2) must be satisfied. The first requirement is that the member *in fact* has no authority to act for the LLP in relation to the particular act in question. The second requirement is that the third party with whom the member acting out with his or her authority was dealing must know that the member had no such authority, or must not know or believe him or her to be a member of the LLP at all.

Duty of good faith

17–12 Of direct relevance to the matter of the agency relationship is the question whether members owe a duty of good faith to each other and/or to the LLP itself. While the 2000 Act does not expressly state that members owe each other or the LLP a general duty of good faith, by creating an agency relationship between members and the LLP, s.6 has resulted in members owing the LLP the common law fiduciary duties[46] which agents owe their principal.[47] What is not clear, however, is whether s.6 has created an

---

[46] Stemming from the fact that the relationship is one of good faith. For example, an agent must obey the principal's instructions, must act with reasonable care and skill, must account to the principal and must refrain from taking secret profits. See *Gloag and Henderson: the Law of Scotland*, edited by HL MacQueen and Lord Eassie, 13th edn (Edinburgh: W. Green, 2012) paras 18.04–18.09 and L. MacGregor, *The Law of Agency in Scotland* (Edinburgh: W. Green, 2013), generally.

[47] There are a few other express provisions in the 2000 Act and the 2001 Regulations which could be considered exceptions to the exclusion of a general duty of good faith. These can be found in reg.7(8) (duty of each member to "render true accounts and full information of all things affecting the LLP to any member ..."); reg.7(9) (duty of each member to account for profits made from a competing business); reg.7(10) (duty of each member to account for any benefit derived from the LLP, a transaction concerning the LLP, or from the use of the property, name or business connection of the LLP without the consent of the LLP). These duties can, however, be excluded by agreement.

agency relationship between and LLP and its members when the members are carrying out internal functions of the business rather than dealing with a third party. It is of course possible that the courts will hold that members *do* owe their fellow members and the LLP a duty of good faith at all times. It is likewise possible that LLPs could chose certainty by expressly providing for such duties in their LLP agreement. Whether such an approach is adopted in the business world remains to be seen having regard to the tensions or conflicts which may arise from time to time between the duties of the members *inter se* and the duties the members owe to the LLP.

Members as employees

Section 4(4) of the 2000 Act states that a member of an LLP is not to be **17–13** regarded as employed by the LLP unless he would be regarded as employed if he was a partner in a traditional partnership.[48] This provision seems somewhat odd since it is trite law, at least in England and Wales, that a partner in a traditional partnership cannot be an employee of the firm since that would make him both employer and employee.[49] There is also doubt as to whether a Scottish partnership can enter into a contract of employment with one of its partners despite its separate legal personality.[50] In any event, the subsection essentially provides that a member of an LLP is not to be regarded as an employee by the LLP. Unfortunately the situation is not that simple, or at least is no longer that simple.

In *Clyde & Co LLP v Bates van Winkelhof*,[51] the Supreme Court, reversing the decision of the Court of Appeal, held that a member of an LLP, while not an employee of the firm was nonetheless a 'worker' within the meaning of s.230(3) of the Employment Rights Act 1996 thus allowing the member to claim the benefit afforded to whistle-blowers by the same Act. As this case was decided very recently, the extent of its ramifications for LLPs is not yet known. What is certain, however, is that by giving members "worker" status, a host of employment rights thought not be to applicable to members of LLPs now apply to them, including the Working Time Regulations,[52] the National Minimum Wage Act 1998 and regulations protecting part-time workers.[53] It must be borne in mind, however, that the rights afforded to this type of "worker" are considerably less extensive than the rights afforded to those working under a

---

[48] s.4(4) of the 2000 Act.
[49] See *Ellis v Joseph Ellis & Co* [1905] 1 K.B. 324 and *Cowell v Quiler Goodison Co Ltd* [1989] I.R.L.R. 392.
[50] See the Joint Consultation Paper of the Law Commissions, *Partnership Law* (Law Commission Consultation Paper No.159, Scottish Law Commission Discussion Paper.No 111) at para 23.21 where reference is made to this "doubt" and to *Allison v Allison's Trustees* (1904) 6 F 496 and *Fife County Council v Minister of National Insurance*, 1947 S.C. 629.
[51] [2014] UKSC 32.
[52] SI 1998/1833.
[53] Part-time Workers (Prevention of Less Favourable Treatment) Regulations 2000 (SI 2000/1551).

contract of employment. In particular, members of an LLP still do not have protection against unfair dismissal.

Salaried members, fixed share members and equity members

17–14 The default position under the 2001 Regulations is that all members are entitled to equal participation in the profits and capital of the LLP.[54] This is also the default position for partners in traditional partnerships.[55] In the vast majority of cases this default position will not apply in practice and questions regarding profit and capital will be governed by the terms of any partnership agreement or LLP agreement.

When a new member joins an LLP, it should be stipulated in writing how this new member is to be remunerated. A full equity member will have a proportion of the distributable profits of the business. A fixed share member is a member who has a nominal percentage of the equity of the LLP and guaranteed minimum drawings, and a salaried member is a member who receives only a salary. It is possible to have a salaried *partner* in an LLP, who is not a member of the LLP, but who is an employee of equivalent standing. This latter species of partner is similar to the salaried partner in the traditional partnership who has no management responsibility in the firm but who nonetheless uses the title of partner. However, it is suggested that the employee of the LLP who uses the title "partner" is less at risk then the salaried partner in the traditional firm who, although *de facto* an employee, holds himself out as a partner and thus renders himself potentially liable to third parties.[56] After all, it will be obvious to any creditor who has conducted the relevant search at Companies House that the salaried partner is not a member of the LLP. Nonetheless, it is suggested the LLP agreement should provide for the category of member or employee who is permitted to use the title "partner" and who will be indemnified by the LLP and the equity members. The LLP is not obliged to disclose which members are full equity members, or fixed share or salaried members to Companies House: that information can be kept secret.

Employee status of salaried or fixed share members

17–15 In light of recent changes to the taxation of members of LLPs, further consideration of the employment status of members is required. Prior to 6 April 2014, HMRC took the view that all members of an LLP, regardless of whether they were full equity members, or fixed-share or salaried members, were to be treated as self-employed for tax purposes.[57] Thus, members of LLPs were taxed in the same way as partners in traditional

---

[54] reg.7(1) of the 2001 Regulations.
[55] s.24(5) of the Partnership Act 1890.
[56] For an analysis of the position of the salaried partner in a traditional partnership, see S.C. Styles, "The salaried partner—liability without profit" (1994) 39(7) J.L.S.S. 254–256.
[57] s.83 of the Income Tax (Trading and Other Income) Act 2005.

partnerships: by way of self-assessment.[58] However, the Finance Act 2014 has introduced salaried members rules which aim to tackle perceived tax avoidance by LLPs whose salaried members, HMRC considered, were akin to employees but who were being taxed as though self-employed. Thus, those members accrued the tax advantages of the self-employed while the LLP itself paid no national insurance contributions on those members' salaries. Detailed consideration of these changes is beyond the scope of this chapter. Put shortly there are three conditions which if met will see members being treated as employees for tax purposes. The three conditions are:

(1) the member receives a disguised salary. A disguised salary is where at least 80 per cent of the member's remuneration is fixed or, if it is variable, is varied without reference to the profits and losses of the LLP as a whole;

(2) the member does not have a significant influence over the affairs of the LLP; and

(3) the member's capital contribution is less than 25 per cent of their disguised salary.[59]

As a result of these changes, many LLPs will be faced with a 13.8 per cent national insurance contribution charge for members who satisfy the salaried members conditions. In order to avoid this contribution, it is expected that many LLPs will now ask those members who would otherwise satisfy the conditions for being deemed an employee for an increase in capital contributions, thus failing the "test" at condition three. However, care should be taken so that the steps taken by the LLP and by the individual do not fall foul of HMRC's anti-avoidance rules.[60] It should however be borne in mind that these changes are unlikely to affect small LLPs whose members, even if salaried, are nonetheless likely to exert significant influence over the affairs of the LLP as a whole.

Key Concept

Members of an LLP are not to be regarded as employees of the LLP. However, in 2014 the Supreme Court held that members were "workers" as defined in the Employment Rights Act 1996. LLPs can have salaried, fixed-share or equity members, but HMRC may treat a salaried member as if he or she were an employee unless certain criteria are met.

---

[58] For more on the taxation of LLPs, see para.17–31 below.

[59] See the guidance from the UK Government: *https://www.gov.uk/government/uploads/ system/uploads/attachment_data/file/283957/140221_RevisedGuidance_SalariedMembers_PartnershipsReview.pdf* [Accessed May 15, 2015].

[60] See further guidance: *https://www.gov.uk/government/publications/salaried-members-rules-revised-technical-note-and-guidance* [Accessed May 15, 2015].

The nature and extent of members' liability

17–16 The principal reason for creating the LLP was to provide a business structure which had the organisational flexibility of a partnership but with limited liability for its members. A consideration of the nature and extent of that limited liability is therefore essential.

In a traditional partnership, the partners are jointly and severally liable with the firm for its debts and obligations.[61] Thus, a third party can raise an action against the firm as well as the individual partners. If the assets of the firm are insufficient to meet the claim, the individual partners are liable in full.[62] It is noteworthy than in an LLP, however, the members are not jointly and severally liable with the LLP for its debts and obligations. Pivotally, if third parties dealing with an LLP are made aware that they are contracting with the LLP alone and not with any individual member thereof, an action in contract can be raised only against the LLP.[63] In such a scenario, the LLP's assets will be used to satisfy any debts or obligations resulting from the claim, and the members themselves risk losing only their capital contributions in the event of a "wipe-out" claim. The position is slightly different, however, in respect of actions in delict.

The personal liability of members for wrongful acts or omissions

17–17 It is not difficult to imagine a situation in which an aggrieved client or third party might also wish to raise an action against an individual member of the LLP, particularly if that member has substantial independent resources. If the client or third party has contracted only with the LLP, the only action open to them will be one founded in delict and the normal principles of delictual liability for such an act or omission will apply. For an individual member to be held personally liable in negligence, the tripartite test of foreseeability of damage, proximity and whether it is fair, just and reasonable to impose a duty of care will apply.[64] However, in addition to the tripartite test, it will almost certainly be necessary for the pursuer to establish that there was an assumption of responsibility by the individual member, that the third party relied upon

---

[61] s.4(2) of the Partnership Act 1890.

[62] If one partner is required to meet the debt, then he has a right of relief against the other partners.

[63] Although it would remain open to a third party to attempt to prove that he was contracting with the individual member.

[64] *Caparo Industries plc v Dickman* [1990] 1 All E.R. 568.

that assumption[65] and that no valid limitation of liability clause was in operation.[66]

The 2000 Act does provide, however, that where a member of an LLP is liable to any person[67] "as a result of a wrongful act or omission of his carried out in the course of business of the [LLP] or with his authority, the [LLP] is liable to the same extent as the member".[68] In addition, protection is available to the member as the 2001 Regulations provide that the LLP must indemnify each member in respect of liabilities incurred "in the ordinary and proper conduct of the business" of the LLP.[69] In the event that the default rules are displaced by an LLP agreement, it would nonetheless be expected that indemnity of this nature would be included in the agreement.[70] It of course remains open to the LLP to argue that the member's wrongful act was not done in the course of the business of the LLP and that only the individual member should be liable.

Key Concept

The extent to which members' liability is limited is arguably the most important aspect of the LLP. Unlike in traditional partnerships where partners could face bankruptcy as a result of the negligence of one of their number, it will normally be the assets of the LLP itself, and not those of the individual members, which are used to satisfy the debts or obligations of the LLP. The members risk losing their capital contributions only in the event of a "wipe-out" claim, or in certain circumstances if they themselves have been negligent.

---

[65] See *Hedley Byrne & Co v Heller & partners* [1964] A.C. 456 and *Henderson v Merrett Syndicates Ltd* [1995] 2 A.C. 145. It is also necessary to consider *Williams v Natural Health Foods Ltd* [1998] 1 W.L.R. 830 on the liability of a company director. This case was specifically referred to in the explanatory notes to the 2000 Act as the likely test for establishing the liability of an individual member although, at the time of writing, there have been no cases in point. See also J. Cooke, "Babb and solicitor's negligence: can LLP status provide complete protection from personal liability?" [2006] *Professional Negligence* 106.

[66] Such a clause would have to satisfy the requirement of reasonableness under the Unfair Contract Terms Act 1977.

[67] Except a fellow member.

[68] s.6(4) of the 2000 Act. It should be noted that the nature of the business being carried out is not qualified with the word "ordinary" or "proper" thus potentially opening up an LLP to a wider range of claims than a traditional partnership. However, whether this difference in wording would in reality make much difference (particularly in light of cases such as *Dubai Aluminium Co Ltd v Salaam* [2002] UKHL 48) is unclear.

[69] reg.7(2) of the 2001 Regulations.

[70] It is suggested that when drafting such an agreement, consideration should be given as to whether the indemnity should extend to "ordinary" *and* "proper" conduct of the business, or whether "ordinary" is sufficient, or whether no qualification as to the nature of the business being carried out is required.

The Management of an LLP

17–18 The members of an LLP have considerable discretion as to how they may manage their business. An LLP does not need to have a limited liability partnership agreement in place and if there is one, it need not be in writing.[71] Like the traditional partnership, the absence of a partnership agreement means that the default rules will apply.[72]

Pre-incorporation agreements

17–19 Before considering the nature of either the default rules or an LLP agreement which would come into force post incorporation, it is important to consider the status of any agreements made pre-incorporation. Section 5(2) of the 2000 Act makes provision for the existence of such agreements and states that "[a]n agreement made before the incorporation of [an LLP] between the persons who subscribe their names to the incorporation document may impose obligations on the [LLP] (to take effect at any time after its incorporation)". It is therefore possible to have an agreement in place which will become effective immediately after incorporation. However, as the date of incorporation will not be known until after the event itself, it would be prudent to indemnify subscriber members against any pre-incorporation liabilities incurred, as it is unlikely that the default indemnity would apply to pre-incorporation acts.

The default provisions

17–20 As already noted, many of the default rules are similar to those found in the Partnership Act 1890. There is, however, a degree of uncertainty as to whether the principles derived from partnership law can be applied by the courts in interpreting the default LLP provisions. Accordingly members drafting an agreement should consider whether the default provisions are beneficial to their LLP before adopting them, and should ensure that they do not impliedly accept them dint of failing to refer to them in their LLP agreement.

Equal division of capital and profits

17–21 Regulation 7(1) provides that members are entitled to share equally in the capital and profits of the LLP. This is similar to s.24(1) of the Partnership Act 1890 although it is of note that reg.7(1) does not deal with apportionment of losses. It should also be noted that "capital" is not defined and therefore, it is suggested, should be taken to include future capital profits *and* ownership of existing capital which is unlikely to be held in equal shares among members, particularly for businesses transferring to LLP status. Furthermore, "profits" is not defined and should therefore be taken to include capital profits as well as operational profits. This is a

---

[71] Although obviously this is advisable.
[72] Found in the 2001 Regulations.

default provision which may not accurately reflect the members' true situations. Accordingly, it is suggested that the LLP agreement should make express provision on these issues to ensure displacement of this default provision.

Members' indemnity

The indemnity provided in reg.7(2) has already been considered briefly **17–22** and is almost identical to that provided in s.24(2) of the 1890 Act. It provides that:

> "The limited liability partnership must indemnify each member in respect of payments made and personal liabilities incurred by him (a) in the ordinary and proper conduct of the business of the limited liability partnership; or (b) in or about anything necessarily done for the preservation of the business or property of the limited liability partnership."

While this provision, in the main, is not problematic, the terms "ordinary" and "proper" merit consideration. Section 6(4) of the 2000 Act provides that the LLP will be liable for the wrongful acts or omissions of a member, to the same extent as the member, as long as the acts or omissions took place in the course of business. However, the indemnity provided for in reg.7(2) qualifies the course (or conduct) of business with the words "ordinary" and "proper". Could the courts interpret this regulation as meaning that there are certain acts which are not so far out with the course of business that the LLP would still be liable, but which are sufficiently out with the course of business that the individual member would not be indemnified? While at present there is no case law in point, it is suggested that these issues should be considered by those tasked with drafting an LLP agreement.

Participation in the management of the firm

Regulation 7(3), which provides that every member is entitled to take **17–23** part in the management of the LLP, mirrors s.24(5) of the 1890 Act. In addition, some of the other default provisions sit alongside this general right to participate in management. Regulation 7(6)[73] provides that decisions on ordinary matters connected with the firm's business may be decided by a majority of members but that no change can be made to the nature of the business of the LLP itself without the consent of all of the members.[74] Regulation 7(7)[75] gives each member the right to inspect the books and records of the LLP at any time. Regulation 7(5)[76] provides that the unanimous consent of all members is required before a new

---

[73] Mirroring s.24(8) of the Partnership Act 1890.
[74] No definition of "ordinary matters" or "nature of the business" is provided. This ought to be clarified in writing in an LLP agreement.
[75] Mirroring s.24(9) of the Partnership Act 1890.
[76] Mirroring, to an extent, s.24(7) of the Partnership Act 1890.

member can be introduced to the LLP or before any member's share in the LLP is assigned.

The implications of these provisions, in particular reg.7(3) and (6) must be considered when drafting the LLP agreement. They are unlikely to be particularly suitable for the larger LLPs.

No remuneration for members

17–24 Regulation 7(4) provides that no member is entitled to remuneration for acting in the business or management of the LLP. The similarly worded s.24(6) of the 1890 Act does not include the word "management", which presumably means acts concerning the running of the business as opposed to those providing the services of the business. This should not be taken to mean that members are to carry out their functions for no return; instead it is clear that members will be remunerated by way of profit share instead of salary. Should an LLP wish to pay members a salary, either because they are salaried members or as a means of pro-viding additional income to those members who have management responsibilities, the LLP agreement should make appropriate provision.

Obligation to disclose information

17–25 Regulation 7(8), which mirrors s.28 of the 1890 Act, provides that "each member shall render true accounts and full information of all things affecting the [LLP] to any member or his legal representatives". This is a somewhat odd provision in that it is the members who have the right to demand such disclosure and not the LLP. It is suggested this provision conflicts somewhat with the general position that members do not owe each other a duty of good faith.[77] Displacing this provision with one giving the LLP the right to make such a demand of members could therefore be considered when drafting an LLP agreement.[78]

Obligation to account for profits from a competing business

17–26 Regulation 7(9) obliges members who without the consent of the LLP are simultaneously involved in a separate similar business, in competition with the LLP, to account and remit to the LLP, their share of profits from that other buisiness.[79] This regulation effectively implies a duty of good faith but it is of note that any implied duty is owed to the LLP as opposed to the other members. This provision is not as restrictive as the provisions made in many partnership agreements which prevent partners or members from carrying on any other business at all, regardless of whether that other business is competing with the firm. Of course a more restrictive provision could be incorporated into any LLP agreement.

---

[77] See para.17–11 above.

[78] Whether that is to the exclusion of the members or along with the members will be up to those drafting the agreement. It is suggested that any decision in that regard should align with any decision made regarding explicit incorporation of duties of good faith.

[79] Mirroring s.30 of the Partnership Act 1890.

Benefits derived from the use of the LLP's name, property or business connection

Regulation 7(10)[80] is similar to reg.7(9) but broader in scope. It obliges **17–27** members to account to the LLP for any benefit they have derived from a transaction concerning the LLP, or from the use of the LLP's property, name or business connection. Like reg.7(9), the obligation to account only arises only if the member has acted without the LLP's consent.

Expulsion

Regulation 8 provides that a majority of members cannot expel another **17–28** member unless such a power has been conferred by express agreement between the members.[81] This is an important provision which offers a form of minority protection, but which can again be excluded by agreement.

Additional provisions

There are many matters not covered by the default provisions which will **17–29** need to be agreed between the members of an LLP. There is no comprehensive list of matters which could or should be included in an LLP agreement and specialist advice should be sought at the drafting stage. It is suggested that, as a minimum, consideration should be given to making provision in the agreement for banking and administrative matters; holiday and sick pay; pensions; members' voting rights; management board structure; designated members' roles and responsibilities; and the insolvency of the LLP.[82]

Key Concept

In the absence of a written LLP agreement, the default provisions contained in the 2001 Regulations will apply. These default provisions are unlikely to be suitable for most LLPs and careful consideration ought to be given to having a written LLP agreement drawn up, and about what ought to be provided for in said written agreement.

TAXATION AND ACCOUNTS

Although detailed consideration of the taxation and accounting and **17–30** auditing requirements of LLPs is beyond the scope of this chapter, a brief introduction to these aspects of the LLP regime is provided here.

---

[80] Mirroring s.29(1) of the Partnership Act 1890.
[81] Mirroring s.25 of the Partnership Act 1890.
[82] A full consideration of what should (and should not) be included in an LLP agreement is beyond the scope of this chapter. Useful guidance can be found in S. Young, *Limited Liability Partnerships Handbook*, 2nd edn (Tottel Publishing, 2007) and G. Morse (ed.), *Palmer's Limited Liability Partnership Law*, 2nd edn (London: Sweet & Maxwell, 2011).

Taxation

17–31 Sections 10 to 13 of the 2000 Act make certain provisions relating to the taxation of LLPs. In essence these sections amend existing tax and national insurance legislation so that it applies to LLPs. There is no single statute governing the tax position of LLPs. However, for those considering converting their traditional partnership to an LLP, taxation should not be unduly burdensome as the tax regime applicable to LLPs is similar in many respects to that which applies to traditional partnerships.

As LLPs are tax transparent entities, it is the members' interests in the LLP which are taxable. Thus, members of LLPs are taxed as if they were partners in a traditional partnership[83] and, notwithstanding the separate legal personality of a partnership in Scotland, the LLP does not pay corporation tax. Thus, the conversion from traditional partnership to LLP should not result in the members of the LLP being taxed differently from the way they were taxed as partners. Furthermore, as long as the requirements set out in Sch.12 to the Land and Buildings Transaction Tax (Scotland) Act 2013 are satisfied,[84] the transfer of the partnership's property from the partners to the LLP should not result in a stamp duty land tax charge.

Key Concept

LLPs are tax transparent entities and thus members are taxed as if they were partners in a traditional partnership. LLPs do not pay corporation tax. The similarities between how traditional partnerships and LLPs are taxed make it very easy for partnerships to incorporate as LLPs.

Accounts and auditing

17–32 The accounting and auditing requirements for LLPs are much closer to those applicable to companies as opposed to partnerships. Indeed, these requirements represent the most significant differences between the two regimes. Although the 2000 Act itself is silent on these requirements, the 2001 Regulations incorporate extensive elements of the Companies Acts which deal with these matters and apply these to LLPs.[85] The obligation to produce an annual return and annual accounts may deter some traditional partnerships from incorporating as an LLP as the financial

---

[83] However regard must be had to the position of salaried partners, as mentioned above.
[84] Principally that: the date of the transfer is not more than one year after the LLP's incorporation and there is no change in membership between incorporation and transfer.
[85] In addition, regard must be had to the Limited Liability Partnerships (Amendment) Regulations 2005 (SI 2005/1989); the Limited Liability Partnerships (Accounts and Audit) (Application of Companies Act 2006) Regulations 2008 (SI 2008/1911); and the Limited Liability Partnerships (Application of Companies Act 2006) Regulations 2009 (SI 2009/1804).

secrecy associated with the partnership is thus lost.[86] However, that is the price which has to be paid if limited liability is to be achieved. The Companies House website provides useful guidance on the minutiae of these requirements.[87] In particular, regard must be had to the obligations placed upon the designated members in ensuring compliance with the requirements. This might inform an LLP's decision as to how many of its members ought to be designated members.

WINDING UP

Another area where the LLP closely mirrors the limited company is in the application of the law of insolvency. This is achieved through the application of the Insolvency Act 1986 with some amendments[88] and allows LLPs to enter into voluntary arrangements, or be subject to administration, receivership and both voluntary and compulsory winding-up. While a considered treatment of the law of insolvency as it relates to LLPs is not provided in this chapter,[89] one particular aspect requires highlighting.

17–33

The "clawback" provision

Section 74 of the Insolvency Act 1986, as amended by the regulations, provides that present and past members of the LLP are liable to contribute to the assets of the LLP in the event of liquidation to the extent previously agreed between themselves and the LLP. However, apart from such an agreement, an individual member may become liable for the debts of the LLP under s.214A of the 1986 Act,[90] which although headed "adjustment of withdrawals", is commonly referred to as the "clawback" provision. This provision states that a member of the LLP, or any person who has been a member in the two years prior to the winding up, may be

17–34

---

[86] Note, however, that there are different accounting requirements depending on whether the LLP is small, medium or large. Small and medium-sized LLPs may submit simpler, abbreviated accounts. There are thresholds for turnover, balance sheet total and the average number of employees which determine whether the LLP is small or medium-sized. If the LLP is not deemed small or medium-sized, it is deemed to be a large LLP. See Small Limited Liability Partnerships (Accounts) Regulations 2008 (SI 2008/1912).

[87] Companies House guidance: *https://www.gov.uk/government/publications/limited-liability-partnership-incorporation-and-names* [Accessed May 15, 2015].

[88] See s.14 of the 2000 Act and reg.5 and Sch.3 to the 2001 Regulations and reg.4 and Sch.2 to the 2001 Scottish Regulations.

[89] However, readers can turn to Young, *Limited Liability Partnerships Handbook*, 2nd edn (2007) and G. Morse (ed.), *Palmer's Limited Liability Partnership Law*, 2nd edn (2011). It should be noted that these texts are no longer up-to-date and principally consider the law as it relates to LLPs in England and Wales. However, they are a useful starting point. For the law on insolvency in general as it applies to Scotland, see *Gloag and Henderson: the Law of Scotland*, edited by H.L. MacQueen and Lord Eassie, 13th edn (Edinburgh: W. Green, 2012) paras 49.01–49.46. The Accountant in Bankruptcy also maintains an excellent website containing useful information on corporate insolvency: *http://www.aib.gov.uk/Services/Corporateinsolvency* [Accessed May 15, 2015].

[90] As amended by reg.4(2) and Sch.3 to the 2001 Scottish Regulations.

liable to contribute to the LLP's assets in the event of liquidation if the member withdrew any property of the LLP during that two-year period.

The withdrawal may be in the form of "a share of profits, salary, repayment of payment of interest on a loan to the limited liability partnership or any other withdrawal of property".[91] In order for a "clawback" to be ordered by the court, the liquidator must prove that, at the time of the withdrawal, the member knew or had reasonable grounds for believing that the LLP was unable to pay its debts,[92] or knew or had reasonable grounds for believing that the LLP would become unable to meet its debts as a result of that withdrawal, taken together with any other withdrawals made (or which were contemplated being made) at the same time.[93] If the liquidator satisfies the court that these conditions have been met, the court may declare that the member in question is liable to make whatever contribution to the assets of the LLP the court thinks proper.[94] However, the court must not make such an order unless it is satisfied that the member knew or ought to have concluded that after each withdrawal there was no reasonable prospect that the LLP would avoid going into insolvent liquidation.[95]

Key Concept

Unlike traditional partnerships, which have complete financial privacy, LLPs must publish their annual accounts. This is the cost of the members having limited liability.

TRANSFERRING AN EXISTING BUSINESS TO AN LLP

17–35 The business vehicle most likely to consider incorporating as an LLP is the traditional partnership, as the tax structures of limited companies and LLPs are so different as to make such a transfer unattractive. However, even traditional partnerships considering incorporating as an LLP must be aware of the issues which can arise from changing business structures. It is suggested that, at the very least, the following must be considered:

- whether the whole of the existing partnership is to be transferred to the LLP or just a part thereof;
- whether the existing partnership will be dissolved at the moment of incorporation or at a later date;

---

[91] s.214A(2)(a) of the Insolvency Act 1986.
[92] See s.123(1)(c) of the Insolvency Act 1986 as amended by reg.4(2) and Sch.3 to the 2001 Scottish Regulations.
[93] s.214A(2)(b) of the Insolvency Act 1986 as amended by reg.4(2) and Sch.3 to the 2001 Scottish Regulations.
[94] s.214A(3) of the Insolvency Act 1986 as amended by reg.4(2) and Sch.3 to the 2001 Scottish Regulations.
[95] s.214A(5) of the Insolvency Act 1986 as amended by reg.4(2) and Sch.3 to the 2001 Scottish Regulations.

- whether all work-in-progress of the existing partnership ought to be billed prior to the transfer or whether it will transfer to the LLP;
- the indemnities which will need to be put in place by the LLP to indemnify the former partners of the old firm against future claims;
- whether the existing partnership is the subject of any ongoing litigation;
- whether approval is required from a regulatory body[96] prior to the transfer, and whether consent is required from clients of the existing partnership to transfer files and communications to the LLP;
- what ought to be included in the transfer agreement, in particular in relation to: the firm's obligations to former partners and their estates; the retirement of members; the valuation of assets; the assignation of debts and liabilities (including pension liabilities); the novation of continuing contracts; the firm's external finance agreements and leases; the firm's professional indemnity insurance; the firm's intellectual property; the firm's goodwill; and banking and staffing matters.

The above list is by no means comprehensive and it is obviously the case that the larger the existing partnership, the more there will be to consider. Like so many aspects of the law relating to LLPs, it is clearly the case that specialist advice must be sought by those considering transferring their business to an LLP.

▼ CHAPTER SUMMARY

MAIN ATTRIBUTES OF AN LLP

(1) A unique business medium often described as a hybrid of a traditional **17–36** partnership and a limited company introduced by the Limited Liability Partnerships Act 2000.

(2) It is a body corporate with separate legal personality from its members which is formed by being incorporated under the 2000 Act.

(3) It can own property in its own name, sue and be sued, grant floating charges and become a partner, shareholder or member in other businesses. An LLP has unlimited capacity and therefore it cannot act ultra vires.

(4) Partners in an LLP are known as members, although in practice members of an LLP are often styled as partners.

(5) Much of the meat of the law on LLPs is found in regulations promulgated under the 2000 Act.

---

[96] For example, from the Law Society of Scotland in the case of a Scottish firm of solicitors.

INCORPORATION

(1) To form an LLP, a minimum of two persons must subscribe their names to an incorporation document.

(2) The incorporation document must then be delivered to the registrar who, if satisfied that the application has been completed properly, that the proposed name is acceptable and that the fee has been paid, will issue a certificate of incorporation.

(3) The incorporation document must stipulate which members are to be designated members.

MEMBERS

(1) Membership is automatically conferred on subscriber members.

(2) A new member can be introduced to the LLP with agreement of the existing members in the manner stipulated in the members' agreement or in the manner provided in the 2001 Regulations.

(3) Every member of an LLP is an agent of the LLP but members are not agents of each other.

(4) For an LLP to avoid being bound by the act of a member acting out-with the scope of his authority, both parts of s.6(2) of the 2000 Act must be satisfied.

(5) A member of an LLP is not to be regarded as employed by the LLP unless he would be regarded as employed if he was a partner in a traditional partnership. The Supreme Court recently held that a member of an LLP, while not an employee of the firm was nonetheless a "worker" within the meaning of s.230(3) of the Employment Rights Act 1996 thus allowing the member to claim the benefit afforded to whistle-blowers by the same Act.

(6) The default position under the 2001 Regulations is that all members are entitled to equal participation in the profits and capital of the LLP. In the vast majority of cases this default position will not apply in practice and questions regarding profit and capital will be governed by the terms of any partnership agreement or LLP agreement.

(7) Regard should be had to the salaried members rules introduced by the Finance Act 2014.

MEMBERS' LIABILITY

(1) The principal reason for creating the LLP was to provide a business structure which had the organisational flexibility of a partnership but with limited liability for its members.

(2) The members are not jointly and severally liable with the LLP for its debts and obligations. If third parties dealing with an LLP are made aware that they are contracting with the LLP alone and not with any individual member thereof, an action in contract can be raised only against the LLP. In such a scenario, the LLP's assets will be used to satisfy any debts or obligations resulting from the claim, and the members themselves risk losing only their capital contributions in the event of a "wipe-out" claim.

(3) For an individual member to be held personally liable in negligence, the tripartite test of foreseeability of damage, proximity and whether it is fair, just and reasonable to impose a duty of care will apply. It will also be necessary for the pursuer to establish that there was an assumption of responsibility by the individual member, that the third party relied upon that assumption and no valid limitation of liability clause was in operation.

MANAGEMENT

(1) The members of an LLP have considerable discretion as to how they may manage their business. An LLP does not need to have a limited liability partnership agreement in place and if there is one, it need not be in writing. Like the traditional partnership, the absence of a partnership agreement means that the default rules found in the 2001 Regulations will apply.

TAXATION AND ACCOUNTS

(1) LLPs are tax transparent entities and thus members are taxed as if they were partners in a traditional partnership. LLPs do not pay corporation tax. The similarities between how traditional partnerships and LLPs are taxed make it very easy for partnerships to incorporate as LLPs.
(2) The accounting and auditing requirements for LLPs are much closer to those applicable to companies as opposed to partnerships. The 2001 Regulations incorporate extensive elements of the Companies Acts which deal with these matters and apply these to LLPs including the obligation to produce an annual return and annual accounts. While this may deter some traditional partnerships from incorporating as an LLP, the removal of complete financial secrecy is the price which has to be paid if limited liability is to be achieved.

WINDING UP

(1) The winding up of LLPs closely mirrors the winding up of the limited company by the application of the law of insolvency. The Insolvency Act 1986 with some amendments applies to LLPs and allows LLPs to enter into voluntary arrangements, or be subject to administration, receivership and both voluntary and compulsory winding-up.
(2) Regard should be had to the "clawback" provision in the Insolvency Act which provides that a member of the LLP, or any person who has been a member in the two years prior to the winding up, may be liable to contribute to the LLP's assets in the event of liquidation if the member withdrew any property of the LLP during that two-year period.

? QUICK QUIZ

- What is an LLP?
- Why was there pressure on the government to introduce LLPs?
- How is an LLP formed?
- Explain the statutory framework of LLPs.
- What is a designated member?
- Do members owe a duty of good faith to each other, and/or to the LLP itself?
- Does the law of partnership apply to LLPs?
- How are new members admitted to an LLP?
- What is a designated member?
- Does the law of partnership apply to LLPs?
- How are new members admitted to an LLP?
- To what extent can members bind the firm?
- Do members owe a duty of good faith to each other, and/or to the LLP itself?
- To what extent are members employees of the firm?
- What are differences between salaried, fixed-share and equity members?
- What was the impact of HMRC's 2014 salaried members rules?
- To what extent is members' liability limited and how does this compare to the traditional partnership?
- Does the LLP itself have limited liability?
- Where are the default provisions found for the management of the LLP if there is no written LLP agreement?
- How are members taxed?
- Why are LLPs required to publish accounts?
- What is the "clawback" provision?
- What ought to be considered when transferring a business to an LLP?

📖 FURTHER READING

- ➤ Department for Trade and Industry, *Limited Liability Partnership—A New Form of Business Association for Professions* (Department for Trade and Industry, 1997, URN 97/597).
- ➤ G. Morse (ed.), *Palmer's Limited Liability Partnership Law*, 2nd edn (London: Sweet & Maxwell, 2011).
- ➤ S. Young, *Limited Liability Partnerships Handbook*, 2nd edn (London: Tottel Publishing, 2007).
- ➤ *Gloag and Henderson: the Law of Scotland*, edited by H.L. MacQueen and Lord Eassie, 13th edn (Edinburgh: W. Green, 2012), para.45.31.

🖰 RELEVANT WEBLINKS

➢ *https://www.gov.uk/government/publications/limited-liability-partnership-incorporation-and-names* [Accessed May 15, 2015].
➢ *https://www.gov.uk/government/publications/salaried-members-rules-revised-technical-note-and-guidance* [Accessed May 15, 2015].

Chapter 18   Insurance Law[1]

DAVID CABRELLI[2]

▶ CHAPTER OVERVIEW

18–01 This chapter is concerned with the law of insurance. Individuals and businesses in the UK will arrange insurance on an annual basis to cover them in case certain unfortunate events occur which result in some kind of financial loss. The aim of this chapter is to consider the general principles (including case law and statutory material) relating to the following aspects of insurance law:

- the sources, purposes, core features and regulation of insurance law in the UK;
- the definition of an insurance contract and the legal requirements for its constitution;
- the importance of insurable interest;
- the indemnity and proximate cause principles and how life assurance differs from indemnity insurance;
- the impact of warranties in an insurance policy;
- the consumer insured's duty to take reasonable care not to make a misrepresentation, the commercial insured's duty to supply a fair presentation of the risk to the insurer and the duty not to make a fraudulent claim; and
- the rule that the insured must not deliberately cause the event insured.

✓ OUTCOMES

18–02 At the end of this chapter you should be able to understand:

- ✓ the common law and legislation which governs insurance law;
- ✓ how the common law defines a contract of insurance;
- ✓ the effect of a lack of insurable interest on the part of the insured in the subject-matter of the insurance contract;

---

[1] A version of this chapter previously appeared in D. Cabrelli, *Commercial Law Essentials* (Dundee: Dundee University Press, 2009) and was reproduced with the kind permission of DUP (second edition of *Commercial Law Essentials* by M. Combe (Edinburgh: Edinburgh University Press, 2013)).
[2] Senior Lecturer in Commercial Law, University of Edinburgh.

✓ how the indemnity principle works in practice;
✓ the difference between a "past/present fact" only and "promissory/continuing" warranty and the effect of a breach of such warranties;
✓ the nature of the consumer insured's duty to take reasonable care not to make a misrepresentation, the commercial insured's duty to supply a fair presentation of the risk to the insurer and the duty not to make a fraudulent claim; and
✓ the circumstances in which an insured will be treated as having deliberately caused the event insured.

INTRODUCTION

Insurance is an incredibly important commercial activity in the UK. It generates a great number of jobs for the UK economy and protects those insured against the risks of modern life. Those protected themselves may be engaged in a commercial pursuit or simply seeking to protect themselves in a personal capacity. Since the inception of the insurance market, the law has recognised the need to regulate this sphere of commercial activity. The law achieves this through a mixture of common law and statutory regulation. **18–03**

PURPOSE OF INSURANCE

The aim of insureds in entering into an insurance contract is to protect themselves against the occurrence of a particular misfortune or particular risks. For example, motor insurance protects the insured in the event that their vehicle is damaged or destroyed. The nature of that protection (i.e. whether the insured has a right of repair or a right to be paid compensation for loss) is regulated by the terms of the insurance contract. However, the crucial point is that in some way the insured will be safeguarded in the event that the perils or risks described in the insurance contract occur. **18–04**

THE NATURE OF INSURANCE

The typology of insurance is regulated by the insurance contract. There are essentially two types of insurance: First, there is indemnity insurance which entitles the insured to indemnification from the insurer on the occurrence of an event or peril which is delimited in the contract of insurance, e.g. theft of property, protection from fire damage or destruction, protection of building and contents, etc. The second form of insurance is life assurance. Life assurance can be contrasted with indemnity insurance. In the case of the latter, the indemnified event is uncertain to occur whereas in the case of the former, it is certain that the life assured will come to an end at some point in time. Although there is **18–05** this element of certainty with regard to life assurance, the precise timing of the death is uncertain and it is this uncertainty which is common to all insurance transactions whether indemnity insurance or life assurance.

REGULATION OF INSURANCE

18–06 The activities of insurance companies and insurance intermediaries such as insurance brokers are regulated by the Financial Services and Markets Act 2000 ("FSMA"). FSMA does not directly regulate the obligations and rights of insurers or insureds pursuant to the contract of insurance— that is largely left to the common law, the Consumer Insurance (Disclosure and Representations) Act 2012 ("CI(DR)A"), the Insurance Act 2015 and the Marine Insurance Act 1906 in the specialised field of marine insurance. Instead, FSMA and the secondary rules promulgated pursuant thereto are concerned with the regulation of the conduct of business by insurance companies (in particular, the Insurance Conduct of Business Sourcebook of the Financial Conduct Authority ("FCA") which is referred to as "ICOBS")[3] and the adequate capitalisation of insurance companies. FSMA also seeks to ensure that those at the helm of insurance companies are fit and proper persons to conduct insurance business.

An insured enjoys additional statutory protection by virtue of the Third Parties (Rights against Insurers) Act 2010. The Third Parties (Rights against Insurers) Act 2010 entitles a third party with a claim against an insolvent insured to a direct action against the indemnity insurer of that insolvent insured. Meanwhile, ss.212–217 of FSMA and the compensation rules in the handbook of the FCA[4] provides funds, contributed to by all insurers practising in the UK, with which to discharge 90 per cent (and 100 per cent in some cases) of the liabilities of insolvent insureds.

Key Concepts

An insurance contract protects an insured against the occurrence of certain perils or risks. In return for the payment of a premium, the insurer agrees to indemnify an insured in respect of the financial consequences of certain losses which arise on the occurrence of an insured event. The activities of insurance companies are regulated by the Financial Services and Markets Act 2000.

---

[3] See Financial Conduct Authority, *Insurance: Conduct of Business sourcebook ("ICOBS")*, available at *https://fshandbook.info/FS/html/FCA/ICOBS* [Accessed May 15, 2015].

[4] See Financial Services Authority, *Compensation ("COMP")*, available at *https://fshandbook.info/FS/html/handbook/COMP* [Accessed May 15, 2015].

DEFINITION OF INSURANCE

There have been many attempts by the courts in Scotland and England to **18–07**
define an insurance contract. None have been completely satisfactory.
The nearest approximation to a definition is contained in the case of
Prudential Insurance Co v Inland Revenue Commissioners[5] where Channell
J. remarked:

> "It must be a contract whereby for some consideration, usually but
> not necessarily for periodical payments called premiums, you secure
> to yourself some benefit, usually but not necessarily the payment of a
> sum of money, upon the happening of some event."[6]

Thus, in terms of the above definition, there are four elements that must
be satisfied as follows:

  (1) consideration must pass from the insured to the insurer (which is
      a periodical payment called the premium);
  (2) the insured must secure a benefit, usually the payment of a sum
      of money;
  (3) upon the happening of some event;
  (4) which involves an element of uncertainty as to: (a) whether the
      event will happen or not; or (b) the time at which it will happen.

Added to criterion (4) above is the requirement that the event must be
adverse to the interests of the insured. A good example of what is
intended here is provided by the case of *Department of Trade and Industry
v St Christopher's Motorists Association*.[7] Here, the question was whether
the association was engaged in providing insurance to its members.
Members paid an annual subscription in return for the services of a
chauffeur for a period of 12 months in the event that the member was
unable to drive following an accident or being disqualified from driving
under the newly enacted drink driving laws. The court ruled that there
was a contract of insurance between the association and the members.
First, the benefit of the services of the chauffeur made available to the
members could be valued in money's worth. Secondly, the benefit was
contingent upon the occurrence of an uncertain event, namely an accident or disqualification of the member from driving for infringement of
the drink driving laws. Thirdly, the event was adverse to the interests of
the member. Therefore, since the contract between the association and
the member possessed the hallmarks of a contract of insurance, the
contract was a contract of insurance, and the association fell to be
regulated in accordance with statute.

---

[5] [1904] 2 K.B. 658.
[6] [1904] 2 K.B. 658, 663.
[7] [1974] 1 All E.R. 395.

CONSTITUTION OF CONTRACT OF INSURANCE

18–08 An insurance contract does not require to be reduced to writing in order to be legally valid in terms of Scots law. Section 1(1) of the Requirements of Writing (Scotland) Act 1995 stipulates that writing is not required for the constitution of any contract, including an insurance contract. However, in the context of marine insurance, s.22 of the Marine Insurance Act 1906 provides that a marine policy will not be admissible in court unless it is embodied in written form.

INSURABLE INTEREST

18–09 A party to an insurance contract must have insurable interest in the subject matter of insurance. The requirement of insurable interest is what distinguishes an insurance contract from a wager. In examining the nature of the interest which the insured must possess, it is beneficial to make a distinction between life assurance and indemnity insurance policies.

First, in the context of life assurance, s.1 of the Life Assurance Act 1774 states that an insurance policy will be void where a person takes out a life assurance policy over the life of another person in whom they have no interest. The nature of that interest is stipulated in s.3 of the Life Assurance Act 1774. Here, the fundamental point is made that the interest must be of a pecuniary or financial variety. For example, a son will have insurable interest in the life of his father due to the son's financial right to the payment of aliment. Likewise, s.1 of the Married Women's Policies of Assurance (Scotland) Act 1880 narrates that a wife has the right to effect a policy of assurance on the life of her husband. In the case of *Dalby v India and London Life Assurance Co*,[8] it was ruled by the court that it was sufficient that the insured possesses an insurable interest in the life assured at the date the policy of insurance is effected: there is no additional requirement that the insured have an insurable interest in the person whose life is assured at the date of death.[9] It is worthwhile stressing that an insurable interest of a pecuniary or financial interest in the context of life assurance is not necessarily limited to familial relationships. For example, in the case of *Turnbull & Co v Scottish Provident Institution*,[10] it was ruled by the Outer House of the Court of Session that a firm had a direct financial interest, and, thus, an insurable interest, in the life of its local agent in Iceland.

Secondly, for the purposes of indemnity insurance, the nature of the insurable interest required was outlined in the landmark case of *Macaura*

---

[8] (1854) 15 C.B. 365.
[9] This can be contrasted with indemnity insurance where the insurable interest of the insured in the subject matter of the insurance contract must exist when the indemnity insurance policy is taken out and also when the loss is incurred, on which see *Godsall v Boldero* (1807) 9 East 72.
[10] (1896) 34 S.L.R. 146.

v Northern Assurance Co Ltd.[11] In *Macaura*, the insured was a creditor and sole shareholder of a limited company. The company owned a quantity of timber, much of which was stored on the land of the insured. The timber was insured in the name of the insured, not the name of the company. When the timber was destroyed by fire, the insured made a claim and the insurer rejected liability to indemnify. The court ruled that the insured had no insurable interest in the timber which was the subject matter of the insurance contract. Only the company had an insurable interest in the timber. The court made the point that it is crucial that the insured has a legal or equitable interest in the property insured. Otherwise, the contract of insurance will be void for lack of insurable interest. Therefore, even in circumstances where an insured has an expectation of, or stands to sustain a, loss as a result of the destruction or damage of the subject matter of the insurance contract, this will be insufficient to entitle them to indemnification if they are unable to point to a legal or equitable interest. Indeed, the insurance interest must exist when the indemnity insurance policy is taken out and also when the loss is incurred.[12]

The effect of a lack of insurable interest is severe for the purported insured. In the case of a life assurance policy, the consequences are clear: s.1 of the Life Assurance Act 1774 stipulates that the policy is "null and void". Meanwhile, in the case of indemnity insurance, Scots common law provides that it is an essential element of a contract of insurance that there is a subject in which the insured has an interest.[13] Hence, without that essential element, the contract is void.

Key Concepts

Four elements must be present before it will be held that an insurance contract exists, namely that: (1) consideration has passed from the insured to the insurer (which is a periodical payment called the premium); (2) the insured must secure a benefit, usually the payment of a sum of money; (3) upon the happening of some event which is adverse to the insured; and (4) involving an element of uncertainty as to: (a) whether the event will happen or not; or (b) the time at which it will happen. Moreover, the insured must have an insurable interest in the subject matter of the insurance contract. In the case of life assurance, the insured will be required to establish that it had a financial or pecuniary interest in the life of the person assured at the time the life assurance policy was concluded, whereas in the case of indemnity insurance, the insured must demonstrate that it had a legal or equitable interest in the property insured when the insurance contract was concluded and also when the loss was suffered.

---

[11] [1925] A.C. 619.
[12] *Godsall v Boldero* (1807) 9 East 72.
[13] *The Laws of Scotland* (Stair Memorial Encyclopaedia) Vol.12, para.848, citing Bell's *Principles* s.457.

THE INDEMNITY PRINCIPLE

18–10   A contract of indemnity insurance is a contract of indemnity. That is to say that it entitles the insured to indemnification on the occurrence of certain defined losses (e.g. the costs of rebuilding a house) as a result of certain defined perils (e.g. fire, storm or explosion). The indemnity principle is applicable to all contracts of indemnity. In terms of such a principle, the insured will only be entitled to compensation when they have suffered a loss. Therefore, if there is no loss, there is no right to be indemnified. This can be contrasted with a life insurance contract, which is not technically a contract of indemnity. Instead, it is referred to as contingency insurance in the sense that the stipulated event is certain to occur, but the time when it will occur is uncertain. Here, when the event stipulated occurs (i.e. the death of the person whose life is assured), the assured will not have sustained any financial loss. Instead, the happening of the event of death will activate the right of the assured to receive a particular agreed sum which is expressed in the contract as payable on the occurrence of the loss event.

In the case of indemnity insurance, the general rule is that the insured is only entitled to be reimbursed for the loss which they have sustained. As stated in *Chapman v Pole*,[14] an insured has no right to recover according to the amount represented as insured. Thus, if the value of a painting is warranted in an insurance policy as £1 million, but the extent of the insured's loss on its destruction is £200,000, it is the latter figure which can be recovered. Hence, by virtue of the indemnity principle, over-insurance will be of no assistance to the insured. In other words, the insured has no right to double recovery if the same risk is insured with two insurers and on a claim he can sue one of the insurers only in order to recover his loss. Where an insured object is damaged and the insured suffers a partial loss, the insurer is under an obligation to pay for the costs of its repair or rebuild ("reinstatement") to the pre-damage condition. Where it is not possible to reinstate the damaged object, or the insurer decides not to pay for the repairs, then the standard measure of indemnity is the second hand sale value of the object, i.e. the insured market value of the insured object in its immediate pre-loss condition. However, there are exceptions where the measure of indemnity will not be the reinstatement value of the damaged object. The case of *Leppard v Excess Insurance Co Ltd*[15] demonstrates one of the exceptions to that general principle. The facts are important in this case. The insured purchased a property from his father with the intention of selling it on to a third party. He intended to sell the property at £4,500 and insured the property against fire for £10,000 which was later increased to £14,000. When the property was destroyed by fire, it was agreed that the rebuilding costs were £8,000. This is the sum which the insured claimed. However, the court held that his loss was £3,000, since this was the sum

---

[14] (1870) 22 L.T. 306.
[15] [1979] 2 All E.R. 668.

which he stood to lose if he sold the property, being the market value of the property (£4,500) less the post-fire value of the site (£1,500). Therefore, in a situation where an insured is intending or has contracted to sell a property, the insured will not be entitled to retrieve the rebuilding costs/ reinstatement costs—only the market value—because this is all that the insured stands to lose.

Indemnity insurance can be contrasted with contingency insurance. In **18–11** the case of contingency insurance, the idea of indemnification for loss sustained by the insured makes little sense. For example, in the case of a life assurance contract, the insured cannot meaningfully be said to have been reimbursed in monetary terms for the loss of the life of the person named in the policy. Instead, life assurance contracts are "valued" policies, that is to say policies which enjoin an insurer to pay a particular sum on the occurrence of the death of the person named in the insurance policy. It is also possible for property insurance, fire insurance, home insurance, etc. to be concluded in terms of a "valued" policy, rather than in terms of an "indemnity" policy. However, outside the domain of the insurance of fine art and antiques, such "valued" policies in the case of property insurance are rare.

As a result of the indemnity principle, insurers are afforded the right of subrogation.[16] "Subrogation" enables an insurer who has paid for a loss to "stand in the shoes" of the insured and to exercise (using the insured's name) all rights that he could have exercised himself to recover from any source other than the insurers themselves the whole or part of the financial loss he has sustained and for which he has been indemnified. So in a public liability insurance contract, where an insurer has indemnified the insured in respect of sums paid to a member of the public for losses sustained by that person, the insurer is entitled to recover from a third party the sum which they are legally due to pay to the insured where the loss sustained was caused by that third party. Thus, where the insured enjoys a double recovery, i.e. recovers from the insurer and also from a third party, the case of *Castellain v Preston*[17] is an authority for the proposition that the insurer is entitled to retrieve the sums they have paid to the insured. Otherwise, the insured would enjoy a substantial profit. The whole doctrine of subrogation is premised on the rule that the insured has no right to be more than fully indemnified for their loss. The process operates to the effect that the insurer is subrogated to the rights of the insured against that third party and sues the third party for recovery in the name of the insured. However, an insurer may sue in its own name where the insured has assigned its rights of recovery (against third parties) to the insurer.[18]

---

[16] Subrogation has no part to play in life assurance contracts.
[17] (1883) 11 L.R. Q.B.D. 380.
[18] *Caledonia North Sea Limited v London Bridge Engineering Ltd*, 2000 S.L.T. 1123 (IH); 2002 S.L.T. 278; 2002 S.C. (H.L.) 117 (HL).

Proximate Cause

18–12 Not every loss sustained by the insured will trigger the right to indemnity in the insurance contract. Thus, there must be a causal link to a particular risk or peril. Therefore, in the case of fire insurance, the loss sustained by the insured must have fire damage or destruction as the proximate cause. Likewise, in the case of a policy which insures in respect of damage or destruction caused by flood, loss by sudden and accidental flood will entitle the insured to an indemnity. However, loss by slow seepage will not usually be covered. Naturally, difficulties arise where there are two possible causes for the loss, one of which is provided for under the policy and the other is not. The general rule governing the meaning of the words "proximate cause" is stipulated in the case of *Ionides v The Universal Marine Insurance Co.*[19] Here, Wiles J. stated that the overriding criterion is to search for the immediate, real or dominant cause of the loss, i.e. the cause that is most closely connected with the loss. Where it is impossible to ascertain which of two independent causes represents the immediate, real or dominant cause of the loss, one of which is covered as an insured peril in the policy and the other is not, the rule in *J.J. Lloyd Instruments Ltd v Northern Star Insurance Co Ltd (The "Miss Jay Jay")*[20] will apply to the effect that the insurer will be liable to indemnify the insured. In the Miss Jay Jay case, a ship was lost at sea due to a mixture of unusual sea conditions and defects in its design. The unusual sea conditions were covered in the policy as a "peril of the sea", whereas there was no specific reference to design defects. Since the dominant cause of the loss of the ship could not be determined definitively, it was ruled by the Court of Appeal that the insurers were liable to pay.

Key Concepts

In the case of a contract of indemnity insurance, the general rule is that the insured is only entitled to be reimbursed for the loss which he/she has sustained. Where the subject matter of any indemnity insurance contract is damaged and the insured suffers a partial loss, the insurer is under an obligation to pay for the costs of the repair or rebuild/reinstatement of the property to the pre-damage condition. Where it is not possible to reinstate the damaged property, or the insurer decides not to pay for the repairs, then the standard measure of indemnity is the second hand sale value of the property, i.e. the insured market value of the insured property in its immediate pre-loss condition. The insurer's right of subrogation flows from the indemnity principle, enabling the insurer who has paid an insured sum to the insured for a loss sustained to: (i) "stand in the shoes" of the insured; and (ii) exercise (using the insured's name) all rights that the insured could have exercised himself to recover from any

---

[19] [1863] 14 S.B. (N.S.) 259.
[20] [1987] 1 Lloyd's Rep. 32 (CA).

source other than the insurers themselves the whole or part of the financial loss the insured sustained and for which he has been indemnified. In order for an insurance claim to be valid, the insured must show that there is a causal link between the insured event (e.g. property damage or destruction) and the particular risks or perils insured (e.g. fire, theft, flood, etc.) and this rule is referred to as the "proximate cause" rule.

WARRANTIES

It should be stressed at the outset that the ensuing exposition of the law **18–13** of warranties in insurance contracts assumes that ss.9 to 11 of the Insurance Act 2015 are in force. A warranty is a fundamental term of an insurance policy. It amounts to a promise made by the insured to the insurer. The common law provided (e.g. see *Bank of Nova Scotia v Hellenic Mutual War Risk Association (Bermuda) Ltd ("The Good Luck")*[21] that if the insured breached a warranty, then the insurer was discharged from liability under the insurance contract with effect from the date of the insured's breach of warranty. However, s.10(1) of the Insurance Act 2015 abolishes that common law rule. As such, if an insurer wishes to terminate the insurance contract, it will have to make a conscious choice to accept the insured's breach of warranty (assuming it is a material breach of the insurance contract) and bring the contract to an end, all in accordance with orthodox contractual principles. If the insurer fails to accept the insured's breach of warranty and terminate the insurance contract, then the contract will continue in effect, but s.10(2) of the Insurance Act 2015 directs that the insurer will not be liable for any losses suffered by the insured occurring, or attributable to something happening, after the warranty (express or implied) has been breached but before the breach has been remedied. Another common law rule provided that it was irrelevant that the insured's breach of warranty was unconnected to any loss that the insured subsequently suffered. For example, imagine the situation where an insured suffered fire damage to cars stored on car dealership premises which he operated. If the insured had breached a warranty in the insurance policy to the effect that he operated a car dealership from property which he owns, the fact that there was no connection between the breach of that warranty and the financial loss occasioned to the insured as a result of the car damage was irrelevant. This common law rule was felt to be unjust. As such, s.11 of the Insurance Act 2015 abolished this common law rule, but the onus is on the insured to satisfy the court that the insured's breach of warranty could not have increased the risk of the loss which he/she actually suffered in the circumstances in which the loss occurred.

In an insurance contract, there are essentially two types of warranty:

---

[21] [1992] 1 A.C. 233 (HL).

(1) a statement of fact by the insured as to the past or present (a "past/present fact warranty only"); or

(2) a continuing undertaking that a state of affairs will prevail throughout the duration of the policy, which must be exactly complied with, whether it be material to the risk insured or not (a "continuing/promissory warranty").

It is not always straightforward to ascertain whether a term of the policy amounts to a "past/present fact only warranty" or a "continuing/promissory warranty" and in such circumstances, the ordinary rules on the construction of contracts will apply. For example, in the case of *Hussain v Brown*,[22] after some dispute between the insurer and the insured, the Court of Appeal ruled that the following words amounted to a "past/present fact only warranty" rather than a continuing/promissory warranty:

> "Are the premises fitted with any system of intruder alarm. If yes give name of installing company."

A good example of a continuing warranty is provided by the case of *Seavision Investments v Evennett and Clarkson Puckle (the "Tiburon")*.[23] In an insurance policy, a promissory warranty was granted by the insured to the effect that a vessel was *and would be* "of German flag, or ownership or management". In fact, the vessel was not of German flag, etc. As a result, when the ship was struck by an Exocet missile during the Iran/Iraq war, the breach of the warranty was held to be fatal to the claim.

How is it possible to tell whether a term of the policy is a past/present fact only warranty or a continuing/promissory warranty? No magic or special words are required, i.e. there is no need to specifically stipulate in the contract that the term is a warranty. Indeed, it was once extremely common for insurance policies to provide that every term of the policy represented the "basis of the contract". Prior to the coming into force of s.6 of the CI(DR)A and s.9 of the Insurance Act 2015, such a "basis of the contract" clause automatically elevated every term of an insurance policy into a warranty. So if a term did not state that it was a warranty, but the policy included such a clause, any breach of that term was treated as a breach of warranty, entitling the insurer to negate liability to the insured, e.g. see *Dawsons Ltd v Bonnin*.[24] However, the common law rule recognising the status of these "basis of the contract" clauses was felt to be unfair to insureds and s.6 of the CI(DR)A and s.9 of the Insurance Act 2015 abolished the rule in the case of consumer insurance contracts and commercial insurance contracts. The net effect is that basis of the contract clauses are now invalid and of no effect in the case of all insurance contracts governed by English or Scots law.

[22] [1996] 1 Lloyd's Rep. 627.
[23] [1992] 2 Lloyd's Rep. 26.
[24] [1922] 2 A.C. 413; 1922 S.C. (H.L.) 156.

Key Concepts

A warranty is a fundamental term of an insurance policy amounting to a promise made by the insured to the insurer. If the insured breaches the warranty, the insurer is entitled to terminate the insurance contract if the breach is material, but the insurer is not automatically discharged from liability under the contract with effect from the date of the insured's breach of warranty. Two types of warranty are commonly encountered in insurance contracts, namely "past/present fact warranties only" and "continuing/promissory warranties" and it is a matter of interpretation within which of these two categories a particular warranty falls.

STATUTORY DUTIES OF CONSUMER INSURED AND COMMERCIAL INSURED

At common law a contract of insurance was a contract "uberrimae fidei", **18–14** that is to say that it was a contract of the "utmost good faith"—*Carter v Boehm*[25] and s.17 of the Marine Insurance Act 1906. The effect of the insurance contract being one of the utmost good faith was that the common law imposed two duties on the insured, namely a duty to make full and accurate disclosure of all material facts that would influence the judgment of a prudent insurer and a duty not to misrepresent material facts to the insurer. However, the effect of s.2(5) of the CI(DR)A and s.14 of the Insurance Act 2015 is that these common law rules and s.17 of the Marine Insurance Act 1906 are essentially abolished. They have been replaced by two statutory duties. In the case of a "consumer insurance contract", i.e. an insurance contract entered into between an insurer who carries on the business of insurance and an individual who enters into the contract wholly or mainly for purposes unrelated to the individual's trade, business or profession,[26] s.2(3) of the CI(DR)A imposes a statutory duty on the latter—who is referred to as the "consumer insured"—to exercise reasonable care not to make a misrepresentation. The counterpart of that statutory duty in the case of non-consumer insurance contracts, i.e. commercial insurance contracts, finds its expression in s.3(1) and (2) of the Insurance Act 2015. Here, it is provided that the commercial insured has a statutory obligation to provide the insurer with a fair presentation of the risk. Both of these statutory duties are imposed on the consumer insured and the commercial insured at particular times only, namely immediately before: (i) the insurance contract is formed, i.e. at the negotiation stage and until the contract of insurance is formed; and (ii) the point of renewal of an insurance contract.[27] Each of the two statutory duties will now be considered in turn.

---

[25] (1766) 3 Burr. 1905.
[26] CI(DR)A s.1.
[27] CI(DR)A s.2(1) and the Insurance Act 2015 s.2(2).

THE CONSUMER INSURED'S DUTY TO TAKE REASONABLE CARE NOT TO MAKE A MISREPRESENTATION BEFORE THE CONTRACT IS FORMED OR VARIED

18–15 As stated above, where the consumer insured and insurer enter into a consumer insurance contract, the common law duty of disclosure and duty not to misrepresent material facts and the equivalent statutory duties in the Marine Insurance Act 1906 are replaced by a single duty which obliges the consumer insured to take reasonable care not to make a misrepresentation before the contract is formed or varied.[28] Unlike the position under the common law,[29] the standard of care to be discharged by the consumer insured is that of the reasonable consumer, unless the insurer was, or ought to have been, aware of any particular character-istics or circumstances of the actual consumer, or the representation made by the consumer was dishonest.[30] Section 3(2) of the CI(DR)A sets out a range of factors that are to be taken into account by a court in determining whether the consumer insured has satisfied the reasonable consumer standard, namely (1) the type of consumer insurance contract in question and its target market; (2) any relevant explanatory material or publicity produced or authorised by the insurer; (3) how clear, and how specific, the insurer's questions were; (4) in the case of a failure to respond to the insurer's questions in connection with the renewal or variation of a consumer insurance contract, how clearly the insurer communicated the importance of answering those questions (or the possible consequences of failing to do so); and (5) whether or not an agent was acting for the consumer. The insurer will have a remedy where the consumer insured breaches the duty to take reasonable care not to make a misrepresenta-tion and this misrepresentation has induced the insurer to enter into the contract.[31] The remedy furnished to the insurer depends on whether the consumer insured made a misrepresentation that was (1) deliberate or reckless; or (2) careless. A misrepresentation will be deliberate or reckless if the consumer insured knew that it was untrue or misleading, or did not care whether or not it was untrue or misleading, and knew that the matter to which the misrepresentation related was relevant to the insurer, or did not care whether or it was relevant to the insurer.[32] Meanwhile, a mis-representation will be careless if it is not deliberate or reckless.[33] If the consumer breaches the duty by making a deliberate or reckless mis-representation, the insurer has the remedy of treating the contract as if it never existed i.e. the contract is voidable and the insurer has the right to refuse all claims and retain all of the premiums paid, except to the extent

---

[28] CI(DR)A s.2(2).

[29] *St. Paul Fire & Marine Insurance Co (UK) Ltd v McConnell Dowell Construction Ltd* [1996] 1 All E.R. 96; *Pan-Atlantic Insurance Co Ltd v Pine Top Insurance Co Ltd* [1995] A.C. 501.

[30] CI(DR)A s.3(3), (4) and (5).

[31] CI(DR)A s.4.

[32] CI(DR)A s.5(2).

[33] The onus lies on the insurer to prove that a misrepresentation was deliberate or reckless: CI(DR)A s.5(4) and see also s.5(5).

(if any) that it would be unfair to the consumer to retain them.[34] Meanwhile, if the consumer makes a careless misrepresentation, the nature of the insurer's remedy is dependent on whether the insurer would have entered into the contract on different terms.[35] If the insurer would not have entered into the contract, then it may avoid the contract i.e. the contract is voidable, but it must return all of the premiums paid.[36] However, if it would have entered into the contract, but on different terms, then the contract is treated as if it includes those different terms and if it would have levied a higher premium, the insurer may reduce proportionately the amount to be paid to the consumer on a claim.[37] The impact of the provisions of sections three to five of the CI(DR)A is that there is no longer any burden imposed on the consumer insured to actively disclose facts. As such, it is a matter for the insurer to ask questions that are comprehensive enough to provide a material understanding of the risks involved in entering into the consumer insurance contract with the consumer insured.

The commercial insured's duty to provide a fair presentation of the risk

Section 3(1) of the Insurance Act 2015 encompasses the commercial **18–16** insured's over-riding duty to make to the insurer a fair presentation of the risk involved in entering into the insurance contract. In terms of s.3(4) of the Insurance Act 2015, this duty involves a requirement to disclose every material circumstance which the commercial insured knows or ought to know, or disclosure which gives the insurer sufficient information to put a prudent insurer on notice that it needs to make further enquiries for the purposes of revealing those material circumstances. There is no requirement for the insured to disclose information that diminishes the risk, of which the insurer is aware, that it ought to know or is presumed to know or where the insurer waives the duty of disclosure.[38] The duty of fair presentation of the risk also imposes a requirement that every material representation by the commercial insured as to a matter of fact be substantially correct and that every material representation as to a matter of expectation or belief be made in good faith.[39] The provisions of s.4(6) of the Insurance Act 2015 direct that a commercial insured should know information that should reasonably have been revealed by a reasonable search of information available to the insured, whether by means of making enquiries or by any other means. As such, it is not open to the commercial insured to turn a blind eye to matters which function to increase the risk in entering into the commercial insurance contract. The nature of the remedies available to the insurer for the commercial insured's breach of statutory duty to make a fair presentation of the risk

---

[34] CI(DR)A s.4 and Sch.1(2).
[35] CI(DR)A s.4 and Sch.1(4).
[36] CI(DR)A Sch.1(5).
[37] CI(DR)A Sch.1(6), (7) and (8).
[38] Insurance Act 2015 s.3(5).
[39] Insurance Act 2015 s.3(3).

mirror those which apply in the case of consumer insurance contracts. As such, a distinction is drawn between a breach of duty which is (1) deliberate or reckless; and (2) one which is not deliberate or reckless.[40] A commercial insured's breach will be deliberate or reckless if he/she knew that it was in breach of the duty of fair presentation, or did not care whether or not it was in breach.[41] The remedies available to the insurer then follow the same pattern as those applicable in the case of consumer insurance contracts.[42]

18–17   It should be stressed that a common law duty to disclose material facts is imposed on the insurer throughout the duration of the insurance contract. For example, the insurer is under a common law obligation of good faith in certain circumstances to make disclosure of such material factors to co-insureds or third party beneficiaries *(Bank of Nova Scotia v Hellenic Mutual War Risk Association (Bermuda) Ltd ("The Good Luck")*[43] and *Banque Financiere de la Cite SA v Westgate Insurance Co Ltd.*[44]

Duty not to make a fraudulent claim

18–18 Section 12(1) of the Insurance Act 2015 prescribes that an insurer is under no liability to indemnify an insured where the latter makes a fraudulent claim. If the insured makes a fraudulent claim, the insurer may by notice to the insured treat the contract as having been terminated with effect from the time of the fraudulent act.[45] The insurer is also entitled to recover any sums paid to the insured in respect of that fraudulent claim. Once the insurance contract is terminated, the insurer is no longer liable under the insurance contract in respect of any losses sustained by the insured subsequent to termination, and the insurer is under no obligation to return the premiums paid by the insured.[46] However, the Insurance Act 2015 does not define what is meant by the words "fraudulent claim". As such, assistance can be derived from the pre-existing common law. A good example of a fraudulent claim is provided by the case of *Black King Shipping Corporation v Massie (The "Litsion Pride")*.[47] Here, an insured entered into war zone insurance in respect of ships entering war zones. Prior to the insured entering into particular areas designated as "war zones" (such as the Gulf of Hormuz), the insured was under an obligation to inform the insurer beforehand or as soon as practicable. The vessel insured was destroyed in a cruise missile attack when it entered the Gulf of Hormuz. However, the insured failed to inform the insurer before the vessel entered this "war zone". The insured realised its mistake and concocted letters with backdated dates to make it look as if it had indeed

---

[40] Insurance Act 2015 s.8(4).
[41] Insurance Act 2015 s.8(5).
[42] See Insurance Act 2015 Sch.1(2)–(11) and para.18–15.
[43] [1992] 1 A.C. 233 (HL).
[44] [1991] A.C. 249.
[45] Insurance Act 2015 s.12(1)(c).
[46] Insurance Act 2015 s.12(2).
[47] [1985] 1 Lloyd's Rep. 437.

informed the insurer before the vessel entered the war zone. However, the letters were discovered to be fraudulent and the court held that the insurer was under no duty to indemnify since the claim was fraudulent.

Key Concepts

A consumer insured is under a statutory obligation to take reasonable care not to make a misrepresentation before the contract is formed or varied and a common law duty not to make a fraudulent claim. This can be contrasted with the commercial insured's statutory duty to supply a fair presentation of the risk and his/her common law duty to refrain from making fraudulent claims.

Event Insured

A principle of insurance law stipulates that the insurer will be entitled to **18–19** negate liability to indemnify the insured where it can be demonstrated that the insured deliberately caused the loss suffered. The classic case that provides an excellent example of this rule in action in the context of life assurance is *Beresford v Royal Insurance Company Ltd.*[48] Here, the insured insured his life five times. The insurance contract stipulated an exception from liability whereby the policy would be void where the insured had taken his own life within one year from the date of commencement of the policy. He subsequently committed suicide at a time when suicide was still a criminal offence. When a claim for indemnity was made by the insured's executors under the insurance policy, the insurer resisted liability. The court sided with the insurer and held that there was no justification for the insurer to pay out the proceeds of the insurance policy to the deceased's executors in such circumstances. This decision was premised on the basis of the doctrine of public policy, rather than on the interpretation of the exception clause. However, this begs the question what the outcome in this case might have been if the insurers had failed to specifically provide in the life insurance contract that they would be liable to indemnify the insured where death was caused by suicide. In such circumstances, it is submitted that there would not have been a whole lot of difference and that the common law would apply the doctrine of public policy to relieve the insurer of liability. However, where the insurer specifically provides in the contract that it will pay out in such circumstances, although it is a moot point, it is submitted that it would be unlikely that a court would interfere with such an agreement (to relieve the insurer of liability) for the reason that suicide is no longer a criminal offence and so it is arguable that committing suicide is no longer contrary to public policy.

Difficulties arise where the death is partly caused by the actions of the

---

[48] [1938] A.C. 586.

insured. In the case of *Dhak v Insurance Co of North America (UK) Ltd*,[49] an insured under a life assurance policy began abusing alcohol to relieve the pain caused by a back injury sustained at work. Tragically, she died six months later choking on her own vomit, which resulted in asphyxiation. The insurer resisted liability to indemnify the executors of the deceased on the basis of an exclusion in the life insurance policy in respect of death caused by deliberate means. The court held that the insurer was under no liability to pay out the insurance proceeds where the insured had deliberately engaged in the act of intoxicating herself and had taken a calculated risk. However, matters would have been different had the death been caused by accidental means.

AVERAGE

18–20 The principle of averaging is relevant to insurance and usually a clause in the insurance contract provides that the insured can recover only the proportion of the sum insured which the damage bears. For example, if the value of the subjects is £10,000 and the subjects are insured for £1,000 (i.e. 10 per cent of their value) then, if the loss equals £5,000, the sum recoverable is £500 (i.e. 10 per cent of the loss).

CONTRIBUTION

18–21 Contribution is the term for the right that arises where property is insured under an indemnity insurance contract with more than one insurance company and an insured event (e.g. a fire, flood, explosion, etc.) causes loss which is valued at less than the combined value of the insured sums stipulated in the policies. The general rule is that the insured has the right to recover from any one insurer the whole amount insured by it. However, as between the insurers, the concept of contribution applies to enable the insurer who has indemnified the insured to obtain a contribution in respect of their pro rata share from the remaining insurers on the basis that the insurers are treated as co-obligants in law (even though they are not co-insurers) (*Caledonia North Sea Ltd v London Bridge Engineering Ltd*).[50] In the case of *Sickness and Accident Insurance Association Ltd v General Accident Assurance Corporation Ltd*,[51] it was held that any insurer that has paid more than its rateable share of the total loss has, by implication of law and without any assignation from the insured, a right of contribution, i.e. a right to recover from the other insurer insurance companies, their rateable shares. However, it is standard practice for a "rateable proportion clause" to be included in every insurance contract to the effect that each insurer shall be liable to

---

[49] [1996] 1 W.L.R. 936.
[50] 2000 S.L.T. 1123 (IH); 2002 S.L.T. 278; 2002 S.C. (H.L.) 117 (HL).
[51] (1892) 19 R. 977.

contribute rateably only. This imposes an obligation on the insured to seek a maximum of the relevant pro rata share from each insurer only.

THIRD PARTIES (RIGHTS AGAINST INSURERS) ACT 2010

Where a third party had sustained a loss as a result of the actions of an **18–22** insured, the common law provided that such third party had no right to claim under an insurance policy entered into between an insured and an insurer which protected the insured from losses caused as a result of making good losses occasioned to the third party. This rule was based on the doctrine of "privity of contract". The principal difficulty with such a rule was that the third party would be left uncompensated where the insured had become bankrupt or insolvent prior to the release of the proceeds of the insurance policy. In such circumstances, the policy proceeds would be paid direct to the executors or personal representatives of the insured. The third party would then rank as an ordinary unsecured creditor in the bankruptcy or insolvency of the deceased insured's estate—and might only recover a proportion of the full monetary value of the claim. The Third Parties (Rights against Insurers) Act 2010 is designed to deal with this problem by effecting a statutory assignation of the insured's rights under the insurance policy to the third party. This affords a large degree of protection to the third party since it means that the third party attains a preferential status in comparison with the insured's general body of creditors.

PROTECTION OF POLICY HOLDERS AND INSURANCE CONDUCT OF BUSINESS RULES

Part XV of FSMA and the Compensation Rules of the FCA's handbook **18–23** provide protection for the insured where the insurer is unable to meet their liabilities, e.g. on liquidation. FSMA imposes levies on insurers in order to finance insurer's liabilities and in some cases the insured will be indemnified in full. Part XVI of FSMA also enables the insured to make a complaint regarding the insurer's resolution of a dispute to the Financial Ombudsman Service. This ombudsman right only covers private individuals or businesses with an annual turnover of less than £1 million.

▼ CHAPTER SUMMARY

(1) An insurance contract protects an insured against the occurrence of a **18–24** particular misfortune or particular risks.

(2) An insurance contract does not require to be reduced to writing in order to be legally valid in terms of Scots law: s.1(1) Requirements of Writing (Scotland) Act 1995.

(3) An insurance contract is a contract whereby for some consideration, usually but not necessarily for periodical payments called premiums, a

person secures some benefit, usually but not necessarily the payment of a sum of money, upon the happening of some event, which event is adverse to the interests of that person and which involves an element of uncertainty as to: (a) whether it will happen or not; or (b) the time at which it will happen.

(4) An insured in the case of an indemnity insurance contract must have a legal or equitable interest in the subject matter of the insurance contract. Moreover, an insured in a contingency insurance contract such as a life assurance contract must have some financial or pecuniary interest in the life of the person assured. Otherwise, the insurance contract is void.

(5) In the case of a contract of indemnity insurance, the general rule is that the insured is only entitled to be reimbursed for the loss. The "indemnity principle" only applies to indemnity insurance contracts.

(6) Where the subject matter of any indemnity insurance contract is damaged and the insured suffers a partial loss, the insurer is under an obligation to pay for the costs of the repair or rebuild/reinstatement of the property to the pre-damage condition. Where it is not possible to reinstate the damaged property, or the insurer decides not to pay for the repairs, then the standard measure of indemnity is the second hand sale value of the property, i.e. the insured market value of the insured property in its immediate pre-loss condition.

(7) The insurer's right of subrogation enables the insurer who has paid an insured sum to the insured for a loss sustained to: (i) "stand in the shoes" of the insured; and (ii) exercise (using the insured's name) all rights that the insured could have exercised himself to recover from any source other than the insurers themselves the whole or part of the financial loss the insured sustained and for which he has been indemnified.

(8) A warranty is a fundamental term of an insurance policy and if breached, the insurer is entitled to terminate the insurance contract, but is not discharged from liability under the contract with effect from the date of the breach.

? QUICK QUIZ

- What are the sources of insurance law?
- What are the objectives and purposes of insurance law?
- What is the definition of insurance?
- What is insurable interest?
- What is a warranty and what are the consequences if it is breached?
- What are the consequences if a warranty is breached?
- What are the statutory and common law duties of the consumer insured and the commercial insured?
- In what circumstances will the consumer insured be treated as having complied with his/her statutory obligation?
- In what circumstances will the commercial insured be taken to have conformed to his/her statutory duty to furnish a fair presentation of the risk?
- What is "subrogation"?
- What is the "indemnity principle"?

📖 FURTHER READING:

> J. Birds, *Birds' Modern Insurance Law*, 9th edn (London: Sweet and Maxwell, 2013).
> J. Lowry and P. Rawlings, *Insurance Law: Doctrines and Principles*, 3rd edn (Oxford: Hart Publishing, 2011).
> F. Davidson and L. Macgregor, *Commercial Law in Scotland*, 3rd edn (Edinburgh: W. Green, 2014), Ch.6.
> Gloag and Henderson, *The Law of Scotland*, 13th edn (Edinburgh: W. Green, 2012), Ch.20.

🖱 RELEVANT WEBLINKS

> Association of British Insurers: *https://www.abi.org.uk/* [Accessed May 15, 2015].
> British Insurance Brokers Association: *www.biba.org.uk* [Accessed May 15, 2015].
> British Insurance Law Association: *www.bila.org.uk* [Accessed May 15, 2015].
> Financial Services Authority: *http://www.fsa.gov.uk/pages/handbook/* [Accessed May 15, 2015].
> Lloyd's of London: *http://www.lloyds.com* [Accessed May 15, 2015].

Chapter 19   Insolvency

ALEX GIBB[1]

▶ CHAPTER OVERVIEW

19–01 Insolvency is the state of affairs in which an individual (or any legal entity, such as a company) is unable to pay his, her or its debts. From an accounting point of view, insolvency can be viewed as the situation where an individual's *income* is outweighed by his *expenditure*, and there is no reasonable prospect of this situation improving.

This chapter discusses personal insolvency and corporate insolvency. The material on personal insolvency is divided into three sections: sequestration, alternative procedures and diligence. The material on corporate insolvency is divided into four sections: company voluntary arrangements, administration, receivership and liquidation.

✓ OUTCOMES

19–02 At the end of this chapter you should be able to:

- ✓ explain what is meant by bankruptcy and sequestration;
- ✓ describe how sequestration affects a debtor's estate;
- ✓ outline how a debtor's estate is distributed among his creditors;
- ✓ explain some alternatives to sequestration;
- ✓ explain what is meant by arrestment, attachment and inhibition;
- ✓ outline how company voluntary arrangements operate;
- ✓ explain what is meant by administration, and outline how this procedure operates;
- ✓ explain what is meant by receivership, and outline how this procedure operates;
- ✓ explain what is meant by liquidation and winding up; and
- ✓ distinguish between compulsory and voluntary winding up, and outline how these procedures operate.

---

[1] Lecturer in Law, North East Scotland College.

Personal Insolvency

Sequestration

A great number of people have debts. Indeed, it is difficult to exist in **19–03** modern society without incurring personal debts at some point in one's life. A far lesser—though still considerable—number of people will encounter difficulty in repaying these debts. The reasons for suffering such crises of cash flow are many and varied, and the majority of people who experience debt problems are able to remedy the situation amicably with their creditors. However, others are not so fortunate, and are faced with the difficult decision to accept legal intervention in an effort to address the problem.

When an individual can be legally declared unable to pay his debts, the term commonly used to describe this is "bankruptcy". The legal mechanism by which a person is declared bankrupt and his assets are disposed of in payment of his debts is called "sequestration". An individual whose estate is to be sequestrated is known as the "debtor".

Key Concept

Sequestration is the legal process by which a bankrupt person's estate is disposed of in payment of his debts.

The law of bankruptcy is primarily found in the Bankruptcy (Scotland) Act 1985 ("BSA 1985"), though it must be said that this Act has been heavily amended in the thirty years since its enactment. Major changes were introduced by the Bankruptcy and Diligence etc. (Scotland) Act 2007 ("BDSA 2007"), and more recent amendments were made by the Bankruptcy and Debt Advice (Scotland) Act 2014 ("BADASA 2014"). Certain provisions of the BDSA 2007 have not, to date, been brought into force, although there still appears to be an intention to do so in the future. These matters will be discussed where appropriate.

The Accountant in Bankruptcy

The Accountant in Bankruptcy ("AiB") is an executive agency of the **19–04** Scottish Government, and is responsible for the supervision and registration of sequestrations in Scotland. Its website[2] provides a huge amount of information for anyone who is likely to be affected by bankruptcy. The AiB also regularly plays an active role in the process of sequestration, acting as trustee (see para.19–07) in around 70 per cent of cases.[3] Under the BADASA 2014 and associated legislation, the AiB's role and powers

---

[2] *http://www.aib.gov.uk* [Accessed May 15, 2015].
[3] Accountant in Bankruptcy, *Annual Report and Accounts 2013–2014* (October 23, 2014). Available at *http://www.aib.gov.uk/2013-14-annual-report-accounts* [Accessed May 15, 2015].

are expanding, with the agency taking over a number of responsibilities from the Sheriff Court.

Access to bankruptcy

19–05 Before a person's estate can be sequestrated, it must be demonstrated that he is, in fact, unable to pay his debts. If an individual's total liabilities outweigh his total assets, he is said to be in "absolute insolvency". Whilst this might sound straightforward, it is not as precise a concept as it may seem, so it is not viewed as an appropriate measure of inability to pay debts as they fall due. More useful is the concept of "apparent insolvency", which can be used to justify a sequestration being initiated either by a creditor or by the debtor himself. There are a number of ways in which apparent insolvency can be constituted, including:

(a) if the debtor's estate has already been sequestrated or he has already been declared bankrupt;
(b) if the debtor gives written notice to his business creditors that he has ceased paying his debts;
(c) if the debtor grants a trust deed (see para.19–18); or
(d) if the debtor fails to pay a debt (or aggregated debts) amounting to £750[4] within three weeks of a demand for payment.[5]

An alternative to establishing apparent insolvency is for the debtor to access the "certificate of sequestration route" (or "certified route"). Introduced by the Home Owner and Debtor Protection (Scotland) Act 2010 ("HODPSA 2010"), this allows a debtor to obtain confirmation of his insolvency from an approved "money advisor", such as an insolvency practitioner or other appropriate professional.[6] The granting of such a certificate gives debt relief to the debtor, and allows him to apply for sequestration on the strength of this certificate.[7] The rationale behind the introduction of this procedure was to allow debtors a route into bankruptcy who otherwise would have required the agreement of a creditor, a condition which many debtors had difficulty satisfying in practice.[8] Along with the introduction of the certified route, the sometimes-problematic "creditor concurrence" route was abolished.[9]

It is finally worth noting here that in order to access Scots bankruptcy procedure, the debtor must be habitually resident, or have an established place of business, in Scotland.[10]

---

[4] This figure was increased to £1,500 by the Bankruptcy (Scotland) Regulations 2008 (SSI 2008/82), but that increase has now been revoked by the Bankruptcy (Scotland) Regulations 2014 (SSI 2014/225).
[5] BSA 1985 s.7.
[6] Bankruptcy (Money Advice and Deduction from Income etc.) (Scotland) Regulations 2014 (SSI 2014/296) r.3.
[7] BSA 1985 s.5B, inserted by HODPSA 2010 s.9(2).
[8] Bankruptcy (Certificate for Sequestration) (Scotland) Regulations 2010 (SSI 2010/397) executive note.
[9] HODPSA 2010 s.9(1)(b).
[10] BSA 1985 s.9.

Commencement of sequestration

As alluded to above, the sequestration process itself can be initiated by **19–06** either the debtor or qualifying creditors. If the debtor himself wishes to apply for sequestration, he must first receive advice from an approved money advisor on the nature and consequences of the process.[11] Once this advice has been received, the debtor can make an application for sequestration to the AiB provided that:

(a) the total amount of his debts is not less than £3,000[12];
(b) no award of sequestration has been made against him within the last five years; and
(c) any one of the following conditions is met: the debtor is apparently insolvent; the debtor has been granted a certificate for sequestration; the debtor has granted a trust deed which cannot be converted into a protected trust deed (see para.19–18); or the debtor qualifies for the "minimal asset process".[13]

The "minimal asset process" was introduced by the BADASA 2014 to provide a simplified application for debtors who have little income or assets.[14] To qualify, the debtor must meet a range of criteria relating to his income, assets and liabilities. Among these are:

(a) the debtor must not have surplus income as calculated by the "common financial tool" (see para.19–10);
(b) the sum of his debts must be between £1,500 and £17,000;
(c) the total value of his assets (not considering liabilities) must be £2,000 or less;
(d) he must not own any single asset with a value in excess of £1,000;
(e) he must not own any land;
(f) he must have been granted a certificate for sequestration; and
(g) his estate must not have been sequestrated within the past 10 years under this process, or five years by any other procedure.[15]

In any instance where the debtor initiates the sequestration, he must provide with his application a full statement of his assets and liabilities.[16] New provisions introduced by the BADASA 2014 allow for a debtor to be granted protection against creditor action (a "moratorium") for a period of six weeks, beginning from the point at which the debtor gives notice to the AiB that he intends to apply for sequestration.[17] This also applies to certain alternative statutory debt solutions that might be

---

[11] BSA 1985 s.5C, inserted by BADASA 2014 s.1.
[12] Increased from £1,500 under BDSA 2007 s.25(a).
[13] BSA 1985 s.5(2B).
[14] This replaces the "low income, low asset" application introduced for the same purpose by the BDSA 2007.
[15] BSA 1985 s.5(2ZA), inserted by BADASA 2014, s.5(1)(b).
[16] BSA 1985 s.5(6A).
[17] BSA 1985 ss.4A–D, inserted by BADASA 2014 s.8.

accessed by a debtor (see para.19–17), though only one such moratorium will be granted within any 12 month period.

Qualifying creditors may commence a sequestration by petition to the court.[18] A creditor is entitled to present such a petition if he is owed a debt of at least £3,000 (or if he makes a joint application with another creditor and together they are owed at least £3,000)[19] and the debtor is apparently insolvent as outlined above. Previously, a petition for sequestration could be presented to either the Sheriff Court or the Court of Session, but the BDSA 2007 stipulates that the petition must now be made to the Sheriff Court.[20] Before making such a petition the creditor must provide the debtor with a "debt advice and information package",[21] which is a document (or collection of documents) providing the debtor with relevant information, such as the availability of debt advice in his locality, plus any other information as is stipulated by the Scottish Ministers, or other authorised bodies.[22]

On debtor applications, the sequestration will be granted as long as the AiB is satisfied that the provisions of the BSA 1985 have been complied with. Where a creditor petitions for sequestration, the debtor will be cited to appear in court to show cause as to why the petition should not be granted. If the debtor fails to appear, or if the grounds for the petition are upheld, the court will grant the sequestration.[23]

The trustee in sequestration

19–07 Upon a successful application or petition for sequestration, a trustee will be appointed to take control of the debtor's estate. The trustee must be a qualified insolvency practitioner[24] and will, ultimately, be responsible for disposing of the debtor's estate in payment of his debts, so far as this is possible and appropriate.

Previously, an interim trustee would be appointed immediately upon sequestration being granted, and would be replaced in due course by a permanent trustee. However, the BDSA 2007 amalgamated these two offices into one, that of the trustee in sequestration.[25] An interim trustee might still be appointed when a petition is presented to the court, with the responsibility of safeguarding the debtor's estate pending the court's decision, but upon the petition being granted he will still be replaced by a trustee in sequestration.[26]

---

[18] BSA 1985 s.5(2)(b).
[19] BSA 1985 s.5(4), increased from £1,500 by BDSA 2007 s.25(b).
[20] BDSA 2007 s.16.
[21] This was a creation of the Debt Arrangement and Attachment (Scotland) Act 2002, and is defined in s.10(5) of that Act.
[22] BSA 1985 s.5(2D).
[23] BSA 1985 s.12.
[24] BSA 1985 s.2(3).
[25] BDSA 2007 s.6.
[26] BSA 1985 s.2.

> **Key Concept**
>
> When a debtor is sequestrated, his estate is placed under the control of a trustee in sequestration, to be distributed amongst his creditors.

Notice of the sequestration must be registered. This is done by a copy of the order being sent to the keeper of the Register of Inhibitions and Adjudications[27] and, if necessary, to the AiB.[28] A record of the award will also be made in the Register of Insolvencies,[29] a public register administered by the AiB.[30] Previously, the trustee was required to advertise the sequestration in the *Edinburgh Gazette*, but this requirement has now been removed.[31]

Duties of the trustee in sequestration

The trustee in sequestration has a range of general functions. Among these are: **19–08**

(a) to recover, manage and realise (sell off) the debtor's estate;
(b) to distribute the estate among the debtor's creditors according to their respective entitlements;
(c) to ascertain the reasons for the debtor's insolvency; and
(d) to ascertain the state of the debtor's liabilities and assets.[32]

Within 60 days of the date of sequestration, the trustee must give notice to every known creditor as to whether or not he intends to hold a statutory meeting of creditors.[33] (Previously, this was an obligation imposed on the interim trustee, but is at the trustee's discretion under the BDSA 2007.)[34] If he does intend to hold such a meeting, it must be called within 28 days of the notice.[35] If he does not intend to hold a meeting any creditor can, within seven days, request that a meeting be held. The trustee cannot refuse if a request is made by creditors representing one-quarter of the debtor's liabilities.[36]

Where a statutory meeting of creditors is held, a vote will be taken whereby the creditors may elect an alternative trustee in sequestration, or confirm the appointment of the original trustee.[37]

---

[27] This was to be renamed "The Register of Inhibitions" under BDSA 2007 s.80, but due to Pt 4 of the Act not being fully brought into force, this has not yet happened.
[28] BSA 1985 s.14.
[29] The Register of Insolvencies is available online at *http://roi.aib.gov.uk/ROI* [Accessed May 15, 2015].
[30] BSA 1985 s.1A(1)(b).
[31] HODPSA 2010 s.12.
[32] BSA 1985 s.3.
[33] BSA 1985 s.21A.
[34] BDSA 2007 s.11(1).
[35] BSA 1985 s.21A(6).
[36] BSA 1985 s.21A(5).
[37] BSA 1985 s.24.

Vesting of the debtor's estate

19–09 Once a trustee has been elected (or confirmed) the debtor's estate "vests" in the trustee, subject to certain rules.[38] This means that the debtor effectively loses his rights in respect of the vested property, and the trustee obtains extensive powers over it. The trustee is then required to administer the estate for the benefit of the debtor's creditors.

Any assets that are necessary for the maintenance of the debtor's family life do not vest in the trustee. This would include home furnishings such as beds and kitchen appliances. Any tools that are necessary for the operation of a business can also be kept by the debtor, but the value of such tools cannot exceed £1,000.[39]

The debtor's heritable property (and so, potentially, his home) will also vest in the trustee. The trustee must register a notice of title, and can potentially require the debtor to leave the property in order that it can be sold. However, this may require an application to the Sheriff court,[40] and must be done within a certain time period; if the trustee has not taken steps towards selling the debtor's family home within three years, the property must be returned to the debtor.[41]

Vesting of estate after sequestration

19–10 Assets that are acquired by the debtor after the date of sequestration are known as *acquirenda*. These will vest in the trustee, except where they would have been excluded from vesting at the date of sequestration.[42] The debtor is required to inform the trustee of any assets so acquired, and failure to do so is a criminal offence.[43] The period during which *acquirenda* vest in the trustee is four years from the date of sequestration.[44]

Any ordinary income that the debtor receives after sequestration is generally kept by him,[45] however it has long been the case that he may be required to surrender "surplus" income to the trustee. The most recent mechanism for achieving this is the "debtor contribution order" introduced by BADASA 2014, which stipulates that a debtor contribution amount will be set in each sequestration,[46] calculated using the "common financial tool".[47] This calculation will take into account the income required for reasonable aliment of the debtor and his family, and can be set at zero if appropriate.[48] The contribution amount can be varied in

---

[38] BSA 1985 s.31.

[39] BSA 1985 s.33.

[40] BSA 1985 s.40, amended by HODPSA 2010 s.11.

[41] BSA 1985 s.39A.

[42] BSA 1985 s.32(6). For a recent case considering the practical problems this might give rise to, see *Accountant in Bankruptcy v Grant*, 2010 G.W.D. 40-812.

[43] BSA 1985 s.32(7).

[44] BSA 1985 s.32(10), amended by BADASA 2014 s.16(2).

[45] BSA 1985 s.32(1).

[46] BSA 1985 s.32A, inserted by BADASA 2014 s.4.

[47] Outlined by the Common Financial Tool etc. (Scotland) Regulations 2014 (SSI 2014/ 290).

[48] BSA 1985 s.32A(4).

accordance with changes in the debtor's circumstances,[49] and is subject to appeal by the debtor or any other interested party.[50] It is also possible for the debtor to request a payment break of up to six months.[51] Similarly as with *acquirenda*, the period for which the debtor will be required to make contributions is four years, though this period can be shortened or lengthened if circumstances justify it.[52]

The debtor contribution order replaces the "income payment agreement" and "income payment order" procedures introduced by BDSA 2007. In light of this, "IPAs" and "IPOs" have been abolished, though any currently in force will continue to have effect until their terms are fulfilled by the debtor, or they are otherwise brought to an end.[53]

Transactions made prior to sequestration

An important role of the trustee in sequestration is to protect the interests **19–11** of the debtor's creditors. This is straightforward in terms of property that has vested in the trustee, but is more difficult in respect of property that the debtor disposes of before his sequestration. Therefore, the trustee has the right to examine transactions entered into by the debtor prior to sequestration and, if sufficient reasons exist, such transactions can be challenged and reduced (declared invalid).

Parties that may have a right to challenge include the trustee in sequestration, a trustee acting under a trust deed (see para.19–18), and any creditor owed a debt as of the date of sequestration.

Challengeable transactions 1: gratuitous alienations

A gratuitous alienation is a transaction whereby the debtor has given **19–12** over assets, or surrendered a right, without receiving a reasonable value in return. A common example would be where a debtor decides to give his possessions away to friends and family, rather than see them given over to his creditors. Clearly this is unfair on creditors who have a legitimate claim to the property.

Such a disposal can be challenged if it took place within a two-year period prior to sequestration or within a period of five years if the recipient is an associate of the debtor such as a family member or business partner. Gifts such as birthday, Christmas and wedding presents are exempted, as long as they are reasonable.[54]

If the challenge is successful, the alienation will be reduced. The recipient will be required to return the property to the debtor's estate, or pay the value of the property. The property must be returned even if the recipient did pay some value for the item, although he can claim against the estate as a creditor in respect of what he has lost.

---

[49] BSA 1985 s.32F.
[50] BSA 1985 s.32C.
[51] BSA 1985 s.32G.
[52] BSA 1985 s.32B.
[53] The rules and procedures relevant to IPAs and IPOs can be found in BDSA 2007 s.18.
[54] BSA 1985 s.34.

Challengeable transactions 2: unfair preferences

19–13 An unfair preference is created by a transaction that places certain creditors in an advantageous position over other creditors, without justification. An example would be where a debtor purposefully settles a debt before it is due, in an effort to retain the creditor's goodwill in the future. A transaction can be challenged as an unfair preference if it was agreed within a six-month period prior to the date of sequestration. A number of transactions are exempt from challenge, namely: transactions made in the ordinary course of business; payments made in respect of debts that have become due; transactions involving reciprocal obligations (unless there is evidence of collusion); and the granting of a mandate to pay over arrested funds (see para.19–21).[55]

If the challenge is successful, the transaction will be reduced. The subject of the transaction must be returned to the debtor's estate, or if this is not possible another form of redress will be directed by the court.

Challengeable transactions 3: equalisation of diligence

19–14 Diligence is a process in which a creditor enforces his right to payment by appropriating certain assets of the debtor, following a court order in his favour or on the strength of certain instruments of debt.

Following sequestration, creditors are prevented from carrying out diligence against the debtor. A problem can occur where certain creditors have commenced diligence proceedings in the period immediately preceding the debtor's sequestration, as this would place them in a favourable position compared to other creditors who have been less aggressive in the pursuit of their debt.

To avoid such inequalities, rules exist regarding the "equalisation" of diligence.[56] The basic effect of these is that all diligence procedures commenced during the 60 days preceding sequestration will be deemed to have been effected on the same day, and will rank equally with each other. Any property obtained as a result of such diligences must be given over to the trustee.

Management and distribution of the debtor's estate

19–15 After the trustee has ingathered the debtor's assets, and carried out any of the above procedures as are appropriate, he is responsible for the management of the debtor's estate.[57] This might include the closing down of the debtor's business (or the continuance of it if this will raise more funds for the creditors) or the raising of court actions if this would benefit the estate. For the debtor's part, he must act in good faith with the trustee and can be required by the trustee to give regular accounts of his income and expenditure.[58]

---

[55] BSA 1985 s.36.
[56] BSA 1985 s.37.
[57] BSA 1985 s.39.
[58] BSA 1985 s.43A.

If they have not already done so, creditors will submit their claims to the trustee and, if necessary, provide supporting evidence.[59] The trustee will assess the validity of each claim[60] and, if it is accepted, the creditor will be entitled to receive a dividend from the debtor's estate.[61] A creditor whose claim is rejected can apply for a review of the decision by the AiB,[62] with a further right of appeal to the Sheriff Court.[63]

In distributing the debtor's estate, the trustee must pay debts according to a statutory order. This order does not include secured debts, since secured creditors will first seek to recover their debt by exercising their rights over any secured property (see Chapter 21, "Rights in Security"). Other than these, then, the order in which debts will be paid is as follows:

(a) the outlays and remuneration of the interim trustee (if appointed);

(b) the outlays and remuneration of the trustee in sequestration;

(c) where the debtor is deceased, the reasonable expenses of his funeral and of the administration of his estate;

(d) where a creditor has petitioned for sequestration, his reasonable expenses incurred in making the petition;

(e) preferred debts[64];

(f) ordinary debts (those of unsecured creditors);

(g) interest on preferred and ordinary debts; and

(h) any postponed debt (e.g. loans made to a spouse or business, or the value of a challenged gratuitous alienation).[65]

The trustee will satisfy each debt in full until there are insufficient funds to fully repay all creditors within a certain category; in practice, this is likely to be the "ordinary debts" due to unsecured creditors. Each creditor within this category will be paid proportionately out of the remaining available funds, i.e. they will each receive an equal percentage of what they are owed.

Discharge of the debtor

Under BDSA 2007, the debtor was automatically discharged from bankruptcy after one year.[66] However, BADASA 2014 abolishes automatic discharge in most cases, and instead requires that the debtor be formally discharged by the AiB.[67] The procedure differs slightly **19–16**

---

[59] BSA 1985 s.48.

[60] BSA 1985 s.49.

[61] BSA 1985 s.50.

[62] BSA 1985 s.49(6).

[63] BSA 1985 s.49(6D).

[64] As outlined by BSA 1985 Sch.3 Pt 1, which deals mainly with any outstanding remuneration payments due to employees of the debtor. (This is most likely to be relevant where the debtor is being sequestrated following the failure of a business.)

[65] BSA 1985 s.51.

[66] BDSA 2007 s.1.

[67] BADASA 2014 s.17.

depending on whether or not the AiB is acting as trustee,[68] but in either case a report must be produced detailing the financial position of the debtor and outlining his conduct throughout the sequestration. The AiB will then decide whether or not to grant a certificate discharging the debtor. The earliest point at which the AiB can consider discharge is one year after the date of sequestration, and if discharge is refused, the AiB must review this decision after a further year. The debtor has the right to apply for review of a refusal to discharge, with a further right of appeal to the Sheriff Court.[69]

There is an exception to the above in the case of "minimal asset" debtors (see para.19–06). Under this process, the debtor is automatically discharged six months after the date on which sequestration was awarded.[70]

Even after discharge, it is possible for the debtor to continue to be affected by his sequestration. In addition to the continuation of any debtor contribution order (see para.19–10), it is also possible for certain restrictions to be placed on the debtor's freedom in financial and related matters. Introduced by BDSA 2007, these are known as "bankruptcy restrictions orders"[71] ("BROs").

The AiB (or the Sheriff Court, if necessary) may make a BRO where the debtor's conduct either before or during the sequestration warrants it. Examples of such conduct would be failure to co-operate with the trustee, and the making of gratuitous alienations or the creation of unfair preferences.[72] The order must be made after sequestration but before the date of discharge, except where the sheriff is willing to permit an application after discharge.[73]

The consequences of a BRO being made vary, but might include the debtor being disqualified from acting in certain capacities (such as a company Director), or having to disclose that he is under a BRO when applying for credit. Depending on the severity of the debtor's misconduct, the AiB can impose a BRO for a period of between two and five years, whilst the court can impose a BRO for a period of between two and fifteen years. As in other matters discussed in this paragraph, the debtor can apply for a review of such a decision, and appeal to the court if necessary.[74]

Discharge will serve to free the debtor from all debts and obligations that existed at the time of his sequestration,[75] with certain exceptions such

---

[68] See BSA 1985 ss.54 and 54A.

[69] BSA 1985 s.54B.

[70] BSA 1985 s.54C.

[71] BSA 1985 s.56A, inserted by BDSA 2007 s.2. It is worth noting that the less-formal "bankruptcy restrictions undertakings" that were introduced at the same time have now been abolished under BADASA 2014 s.52.

[72] BSA 1985 s.56B.

[73] BSA 1985 s.56D.

[74] BSA 1985 s.56E.

[75] BSA 1985 s.55(1).

as fines[76] and student loans.[77] Recent case law affirms that the statutory exceptions are clear and unambiguous, and that there is limited scope for creative interpretation by disappointed creditors.[78] Once discharged, the debtor may, subject to any contribution or restrictions orders, acquire assets and property, and effectively continue with his life.

Key Concept

Once a sequestration is complete, the debtor is "discharged" and is freed from most of his previous debts. However, measures can be put in place that will affect him even after he is discharged.

Alternative procedures

Sequestration can be a lengthy process, and certainly has important **19–17** implications for a person's life. As with other areas of insolvency, it might be possible to remedy an individual's problematic situation without recourse to such an onerous procedure. It is possible, therefore, for an insolvent individual to enter into certain arrangements with his creditors, as an alternative to sequestration proceedings. Two such alternatives are the granting of a "trust deed" and accessing the "debt arrangement scheme".

Trust deeds

A trust deed is a voluntary agreement entered into between a debtor and **19–18** his creditors, whereby a portion of the debtor's estate is put in the hands of a trustee, to be administered for the benefit of the creditors. The trustee can raise funds from the sale of the debtor's property, and the debtor will usually be expected to make a contribution from his income. All monies raised will be used to repay the creditors as much of what they are owed as possible. If the debtor fails to comply with the conditions of a trust deed, the trustee can petition for the debtor's estate to be sequestrated.[79]

Key Concept

A trust deed is an alternative to sequestration, and involves an agreement being made between the debtor and his creditors. It is a less formal process, with fewer legal implications for the debtor.

The most significant drawback of a voluntary trust deed is that its success

---

[76] BSA 1985 s.55(2).
[77] BDSA 2007 s.34.
[78] See e.g. *Grimshaw v Bruce* [2011] CSOH 212.
[79] BSA 1985 s.5(2C).

depends largely on all creditors acceding (agreeing) to it. This is because any creditors who do not accede to the trust deed are not bound by its terms, and neither are new creditors bound by it. Such creditors may still effect diligence against the debtor (see para.19–20), which is clearly to the disadvantage of the creditors who are party to the trust deed.

As a result of such failings, voluntary trust deeds have proved unpopular in practice.[80] However, a more favourable alternative exists in the form of the protected trust deed. This is a deed which, provided it conforms to statutory criteria, will provide additional layers of protection against action by creditors.

Protected trust deeds are currently regulated by the Protected Trust Deeds (Scotland) Regulations 2013 ("PTDSR 2013").[81] These came into force on November 28, 2013, with any deeds created before this date continuing to be regulated by the older legislation.[82]

There are a number of conditions that must be met in order for a trust deed to become protected. The debtor must owe debts totalling at least £5,000, and his estate must not already be subject to sequestration procedure.[83] The trustee must be a suitably qualified person,[84] and must provide advice to the debtor as to the potential consequences of his granting a trust deed.[85]

The trust deed itself must state the following:

 (a) that all the debtor's estate, other than that excluded under statute, is conveyed to trustee;
 (b) that the debtor agrees to convey to the trustee any qualifying estate acquired during the subsequent four years; and
 (c) that the debtor will, if appropriate, make a contribution payment from his income.[86]

Upon the debtor granting the trust deed the trustee must, without delay, arrange with the AiB for notice of this to be published in the Register of Insolvencies.[87] He must then, within seven days, provide every creditor who has an interest in the affected estate with a copy of the trust deed, a statement of the debtor's financial affairs, and a statement of the anticipated funds that will be realised including any dividend that the creditors will be likely to receive.[88] Creditors then have five weeks within which to accede to the trust deed or raise an objection, with accession being presumed if no response is made. Provided a majority in number or

---

[80] See e.g. Protected Trust Deeds (Scotland) Regulations 2008 (SSI 2008/173) executive note.
[81] SSI 2013/318.
[82] This being either the Protected Trust Deeds (Scotland) Regulations 2008 (SSI 2008/173) or BSA 1985 Sch.5, as applicable.
[83] PTDSR 2013 r.4.
[84] PTDSR 2013 r.5.
[85] PTDSR 2013 r.7(3).
[86] PTDSR 2013 r.7(1).
[87] PTDSR 2013 r.9.
[88] PTDSR 2013 r.10(1).

two-thirds in value of the debtor's creditors accede (or fail to object), the trust deed will be granted protected status.[89] As soon as is reasonably practicable thereafter the trustee must provide all relevant documentation to the AiB for registration in the Register of Insolvencies.[90]

The effect of a trust deed becoming protected is that creditors are prevented from taking action against the debtor to enforce their debts, or to execute diligence against his assets, except in very limited circumstances.[91] The trustee will administer the affected estate and give annual accounts of his activities to the debtor, creditors and the AiB.[92] If there are sufficient funds, the trustee must make a dividend payment to creditors two years after the granting of the trust deed, and will make further dividend payments at six-monthly intervals.[93] This will continue until the end of the period during which the debtor is required to make a contribution from income payment, which is normally four years, though this can be shortened or lengthened as appropriate.[94]

Provided the debtor has complied with his obligations under the trust deed, the trustee will apply to the AiB seeking his discharge. Once discharged, the debtor will be free from all debts and obligations he was under at the time the deed was granted, subject to certain exceptions.[95]

Debt arrangement scheme

It is also possible for a debtor to access a statutory mechanism called the **19–19** "debt arrangement scheme",[96] which provides a facility for the orderly repayment of debts. Debtors who are unable to pay debts as they fall due, but who have a reasonable surplus income after meeting their basic living costs, can enter into a "debt payment programme" in order to spread their repayments over an agreed period. Creditors are prevented from enforcing debts whilst the debtor is participating in the programme and, subject to certain exceptions, prevented from executing diligence (see para.19–20) against the debtor's property.[97] The agreement of all creditors is usually required for a programme to be approved,[98] though this can be circumvented if the programme is considered fair and reasonable by the scheme administrator (in practice, this is usually the AiB).[99]

Under an approved debt payment programme, the debtor ceases making payments to individual creditors, and instead makes a single

---

[89] PTDSR 2013 r.10(2).
[90] PTDSR 2013 r.11(1).
[91] PTDSR 2013 rr.12–13.
[92] PTDSR 2013 r.21.
[93] PTDSR 2013 r.16.
[94] PTDSR 2013 r.8.
[95] PTDSR 2013 r.24.
[96] Governed by the Debt Arrangement and Attachment (Scotland) Act 2002 ("DAA 2002") and associated Regulations.
[97] DAA 2002 s.4.
[98] DAA 2002 s.2(4).
[99] Debt Arrangement Scheme (Scotland) Regulations 2011 (SSI 2011/141) r.25.

payment to an approved distributor, who is then responsible for the fair distribution of that payment among the debtor's creditors.[100]

In recent years, the debt arrangement scheme has proven to be an increasingly popular debt management solution.[101] It has also now been extended to include businesses, and can be accessed by certain "non-natural" legal persons, such as partnerships.[102]

Diligence

19–20 The law of diligence provides creditors with a range of legal procedures under which debts can be enforced. Most forms of diligence involve some exercise of control over certain assets of the debtor, a common example being seizure and sale of property. In order to be lawful, these procedures must be commenced only on the authority of a court order or, perhaps less commonly, on the terms of an instrument of debt. A creditor must usually make a final demand for payment, and must often (but not always) issue the debtor with a "debt advice and information package" (see para.19–06), before executing diligence.

Key Concept

Diligence is an area of the law that provides a range of procedures under which a creditor can force payment of a debt.

Arrestment

19–21 Arrestment is a process of diligence executed against property that belongs to the debtor, but is in the hands of a third party. A common example would be the funds in a debtor's bank account; these belong to the debtor, but are of course under the immediate control of the bank.

The effect of a successful arrestment is that the arrested assets are "frozen", and can be disposed of by neither the debtor nor the third party (who is known as the "arrestee"). The arrested assets remain in the possession of the arrestee, and will be given over to the creditor either upon the signing of a mandate to this effect by the debtor, or upon the raising of a successful action of furthcoming by the creditor. An action of furthcoming is an application made by the creditor to the court, for the passing of arrested assets into his ownership, or for the selling of arrested assets so that the proceeds can be given over to him.

Arrestment is governed in large part by the Debtors (Scotland) Act 1987 ("DSA 1987"), as amended. The rules and procedures of arrestment have undergone some changes in recent years, mainly due to criticisms

---

[100] Debt Arrangement Scheme (Scotland) Regulations 2011 r.16.

[101] Accountant in Bankruptcy, *Debt Arrangement Scheme Review* (2012). Available at *http://www.aib.gov.uk/publications/debt-arrangement-scheme-review-2012* [Accessed May 15, 2015].

[102] Debt Arrangement Scheme (Scotland) Amendment Regulations 2014 (SSI 2014/294).

that were levelled against the DSA 1987 as originally enacted.[103] The first of these was that creditors faced difficulty in ascertaining the value of the arrested assets, or indeed in ascertaining whether any assets had been arrested at all; for example, a debtor's bank account might already be devoid of funds. The second criticism was that the process could be somewhat cumbersome, as it potentially involved two separate legal actions.

These issues were addressed by the BDSA 2007. In terms of creditor uncertainty regarding arrested assets, a duty of disclosure is now placed on the arrestee. Under this duty the arrestee must inform the creditor of the nature and value of the arrested assets.[104] In addition, provisions allow for any arrested funds to be released to a creditor automatically after 14 weeks,[105] although this is subject to certain restrictions.[106]

It should be noted that the term "arrestment" is also used in relation to certain diligences done against a debtor's earnings, whereby an employer can be compelled to make deductions at source from a debtor's income. These involve quite different procedures, are separately regulated.[107]

Attachment

Attachment is a form of diligence executed against goods that are in the **19–22** possession of the debtor. It was introduced in 2002[108] as a replacement for the widely criticised "poinding and sale" procedure which, as well as being objectionable to many by its nature, was largely an ineffective method of recovering a debt.[109] A crucial difference between attachment and poinding is that attachment is less likely to involve the removal of property from a debtor's home, which was a central aspect of poinding's unpopularity.

Before a creditor can proceed with attachment, three conditions must be met. These are:

(a) that the debtor has been charged to pay the debt;
(b) that the period for payment has expired without payment being made; and
(c) that the creditor has provided the debtor with a debt advice and information package (see para.19–06).[110]

Certain restrictions apply to attachment. The procedure is only relevant in respect of corporeal moveable property (see Ch.11, "Property"),[111] and

---

[103] See e.g. E. Baijal, "The Bankruptcy and Diligence etc. (Scotland) Act 2007: The New Jewel in the Creditor's Crown" (2007) 9 S.L.T. 55–59.
[104] DSA 1987 s.73G, inserted by BDSA 2007 s.206.
[105] DSA 1987 s.73J, inserted by BDSA 2007 s.206.
[106] DSA 1987 s.73L, inserted by BDSA 2007 s.206
[107] See DSA 1987 Pt III.
[108] By the DAA 2002.
[109] See e.g. Scottish Law Commission, D. Nichols, *Poinding and Sale: Effective Enforcement and Debtor Protection* (1999), Scot. Law Com. No.110.
[110] DAA 2002 s.10(3).
[111] DAA 2002 s.10(1).

should not be confused with certain newer diligences such as "money attachment" (see para.19–24). Under the form of attachment being considered here, a range of items are exempt, including:

(a) tools and other items that are necessary for the debtor's profession, up to a combined value of £1,000;
(b) any vehicle reasonably required by the debtor, up to a value of £3,000[112];
(c) a mobile home that is the debtor's only or primary residence; and
(d) any tools or equipment reasonably required for keeping the garden or yard of a dwellinghouse in good order.[113]

It is not generally competent to execute attachment on a Sunday, or on a public holiday, or outwith the times of 08.00 and 20.00.[114] As mentioned above, attachment does not tend to involve the removal of property from a debtor's home, though this is possible in exceptional circumstances.[115] It is far more common for attachment to be executed against items being kept outwith the debtor's home.

Once attached, the property will then be valued, by a suitably skilled person if necessary, within 14 days.[116] The property may be "redeemed" (bought back) by the debtor at the valuation reached upon,[117] else the property will be removed and put up for auction.[118]

Inhibition

19–23 Inhibition is a form of diligence executed against a debtor's heritable property. It differs significantly from arrestment and attachment in that it does not involve the creditor taking control of the debtor's assets. Instead, it puts restrictions on the debtor's use of the inhibited property. It is therefore perhaps better viewed as a defensive measure to encourage settlement of a debt by the debtor, rather than as a positive remedy exercised by the creditor to recover his debt. Historically, inhibition was regulated largely by common law, but the BDSA 2007 made extensive statutory provision in relation to this area.

A creditor can execute an inhibition on the authority of a relevant decree or document of debt.[119] The debtor must be served with a "schedule of inhibition" and must also be provided with a debt advice and

---

[112] Increased from £1,000 by the Bankruptcy (Scotland) Amendment Regulations 2010 (SSI 2010/367) s.4.
[113] DAA 2002 s.11(1).
[114] DAA 2002 s.12.
[115] DAA 2002 Pt 3.
[116] DAA 2002 s.15(2) and (3).
[117] DAA 2002 s.18.
[118] DAA 2002 s.19.
[119] BDSA 2007 s.146.

information package (see para.19–06).[120] The inhibition must then be registered in the Register of Inhibitions and Adjudications.[121]

The effect of an inhibition is that the debtor is prohibited from voluntarily selling the property, and from using it for certain purposes, e.g. as security. If the debtor does undertake any prohibited act in respect of the inhibited property, he will be held in breach of the inhibition.[122]

An inhibition will generally be effective for five years,[123] or shorter if the matter resulting in the inhibition is resolved. The BDSA 2007 makes it clear that an inhibition will cease to have effect if the amount due (plus interest and expenses) is paid in full,[124] or if any other relevant obligation is complied with.[125]

Money attachment

This is a new form of diligence introduced by the BDSA 2007,[126] which **19–24** allows for the attachment (see para.19–22) of money owned by the debtor. "Money" for these purposes is taken to mean cash in any currency, or banking instruments such as cheques and promissory notes.[127] An important exception is that any coins or banknotes that have a higher intrinsic value than their face value (i.e. those that are collectable) cannot be attached.[128]

A number of other restrictions apply to money attachment. It is not possible to attach money that is being kept within a dwelling,[129] and it is also not competent to attach money that would be capable of being arrested.[130] Similarly with attachment of corporeal moveable property, money attachment generally cannot be carried out on a Sunday, on a public holiday or outwith the times of 08.00 and 20.00.[131]

Land attachment

This is another new form of diligence, introduced by the BDSA 2007 to **19–25** replace the older (and of late rarely seen) diligence of adjudication.[132] At the time of writing, the relevant Part of the Act[133] has not yet been brought into force; if and when it is, adjudication will thereafter be abolished.[134]

---

[120] BDSA 2007 s.147.
[121] BDSA 2007 s.148.
[122] BDSA 2007 s.160.
[123] Conveyancing (Scotland) Act 1924 s.44(3)(aa).
[124] BDSA 2007 s.157.
[125] BDSA 2007 s.158.
[126] BDSA 2007 Pt 8.
[127] BDSA 2007 s.175(1).
[128] BDSA 2007 s.175(1).
[129] BDSA 2007 s.174(3).
[130] BDSA 2007 s.174(3).
[131] BDSA 2007 s.176(1) and (2).
[132] A rare modern example of adjudication can be found in *Hull v Campbell* [2011] CSOH 24.
[133] BDSA 2007 Pt 4 Ch.2.
[134] BDSA 2007 s.79.

The process of land attachment is similar to that of attachment of moveable property (see para.19–22), but instead the subject of the attachment is land. This can be land owned by the debtor, or land of which the debtor is a tenant under an assignable long lease.[135] Land attachment is only competent to enforce a debt exceeding £3,000.[136]

The effect of land attachment is that the creditor is given a subordinate real right over the land, as security (see Chapter 21, "Rights in Security") for the outstanding debt plus any accrued interest and expenses.[137] After a period of six months has elapsed since registration of the notice of land attachment, if the outstanding debt is still in excess of £3,000, the creditor can apply for a warrant to sell the attached land.[138]

Residual attachment

19–26 A final new form of diligence introduced by the BDSA 2007 is that of residual attachment,[139] though like land attachment (see para.19–25) the relevant provisions have not yet been brought into force. The intention here is to allow the attachment of certain types of property that cannot be attached by any other form of diligence. The BDSA 2007 gives power to the Scottish Ministers to specify what property may be attached in this way, subject to certain rules and exemptions.[140]

If a creditor wishes to execute residual attachment, he must apply to the court for sanction.[141] If a residual attachment order is granted, this will confer on the creditor a right in security over the attached property.[142] If the debt (plus interest and expenses) remains unpaid, the creditor can then apply to the court for a satisfaction order. If granted, this will allow provisions to be made for satisfaction of the debt by, for example, sale of the property, or transfer of the property to the creditor.[143]

CORPORATE INSOLVENCY

Company voluntary arrangements

19–27 When a company is facing serious financial difficulty—or indeed if it is already insolvent—steps can be taken in an attempt to remedy the situation and prevent the company from collapsing. Under the Insolvency Act 1986 ("IA 1986"), an agreement can be entered into between the company and its creditors, whereby existing debts are frozen, and the company is allowed to continue trading. Over a stipulated time period,

---

[135] BDSA 2007 s.82.
[136] BDSA 2007 s.83(2) and (3).
[137] BDSA 2007 s.86(5) and (6).
[138] BDSA 2007 s.92.
[139] BDSA 2007 Pt 4 Ch.3.
[140] BDSA 2007 s.129.
[141] BDSA 2007 s.130.
[142] BDSA 2007 s.134(2).
[143] BDSA 2007 s.136(4).

which is commonly between three and five years, regular payments are made to creditors, with a view to eventually repaying the outstanding debts. These agreements are known as "company voluntary arrangements", although they are sometimes referred to as CVAs or, simply, voluntary arrangements.

> **Key Concept**
>
> A company voluntary arrangement is where a company enters into an agreement with its creditors outlining how debts are to be repaid.

Initiating the procedure

A proposal for voluntary arrangements can be made by the company's **19–28** directors,[144] regardless of whether or not the company is insolvent, but not if the company is already in liquidation (see para.19–45) or administration (see para.19–31). In the latter situation, a liquidator or administrator is empowered to make the proposal.[145]

In either case, the voluntary arrangement must be supervised by a "nominee". Where the directors have made the proposal, they will appoint the nominee, who must be a licensed insolvency practitioner[146] or a member of a body recognised for this purpose.[147] If a liquidator or administrator makes the proposal, he will act as nominee.

After investigating the proposals the nominee must, within 28 days, make a report to the court giving his opinion as to whether the scheme is viable.[148] (A court report is not required if the nominee is already a liquidator or an administrator.) The nominee will then order separate meetings of the company members and the creditors, so that the proposals can be considered and voted on.[149]

Approval of the scheme

At the meeting of the company members, approval of the scheme requires **19–29** a simple majority in value; i.e. members representing more than half of the total votes must be in favour of the proposals. At the meeting of company creditors, approval requires a qualified majority of three-quarters support.[150]

If the scheme is approved, the arrangement will be binding on all ordinary creditors. The arrangement cannot involve any proposal

---

[144] IA 1986 s.1(1).
[145] IA 1986 s.1(3).
[146] IA 1986 s.1(2).
[147] As outlined under IA 1986 s.389A.
[148] IA 1986 s.2.
[149] IA 1986 s.3.
[150] Insolvency (Scotland) Rules 1986 (SI 1986/1915) rr.1.16A & B.

Business Law in Scotland

affecting the rights of secured and preferential creditors, unless they agree to the contrary.[151]

Subsequent procedure

19–30 If the scheme is approved, the nominee's function is to act as supervisor of the scheme and to oversee its implementation.[152] As supervisor, the nominee has a range of decision-making powers, but any decisions he makes are subject to potential challenge by the creditors.[153]

The intention behind these voluntary arrangements is, as outlined above, that debts are repaid, thus preventing the company from being wound up. It is possible, of course, that in spite of the scheme being put in place, the company's financial position will not improve, and it will ultimately be forced into winding up regardless.

Administration

19–31 Administration is a process by which a specialist individual is given the task of managing a company's affairs, with a view to improving the company's financial position. The primary function of this "administrator" is to rescue the company from financial difficulty, allowing it to continue as a going concern. However, if this is not possible, then there are a number of secondary functions, which involve facilitating a more favourable position for the company's creditors.

Key Concept

Administration is where a specialist takes control of a company's affairs, usually in an effort to rescue it from insolvency.

The area of administration is governed largely by the IA 1986, although significant additions to this Act were made by the Enterprise Act 2002 ("EA 2002"). Under the IA 1986, the courts have the power to make an administration order in relation to any company that is already insolvent, or is likely to soon become insolvent. The EA 2002 introduced an additional simpler process, by which an administrator could be appointed without the need to go to court.

The EA 2002 also introduced two important new concepts relating to floating charges (see Chapter 21, "Rights in Security"). These are the "qualifying floating charge" ("QFC") and the "qualifying floating charge holder" ("QFCH").[154] A QFC is one to which the EA 2002 applies, while

---

IA 1986 s.4.
IA 1986 s.7(2).
IA 1986 s.7(3).
EA 2002 Pt 10.

a QFCH is a person who holds a QFC that relates to the whole or substantially the whole of the company's property.[155]

The purposes of administration

As stated above, the primary function of an administrator is to improve **19–32** the company's financial position. However, the purpose of an adminis- tration order can go beyond this remit, and indeed it may not be possible to rescue the company from insolvency at all. An administrator must therefore perform his functions with the following objectives:

(a) to rescue the company as a going concern;
(b) to achieve a better result for the company's creditors as a whole than would be likely if the company were wound up; or
(c) to realise property in order to make a distribution to one or more secured or preferential creditors, provided this can be done without unnecessarily harming the interests of the creditors as a whole.[156]

Court appointment of an administrator

The court route to administration is commenced by petition to court, **19–33** which can be presented by the company members, the directors or any creditor.[157] The court will grant the order if:

(a) it is satisfied that the company is unable to pay its debts, or likely to soon become unable to pay its debts; and
(b) it is of the opinion that the order would be likely to achieve at least one of the statutory purposes of administration.[158]

It is also possible for a QFCH to make the petition. In this case the court need only be satisfied that the charge is indeed a QFC, and that it is enforceable.[159]

Upon successful application, an administrator will be appointed. He must, as soon as is reasonably practicable, send notice of his appointment to the company and each of its creditors, and must advertise his appointment in the *Edinburgh Gazette*. He must also, within seven days, give notice of the court order to the Registrar of Companies.[160]

Out of court appointment

The EA 2002 also introduced provisions allowing an administrator to be **19–34** appointed without the need to go to court. This simplifies the process somewhat, and also avoids the expense of a court application. The

---

[155] IA 1986 Sch.B1 para.14.
[156] IA 1986 Sch.B1 para.3.
[157] IA 1986 Sch.B1 para.12.
[158] IA 1986 Sch.B1 para.11.
[159] IA 1986 Sch.B1 para.35.
[160] IA 1986 Sch.B1 para.46.

purposes of administration remain the same when an out of court appointment is made.

An out of court appointment can be made by either a QFCH, or by the company or its directors. The procedure to be followed differs depending on who is making the appointment.

Out of court appointment by a QFCH

19-35 When a QFCH intends to appoint an administrator using the out of court route, he must give two business days' written notice to (or otherwise secure the consent of) any QFCH who has priority.[161] The QFCH must then file with the court the following:

(a) a notice of appointment;
(b) a relevant statutory declaration; and
(c) a statement of consent made by the administrator.[162]

Upon satisfaction of the above requirements, the appointment is effective.

Out of court appointment by the company or the directors

19-36 Where an out of court appointment is to be made by the company or directors, at least five business days' notice in writing must be given to any person who is entitled to appoint an administrator as a QFCH.[163] This written notice must be filed with the court as soon as is reasonably practicable, and must be accompanied by a statutory declaration by the person who proposes to make the appointment that:

(a) the company is or is likely to become unable to pay its debts;
(b) the company is not in liquidation; and
(c) as far as can be ascertained, appointment of an administrator is not otherwise prevented.[164]

Upon expiry of the notice period, the person seeking to make the appointment must then file with the court a notice of the appointment and a statutory declaration of compliance. The notice of appointment must identify the administrator, and must be accompanied by a statement of consent made by him.[165]

Upon satisfaction of the above requirements, the appointment is effective.

---

[161] IA 1986 Sch.B1 para.15(1).
[162] IA 1986 Sch.B1 para.18.
[163] IA 1986 Sch.B1 para.26(1).
[164] IA 1986 Sch.B1 para.27.
[165] IA 1986 Sch.B1 para.29.

Effect of administrator's appointment

Regardless of how the administrator has been appointed, once the rele- **19–37** vant procedure has been completed, the company is said to be "in administration". This fact must be publicised on every business document issued by or on behalf of the company.[166]

The appointment of an administrator affords the company certain protections against action by its creditors. A "moratorium" is enforced which prevents creditors initiating insolvency proceedings (subject to certain exceptions)[167] or any other legal process such as the enforcement of securities and repossession of goods, except with the consent of the administrator or the court.[168] These restrictions on creditor action remain in place for the duration of the administration.

The administration process

Following his appointment, the administrator will request of the com- **19–38** pany's officers a statement of the company's affairs. This statement of affairs is the starting point for the administration, and must be supplied within 11 days of the administrator making the request.[169] The statement details the company's assets and liabilities, and will often have been prepared by the company's accountant.

The administrator is then generally empowered to do anything he feels is necessary to achieve the purpose of the administration. This includes the power to:

(a) sell company property;
(b) raise or borrow money on behalf of the company;
(c) bring or defend legal action in the company's name;
(d) call meetings of the creditors or members; and
(e) remove and appoint directors as appropriate.[170]

Within eight weeks of the administration order having been made, the administrator must make a statement of his proposals as to how the purpose of the administration order is to be achieved. This must be sent to the Registrar of Companies, the members of the company and to all creditors of whom the administrator is aware.[171]

The proposals must also be laid before a meeting of the creditors, to be held within 10 weeks of the company going into administration.[172] At this meeting, the creditors will vote, by a simple majority in value, on whether or not they wish to approve the proposals.[173]

The administrator must report the result of the meeting to the court

---

[166] IA 1986 Sch.B1 para.45.
[167] IA 1986 Sch.B1 para.42.
[168] IA 1986 Sch.B1 para.43.
[169] IA 1986 Sch.B1 para.48.
[170] IA 1986 Sch.B1 Pt 8.
[171] IA 1986 Sch.B1 para.49.
[172] IA 1986 Sch.B1 para.51.
[173] IA 1986 Sch.B1 para.53.

and must also notify the Registrar of Companies. If the creditors refuse to approve the proposals, the court may either discharge the administration order or make any other order as it sees fit in the circumstances.[174]

Ending of the administration

19–39 The administrator must complete the administration within 12 months of the date of appointment, at which time his appointment will automatically come to an end. This date may be extended by a further six months with the consent of the creditors, or by any such period as is deemed necessary by the court.[175]

There are several possible outcomes of administration. Assuming the administrator's proposals are accepted by the creditors, any payments due will be made, subject to statutory rules.[176] The most desirable scenario is, of course, that the purpose of the administration order will have been achieved, though in practice this is not always the case. Where a company cannot be rescued, the administrator may be required to petition for the company to be liquidated and wound up (see para.19–45).[177]

Two alternative courses of action are available to an out-of-court appointed administrator. If, at any time during the process, he is of the opinion that the administration has been successful to the point where the company has been rescued, he can file a notice to this effect with the court and the Registrar of Companies.[178] He must also send copies of this notice to the creditors. Upon filing of the notice in court, the administration ends. If, on the other hand, he is at any point of the opinion that the purpose of the administration *cannot* be achieved, he may apply to the court for a discharge of the order.[179] This will likely result in the same outcome as above, i.e. a petition for liquidation and winding up.

Receivership

19–40 Receivership is not a procedure that seeks to rescue the company, as administration or company voluntary arrangements might. It is a process whereby a creditor who holds a floating charge (see Chapter 21, "Rights in Security") over the company's assets arranges for these to be seized, and sold off ("realised") with a view to repaying the debt. The individual appointed to seize and realise these assets is known as a "receiver".

---

[174] IA 1986 Sch.B1 para.55.
[175] IA 1986 Sch.B1 para.76.
[176] IA 1986 Sch.B1 para.65.
[177] IA 1986 Sch.B1 paras 83–84.
[178] IA 1986 Sch.B1 para.80.
[179] IA 1986 Sch.B1 para.79.

> **Key Concept**
>
> Receivership is where an individual takes control of certain company assets, which he will sell with a view to repaying the creditor who appointed him.
>
> Receivership became unpopular towards the end of the twentieth century, mainly due to the fact that arbitrary seizure and sale of a company's assets tends to have a detrimental effect on the company as a whole.[180] The law regulating receivership was changed significantly by the EA 2002, which came into force in September 2003 and generally prohibits the appointment of receivers in respect of charges created after this date. However, it is still legitimate to appoint a receiver in respect of charges created before the EA 2002 came into force.

Appointment of a receiver

A receiver may be appointed by a creditor who holds a floating charge **19–41** over any part of a company's assets. It is also possible for the court to appoint a receiver on application from a floating charge holder.[181]

A floating charge holder is justified in appointing a receiver on the happening of any event specified in the instrument of charge as entitling such appointment. A common example of such an event would be failure by the company to repay a debt by a specified date. It is also possible for a receiver to be appointed on the following statutory grounds:

(a) the expiry of 21 days after the making of a demand for payment, without payment being made;
(b) the expiry of two months during the whole of which interest due under the charge has been in arrears;
(c) the making of an order or the passing of a resolution to wind up the company; and
(d) the appointment of a receiver by virtue of any other floating charge created by the company.[182]

Notification must be given to the Registrar of Companies within seven days of the appointment.[183]

When a receiver is appointed, he must immediately notify the company and publish the fact that he has been appointed. He must also, within 28

---

[180] See e.g. M. Hunter, "The Nature and Functions of a Rescue Culture" (1999) Nov J.B.L. 491–520.
[181] IA 1986 s.51.
[182] IA 1986 s.52.
[183] IA 1986 s.53.

days, notify all the company's creditors of his appointment.[184] In addition, every business document issued by or on behalf of the company must include a statement that a receiver has been appointed.[185]

Receiver's powers

19–42 A receiver's powers are essentially limited to those outlined in the Instrument of Charge, and those powers granted by statute. Among a receiver's most significant statutory powers are:

    (a) to take possession of company property;
    (b) to sell company property;
    (c) to appoint a solicitor or accountant, or other professional person to assist him in performance of his functions;
    (d) to do all such things as may be necessary for the realisation of the property; and
    (e) to call up any uncalled capital of the company.[186]

Distribution of monies

19–43 Although the receiver's duty is to the creditor who appointed him, and indeed his function is to repay that creditor, he cannot be ignorant as to the rights of other creditors. Some of these creditors will have debts that rank higher than that of the floating charge holder and, when distributing realised assets, the receiver is bound to recognise these prior-ranking claims before paying over any monies to the floating charge holder who appointed him. Therefore, the distribution of monies must be made in the following order:

    (a) any creditor who holds a fixed security over property which is also the subject of the floating charge and which ranks prior to, or equally with, the floating charge;
    (b) any creditor who, before the receiver's appointment, has effectually executed diligence against property of the company that is also the subject of the floating charge;
    (c) debts incurred by the receiver in the course of the receivership;
    (d) expenses of the receivership and the remuneration of the receiver;
    (e) preferential creditors who have intimated their claims within six months; and
    (f) the holder of the floating charge by virtue of which the receiver was appointed.[187]

---

[184] IA 1986 s.65.
[185] IA 1986 s.64.
[186] IA 1986 Sch.2.
[187] IA 1986 s.60(1).

Termination of receivership

Once the receiver has completed the purpose for which he was appointed, **19–44** the receivership will come to an end. Notice of termination of the receivership must be given, within 14 days, to the Registrar of Companies.[188]

Liquidation

Liquidation is the process by which all of a company's assets are **19–45** ingathered, and used to repay existing debts. The company's affairs are "wound up" and, after the process is complete and notice has been given to the Registrar of Companies, the company is dissolved and ceases to exist. Any outstanding debts not satisfied by the distribution of the company's assets will expire along with the company.

Key Concept

Liquidation is where a company's assets are sold off, after which the company is dissolved and ceases to exist.

It is most commonly the case that a company is wound up because it cannot be rescued from insolvency. In such a case, circumstance more than choice has determined the company's fate. However, there are various other reasons why a company might be wound up, so it is worth bearing in mind that insolvency is *not* a prerequisite of liquidation.

Broadly, a company may be wound up by one of two methods: compulsory liquidation and voluntary liquidation. In practice, voluntary liquidation is more common.

Liquidation 1: compulsory winding up

A compulsory liquidation is commenced by the presentation of a petition **19–46** for a winding up to the court. There are a number of situations that justify such a petition being presented,[189] the most common ground being that the company is unable to pay its debts. The court is not bound to grant the petition, regardless of the reason for it being presented.

Making the petition

A petition for winding up can be presented by a number of parties. **19–47** Among the most common are the company itself, the directors, creditors and "contributories", i.e. any person who is liable to contribute to the assets of the company upon winding up.[190] It is also possible for an

---

[188] IA 1986 s.62(5).
[189] IA 1986 s.122.
[190] IA 1986 s.124.

administrator (see para.19–31)[191] or (in Scotland) a receiver (see para.19–40)[192] to present the petition.

Such a petition may be presented if:

(a) the company has passed a special resolution to that effect;
(b) the company is a Plc that has failed to obtain a trading certificate within 12 months of incorporation;
(c) the company has not commenced its business within one year of incorporation, or has suspended its business for an entire year;
(d) the company is unable to pay its debts; and
(e) the court is of the opinion that it is just and equitable that the company should be wound up.[193]

In addition to these grounds, it is also possible to present a petition for winding up of a Scottish company if there is a floating charge over the company's assets, and the court is satisfied that the security of the creditor is in jeopardy.[194]

A company is deemed to be unable to pay its debts if it can be proved that the value of its assets is less than the extent of its liabilities, or if:

(a) a creditor for £750 or more serves a written demand for payment, and the debt is not satisfied within three weeks;
(b) payment is not made within the time allowed following a court order to repay the debts; or
(c) it is proved to the satisfaction of the court that the company is unable to pay its debts as they fall due.[195]

Effects of a winding up order

19–48 Upon the making of a winding up order by the court, the company is said to be "in liquidation", as from the date on which the petition was presented. The Registrar of Companies and AiB must be notified as to this fact within seven days.[196] Any records held pertaining to the company will be amended accordingly, and all business documents issued from then on by or on behalf of the company must state that the company is in liquidation.[197]

The winding up order has a number of important consequences, for example:

(a) no legal action may be commenced against the company without the leave of the court[198];

---

[191] IA 1986 s.14(1).
[192] IA 1986 s.55(2).
[193] IA 1986 s.122(1).
[194] IA 1986 s.122(2).
[195] IA 1986 s.123.
[196] IA 1986 s.130(1).
[197] IA 1986 s.188.
[198] IA 1986 s.130(2).

(b) all sales or other dispositions of the company's property and all transfers of the company's shares are void unless the court orders otherwise[199]; and

(c) all diligences executed within 60 days prior to the winding up order being made are rendered ineffectual.[200]

Appointment of the liquidator

It is open to the courts, upon the presentation of a petition for winding up, to take charge of the company's affairs by appointing a "provisional" liquidator. His function is to protect the interests of the creditors, pending the outcome of the court hearing. To this end, he will have such powers as are conferred on him by the court.[201]　　**19–49**

Where the court makes a winding up order, it will at the same time appoint an "interim" liquidator, who must hold a meeting of the creditors and, if appropriate, a meeting of the contributories.[202] The purpose of this meeting is to select a person to take over as the company's "liquidator" and oversee the winding up in full. If no appropriate person is identified at the meeting, the courts will appoint a liquidator.[203]

It is also possible for a liquidation committee to be established, to advise and assist the liquidator in his functions, and to sanction certain powers the liquidator might wish to exercise. The committee may consist of both creditors and contributories, except where the company is being wound up due to an inability to pay its debts, in which case the committee will be composed entirely of creditors.[204]

Liquidator's function and powers

The primary functions of the liquidator are to ingather the company's assets, and apply those assets in satisfaction of the company's liabilities.[205] The liquidator has a range of powers, which are divided broadly into those that can be exercised without prior sanction of the court (or liquidation committee, if applicable), and those that do require prior sanction.　　**19–50**

Powers that require sanction include:

(a) the power to pay any class of creditor in full;

(b) the power to bring or defend certain legal proceedings; and

(c) the power to carry on the business of the company so far as may be necessary for its beneficial winding up.[206]

---

[199] IA 1986 s.127.
[200] IA 1986 s.185.
[201] IA 1986 s.135.
[202] IA 1986 s.138.
[203] IA 1986 s.139.
[204] IA 1986 s.142.
[205] IA 1986 s.143.
[206] IA 1986 Sch.4 Pts 1 and 2.

(The powers to defend legal actions and to carry on company business require no prior sanction in a voluntary winding up—see para.19–53.)
Powers that require no prior sanction include:

(a) the power to sell any of the company's property;
(b) the power to raise money on the security of the company's assets; and
(c) the power to do all such other things as may be necessary for winding up the company's affairs and distributing its assets.[207]

Distribution of monies

19–51 Once the liquidator has ingathered all the company's assets, he must then apply those assets to the company's debts. All proven creditor claims must be ranked against each other to determine the order of payment. The liquidator must apply assets according to the following ranking:

(a) holders of fixed securities;
(b) costs of liquidation, including the liquidator's remuneration;
(c) preferential creditors (most commonly, unpaid employees of the company)[208];
(d) floating charge holders, subject to the rule that any floating charge created within 12 months prior to commencement of the winding up is void; and
(e) ordinary creditors.[209]

Ordinary creditors rank equally with each other, and might not be paid at all if the funds by this point have been exhausted. Any surplus (i.e. if the company was solvent) is distributed among the members proportionately to their shareholding.

Dissolution of the company

19–52 Once all assets have been applied to proven debts, and any surplus monies distributed among the company members, the liquidation is complete.[210] The liquidator, having held a final meeting of the creditors to present his report on the winding up, must inform the Registrar of Companies. After a period of three months the company is dissolved and ceases to exist.[211]

Liquidation 2: voluntary winding up

19–53 The process of going to court can be expensive and time consuming. Therefore, a more straightforward procedure can be utilised when there is a broad agreement that the company has no viable future. This procedure

---

[207] IA 1986 Sch.4 Pt 3.
[208] IA 1986 Sch.6.
[209] Insolvency (Scotland) Rules 1986 r.4.66.
[210] IA 1986 s.146.
[211] IA 1986 s.205.

is available in the form of voluntary winding up, which allows the company's affairs to be settled without the formality of petitioning the court.

There are two distinct situations in which a company might be wound up voluntarily. The first is where there is no doubt as to the company's solvency. In this situation, the creditors need not be involved, as there is no risk of their debts being left unsatisfied. The liquidation can therefore proceed as a "members' voluntary winding up". However, if there *is* some doubt as to whether all debts of the company will be paid, the creditors will likely wish to supervise the process, and so the liquidation must proceed as a "creditors' voluntary winding up".

Key Concept

If a solvent company is to be wound up voluntarily, this can be done as a members' voluntary winding up. If the company is not solvent, the procedure employed must be a creditors' voluntary winding up.

Other than where specifically highlighted, the rules outlined above for compulsory winding up (e.g. the effects of the winding up and the ranking of creditors' claims) remain the same.

Commencement of a voluntary winding up

Regardless of whether or not the creditors will supervise the liquidation, a **19–54** voluntary winding up is commenced by the passing of a resolution to that effect by the members of the company at a general meeting. A company can be wound up by ordinary resolution on the expiry of a fixed period for the duration of the company (or on the occurrence of a specified event), or by special resolution if the company cannot, by reason of its liabilities, continue its business.[212]

Within 15 days, the company must send a copy of the resolution to the Registrar of Companies[213] and must give notice in the *Edinburgh Gazette* within 14 days.[214] The winding up is deemed to have commenced at the time of the passing of the resolution.[215]

Members' voluntary winding up

The essential feature of a members' voluntary winding up is that the **19–55** company must be in a position to pay off all outstanding debts. The directors must make a "declaration of solvency" to this effect, stating that they have made a full investigation of the company's affairs and are

---

[212] IA 1986 s.84(1).
[213] IA 1986 s.84(3).
[214] IA 1986 s.85.
[215] IA 1986 s.86.

of the opinion that the company will, within a period not exceeding 12 months, be able to pay all its debts.[216]

The liquidator in this case is appointed by the members,[217] and there is no liquidation committee. The liquidator must keep the members informed as to the progress of the winding up, and must call meetings for this purpose. If at any point the liquidator becomes of the opinion that the company will *not* after all be able to pay its debts in full, he must call a meeting of the creditors to notify them of this[218]; from the date of the meeting, the liquidation will proceed as a creditors' voluntary winding up.[219]

Once the winding up is complete, a final meeting of the members must be called by the liquidator.[220] His final report and accounts will be given at this meeting, after which he must notify the Registrar that the company's affairs have been wound up. The company will then be dissolved as of three months from the date of notification.[221]

Creditors' voluntary winding up

19–56 If there is any doubt as to the company's ability to repay its debts the directors will, of course, be unable to make a statutory declaration of solvency. In such a case, the winding up must proceed as a creditors' voluntary winding up. The decision to commence a winding up must still be taken by the company members at a general meeting, but there must be an additional meeting of the creditors called within 14 days of the resolution being passed.[222]

At this meeting, a full statement of the company's affairs must be placed before the creditors.[223] The creditors may appoint a liquidator, or may accept a nominee of the company as liquidator.[224] They may also establish a liquidation committee.[225]

The liquidator in this case is answerable to the creditors, and must hold meetings to keep them informed of the progress of the winding up.[226] Once the winding up is complete and a final meeting of the creditors has been called,[227] the Registrar must be notified that the company has been wound up. The company will then be dissolved as of three months from the date of notification.[228]

---

[216] IA 1986 s.89.
[217] IA 1986 s.91.
[218] IA 1986 s.95.
[219] IA 1986 s.96.
[220] IA 1986 s.94.
[221] IA 1986 s.201.
[222] IA 1986 s.98.
[223] IA 1986 s.99.
[224] IA 1986 s.100.
[225] IA 1986 s.101.
[226] IA 1986 s.105.
[227] IA 1986 s.106.
[228] IA 1986 s.201.

▼ CHAPTER SUMMARY

PERSONAL INSOLVENCY

(1) Sequestration of a debtor's estate can be commenced by the debtor, his **19–57**
creditors, or a trustee acting under a trust deed.

(2) A trustee in sequestration is appointed to recover, manage and realise
the debtor's assets, and distribute them amongst the debtor's creditors.

(3) Property that is essential for the maintenance of the debtor's family life,
or for the operation of the debtor's business (up to £1,000) do not vest
in the trustee.

(4) To protect creditors, certain transactions of the debtor prior to his
sequestration can be challenged by the trustee. Challengeable transactions include gratuitous alienations, unfair preferences and diligences
commenced within 60 days prior to sequestration.

(5) The trustee must pay debts according to a statutory order, laid down by
the Bankruptcy (Scotland) Act 1985 s.51.

(6) A debtor will be eligible for discharge from bankruptcy after one year,
but this is dependent upon his conduct during the sequestration.

(7) As an alternative to sequestration, a debtor can enter into a trust deed
with his creditors, or access the statutory debt arrangement scheme.

(8) Arrestment is where assets of the debtor being held by third parties are
"frozen", and in time are handed over to the creditor to be sold for
repayment of a debt.

(9) Attachment is where assets of the debtor that are in his possession are
removed, valued and sold for repayment of a debt.

(10) Inhibition is where restrictions are put on the debtor's use of his
property, to encourage repayment of a debt.

CORPORATE INSOLVENCY

(1) A company facing financial difficulty can enter into a voluntary
arrangement with its creditors whereby a schedule for repayment of
debts is agreed.

(2) Administration is a process whereby a specialist takes control of a
company's affairs, in an effort to improve its financial position.

(3) An administrator can be appointed either by the court, or by a qualifying floating charge holder, or by the company.

(4) When a company is in administration, it is protected against a range of
legal proceedings that might otherwise be taken by creditors.

(5) An administrator has a wide range of powers, including the power to
sell company property, and raise or borrow money on the company's
behalf.

(6) Receivership is a process by which a creditor who holds a floating
charge can appoint a receiver to take control of the charged assets, and
sell them with a view to recovering a debt.

(7) A receiver has a range of powers, but he must exercise these powers
subject to the rights of any prior-ranking creditors.

(8) Liquidation is a process by which the assets of a company are sold off,
and the money used to repay as much of the company's debt as possible.

At the end of this "winding up" process the company will be dissolved and will cease to exist.

(9) Winding up can either be compulsory, which requires a petition to the court, or voluntary, where the company members decide that the company should be wound up.

(10) If the company is solvent when the decision is made to commence a voluntary winding up, this can be done as a members' voluntary winding up. If the company is insolvent, the procedure will proceed as a creditors' voluntary winding up.

? QUICK QUIZ

- Explain briefly what is meant by insolvency.
- What is a trustee in sequestration's main function?
- Briefly outline the rules regulating the debtor's discharge from bankruptcy.
- Explain briefly the diligences of arrestment, attachment and inhibition.
- What are the benefits of a company voluntary arrangement to a company that is facing financial difficulty?
- What is the main purpose of administration?
- Under what circumstances can a creditor of a company appoint a receiver?
- In terms of insolvency procedures, why is administration often seen as a preferable alternative to receivership?
- Briefly outline any *two* circumstances that might justify a company being put into liquidation.
- What is the essential difference between a members' voluntary winding up and a creditors' voluntary winding up?

📖 FURTHER READING

Books: Personal Insolvency

➤ A. Adie, *Bankruptcy* (Edinburgh: W. Green, 2012).
➤ F. Davidson and L. Macgregor, *Commercial Law in Scotland*, 3rd edn (Edinburgh: W. Green, 2014).
➤ G. Maher, *The Law and Practice of Diligence*, 2nd edn (London: Bloomsbury, 2011).
➤ N. Grier, *Debt* (Edinburgh: W. Green, 1998).
➤ W. McBryde, *Bankruptcy*, 2nd edn (Edinburgh: W. Green, 1995).

Books: Corporate Insolvency

➤ D. Keenan and J. Bisacre, *Smith and Keenan's Company Law (Scottish Edition)*, 14th edn (London: Pearson/Longman, 2009).
➤ D. McKenzie Skene, *Insolvency Law in Scotland* (Edinburgh: Tottel Publishing, 2000).

> L. Sealy and D. Milman, *Annotated Guide to the Insolvency Legislation* (London: Sweet & Maxwell, 2010).
> L. Sealy, *Cases and Materials in Company Law*, 10th edn (Oxford: Oxford University Press, 2013).
> N. Grier, *Company Law*, 4th edn (Edinburgh: W. Green, 2014).
> St Clair and Lord Drummond Young, *The Law of Corporate Insolvency in Scotland*, 4th edn (Edinburgh: W. Green, 2011).

⌨ RELEVANT WEBLINKS

> The Accountant in Bankruptcy: *www.aib.gov.uk* [Accessed May 15, 2015].
> The Registrar of Companies: *https://www.gov.uk/government/organisations/companies-house* [Accessed May 15, 2015].
> The Register of Insolvencies: *http://roi.aib.gov.uk/roi* [Accessed May 15, 2015].
> UK Legislation Database: *www.legislation.gov.uk* [Accessed May 15, 2015].

Chapter 20　Negotiable Instruments

FIONA GRANT[1]

► CHAPTER OVERVIEW

20–01 This chapter explains the law on negotiable instruments. A negotiable instrument is a signed document[2] detailing the ownership of a debt which can be used by debtors as a method of paying for goods or services. A negotiable instrument may be used as an alternative to payment in cash or via electronic transfer of funds. The benefit of settling a debt by means of a negotiable instrument is that the signed document in question can be *negotiated*, which means that it can be transferred from one person to another before the debt it details is due to be paid. In essence, a negotiable instrument is equivalent to cash, given that it can change hands many times in its lifetime in exactly the same way as money does. Although negotiable instruments are not used as frequently as they were in the past, they still have a part to play in modern day commercial transactions when an immediate cash payment is not required or desired by the creditor. Negotiable instruments include: bills of exchange; cheques (which are a distinct type of bill of exchange); and promissory notes. The law relating to negotiable instruments is mainly found in the Bills of Exchange Act 1882 (hereinafter referred to as the "BOEA") as amended by the Cheques Act 1957 and the Cheques Act 1992.

✓ OUTCOMES

20–02 By the end of this chapter you will be able to:

✓　recognise the essential features of a bill of exchange;
✓　recognise the parties to a bill of exchange;
✓　understand who is liable on a bill of exchange;
✓　understand how a bill of exchange is *negotiated*; and
✓　recognise where and why cheques and promissory notes differ from bills of exchange.

---

[1] Lecturer in Law, Abertay University.
[2] At the time of writing, a bill of exchange is a paper document. However, as discussed in para.20–17, its definition may be extended in due course to include scanned documents which are transferred by mobile and fixed communications technology.

INTRODUCTION

Origins of bills of exchange

History suggests that the origins of such an enterprising instrument to **20–03** facilitate and enforce payment of a debt can be traced back to the Order of the Temple, a religious order sanctioned by the Pope in the twelfth century. The Knights of the Order of the Temple devised the concept of the transfer of cash funds by "note of hand". One duty undertaken by the Templars was to house and protect pilgrims on their way to and from the Holy Land. For obvious reasons, a pilgrim navigating unknown and often hostile territory would not wish to travel thousands of miles carrying large sums in cash. So, before the journey began, funds would be deposited with a Templar representative in the pilgrim's homeland and, in return, the pilgrim would receive a "coded note" detailing the amount deposited. At each stop along the way, the pilgrim would hand this note to the local Templar representative who would then pay the cash required in local currency and record the transaction, again in code, on the note. When the pilgrim returned home, the note was presented to the Templar who had issued it, with any balance being returned or overspend cleared at that time. Bills of exchange, as we understand them today, were popularised on a commercial scale by the business practices of Lombardy merchants in Northern Italy in the fourteenth century who, when enjoying a rising volume of overseas trade, wished to avoid the perils of sending large sums of cash to and from foreign shores.[3]

Benefits of bills of exchange

A bill of exchange may be the preferred method of payment for goods or **20–04** services if payment is to occur at some point after the goods or services have been provided. For example, the seller of goods may operate an open trading account with either a domestic or foreign buyer, with usual practice being that an invoice for payment is sent after the goods have been shipped. If the buyer fails to pay, the seller's only recourse is to raise a court action to seek an order for payment. If, however, the seller has been provided with a properly constituted bill of exchange from the buyer, ordering a *third party* to make payment, this would ensure payment, irrespective of the solvency or otherwise of the buyer at the time payment fell due. Thus, the prime benefit of being paid via a bill of exchange is that the seller can *negotiate* the bill, that is to say, sell the bill on to a third party for less than its face value and get paid sooner if the bill falls due weeks, months or even years hence. The profit to the third party buying the negotiated bill is the difference between what s/he paid to the seller and the face value of the bill. An obvious advantage of making payment with a bill of exchange which falls due at some future

---

[3] Transactions with clients were "conducted on benches or bancos and it is from that work that our 'bank' is said to be derived". See *http://www.banking-history.co.uk/history.html* [Accessed June 5, 2015].

point in time is that it allows a trader to carry on his/her business on credit.

The following examples illustrate how a bill of exchange operates in practice:

Example 1

Robin is a trader based in Edinburgh. Caroline is a trader based in St Andrews. Horst is a trader based in Munich.
Horst owes Robin £10,000. Caroline owes Horst £10,000.
Instead of Horst sending cash to Robin and Caroline sending cash to Horst, Horst will *draw a bill* for £10,000 on his debtor who is Caroline.

If Caroline accepts the bill it will be sent to Robin, Horst's creditor. Robin will then obtain payment from Caroline at the time stipulated on the face of the bill.
In this way both transactions are settled without any cash being sent to or from Munich.

Such a bill is known as a *foreign bill*, given one of the parties is based overseas, which is of significance should the bill be *dishonoured*—that is to say, the party accepting the bill ultimately fails to pay the debt. *Dishonourment* of a bill is discussed below at para.20–13.

Example 2

Charlotte, Ellen and Nick are all traders based in Scotland.
Charlotte buys goods from Ellen for £2,000.
Charlotte is experiencing cash-flow problems and cannot pay for the goods on the date of purchase. However, she is owed £2,500 by Nick two months hence.
If Ellen agrees to wait for payment, Charlotte can *draw a bill* ordering Nick to pay Ellen £2,000 in two months time. If Nick accepts the bill it will be delivered to Ellen and Nick will pay the £2,000 he owes Charlotte two months hence to Ellen instead.
However, if Ellen requires to realise funds before the bill falls due for payment, she can *negotiate* the bill—that is to say, sell it on to Ben for say £1,700. Ben in turn can negotiate the bill by selling it on to Jennifer for £1,500. Jennifer will then present the bill to Nick for payment on the due date.

Such a bill is known as an *inland bill* given all the parties are domiciled in the same country.[4]

---

[4] Bills of Exchange Act 1882 ("the BOEA") s.4(1).

Parties to a bill

The party drawing the bill is known as the *drawer* (debtor). The party **20–05** ordered to pay the specified sum is known as the *drawee*. This could be a bank or a private individual. If a bank is the drawee, the document is known as a *bank draft*. The party who is due the sum specified in the bill is known as the *payee* (creditor).

Terminology

The reader will quickly become aware of alternative names for the parties **20–06** to a bill of exchange, depending upon the stage the transaction has reached. To properly explain the legal significance of such designations, the use of these alternatives is unavoidable.

Definition of a bill of exchange—BOEA, as amended

The BOEA, as amended, dictates whether a document ordering a party to **20–07** make payment *upon demand* or *on sight* or at some stated time in the future is a valid bill of exchange.[5] To be such, the document must comply with the relevant sections of the act; primarily the document must conform to the statutory definition of a bill to ensure its *negotiability* which is the ability to transfer the bill between parties, as detailed above in para.20–04.

Section 3(1) of the BOEA states that a bill of exchange is:

> "[A]n unconditional order in writing, addressed by one person to another, signed by the person giving it, requiring the person to whom it is addressed to pay on demand, or at a fixed or determinable future time a sum certain in money, or to the order of a specified person or to bearer."

It is therefore clear that the bill must:

- be an *unconditional order* to pay, meaning that the words used must emphatically instruct payment[6] and there must be no conditions on the face of the bill restricting the right to payment[7];
- be in writing in any recognised language[8] and on any durable medium[9];

---

[5] A bill may also become payable upon the occurrence of a specified event which is certain to happen, e.g. death, but not marriage.

[6] In *Hamilton v Spottiswoode* (1849) 154 E.R. 1182 it was held that the words "We hereby authorise you to pay" was not an order to pay per s.3(1) of the BOEA.

[7] In *Bavins Jnr & Sims v London & South Western Bank Ltd* [1901] 1 Q.B. 270 a stipulation that the payee was to sign a receipt prior to receiving payment appeared on the face of the bill. This condition meant the document was not a bill of exchange per s.3(1) of the BOEA.

[8] *Arab Bank Ltd v Ross* [1952] 2 Q.B. 216 where both Arabic and English words were used on the face of the bills which were in the form of promissory notes.

[9] Except metal to comply with the terms of s.5 of the Coinage Act 1870.

- be addressed by one person to another, that is by the *drawer* to the *drawee*, and signed by the person drawing the bill;
- be payable on demand or at a fixed or determinable future time[10];
- be a sum certain in money[11];
- be payable to the order of a specified person or to the *bearer* who is the person in possession of the bill when it falls due for payment.

A document which fails to comply with *all* the requirements of s.3(1) is not a bill of exchange and, accordingly, cannot be negotiated.

FORM OF THE BILL

20–08 There is no prescribed statutory form of a bill of exchange but a *foreign bill*, as detailed in Example 1 in para.20–04 above, would look like this:

£16,000   Ruritania, May 6, 2015
At thirty (30) days after date pay X *or order* the sum of sixteen thousand pounds Sterling for value received.
To Y   (Signed) Z
3 Marine Avenue,
Atlantis

The bill will be sent by Z to Y who will write *accepted* on the face of the bill and add his/her signature. The bill is said to be *drawn upon* Y, who is now called the *acceptor* of the bill.[12]

£16,000   Ruritania, May 6, 2015
At thirty (30) days after date pay X *or order* the sum of sixteen thousand pounds Sterling for value received.
To Y   (Signed) Z
3 Marine Avenue,
Atlantis
ACCEPTED Y

The bill will then be sent to X, who can if s/he so chooses *negotiate* the bill, that is, to sell the bill to another party who will then be entitled to

---

[10] Bills payable at a future date are generally made payable in periods of 30 days. If a bill is undated, s.12 of the BOEA permits the payee to insert a date.

[11] *Dixon v Bovill* (1856) 3 Macq. (HL) 1.

[12] The drawee does not need to accept at this point, but it is clearly wise to confirm that the drawee will pay the debt. Upon acceptance, the acceptor becomes the principal debtor under the bill.

payment from Y on the due date. A bill made out *to order* is transferred by *indorsement and delivery*. In the above example the words *or order* appear after X's name. However, if these words had been omitted, X could still sell the bill on as the law deems a bill made payable to a named individual should be read as to include the words *or order*.[13] Where a bill is made out *to bearer*, the bill is transferred from party to party purely by delivery.[14] The word *bearer* simply means the party who has possession of the bill at the relevant time.

Indorsement

To transfer a bill made payable *to order*, the payee will sign his/her name **20–09** on the back of the bill. His/her signature acts as *indorsement*, signifying that a new payee has been nominated. The name of the new payee, now known as the *indorsee*, can also be written on the back of the bill. This is known as a *special indorsement*.[15]

> *Example of a Special Indorsement*
>
> **Thomas Glen (existing payee/indorser)**
> **Pay Margaret Douglas (new payee/indorsee)**

Although at this point the transfer of the bill is restricted to Margaret Douglas, she is not prohibited from indorsing the bill herself and transferring it to a new indorsee thereafter. A *special indorsement* is to be distinguished from a *restrictive indorsement*. This is achieved by adding the word *only* after the name of the new indorsee. If this happens, the bill cannot be negotiated beyond the named indorsee.[16]

> *Example of a Restrictive Indorsement*
>
> **Thomas Glen**
> **Pay Margaret Douglas only**

If the name of the indorsee is not stated, a *blank indorsement* has been given by the indorser. The bill then automatically becomes a *bearer bill* which can be negotiated by delivery alone.[17] However, the recipient of a *blank indorsement* is entitled to sign his name above that of the indorser's. If this is done, the *blank indorsement* is converted into a *special indorsement* which can then be negotiated by future indorsement in favour of a new indorsee or bearer.[18] Negotiation is complete when the indorsee receives the bill.[19] For obvious reasons, an *order bill* is always to be

---

[13] BOEA s.8(2), (4).
[14] BOEA s.31(2).
[15] BOEA s.34(2).
[16] BOEA ss.8(1), 35(2).
[17] BOEA s.34(1).
[18] BOEA s.34(4).
[19] BOEA s.31(3).

preferred to a *bearer bill* given that a thief in possession of a *bearer bill* can sell it on without indorsement or simply present it for payment to the acceptor.

Holders

20–10 When the bill is transferred, either by *indorsement and delivery*, or by delivery alone in the case of a *bearer bill*, the recipient is then known as the *holder* of the bill. Only the holder is entitled to negotiate the bill[20] and this status also enables him/her to present the bill to the drawee/acceptor for payment when it falls due.[21] However, to be sure of realising payment a holder must also be both a *holder for value* and a *holder in due course*.

Before explaining the meaning of the above terms it is necessary to further explore the legal effect of negotiability.

The ability to transfer a bill of exchange from party to party without the knowledge or agreement of the drawee/acceptor stems from the fact that the bill is treated as a cash equivalent, as stated in para.20–01 above. Accordingly, a bill *stands on its own two feet* and differs from other forms of incorporeal moveable property, such as shares or rights under an insurance policy, where, to effect a legally enforceable transfer of the benefit of the property between the parties, *assignation and intimation* must occur.[22] If this does not happen, the assignee gains no right to or benefit in the property at all.

> Accordingly, "The privilege of a negotiable document is that it passes in its own corpus the thing it represents without intimation."[23]

However, if a bill of exchange is *negotiated for value* and the indorsee holds it in good faith and in ignorance of any defect attaching to it, for example the bill was stolen by the party who indorsed it in his/her favour, s/he is in the fortunate position of being a *holder for value* and a *holder in due course* respectively.

Holder for value

20–11 The requirement that the indorsee has actually paid for the bill, rather than have been given it as a gift, must be met to satisfy a rule of English, not Scots, contract law.[24] As the BOEA applies throughout the UK, this requirement must be met in Scotland too if the indorsee is to enforce payment of the bill.

---

[20] BOEA s.31.

[21] BOEA s.45(3).

[22] See para.21–31.

[23] *Connal & Co v Loder* (1868) 6 M. 1095, per Lord Neaves at 1102.

[24] BOEA s.27(1) and (2). English law requires consideration. See para.4–05, above.

Holder in due course

To meet the requirements of the BOEA, the bill must appear on the face **20–12** of things to have been executed in proper form,[25] taken in good faith from the previous holder by the *holder for value*[26] whilst unaware of any defect in the title of the bill at that time or previous dishonour of the bill.[27] The bill must also not be overdue.[28] If it is overdue the indorsee who takes such a bill gets no better title than the indorser who negotiated it to him/her. Dishonoured bills and overdue bills are discussed at para.20–13.

If these stipulations are met, a *holder in due* course is entitled to be paid by the drawee/acceptor notwithstanding the fact that the title of the previous indorsee is defective because the bill was obtained by him/her though nefarious means such as theft, duress, force or fear or by fraud.

Key Concept

For a holder to gain good title to the debt, irrespective of any defect in his/her title, s/he must also be a *holder for value* and a *holder in due course*.

The legal protection afforded by a negotiable instrument as a means of receiving payment of a debt is succinctly stated by Willes J. in *Whistler v Forster*,[29] "[t]he general rule of law is undoubted that no-one can acquire a better title than he himself possesses.[30] To this there are some exceptions; one of which arises out of the rule of [the] law-merchant as to negotiable instruments. These, being part of the currency, are subject to the same rule as money: and if such an instrument be transferred in good faith, for value, before it is overdue, it becomes available in the hands of the holder, notwithstanding fraud which would have rendered it unavailable in the hands of a previous holder."

Parties liable on a bill

In an ideal world the drawee will have accepted the bill in advance of the **20–13** due date for payment. The holder will then simply present it and get paid. However, as stated above, a drawee may not have accepted the bill and until s/he does so, which may be as late as the time it is presented for payment, s/he is not a party to the bill. If the drawee refuses to accept the bill this is known as *dishonour by non-acceptance* and the drawer of the bill is liable to make payment to the holder. In addition, if the bill has been negotiated by indorsement each indorsee is also potentially liable to

---

[25] BOEA s.29(1).
[26] BOEA s.90.
[27] BOEA s.36(5).
[28] BOEA s.36(2).
[29] (1863) 14 C.B. (NS) 248 at 257.
[30] This is expressed in the Latin maxim *Nemo dat quod non habet* which roughly translated means "you cannot give that which you do not have".

the holder.[31] This liability is clearly stated in BOEA s.43(2) and elaborated on in s.55:

> "(1) The drawer of a bill by drawing it—
>
>> (a) Engages that on due presentment it shall be accepted and paid according to its tenor, and that if it be dishonoured he will compensate the holder or any indorser who is compelled to pay it, provided that the requisite proceedings on dishonour be duly taken;
>>
>> ...
>
> (2) The indorser of a bill by indorsing it—
>
>> (a) Engages that on due presentment it shall be accepted and paid according to its tenor, and that if it be dishonoured he will compensate the holder or a subsequent indorser who is compelled to pay it, provided that the requisite proceedings on dishonour be duly taken ...".

If, however, the acceptor has insufficient funds to pay the bill or refuses to pay the bill it is said to be *dishonoured by non-payment*.[32] The holder must inform the drawer and every endorser that the bill has been dishonoured in this way.[33] If the bill is a foreign bill, it must also be *noted and protested*, which means that a *notary public*[34] must certify that the acceptor has failed to honour the bill. This should be done no later than the next business day after the bill has been dishonoured.[35] An inland bill may be *noted and protested* but this is not a requirement under the BOEA.

The drawer and any party who indorses a bill may be held liable to the holder if the acceptor refuses to honour the bill when it is presented for payment, unless, that is, any individual's signature has been forged.[36] However, as stated in para.20–12, the *holder for value* gains good title to have the debt discharged irrespective of any fraud or irregularity. Thus, if one indorser's signature has been forged and/or the bill was transferred to the holder by another indorser, who him/herself did not hold good title, the bill remains valid and the holder for value can sue any party for payment, save the party whose signature has been forged. Section 58 of the BOEA states that where the holder of a bill payable to *bearer*

---

[31] BOEA s.43(2).

[32] BOEA s.47.

[33] BOEA s.48.

[34] BOEA s.51(2). Noting is achieved by the notary stating the date of dishonour on the bill with the addition of his/her initials and the letters NP to mark his/her office. Notaries are solicitors who have authority from the Court of Session to, amongst other duties, administer oaths and to witness and authenticate documents.

[35] BOEA s.49(12).

[36] BOEA s.47(2) and (24).

negotiates it by delivery without indorsing it s/he is not liable on the instrument.[37]

Material alterations to a bill

If a bill has been materially altered in some way without the agreement of **20–14** all the parties liable on the bill, for example the sum payable on the face of the bill has been changed from £7,000 to £70,000, parties to the bill before the material alteration occurred are not liable to pay the £70,000 fraudulently stated on the bill.[38] They are, however, potentially liable for the original sum of £7,000 if the alteration was not apparent to the holder. The party who actually altered the bill and subsequent indorsers are all potentially liable to pay £70,000 to the holder.

Overdue bills

When a bill falls due for payment the holder must present it to the drawer **20–15** or acceptor for payment on the day it actually falls due. Failure to do this sees the holder lose the right to claim against the drawer and any indorsers, unless the delay in making presentation is beyond his/her control.[39] In *Hamilton Finance Co Ltd v Coverley Westray Walbaum & Tosetti Ltd*[40] the court accepted that a bill delayed for presentment by the inefficiency of the postal service met the terms of s.46(1) of the BOEA. A bill *payable on demand* is held to be overdue when it has been in circulation for an unreasonable length of time. In determining what is "reasonable" a court will look to the facts of the individual case and also usual trade practice. If a bill *payable on demand* is held to be overdue the drawer and indorsers are discharged from making payment.[41]

In any event, if a bill is not presented for payment within five years it will *prescribe*.[42] This means that if five years from the appropriate date of payment have elapsed without the bill being presented to the acceptor for payment, or any relevant claim being made in connection to the bill via a court action, the holder has no further mechanism by which to enforce payment.

---

[37] Where the holder of a bill payable to bearer negotiates it by delivery without indorsing it s/he is called a transferor by delivery. However, a transferor by delivery who negotiates a bill thereby warrants to his/her immediate transferee being a holder for value that the bill is what it purports to be, that s/he has a right to transfer it, and that at the time of transfer s/he is not aware of any fact which renders it valueless (s.58(1), (2), (3)).

[38] BOEA s.64(1).

[39] BOEA s.45(1) and s.46(1). However, the acceptor will still be liable to the drawer.

[40] [1969] 1 L.R. 53.

[41] BOEA s.74.

[42] Prescription and Limitation (Scotland) Act 1973 s.6(1), Sch.1 para.1(e).

Lost bills

20–16   If a bill is lost before it is overdue the person who was the holder of it at the relevant time may require the drawer to provide a duplicate bill for the purpose of indemnifying the holder in case the missing bill subsequently reappears in the hands of another person.[43]

CHEQUES

20–17   A cheque is a type of bill of exchange. Section 73 of the BOEA states that a cheque is a bill of exchange "drawn on a banker and payable on demand". In essence, a cheque is a written document giving an order to a bank from one of its customers to pay money, held by the bank on behalf of the customer, to a third party, or to the customer him/herself if s/he wishes to withdraw cash. Whilst it is still true to say that a cheque is nowadays the most commonly used bill of exchange, the availability of near instant payment by means of electronic transfer of cash via debit cards, PayPal or developing mobile phone technology led the non-statutory body the UK Payments Council to announce in 2009 that cheques, after more than 350 years of use, would be phased out by October 31, 2018, subject to the caveat that adequate and secure paperless alternatives were to be developed by that date.[44] However, on July 12, 2011 the Payments Council announced that, "cheques will continue for as long as customers need them and the target for possible closure of the cheque clearing in 2018 has been cancelled".[45] This decision was directly presaged by a public consultation exercise undertaken by the Payments Council and comments made by the then Financial Secretary to the UK Treasury to the effect that that the industry had failed to carry out a cost/benefit analysis and had yet to propose a viable alternative to cheques. Then, on March 6, 2014, the UK government announced that it now intends to secure the use of cheques for the foreseeable future by introducing legislation to permit *cheque imaging* whereby an electronic image of the cheque rather than the paper original will be sent for *clearing*. See paras 19–21 and 19–22, below. It is anticipated that by introducing *cheque imaging*, using both mobile and fixed communications technology, payment will be swifter than at present with the time period for actual payment of the sum stipulated on the cheque (from presentment to the

---

[43] BOEA s.69.

[44] Research undertaken in 2007 indicated that personal cheques accounted for only 6% of cashless transactions (see *http://news.bbc.co.uk/1/hi/business/7850945.stm* [Accessed June 5, 2015]) a position likely reached, in part, by the decision at that time by many major retailers to stop accepting personal cheques (see *http://www.paymentscouncil.org.uk/files/payments_files/cheque_guarantee_report_june_2009.pdf* [Accessed June 5, 2015]). However, in 2012, £840 billion of cheques were processed in the relevant accounting period accounting for 10% of all payments made by individuals (see *https://www.gov.uk/government/news/cheque-payments-to-become-quicker-and-easier* [Accessed June 5, 2015].

[45] See *http://www.paymentscouncil.org.uk/files/payments_council/the_future_of_cheques_final_version.pdf* [Accessed June 5, 2015] and *http://www.chequeandcredit.co.uk/files/candc/press/cheques_the_facts_2012.pdf* [Accessed June 5, 2015].

funds being credited to an individual account), being reduced from five days to two days in most instances.[46]

In the meantime, the law as stated in the BOEA applies to cheques in the same way as bills, albeit with some minor differences. These differences are highlighted in the following paragraphs.

Parties to a cheque

The parties to a cheque comprise the *drawer*, the person who signs the **20–18** cheque, the *drawee*, the bank to whom the cheque is addressed and the *payee*, the party to whom, or to whose order, the money is to be paid. The first discernible difference between a bill of exchange as detailed in the preceding paragraphs and a cheque is that a cheque is *payable on demand*, thus the bank (the drawee), does not need to "accept" the cheque which will only ever be presented to it for the purpose of payment.

Stale and undated cheques

As with any other bill of exchange, the cheque must be delivered to the **20–19** payee before it reaches the status of a negotiable instrument and s.45(2) of the BOEA states that the drawer and any indorser will be discharged if the cheque is not presented for payment within a "reasonable" time. However, banking practice dictates that a cheque will not be honoured if it is presented for payment six months after it was signed by the drawer. Banks treat such cheques as *stale*. In addition, although under s.3(4) of the BOEA a cheque is valid even if it is undated, in practice banks refuse to pay such cheques. This practice has been upheld by the courts.

> ### Griffiths v Dalton
> #### [1940] 2 K.B. 264
>
> Dalton gave Griffiths an undated cheque and 18 months later Griffiths filled in the date as February 20, 1933. By that date, however, Dalton was dead and Griffiths raised an action to recover the sum through Dalton's executors. The court held that a bill, in incomplete form, must be rectified (the date added) within a reasonable time, per s.20(2) of the BOEA, and that by February 20, 1933 that period had expired. Accordingly, Dalton's estate was not liable on the cheque.[47]

---

[46] *https://www.gov.uk/government/uploads/system/uploads/attachment_data/file/322753/ PU1680_final__2_.pdf* [Accessed June 5, 2015].

[47] The Cheque and Credit Clearing Company recommends that holders of cheques that are over six months old obtain a replacement. See para.20–22.

Crossed cheques

20–20 The main distinction between a bill and a cheque is that a cheque may be *crossed.* Crossing a cheque is achieved by drawing two parallel across the face of the cheque. A *general crossing* occurs when the words *account payee* or *account payee only* are added. A generally crossed cheque must be presented for payment via the payee's bank account. Modern banking practice dictates that cheques are now pre-printed, and supplied to customers pre-crossed which means that such a cheque cannot be transferred by indorsement and is thus only valid between the parties concerned.[48] Section 78 of the BOEA states that a crossing is a material part of the cheque and that it is unlawful for any person to obliterate or, except as authorised by the act, to add to or alter the crossing. However, the drawer can *open* the crossing, that is to say, before delivery to the payee, write the words *Pay Cash* on the face of the cheque and add his/her initials or signature next to the words. This does not amount to a material alteration and the payee can then present the cheque for cash payment or transfer it by indorsement and delivery in the usual way. It will be recalled that a cheque, as a species of bill of exchange, does not achieve that status until it has been delivered to the payee.

A *special crossing* is given if the name of the bank at which payment will be made is stipulated on the face of the cheque.[49] Special crossings are rare in practice. In the event that a signed cheque is uncrossed it may be crossed by the drawer or any holder.[50] In addition, if a cheque is crossed and the words *not negotiable* alone appear on the face of the cheque, the cheque may be transferred, but not negotiated. Thus the holder can assign the right to another party to receive the sum stated on the face of the cheque. However, the assignee will only obtain as good a title to the cheque as the assignor had him/herself.[51] If there is any taint attached to the cheque the assignee will not qualify as a holder in due course, making his/her right to payment void.[52]

Key Concept

A cheque is to be regarded as a negotiable instrument so long as it contains no words or markings prohibiting its transfer or indicating an intention that it should not be transferred.

Section 81(1) of the BOEA makes it clear that where a cheque is crossed and the words *account payee* or *a/c payee* are added either with or without the word *"only"* the cheque is not transferable.

---

[48] BOEA s.81A(1).
[49] BOEA s.76(2).
[50] BOEA s.77.
[51] *Great Western Railway Co v London and County Banking Co* [1900] 2 Q.B. 464.
[52] BOEA s.81.

Clearing

Liability of the parties

The rationale behind issuing crossed cheques is simply to better protect **20–21** the parties against fraud given that an uncrossed cheque obtained by theft could simply be presented for payment in cash. If a bank pays in cash a cheque bearing the words *a/c payee only* when presented by a thief, the bank is liable to the true owner of cheque and will have to reimburse that party.[53] On the other hand, if a bank pays a cheque into an account, in accordance with its crossing, and does so without being negligent and in good faith, s.80 of the BOEA states that the bank is deemed to have paid the cheque to its lawful owner notwithstanding the fact that the cheque was non-transferable under s.81A. Accordingly, the drawer's bank account can be lawfully debited, even if it transpires that the cheque has been stolen. In similar vein, if a bank credits a customer account with a cheque received by it but which the customer has no title to (a stolen cheque) and thereafter debits any charges due by the customer to the bank, the bank will not be held liable to the lawful owner of the cheque.

Clearing

Upon presentment of the cheque, the paying bank will pay the proceeds **20–22** to the holder's bank once the cheque has *cleared*. Clearing is the process by which banks resolve their indebtedness to one another.[54] Once a cheque has been presented to a bank for payment the bank will send it, in a batch along with other cheques which have been presented to it, to a *clearing house*. In this way, debits and credits between specific banks are recorded and settled thereby avoiding the cumbersome process of presenting a single cheque to one another for individual attention. Historically, there was no stipulated time for clearing to occur. However, in November 2007 the industry body the Cheque and Credit Clearing Company announced that cheques are deemed to have cleared at the end of the sixth working day after being paid in to a bank or building society account.[55] If a cheque is dishonoured or "bounces" (is returned unpaid due to its author having insufficient funds in their account) after this time the holder, unless party to a fraud, will be protected from any loss.[56] This arises through agreement within the banking sector, not as a matter of law. Section 254 of the Banking Act 2009 amends s.53(2) of the BOEA by abolishing, in relation to cheques but not bills of exchange, a rule of Scots

---

[53] BOEA s.79(2).

[54] The clearing system in Great Britain is managed by the Cheque and Credit Clearing Company. *http://www.chequeandcredit.co.uk* [Accessed June 5, 2015].

[55] At the time of writing, this remains the industry standard. However, as discussed in para.20–17, the introduction of *cheque imaging* would potentially see payment being made within two days.

[56] *http://www.paymentscouncil.org.uk/media_centre/press_releases/2011_archive/-/page/2996/* [Accessed June 5, 2015]. See *http://www.chequeandcredit.co.uk/files/candc/flash_files/ 246._updated.swf* [Accessed June 5, 2015] for a more detailed explanation of the presentment/payment process known as "2, 4, 6".

law known as the *funds attached* rule. Previously, when a cheque was presented for payment in Scotland, the amount stated on its face was said to be assigned to the holder.[57] Where insufficient funds were available to satisfy the sum stated, such lesser amount as was available was then assigned to the holder. Section 53(2) of the BOEA now reads as follows:

> "[W]here the drawee of a bill [other than a cheque] has in his hands funds available for the payment thereof, the bill operates as an assignment of the sum for which it is drawn in favour of the holder, from the time when the bill is presented to the drawee."

PROMISSORY NOTES

20–23 The BOEA recognises one further form of negotiable instrument—the promissory note. A promissory note is defined in s.83(1) of the BOEA as:

> "[A]n unconditional promise in writing made by one person to another signed by the maker, engaging to pay, on demand or at a fixed or determinable future time, a sum certain in money, to, or to the order of, a specified person or to bearer."

It is clear from the above that a promissory note is a *personal promise* to pay with no order being given to a third party to make payment to the *promissee*. As there is no drawer or acceptor, s.89(3) of the BOEA states that any provisions within the act dealing with acceptance do not apply to promissory notes. As with bills and cheques, delivery is necessary[58] and a promissory note may be negotiated in exactly the same way as a bill. The *promissor* is primarily liable on the note and any indorser is in exactly the same legal position as an indorser to a bill of exchange. There is no statutory form of promissory note and the word *"promise"* need not appear at all on the face of the document. However, the words used must give rise to an inference that a promise to pay has been made.[59] It is the unequivocal "promise to pay" that distinguishes a promissory note from an IOU—which is simply a document stating that a certain sum of money is owed by one party to another.

▼ CHAPTER SUMMARY

20–24 A negotiable instrument is a signed document detailing the ownership of a debt. The benefit of settling a debt by means of a negotiable instrument is that the signed document in question can be negotiated meaning that it can be transferred

---

[57] *Bank of Scotland v Richmond & Co* [1997] 6 Bank. L.R. 378.
[58] BOEA s.84.
[59] *Akbar Khan v Attar Singh* [1936] 2 All E.R. 545.

from one person to another before the debt is due to be paid. Negotiable instruments include: bills of exchange, cheques and promissory notes. The law relating to negotiable instruments is mainly found in the BOEA 1882, as amended by the Cheques Act 1957 and the Cheques Act 1992.

(1) The party drawing the bill is known as the *drawer*, the party ordered to pay the specified sum is known as the *drawee* and the party who is due the sum specified in the bill is known as the *payee* (creditor).

(2) To qualify as a bill of exchange the signed document in question must be an unconditional order in writing, addressed by one person to another, signed by the person giving it, requiring the person to whom it is addressed to pay on demand, or at a fixed or determinable future time a sum certain in money, or to the order of a specified person (an *order bill*) or to bearer (a *bearer bill*):

> ➤ BOEA s.3(1); *Hamilton v Spottiswoode* (1849) 154 E.R. 1182; *Bavins Jnr & Sims v London & South Western Bank Ltd* [1901] 1 Q.B. 270; *Arab Bank Ltd v Ross* [1952] 2 Q.B. 216.

(3) To transfer a bill made payable to order the current payee will sign his/her name on the back of the bill. His/her signature acts as a *special indorsement*, signifying that a new named payee has been nominated. Negotiation is complete when the indorsee receives the bill. A *bearer bill* is transferred by delivery alone:

> ➤ BOEA ss.31(2) and 34(2).

(4) If the name of the indorsee is not stated a *blank indorsement* has been given and the bill then automatically becomes a *bearer bill*:

> ➤ BOEA s.34(1).

(5) When the bill is transferred, either by *indorsement and delivery*, or by *delivery* alone, in the case of a *bearer bill*, the recipient is then known as the *holder of the bill*. Only the holder is entitled to negotiate the bill:

> ➤ BOEA s.31.

(6) To be entitled to payment a holder must also be a *holder for value* (having paid for the bill) and a *holder in due course*; the bill must appear to have been executed in proper form, taken in good faith whilst unaware of any defect in the title of the bill at that time. If these stipulations are met, the holder is entitled to be paid by the drawee/acceptor notwithstanding the fact that the title of the previous indorsee is defective:

> ➤ BOEA ss.27(1) and (2), 29(1), 36(5) and 90; *Connal & Co v Loder* (1868) 6 M. 1095; *Whistler v Forster* (1863) 14 C.B. (NS) 248.

(7) If the drawee refuses to accept the bill this is known as *dishonour by non-acceptance* and the drawer of the bill is liable to make payment to the holder. In addition, if the bill has been *negotiated by indorsement* each indorsee is potentially liable to the holder:

> ➤ BOEA ss.43(2) and 55.

(8) If the bill has been accepted and the acceptor refuses to pay the bill it is said to be *dishonoured by non-payment*. The holder must inform the drawer and every endorser that the bill has been dishonoured in this

way. If the bill is a *foreign bill*, it must also be noted and protested. The drawer and any indorser of the bill are potentially liable to the holder:

➢ BOEA ss.24, 47(2), 48 and 51(2).

(9) When a bill falls due for payment the holder must present it to the drawer or acceptor for payment on the day it actually falls due. Failure to do this sees the holder lose the right to claim against the drawer and any indorsers, unless the delay in making presentation is beyond his/her control:

➢ BOEA s.46(1); *Hamilton Finance Co Ltd v Coverley Westray Walbaum & Tosetti Ltd* [1969] 1 L.R. 53.

(10) A cheque is a bill of exchange drawn on a banker and payable on demand:

➢ BOEA s.73.

(11) The parties to a cheque comprise the *drawer*, the *drawee* and the *payee*.

(12) Banking practice dictates that a cheque will be treated as *stale* if not presented for payment within six months of being signed by the drawer. This practice has been upheld by the courts:

➢ *Griffiths v Dalton* [1940] 2 K.B. 264.

(13) An undated cheque will not be honoured by a bank irrespective of the fact that s.3(4) of the BOEA states an undated cheque is valid.

(14) If a cheque is crossed it must be paid into the payee's bank account and cannot be transferred by indorsement. It is valid between the drawer and payee only:

➢ BOEA s.81A(1).

(15) A promissory note is an unconditional promise in writing made by one person to another signed by the maker, engaging to pay on demand or at a specified time in the future a sum certain in money to, or to the order of, a specified person or to bearer:

➢ BOEA s.83(1).

(16) As a promissory note is a personal promise to pay another person, there is no drawer or acceptor thus s.89(3) of the BOEA does not apply to promissory notes.

(17) A promissory note can be negotiated in exactly the same way as a bill.

? QUICK QUIZ

True or False?

- A bill of exchange is always payable on demand.
- A bearer bill cannot be negotiated.
- A holder who is also a holder for value and a holder in due course is entitled to be paid even if the person he bought the bill from came by it dishonestly.
- Overdue bills cannot be paid in any circumstance.
- A crossed cheque must be paid into the payee's bank account.

📖 FURTHER READING

> C. Ashton et al., *Understanding Scots Law*, 2nd edn (Edinburgh: W. Green, 2012), Ch.10.
> F. Davidson and L. Macgregor, *Commercial Law in Scotland*, 3rd edn (Edinburgh: W. Green, 2014), Ch.5.

🖱 RELEVANT WEBLINKS

> A fully revised version of the Bills of Exchange Act 1882 can be accessed at: *http://www.legislation.gov.uk/ukpga/Vict/45-46/61* [Accessed June 5, 2015].
> *http://www.banking-history.co.uk/history.html* [Accessed June 5, 2015].
> *http://www.chequeandcredit.co.uk* [Accessed June 5, 2015].
> *http://www.chequeandcredit.co.uk/files/candc/flash_files/ 246._updated.swf* [Accessed June 5, 2015].
> *http://news.bbc.co.uk/1/hi/business/7850945.stm* [Accessed June 5, 2015].
> *https://www.gov.uk/government/news/cheque-payments-to- become-quicker-and-easier* [Accessed June 5, 2015].
> *https://www.gov.uk/government/uploads/system/uploads/attach- ment_data/file/322753/PU1680_final__2_.pdf* [Accessed June 5, 2015].
> *http://www.paymentscouncil.org.uk/files/payments_files/cheque_ guarantee_report_june_2009.pdf* [Accessed June 5, 2015].
> *http://www.paymentscouncil.org.uk/files/payments_council/the_ future_of_cheques_final_version.pdf* [Accessed June 5, 2015].
> *http://www.chequeandcredit.co.uk/files/candc/press/cheques_the_ facts_2012.pdf* [Accessed June 5, 2015].
> *http://www.paymentscouncil.org.uk/media_centre/press_releases/ 2011_archive/-/page/2996/* [Accessed June 5, 2015].

Chapter 21   Rights in Security

Fiona Grant[1]

▶ CHAPTER OVERVIEW

21–01 This chapter is concerned with rights in security for the repayment of debt. A right in security confers a legal right which the creditor may enforce should the debtor fail to pay the sum(s) owed. A right in security exists in tandem with, but is distinct from, the creditor's right of action against the debtor under any contractual obligation to repay the debt. Rights in security can be subdivided into *personal* rights, which are traditionally known as cautionary[2] obligations and *real* rights. This chapter begins by outlining the key differences between the two types of right. It then explains how a cautionary obligation is constituted and how it operates. It details real rights in security over heritage (land and buildings) and moveable property.[3] Moveable property may be either corporeal, something that has a physical existence and can be moved from one place to another, or incorporeal, for example shares in a company, the existence of which may be proved by the issue of a share certificate but otherwise has no tangible existence.

✓ OUTCOMES

21–02 At the end of this chapter the reader should be able to:

  ✓ understand the difference between a *personal* right and a *real* right in security;
  ✓ understand the rules underpinning the creation of a contract of caution(guarantee);
  ✓ distinguish the respective rights and duties of the creditor, debtor and cautioner (guarantor);
  ✓ appreciate the general principles underpinning the creation of a *real* right in security;
  ✓ understand the different methods by which a *real* right can be created and enforced;
  ✓ distinguish heritable, corporeal and incorporeal moveable property; and

---

[1] Lecturer in Law, Abertay University.
[2] Pronounced *kay-shun-ary*.
[3] For further consideration of heritable and moveable property, see Ch.11, "Property".

  ✓ develop understanding of core principles of contract and property law.

INTRODUCTION

A creditor may demand a right in security for a debt to increase the **21–03** likelihood that s/he will recover his/her outlay should the debtor fail to make payment when it falls due. In Scots law, a right in security gives rise to either a *personal* right (*jus in personam*) or a *real* right (*jus in re*). The distinction is important.

Where the right in security is a *personal* right this allows the creditor to recover the debt from a specified third party, other than the debtor, or to force that third party to carry out some other obligation on behalf of the debtor. The obligation is generally to pay the sum(s) due by the debtor. If the third party, often known as the guarantor, becomes insolvent, however, the creditor has no preferential right to any property or assets belonging to the guarantor and is thus in no better position than any of the guarantor's ordinary creditors.

Where the right in security is a *real* right, this gives the creditor the right to claim identified property belonging to the debtor, or the right to withhold certain property from him/her, in satisfaction of the debt. In most cases, the holder of a *real* right in security will defeat the claims of all other creditors to the property in question. Thus, " ...rights in security provide creditors with some extra security beyond the personal obligation of the debtor that repayment will be made...no personal obligation undertaken by the debtor, however expressed, can ever create a right in security."[4]

Key Concept

A *personal* right in security is inferior to that of a *real* right, given it is only of any practical effect if the guarantor is solvent and in a position to honour the debtor's liability to the creditor.

THE CONTRACT OF CAUTION (GUARANTEE)

A cautionary obligation is a *personal* right in security that gives the **21–04** creditor the right to recover the sum(s) owed him/her by the debtor, who is known as the principal debtor, from another person who has undertaken to pay the debt if the debtor fails to do so. This other person is known traditionally in Scots law as the cautioner but now, more commonly, as the guarantor. A contract of caution (guarantee) is an *accessory* obligation which means that the principal debt must exist or be in

---

[4] F. Davidson and L.J. Macgregor, *Commercial Law in Scotland*, 3rd edn (Edinburgh: W Green, 2014), p.172.

the contemplation of the parties, before it can be enforced against the cautioner (guarantor). It follows that the cautioner's (guarantor's) liability to the creditor is in addition to that of the principal debtor and can only be enforced if the debtor fails to pay his/her debt(s). Contracts of caution (guarantee) are generally sought and drafted by financial institutions. In the interests of consistency, the word "caution" and its derivatives are preferred to that of guarantee, etc. for the purposes of this chapter.

CONSTITUTION OF THE CAUTIONARY OBLIGATION

21–05 A contract of caution need not be in writing unless it is *gratuitous* and *unilateral* obligation and entered into in a personal, rather than business, capacity.[5] Such an obligation arises where one party undertakes to do something for another party with that other party having no corresponding obligation to do or give anything in return.[6] In most cases, the cautioner and debtor are clearly identifiable as such—this is known as *proper* caution. This enables the creditor to enforce the cautionary obligation against the cautioner as soon as the debtor defaults, unless a contractual term states otherwise. *Improper* caution, on the other hand, arises where the two parties appear, on the face of things, to be co-debtors of the creditor thus *jointly and severally* liable for the debt, enabling the creditor to proceed against a co-debtor of choice for the whole sum due. This may occur where the creditor is unaware that the two parties have agreed *inter se* (between themselves) that one will act as cautioner, the other being the principal debtor. However, if the true nature of the relationship between the two parties can be determined then the party identified as the cautioner will be entitled to exercise the legal rights such a designation confers. These rights are discussed in paras 21–07 and 21–08.

EXTENT OF THE CAUTIONER'S LIABILITY

21–06 It is in order for the cautioner to agree with the debtor alone that s/he will guarantee debts to unspecified creditors, either for a fixed period of time or for a stated sum of money. If this is the case, the creditor(s) concerned must subsequently show:

 (i) that they knew of the existence of the contract of caution at the time the contract was entered into with the debtor, and
 (ii) that they placed reliance on it, otherwise the cautioner will not be bound.

---

[5] Requirements of Writing (Scotland) Act 1995 s.1(2)(a)(ii).
[6] Such obligations are further discussed in Chapter 4, para.4–10.

> **Key Concepts**
>
> - As a contract of caution (guarantee) is an *accessory* obligation the cautioner cannot be held liable for more than the principal debt itself.[7]
> - If the debtor dies, the cautioner will only be liable for any debt due at the date of the debtor's death.
> - If the creditor dies, the position of the cautioner remains unchanged in relation to the cautionary obligation s/he originally entered into.
> - If the cautioner dies, his/her liability to existing creditors lives on and will be charged as a debt on his/her estate.

CAUTIONER'S RIGHTS

Right of relief against the debtor

The cautioner who has paid the debt has a *right of relief*, which is the right to claim the sum paid, including expenses, from the debtor. This right will exist for a period of five years after the debt has been paid. Thereafter, it will *prescribe*, meaning that the cautioner is no longer able to raise a court action against the debtor to recover the sum s/he paid to the creditor.[8] **21–07**

Right of relief against co-cautioners

Where there are several cautioners, each is generally only liable for his/ her *pro rata* (proportionate) share of the debt if all co-cautioners are solvent. If any co-cautioner is insolvent the deficit is made up by the other co-cautioners. This right is styled the *benefit of division*. It is important to note that a co-cautioner cannot be asked to pay his/her *pro rata* share unless the creditor requires all co-cautioners to do likewise. However, if the contract of caution states that co-cautioners are bound *jointly and severally* the creditor may proceed against a co-cautioner of choice for the whole sum due. If a co-cautioner is required to pay more than his/her *pro rata* share, s/he can subsequently claim *pro rata* relief from his/her co-cautioner(s) for any additional sum s/he has paid to the creditor or other loss incurred. For this reason *joint and several* liability is best avoided. **21–08**

---

[7] *Struthers v Dykes* (1847) 9 D. 1437.
[8] Prescription and Limitation (Scotland) Act 1973 s.6.

Marshall & Co v Pennycook
1908 S.C. 276

Messrs Marshall and Pennycook agreed to be bound jointly and severally as co-guarantors for Mr McDonald who had entered into an engineering contract with a local authority. When Mr McDonald found himself unable to complete the contract, Mr Marshall, with the agreement of Mr Pennycook, took over the contract and completed the works, but at a loss. Applying the principle that co-guarantors are only liable pro rata, the court held that Mr Penny-cook was liable to pay Mr Marshall 50 per cent of the loss he had incurred.

CONTRA PROFERENTEM RULE

21–09 Most contracts of caution will clearly set out the extent of the cautioner's liability and also include a clause allowing for immediate steps to be taken against the cautioner (do summary diligence) to recover the sum(s) owed without the need for the creditor to go to court. However, if the contract of caution is worded imprecisely or is ambiguous in any way, the court will invoke the *contra proferentem* rule. This sees the court interpret ambiguous phrases or words contrary to the interests of the party seeking to rely upon any such ambiguity. This will invariably be the creditor.

Fortune v Young
1917 2 S.L.T. 150

Mr Young wrote a letter which stated:

> "The bearer, Mr Fortune, we have known for a long number of years, and have pleasure in testifying as to his good and straightforward character, and guarantee that his financial standing is all in order, in accordance with his statement to the extent of from sixteen to eighteen hundred pounds stg."[9]

Young subsequently disputed that the letter gave a guarantee arguing that it was merely a testimonial as to Fortune's creditworthiness. The court disagreed.

> "From the terms of the document itself I think the evidence makes it abundantly clear, that the defender having given what was a perfectly good testimonial was asked if he could not say

---

[9] *Fortune v Young*, 1917 2 S.L.T. 150, per L.J.C. Dickson at 154.

something more, and he accordingly added the words 'and guarantee that his financial standing is all in order in accordance with his statement to the extent of from sixteen to eighteen hundred pounds'. I cannot read that as amounting to anything else than a very clear, distinct, and specific guarantee to the extent of from sixteen to eighteen hundred pounds."[10]

GROUNDS TO INVALIDATE A GUARANTEE

Void or voidable contracts of caution

If the contract of caution is held to be invalid due to the creditor or **21–10** principal debtor lacking contractual capacity at the time the contract was entered into or the substance of the contract is or becomes illegal (*pacta illicitum*) the contract will be void, meaning it is viewed as never having come into existence. A contract of caution may also be void or voidable,[11] if the cautioner entered into the contract on the basis of a misrepresentation made by the creditor or was put under pressure to do so. However, a contract of caution is not considered a contract *uberrimae fidei* (of utmost good faith), therefore there is no general legal duty placed on the creditor to disclose all material facts concerning the debtor's affairs or financial standing to the cautioner.

Young v Clydesdale Bank
(1889) 17 R. 231

Young gave guarantee on behalf of his brother for, "payment of any advances made and which may hereafter be made".

The bank did not inform Young that his brother's account was heavily overdrawn at the time and Young failed to read the guarantee before he signed it.

"It is well settled that it is not the duty of the bank to give any information to a proposed cautioner as to the state of the accounts with the principal. If the cautioner desires to know it is his duty to ask and inform himself but no duty lies upon a party seeking security to give any information of that kind."[12]

If, however, the cautioner actively seeks information from the creditor about the debtor's financial standing the creditor must answer all

---

[10] *Fortune v Young*, 1917 2 S.L.T. 150, per Lord (Ordinary) Hunter quoted at 151. See also *Aitken's Trustees v Bank of Scotland*, 1944 S.C. 270 and *McLaughlin, Petitioner* [2010] CSIH 24.

[11] Meaning the court may set the guarantee aside if challenged by one of the parties to it.

[12] (1889) 17 R. 231 at 240.

questions posed truthfully. If the creditor fails to do so by mis-representing, even innocently, the facts, and the cautioner then relies on his/her response to enter into the contract, the cautioner has the right to resile (withdraw) from the contract which means s/he can treat the cautionary obligation as at an end, without going to court.[13] The debtor is also under an obligation not to mislead the cautioner by misrepresenting his/her actual financial situation. If the misrepresentation is fraudulent, the cautioner may seek to have the contract of caution set aside, if s/he is aware of the fraud. Otherwise, the contract of caution will stand. However, there is a significant exception to this general rule.

Creditors' duty of good faith

21-11 In *Smith v Bank of Scotland*[14] it was held by the House of Lords (the predecessor of the Supreme Court)[15] that where a "proximate" relationship[16] exists between the debtor and the cautioner and the creditor is aware of the nature of the relationship between the parties, then the creditor is under a duty to act in good faith and to take "reasonable" steps to enquire whether the party with no financial interest in the venture guaranteed (in *Smith* this was a wife who had guaranteed her husband's commercial debts) has entered into the cautionary obligation in full knowledge of the risk(s) involved, without undue influence being exerted, or through any misrepresentation made, by the debtor:

> Lord Clyde: "He (the creditor) should take reasonable steps to secure that in relation to the proposed contract he acts throughout in good faith it seems to me that it would be sufficient for the creditor to warn the potential cautioner of the consequences of entering into the proposed cautionary obligation and to advise him or her to take independent advice. But apart from that it seems to me that the giving of the warning and the advice should be sufficient so far as Scots law is concerned to fulfil the duty on the creditor and secure that he remains in good faith in relation to the proposed transaction."[17]

In *Smith* the guarantee was set aside by the court as the creditor had failed to take the "reasonable" steps outlined by Lord Clyde. The subsequent case of Braithwaite v Bank of Scotland clarified that a cautionary

---

[13] See Chapter 4, para.4–84.
[14] *Smith v Bank of Scotland*, 1997 S.C. (H.L.) 111.
[15] See Chapter 2, para.2–22.
[16] The debtor and guarantor are connected by close personal (non-commercial) relationship.
[18] *Braithwaite v Bank of Scotland*, 1999 S.L.T. 25.

obligation should only be set aside if the cautioner could show, in addition to the failure of the creditor to take the aforementioned "reasonable steps", that the debtor had mislead him/her in a material way, i.e. the debtor him/herself had committed an actionable wrong to induce the cautioner to enter the contract of caution.

Unenforceable contracts of caution

The law implies, as a condition of the contract, that if there is more than **21–12** one cautioner each has agreed to undertake liability on the basis that his/ her co-cautioners have also accepted liability.[18] Therefore, if there is more than one cautioner it is imperative that the creditor has ensured that all co-cautioners have agreed to undertake liability. If it proves to be otherwise, the contract cannot be enforced by the creditor. This rule is illustrated in *Scottish Provincial Insurance Co v Pringle*[19] where the signature of one of the cautioners was forged by the debtor on the contract of caution. The contract was held to be unenforceable as it had been stipulated by the creditor that the sums advanced to the debtor were only being released on the condition that the four individuals named on the contract of caution had agreed to act as co-cautioners.

EXTINCTION OF THE CAUTIONARY OBLIGATION

The obligation will expire if any of the following events occur: **21–13**

- the principal debt is repaid;
- the debtor dies (the cautioner will only be held liable for debts due at the date of death);
- where *joint and several* liability applies, if a co-cautioner is discharged (relieved of liability) without the consent of the other co-cautioners or without them also being relieved of liability all fellow cautioners are deemed to be discharged also[20];
- the cautionary obligation *prescribes*. s.6 of the Prescription and Limitation (Scotland) Act 1973 states that a cautionary obligation *prescribes* five years after the "appropriate date", if no claim has been made by the creditor before that time. Appropriate dates for certain types of obligations are listed in Sch.2 to the 1973 Act; however, the statute is silent on the "appropriate date" for a cautionary obligation. Courts have taken the view that the "appropriate date" for a cautionary obligation to *prescribe* is five years from the date of default by the debtor. If the creditor fails to raise a court action or to do diligence against the cautioner within this period, s/he loses his/her right to recompense. On the other

---

[18] *Paterson v Bonar* (1844) 6 D. 987.
[19] *Scottish Provincial Insurance Co v Pringle* (1858) 20 D. 465.
[20] Mercantile Law Amendment Scotland Act 1856 s.9. However, the guarantee may dictate otherwise avoiding the effect of s.9.

hand, if a contract of caution is worded in such a way as to be "payable on demand" the prescriptive period will only begin to run when the creditor demands payment.

> ### Royal Bank of Scotland Ltd v Brown
> #### 1982 S.C. 89
>
> The bank raised an action on May 23, 1979 against co-guarantors for a loan made to a company that went into liquidation in 1969. The bank argued that the prescriptive period did not start running until May 27, 1974, which was the day the bank contacted the co-guarantors, demanding payment. The co-guarantors argued that their obligation had prescribed given that the "appropriate date" was September 1, 1969 when the bank first raised a claim in the liquidation of the company. The court held that such payment on demand guarantees prescribe five years from the date of demand not the date of the debtor's default.
>
> As the "appropriate date" was held to be the date of demand, the bank was entitled to enforce the guarantee as it had demanded payment four years and 361 days before the expiry of the deemed five-year prescriptive period.[21]

REAL RIGHTS IN SECURITY OVER PROPERTY

> **Key Concept**
>
> A *real* right in security differs from a *personal* right in that it gives the creditor a right, often referred to as a *nexus* or a *bond*, over heritable property (land and buildings) or moveable property belonging to the debtor if the debt remains unpaid, or some specified event occurs. The holder of a *real* right will, in general terms, defeat the claims of the debtor's other creditors to the property concerned if the debtor is sequestrated or, in the case of a company, becomes insolvent.

21–14 A *real* right in security, as with a contract of caution, is an *accessory* obligation. However, a real right can only generally be created if there is "delivery" by the debtor to the creditor of the property that is subject to the security. It is therefore not sufficient for the debtor to identify a particular item of property then set it aside for the benefit of the creditor at some point in the future. However, as suggested above, there are exceptions to this general principle of Scots law and these exceptions are discussed first.

---

[21] See also *Bank of Scotland v Laverock*, 1991 S.C. 117.

REAL RIGHTS IN SECURITY WHERE DELIVERY IS NOT REQUIRED

Hypothecs

Hypothec is the legal term used to describe a right in security over cor- **21–15** poreal moveable property where delivery is not required. At common law, hypothecs may either be created by contract, these are known as *conventional* hypothecs, or created by the operation of law where the term *legal* hypothecs is used.

Conventional hypothecs

Conventional hypothecs are restricted to *bonds of bottomry* and *bonds of* **21–16** *respondentia* which can be granted over, respectively, a ship or its cargo. Such hypothecs can be granted either by the owner of the ship, the owner of the cargo or an agent of either party to raise funds, which cannot be found by any other means, to enable the ship to reach its destination. The law will also imply that the master of a ship who is unable to make contact with the owner of the ship/cargo it is carrying may, if the ship is berthed in a foreign port, grant a bond of either type to enable the ship to reach its home port. The holder of either type of bond who remains unpaid when the ship reaches its destination can apply to the court for an order to sell either the ship or its cargo. *Conventional* hypothecs are now likely to be of historic interest given modern methods of communication.

Legal hypothecs

The *solicitor's* hypothec may be exercised in relation to outlays incurred **21–17** whilst bringing a court action on behalf of a client. The hypothec, at common law, is over the award of any damages or costs to the client and, under statute, to property belonging to the client which is recovered during litigation.[22]

At common law, a *landlord's* hypothec originally enabled the landlord to raise an action in the sheriff court known as sequestration for rent to claim the value of up to one year's rent due by seeking to take possession of certain moveable property of the tenant located within the leased property. If the court action succeeded, the landlord could lawfully remove the goods then sell them. The Bankruptcy and Diligence etc. (Scotland) Act 2007 abolished both the common law diligence of sequestration for rent and the landlord's hypothec over goods in dwelling houses or kept on agricultural land or in a croft.[23] Although the landlord's hypothec has been retained by the 2007 Act its effect is now somewhat limited.[24]

---

[22] Solicitors (Scotland) Act 1980 s.62(1).
[23] Bankruptcy and Diligence etc. (Scotland) Act 2007 s.208.
[24] Moveable property kept in residential garages, lock-ups, sheds, outbuildings, etc. and property in commercial premises only will now be subject to landlord's hypothec. The hypothec is now not limited to one year's rent, thus, it subsists for as long as rent due remains unpaid.

Floating charges

21–18 A floating charge is a statutory form of security granted over the heritable and moveable property of a registered company but not those of individuals or partnerships. The applicable law is contained in the Companies Act 1985, the Companies Act 2006,[25] the Insolvency Act 1986 and the Enterprise Act 2002. A floating charge is just that—it "floats" over the assets of a company and if the repayments to the charge holder are up to date the charge will continue to float undisturbed enabling the company to use the property, dispose of it and also add further assets to its holdings.

As of September 15, 2003, when the relevant sections of the Enterprise Act 2002 came into force, the law relating to floating charges has to be understood with regard to charges granted before and on or after that date.

Charges granted before September 15, 2003

21–19 To be valid, a floating charge granted before September 15, 2003 must be in writing and registered with the Registrar of Companies in Scotland within 21 days of the date of the execution (creation) of the deed.[26] However, the floating charge would actually have taken effect from the date of execution if registration was completed within the statutory period. A pre-Enterprise Act 2002 floating charge will *crystallise* (attach to the assets in the company's ownership at that time) if the company goes into liquidation[27] or the floating charge holder appoints a receiver. It is at the point of crystallisation that the *real* right in security is constituted. In essence, the charge becomes a fixed one.

Company in liquidation

21–20 When a company goes into liquidation a floating charge attaches to the relevant property, subject to the legal rights of any person who has:

    (i) Executed diligence on the property.
    (ii) Holds a fixed security over the property.
    (iii) Holds over the property a floating charge with prior ranking. Ranking is determined in order of the date of execution of the deed creating the charge.[28] Section 464(1) of the Companies Act 1985 allows, however, for a deed executing a floating charge to contain a ranking agreement setting out the actual and agreed ranking of the floating charge in relation to any future securities granted over the same property. Where a ranking agreement exists, a fixed security arising by the operation of law,[29] such as a

---

[25] Sections 878–892 of the Companies Act 2006 apply to floating charges.
[26] Companies Act 1985 s.410(2).
[27] Companies Act 1985 s.463(1).
[28] Companies Act 1985 s.464(3) and (4).
[29] A pre-existing implied legal right that cannot be negated by a subsequent agreement.

hypothec, will have priority over the claim of the floating charge holder concerned.

Appointment of a receiver

A receiver may be appointed if a contractually specified event occurs, **21–21** usually non-payment of the debt, or an event stipulated in s.52(1) of the Insolvency Act 1986 comes to pass. A floating charge will *crystallise* under s.52(1) if any of the following occur:

(i) when asked to do so by the floating charge holder the company fails to repay the sum due within 21 days[30];

(ii) the company is two months in arrears of interest due[31]; the company is wound up[32]; and

(iii) another holder of a floating charge over the same property appoints a receiver.[33]

The role of the receiver is to act primarily in the interests of the floating charge holder who appointed him/her to ensure the repayment of the debt. This can be achieved by keeping the company running as a going concern or by selling all or part of the company. To discharge the duty owed to the charge holder the receiver will ingather all monies or assets owed to the company prior to settling the claims of debtors, according to their ranking. s.60 of the Insolvency Act 1986 details the ranking of creditors.

The ranking is as follows:

(i) the holder of any fixed charge that is over property subject to the floating charge and which ranks prior to or *pari passu* (equal to) the floating charge;

(ii) individuals or bodies who have executed diligence on any part of the property of the company which is subject to the charge;

(iii) creditors in respect of all liabilities, charges and expenses incurred by or on behalf of the receiver;

(iv) the receiver in respect of his/her liabilities, expenses and remuneration; and

(v) preferential creditors entitled to payment such as HM Revenue and Customs (HMRC) per outstanding taxes and employees owed wages/salaries.

Only after the above five categories of creditor have been paid can the receiver lawfully pay the holder of the floating charge who appointed him/her.

---

[30] Insolvency Act 1986 s.52(1)(a).
[31] Insolvency Act 1986 s.52(1)(b).
[32] Insolvency Act 1986 s.52(1)(c).
[33] Insolvency Act 1986 s.52(1)(d).

Limitations on the receiver's powers

21–22 Certain statutory and non-statutory rules of law may restrict the receiver's powers to satisfy the claim of the floating charge holder who appointed him, for example:

> (i) the floating charge was not registered within the 21-day statutory period;
>
> (ii) the floating charge was created or granted in breach of ss.243–245 of the Insolvency Act 1986; and
>
> (iii) the House of Lords ruling in *Sharp v Thomson*.[34]

In *Sharp v Thomson*, a company granted a floating charge over certain property and thereafter entered into missives for the sale of a flat, subject to the floating charge. A disposition was delivered to the purchasers but the following day a receiver was appointed. The disposition was not recorded in the Register of Sasines at that point. The receiver argued that at the time of *crystallisation* the flat still belonged to the company given heritage in Scotland only passes to the buyer when the disposition is recorded. Although the House of Lords agreed that delivery of a disposition cannot create a real right in property, it held that the Insolvency Act 1986 did not allow the receiver to lay claim to the flat. If the receiver had been entitled to the flat he/she would have been granted legal authority to do something which, if it had been carried out by the company, would amount to fraud given that the purchasers had paid for the flat. The House of Lords concluded by stating that the heritable property to which a floating charge attaches is the 'beneficial interest' in the property and not the title to it. Therefore, once a disposition is delivered the seller loses beneficial interest.

Charges granted on or after September 15, 2003

21–23 Section 250(2) of the Enterprise Act 2002 inserts a new section into the Insolvency Act 1986[35] that stipulates that the holder of a floating charge may not appoint a receiver unless one of the exceptions detailed in ss.72B–72G of the Insolvency Act 1986 Act, as amended apply.[36] Instead, an administrator will be appointed who is under a statutory duty to manage the company's affairs, business and property with the objective of rescuing the company as a going concern, or, if that proves impossible, achieving a better result for all the company's creditors than would be likely if the company were to be wound up immediately. Accordingly, an administrator does not just act for the benefit of the holder of the floating

---

[34] 1997 S.C. (H.L.) 66.

[35] Insolvency Act 1986 s.72A.

[36] The Insolvency Act 1986 Amendment (Appointment of Receivers) (Scotland) Regulations 2011 (SSI 2011/140) amended s.51(1) of the 1986 Act to allow for the appointment of a receiver where an EU Member State court has jurisdiction to authorise insolvency proceedings regarding property situated in Scotland and the Court of Session does not.

charge who appointed him/her.[37] The Enterprise Act 2002 also removes the preferential status of HMRC excepting the preferential right of employees for unpaid wages.[38] These debts will now rank alongside other unsecured debts. s.252 of the Enterprise Act 2002 also introduces a procedure under which a set percentage of the company's net property is to be set aside for distribution to unsecured creditors and the administrator is prohibited by law from distributing this *prescribed part* to the holder of a floating charge unless it exceeds the amount required for the satisfaction of unsecured debts.[39]

BANKRUPTCY AND DILIGENCE ETC. (SCOTLAND) ACT 2007

The relevant sections of the Bankruptcy and Diligence etc. (Scotland) Act **21–24** 2007 as detailed below are currently prospective[40] but will impact upon the registration and ranking of floating charges created on or after September 15, 2003 if ever brought into force with a commencement order.

Prospective registration requirements

Section 37 of the 2007 Act provides for a new registration regime under **21–25** the auspices of the Keeper of the Registers of Scotland.[41] It is proposed that the date of registration of a floating charge will be when the relevant registration documents or notice of registration is received by the Keeper, rather than when the floating charge is executed as is presently the case. Unless, or until, this part of s.37 is brought in to effect, floating charges will still require to be registered with the Registrar of Companies at Companies House.

Section 39 of the 2007 Act allows a creditor and debtor to jointly lodge an advance notice of a floating charge. If the charge is registered within 21 days of advance notice being received by the Keeper, the date of the creation of the floating charge will be that of the date of the registration of the advance notice. This would mean that there would no longer be a period during which a floating charge exists but its existence is not within the public domain.

The likelihood of the prospective provisions of the Bankruptcy and Diligence etc. (Scotland) Act 2007, as detailed above, being brought into

---

[37] Insolvency Act 1986 Sch.B1.

[38] Enterprise Act 2002 s.251.

[39] Articles 1–3 of the Insolvency Act 1986 (Prescribed Part) Order 2003 (SI 2003/2097) detail how the prescribed part is to be calculated. If the minimum value of the company's net property is £10,000, the prescribed part is 50% of the first £10,000 and 20% of the part of the company's net property in excess of £10,000 up to a ceiling of £600,000.

[40] With the exception of s.37 of the 2007 Act, which is partly in force for the purpose of making orders or regulations. See the Bankruptcy and Diligence etc. (Scotland) Act 2007 (Commencement No.3, Savings and Transitionals) Order 2008 (SSI 2008/115).

[41] s.37(1) of the Bankruptcy and Diligence etc. (Scotland) Act 2007 Act requires the Keeper of the Registers of Scotland to establish and maintain a register to be known as the Register of Floating Charges. See Registers of Scotland, *https://www.ros.gov.uk/* [Accessed May 15, 2015].

force in the foreseeable future must be considered somewhat remote in light of subsequent pieces of legislation:

(i) The Financial Markets and Insolvency (Settlement Finality and Financial Collateral Arrangements) (Amendment) Regulations 2010 came into force on April 6, 2011.[42] These Regulations were enacted to comply with EU Directive 2009/44/EC.[43] Regulation 5(2) states that if a floating charge "is created or otherwise arises under a security financial collateral arrangement", it is created when the document granting the floating charge is executed by the company granting the charge and without registration in the Register of Floating Charges. This requirement clearly conflicts with the effect of the prospective sections of the Bankruptcy and Diligence etc. (Scotland) Act 2007 discussed above. The Scottish Government convened a working group in 2010, under the auspices of the Registers of Scotland to bring forward proposals for the operation of the proposed Register of Floating Charges in light of the impact of the Financial Markets and Insolvency (Settlement Finality and Financial Collateral Arrangements) (Amendment) Regulations 2010. The working group reported in 2011,[44] setting out possible options, ranging from bringing the prospective provisions for floating charges in the Bankruptcy and Diligence etc. (Scotland) Act 2007 fully into force, with further consideration then being given to compliance with EU law, or to abandon the aforementioned 2007 provisions in their entirety. At the time of writing, the Scottish Government is still considering the working group's recommendations.

(ii) The Companies Act 2006 (Amendment of Part 25) Regulations 2013,[45] which came into force on April 30, 2013, introduced a uniform and UK-wide registration scheme for registrable securities created over UK companies. Thus, for the purposes of registration, where a company is registered, (i.e. Scotland, England, Wales or Northern Ireland), is no longer of any practical or legal significance. The 2012 Regulations stipulate that charges created on or after April 30, 2013 must be registered with the Registrar of Companies at Companies House within 21 days of the date of the charge being "created" with s.859E(1) of the Companies Act 2006, as amended, now stating that the 21-day period will normally commence when the instrument creating the charge is delivered to the creditor.

---

[42] Financial Markets and Insolvency (Settlement Finality and Financial Collateral Arrangements) (Amendment) Regulations 2010 (SI 2010/2993).

[43] Directive 2009/44/EC of the European Parliament and the Council on Settlement Finality and Financial Collateral Arrangements (2009). This requirement is also reflected in s.253 of the Banking Act 2009.

[44] Register of Floating Charges Technical Working Group; Report to Scottish Government (August 2011), available at *http://www.scotland.gov.uk/Resource/Doc/254430/0121799.pdf* [Accessed May 15, 2015].

[45] SI 2013/600.

Prospective ranking of floating charges

Section 40 of the 2007 Act prospectively amends the law as follows: **21–26**

(i) A floating charge will rank with any other floating charge which has attached to that property or any fixed security over that property or any part of it according to date of creation, which is the date of registration with the Keeper.

(ii) A floating charge will also rank equally with a floating charge or fixed security which was created on the same date as the floating charge.[46] For the time being, however, the existing statutory provisions with regard to the ranking of floating charges discussed in paras 21–21—21–23 will continue to apply.

RIGHTS IN SECURITY WHERE DELIVERY IS REQUIRED

As detailed in para.21–14, with the exception of hypothecs and floating **21–27** charges, it is a general principle of Scots law that a *real* right can only be created if there is "delivery", from the debtor to the creditor, of the property that is subject to the security. It is the act of "delivery", putting the property beyond the reach of the debtor, that creates the *real* right to the property itself and confers on the creditor an additional and more secure right to payment if the debtor defaults. The Latin maxim *traditionibus, non nudis pactis, transferunter rerum dominia* (by delivery not mere agreements are *real* rights in property transferred) applies, although in certain cases, actual delivery of the property will not be possible so *symbolic* or *constructive* delivery of the property will be sufficient to effect the security.

RIGHTS IN SECURITY OVER HERITABLE PROPERTY

The standard security

The only means of granting a right of security over heritable property is **21–28** by entering into a contract of *standard security*, which must be in the form prescribed by the Conveyancing and Feudal Reform Act 1970 and registered in the Land Register or the Register of Sasines kept by the

---

[46] s.40 of the Bankruptcy and Diligence etc. (Scotland) Act 2007 also prospectively restates the rule that where the property is subject to both a floating charge and a security arising by operation of law, such as a hypothec, the fixed security has priority over any floating charge and, at s.41, that ranking agreements may displace the statutory ranking contained within s.40—with the exception that a security arising by the operation of law, for example, a *solicitor's* hypothec, (see para.21–17) cannot be displaced by such an agreement.

Keeper of the Registers of Scotland.[47] The security becomes effective on the date it is recorded in either Register.[48]

Registration amounts to *constructive* delivery of the property. On registration, the creditor, usually a bank, gains a *real* right to the property and is known as the standard security holder. If the debtor fails to make the loan repayments as agreed, or abide by other conditions set out in the *standard security*, the holder can ultimately enforce the sale of the property.

The holder of a *standard security* (heritable creditor) also currently has the comfort of knowing that his/her security acts as a fixed charge, meaning that if the debtor is sequestrated or goes into liquidation, all proceeds of the sale of the property concerned will be made over to him/her in preference to other creditors.

However, as detailed in para.21–26 above, if s.40(2) of the Bankruptcy and Diligence etc. (Scotland) Act 2007 comes into force, a floating charge will rank with any fixed security over that property or any part of it according to date of creation, which is the date of registration with the Keeper. A floating charge would also rank equally with a fixed security which was created on the same date as the floating charge. However, a ranking agreement between charge holders would displace the statutory ranking contained within s.40(2), with the exception that a security arising by the operation of law could not be displaced.[49]

RIGHTS IN SECURITY OVER CORPOREAL MOVEABLE PROPERTY

Pledge

21–29 It is generally a straightforward matter to effect delivery of corporeal moveable property by simply handing it over to the creditor. Where this is possible the security created is known as *pledge* and the *pledger* is under a contractual obligation to deliver the property to the *pledgee* as security for the personal obligation s/he has entered into. When the obligation is fulfilled, usually the repayment of a loan, the *pledgee* must return the property to the *pledger*. Most contracts of *pledge* will permit the *pledgee* to sell the property if the *pledger* defaults. Pawn broking is a form of *pledge* and is regulated by ss.114–122 of the Consumer Credit Act 1974. Pledge can also be created by *constructive*[50] or *symbolic*[51] delivery of the property to the pledgee.

---

[47] Conveyancing and Feudal Reform Act 1970 s.9.

[48] Companies Act 2006 (Amendment of Part 25) Regulations 2013 (SI 2013/600), as detailed in para.21–25, restates this position in s.859E. Registers of Scotland will be required to confirm the relevant date to Companies House.

[49] Bankruptcy and Diligence etc. (Scotland) Act 2007 s.41(1).

[50] For example, where the property is in the safekeeping of a third party who has been made aware that he is holding the goods on behalf of the pledgee: *HD Pochin & Co v Robinows & Marjoribanks* (1869) 7 M. 622.

[51] A bill of lading, which indicates that goods have been shipped, is a pledge of the goods themselves if it has been delivered to the pledgee: *Hayman & Son v McLintock*, 1907 S.C. 936.

Lien

A lien (pronounced lean) is a right of security created by the operation of **21–30** law and enables the party in possession of the property to retain it until the owner of the property fulfils his/her obligation, which is generally to pay money. Liens are classified as either *general* or *special* liens. A *general* lien allows the person holding the property to exercise it in relation to all his/her transactions with the debtor. An innkeeper, as defined in s.1 of the Innkeepers Act 1878, has a *general* lien over property (except clothing) brought into his establishment by a guest who fails to pay his/her bill, as does a solicitor over the property of a client who has failed to pay fees and expenses incurred on his/her behalf. A *special* lien, on the other hand, may only be exercised in relation to a single transaction with the debtor. A *special* lien will arise, for example, when property has been handed over for repair or safekeeping. The party in possession of the property has no right to sell the property, unless s/he is successful in seeking a court order to dispose of it, or s.39 of the Sale of Goods Act 1979, applies.[52]

RIGHTS IN SECURITY OVER INCORPOREAL MOVEABLE PROPERTY

Incorporeal moveable property, which includes royalties, shares, patents, **21–31** copyright, trade marks and rights arising under insurance policies, has in itself no physical existence, therefore mere "delivery" to the creditor of a document detailing the existence and extent of the right concerned does not create a *real* right in security. To effect "delivery" a two-stage process must be followed:

(i) *assignation* of the right by the property owner (*assignor*) to the party providing the security (*assignee*); and
(ii) *intimation* to the debtor that the property has been assigned and that all benefits arising from it are now payable to the *assignee*.

Assignation by itself only creates a contractual right (that is to say, a *personal* right) against the *assignor* who is borrowing money on the strength of the value of, or the income generated by, the property concerned. Generally, for a *real* right to be created in favour of the *assignee*, the *assignor's* debtor must be informed that *assignation* has taken place. It is when this step (*intimation*) has been taken by the *assignee* that 'delivery' is complete.[53]

---

[52] If the seller remains unpaid s/he may resell the goods if s/he gives the debtor reasonable notice of his/her intention to do so.
[53] *Gallemos Ltd v Barratt Falkirk Ltd*, 1990 S.L.T. 98.

SITUATIONS WHERE INTIMATION IS NOT POSSIBLE—EXCEPTIONS TO THE GENERAL RULE

21–32 The bare act of *assignation* of certain types of incorporeal property, for example patents and shares is capable of creating a *real* right. This exception arises because there is no actual debtor to inform that *assignation* has taken place. However, the *real* right will not be constituted until the *assignation* is registered, if registration is required by law. Thus, to effect a valid assignation of a patent this must be registered in the Register of Patents[54] and the assignation of shares in a company will only be effected when the transfer of the shares is registered in that company's register of shareholders.

▼ CHAPTER SUMMARY

21–33 A creditor may demand a right in security for a debt to increase the likelihood that s/he will recover his/her outlay should the debtor fail to make payment when it falls due. In Scots law, a right in security gives rise to either a *personal* right (*jus in personam*) or a *real* right (*jus in re*).

PERSONAL RIGHTS IN SECURITY

(1) A cautionary obligation is a *personal* right in security which gives the creditor the right to recover the sum owed him/her by the debtor from another person.

(2) A contract of caution is an *accessory* obligation which means that the debt must exist before it can be enforced against the cautioner.

(3) The cautioner cannot be held liable for more than the principal debt itself:

➢   *Struthers v Dykes*.

(4) If the cautioner has paid the debt s/he has a right of relief, which is to claim the sum paid, including expenses, from the debtor.

(5) Where there are several cautioners, each is only liable for his/her *pro rata* share of the debt if all co-cautioners are solvent and *joint and several* liability does not apply. If any co-cautioner is insolvent the deficit is made up by the other co-cautioners.

(6) If the contract of caution states that co-cautioners are bound *jointly and severally* the creditor may proceed against a co-cautioner of choice for payment. If a co-cautioner is required to pay more than his/her *pro rata* share, s/he can subsequently claim *pro rata* relief from his/her co-cautioners:

➢   *Marshall & Co v Pennycook*, 1908 S.C. 276.

(7) If the contract of caution is worded imprecisely or is ambiguous a court will apply the *contra proferentem* rule:

---

[54] Patents Act 1977 ss.31–33. There is also a register for trade marks under the terms of ss.22–24 of the Trade Marks Act 1994.

➢ *Fortune v Young*, 1917 2 S.L.T. 150.

(8) A contract of caution is not considered a contract *uberrimae fidei* therefore there is no general duty on the creditor to disclose all material facts concerning the debtor's affairs to the cautioner:

➢ *Young v Clydesdale Bank* (1889) 17 R. 231.

(9) The exception to this rule is where a "proximate" relationship exists between the debtor and the cautioner. If the creditor is aware of the nature of the relationship between the parties, there exists a duty to act in good faith:

➢ *Smith v Bank of Scotland*, 1997 S.C (H.L.) 111.

REAL RIGHTS IN SECURITY OVER PROPERTY

A *real* right in security differs from a *personal* right in that it gives the creditor a right, often referred to as a *nexus* or a bond, over heritable property or moveable property belonging to the debtor. A *real* right can generally only be created if there is delivery from the debtor to the creditor of the property that is subject to the security. The exceptions to this rule are as follows:

Hypothecs

(1) Hypothecs are either *conventional*, or implied by law where the term *legal* hypothecs is used. *Conventional* hypothecs are restricted to *bonds of bottomry* and *bonds of respondentia*. *Legal* hypothecs include the *solicitor's* hypothec which, at common law, is over the award of any damages or costs to the client and, under statute, to property belonging to the client which is recovered during litigation:

➢ Solicitor's (Scotland) Act 1980 s.62(1).

(2) The *landlord's legal* hypothec can now only be exercised in relation to goods kept outwith domestic premises and those in commercial premises:

➢ Bankruptcy and Diligence etc. (Scotland) Act 2007 s.208.

Floating charges

A floating charge is a statutory form of security which can be created by contract over the heritable and moveable property of a registered company but not those of individuals or partnerships. The charge "floats" over the assets of a company and if the repayments to the charge holder are up to date the charge will continue to float undisturbed. If the debt is not repaid the charge is said to *crystallise*.

(1) A charge granted before September 15, 2003 enables the charge holder to appoint a receiver to recover the debt.
(2) A charge granted on or after September 15, 2003 requires, in most circumstance, the charge holder to appoint an administrator, who unlike a receiver, is under a statutory duty to achieve the best result for all the company's creditors:

> ➢ Companies Act 1985; the Insolvency Act 1986; the Enterprise Act
> 2002.

RIGHTS IN SECURITY WHERE DELIVERY IS REQUIRED

With the exception of hypothecs and floating charges, it is a general principle of
Scots law that a *real* right can only be created if there is "delivery" from the
debtor to the creditor, of the property that is subject to the security. In certain
cases, physical delivery of the property will not be possible, so *symbolic* or *constructive* "delivery" of the property will suffice.

STANDARD SECURITY

> (1) Since 1970 the only competent means of granting a right of security over
> heritable property is by entering into a contract of *standard security*:
>
> ➢ Conveyancing and Feudal Reform Act 1970.
>
> (2) If the debtor fails to make the loan repayments as agreed the *standard
> security* holder can ultimately enforce the sale of the property.

RIGHTS IN SECURITY OVER CORPOREAL MOVEABLE PROPERTY

> (1) Pledge usually occurs where corporeal moveable property is delivered
> by the *pledger* to the *pledgee*. However, pledge can also be created by
> actual, *constructive* or *symbolic* delivery of the property:
>
> ➢ *HD Pochin & Co v Robinows & Marjoribanks* (1869) 7 M. 622;
> *Hayman & Son v McLintock*, 1907 S.C. 936.
>
> (2) A lien is created by the operation of law enabling the party in possession
> of the property to retain it until the owner of the property fulfils his/her
> obligation which is generally to pay money. Liens are classified as either
> *general* or *special*.

RIGHTS IN SECURITY OVER INCORPOREAL MOVEABLE PROPERTY

> (1) Incorporeal moveable property enjoys no physical existence and mere
> "delivery" to the creditor of a document detailing the existence and
> extent of the right concerned will not generally create a *real* right in
> security. To effect "delivery" of such a property right *assignation* and
> *intimation* are generally required.

? QUICK QUIZ

True or False?

- A *real* right in security is always to be preferred to a *personal*
  right.

- A contract of caution is a principal obligation.
- The cautioner enjoys no right of relief against the debtor if required to pay the creditor on his/her behalf.
- A contract of caution is considered a contract *uberrimae fidei.*
- A *real* right in security can only be created where there is "delivery" of the property subject to the security.
- A floating charge is said to *crystallise* if the company concerned goes into liquidation or a receiver/administrator is appointed.
- Pledge may only be constituted by actual "delivery" of the property concerned.
- A *real* right in security over incorporeal moveable property can only be created via *assignation* and *intimation.*

📖 FURTHER READING

> - C. Ashton et al., *Understanding Scots Law* (Edinburgh: W. Green, 2007), Ch.10.
> - F. Davidson and L. Macgregor, *Commercial Law in Scotland*, 3rd edn (Edinburgh: W. Green, 2014), Ch.5.
> - N. Grier, *Commercial Law Basics* (Edinburgh: W. Green, 2010), Ch.10.

🖱 RELEVANT WEBLINKS:

> - *http://www.hmrc.gov.uk/* [Accessed May 15, 2015].
> - *http://www.legislation.gov.uk* [Accessed May 15, 2015].
> - *http://www.scotland.gov.uk/Resource/Doc/254430/0121799.pdf* [Accessed May 15, 2015].

Chapter 22   Dispute Resolution

HONG-LIN YU[1]

▶ CHAPTER OVERVIEW

22–01 This chapter is concerned with different forms of dispute resolution in business, both domestic and international in nature. It starts by presenting the practice of negotiation and mediation. The chapter goes on to discuss the operation of commercial arbitration involving Scottish or international businesses. The chapter then turns to consider the use of adjudication in construction disputes. Finally, the topic of court actions will be examined.

✓ OUTCOMES

22–02 At the end of this chapter you should be able to:

- ✓ understand the reasons for the popularity of alternative dispute resolution;
- ✓ identify the advantages and disadvantages of different forms of dispute resolution;
- ✓ understand the practice of negotiation;
- ✓ understand the practice of mediation;
- ✓ understand the different aspects of commercial arbitration;
- ✓ appreciate the different rules governing commercial arbitration involving a Scottish company in foreign trade;
- ✓ understand the laws relating to adjudication; and
- ✓ identify the courts to which disputes can be submitted.

ADVANTAGES AND DISADVANTAGES OF ADR

22–03 In the business world, disputes arise every day and various ways have been devised to resolve them. These methods fall into two broad categories: public resolution through the civil courts; and private dispute resolution through devices such as negotiation, mediation, arbitration and adjudication, collectively known as alternative dispute resolution ("ADR"). While court processes are public, ADR is private. The

---

[1] Reader in Law, University of Stirling.

advantages of a public resolution are that the parties will receive a binding decision from the court and the court can exercise coercive powers over the parties or relevant third parties. However, this method may cause difficulties such as slow process and exposure of the disputes in the public domain.

The second type of dispute resolution that is popular in business is to resolve the dispute in a closed-door environment. This is alternative dispute resolution which covers the areas of negotiation, mediation, arbitration and adjudication. The advantages of ADR are privacy, speed, specialised decision makers, confidentiality and flexibility. However, due to its private nature, ADR is often criticised for its lack of coercive powers and lack of binding force decision (apart from arbitration).

In Scotland, the importance of the role played by ADR has increased. It is highlighted in the Consultation Paper on the Scottish Civil Court Review that the review team, led by Lord Gill, will look into, "the role of mediation and other methods of dispute resolution in assisting people to resolve disputes with resort to the courts".[2] Therefore, it is essential to discuss the different types of dispute resolution in this chapter. They include negotiation, mediation, arbitration, adjudication and finally, traditional court actions.

NEGOTIATION

Negotiation is a form of ADR, "which can be informal, economic and **22–04** quick, and which encourages the parties to work out a resolution for themselves".[3] Negotiation sees the parties discussing means of settling a dispute that will lead to a satisfactory outcome for both parties. It is often the first step parties may take to resolve a dispute. It may take the form of telephone calls, face-to-face meetings between the parties or, more formally, meetings between the parties' lawyers. Frequently, disputes will end after the parties engage in negotiation. However it is said that whatever type of negotiation one is involved in:

> "There must be thorough preparation and careful assessment of the different issues. The presentation involves knowing your own case, your opponent's case, how the process will develop, what conventions will apply, where they will take place and who should make the opening offer."[4]

Yet sometimes negotiations will break down, so that parties may look to a third party to determine the disputes. This leaves the parties to choose

---

[2] Court of Session, *Scottish Civil Court Review Consultation Paper* (November 2007), para.2.6.
[3] S. Moody and R. Mackay (eds), *Green's Guide to Alternative Dispute Resolution in Scotland* (Edinburgh: W. Green, 1995), p.2.
[4] A. Bevan, *Alternative Dispute Resolution* (London: Sweet and Maxwell, 1992), pp.4–5.

between mediation, arbitration, adjudication or litigation, all of which will be discussed in detail in the following sections.

MEDIATION

Introduction

22–05 Mediation involves an independent third party—a mediator—whose job is to help the parties resolve their dispute. A mediator may help the parties evaluate their position, and can often be proactive in suggesting ways in which the dispute might be resolved.

Mediation process

22–06 It is said that:

> "Mediation is forward-looking; the goal is for all parties to work out a solution they can live with and trust. It focuses on solving problems, not uncovering the truth or imposing legal rules. This, of course, is a far different approach than courts take. In court, a judge or jury looks back to determine who was right and who was wrong, then imposes a penalty or award based on its decision."[5]

This emphasises the fact that the process focuses not on the legal rights of the parties, but on their interests and thus looks to arrive at a resolution which is mutually beneficial. While going to court (or indeed arbitration) produces a winner and a loser, mediation allows both parties to emerge as winners.

During the mediation process the parties can either choose to represent themselves or send representatives with their full authority to resolve the dispute. It is not unusual to have lawyers acting on behalf of their clients participate in the proceedings. Once the mediation starts, parties will be asked to explain the case and their positions to the mediator who may probe in order to find out what the parties really want out of the process. While sometimes mediators are little more than intermediaries, or do little more than point out the strengths and weaknesses of the respective positions, others may seize the initiative and offer innovative solutions to the parties' problems. It is important to understand that even if a mediator puts forward a specific solution, the parties are free to take it or leave it. In other words, mediation is not binding, although if the parties reach a formal agreement as a result of the mediation, that is binding. The non-binding character of mediation is sometimes seen as a weakness, since although it is private, flexible, speedy and informal, if mediation fails then the parties will not have a resolution for their dispute. For that reason many prefer to resort to a process which results in the imposition of a binding decision, such as going to court or arbitration.

---

[5] *http://www.nolo.com* [Accessed June 24, 2015].

For the past decade, mediation is recognised as consensus and involving process[6] in resolving disputes.[7] Such dispute resolution mechanism has attracted the attention of the EU invoking the important role mediation can play in commercial and civil disputes in aid of reducing court efficiency in terms of costs and resources. This development can be seen in the EU Directive[8] and the Woolf Reform on Access to Justice,[9] the Jackson Report[10] on civil litigation costs in England and Wales and the Gill Report in Scotland.[11] They all highlight mediation as a means of achieving costs savings and delivering value in the dispute management process[12] in large insurance cases,[13] personal injury cases,[14] pre-action protocol for personal injury claims,[15] bodily injury claims,[16] small business dispute,[17] housing claims[18] and construction disputes. [19]

In England, the intention to use mediation better deploy of court resources is clear. One saw Brooke LJ *Dunnett v Railtrack plc*[20] and *Halsey*[21] applying r.1.4 of the CPR and political pledges issued by the

---

[6] Tony Allen, "Successful Defendant Can be Deprived of Costs: Another Reading of *Daniels v Metropolitan Police Commissioner*" (2006) 2(4) *Kemp News* 2.

[7] John Sturrock, "The Role of Mediation in A Modern Civil Justice System" (2010) 21 S.L.T. 111, 112; Leonard Riskin, "Understanding Mediators' Orientations, Strategies and Techniques: A Grid for the Perplexed" (1996) 1 *Harvard Negotiation Law Review* 7 at 23.

[8] The EU Directive 2008/52/EC of the European Parliament and the Council of 21 May 2008 on certain aspects of mediation in civil and commercial matters ("Mediation Directive") was introduced to provide for mediation in cross-border disputes as well as internal mediation process among the Member States (Recital 8). It was implemented by the UK Government in the Cross-Border Mediation (EU Directive) Regulations 2011 (SI 2011/1133). Also see Karen Akinc, "Mediation in Turkey and the Mediation Bill" (2012) 78(3) *Arbitration* 269.

[9] Lord Woolf, *Access to Justice* (1996), Ch.13, para.39, available at *http://webarchive.nationalarchives.gov.uk/+/http:/www.dca.gov.uk/civil/final/index.htm* [Accessed June 24, 2015].

[10] Lord Justice Jackson, *Review of Civil Litigation Costs: Final Report* (Courts and Tribunals Judiciary/TSO, 2010).

[11] Scottish Executive, *Modern Laws for a Modern Scotland* (Edinburgh: Scottish Executive, 2007), para.3.5.

[12] Lord Justice Jackson, *Review of Civil Litigation Costs: Final Report* (Courts and Tribunals Judiciary/TSO, 2010), Ch.6, Pt 6.

[13] As above, Ch.22, para.2.1 (p.216).

[14] As above, Ch.16, para.2.6 (p.175).

[15] As above, Ch.22, para.3.13 (p.223).

[16] As above, Ch.22, para.6.2 (p.228).

[17] As above, Ch.25.

[18] As above, Ch.26, para.4.1 (p.286).

[19] As above, Ch.30, para.4.6 (p.299).

[20] [2002] EWCA Civ 303.

[21] *Halsey v Milton Keynes General NHS Trust* [2004] EWCA Civ 576, [2004] 1 W.L.R. 3002.

Lord Chancellor and the Department for Constitutional Affairs[22] as the starting point, "encourage the parties to use an alternative dispute resolution procedure if the court considers that appropriate and facilitating the use of such procedure".[23] The English Court of Appeal established that the court may use its discretion to depart from the usual rule[24] stipulated in CPR r.36(10)(5) and confirmed that the successful party should not recover its costs if it can be shown that the successful party unreasonably refused to engage in ADR.[25] A further step was taken in *PGF II*[26] in 2013 where Lord Briggs concluded that silence to the invitation is viewed as unreasonable behaviour which will deprive the winning part the costs.

ARBITRATION—THE ARBITRATION (SCOTLAND) ACT 2010

22–07 With an ambition to put Scotland on the map of international arbitration and attract international businessmen to choose Scotland as the place of their arbitration in order to generate revenue, the Scottish Government promulgate the Arbitration (Scotland) Act 2010 ("the 2010 Act") which is designed to provide a one stop shop with a single track of arbitration law corresponding with the modern trends in arbitration to cover both domestic and international arbitration.[27] The four objectives of the 2010 Act are:

- to clarify and consolidate Scottish arbitration law, filling in gaps where these exist;
- to provide a statutory framework for arbitrations which will operate in the absence of agreement to the contrary;
- to ensure fairness and impartiality in the process; and
- to minimise expense and ensure that the process is efficient.[28]

---

[22] *Halsey*, above, at [7]. The Court expressed that "We are also mindful of the position which had been taken by government on this issue. Thus, in March 2001, the Lord Chancellor announced an 'ADR Pledge' by which all government departments and Agencies made a number of commitments including that: 'Alternative Dispute Resolution will be considered and used in all suitable cases wherever the other party accepts it.' In July 2002, the Department for Constitutional Affairs published a report stated that the pledge as to the effectiveness of the Government's commitment to the ADR pledge ... following initiative on the part of the National Health Service Litigation Authority".

[23] CPR r.1.4(2)(e), *Halsey*, above, at [4].

[24] CPR r.36.10(5).

[25] A refusal can be deemed as unreasonable according to (1) the nature of the dispute, (2) the merits of the case, (3) the extent to which other settlement methods have been attempted, (4) whether the costs of ADR would be disproportionately high, (5) whether any delay in setting up and attending ADR would have been prejudicial, and (6) whether ADR had a reasonable prospect of success.

[26] *PGF II SA v OMFS Company 1 Ltd* [2013] EWCA Civ 1288.

[27] As stated in its policy memorandum, January 29, 2009, at para.28, "[i]t is hoped that the Bill—one enacted—will encourage the use of arbitration domestically and will attract international arbitration business to Scotland".

[28] Policy Memorandum, January 29, 2009, at para.26.

Structure of the 2010 Act

The 2010 Act contains 37 sections outlining the general principles applied **22–08** in the Scottish arbitration in the main part and 84 rules providing detailed arbitration procedure rules to be followed in Sch.1. Interestingly, the structure of the 2010 Act is such that the main part only provides the general principles to be followed by both courts and arbitral tribunals. The detailed procedure rules regulating arbitration seated in Scotland or subject to the 2010 Act are provided in the Scottish Arbitration Rules ("the Rules"), containing both mandatory[29] and default rules.[30] Both the main body of the 2010 Act and the Rules form the primary legislation of Scotland. The rules are a "ready-made framework"[31] for the parties to use in conducting the arbitral proceedings, if they choose to. There are also mandatory rules, which must be followed. These are set out in s.8 of the 2010 Act.

Key features of the 2010 Act

Founding principles—s.1

Three principles ensuring arbitration to be an effective dispute resolution **22–09** mechanism are listed in s.1 of the 2010 Act; they are:

"(a) that the object of arbitration is to resolve disputes fairly, impartially and without unnecessary delay or expense,

(b) that parties should be free to agree how to resolve disputes subject only to such safeguards as are necessary in the public interest,

(c) that the court should not intervene in an arbitration except as provided by this Act.

Anyone construing this Act must have regard to the founding principles when doing so."

Types of arbitration and dispute—s.2

To ensure a single track of the arbitration law, according to s.2(1) of the **22–10** 2010 Act, "arbitration" includes domestic arbitration,[32] international arbitration,[33] and arbitration between parties residing or carrying on business, anywhere in the UK.[34] An inclusive definition[35] can be seen in the definition of "dispute" in s.2(1) which provides "'dispute' includes: (a) any refusal to accept a claim; and (b) any other difference (whether contractual or not)".

---

[29] Arbitration (Scotland) Act 2010 s.8.
[30] Arbitration (Scotland) Act 2010 s.9(1).
[31] Policy Memorandum, para.88.
[32] Arbitration (Scotland) Act 2010 s.2(1)(a).
[33] Arbitration (Scotland) Act 2010 s.2(1)(c).
[34] Arbitration (Scotland) Act 2010 s.2(1)(b).
[35] Arbitration (Scotland) Act 2010 revised explanatory notes 2009, para.21.

Seat of arbitration—s.3

22–11 As s.3 provides that an arbitration will be regarded as being seated in Scotland if: Scotland is designated as the juridical seat of the arbitration by the parties; by any party to whom the parties give power to so designate; or where the parties fail to designate or so authorise a third party; by the tribunal; or in the absence of any such designation, the court determines that Scotland is to be the juridical seat of the arbitration. Once the juridical seat of arbitration is deemed to be in Scotland, the arbitration is subjected to the 2010 Act and the mandatory rules listed in the Rules will apply. Nevertheless, it is worth noting that the choice of Scotland as the juridical seat of arbitration does not affect the choice and the application of the substantive law to be used to decide the dispute.[36]

Repeal—s.29

22–12 To achieve the aim of modernising the Scottish arbitration law providing a single track and one stop shop Act, s.29 of and Sch.2 to the 2010 Act repeals the various relevant arbitration laws; namely, Arbitration (Scotland) Act 1894 (c.13); Arbitration Act 1950 (c.27); Arbitration Act 1975 (c.3); s.3 of the Administration of Justice (Scotland) Act 1972 (c.59); ss.17, 66 of and Sch.7 to the Law Reform (Miscellaneous provisions) (Scotland) Act 1990 (c.55).

Party autonomy and its restrictions—ss.1 and 9

22–13 The principle of party autonomy is manifested in the parties' freedom in designing the arbitration procedures to suit their needs. Such principle is firmly rooted in s.1, of the 2010 Act which stipulates that, "parties should be free to agree how to resolve disputes subject only to such safeguards as are necessary in the public interest". Additionally, s.9 of the 2010 Act offers the parties the freedom to modify or disapply the default rules contained in the Scottish Arbitration Rules. In general, s.9 is a reflection of the belief that the parties and the arbitrators can adopt procedures that are most appropriate to deal with the circumstances of the particular case. Consequently, arbitration under the 2010 Act can provide flexible procedures allowing the parties to make arrangements suit their particular needs.[37] However, it shall be borne in mind that party autonomy is not unlimited. It can be restricted by mandatory rules listed in s.8 of the 2010 Act and public policy which was used to ensure that arbitration is carried out according to a minimum level of standard.

---

[36] Arbitration (Scotland) Act 2010 s.3(2).
[37] Policy Memorandum, January 29, 2010, para.86.

Arbitrators—ss.24–25 of the 2010 Act and rr.2–18 of the Rules

Method of appointment—r.6

An arbitrator can be appointed by the parties, the appointed arbitrators **22–14** or any third party who is given the authority to make such an appointment. An arbitrator may be chosen from any field as diverse as farming, construction, forestry, trade, commodities, engineering, legal or accounting professions. If the parties agree to have multiple arbitrators, each party must appoint an eligible individual as an arbitrator within 28 days of receiving the request from the other party[38] and where more arbitrators are to be appointed, the arbitrators appointed by the parties must appoint eligible individuals as the remaining arbitrators.[39]

Eligibility, number of arbitrators and duty of disclosure—rr.3, 4, 5 and 8

It is mandatory that an arbitrator is a natural person[40] who is over the age **22–15** of 16[41] and is not declared as having lack of legal capacity[42] within the meaning of s.1(6) of the Adults with Incapacity (Scotland) Act 2000. An individual must declare any conflict of interest known to him which might reasonably be considered relevant when considering the issue of independence or impartiality.[43]

Arbitrator's duties

The arbitrator has a number of duties, including: **22–16**

- The duty to disclose a conflict of interest—r.8

An individual who is an arbitrator or has been contacted about his willingness to act as an arbitrator must disclose to the parties any circumstances known to the individual that might reasonably be considered as conflict of interests to the arbitral appointment referee, other third party or court empowered to make appointments.[44]

- The duty of impartiality and independence, efficiency and fair treatment—rr.24, 77, 78, and 81

Apart from disclosing any reasonably suspected conflict of interests, the tribunal is also required by law to act impartially and independently,[45] conduct the arbitration procedures without necessary delay or incurring

---

[38] Scottish Arbitration Rules r.6(b)(i).
[39] Scottish Arbitration Rules r.6(b)(ii).
[40] Scottish Arbitration Rules r.3.
[41] Scottish Arbitration Rules r.4(a).
[42] Scottish Arbitration Rules r.4(b).
[43] Scottish Arbitration Rules r.8.
[44] Scottish Arbitration Rules r.8(2).
[45] Scottish Arbitration Rules r.24(1)(a).

unnecessary expense[46] and treat the parties fairly by giving each party a reasonable opportunity to present his case.[47] To avoid any ambiguity arising from the issue of independence, r.77 provides a mandatory list of circumstances in which an arbitrator is not independent.

• The duty of confidentiality—r.26

As a default rule, r.26 imposes the arbitrator(s) and the parties a legal duty not to disclose any confidential information[48] relating to the arbitration. A breach of confidence is actionable by the party or parties to whom the duty was owed. In the case where a breach leads to substantial injustice, the arbitrator(s) involved in the breach will be subject to removal under r.12. A breach of confidentiality allows the party or parties to seek remedy in the forms of interdict or damages.[49]

However, the duty of confidentiality is subject to a few exceptions listed in r.26(1). In accordance with this provision, first, confidential information can be revealed: (a) with the parties' expressed or implied authorisation[50]; (b) if such disclosure is required by the tribunal or is for the conduct of the arbitration proceedings[51]; (c) if it is required by the enactment or rule of law[52] for the discharge of the public functions performed by the discloser's[53] or the public body or office[54]; and (d) on the grounds of public interest,[55] the interest of public justice[56] as well as a defence of absolute privilege in a defamation action.[57] Arbitrators also have a duty to inform the arbitrating parties of any proceedings deemed confidential.[58]

Right to resign—r.15

22–17 Rule 15 allows the arbitrator to resign in certain circumstances. An arbitrator is allowed to resign if both parties consent to his resignation[59] or if he already secured a contractual right to resign in the circumstances listed in the appointment agreement.[60] Apart from consensual agreement,

---

[46] Scottish Arbitration Rules r.24(1)(c). Similar mandatory duty is imposed upon the parties under r.25.

[47] Scottish Arbitration Rules rr.24(1)(b) and 24(2).

[48] Scottish Arbitration Rules r.26(4). Confidential information is defined as any information related to the dispute, the arbitral proceedings, the award or any civil proceedings relating to the arbitration in respect of which an order has been granted under s.15 of the Arbitration (Scotland) Act 2010 which is not, and had never been, in the public domain.

[49] Arbitration (Scotland) Act 2010 revised explanatory notes 2009, para.142.

[50] Scottish Arbitration Rules r.26(1)(a).

[51] Scottish Arbitration Rules r.26(1)(b).

[52] Scottish Arbitration Rules r.26(1)(c)(i).

[53] Scottish Arbitration Rules r.26(1)(c)(ii).

[54] Scottish Arbitration Rules r.26(1)(c)(iii).

[55] Scottish Arbitration Rules r.26(1)(e).

[56] Scottish Arbitration Rules r.26(1)(f).

[57] Scottish Arbitration Rules r.26(1)(g).

[58] Scottish Arbitration Rules r.26(3).

[59] Scottish Arbitration Rules r.15(1)(a).

[60] Scottish Arbitration Rules r.15(1)(b).

an arbitrator may also resign if his appointment is challenged on the grounds of lacking impartiality, independence or fair treatment under rr.10 or 12.[61] An arbitrator is also allowed to resign if he has accepted the appointment on the basis that he or she would be assisted by an expert during the course of the arbitration under r.34(1) but the parties subsequently refused to pay for such an expert.[62] In other situations, the arbitrator can be removed in terms of rr.12 and 14 on the application by any party to the court where the arbitrator has failed his duty to be impartial and independent[63] or to treat the parties fairly.[64] The Outer House of the Court of Session may also remove the arbitral party if a party can prove that substantial injustice has been caused because of a failure to conduct the arbitration in accordance with the arbitration agreement.

Arbitrator's entitlement or liability—r.16

On the application by any party, the Outer House has the mandatory **22–18** power to order the parties to pay any outstanding fees or expenses due to the arbitrator whose tenure ended.[65] On the other hand, if the court considers it is reasonable, it may order the arbitrators who ended the tenure to repay the fees or expenses that have already been made.[66]

Arbitrator's fees and expenses—rr.59, 60–66

In Scotland, by carrying out the tasks of resolving the parties' dispute, **22–19** arbitrators are entitled to fees and expenses incurred personally or as a member of the tribunal for the purpose of conducting the arbitration. It is up to the parties to reach an agreement between themselves and the arbitrator(s) or the arbitral appointment referees on the amount of fees and expenses payable.[67] Failing to reach any agreement, the amounts are to be determined by the Auditor of the Court of Session.[68] Once the amounts are agreed, r.60, a mandatory rule, makes the parties severally liable to the fees of the arbitrators, the arbitral appointments referee or any other third party to whom the parties give powers in relation to the arbitration.[69]

Accordingly, the parties have to pay the arbitrators: (a) the arbitrators' fees and expenses[70]; and (b) expenses incurred by the tribunal when conducting the arbitration.[71] The expenses include the fees and expenses of any clerk, agent, employee or other person appointed by the tribunal

---

[61] Scottish Arbitration Rules r.15(1)(c).
[62] Scottish Arbitration Rules r.15(1)(d).
[63] Scottish Arbitration Rules r.12(a).
[64] Scottish Arbitration Rules r.12(b).
[65] Scottish Arbitration Rules r.16(1)(a).
[66] Scottish Arbitration Rules r.16(1)(b).
[67] Scottish Arbitration Rules r.60(3).
[68] Scottish Arbitration Rules r.60(3)(b).
[69] Scottish Arbitration Rules r.60(1)–60(2).
[70] Scottish Arbitration Rules r.60(1)(a)(i)–(ii).
[71] Scottish Arbitration Rules r.60(1)(b).

to assist it in conducting the arbitration, the fees and expenses of any expert from whom the tribunal obtains an opinion, any expenses in respect of meeting and hearing facilities, and any expenses incurred in determining recoverable arbitration expenses.[72]

Death of arbitrator and party—rr.79 and 80

22–20 The death of arbitrator will discharge his contractual obligations owed to the parties to act as an arbitrator because his authority is personal and such authority ceases on his death.[73] However, the death of a party does not discharge the arbitration agreement. A valid arbitration agreement allows the other party to enforce the agreement against the executor or other representative of that party.[74]

Immunity—rr.73–75

22–21 Rule 73(1) provides that arbitrators are not liable for anything done or omitted in the performance or purported performance, of the tribunal's functions. However their immunity is subject to the exceptions of bad faith[75] or liability arising from an arbitrator's resignation.[76] Such immunity is also extended to any clerk, agent, employee or other person assisting the tribunal to perform its functions,[77] arbitral appointment referees, other third party empowered to make nomination of arbitrators,[78] agents or employees of arbitral appointment referees or other third party empowered to make nomination of arbitrators,[79] as well as experts, witnesses and legal representatives participating in arbitration.[80]

Procedural law

22–22 It is settled that the choice of a procedural law can be different from the choice of the substantive law. This can be seen in s.3(2) of the 2010 Act, which stipulates: "[t]he fact that an arbitration is seated in Scotland does not affect the substantive law to be used to decide the dispute".

The parties' chosen procedural law regulates all procedural matters which have to be followed by the arbitrators. However, parties' freedom in the choice of procedural law is limited by the exceptions of mandatory rules and public policy.

---

[72] Scottish Arbitration Rules r.60(1)(b)(i)–(iv).
[73] Scottish Arbitration Rules r.79.
[74] Scottish Arbitration Rules r.80(1).
[75] Scottish Arbitration Rules r.73(2)(a).
[76] Scottish Arbitration Rules r.73(2)(b).
[77] Scottish Arbitration Rules r.73(3).
[78] Scottish Arbitration Rules r.74(1).
[79] Scottish Arbitration Rules r.74(2).
[80] Scottish Arbitration Rules r.75 and Policy Memorandum, para.213.

Seat of arbitration—s.3

In accordance with s.3 of the 2010 Act, the seat of arbitration can be **22–23** decided by the parties, the arbitrators, the third parties authorised to so designated or by the court. Accordingly, Scotland is regarded as the juridical seat of arbitration if Scotland is designated as the seat of the arbitration by the parties directly or by any third parties, such as an institution or an individual, where authorised explicitly by the parties or by the arbitral tribunal. Failing to decide on the seat of arbitration,[81] according to s.3(1)(a), the seat of the arbitration may also be decided by the tribunal[82] or the courts[83] in accordance with the rules of private international law. Apart from the relevant provisions on the juridical seat of arbitration, for convenience, r.28(2)(a) allows the tribunal to meet and otherwise conduct the arbitration anywhere it chooses (in or outwith Scotland). Once Scotland is designated as the seat of arbitration, both parties and the tribunal will have to observe the mandatory rules listed in the Scottish Arbitration Rules to ensure the enforceability of arbitral awards at the later stage.

Choice and the determination of the proper law—r.47

Subject to the parties' agreement, if an agreed choice of proper law can be **22–24** established then the tribunal must apply the parties' choice of proper law to resolve the dispute. This choice can be made either expressly or by implication. The parties' freedom to have their disputes governed by the law they desire is based on the theory of party autonomy which was provided in r.47(1)(a). It reads, "the tribunal must decide the dispute in accordance with the law chosen by the parties as applicable to the substance of the dispute".

If no such choice is made or the purported choice is unlawful, the arbitral tribunal will have to follow the appropriate conflict of law rules, i.e. implied choice of law test or the closest and most real test to determine the proper law. Rule 47(3) also requires the arbitrators to take commercial and trade usage, custom, or practices into consideration when deciding the disputes. However, regarding the international practice of *"ex bono et aequo"* and *"amiable compositeur"*, r.47(2) provides that an arbitrator is only allowed to disregard the law and rely solely on what he or she considers to be fair and equitable if that forms part of the law concerned or is expressly authorised by the agreement between the parties.

---

[81] Arbitration (Scotland) Act 2010 s.3(1)(a)(i)–(iii).
[82] Arbitration (Scotland) Act 2010 s.3(1)(a).
[83] Arbitration (Scotland) Act 2010 explanatory notes, para.22 and Arbitration (Scotland) Act 2010 s.3(1)(b).

Arbitral proceedings—part four of the Scottish Arbitration Rules

22–25 Part four of the Rules set out rules relating to procedure and evidence, and administrative duties. Unless modified or disapplied by the parties' agreement, r.28, a default rule, offers the arbitrator the power to decide the procedure to be followed and also the evidential matters.[84] Where a party fails to comply with a direction given by the tribunal or breaches the agreement or Rules, then the tribunal has the power under r.39 to make an order relating to the conduct of the arbitration. The orders a tribunal is empowered to make include: direction that the party is not entitled to rely on any allegation or material which was the subject matter of the order; draw adverse inferences from the non-compliance; proceed with the arbitration and make its award; or make such provisional award (including an award on expenses) as it considers appropriate in consequence of the non-compliance.[85]

Powers of court in relation to arbitral proceedings

Power to determine points of Scots law—rr.41 and 42

22–26 Rule 41 expressly offers the Outer House the power to determine any points of Scots law arising in arbitration, although this power is restricted in practice under r.42. The stated case application is only valid if the parties have agreed that the application may be made,[86] or the parties have consented to it being made and the court is satisfied that determining the question is likely to produce substantial savings in expenses, the application was made without delay, and there is a good reason why the question should be determined by the court. The Outer House's decision on the point of Scots law is final.[87]

Arbitral awards

Remedies awarded in the award—rr.48–50

22–27 Rule 48(1) provides a mandatory provision granting the tribunal the power to order the payment of a sum of money as well as a sum in damages. The currency of the sum ordered by the tribunal has to be the one agreed between the parties or, in the absence of such agreement, in such a currency as the tribunal considers appropriate.[88] Other remedies available to the tribunal though can be modified or disapplied by the parties' agreement, include a declaratory award, an award ordering a

---

[84] Scottish Arbitration Rules r.28(1).
[85] Scottish Arbitration Rules r.39(2)(a)–(d).
[86] Scottish Arbitration Rules r.42(2)(a).
[87] Scottish Arbitration Rules r.42(4). However, it is important to point out that r.41 is a default rule; therefore the courts will not be able to exercise the power on referral of point of law if the parties agree to exclude the application of r.41. It has to be noted that r.69 allows "legal error appeal", which grants the parties the right to appeal to the Outer House against the tribunal's award on the ground that the tribunal erred on a point of Scots law.
[88] Scottish Arbitration Rules r.48(2).

party to do or refrain from doing something or an award ordering the rectification or reduction of any deed or other document allowed by the applicable laws.[89] However, if a court decree is involved in the decision making process, it is not possible for the tribunal to reduce a court decree.

Forms of award—r.51

As a default rule, r.51 provides that an award must be signed by all **22–28** arbitrators or all those assenting to the award.[90] An award shall contain reasons and, if any, any other provisional or partial awards in relation to the particular arbitration shall also be stated in an award.[91] Once an award is made, it has to be in writing and delivered (by hand, post, electronic transmissions or any other methods).[92]

Types of award—rr.53–55

Under the 2010 Act, arbitrators are allowed to make different types of **22–29** award, such as provisional awards, partial awards, draft awards and final awards in order to dispose of all the issues submitted to the tribunal and complete the arbitration process.

Correction of awards—r.58

From time to time, arbitral tribunals may make some clerical, typo- **22–30** graphical or accidental errors or omission in the awards. Instead of invalidating such awards, r.58 of the Rules, a default rule, allows the tribunal to correct such errors or omissions in order to clarify or remove any ambiguity in the awards.[93]

Withholding of an award for non-payment—r.56

Rule 56 provides the tribunal a mandatory power to withhold an award **22–31** until all the fees and expenses incurred by the tribunal have been paid in full,[94] subject to a right of appeal by the parties.

When does an arbitration end—r.57

Arbitration ends when the tribunal delivers the last and final award.[95] **22–32** However, arbitration may end prematurely if the tribunal determines to end the arbitration as a result of a justified objection to his jurisdiction[96] being made, or parties fail to submit a claim or defence for the tribunal to

---

[89] Scottish Arbitration Rules r.49(a)–(c).
[90] Scottish Arbitration Rules r.51(1).
[91] Scottish Arbitration Rules r.51(2)(c)–(d).
[92] Scottish Arbitration Rules rr.51(3) and 83 in relation to formal communication.
[93] Scottish Arbitration Rules r.58(1).
[94] Scottish Arbitration Rules r.56(1).
[95] Scottish Arbitration Rules r.57(1).
[96] Scottish Arbitration Rules rr.57(2) and 20(3).

consider the disputes submitted.[97] Arbitration may also be brought to an end by the parties if an early settlement is reached between them.[98] In the case of a settlement, the parties can request the tribunal to make a final and binding award recording the terms of the settlement.[99]

Enforcement and challenge of arbitral awards—ss.11–15

22–33 To ensure arbitration remains a speedy and efficient method of alternative dispute resolution, the arbitral award will be final and binding on the parties and be capable of being recognised or enforced, in terms of s.11(1) of the 2010 Act.

Challenge of arbitral awards

22–34 The finality of an arbitral award does not mean that the arbitrating parties must carry out the award according to the tribunal's decision immediately if substantial injustice has been caused because the arbitrators or oversman has failed in his duty towards the parties. The challenge procedures available within the 2010 Act are limited to the grounds of lack of substantive jurisdiction, serious irregularity or legal errors.[100] The court's task is to review the process on how the arbitrator came to a decision, rather than review the merits of the award. Furthermore, a challenge on these grounds is only competent if the applicant party has exhausted any available arbitral process of appeal or review of the award,[101] and made the application within the 28 days after the award, the correction or review of the award was made available.[102]

Challenge based on lack of substantive jurisdiction—r.67

22–35 A party who wishes to challenge the tribunal's award on the ground of lack of jurisdiction may appeal to the Outer House against such an award.[103]

Challenge based on serious irregularities— r.68

22–36 If a party can prove and satisfy the Outer House that substantial injustice[104] has been caused by the tribunal's failure in conducting the arbitration in accordance with the arbitration agreement, the applicable Rules or any agreed conduct of the arbitration between the parties, the affected party may appeal to the Outer House against the award on the basis of serious irregularity contained in r.68(1) of the Rules.

---

[97] Scottish Arbitration Rules rr.57(2) and 37(1).
[98] Scottish Arbitration Rules r.57(3).
[99] Scottish Arbitration Rules r.57(4). It is important to point out that the relevant Scottish Arbitration Rules still apply to matters connected with the arbitration even if there is an early termination of arbitration proceedings.
[100] Arbitration (Scotland) Act 2010 s.11(3).
[101] Scottish Arbitration Rules r.71(2).
[102] Scottish Arbitration Rules r.71(4).
[103] Scottish Arbitration Rules r.67(1).
[104] Scottish Arbitration Rules r.68(2)(a).

Legal errors appeal—r.69

A party may appeal to the Outer House against the tribunal's award on **22–37** the grounds that the tribunal erred on a point of Scots law.[105]

Enforcement of arbitral awards—ss.12–15

Generally speaking, once a party receiving an award in his favour applies **22–38** to the sheriff courts or the Court of Session[106] in Scotland, the courts have the discretion to order the enforcement of an arbitral award made by a tribunal as if it were an extract registered decree bearing a warrant for execution granted by the court.[107]

To avoid the characteristics of confidentiality being undermined during the court proceedings, the 2010 Act allows parties to request anonymity in the court legal proceedings.

Arbitration expenses—r.59

Rule 59 contains a default provision defining the term arbitration **22–39** expenses incurred in arbitration proceedings. In accordance with r.59, arbitration expenses means the arbitrators' fees and expenses for which the parties are liable under r.60,[108] any expenses incurred by the tribunal when conducting the arbitration for which the parties are liable under r.60,[109] the parties' legal and other expenses,[110] and the fees and expenses of any arbitral appointments referee, and any other third party to whom the parties give powers in relation to the arbitration for which the parties are liable under r.60.[111]

Arbitrator's fees and expenses—r.60

To protect the arbitrators' entitlements to payment, r.60 is a mandatory **22–40** rule stipulating that the parties are severally liable to any fees and expenses incurred by the tribunal when conducting the arbitration.[112]

The amounts of fees and expenses payable shall be agreed between the parties and the arbitrators, or the arbitral appointment referee or other third party.[113] In the absence of any agreement, the level of the fees and expenses shall be decided by the Auditor of the Court of Session.[114]

---

[105] Scottish Arbitration Rules r.69(1).
[106] Arbitration (Scotland) Act 2010 s.12(8).
[107] Arbitration (Scotland) Act 2010 s.12(1).
[108] Scottish Arbitration Rules r.59(a).
[109] Scottish Arbitration Rules r.59(b).
[110] Scottish Arbitration Rules r.59(c).
[111] Scottish Arbitration Rules r.59(d)(i)–(ii).
[112] Scottish Arbitration Rules r.60(1).
[113] Scottish Arbitration Rules r.60(3)(a).
[114] Scottish Arbitration Rules r.60(3)(b).

Recoverable arbitration expenses—r.61

22–41 Further stipulated than r.59 regarding the parties' liability to the arbitrators' fees and expenses, r.61 provides a list of arbitration expenses which may be recoverable. They are: the arbitrators' fees and expenses for which the parties are liable under r.60[115]; any expenses incurred by the tribunal when conducting the arbitration for which the parties are liable under r.60[116]; and the fees and expenses of any arbitral appointments referee (or any other third party to whom the parties give powers in relation to the arbitration) for which the parties are liable under r.60.[117]

ADJUDICATION

22–42

> **Key Concept**
>
> Adjudication is widely used in construction disputes under the Housing Grants, Construction and Regeneration Act 1996.

Adjudication is a decision-making process involving a neutral third party, called an adjudicator, with the authority to make a binding decision on the parties. To reduce the caseloads of the courts and arbitration, since May 1, 1998, adjudication as an ADR to resolve disputes arising under the construction, telecommunications, security installation and engineering contracts has been introduced by the Housing Grants, Construction and Regeneration Act 1996 ("HGCRA"). Since then adjudication has been receiving full support from the construction industry. Based on its mandatory provision, adjudication has become a standard form of dispute resolution settling differences between parties to a construction contract. According to the 2010 Act, to submit disputes arising from the contract to adjudication, the construction contract between the parties must be in writing, made by exchange of correspondence or otherwise evidenced in writing. Different types of dispute which can be submitted to adjudication include money claims, delay and disruption, extension of time, declarations, specific performance and defect claims.

Legal framework

22–43 Alongside the HGCRA, in Scotland, there are statutes affecting the adjudication process. They are:

- the Scheme for Construction Contracts (Scotland) Regulations 1998;

---

[115] Scottish Arbitration Rules r.61(1)(a).
[116] Scottish Arbitration Rules r.61(1)(b).
[117] Scottish Arbitration Rules r.61(1)(c).

- the Construction Contracts (Scotland) Exclusion Order 1998; and
- the Housing Grants, Construction and Regeneration Act 1996 (Scotland) (Commencement No.5) Order 1998.

Section 108(1) of the HGCRA sets out the right to refer disputes to adjudication. It reads:

"A party to a construction contract has the right to refer a dispute arising under the contract for adjudication under a procedure complying with this section. For this purpose 'dispute' includes any difference."

Following this provision, the parties have the right to give notice of intention to refer a dispute to adjudication[118] and the dispute must be referred to the adjudicator so appointed within seven days of such notice.[119] Once the dispute is submitted to the adjudicator, he is required to reach a decision within 28 days,[120] extendable to 42 days in total.[121] The appointed adjudicator is required by law to act in an impartial manner[122] and take his initiative in ascertaining the facts and the law.[123] The binding nature of adjudicator's decision is usually upheld by arbitral tribunal or the courts.[124] It is furthermore enforced by the courts by means of summary proceedings. Once the decision turns into a court order, then the court, upon the application of the party, will be able to enforce the award against the losing party. It is also noted that the right to adjudication is not affected by the discharge or termination of the main contract. Unless acting in bad faith, the adjudicator is not liable for anything done or omitted in the discharge or purported discharge of his function as adjudicator.[125] Similar protection is also afforded to the agents or employee of the adjudicator.[126]

---

[118] HGCRA s.108(2)(a).
[119] HGCRA s.108(2)(b).
[120] HGCRA s.108(2)(c).
[121] HGCRA s.108(2)(d).
[122] HGCRA s.108(2)(e).
[123] HGCRA s.108(2)(f).
[124] HGCRA s.108(3).
[125] HGCRA s.108(4).
[126] In any case, if the contract does not comply with the requirements of s.108(1)–(4), the parties to a construction contract are unable to reach agreement regarding entitlement to stage payment, notice of intention to withhold payment and prohibition of conditional payment, or a construction contract does not make provisions about date of payment, the provisions of the Scheme for Construction Contracts apply to adjudication.

COURT ACTIONS

22–44 | **Key Concept**

The value of the claim determines which court the pursuer shall submit the dispute to.

- Court of Session—£5,000 or above;
- Sheriff Court—ordinary causes action—£5,000 or above;
- Sheriff Court—Simple procedure £5,000 or less.

Jurisdiction under the Civil Jurisdiction and Judgments Act 1982

22–45 If the parties decide to resolve their business disputes in Scotland, it is paramount for the parties to find out whether the Scottish courts have jurisdiction over the dispute. The general principle to determine whether a court has jurisdiction over the dispute depends on whether the individual or the corporate is domiciled within the court jurisdiction. An individual is domiciled in Scotland if and only if: (a) he is resident in Scotland; and (b) the nature and circumstances of his residence indicate that he has a substantial connection with Scotland.[127] For a legal person, the seat of a corporation or association shall be treated as its domicile in Scotland[128] if it was incorporated or formed under the Scottish law, or its central management and control is exercised in Scotland, or it has its registered office or some other official address in Scotland, or it has a place of business in Scotland.[129]

Subject to Pts I and II of the Civil Jurisdiction and Judgments Act 1982 Sch.8 has effects to determine in what circumstances a person may be sued in civil proceedings in the Court of Session or in a Sheriff Court in Scotland. Under Sch.8, if the parties agree in writing that a court is to have jurisdiction to settle any disputes that have arisen or that may arise in connection with a particular legal relationship, that court shall have jurisdiction.[130] A Scottish court also has exclusive jurisdiction: (a) in proceedings that have as their object rights in rem in, or tenancies of, immovable property, the courts for the place where the property is situated in Scotland; (b) in proceedings which have as their object the validity of the constitution, the nullity or the dissolution of companies or other legal persons or associations of natural or legal persons, the courts for the place where the company, legal person or association has its seat in Scotland; (c) in proceedings that have as their object the validity of entries in public registers, the courts for the place where the register is kept in Scotland; and (d) in proceedings concerned with the enforcement of judgments, the courts for the place where the judgment has been or is

---

[127] Civil Jurisdiction and Judgments Act 1982 s.41(3).
[128] Civil Jurisdiction and Judgments Act 1982 s.42(1).
[129] Civil Jurisdiction and Judgments Act 1982 s.42(3)–(5).
[130] Civil Jurisdiction and Judgments Act 1982 s.41(3) and Sch.8 r.6.

to be enforced in Scotland.[131] Regarding jurisdiction over consumer contracts, such as a contract for sale of goods on instalment credit term or a contract for a loan repayable by instalments or other financial arrangements or other similar types consumer contract, the Scottish court has jurisdiction if the consumer or the defender or both of them is domiciled in Scotland.[132]

Value of the claim determining which court has the jurisdiction[133]

Apart from the issue of domicile, the value of the claims the purser raises **22–46** is also a factor to consider about which court has jurisdiction over the dispute.

Court of Session

According to s.7 of the Sheriff Courts (Scotland) Act 1907,[134] a claim over **22–47** £10,000[135] excluding expenses and interest, the parties can submit to either the Court of Session. Parties can also raise a commercial action if the dispute arising from the construction of a commercial or mercantile document, the sale or hire purchase of goods, the export or import of merchandise, the carriage of goods by land, air or sea (other than an Admiralty action within the meaning of r.46.1), insurance, banking, the provision of financial services, mercantile agency, mercantile usage or a custom of trade, a building, engineering or construction contract, a commercial lease, or any matters not falling into this list but relating to a dispute of a business or commercial nature.[136]

Sheriff Court

Ordinary Cause Actions

With the intentions to make provision about the sheriff courts; to **22–48** establish a Sheriff Appeal Court; to make provision about civil court procedure; to make provision about appeals in civil proceedings; to make provision about appeals in criminal proceedings; to make provision about justice of the peace courts; to rename the Scottish Court Service and give it functions in relation to tribunals, the Courts Reform (Scotland) Act 2014 was promulgated and received Royal Assent on November 10, 2014. The Act consolidates the Sheriff Court Acts of 1907 and 1971 and removes summary causes and small claims as well as further creates the sheriff appeal court dealing with all appeal civil cases.[137]

---

[131] Civil Jurisdiction and Judgments Act 1982 s.41(3) and Sch.8 r.5.
[132] Civil Jurisdiction and Judgments Act 1982 s.41(3) and Sch.8 rr.3–6. The Civil Jurisdiction and Judgments Act 1982 also lists the grounds where a person may be sued in Scottish courts.
[133] For detailed discussion, see Ch.2, "Structure of the Scottish Legal System".
[134] For actions commenced on or after January 1, 1994, the issue will be regulated by SI 1993/1956 as amended by SI 1996/2167, SI 1996/2445 and SI 1996/2586.
[135] Court Reform (Scotland) Act 2014 s.39.
[136] Act of Sederunt (Rules of the Court of Session) 1994 (SI 1994/1443) rr.47.1.
[137] Court Reform (Scotland) Act 2014 s.46.

Part 3 (Civil Procedure) of the 2010 Act makes provision for civil jury trials in an all-Scotland sheriff court as well as includes provisions for simple procedure which will replace small claims and summary cause procedures. It also raises the financial limit for higher claims to be dealt with by the sheriff to £100,000 in order to free up the Court of Session.[138] According to s.39 of the 2010 Act, the Sheriff has the power to hear a dispute with the aggregate total value of all such orders sought, exclusive of interest and expenses, under £100,000.[139]

Simple procedure

22–49 With the intentions to make provision about the sheriff courts; to establish a Sheriff Appeal Court; to make provision about civil court procedure; to make provision about appeals in civil proceedings; to make provision about appeals in criminal proceedings; to make provision about justice of the peace courts; to rename the Scottish Court Service and give it functions in relation to tribunals, the Courts Reform (Scotland) Act 2014 was promulgated and received Royal Assent on November 10, 2014. The Act consolidates the Sheriff Court Acts of 1907 and 1971 and removes summary causes and small claims as well as further creates the sheriff appeal court dealing with all appeal civil cases.[140] Part 3 (Civil Procedure) of the 2010 Act makes provision for civil jury trials in an all-Scotland sheriff court as well as includes provisions for simple procedure which will replace small claims and summary cause procedures.

The simple procedure is stipulated in s.72 of the 2010 Act. The explanatory notes of the 2010 Act confirmed the need for a distinct procedure for low value claims. The financial limit for low value claims is set as £5,000. For cases under £5,000 are now to be dealt with primarily by summary sheriffs which is referred as simple procedure. Under the simple procedure, five types of proceedings may only be brought subject to such procedure. They are: (a) proceedings for payment of a sum of money not exceeding £5,000[141]; (b) actions of multiplepoinding where the value of the fund or property that is the subject of the action does not exceed £5,000[142]; (c) actions of furthcoming where the value of the arrested fund or subject does not exceed £5,000[143]; (d) actions ad factum praestandum, other than actions in which there is claimed, in addition or as an alternative to a decree ad factum praestandum, a decree for payment of a sum of money exceeding £5,000[144]; (e) proceedings for the recovery of possession of heritable property or moveable property, other than proceedings in which there is claimed, in addition or as an

---

[138] Court Reform (Scotland) Act 2014 s.39.
[139] Court Reform (Scotland) Act 2014 s.39(1)(b)(ii).
[140] Court Reform (Scotland) Act 2014 s.46.
[141] Court Reform (Scotland) Act 2014 s.72(3)(a).
[142] Court Reform (Scotland) Act 2014 s.72(3)(b).
[143] Court Reform (Scotland) Act 2014 s.72(3)(c).
[144] Court Reform (Scotland) Act 2014 s.72(3)(d).

alternative to a decree for such recovery, a decree for payment of a sum of money exceeding £5,000.[145]

In a case where the civil proceedings in the sheriff court that are being conducted otherwise than as a simple procedure case, the parties can make a joint application to the sheriff for the proceedings to continue subject to simple procedure.[146] Likewise, a party to a simple procedure case may, at any stage, make an application for the case not to proceed subject to simple procedure.[147] Where such an application is made, the sheriff has the discretion to decide whether the case shall be transferred from simple procedure.

Transfer of cases to and from simple procedure and appeals

In a case where the civil proceedings in the sheriff court that are being **22–50** conducted otherwise than as a simple procedure case, the parties can make a joint application to the sheriff for the proceedings to continue subject to simple procedure.[148] Likewise, a party to a simple procedure case may, at any stage, make an application for the case not to proceed subject to simple procedure.[149] Where such an application is made, the sheriff has the discretion to decide whether the case shall be transferred from simple procedure.[150] An appeal may be made to the Sheriff Appeal Court under s.110 of the 2010 Act on a point of law only against a decision of the sheriff constituting final judgment in a simple procedure case.[151]

Commercial litigation

Both r.47.1(2) of the Rules of the Court of Session 1994 and r.40.1(2)(a) **22–51** of the Ordinary Cause Rule 1993 define commercial action as an action arising out of, or concerned with, any transaction or dispute of a commercial or business nature including, but not limited to, actions relating to the construction of a commercial document, the sale or hire purchase of goods, the export or import of merchandise, the carriage of goods by land, air or sea, insurance, banking, the provision of services, building, engineering or construction contract, or a commercial lease.

In the Court of Session, all commercial actions shall be brought to the commercial judges in the Outer House.[152] The defender has the right to defend himself, however, the defences in a commercial action shall be in the form of answers to the summons with any additional statement of facts or legal grounds on which it is intended to rely.[153] Both preliminary and procedural hearing will be arranged then a debate will be ordered by

---

[145] Court Reform (Scotland) Act 2014 s.72(3)(e).
[146] Court Reform (Scotland) Act 2014 s.78(2).
[147] Court Reform (Scotland) Act 2014 s.80(1).
[148] Court Reform (Scotland) Act 2014 s.78(2).
[149] Court Reform (Scotland) Act 2014 s.80(1).
[150] Court Reform (Scotland) Act 2014 s.80(2).
[151] Court Reform (Scotland) Act 2014 s.82.
[152] Rules of the Court of Session 1994 r.47.2.
[153] Rules of the Court of Session 1994 r.47.6(1).

the judge.[154] Also, any document required for any proof in a commercial action shall be lodged as a production not less than seven days before the date fixed for the proof.[155] Finally, the judge may: (a) refuse to extend any period for compliance with a provision in these Rules or an order of the court; (b) dismiss the action or counterclaim, as the case may be, in whole or in part; (c) grant a decree in respect of all or any of the conclusions of the summons or counterclaim, as the case may be; or (d) make an award of expenses if any party fails to comply with the Rules or any order made by the judge.[156]

For a commercial action raised in the sheriff court, it was regulated in the Ordinary Cause Rule 1993 where similar definition is provided in r.40.1(2)(a). In the appropriate cases, the proceeding can be initiated by the pursuer electing to adopt the commercial action procedure by bringing an action[157] or providing no election by the pursuer, based on the application made by any party to have the cause appointed as commercial action.[158] Alternatively, the sheriff court may, on its own initiative, order the case to be decided in commercial action to achieve justice or transfer the dispute to commercial action on the basis of the joint motion between the parties.[159] To commence a commercial action proceeding in a sheriff court, a writ must be submitted by the pursuer to the court.[160] The defender must lodge defence within seven days after a notice of intention to defend is lodged with the sheriff clerk if he wishes to challenge the jurisdiction of the court, state a defence or make a counterclaim.[161] On the lodging of defences, the sheriff clerk shall fix a date and time and the first suitable court day shall be not sooner than 14 days, nor later than 28 days, after the date of expiry of the period of notice.[162] The parties shall lodge any proofs which are necessary for the judge to decide the case[163] and the judge can arrange a hearing if he deems it necessary.[164] Any failure of a party to comply with the Rules or any order made by the sheriff, the sheriff has the power to: (a) refuse to extend any period for compliance with a provision in these Rules or an order of the court; (b) dismiss the action or counterclaim, as the case may be, in whole or in part; (c) grant decree in respect of all or any of the craves of the initial writ or counterclaim, as the case may be; or (d) make an award of expenses.[165]

---

[154] Rules of the Court of Session 1994 r.47.11–13.
[155] Rules of the Court of Session 1994 r.47.14.
[156] Rules of the Court of Session 1994 r.47.16.
[157] Ordinary Cause Rules 1993 r.40.4.
[158] Ordinary Cause Rules 1993 r.40.5(1).
[159] Ordinary Cause Rules 1993 r.40.6.
[160] Ordinary Cause Rules 1993 r.40.7.
[161] Ordinary Cause Rules 1993 r.40.8.
[162] Ordinary Cause Rules 1993 r.40.10.
[163] Ordinary Cause Rules 1993 r.40.13.
[164] Ordinary Cause Rules 1993 r.40.14.
[165] Ordinary Cause Rules 1993 r.40.15.

CONCLUSION

ADR such as negotiation and mediation, has the advantages of low costs, **22–52** speed, flexibility and confidentiality in terms of resolving disputes. However, they do not provide the parties with a binding decision. This may leave the parties involved in such types of ADR in a vulnerable situation. To obtain a binding decision, the parties will have to consider the possibilities of arbitration and court actions. The parties must consider the types of dispute and their expectations and needs before deciding which mechanism is the most suitable choice for them.

▼ CHAPTER SUMMARY

NEGOTIATION

Negotiation is the first step to take to resolve disputes. It can be carried out by the **22–53** parties or their legal representatives.

MEDIATION

Mediation is an informal method of ADR, where a third party is appointed as a mediator. His task is to guide the parties to reach a mutually acceptable resolution without damaging the business relationship. The main advantages of mediation are informality and lower costs. The disadvantages of mediation include the facts that the parties can leave the process at any time, the agreement is not binding and the evidence used in the mediation process may compromise the case if the parties submit their disputes to the court or arbitration at a later stage.

ARBITRATION

Commercial arbitration is a more formal form of ADR used in business. In Scotland, both domestic and international arbitrations are governed by the Arbitration (Scotland) Act 2010. The arbitration process is private, confidential, speedy and can be controlled by parties' agreement. Parties are given control over the choice of law, language, place, arbitrators and applicability. The arbitral award is binding.

ADJUDICATION

Adjudication is a decision-making process involving a neutral third party with the authority to make a binding decision on the parties. It is the main dispute resolution method used in construction disputes under the Housing Grants, Construction and Regeneration Act 1996.

COURT ACTIONS

Under the Court Reform (Scotland) Act 2014, summary causes and small claims were removed and a sheriff appeal court is created to deal with all appeal civil cases for cases for £5,000 or less for better deployment of court resouce for low value claims. For a claim over £5,000, excluding expenses and interest, the parties can submit to the Court of Session (SSI 2007/507).

? QUICK QUIZ

- Do the parties to a business dispute have to hire lawyers in the negotiation process?
- What are the main features of mediation?
- What are the advantages and disadvantages of using commercial arbitration to resolve business disputes?
- What statutes regulate arbitration in Scotland?
- What duties does an arbitrator have?
- What is the legal effect of an arbitral award?
- Which form of alternative dispute resolution is widely adopted for construction disputes and which statute provides the legal framework for such method?
- What is the limit of claim for the Court of Session?
- What is the limit of claim for the simple procedure?
- What is the function of a sheriff appeal court?

FURTHER READING

- A. Bevan, *Alternative Dispute Resolution* (London: Sweet & Maxwell, 1992).
- A.D.M. Forte, *Scots Commercial Law* (Edinburgh: LexisNexis/Butterworths, 1997).
- A. Redfern and M. Hunter, *International Commercial Arbitration*, 5th edn (Oxford: OUP, 2009). (6th edition due September 2015.)
- F. Davidson and L. Macgregor, *Commercial Law in Scotland*, 3rd edn (Edinburgh: W. Green, 2014).
- Andrew Agapiou and Bryan Clark, "An Empirical Analysis of Scottish Construction Lawyers' Interaction with Mediation: A Qualitative Approach" (2012) 31(4) C.J.Q. 494.
- Andrew Agapiou and Bryan Clark, "A Follow-Up Empirical Analysis of Scottish Construction Clients Interaction with Mediation" (2013) 32(3) C.J.Q. 349.
- Tony Bennett, "The Role of Mediation: A Critical Analysis of the Changing Nature of Dispute Resolution in the Workplace" (2012) 41(4) I.L.J. 479.
- Lord Neuberger of Abbotsbury M.R., "Has Mediation Had Its Day?", The Gordon Slynn Memorial Lecture 2010, November

10, 2010, available at: *http://www.judiciary.gov.uk/* [Accessed June 24, 2015].

➤ Derek Roebuck, "Keeping An Eye on Fundamentals" (2012) 78(4) *Arbitration* 375.

➤ Anthony Connerty, "ADR as A 'Filter' Mechanism: The Use of ADR in the Context of International Disputes" (2013) 79(2) *Arbitration* 120.

➤ Markus Petsche, "Mediation as the Preferred Method to Solve International Business Disputes? A Look into the Future" (2013) 4 I.B.L.J. 251.

➤ S. Moody and R. Mackay (eds), *Green's Guide to Alternative Dispute Resolution in Scotland* (Edinburgh: W. Green, 1995).

➤ Scottish Executive, MRUK research Civil & International Analytical Team within Scottish Government, *Public Awareness and Perceptions of Mediation in Scotland (Social Research: Civil Justice)*, (Scottish Parliament, December 2007) ISBN 978 0 7559 6888 6.

➤ John Sturrock, "Reflections on Commercial Mediation in Scotland Arbitration" (2007) 73(1) *Journal of the Chartered Institute of Arbitrators* 77.

➤ Hong-Lin Yu, *Commercial Arbitration: Scottish and International Perspectives*, (Dundee: DUP, 2011).

⌨ RELEVANT WEBLINKS

➤ Chartered Institute of Arbitrators: *http://www.ciarb.org/branches/great-britain/scotland/arbitration* [Accessed June 24, 2015].

➤ Scottish Law Online: *http://www.scottishlaw.org.uk/scotlaw/* [Accessed June 24, 2015].

➤ Negotiation skills:

  • *http://www.skillsyouneed.com/ips/negotiation.html* (in general) [Accessed June 24, 2015].

  • *http://www.smallbusiness.co.uk/running-a-business/business-management/2137753/why-negotiation-is-an-important-skill-to-learn.thtml* (UK perspective) [Accessed June 24, 2015].

  • *http://www.justice.gc.ca/eng/rp-pr/csj-sjc/dprs-sprd/res/drrg-mrrc/03.html* (Canadian perspective) [Accessed June 24, 2015].

  • *https://www.business.qld.gov.au/business/running/managing-business-relationships/negotiating-successfully* (Australian perspective) [Accessed June 24, 2015].

➤ Scottish Courts: *http://www.scotcourts.gov.uk/* [Accessed June 24, 2015].

➤ Scottish Executive, *Improving Adjudication in the Construction Industry, A Consultation Document*: *http://www.gov.scot/Publications/2003/01/16130/16352* [Accessed June 24, 2015].

➢ Scottish Executive: *Improving Adjudication in the Construction Industry—Report of Consultation and Proposals*: *http://www.gov.scot/Publications/2004/05/19360/37122* [Accessed June 24, 2015].

➢ Scottish Mediation Network: *http://www.scottishmediation.org.uk/* [Accessed June 24, 2015].

➢ United Nations Commission on International Trade Law: *http://www.uncitral.org/* [Accessed June 24, 2015].

➢ Wolters Kluwer: *http://www.kluwerarbitration.com* [Accessed June 24, 2015].

➢ Scottish Government, *Making Justice Work: Enabling Access to Justice Project—Overview report of Alternative Dispute Resolution in Scotland* (November 2014): *slab.kraya.net/permalink/6f0ed95a-7c66-11e4-994a-0015c5f5117d.docx* [Accessed June 24, 2015].

Chapter 23 Introduction to Legal Writing and Problem Solving Techniques

► CHAPTER OVERVIEW

This chapter is intended to help students with the demands of legal essay **23–01** writing and exams. Writing essays and sitting exams can be daunting tasks, especially in a new subject which has its own vocabulary and rules. Citing legal authority, using the right terminology and dealing with different types of questions present problems and pitfalls for students who are new to the study of law. The following guide aims to provide some advice and suggest ways to help you demonstrate and communicate your legal knowledge as clearly and confidently as possible.

The guide is split into three sections:

- writing legal essays;
- answering problem questions; and
- exam hints.

WRITING LEGAL ESSAYS

In any law course, it is likely that you will have to write essays. These may **23–02** be course assignments or part of the final exam. The guide below is intended to help with essay structure and to explain some technical elements of legal authorities, which are critically important in any legal work.

Essays in law are expected to exhibit:

- good structure: have a clear beginning, middle and end—state the problem, argue for an answer, refute counter-arguments, then state your conclusion;
- relevance: stick to the point at issue and do not digress;
- clarity: avoid obscurity and undue complexity;

---

[1] Senior Lecturer in Law, University of Edinburgh. The author wishes to thank Professor George Gretton, Professor Burkhard Schafer and Mr Scott Wortley for their generous consent to use their study technique guide as a basis for this chapter, the glossary and abbreviations in Appendix 1. The original guide was produced for the Scottish Legal System course offered by the School of Law at the University of Edinburgh, and has been modified for this chapter.

- good style: write in formal English, with the tone and register that you find in good law journals and textbooks, and stick to plain English; and
- proper citation of legal authorities (cases and statutes) and of academic or other sources that support key points you are making. Also cite any work you have used in building up your argument (but note that neither the course handout nor Wikipedia are acceptable reference works).

In all prepared written work (although much less so in unseen examinations) it is necessary to acknowledge the authorship of quotations and to refer to any authority on which a statement of law is based. Both in relation to cases and statutes and in relation to textbooks and articles you need to develop the skill of presenting in a concise way and in your own words your understanding of the main point of authorities or learned works on which you base your own argument. This is true whether you take a critical or a supportive line towards the material you are using. Careful and accurate acknowledgement of sources, and appropriate marking of quotations, helps to ensure you keep clear of all suspicion of plagiarism.

Using correct methods for referencing and citation is a crucial part of writing an essay. You have to master two skills for this: *what* to reference, and *how* to do it.

(1) What to reference

23–03 To get this question right is crucial to avoid accusations of plagiarism, which in minor cases can cost you marks and in more serious cases may even result in disciplinary proceedings. Not everything you write will need referencing though. Some facts are so generally known that it is not necessary to attribute a source. You may have read, for instance, that Scotland has trial by jury. If you want to use this information in an essay, you would not need to find out where you first read it. However, if you come across an academic article that states, "trial by jury never developed the same social significance in Scotland as it did in England or the US" and you want to use this idea, you have to acknowledge where it came from. As a general rule, if in doubt, reference it.

For students on a law course, using the right *legal authority* is of crucial importance to make a valid legal argument. In most cases in Scots law, the appropriate legal authority for a statement of law will be a statute or a judicial decision (case law). When you write a legal essay, you will have to show which authority you are using. To know that the age of legal capacity in Scots law is 16 years is not enough. You will also have to state what the authority for this rule is, in this particular case a statute (Act of Parliament). Examples on how to do this properly are given below.

(2) How to reference

Unfortunately, there are several different standards for referencing in **23–04** existence, which often creates confusion. They are created by influential journals, universities or academic societies. Whichever one you use though, you must use it consistently. Once you have chosen a style, all references in that essay should follow it.

All these standards have something in common. They tell the reader:

- **who** wrote the work;
- **when** the book or article was written, or the case was decided;
- **what** is the title of the work; and
- **where** it can be found.

In addition to acknowledging the author, they allow the readers to find or check for themselves the sources you use, in as easy a way as possible. Giving a date also ensures that the reader can check if your information is up-to-date.

There are two very different ways in which you can use ideas, facts or theories from other authors. BOTH of them need referencing.

(i) Direct quotations

Sometimes an idea is so crucial, or so well worded by the original author, **23–05** that you want to *quote* it word by word. If you want to quote a passage directly, you have to put it into quotation marks and, especially with longer quotations, it is helpful to indent it. If you wish to omit a section from the passage you are quoting, you can do this with an ellipsis: these three dots "..." mark the place of the omitted text.

You can see examples of direct quotations throughout this textbook.

(ii) Paraphrasing

Alternatively, you may want to rephrase the author's statement in your **23–06** own words. This is perfectly acceptable, but it STILL requires a reference.

Note that only minor changes, e.g. from "uncivilised and inhuman" to "inhumane and uncivilised", or simply replacing words by synonyms, e.g. "have been wrongly sentenced" changed to "have been mistakenly sentenced" is not a paraphrase. You should either quote literally, or express the idea entirely in your own words.

A detailed guide to citing legal materials is given at the end of this chapter. However, you would only need to cite sources in this manner in course work or take home assessments: in an exam, it is acceptable to use a briefer form of citation. For example, if you are discussing the law relating to formation of contract, you may wish to cite *Mathieson Gee v Quigley*, and it would generally be sufficient to give the name of the case, without providing the year or full case citation.

ANSWERING PROBLEM QUESTIONS

23-07 Broadly, a legal "problem question" involves a scenario containing a given set of facts, followed by an instruction to you—usually to advise one or both of the parties on their rights and any legal remedies they may have. Problem questions really test your understanding of a particular section of law. This is because problems force you to *apply* the law that you have learnt to those facts.

As with essay writing, there are varied approaches to legal problem solving. In general examiners want to see that you are alive to all the possibilities that a set of facts throws up. This means that you are able to see all the issues that arise for consideration and are able to deal with them in a legally accurate and structured way. This ability generally is what distinguishes a good student from an average one. The aim of this guide is to give you a suggested framework to help you develop your legal skills in answering problem questions.

It is helpful to take a relatively simple four-step structure when approaching legal problems: issue, law, application and conclusion ("ILAC"). What do these steps entail?

1. The issue

23-08 The first step to solving a legal problem is to work out what the issues are that arise out of the set of facts. Of course the better you know the law the easier it is to spot the issues.

You should first read the problem *carefully* to get an overall idea of the area(s) of law involved. Lots of students lose marks because they misread the question and their answer is correspondingly wrong. You should then pay close attention to the question that is posed at the end of the problem. In general you will be asked to advise one or more of the respective parties that appear in the problem. If that is the case, ask yourself what that party would really want to know. The answer to this question will reveal the legal issue for determination. It is vitally important for your own clarity (and it usually impresses the examiners) if you can accurately and clearly identify the issues in this way.

When writing your answer, there is no need to start by repeating the facts: instead, you should set out in the introduction the salient points that you will address in the rest of your response and the area(s) of law involved.

2. The applicable law

23-09 Once you have identified the issues for determination, the next step is to set out the law applicable to these issues. You will need to cite the relevant authority in support of the current legal position in respect of the issues raised. *It cannot be stressed strongly enough how important it is for you to cite authority for your statements relating to the law*. In general this entails citing one of the authoritative sources of law, such as case law or statute. Where there is no authoritative source then you should acknowledge this and cite one of the persuasive sources such as an obiter dicta judgment or a textbook/article.

Although there is frequently a clear and settled point of law that will decide a case, this is not always so. Sometimes there is conflicting authority with the result that the law is unclear. In these situations it is usually helpful if you acknowledge this lack of clarity and argue the point both ways when it comes to applying the law to the facts. Don't be afraid to express your (substantiated) opinion if you think that one view is preferable to another.

3. Applying the law to the facts

After you have identified the issues and clearly set out the applicable law, **23–10** you then need to apply the law to the facts of the problem at hand. Sometimes the facts of the problem will closely track a particular case and this will provide you with a clear starting point (and sometimes a suggested conclusion) when applying the law to the facts. However, where this is not the case, you will have to argue by analogy, or reason from scratch, and come to a decision as to how the current problem should be decided. You should try to find evidence in the facts given to you which supports your conclusions.

It is not unusual for the problem question to provide an incomplete set of facts. This lack of detail may well make it impossible to say for certain what the outcome of a particular problem might be. For example, a question on contract issues might disclose that the defender had been drinking alcohol, but not specify how much or whether this resulted in the defender lacking capacity at the point of conclusion of contract. Whether or not the defender had capacity is therefore unclear. In these situations you need to explain what information is missing, and what you would need to give a definitive answer. In the absence of such information, you should also mount contingency arguments. This means you should explore the reasonable possibilities. So, in the example just given, you would ideally argue the point both ways, and say: (a) if the party had drunk 25 shots of vodka, then he would be likely to lack capacity by reason of intoxication; but you would also have to point out that (b) if it was proved that he had only had one glass of wine then he would be likely to have full capacity.

Another manifestation of this problem arises where you are given all the facts, but it is difficult to reach a conclusion as to the *impact* of these facts. To take another example from the field of contract law, the law of contract tells us that a contract can be terminated only if a breach is material. The law also states that a breach is material if it is serious (or goes to the root of the contract). Whether a breach is material may be unclear from the facts that have been given to you in the problem question. Again, in this situation you would have to argue: (a) that should the court find that the breach is material then x; but (b) in the event that the court should find that the breach is not material then y. However, if the facts lean a particular way or if you think you can substantiate one or other conclusion, then you should not shy away from saying so.

4. Conclusion

23–11 Once you have: (i) identified the issue; (ii) set out the law; and (iii) applied the law to the facts, you need to conclude. In general it is useful to frame the conclusion in relation to the issues that you have identified, as well as in relation to the question that you have been asked. For example, if you have said that the issue for determination is whether there is a valid contract between X and Y and you have been asked to advise X, you might conclude that there is a valid contract between X and Y and, accordingly, you advise X to sue Y on the contract.

The most important thing is to **remember to answer the question you have been asked**.

5. Tackling problem questions in an exam

23–12 Remember, the examiners are looking for the ability to *apply* legal knowledge, not a *recitation* of that knowledge. When you look at a law book or a statute it seems that law is a set of rules, and therefore that to learn the law is to learn those rules. In a sense that is true. But in reality there are far too many rules for anyone to learn. In addition, lawyers and judges do not start with the rules, but with problems. Law is largely about problem-solving.

The following pointers should help you apply your legal knowledge to solve the problem you are faced with in the exam:

(1) Sometimes a problem has a clear answer, and sometimes no clear answer, and sometimes partly both. Identifying where the law is clear and where it is not is one of the skills being tested.

(2) Sometimes a problem question will contain *irrelevant facts*. That is like real life. One of the skills of a lawyer is to perceive which facts are legally relevant and which are not.

(3) Conversely, a problem question may leave out some vital piece of information. Again, this is like real life. One of the skills of the lawyer is to identify missing information which will enable him to solve a problem.

(4) Credit is given for identifying relevant issues, even if the wrong answer is given. This is probably the single most important skill in tackling a law exam. You may know everything there is to know about directors' duties in company law, for example, but your knowledge is useless if you cannot spot such an issue hiding in a set of facts.

(5) Do not *waffle*. Irrelevancy counts against you. To put in background information is legitimate. Learning to draw the line between background information and sheer waffle is one of the skills being tested.

(6) However, if some aspect of the problem might be relevant but in your view is in fact irrelevant, you should of course say why.

Address the question that is posed. If you are asked whether Smith is liable to Robertson, answer that question, whether your answer is a yes or a no or a maybe. This may seem obvious, but each year numerous students get nowhere near actually offering an answer to the question asked. You may be reluctant to give an answer in case it is the wrong answer, but the truth is that nothing can be worse than no answer at all.

Exam Hints

The chances are that you will not be sitting an exam on business law: you **23–13** will be sitting an cxam on business law as taught in your University/ College/course by Ms A, Dr B, Professor C and so on. The lecturer has a limited time to decide what to teach and what to leave out, and also a limited time in which to examine the course. Inevitably the exam will tend to be an exam on the course as taught. (Which is not to say that questions will not sometimes require knowledge beyond that which was covered in lectures and tutorials.)

Exam questions can comprise a number of different types:

- problem questions;
- essay questions;
- "notes" questions; and
- multiple choice questions.

This section will contain some general hints on improving your exam performance. It will also contain a brief section on notes questions and multiple choice questions: for guidance on problems and essays you should refer to the sections above.

Revision

Before we turn to guidance on the exam, it is helpful to think about **23–14** revision. Remember to plan your revision carefully. Find out as soon as possible what the format of the exam paper will be. Is the whole course examinable, or just certain sections? What types of questions will be in the paper? (For example, multiple choice; essay; problem; short notes?) If you will have to answer three questions on contract law and only one question on partnership, for example, then this suggests that you need to know contract law in much greater detail—and therefore you will need to dedicate more time to it in your revision. If you devise a revision schedule, this will help you manage your time and ensure you allocate enough time to different topics.

When you are revising, you should also work out what you need to learn from each section: do you need to memorise cases and statutory material? Will you have access to statutes in the exam?

One of the best ways to put your revision into practice is to do past exam papers in exam conditions. After you have revised one part of the course, sit down with a past paper and try a question from that part of the course. Make sure you answer it as fully as possible, but only using any materials that you will have with you in the exam. Can you write an answer in the allotted time period? A structured approach to revision and practice exam papers will help ensure you are well prepared for the exam.

General exam advice

23–15 *Time management is crucial*

No matter how much you know, you cannot and will not get a good mark if you do not leave yourself enough time to answer the necessary questions. If you are required to write three essays, then composing two excellent ones will not compensate for running out of time on the third one. You should know before you start the exam how much time you have for each question—and make sure you stick to it.

One of the most important elements in any exam is the ability to communicate. You need to be able to communicate your answer *clearly*, *concisely*, *correctly* and *unambiguously*. Don't forget presentation, especially:

- spelling;
- grammar;
- punctuation; and
- handwriting (examiners cannot give marks for what they cannot read).

Poor English makes a bad impression and may make it difficult to understand what you are trying to say. Thus, "the contract between A and B is subject to C's right. So he can sue". Who can sue? A, B or C? How many mistakes can you spot in the following?

"Bank of Edinburgh credits a/c when they recieve the cheque so b/c a banker has lien & so becomes holder if it's customer has got an overdraft, (s.2 of 1882 act) he may be able to sue, b/c he does have overdraft there is a lien therefore the chq must be payed, this is, basically an unsatisfactary senario if they get liquidated."

Here it is again, with the errors highlighted in bold:

"Bank of Edinburgh credits a/c when they **recieve** the cheque so **b/c** a banker has lien & so becomes holder if **it's** customer has got an overdraft, (s.2 of 1882 **act) he** [who?] may be able to sue**, b/c he** [who?] does have **[an]** overdraft there is a lien therefore the **chq** must be **payed**, this is, basically an **unsatisfactary senario** if **they** [who?] get liquidated."

Beware of abbreviations. Conventional abbreviations are acceptable. Thus, in the above example "a/c" for "account" is acceptable, as is "&" for "and". But unconventional abbreviations, such as "b/c" for "because" make a bad impression and sometimes entirely baffle the examiner as to their meaning, especially if the handwriting is poor.

Beware of colloquialisms: you are supposed to be writing a legal brief. Write complete sentences, in formal English. Do not write notes. Do not use txt spk.

In a problem question there will usually be various parties. If you mean "Jones" do not write "Smith". This may seem obvious, but it is a common error. The examiner can judge you only on what you have written.

Perhaps the most careless error to make is to talk of Scot's law. Or Scots' law. Or scots law. Or Scott's law. **The term is "Scots law"**. No apostrophes. Only one "t". And an upper case initial "S".

It helps the examiner if you underline cases and statutes.

Re-read your answers, to correct blunders

Many students feel an overwhelming disinclination to do this: they **23–16** cannot bear to look again at what they have said. Do it. It can save many lost marks.

Give authority

You have to tread a middle path in this respect. Excessive citation of **23–17** authority is often a symptom of irrelevance, and is often an attempt to cover up a failure to understand the issues. But equally an answer on company law which suggests that you have not heard of the Companies Act 2006 is likely to attract a fail mark. If the exam is an open-folder one, you do not need to cite authority merely to impress. Cite authority where it is needed in the development of your argument or analysis, but not otherwise.

Look at exam papers for the same course for the past three or four years to get an idea of the format and of the sort of questions that are likely to be asked.

Students often fear that if they develop a line of reasoning not given in the lectures they will make fools of themselves. On the contrary, *you should not be afraid to argue*. An interesting line of argument will often attract several additional marks even if the examiner disagrees with it.

Spend time reading the exam questions carefully. Do not be intimidated by the fact that the person at the next desk is already on page two of the answer book before you have started writing.

Leading on from the last point, examiners are looking for quality rather than quantity. You are not marked by the number of pages you have managed to fill up. Shorter answers can attract a higher mark than longer ones.

It is usually helpful to make notes on a question before answering it. If you do this, do not forget to cross out your notes at the end, for otherwise the examiner has to assume that your notes form part of your answer.

If part of a question baffles you, you should nevertheless write something about it. For silence you can be awarded no marks, but even a bad answer will normally pick up a few marks.

Read the instructions on the front of the script book. This will often advise you to start each answer on a new page, for example, and complete the front of the script book. FOLLOW THESE INSTRUCTIONS.

Do not begin by copying out the question or narrating the facts of the problem. This is a sheer waste of time. The examiner has the question paper to hand while marking.

Likewise, there is normally no point in copying out a statutory provision, unless it is very brief. In general, a simple reference is enough. Longer quotation from a statutory provision makes sense only if you need to discuss its precise wording.

Avoid non-sequiturs. Avoid self-contradictions. What happens all too often is that a student says one thing in one sentence and the opposite a few lines later. Sometimes this is because he has changed his mind in the course of writing. You can lessen the danger of this by making notes for an answer first. You can also save yourself by re-reading what you have written to pick up errors and contradictions.

In an open-folder exam, no credit is given just for copying out chunks of the handouts or lectures. In other exams (the majority) some credit is given for memory work, but it is not the most important aspect of the examination: the real test is the correct application of law.

Finally, remember the guidance of Eric Blair (George Orwell) who in an essay on "Politics and the English Language" (available in his collected essays) proposed five rules for clear writing:

"(i) Never use a metaphor, simile, or other figure of speech which you are used to seeing in print.
(ii) Never use a long word where a short one will do.
(iii) If it is possible to cut a word out, always cut it out.
(iv) Never use the passive where you can use the active.
(v) Never use a foreign phrase, a scientific word, or a jargon word if you can think of an everyday English equivalent.
(vi) Break any of these rules sooner than say anything outright barbarous."

Notes questions

23–18 A notes style question will ask you to write short notes on a particular case or statutory provision, or perhaps a particular legal doctrine. Typically, it will ask you to write short notes on a number of these, not just one.

It can be too easy to answer these questions by simply repeating the facts of the case or the effect of the statutory provision. This may attract some marks, but it is unlikely that it will be enough to pass.

Instead, you need to tell the examiner not only what the case/statute/doctrine says, but also why it is so important. Think about why the examiner might have selected that case/statutory provision, etc. for inclusion in the exam paper, instead of another. The sort of things you may wish to comment on are:

- Has it changed a previous rule of law?
- Have there been subsequent cases regarding it?
- Is it controversial?

- How does it interact with other legal provisions?

A good answer will discuss wider issues—perhaps not in too much detail, but it will certainly not be restricted to only the precise point on which you have been asked to comment.

Multiple choice questions

There are three secrets to success with multiple choice questions: know **23–19** the law, read the question carefully, and read the answers carefully. If you have not learnt the relevant law, then this type of exam question will really catch you out: you cannot hide partial or incomplete knowledge in waffle. All you can do is pick one answer, and you need to make sure it's the right one.

However, even if you know the law, it's all too easy to get it wrong by misreading the question and the choice of answers. Examiners will usually select the wrong answers (known as "distractors") very carefully. For example, if you are asked to calculate the value of *unpaid* shares in a given scenario, the choice of wrong answers may well be plausible figures, such as the total value of the shareholding, or the value of the *paid* shares instead. Not only do you need to know how to calculate the value of the unpaid shares, you need to make sure you are not distracted by the distractors.

A final tip is to be clear whether the multiple choice questions will be negatively marked or not. Negative marking is where you lose marks if you give the wrong answer: a common scheme might be +2 marks for a correct answer, 0 marks for no answer, and -1 marks for a wrong answer. In this case, it is often better not to answer a question (thus attracting 0 marks), rather than guessing and getting it wrong (thereby losing 1 mark). (However, you cannot pass the exam without answering some of the questions, so you cannot play safe by leaving them all blank!) Where negative marking does not apply, then it is common to get +1 mark for a correct answer and 0 marks for a blank or a wrong answer. In these exams, there is more to be gained by guessing, even if you are not sure. However, whichever tactical approach you take, you must be 100 per cent sure of the marking scheme, i.e. whether it is negatively marked or not.

A style guide to citing legal works

Case citations

A case name should be given as it appears in the most authoritative **23–20** report of the case. Citations should follow the conventions established in the Oxford Standard Citation of Legal Authorities. In submitted work, such as essays, a full citation need only be given at the first reference to the case, which should also provide the shorthand reference to be used in subsequent citations, e.g.:

> *Junior Books Ltd v The Veitchi Co Ltd*, 1982 S.C. (H.L.) 244 (henceforth *Junior Books*).

Such shorthand references should enable ready recognition of the case referred to.

If you refer to dicta (judicial speeches) within the case, your footnote should state the page number and the name of the judge who made that speech. For example:

> *Robertson v Forth Road Bridge Joint Board*, 1996 S.L.T. 263 at 265 per Lord President Hope.

Where a neutral case citation (such as [2007] UKHL 21) is available, this should be given, and paragraph rather than page numbering should be used to identify dicta within the case.

Cite ECJ cases thus:

> Case 6/60 *Humblet v Belgium* [1960] ECR 559.
> Case C-213/89 *R v Secretary of State for Transport, ex parte Factortame* [1991] ECR I-3905.

As noted above, these detailed citations are only required in written work which is submitted, rather than exam work. In an exam, it would be acceptable to give simply the common name of the case, for example, "*Junior Books v Veitchi*".

Statute citations

23–21 Statutes should normally be referred to by their short titles only, together with the calendar year, as in the example below. No comma should be inserted between the word "Act" and the date. The following abbreviations are permissible:

(1) "Section" becomes "s.", except where it is the first word in a sentence or footnote.
(2) "Sections" can be abbreviated as "ss.".
(3) "Schedule" becomes "Sch." unless the Act contains only one Schedule.
(4) "Chapter" is abbreviated as "Ch.".
(5) "Part" should be left in full or may be abbreviated to Pt.

To show these in practice, two examples are given:

> ➤ Finance Act 1965 s.19(1) Sch.7.
> ➤ Companies Act 2006 Part V Ch.I.

Cite Acts of the Scottish Parliament thus:

> ➤ Mental Health (Public Safety and Appeals) (Scotland) Act 1999 (asp 1).

Statutory instruments should be referred to by name and date, followed by their number, thus:

> ➢ Duration of Copyright and Rights in Performances Regulations 1995 (SI 1995/3297).
> ➢ The Parking Attendants (Wearing of Uniforms) (City of Glasgow Parking Area) Regulations 1999 (SSI 1999/62).

EU legislation

Cite Treaty articles thus: **23–22**
  For example, for the Treaty on the Functioning of the European Union:

> ➢ Article 288 TFEU.

Paragraphs of articles should be cited thus:

> ➢ Article 288(1) TFEU.

Cite Directives thus:

> ➢ Council Directive 2001/89/EC of October 23, 2001 on Community measures for the control of classical swine fever OJ 2001 L 316/5.

Cite Decisions thus:

> ➢ Commission Decision 239/96/EC on emergency measures to protect against bovine spongiform encephalopathy OJ 1996 L78/47.

Cite Regulations thus:

> ➢ Commission Regulation (EC) 3223/94/EC of December 21, 1994 on detailed rules for the application of the import arrangements for fruit and vegetables OJ 1994 L 337/66.

Note that OJ stands for the Official Journal.

Citation of the Stair Memorial Encyclopaedia

The first reference to this work in an article should be as follows: *The* **23–23** *Laws of Scotland: Stair Memorial Encyclopaedia* (henceforth "SME").
  Citation should then be by volume number (Vol.18), year of publication in brackets, and paragraph number (para.16). The names of editors and authors in this work should not be cited, although they may be referred to in the text as holding the views expressed in their contributions to the Encyclopaedia. Similar principles should be applied to other encyclopaedic works.

Citation of books

23–24 Give the author's initial(s) and surname, the title (in italics) and the year
of publication in round brackets. If it is not the first edition, you should
also state to which edition number you are referring ("edition" is usually
abbreviated as "edn"):

> ➤ T.B. Smith, *A Short Commentary on the Law of Scotland* (1962).
> ➤ E.M. Clive, *The Law of Husband and Wife in Scotland*, 4th edn
> (1997).

For edited books, give the editor's name(s) as above for the author, with
"ed" or "eds" following immediately in round brackets.

> ➤ D.L. Carey Miller and D.W. Meyers (eds), *Comparative and
> Historical Essays in Scots Law: a Tribute to Sir Thomas Smith
> QC* (1992).

At the first of repeated references to a book, give a shorthand reference
consisting of author's surname and keywords from the title, introduced
by "hereafter referred to as":

> ➤ T.B. Smith, *A Short Commentary on the Law of Scotland* (1962)
> (hereafter referred to as Smith, *Short Commentary*).

Citation of articles

23–25 Give the author's initials and surname, the full title of the article within
double quotation marks but with minimum necessary capitalisation, the
location, publisher and year of publication (in round brackets unless
there is no volume number), the volume number in Arabic numerals, the
full name of the journal in italics, the first page of the article:

> ➤ A.D.M. Forte, "Marine insurance and risk distribution in
> Scotland before 1800" (1987) 4 *Law and History Review* 394.

If a more specific page reference is being given, include the page num-
ber(s) in the form "at 397", for example:

> ➤ A.D.M. Forte, "Marine insurance and risk distribution in
> Scotland before 1800" (1987) 4 *Law and History Review* 394 at
> 397.

At the first of repeated references to an article, give a shorthand reference
consisting of author's surname and keywords from the title, introduced
by "hereafter referred to as", as with book citations above.

Multiple authors

For publications that have multiple authors, you should use the last name **23–26** and initial(s) for up to three authors, separated by a comma and "and", thus:

> ➢ E.P. Ellinger, E. Lomnicka and R. Hooley, *Modern Banking Law* (2002).

For more than three authors use the last name and initials of the first author, and then "et al", thus:

> ➢ R. Anderson, et al, *Universal Access to Email: Feasibility and Societal Implications* (1995).

Citation from websites

URLs should be italicised and placed within brackets. You should always **23–27** include the date when you last visited the website.

When a case or article available in printed form is cited, reference should always be made to the printed source. If there is no printed equivalent, e.g. for a recent case obtained from the Scottish Courts Administration website, give the date of the judgment and the relevant URL.

Health warning: websites can be a useful source of information, but they are not always accurate or up-to-date. It is also likely that an online search for material will produce legal material *for other jurisdictions*: remember that your authority must usually be relevant to the jurisdiction that you have been asked to write about (e.g. Scotland or England).

Appendix 1   Glossary and Abbreviations

This is only a selection of terms which you may come across. If you encounter unfamiliar terms and do not find them here, there are various books in the library that will help, for instance the *Glossary: Scottish and European Union Legal Terms* and Trayner's *Latin Maxims*.

Glossary

ADVOCATE Member of Faculty of Advocates, who represents litigants in Court of Session and High Court work. Similar to English barrister.

AUDIENCE If a lawyer has the "right of audience" in a court that means they can appear there for a client. Advocates and solicitor-advocates have rights of audience in all courts. Other solicitors only have a right of audience in lower courts.

APPELLANT Person appealing to higher court from decision of lower court.

AVER To aver is to claim the truth of certain facts. Noun is averment.

AVIZANDUM If a court "makes avizandum" that means that it will not give judgment at once but will take time to consider.

BARRISTER English equivalent of advocate.

BLACKLETTER LAW Blackletter law means technical legal doctrine as opposed, for example, to questions of public policy or legal philosophy. So called because law texts were formerly often printed in blackletter typeface.

BONA FIDES Good faith. (*Fide* is the ablative form, e.g. "The purchaser was in bona fide".) To be in good faith is to act honestly, to be unaware of any irregularity or wrongdoing. For example, a purchaser from a thief is in good faith if he has no reason to suspect that the goods are stolen.

CAPACITY The ability to have rights and enter into juristic acts. Some persons have restricted capacity. Thus a person with severe mental impairment could own property (passive capacity) but not, on their own, sell it. Again, a company has legal capacity for most things but not, for example, marriage.

CAUTION (Pronounced "cayshun".) A guarantee for someone else's debt.

CIVIL As well as being the opposite of criminal, civil also means Roman. "Civil law" = Roman law. A "civilian" legal system is one much influenced by Roman law.

CLAIMANT Modern English term for plaintiff.

CODE (1) Part of the *Corpus Juris Civilis*. (2) A statute which systematically sets forth the whole of a large area of law. The two most famous codes are the French *Code Civil* (also called the *Code Napoleon*) and the German *Bürgerliches Gesetzbuch* (the BGB). They have had international influence.

802

COMMON LAW (1) Unenacted law. (2) A collective term for the Anglo-American legal systems.

CONSENSUS IN [or AD] IDEM PLACITUM Agreement on the same proposition: a meeting of the minds. In a contract, the two parties must understand each other aright.

CORPORATION Any juristic person other than a partnership.

COUNSEL An advocate. Senior counsel = Queen's Counsel. Junior counsel = any advocate other than a QC.

COURT OF SESSION Established 1532. Sits in Edinburgh only. Divided into Outer House and Inner House. Outer House is a court of first instance. Inner House hears appeals from Outer House and other lower courts. Judges are called "Lords of Council and Session" or "Senators of the College of Justice".

CROWN Term used to mean the state, which the Queen personifies.

CULPA Fault.

CURATOR BONIS A type of judicial factor, appointed to look after the affairs of an incapax.

DAMAGES (always plural) means not harm but the right to compensation for harm.

DAMNUM Loss. *Damnum injuria datum* means loss caused by wrongdoing (that is, by another person).

DECLARATOR Decree setting forth existence of rights without necessarily seeking to enforce them.

DECREE (Stress is on first syllable.) The order of a court disposing of a case, in favour of the pursuer or the defender. The three main types of decree are: (a) condemnator, in which the pursuer's case is upheld; (b) absolvitor, in which the defender's case is upheld; and (c) dismissal, in which no decision is reached, for example because the pursuer has abandoned the action or because the pursuer has sued in the wrong court, etc. Dismissal is decree effectively in favour of defender, but since no determination of the dispute it is not *res judicata*. A decree in absence is where defender has not appeared. Decree *in foro contentioso* is where defender has appeared.

DEFENDANT English term for defender.

DEFENDER Person against whom an action is raised, opposite of pursuer.

DELEGATED LEGISLATION *See* STATUTORY INSTRUMENT.

DELICT A civil wrong other than breach of contract. Also called law of reparation.

DISTINGUISH To distinguish a precedent is to show that the precedent in fact deals with a different situation and so is not a true precedent.

EQUITY Slippery word with many meanings. (1) Special branch of English law. (2) Fairness, to be applied where law is silent or too rigid. (3) Share capital of company. (4) Value of land or buildings minus debt secured thereon.

GOOD FAITH *See* BONA FIDES.

HERITABLE Heritable or immoveable property means land and buildings.

Everything else is moveable property. Heritable security means a security over heritable property, securing a loan. (It is often referred to by its name in English law: a mortgage.)

HIGH COURT OF JUSTICIARY Highest criminal court, which hears both trials and appeals. Based in Edinburgh but goes "on circuit" around the country. The judges (Commissioners of Justiciary) are same persons as Court of Session judges.

HOUSE OF LORDS (1) The upper House of Parliament, whose members are unelected. Limited powers since the House of Commons can override its veto. (2) Until October 2009, the highest court of appeal in civil matters (and, in England, in criminal matters also). Now replaced by the Supreme Court of the United Kingdom.

INCAPAX Someone not able to look after their affairs; lacking in full legal capacity, e.g. through severe mental impairment.

INJURIA Wrongdoing, delict. Does not mean "injury".

INNER HOUSE of Court of Session. Highest appeal court (except Supreme Court and ECJ) for civil matters. Normally sits in two "divisions" to double throughput. Occasionally a third "extra" division is added.

INTER VIVOS Between living persons. Opposite of *mortis causa*.

INTERDICT A court order forbidding someone from doing something. The English equivalent is an injunction.

INTERLOCUTOR Any order made by court. The final interlocutor disposing of the case is called the decree. A court is said to "pronounce" an interlocutor.

JOINT AND SEVERAL Joint and several liability, or solidary (*in solido*) liability, is where two or more persons are liable for the same debt, in full. Creditor can claim the full sum from either debtor, but of course cannot recover more than the total due. Where one debtor pays the full debt, they then have a right of recovery against the other debtors for their pro rata share.

JUDICIAL FACTOR A person appointed by the court to administer property, investments, etc. for some special reason, e.g. curator bonis.

JURISPRUDENCE (1) Law or legal system, e.g. "jurisprudence of Italy" = Italian law. (2) Philosophy of law. (3) Case law.

JURIDICAL ACT (Also called juristic act.) A lawful act which changes the legal situation, such as the making of a contract, the raising of an action, getting married. Only a person with legal or juristic capacity can do juristic acts. (Contrast a juristic event, which is an event which changes the legal situation but is not a deliberate act, for example, death. Also contrast illicit acts, such as delicts.)

JURISTIC PERSON Also called artificial or legal or moral person. Law divides persons into natural (i.e. human beings) and juristic. Some juristic persons exist in public law (e.g. City of Edinburgh Council) and others in private law (e.g. Royal Bank of Scotland).

LAW SOCIETY OF SCOTLAND Professional body to which all solicitors belong.

LORD ADVOCATE Government minister. Advises Government on matters of

Scots law. Represents the Crown in litigation. In criminal cases called "Her Majesty's Advocate".

MORTIS CAUSA By reason of death. A *mortis causa* act takes full effect on death. Main example is a will.

MOVEABLE PROPERTY All property other than land and buildings. Opposite of heritable.

NOBILE OFFICIUM The power of the Court of Session and High Court to modify the law in technical points, adhering to the spirit of the law. Used rarely.

NOTARY Or notary public. Person authorised to take sworn statements (affidavits) and to authenticate some types of document. Notaries exist in all legal systems. In Scotland all notaries are solicitors.

NULLITY Something is absolutely null (void) if it appears valid but in fact has no legal effect at all, for instance a forged testament, or a contract signed at gunpoint. A thing is relatively null (voidable) if it is valid but can be made null at the option of someone. Thus, a contract entered into by fraud is voidable and the defrauded party can annul (avoid) the contract or not at his option.

OBITER DICTA "Things said by the way." Singular is obiter dictum. Things said by judge which are not necessary to reach her/his decision. Opposite of ratio.

OPINION (1) Of judge, explaining her/his decision. Sometimes called judgment. (2) In some cases a law firm will seek opinion of advocate or other independent party to assist with a particular legal problem.

OUTER HOUSE of Court of Session. Judges sit singly to hear cases at first instance.

OVERRULE Where an appellate court says that a decision of a lower court in another earlier unconnected case was wrong.

PERSONAL RIGHT A right against a person, for e.g. a right to sue someone for breach of contract, as opposed to a real right.

PLAINTIFF Former English term for pursuer. (Modern term is claimant.)

POINT To be "in point" means to be relevant. Thus if a court "distinguishes" an earlier case it does so because it is not "in point".

PRECEDENT The doctrine of precedent, also called the doctrine of stare decisis, is that where the law has been settled in a case, later cases should follow same rule. A "precedent" is a prior case on which reliance is placed. A "binding precedent" is one which the court must follow. A "persuasive precedent" is one which has weight but is not binding. (For example, English cases are usually only persuasive precedents in Scots law.)

PRESCRIPTION (1) Negative or extinctive prescription means the loss of rights by non-enforcement for a certain period of years. Thus, a debt not claimed will eventually prescribe. (2) Positive or acquisitive prescription means acquisition of ownership by possession over a certain period of years.

PRIVATE LAW All law except public law.

PRIVY COUNCIL (1) A body which, in theory, advises the Queen. "Order in Council" is a royal decree to which this body has nominally assented: in practice a type of government order. (2) Appeal court for certain Commonwealth countries.

PROOF Court hearing in which the facts are investigated. A "proof before answer" is a proof where disputed points of law are left open until after the proof.

PUBLIC LAW Law concerning the state (Crown) and state organisations (e.g. local authorities). Examples: tax law, planning law, constitutional law, criminal law. Opposite of private law.

PURSUER The person who raises an action, opposite of defender.

QUANTUM "How much." The extent of a loss suffered, in money terms.

QUASI-CONTRACT Another name for the law of unjustified enrichment.

RATIO DECIDENDI Or ratio for short. Reason or rule of law on which decision is based. (A case which turns purely on disputed facts will not have any ratio.) Contrast obiter dicta.

REAL RIGHT A right in a thing, as opposed to a right against a person (personal right). Examples are ownership and servitude.

RELEVANCY One possible defence to an action is that, as stated, it is "irrelevant" that is to say, even if the pursuer can prove all their alleged facts it still would not entitle them to the remedy they seek.

RESCIND To withdraw from a contract on the ground of the other party's breach of it.

RESILE (1) To withdraw from an agreement before it has become a binding contract. (2) To withdraw from a contract.

RESPONDENT (1) In an appeal, the non-appealing party, i.e. opposite of appellant. (2) In a petition, the respondent corresponds to the defender in an ordinary action.

SEQUESTRATION Main meaning is formal bankruptcy.

SERVITUDE A right held by one landowner in relation to neighbouring property. Thus, a servitude of way is private right of way across someone else's land.

SHERIFF Judge in the Sheriff Court, who has jurisdiction on most matters, civil and criminal.

SIST (Noun and verb.) (1) To sist an action is to suspend all further procedure for the time being. But the action remains in existence, and the sist can be recalled. (2) To sist a party in an action is to bring that party in as additional party. For example, if a pursuer dies, their executor may be "sisted" to carry on action.

SOLATIUM Damages to compensate for suffering, as opposed to patrimonial loss.

SOLICITOR Lawyer qualified to do all legal work but with no right of audience in the Court of Session or High Court. But some solicitors, called solicitor-advocates, have such rights.

SPECIFIC IMPLEMENT Remedy of getting someone to perform their obligation, as opposed to an award of damages for their non-performance.

STARE DECISIS "To stand by the decisions." *See* PRECEDENT.

STATUTORY INSTRUMENT An SI is subordinate (delegated) legislation, passed not by Act of Parliament but by a procedure authorised by some Act of

Parliament. Thus procedural rules of the Court of Session ("Acts of Sederunt") are SIs authorised by the Acts of Parliament regulating the Court of Session.

SUBORDINATE LEGISLATION *See* STATUTORY INSTRUMENT.

SUPREME COURT OF THE UNITED KINGDOM The final court of civil appeal from all courts in the UK, and the final court of criminal appeal from the courts in England, Wales and Northern Ireland. The Supreme Court replaced the House of Lords as the final court of appeal, and came into being in October 2009 by virtue of the Constitutional Reform Act 2005.

THIRD PARTY (Also called a *tertius*.) Legal transactions are often between two persons. In that case anyone else is called a third party. For example, third party motor insurance is where an insurance contract between a motorist and an insurance company covers claims against the motorist by third parties (perhaps an injured pedestrian).

TITLE TO SUE One possible defence to a claim is that the pursuer has no title to sue. Thus, even if the defender has acted unlawfully, the right to object is vested in someone else, not in the pursuer. Also called locus standi.

TORT English term for delict.

ULTRA VIRES "Beyond the powers". Corporations are often restricted in what they can do. Acts outwith these powers are ultra vires and may thus be null. A statutory instrument can also be ultra vires if it goes beyond what was authorised by the Act of Parliament in question.

UNJUSTIFIED ENRICHMENT A branch of the law of obligations. In certain cases a person who is "unjustifiably enriched" can be required to return the benefit. To give an example, if A mistakenly pays a bill twice to B, B is unjustifiably enriched and must return the second payment to A. B's obligation to do so is not contractual or delictual, but belongs to this branch of law. Known as unjust enrichment in English law.

VOID, VOIDABLE *See* NULLITY.

Abbreviations

AG: Attorney General

All E.R.: All England Reports

asp: Act of the Scottish Parliament

c or **ch.** or **cap**: Chapter (statute number)

CAB[x]: Citizens Advice Bureau[x]

CB: Curator Bonis

ECHR: European Convention on Human Rights

ECtHR: European Court of Human Rights

ECJ: European Court of Justice

HL: House of Lords

JF: Judicial Factor

LA (or **Ld Adv**): Lord Advocate

LLP: Limited liability partnership

LJC: Lord Justice Clerk

LP: Lord President

Mor: Morison's Dictionary of Decisions

MR: Master of the Rolls (the presiding officer of the Civil Division of the Court of Appeal in England and Wales)

OJ: Official Journal of the European Communities

PC: Privy Council

QC: Queen's Counsel

s.: section

SC: (1) the Supreme Court of the United Kingdom (also referred to as UKSC); (2) Session Cases

Sch.: Schedule

SCLR: Scottish Civil Law Reports

SI: Statutory Instrument

SSI: Scottish Statutory Instrument

SME: *Stair Memorial Encyclopaedia*

S.L.T.: Scots Law Times

UKSC: the Supreme Court of the United Kingdom

W.L.R.: Weekly Law Reports

Appendix 2   Quick Quiz Answers

Chapter 1—Introduction to the Nature and Sources of Scots Law

- *Why is it important that a business or accountancy student should know something about business law?*
  Students of other disciplines such as business or accountancy may be surprised when they find business or commercial law subjects on their curriculum. Although business and accountancy students are not going to become professional lawyers, business managers will have to work within the legal framework of business, and need to know about certain areas of law that are important for them. Accountants have to have quite a wide knowledge of law, in addition to specialist areas such as the statutory rules for the contents of company annual accounts, as their business clients will seek advice on areas of law that apply to them, such as the differences between operating as a business as a partnership or as a company.
- *What is the essential difference between public law and private law?*

  —Public law governs the relationship between the state and the citizen (constitutional law, administrative law and criminal law).
  —Private law governs relationships between citizens, and has several branches (including the law of contract, the law of delict and the law of persons).

- *Explain the procedure for the enactment of a public Bill in the UK Parliament.*
  A Bill is drafted by Parliamentary draftsmen and introduced to one of the Houses of Parliament by a government minister or other sponsor of the Bill. At the First Reading the title is read out and the Bill is printed. At the Second Reading the general principles of the Bill are debated. At the Committee Stage the Bill is examined clause by clause and amendments are often made. At the Report Stage the Committee reports back to the House with proposed amendments, which are voted on. At the Third Reading a final discussion will take place and the Bill is passed. Once the Bill has been passed in one House, it goes to the other House and is put through the same procedures. It then obtains the Royal assent and becomes an Act.
- *If you wanted to look up a section of an Act of the UK Parliament, where would you look?*
  You could purchase a hard copy of the Act at the Stationery Office. Alternatively, you could look the statute up in Public General Statutes and Measures. In these places you could find the Act as it was originally enacted, and not with any later amendments incorporated. It is a good idea to look for the section of the Act in a source that gives you the law as updated including any amendments. You can use the UK Statute Law Database provided by the National Archives *http://www.legislation.gov.uk* [Accessed May 12, 2015] or one of the subscription databases such as Westlaw.

- *What are the provisions in the Scotland Act 1998 which fix the boundaries of the legislative competence of the Scottish Parliament?*
  Sections 29–30 of and Sch.5 to the Scotland Act 1998.
  The Scottish Parliament may legislate on any matters that are not reserved to the Westminster Parliament. It may not legislate in ways that are incompatible with the European Convention on Human Rights and Fundamental Freedoms or EU law. Also it may not enact legislation with extra-territorial scope. And it may not legislate so as to remove the Lord Advocate as head of the system of criminal prosecution or of the investigation of deaths in Scotland.
- *Name one new area of legislative competence granted to the Scottish Parliament in the Scotland Act 2012*
  The power to regulate air weapons—s.10; the power to set a Scottish rate of income tax—s.25; the power to levy a tax on transactions involving interests in land—s.28; the power to levy a tax on disposals to landfill—s.30.
- *What role does the UK Parliament and the Scottish Parliament play in relation to delegated legislation?*
  The UK Parliament and the Scottish Parliament must pass an Act authorising another body to make delegated legislation, within set limits (usually a government department). Depending on what that parent Act provides, whichever Parliament enacted the parent Act will have a role in scrutinising the delegated legislation before it comes into effect, but will not have power to amend it. In the case of some Scottish delegated legislation, both parliaments will scrutinise the delegated legislation.
- *What are the advantages and disadvantages of having a system of binding precedent?*
  Advantages:

  —It helps to promote justice by treating like cases alike.
  —It makes the outcomes of litigation more predictable.
  —It provides scope for the law to develop slowly as society's needs change by forcing judges to take previous cases into account.

  Disadvantages:

  —Bad decisions can hold back the development of the law.
  —There may be a lack of relevant case law in a particular area of law, making the law doubtful.
  —There may be conflicting precedents.
  —A precedent may be difficult to interpret because it may be badly reported.
  —A court may be overloaded with precedents.

- *In what circumstances must a later court follow the decision of an earlier court in Scotland?*

  —The precedent must be: (1) in point; and (2) binding.
  —A precedent is in point if the ratio decidendi (issue of law on which the earlier case was decided) is the same as the current case.
  —A precedent is binding if it comes from a court whose judgments bind the current court (generally courts of appeal bind courts of first instance and higher courts bind lower).

- *To what extent are the institutional writers still of relevance to the decisions of the courts today?*

The institutional writers did their work over a long period between roughly 1600–1800, and were responsible for crafting a modern legal system for Scotland from old Scots customary law, mediaeval writings, Acts of the old Scots Parliament, decisions of the courts, and borrowings from Roman law. Their works were regarded as themselves being formal sources of law, rather than secondary sources.

Nowadays their influence is declining as their works become superseded by legislation or developments in case law. However, their writings will still be cited in today's courts where still relevant.

- *In what circumstances is custom regarded as a formal source of Scots law?*
  Some old customs are already part of the law because they have been recognised as law by the courts. Their formal source then becomes judicial precedent. Where this has not occurred, the custom must be proved to the court: (1) to have been acquiesced in as representing law for a long though undefined period of time; (2) to be definite and certain; (3) to be fair and reasonable; and (4) to be consistent with legal principle.
- *Explain what is meant by the nobile officium of the Court of Session and High Court of Justiciary.*
  The Court of Session and the High Court of Justiciary have an extra-ordinary equitable jurisdiction to fill in the gaps in the law to provide a remedy if one is not otherwise available.
- *When writing about the law in an essay or an examination, you have to give the formal source of a legal rule. Why would it not usually be correct to refer to a textbook as your authority?*
  When you write about the law, you must give authority for what you say. When you are explaining how a legal rule works, you will need to refer to statutory or case law as authority for what you are asserting. These are the formal sources. A textbook might write about a statute or a case, and the writer might have worthwhile things to say, but is a secondary source. However, you should refer directly to the statute or the case, and only refer to the textbook if you want to refer to the particular opinion of the textbook writer. Never use the textbook as your authority in place of naming the section and the statute, or giving the citation of the case.

Chapter 2—Structure of the Scottish Legal System

- *What does "privative jurisdiction" mean?*
  Cases or issues restricted to a specific court, e.g. the High Court of Justiciary has privative jurisdiction to try cases of murder.
- *What three criteria define the civil jurisdiction of the sheriff court?*
  Location; persons; and subject matter.
- *Which court hears applications for judicial review?*
  The Court of Session.
- *What is the maximum prison sentence that can be imposed by the JP court?*
  60 days.
- *How many years must a JP have practised as a lawyer?*
  None, JPs are lay justices and not legally qualified.
- *What is the ultimate court of civil appeal?*
  The Supreme Court of the United Kingdom (formerly the House of Lords).
- *What is the ultimate court of criminal appeal?*
  The High Court of Justiciary sitting as a Court of Appeal.
- *What is the maximum fine a sheriff can impose after conviction in a solemn trial?*

There is no maximum amount, the level is unlimited.
- *How many people sit in a Scottish criminal jury?*
15
- *What is a judge of the High Court called?*
Lord Commissioner of Justiciary.
- *What does an Advocate depute do?*
Prosecute in the High Court of Justiciary.
- *Name the offices of the highest civil and criminal judiciary in Scotland?*
The Lord President of the Court of Session (civil) and The Lord Justice-General (criminal).

Chapter 3—Business Regulation

- *Is the criminal law a branch of public or private law?*
It is a branch of public law. Although victims' rights are increasingly recognised in the system, the criminal law is essentially concerned with the state exercising the public interest in preventing, resolving and punishing harmful behaviour.
- *What are the elements of a common law offence?*
Common law offences can only be committed if the accused has engaged in some manner of prohibited behaviour (i.e. carried out the actus reus of the crime) while possessing a criminal or blameworthy state of mind (mens rea).
- *What kinds of state of mind are capable of satisfying the requirement of mens rea?*
The mens rea differs depending on the particular crime that the accused is charged with. Some crimes require intention; for others, the requirement is satisfied through recklessness, negligence, or possession of a particular state of knowledge.
- *What is strict liability?*
A strict liability crime is one which does not require proof of mens rea. Thus one can commit a strict liability crime merely by carrying out its actus reus. Mens rea is required for all common law crimes, but not all statutory ones. The consequences of imposing strict liability can be very harsh. As a result the courts are somewhat reluctant to hold that a crime is one of strict liability, and parliament will often temper the effect of strict liability crimes by providing the accused with a "due diligence" defence.
- *What is vicarious liability?*
Vicarious liability arises when the courts hold someone guilty of a criminal offence because of something done by someone else, even though the two persons involved did not share a common purpose. Vicarious liability does not arise at common law but can arise in the context of statutory offences. For example, the proprietor of a business may in certain circumstances be made criminally liable for the criminal conduct of his employees.
- *Can corporations be found guilty of a crime?*
Yes. Corporations can be found vicariously liable for the actings of their employees in appropriate circumstances. In addition, corporations can themselves be found guilty of breaching the criminal law, albeit it can be difficult to establish mens rea, particularly against large corporations.
- *What is the mens rea of theft?*
An intention to deprive the owner of his/her property.
- *What are the elements of the crime of fraud?*

The actus reus of fraud is the use of a false pretence that: (a) deceives another; and (b) causes a definite practical result. The mens rea of the offence is comprised of knowing that the statement made is false, and intending to deceive the person to whom the statement was made.

- *How can a business defend itself against a charge of failing to prevent bribery?*
The Bribery Act 2010 provides a statutory defence for organisations that can prove that they have adequate procedures in place to prevent persons associated with it from offering bribes.
- *What does the expression "regulatory law" mean?*
Regulatory law can be defined as the body of law whereby public authorities seek to exercise control over activities which are of importance to the community. This can involve making certain types of activities criminal offences, but also includes other forms of regulatory controls such as demanding that persons obtain a licence before carrying out certain activities.
- *The Health and Safety at Work etc. Act 1974 is the main piece of occupational health legislation in the UK. What are the essential features of HSWA?*
The HSWA itself imposes duties upon employers—most notably the duties to ensure "so far as is reasonably practicable" the health, safety and welfare at work of all his employees and to ensure that persons not in his employment who may be affected by it are not exposed to risks to their health or safety. HWSA also allows regulations to be issued which impose more detailed and specific duties upon employers. HSWA also created the Health and Safety Executive, which can enforce HSWA by using a range of powers, including prosecution for breaches of the Act.
- *What is the purpose of the Corporate Manslaughter and Corporate Homicide Act 2007?*
The Act creates the offence of corporate homicide. This offence gives the court no more sentencing power than HSWA, but, given the difficulties that have occurred in convicting large corporations of common law homicide, Parliament felt that the Act would satisfy the public's desire to see companies that kill as a result of a serious breach of duty convicted of an offence which obviously carries a serious degree of blameworthiness.
- *What are the essential features of the Data Protection Act 1998?*
The DPA regulates the way in which personal data may be collected and used. It requires organisations which hold personal data to register with the regulator and to abide with a series of data protection principles when holding or making use of that data. Data subjects (i.e. the person the held data concerns) have certain rights and can, e.g. ensure that the data held about them is correct; the Information Commissioner's office also has a range of powers, including, in certain cases, the right to prosecute, to ensure that the Act is complied with.
- *Why do we regulate competition between businesses? Which anti-competitive behaviours are regulated by competition law? What are the consequences of breaching the prohibitions?*
Competition between businesses is widely believed to bring benefits to consumers and society as a whole. Any illegitimate manipulation of free markets, making them less competitive, is therefore seen as a serious matter. Competition law regulates anti-competitive agreements (such as price-fixing agreements) and the abuse of a dominant position. Breaching the rules can result in civil penalites of up to 10 per cent of a company

group's annual worldwide turnover. Criminal sanctions are also available in very serious cases, anti-competitive agreements will be unenforceable, and third parties who have suffered a loss as a result of a breach of competition law may be able to claim damages against the wrongdoing parties.

Chapter 4—The Law of Contract

- *What is a contract?*
  At its most basic, a contract is as described by Gloag: "an agreement intended to create a legal obligation between the parties".
- *Are all agreements contractually binding?*
  No; not *all* agreements are intended to create legal obligations. See, e.g. the case of social and domestic arrangements. Most agreements entered into in a business context will be intended to create legal obligations, and therefore binding. However even here there are exceptions. See para.4–09.
- *Is a unilateral gratuitous promise a contract?*
  No, but under Scots law promises will be legally binding if the conditions set out in RSWA are met: see para.4–10.
- *What is consensus in idem? What is its legal significance?*
  A *consensus in idem* is a meeting of the minds; agreement by the parties on the essential elements of a contract. The moment that *consensus* is reached, a contract comes into existence.
- *What kind of test do the courts use to assess if consensus in idem has been reached?*
  An objective test. In other words, whether the parties themselves think they have agreement is irrelevant; what matters is what an objective bystander witnessing their discussions and negotiations would think.
- *What is the identifying feature of an offer?*
  An offer must "contemplate acceptance". If a proposition or statement is not of such a nature that it can be met with an unqualified agreement, it is not an offer.
- *What is an invitation to treat? Give examples of common invitations to treat.*
  An invitation to treat is an invitation for someone else to make an offer. Examples include shop displays and their online equivalent and (usually) advertisements and invitations to tender.
- *Does an offer not stated to be subject to a time limit remain open indefinitely?*
  No. It will lapse after the expiry of a reasonable time. It may also be capable of being revoked.
- *What is the identifying feature of an acceptance?*
  It must be an unqualified agreement to an offer.
- *What is the legal effect of a counter-offer?*
  A counter-offer revokes the offer to which it responds, and puts in place a new offer which the original offeror can either accept or decline as he/she chooses.
- *When will the law consider an acceptance to have been effectually communicated to the offeror?*
  In the case of instantaneous forms of communication, when the acceptance is actually received. In the case of delayed forms of communication, upon despatch of the acceptance.

- *"Contracts relating to _____ form the most significant exception to the rule that contracts do not require to be in writing." What is the missing word?*
Land.
- *A and B intend to enter into a contract. A brings a document containing contractual terms and conditions to B's attention before the contract is concluded. B doesn't understand what the terms mean, but reckons that as long he doesn't sign anything they can't become part of the contract anyway. Is B's analysis correct?*
No, his analysis is incorrect and unsafe. Although he would be bound by the terms if he signed them, that is not the only way in which they can be incorporated into a contract. They will also be incorporated without signature if: (i) the offeror brings them to the offerees attention in time; (ii) they are contained in a contractual document; and (iii) the notice is adequate. The fact that B doesn't understand what they mean is irrelevant to the question of whether they have been incorporated into the contract. However, if they are not written in plain English, and if B is a consumer, then the Consumer Rights Act 2015 means that any ambiguity will be resolved in B's favour.
- *Name the two major statutory regimes which regulate contractual terms. Outline their essential features.*
The Unfair Contract Terms Act 1977 ("UCTA") and Pt 2 of the Consumer Rights Act 2015 ("CRA"). UCTA does not apply to consumer contracts. It controls the circumstances in which the courts will enforce exemption clauses in business to business contracts. The CRA applies to consumer contracts only. It provides the consumer with a legal right to challenge terms in a consumer contract which the consumer believes to be unfair. This right applies to all provisions other than those which set out the subject-matter of the agreement or its price. Certain types of provision (e.g. attempts to exclude liability for negligently-caused personal injury or death) will be deemed to be unfair, and are thus unenforceable against the consumer. Certain other types of provision (e.g. ones which provide the trader with the right to unilaterally determine the price of the contract after the consumer has already become contractually bound) are on a statutory "greylist", meaning that they will not be automatically held to be unfair, but will be subjected to close scrutiny by the court. The court's oversight is not, however, restricted to the types of provision which appear on the greylist; other provisions which, contrary to the requirement of good faith, causes a significant imbalance in the parties' rights and obligations to the detriment of the consumer will be held to be unfair. The CRA is in addition enforced and overseen by the Competition and Markets Authority, which can take action to prevent traders from including unfair terms in their consumer contracts.
- *Is a contract entered into between a record company and an 8-year old child prodigy legally binding? What about one between a record company and a 17-year old?*
No. The 8-year old lacks capacity. The record company would have to contract with their legal guardian. The 17-year old has capacity but could subsequently challenge the contract if it was entered into on prejudicial terms. The record company could exclude the possibility of challenge by having the court ratify the contract.
- *If a person suffering from a mental illness, while on a euphoric high, decides to spend £100,000 on designer clothes, is the contract of purchase they have apparently entered into legally binding?*

Yes, unless the purchaser could demonstrate that they satisfied the legal test of insanity, and therefore lacked capacity at the time. This would involve demonstrating that they were incapable of understanding the legal obligations the contract entailed.

- *A is a fan of the band Fleet Foxes. He learns from friends that "The Foxes" are to be appearing live at SECC, and phones the ticket hotline to buy a ticket for the event. When the ticket arrives, he sees that it is for a concert being given by a different band simply called "The Foxes", who he hadn't heard of before and doesn't wish to go and see. Is A bound by the contract?*
Yes. This is a unilateral, uninduced error. The ticket purchaser is therefore bound. Matters would be different if the purchaser of the tickets had been tricked into buying the tickets by misrepresentation on the part of the seller. That would have satisfied the "error plus" requirement and rendered the contract susceptible to being set aside by the purchaser.

- *A places a large bet on a horse-race. His horse loses. Disappointed, he decides to cheer himself up by buying a knighthood from a corrupt public official. Happy now, he celebrates by buying a case of vintage champagne and hiring a prostitute. How many binding contracts has A entered into in this sequence of events?*
Two: the bet is (now, since the Gambling Act 2005 Act entered into legal force) a valid legal contract; so too is the purchase of the champagne. The other two agreements are *pacta illicita*.

- *What is a restrictive covenant? Will such contractual terms be enforced by the courts?*
A restrictive covenant is a contractual term by which one of the parties agrees that they will in some way refrain from competing with the other. They are commonly inserted into contracts of employment and contracts for the sale of a business. Such terms are unenforceable unless the party seeking to enforce it has a legitimate interest to protect, the clause is reasonable in its scope and extent and it is in the public interest.

- *What is a material breach of contract? Which contractual remedies available to someone suffering a material breach of contract are not available to the innocent party in the case of a non-material breach?*
A material breach of contract is a particularly significant breach of contract—one which goes "to the root of the contract." The additional remedies available in the case of a material breach are the self-help remedies: rescission, retention and lien.

- *What is meant by "the duty to mitigate loss"?*
The legal duty imposed upon the innocent party to take reasonable steps to reduce the loss he/she has suffered as a result of the breach of contract.

- *What is meant by "remoteness of damages"?*
An innocent party is only entitled to recover such damages as arise naturally from the breach of contract or such as may reasonably supposed to have been in the contemplation of both parties at the time they made the contract. Any other losses will be deemed "too remote" and will not be legally recoverable.

- *What are liquidate damages, and are they legally enforceable?*
Liquidate damages clauses are terms inserted into contracts by which the parties agree the amount of damages which will be paid in the event of a particular type of breach. They are legally enforceable if they are a genuine attempt at pre-estimating loss but not if they are punitive in nature.

- *After what period of time will the right to enforce a contractual obligation be lost?*
  Five years from the date when the obligation became enforceable unless the contract is one pertaining to land, in which case the relevant period is 20 years.
- *In which circumstances will a contract be brought to an end by "frustration"?*
  If the contract becomes:

  (i) physically impossible to perform, e.g. as a result of the destruction of the contractual subject matter;
  (ii) practically impossible to perform; or
  (iii) illegal to perform.

Chapter 5—Commercial Sale and Supply of Goods

- *Name three types of contract dealing with the supply of goods.*
  Sale, barter, hire-purchase, hire and contracts for services where goods also are supplied.
- *Which Act of Parliament governs commercial contracts of sale?*
  Sale of Goods Act 1979.
- *How is a contract of sale different from other contracts for the supply of goods?*
  It involves a money consideration called the price and transfers ownership.
- *There are exceptions to the rule that someone who is not the legal owner of goods cannot pass on a good title to them. State two of them.*

  —Personal bar.
  —Sale by a mercantile agent.
  —Sale under a voidable title.
  —Sale by a seller in possession after a sale.
  —Sale by a buyer in possession after a sale.
  —Sales of motor vehicles subject to hire-purchase or conditional sale.

- *What terms are implied in contracts of sale?*
  Terms about title, description, satisfactory quality, fitness for a specified purpose, conformity of bulk with sample.
- *When are goods of satisfactory quality?*
  See the general definition in s.14(2A) and the factors set out in s.14(2B) of the Sale of Goods Act 1979.
- *When does the satisfactory quality test not apply?*
  Where defects have been specifically drawn to the attention of the buyer before sale and, where the buyer has examined the goods, defects which that examination ought to have revealed.
- *What remedies are available to a purchaser who buys defective goods?*
  Rejection, damages, specific implement
- *What remedies are available to a seller if the buyer breaks the contract?*

  1. Action for the price—s.49.
  2. Damages for non-acceptance—s.50.
  3. In some circumstances:
     (a) right of lien over goods—ss.39(1)(a) and 41;
     (b) stoppage in transit—ss.44–46; and
     (c) right of resale—ss.39(1)(a) and 48.

- *What terms are implied in contracts for the transfer of goods governed by the Supply of Goods and Services Act 1982?*
  The same types as are implied in contracts of sale, i.e. title, description, satisfactory quality, fitness for specified purpose and correspondence of bulk with sample.

Chapter 6—Consumer Protection

- *Which Act would you consult if you bought digital content which turned out to be defective?*
  The Consumer Rights Act 2015.
- *What are your remedies if a TV you have bought has a fault?*
  The principal remedies in the Consumer Rights Act 2015 are:

  —short term right to reject;
  —repair or replacement; and
  —price reduction or final right to reject.

  In some circumstances you might, in addition or as an alternative:

  —claim damages;
  —seek an order for specific implement;
  —rely on the breach to defend a claim by the trader for the unpaid price; or
  —for breach of an express term, exercise a right to treat the contract as at an end.

- *Which are the main statutes governing consumer credit?*
  Consumer Credit Act 1974 and the Financial Services and Markets Act 2000.
- *Which two categories of agreement do the Acts referred to in the previous question cover?*
  Credit agreement and hire agreements.
- *Name two ways in which the activities of traders in the credit industry are controlled.*
  Authorisation, advertising controls, a ban on canvassing off trade premises, a ban on circulars to minors, and a ban on unsolicited distribution of credit cards.
- *Who runs the system for authorising involvement in the credit industry?*
  The Financial Services Authority.
- *What is connected lender liability?*
  This describes a situation where a person providing credit is liable for acts or omissions of the person who supplied the goods or services purchased on credit. Examples are in ss.56 and 75 of the Consumer Credit Act 1974.
- *Why were the Consumer Protection from Unfair Trading Regulations 2008 introduced?*
  To implement the EU's Unfair Commercial Practices Directive.
- *As well as a general ban on unfair practices the CPRs ban four different types of unfair practice. Name them.*
  Misleading actions, misleading omissions, aggressive practices and those on the banned list in Sch.1.
- *Describe a specific practice banned by the CPRs.*
  See the list of 31 practices referred to in the text.
- *What is meant in the CPRs by the "average consumer"?*
  In general it means someone, "who is reasonably well-informed, reasonably observant and circumspect ". In addition, where a practice is

aimed at a particular group of consumers it is the average member of that group; and the average member of a group who are particularly vulnerable.

- *What methods are used to enforce the Consumer Protection from Unfair Trading Regulations 2008?*
  Informal means, enforcement orders, criminal prosecutions and civil actions by individual consumers who have suffered loss.
- *Name other legislation controlling a trade practice.*
  Consumer Protection (Cancellation of Contracts Concluded away from Business Premises) Regulations 1987 (SI 1987/2117); Consumer Contracts (Information, Cancellation and Additional Charges) Regulations 2013 (SI 2013/3134); Timeshare, Holiday Products, Resale and Exchange Contracts Regulations 2010 (SI 2010/2960); and the Estate Agents Act 1979.

Chapter 7—E-commerce

- *Can a contract be concluded electronically in Scots law? What is your authority for this?*
  Yes: the Requirements of Writing (Scotland) Act 1995 Pt 3 as amended by the Land Registration etc. (Scotland) Act 2012.
- *When is the contract concluded?*
  In accordance with the normal principle of Scots contract law, a contract is concluded when there is an offer which has been met by an unqualified acceptance. There are, however, four potential points when this could be said to occur online. Sadly, no clear answer emerges from the E-Commerce Regulations or the CC Regulations as to which is correct. Therefore, instead each factual situation must be analysed to determine at what point an offer was met by an unqualified acceptance.
- *What are "information society services"?*
  The term is defined by the E-Commerce Directive, as: "any service normally provided for remuneration, at a distance, by means of electronic equipment for the processing (digital compression) and storage of data, and at the individual request of a recipient of the service". It therefore covers online services such as email and webhosting as well as the sale of goods and services online.
- *What legislation regulates the provision of information society services?*
  The Electronic Commerce (EC Directive) Regulations 2002 (SI 2002/2013), which implements the Electronic Commerce Directive 2000/31/EC.
- *What obligations are imposed on providers of information society services? (Hint: what information is required?)*
  Regulation 6 requires the provision of certain information including details as to the geographical location of the service provider and his contact details.
  Regulations 7 and 8 require all "commercial communications", such as an email from an online retailer, to be marked as such.
  Regulation 9 requires the service provider to specify the different technical steps required to conclude the contract online
- *What is a "distance contract"? (Your definition should contain five elements.)*
  A distance contract is defined by reg.5: it must have the following five elements: (i) it is a concluded contract; (ii) between a trader and a consumer; (iii) there is an organised distance sales or service provision

scheme; (iv) the parties were not together and physically present when the contract was concluded; and (v) it was concluded using one or more means of distance communication.

- *What legislation regulates distance contracts?*

The Consumer Contract (Information, Cancellation and Additional Charges) Regulations 2013 (SI 2013/3134), implementing the Consumer Rights Directive 2011/83/EU.

- *What is a sales contract? Give an example.*

A sales contract is defined by reg.5 as a contract where the trader transfers or agrees to transfer ownership of goods to a consumer in return for payment of a price. Importantly, a sales contract can have service elements, so long as the main purpose of the contract is still the transfer of ownership.

An example of a sales contract is a wedding dress purchased from an online store.

- *What is service contract? Give an example.*

A service contract is again defined by reg.5 as a contract where the trader supplies or agrees to supply a service to the consumer in return for a price. Importantly a service contract cannot also be a sales contract. If, however, the main purpose of the contract is the provision of a service, then the fact there are some elements involving the transfer of ownership in goods will not bar it from being classed as a service contract.

An example of this more complex situation is a cookery class, where the price includes the ingredients, but the main purpose is the provision of a service in the form of cookery tuition.

A simpler example of a pure service contract would be an online course, where the tuition is provided in return for a fee.

- *When is a contract a contract for the supply of digital content not on a tangible medium?*

This is the third, and newly recognised, type of contract under the CC Regulations. Although not explicitly defined in the Regulations, at its simplest it is a contract which provides data in a digital form, for example an online newspaper subscription. Importantly the digital content must not be in a tangible medium, which means it cannot be provided on a CD or DVD. If it is, then it is a sales contract, the contract relating to the transfer of ownership in the CD or DVD.

Finally, unlike sales and service contracts there is no requirement in the Regulations for a price to be paid in order for the contract to be classed as a contract for the supply of digital content not on a tangible medium. This means, in theory, free downloadable apps are within the definition.

- *What information must be provided by sellers under a distance contract? (Hint: don't forget the additional requirements when the contract is concluded by "electronic means")*

Regulation 13 requires the following information to be provided before the contract is concluded:

—The information listed in Schedule 2 of the Regulations.
—The Model Cancellation Form as set out in Part B of Schedule 3 of the Regulations.

When the contract is concluded by "electronic means", under Regulation 14 the trader must also:

—Inform the consumer of any delivery restrictions and which means of payment are accepted.

—Make sure the information listed in Sch.2 paras (a), (f), (g), (h), (s) and (t) have been provided. (Which of course it should have been under reg.13.)

Regardless of whether the contract is concluded by electronic means, once the contract is concluded the trader must confirm the contract in line with reg.16, this requires:

—The information in Sch.2 to be provided in a "durable medium".

The aim being to ensure the parties have a record of the information, if the information has already been provide in a durable medium there is no need to send it again.

- *When does the consumer's right to cancel arise? How does this cancellation affect ancillary contracts?*
  All consumers have a right to cancel, without giving any reason, so long as they are within the cancellation period. Under reg.38 if the consumer cancels the main contract then any ancillary contracts associated with it are also cancelled.
- *How can the CC Regulations be enforced by a consumer?*

  —By complaining to the enforcement authorities—in Scotland this means the local council—who will notify the Competition and Markets Authority (the replacement for the OFT).
  —Raise an action for breach of contract, relying on the normal principles of contract law. This is a viable option because the Regulations make many of their terms implied terms in the contract between the trader and the consumer. Therefore where the trader fails to comply, there are not only failing to comply with the Regulations, they are breaching an implied term of the contract.

Chapter 8—Employment Law

- *What are the key ingredients for a contract of service?*
  Sufficient mutuality of obligation, personal service, control and other terms being consistent with employment.
- *Can a director who has a controlling shareholder also be an employee?*
  Yes—but only if this genuinely reflects the reality of the situation and is not a sham—the extent of shareholding is a relevant but not decisive factor.
- *When does a written statement of employment particulars have to be provided by an employer?*
  Within two months of employment commencing.
- *What is a collective agreement? How can such agreements be sources of terms and conditions of employment?*
  An agreement between one or more employers (or employers associations) with one or more trade unions. Whilst such agreements are presumed not to be binding as between employer and trade union they can contain terms and conditions of employment which become incorporated in individual contracts of employment.
- *What limit does the Working Time Regulations 1998 place on maximum weekly working hours? Can employees waive their rights to this limit?*
  The Regulations provide for a maximum weekly average of 48 hours calculated over a default 17-week reference period. Individuals can opt-out of this average limit by signing opt-out agreements.
- *What is wrongful dismissal and how is this different from unfair dismissal?*

Wrongful dismissal is essentially a termination of employment in breach of contract by the employer. The remedy of the employee is to claim damages under common law principles. Unfair dismissal is a separate statutory right not to be unfairly dismissed involving a claim to an employment tribunal.

- *What are the five potentially fair reasons for dismissal in unfair dismissal law?*
  The five potentially fair reasons are: capability/qualifications; conduct; redundancy; inability to continue working without contravening an enactment; and some other substantial reason.
- *How much continuous service is required to be eligible to claim a redundancy payment?*
  Two years continuous service.
- *Can direct sex discrimination ever be justified?*
  No—direct sex discrimination can never be justified although there are certain occupational requirements which permit employing one gender for certain roles in exceptional circumstances.
- *What is the general test for "disability" under the Equality Act 2010?*
  The Act generally requires a claimant to establish a physical or mental impairment which has a substantial and long-term adverse effect on their ability to carry out normal day-to-day activities.

Chapter 9—Agency

- *What is the purpose of agency?*
  Agency is a mechanism which is often used in business (but is not restricted to business use) which allows one party (the principal) to use an intermediary (the agent) to enter into binding contractual arrangements with third parties. It is often used when the principal requires expertise or advice from the agent or where the principal is too busy or simply prefers that someone else looks after their commercial arrangements.
- *What are the main categories and types of agency?*
  There are many differing types and categories of agency and the labels used are not always a definitive guide to the actual agency involved. The main labels and descriptions used general and special agency, the less common mercantile and *del credere* agency, and the newer commercial agency.
- *What are the main ways that agency can be created?*
  Agency can be created:

  —expressly;
  —by implication;
  —by ratification;
  —by necessity; and
  —by holding out.

- *Give an example of agency created by implication*
  A good example arises in partnership where s.5 of the Partnership Act 1890 contains a rule of law that implies agency. If someone can be shown to factually be a partner then that factual situation combined with the rule of law in s.5 impliedly creates agency.
- *What are the conditions needed to establish agency by ratification?*

  —The agent must have been acting as an agent and disclosed this to the third party.

—The principal must have been in existence at the time of the agent's actions.
—The principal must have had the necessary legal capacity to take the action in question.
—The principal must have known all the facts behind the agent's actions.
—The ratification has to have taken place within any relevant time limits.
—The action being ratified must itself have been legal.

- *What is needed for agency to exist on the basis of holding out?*
  The third party needs to believe that the "agent" is acting as an agent and has this belief either on the basis of positive encouragement from the principal or because the principal takes no action to contradict this belief.
- *What are the main types of authority an agent may have?*

  —Express.
  —Implied.
  —Apparent or ostensible.

- *How does apparent or ostensible authority differ from implied authority?*
  Apparent or ostensible authority will involve an impression being given to third parties that the "agent" has authority to act on the basis of action or inaction on the part of the principal. Implied authority can come out on the basis of a broader range of circumstances which simply imply that authority exists.
- *What are the duties owed by an agent to a principal?*

  —The duty to perform instructions.
  —A good faith/fiduciary duty.
  —The duty to exercise skill and care.
  —The duty to keep accounts.

- *What rights does an agent enjoy?*

  —To be remunerated and reimbursed.
  —To be relieved of liabilities.
  —To enjoy rights of lien and security.

- *When might an agent become liable to a third party?*
  The main situations when this can arise are when the agent acts in a way which exceeds the authority the agent has been given or the agent acts but does not disclose that they is acting as an agent.
- *What happens if an agent exceeds the authority given by a principal?*
  There will be no binding contract between the principal and the third party unless the principal decides to ratify the agent's actions and the agent will almost certainly be liable to the third party.
- *What is a commercial agent?*
  A commercial agent is a self employed intermediary who negotiates the sale or purchase of goods on behalf of a principal.
- *What rights do the Commercial Agents (Council Directive) Regulations give to a commercial agent?*

  —To be provided by the principal with all necessary documentation.
  —To be provided by the principal with all information needed to perform the contract.

—To be notified by the principal if it is anticipated if the volume of transactions will be significantly less than the agent could have anticipated.

—To be informed by the principal within a reasonable time of the principal's acceptance or refusal of a transaction which the agent has arranged.

- *What duties are owed to a principal by a commercial agent?*
A commercial agent must act dutifully for the principal and act in good faith and look after the principal's interests.
- *How can commercial agency be terminated?*
The most straightforward to terminate commercial agency is on the basis of notice given by either the principal or the agent. The Regulations set out the periods of notice which require to be given.

Chapter 10—Delict

- *Explain what is meant by damnum injuria datum?*
This literally means a loss caused by a legal wrong. This is the essence of delict; the legal obligation to take responsibility for harm caused to another.
- *Which case set out the criteria for the delict of passing off?*

  ➤ *Erven Warnink BV v J Townend & Sons (Hull) Ltd (No.1).*

- *State the five steps used to establish a case of liability for unintentional harm?*

  —There must be a duty of care between pursuer and defender.
  —The defender must have breached the duty of care by falling below the standard of care exercised by the reasonable man.
  —The pursuer must have sustained a loss.
  —The breach of duty of care must have been the factual and legal cause of the loss to the pursuer.
  —The loss must not be too remote.

- *What is a duty of care and what is the test for identifying whether a duty exists?*
A duty of care is the responsibility owed by each person to take care in their acts and omissions so as not to cause harm to others. A duty of care can be established where there is foreseeability, proximity and it is fair, just and reasonable to impose a duty. This is the tripartite test set out in *Caparo Industries Plc v Dickman.*
- *How will the court determine whether a duty of care has been breached?*
The court will ascertain whether a pursuer has exercised less care then the reasonable man would in the same situation by applying the calculus of risk.
- *What types of loss will give rise to recovery in delict?*
Physical injury and financial losses resulting from it will give rise to a claim, as will property damage. Psychiatric injury will give rise to a claim for primary victims and for secondary victims where the three criteria set out in *Alcock v Chief Constable of South Yorkshire Police* are fulfilled. Pure economic loss will not give rise to recovery except in very limited circumstances of cases such as *Henderson v Merrett Syndicates Ltd.*
- *Explain the meaning of the term causa causans?*

The *causa causans* is the legal cause, or the dominant, effective or immediate cause, of the pursuer's loss.

- *What is the correct test for remoteness of damage?*
  The correct test, following *Simmons v British Steel*, is probably the reasonable foreseeability test set out in *Overseas Tankship (UK) Ltd v Morts Dock & Engineering Co Ltd (The Wagon Mound)*.
- *What will be the effect of a finding of contributory negligence in a case of liability for unintentional harm?*
  A finding of contributory negligence will reduce the pursuer's damages by the percentage by which they were found to be contributorily negligent.
- *Name the two conditions which must be satisfied before an employer will be found vicariously liable for the actions of his employee?*
  A contract of employment must exist between the two parties and the employee must have been acting in the course of his duties at the time the delictual act took place.
- *What rule was set out by the case of Hunter v Hanley?*
  This case set out the test of professional negligence, which is that the professional must have taken a course of action that no other reasonable professional in the same circumstances would have followed.
- *What is an interdict?*
  An interdict is a court order prohibiting specific conduct which is either anticipated or ongoing.

Chapter 11—Property

- *What are the main ways in which property can be classified?*
  Property may be classified into heritable property (mainly land and buildings) and moveable property (everything else). Moveable property may be classified into corporeal moveable property (things in the physical world that can be seen or touched) and incorporeal moveable property (rights).
- *What is the difference between real rights and personal rights?*
  Real rights (e.g. ownership) can be enforced against anyone in the world, whereas personal rights (e.g. contractual rights) can only be enforced against a particular person, the one who owes the corresponding obligation.
- *What are the main characteristics of registration of title?*

  —the title is registered as a whole and not as a series of individual documents;
  —the validity of the title is backed by a warranty from the Keeper of the Registers of Scotland;
  —each property is identified on a master plan; and
  —records are held electronically, and some transactions can be carried out electronically, by —a system of automated registration of title to land ("ARTL").

- *What are the main rights of ownership?*

  —the right to exclusive possession;
  —the right to freedom from interference by neighbours; and
  —rights of support.

- *In what circumstances can a person raise an action under the common law of nuisance and what remedies may be available to him or her?*

The most common cases of nuisance arise where a person's activities interfere with the peaceful enjoyment of neighbour's property (e.g. by the creation of noise, vibration, smoke or fumes). A nuisance must be continuing and substantial and it makes no difference that it may have predated the arrival of the complaining owner. The main remedy is interdict. Damages may also be claimed where *culpa* (blame) can be established.

- *In what respects has the law of trespass been modified by the Land Reform (Scotland) Act 2003?*
  Members of the public now have a statutory right of access to private land for recreational, educational and commercial purposes, and the also the right to cross land, though subject to certain exceptions. Guidance can be found in the *Scottish Outdoor Access Code*.

- *What are the rules for determining whether or not an item is a heritable fixture?*
  An item may be a heritable fixture:

  —if it cannot be removed without damaging itself or damaging the soil or building to which it is attached;
  —if it was intended to be permanent;
  —if the building or land has been specially adapted to it;
  —if its removal would substantially affect the use and enjoyment of the property; or
  —if it is particularly heavy.

- *What are the main rules of the law of the tenement?*
  The statutory law of the tenement under the Tenements (Scotland) Act 2004 provides:

  —the boundary between adjacent flats, etc. is the mid point;
  —a door or window serving one flat only is the sole property of that flat's owner;
  —a top flat includes the roof over that flat and the air space up to the roof's highest point;
  —a bottom flat includes the solum (the site) under the flat;
  —the close, stair and landings are common property;
  —a lift is normally common property;
  —ground is owned by the owner of the immediately adjacent bottom flat; and
  —chimney stacks are common property.

  The owner of each flat is obliged to provide shelter for any flat below it and support for any flat above.
  Strategic parts of the tenement have to be maintained by all owners on an equitable basis.

- *What are the main legal restrictions upon ownership?*
  —servitudes;
  —real burdens;
  —securities; and
  —statutory controls, such as planning or building control.

- *What is meant by saying that a lease confers a real right upon a tenant?*
  A tenant's real right to a property means that, should the landlord sell the property, the lease can be enforced against the new owner.

- *What are the main legal remedies of the parties to a lease in the event of a breach of the lease contract?*
  The main breach of contract remedies of the parties to a lease are:

  —specific implement or interdict;
  —court action for debt;
  —rescission;
  —damages;
  —rent retention (tenant only);
  —hypothec (landlord only, and only in commercial leases); and
  —irritancy (landlord only, and only in commercial leases).

- *What are the main categories of lease and the statutes regulating them?*

  —residential leases, including private sector assured and short assured tenancies (regulated by the Housing (Scotland) Acts 1988 and 2006) and social tenancies (regulated by the Housing (Scotland) Act 2001);
  —agricultural leases (regulated by the Agricultural Holdings (Scotland) Acts 1991 and 2003); and
  —commercial leases (i.e. of shops, offices, factories or other business premises) which are largely free of statutory regulation in Scotland, apart from the right of shop tenants to apply to the sheriff court for up to one year's extension to their lease under the Tenancy of Shops (Scotland) Act 1949.

Chapter 12—Intellectual Property

- *What are the elements that a pursuer must establish to constitute the action of passing off?*

  —Goodwill.
  —Misrepresentation.
  —Damage.

- *What are the advantages of registering trade marks?*

  —UK registered trade mark protection extends UK-wide and is not limited by the geographical scope of goodwill.
  —A mark need not have been used or acquired goodwill before registration.
  —The registered trade mark owner may save costs relative to the costs of having to prove all of the elements of a claim in passing off every time there is an infringement.
  —Once registered the protection against infringement may be wider for a registered mark than under passing off.

- *Are written responses to this quick quiz protected by copyright? How?*

  —The written responses originated from the responder (hopefully).
  —They are recorded.
  —They are considered "literary works" as a subject matter which attracts copyright.

- *What intellectual property rights may exist in the THOMSON REUTERS logo?*

  —Trade mark.
  —Right against passing off.

—Copyright (both economic and moral rights).

- *What are the advantages to registering design rights?*

    —Registered design rights last longer (up to 25 years) than CDPA unregistered design rights (up to 15 years).
    —Registration provides evidence to the existence and priority of the right.
    —CDPA rights are only infringed where copying is shown. Copying is not necessary as an element of registered design right infringement.

- *What are the basic criteria in determining the patentability of an invention?*

    —Novelty.
    —Inventive step.
    —Capable of industrial application.
    —Not excluded from patentability on any relevant grounds.

- *What are two basic types of patent claims?*

    —A product patent.
    —A process patent.

Chapter 13—Trusts

- *What is a trust?*
  A trust exists where a truster transfers property to a trustee, who is under no obligation to apply that property for the benefit of the beneficiary.
- *Who owns trust property?*
  The trustee.
- *How is a voluntary trust created?*
  By declaring the trust purposes and transferring the property from the truster to the trustee.
- *What restrictions does Scots law place on the validity of trust purposes?*
  They must not be criminal, "directly prohibited", *contra bonos mores* or contrary to public policy.
- *Must trust decisions be taken unanimously?*
  No, they can be taken by a majority.
- *What general duties does the law impose on trustees?*
  A general duty of care, along with duties not to delegate the trust, to secure trust property, to invest trust property, to take advice where appropriate, to meet existing debts and obligations, to keep accounts and to pay the correct beneficiaries.
- *What is meant by the rule against auctor in rem suam?*
  A trustee must not place themself in a position where their position as trustee and their interests as an individual conflict.
- *What are the sources of trustees' powers?*
  The trust deed, along with the statutory powers implied under s.4 of the Trusts (Scotland) Act 1921. It is possible to apply to the court for additional powers in some cases.
- *When a trustee has been in breach of trust, what remedies are open to the beneficiaries?*
  The principal remedies are an action for interdict, damages, or "count, reckoning and payment" ("accounting").
- *How may trustees be protected from liability for breach of trust?*

By an immunity clause in the trust deed, or by relying on statutory defences available to trustees who act honestly and reasonably or commit a breach of trust at a beneficiary's instigation.

- *Are trustees personally liable on trust contracts?*
  Yes, unless there is an agreement to the contrary.
- *What requirements must be satisfied before the terms of a private trust can be varied? To what extent is the court involved in this process?*
  All the beneficiaries must consent. The court has a power to consent on behalf of beneficiaries who are incapable of doing so if certain conditions are met.

Chapter 14—Choice of Business Medium

- *What is a sole trader?*
  A sole trader is an individual involved in the management and control of his/her own business.
- *What is a partnership?*
  A partnership is the relation which subsists between persons carrying on a business in common with a view of profit.
- *How are the sole trader, partnership, LLP and incorporated company distinct?*
  Companies and LLPs are both bodies corporate whereas sole traders and partnerships are not. Partnerships and companies possess legal personality and are legally distinct from their partners, members and managers/directors. This can be contrasted with the sole trader who has no separate legal personality.
- *What is meant by personal liability in this context?*
  Personal liability means that the owners or members of an organisation are fully liable for the debts of that organisation.
- *What is meant by limited liability?*
  Limited liability means that the owners or members of an organisation enjoy limited liability for the debts of that organisation. The extent of the limitation is regulated by the limited liability partnership agreement in the case of an LLP and in the case of an incorporated company limited by shares, the shareholder's liability is limited to the value which remains unpaid on their shares. In the case of an incorporated company limited by guarantee, the extent of a member's liability is limited to the monetary value which he/she has agreed to contribute towards the debts of the company on a winding up in terms of the memorandum of association.
- *What does separate legal personality mean?*
  An organisation has separate legal personality when it is an organisation which is distinct from its members, partners or owners.
- *What is perpetual succession?*
  If an organisation possesses perpetual succession, this means that it is not dissolved or terminated by a change in the composition of its membership or management. In other words, it continues to exist notwithstanding such changes.
- *What is meant by a division of ownership and control?*
  If an organisation exhibits a separation between ownership and control, this means that a manager of the organisation does not require to be an owner or vice versa and, thus, it is easier to obtain outside capital investment since investors know that they do not necessarily need to participate in the management of the business.

Chapter 15—The Law of Partnership

- *What is a partnership and what are its main attributes?*
  A partnership is the relation which subsists between persons carrying on
  a business in common with a view of profit. It is a separate legal person
  distinct from its partners in terms of Scots law—s.4(2) of the Partnership
  Act 1890. A partnership can be constituted in writing or orally. It may
  also be inferred from the actions of the parties and in particular the
  attributes of their relationship towards each other. Where the relationship between partners amounts to a partnership, they are deemed to be
  fiduciaries.
- *What are the rules for determining whether the partnership or other partners are liable for wrongs, delicts or omissions of a partner which have
  caused injury or loss to a third party?*

  1. Where a partner commits a wrongful act or omits to act in the
     ordinary course of the business of the partnership, or with the
     authority of their co-partners, loss or injury is caused to a third
     party, or any penalty is incurred, the partnership is liable to the
     same extent as the partner so acting or omitting to act.
  2. Where a partner in a firm of solicitors dishonestly assists a client in
     perpetrating a fraud by drafting bogus agreements, this will amount
     to the ordinary course of the business of the partnership, since
     drafting and advising on agreements is part and portion of the
     business of a firm of solicitors—*Dubai Aluminium v Salaam* [2003] 2
     A.C. 366.

- *Which rules in the 1890 Act regulate partnership property?*
  Property purchased with the money of the partnership or on account of
  the partnership in the ordinary course of the business of the partnership,
  is deemed to be partnership property. Such property must be held by the
  partners exclusively for the purposes of the partnership and in accordance with the partnership agreement—s.20(1) of the 1890 Act.
- *Can the partners dismiss a partner by majority vote?*
  No. Section 25 of the 1890 Act states that unanimity is required. However, the partnership agreement may provide otherwise.
- *Is a partnership legally bound where a third party enters into a contract
  with the partnership knowing that the partner has no authority to bind the
  partnership?*
  No. See s.5 of the 1890 Act.
- *Is a partner entitled to retain a personal profit?*
  No. A partner is a fiduciary and owes fiduciary obligations to the partnership which involve full disclosure and accounting to the partnership
  for private profits. See s.29 of the 1890 Act.
- *Is a provision in the partnership agreement which provides that the partnership will continue notwithstanding the death of a partner a lawful provision which will be upheld by the courts?*
  Yes. The general rule in s.33(1) of the 1890 Act is that the death of a
  partner automatically dissolves the partnership. However, this rule may
  be disapplied by the partnership agreement. A prime example of this
  technique is provided by *WS Gordon & Co Ltd v Thomson Partnership*,
  1985 S.L.T. 122.
- *Section 35(f) of the 1890 Act stipulates that a partnership can be dissolved
  by the court where it is "just and equitable". What does this mean?*

There is no straightforward answer to this question. The concept of "just and equitable" is very wide and flexible. However, one can point to past case law and in particular the case of *Sutherland v Barnes* (Unreported, October 8, 1997, Vinelott J. (CA)) for examples of what the courts have considered to be "just and equitable" grounds for dissolution. Here it was held that it was "just and equitable" to dissolve a partnership in circumstances where the relationship of trust and confidence had irrevocably broken down between the partners of the partnership.

- *I don't understand the case of Dubai Aluminium v Salaam [2003] 2 A.C. 366. How can it be logical that a partnership is liable to third parties under s.10 of the 1890 Act for the fraudulent activities of a partner?*
  The relevant question is not whether fraud is "in the ordinary course of the business of the 'partnership'" in terms of s.10 of the 1890 Act. Instead, one must focus on the general acts of the partner in perpetrating the fraud and ask whether they were so closely connected with the acts which that partner was authorised to do that those actions might fairly and properly be considered as done by the partner whilst acting in the ordinary course of the firm's business. In *Dubai Aluminium*, the House of Lords held that the general acts of the partner in perpetrating the fraud were the drafting and negotiation of bogus agreements. Since the drafting of the agreements were acts which partners in law firms were authorised to do as part of the partnership's business, such acts were within the ordinary course of the firm's business and so the partnership was liable to third parties for losses which the latter had sustained as a result of the perpetration of the fraud.

- *What is joint and several liability?*
  Partners are jointly and severally liable for the debts of the partnership. This means that an injured third party may sue one partner, some partners or all of the partners to recover debts, damages or compensation which is due to them by the partnership. The third party also has the right to sue such partners for different amounts and if they do so, s.4(2) of the 1890 Act applies to settle matters amongst the partners.

Chapter 16—Company Law

- *What are the sources of company law?*
  The sources of company law may be divided into a number of categories, as follows:

    —primary legislation;
    —subordinate legislation;
    —the common law; and
    —extra-legal rules.

- *What are the objectives and purposes of company law?*
  Company law is concerned with the regulation of the power, rights, duties and liabilities of companies and constituencies that are closely connected with the company, namely the company's directors, managers, members/shareholders and creditors.

- *What are the core features of companies?*

    —The shareholders of limited liability companies enjoy limited liability for the debts of the company.
    —A company is a body corporate having separate legal personality distinct from its constituent members and so can be sued, sue third

parties in its own name, enter into contracts, own property in its own name, etc.

—Companies have the power to issue transferable shares to share-holders/investors as a means of raising corporate finance.

—There is a natural division between ownership of the company and its control:

    (i) the ease with which a company can replace poorly per-forming directors with specialised management as a means of turning around the fortunes of the company;

    (ii) a company enjoys the attribute of perpetual succession and only on the completion of a liquidation in terms of the Insolvency Act 1986 or the implementation of a striking out in terms of the Companies Act 2006 will a company cease to exist; and

    (iii) a company has the ability to grant a floating charge which is a kind of enterprise security which can be granted over the entirety of the assets and undertaking of a company to a lender in exchange for debt funding.

- *What are the main types of company?*
Companies may be divided into three different categories:

    (i) limited liability companies v unlimited companies;
    (ii) companies limited by shares v companies limited by guarantee; and
    (iii) private companies v public.

- *What documentation is required to incorporate a company?*

    (i) The company's memorandum of association—s.8 of the 2006 Act.
    (ii) The company's articles of association, unless the company is proposing to adopt the model articles of association referred to in s.20 of the 2006 Act—s.9(5)(b) of the 2006 Act.
    (iii) A statement of compliance—ss.9(1) and 13 of the 2006 Act.
    (iv) An application for registration—s.9 of the 2006 Act.

- *What are the constitutional documents of the company?*

    1. Memorandum of Association.
    2. Articles of Association.

- *What is the memorandum of association?*
The memorandum of association of a company is a document which states that the subscribers: (i) wish to form a company under the 2006 Act; and (ii) agree to become members of the company and, in the case of a company that is to have a share capital, to take at least one share each. It must be subscribed by each member on incorporation of the com-pany—s.8 of the 2006 Act.

- *What are the articles of association of the company?*
The articles regulate the internal affairs of the company and contain provisions on the division of authority between the directors and the members, the powers and responsibilities of directors, decision-making by directors, the appointment of directors, the organisation of, and voting at, general meetings, provisions on shares, transfers of shares and distributions of income amongst the members.

- *What is the legal effect of the articles of association?*

Section 33 of the 2006 Act provides that the articles represent a "contract" entered into between the members and the company and the members inter se. Accordingly, the members of the company can enforce the articles as a "contract" against the company and the company can enforce the articles against the members.

- *What are trading disclosures?*
Trading disclosures enjoin a company to display, state and provide information about itself in certain locations and communications (e.g. business letters, letters of credit, licences, business correspondence, business communications, invoices, bills of exchange, etc.), including its name and registered office.

- *Through what organs can a company act?*
The company can act through two organs, namely its board of directors and the members in: (a) general meeting; and (b) in the case of a private company, outwith general meeting by written resolution procedure under the 2006 Act.

- *Explain the role of the company secretary?*
The company secretary performs an administrative role, dealing with official correspondence on behalf of the company, maintaining the statutory registers and ensuring that the filing and other administrative obligations imposed on the company are complied with in accordance with the terms of the 2006 Act.

- *What is the role of a company director?*
A director is the agent of the company and is responsible for the management and direction of the company.

- *How many directors must a company have?*
Every private company must have at least one director and a public company must have no less than two directors—s.154 of the 2006 Act.

- *Are there any restrictions on who can be a director?*
Persons under 16 years of age are not eligible for appointment as a director and an undischarged bankrupt cannot be appointed as a director of a company without the prior leave of the court—s.157(1) of the 2006 Act and s.11 of the Company Directors Disqualification Act 1986.

- *List the different types of directors.*
Directors may be:

  (i) executive directors who are involved in the "day-to-day" management of the business, take executive decisions on behalf of the company; and

  (ii) non-executive directors who do not directly run or manage the business of the company. Directors may also be shadow directors.

- *Explain how directors can be removed in terms of the law?*
Directors may be removed by an ordinary resolution of the members of the company by special notice procedure—ss.168(1) and 312 of the 2006 Act. At a general meeting, the director has the right to protest his/her removal and has a right to be heard—s.169 of the 2006 Act.

- *To whom do directors owe their duties?*
Directors owe their duties to the company—s.170(1) of the 2006 Act. Having said that, the directors will owe their duties to the creditors of the company in terms of the common law where the company is of doubtful solvency or is insolvent.

- *What is the general meeting and what is its purpose?*

The general meeting is the place where the members of the company can come together to consider the performance of the directors of the company and vote on matters which the 2006 Act and the articles of association of the company specify must be passed by ordinary or special resolution.

- *Who has the power to call general meetings?*
  The directors, 10 per cent of the members (in voting terms) and the court have the power to call a general meeting—ss.302, 303 and 306 of the 2006 Act.
- *How much notice must be given of general meetings?*
  Subject to any longer period of notice stipulated in the articles, a general meeting of a private company requires 14 days' prior notice to the members. In the case of a plc, a general meeting must be called by 21 days' prior notice to the members in the case of an AGM or 14 days' prior notice to the members in the case of any other general meeting.
- *What information must be included in a notice of a general meeting?*
  The time, date and place of the meeting must be detailed, including the general nature of the business to be dealt with at the meeting, but this is subject to any provision in the company's articles—s.311 of the 2006 Act. In the case of an AGM of a public company, it is legal requirement for the plc to specify in the notice that the meeting is an annual general meeting—ss.307 and 337 of the 2006 Act.
- *What is a proxy?*
  A proxy is a person who attends a general meeting on behalf of a member and has the right to speak and vote at a general meeting on behalf of his appointing member on a show of hands or on a poll. A proxy also has the right to demand a vote on a poll and to be appointed as the chairman of the meeting—ss.324, 328 and 329 of the 2006 Act.
- *What is an ordinary resolution?*
  An ordinary resolution of the members of a company or of a class of members of a company means a resolution that is passed by a simple majority of the members—s.282 of the 2006 Act.
- *What is a special resolution?*
  A special resolution of the members of a company or of a class of members of a company means a resolution that is passed by a majority of not less than 75 per cent—s.283 of the 2006 Act.
- *What is a written resolution?*
  In the case of a private company only, an ordinary resolution or special resolution may be passed as a written resolution outwith a general meeting of the company in accordance with the written resolution procedure contained in the Act—s.288 of the 2006 Act.
- *What is a share?*
  A share is the interest of a shareholder in the company measured by a sum of money, for the purpose of liability in the first place, and of interest in the second, but also consisting of a series of mutual covenants entered into by all the shareholders inter se in accordance with the 2006 Act—*Borland's Trustee v Steel Bros & Co Ltd* [1901] 1 Ch. 279, per Farwell J at 288.
- *What is meant by different classes of shares?*
  A share belongs to a class where the articles of association attach certain rights to that class which can be distinguished from rights attaching to shares of another class.

- *How can shares be acquired?*
  Shares may be acquired by original acquisition, i.e. by an allotment and issue of fresh shares or derivative acquisition, i.e. by the transfer or transmission of shares.
- *What is a prospectus?*
  A prospectus is a document which a public company must issue if it is seeking to offer its shares to the public in return for capital investment.
- *What is a debenture?*
  A debenture is a debt instrument, sometimes also known as a bond, loan stock or loan notes issued by a company in return for capital investment.
- *What protections are available to minority shareholders?*
  Minority shareholders may: (i) raise statutory derivative proceedings; or (ii) present a petition to the court on the basis that they are suffering from unfair prejudice.

Chapter 17—Limited Liability Partnerships

- *What is an LLP?*
  A unique business entity with separate legal personality from its members often described as a hybrid between a traditional partnership and a limited company.
- *Why was there pressure on the government to introduce LLPs?*
  The twentieth century saw a significant increase in the size of partnerships which led to concerns about the appropriateness of unlimited liability of partners in many hundred partner firms. They had already been introduced in the USA and Jersey.
- *How is an LLP formed?*
  By completing the incorporation document and delivering same to the Registrar (with appropriate fee) who will issue an incorporation document.
- *Explain the statutory framework of LLPs.*
  See in general para.17–03. The Limited Liability Partnerships Act 2000 created the LLP regime but much of the detail is provided for in statutory instruments.
- *What is a designated member?*
  A designated member of an LLP is one who has additional administrative responsibilities to those imposed on other members. Among the designated members' duties is a responsibility to ensure that the LLP complies with the statutory regime; the duty to inform the registrar of any changes to the membership of the LLP; the duty to prepare the annual return, sign the annual accounts and deliver them to the registrar; and the duty to act on the LLP's behalf during winding up or dissolution.
- *Do members owe a duty of good faith to each other, and/or to the LLP itself?*
  The Act does not expressly state that members owe each other or the LLP a general duty of good faith however the agency relationship between members and the LLP has resulted in members owing the LLP the common law fiduciary duties which agents owe their principal. It is not clear if s.6 of the 2000 Act has created an agency relationship between an LLP and its members when the members are carrying out internal functions of the business rather than dealing with a third party.
- *Does the law of partnership apply to LLPs?*
  At first glance, no. However, see para.17–07 for a discussion.

- *How are new members admitted to an LLP?*
  A new member can be introduced to the LLP with agreement of the existing members in the manner stipulated in the members' agreement or in the manner provided in the Regulations.
- *To what extent can members bind the firm?*
  Every member of an LLP is agent of the LLP and the LLP is bound by the actions of the member unless the member had no authority to act and the person with whom he was dealing either knew him or her not to have authority or did not believe him or her to be a member at all.
- *To what extent are members employees of the firm?*
  Section 4(4) of the 2000 Act states that a member is not to be regarded as employed by the LLP unless he would be regarded as employed if he was a partner in a traditional partnership. However, see *Clyde & Co LLP v Bates van Winkelhof.*
- *What are differences between salaried, fixed-share and equity members?*
  A full equity member will have a proportion of the distributable profits of the business. A fixed share member is a member who has a nominal percentage of the equity of the LLP and guaranteed minimum drawings, and a salaried member is a member who receives only a salary.
- *What was the impact of HMRC's 2014 salaried members rules?*
  The Finance Act 2014 introduced salaried members rules which aim to tackle perceived tax avoidance by LLPs whose salaried members, HMRC considered, were akin to employees but who were being taxed as though self-employed. There are three conditions which if met will see members being treated as employees for tax purposes. As a result of these changes, many LLPs will be faced with a 13.8 per cent national insurance contribution charge for members who satisfy the salaried members conditions.
- *To what extent is members' liability limited and how does this compare to the traditional partnership?*
  The members are not jointly and severally liable with the LLP for its debts and obligations. If third parties dealing with an LLP are made aware that they are contracting with the LLP alone and not with any individual member thereof, an action in contract can be raised only against the LLP. In such a scenario, the LLP's assets will be used to satisfy any debts or obligations resulting from the claim, and the members themselves risk losing only their capital contributions in the event of a "wipe-out" claim. For an individual member to be held personally liable in negligence, the tripartite test of foreseeability of damage, proximity and whether it is fair, just and reasonable to impose a duty of care will apply. It will also be necessary for the pursuer to establish that there was an assumption of responsibility by the individual member, that the third party relied upon that assumption and no valid limitation of liability clause was in operation. In a traditional partnership, the partners are jointly and severally liable with the firm for its debts and obligations.
- *Does the LLP itself have limited liability?*
  No.
- *Where are the default provisions found for the management of the LLP if there is no written LLP agreement?*
  Reg.7 of the 2001 Regulations.
- *How are members taxed?*
  LLPs are tax transparent entities and it is the members' interests in the LLP which are taxable. Members of LLPs are taxed as if they were

partners in a traditional partnership and the LLP does not pay corporation tax.
- *Why are LLPs required to publish accounts?*
  It is the price which is paid for receiving limited liability.
- *What is the "clawback" provision?*
  The "clawback" provision in the Insolvency Act which provides that a member of the LLP, or any person who has been a member in the two years prior to the winding up, may be liable to contribute to the LLP's assets in the event of liquidation if the member withdrew any property of the LLP during that two-year period.
- *What ought to be considered when transferring a business to an LLP?*
  Many, many things! See para.17–35.

Chapter 18—Insurance Law

- *What are the sources of insurance law?*
  The sources of insurance law may be divided into a number of categories, as follows:

  —primary legislation, such as the Consumer Insurance (Disclosure and Representations) Act 2012 ("CI(DR)A"), the Insurance Act 2015 and the Marine Insurance Act 1906;
  —the common law; and
  —extra-legal rules

- *What are the objectives and purposes of insurance law?*
  Insurance law is concerned with the regulation of the insurance contract, which is a contract that protects those insured against the risks of modern life.
- *What is the definition of insurance?*
  Insurance is a contract whereby for some consideration, usually but not necessarily for periodical payments called premiums, an insured secures to him/herself some benefit, usually but not necessarily the payment of a sum of money, upon the happening of some event that is adverse to the insured, involving an element of uncertainty as to (a) whether the event will happen or not; or (b) the time at which it will happen.
- *What is insurable interest?*
  Insurance law prescribes that the insured must have an insurable interest in the subject matter of the insurance contract. In the case of life assurance, the insured must have a pecuniary or financial interest in the life or lives assured. As for indemnity insurance, there is a requirement that the insured has a legal or equitable interest in the property insured.
- *What is a warranty and what are the consequences if it is breached?*
  A warranty is a fundamental term of an insurance policy amounting to a promise made by the insured to the insurer. Warranties can be divided into two camps, namely a term of the insurance contract comprising (a) a statement of fact by the insured as to the past or present (a "past/present fact warranty only"); or (b) a continuing undertaking that a state of affairs will prevail throughout the duration of the policy, which must be exactly complied with, whether it be material to the risk insured or not (a "continuing/promissory warranty").
- *What are the consequences if a warranty is breached?*
  If the insured breaches a past/present fact warranty or a continuing/promissory warranty, then s.10 of the Insurance Act 2015 provides that the insurer has the right to terminate the insurance contract if the breach

is material, but the insurer is not automatically discharged from liability under the contract with effect from the date of the insured's breach of warranty. It is irrelevant that there is no connection between the breach and any loss that subsequently occurs.

- *What are the statutory and common law duties of the consumer insured and the commercial insured?*
A consumer insured is under a statutory obligation to take reasonable care not to make a misrepresentation before the contract is formed or varied and a common law duty not to make a fraudulent claim. This can be contrasted with the commercial insured's statutory duty to supply a fair presentation of the risk and his/her common law duty to refrain from making fraudulent claims.

- *In what circumstances will the consumer insured be treated as having complied with his/her statutory obligation?*
Section 3 of the CI(DR)A directs that the consumer insured must meet the standard of the reasonable consumer, unless the insurer was, or ought to have been, aware of any particular characteristics or circumstances of the actual consumer, or the representation made by the consumer was dishonest.

- *In what circumstances will the commercial insured be taken to have conformed to his/her statutory duty to furnish a fair presentation of the risk?*
In terms of s.3(4) of the Insurance Act 2015, this duty involves a requirement to disclose every material circumstance which the commercial insured knows or ought to know, or disclosure which gives the insurer sufficient information to put a prudent insurer on notice that it needs to make further enquiries for the purposes of revealing those material circumstances.

- *What is "subrogation"?*
The right of subrogation enables the insurer who has paid an insured sum to the insured for a loss sustained to: (i) "stand in the shoes" of the insured; and (ii) exercise (using the insured's name) all rights that the insured could have exercised himself to recover from any source other than the insurers themselves the whole or part of the financial loss the insured sustained and for which he has been indemnified.

- *What is the "indemnity principle"?*
This is the idea that the insured is only entitled to be reimbursed for the loss sustained as a result of the occurrence of the insured event, peril or loss.

Chapter 19—Insolvency

- *Explain briefly what is meant by insolvency.*
Insolvency is the situation where an individual or other legal entity is incapable of paying its debts.

- *What is a trustee in sequestration's main function?*
The main function of the trustee in sequestration is to ingather the assets of an individual who has been declared bankrupt and, as far as possible, to use these assets to pay off the individual's debts.

- *Briefly outline the rules regulating the debtor's discharge from bankruptcy.*
Under s.17 of the Bankruptcy and Debt Advice (Scotland) Act 2014, a debtor will be eligible for discharge from bankruptcy after one year. However, discharge must be formally granted by the Accountant in Bankruptcy, and can be refused if the debtor's conduct during

sequestration has been unacceptable. Refusal to discharge must be reviewed after a further year.

- *Explain briefly the diligences of arrestment, attachment and inhibition.*
Arrestment is a process by which certain assets of the debtor being held by third parties are "frozen", and will be handed over in time to the relevant creditor. Attachment is a process by which certain assets of the debtor are seized and sold, with a view to paying off the creditor executing the attachment. Inhibition is where restrictions are put on the debtor's use of his property, with a view to encouraging repayment of a debt.

- *What are the benefits of a company voluntary arrangement to a company that is facing financial difficulty?*
A company voluntary arrangement ("CVA") allows a company to agree, with its creditors, a scheme for repayment of its debts. This is beneficial because it allows the company to continue trading, and affords an opportunity to remedy its financial problems without the formality of other procedures.

- *What is the main purpose of administration?*
The main purpose of administration is to improve a company's financial position. The ideal situation is that the company is rescued from its financial problems and allowed to continue as a going concern, but this is not always possible.

- *Under what circumstances can a creditor of a company appoint a receiver?*
A creditor can only appoint a receiver if he holds a floating charge over any part of the company's assets. (Since September 2003 and the coming into force of the Enterprise Act 2002, many floating charge holders will now be required to appoint an administrator rather than a receiver.)

- *In terms of insolvency procedures, why is administration often seen as a preferable alternative to receivership?*
Administration is generally seen as preferable to receivership because it involves an attempt to improve the company's financial position, which is to the benefit of all creditors. Receivership does not have this objective, and aims instead to repay only the floating charge holder.

- *Briefly outline any two circumstances that might justify a company being put into liquidation.*
There are a number of circumstances that would justify a company being put into liquidation. The most common reason is that the company is unable to pay its debts. Other circumstances include: if the company passes a special resolution to this effect; if a Plc fails to obtain a trading certificate within 12 months of incorporation; if the company has not commenced its business within one year of incorporation, or suspends its business for a year; if the court is of the opinion that it is just and equitable that the company should be wound up.

- *What is the essential difference between a members' voluntary winding up and a creditors' voluntary winding up?*
The essential difference between a members' voluntary winding up and a creditors' voluntary winding up is the *declaration of solvency*. Essentially, if there is no doubt that the company will be able to pay off all its existing debt, the creditors need not be involved, and the liquidation can proceed as a members' voluntary winding up. However, if there is a possibility that not all debts will be paid, the liquidation must proceed as a creditors' voluntary winding up.

Chapter 20—Negotiable Instruments

- *A bill of exchange is always payable on demand.*

  ➢ True/False

  Commercial bills and promissory notes may be payable at a specified date in the future or on demand or on sight. However, a cheque is payable on demand, unless it is post-dated.

- *A bearer bill cannot be negotiated.*

  ➢ False

  A bearer bill is negotiated by delivery. On the other hand, a bill made payable to order is negotiated by indorsement and delivery. If no indorsee is named on the bill this is known as a blank indorsement and the bill then becomes a bearer bill.

- *A holder who is also a holder for value and a holder in due course is entitled to be paid even if the person they bought the bill from came by it dishonestly.*

  ➢ True

  A bill "stands on its own two feet" and is treated as a cash equivalent. If the holder in due course is unaware of any defect in the title he can enforce payment against the drawer and any indorser. This is an exception to the *nemo dat quem non habet* rule.

- *Overdue bills cannot be paid in any circumstance.*

  ➢ False

  Although a commercial bill should be presented for payment on the date specified on the face of the bill if the delay is due to circumstances beyond the control of the bearer they will still be entitled to payment. In the case or a bill payable on demand it will be held to be overdue if it has been in circulation for an unreasonable length of time. Banking practice, however, sees banks treat a cheque which has not been presented within six months as stale.

- *A crossed cheque must be paid into the payee's bank account.*

  ➢ True

  Section 79(2) of the 1882 Act applies. If a bank fails to abide by this stipulation and pays in cash a cheque bearing the words account payee the bank will be liable to the true owner of the cheque if it turns out that the cheque has been stolen.

Chapter 21—Rights in Security

- *A real right in security is always to be preferred to a personal right.*

  ➢ True

  A real right in security differs from a personal right in that it gives the creditor a nexus or a bond, over heritable or moveable property belonging to the debtor. A personal right in security is inferior to that of a real right, given it is only of any practical effect if the guarantor is solvent and in a position to honour the debtor's liability to the creditor.

- *A contract of guarantee is a principal obligation.*

  ➢ False

  A contract of guarantee is an accessory obligation which means that the principal debt must exist or be in the contemplation of the parties, before it can be enforced against the guarantor. It follows that the guarantor's liability to the creditor is in addition to that of the principal debtor and can only be enforced if the debtor fails to pay.

- *The guarantor enjoys no right of relief against the debtor if required to pay the creditor on his behalf.*

  ➢ False

  The guarantor who has paid the debt has a right of relief, which is to claim the sum paid, including expenses, from the debtor. This right will exist for a period of five years after the debt has been paid.

- *A guarantee is considered a contract uberrimae fidei.*

  ➢ False

  There is no general duty placed on the creditor to disclose the financial standing of the debtor to the creditor. However, a creditor will be under a duty to act in good faith where a proximate relationship exists between the debtor and the guarantor and the creditor is aware of the nature of the relationship between the parties. This duty is discharged if the creditor takes reasonable steps to enquire whether the party with no financial interest in the venture guaranteed has entered into the guarantee in full knowledge of the risk involved and without undue influence being exerted, or through any misrepresentation made, by the debtor.

- *A real right in security can only be created where there is delivery of the property subject to the security.*

  ➢ False

  It is a general rule of Scots law that a real right can only be created if there is delivery from the debtor to the creditor; however there are exceptions to this rule, namely hypothecs and floating charges.

- *A floating charge is said to crystallise if the company concerned goes into liquidation or a receiver is appointed.*

  ➢ True

  Until this occurs, the charge floats over the assets of the company undisturbed enabling the company to use the property, dispose of it or add further assets to its holdings.

- *Pledge may only be constituted by actual delivery of the property concerned.*

  ➢ False

  Pledge can also be created by constructive or symbolic delivery of the property to the pledgee.

- *A real right in security over incorporeal moveable property can only be created via assignation and intimation.*

  ➢ False

  Although this is the general rule, intimation is not always possible. This will arise where there is no actual debtor to inform that assignation has taken place. However, the real right will not be constituted until the assignation is registered, if registration is required by law.

Chapter 22—Dispute Resolution

- *Do the parties to a business dispute have to hire lawyers in the negotiation process?*
  No.
- *What are the main features of mediation?*
  Mediation is an informal dispute resolution where the parties try to reach an agreement with the help of mediator. However, the decision made by the mediator has no binding force on the parties.
- *What are the advantages and disadvantages of using commercial arbitration to resolve business disputes?*
  Advantages: Speed, confidentiality, privacy, party autonomy and the binding effect of the arbitral awards.
  Disadvantages: Arbitrator's lack of coercive power.
- *What statutes regulate arbitration in Scotland?*
  Arbitration (Scotland) Act 2010.
- *What duties does an arbitrator have?*
  To act independently, impartially and with due diligence to resolve the disputes.
- *What is the legal effect of an arbitral award?*
  An arbitral award has binding force on the parties.
- *Which form of alternative dispute resolution is widely adopted for construction disputes and which statute provides the legal framework for such method?*
  Adjudication: the Housing, Grants, Construction and Regeneration Act 1996.
- *What is the limit of claim for the Court of Session?*
  A claim over £5,000.
- *What is the limit of claim for the simple procedure?*
  A claim under £5,000.
- *What is the function of a sheriff appeal court?*
  A sheriff appeal court is created under the Court Reform (Scotland) Act 2014 to deal with all appeal civil cases for cases for £5,000 or less for better deployment of court resource for low value claims.

Index